Social Security Tax—2017

Category	Rate	Dollar Limit
OASDI	6.2%	$127,200
Medicare*	1.45%	First $200,000 c for joint returns,
	2.35%	Wages greater th ($250,000 for joi

*Only the employee is required to pay the additional Me wages above $200,000 ($250,000 for joint returns). The e ployer pays Medicare tax of 1.45% on all wages.

Self-Employment Tax—2017

Categ	Rate	Dollar Limit
	12.4%	$127,200
	2.9%	First $200,000 of self-employment income ($250,000 combined self-employment income for joint returns)
	3.8%	Self-employment income greater than $200,000 ($250,000 for joint returns)

Alternative Minimum Tax—2017

If AMTI minus the exemption amount is:		The tax is:	
Over—	But Not Over—		Of the Amount Over—
$0	$187,800*	26%	$0
$187,800*		$48,828* + 28%	$187,800

*$93,900 and $24,414 for married taxpayers filing separately.

AMT exemption amounts (before phase-outs and other adjustments):

Unmarried individuals (other than surviving spouses and heads of households)	$54,300
Married individuals filing joint returns and surviving spouses	84,500
Married individuals filing separate returns	42,250
Estates and trusts	24,100

STANDARD DEDUCTION

Filing Status	
Married individuals filing joint returns and surviving spouses	$12,700
Heads of households	9,350
Unmarried individuals (other than surviving spouses and heads of households)	6,350
Married individuals filing separate returns	6,350
Additional standard deduction for the aged and the blind	
Individual who is married and surviving spouses	1,250*
Individual who is unmarried and not a surviving spouse	1,550*
Taxpayer claimed as dependent on another taxpayer's return: Greater of (1) earned income plus $350, or (2) $1,050.	

*These amounts are $2,500 and $3,100, respectively, for a taxpayer who is both aged and blind.

PERSONAL AND DEPENDENCY EXEMPTION AND PHASE-OUTS

Personal and dependency exemption $ 4,050

Phase-outs for high income taxpayers:

Personal and dependency exemptions are reduced by 2% for each $2,500 increment (or part of increment) for AGI above the threshold amount.

Itemized deductions are reduced by 3% for each dollar of AGI above the threshold amounts (taxpayers cannot lose more than 80% of their allowable itemized deductions).

For both provisions, the AGI threshold amounts are:

Married individuals filing joint returns and surviving spouses	$313,800
Heads of households	287,650
Unmarried individuals (other than surviving spouses and heads of households)	261,500
Married individuals filing separate returns	156,900

Vice President, Business Publishing: Donna Battista
Director of Portfolio Management: Adrienne D'Ambrosio
Specialist Portfolio Manager: Lacey Vitetta
Editorial Assistant: Elisa Marks
Vice President, Product Marketing: Roxanne McCarley
Director of Strategic Marketing: Brad Parkins
Strategic Marketing Manager: Deborah Strickland
Product Marketer: Tricia Murphy
Field Marketing Manager: Natalie Wagner
Field Marketing Assistant: Kristen Compton
Product Marketing Assistant: Jessica Quazza
Vice President, Production and Digital Studio, Arts and Business: Etain O'Dea
Director of Production, Business: Jeff Holcomb
Managing Producer, Business: Ashley Santora
Content Producer: Mary Kate Murray
Project Manager: Melissa Pellerano
Operations Specialist: Carol Melville
Creative Director: Blair Brown
Manager, Learning Tools: Brian Surette
Content Developer, Learning Tools: Sarah Peterson
Managing Producer, Digital Studio, Arts and Business: Diane Lombardo
Digital Studio Producer: Regina DaSilva
Digital Studio Producer: Alana Coles
Digital Content Team Lead: Noel Lotz
Digital Content Project Lead: Martha LaChance
Full-Service Project Management, Composition, and Cover Design:
Integra Software Services
Cover Art: Klaru686/Shutterstock
Printer/Binder: LSC Communications, Inc./Willard
Cover Printer: Phoenix Color/Hagerstown

Photo credits: chapter openers dgrilla/Fotolia, Rabbit75_fot/Fotolia

1 17

www.pearsonhighered.com

ISBN-10: 0-13-455092-7
ISBN-13: 978-0-13-455092-3

PEARSON'S FEDERAL TAXATION 2018

CORPORATIONS, PARTNERSHIPS, ESTATES & TRUSTS

EDITORS

KENNETH E. ANDERSON
University of Tennessee

THOMAS R. POPE
University of Kentucky

TIMOTHY J. RUPERT
Northeastern University

CONTRIBUTING AUTHORS

ANNA C. FOWLER
University of Texas at Austin (Emeritus)

RICHARD J. JOSEPH
Bryant University

DAVID S. HULSE
University of Kentucky

LEANN LUNA
University of Tennessee

WILLIAM J. MOSER
Miami University

MICHAEL S. SCHADEWALD
University of Wisconsin–Milwaukee

330 Hudson Street, New York, NY 10013

CONTENTS

CHAPTER 14

CHAPTER 15

ABOUT THE EDITORS

KENNETH E. ANDERSON

Kenneth E. Anderson is the Pugh CPAs Professor of Accounting at the University of Tennessee. He earned a B.B.A. from the University of Wisconsin–Milwaukee and subsequently attained the level of tax manager with Arthur Young (now part of Ernst & Young). He then earned a Ph.D. from Indiana University. He teaches corporate taxation, partnership taxation, and tax strategy. Professor Anderson also is the Director of the Master of Accountancy Program. He has published articles in *The Accounting Review, The Journal of the American Taxation Association, Advances in Taxation,* the *Journal of Accountancy,* the *Journal of Financial Service Professionals,* and a number of other journals.

THOMAS R. POPE

Thomas R. Pope is the Ernst & Young Professor of Accounting at the University of Kentucky. He received a B.S. from the University of Louisville and an M.S. and D.B.A. in business administration from the University of Kentucky. He teaches international taxation, partnership and S corporation taxation, tax research and policy, and introductory taxation and has won outstanding teaching awards at the University, College, and School of Accountancy levels. He has published articles in *The Accounting Review,* the *Tax Adviser, Taxes, Tax Notes,* and a number of other journals. Professor Pope's extensive professional experience includes eight years with Big Four accounting firms. Five of those years were with Ernst & Whinney (now part of Ernst & Young), including two years with their National Tax Department in Washington, D.C. He subsequently held the position of Senior Manager in charge of the Tax Department in Lexington, Kentucky. Professor Pope also has been a leader and speaker at professional tax conferences all over the United States and is active as a tax consultant.

TIMOTHY J. RUPERT

Timothy J. Rupert is a Professor at the D'Amore-McKim School of Business at Northeastern University. He received his B.S. in Accounting and his Master of Taxation from the University of Akron. He also earned his Ph.D. from Penn State University. Professor Rupert's research has been published in such journals as *The Accounting Review, The Journal of the American Taxation Association, Behavioral Research in Accounting, Advances in Taxation, Applied Cognitive Psychology, Advances in Accounting Education,* and *Journal of Accounting Education.* He currently is the co-editor of *Advances in Accounting Education.* In 2010, he received the Outstanding Educator Award from the Massachusetts Society of CPAs. He also has received the University's Excellence in Teaching Award and the D'Amore-McKim School's Best Teacher of the Year award multiple times. He is active in the American Accounting Association and the American Taxation Association (ATA) and has served as president, vice president, and secretary of the ATA.

ABOUT THE AUTHORS

Anna C. Fowler is the John Arch White Professor Emeritus in the Department of Accounting at the University of Texas at Austin. She received her B.S. in accounting from the University of Alabama and her M.B.A. and Ph.D. from the University of Texas at Austin. Active in the American Taxation Association throughout her academic career, she served on the editorial board of its journal and held many positions, including president. She is a former member of the American Institute of CPA's Tax Executive Committee and a former chair of the AICPA's Regulation/Tax Subcommittee for the CPA exam. She has published a number of articles, most of which have dealt with estate planning or real estate transaction issues. In 2002, she received the Ray M. Sommerfeld Outstanding Educator Award, co-sponsored by the American Taxation Association and Ernst & Young.

Richard J. Joseph is Executive Director of Babson Global, Inc., an international education subsidiary of Babson College. He is the former Provost-for-Term and Chief Academic Officer of Bryant University in Smithfield, Rhode Island. Before joining Bryant, he served on the administration and tax faculty of The University of Texas at Austin. He also has worked as an international banker at Citibank, Riyadh; an investment banker at Lehman Brothers, New York; a securities trader at Becker Paribas, Dallas, and Bear Stearns, New York; and a mergers and acquisitions lawyer for the Bass Group, Fort Worth. He is a graduate *magna cum laude* of Harvard College, Oxford University, and The University of Texas at Austin School of Law. Dr. Joseph is co-editor of the *Handbook of Mergers and Acquisitions* (Oxford University Press) and author of *The Origins of the American Income Tax* (Syracuse University Press). He has written numerous commentaries in the *Financial Times*, *The Christian Science Monitor*, *Tax Notes*, and *Tax Notes International*.

David S. Hulse is an Associate Professor of Accountancy at the University of Kentucky, where he teaches introductory and corporate taxation courses. He received an undergraduate degree from Shippensburg University, an M.S. from Louisiana State University, and a Ph.D. from the Pennsylvania State University. Professor Hulse has published a number of articles on tax issues in academic and professional journals, including *The Journal of the American Taxation Association, Advances in Taxation,* the *Journal of Financial Service Professionals,* the *Journal of Financial Planning*, and *Tax Notes.*

LeAnn Luna is a Professor of Accounting at the University of Tennessee. She is a CPA and holds an undergraduate degree from Southern Methodist University, an M.T. from the University of Denver College of Law, and a Ph.D. from the University of Tennessee. She has taught introductory taxation, corporate and partnership taxation, and tax research. Professor Luna also holds a joint appointment with the Center for Business and Economic Research at the University of Tennessee, where she interacts frequently with state policymakers on a variety of policy-related issues. She has published articles in the *Journal of Accounting and Economics, National Tax Journal, The Journal of the American Taxation Association,* and *State Tax Notes.*

William J. Moser is an Assistant Professor in the Department of Accountancy at the Farmer School of Business at Miami University. He received his B.S. in Accountancy from Miami University in 1995, his Masters in Accountancy with an emphasis in taxation from Northern Illinois University in 1997, and his Ph.D. from the University of Arizona in 2005. He teaches taxation of individuals, property transactions, business entities, estates, gifts, and trusts, and he has received numerous teaching awards during his academic career. He has co-authored articles in the *Journal of Accounting Research,* the *Journal of Financial and Quantitative Analysis, Review of Accounting Studies,* and *The Journal of the American Taxation Association.*

Michael S. Schadewald, Ph.D., CPA, is on the faculty of the University of Wisconsin–Milwaukee, where he teaches graduate and undergraduate courses in business taxation. A graduate of the University of Minnesota, Professor Schadewald is a co-author of several books on multistate and international taxation and has published more than 40 articles in academic and professional journals, including *The Accounting Review, Journal of Accounting Research, Contemporary Accounting Research, The Journal of the American Taxation Association, CPA Journal, Journal of Taxation*, and *The Tax Adviser*. Professor Schadewald also has served on the editorial boards of *The Journal of the American Taxation Association, Journal of State Taxation, International Tax Journal, The International Journal of Accounting, Issues in Accounting Education*, and *Journal of Accounting Education*.

PREFACE

Why is the Rupert/Pope/Anderson series the best choice for you and your students?

The Rupert/Pope/Anderson 2018 Series in Federal Taxation is appropriate for use in any first course in federal taxation, and comes in a choice of three volumes:

Federal Taxation 2018: Individuals
Federal Taxation 2018: Corporations, Partnerships, Estates & Trusts (the companion book to *Individuals*)
Federal Taxation 2018: Comprehensive (14 chapters from *Individuals* and 15 chapters from *Corporations*)
** For a customized edition of any of the chapters for these texts, contact your Pearson representative and they can create a custom text for you.

- The *Individuals* volume covers *all* entities, although the treatment is often briefer than in the *Corporations* and *Comprehensive* volumes. The *Individuals* volume, therefore, is appropriate for colleges and universities that require only one semester of taxation as well as those that require more than one semester of taxation. Further, this volume adapts the suggestions of the Model Tax Curriculum as promulgated by the American Institute of Certified Public Accountants.
- The *Corporations, Partnerships, Estates & Trusts* and *Comprehensive* volumes contain three comprehensive tax return problems whose data change with each edition, thereby keeping the problems fresh. Problem C:3-66 contains the comprehensive corporate tax return, Problem C:9-58 contains the comprehensive partnership tax return, and Problem C:11-64 contains the comprehensive S corporation tax return, which is based on the same facts as Problem C:9-58 so that students can compare the returns for these two entities.
- The *Corporations, Partnerships, Estates & Trusts* and *Comprehensive* volumes contain sections called Financial Statement Implications, which discuss the implications of Accounting Standards Codification (ASC) 740. The main discussion of accounting for income taxes appears in Chapter C:3. The financial statement implications of other transactions appear in Chapters C:5, C:7, C:8, and C:16 (*Corporations* volume only).

What's New to this Edition?

INDIVIDUALS

- Complete updating of significant court cases and IRS rulings and procedures during 2016 and early 2017.
- Complete updating for the Protecting Americans from Tax Hikes Act of 2015 and the 2016 Consolidated Appropriations Act.
- Discussion of the expiration of certain deductions and credits in 2017.
- All tax rate schedules have been updated to reflect the rates and inflation adjustments for 2017.
- Whenever new updates become available, they will be accessible via MyAccountingLab.

CORPORATIONS

- The comprehensive corporate tax return, Problem C:3-66, has all new numbers for the 2016 forms.
- The comprehensive partnership tax return, Problem C:9-58, has all new numbers for the 2016 forms.
- The comprehensive S corporation tax return, Problem C:11-64, has all new numbers for the 2016 forms.
- Changes affecting 2017 tax law have been incorporated into the text where appropriate, including the tax legislation listed in the second Individuals bullet item above.
- All tax rate schedules have been updated to reflect the rates and inflation adjustments for 2017.
- Whenever new updates become available, they will be accessible via MyAccountingLab.

MyAccountingLab

MyAccountingLab is an online homework, tutorial, and assessment program designed to work with *Pearson's Federal Taxation 2018* to engage students and improve results. MyAccountingLab's homework and practice questions are correlated to the textbook, they regenerate algorithmically to give students unlimited opportunity for practice and mastery, and they offer helpful feedback when students enter incorrect answers. Combining resources that illuminate content with accessible self-assessment, MyAccountingLab with eText provides students with a complete digital learning experience—all in one place. To register, go to http://www.pearsonmylabandmastering.com.

For Instructors

MyAccountingLab provides instructors with a rich and flexible set of course materials, along with course-management tools that make it easy to deliver all or a portion of your course online.

- **Powerful Homework and Test Manager** Create, import, and manage online homework and media assignments, quizzes, and tests. Create assignments from online questions directly correlated to this and other textbooks. Homework questions include "Help Me Solve This" guided solutions to help students understand and master concepts. You can choose from a wide range of assignment options, including time limits and maximum number of attempts allowed. In addition, you can create your own questions—or copy and edit ours—to customize your students' learning path.
- **Comprehensive Gradebook Tracking** MyAccountingLab's online gradebook automatically tracks your students' results on tests, homework, and tutorials and gives you control over managing results and calculating grades. All MyAccountingLab grades can be exported to a spreadsheet program, such as Microsoft® Excel. The MyAccountingLab Gradebook provides a number of student data views and gives you the flexibility to weight assignments, select which attempts to include when calculating scores, and omit or delete results for individual assignments.
- **Department-Wide Solutions** Get help managing multiple sections and working with Teaching Assistants using MyAccountingLab Coordinator Courses. After your MyAccountingLab course is set up, it can be copied to create sections or "member courses." Changes to the Coordinator Course flow down to all members, so changes only need to be made once.

We will add the most current tax information to MyAccountingLab as it becomes available.

For Students

MyAccountingLab provides students with a personalized interactive learning environment, where they can learn at their own pace and measure their progress.

- **Interactive Tutorial Exercises** MyAccountingLab's homework and practice questions are correlated to the textbook, and "similar to" versions regenerate algorithmically to give students unlimited opportunity for practice and mastery. Questions offer helpful feedback when students enter incorrect answers, and they include "Help Me Solve This" guided solutions as well as other learning aids for extra help when students need it.
- **Study Plan** The Study Plan acts as a tutor, providing personalized recommendations for each of your students based on his or her ability to master the learning objectives in your course. This allows students to focus their study time by pinpointing the precise areas they need to review, and allowing them to use customized practice and learning aids—such as videos, eText, tutorials, and more—to get them back on track. Using the report available in the Gradebook, you can then tailor course lectures to prioritize the content where students need the most support—offering you better insight into classroom and individual performance.
- **Dynamic Study Modules** Dynamic Study Modules help students study effectively on their own by continuously assessing their activity and performance in real time. Here's how it works: students complete a set of questions with a unique answer format that also asks them to indicate their confidence level. Questions repeat until the student can answer them all correctly and confidently. Once completed, Dynamic Study Modules explain the concept using materials from the text. These are available as graded assignments prior to class, and accessible on smartphones, tablets, and computers. NEW! Instructors can now remove questions from Dynamic Study Modules to better fit their course. Available for select titles.

Strong Pedagogical Aids

- Appropriate blend of technical content of the tax law with a high level of readability for students.
- Focused on enabling students to apply tax principles within the chapter to real-life situations.

Real-World Example

These comments relate the text material to events, cases, and statistics occurring in the tax and business environment. The statistical data presented in some of these comments are taken from the IRS's Statistics of Income at www.irs.gov.

Book-to-Tax Accounting Comparison

These comments compare the tax discussion in the text to the accounting and/or financial statement treatment of this material. Also, the last section of Chapter C:3 discusses the financial statement implications of federal income taxes.

What Would You Do in This Situation?

Unique to the Rupert/Pope/Anderson series, these boxes place students in a decision-making role. The boxes include many *controversies* that are as yet unresolved or are currently being considered by the courts. These boxes make extensive use of **Ethical Material** as they represent choices that may put the practitioner at odds with the client.

Stop & Think

These "speed bumps" encourage students to pause and apply what they have just learned. Solutions for each issue are provided in the box.

Ethical Point

These comments provide the ethical implications of material discussed in the adjoining text. Apply what they have just learned.

Tax Strategy Tip

These comments suggest tax planning ideas related to material in the adjoining text.

Additional Comment

These comments provide supplemental information pertaining to the adjacent text.

Program Components

Materials for the instructor may be accessed at the Instructor's Resource Center (IRC) online, located at **www.pearsonhighered.com/pearsontax** or within the Instructor Resource section of MyAccountingLab. You may contact your Pearson representative for assistance with the registration process.

- ***TaxAct 2016 Software:*** Available via online purchase with Individuals, Corporations, and Comprehensive Texts. This user-friendly tax preparation program includes more than 80 tax forms, schedules, and worksheets. TaxAct calculates returns and alerts the user to possible errors or entries. Consists of Forms 990, 1040, 1041, 1065, 1120, and 1120S.
- ***Instructor's Resource Manual:*** Contains sample syllabi, instructor outlines, and information regarding problem areas for students. It also contains solutions to the tax form/tax return preparation problems.
- ***Solutions Manual:*** Contains solutions to discussion questions, problems, and comprehensive and tax strategy problems. It also contains all solutions to the case study problems, research problems, and "What Would You Do in This Situation?" boxes.
- ***Test Bank:*** Offers a wealth of true/false, multiple-choice, and calculative problems. A computerized program is available to adopters.
- ***PowerPoint Slides:*** Consists of chapter outlines, featuring images, examples, and problems throughout, to aid in class lectures.
- ***Image Library:*** Figures, tables, and tax forms featured in the book are provided as individual files for the convenience of instructors and students.
- ***Multi-State Tax Chapter:*** An entire chapter, complete with problems (and solutions) dedicated to multi-state tax practices.

Acknowledgments

Our policy is to provide annual editions and to prepare timely updated supplements when major tax revisions occur. We are most appreciative of the suggestions made by outside reviewers because these extensive review procedures have been valuable to the authors and editors during the revision process.

We also are grateful to the various graduate assistants, doctoral students, and colleagues who have reviewed the text and supplementary materials and checked solutions to maintain a high level of technical accuracy. In particular, we would like to acknowledge the following colleagues who assisted in the preparation of supplemental materials for this text:

Ann Burstein Cohen	SUNY at Buffalo
Craig J. Langstraat/Joshua G. Coyne	University of Memphis
Kate Demarest	Carroll Community College
Allison McLeod	University of North Texas
Mitchell Franklin	LeMoyne College
Anthony Masino	East Tennessee State University

In addition, we want to thank Myron S. Scholes, Mark A. Wolfson, Merle M. Erickson, M. L. Hanlon, Edward L. Maydew, and Terry J. Shevlin for allowing us to use the model discussed in their text, *Taxes and Business Strategy: A Planning Approach*, as the basis for material in Chapter I:18.

Please send any comments to Kenneth E. Anderson or Timothy J. Rupert.

CHAPTER

1

TAX RESEARCH

LEARNING OBJECTIVES

After studying this chapter, you should be able to

1. Distinguish between closed fact and open fact tax situations
2. Describe the steps in the tax research process
3. Explain how the facts influence tax consequences
4. Identify the sources of tax law and assess the authoritative value of each
5. Consult tax services to research an issue
6. Apply the basics of Internet-based tax research
7. Use a citator to assess tax authorities
8. Describe the professional guidelines that CPAs in tax practice should follow
9. Prepare work papers and communicate to clients

CHAPTER OUTLINE

This chapter introduces the reader to the tax research process. Its major focus is the sources of the tax law (i.e., the Internal Revenue Code and other tax authorities) and the relative weight given to each source. The chapter describes the steps in the tax research process and places particular emphasis on the importance of the facts to the tax consequences. It also describes the features of frequently used tax services and computer-based tax research resources. Finally, it explains how to use a citator.

The end product of the tax research process—the communication of results to the client—also is discussed. This text uses a hypothetical set of facts to provide a comprehensive illustration of the process. Sample work papers demonstrating how to document the results of research are included in Appendix A. The text also discusses two types of professional guidelines for CPAs in tax practice: the American Institute of Certified Public Accountants' (AICPA's) *Statements on Standards for Tax Services* (reproduced in Appendix E) and Treasury Department *Circular 230*.

Overview of Tax Research

OBJECTIVE 1

Distinguish between closed fact and open fact tax situations

Tax research is the process of solving tax-related problems by applying tax law to specific sets of facts. Sometimes it involves researching several issues and often is conducted to formulate tax policy. For example, policy-oriented research would determine how far the level of charitable contributions might decline if such contributions were no longer deductible. Economists usually conduct this type of tax research to assess the effects of government policy.

Tax research also is conducted to determine the tax consequences of transactions to specific taxpayers. For example, client-oriented research would determine whether Smith Corporation could deduct a particular expenditure as a trade or business expense. Accounting and law firms generally engage in this type of research on behalf of their clients.

ADDITIONAL COMMENT

Closed-fact situations afford the tax advisor the least amount of flexibility. Because the facts are already established, the tax advisor must develop the best solution possible within certain predetermined constraints.

This chapter deals only with client-oriented tax research, which occurs in two contexts:

1. **Closed fact or tax compliance situations:** The client contacts the tax advisor after completing a transaction or while preparing a tax return. In such situations, the tax consequences are fairly straightforward because the facts cannot be modified to obtain different results. Consequently, tax saving opportunities may be lost.

EXAMPLE C:1-1 ▶ Tom informs Carol, his tax advisor, that on November 4 of the current year, he sold land held as an investment for $500,000 cash. His basis in the land was $50,000. On November 9, Tom reinvested the sales proceeds in another plot of investment property costing $500,000. This is a closed fact situation. Tom wants to know the amount and the character of the gain (if any) he must recognize. Because Tom solicits the tax advisor's advice after the sale and reinvestment, the opportunity for tax planning is limited. For example, the possibility of deferring taxes by using a like-kind exchange or an installment sale is lost. ◀

ADDITIONAL COMMENT

Open-fact or tax-planning situations give a tax advisor flexibility to structure transactions to accomplish the client's objectives. In this type of situation, a creative tax advisor can save taxpayers dollars through effective tax planning.

2. **Open fact or tax planning situations:** Before structuring or concluding a transaction, the client contacts the tax advisor to discuss tax planning opportunities. Tax-planning situations generally are more difficult and challenging because the tax advisor must consider the client's tax and nontax objectives. Most clients will not engage in a transaction if it is inconsistent with their nontax objectives, even though it produces tax savings.

EXAMPLE C:1-2 ▶ Diane is a widow with three children and five grandchildren and at present owns property valued at $30 million. She seeks advice from Carol, her tax advisor, about how to minimize her estate taxes and convey the greatest value of property to her descendants. This is an open-fact situation. Carol could advise Diane to leave all but $5.49 million of her property to a charitable organization so that her estate would owe no estate taxes. Although this recommendation would eliminate Diane's estate taxes, Diane is likely to reject it because she wants her children or grandchildren to be her primary beneficiaries. Thus, reducing estate taxes to zero is inconsistent with her objective of allowing her descendants to receive as much after-tax wealth as possible. ◄

TAX STRATEGY TIP

Taxpayers should make investment decisions based on after-tax rates of return or after-tax cash flows.

When conducting research in a tax planning context, the tax professional should keep a number of points in mind. First, the objective is not to minimize taxes per se but rather to maximize a taxpayer's after-tax return. For example, if the federal income tax rate is a constant 30%, an investor should not buy a tax-exempt bond yielding 5% when he or she could buy a corporate bond of equal risk that yields 9% before tax and 6.3% after tax. This is the case even though his or her explicit taxes (actual tax liability) would be minimized by investing in the tax-exempt bond.[1] Second, taxpayers typically do not engage in unilateral or self-dealing transactions; thus, the tax ramifications for all parties to the transaction should be considered. For example, in the executive compensation context, employees may prefer to receive incentive stock options (because they will not recognize income until they sell the stock), but the employer may prefer to grant a different type of option (because the employer cannot deduct the value of incentive stock options upon issuance). Thus, the employer might grant a different number of options if it uses one type of stock option versus another type as compensation. Third, taxes are but one cost of doing business. In deciding where to locate a manufacturing plant, for example, factors more important to some businesses than the amount of state and local taxes paid might be the proximity to raw materials, good transportation systems, the cost of labor, the quantity of available skilled labor, and the quality of life in the area. Fourth, the time for tax planning is not restricted to the beginning date of an investment, contract, or other arrangement. Instead, the time extends throughout the duration of the activity. As tax rules change or as business and economic environments change, the tax advisor must reevaluate whether the taxpayer should hold onto an investment and must consider the transaction costs of any alternatives.

ADDITIONAL COMMENT

It is important to consider nontax as well as tax objectives. In many situations, the nontax considerations outweigh the tax considerations. Thus, the plan eventually adopted by a taxpayer may not always be the best when viewed strictly from a tax perspective.

One final note: the tax advisor should always bear in mind the financial accounting implications of proposed transactions. An answer that may be desirable from a tax perspective may not always be desirable from a financial accounting perspective. Though interrelated, the two fields of accounting have different orientations and different objectives. Tax accounting is oriented primarily to the Internal Revenue Service (IRS). Its objectives include calculating, reporting, and predicting one's tax liability according to legal principles. Financial accounting is oriented primarily to shareholders, creditors, managers, and employees. Its objectives include determining, reporting, and predicting a business's financial position and operating results according to Generally Accepted Accounting Principles. Because tax and financial accounting objectives may differ, planning conflicts could arise. For example, management might be reluctant to engage in tax reduction strategies that also reduce book income and reported earnings per share. Success in any tax practice, especially at the managerial level, requires consideration of both sets of objectives and orientations.

STEPS IN THE TAX RESEARCH PROCESS

OBJECTIVE 2

Describe the steps in the tax research process

In both open- and closed-fact situations, the tax research process involves six basic steps:

1. Determine the facts.
2. Identify the issues (questions).
3. Locate the applicable authorities.
4. Evaluate the authorities and choose those to follow where the authorities conflict.
5. Analyze the facts in terms of the applicable authorities.
6. Communicate conclusions and recommendations to the client.

[1] For an excellent discussion of explicit and implicit taxes and tax planning see M. S. Scholes, M. A. Wolfson, M. Erickson, M. Hanlon, L. Maydew, and T. Shevlin, *Taxes and Business Strategy: A Planning Approach,* fifth edition (Upper Saddle River, NJ: Pearson Prentice Hall, 2015). Also see Chapter I:18 of the *Individuals* volume. An example of an implicit tax is the excess of the before-tax earnings on a taxable bond over the risk-adjusted before-tax earnings on a tax-favored investment (e.g., a municipal bond).

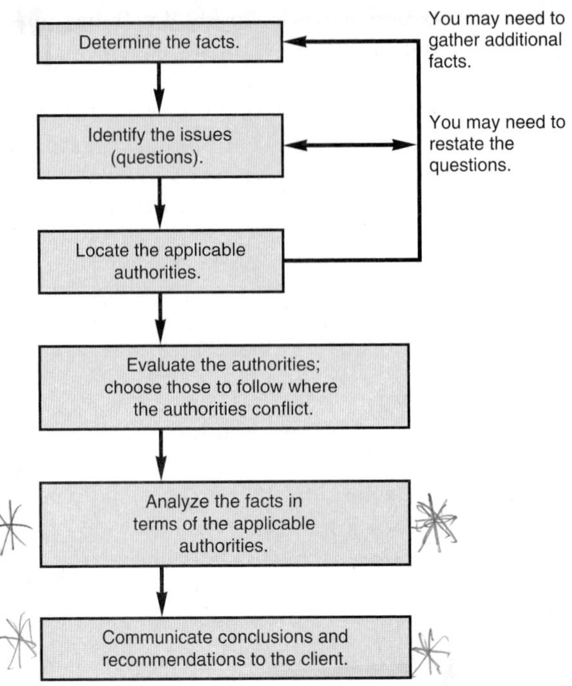

FIGURE C:1-1 ▶ STEPS IN THE TAX RESEARCH PROCESS

ADDITIONAL COMMENT

The steps of tax research provide an excellent format for a written tax communication. For example, a good format for a client memo includes (1) statement of facts, (2) list of issues, (3) discussion of relevant authority, (4) analysis, and (5) recommendations to the client of appropriate actions based on the research results.

Although the above outline suggests a linear approach, the tax research process often is circular. That is, it does not always proceed step-by-step. Figure C:1-1 illustrates a more accurate process, and Appendix A provides a comprehensive example of this process.

In a closed-fact situation, the facts have already occurred, and the tax advisor's task is to analyze them to determine the appropriate tax treatment. In an open-fact situation, by contrast, the facts have not yet occurred, and the tax advisor's task is to plan for them or shape them so as to produce a favorable tax result. The tax advisor performs the latter task by reviewing the relevant legal authorities, particularly court cases and IRS rulings, all the while bearing in mind the facts of those cases or rulings that produced favorable results compared with those that produced unfavorable results. For example, if a client wants to realize an ordinary loss (as opposed to a capital loss) on the sale of several plots of land, the tax advisor might consult cases involving similar land sales. The advisor might attempt to distinguish the facts of those cases in which the taxpayer realized an ordinary loss from the facts of those cases in which the taxpayer realized a capital loss. The advisor then might recommend that the client structure the transaction based on the fact pattern in the ordinary loss cases.

TYPICAL MISCONCEPTION

Many taxpayers think the tax law is all black and white. However, most tax research deals with gray areas. Ultimately, when confronted with tough issues, the ability to develop strategies that favor the taxpayer and then to find relevant authority to support those strategies will make a successful tax advisor. Thus, recognizing planning opportunities and avoiding potential traps is often the real value added by a tax advisor.

Often, tax research involves a question to which no clearcut, unequivocally correct answer exists. In such situations, probing a related issue might lead to a solution pertinent to the central question. For example, in researching whether the taxpayer may deduct a loss as ordinary instead of capital, the tax advisor might research the related issue of whether the presence of an investment motive precludes classifying a loss as ordinary. The solution to that issue might be relevant to the central question of whether the taxpayer may deduct the loss as ordinary.

Identifying the issue(s) to be researched often is the most difficult step in the tax research process. In some instances, the client defines the issue(s) for the tax advisor, such as where the client asks, "May I deduct the costs of a winter trip to Florida recommended by my physician?" In other instances, the tax advisor, after reviewing the documents submitted to him or her by the client, identifies and defines the issue(s) himself or herself. Doing so presupposes a firm grounding in tax law.[2]

[2] Often, in an employment context, supervisors define the questions to be researched and the authorities that might be relevant to the tax consequences.

Once the tax advisor locates the applicable legal authorities, he or she might have to obtain additional information from the client. Example C:1-3 illustrates the point. The example assumes that all relevant tax authorities are in agreement.

EXAMPLE C:1-3 ▶ Mark calls his tax advisor, Al, and states that he (1) incurred a loss on renting his beach cottage during the current year and (2) wonders whether he may deduct the loss. He also states that he, his wife, and their minor child occupied the cottage only eight days during the current year.

This is the first time Al has dealt with the Sec. 280A vacation home rules. On reading Sec. 280A(d), Al learns that a loss is *not* deductible if the taxpayer used the residence for personal purposes for longer than the greater of (1) 14 days or (2) 10% of the number of days the unit was rented at a fair rental value. He also learns that the property is *deemed* to be used by the taxpayer for personal purposes on any days on which it is used by any member of his or her family (as defined in Sec. 267(c)(4)). The Sec. 267(c)(4) definition of family members includes brothers, sisters, spouse, ancestors (e.g., parents and grandparents), or lineal descendants (e.g., children and grandchildren).

Mark's eight-day use is not long enough to make the rental loss nondeductible. However, Al must inquire about the number of days, if any, Mark's brothers, sisters, or parents used the property. (He already knows about use by Mark, his spouse, and his lineal descendants.) In addition, Al must find out how many days the cottage was rented to other persons at a fair rental value. Upon obtaining the additional information, Al proceeds to determine how to calculate the deductible expenses. Al then derives his conclusion concerning the deductible loss, if any, and communicates it to Mark. (This example assumes the passive activity and at-risk rules restricting a taxpayer's ability to deduct losses from real estate activities will not pose a problem for Mark. See Chapter I:8 for a comprehensive discussion of these topics.) ◀

Many firms require that a researcher's conclusions be communicated to the client in writing. Members or employees of such firms may answer questions orally, but their oral conclusions should be followed by a written communication. According to the AICPA's *Statements on Standards for Tax Services* (reproduced in Appendix E),

> Although oral advice may serve a taxpayer's needs appropriately in routine matters or in well-defined areas, written communications are recommended in important, unusual, substantial dollar value, or complicated transactions. The member may use professional judgment about whether, subsequently, to document oral advice.[3]

In addition, Treasury Department *Circular 230* covers all written advice communicated to clients. These requirements are more fully discussed at the end of this chapter and in Chapter C:15.

IMPORTANCE OF THE FACTS TO THE TAX CONSEQUENCES

OBJECTIVE 3

Explain how the facts influence tax consequences

Many terms and phrases used in the Internal Revenue Code (IRC) and other tax authorities are vague or ambiguous. Some provisions conflict with others or are difficult to reconcile, creating for the researcher the dilemma of deciding which rules are applicable and which tax results are proper. For example, as a condition to claiming another person as a dependent, the taxpayer must provide a certain level of support for such person.[4] Neither the IRC nor the Treasury Regulations define "support." This lack of definition could be problematic. For example, if the taxpayer purchased a used automobile costing $8,000 for an elderly parent whose only source of income is $7,800 in Social Security benefits, the question of whether the expenditure constitutes support would arise. The tax advisor would have to consult court opinions, revenue rulings, and other IRS pronouncements to ascertain the legal meaning of the term "support." Only after thorough research would the meaning of the term become clear.

3 AICPA, *Statement on Standards for Tax Services,* No. 7, "Form and Content of Advice to Taxpayers," 2010, Para. 6.

4 Sec. 152(e)(1)(A) and Sec. 152(d)(1)(C).

In other instances, the legal language is quite clear, but a question arises as to whether the taxpayer's transaction conforms to a specific pattern of facts that gives rise to a particular tax result. Ultimately, the peculiar facts of a transaction or event determine its tax consequences. A change in the facts can significantly change the consequences. Consider the following illustrations:

Illustration One
Facts: A holds stock, a capital asset, that he purchased two years ago at a cost of $1,000. He sells the stock to B for $920. What are the tax consequences to A?
Result: Under Sec. 1001, A realizes an $80 capital loss. He recognizes this loss in the current year. A must offset the loss against any capital gains recognized during the year. Any excess loss is deductible from ordinary income up to a $3,000 annual limit.
Change of Facts: A is B's son.
New Result: Under Sec. 267, A and B are related parties. Therefore, A may not recognize the realized loss. However, B may use the loss if she subsequently sells the stock at a gain.

Illustration Two
Facts: C donates to State University ten acres of land that she purchased two years ago for $10,000. The fair market value (FMV) of the land on the date of the donation is $25,000. C's adjusted gross income is $100,000. What is C's charitable contribution deduction?
Result: Under Sec. 170, C is entitled to a $25,000 charitable contribution deduction (i.e., the FMV of the property unreduced by the unrealized long-term gain).
Change of Facts: C purchased the land 11 months ago.
New Result: Under the same IRC section, C is entitled to only a $10,000 charitable contribution deduction (i.e., the FMV of the property reduced by the unrealized short-term gain).

Illustration Three
Facts: Acquiring Corporation pays Target Corporation's shareholders one million shares of Acquiring voting stock. In return, Target's shareholders tender 98% of their Target voting stock. The acquisition is for a bona fide business purpose. Acquiring continues Target's business. What are the tax consequences of the exchange to Target's shareholders?
Result: Because the transaction qualifies as a reorganization under Sec. 368(a)(1)(B), Target's shareholders are not taxed on the exchange, which is solely for Acquiring voting stock.
Change of Facts: In the transaction, Acquiring purchases the remaining 2% of Target's shares with cash.
New Result: Under the same IRC provision, Target's shareholders are now taxed on the exchange, which is not solely for Acquiring voting stock.

CREATING A FACTUAL SITUATION FAVORABLE TO THE TAXPAYER

TYPICAL MISCONCEPTION

Many taxpayers believe tax practitioners spend most of their time preparing tax returns. In reality, providing tax advice that accomplishes the taxpayer's objectives is one of the most important responsibilities of a tax advisor. This latter activity is tax consulting as compared to tax compliance.

Based on his or her research, a tax advisor might recommend to a taxpayer how to structure a transaction or plan an event so as to increase the likelihood that related expenses will be deductible. For example, suppose a taxpayer is assigned a temporary task in a location (City Y) different from the location (City X) of his or her permanent employment. Suppose also that the taxpayer wants to deduct the meal and lodging expenses incurred in City Y as well as the cost of transportation thereto. To do so, the taxpayer must establish that City X is his or her tax home and that he or she temporarily works in City Y. (Section 162 provides that a taxpayer may deduct travel expenses while "away from home" on business. A taxpayer is deemed to be "away from home" if his or her employment at the new location does not exceed one year, i.e., it is "temporary.") Suppose the taxpayer wants to know the tax consequences of his or her working in City Y for ten months and then, within that ten-month period, finding permanent employment in City Y. What is tax research likely to reveal?

Tax research will lead to an IRS ruling stating that, in such circumstances, the employment will be deemed to be temporary until the date on which the realistic expectation about the temporary nature of the assignment changes.[5] After this date, the employment

[5] Rev. Rul. 93-86, 1993-2 C.B. 71.

will be deemed to be permanent, and travel expenses relating to it will be nondeductible. Based on this finding, the tax advisor might advise the taxpayer to postpone his or her permanent job search in City Y until the end of the ten-month period and simply treat his or her assignment as temporary. So doing would lengthen the time he or she is deemed to be "away from home" on business and thus increase the amount of meal, lodging, and transportation costs deductible as travel expenses. The taxpayer should compare the tax savings to any additional personal costs of maintaining two residences.

The Sources of Tax Law

OBJECTIVE 4

Identify the sources of tax law and assess the authoritative value of each

The language of the IRC is general; that is, it prescribes the tax treatment of broad categories of transactions and events. The reason for the generality is that Congress can neither foresee nor provide for every conceivable transaction or event. Even if it could, doing so would render the statute narrow in scope and inflexible in application. Accordingly, interpretations of the IRC—both administrative and judicial—are necessary. Administrative interpretations are provided in Treasury Regulations, revenue rulings, revenue procedures, and several other pronouncements discussed later in this chapter. Judicial interpretations are presented in court opinions. The term *tax law* as used by most tax advisors encompasses administrative and judicial interpretations in addition to the IRC. It also includes the meaning conveyed in reports issued by Congressional committees involved in the legislative process.

THE LEGISLATIVE PROCESS

Tax legislation begins in the House of Representatives. Initially, a tax proposal is incorporated in a bill. The bill is referred to the House Ways and Means Committee, which is charged with reviewing all tax legislation. The Ways and Means Committee holds hearings in which interested parties, such as the Treasury Secretary and IRS Commissioner, testify. At the conclusion of the hearings, the Ways and Means Committee votes to approve or reject the measure. If approved, the bill goes to the House floor where it is debated by the full membership. If the House approves the measure, the bill moves to the Senate where it is taken up by the Senate Finance Committee. Like Ways and Means, the Finance Committee holds hearings in which Treasury officials, tax experts, and other interested parties testify. If the committee approves the measure, the bill goes to the Senate floor where it is debated by the full membership. Upon approval by the Senate, it is submitted to the President for his or her signature. If the President signs the measure, the bill becomes public law. If the President vetoes it, Congress can override the veto by at least a two-thirds majority vote in each chamber.

Generally, at each stage of the legislative process, the bill is subject to amendment. If amended, and if the House version differs from the Senate version, the bill is referred to a House-Senate conference committee.[6] This committee attempts to resolve the differences between the House and Senate versions. Ultimately, it submits a compromise version of the measure to each chamber for its approval. Such referrals are common. For example, in 1998 the House and Senate disagreed over what the taxpayer must do to shift the burden of proof to the IRS. The House proposed that the taxpayer assert a "reasonable dispute" regarding a taxable item. The Senate proposed that the taxpayer introduce "credible evidence" regarding the item. A conference committee was appointed to resolve the differences. This committee ultimately adopted the Senate proposal, which was later approved by both chambers.

ADDITIONAL COMMENT

Committee reports can be helpful in interpreting new legislation because they indicate the intent of Congress. With the proliferation of tax legislation, committee reports have become especially important because the Treasury Department often is unable to draft the needed regulations in a timely manner.

After approving major legislation, the Ways and Means Committee and Senate Finance Committee usually issue official reports. These reports, published by the U.S. Government Printing Office (GPO) as part of the *Cumulative Bulletin* and as separate documents, explain the committees' reasoning for approving (and/or amending) the legislation.[7] In addition, the GPO publishes both records of the committee hearings and transcripts of the floor debates. The records are published as separate House or Senate documents. The transcripts are incorporated in the *Congressional Record* for the day of the

[6] The size of a conference committee can vary. It is made up of an equal number of members from the House and the Senate.

[7] The *Cumulative Bulletin* is described in the discussion of revenue rulings on page C:1-12.

debate. In tax research, these records, reports, and transcripts are useful in deciphering the meaning of the statutory language. Where this language is ambiguous or vague, and the courts have not interpreted it, the documents can shed light on **Congressional intent**, i.e., what Congress *intended* by a particular term, phrase, or provision.

EXAMPLE C:1-4 ▶ In 1998, Congress passed legislation concerning shifting the burden of proof to the IRS. This legislation was codified in Sec. 7491. The question arises as to what constitutes "credible evidence" because the taxpayer must introduce such evidence to shift the burden of proof to the IRS. Section 7491 does not define the term. Because the provision was relatively new, few courts had an opportunity to interpret what "credible evidence" means. In the absence of relevant statutory or judicial authority, the researcher might have looked to the committee reports to ascertain what Congress intended by the term. Senate Report No. 105-174 states that "credible evidence" means evidence of a quality, which, "after critical analysis, the court would find sufficient upon which to base a decision on the issue if no contrary evidence were submitted."[8] This language suggests that Congress intended the term to mean evidence of a kind sufficient to withstand judicial scrutiny. Such a meaning should be regarded as conclusive in the absence of other authority. ◀

THE INTERNAL REVENUE CODE

The IRC, which comprises Title 26 of the United States Code, is the foundation of all tax law. First codified (i.e., organized into a single compilation of revenue statutes) in 1939, the tax law was recodified in 1954. The IRC was known as the Internal Revenue Code of 1954 until 1986, when its name was changed to the Internal Revenue Code of 1986. Whenever changes to the IRC are approved, the old language is deleted and new language added. Thus, the IRC is organized as an integrated document, and a researcher need not read through the relevant parts of all previous tax bills to find the current version of the law. Nevertheless, a researcher must be sure that he or she is working with the law in effect when a particular transaction occurred.

ADDITIONAL COMMENT

The various tax services, discussed later in this chapter, provide IRC histories for researchers who need to work with prior years' tax law.

The IRC contains provisions dealing with income taxes, estate and gift taxes, employment taxes, alcohol and tobacco taxes, and other excise taxes. Organizationally, the IRC is divided into subtitles, chapters, subchapters, parts, subparts, sections, subsections, paragraphs, subparagraphs, and clauses. Subtitle A contains rules relating to income taxes, and Subtitle B deals with estate and gift taxes. A set of provisions concerned with one general area constitutes a subchapter. For example, the topics of corporate distributions and adjustments appear in Subchapter C, and topics relating to partners and partnerships appear in Subchapter K. Figure C:1-2 presents the organizational scheme of the IRC.

An IRC section contains the operative provisions to which tax advisors most often refer. For example, they speak of "Sec. 351 transactions," "Sec. 306 stock," and "Sec. 1231 gains and losses." Although a tax advisor need not know all the IRC sections, paragraphs, and parts, he or she must be familiar with the IRC's organizational scheme to read and interpret it correctly. The language of the IRC is replete with cross-references to titles, paragraphs, subparagraphs, and so on.

EXAMPLE C:1-5 ▶ Section 7701, a definitional section, begins, "When used in this title . . ." and then provides a series of definitions. Because of this broad reference, a Sec. 7701 definition applies for all of Title 26; that is, it applies for purposes of the income tax, estate and gift tax, excise tax, and other taxes governed by Title 26. ◀

EXAMPLE C:1-6 ▶ Section 302(b)(3) allows taxpayers whose stock holdings are completely terminated in a redemption (a corporation's purchase of its stock from one or more of its shareholders) to receive capital gain treatment on the excess of the redemption proceeds over the stock's basis instead of ordinary income treatment on the entire proceeds. Section 302(c)(2)(A) states, "In the case of a distribution described in subsection (b)(3), section 318(a)(1) shall not apply if. . . ." Further, Sec. 302(c)(2)(C)(i) indicates "Subparagraph (A) shall not apply to a distribution to any entity unless. . . ." Thus, in determining whether a taxpayer will receive capital gain treatment in a stock redemption, a tax advisor must be able to locate and interpret various cross-referenced IRC sections, subsections, paragraphs, subparagraphs, and clauses. ◀

[8] S. Rept. No. 105-174, 105th Cong., 1st Sess. (unpaginated) (1998).

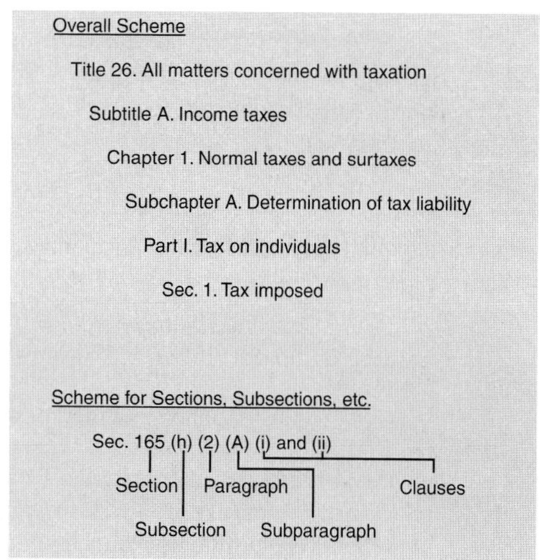

FIGURE C:1-2 ▶ ORGANIZATIONAL SCHEME OF THE INTERNAL REVENUE CODE

TREASURY REGULATIONS

The Treasury Department issues regulations that expound upon the IRC. Treasury Regulations often provide examples with computations that assist the reader in understanding how IRC provisions apply. Treasury Regulations are formulated on the basis of Treasury Decisions (T.D.s). The numbers of the Treasury Decisions that form the basis of a Treasury Regulation usually are found in the notes at the end of the regulation.

Because of frequent IRC changes, the Treasury Department does not always update the regulations in a timely manner. Consequently, when consulting a regulation, a tax advisor should check its introductory or end note to determine when the regulation was adopted. If the regulation was adopted before the most recent revision of the applicable IRC section, the regulation should be treated as authoritative to the extent consistent with the revision. Thus, for example, if a regulation issued before the passage of an IRC amendment specifies a dollar amount, and the amendment changed the dollar amount, the regulation should be regarded as authoritative in all respects except for the dollar amount.

Proposed, Temporary, and Final Regulations. A Treasury Regulation is first issued in proposed form to the public, which is given an opportunity to comment on it. Parties most likely to comment are individual tax practitioners and representatives of organizations such as the American Bar Association, the Tax Division of the AICPA, and the American Taxation Association. The comments may suggest that the proposed rules could affect taxpayers more adversely than Congress had anticipated. In drafting a final regulation, the Treasury Department generally considers the comments and may modify the rules accordingly. If the comments are favorable, the Treasury Department usually finalizes the regulation with minor revisions. If the comments are unfavorable, it usually finalizes the regulation with major revisions or allows the proposed regulation to expire.

Proposed regulations are just that—proposed. Consequently, they carry no more authoritative weight than do the arguments of the IRS in a court brief. Nevertheless, they represent the Treasury Department's official interpretation of the IRC. By contrast, **temporary regulations** are binding on the taxpayer. Effective as of the date of their publication, they often are issued immediately after passage of a major tax act to guide taxpayers and their advisors on procedural or computational matters. Regulations issued as temporary are concurrently issued as proposed. Because their issuance is not preceded by a public comment period, they are regarded as somewhat less authoritative than final regulations.

Once finalized, regulations can be effective the earliest of (1) the date they were filed with the *Federal Register*, a daily publication that contains federal government pronouncements; (2) the date temporary regulations preceding them were first published in the *Federal Register*; or (3) the date on which a notice describing the expected contents of the regulation was issued to the public.[9] For changes to the IRC enacted after July 29, 1996, the Treasury Department generally cannot issue regulations with retroactive effect.

Interpretative and Legislative Regulations. In addition to being officially classified as proposed, temporary, or final, Treasury Regulations are unofficially classified as interpretative or legislative. **Interpretative regulations** are issued under the general authority of Sec. 7805 and, as the name implies, merely make the IRC's statutory language easier to understand and apply. In addition, they often illustrate various computations. **Legislative regulations,** by contrast, arise where Congress delegates its rule-making authority to the Treasury Department. When Congress believes it lacks the expertise necessary to deal with a highly technical matter, it instructs the Treasury Department to set forth substantive tax rules relating to the matter.

Whenever the IRC contains language such as "The Secretary shall prescribe such regulations as he may deem necessary" or "under regulations prescribed by the Secretary," the regulations interpreting the IRC provision are legislative. The consolidated tax return regulations are an example of legislative regulations. In Sec. 1502, Congress delegated to the Treasury Department authority to issue regulations that determine the tax liability of a group of affiliated corporations filing a consolidated tax return. As a precondition to filing such a return, the corporations must consent to follow the consolidated return regulations.[10] Such consent generally precludes the corporations from later arguing in court that the regulatory provisions are invalid.

Authoritative Weight. Final Treasury Regulations are presumed to be valid and have almost the same authoritative weight as the IRC. Despite this presumption, taxpayers occasionally argue that a regulation is invalid and, consequently, should not be followed.

Prior to 2011, courts held interpretive and legislative regulations to different standards, giving more authority to legislative regulations that Congress specifically delegated to the Treasury Department to draft. The difference in authoritative weight largely disappeared, however, in 2011 with the Supreme Court decision in *Mayo Foundation.*[11] Going forward, both types of regulations will have the same authoritative weight and will be overturned only in very limited cases such as when, in the Court's opinion, the regulations exceed the scope of power delegated to the Treasury Department,[12] are contrary to the IRC,[13] or are unreasonable.[14]

KEY POINT

The older a Treasury Regulation becomes, the less likely a court is to invalidate the regulation. The legislative reenactment doctrine holds that if a regulation did not reflect the intent of Congress, lawmakers would have changed the statute in subsequent legislation to obtain their desired objectives.

In assessing the validity of long-standing Treasury Regulations, some courts apply the **legislative reenactment doctrine.** Under this doctrine, a regulation is deemed to receive congressional approval whenever the IRC provision under which the regulation was issued is reenacted without amendment.[15] Underlying this doctrine is the rationale that, if Congress believed that the regulation offered an erroneous interpretation of the IRC, it would have amended the IRC to conform to its belief. Congress's failure to amend the IRC signifies approval of the regulation.[16] This doctrine is predicated on Congress's constitutional authority to levy taxes. This authority implies that, if Congress is dissatisfied with the manner in which either the executive or the judiciary has interpreted the IRC, it can invalidate these interpretations through new legislation.

Question: You are researching the manner in which a deduction is calculated. You consult Treasury Regulations for guidance because the IRC states that the calculation is to be done "in a manner prescribed by the Secretary." After reviewing these authorities, you

[9] Sec. 7805(b).

[10] Sec. 1501.

[11] *Mayo Foundation for Medical Education & Research, et al. v. U.S.*, 107 AFTR 2d 2011-341, 131 S.Ct. 704 (2011).

[12] *McDonald v. CIR*, 56 AFTR 2d 85-5318, 85-2 USTC ¶9494 (5th Cir., 1985).

[13] *Jeanese, Inc. v. U.S.*, 15 AFTR 2d 429, 65-1 USTC ¶9259 (9th Cir., 1965).

[14] *United States v. Vogel Fertilizer Co.*, 49 AFTR 2d 82-491, 82-1 USTC ¶9134 (USSC, 1982).

[15] *United States v. Homer O. Correll*, 20 AFTR 2d 5845, 68-1 USTC ¶9101 (USSC, 1967).

[16] One can rebut the presumption that Congress approved of the regulation by showing that Congress was unaware of the regulation when it reenacted the statute.

conclude that another way of doing the calculation arguably is correct under an intuitive approach. This approach would result in a lower tax liability for the client. Should you follow the Treasury Regulations, or should you use the intuitive approach and argue that the regulations are invalid?

Solution: Because of the language "in a manner prescribed by the Secretary," the Treasury Regulations dealing with the calculation are legislative. Whenever Congress calls for legislative regulations, it explicitly authorizes (directs) the Treasury Department to write the "rules." Thus, a challenge based on the existence of a reasonable alternative method is unlikely to succeed in court. Under the *Mayo Foundation* decision, you should reach the same conclusion even if dealing with an interpretive Treasury Regulation.

ADDITIONAL COMMENT

Citations serve two purposes in tax research: first, they substantiate propositions; second, they enable the reader to locate underlying authority.

Citations. Citations to Treasury Regulations are relatively easy to understand. One or more numbers appear before a decimal place, and several numbers follow the decimal place. The numbers immediately following the decimal place indicate the IRC section being interpreted. The numbers preceding the decimal place indicate the general subject of the regulation. Numbers that often appear before the decimal place and their general subjects are as follows:

Number	*General Subject Matter*
1	Income tax
20	Estate tax
25	Gift tax
301	Administrative and procedural matters
601	Procedural rules

The number following the IRC section number indicates the numerical sequence of the regulation, such as the fifth regulation. No relationship exists between this number and the subsection of the IRC being interpreted. An example of a citation to a final regulation is as follows:

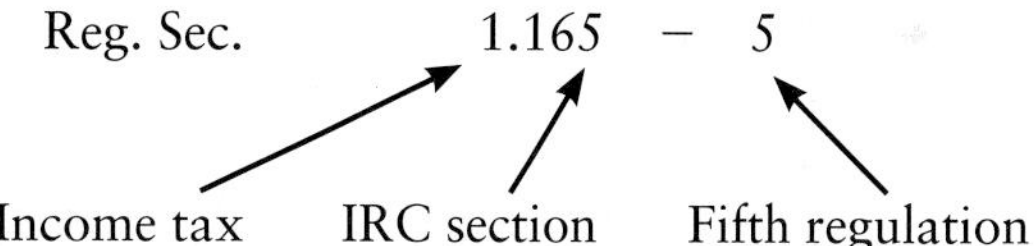

Citations to proposed or temporary regulations follow the same format. They are referenced as Prop. Reg. Sec. or Temp. Reg. Sec. For temporary regulations the numbering system following the IRC section number always begins with the number of the regulation and an upper case T (e.g., -1T).

Section 165 addresses the broad topic of losses and is interpreted by several regulations. According to its caption, the topic of Reg. Sec. 1.165-5 is worthless securities, which also is addressed in subsection (g) of IRC Sec. 165. Parenthetical information following the text of the Treasury Regulation indicates that the regulation was last revised on March 11, 2008, by Treasury Decision (T.D.) 9386. Section 165(g) was last amended in 2000. A researcher must always check when the regulations were last amended and be aware that an IRC change may have occurred after the most recent regulation amendment, potentially making the regulation inapplicable.

When referencing a regulation, the researcher should fine-tune the citation to indicate the precise passage that supports his or her conclusion. An example of such a detailed citation is Reg. Sec. 1.165-5(j), Ex. 2(i), which refers to paragraph (i) of Example 2, found in paragraph (j) of the fifth regulation interpreting Sec. 165.

ADMINISTRATIVE PRONOUNCEMENTS

The IRS interprets the IRC through **administrative pronouncements**, the most important of which are discussed below. After consulting the IRC and Treasury Regulations, tax advisors are likely next to consult these pronouncements.

TYPICAL MISCONCEPTION

Even though revenue rulings do not have the same weight as Treasury Regulations or court cases, one should not underestimate their importance. Because a revenue ruling is the official published position of the IRS, in audits the examining agent will place considerable weight on any applicable revenue rulings.

Revenue Rulings. In **revenue rulings**, the IRS indicates the tax consequences of specific transactions encountered in practice. For example, in a revenue ruling, the IRS might indicate whether the exchange of stock for stock derivatives in a corporate acquisition is tax-free.

The IRS issues more than 50 revenue rulings a year. These rulings do not rank as high in the hierarchy of authorities as do Treasury Regulations or federal court cases. They simply represent the IRS's view of the tax law. Taxpayers who do not follow a revenue ruling will not incur a substantial understatement penalty if they have substantial authority for different treatment.[17] Nonetheless, the IRS presumes that the tax treatment specified in a revenue ruling is correct. Consequently, if an examining agent discovers in an audit that a taxpayer did not adopt the position prescribed in a revenue ruling, the agent will contend that the taxpayer's tax liability should be adjusted to reflect that position.

A revenue ruling appears in the weekly *Internal Revenue Bulletin* (cited as I.R.B.), published by the U.S. Government Printing Office (GPO). Prior to 2009, revenue rulings appeared in the *Cumulative Bulletin* (cited as C.B.), a bound volume issued semiannually by the GPO. An example of a citation to a revenue ruling appearing in the *Cumulative Bulletin* is as follows:

Rev. Rul. 97-4, 1997-1 C.B. 5.

This is the fourth ruling issued in 1997, and it appears on page 5 of Volume 1 of the 1997 *Cumulative Bulletin.* For rulings after 2008, researchers should use citations to the *Internal Revenue Bulletin.* An example of such a citation follows:

Rev. Rul. 2013-8, 2013-15 I.R.B. 763.

For revenue rulings (and other IRS pronouncements) issued after 1999, the full four digits of the year of issuance are set forth in the title. For revenue rulings (and other IRS pronouncements) issued before 2000, only the last two digits of the year of issuance are set forth in the title. The above citation represents the eighth ruling for 2013. This ruling is located on page 763 of the *Internal Revenue Bulletin* for the fifteenth week of 2013. Once a revenue ruling is published in the *Cumulative Bulletin,* only the citation to the *Cumulative Bulletin* should be used. Thus, a citation to the I.R.B. is temporary.

Revenue Procedures. As the name suggests, **revenue procedures** are IRS pronouncements that usually deal with the procedural aspects of tax practice. For example, one revenue procedure deals with the manner in which tip income should be reported. Another revenue procedure describes the requirements for reproducing paper substitutes for informational returns such as Form 1099.

As with revenue rulings, revenue procedures are published in the *Internal Revenue Bulletin* and, prior to 2009, in the *Cumulative Bulletin.* For revenue procedures issued after 2008, the I.R.B. is the final reference. An example of a citation to a revenue procedure appearing in the *Internal Revenue Bulletin* is as follows:

SELF-STUDY QUESTION

Are letter rulings of precedential value for third parties?

ANSWER

No. A letter ruling is binding only on the taxpayer to whom the ruling was issued. Nevertheless, letter rulings can be very useful to third parties because they provide insight as to the IRS's opinion about the tax consequences of various transactions.

Rev. Proc. 2017-4, 2017-1 I.R.B. 146.

This pronouncement is found in the first issue of the *Internal Revenue Bulletin* on page 146. It is the fourth revenue procedure issued in 2017.

In addition to revenue rulings and revenue procedures, the *Cumulative Bulletin* contains IRS notices, as well as the texts of proposed regulations, tax treaties, committee reports, and U.S. Supreme Court decisions.

Letter Rulings. **Letter rulings** are initiated by taxpayers who ask the IRS to explain the tax consequences of a particular transaction.[18] The IRS provides its explanation in the form of a letter ruling, a response personal to the taxpayer requesting an answer. Only the

[17] Chapter C:15 discusses the authoritative support taxpayers and tax advisors should have for positions they adopt on a tax return.

[18] Chapter C:15 further discusses letter rulings.

taxpayer to whom the ruling is addressed may rely on it as authority. Nevertheless, letter rulings are relevant for other taxpayers and tax advisors because they offer insight into the IRS's position on the tax treatment of particular transactions.

Originally the public did not have access to letter rulings issued to other taxpayers. As a result of Sec. 6110, enacted in 1976, letter rulings (with confidential information deleted) are accessible to the general public and have been reproduced by major tax services. An example of a citation to a letter ruling appears below:

Ltr. Rul. 200130006 (July 30, 2001).

The first four digits (two if issued before 2000) indicate the year in which the ruling was made public, in this case, 2001.[19] The next two digits denote the week in which the ruling was made public, here the thirtieth. The last three numbers indicate the numerical sequence of the ruling for the week, here the sixth. The date in parentheses denotes the date of the ruling.

ADDITIONAL COMMENT

A technical advice memorandum is published as a letter ruling. Whereas a taxpayer-requested letter ruling deals with prospective transactions, a technical advice memorandum deals with past or consummated transactions.

Other Interpretations

Technical Advice Memoranda. When the IRS audits a taxpayer's return, the IRS agent might ask the IRS national office for advice on a complicated, technical matter. The national office will provide its advice in a **technical advice memorandum**, released to the public in the form of a letter ruling.[20] Researchers can identify which letter rulings are technical advice memoranda by introductory language such as, "In response to a request for technical advice. . . ." An example of a citation to a technical advice memorandum is as follows:

T.A.M. 9801001 (January 2, 1998).

This citation refers to the first technical advice memorandum issued in the first week of 1998. The memorandum is dated January 2, 1998.

News Releases. If the IRS wants to disseminate information to the general public, it will issue a **news release**. News releases are written in lay terms and are dispatched to thousands of newspapers throughout the country. The IRS, for example, may issue a news release to announce the standard mileage rate for business travel. An example of a citation to a news release is as follows:

I.R. News Release 2012-25 (February 17, 2012).

This citation is to the twenty-fifth news release issued in 2012. The release is dated February 17, 2012.

ADDITIONAL COMMENT

Announcements are used to summarize new tax legislation or publicize procedural matters. Announcements generally are aimed at tax practitioners and are considered to be "substantial authority" [Rev. Rul. 90-91, 1990-2 C.B. 262].

Announcements and Notices. The IRS also disseminates information to tax practitioners in the form of **announcements** and **notices**. These pronouncements generally are more technical than information releases and frequently address current tax developments. After passage of a major tax act, and before the Treasury Department has had an opportunity to issue proposed or temporary regulations, the IRS may issue an announcement or notice to clarify the legislation. The IRS is bound to follow the announcement or notice just as it is bound to follow a revenue procedure or revenue ruling. Examples of citations to announcements and notices are as follows:

Announcement 2007-3, 2007-1 C.B. 376.
Notice 2007-9, 2007-1 C.B. 401.

The first citation is to the third announcement issued in 2007. It can be found on page 376 of the first *Cumulative Bulletin* for 2007. The second citation is to the ninth

---

[19] Sometimes a letter ruling is cited as PLR (private letter ruling) instead of Ltr. Rul.

[20] Technical advice memoranda are discussed further in Chapter C:15.

notice issued in 2007. It can be found on page 401 of the first *Cumulative Bulletin* for 2007. Notices and announcements issued prior to 2009 appear in both the *Internal Revenue Bulletin* and the *Cumulative Bulletin,* but after 2008 they appear only in the *Internal Revenue Bulletin.*

JUDICIAL DECISIONS

Judicial decisions are an important source of tax law. Judges are reputed to be unbiased individuals who decide questions of fact (the existence of a fact or the occurrence of an event) or questions of law (the applicability of a legal principle or the proper interpretation of a legal term or provision). Judges do not always agree on the tax consequences of a particular transaction or event. Therefore, tax advisors often must derive conclusions against a background of conflicting judicial authorities. For example, a U.S. district court might disagree with the Tax Court on the deductibility of an expense. Likewise, one circuit court might disagree with another circuit court on the same issue.

Overview of the Court System. A taxpayer may begin tax litigation in any of three courts: the U.S. Tax Court, the U.S. Court of Federal Claims (formerly the U.S. Claims Court), or U.S. district courts. Court precedents are important in deciding where to begin such litigation (see page C:1-21 for a discussion of precedent). Also important is when the taxpayer must pay the deficiency the IRS contends is due. A taxpayer who wants to litigate either in a U.S. district court or in the U.S. Court of Federal Claims must first pay the deficiency. The taxpayer then files a claim for refund, which the IRS is likely to deny. Following this denial, the taxpayer must petition the court for a refund. If the court grants the taxpayer's petition, he or she receives a refund of the taxes in question plus accrued interest. If the taxpayer begins litigation in the Tax Court, on the other hand, he or she need not pay the deficiency unless and until the court decides the case against him or her. In that event, the taxpayer also must pay interest and penalties.[21] A taxpayer who believes that a jury would be sympathetic to his or her case should litigate in a U.S. district court, the only forum where a jury trial is possible.

SELF-STUDY QUESTION

What are some of the factors that a taxpayer should consider when deciding in which court to file a tax-related claim?

ANSWER

(1) Each court's published precedent pertaining to the issue, (2) desirability of a jury trial, (3) tax expertise of each court, and (4) when the deficiency must be paid.

If a party loses at the trial court level, it can appeal the decision to a higher court. Appeals of Tax Court and U.S. district court decisions are made to the court of appeals for the taxpayer's circuit. The appeals court system is comprised of 11 geographical circuits designated by numbers, the District of Columbia Circuit, and the Federal Circuit.[22] Table C:1-1 shows the states that lie in the various circuits. California, for example, lies in the Ninth Circuit. When referring to these appellate courts, instead of saying, for example, "the Court of Appeals for the Ninth Circuit," one generally says "the Ninth Circuit." All decisions of the U.S. Court of Federal Claims are appealable to one court—the Court of Appeals for the Federal Circuit—irrespective of where the taxpayer resides or does business.[23] The only cases the Federal Circuit hears are those that originate in the U.S. Court of Federal Claims.

The party losing at the appellate level can petition the U.S. Supreme Court to review the case under a **writ of certiorari.** If the Supreme Court agrees to hear the case, it grants certiorari.[24] If it refuses to hear the case, it denies certiorari. In recent years, the Court has granted certiorari in only about six to ten tax cases per year. Figure C:1-3 and Table C:1-2 provide an overview and summary of the court system with respect to tax matters.

ADDITIONAL COMMENT

Because the Tax Court deals only with tax cases, it presumably has a higher level of tax expertise than do other courts. Tax Court judges are appointed by the President, in part, due to their considerable tax experience. The Tax Court typically maintains a large backlog of tax cases, sometimes numbering in the tens of thousands.

The U.S. Tax Court. The U.S. Tax Court was created in 1942 as a successor to the Board of Tax Appeals. It is a court of national jurisdiction that hears only tax-related cases. All taxpayers, regardless of their state of residence or place of business, may litigate in the Tax Court. It has 19 judges, including one chief judge.[25] The President, with the consent of the Senate, appoints the judges for a 15-year term and may reappoint them for an additional

[21] Revenue Procedure 2005-18, 2005-1 C.B. 798, provides procedures for taxpayers to make remittances or apply overpayments to stop the accrual of interest on deficiencies.

[22] The Federal Circuit has nationwide jurisdiction to hear appeals in specialized cases, such as those involving patent laws.

[23] The Court of Claims was reconstituted as the United States Court of Claims in 1982. In 1992, this court was renamed the U.S. Court of Federal Claims.

[24] The granting of certiorari signifies that the Supreme Court is granting an appellate review. The denial of certiorari does not necessarily mean that the Supreme Court endorses the lower court's decision. It simply means the court has decided not to hear the case.

[25] The Tax Court also periodically appoints, depending on budgetary constraints, a number of trial judges and senior judges who hear cases and render decisions with the same authority as the regular Tax Court judges.

▼ TABLE C:1-1
Federal Judicial Circuits

Circuit	States Included in Circuit
First	Maine, Massachusetts, New Hampshire, Rhode Island, Puerto Rico
Second	Connecticut, New York, Vermont
Third	Delaware, New Jersey, Pennsylvania, Virgin Islands
Fourth	Maryland, North Carolina, South Carolina, Virginia, West Virginia
Fifth	Louisiana, Mississippi, Texas
Sixth	Kentucky, Michigan, Ohio, Tennessee
Seventh	Illinois, Indiana, Wisconsin
Eighth	Arkansas, Iowa, Minnesota, Missouri, Nebraska, North Dakota, South Dakota
Ninth	Alaska, Arizona, California, Hawaii, Idaho, Montana, Nevada, Oregon, Washington, Guam, Northern Marina Islands
Tenth	Colorado, Kansas, New Mexico, Oklahoma, Utah, Wyoming
Eleventh	Alabama, Florida, Georgia
D.C.	District of Columbia
Federal	All jurisdictions (for taxpayers appealing from the U.S. Court of Federal Claims)

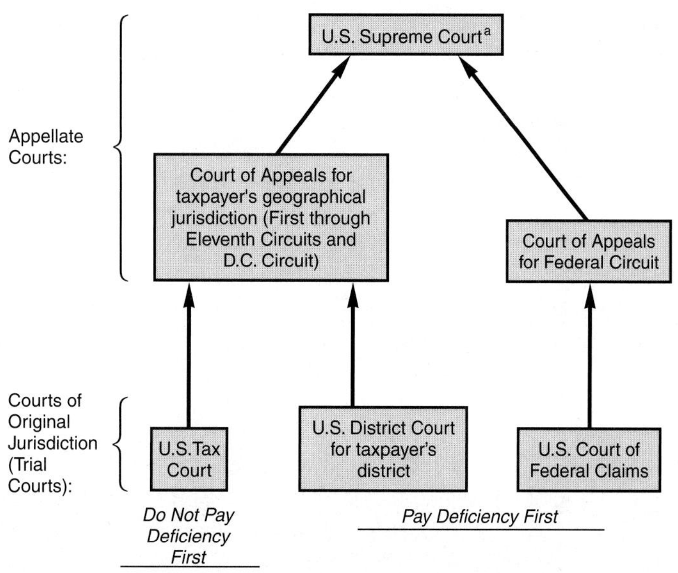

FIGURE C:1-3 ▶ OVERVIEW OF COURT SYSTEM—TAX MATTERS

term. The judges, specialists in tax-related matters, periodically travel to roughly 100 cities throughout the country to hear cases. In most instances, only one judge hears a case.

The Tax Court issues both regular and memorandum (memo) decisions. Generally, the first time the Tax Court decides a legal issue, its decision appears as a **regular decision. Memo decisions,** on the other hand, usually deal with factual variations of previously decided cases. Nevertheless, regular and memo decisions carry the same authoritative weight.

At times, the chief judge determines that a particular case concerns an important issue that the entire Tax Court should consider. In such a situation, the words *reviewed by the court* appear at the end of the majority opinion. Any concurring or dissenting opinions follow the majority opinion. A judge who issues a concurring opinion agrees with the basic outcome of the majority's decision but not with its rationale. A judge who issues a dissenting opinion believes the majority reached an erroneous conclusion.

▼ **TABLE C:1-2**
Summary of Court System—Tax Matters

Court(s) (Number of)	Number of Judges on Each	Personal Jurisdiction	Subject Matter Jurisdiction	Determines Questions of Fact	Trial by Jury	Precedents Followed	Where Opinions Published
U.S. district courts (over 95)	1–28*	Local	General	Yes	Yes	Same court Court for circuit where situated U.S. Supreme Court	*Federal Supplement* *American Federal Tax Reports* *United States Tax Cases*
U.S. Tax Court (1)	19	National	Tax	Yes	No	Same court Court for taxpayer's circuit U.S. Supreme Court	*Tax Court of the U.S. Reports* *CCH Tax Court Memorandum Decisions* *RIA Tax Court Memorandum Decisions*
U.S. Court of Federal Claims (1)	16	National	Claims against U.S. Government	Yes	No	Same court Federal Circuit Court U.S. Supreme Court	*Federal Reporter* (pre-1982) *U.S. Court of Federal Claims* *American Federal Tax Reports* *United States Tax Cases*
U.S. Courts of Appeals (13)	About 20	Regional	General	No	No	Same court U.S. Supreme Court	*Federal Reporter* *American Federal Tax Reports* *United States Tax Cases*
U.S. Supreme Court (1)	9	National	General	No	No	Same court	*U.S. Supreme Court Reports* *Supreme Court Reporter* *United States Reports, Lawyers' Edition* *American Federal Tax Reports* *United States Tax Cases*

*Although the number of judges assigned to each court varies, only one judge hears a case.

Another phrase sometimes appearing at the end of a Tax Court opinion is *Entered under Rule 155*. This phrase signifies that the court has reached a decision concerning the tax treatment of an item but has left computation of the deficiency to the two litigating parties.

SELF-STUDY QUESTION

What are some of the considerations for litigating under the small cases procedure of the Tax Court?

ANSWER

The small cases procedure gives the taxpayer the advantage of having his or her "day in court" without the expense of an attorney. But if the taxpayer loses, the decision cannot be appealed. On the other hand, the IRS also cannot appeal if *it* loses.

Small Cases Procedure. Taxpayers have the option of having their cases heard under the **small cases procedure** of the Tax Court if the amount in controversy on an annual basis does not exceed $50,000.[26] This procedure is less formal than the regular Tax Court procedure, and taxpayers can represent themselves without an attorney.[27] The cases are heard by special commissioners instead of by one of the 19 Tax Court judges. A disadvantage of the small cases procedure for the losing party is that the decision cannot be appealed. The opinions of the commissioners generally are not published and have no precedential value.

Acquiescence Policy. The IRS has adopted a policy of announcing whether, in future cases involving similar facts and similar issues, it will follow federal court decisions that are adverse to it. This policy is known as the IRS **acquiescence policy**. If the IRS wants taxpayers to know that it will follow an adverse decision in future cases involving similar facts and issues, it will announce its "acquiescence" in the decision. Conversely, if it wants taxpayers to know that it will not follow the decision in such future cases, it will announce its "nonacquiescence." The IRS does not announce its acquiescence or nonacquiescence in every decision it loses.

ADDITIONAL COMMENT

The only cases with respect to which the IRS will acquiesce or nonacquiesce are decisions that the government loses. Because the majority of cases, particularly Tax Court cases, are won by the government, the IRS will potentially acquiesce in only a small number of cases.

The IRS publishes its acquiescences and nonacquiescences as "Actions on Decision" first in the *Internal Revenue Bulletin,* then in the *Cumulative Bulletin.* Before 1991, the IRS acquiesced or nonacquiesced in regular Tax Court decisions only. In 1991, it broadened the scope of its policy to include adverse U.S. Claims Court, U.S. district court, and U.S. circuit court decisions.

In cases involving multiple issues, the IRS may acquiesce in some issues but not others. In decisions supported by extensive reasoning, it may acquiesce in the result but not the rationale (*acq. in result*). Furthermore, it may retroactively revoke an acquiescence or nonacquiescence. The footnotes to the relevant announcement in the *Internal Revenue Bulletin* and *Cumulative Bulletin* indicate the nature and extent of IRS acquiescences and nonacquiescences.

These acquiescences and nonacquiescences have important implications for taxpayers. If a taxpayer bases his or her position on a decision in which the IRS has nonacquiesced, he or she can expect an IRS challenge in the event of an audit. In such circumstances, the taxpayer's only recourse may be litigation. On the other hand, if the taxpayer bases his or her position on a decision in which the IRS has acquiesced, he or she can expect little or no challenge. In either case, the examining agent will be bound by the IRS position.

ADDITIONAL COMMENT

If a particular case is important, the chief judge will instruct the other judges to review the case. If a case is reviewed by the entire court, the phrase *reviewed by the court* is inserted immediately after the text of the majority opinion. A reviewed decision provides an opportunity for Tax Court judges to express their dissenting opinions.

Published Opinions and Citations. Regular Tax Court decisions are published by the U.S. Government Printing Office in a bound volume known as the *Tax Court of the United States Reports*. Soon after a decision is made public, Research Institute of America (RIA) and Commerce Clearing House (CCH) each publish the decision in its respective reporter of Tax Court decisions. An official citation to a Tax Court decision is as follows:[28]

MedChem Products, Inc., 116 T.C. 308 (2001).

The citation indicates that this case appears on page 308 in Volume 116 of *Tax Court of the United States Reports* and that the case was decided in 2001.

---

[26] Sec. 7463. The $50,000 amount includes penalties and additional taxes but excludes interest.

[27] Taxpayers also can represent themselves in regular Tax Court proceedings even though they are not attorneys. Where taxpayers represent themselves, the words *pro se* appear in the opinion after the taxpayer's name. The Tax Court is the only federal court before which non-attorneys, including CPAs, may practice.

[28] In a citation to a case decided by the Tax Court, only the name of the plaintiff (taxpayer) is listed. The defendant is understood to be the Commissioner of Internal Revenue whose name usually is not shown in the citation. In cases decided by other courts, the name of the plaintiff is listed first and the name of the defendant second. For non-Tax Court cases, the Commissioner of Internal Revenue is referred to as *CIR* in our footnotes and text.

From 1924 to 1942, regular decisions of the Board of Tax Appeals (predecessor of the Tax Court) were published by the U.S. Government Printing Office in the *United States Board of Tax Appeals Reports*. An example of a citation to a Board of Tax Appeals case is as follows:

J.W. Wells Lumber Co. Trust A., 44 B.T.A. 551 (1941).

This case is found in Volume 44 of the *United States Board of Tax Appeals Reports* on page 551. It is a 1941 decision.

ADDITIONAL COMMENT

Once the IRS has acquiesced in a federal court decision, other taxpayers generally will not need to litigate the same issue. However, the IRS can change its mind and revoke a previous acquiescence or nonacquiescence. References to acquiescences or nonacquiescences in federal court decisions can be found in the citators.

If the IRS has acquiesced or nonacquiesced in a federal court decision, the IRS's action should be denoted in the citation. At times, the IRS will not announce its acquiescence or nonacquiescence until several years after the date of the decision. An example of a citation to a decision in which the IRS has acquiesced is as follows:

Security State Bank, 111 T.C. 210 (1998), *acq.* 2001-1 C.B. xix.

The case appears on page 210 of Volume 111 of the *Tax Court of the United States Reports* and the acquiescence is reported on page xix of Volume 1 of the 2001 *Cumulative Bulletin.* In 2001, the IRS acquiesced in this 1998 decision. A citation to a decision in which the IRS has nonacquiesced is as follows:

Estate of Algerine Allen Smith, 108 T.C. 412 (1997), *nonacq.* 2000-1 C.B. xvi.

KEY POINT

To access all Tax Court cases, a tax advisor must refer to two different publications. The regular opinions appear in the T*ax Court of the United States Reports,* published by the U.S. Government Printing Office, and the memo decisions are published by both RIA (formerly PH) and CCH in their own court reporters.

The case appears on page 412 of Volume 108 of the *Tax Court of the United States Reports*. The nonacquiescence is reported on page xvi of Volume 1 of the 2000 *Cumulative Bulletin.* In 2000, the IRS nonacquiesced in this 1997 decision.

Tax Court memo decisions are not published by the U.S. Government Printing Office. They are, however, published by RIA in *RIA T.C. Memorandum Decisions* and by CCH in *CCH Tax Court Memorandum Decisions.* In addition, shortly after its issuance, an opinion is made available electronically and in loose-leaf form by RIA and CCH in their respective tax services. The following citation is to a Tax Court memo decision:

Edith G. McKinney, 1981 PH T.C. Memo ¶81,181 (T.C. Memo 1981-181), 41 TCM 1272.

ADDITIONAL COMMENT

In its Internet-based tax service (see Page C:1-26), RIA uses a different format for its Tax Court Memorandum Decisions, which in this textbook appear in parentheses after the "official" RIA citation.

McKinney is found at Paragraph 81,181 of Prentice Hall's (now RIA's)[29] 1981 *PH T.C. Memorandum Decisions* reporter, and in Volume 41, page 1272, of CCH's *Tax Court Memorandum Decisions.* The 181 in the PH citation indicates that the case is the Tax Court's 181st memo decision of the year. A more recent citation is formatted in the same way but refers to RIA memo decisions.

Paul F. Belloff, 1992 RIA T.C. Memo ¶92,346 (T.C. Memo 1992-346), 63 TCM 3150.

U.S. District Courts. Each state has at least one U.S. district court, and more populous states have more than one. Each district court is independent of the others and is thus free to issue its own decisions, subject to the precedential constraints discussed later in this chapter. Different types of cases—not just tax-related—are adjudicated in this forum. A district court is the only forum in which the taxpayer may have a jury decide questions of fact. Depending on the circumstances, a jury trial might be advantageous for the taxpayer.[30]

District court decisions are officially reported in the *Federal Supplement* (cited as F. Supp.) published by West®. Some decisions are not officially reported and are referred

[29] Several ownership changes have occurred for publishers of tax service materials. Thomson Reuters added the former Prentice Hall tax materials to the product line of its RIA tax publishing division. RIA and West® are members of Thomson Reuters, Tax and Accounting Division, and CCH is a member of the Wolters Kluwer Tax, Accounting and Legal Division.

[30] Taxpayers might prefer to have a jury trial if they believe a jury will be sympathetic to their case.

to as **unreported decisions**. Decisions by U.S. district courts on the topic of taxation also are published by RIA and CCH in secondary reporters that contain only tax-related opinions. RIA's reporter is *American Federal Tax Reports* (cited as AFTR).[31] CCH's reporter is *U.S. Tax Cases* (cited as USTC). A case not officially reported nevertheless might be published in the AFTR and USTC. An example of a complete citation to a U.S. district court decision is as follows:

> *Alfred Abdo, Jr. v. IRS,* 234 F. Supp. 2d 533, 90 AFTR 2d 2002-7484, 2003-1 USTC ¶50,107 (DC North Carolina, 2002).

ADDITIONAL COMMENT

A citation, at a minimum, should contain the following information: (1) the name of the case, (2) the reporter that publishes the case along with both a volume and page (or paragraph) number, (3) the year the case was decided, and (4) the court that decided the case.

In the example above, the **primary citation** is to the *Federal Supplement*. The case appears on page 533 of Volume 234 of the second series of this reporter. **Secondary citations** are to *American Federal Tax Reports* and *U.S. Tax Cases*. The same case is found in Volume 90 of the second series of the AFTR, page 2002-7484 (meaning page 7484 in the volume containing 2002 cases) and in Volume 1 of the 2003 USTC at Paragraph 50,107. The parenthetical information indicates that the case was decided in 2002 by the U.S. District Court for North Carolina. Because some judicial decisions have greater precedential weight than others (e.g., a Supreme Court decision versus a district court decision), information relating to the identity of the adjudicating court is useful in evaluating the authoritative value of the decision.

ADDITIONAL COMMENT

The U.S. Court of Federal Claims adjudicates claims (including suits to recover federal income taxes) against the U.S. Government. This court usually hears cases in Washington, D.C., but will hold sessions in other locations as the court deems necessary.

U.S. Court of Federal Claims. The U.S. Court of Federal Claims, another court of first instance that addresses tax matters, has nationwide jurisdiction. Originally, this court was called the U.S. Court of Claims (cited as Ct. Cl.), and its decisions were appealable to the U.S. Supreme Court only. In a reorganization, effective October 1, 1982, the reconstituted court was named the U.S. Claims Court (cited as Cl. Ct.), and its decisions became appealable to the Circuit Court of Appeals for the Federal Circuit. In October 1992, the court's name was again changed to the U.S. Court of Federal Claims (cited as Fed. Cl.).

Beginning in 1982, U.S. Claims Court decisions were reported officially in the *Claims Court Reporter,* published by West® from 1982 to 1992.[32] An example of a citation to a U.S. Claims Court decision appears below:

> *Benjamin Raphan v. U.S.,* 3 Cl. Ct. 457, 52 AFTR 2d 83-5987, 83-2 USTC ¶9613 (1983).

The *Raphan* case appears on page 457 of Volume 3 of the *Claims Court Reporter*. Secondary citations are to Volume 52, page 83-5987 of the AFTR, Second Series, and to Volume 2 of the 1983 USTC at Paragraph 9613.

Effective with the 1992 reorganization, decisions of the U.S. Court of Federal Claims are now reported in the *Federal Claims Reporter.* An example of a citation to an opinion published in this reporter is presented below:

> *Jeffrey G. Sharp v. U.S.,* 27 Fed. Cl. 52, 70 AFTR 2d 92-6040, 92-2 USTC ¶50,561 (1992).

The *Sharp* case appears on page 52 of Volume 27 of the *Federal Claims Reporter,* on page 6040 of the 70th volume of the AFTR, Second Series, and at Paragraph 50,561 of Volume 2 of the 1992 USTC reporter. Note that, even though the name of the reporter published by West® has changed, the volume numbers continue in sequence as if no name change had occurred.

---

[31] The *American Federal Tax Reports* (AFTR) is published in two series. The first series, which includes opinions issued up to 1957, is cited as AFTR. The second series, which includes opinions issued after 1957, is cited as AFTR 2d. The *Alfred Abdo, Jr.* decision cited as an illustration of a U.S. district court decision appears in the second *American Federal Tax Reports* series.

[32] Before the creation in 1982 of the U.S. Claims Court (and the *Claims Court Reporter*), the opinions of the U.S. Court of Claims were reported in either the *Federal Supplement* (F. Supp.) or the *Federal Reporter, Second Series* (F.2d). The *Federal Supplement* is the primary source of U.S. Court of Claims opinions from 1932 through January 19, 1960. Opinions issued from January 20, 1960, to October 1982 are reported in the *Federal Reporter, Second Series.*

Circuit Courts of Appeals. Lower court decisions are appealable by the losing party to the court of appeals for the circuit in which the litigation originated. Generally, if the case began in the Tax Court or a U.S. district court, the case is appealable to the circuit for the individual's residence as of the appeal date. For a corporation, the case is appealable to the circuit for the corporation's principal place of business. The Federal Circuit hears all appeals of cases originating in the U.S. Court of Federal Claims.

As mentioned earlier, there are 11 geographical circuits designated by numbers, the District of Columbia Circuit, and the Federal Circuit. In October 1981, the Eleventh Circuit was created by moving Alabama, Georgia, and Florida from the Fifth to a new geographical circuit. The Eleventh Circuit has adopted the policy of following as precedent all decisions of the Fifth Circuit during the time the states currently constituting the Eleventh Circuit were part of the Fifth Circuit.[33]

EXAMPLE C:1-7 ▶ In the current year, the Eleventh Circuit first considered an issue in a case involving a Florida taxpayer. In 1980, the Fifth Circuit had ruled on the same issue in a case involving a Louisiana taxpayer. Because Florida was part of the Fifth Circuit in 1980, under the policy adopted by the Eleventh Circuit, it will follow the Fifth Circuit's earlier decision. Had the Fifth Circuit's decision been rendered in 1982—after the creation of the Eleventh Circuit—the Eleventh Circuit would not have been bound by the Fifth Circuit's decision. ◀

As the later discussion of precedent points out, different circuits may reach different conclusions concerning similar facts and issues.

Circuit court decisions—regardless of topic (e.g., civil rights, securities law, and taxation)—are now reported officially in the *Federal Reporter, Third Series* (cited as F.3d), published by West®. The third series was created in October 1993 after the volume number for the second series reached 999. The primary citation to a circuit court opinion should be to the *Federal Reporter*. Tax decisions of the circuit courts also appear in the *American Federal Tax Reports* and *U.S. Tax Cases*. Below is an example of a citation to a 1994 circuit court decision:

> *Leonard Greene v. U.S.*, 13 F.3d 577, 73 AFTR 2d 94-746, 94-1 USTC ¶50,022 (2nd Cir., 1994).

The *Greene* case appears on page 577 of Volume 13 of the *Federal Reporter, Third Series*. It also is published in Volume 73, page 94-746 of the AFTR, Second Series, and in Volume 1, Paragraph 50,022, of the 1994 USTC. The parenthetical information indicates that the Second Circuit decided the case in 1994. (A *Federal Reporter, Second Series* reference is found in footnote 33 of this chapter.)

ADDITIONAL COMMENT

A judge is not required to follow judicial precedent beyond his or her jurisdiction. Thus, the Tax Court, the U.S. district courts, and the U.S. Court of Federal Claims are not required to follow the others' decisions, nor is a circuit court required to follow the decision of a different circuit court.

U.S. Supreme Court. Whichever party loses at the appellate level can request that the U.S. Supreme Court hear the case. The Supreme Court, however, hears very few tax cases. Unless the circuits are divided on the tax treatment of an item, or the issue is deemed to be of great significance, the Supreme Court probably will not hear the case.[34] Supreme Court decisions are the law of the land and take precedence over all other court decisions, including the Supreme Court's earlier decisions. As a practical matter, a Supreme Court interpretation of the IRC is almost as authoritative as an act of Congress. If Congress does not agree with the Court's interpretation, it can amend the IRC to achieve a different result and has in fact done so on a number of occasions. If the Supreme Court declares a tax statute to be unconstitutional, the statute is invalid.

All Supreme Court decisions, regardless of subject, are published in the *United States Supreme Court Reports* (cited as U.S.) by the U.S. Government Printing Office, the *Supreme Court Reporter* (cited as S. Ct.) by West®, and the *United States Reports, Lawyers' Edition* (cited as L. Ed.) by LexisNexis®. In addition, the AFTR and USTC

[33] *Bonner v. City of Prichard*, 661 F.2d 1206 (11th Cir., 1981).

[34] *Vogel Fertilizer Co. v. U.S.*, 49 AFTR 2d 82-491, 82-1 USTC ¶9134 (USSC, 1982), is an example of a case the Supreme Court heard to settle a split in judicial authority. The Fifth Circuit, the Tax Court, and the Court of Claims had reached one conclusion on an issue, while the Second, Fourth, and Eighth Circuits had reached another.

reporters published by RIA and CCH, respectively, contain Supreme Court decisions concerned with taxation. An example of a citation to a Supreme Court opinion appears below:

> *Boeing Company v. U.S.,* 537 U.S. 437, 91 AFTR 2d 2003-1088, 2003-1 USTC ¶50,273 (USSC, 2003).

According to the primary citation, this case appears in Volume 537, page 437, of the *United States Supreme Court Reports*. According to the secondary citation, it also appears in Volume 91, page 2003-1088, of the AFTR, Second Series, and in Volume 1, Paragraph 50,273, of the 2003 USTC.

Table C:1-3 provides a summary of how the IRC, court decisions, revenue rulings, revenue procedures, and other administrative pronouncements should be cited. Primary citations are to the reporters published by West® or the U.S. Government Printing Office, and secondary citations are to the AFTR and USTC.

SELF-STUDY QUESTION

Is it possible for the Tax Court to intentionally issue conflicting decisions?

ANSWER

Yes. If the Tax Court issues two decisions that are appealable to different circuit courts and these courts have previously reached different conclusions on the issue, the Tax Court follows the respective precedent in each circuit and issues conflicting decisions. This is a result of the *Golsen* Rule.

Precedential Value of Various Decisions.

Tax Court. The Tax Court is a court of national jurisdiction. Consequently, it generally rules uniformly for all taxpayers, regardless of their residence or place of business. It follows U.S. Supreme Court decisions and its own earlier decisions. It is not bound by cases decided by the U.S. Court of Federal Claims or a U.S. district court, even if the district court has jurisdiction over the taxpayer.

In 1970, the Tax Court adopted what is known as the *Golsen* Rule.[35] Under this rule, the Tax Court departs from its general policy of adjudicating uniformly for all taxpayers and instead follows the decisions of the court of appeals to which the case in question is appealable. Stated differently, the *Golsen* Rule mandates that the Tax Court rule consistently with decisions of the court for the circuit where the taxpayer resides or does business.

EXAMPLE C:1-8 ▶ In the year in which an issue was first litigated, the Tax Court decided that an expenditure was deductible. The government appealed the decision to the Tenth Circuit Court of Appeals and won a reversal. This is the only appellate decision regarding the issue. If and when the Tax Court addresses this issue again, it will hold, with one exception, that the expenditure is deductible. The exception applies to taxpayers in the Tenth Circuit. Under the *Golsen* Rule, these taxpayers will be denied the deduction. ◀

U.S. District Court. Because each U.S. district court is independent of the other district courts, the decisions of each have precedential value only within its own jurisdiction (i.e., only with respect to subsequent cases brought before that court). District courts must follow decisions of the U.S. Supreme Court, the circuit court to which the case is appealable, and the district court's own earlier decisions regarding similar facts and issues.

EXAMPLE C:1-9 ▶ The U.S. District Court for Rhode Island, the Tax Court, and the Eleventh Circuit have decided cases involving similar facts and issues. Any U.S. district court within the Eleventh Circuit must follow that circuit's decision in future cases involving similar facts and issues. Likewise, the U.S. District Court for Rhode Island must decide such cases consistently with its previous decision. Tax Court decisions are not binding on the district courts. Thus, all district courts other than the one for Rhode Island and those within the Eleventh Circuit are free to decide such cases independently. ◀

U.S. Court of Federal Claims. In adjudicating a case, the U.S. Court of Federal Claims must rule consistently with U.S. Supreme Court decisions, decisions of the Circuit Court of Appeals for the Federal Circuit, and its own earlier decisions, including those rendered when the court had a different name. It need not follow decisions of other circuit courts, the Tax Court, or U.S. district courts.

---

[35] The *Golsen* Rule is based on the decision in *Jack E. Golsen,* 54 T.C. 742 (1970).

▼ **TABLE C:1-3**
Summary of Tax-Related Primary Sources—Statutory and Administrative

Source Name	Publisher	Materials Provided	Citation Example
U.S. Code, Title 26	Government Printing Office	Internal Revenue Code	Sec. 441(b)
Code of Federal Regulations, Title 26	Government Printing Office	Treasury Regulations (final)	Reg. Sec. 1.461-1(c)
		Treasury Regulations (temporary)	Temp. Reg. Sec. 1.62-1T(e)
Internal Revenue Bulletin	Government Printing Office	Treasury Regulations (proposed)	Prop. Reg. Sec. 1.671-1(h)
		Treasury decisions	T.D. 8756 (January 13, 1998)
		Revenue rulings	Rev. Rul. 2009-33, 2009-40 I.R.B. 447
		Revenue procedures	Rev. Proc. 2009-52, 2009-49 I.R.B. 744
		Committee reports	S.Rept. No. 105-33, 105th Cong., 1st Sess., p. 308 (1997)
		Public laws	P.L. 105-34, Sec. 224(a), enacted August 6, 1997
		Announcements	Announcement 2007-3, 2007-4 I.R.B. 376
		Notices	Notice 2009-21, 2009-13 I.R.B. 724
Cumulative Bulletin	Government Printing Office	Treasury Regulations (proposed)	Prop. Reg. Sec. 1.671-1(h)
		Treasury decisions	T.D. 8756 (January 12, 1998)
		Revenue rulings	Rev. Rul. 84-111, 1984-2 C.B. 88
		Revenue procedures	Rev. Proc. 77-28, 1977-2 C.B. 537
		Committee reports	S.Rept. No. 105-33, 105th Cong., 1st Sess., p. 308 (1997)
		Public laws	P.L. 105-34, Sec. 224(a), enacted August 6, 1997
		Announcements	Announcement 2006-8, 2006-1 C.B. 344
		Notices	Notice 88-74, 1988-2 C.B. 385

Summary of Tax-Related Primary and Secondary Sources—Judicial

Reporter Name	Publisher	Decisions Published	Citation Example
U.S. Supreme Court Reports	Government Printing Office	U.S. Supreme Court	*Boeing Company v. U.S.*, 537 U.S. 437 (2003)
Supreme Court Reports	Thomson Reuters/West	U.S. Supreme Court	*Boeing Company v. U.S.*, 123 S. Ct. 1099 (2003)
Federal Reporter (1st–3rd Series)	Thomson Reuters/West	U.S. Court of Appeal Pre-1982 Court of Claims	*Leonard Greene v. U.S.*, 13 F.3d 577 (2nd Cir., 1994)
Federal Supplement Series	Thomson Reuters/West	U.S. District Court	*Alfred Abdo, Jr. v. IRS*, 234 F. Supp. 2d 553 (DC North Carolina, 2002)
U.S. Court of Federal Claims	Thomson Reuters/West	Court of Federal Claims	*Jeffery G. Sharp v. U.S.*, 27 Fed. Cl. 52 (1992)
Tax Court of the U.S. Reports	Government Printing Office	U.S. Tax Court regular	*Security State Bank*, 111 T.C. 210 (1998), acq. 2001-1 C.B. xix
Tax Court Memorandum Decisions	Wolters Kluwer/CCH	U.S. Tax Court memo	*Paul F. Belloff*, 63 TCM 3150 (1992)
RIA Tax Court Memorandum Decisions	Thomson Reuters/RIA	U.S. Tax Court memo	*Paul F. Belloff*, 1992 RIA T.C. Memo ¶92,346 (T.C. Memo 1992-346)
American Federal Tax Reports	Thomson Reuters/RIA	Tax: all federal courts except Tax Court	*Boeing Company v. U.S.*, 91 AFTR 2d 2003-1 (USSC, 2003)
U.S. Tax Cases	Wolters Kluwer/CCH	Tax: all federal courts except Tax Court	*Ruddick Corp. v. U.S.*, 81-1 USTC ¶9343 (Ct. Cls., 1981)

EXAMPLE C:1-10 ▶ Assume the same facts as in Example C:1-9. In a later year, a case involving similar facts and issues is heard by the U.S. Court of Federal Claims. This court is not bound by precedents set by any of the other courts. Thus, it may reach a conclusion independently of the other courts. ◀

Circuit Courts of Appeals. A circuit court is bound by U.S. Supreme Court decisions and its own earlier decisions. If neither the Supreme Court nor the circuit in question has already decided an issue, the circuit court has no precedent that it must follow, regardless of whether other circuits have ruled on the issue. In such circumstances, the circuit court is said to be writing on a clean slate. In rendering a decision, the judges of that court may adopt another circuit's view, which they are likely to regard as relevant.

EXAMPLE C:1-11 ▶ Assume the same facts as in Example C:1-9. Any circuit other than the Eleventh would be writing on a clean slate if it adjudicated a case involving similar facts and issues. After reviewing the Eleventh Circuit's decision, another circuit might find it relevant and rule in the same way. ◀

In such a case of "first impression," when the court has had no precedent on which to base a decision, a tax practitioner might look at past opinions of the court to see which other judicial authority the court has found to be "persuasive."

Forum Shopping. Not surprisingly, courts often disagree on the tax treatment of the same item. This disagreement gives rise to differing precedents within the various jurisdictions (what is called a "split in judicial authority"). Because taxpayers have the flexibility of choosing where to file a lawsuit, these circumstances afford them the opportunity to **forum shop.** Forum shopping involves choosing where among the courts to file a lawsuit based on differing precedents.

An example of a split in judicial authority concerned the issue of when it became too late for the IRS to question the tax treatment of items that "flowed through" an S corporation's return to a shareholder's return. The key question was this: if the time for assessing a deficiency (limitations period) with respect to the corporation's, but not the shareholder's, return had expired, was the IRS precluded from collecting additional taxes from the shareholder? In *Kelley,*[36] the Ninth Circuit Court of Appeals ruled that the IRS would be barred from collecting additional taxes from the shareholder if the limitations period for the *S corporation's* return had expired. In *Bufferd,*[37] *Fehlhaber,*[38] and *Green,*[39] three other circuit courts ruled that the IRS would be barred from collecting additional taxes from the shareholder if the limitations period for the *shareholder's* return had expired. The Supreme Court affirmed the *Bufferd* decision,[40] establishing that the statute of limitations for the shareholder's return governed. This action brought about certainty and uniformity within the judicial system.

Dictum. At times, a court may comment on an issue or a set of facts not central to the case under review. A court's remark not essential to the determination of a disputed issue, and therefore not binding authority, is called *dictum.* An example of dictum is found in *Central Illinois Public Service Co.*[41] In this case, the U.S. Supreme Court addressed whether lunch reimbursements received by employees constitute wages subject to withholding. Justice Blackman remarked in passing that earnings in the form of interest, rents, and dividends are not wages. This remark is dictum because it is not essential to the determination of whether lunch reimbursements are wages subject to withholding. Although not authoritative, dictum may be cited by taxpayers to bolster an argument in favor of a particular tax result.

[36] *Daniel M. Kelley v. CIR,* 64 AFTR 2d 89-5025, 89-1 USTC ¶9360 (9th Cir., 1989).
[37] *Sheldon B. Bufferd v. CIR,* 69 AFTR 2d 92-465, 92-1 USTC ¶50,031 (2nd Cir., 1992).
[38] *Robert Fehlhaber v. CIR,* 69 AFTR 2d 92-850, 92-1 USTC ¶50,131 (11th Cir., 1992).
[39] *Charles T. Green v. CIR,* 70 AFTR 2d 92-5077, 92-2 USTC ¶50,340 (5th Cir., 1992).
[40] *Sheldon B. Bufferd v. CIR,* 71 AFTR 2d 93-573, 93-1 USTC ¶50,038 (USSC, 1993).
[41] *Central Illinois Public Service Co. v. CIR,* 41 AFTR 2d 78-718, 78-1 USTC ¶9254 (USSC, 1978).

Question: You have been researching whether an amount received by your new client can be excluded from her gross income. The IRS is auditing the client's prior year tax return, which another firm prepared. In a similar case decided a few years ago, the Tax Court allowed an exclusion, but the IRS nonacquiesced in the decision. The case involved a taxpayer in the Fourth Circuit. Your client is a resident of Maine, which is in the First Circuit. Twelve years ago, in a case involving another taxpayer, the federal court for the client's district ruled that this type of receipt is not excludable. No other precedent exists. To sustain an exclusion, must your client litigate? Explain. If your client litigates, in which court of first instance should she begin her litigation?

Solution: Because of its nonacquiescence, the IRS is likely to challenge your client's tax treatment. Thus, she may be compelled to litigate. She would not want to litigate in her U.S. district court because it would be bound by its earlier decision, which is unfavorable to taxpayers generally. A good place to begin would be the Tax Court because it is bound by appellate court, but not district court, decisions and because of its earlier pro-taxpayer position. No one can predict how the U.S. Court of Federal Claims would rule because no precedent that it must follow exists.

ADDITIONAL COMMENT

A tax treaty carries the same authoritative weight as a federal statute (IRC). A tax advisor should be aware of provisions in tax treaties that will affect a taxpayer's worldwide tax liability.

TAX TREATIES

The United States has concluded **tax treaties** with numerous foreign countries. These treaties address the alleviation of double taxation and other matters. A tax advisor exploring the U.S. tax consequences of a U.S. corporation's operations in another country should determine whether a treaty between that country and the United States exists. If one does, the tax advisor should ascertain the applicable provisions of the treaty. (See Chapter C:16 for a more extensive discussion of treaties.)

KEY POINT

Tax articles can be used to help *find* answers to tax questions. Where possible, the underlying statutory, administrative, or judicial sources referenced in the tax article should be cited as authority and not the author of the article. The courts and the IRS will place little, if any, reliance on mere editorial opinion.

TAX PERIODICALS

Tax periodicals assist the researcher in tracing the development of, and analyzing tax law. These periodicals are especially useful when they discuss the legislative history of a recently enacted IRC statute that has little or no administrative or judicial authority on point.

Tax experts write articles on landmark court decisions, proposed regulations, new tax legislation, and other matters. Frequently, those who write articles of a highly technical nature are attorneys, accountants, or professors. Among the periodicals that provide in-depth coverage of tax-related matters are the following:

The Journal of Taxation
The Tax Adviser
Practical Tax Strategies
Taxes—The Tax Magazine
Tax Law Review
Tax Notes
Corporate Taxation
Business Entities
Real Estate Taxation
Estate Planning

The first six journals are generalized; that is, they deal with a variety of topics. As their titles suggest, the next four are specialized; they deal with specific subjects. All these publications (other than *Tax Notes*, which is published weekly) are published monthly, bi-monthly, or quarterly. Daily newsletters, such as the *Daily Tax Report*, published by Bloomberg BNA in print and electronic formats, are used by tax professionals when they need updates more timely than can be provided by monthly or quarterly publications.

Tax periodicals and tax services are secondary authorities. The IRC, Treasury Regulations, IRS pronouncements, and court opinions are primary authorities. In presenting research results, the tax advisor should always cite primary authorities.

TAX SERVICES

OBJECTIVE 5

Consult tax services to research an issue

Various publishers provide multivolume commentaries on the tax law in what are familiarly referred to as **tax services**. Researchers often consult tax services at the beginning of the research process because a tax service helps identify the tax authorities pertaining to a particular tax issue. The actual tax authorities (e.g., IRC, Treasury Regulations, IRS pronouncements, and court cases), and not the tax services, are generally cited as support for a particular tax position. The services are available in print form via the publishers and electronic form via the Internet. (See further discussion at "The Internet as a Research Tool" later in this chapter). Although each major tax service is an outstanding resource, significant differences exist in the content and organizational scheme from one publisher to the next. For example, each service has its own special features and editorial approach to tax issues along with a great deal of proprietary content. The best way to acquaint oneself with the various tax services and the advantages and disadvantages of each is to use them in researching hypothetical or actual problems.

Organizationally, tax services fall into two types: annotated and topical (although this distinction has become somewhat blurred in the Internet version of these services). An **annotated tax service** is organized by IRC section. The IRC-arranged subdivisions of this service are likely to encompass several topics. The annotations accompany editorial commentaries and include digests or summaries of IRS pronouncements and court opinions that interpret a particular IRC section. They are classified by subtopic and cite pertinent primary authorities. A **topical tax service**, on the other hand, is organized by broad topic, including income taxes, estate and gift taxes, and excise taxes. The topically arranged subdivisions of this service are likely to encompass several IRC sections.

Annotated tax services include the *United States Tax Reporter* and the *Standard Federal Income Tax Reporter* services, both of which are organized by IRC section. Many tax advisors find these reporters easy to use because of their extensive indexing system. Topical tax services include RIA's *Federal Tax Coordinator 2d* and Bloomberg BNA's *Tax Management Portfolios*. *Tax Management Portfolios* are popular with many tax advisors because they are very readable yet still provide a comprehensive discussion of a broad range of tax issues. Each portfolio (e.g., Passive Loss Rules, Portfolio 549) covers a particular topic in great detail. However, because the published portfolios do not cover all areas of the tax law, another service may be necessary to supplement the gaps in a portfolio's coverage. Table C:1-4 summarizes the organization and key features of the major tax services.

▼ TABLE C:1-4
Summary of Key Features of Tax Services

Name	Publisher	Organization	Key Features
United States Tax Reporter	Thomson Reuters/RIA	IRC section number	• Editorial commentary • Index and findings list • Annotations
Standard Federal Income Tax Reporter	Wolters Kluwer/CCH	IRC section number	• Editorial commentary • Index and findings list • Annotations
Federal Tax Coordinator 2d	Thomson Reuters/RIA	Tax topic (income tax by topic, estate and gift taxes, excise taxes)	• Commentary organized by topic with references to primary authority and tabbed access to IRC and Treasury Regulations.
Tax Management Portfolios	Bloomberg BNA	U.S. income, foreign income, state tax, estate and gift tax	• Over 400 specialized booklets with extensive commentary by topic, heavily footnoted and referenced to primary authority.

THE INTERNET AS A RESEARCH TOOL

OBJECTIVE 6

Apply the basics of Internet-based tax research

Internet databases are rapidly replacing print-based services as the principal source of tax related information. These databases encompass not only the IRC, Treasury Regulations, court cases, state laws, and other primary authorities, but also citators and secondary sources such as tax service reporters, treatises, journals, and newsletters. The principal advantages of using Internet-based tax services are ease and speed of access. These services eliminate the need for searching through several volumes of text, the need for consulting numerous cumulative supplements, and the time required to regularly update a print-based library. In addition, Internet based research tools put a vast amount of information in the hands of a tax practitioner without the cost and space requirements of a well equipped print-based tax library.

ADDITIONAL COMMENT

To apply the online research tools discussed in this chapter, textbook users must have access to the described Internet-based tax services at their institution.

Because of these advantages, the Internet has become the principal medium for conveying tax related information to professionals. The most widely used Internet-based research services are RIA's Checkpoint™ (hereafter CHECKPOINT) and CCH IntelliConnect™. Westlaw®[42] and LexisNexus are online legal research services that are predominately used by legal professionals.[43] This chapter discusses the use of internet-based tax services in general and uses CHECKPOINT for illustrative purposes. Similar features will exist for other major tax services.

The tax services include a variety of libraries that will vary by vendor (e.g., CCH or RIA) and by subscription type (limited or comprehensive). The core of any tax service covers federal taxes but also can cover state and local taxes, estate planning, payroll taxes, pensions, international tax, and financial planning. The federal libraries will include text of the IRC, Treasury Regulations, IRS pronouncements, court opinions, and other primary sources. In addition, the Internet services will include a section containing daily updates for important tax developments in the subscribed practice areas as well as the annotated and/or topical tax services discussed previously, such as the *United States Tax Reporter* (CCH) and the *Federal Tax Coordinator 2d* (RIA). State and local libraries will include tax reporters for all 50 states as well as various multi-state tax guides that provide useful state-by-state comparisons for selected state tax topics (e.g., combined reporting and apportionment methods). Other libraries, such as those covering estate and gift taxes, pensions, and payroll taxes, provide detailed information for professionals heavily engaged in these specialized areas of tax practice.

Libraries and databases in Internet services can be searched in three basic ways:

- By keyword
- By citation
- By index

EXAMPLE C:1-12 ▶ Rhonda Researcher's client is a real estate developer and wants to exchange an office building for a residential condominium in the same town. The client wants to know if he can structure the transaction in a tax advantaged way. Rhonda immediately recognizes the situation as a potential like-kind exchange of real property. Therefore, she undertakes a keyword search using the term *like-kind exchange* to quickly uncover potentially applicable documents. She also knows that Sec. 1031 is the relevant IRC section and can search the IRC or Treasury Regulations by citation. On the other hand, if she were unfamiliar with the topic, she could employ several other options. For example, she may browse the index, which is arranged alphabetically by topic. The index entries under "like-kind exchange" direct Rhonda to a number of entries potentially applicable to the transaction. ◀

Most tax professionals conduct tax research using the keyword and citation methods. We discuss these two methods in more detail below.

[42] Westlaw® is owned by Thomson Reuters.

[43] The research products discussed in this section (e.g., RIA Checkpoint, CCH IntelliConnect™, Westlaw®, and LexisNexus) generally are available only to paid subscribers.

KEYWORD SEARCHES

Searching tax services by keyword is relatively simple, particularly if the researcher is familiar with the Internet. The first step is to select which source (e.g., IRC or editorial materials) to search, perform an initial keyword search, and refine the results after the initial query. The researcher can choose to search across any combination of the available databases. The CHECKPOINT Federal databases include primary sources such as the Internal Revenue Code, Treasury Regulations, and Federal Tax Cases along with editorial databases such as RIA's *Federal Tax Coordinator 2d*. Deciding which database to include in the search depends partly on the expected complexity of the research question and on the researcher's familiarity with the topic.

The search engines within the services look for the terms selected and many variations of the terms. For example, the search for *auto* will return documents with auto, car, automobile, motor vehicle, passenger vehicle, sedan, and others.[44] Searches will include both singular and plural variations. Any document with the term or terms is returned and ranked by best match according to the search. If two terms are used, the best matches generally are documents where the terms are close together. Choosing effective search terms is critical to success. The search must be broad enough to include relevant documents but not so broad to include hundreds or thousands of documents unlikely to be on point.

For example, if the researcher selects the database containing court cases, the term *property exchange* returns thousands of results that have both the words *property* and *exchange* somewhere in the document. Clearly, this outcome is too broad for a researcher just beginning his or her research. Fortunately, several methods of narrowing the search exist. For example, the keyword search "property exchange" that uses quotation marks around the search phrase will return documents only with that exact phrase. Thus, quotation marks should be used sparingly and only when the researcher knows the precise phrase. Using Boolean connectors is helpful as well. These connectors force the search engine to narrow the search based on the parameters set. Table C:1-5 provides a partial list of connectors available in CHECKPOINT.

Another way to narrow a search is to focus on terms unique to the research question at hand. The goal is to identify tax related terms likely to appear only in relevant tax

▼ TABLE C:1-5
Connectors Used in CHECKPOINT

Connector	Description	Examples
&, and	Retrieves documents with both terms.	property & exchange
|, or	Retrieves documents with either term.	property | exchange
^, not	Retrieves documents with one term but not the other.	property ^ exchange
/n	Retrieves documents in which the first term is separated from the second term by no more than n number of words.	property /5 exchange Locates property within 5 words of exchange
/s	Retrieves documents that contain the first term within 20 words of the second term (or within the same sentence for RIA).	property /s exchange
/p	Retrieves documents that contain the first term within 80 words of the second term (or within the same paragraph for RIA).	property /p exchange
" "	Exact phrase.	"property exchange"
*	Keyword variation.	Deprecia* returns depreciation, depreciate, depreciated, depreciating
?	Keyword variation.	Advis?r returns advisor and adviser

44 Tax services provide a thesaurus tool, which can identify synonyms and suggest alternative terms related to search terms used by the researcher. The search engine automatically searches for synonyms unless the researcher restricts the search to specific terms using Boolean connectors or quotation marks. For example, a search for the specific phrase "automobile depreciation" will not return documents that refer to *auto*, *car*, or *vehicle*.

authorities. For example, stamps are a type of collectible, but the term also will appear in documents discussing taxation of distilled spirits, food stamps, and store stamps and coupons. The researcher should begin the search with limiting terms such as *collectible* rather than the broader term *stamps*. Also, researchers with a good working knowledge of the IRC quickly learn that using IRC sections in search terms is a great way to obtain relevant documents. Browsing the index containing editorial content can identify helpful keywords.

Searching using key words is a skill that improves with practice. Researchers becoming familiar with using the databases will learn to craft search terms that include the most relevant elements of the question at hand. Once the researcher finds a document on point, the information within that document often can be used to narrow future searches. The search can be repeated by adding terms, or the documents returned originally can be searched using a new set of terms. Also, the "search within results" feature offered by major tax services is helpful when the search returns too many documents. However, if searches by keyword search do not return the desired results, other options exist.

SEARCH BY CITATION

Often the desired document is a specific IRC section, Treasury Regulation, court case, IRS pronouncement, or other document. If so, tax services offer searches by specific citation. Researchers must be careful to use exact citations using this tool because close matches will not return the desired document.

Within tax services, the citation search tools provide dedicated boxes in which to type the specific type of document requested. For example, to search for IRC Sec. 267, the researcher simply types 267 in the box labeled Current Code in CHECKPOINT under the "Find by Citation" link. Specific boxes also exist for various Treasury Regulations, court decisions, revenue rulings, revenue procedures, and other IRS pronouncements.

NONCOMMERCIAL INTERNET SERVICES

Many noncommercial institutions, such as governments and universities, allow access to their tax-related databases via the Internet. In "tax-surfing" the Internet, the researcher might first visit the IRS site located at *www.irs.gov*. Although oriented to the layman, this site contains a wealth of information useful to the tax professional. Such information includes guidelines for electronic filing, IRS forms and instructions, the full text of Treasury Regulations, and recent issues of the *Internal Revenue Bulletin*. Other useful sites include those maintained by the Library of Congress at *www.loc.gov* and the U.S. Government Publishing Office Federal Digital System at *www.gpo.gov/fdsys/*. From these sites, the researcher can retrieve the text of recent court opinions, tax legislation, committee reports, state and federal tax laws, and much more.

An excellent gateway for starting tax related research is the Tax, Accounting, and Payroll Sites Directory at *www.taxsites.com*, maintained by AccountantsWorld, LLC. This site provides hundreds of hyperlinks to federal, state, and international tax law and tax form databases. Instrumental in financial accounting searches is the Electronic Data Gathering, Analysis, and Retrieval (EDGAR) site at *www.sec.gov/edgar.shtml*. EDGAR is a document filing and retrieval service sponsored by the U.S. Securities and Exchange Commission (SEC). It provides access to the full text of documents filed with the SEC by publicly traded companies. These documents include annual financial statements on Form 10-K, quarterly financial statements on Form 10-Q, proxy statements, and prospectuses. The EDGAR database extends from January 1994 to the present and is accessible by company name, central index key, document file number, and keyword.

CITATORS

OBJECTIVE 7

Use a citator to assess tax authorities

Citators serve two functions. First, they trace the judicial history of a particular case (e.g., if the case under analysis is an appeals court decision, the citator indicates the lower court that heard the case and whether the Supreme Court reviewed the case). Second, they list other authorities (e.g., cases and IRS pronouncements) that cite the case or authority in question. These listed authorities are called *citing cases* or *citing rulings*. The judicial history also indicates whether the case is affirmed, reversed or remanded.[45]

Because tax law relies heavily on precedent, the citator provides an index of citing cases and rulings that help the researcher determine the strength of the case or ruling he or she is evaluating. The citator gives full citations for the citing case and lists where the citing cases can be found. It is important to note that the same case may have as many as three decisions (i.e., lower court, court of appeals, and Supreme Court) with each listing having its own list of citing cases. Therefore, if a citing case cites only the Supreme Court decision, the citator will list it only under the Supreme Court cite. The citator allows the researcher to enter case names or case citations. The discussion in this section focuses on the electronic version of the citators, although print versions also exist.

The basic function of a citator is to provide the history of each authority and list cases and pronouncements that have cited the authority. Also, the citator often provides additional information about the citing case, showing whether the citing authorities comment favorably or unfavorably on the cited case or whether they can be distinguished from the cited case.[46]

In addition to tax cases, the citator evaluates revenue rulings and other IRS pronouncements and lists any status changes. Before relying on a revenue ruling or pronouncement, a researcher must confirm that the pronouncement reflects the current position of the IRS. For example, a revoked ruling is one in which the ruling is no longer correct and the correct position is being stated in the new ruling. The IRS does not remove the old ruling from the *Internal Revenue Bulletin* or *Cumulative Bulletin*, but the old ruling does not have authority regarding a transaction occurring after the revocation. Thus, failure to confirm its status could result in an incorrect conclusion. Table C:1-6 provides a list of terms the IRS uses to describe changes in the status of a ruling.

▼ TABLE C:1-6
Terms to Describe Status Changes to IRS Rulings

Term	Description of Term
Amplified	No change in the prior published position has occurred, but the prior position is extended to cover a variation of the fact situation previously addressed.
Clarified	Language used in a prior published position is being made clear because the previous language has caused or could cause confusion.
Distinguished	The ruling mentions a prior ruling but points out an essential difference between the two rulings.
Modified	The substance of a previously published ruling is being changed, but the prior ruling remains in effect.
Obsoleted	A previously published ruling is no longer determinative with respect to future transactions, e.g., because laws or regulations have changed, or the substance of the ruling has been adopted into regulations.
Revoked	A previously published ruling has been determined to be incorrect, and the correct position is being stated in the new ruling.
Superseded	The new ruling merely restates the substance of a previously published ruling or series of rulings.
Supplemented	The ruling expands a previous ruling, e.g., by adding items to a list.
Suspended	The previously published ruling will not be applied pending some future action, such as the issuance of new or amended regulations.

Source: Appendices in IRS Internal Revenue Bulletins.

[45] If a case is *affirmed*, the decision of the lower court is upheld. *Reversed* means the higher court invalidated the decision of the lower court because it reached a conclusion different from that derived by the lower court. *Remanded* signifies that the higher court sent the case back to the lower court with instructions to address matters consistent with the higher court's ruling.

[46] When a court distinguishes the facts of one case from those of an earlier case, it suggests that its departure from the earlier decision is justified because the facts of the two cases are different.

USING THE CITATOR

Internet-based versions of the citators are easier to use than print-based citators. For example, assume the researcher is currently reading *Leonarda C. Diaz v. Commissioner of Internal Revenue*, 70 TC 1067 (1978). The researcher can click on the citator, and the service opens up a new tab with a summary of activity of the case. The information provided indicates that the *Diaz* case was first decided by the Tax Court (i.e., TC), and then by the Second Circuit Court of Appeals (i.e., CA-2). It shows that the Second Circuit affirmed (upheld) the Tax Court's decision. Cases underneath the Second Circuit decision cite the *Diaz* decision and might be useful for the researcher to better understand the impact of the case. Cases listed beneath the Tax Court decision cite the Tax Court's opinion.

PROFESSIONAL GUIDELINES FOR TAX SERVICES

OBJECTIVE 8

Describe the professional guidelines that CPAs in tax practice should follow

Professional guidelines for tax services are contained in both government-imposed and professional-imposed tax standards. The following sections briefly describe two types of guidelines—Treasury Department ***Circular 230*** (Rev. 6-2014) and the American Institute of Certified Public Accountants (AICPA) ***Statements on Standards for Tax Services (SSTSs)***. A fuller discussion of these standards appears in Chapter C:15.

TREASURY DEPARTMENT *CIRCULAR 230*

Circular 230 sets forth rules to practice before the Internal Revenue Service and pertains to certified public accountants, attorneys, enrolled agents, and other persons representing taxpayers before the IRS. It presents the duties and restrictions relating to such practice and prescribes sanctions and disciplinary proceedings for violating these regulations.

Circular 230 rules, however, are not ethical standards. Instead, the document focuses on the right to represent clients before the IRS. These standards differ from the AICPA's SSTSs in the following ways:

- They apply only to federal tax issues and not state authorities.
- They generally apply only to federal income tax practice.
- They do not provide the depth of guidance found in the SSTSs.
- They give the government the authority to impose monetary penalties for violations of the rules.

Circular 230 provides guidelines for written advice to taxpayers. In June 2014, the IRS substantially revised and simplified the rules and eliminated the distinction between covered opinions and other written advice. Under the new rules, all written advice is held to a "reasonable practitioner standard" that will vary based on the nature and extent of the advice. An email to a client answering a routine tax question will be held to a different standard than will an opinion on the tax effects of a complex transaction. The written advice rules do not apply to training or educational presentations but do apply to marketing and sales presentations.

For all written advice, the practitioner is expected to base the advice on reasonable assumptions, consider relevant facts and circumstances, identify the facts relevant to the advice, be properly skeptical of representations by the taxpayer and others, relate applicable law and authority to the facts, and not base an opinion on the chances that a transaction will or will not be identified by IRS and subject to audit. The revised Section 10.37 of *Circular 230* does note that the IRS representative will consider the "additional risk" associated with opinions related to tax shelters.

AICPA'S STATEMENTS ON TAX STANDARDS

Tax advisors confronted with ethical issues frequently turn to a professional organization for guidance. Although the guidelines set forth by such organizations are not *legally* enforceable, they carry significant moral weight, and may be cited in a negligence lawsuit as the proper "standard of care" for tax practitioners. They also may provide grounds for the termination or suspension of one's professional license. One such set of guidelines is the *Statements on Standards for Tax Services* (SSTSs),[47] issued by the American Institute of Certified Public Accountants (AICPA) and reproduced in Appendix E.

The SSTSs provide an ethical framework to govern the normative relationship between a tax advisor and his or her client, where, unlike an auditor, a tax advisor acts as the client's advocate. Thus, his or her primary duty is to the client, not the IRS. In fulfilling this duty, the advisor is bound by the highest standards of care. The most recent version of the SSTSs includes seven standards that provide guidance for AICPA members in their professional tax practice.

SSTS No. 1—Tax Return Positions. Tax professionals often provide tax advice in situations where the authority is unclear or evolving. Frequently this advice involves recommending positions that could be reversed upon audit. This statement describes the minimum level of confidence a CPA must achieve to recommend a tax return position to a taxpayer. Members first must determine and comply with all standards imposed by the various taxing authorities. Regardless of those standards, a member should not recommend a position unless he or she has a good faith belief that the position has a "realistic possibility" of being sustained administratively or judicially on its merits if challenged. Members are not permitted to take the probability of audit into account.

If the position does not meet the realistic probability standard, a member still may recommend a tax return position if he or she concludes that the position has a "reasonable basis" and the position is properly disclosed. When recommending a tax return position and when preparing or signing a return on which a tax return position is taken, a member should, when relevant, advise the taxpayer regarding potential penalty consequences of such tax return position and the opportunity, if any, to avoid such penalties through disclosure. The member also may consider any GAAP requirements to disclose aggressive tax positions under the portion of Accounting Standards Codification 740 formerly known as FIN 48.

The standard highlights the dual responsibility of the member. The U.S. tax system can function only when taxpayers file "true, correct, and complete" returns, but taxpayers also have no obligation to pay more in tax than they legally owe. The tax professional's duty is to meet his or her responsibilities to both the tax system and the taxpayer client.

SSTS No. 2—Answers to Questions on Returns. Return preparers often must sign a declaration that the return is "true, correct, and complete." A member should make a reasonable effort to obtain from the taxpayer the information necessary to provide appropriate answers to all questions on a tax return before signing as preparer. However, in certain circumstances, questions or information applicable to the taxpayer may be omitted. Reasonable grounds include the following situations:

- The omitted information is not readily available or is immaterial and has little effect on taxable income or loss or the tax liability.
- The meaning of the question as it relates to the taxpayer is uncertain.
- The requested information is voluminous, in which case the taxpayer can attach a statement indicating that the requested information will be supplied upon request.

[47] AICPA, *Statements on Standards for Tax Services*, 2009, effective January 1, 2010.

SSTS No. 3—Certain Procedural Aspects of Preparing Returns. Tax returns are based on information provided by the client. This statement sets forth the applicable standards for members concerning this information. Specifically, in preparing or signing a return, members are not required to examine or verify a client's supporting data. A member may rely on information supplied by the taxpayer unless the information appears to be incorrect, incomplete, inconsistent, or unreasonable under the circumstances. However, if the applicable law or regulations impose a specific record keeping requirement to claim a deduction, the member should inquire and satisfy himself or herself that the required records do exist.

Members are specifically encouraged to make use of a taxpayer's returns for one or more prior years in preparing the current return, whenever feasible. The practice should help avoid the omission or duplication of items and provide a basis for the treatment of similar or related transactions.

SSTS No. 4—Use of Estimates. For various reasons, precise information about an amount required on a tax return might not be available at the time the tax return is prepared. For example, the taxpayer might not have a record of small transactions or might be missing certain records. In such cases, a member may advise on estimates used in the preparation of the tax return, but the taxpayer has the responsibility to provide the estimated data. Appraisals and valuations are not considered estimates.

If estimates are used, they generally need not be labeled as estimates, but they should not be presented in a manner that provides a misleading impression about the degree of factual accuracy. However, disclosure that estimates were used should be made in some unusual situations, including:

- A taxpayer has died or is ill at the time the return is prepared.
- A taxpayer has not received a schedule K-1 at the time the tax return is to be filed.
- Litigation is pending that affects the return.
- Fire, computer failure, or a natural disaster has destroyed the relevant records.

Notwithstanding this statement, the tax practitioner may not use estimates when such use is implicitly prohibited by the IRC. For example, Sec. 274(d) disallows deductions for certain expenses (e.g., meals and entertainment) unless the taxpayer can substantiate the expenses with adequate records or sufficient corroborating information. The documentation requirement effectively precludes the taxpayer from estimating such expenses and the practitioner from using such estimates.

SSTS No. 5—Departure from a Position Previously Concluded in an Administrative Proceeding or Court Decisions. Members can take positions that differ from a position determined in an administrative proceeding with respect to the taxpayer's prior return (such as an IRS audit, IRS appeals conference, or a court decision.) Departure might be warranted because of a change in the law or regulations, or favorable court decisions. In any event, if the member can otherwise meet the standards of SSTS No. 1, departure from previous positions is permissible.

SSTS No. 6—Knowledge of Error: Return Preparation and Administrative Proceedings. For purposes of this standard, the definition of an error has the common meaning, including a mathematical error, but the definition also encompasses any position that does not meet the standards of SSTS No. 1. A position also qualifies as an error if it met the standard when a return was originally filed but no longer does because of a retroactive legislative or legal proceeding. An error for this purpose does not include immaterial items.

A member should inform the taxpayer promptly upon becoming aware of (1) an error in a previously filed return, (2) an error in a return that is the subject of an administrative proceeding (e.g., an IRS audit or appeals conference), or (3) a taxpayer's failure to file a required return. A member should advise the taxpayer of the potential consequences of the error and recommend corrective measures to be taken. This advice can be given orally.

The member is not obligated to inform the taxing authority of an error and, in fact, may not do so without the taxpayer's permission except when required by law.

However, if the taxpayer requests that a member prepare the current year's return and the taxpayer has not taken appropriate action to correct an error in a prior year's return, the member should consider whether to withdraw from preparing the return and whether to continue a professional or employment relationship with the taxpayer.

The standard recognizes that conflicts can arise between the member's interests and those of the client. For example, withdrawal from an engagement could have an adverse impact on the taxpayer. In some situations, the member should consult his or her own legal counsel before deciding on recommendations to the taxpayer and whether to continue the engagement. In situations involving potential fraud or criminal charges, the member should advise the client to consult with an attorney before taking any action.

SSTS No. 7—Form and Content of Advice to Taxpayers. A member should use professional judgment to ensure that tax advice provided to a taxpayer reflects competence and appropriately serves the taxpayer's needs. The advice can be communicated in writing or orally. When communicating tax advice to a taxpayer in writing, a member should comply with relevant taxing authorities' standards applicable to written tax advice. A member should use professional judgment about any need to document oral advice.

In deciding on the form of advice provided to a taxpayer, a member should consider factors such as:

- The importance of the transaction and the amounts involved
- The technical complexity involved
- The existence of authorities and precedents
- The tax sophistication of the taxpayer
- The need to seek other professional advice
- The potential penalty consequences of a tax return position and whether any penalties can be avoided through disclosure

This statement implies that practitioner-taxpayer dealings should not be casual, non-consensual, or open ended. Rather, they should be professional, contractual, and definite. Oral advice may be appropriate in routine matters, but written communications are recommended in important, complicated, or significant dollar value transactions.

In addition to these obligations, the tax advisor has a strict duty of confidentiality to the client. Although not encompassed under the SSTSs, this duty is implied in the accountant client privilege. (For a discussion of this privilege, see Chapter C:15.)

? STOP & THINK

Question: As described in the Stop & Think box on pages C:1-10 and C:1-11, you are researching the manner in which a deduction is calculated. The IRC states that the calculation is to be made "in a manner prescribed by the Secretary." After studying the IRC, Treasury Regulations, and committee reports, you conclude that another way of doing the calculation is arguably correct under an intuitive approach. This approach would result in a lower tax liability for the client. According to the *Statements on Standards for Tax Services*, may you take a position contrary to final Treasury Regulations based on the argument that the regulations are not valid?

Solution: You should not take a position contrary to the Treasury Regulations unless you have a "good-faith belief that the position has a realistic possibility of being sustained administratively or judicially on its merits." However, you can take a position that does not meet the above standard, provided you adequately disclose the position, and the position has a reasonable basis. Whether or not you have met the standard depends on all the facts and circumstances. Chapter C:15 discusses tax return preparer positions contrary to Treasury Regulations.

WHAT WOULD YOU DO IN THIS SITUATION?

Regal Enterprises and Macon Industries, unaffiliated corporations, have hired you to prepare their respective income tax returns. In preparing Regal's return, you notice that Regal has claimed a depreciation deduction for equipment purchased from Macon on February 22 at a cost of $2 million. In preparing Macon's return, you notice that Macon has reported sales proceeds of $1.5 million from the sale of equipment to Regal on February 22. One of the two figures must be incorrect. How do you proceed to correct it? Hint: See SSTS No. 3 in Appendix E.

SAMPLE WORK PAPERS AND CLIENT LETTER

OBJECTIVE 9

Prepare work papers and communicate to clients

Appendix A presents a set of sample work papers, including a draft of a client letter and a memo to the file. The work papers indicate the issues to be researched, the authorities addressing the issues, and the researcher's conclusions concerning the appropriate tax treatment, with rationale therefor.

The format and other details of work papers differ from firm to firm. The sample in this text offers general guidance concerning the content of work papers. In practice, work papers may include less detail.

PROBLEM MATERIALS

Note: To complete the online research problems for this chapter, textbook users must have access to an Internet-based service.

DISCUSSION QUESTIONS

C:1-1 Explain the difference between closed-fact and open-fact situations.

C:1-2 According to the AICPA's *Statements on Standards for Tax Services,* what duties does the tax practitioner owe the client?

C:1-3 Explain what is encompassed by the term *tax law* as used by tax advisors.

C:1-4 The U.S. Government Printing Office publishes both hearings on proposed legislation and committee reports. Distinguish between the two.

C:1-5 Explain how committee reports can be used in tax research. What do they indicate?

C:1-6 A friend notices that you are reading the Internal Revenue Code of 1986. Your friend inquires why you are consulting a 1986 publication, especially when tax laws change so frequently. What is your response?

C:1-7 Does Title 26 contain statutory provisions dealing only with income taxation? Explain.

C:1-8 Refer to IRC Sec. 301.
a. Which subsection discusses the general rule for the tax treatment of a property distribution?
b. Where should one look for exceptions to the general rule?
c. What type of Treasury Regulations would relate to subsection (e)?

C:1-9 Why should tax researchers note the date on which a Treasury Regulation was adopted?

C:1-10 a. Distinguish between proposed, temporary, and final Treasury Regulations.
b. Distinguish between interpretative and legislative Treasury Regulations.

C:1-11 In 2011, there was a change in the authoritative weight of interpretive versus legislative regulations. Briefly explain what changed and why.

C:1-12 Explain the legislative reenactment doctrine.

C:1-13 a. Discuss the authoritative weight of revenue rulings.

b. As a practical matter, what consequences are likely to ensue if a taxpayer does not follow a revenue ruling and the IRS audits his or her return?

C:1-14 a. In which courts may litigation dealing with tax matters begin?
b. Discuss the factors that might be considered in deciding where to litigate.
c. Describe the appeals process in tax litigation.

C:1-15 May a taxpayer appeal a case litigated under the Small Cases Procedure of the Tax Court?

C:1-16 Explain whether the following decisions are of the same precedential value: (1) Tax Court regular decisions, (2) Tax Court memo decisions, and (3) decisions under the Small Cases Procedures of the Tax Court.

C:1-17 Does the IRS acquiesce in decisions of U.S. district courts?

C:1-18 The decisions of which courts are reported in the AFTR? In the USTC?

C:1-19 Why do some revenue ruling citations refer to the *Internal Revenue Bulletin* (I.R.B.) and others to a *Cumulative Bulletin* (C.B.)?

C:1-20 Explain the *Golsen* Rule. Give an example of its application.

C:1-21 Assume that the only precedents relating to a particular issue are as follows:

Tax Court—decided for the taxpayer
Eighth Circuit Court of Appeals—decided for the taxpayer (affirming the Tax Court)
U.S. District Court for Eastern Louisiana—decided for the taxpayer
Fifth Circuit Court of Appeals—decided for the government (reversing the U.S. District Court of Eastern Louisiana)

a. Discuss the precedential value of the foregoing decisions for your client, who is a California resident.
b. If your client, a Texas resident, litigates in the Tax Court, how will the court rule? Explain.

C:1-22 Which official publication(s) contain(s) the following:
a. Transcripts of Senate floor debates
b. IRS announcements
c. Tax Court regular opinions
d. Treasury decisions
e. U.S. district court opinions
f. Technical advice memoranda

C:1-23 Under what circumstances might a tax advisor find the provisions of a tax treaty useful?

C:1-24 What two functions does a citator serve?

C:1-25 Name three primary sources of authority that tax professionals should check against the citator before relying on those sources for important matters.

C:1-26 List three methods of searching the major tax service databases.

C:1-27 Use any major tax service to answer the following questions:
a. What are the principal primary sources?
b. What are the principal secondary sources?

C:1-28 Compare the features of the computerized tax services with those of Internet sites maintained by noncommercial institutions. What are the relative advantages and disadvantages of each? Could the latter sites serve as a substitute for a commercial tax service?

C:1-29 According to the *Statements on Standards for Tax Services,* what belief should a CPA have before taking a pro-taxpayer position on a tax return?

C:1-30 List an advisor's duties that are excluded under the AICPA's *Statements on Standards for Tax Services.*

C:1-31 List three requirements that apply to written advice under Treasury Department *Circular 230.*

C:1-32 Explain how Treasury Department *Circular 230* differs from the AICPA's *Statements on Standards for Tax Services.*

PROBLEMS

C:1-33 *Interpreting the IRC.* Under a divorce agreement executed in the current year, an ex-wife receives from her former husband cash of $25,000 per year for eight years. The agreement does not explicitly state that the payments are excludable from gross income.
a. Does the ex-wife have gross income? If so, how much?
b. Is the former husband entitled to a deduction? If so, is it for or from AGI?
Refer only to the IRC in answering this question. Start with Sec. 71.

C:1-34 *Interpreting the IRC.* Refer to Sec. 385 and answer the questions below.
a. Whenever Treasury Regulations are issued under this section, what type are they likely to be: legislative or interpretative? Explain.
b. Assume Treasury Regulations under Sec. 385 have been finalized. Will they be relevant to estate tax matters? Explain.

C:1-35 *Using IRS Rulings.* Locate PLR 8733007 and Rev. Rul. 81-219.
a. Briefly summarize the tax issue and conclusion of each ruling.
b. Under what circumstances can a researcher rely on the private letter ruling?
c. Under what circumstances can a researcher rely on the revenue ruling?

C:1-36 *Using Treasury pronouncements.* Which IRC section(s) does Rev. Rul. 2001-29 interpret? (Hint: consult the official pronouncement of the IRS.)

C:1-37 *Using a Major Tax Service for a Keyword Search.* The objective is to locate a general overview of available home office deductions. On the main research tab, select the *United States Tax Reporter—Explanations* database. How many results does the search return for each search term if the terms and connectors option is selected?
a. Search term: home office deduction.
b. Search term: "home office" deduction.
c. Search term: "home office" /5 deduction.

C:1-38 *Using a Major Tax Service for a Citation Search.* The objective is to locate a general overview of available home office deductions. You have previously researched the issue and know that Sec. 280A is the primary authority for this issue. In the Keyword Search box, enter 280A and check the IRS Rulings and Releases database and answer the following questions.
a. How many results for Revenue Rulings does the search return for the search term: 280A?
b. Using the search within results function, use the new term: home office. How many results does the search return?
c. Does using the search within results function improve your results? Explain why.

C:1-39 *Determining Acquiescence.*
a. What official action (acquiescence or nonacquiescence) did the IRS Commissioner take regarding the 1985 Tax Court decision in *John McIntosh*, 85 T.C. 31 (1985)? (Hint: Consult Actions on Decisions.)
b. Did this action concern *all* issues in the case? If not, explain. (Before answering this question, consult the headnote to the court opinion.)

C:1-40 *Determining Acquiescence.*
a. What original action (acquiescence or nonacquiescence) did the IRS Commissioner take regarding the 1952 Tax Court decision in *Streckfus Steamers, Inc.*, 19 T.C.1 (1952)? (Hint: Consult Actions on Decisions.)
b. Was the action complete or partial?
c. Did the IRS Commissioner subsequently change his mind? If so, when?

C:1-41 *Determining Acquiescence.*
a. What original action (acquiescence or nonacquiescence) did the IRS Commissioner take regarding the 1982 Tax Court decision in *Doyle, Dane, Bernbach, Inc.*, 79 T.C. 101 (1982)? (Hint: Consult Actions on Decisions.)
b. Did the IRS Commissioner subsequently change his mind? If so, when?

C:1-42 *Evaluating a Case.* Look up *James E. Threlkeld*, 87 T.C. 1294 (1988) and answer the questions below.
a. Was the case reviewed by the court? If so, was the decision unanimous? Explain.
b. Was the decision entered under Rule 155?
c. Consult a citator. Was the case reviewed by an appellate court? If so, which one?

C:1-43 *Evaluating a Case.* Look up *Bush Brothers & Co.*, 73 T.C. 424 (1979) and answer the questions below.
a. Was the case reviewed by the court? If so, was the decision unanimous? Explain.
b. Was the decision entered under Rule 155?
c. Consult a citator. Was the case reviewed by an appellate court? If so, which one?

C:1-44 *Writing Citations.* Provide the proper citations (including both primary and secondary citations where applicable) for the authorities listed below. (For secondary citations, reference both the AFTR and USTC.)
a. *National Cash Register Co.*, a 6th Circuit Court decision
b. *Thomas M. Dragoun v. CIR*, a Tax Court memo decision
c. *John M. Grabinski v. U.S.*, a U.S. district court decision
d. *John M. Grabinski v. U.S.*, an Eighth Circuit Court decision
e. *Rebekah Harkness*, a 1972 Court of Claims decision
f. *Hillsboro National Bank v. CIR*, a Supreme Court decision
g. Rev. Rul. 78-129

C:1-45 *Writing Citations.* Provide the proper citations (including both primary and secondary citations where applicable) for the authorities listed below. (For secondary citations, reference both the AFTR and USTC.)

a. Rev. Rul. 99-7
b. *Frank H. Sullivan,* a Board of Tax Appeals decision
c. *Tate & Lyle, Inc.,* a 1994 Tax Court decision
d. *Ralph L. Rogers v. U.S.,* a U.S. district court decision
e. *Norman Rodman v. CIR,* a Second Circuit Court decision

C:1-46 *Interpreting Citations.* Indicate which courts decided the cases cited below. Also indicate on which pages and in which publications the authority is reported.

a. *Lloyd M. Shumaker v. CIR,* 648 F.2d 1198, 48 AFTR 2d 81-5353 (9th Cir., 1981)
b. *Xerox Corp. v. U.S.,* 14 Cl. Ct. 455, 88-1 USTC ¶9231 (1988)
c. *Real Estate Land Title & Trust Co. v. U.S.,* 309 U.S. 13, 23 AFTR 816 (USSC, 1940)
d. *J. B. Morris v. U.S.,* 441 F. Supp. 76, 41 AFTR 2d 78-335 (DC TX, 1977)
e. Rev. Rul. 83-3, 1983-1 C.B. 72
f. *Malone & Hyde, Inc. v. U.S.,* 568 F.2d 474, 78-1 USTC ¶9199 (6th Cir., 1978)

C:1-47 *Using a Tax Service.* Use the index of any tax service to locate authorities dealing with the deductibility of the cost of a facelift.

a. Cite the authority you find.
b. List the primary IRC section cited as authority.
c. May a taxpayer deduct the cost of a facelift paid in the current year? Explain.

C:1-48 *Using a Tax Service.* Using any tax service, locate Reg. Sec. 1.302-1. Does this Treasury Regulation reflect recent amendments to the IRC? Explain.

C:1-49 *Using a Tax Service.* Using the index of any tax service, search the editorial materials to locate authorities addressing whether termite damage constitutes a casualty loss.

a. Cite the authority you found.
b. Cite at least two primary authorities.

C:1-50 *Using a Tax Service.*

a. Using any tax service, locate Sec. 303. This section states that Sec. 303(a) applies only if the stock in question meets a certain percentage test. What is the applicable percentage?
b. Locate Reg. Sec. 1.303-2(a) in the same service. Does this Treasury Regulation reflect recent amendments to the IRC with respect to the percentage test addressed in Part a? Explain.

C:1-51 *Using a Tax Service.* Using the BNA tax service, identify the number of the BNA portfolio for the following subjects.

a. Innocent spouse relief.
b. Accounting methods.
c. Involuntary conversions.
d. IRAs.
e. Deductibility of legal and accounting fees, bribes, and illegal payments.

C:1-52 *Using a Keyword Search.* Using a keyword search of editorial materials in any tax service, locate authorities dealing with the deductibility of the cost of work clothing by a firefighter. List a revenue ruling addressing this question.

C:1-53 *Using a Citator.* Trace *Biltmore Homes, Inc.,* a 1960 Tax Court memo decision, in the citator.

a. According to the citator, how many times has the Tax Court decision been cited by other courts?
b. How many issues did the lower court address in its opinion? (Hint: Refer to the case headnote numbers.)
c. Did an appellate court review the case? If so, which one?

C:1-54 *Using a Citator.* Trace *Stephen Bolaris,* 776 F.2d 1428, in the citator.

a. According to the citator, how many times has the Ninth Circuit's decision been cited?
b. Did the decision address more than one issue? Explain.
c. Was the decision ever cited unfavorably? Explain.

C:1-55 *Interpreting a Case.* Using any tax service, refer to the *Holden Fuel Oil Company*, RIA T.C. Memo ¶72,045 (T.C. Memo 1972-45), 31 TCM 184.
a. In which year was the case decided?
b. What controversy was litigated?
c. Who won the case?
d. Was the decision reviewed at the lower court level?
e. Was the decision appealed?
f. Has the decision been cited in other cases?

C:1-56 *Internet Research.* Access the IRS Internet site at *www.irs.gov* and answer the following questions:
a. How does one file a tax return electronically?
b. How can the taxpayer transmit funds electronically?
c. What are the advantages of electronic filing?

C:1-57 *Internet Research.* Access the IRS Internet site at *www.irs.gov* and indicate the titles of the following IRS forms:
a. Form 4506
b. Form 973
c. Form 8725

C:1-58 *Internet Research.* Access the Federation of Tax Administrators Internet site at *www.taxadmin.org/state-tax-forms* and indicate the titles of the following state tax forms and publications:
a. Minnesota Form M-100
b. Illinois Individual Schedule CR
c. North Carolina Form D-403

C:1-59 *Internet Research.* Access the Urban Institute and Brookings Institution Tax Policy Center at *taxpolicycenter.org*. On the home page, search for *state individual income tax rates* and locate the Tax Policy Center's latest summary of each state's rates. Researchers also can locate the file by looking under the TAX FACTS tab and then the *State* tab, *Main Features of State Tax Systems*.
a. How many states do not have a state individual income tax?
b. How many states tax only interest and dividends for individuals?
c. What is the top marginal individual income tax rate in Oregon?
d. Of those that do impose an income tax, which state's top marginal rate is lowest?

COMPREHENSIVE PROBLEM

C:1-60 Your client, a physician, recently purchased a yacht on which he flies a pennant with a medical emblem on it. He recently informed you that he purchased the yacht and flies the pennant to advertise his occupation and thus attract new patients. He has asked you if he may deduct as ordinary and necessary business expenses the costs of insuring and maintaining the yacht. In search of an answer, consult the editorial materials in any tax service. Explain the steps taken to find your answer.

TAX STRATEGY PROBLEM

C:1-61 Your client, Home Products Universal (HPU), distributes home improvement products to independent retailers throughout the country. Its management wants to explore the possibility of opening its own home improvement centers. Accordingly, it commissions a consulting firm to conduct a feasibility study, which ultimately persuades HPU to expand into retail sales. The consulting firm bills HPU $150,000, which HPU deducts on its current year tax return. The IRS disputes the deduction, contending that, because the cost relates to entering a new business, it should be capitalized. HPU's management, on the other hand, firmly believes that, because the cost relates to expanding HPU's existing business, it should be deducted. In contemplating legal action against the IRS, HPU's management considers the state of judicial precedent: The federal court for HPU's district has ruled that the cost of expanding from distribution into retail sales should be capitalized. The appellate court for HPU's circuit has stated in *dictum* that, although in some circumstances switching from product distribution to product sales entails entering a new trade or business, improving customer access to one's existing products generally does not. The

Federal Circuit Court has ruled that wholesale distribution and retail sales, even of the same product, constitute distinct businesses. In a case involving a taxpayer from another circuit, the Tax Court has ruled that such costs invariably should be capitalized. HPU's Chief Financial Officer approaches you with the question, "In which judicial forum should HPU file a lawsuit against the IRS: (1) U.S. district court, (2) the Tax Court, or (3) the U.S. Court of Federal Claims?" What do you tell her?

CASE STUDY PROBLEM

C:1-62 A client, Mal Manley, fills out his client questionnaire for the previous year and on it provides information for the preparation of his individual income tax return. The IRS has never audited Mal's returns. Mal reports that he made over 100 relatively small cash contributions totaling $24,785 to charitable organizations. In the last few years, Mal's charitable contributions have averaged about $15,000 per year. For the previous year, Mal's adjusted gross income was roughly $350,000, about a 10% increase from the year before.

Required: Applying *Statements on Standards for Tax Services* No. 3, determine whether you can accept at face value Mal's information concerning his charitable contributions. Now assume that the IRS recently audited Mal's tax return for two years ago and denied 75% of that year's charitable contribution deduction because the deduction was not substantiated. Assume also that Mal indicates that, in the previous year, he contributed $25,000 (instead of $24,785). How do these changes of fact affect your earlier decision?

TAX RESEARCH PROBLEMS

C:1-63 The purpose of this problem is to enhance your skills in interpreting the authorities that you locate in your research. In answering the questions that follow, refer only to *Thomas A. Curtis, M.D., Inc.*, 1994 RIA TC Memo ¶94,015 (T.C. Memo 1994-15), 67 TCM 1958.

a. What was the principal controversy litigated in this case?
b. Which party—the taxpayer or the IRS—won?
c. Why is the corporation instead of Dr. and/or Ms. Curtis listed as the plaintiff?
d. What is the relationship between Ellen Barnert Curtis and Dr. Thomas A. Curtis?
e. Approximately how many hours a week did Ms. Curtis work, and what were her credentials?
f. For the fiscal year ending in 1989, what salary did the corporation pay Ms. Curtis? What amount did the court decide was reasonable?
g. What dividends did the corporation pay for its fiscal years ending in 1988 and 1989?
h. To which circuit would this decision be appealable?
i. According to *Curtis*, what five factors did the Ninth Circuit mention in *Elliotts, Inc.* as relevant in determining reasonable compensation?

C:1-64 Josh contributes $5,000 toward the support of his widowed mother, aged 69, a U.S. citizen and resident. She earns gross income of $2,000 and spends it all for her own support. In addition, Medicare pays $3,200 of her medical expenses. She does not receive financial support from sources other than those described above. Must the Medicare payments be included in the support that Josh's mother is deemed to provide for herself?

Prepare work papers and a client letter (to Josh) dealing with the issue.

C:1-65 Amy owns a vacation cottage in Maine. She predicts that the time during which the cottage will be used in the current year is as follows:

By Amy, solely for vacation	12 days
By Amy, making repairs ten hours per day and vacationing the rest of the day	2 days
By her sister, who paid fair rental value	8 days
By her cousin, who paid fair rental value	4 days
By her friend, who paid a token amount of rent	2 days
By three families from the Northeast, who paid fair rental value for 40 days each	120 days
Not used	217 days

Calculate the ratio for allocating the following expenses to the rental income expected to be received from the cottage: interest, taxes, repairs, insurance, and depreciation. The ratio will be used to determine the amount of expenses that are deductible and, thus, Amy's taxable income for the year.

For the tax manager to whom you report, prepare work papers in which you discuss the calculation method. Also, draft a memo to the file dealing with the results of your research.

C:1-66 Look up *Summit Publishing Company*, 1990 PH T.C. Memo ¶90,288 (T.C. Memo 1990-288), 59 TCM 833, and *J.B.S. Enterprises*, 1991 PH T.C. Memo ¶91,254 (T.C. Memo 1991-254), 61 TCM 2829, and answer the following questions:

a. What was the principal issue in these cases?
b. What factors did the Tax Court consider in resolving the central issue?
c. How are the facts of these cases similar? How are they dissimilar?

C:1-67 Your supervisor would like to set up a single Sec. 401(k) plan exclusively for the managers of your organization. Concerned that this arrangement might not meet the requirements for a qualified plan, he has asked you to request a determination letter from the IRS. In a brief memorandum, address the following issues:

a. What IRS pronouncements govern requests for determination letters?
b. What IRS forms must be filed with the request?
c. What information must be provided in the request?
d. What actions must accompany the filing?
e. Where must the request be filed?

CHAPTER

2

CORPORATE FORMATIONS AND CAPITAL STRUCTURE

LEARNING OBJECTIVES

After studying this chapter, you should be able to

1. Discuss the tax advantages and disadvantages of alternative business forms
2. Apply the check-the-box regulations to partnerships, corporations, and trusts
3. Recognize the legal requirements and tax considerations related to forming a corporation
4. Discuss the requirements for deferring gain or loss upon incorporation
5. Explain the tax implications of alternative capital structures
6. Determine the tax consequences of worthless stock or debt obligations
7. Identify tax planning opportunities in corporate formations
8. Comply with procedural rules for corporate formations

CHAPTER OUTLINE

When starting a business, entrepreneurs must decide whether to organize it as a sole proprietorship, partnership, corporation, limited liability company, or limited liability partnership. This chapter discusses the advantages and disadvantages of each form of business association. Because many entrepreneurs find organizing their business as a corporation advantageous, the chapter looks at the definition of a corporation for federal income tax purposes. It also discusses the tax consequences of incorporating a business. The chapter closes by examining the tax implications of capitalizing a corporation with equity and/or debt and describing the advantages and disadvantages of alternative capital structures.

This textbook takes a life-cycle approach to corporate taxation. The corporate life cycle starts with corporate formation, discussed in this chapter. Once formed and operating, the corporation generates taxable income (or loss), incurs federal income tax and other liabilities, and makes distributions to its shareholders. Finally, at some point, the corporation might outlive its usefulness and be liquidated and dissolved. The corporate life cycle is too complex to discuss in one chapter. Therefore, additional coverage follows in Chapters C:3 through C:8.

ORGANIZATION FORMS AVAILABLE

OBJECTIVE 1

Discuss the tax advantages and disadvantages of alternative business forms

Businesses can be organized in several forms including

- Sole proprietorships
- Partnerships
- Corporations
- Limited liability companies
- Limited liability partnerships

A discussion of the tax implications of each form is presented below.

ADDITIONAL COMMENT

The income/loss of a sole proprietorship reported on Schedule C carries to page 1 of Form 1040 and is included in the computation of the individual's taxable income. Net income, if any, also carries to Schedule SE of Form 1040 for computation of the sole proprietor's self-employment tax.

SOLE PROPRIETORSHIPS

A **sole proprietorship** is an unincorporated business owned by one individual. It often is selected by entrepreneurs who are beginning a new business with a modest amount of capital. From a tax and legal perspective, a sole proprietorship is not a separate entity. Rather, it is a legal extension of its individual owner. Thus, the individual owns all the business assets and reports income or loss from the sole proprietorship directly on his or her individual tax return. Specifically, the individual owner (proprietor) reports all the business's income and expenses for the year on Schedule C (Profit or Loss from Business) or Schedule C-EZ (Net Profit from Business) of Form 1040. A completed Schedule C is included in Appendix B, where a common set of facts (with minor modifications) illustrates the similarities and differences in sole proprietorship, C corporation, partnership, and S corporation tax reporting.

If the business is profitable, the profit is included in the proprietor's other income.

EXAMPLE C:2-1 ▶ John, a single taxpayer, starts a new computer store, which he operates as a sole proprietorship. John reports a $15,000 profit from the business in its first year of operation. Assuming his marginal tax rate is 33%, John's tax on the $15,000 of profit from the business is $4,950 (0.33 × $15,000).[1] ◀

If the business is unprofitable, the loss reduces the proprietor's total taxable income, thereby generating tax savings.

EXAMPLE C:2-2 ▶ Assume the same facts as in Example C:2-1 except John reports a $15,000 loss instead of a $15,000 profit in the first year of operation. Assuming he still is taxed at a 33% marginal tax rate, the $15,000 loss produces tax savings of $4,950 (0.33 × $15,000). ◀

---

[1] The $15,000 Schedule C profit in Example C:2-1 will increase adjusted gross income (AGI). The AGI level affects certain deduction calculations (e.g., medical, charitable contributions, and miscellaneous itemized) and, because of limitations, may result in a taxable income increase different from the $15,000 AGI increase.

ADDITIONAL COMMENT

Although this chapter emphasizes the tax consequences of selecting the entity in which a business will be conducted, other issues also are important in making such a decision. For example, the amount of legal liability assumed by an owner is important and can vary substantially among the different business entities.

Tax Advantages. The tax advantages of conducting business as a sole proprietorship are as follows:

- The sole proprietorship is not subject to taxation as a separate entity. Rather, the sole proprietor, as an individual, is taxed at his or her marginal rate on income earned by the business.
- The proprietor's marginal tax rate may be lower than the marginal tax rate that would have applied had the business been organized as a corporation.
- The owner may contribute cash to, or withdraw profits from, the business without tax consequences.
- Although the owner usually maintains separate books, records, and bank accounts for the business, the money in these accounts belongs to the owner personally.
- The owner may contribute property to, or withdraw property from, the business without recognizing gain or loss.
- Business losses may offset nonbusiness income, such as interest, dividends, and any salary earned by the sole proprietor or his or her spouse, subject to the passive activity loss rules.

Tax Disadvantages. The tax disadvantages of conducting business as a sole proprietorship are as follows:

- The profits of a sole proprietorship are currently taxed to the individual owner, whether or not the profits are retained in the business or withdrawn for personal use. By contrast, the profits of a corporation are taxed to its shareholders only if and when the corporation distributes the earnings as dividends.
- At times, corporate tax rates have been lower than individual tax rates. In such times, businesses conducted as sole proprietorships have been taxed more heavily than businesses organized as corporations.
- A sole proprietor must pay the full amount of Social Security taxes because he or she is not considered to be an employee of the business. By contrast, shareholder-employees must pay only half their Social Security taxes; the corporate employer pays the other half. (The employer, however, might pass this half onto employees in the form of lower wages or fewer employees hired.)
- Sole proprietorships may not deduct compensation paid to owner-employees. By contrast, corporations may deduct compensation paid to shareholder-employees.
- Certain tax-exempt benefits (e.g., premiums for group term life insurance) available to shareholder-employees are not available to owner-employees.[2]
- A sole proprietor must use the same accounting period for business and personal purposes. Thus, he or she cannot defer income by choosing a business fiscal year that differs from the individual's calendar year. By contrast, a corporation may choose a fiscal year that differs from the shareholders' calendar years.

ADDITIONAL COMMENT

In 2016 and 2017, the employee's half of Social Security taxes is 6.2%, and the employee's half of the Medicare tax is 1.45%, for a total of 7.65%. The employer pays the same percentages for its half of these items. In addition, the employee (but not the employer) is subject to an additional 0.9% Medicare tax if the employee's wages exceed a threshold amount ($200,000 unmarried; $250,000 for married filing jointly; $125,000 for married filing separately).

PARTNERSHIPS

A **partnership** is an unincorporated business carried on by two or more individuals or entities for profit. The partnership form often is used by friends or relatives who engage in a business and by groups of investors who want to share the profits, losses, and expenses of an investment such as a real estate project.

A partnership is a tax reporting, but not taxpaying, entity. The partnership acts as a conduit for its owners. Its income, expenses, losses, credits, and other tax-related items pass through to the partners who report these items on their separate tax returns.

Each year a partnership must file a tax return (Form 1065—U.S. Partnership Return of Income) to report the results of its operations. When the partnership return is filed, the preparer must send each partner a statement (Schedule K-1, Form 1065) that reports the

REAL-WORLD EXAMPLE

Entities filed the following number of tax returns in 2015:

Entity	Number
Partnership	3.8 million
C corporation	2.2 million
S corporation	4.7 million

[2] Section 162(l) permits self-employed individuals to deduct as a trade or business expense all of the health insurance costs incurred on behalf of themselves, their spouses, and their dependents.

partner's allocable share of partnership income, expenses, losses, credits, and other tax-related items. The partner then must report these items on his or her separate tax return. As with a sole proprietorship, the partner's allocable share of business profits is added to the partner's other income and taxed at that partner's marginal tax rate. A completed Form 1065 appears in Appendix B.

EXAMPLE C:2-3 ▶ Bob, a single taxpayer, owns a 50% interest in the BT Partnership, a calendar year entity. The BT Partnership reports a $30,000 profit in its first year of operation. Bob's $15,000 share passes through from the partnership level to Bob's individual tax return. Assuming Bob is taxed at a 33% marginal rate, his tax on the $15,000 is $4,950 (0.33 × $15,000). Bob must pay the $4,950 tax whether or not the BT Partnership distributes any of its profits to him. ◀

If a partnership reports a loss, the partner's allocable share of the loss reduces that partner's other income and provides tax savings based on the partner's marginal tax rate. The passive activity loss rules, however, may limit the amount of any loss deduction available to the partner. (For a discussion of these rules, see Chapter C:9 of this textbook.)

EXAMPLE C:2-4 ▶ Assume the same facts as in Example C:2-3 except that, instead of a profit, the BT Partnership sustains a $30,000 loss in its first year of operation. Assuming Bob is taxed at a 33% marginal rate, his $15,000 share of the first year loss produces a tax savings of $4,950 (0.33 × $15,000). ◀

TAX STRATEGY TIP

In a limited partnership, the general partner could be a corporation, thereby affording the general owners (shareholders) of the corporation added liability protection.

Organizationally, a partnership can be either general or limited. In a general partnership, the liability of each partner for partnership debts is unlimited. Thus, these partners are at risk for more than the amount of their capital investment in the partnership. In a limited partnership, at least one partner must be a general partner, and at least one partner must be a limited partner. As in a general partnership, the general partners are liable for all partnership debts, and the limited partners are liable only to the extent of their capital investment in the partnership, plus any amount they are obligated to contribute under their partnership agreement. Unless specified in that agreement, limited partners generally may not participate in the management of the partnership business.

Tax Advantages. The tax advantages of doing business as a partnership are as follows:

- The partnership as an entity pays no tax. Rather, the income of the partnership passes through to the separate returns of the partners and is taxed directly to them.
- A partner's tax rate may be lower than a corporation's tax rate for the same level of taxable income.
- Partnership income is not subject to double taxation. Although partnership profits are accounted for at the partnership level, they are taxed only at the partner level.
- Additional taxes generally are not imposed on distributions to the partners. With limited exceptions, partners can contribute money or property to, or withdraw money or property from, the partnership without recognizing gain or loss.
- Subject to limitations, partners can use losses to offset income from other sources.
- A partner's basis in a partnership interest is increased by his or her share of partnership income. This basis adjustment reduces the amount of gain recognized when the partner sells his or her partnership interest, thereby avoiding double taxation.

Tax Disadvantages. The tax disadvantages of doing business as a partnership are as follows:

ADDITIONAL COMMENT

If two or more owners exist, a business cannot be conducted as a sole proprietorship. From a tax compliance and recordkeeping perspective, conducting a business as a partnership is more complicated than conducting the business as a sole proprietorship.

- All the partnership's profits are taxed to the partners when earned, even if not distributed.
- A partner's tax rate could be higher than a corporation's tax rate for the same level of taxable income.
- A partner is not considered to be an employee of the partnership. Therefore, he or she must pay the full amount of self-employment taxes on his or her share of partnership

income. Some tax-exempt fringe benefits (e.g., premiums for group term life insurance) are not available to partners.[3]

- Partners generally cannot defer income by choosing a fiscal year for the partnership that differs from the tax year of the principal partner(s). However, if the partnership demonstrates a business purpose, or if it makes a special election, it may use a fiscal year in general.

Chapters C:9 and C:10 of this volume discuss partnerships in greater detail.

CORPORATIONS

Corporations fall into two categories: C corporations and S corporations. Both have limited liability. A C corporation is subject to double taxation. Its earnings are taxed first at the corporate level when earned, then again at the shareholder level when distributed as dividends. An S corporation, by contrast, is subject to single-level taxation, much like a partnership. Its earnings are accounted for at the corporate level but are taxed only at the shareholder level.

ADDITIONAL COMMENT

Unlike a sole proprietorship and a partnership, a C corporation is a separate taxpaying entity. This form can be advantageous because corporate rates start at 15%, which may be much lower than an individual shareholder's rate, which might be as high as 39.6%.

C Corporations. A **C corporation** is a separate entity taxed on its income at rates ranging from 15% to 35%.[4] A C corporation must report all its income and expenses and compute its tax liability on Form 1120 (U.S. Corporation Income Tax Return). A completed Form 1120 appears in Appendix B. Shareholders are not taxed on the corporation's earnings unless these earnings are distributed as dividends. After 2012, the applicable capital gains tax rate for net capital gains and qualified dividends of noncorporate taxpayers is 0% for taxpayers in tax brackets of 15% and below, 15% for taxpayers in the 25% through 35% tax brackets, and 20% for taxpayers in the 39.6% tax bracket. Also, 25% and 28% rates apply for gains on certain types of property. In addition, an incremental 3.8% rate applies to net investment income for taxpayers whose modified AGI exceeds $200,000 ($250,000 for married filing jointly). Net investment income includes, among other things, interest, dividends, annuities, royalties, rents, and net gains from the disposition of property not used in a trade or business, all reduced by deductions allocable to such income or gains.

EXAMPLE C:2-5 ▶ Jane owns 100% of York Corporation stock. York reports taxable income of $50,000 for the current year. The first $50,000 of taxable income is taxed at a 15% rate, so York pays a corporate income tax of $7,500 (0.15 × $50,000). If the corporation distributes none of its earnings to Jane during the year, she pays no tax on York's earnings. However, if York distributes its current after-tax earnings to Jane, she must pay tax on $42,500 ($50,000 − $7,500) of dividend income. Assuming Jane's capital gains tax rate is 15%, her tax on the dividend income is $6,375 (0.15 × $42,500). The total tax on York's $50,000 of profits is $13,875 ($7,500 paid by York + $6,375 paid by Jane). ◀

TAX STRATEGY TIP

If a shareholder is also an employee of the corporation, the corporation can avoid double taxation by paying a deductible salary instead of a dividend. The salary, however, must be reasonable in amount. See Tax Planning Considerations in Chapter C:3 for further discussion of this technique along with an example demonstrating how the lower tax rate on dividends reduces the difference between salary and dividend payments.

Even when a corporation does not distribute its profits, double taxation may result. The profits are taxed to the corporation when they are earned. Then, effectively, they may be taxed a second time (as capital gains) when the shareholder sells appreciated stock or when the corporation liquidates.

EXAMPLE C:2-6 ▶ On January 2 of the current year, Carl purchases 100% of York Corporation stock for $60,000. In the same year, York reports taxable income of $50,000, on which it pays tax of $7,500. The corporation distributes none of the remaining $42,500 to Carl. On January 3 of the next year, Carl sells his stock to Mary for $102,500 (his initial investment plus the current year's accumulated earnings). Carl must report a capital gain of $42,500 ($102,500 − $60,000). Thus, York's profit is effectively taxed twice—first at the corporate level when earned and again at the shareholder level when Carl sells the appreciated stock at a gain. ◀

TAX STRATEGY TIP

By having a corporation retain earnings instead of paying dividends, the shareholder converts current ordinary income into deferred capital gains. The corporation, however, must avoid the accumulated earnings tax (see Chapter C:5).

Tax Advantages. The tax advantages of doing business as a C corporation are as follows:

- A C corporation is an entity separate and distinct from its owners. Its marginal tax rate may be lower than its owners' marginal tax rates. So long as these earnings are not distributed and taxed to both the shareholders and the corporation, aggregate tax savings may result. If retained in the business, the earnings may be used for reinvestment and the retirement of debt. This advantage, however, may be limited by the accumulated earnings tax and the personal holding company tax. (See Chapter C:5 for a discussion of these two taxes.)

[3] Partners are eligible to deduct their health insurance costs in the same manner as a sole proprietor. See footnote 2 for details.

[4] As discussed in Chapter C:3, the corporate tax rate is 39% and 38% for certain levels of taxable income.

- Shareholders employed by the corporation are considered to be employees for tax purposes. Consequently, they are liable for only half their Social Security taxes, while their corporate employer is liable for the other half.
- Shareholder-employees are entitled to nontaxable fringe benefits (e.g., premiums paid on group term life insurance and accident and health insurance). The corporation can provide these benefits with before-tax dollars (instead of after-tax dollars). By contrast, because sole proprietors and partners are not considered to be employees for tax purposes, they are ineligible for certain tax-free fringe benefits, although they are permitted to deduct their health insurance premiums.
- A corporation may deduct as an ordinary and necessary business expense compensation and certain benefits paid to shareholder-employees. Within reasonable limits, it may adjust this compensation and these benefits upward to shelter corporate taxable income.
- A C corporation can use a fiscal instead of a calendar year as its reporting period. A fiscal year could permit a corporation to defer income to a later reporting period. (A personal service corporation, however, generally must use a calendar year as its tax year.[5])
- Special rules allow a shareholder to exclude 50% of the gain realized on the sale or exchange of stock held more than five years, provided the corporation meets certain requirements.

SELF-STUDY QUESTION

How are corporate earnings subject to double taxation?

ANSWER

Corporate earnings initially are taxed to the corporation. In addition, once these earnings are distributed to the shareholders as dividends, they are taxed again. Because the corporation does not receive a deduction for the distribution, these earnings have been taxed twice. Also, double taxation can occur when a shareholder sells his or her stock at a gain. In either case, the dividends or capital gains are taxed at the applicable capital gains rate.

Tax Disadvantages. The tax disadvantages of doing business as a C corporation are as follows:

- Double taxation of income results when the corporation distributes its earnings as dividends to shareholders or, effectively, when shareholders sell or exchange appreciated stock.
- Shareholders generally cannot withdraw money or property from the corporation without recognizing income. A distribution of cash or property to a shareholder generally is taxable as a dividend if the corporation has sufficient earnings and profits (E&P). (See Chapter C:4 for a discussion of E&P.)
- Net operating losses confer no tax benefit to the owners in the year the corporation incurs them. They can be carried back or carried forward to offset the corporation's income in other years. For start-up corporations, these losses provide no tax benefit until the corporation earns a profit in a subsequent year. Shareholders cannot use these losses to offset income from other sources.
- Capital losses confer no tax benefit to the owners in the year the corporation incurs them. They cannot offset the ordinary income of either the corporation or its shareholders. These losses must be carried back or carried forward to offset corporate capital gains realized in other years.

S Corporations. An **S corporation** is so designated because special rules governing its tax treatment are found in Subchapter S of the IRC. Nevertheless, the general corporate tax rules apply unless overridden by the Subchapter S provisions. Like a partnership, an S corporation is a pass-through entity. Income, deductions, losses, and credits are accounted for by the S corporation, which generally is not subject to taxation. They pass through to the separate returns of its owners, who generally are subject to taxation. An S corporation offers its owners less planning flexibility than does a partnership. For example, the number and type of S corporation shareholders are limited, and the shareholders cannot allocate income, deductions, losses, and credits in a way that differs from their proportionate ownership. As mentioned before, like C corporation shareholders, S corporation shareholders enjoy limited liability.

To obtain S corporation status, a corporation must make a special election, and its shareholders must consent to that election. Each year, an S corporation files an information return, Form 1120S (U.S. Income Tax Return for an S Corporation), which reports the results of its operations and indicates the items of income, deduction, loss, and credit that pass through to the separate returns of its shareholders.

[5] Sec. 441. See Chapter C:3 for the special tax year restrictions applying to personal service corporations.

EXAMPLE C:2-7 ▶ Chuck owns 50% of the stock in Maine, an S corporation that uses the calendar year as its tax year. In its first year of operation, Maine reports $30,000 of taxable income, all ordinary in character. Maine pays no corporate income tax. Chuck, however, must pay tax on his $15,000 (0.50 × $30,000) share of Maine's income whether or not the corporation distributes this income to him. If his marginal rate is 33%, Chuck pays a tax of $4,950 (0.33 × $15,000) on this share. If Maine instead reports a $30,000 loss, Chuck's $15,000 share of the loss reduces his tax liability by $4,950 (0.33 × $15,000). ◀

TAX STRATEGY TIP

If a corporation anticipates losses in its early years, it might consider operating as an S corporation so that the losses pass through to the shareholders. When the corporation becomes profitable, it can revoke the S election if it wishes to accumulate earnings for growth.

Tax Advantages. The tax advantages of doing business as an S corporation are as follows:

- S corporations generally pay no tax. Instead, corporate income passes through and is taxed to the shareholders.
- The shareholders' marginal tax rates may be lower than a C corporation's marginal tax rate, thereby producing overall tax savings.
- Corporate losses flow through to the separate returns of the shareholders and may be used to offset income earned from other sources. (Passive loss and basis rules, however, may limit loss deductions to shareholders. See Chapter C:11.) This treatment can be beneficial to owners of start-up corporations that generate losses in their early years of operation.
- Because capital gains, as well as other tax-related items, retain their character when they pass through to the separate returns of shareholders, the shareholders are taxed on these gains as though they directly realized them. Consequently, they can offset the gains against capital losses from other sources. Furthermore, they are taxed on these gains at their own capital gains rates.

- Shareholders generally can contribute money to or withdraw money from an S corporation without recognizing gain.
- Corporate profits are taxed only at the shareholder level in the year earned. Generally, the shareholders incur no additional tax liability when the corporation distributes the profits.
- A shareholder's basis in S corporation stock is increased by his or her share of corporate income. This basis adjustment reduces the shareholder's gain when he or she later sells the stock, thereby avoiding double taxation.

TAX STRATEGY TIP

Relatively low individual tax rates may increase the attractiveness of an S corporation relative to the C corporation form of doing business.

Tax Disadvantages. The tax disadvantages of doing business as an S corporation are as follows:

- Shareholders are taxed on all of an S corporation's current year profits whether or not the corporation distributes these profits and whether or not the shareholders have the wherewithal to pay the tax on these profits.
- If the shareholders' marginal tax rates exceed those for a C corporation, the overall tax burden may be heavier, and the after-tax earnings available for reinvestment and debt retirement may be reduced.
- Nontaxable fringe benefits generally are not available to S corporation shareholder-employees.[6] Ordinarily, fringe benefits provided by an S corporation are deductible by the corporation and taxable to the shareholder. On the other hand, S corporation shareholder-employees pay half of Social Security taxes while the S corporation employer pays the other half.
- S corporations generally cannot defer income by choosing a fiscal year other than a calendar year unless the S corporation can establish a legitimate business purpose for a fiscal year or unless it makes a special election.

Chapter C:11 discusses S corporations in greater detail. In addition, Appendix F compares the tax treatment of C corporations, partnerships, and S corporations.

---

[6] S corporation shareholders may deduct their health insurance costs in the same manner as sole proprietors and partners. See footnotes 2 and 3 for details.

ADDITIONAL COMMENT

All 50 states have adopted statutes providing for LLCs.

LIMITED LIABILITY COMPANIES

A **limited liability company** (LLC) combines the best features of a partnership with those of a corporation even though, from a legal perspective, it is neither. While offering its owners the limited liability of a corporation, an LLC with more than one owner generally is treated as a partnership for tax purposes. This limited liability extends to all the LLC's owners. In this respect, the LLC is analogous to a limited partnership with no general partners. Unlike an S corporation, an LLC may have an unlimited number of owners who can be individuals, corporations, estates, and trusts. As discussed below, under the check-the-box regulations, the LLC may elect to be taxed as a corporation or be treated by default as a partnership. If treated as a partnership, the LLC files Form 1065 (U.S. Partnership Return of Income) with the IRS.

REAL-WORLD EXAMPLE

All the Big 4 accounting firms have converted general partnerships into LLPs.

LIMITED LIABILITY PARTNERSHIPS

The **limited liability partnership** (LLP) business form is attractive to owners of professional service organizations, such as public accounting firms, that adopt LLP status primarily to limit their legal liability. Under state LLP laws, partners are liable for their own acts and omissions as well as the acts and omissions of individuals under their direction. On the other hand, LLP partners are not liable for the negligence or misconduct of the other partners. Thus, from a legal liability perspective, an LLP partner is like a limited partner with respect to other partners' acts but like a general partner with respect to his or her own acts, as well as the acts of his or her agents. Like a general partnership or LLC with more than one owner, an LLP can elect to be taxed as a corporation under the check-the-box regulations. If treated as a partnership by default, the LLP files Form 1065 (U.S. Partnership Return of Income) with the IRS.

CHECK-THE-BOX REGULATIONS

OBJECTIVE 2

Apply the check-the-box regulations to partnerships, corporations, and trusts

Most unincorporated businesses may choose to be taxed as a partnership or a corporation under rules commonly referred to as the **check-the-box regulations**. According to these regulations, an unincorporated business with two or more owners is treated by default as a partnership for tax purposes unless it elects to be taxed as a corporation. An unincorporated business with one owner is disregarded as a separate entity and thus treated as a sole proprietorship by default unless it elects to be taxed as a corporation.[7]

TAX STRATEGY TIP

When applying the federal check-the-box regulations, taxpayers also must check to see whether or not their state will treat the entity in a consistent manner for state tax purposes.

An eligible entity (i.e., an unincorporated business) may elect its classification by filing Form 8832 (Entity Classification Election) with the IRS. The form must be signed by each owner of the entity, or any officer, manager, or owner of the entity authorized to make the election. The signatures must specify the date on which the election will be effective. The effective date cannot be more than 75 days before or 12 months after the date the entity files Form 8832. A copy of the form must be attached to the entity's tax return for the election year.

EXAMPLE C:2-8 ▶ On January 10 of the current year, a group of ten individuals organizes an LLC to conduct a bookbinding business in Texas. In the current year, the LLC is an eligible entity under the check-the-box regulations and thus may elect (with the owners' consent) to be taxed as a corporation. If the LLC does not make the election, the LLC, for tax purposes, will be treated as a partnership by default. ◀

EXAMPLE C:2-9 ▶ Assume the same facts as in Example C:2-8 except only one individual organized the LLC. Unless the LLC elects to be taxed as a corporation, the LLC, For tax purposes, will be disregarded by default. Consequently, its income will be taxed directly to the owner as if it were a sole proprietorship. ◀

---

[7] This rule does not apply to corporations, trusts, or certain special entities such as real estate investment trusts, real estate mortgage investment conduits, or publicly traded partnerships. Reg. Sec. 301.7701-2(b)(8). Publicly traded partnerships are discussed in Chapter C:10. Special check-the-box rules apply to foreign corporations. These rules are beyond the scope of this text.

If an entity elects to change its tax classification, it cannot make another election until 60 months after the effective date of the initial election. Following the election, certain tax consequences ensue. For example, following a partnership's election to be taxed as a corporation, the partnership is deemed to distribute its assets to the partners, who are then deemed to contribute the assets to a new corporation in a nontaxable exchange for stock. If an eligible entity that previously elected to be taxed as a corporation subsequently elects to be treated as a partnership or a disregarded entity, it is deemed to have distributed its assets and liabilities to its owner(s) in a liquidation as described in Chapter C:6. In the case of a partnership, the deemed distribution is followed by a deemed contribution of assets and liabilities to a newly formed partnership.[8]

LEGAL REQUIREMENTS AND TAX CONSIDERATIONS RELATED TO FORMING A CORPORATION

OBJECTIVE 3

Recognize the legal requirements and tax considerations related to forming a corporation

LEGAL REQUIREMENTS

State or jurisdictional laws dictate the legal requirements for forming a corporation. These requirements usually include

- Investing a minimum amount of capital
- Filing articles of incorporation
- Issuing stock
- Paying incorporation fees to the state or other jurisdiction

One of the first decisions an entrepreneur must make when organizing a corporation is choosing a state of incorporation. Although most entrepreneurs incorporate in the state where they conduct business, many incorporate in other states with more favorable corporation laws. Such laws might provide for little or no income, sales, or use taxes; low minimum capital requirements; and modest incorporation fees. Regardless of the state of incorporation, the entrepreneur must follow the incorporation procedure set forth in the applicable state statute. Typically, under this procedure, the entrepreneur must file articles of incorporation with the appropriate state agency. The articles must specify certain information, such as the formal name of the corporation; its purpose; the par value, number of shares, and classes of stock it is authorized to issue; and the names of the individuals who will initially serve on the corporation's board of directors. The state usually charges a fee for incorporation or filing. In addition, it periodically may assess a franchise tax for the privilege of doing business in the state. These fees and taxes could be substantial.

ADDITIONAL COMMENT

States are not consistent in how they tax corporations. Certain states have no state income taxes. Other states do not recognize an S corporation election, thereby taxing an S corporation as a C corporation.

TAX CONSIDERATIONS

Once the entrepreneur decides on the corporate form, he or she must transfer cash, property (e.g., equipment, furniture, inventory, and receivables), or services (e.g., accounting, legal, or architectural services) to the corporation in exchange for its debt or equity. These transfers may have tax consequences for both the transferor investor and the transferee corporation. For instance, the sale of property for stock usually is taxable to the transferor.[9] However, if Sec. 351(a) (which treats an investor's interest in certain transferred business assets to be "changed in form" rather than "disposed of") applies, any gain or loss realized on the exchange may be deferred. In determining the tax consequences of incorporation, one must answer the following questions:

- What property should be transferred to the corporation?
- What services should the transferors or third parties provide for the corporation?

[8] Reg. Sec. 301.7701-3(g). An alternative way for a corporation to be taxed as a pass-through entity is to make an election to be taxed as an S corporation. See Chapter C:11.

[9] Sec. 1001.

▶ What liabilities, in addition to property, should be transferred?

▶ How should the property be transferred (e.g., sale, contribution to capital, or loan)?

Example C:2-10 and Table C:2-1 compare the tax consequences of taxable and nontaxable property transfers.

EXAMPLE C:2-10 ▶ For several years Brad has operated a successful manufacturing business as a sole proprietorship. To limit his liability, he decides to incorporate his business as Block Corporation. Immediately preceding the incorporation, he reports the following balance sheet for his sole proprietorship, which uses the accrual method of accounting:

		Adjusted Basis	*Fair Market Value*
Assets:			
Cash		$ 10,000	$ 10,000
Accounts receivable		15,000	15,000
Inventory		20,000	25,000
Equipment	$120,000		
Minus: Depreciation	(35,000)	85,000	100,000
Total		$130,000	$150,000
Liabilities and owner's equity:			
Accounts payable		$ 30,000	$ 30,000
Note payable on equipment		50,000	50,000
Owner's equity		50,000	70,000
Total		$130,000	$150,000

When Brad transfers the assets to Block in exchange for its stock, he realizes a gain because the value of the stock received exceeds his basis in the assets. If the exchange is taxable, Brad recognizes $5,000 of ordinary income on the transfer of the inventory ($25,000 FMV – $20,000 basis) and, because of depreciation recapture, $15,000 of ordinary income on the transfer of the equipment ($100,000 FMV – $85,000 basis). However, if the exchange meets the requirements of Sec. 351(a), it is nontaxable. In other words, Brad recognizes none of the income or gain realized on the transfer of assets and liabilities to Block. ◀

STOP & THINK

Question: Joyce has conducted a business as a sole proprietorship for several years. She needs additional capital and wants to incorporate her business. The assets of her business (building, land, inventory, etc.) have a $400,000 adjusted basis and a $1.5 million FMV. Joyce is willing to exchange the assets for 1,500 shares of Ace Corporation stock, each having a $1,000 fair market value. Bill and John each are willing to invest $500,000 in Joyce's business for 500 shares of stock. Why is Sec. 351 relevant to Joyce? Does it matter to Bill and John?

Solution: If not for Sec. 351, Joyce would recognize gain on the incorporation of her business. She realizes a gain of $1.1 million ($1,500,000 – $400,000) on her contribution of proprietorship assets to a new corporation in exchange for 60% of its outstanding shares (1,500 ÷ [1,500 + 500 + 500] = 0.60). However, she recognizes none of this gain because she meets the requirements of Sec. 351. Section 351 does not affect Bill or John because each is simply purchasing 20% of the new corporation's stock for $500,000 cash. They will not realize or recognize gain or loss unless they subsequently sell their stock at a price above or below the $500,000 cost.

If all exchanges of property for corporate stock were taxable, many entrepreneurs would find the tax cost of incorporating their business prohibitively high. In Example C:2-10, for example, Brad would recognize a $20,000 gain on the exchange of his assets for the corporate stock. Moreover, because losses also are realized in an exchange, without special rules, taxpayers could exchange loss property for stock and recognize the loss while maintaining an equity interest in the property transferred.

▼ **TABLE C:2-1**
Overview of Corporate Formation Rules

Tax Treatment for:	Taxable Property Transfer	Nontaxable Property Transfer
Transferors: 1. Gain realized	FMV of stock received Money received FMV of noncash boot property (including securities) received Amount of liabilities assumed by transferee corporation Minus: Adjusted basis of property transferred Realized gain (Sec. 1001(a))	Same as in a taxable transaction
2. Gain recognized	Transferors recognize the entire amount of realized gain (Sec. 1001(c)) Losses may be disallowed under related party rules (Sec. 267(a)(1)) Installment sale rules may apply to the realized gain (Sec. 453)	Transferors recognize none of the realized gain unless one of the following exceptions applies (Sec. 351(a)): a. Boot property is received (Sec. 351(b)) b. Liabilities are transferred to the corporation for a nonbusiness or tax avoidance purpose (Sec. 357(b)) c. Liabilities exceeding basis are transferred to the corporation (Sec. 357(c)) d. Services, certain corporate indebtedness, and interest claims are transferred to the corporation (Sec. 351(d)) The installment method may defer recognition of gain when a shareholder receives a corporate note as boot (Sec. 453)
3. Basis of property received	FMV (Cost) (Sec. 1012)	Basis of property transferred to the corporation Plus: Gain recognized Minus: Money received (including liabilities treated as money) FMV of noncash boot property Total basis of stock received (Sec. 358(a)) Allocation of total stock basis is based on relative FMVs Basis of noncash boot property is its FMV
4. Holding period of property received	Day after the exchange date	Holding period of stock received includes holding period of Sec. 1231 property or capital assets transferred; otherwise it begins the day after the exchange date
Transferee Corporation: 1. Gain recognized	The corporation recognizes no gain or loss on the receipt of money or other property in exchange for its stock (including treasury stock) (Sec. 1032)	Same as taxable transaction except the corporation may recognize gain under Sec. 311 if it transfers appreciated noncash boot property (Sec. 351(f))
2. Basis	FMV (Cost) (Sec. 1012)	Generally, same as in transferor's hands plus any gain recognized by transferor (Sec. 362) If the total adjusted basis of all transferred property exceeds the total FMV of the property, the total basis to the transferor is limited to the property's total FMV
3. Holding period	Day after the exchange date	Transferor's carryover holding period for the property transferred regardless of the property's character (Sec. 1223(2)) Day after the exchange date if basis is reduced to FMV

To allow taxpayers to incorporate without incurring a high tax cost and to prevent taxpayers from recognizing losses while maintaining an equity claim to the loss assets, Congress enacted Sec. 351.

SECTION 351: DEFERRING GAIN OR LOSS UPON INCORPORATION

OBJECTIVE 4

Discuss the requirements for deferring gain or loss upon incorporation

Section 351(a) provides that transferors recognize no gain or loss when they transfer property to a corporation solely in exchange for the corporation's stock if immediately after the exchange, the transferors are in control of the corporation. Section 351 does not apply to a transfer of property to an investment company, nor does it apply in certain bankruptcy cases.

This rule is based on the premise that, when property is transferred to a controlled corporation, the transferors merely exchange direct ownership for indirect ownership through stock in the transferee corporation, which gives them an equity interest in the underlying assets. In other words, the transferors maintain a continuity of interest in the transferred property. Furthermore, if the only consideration the shareholders receive is stock, they have not generated cash with which to pay their taxes. If the transferors of property receive other consideration in addition to stock, such as cash or debt instruments, they will have the wherewithal to pay taxes and, under Sec. 351(b), may have to recognize some or all of their realized gain.

TAX STRATEGY TIP

A transferor who wishes to recognize gain or loss must take steps to avoid Sec. 351 by deliberately failing at least one of its requirements or by engaging in sales transactions. See Tax Planning Considerations at the end of this chapter for details.

A transferor's realized gain or loss that is unrecognized for tax purposes is not exempt from taxation. It is only *deferred* until the shareholder sells or exchanges the stock received in the Sec. 351 exchange. Shareholders who receive stock in such an exchange take a stock basis that reflects the deferred gain or loss. For example, if a shareholder receives stock in exchange for property and recognizes no gain or loss, the stock basis equals the basis of property transferred less liabilities assumed by the corporation (see Table C:2-1). This tax treatment is discussed later in this chapter. Under an alternative approach, the stock basis can be calculated as follows: FMV of qualified stock received, minus any deferred gain (or plus any deferred loss). This latter approach highlights the deferral aspect of this type of transaction. If the shareholder later sells the stock, he or she will recognize the deferred gain or loss inherent in the basis adjustment.

EXAMPLE C:2-11 ▶ Assume the same facts as in Example C:2-10. If Brad satisfies the conditions of Sec. 351, he will not recognize the $20,000 realized gain ($15,000 gain on equipment + $5,000 gain on inventory) when he transfers the assets and liabilities of his sole proprietorship to Block Corporation. Under the alternative approach, Brad's basis in the Block stock is decreased to reflect the deferred gain. Thus, Brad's basis in the Block stock is $50,000 ($70,000 FMV − $20,000 deferred gain). If Brad later sells his stock for its $70,000 FMV, he will recognize the $20,000 gain at the time of sale. ◀

The specific requirements for deferral of gain and loss under Sec. 351(a) are

- ▶ The transferors must transfer property to the corporation.
- ▶ They must receive stock of the transferee corporation in exchange for their property.
- ▶ They must be in control of the corporation immediately after the exchange.

Each of these requirements is explained below.

THE PROPERTY REQUIREMENT

The rule of gain or loss nonrecognition applies only to transfers of property to a corporation in exchange for the corporation's stock. Section 351 does not define the term *property*. However, the courts and the IRS have defined *property* to include cash and almost any other asset, including installment obligations, accounts receivable, inventory, equipment, patents and other intangibles representing know-how, trademarks, trade names, and computer software.[10]

Excluded from the statutory definition of property are[11]

- Services (such as legal or accounting services) rendered to the corporation in exchange for its stock
- Indebtedness of the transferee corporation not evidenced by a security
- Interest on transferee corporation debt that accrued on or after the beginning of the transferor's holding period for the debt

The first of these exclusions perhaps is the most important. A person receiving stock in compensation for services must recognize the stock's FMV as ordinary income for tax purposes. In other words, an exchange of services for stock is a taxable transaction even where concurrent transfers of property for stock are nontaxable under Sec. 351.[12] A shareholder's basis in the stock received in compensation for services is the stock's FMV (not necessarily the FMV of the services).

EXAMPLE C:2-12 ► Amy and Bill form West Corporation. Amy exchanges property for 90 shares (90% of the outstanding shares) of West stock. Amy's exchange is nontaxable because Amy has exchanged property for stock and controls West immediately after the exchange. Bill performs accounting services that he normally bills for $12,000 in exchange for ten shares of West stock worth $10,000. Bill's exchange is taxable because he has provided services in exchange for stock. Thus, Bill recognizes $10,000 of ordinary income—the FMV of the stock—as compensation for his services. Bill's basis in the stock is its $10,000 FMV. ◄

THE CONTROL REQUIREMENT

Section 351 requires the transferors, as a group, to be in control of the transferee corporation immediately after the exchange. A transferor may be an individual or any type of entity (such as a partnership, another corporation, or a trust). Section 368(c) defines *control* as ownership of at least 80% of the total combined voting power of all classes of stock entitled to vote and at least 80% of the total number of shares of all other classes of stock (e.g., nonvoting preferred stock).[13] The minimum ownership levels for nonvoting stock apply to each class of stock rather than to the nonvoting stock in total.[14]

EXAMPLE C:2-13 ► Dan exchanges property having a $22,000 adjusted basis and a $30,000 FMV for 60% of newly created Sun Corporation's single class of stock. Ed exchanges $20,000 cash for the remaining 40% of Sun stock. The transaction qualifies as a nontaxable exchange under Sec. 351 because the transferors, Dan and Ed, together own at least 80% of the Sun stock immediately after the exchange. Therefore, Dan defers recognition of his $8,000 ($30,000 − $22,000) realized gain. (Ed realizes no gain because he contributes cash.) ◄

Because services do not qualify as property, stock received by a person who exclusively provides services does not count toward the 80% control threshold. Unless transferors of property own at least 80% of the corporation's stock immediately after the exchange, the control requirement will not be met, and the entire transaction will be taxable.

EXAMPLE C:2-14 ► Dana transfers property having an $18,000 adjusted basis and a $35,000 FMV to newly created York Corporation for 70 shares of York stock. Ellen provides legal services for the remaining 30 York shares valued at $15,000. Because Ellen does not transfer property to York, her stock is not counted toward the 80% ownership threshold. On the other hand, because Dana transfers property to York, his stock is counted toward this threshold. However, Dana is not in control of York immediately after the exchange because he owns only 70% of York stock. Therefore, Dana recognizes all $17,000 ($35,000 − $18,000) of his gain realized on the exchange. Dana's basis in his York stock is its $35,000 FMV. Ellen recognizes $15,000 of ordinary income, the FMV of stock received for her services. Ellen's basis in her York stock is $15,000. The tax consequences to Ellen are the same whether or not Dana meets the control requirement. ◄

---

[10] For an excellent discussion of the definition of *property*, see footnote 6 of *D.N. Stafford v. U.S.*, 45 AFTR 2d 80-785, 80-1 USTC ¶9218 (5th Cir., 1980).

[11] Sec. 351(d).

[12] Secs. 61 and 83.

[13] In determining whether the 80% requirements are satisfied, the constructive ownership rules of Sec. 318 do not apply (see Rev. Rul. 56-613, 1956-2 C.B. 212). See Chapter C:4 for an explanation of Sec. 318.

[14] Rev. Rul. 59-259, 1959-2 C.B. 115, as modified by Rev. Rul. 81–17, 1981-1 C.B. 75.

If the property transferors own at least 80% of the stock immediately after the exchange, they, but not the provider of services, will be in control of the transferee corporation.

EXAMPLE C:2-15 ▶ Assume the same facts as in Example C:2-14, except a third individual, Fred, contributes $35,000 in cash for 70 shares of York stock. Now Dana and Fred together own more than 80% of the York stock (140 ÷ 170 = 0.82) immediately after the exchange. Therefore, the transaction meets the Sec. 351 control requirement, and neither Dana nor Fred recognizes gain on the exchange. Ellen still must recognize $15,000 of ordinary income, the FMV of the stock she receives for her services. ◀

Transferors of Both Property and Services. If a person transfers both services *and* property to a corporation in exchange for the corporation's stock, all the stock received by that person, including stock received in exchange for services, is counted toward the 80% control threshold.[15]

EXAMPLE C:2-16 ▶ Assume the same facts as in Example C:2-14 except that, in addition to providing legal services in exchange for stock worth $15,000, Ellen contributes property worth at least $1,500. In this case, all of Ellen's stock counts toward the 80% ownership threshold. Because Dana and Ellen together own 100% of the York stock, the exchange meets the Sec. 351 control requirement. Therefore, Dana recognizes no gain on his property exchange. However, Ellen still must recognize $15,000 of ordinary income, the FMV of the stock received as compensation for services. ◀

When a person transfers both property and services in exchange for a corporation's stock, the property must have more than nominal value for that person's stock to count toward the 80% control threshold.[16] The IRS generally requires that the FMV of the stock received for transferred property be at least 10% of the value of the stock received for services provided. If the value of the stock received for the property is less than 10% of the value of the stock received for the services, the IRS will not issue an advance ruling to the effect that the transaction meets the requirements of Sec. 351.[17]

EXAMPLE C:2-17 ▶ Assume the same facts as in Example C:2-16 except that Ellen contributes only $1,000 worth of property in addition to the legal services. In this case, the IRS will not issue an advance ruling that the transaction meets the Sec. 351 requirements because the FMV of stock received for the property ($1,000) is less than 10% of the value of the stock received for the services ($1,500 = 0.10 × $15,000). Consequently, if the IRS audits Ellen's tax return for the year of transfer, it probably will challenge Dana's and Ellen's position that the transfer is nontaxable under Sec. 351. ◀

Transfers to Existing Corporations. Section 351 applies to transfers to an existing corporation as well as transfers to a newly created corporation. The same requirements must be met in both cases. Property must be transferred in exchange for stock, and the property transferors must be in control of the corporation immediately after the exchange.

EXAMPLE C:2-18 ▶ Jack and Karen own 75 and 25 shares, respectively, of Texas Corporation stock. Jack transfers property with a $15,000 adjusted basis and a $25,000 FMV to the corporation in exchange for an additional 25 shares of Texas stock. The transaction meets the Sec. 351 control requirement because, immediately after the exchange, Jack owns 80% (100 ÷ 125 = 0.80) of Texas stock. Therefore, Jack recognizes no gain. ◀

If a shareholder transfers property to an existing corporation for additional stock but does not own at least 80% of the stock immediately after the exchange, the control requirement is not met. Thus, Sec. 351 denies tax-free treatment for many transfers of property to an existing corporation by a new shareholder. A new shareholder's transfer of property to an existing corporation is nontaxable only if that shareholder acquires at least 80% of the corporation's stock, or if enough existing shareholders also transfer additional property so that the transferors as a group, including the new shareholder, control the corporation immediately after the exchange.

[15] Reg. Sec. 1.351-1(a)(2), Ex. (3).
[16] Reg. Sec. 1.351-1(a)(1)(ii).
[17] Rev. Proc. 77-37, 1977-2 C.B. 568, Sec. 3.07, as modified by T.D. 8761, 1998-1 C.B. 812.

EXAMPLE C:2-19 ▶ Alice owns all 100 shares of Local Corporation stock, valued at $100,000. Beth owns property with a $15,000 adjusted basis and a $100,000 FMV. Beth contributes the property to Local in exchange for 100 shares of newly issued Local stock. The transaction does not meet the Sec. 351 control requirement because Beth owns only 50% of Local stock immediately after the exchange. Consequently, Beth recognizes an $85,000 ($100,000 − $15,000) gain. ◀

If an existing shareholder exchanges property for additional stock to enable another shareholder to qualify for tax-free treatment under Sec. 351, the stock received must be of more than nominal value.[18] For advance ruling purposes, the IRS requires that this value be at least 10% of the value of the stock already owned.[19]

EXAMPLE C:2-20 ▶ Assume the same facts as in Example C:2-19 except that Alice transfers additional property worth $10,000 for an additional ten shares of Local stock. Now both Alice and Beth are transferors, thereby satisfying the Sec. 351 control requirement. Consequently, neither Alice nor Beth recognizes gain on the exchange. If Alice receives fewer than ten shares, the IRS will not issue an advance ruling that the exchange is tax-free under Sec. 351. ◀

STOP & THINK

Question: Matthew and Michael each own 50 shares of Main Corporation stock having a $250,000 FMV. Matthew wants to transfer property with a $40,000 adjusted basis and a $100,000 FMV to Main in exchange for an additional 20 shares. Can Matthew avoid recognizing $60,000 ($100,000 − $40,000) of the gain realized on the transfer?

Solution: If Matthew simply exchanges the property for additional stock, he must recognize the gain. The Sec. 351 control requirement will not have been met because Matthew will own only 70 of the 120 outstanding shares (or 58.33%) immediately after the exchange.

Gain recognition can be avoided in two ways:

1. Matthew can transfer sufficient property (i.e., $750,000 worth) to Main to receive 150 additional shares so that, immediately after the exchange, he will own 80% (200 out of 250 shares) of Main stock.
2. Alternatively, Michael also can contribute additional property to qualify as a transferor. Specifically, he can contribute to the corporation at least $25,000, or 10% of the $250,000 value of the Main stock that he already owns so that together the two transferors will own 100% of Main stock immediately after the exchange.

Disproportionate Exchanges of Property and Stock. Section 351 does not require that the value of the stock received by the transferors be proportionate to the value of the property transferred. However, if the value of the stock received is *not* proportionate to the value of the property transferred, the exchange may be treated in accordance with its economic effect, that is, a proportional exchange followed by a constructive gift, compensation payment, or extinguishment of a liability owed by one shareholder to another.[20] If the deemed effect of the transaction is a gift from one transferor to another, for example, the "donor" will be treated as though he or she received stock equal in value to that of the property contributed and then gave some of the stock to the "donee."

EXAMPLE C:2-21 ▶ Don and his son John transfer property worth $75,000 (adjusted basis of $42,000 to Don) and $25,000 (adjusted basis of $20,000 to John), respectively, to newly formed Star Corporation in exchange for all 100 shares of Star stock. Don and John receive 25 and 75 Star shares, respectively. Because Don and John are in control of Star immediately after the exchange, they recognize no gain or loss. However, because Don and John did not receive the stock in proportion to the FMV of their respective property contributions, Don might be deemed to have received 75 shares (worth $75,000), then to have given 50 shares (worth $50,000) to John. If the IRS deems such a gift, it might require Don to pay gift taxes. Don's basis in his remaining 25 shares is $14,000 [(25 ÷ 75) × $42,000 basis in the property transferred]. John's basis in the 75 shares is $48,000 [$20,000 basis in the property transferred by John + ($42,000 − $14,000) basis in the shares deemed to have been gifted by Don]. ◀

---

[18] Reg. Sec. 1.351-1(a)(1)(ii).

[19] Rev. Proc. 77-37, 1977-2 C.B. 568, Sec. 3.07, as modified by T.D. 8761, 1998-1 C.B. 812.

[20] Reg. Sec. 1.351-1(b)(1).

Immediately After the Exchange. Section 351 requires that the transferors be in control of the transferee corporation "immediately after the exchange." This requirement does not mean that all transferors must simultaneously exchange their property for stock. It does mean, however, that all the exchanges must be agreed to beforehand, and the agreement must be executed in an expeditious and orderly manner.[21]

EXAMPLE C:2-22 ▶ Art, Beth, and Carlos form New Corporation. Art and Beth each transfer noncash property worth $25,000 in exchange for one-third of the New stock. Carlos contributes $25,000 cash for another one-third of the New stock. On January 10, Art and Carlos transfer their property and cash, respectively. Beth transfers her property on March 3. Because all three transfers are part of the same prearranged transaction, the transferors are deemed to be in control of the corporation immediately after the exchange. ◀

TAX STRATEGY TIP

If one shareholder has a prearranged plan to dispose of his or her stock, and the disposition reduces the ownership of the transferor shareholders below the required 80% control, such disposition can disqualify the Sec. 351 transaction for all the shareholders. As a precaution, all shareholders should provide a written representation that they do not currently have a plan to dispose of their stock.

Section 351 does not require the transferors to retain control of the transferee corporation for any specific length of time after the exchange. Control is required only "immediately after the exchange." The IRS has interpreted this phrase to mean that the transferors must not have a prearranged plan to dispose of their stock outside the control group. If they do have such a plan, they are not considered to be in control immediately after the exchange.[22]

EXAMPLE C:2-23 ▶ Amir, Bill, and Carl form White Corporation. Each contributes to White appreciated property worth $25,000 in exchange for one-third of White stock. Before the exchange, Amir arranges to sell his stock to Dana as soon as he receives it. This prearranged plan implies that Amir, Bill, and Carl do *not* have control immediately after the exchange because Bill and Carl own only 66.7% of the stock while Amir has disposed of his interest. Therefore, each must recognize gain on the exchange. ◀

THE STOCK REQUIREMENT

Under Sec. 351, transferors who exchange property solely for transferee corporation qualified stock recognize no gain or loss if they control the corporation immediately after the exchange. For this purpose, qualified stock may be voting or nonvoting and may be common stock or qualified preferred stock. On the other hand, *nonqualified* preferred stock is treated as boot. Preferred stock generally has a preferred claim to dividends and liquidating distributions. Such stock, however, is nonqualified if

- The shareholder can require the corporation to redeem it,
- The corporation either is required to redeem the stock or is likely to exercise a right to redeem it, or
- The dividend rate on the stock varies with interest rates, commodity prices, or other similar indices.

These features render the preferred stock more like cash or debt than like equity. Thus, it is treated as boot subject to the rules discussed below. In addition, stock rights or stock warrants are not considered stock for purposes of Sec. 351.[23]

Topic Review C:2-1 summarizes the major requirements for a nontaxable exchange under Sec. 351.

ADDITIONAL COMMENT

Nonqualified preferred stock is preferred stock that has one of the following characteristics: (1) the shareholder can require the corporation to redeem the stock, (2) the corporation is required to redeem the stock, (3) the corporation has the right to redeem the stock and is more likely than not to do so, or (4) the dividend rate on the stock varies in relation to interest rates or other such indices [see Sec. 351(g)].

EFFECT OF SEC. 351 ON THE TRANSFERORS

If all Sec. 351 requirements are met, the transferors recognize no gain or loss on the exchange of their property for stock in the transferee corporation. The receipt of property other than stock does not necessarily render the entire transaction taxable. Rather, it could result in the recognition of all or part of the transferors' realized gain.

Receipt of Boot. If a transferor receives any money or property other than stock in the transferee corporation, the additional money or property is considered to be **boot**. Boot may include cash, notes, securities, nonqualified preferred stock, or stock in another corporation. Upon receiving boot, the transferor recognizes gain to the extent of the lesser of the transferor's realized

[21] Reg. Sec. 1.351-1(a)(1).

[22] Rev. Rul. 79-70, 1979-1 C.B. 144.

[23] Reg. Sec. 1.351-1(a)(1)(ii).

TOPIC REVIEW C:2-1

Major Requirements of Sec. 351

1. The nonrecognition of gain or loss rule applies only to transfers of property in exchange for a corporation's stock. It does not apply to an exchange of services for stock.
2. The property transferors must be in control of the transferee corporation immediately after the exchange. Control means ownership of at least 80% of the voting power and at least 80% of the total number of shares of all other classes of stock. Stock disposed of after the exchange pursuant to a prearranged plan does not meet the "immediately after the exchange" requirement.
3. The nonrecognition rule applies only to the gain realized in an exchange of property for stock. If the transferor receives property other than stock, such property is considered to be boot. The transferor recognizes gain to the extent of the lesser of the FMV of any boot received or the realized gain.

gain or the FMV of the boot property received.[24] A transferor never recognizes a loss in an exchange qualifying under Sec. 351 whether or not he or she receives boot.

The character of the recognized gain depends on the type of property transferred. For example, if the shareholder transfers a capital asset such as stock in another corporation, the recognized gain is capital in character. If the shareholder transfers Sec. 1231 property, such as equipment or a building, the recognized gain is ordinary in character to the extent of any depreciation recaptured under Sec. 1245 or 1250.[25] Thus, depreciation is not recaptured unless the transferor receives boot and recognizes a gain on the depreciated property transferred.[26] If the shareholder transfers inventory, the recognized gain is entirely ordinary in character.

EXAMPLE C:2-24 ▶ Pam, Rob, and Sam form East Corporation and transfer the following property:

Transferor	*Asset*	*Transferor's Adj. Basis*	*FMV*	*Consideration Received*
Pam	Machinery	$ 10,000	$12,500	25 shares East stock
Rob	Land	18,000	25,000	40 shares East stock and $5,000 East note
Sam	Cash	17,500	17,500	35 shares East stock

The machinery is Sec. 1231 property, and the land is a capital asset. The exchange meets the requirements of Sec. 351 except that, in addition to East stock, Rob receives boot of $5,000 (the FMV of the note). Rob realizes a $7,000 ($25,000 − $18,000) gain, of which he recognizes $5,000—the lesser of the $7,000 realized gain or the $5,000 boot received. The gain is capital in character because the property transferred was a capital asset in Rob's hands. Pam realizes a $2,500 gain on her exchange of machinery. However, even though Pam would have been required to recapture depreciation had she sold or exchanged the machinery, she recognizes no gain because she received no boot. Sam neither realizes nor recognizes gain on his cash purchase of East stock. ◀

ADDITIONAL COMMENT

If multiple assets were aggregated into one computation, any built-in losses would be netted against the gains. Such a result is inappropriate because losses cannot be recognized in a Sec. 351 transaction.

Computing Gain When Several Assets Are Transferred. Revenue Ruling 68-55 adopts a "separate properties approach" for computing gain or loss when a shareholder transfers more than one asset to a corporation.[27] Under this approach, the gain or loss realized and recognized is computed separately for each property transferred. The transferor is deemed to have received a proportionate share of stock, securities, and boot in exchange for each property transferred, based on the assets' relative FMVs.

EXAMPLE C:2-25 ▶ Joan transfers two assets to newly formed North Corporation in a transaction qualifying in part for tax-free treatment under Sec. 351. The total FMV of the assets is $100,000. The consideration

[24] Sec. 351(b).

[25] Section 1239 also may require some gain to be characterized as ordinary income. Section 1250 ordinary depreciation recapture will not apply to real property placed in service after 1986 because MACRS mandates straight-line depreciation.

[26] Secs. 1245(b)(3) and 1250(c)(3).

[27] 1968-1 C.B. 140, as amplified by Rev. Rul. 85-164, 1985-2 C.B. 117.

received by Joan consists of $90,000 of North stock and $10,000 of North notes. The following data illustrate how Joan determines her realized and recognized gain under the procedure set forth in Rev. Rul. 68-55.

	Asset 1	*Asset 2*	*Total*
Asset's FMV	$40,000	$60,000	$100,000
Percent of total FMV	40%	60%	100%
Consideration received in exchange for asset:			
Stock (Stock × percent of total FMV)	$36,000	$54,000	$ 90,000
Notes (Notes × percent of total FMV)	4,000	6,000	10,000
Total proceeds	$40,000	$60,000	$100,000
Minus: Adjusted basis	(65,000)	(25,000)	(90,000)
Realized gain (loss)	($25,000)	$35,000	$ 10,000
Boot received	$ 4,000	$ 6,000	$ 10,000
Recognized gain (loss)	None	$ 6,000	$ 6,000

Under the separate properties approach, the loss realized on the transfer of Asset 1 does not offset the gain realized on the transfer of Asset 2. Therefore, Joan recognizes $6,000 of the total $10,000 realized gain, even though she receives $10,000 of boot. Joan's selling Asset 1 to North so as to recognize the loss might be advisable. However, the Sec. 267 loss limitation rules may apply to Joan if she is a controlling shareholder (see pages C:2-34 and C:2-35). ◀

Computing a Shareholder's Basis.

Boot Property. A transferor's basis in any boot property received is the property's FMV.[28]

Stock. A shareholder computes his or her adjusted basis in stock received in a Sec. 351 exchange as follows:[29]

Adjusted basis of property transferred to the corporation	
Plus:	Any gain recognized by the transferor
Minus:	FMV of boot received from the corporation
	Money received from the corporation
	Liabilities assumed by the corporation
Adjusted basis of stock received	

EXAMPLE C:2-26 ▶ Bob transfers a capital asset having a $50,000 adjusted basis and an $80,000 FMV to South Corporation. He acquired the property two years ago. Bob receives all 100 shares of South stock, having a $70,000 FMV, plus a $10,000 90-day South note (boot property). Bob realizes a $30,000 gain on the exchange, computed as follows:

FMV of stock received	$70,000
Plus: FMV of 90-day note	10,000
Amount realized	$80,000
Minus: Adjusted basis of property transferred	(50,000)
Realized gain	$30,000

Bob's recognized gain is $10,000, i.e., the lesser of the $30,000 realized gain or the $10,000 FMV of the boot property. This gain is long-term and capital in character. The Sec. 351 rules effectively require Bob to defer $20,000 ($30,000 – $10,000) of his realized gain. Bob's basis in the South stock is $50,000, computed as follows:

Adjusted basis of property transferred	$50,000
Plus: Gain recognized by Bob	10,000
Minus: FMV of boot received	(10,000)
Adjusted basis of Bob's stock	$50,000 ◀

ADDITIONAL COMMENT

Because Sec. 351 is a deferral provision, any unrecognized gain must be reflected in the basis of the stock received by the transferor shareholder and is accomplished by substituting the shareholder's basis in the property transferred for the basis of the stock received. This substituted basis may be further adjusted by gain recognized and boot received.

[28] Sec. 358(a)(2).

[29] Sec. 358(a)(1).

If a transferor receives more than one class of qualified stock, his or her basis must be allocated among the classes according to their relative FMVs.[30]

EXAMPLE C:2-27 ▶ Assume the same facts as in Example C:2-26 except Bob receives 100 shares of South common stock with a $45,000 FMV, 50 shares of South qualified preferred stock with a $25,000 FMV, and a 90-day South note with a $10,000 FMV. The total adjusted basis of the stock is $50,000 ($50,000 basis of property transferred + $10,000 gain recognized − $10,000 FMV of boot received). This basis must be allocated between the common and qualified preferred stock according to their relative FMVs, as follows:

$$\text{Basis of common stock} = \frac{\$45{,}000}{\$45{,}000 + \$25{,}000} \times \$50{,}000 = \$32{,}143$$

$$\text{Basis of preferred stock} = \frac{\$25{,}000}{\$45{,}000 + \$25{,}000} \times \$50{,}000 = \$17{,}857$$

Bob's basis in the note is its $10,000 FMV. ◀

SELF-STUDY QUESTION

What is an alternative method for determining the basis of the assets received by the transferor shareholder? How is this method applied to Bob in Example C:2-26?

ANSWER

The basis of all boot property is its FMV, and the basis of qualified stock received is the stock's FMV minus any deferred gain or plus any deferred loss. Bob's stock basis under the alternative method is $50,000 ($70,000 FMV of stock − $20,000 deferred gain).

Transferor's Holding Period. The transferor's holding period for any stock received in exchange for a capital asset or Sec. 1231 property includes the holding period of the property transferred.[31] If the transferor exchanged any other kind of property (e.g., inventory) for the stock, the transferor's holding period for the stock begins on the day after the exchange. Likewise, the holding period for boot property begins on the day after the exchange.

EXAMPLE C:2-28 ▶ Assume the same facts as in Example C:2-26. Bob's holding period for the stock includes the holding period of the capital asset transferred. His holding period for the note starts on the day after the exchange. ◀

Question: The holding period for stock received in exchange for a capital asset or Sec. 1231 property includes the holding period of the transferred item. The holding period for inventory or other assets begins on the day after the exchange. Why the difference?

Solution: Because stock received in a Sec. 351 exchange represents a "continuity of interest" in the property transferred, logically the stock should not only be valued and characterized in the same manner as the asset exchanged for the equity claim, but also accorded the same tax attributes. Because the holding period of a capital asset is relevant in determining the character of gain or loss realized (i.e., long-term or short-term) on the asset's subsequent sale, stock received in a tax-free exchange of the asset should be accorded the same holding period for the purpose of determining the character of gain or loss realized on the stock's subsequent sale. By the same token, because the holding period of a noncapital asset is less relevant in determining the character of gain or loss realized on the asset's subsequent sale, stock received in a tax-free exchange of the asset need not be accorded the same holding period for the purpose of determining the character of gain or loss realized on the stock's subsequent sale. Given the very nature of a noncapital asset, this gain or loss generally is ordinary in character, in any event. Moreover, if stock received in exchange for a noncapital asset were accorded a holding period that includes that of the transferred property, a transferor could sell the stock in a short time to realize a long-term capital gain, thereby converting ordinary income (potentially from the sale of the noncapital asset) into capital gain from the sale of stock.

Topic Review C:2-2 summarizes the tax consequences of a Sec. 351 exchange to the transferor(s) and the transferee corporation.

[30] Sec. 358(b)(1) and Reg. Sec. 1.358-2(b)(2).

[31] Sec. 1223(1). Revenue Ruling 85-164 (1985-2 C.B. 117) provides that a single share of stock may have two holding periods: a carryover holding period for the portion of such share received in exchange for a capital asset or Sec. 1231 property and a holding period that begins on the day after the exchange for the portion of such share received for inventory or other property. The split holding period is relevant only if the transferor sells the stock received within one year of the transfer date.

TOPIC REVIEW C:2-2

Tax Consequences of a Sec. 351 Exchange

To Transferor(s):

1. Transferors recognize no gain or loss when they exchange property for stock. Exception: A transferor recognizes gain equal to the lesser of the realized gain or the sum of any money received plus the FMV of any non-cash property received. The character of the gain depends on the type of property transferred.
2. The basis of the stock received equals the adjusted basis of the property transferred plus any gain recognized by the transferor minus the FMV of any boot property received minus any money received (including liabilities assumed or acquired by the transferee corporation).
3. The holding period of stock received in exchange for capital assets or Sec. 1231 property includes the holding period of the transferred property. The holding period of stock received in exchange for any other property begins on the day after the exchange.

To Transferee Corporation:

1. A corporation recognizes no gain or loss when it exchanges its own stock for property or services.
2. The corporation's basis in property received is the transferor's basis plus any gain recognized by the transferor. However, if the total adjusted basis of all transferred property exceeds the total FMV of the property, the total basis to the transferee is limited to the property's total FMV.
3. The corporation's holding period for property received includes the transferor's holding period.

ADDITIONAL COMMENT

The nonrecognition rule for corporations that issue stock for property applies whether or not the transaction qualifies the transferor shareholder for Sec. 351 treatment.

TAX CONSEQUENCES TO TRANSFEREE CORPORATION

A corporation that issues stock or debt for property or services is subject to various IRC rules for determining the tax consequences of that exchange.

Gain or Loss Recognized by the Transferee Corporation. Corporations recognize no gain or loss when they issue their own stock in exchange for property or services.[32] This result ensues whether or not Sec. 351 governs the exchange and whether or not the corporation issues new stock or treasury stock.

EXAMPLE C:2-29 ▶ West Corporation pays $10,000 to acquire 100 shares of its own stock from existing shareholders. The next year, West reissues these 100 treasury shares in exchange for land having a $15,000 FMV. West realizes a $5,000 ($15,000 − $10,000) gain on the exchange but recognizes none of this gain. ◀

Corporations also recognize no gain or loss when they exchange their own debt instruments for property or services. On the other hand, a corporation recognizes gain (but not loss) if it transfers appreciated property to a transferor as part of a Sec. 351 exchange. The amount and character of the gain are determined as though the property had been sold by the corporation immediately before the transfer.

EXAMPLE C:2-30 ▶ Alice, who owns 100% of Ace Corporation stock, transfers to Ace land having a $100,000 FMV and a $60,000 adjusted basis. In exchange, Alice receives 75 additional shares of Ace common stock having a $75,000 FMV, and Zero Corporation common stock having a $25,000 FMV. Ace's basis in the Zero stock, a capital asset, is $10,000. Alice realizes a $40,000 gain [($75,000 + $25,000) − $60,000] on the land transfer, of which she recognizes $25,000 (i.e., the FMV of the boot property received). In addition, Ace recognizes a $15,000 capital gain ($25,000 − $10,000) upon transferring the Zero stock to Alice. ◀

Transferee Corporation's Basis for Property Received. A corporation that acquires property in exchange for its stock in a transaction that is taxable to the transferor takes a current cost (i.e., its FMV) basis in the property. On the other hand, if

[32] Sec. 1032.

ADDITIONAL COMMENT

If a shareholder transfers built-in gain property in a Sec. 351 transaction, the built-in gain actually is duplicated. This duplication occurs because the transferee corporation assumes the potential gain through its carryover basis in the assets it receives, and the transferor shareholder assumes the potential gain through its substituted basis in the transferee corporation stock. A similar duplication occurs for built-in loss property. This result reflects the double taxation characteristic of C corporations.

the exchange qualifies for nonrecognition treatment under Sec. 351 and is wholly or partially tax-free to the transferor, the corporation's basis in the property is computed as follows:[33]

Transferor's adjusted basis in property transferred to the corporation
Plus: Gain (if any) recognized by transferor
Minus: Reduction for loss property (if applicable)
Transferee corporation's basis in property

The transferee corporation's holding period for property acquired in a transaction satisfying the Sec. 351 requirements includes the period during which the property was held by the transferor.[34] This general rule applies to all types of property without regard to their character in the transferor's hands or the amount of gain recognized by the transferor. However, if the corporation reduces a property's basis to its FMV under the loss property limitation rule discussed below, the holding period will begin the day after the exchange date because no part of the new basis references the transferor's basis.

EXAMPLE C:2-31 ▶ Top Corporation issues 100 shares of its stock for land having a $15,000 FMV. Tina, who transferred the land, had a $12,000 basis in the property. If the exchange satisfies the Sec. 351 requirements, Tina recognizes no gain on the exchange. Top's basis in the land is $12,000, the same as Tina's. Top's holding period includes Tina's holding period. However, if the exchange does *not* satisfy the Sec. 351 requirements, Tina recognizes $3,000 of gain. Top's basis in the land is its $15,000 acquisition cost, and its holding period begins on the day after the exchange date. ◀

Reduction for Loss Property. Section 362(e)(2) prevents shareholders from generating double losses by transferring loss property to a corporation. The double loss potential exists because the corporation would hold property with a built-in loss, and the shareholders would hold stock with a built-in loss. Accordingly, if a corporation's total adjusted basis (including any increase for gain recognized by the shareholder) for all properties transferred by the shareholder exceeds the properties' total FMV, the basis to the corporation of the properties must be reduced by this excess. The reduction in basis is allocated among the properties in proportion to their respective built-in losses. The limitation applies on a shareholder-by-shareholder basis. In other words, the property values and built-in losses of all shareholders are not aggregated.

EXAMPLE C:2-32 ▶ John transfers the following assets to Pecan Corporation in exchange for all of Pecan's stock worth $26,000.

Assets	*Adjusted Basis to John*	*FMV*
Inventory	$ 5,000	$ 8,000
Equipment	15,000	11,000
Furniture	9,000	7,000
Total	$29,000	$26,000

Although the transaction meets the requirements of Sec. 351, the total basis of the assets transferred ($29,000) exceeds their total FMV. Consequently, the total basis to Pecan is limited to the assets' FMV ($26,000). The $3,000 ($29,000 – $26,000) reduction in basis must be allocated among the assets in proportion to their respective built-in losses as follows:

Assets	*Built-in Losses*	*Allocated Reduction*
Equipment	$4,000	$2,000
Furniture	2,000	1,000
Total	$6,000	$3,000

[33] Sec. 362.

[34] Sec. 1223(2).

Thus, Pecan's bases for the assets transferred by John are:

Inventory	$ 5,000
Equipment ($15,000 − $2,000)	13,000
Furniture ($9,000 − $1,000)	8,000
Total	$26,000

Because each property's basis was not reduced to the property's FMV, the holding period of each property includes the transferor's holding period. ◀

A corporation subject to the basis reduction rules described above can avoid this result if the corporation and all its shareholders so elect. Under the election, the corporation need not reduce the bases of the assets received, but the affected shareholder's basis in stock received for the property is reduced by the amount by which the corporation would have reduced its basis absent the election.

EXAMPLE C:2-33 ▶ Assume the same facts as in Example C:2-32 except John and Pecan elect not to reduce the bases of the assets Pecan received. Under the election, John's basis in his Pecan stock is reduced to $26,000 ($29,000 − $3,000). ◀

A corporation and its shareholders can avoid the basis reduction rules altogether if each shareholder transfers enough appreciated property to offset any built-in losses of other property transferred. This avoidance opportunity exists because in making the comparison, each shareholder aggregates the adjusted bases and FMVs of his or her property transferred.

EXAMPLE C:2-34 ▶ Assume the same facts as in Example C:2-32 except the inventory's FMV is $12,000. In this case, total basis equals $29,000 and total FMV equals $30,000. Because total basis does not exceed total FMV, the limitation does not apply. Consequently, the corporation takes a carryover basis in each asset even though some assets have built-in losses. ◀

ASSUMPTION OF THE TRANSFEROR'S LIABILITIES

When a shareholder transfers property to a controlled corporation, the corporation often assumes the transferor's liabilities. The question arises as to whether the transferee corporation's assumption of liabilities is equivalent to a cash (boot) payment to the transferor. In certain types of transactions, the transferee's assumption of a transferor's liability is treated as a payment of cash to the transferor. For example, in a like-kind exchange, if a transferee assumes a transferor's liability, the transferor is treated as though he or she received a cash payment equal to the amount of the liability assumed. By contrast, if a transaction satisfies the Sec. 351 requirements, Sec. 357 provides relief from such treatment.

General Rule—Sec. 357(a). For the purpose of determining gain recognition, the transferee corporation's assumption of liabilities in a property transfer qualifying under Sec. 351 is *not* considered equivalent to the transferor's receipt of money. Consequently, the transferee corporation's assumption of liabilities does not result in the transferor's recognizing part or all of his or her realized gain. For the purpose of calculating the transferor's stock basis, however, the transferee corporation's assumption of liabilities *is* treated as money received and thus decreases the transferor's stock basis. Moreover, for the purpose of calculating the transferor's *realized* gain, the transferee corporation's assumption of liabilities is treated as part of the transferor's amount realized.[35]

EXAMPLE C:2-35 ▶ Roy and Eduardo transfer the following assets and liabilities to newly formed Palm Corporation:

[35] Sec. 358(d)(1).

Transferor	Asset/ Liability	Transferor's Adj. Basis	FMV	Consideration Received
Roy	Machinery	$15,000	$32,000	50 shares Palm stock
	Mortgage	8,000	—	Assumed by Palm
Eduardo	Cash	24,000	24,000	50 shares Palm stock

The transaction meets the requirements of Sec. 351. Roy's recognized gain is determined as follows:

FMV of stock received	$24,000
Plus: Palm's assumption of the mortgage liability	8,000
Amount realized	$32,000
Minus: Basis of machinery	(15,000)
Realized gain	$17,000
Boot received	$ –0–
Recognized gain	$ –0–

Although Palm's assumption of the mortgage liability increases Roy's amount realized, Roy recognizes none of his realized gain because the mortgage assumption is not considered to be boot (i.e., a cash equivalent). Eduardo recognizes no gain because he transferred only cash. Roy's stock basis is $7,000 ($15,000 basis of property transferred − $8,000 liability assumed by Palm). Eduardo's stock basis is $24,000. ◀

ADDITIONAL COMMENT

If any of the assumed liabilities are created for tax avoidance purposes, *all* the assumed liabilities are tainted.

The general rule of Sec. 357(a), however, has two exceptions. These exceptions, discussed below, relate to (1) transfers for the purpose of tax avoidance or without a bona fide business purpose and (2) transfers where the liabilities assumed by the corporation exceed the total basis of the property transferred.

ETHICAL POINT

Information about any transferor liabilities assumed by the transferee corporation must be reported with the transferee and transferor's tax returns for the year of transfer (see page C:2-36). Where a client asks a tax practitioner to ignore the fact that tax avoidance is the primary purpose for transferring a liability to a corporation, the tax practitioner must examine the ethical considerations of continuing to prepare returns and provide tax advice for the client.

Tax Avoidance or No Bona Fide Business Purpose—Sec. 357(b). All liabilities assumed by a controlled corporation *are* considered to be money received by the transferor, and therefore boot, if the principal purpose of the transfer of any portion of such liabilities is tax avoidance or if the liability transfer has no bona fide business purpose.

The transfer of liabilities might be considered to be motivated principally by tax avoidance where the transferor incurred the liabilities shortly before the transfer. Thus, the most important factor in determining whether a tax avoidance purpose exists may be the length of time between the incurrence of the liability and its transfer to, or assumption by, the corporation.

The assumption of liabilities normally is considered to have a business purpose if the transferor incurred the liabilities in the normal course of business or in the course of acquiring business property. Examples of liabilities without a bona fide business purpose and whose transfer would cause *all* liabilities transferred to be considered boot are personal obligations of the transferor, including a home mortgage or any other loans of a personal nature.

EXAMPLE C:2-36 ▶ David owns land having a $100,000 FMV and a $60,000 adjusted basis. The land is not encumbered by any liabilities. To obtain cash for his personal use, David transfers the land to his wholly owned corporation in exchange for additional stock and $25,000 cash. Because the cash is considered to be boot, David must recognize $25,000 of gain. Assume instead that David mortgages the land for $25,000 to obtain the needed cash. If shortly thereafter David transfers the land and the mortgage to his corporation for additional stock, the $25,000 mortgage assumed by the corporation will be considered to be boot because the transfer of the mortgage appears to have no bona fide business purpose. David's recognized gain will be $25,000, i.e., the lesser of the boot received ($25,000) or his realized gain ($40,000). This special liability rule prevents David from obtaining cash without boot recognition. ◀

Liabilities in Excess of Basis—Sec. 357(c). Under Sec. 357(c), if the total amount of liabilities transferred to a controlled corporation exceeds the total adjusted basis of all property transferred, the excess liability is taxed as a gain to the transferor.

This rule applies regardless of whether the transferor realizes any gain or loss. The rationale for the rule is that the transferor has received a benefit (in the form of a release from liabilities) that exceeds his or her original investment in the transferred property. Therefore, the transferor should be taxed on this benefit. The character of the recognized gain depends on the type of property transferred to the corporation. The transferor's basis in any stock received is zero.

EXAMPLE C:2-37 ▶ Judy transfers $10,000 cash and land, a capital asset, to Duke Corporation in exchange for all its stock. At the time of the exchange, the land has a $70,000 adjusted basis and a $125,000 FMV. Duke assumes a $100,000 mortgage on the land for a bona fide business purpose. Although Judy receives no boot, Judy must recognize a $20,000 ($100,000 − $80,000) capital gain, the amount by which the liabilities assumed by Duke exceed the basis of the land and the cash. Judy's basis in the Duke stock is zero, computed as follows:

Judy's basis in the land transferred		$ 70,000
Plus:	Cash transferred	10,000
	Gain recognized	20,000
Minus:	Liabilities assumed by Duke	(100,000)
Judy's basis in the Duke stock		$ -0-

Note that, without the recognition of the $20,000 gain, Judy's basis in the Duke stock would be a negative $20,000 ($80,000 – $100,000). ◀

STOP & THINK

Question: What are the fundamental differences between the liability exceptions of Sec. 357(b) and Sec. 357(c)?

Solution: Section 357(b) treats all "tainted" liabilities as boot so that gain recognition is the lesser of gain realized or the amount of boot. Excess liabilities under Sec. 357(c) are not treated as boot; they require gain recognition whether or not the transferor realizes any gain. Section 357(b) tends to be punitive in that the "tax avoidance" liabilities cause all the "offending" shareholder's transferred liabilities to be treated as boot even if the transfer of some liabilities do not have a tax avoidance purpose. Section 357(c) is not intended to be punitive. It recognizes that the shareholder has received an economic benefit to the extent of excess liabilities, and it prevents the occurrence of a negative stock basis. In short, Section 357(b) deters or punishes tax avoidance while Sec. 357(c) taxes an economic gain.

KEY POINT

Because of the "liabilities in excess of basis" exception, many cash basis transferor shareholders might inadvertently create recognized gain in a Sec. 351 transaction. However, a special exception exists that protects cash basis taxpayers. This exception provides that liabilities that would give rise to a deduction when paid are not treated as liabilities for purposes of Sec. 357(c).

Liabilities of a Cash Method Taxpayer—Sec. 357(c)(3). In a Sec. 351 tax-free exchange, special problems arise when a taxpayer using the cash or hybrid method of accounting transfers property and liabilities of an ongoing business to a corporation.[36] Often, the principal assets transferred are accounts receivable having a zero basis. Liabilities usually are transferred as well. Consequently, the amount of liabilities transferred may exceed the total basis (but not the FMV) of the property transferred.

Under the general rule of Sec. 357(c), the transferor recognizes gain equal to the amount by which the liabilities assumed exceed the total basis of the property transferred. Section 357(c)(3), however, provides that, in applying the general rule, the term *liabilities* does *not* include any amount that would give rise to a deduction when paid (e.g., accounts payable of a cash basis taxpayer). These amounts also are not considered liabilities for the purpose of determining the shareholder's basis in stock received.[37] Therefore, they generally do not reduce this basis. However, if after all other adjustments the stock's basis exceeds its FMV, these liabilities could reduce stock basis, but not below the stock's FMV.[38]

EXAMPLE C:2-38 ▶ Tracy operates a cash basis accounting practice as a sole proprietorship. She transfers the assets of her practice to Prime Corporation in exchange for all the Prime stock. The balance sheet for the transferred practice is as follows:

[36] Sec. 357(c)(3).
[37] Sec. 358(d)(2).
[38] Sec. 358(h)(1).

Assets and Liabilities	Adjusted Basis	FMV
Cash	$ 5,000	$ 5,000
Furniture	5,000	8,000
Accounts receivable	-0-	50,000
Total	$10,000	$63,000
Accounts payable (deductible expenses)	$ -0-	$25,000
Note payable (on office furniture)	2,000	2,000
Owner's equity	8,000	36,000
Total	$10,000	$63,000

If, for purposes of Sec. 357(c), the accounts payable were considered liabilities, the $27,000 of liabilities transferred (i.e., the $25,000 of accounts payable and the $2,000 note payable) would exceed the $10,000 total basis of assets transferred, and Troy would recognize a $17,000 gain. Because paying the $25,000 of accounts payable gives rise to a deduction, however, they are not considered liabilities for purposes of Sec. 357(c). On the other hand, the $2,000 note payable *is* considered a liability for this purpose because paying it would not give rise to a deduction. Thus, the total liabilities transferred to Prime amount to only $2,000. Because that amount does not exceed the $10,000 total basis of the assets transferred, Tracy recognizes no gain. Moreover, the accounts payable are not considered liabilities for purposes of computing Tracy's basis in her stock because the stock's basis ($8,000) does not exceed its FMV ($36,000). Thus, her basis in the Prime stock is $8,000 ($10,000 – $2,000). ◀

Topic Review C:2-3 summarizes the liability assumption and acquisition rules of Sec. 357.

OTHER CONSIDERATIONS IN A SEC. 351 EXCHANGE

Recapture of Depreciation. If a Sec. 351 exchange is completely nontaxable (i.e., the transferor receives no boot), no depreciation is recaptured. Instead, the corporation inherits the entire amount of the transferor's recapture potential. Where the transferor recognizes some depreciation recapture as ordinary income (e.g., because of boot recognition), the transferee inherits the remaining recapture potential. If the transferee corporation subsequently disposes of the depreciated property, the corporation is subject to recapture rules on depreciation it claimed subsequent to the transfer, plus the recapture potential it inherited from the transferor.

EXAMPLE C:2-39 ▶ Azeem transfers machinery having a $25,000 original cost, an $18,000 adjusted basis, and a $35,000 FMV for all 100 shares of Wheel Corporation stock. Before the transfer, Azeem used the machinery in his business and claimed $7,000 of depreciation. In the transfer, Azeem recaptures no depreciation, and Wheel inherits the $7,000 recapture potential. After claiming an additional $2,000 of depreciation, Wheel has a $16,000 adjusted basis in the machinery. If

TOPIC REVIEW C:2-3

Liability Assumption and Acquisition Rules of Sec. 357

1. *General Rule (Sec. 357(a)):* A transferee corporation's assumption of liabilities in a Sec. 351 exchange is not treated as boot by the shareholder for gain recognition purposes. On the other hand, the assumption of liabilities is treated as the receipt of money for purposes of determining the transferor's stock basis and amount realized.
2. *Exception 1 (Sec. 357(b)):* All liabilities assumed by a transferee corporation are considered to be money/boot received by the transferor if the principal purpose of the transfer of any of the liabilities is tax avoidance or if no bona fide business purpose exists for the transfer.
3. *Exception 2 (Sec. 357(c)):* If the total amount of liabilities assumed by a transferee corporation exceeds the total basis of property transferred, the transferor recognizes the excess as gain.
4. *Special Rule (Sec. 357(c)(3)):* For purposes of Exception 2, the term liabilities for a transferor using a cash or hybrid method of accounting does not include any amount that would give rise to a deduction when paid.

Wheel now sells the machinery for $33,000, it must recognize a $17,000 ($33,000 − $16,000) gain. Of this gain, $9,000 is ordinary income recaptured under Sec. 1245. The remaining $8,000 is a Sec. 1231 gain. ◀

Computing Depreciation. When a shareholder transfers depreciable property to a corporation in a nontaxable Sec. 351 exchange and the shareholder has not fully depreciated the property, the corporation must use the depreciation method and recovery period used by the transferor.[39] For the year of the transfer, the depreciation must be allocated between the transferor and the transferee corporation according to the number of months each party held the property. The transferee corporation is assumed to have held the property for the entire month in which the property was transferred.[40]

EXAMPLE C:2-40 ▶ On June 10 of Year 1, Carla paid $6,000 for a computer (five-year property for MACRS purposes), which she used in her sole proprietorship business. In Year 1, she claimed $1,200 (0.20 × $6,000) of depreciation. She did not elect Sec. 179 expensing and did not claim any bonus depreciation. On February 10 of Year 2, she transfers the computer and other sole proprietorship assets to King Corporation in exchange for King stock. Because Sec. 351 applies, she recognizes no gain or loss. King must use the same MACRS recovery period and method that Carla used. Depreciation for Year 2 is $1,920 (0.32 × $6,000). That amount must be allocated between Carla and King. The computer is considered to have been held by Carla for one month and by King for 11 months (including the month of transfer). The Year 2 depreciation amounts claimed by Carla and King are calculated as follows:

Carla	$6,000 × 0.32 × 1/12 = $ 160
King Corporation	$6,000 × 0.32 × 11/12 = $1,760

King's basis in the computer is calculated as follows:

Original cost	$6,000
Minus: Year 1 depreciation claimed by Carla	(1,200)
Year 2 depreciation claimed by Carla	(160)
Adjusted basis on transfer date	$4,640

King's depreciation for Year 2 and subsequent years is as follows:

Year 2 (as computed above)	$1,760
Year 3 ($6,000 × 0.1920)	1,152
Year 4 ($6,000 × 0.1152)	691
Year 5 ($6,000 × 0.1152)	691
Year 6 ($6,000 × 0.0576)	346
Total	$4,640

◀

If the transferee corporation's basis in the depreciable property exceeds the transferor's basis (e.g., as a result of an upward adjustment to reflect gain recognized by the transferor), the corporation treats the excess amount as newly purchased MACRS property and uses the recovery period and method applicable to the class of property transferred.[41]

EXAMPLE C:2-41 ▶ Assume the same facts as in Example C:2-40 except that, in addition to King stock, Carla receives a King note. Consequently, she must recognize $1,000 of gain on the transfer of the computer. King's basis in the computer is calculated as follows:

Original cost	$6,000
Depreciation claimed by Carla	(1,360)
Adjusted basis on transfer date	$4,640
Plus: Gain recognized by Carla	1,000
Basis to King on transfer date	$5,640

The additional $1,000 of basis is depreciated as though it were separate, newly purchased five-year MACRS property. Thus, King claims depreciation of $200 (0.20 × $1,000) on this portion of

[39] Sec. 168(i)(7).

[40] Prop. Reg. Secs. 1.168-5(b)(2)(i)(B), 1.168-5(b)(4)(i), and 1.168-5(b)(8).

[41] Prop. Reg. Sec. 1.168-5(b)(7).

the basis in addition to the $1,760 of depreciation on the $4,640 carryover basis. Alternatively, King could elect to expense the $1,000 "new" basis under Sec. 179. ◀

ADDITIONAL COMMENT

Currently, we have no clear guidance on how the corporation depreciates transferred property that has a reduced basis under the loss property limitation rule discussed on page C:2-21. For now, taxpayers probably should rely on Prop. Reg. 1.168-2(d)(3), which provides a method for calculating depreciation when the transferee's basis is less than the transferor's basis.

Assignment of Income Doctrine. The **assignment of income doctrine** holds that income is taxable to the person who earned it and that it may not be assigned to another person for tax purposes.[42] The question arises as to whether the assignment of income doctrine applies where a cash method taxpayer transfers uncollected accounts receivable to a corporation in a Sec. 351 exchange. Specifically, who must recognize the income when it is collected—the taxpayer who transferred the receivable or the corporation that now owns and collects on the receivable? The IRS has ruled that the doctrine does *not* apply in a Sec. 351 exchange if the taxpayer transfers substantially all the business assets and liabilities, and a bona fide business purpose exists for the transfer. Instead, the accounts receivable take a zero basis in the corporation's hands, and the corporation includes their value in its income when it collects on the receivables.[43]

EXAMPLE C:2-42 ▶ For a bona fide business purpose, Ruth, a cash basis taxpayer, transfers all the assets and liabilities of her legal practice to Legal Services Corporation in exchange for all of Legal Services stock. The assets include $30,000 of accounts receivable that will generate earnings that Ruth has not included in her gross income. Because Ruth transfers substantially all the business assets and liabilities for a bona fide business purpose, the assignment of income doctrine does not apply to the receivables transferred, and Legal Services takes a zero basis in the receivables. Subsequently, Legal Services includes the value of the receivables in its income as it collects on them. ◀

The question of whether a transferee corporation can deduct the accounts payable transferred to it in a nontaxable transfer has frequently been litigated.[44] Most courts have held that ordinarily expenses are deductible only by the party that incurred those liabilities in the course of its trade or business. However, the IRS has ruled that in a nontaxable exchange the transferee corporation may deduct the payments it makes to satisfy the transferred accounts payable even though they arose in the transferor's business.[45]

CHOICE OF CAPITAL STRUCTURE

OBJECTIVE 5

Explain the tax implications of alternative capital structures

When a corporation is formed, the way it is financed will determine its capital structure. The corporation may obtain capital from shareholders, nonshareholders, and creditors. In exchange for their capital, shareholders may receive common or preferred stock; nonshareholders may receive benefits such as employment or special rates on products sold by the corporation; and creditors may receive long- or short-term debt. As explained below, each of these alternatives has tax advantages and disadvantages for the shareholders, creditors, and corporation.

CHARACTERIZATION OF OBLIGATIONS AS DEBT OR EQUITY

The deductibility of interest payments creates an incentive for corporations to incur as much debt as possible. Because debt financing often resembles equity financing (e.g., preferred stock), the IRS and the courts have refused to accept the form of the security as controlling.[46] In some cases, debt obligations that possess equity characteristics have been treated as common or preferred stock for tax purposes. In determining the appropriate tax treatment, the courts have relied on a number of factors.

[42] See, for example, *Lucas v. Guy C. Earl*, 8 AFTR 10287, 2 USTC ¶496 (USSC, 1930).

[43] Rev. Rul. 80-198, 1980-2 C.B. 113.

[44] See, for example, *Wilford E. Thatcher v. CIR*, 37 AFTR 2d 76-1068, 76-1 USTC ¶9324 (9th Cir., 1976), and *John P. Bongiovanni v. CIR*, 31 AFTR 2d 73-409, 73-1 USTC ¶9133 (2nd Cir., 1972).

[45] Rev. Rul. 80-198, 1980-2 C.B. 113.

[46] See, for example, *Aqualane Shores, Inc. v. CIR*, 4 AFTR 2d 5346, 59-2 USTC ¶9632 (5th Cir., 1959) and *Sun Properties, Inc. v. U.S.*, 47 AFTR 273, 55-1 USTC ¶9261 (5th Cir., 1955).

Congress enacted Sec. 385 to establish a standard for determining whether a security is debt or equity. Section 385 provides that the following factors be considered in the determination:

HISTORICAL NOTE

The Treasury Department at one time issued proposed and final regulations covering Sec. 385. These regulations were the subject of so much criticism that the Treasury Department eventually withdrew them. Section 385, however, makes it clear that Congress wants the Treasury Department to make further attempts at clarifying the debt-equity issue. So far, the Treasury Department has issued no "new" proposed or final regulations.

- Whether there is a written unconditional promise to pay on demand or on a specified date a certain sum of money in return for adequate consideration in the form of money or money's worth, in addition to an unconditional promise to pay a fixed rate of interest
- Whether the debt is subordinate to, or preferred over, other indebtedness of the corporation
- The ratio of corporate debt to equity
- Whether the debt is convertible into stock of the corporation
- The relationship between holdings of stock in the corporation and holdings of the interest in question[47]

DEBT CAPITAL

Various provisions govern the tax treatment of (1) the issuance of debt; (2) the payment of interest on debt; and (3) the extinguishment, retirement, or worthlessness of debt. The tax implications of each of these events are examined below.

SELF-STUDY QUESTION

From a tax perspective, why is the distinction between debt and equity important?

ANSWER

Interest paid with respect to a debt instrument is deductible by the payor corporation. Dividends paid with respect to an equity instrument are not deductible by the payor corporation. Thus, the determination of whether an instrument is debt or equity can provide different results to the payor corporation. Different results apply to the payee as well. Qualified dividends are subject to the applicable capital gains tax rate while interest is taxed as ordinary income.

Issuance of Debt. If a transferor transfers appreciated property in exchange for stock, the transfer will be nontaxable, provided the Sec. 351 requirements have been met. On the other hand, if the transferor transfers appreciated property in exchange for corporate debt as part of a Sec. 351 exchange, the FMV of the debt received will be treated as boot, possibly leading to gain recognition.

Payment of Interest. Interest paid on indebtedness is deductible by the corporation in deriving its taxable income.[48] Moreover, a corporation is not subject to the investment interest deduction limitation applicable to individual taxpayers. By contrast, the corporation cannot deduct dividends paid on equity securities.

If a corporation issues a debt instrument at a discount, Sec. 1272 requires the holder to amortize the original issue discount over the term of the obligation and treat the accrual as interest income. The debtor corporation amortizes the original issue discount over the term of the obligation and treats the accrual as an additional cost of borrowing.[49] If the corporation repurchases the debt instrument for more than the issue price (plus any original issue discount deducted as interest), the corporation deducts the excess of the purchase price over the issue price (adjusted for any amortization of original issue discount) as interest expense.[50]

Under Sec. 171, if a corporation issues a debt instrument at a premium, the holder may elect to amortize the premium over the term of the obligation and treat the accrual as a reduction in interest income earned on the obligation. For the debtor corporation, the premium reduces the amount of deductible interest.[51] If the corporation repurchases the debt instrument at a price greater than the issue price (minus any premium treated as income), the corporation deducts the excess of the purchase price over the issue price (adjusted for any amortization of premium) as interest expense.[52]

Extinguishment of Debt. Generally, the retirement of debt is not a taxable event. Thus, a debtor corporation's extinguishing an obligation at face value does not result in the creditor's recognizing gain or loss. However, amounts received by the holder

[47] See also *O.H. Kruse Grain & Milling v. CIR*, 5 AFTR 2d 1544, 60-2 USTC ¶9490 (9th Cir., 1960), which lists additional factors that the courts might consider.

[48] Sec. 163(a).

[49] Sec. 163(e).

[50] Reg. Sec. 1.163-7(c).

[51] Reg. Sec. 1.163-12.

[52] Reg. Sec. 1.163-7(c).

of a debt instrument (e.g., note, bond, or debenture) at the time of its retirement are deemed to be "in exchange for" the obligation. Thus, if the obligation is a capital asset in the holder's hands, the holder must recognize a capital gain or loss if the amount received differs from its face value or adjusted basis, unless the difference is due to original issue or market discount.

EXAMPLE C:2-43 ▶ Titan Corporation issues a ten-year note at its $1,000 face amount. On the date of issuance, Rick purchases the note for $1,000. Because of a decline in interest rates, Titan calls the note at a price of $1,050 payable to each note holder. Rick reports the premium as a $50 capital gain, and Titan deducts as interest expense total premiums paid to all its note holders. ◀

ADDITIONAL COMMENT

Even though debt often is thought of as a preferred instrument because of the deductibility of the interest paid, the debt must be repaid at its maturity, whereas stock has no specified maturity date. Also, interest usually must be paid at regular intervals, whereas dividends do not have to be declared if sufficient funds are not available to pay them or if the corporation needs to retain funds for operations or growth.

Table C:2-2 presents a comparison of the tax advantages and disadvantages of a corporation's using debt in its capital structure.

EQUITY CAPITAL

Corporations can raise equity capital through the issuance of various types of stock. Some corporations issue only a single class of stock, whereas others issue numerous classes of stock. Reasons for the use of multiple classes of stock include

- ▶ Permitting nonfamily employees of family owned corporations to obtain an equity interest in the business while keeping voting control in the hands of family members.
- ▶ Financing a **closely held corporation** through the issuance of preferred stock to an outside investor, while leaving voting control in the hands of existing common stockholders.

Table C:2-3 lists some of the major tax advantages and disadvantages of using common and preferred stock in a corporation's capital structure.

SELF-STUDY QUESTION

Does the transferee corporation recognize gain on the receipt of appreciated property from a shareholder?

ANSWER

No. A corporation does not recognize gain when it receives property from its shareholders, whether or not it exchanges its own stock. However, the transfer must qualify as a Sec. 351 exchange or the transaction will be taxable to the shareholders.

CAPITAL CONTRIBUTIONS BY SHAREHOLDERS

A corporation recognizes no income when it receives cash or noncash property as a capital contribution from a shareholder.[53] If the shareholders make voluntary pro rata payments to a corporation but do not receive any additional stock, the payments are treated as additional consideration for the stock already owned.[54] The shareholders' respective bases in their stock are increased by the amount of cash contributed, plus the basis of any noncash property contributed, plus any gain recognized by the shareholders. The

▼ TABLE C:2-2

Tax Advantages and Disadvantages of Using Debt in a Corporation's Capital Structure

Advantages:

1. A corporation can deduct interest paid on a debt obligation.
2. Shareholders do not recognize income in a debt retirement as they would in a stock redemption.

Disadvantages:

1. If at the time the corporation is formed or later when a shareholder makes a capital contribution, the shareholder receives a debt instrument in exchange for property, the debt is treated as boot, and the shareholder recognizes gain to the extent of the lesser of the boot's FMV or the realized gain.
2. If debt becomes worthless or is sold at less than its face value, the loss generally is a nonbusiness bad debt (treated as a short-term capital loss) or a capital loss. Section 1244 ordinary loss treatment applies only to stock (see pages C:2-32 and C:2-33).

[53] Sec. 118(a).

[54] Reg. Sec. 1.118-1.

▼ TABLE C:2-3

Tax Advantages and Disadvantages of Using Equity in a Corporation's Capital Structure

Advantages:

1. A 70%, 80%, or 100% dividends-received deduction is available to a corporate shareholder who receives dividends. A similar deduction is not available for the receipt of interest (see Chapter C:3).
2. A shareholder can receive common and preferred stock in a tax-free corporate formation under Sec. 351 or a nontaxable reorganization under Sec. 368 without recognizing gain (see Chapters C:2 and C:7, respectively). Receipt of debt securities in each of these two types of transactions generally results in the shareholder's recognizing gain.
3. Common and preferred stock can be distributed tax-free to the corporation's shareholders as a stock dividend. Some common and preferred stock distributions, however, may be taxable as dividends under Sec. 305(b). Distributions of debt obligations generally are taxable as a dividend (see Chapter C:4).
4. Under Sec. 1244, common or preferred stock that the shareholder sells or exchanges or that becomes worthless is eligible for ordinary loss treatment, subject to limitations (see pages C:2-32 and C:2-33). The loss recognized on similar transactions involving debt securities generally is treated as capital in character.
5. Section 1202 excludes 50% of capital gains realized on the sale or exchange of qualified small business (C) corporation stock that has been held for more than five years. For qualified stock acquired after February 17, 2009 and before September 28, 2010, the exclusion is 75%, and for qualified stock acquired after September 27, 2010, the exclusion is 100%.
6. Qualified dividends are taxed at the applicable capital gains rate.

Disadvantages:

1. Dividends are not deductible in determining a corporation's taxable income.
2. Redemption of common or preferred stock generally is taxable to the shareholders as a dividend. Under the general rule, none of the redemption distribution offsets the shareholder's basis for the stock investment. Redemption of common and preferred stock is eligible for exchange treatment only in situations specified in Secs. 302 and 303 (see Chapter C:4).
3. Preferred stock issued to a shareholder as a dividend might meet the definition of Sec. 306 stock. Sale, exchange, or redemption of such stock can result in the recognition of ordinary income instead of capital gain (see Chapter C:4). This ordinary income is taxed as a "deemed dividend" at the applicable capital gains rate.

TYPICAL MISCONCEPTION

The characteristics of preferred stock can be similar to those of a debt security. Often, a regular dividend is required at a stated rate, much like what would be required with respect to a debt obligation. The holder of preferred stock, like a debt holder, may have preferred liquidation rights over holders of common stock. Also, preferred stock is not required to possess voting rights. However, differences remain. A corporation can deduct its interest expense but not dividends. Interest income is ordinary income to shareholders, but qualified dividends are subject to the applicable capital gains tax rate.

corporation's basis in any property received as a capital contribution from a shareholder equals the shareholder's basis, plus any gain recognized by the shareholder.[55] Normally, the shareholders recognize no gain when they transfer property to a controlled corporation as a capital contribution.

EXAMPLE C:2-44 ▶ Dot and Fred each own 50% of the stock in Trail Corporation, and each has a $50,000 basis in that stock. Later, as a voluntary contribution to Trail's capital, Dot contributes $40,000 in cash and Fred contributes property having a $25,000 basis and a $40,000 FMV. As a result of the contributions, Trail recognizes no income. Dot's basis in her stock is increased to $90,000 ($50,000 + $40,000), and Fred's basis in his stock is increased to $75,000 ($50,000 + $25,000). Trail's basis in the property contributed by Fred is $25,000—the same as Fred's basis in the property. ◀

If a shareholder-lender gratuitously forgives corporate debt, the debt forgiveness might be treated as a capital contribution equal to the principal amount of the forgiven debt. A determination of whether debt forgiveness is a capital contribution is based on the facts and circumstances surrounding the event.

[55] Sec. 362(a).

WHAT WOULD YOU DO IN THIS SITUATION?

Your corporate client wants to issue 100-year bonds. The corporation's CEO reads *The Wall Street Journal* regularly and has observed that similar bonds have been issued by several companies, including several Fortune 500 companies. He touts the fact that the interest rate on these bonds is slightly more than that for 30-year U.S. Treasury bonds. In addition, he expresses the belief that interest on the bonds would be deductible, whereas dividends on preferred or common stock would be nondeductible. You are concerned that the IRS might treat the bonds as equity because of their extraordinarily long term. If the IRS does treat the bonds as such, it might recharacterize the "interest" as dividends and deny your client an interest deduction.

What advice would you give the client now regarding the bond issue? What advice would you give it when it prepares its tax return after the new bonds have been issued?

CAPITAL CONTRIBUTIONS BY NONSHAREHOLDERS

Nonshareholders sometimes contribute capital to a corporation in the form of cash or other property. For example, a city government might contribute land to a corporation to induce the corporation to locate within the city and provide jobs for citizens of the municipality. Such contributions are excluded from the corporation's gross income if the money or property contributed is neither a payment for goods or services nor a subsidy to induce the corporation to limit production.[56]

BOOK-TO-TAX ACCOUNTING COMPARISON

The IRC requires capital contributions of property other than money made by a nonshareholder to be reported at a zero basis. Financial accounting rules, however, require donated capital to be reported at the FMV of the asset on the financial accounting books. Neither set of rules requires the property's value to be included in income.

If a nonshareholder contributes noncash property to a corporation, the corporation's basis in such property is zero.[57] The zero basis precludes the corporation from claiming either a depreciation deduction or capital recovery offset with respect to the contributed property.

If a nonshareholder contributes cash, the basis of any property acquired with the cash during a 12-month period beginning on the day the corporation received the contribution is reduced by the cash amount. This rule limits the corporation's deduction to the amount of funds it invested in the property. The amount of any cash received from nonshareholders that the corporation did not spend to purchase property during the 12-month period reduces the basis of any noncash property held by the corporation on the last day of the 12-month period.[58]

The basis reduction applies to the corporation's property in the following order:

1. Depreciable property
2. Amortizable property
3. Depletable property
4. All other property

In the sequence of these downward adjustments, however, a property's basis may not be reduced below zero.

EXAMPLE C:2-45 ►

To induce the company to locate in the municipality, the City of San Antonio contributes to Circle Corporation $100,000 in cash and a tract of land having a $500,000 FMV. Because of a downturn in Circle's business, the company spends only $70,000 of the contributed funds over a 12-month period. Circle recognizes no income as a result of the contribution. Circle's bases in the land and other property purchased with the contributed funds are zero. The basis of Circle's remaining assets, starting with its depreciable property, must be reduced by the $30,000 ($100,000 − $70,000) contributed but not spent. ◄

[56] Reg. Sec. 1.118-1.
[57] Sec. 362(c)(1).
[58] Sec. 362(c)(2).

Worthlessness of Stock or Debt Obligations

OBJECTIVE 6

Determine the tax consequences of worthless stock or debt obligations

Investors who purchase stock in, or lend money to, a corporation usually want to earn a profit and recover their investment. Some investments, however, do not offer an adequate return on capital, and an investor may lose part or all of the investment. In this event, the securities evidencing the investment become worthless. This section examines the tax consequences of stock or debt securities becoming worthless.

SECURITIES

A debt or equity **security** that becomes worthless results in a capital loss for the investor as of the last day of the tax year in which the security becomes worthless. For purposes of this rule, the term *security* includes (1) a share of stock in a corporation; (2) a right to subscribe for, or the right to receive, a share of stock in a corporation; or (3) a bond, debenture, note, or other evidence of indebtedness with interest coupons or in registered form issued by a corporation.[59]

TYPICAL MISCONCEPTION

Probably the most difficult aspect of deducting a loss on a worthless security is establishing that the security is actually worthless. A mere decline in value is not sufficient to create a loss. The burden of proof of establishing total worthlessness rests with the taxpayer.

In some situations, investors recognize an ordinary loss when a security becomes worthless. Investors who contribute capital, either in the form of equity or debt to a corporation that later fails, generally prefer ordinary losses because such losses are deductible against ordinary income. Ordinary losses that generate an NOL can be carried back two years or forward up to 20 years. In general, ordinary loss treatment is available in the following circumstances:

- *Securities that are noncapital assets.* An ordinary loss occurs when a security that is a noncapital asset in the hands of the taxpayer is sold or exchanged or becomes totally worthless. Securities in this category include those held as inventory by a securities dealer.
- *Affiliated corporations.* A domestic corporation can claim an ordinary loss for any affiliated corporation's security that becomes worthless during the tax year. The domestic corporation must own at least 80% of the total voting power of all classes of stock entitled to vote, and at least 80% of each class of nonvoting stock (other than stock limited and preferred as to dividends). At least 90% of the aggregate gross receipts of the loss corporation for all tax years must have been derived from nonpassive income sources.
- *Section 1244 stock.* Section 1244 permits a shareholder to claim an ordinary loss if qualifying stock issued by a small business corporation is sold or exchanged or becomes worthless. This treatment is available only to an individual who was issued the qualifying stock or who was a partner in a partnership at the time the partnership acquired the qualifying stock. In the latter case, the partner's distributive share of partnership losses includes the loss sustained by the partnership on such stock. Ordinary loss treatment is not available for stock inherited, received as a gift, or purchased from another shareholder. The ordinary loss is limited to $50,000 per year (or $100,000 if the taxpayer is married and files a joint return). Losses exceeding the dollar ceiling in any given year are considered capital in character.

SELF-STUDY QUESTION

Why would a shareholder want his or her stock to qualify as Sec. 1244 stock?

ANSWER

Section 1244 is a provision that may help the taxpayer but that can never hurt. If the Sec. 1244 requirements are satisfied, the individual shareholders of a small business corporation may treat losses from the sale or worthlessness of their stock as ordinary rather than capital in character. If the Sec. 1244 requirements are not satisfied, such losses generally are treated as capital in character.

EXAMPLE C:2-46 ▶ For $175,000, Tammy and her husband Cole purchased 25% of Minor Corporation's initial offering of a single class of stock. Minor is a small business corporation, and the Minor stock satisfies all Sec. 1244 requirements. On September 1 of the current year, Minor filed for bankruptcy. Two years later, the bankruptcy court notifies shareholders that the Minor stock is worthless. In that year, Tammy and Cole can deduct $100,000 of their initial investment as an ordinary loss. The remaining $75,000 loss is treated as capital in character. ◀

If a corporation issues Sec. 1244 stock for property whose adjusted basis exceeds its FMV immediately before the exchange, the stock's basis is reduced to the property's FMV for the purpose of determining the ordinary loss amount.

[59] Sec. 165(g).

EXAMPLE C:2-47 ▶ In a Sec. 351 nontaxable exchange, Penny transfers to Small Corporation property having a $40,000 adjusted basis and a $32,000 FMV for 100 shares of Sec. 1244 stock. Ordinarily, Penny's basis in the stock would be $40,000. However, for Sec. 1244 purposes, her stock basis is the property's FMV, or $32,000. If Penny sells the stock for $10,000, her recognized loss is $30,000 ($10,000 − $40,000). Her ordinary loss under Sec. 1244 is $22,000 ($10,000 − $32,000 Sec. 1244 basis). The remaining $8,000 loss is treated as capital in character. (Note also that, under Sec. 362(e)(2), Small would reduce its basis in the transferred property to its $32,000 FMV.) ◀

Section 1244 loss treatment requires no special election. Investors, however, should be aware that, if they fail to satisfy certain requirements, ordinary loss treatment will be unavailable, and their loss will be treated as capital in character. The requirements are as follows:

- The issuing corporation must be a small business corporation at the time it issues the stock. A small business corporation is a corporation that receives in the aggregate $1 million or less in money or noncash property (other than stock and securities) in exchange for its stock.[60]
- The issuing corporation must have derived more than 50% of its aggregate gross receipts from "active" sources (i.e., other than royalties, rents, dividends, interest, annuities, and gains on sales of stock and securities) during the five most recent tax years ending before the date on which the shareholder sells or exchanges the stock or the stock becomes worthless.

TAX STRATEGY TIP

If a shareholder contributes additional money or property to an existing corporation, he or she should be sure to receive additional stock in the exchange so that it will qualify for Sec. 1244 treatment if all requirements are met. If the shareholder does not receive additional stock, the increased basis of existing stock resulting from the capital contribution will not qualify for Sec. 1244 treatment.

If a shareholder contributes additional cash or property to a corporation after acquiring Sec. 1244 stock, the amount of ordinary loss recognized on the sale, exchange, or worthlessness of the Sec. 1244 stock is limited to the shareholder's capital contribution at the time the corporation issued the stock.

UNSECURED DEBT OBLIGATIONS

In addition to holding an equity interest, shareholders may lend funds to the corporation. The type of loss allowed if the corporation does not repay the borrowed funds depends on the nature of the loan or advance.

If the unpaid loan was not evidenced by a security (i.e., an unsecured debt obligation), it is considered to be either business or nonbusiness bad debt. Nonbusiness bad debts are treated less favorably than business bad debts. Under Sec. 166, nonbusiness bad debts are deductible as short-term capital losses (up to the $3,000 annual limit for net capital losses) when they become totally worthless. Business bad debts are deductible as ordinary losses without limitation when they become either partially or totally worthless. The IRS generally treats a loan made by a shareholder to a corporation in connection with his or her stock investment as nonbusiness in character.[61] It is understandable why a shareholder might attempt to rebut this presumption with the argument that a business purpose exists for the loan.

An advance in connection with the shareholder's trade or business, such as a loan to protect the shareholder's employment at the corporation, may be treated as an ordinary loss under the business bad debt rules. Regulation Sec. 1.166-5(b) states that whether a bad debt is business or nonbusiness related depends on the taxpayer's motive for making the advance. The debt is business related if the necessary relationship between the loss and the conduct of the taxpayer's trade or business exists at the time the debt was incurred, acquired, or became worthless.

In *U.S. v. Edna Generes,* the U.S. Supreme Court held that where multiple motives exist for advancing funds to a corporation, such as where a shareholder-employee advances funds to protect his or her employment, determining whether the advance is business or nonbusiness related must be based on the "dominant motivation" for the

[60] Regulation Sec. 1.1244(c)-2 provides special rules for designating which shares of stock are eligible for Sec. 1244 treatment when the corporation has issued more than $1 million of stock.

[61] Here, it is assumed that the loan is not considered to be an additional capital contribution. In such a case, the Sec. 165 worthless security rules apply instead of the Sec. 166 bad debt rules.

KEY POINT

In many closely held corporations, the shareholders are also employees. Thus, when a shareholder-employee makes a loan to the corporation, a question arises as to whether the loan is being made in the individual's capacity as an employee or a shareholder. The distinction is important because an employee loan that is worthless is entitled to ordinary loss treatment, whereas a shareholder loan that is worthless is treated as a nonbusiness bad debt (short-term capital loss).

advance.[62] If the advance is only "significantly motivated" by considerations relating to the taxpayer's trade or business, such motivation will not establish a proximate relationship between the bad debt and the taxpayer's trade or business. Therefore, it may result in a nonbusiness bad debt characterization. On the other hand, if the advance is "dominantly motivated" by considerations relating to the taxpayer's trade or business, such motivation usually is sufficient to establish such a proximate relationship. Therefore, it may result in a business bad debt characterization.

Factors deemed important in determining the character of bad debt include the taxpayer's equity in the corporation relative to compensation paid by the corporation. For example, a modest salary paid by the corporation relative to substantial stockholdings in the corporation suggests an investment motive for the advance. Conversely, a substantial salary paid by the corporation relative to modest stockholdings suggests a business motive for the advance. The business motive at issue is the protection of the employee-lender's employment because the advance may help save the business from failing. Reasonable minds may differ on what is substantial and what is modest, and monetary stakes often are high in these cases. Consequently, the determination frequently involves litigation.

EXAMPLE C:2-48 ▶

Top Corporation employs Mary as its legal counsel. It pays Mary an annual salary of $100,000. In March of the current year, Mary advances the corporation $50,000 to assist it financially. In October of the current year, Top declares bankruptcy and liquidates. In the liquidation, Mary and other investors receive 10 cents on every dollar advanced. If Mary can show that her advance was dominantly motivated by a desire to preserve her employment, her $45,000 ($50,000 × 0.90) loss will be treated as business bad debt, ordinary in character, and fully deductible in the current year. On the other hand, if Mary shows that the advance was only significantly motivated by a desire to preserve her employment, her $45,000 loss will be treated as nonbusiness bad debt, capital in character, and deductible in this year and in subsequent years only to the extent of $3,000 in excess of any capital gains she recognizes. ◀

ADDITIONAL COMMENT

For the act of lending money to a corporation to be considered the taxpayer's trade or business, the taxpayer must show that he or she was individually in the business of seeking out, promoting, organizing, and financing business ventures. *Ronald L. Farrington v. CIR,* 65 AFTR 2d 90-616, 90-1 USTC ¶50,125 (DC Okla., 1990).

A loss sustained by a shareholder who guarantees a loan made by a third party to the corporation generally is treated as a nonbusiness bad debt. The loss can be claimed only to the extent the shareholder actually pays the third party and is unable to recover the payment from the debtor corporation.[63] Occasionally, the IRS treats the amount of a shareholder advance as additional paid-in capital. In such circumstances, any worthless security loss the shareholder claims for his or her equity investment may be increased by this amount.

TAX PLANNING CONSIDERATIONS

OBJECTIVE 7

Identify tax planning opportunities in corporate formations

AVOIDING SEC. 351

Section 351 is not an elective provision. If its conditions are met, a corporate formation is tax-free, even if the taxpayer does not want it to be. Most often, taxpayers desire Sec. 351 treatment because it allows them to defer gains when transferring appreciated property to a corporation. In some cases, however, shareholders find such treatment disadvantageous because they would like to recognize gain or loss on the property transferred.

Avoiding Nonrecognition of Losses Under Sec. 351. If a shareholder transfers to a corporation property that has declined in value, the shareholder may want to recognize the loss so it can offset income from other sources. The shareholder can recognize the loss only if the Sec. 351 nonrecognition rules and the Sec. 267 related party rules do not apply to the exchange.

Avoiding Sec. 351 treatment requires that one or more of its requirements not be met. The simplest way to accomplish this objective is to ensure that the transferors of property do not receive 80% of the voting stock.

[62] 29 AFTR 2d 72-609, 72-1 USTC ¶9259 (USSC, 1972).

[63] Reg. Sec. 1.166-8(a).

Even if a shareholder avoids Sec. 351 treatment, he or she still may not be able to recognize the losses because of the Sec. 267 related party loss rules. Under Sec. 267(a)(1), if the shareholder owns more than 50% of the corporation's stock, directly or indirectly, he or she is a related party and therefore cannot recognize loss on an exchange of property for the corporation's stock or other property. If the transferors of property receive less than 80% of the corporation's voting stock and if the transferor of loss property does not own more than 50% of the stock, the transferor of loss property may recognize the loss.

EXAMPLE C:2-49 ▶ Lynn owns property having a $100,000 basis and a $60,000 FMV. If Lynn transfers the property to White Corporation in a nontaxable exchange under Sec. 351, she will not recognize a loss, which will be deferred until she sells her White stock. If the Sec. 351 requirements are not met, she will recognize a $40,000 loss in the year she transfers the property. If Lynn receives 50% of the White stock in exchange for her property, Cathy, an unrelated individual, receives 25% of the stock in exchange for $30,000 cash, and John, another unrelated individual, receives the remaining 25% for services performed, the Sec. 351 control requirement will not be met because the transferors of property acquire less than 80% of the White stock. Moreover, Lynn will not be a related party under Sec. 267 because she will not own more than 50% of the stock either directly or indirectly. Therefore, Lynn will recognize a $40,000 loss on the exchange. ◀

SELF-STUDY QUESTION

Which tax provisions may potentially limit a transferor shareholder from recognizing a loss on the transfer of property to a corporation?

ANSWER

Such transfer cannot be to a controlled corporation, or Sec. 351 will defer the loss. Even if Sec. 351 can be avoided, losses on sales between a corporation and a more-than-50% shareholder are disallowed under Sec. 267. Thus, to recognize a loss on the sale of property, such shareholder must, directly or indirectly, own 50% or less of the transferee corporation's stock.

Avoiding Nonrecognition of Gain Under Sec. 351. Sometimes a transferor would like to recognize gain when he or she transfers appreciated property to a corporation so the transferee corporation can get a stepped-up basis in the transferred property. Some other reasons for recognizing gain are as follows:

- If the transferor's gain is capital in character, he or she can offset this gain with capital losses from other transactions.
- Individual long-term capital gains are taxed at the applicable capital gains rate, which may be lower than the 35% top tax rate applicable to corporate-level capital gains.
- The corporation's marginal tax rate may be higher than a noncorporate transferor's marginal tax rate. In such case, it might be beneficial for the transferor to recognize gain so the corporation can get a stepped-up basis in the property. A stepped-up basis would either reduce the corporation's gain when it later sells the property or allow the corporation to claim greater depreciation deductions when it uses the property.

ADDITIONAL COMMENT

Any potential built-in gain on property transferred to the transferee corporation is duplicated because such gain may be recognized at the corporate level and at the shareholder level. This double taxation may be another reason for avoiding the nonrecognition of gain under Sec. 351.

A transferor who wishes to recognize gain on the transfer of appreciated property to a corporation can avoid Sec. 351 treatment through one of the following planning techniques:

- The transferor can sell the property to the controlled corporation for cash.
- The transferor can sell the property to the controlled corporation for cash and debt. This transaction involves relatively less cash than the previous transaction. However, the sale may be treated as a nontaxable exchange if the IRS recharacterizes the debt as equity.[64]
- The transferor can sell the property to a third party for cash and have the third party contribute the property to the corporation for stock.
- The transferor can have the corporation distribute sufficient boot property so that, even if Sec. 351 applies to the transaction, he or she will recognize gain.
- The transferors can fail one or more of the Sec. 351 tests. For example, if the transferors do not own 80% of the voting stock immediately after the exchange, the Sec. 351 control requirement will not have been met, and they will recognize gain.
- To trigger gain recognition under Sec. 357(c), the transferors may transfer to the corporation debt that exceeds the basis of all property transferred.

---

[64] See, for example, *Aqualane Shores, Inc. v. CIR*, 4 AFTR 2d 5346, 59-2 USTC ¶9632 (5th Cir., 1959) and *Sun Properties, Inc. v. U.S.*, 47 AFTR 273, 55-1 USTC ¶9261 (5th Cir., 1955).

EXAMPLE C:2-50 ▶ Ten years ago, James purchased land as an investment for $100,000. The land is now worth $500,000. James plans to transfer the land to Bell Corporation in exchange for all its stock. Bell will subdivide the land and sell individual tracts. Because the land is inventory, Bell's gain on the land sales will be ordinary income. James has realized a large capital loss in the current year and would like to recognize capital gain on the transfer of the land to Bell. One way for James to accomplish this objective is to transfer the land to Bell in exchange for all the Bell stock plus a note for $400,000. Because the note is boot, James will recognize $400,000 of gain even though Sec. 351 applies to the exchange. However, if the note is due in a subsequent year, James's gain will be deferred until collection unless he elects out of the installment method. ◀

COMPLIANCE AND PROCEDURAL CONSIDERATIONS

OBJECTIVE 8

Comply with procedural rules for corporate formations

REPORTING REQUIREMENTS UNDER SEC. 351

A taxpayer who receives stock or other property in a Sec. 351 exchange must attach a statement to his or her tax return for the period encompassing the date of the exchange.[65] The statement must include all facts pertinent to the exchange, including:

- A description of the property transferred and its adjusted basis to the transferor
- A description of the stock received in the exchange, including its type, number of shares, and FMV
- A description of any other securities received in the exchange, including principal amount, terms, and FMV
- The amount of money received
- A description of any other property received, including its FMV
- A statement of the liabilities transferred to the corporation, including the nature of the liabilities, when and why they were incurred, and the business reason for their transfer

ADDITIONAL COMMENT

The required information provided to the IRS by both the transferor-shareholders and the transferee corporation should be consistent. For example, the FMVs assigned to the stock and other properties included in the exchange should be the same for all parties to the transaction.

The transferee corporation must attach a statement to its tax return for the year in which the exchange took place. The statement must include

- A complete description of all property received from the transferors
- The transferors' adjusted bases in the property
- A description of the stock issued to the transferors
- A description of any other securities issued to the transferors
- The amount of money distributed to the transferors
- A description of any other property distributed to the transferors
- Information regarding the transferor's liabilities assumed by the corporation

[65] Reg. Sec. 1.351-3.

Problem Materials

DISCUSSION QUESTIONS

C:2-1 What entities or business forms are available for a new enterprise? Explain the advantages and disadvantages of each.

C:2-2 Alice and Bill plan to go into business together. For the first two or three years of operations, they anticipate losses, which they would like to use to offset income from other sources. They also are concerned about exposing their personal assets to business liabilities. Advise Alice and Bill as to what business form would best meet their needs.

C:2-3 Bruce and Bob organize Black LLC on May 10 of the current year. What is the entity's default tax classification? Are any alternative classification(s) available? If so, (1) how do Bruce and Bob elect the alternative classification(s) and (2) what are the tax consequences of doing so?

C:2-4 John and Wilbur form White Corporation on May 3 of the current year. What is the entity's default tax classification? Are any alternative classification(s) available? If so, (1) how do John and Wilbur elect the alternative classification(s) and (2) what are the tax consequences of doing so?

C:2-5 Barbara organizes Blue LLC on May 17 of the current year. What is the entity's default tax classification? Are any alternative classification(s) available? If so, (1) how does Barbara elect the alternative classification(s) and (2) what are the tax consequences of doing so?

C:2-6 Debate the following proposition: All corporate formation transactions should be taxable events.

C:2-7 What are the tax consequences for the transferor and transferee when property is transferred to a newly created corporation in an exchange qualifying as nontaxable under Sec. 351?

C:2-8 What items are considered to be property for purposes of Sec. 351(a)? What items are not considered to be property?

C:2-9 How is "control" defined for purposes of Sec. 351(a)?

C:2-10 Explain how the IRS has interpreted the phrase "in control immediately after the exchange" for purposes of a Sec. 351 exchange.

C:2-11 John and Mary each exchange property worth \$50,000 for 100 shares of New Corporation stock. Peter exchanges services for 98 shares of New stock and \$1,000 in cash for two shares of New stock. Are the Sec. 351 requirements met? Explain why or why not. What advice would you give the shareholders?

C:2-12 Does Sec. 351 require shareholders to receive stock equal in value to the property transferred? Suppose Fred and Susan each transfer property worth \$50,000 to Spade Corporation. In exchange, Fred receives 25 shares of Spade stock and Susan receives 75 shares. Are the Sec. 351 requirements met? Explain the tax consequences of the exchange.

C:2-13 Does Sec. 351 apply to property transfers to an existing corporation? Suppose Carl and Lynn each own 50 shares of North Corporation stock. Carl transfers property worth \$50,000 to North for an additional 25 shares. Does Sec. 351 apply? Explain why or why not. If not, what can be done to qualify the transaction for Sec. 351 treatment?

C:2-14 How are a transferor's basis and holding period determined for stock and other property (boot) received in a Sec. 351 exchange? How does the transferee corporation's assumption of liabilities affect the transferor's basis in the stock?

C:2-15 Under what circumstances is a corporation's assumption of liabilities considered boot in a Sec. 351 exchange?

C:2-16 What factor(s) would the IRS likely consider to determine whether the transfer of a liability to a corporation in a Sec. 351 exchange was motivated by a business purpose?

C:2-17 Mark transfers all the property of his sole proprietorship to newly formed Utah Corporation in exchange for all the Utah stock. Mark has claimed depreciation on some of the property. Under what circumstances is Mark required to recapture previously claimed depreciation deductions? How is the depreciation deduction for the year of transfer calculated? What are the tax consequences if Utah sells the depreciable property?

C:2-18 How does the assignment of income doctrine apply to a Sec. 351 exchange?

C:2-19 What factors did Congress mandate to be considered in determining whether indebtedness is classified as debt or equity for tax purposes?

C:2-20 What are the advantages and disadvantages of using debt in a firm's capital structure?

C:2-21 What are the advantages of Sec. 1244 loss treatment when a stock investment becomes worthless? What conditions must be met to qualify for this treatment?

C:2-22 What are the advantages of business bad debt treatment when a shareholder's loan or advance to a corporation cannot be repaid? What must the debtholder show to claim a business bad debt deduction?

C:2-23 Why might shareholders avoid Sec. 351 treatment? Explain three ways they can accomplish this end.

C:2-24 What are the Sec. 351 reporting requirements?

ISSUE IDENTIFICATION QUESTIONS

C:2-25 Peter Jones has owned all 100 shares of Trenton Corporation stock for the past five years. This year, Mary Smith contributes property with a $50,000 basis and an $80,000 FMV for 80 newly issued Trenton shares. At the same time, Peter contributes $15,000 in cash for 15 newly issued Trenton shares. What tax issues regarding the exchanges should Mary and Peter consider?

C:2-26 Carl contributes equipment with a $50,000 adjusted basis and an $80,000 FMV to Cook Corporation for 50 of its 100 shares of stock. His son, Carl Jr., contributes $20,000 cash for the remaining 50 Cook shares. What tax issues regarding the exchanges should Carl and his son consider?

C:2-27 Several years ago, Bill acquired 100 shares of Bold Corporation stock directly from the corporation for $100,000 in cash. This year, he sold the stock to Sam for $35,000. What tax issues regarding the stock sale should Bill consider?

PROBLEMS

C:2-28 *Organizational Forms Available.* Lucia, a single taxpayer, operates a florist business. She is considering either continuing the business as a sole proprietorship or reorganizing it as either a C corporation or an S corporation. Her goal is to withdraw $20,000 of profits from the business annually while minimizing her total tax liability. She expects the business to generate annually $50,000 of taxable income before considering a deductible salary expense (see below). Which business form(s) can best achieve Lucia's goals? Remember that a shareholder is taxed on S corporation income whether withdrawn or not and is not taxed on the actual withdrawals or distributions. Assume that the C corporation is in the 15% corporate tax bracket, Lucia is in the 25% individual tax bracket for ordinary income, and Lucia is taxed at 15% on dividend income. When considering either corporate option, perform the analysis first by treating any withdrawals as deductible salary payments of the corporation. Then do the analysis by treating them as nondeductible dividends or distributions. Ignore employment taxes.

C:2-29 *Transfer of Property and Services to a Controlled Corporation.* In the current year, Dick, Evan, and Fran form Triton Corporation. Dick contributes land (a capital asset) having a $50,000 FMV in exchange for 50 shares of Triton stock. He purchased the land three years ago for $60,000. Evan contributes machinery (Sec. 1231 property purchased four years ago) having a $45,000 adjusted basis and a $30,000 FMV in exchange for 30 shares of Triton stock. Fran contributes services worth $20,000 in exchange for 20 shares of Triton stock.

a. What is the amount of Dick's recognized gain or loss?
b. What is Dick's basis in his Triton shares? When does his holding period begin?
c. What is the amount of Evan's recognized gain or loss?
d. What is Evan's basis in his Triton shares? When does his holding period begin?
e. How much income, if any, does Fran recognize?
f. What is Fran's basis in her Triton shares? When does her holding period begin?
g. What is Triton's basis in the land and the machinery? When does its holding period begin? How does Triton treat the amount paid to Fran for her services?

C:2-30 *Transfer of Property and Services to a Controlled Corporation.* In the current year, Ed, Fran, and George form Jet Corporation. Ed contributes land (a capital asset) having a $35,000 FMV purchased as an investment four years ago for $15,000 in exchange for 35 shares of Jet stock. Fran contributes machinery (Sec. 1231 property) purchased four years ago and used in her business in exchange for 35 shares of Jet stock. Immediately before the exchange, the machinery had a $45,000 adjusted basis and a $35,000 FMV. George contributes services worth $30,000 in exchange for 30 shares of Jet stock.

a. What is the amount of Ed's recognized gain or loss?
b. What is Ed's basis in his Jet shares? When does his holding period begin?
c. What is the amount of Fran's recognized gain or loss?
d. What is Fran's basis in her Jet shares? When does her holding period begin?
e. How much income, if any, does George recognize?
f. What is George's basis in his Jet shares? When does his holding period begin?
g. What is Jet's basis in the land and the machinery? When does its holding period begin? How does Jet treat the amount paid to George for his services?
h. How would your answers to Parts a through g change if George instead contributed $5,000 in cash and services worth $25,000 for his 30 shares of Jet stock?

C:2-31 *Control Requirement.* In which of the following independent situations is the Sec. 351 control requirement met?

a. Olive transfers property to Quick Corporation for 75% of Quick stock, and Mary provides services to Quick for the remaining 25% of Quick stock.
b. Pete transfers property to Target Corporation for 60% of Target stock, and Robert transfers property worth $15,000 and performs services worth $25,000 for the remaining 40% of Target stock.
c. Herb and his wife, Wilma, each have owned 50 of the 100 outstanding shares of Vast Corporation stock since it was formed three years ago. In the current year, their son, Sam, transfers property to Vast for 50 newly issued shares of Vast stock.
d. Charles and Ruth develop a plan to form Tiny Corporation. On June 3 of this year, Charles transfers property worth $50,000 for 50 shares of Tiny stock. On August 1, Ruth transfers $50,000 cash for 50 shares of Tiny stock.
e. Assume the same facts as in Part d except that Charles has a prearranged plan to sell 30 of his shares to Sam on October 1.

C:2-32 *Control Requirement.* In which of the following unrelated exchanges is the Sec. 351 control requirement met? If the transaction does not meet the Sec. 351 requirements, suggest ways in which the transaction can be structured so as to meet these requirements.

a. Fred exchanges property worth $50,000 and services worth $50,000 for 100 shares of New Corporation stock. Greta exchanges $100,000 cash for the remaining 100 shares of New stock.
b. Maureen exchanges property worth $2,000 and services worth $48,000 for 100 shares of Gemini Corporation stock. Norman exchanges property worth $50,000 for the remaining 100 shares of Gemini stock.

C:2-33 *Control Requirement.* Sam and Veronica own 300 and 200 shares, respectively, of Poly-Electron Corporation stock, which represent all the shares outstanding. The current market value per share is $25. Poly-Electron needs capital to expand its operations, and Veronica is willing to contribute to Poly-Electron silver bullion against which the corporation can borrow operating funds. Veronica purchased the bullion 12 years ago, when its cost was a fraction of its current market value. If Veronica wants to avoid recognizing a gain upon transferring the bullion to the corporation, how many additional shares must she receive in exchange for the bullion, and what value of silver bullion should she contribute to Poly-Electron in exchange for additional shares? Hint: Veronica needs to achieve 80% control of the corporation.

C:2-34 *Sec. 351 Requirements.* Al, Bob, and Carl form West Corporation and transfer the following items to West:

		Item Transferred		
Transferor	*Item*	*Transferor's Basis*	*FMV*	*Shares Received by Transferor*
Al	Patent	–0–	$25,000	1,000 common
Bob	Cash	$25,000	25,000	250 preferred
Carl	Services	–0–	7,500	300 common

The common stock has voting rights. The preferred stock does not.

a. Is the exchange nontaxable under Sec. 351? Explain the tax consequences of the exchange to Al, Bob, Carl, and West.

b. How would your answer to Part a change if Bob instead had received 200 shares of common stock and 200 shares of preferred stock?
c. How would your answer to Part a change if Carl instead had contributed $800 cash as well as services worth $6,700?

C:2-35 *Incorporating a Sole Proprietorship.* Tom incorporates his sole proprietorship as Total Corporation and transfers its assets to Total in exchange for all 100 shares of Total stock and four $10,000 interest-bearing notes. The stock has a $125,000 FMV. The notes mature consecutively on the first four anniversaries of the incorporation date. The assets transferred are as follows:

Assets		*Adjusted Basis*	*FMV*
Cash		$ 5,000	$ 5,000
Equipment	$130,000		
Minus: Accumulated depreciation	(70,000)	60,000	90,000
Building	$100,000		
Minus: Accumulated depreciation	(49,000)	51,000	40,000
Land		24,000	30,000
Total		$140,000	$165,000

a. What are the amounts and character of Tom's recognized gains or losses?
b. What is Tom's basis in the Total stock and notes?
c. What is Total's basis in the property received from Tom?

C:2-36 *Transfer to an Existing Corporation.* For the last five years, Ann and Fred each have owned 50 of the 100 outstanding shares of Zero Corporation stock. Ann transfers land having a $10,000 basis and a $25,000 FMV to Zero for an additional 25 shares of Zero stock. Fred transfers $1,000 cash to Zero for one additional share of Zero stock. What amount of the gain or loss must Ann recognize on the exchange? If the transaction does not meet the Sec. 351 requirements, suggest ways in which it can be structured so as to meet these requirements.

C:2-37 *Transfer to an Existing Corporation.* For the last three years, Lucy and Marvin each have owned 50 of the 100 outstanding shares of Lucky Corporation stock. Lucy transfers property having an $8,000 basis and a $12,000 FMV to Lucky for an additional ten shares of Lucky stock. How much gain or loss must Lucy recognize on the exchange? If the transaction does not meet the Sec. 351 requirements, suggest ways in which it can be structured so as to meet these requirements.

C:2-38 *Disproportionate Receipt of Stock.* Jerry transfers property with a $28,000 adjusted basis and a $50,000 FMV to Texas Corporation for 75 shares of Texas stock. Frank, Jerry's father, transfers property with a $32,000 adjusted basis and a $50,000 FMV to Texas for the remaining 25 shares of Texas stock.
a. What is the amount of each transferor's recognized gain or loss?
b. What is Jerry's basis in his Texas stock?
c. What is Frank's basis in his Texas stock?

C:2-39 *Sec. 351: Boot Property Received.* Sara transfers land (a capital asset) having a $30,000 adjusted basis to Temple Corporation in a Sec. 351 exchange. In return, Sara receives the following consideration:

Consideration	*FMV*
100 shares of Temple common stock	$100,000
50 shares of Temple qualified preferred stock	50,000
Temple note due in three years	20,000
Total	$170,000

a. What are the amount and character of Sara's recognized gain or loss?
b. What is Sara's basis in her common stock, preferred stock, and note?
c. What is Temple's basis in the land?

C:2-40 *Receipt of Bonds for Property.* Joe, Karen, and Larry form Gray Corporation. Joe contributes land (a capital asset) having an $8,000 adjusted basis and a $15,000 FMV to

Gray in exchange for Gray ten-year notes having a $15,000 face value. Karen contributes equipment (Sec. 1231 property) having an $18,000 adjusted basis and a $25,000 FMV for 50 shares of Gray stock. She previously claimed $10,000 of depreciation on the equipment. Larry contributes $25,000 cash for 50 shares of Gray stock.

a. What are the amount and character of Joe's, Karen's, and Larry's recognized gains or losses?

b. What basis do Joe, Karen, and Larry take in the stock or notes they receive?

c. What basis does Gray take in the land and equipment? What happens to the $10,000 of depreciation recapture potential on the equipment?

C:2-41 *Transfer of Depreciable Property.* Nora transfers to Needle Corporation depreciable machinery originally costing $18,000 and now having a $15,000 adjusted basis. In exchange, Nora receives all 100 shares of Needle stock having an $18,000 FMV and a three-year Needle note having a $4,000 FMV.

a. What are the amount and character of Nora's recognized gain or loss?

b. What are Nora's bases in the Needle stock and note?

c. What is Needle's basis in the machinery?

C:2-42 *Transfer of Personal Liabilities.* Jim owns 80% of Gold Corporation stock. He transfers a business automobile to Gold in exchange for additional Gold stock worth $5,000 and Gold's assumption of both his $1,000 automobile debt and his $2,000 education loan. The automobile originally cost Jim $12,000 and, on the transfer date, has a $4,500 adjusted basis and an $8,000 FMV.

a. What are the amount and character of Jim's recognized gain or loss?

b. What is Jim's basis in his additional Gold shares?

c. When does Jim's holding period for the additional shares begin?

d. What basis does Gold take in the automobile?

C:2-43 *Liabilities in Excess of Basis.* Barbara transfers to Moore Corporation $10,000 cash and machinery having a $15,000 basis and a $35,000 FMV in exchange for 50 shares of Moore stock. The machinery was used in Barbara's business, originally cost Barbara $50,000, and is subject to a $28,000 liability, which Moore assumes. Sam exchanges $17,000 cash for the remaining 50 shares of Moore stock.

a. What are the amount and character of Barbara's recognized gain or loss?

b. What is Barbara's basis in the Moore stock?

c. What is Moore's basis in the machinery?

d. What are the amount and character of Sam's recognized gain or loss?

e. What is Sam's basis in the Moore stock?

f. When do Barbara and Sam's holding periods for their stock begin?

g. How would your answers to Parts a through f change if Sam received $17,000 of Moore stock for legal services (instead of cash)?

C:2-44 *Transfer of Business Properties.* Jerry transfers to Emerald Corporation property having a $32,000 adjusted basis and a $50,000 FMV in exchange for all of Emerald's stock worth $15,000 and Emerald's assumption of a $35,000 mortgage on the property.

a. What is the amount of Jerry's recognized gain or loss?

b. What is Jerry's basis in the Emerald stock?

c. What is Emerald's basis in the property?

d. How would your answers to Parts a through c change if the mortgage assumed by Emerald were $15,000 and the Emerald stock were worth $35,000?

C:2-45 *Incorporating a Cash Basis Proprietorship.* Ted decides to incorporate his medical practice. He uses the cash method of accounting. On the date of incorporation, the practice reports the following balance sheet:

	Basis	*FMV*
Assets:		
Cash	$ 5,000	$ 5,000
Accounts receivable	–0–	65,000
Equipment (net of $15,000 depreciation)	35,000	40,000
Total	$40,000	$110,000

Liabilities and Owner's Equity:		
Current liabilities	$ -0-	$ 35,000
Note payable on equipment	15,000	15,000
Owner's equity	25,000	60,000
Total	$40,000	$110,000

All the current liabilities would be deductible by Ted if he paid them. Ted transfers all the assets and liabilities to a professional corporation in exchange for all of its stock.

a. What are the amount and character of Ted's recognized gain or loss?
b. What is Ted's basis in the stock?
c. What is the corporation's basis in the property?
d. Who recognizes income on the receivables upon their collection? Can the corporation obtain a deduction for the liabilities when it pays them?

C:2-46 *Transfer of Depreciable Property.* On January 10 of the current year, Mary transfers to Green Corporation a machine purchased three years ago for $100,000. On the transfer date, the machine has a $60,000 adjusted basis and a $110,000 FMV. Mary receives all 100 shares of Green stock, worth $100,000, and a two-year Green note worth $10,000.

a. What are the amount and character of Mary's recognized gain or loss?
b. What is Mary's basis in the stock and note? When does her holding period begin?
c. What are the amount and character of Green's gain or loss?
d. What is Green's basis in the machine? When does Green's holding period begin?

C:2-47 *Contribution to Capital by a Nonshareholder.* The City of Omaha donates land worth $500,000 to Ace Corporation to induce it to locate in Omaha and create an estimated 2,000 jobs for its citizens.

a. How much income, if any, must Ace report on the land contribution?
b. What basis does Ace take in the land?
c. Assume the same facts except the City of Omaha also donated to Ace $100,000 cash, which the corporation used to pay a portion of the $250,000 cost of equipment that it purchased six months later. How much income, if any, must Ace report on the cash contribution? What basis does Ace take in the equipment?

C:2-48 *Choice of Capital Structure.* Kobe transfers $500,000 in cash to newly formed Bryant Corporation for 100% of Bryant's stock. In the first year of operations, Bryant's taxable income before any payments to Kobe is $120,000. What total amount of taxable income must Kobe and Bryant each report in the following two scenarios?

a. Bryant pays a $70,000 dividend to Kobe.
b. Assume that when Bryant was formed, Kobe transferred his $500,000 to the corporation for $250,000 of Bryant stock and $250,000 in Bryant notes. The notes are repayable in five annual installments of $50,000 plus 8% annual interest on the unpaid balance. During the current year, Bryant gives Kobe $50,000 in repayment of the first note plus $20,000 interest.

C:2-49 *Worthless Stock or Securities.* Tom and Vicki are married and file a joint income tax return. They each purchase 50% of the stock in Guest Corporation from Al for $75,000. Tom is employed full-time by Guest and earns $100,000 in annual salary. Because of Guest's financial difficulties, Tom and Vicki each lend Guest an additional $25,000. The $25,000 is secured by bonds and is repayable in five years, with interest accruing at the prevailing market rate. Guest's financial difficulties escalate, and it eventually declares bankruptcy. Tom and Vicki receive nothing for their Guest stock or Guest bonds.

a. What are the amount and character of each shareholder's loss on the worthless stock and bonds?
b. How would your answer to Part a change if the liability were not secured by bonds?
c. How would your answer to Part a change if Tom and Vicki had purchased their stock for $75,000 each at the time Guest was formed?

C:2-50 *Worthless Stock.* Duck Corporation is owned equally by Harry, Susan, and Big Corporation. Harry and Susan are single. Eight years ago, Harry, Tom, and Big, the original investors in Duck, each paid $125,000 for their Duck stock. Susan purchased her stock from Tom five years ago for $175,000. No adjustments to basis occur after the stock acquisition date. Duck encounters financial difficulties as a result of a lawsuit brought by a customer who suffered personal injuries from using a defective product. Duck files for bankruptcy, and uses all its assets to pay its creditors in the current year. What are the amount and character of each shareholder's loss?

C:2-51 *Sale of Sec. 1244 Stock.* Lois, who is single, transfers property with an $80,000 basis and a $120,000 FMV to Water Corporation in exchange for all 100 shares of Water stock. The shares qualify as Sec. 1244 stock. Two years later, Lois sells the shares for $28,000.

a. What are the amount and character of Lois's recognized gain or loss?

b. How would your answer to Part a change if the FMV of the property were $70,000?

C:2-52 *Transfer of Sec. 1244 Stock.* Assume the same facts as in Problem C:2-51 except that Lois gave the Water stock to her daughter, Sue, six months after she received it. The stock had a $120,000 FMV when Lois acquired it and when she made the gift. Sue sold the stock two years later for $28,000. How is the loss treated for tax purposes?

C:2-53 *Avoiding Sec. 351 Treatment.* Six years ago, Donna purchased land as an investment. The land cost $150,000 and is now worth $480,000. Donna plans to transfer the land to Development Corporation, which will subdivide it and sell individual tracts. Development's income on the land sales will be ordinary in character.

a. What are the tax consequences of the asset transfer and land sales if Donna contributes the land to Development in exchange for all its stock?

b. In what alternative ways can the transaction be structured to achieve more favorable tax results? Assume Donna's marginal tax rate is 39.6%, and Development's marginal tax rate is 34%.

COMPREHENSIVE PROBLEMS

C:2-54 On March 1 of the current year, Alice, Bob, Carla, and Dick form Bear Corporation and transfer the following items:

	Property Transferred			
Transferor	*Asset*	*Basis to Transferor*	*FMV*	*Number of Common Shares Issued*
Alice	Land	$12,000	$30,000	
	Building	38,000	70,000	400
	Mortgage on the land and building	60,000	60,000	
Bob	Equipment	25,000	40,000	300
Carla	Van	15,000	10,000	50
Dick	Accounting services	–0–	10,000	100

Alice purchased the land and building several years ago for $12,000 and $50,000, respectively. Alice has claimed straight-line depreciation on the building. Bob also receives a Bear note for $10,000 due in three years. The note bears interest at the prevailing market rate. Bob purchased the equipment three years ago for $50,000. Carla also receives $5,000 cash. Carla purchased the van two years ago for $20,000.

a. Does the transaction satisfy the requirements of Sec. 351?

b. What are the amount and character of the gains or losses recognized by Alice, Bob, Carla, Dick, and Bear?

c. What is each shareholder's basis in his or her Bear stock? When does the holding period for the stock begin?

d. What is Bear's basis in its property and services? When does the holding period for each property begin?

C:2-55 Ed and Fay together own 100% of the common stock of an existing corporation. On January 2 of the current year, they made the following additional transfers to the corporation, which qualify under Sec. 351. Ed transferred equipment (having a $55,000 FMV and $36,000 adjusted basis) in exchange for additional common stock worth $40,000, qualified preferred stock worth $9,000, and nonqualified preferred stock worth $6,000. Ed acquired the equipment on March 14 three years ago and claimed $46,000 of depreciation before contributing it to the corporation. Fay transferred inventory (having a $40,000 FMV and $14,000 adjusted basis) and land (a capital asset having a $20,000 FMV and $50,000 adjusted basis) in exchange for additional common stock worth $33,000 and $24,000 cash. Fay acquired the land on February 3 eight years ago. In addition, the corporation assumed $3,000 of Fay's liabilities, which were bona fide business debts with no tax avoidance purpose. These liabilities are general liabilities not associated with any particular asset. For each transferor shareholder, determine the amount realized, gain or loss realized, gain or loss recognized (if any), character of gain or loss recognized, basis of stock received, and holding period of stock received. For the corporation, determine the gain or loss recognized (if any), basis of each property received, and holding period of *each* property received.

TAX STRATEGY PROBLEMS

C:2-56 Assume the same facts as in Problem C:2-55.

a. Under what circumstances is the tax result in Problem C:2-55 beneficial, and for which shareholders? Are the shareholders likely to be pleased with the result?

b. If the shareholders decide that meeting the Sec. 351 requirements would generate a greater tax benefit, how might they proceed?

C:2-57 Paula Green owns and operates the Green Thumb Nursery as a sole proprietorship. The business has total assets with a $260,000 adjusted basis and a $500,000 FMV. Paula wants to expand into the landscaping business. She views this expansion as risky and therefore wants to incorporate so as not to put her personal assets at risk. Her friend, Mary Brown, is willing to invest $250,000 in the enterprise.

Although Green Thumb has earned approximately $55,000 per year, Paula and Mary expect that, when the landscaping business is launched, the new corporation will incur annual losses of $50,000 for the next two years. They expect profits of at least $80,000 annually, beginning in the third year. Paula and Mary earn approximately $50,000 from other sources. They are considering the following alternative capital structures and elections:

a. Green Thumb issues 50 shares of common stock to Paula and 25 shares of common stock to Mary.

b. Green Thumb issues 50 shares of common stock to Paula and a $250,000 ten-year note bearing interest at 8% to Mary.

c. Green Thumb issues 40 shares of common stock to Paula plus a $100,000 ten-year note bearing interest at 6% and 15 shares of common stock to Mary, plus a $100,000 ten-year note bearing interest at 6%.

d. Green Thumb issues 50 shares of common stock to Paula and 25 shares of preferred stock to Mary. The preferred stock is nonparticipating but pays a cumulative preferred dividend at 8% of its $250,000 stated value.

What are the advantages and disadvantages of each of these alternatives? What considerations are relevant for determining the best alternative?

C:2-58 Assume the same facts as in Problem C:2-57.

a. Given the nursery's operating prospects, what business forms might Paula and Mary consider and why?

b. In light of their proposed use of debt and equity, how might Paula and Mary structure a partnership to achieve their various business and investment objectives?

CASE STUDY PROBLEMS

C:2-59 Bob Jones has a small repair shop that he has run for several years as a sole proprietorship. The proprietorship uses the cash method of accounting and the calendar year as its tax year. Bob needs additional capital for expansion and knows two people who might be interested in investing in the business. One would like to work for the business. The other would only invest.

Bob wants to know the tax consequences of incorporating the business. His business assets include a building, equipment, accounts receivable, and cash. Liabilities include a mortgage on the building and a few accounts payable, which are deductible when paid. Assume that Bob's ordinary tax rate is greater than 25%.

Required: Write a memorandum to Bob explaining the tax consequences of the incorporation. As part of your memorandum examine the possibility of having the corporation issue common and preferred stock and debt for the shareholders' property and money.

C:2-60 Eric Wright conducts a dry cleaning business as a sole proprietorship. The business operates in a building that Eric owns. Last year, Eric mortgaged for $150,000 the building and the land on which the building sits. He used the money for a down payment on his personal residence and college expenses for his two children. He now wants to incorporate his business and transfer the building and the mortgage to a new corporation, along with other assets and some accounts payable. The amount of the unpaid mortgage balance will not exceed Eric's adjusted basis in the land and building at the time he transfers them to the corporation. Eric is aware that Sec. 357(b) could impact the tax consequences of the transaction because no bona fide business purpose exists for the mortgage transfer, which the IRS might consider to have been for a tax avoidance purpose. However, Eric refuses to acknowledge this possibility when you confront him. He maintains that many taxpayers play the audit lottery and that, in the event of an audit, invoking this issue could be a bargaining ploy.

Required: What information about the transaction must be provided with the transferor and transferee's tax returns for the year in which the transfer takes place? Discuss the ethical issues raised by the AICPA's *Statements on Standards for Tax Services No. 1, Tax Return Positions* (which can be found in Appendix E) as it relates to this situation. Should the tax practitioner act as an advocate for the client? Should the practitioner sign the return?

TAX RESEARCH PROBLEMS

C:2-61 Anne and Michael own and operate a successful mattress business. They have decided to take the business public. They contribute all the assets of the business to newly formed Spring Corporation each in exchange for 20% of the stock. The remaining 60% is issued to an underwriting company that will sell the stock to the public and charge 10% of the sales proceeds as a commission. Prepare a memorandum for your tax manager explaining whether or not this transaction meets the tax-free requirements of Sec. 351.

C:2-62 Bob and Carl transfer property to Stone Corporation for 90% and 10% of Stone stock, respectively. Pursuant to a binding agreement concluded before the transfer, Bob sells half of his stock to Carl. Prepare a memorandum for your tax manager explaining why the exchange does or does not meet the Sec. 351 control requirement. Your manager has suggested that, at a minimum, you consult the following authorities:

- IRC Sec. 351
- Reg. Sec. 1.351-1

C:2-63 In an exchange qualifying for Sec. 351 tax-free treatment, Greta receives 100 shares of White Corporation stock plus a right to receive another 25 shares. The right is contingent on the valuation of a patent contributed by Greta. Because the patent license is pending, the patent cannot be valued for several months. Prepare a memorandum for your tax manager explaining whether the underlying 25 shares are considered "stock" for purposes of Sec. 351 and what tax consequences ensue from Greta's receipt of the 100 shares now and 25 shares later upon exercise of the right.

C:2-64 Your clients, Lisa and Matthew, are planning to form Lima Corporation. Lisa will contribute $50,000 cash to Lima for 50 shares of its stock. Matthew will contribute land having a $35,000 adjusted basis and a $50,000 FMV for 50 shares of Lima stock. Lima will borrow additional capital from a bank and then will subdivide and sell the land. Prepare a memorandum for your tax manager outlining the tax treatment of the corporate formation. In your memorandum, compare tax and financial accounting for this transaction. References:

- IRC Sec. 351
- Accounting Standards Codification (ASC) 845 (Nonmonetary Transactions), formerly APB No. 29

C:2-65 John plans to transfer the assets and liabilities of his business to Newco in exchange for all of Newco's stock. The assets have a $250,000 basis and an $800,000 FMV. John also plans to transfer $475,000 of business related liabilities to Newco. Under Sec. 357(c), can John avoid recognizing a $175,000 gain (the excess of liabilities over the basis of assets transferred) by transferring a $175,000 personal promissory note along with the assets and liabilities?

C:2-66 Six years ago, Leticia, Monica, and Nathaniel organized Lemona Corporation to develop and sell computer software. Each individual contributed $10,000 to Lemona in exchange for 1,000 shares of Lemona stock (for a total of 3,000 shares issued and outstanding). The corporation also borrowed $250,000 from Venture Capital Associates to finance operating costs and capital expenditures.

Because of intense competition, Lemona struggled in its early years of operation and sustained chronic losses. This year, Leticia, who serves as Lemona's president, decided to seek additional funds to finance Lemona's working capital.

Venture Capital Associates declined Leticia's request for additional capital because of the firm's already high credit exposure to the software corporation. Hi-Tech Bank proposed to lend Lemona $100,000, but at a 10% premium over the prime rate. (Other software manufacturers in the same market can borrow at a 3% premium.) Investment Managers LLC proposed to inject $50,000 of equity capital into Lemona, but on the condition that the investment firm be granted the right to elect five members to Lemona's board of directors. Discouraged by the "high cost" of external borrowing, Leticia turned to Monica and Nathaniel.

She proposed to Monica and Nathaniel that each of the three original investors contribute an additional $25,000 to Lemona, each in exchange for five 20-year debentures. The debentures would be unsecured and subordinated to Venture Capital Associates debt. Annual interest on the debentures would accrue at a floating 5% premium over the prime rate. The right to receive interest payments would be cumulative; that is, each debenture holder would be entitled to past and current interest payments before Lemona's board could declare a common stock dividend. The debentures would be both nontransferable and noncallable.

Leticia, Monica, and Nathaniel have asked you, their tax accountant, to advise them on the tax implications of the proposed financing arrangement. After researching the issue, set forth your advice in a client letter. At a minimum, you should consult the following authorities:

- IRC Sec. 385
- *Rudolph A. Hardman*, 60 AFTR 2d 87-5651, 87-2 USTC ¶9523 (9th Cir., 1987)
- *Tomlinson v. The 1661 Corporation*, 19 AFTR 2d 1413, 67-1 USTC ¶9438 (5th Cir., 1967)

CHAPTER

3

THE CORPORATE INCOME TAX

LEARNING OBJECTIVES

After studying this chapter, you should be able to

1. Select tax years and accounting methods for C corporations
2. Calculate deductions particular to corporations and arrive at corporate taxable income
3. Compute a corporation's regular income tax liability
4. Recognize what a controlled group is and determine the tax consequences of being a controlled group
5. Identify planning strategies to reduce taxes for corporations and their shareholders
6. Comply with corporate tax filing requirements
7. Determine the financial statement implications of corporate federal income taxes

CHAPTER OUTLINE

A **corporation** is a separate taxpaying entity that must file an annual tax return even if it has no income or loss for the year. This chapter covers the tax rules for **domestic corporations** (i.e., corporations incorporated in one of the 50 states or under federal law) and other entities taxed as domestic corporations under the check-the-box regulations.[1] It explains the rules for determining a corporation's taxable income, loss, and tax liability and for filing corporate tax returns. See Table C:3-1 for the general formula for determining the corporate tax liability. It also discusses the financial implications of federal income taxes. Some of these implications appear briefly in the Book-to-Tax Accounting Comparisons, and a more detailed discussion appears at the end of this chapter.

The corporations discussed in this chapter are sometimes referred to as regular or C corporations because Subchapter C of the Internal Revenue Code (IRC) dictates much of their tax treatment. Corporations that have a special tax status include S corporations (see Chapter C:11) and affiliated groups of corporations that file consolidated returns (see Chapter C:8). A comparison of the tax treatments of C corporations, partnerships, and S corporations appears in Appendix F.

CORPORATE ELECTIONS

OBJECTIVE 1

Select tax years and accounting methods for C corporations

Once formed, a corporation must make certain elections, such as selecting its **tax year** and its accounting methods. The corporation makes these elections on its first tax return. They are important and should be considered carefully because, once made, they generally can be changed only with permission from the Internal Revenue Service (IRS).

CHOOSING A CALENDAR OR FISCAL YEAR

A new corporation may elect to use either a calendar year or a fiscal year as its accounting period. The corporation's tax year must be the same as the annual accounting period used for financial accounting purposes. The corporation makes the election by filing its first tax return for the selected period. A calendar year is a 12-month period ending on December 31. A fiscal year is a 12-month period ending on the last day of any month other than December. Examples of acceptable fiscal years are February 1, 2017, through January 31, 2018, and October 1, 2017, through September 30, 2018. A fiscal year that runs from September 16, 2017, through September 15, 2018, however, is not an acceptable tax year because it does not end on the last day of the month. The IRS requires that a corporation using an unacceptable tax year change to a calendar year.[2]

KEY POINT

Whereas partnerships and S corporations generally must adopt a calendar year, C corporations (other than personal service corporations) have the flexibility of adopting a fiscal year. The fiscal year must end on the last day of the month.

Short Tax Period. A corporation's first tax year might not cover a full 12-month period. If, for example, a corporation begins business on March 10, 2017, and elects a fiscal year ending on September 30, its first tax year covers the period from March 10, 2017, through September 30, 2017. Its second tax year covers the period from October 1, 2017, through September 30, 2018. The corporation must file a **short-period tax return** for its first tax year.[3] From then on, its tax returns will cover a full 12-month period. The last year of a corporation's life, however, also may be a short period covering the period from the beginning of the last tax year through the date the corporation ceases to exist.

Restrictions on Adopting a Tax Year. A corporation may be subject to restrictions in its choice of a tax year. For example, an S corporation generally must use a calendar year (see Chapter C:11), and members of an affiliated group filing a consolidated return must use the same tax year as the group's parent corporation (see Chapter C:8).

A **personal service corporation** (PSC) generally must use a calendar year as its tax year. This restriction prevents a personal service corporation with, for example, a January 31 year-end from distributing a large portion of its income earned during the February through December portion of 2017 to its calendar year shareholder-employees in January

[1] Sec. 7701(a)(4). Corporations that are not classified as domestic are foreign corporations. Foreign corporations are taxed like domestic corporations if they conduct a trade or business in the United States.

[2] Sec. 441. Section 441 also permits accounting periods of either 52 or 53 weeks that always end on the same day of the week (such as Friday).

[3] Sec. 443(a)(2).

▼ **TABLE C:3-1**
General Rules for Determining the Corporate Tax Liability

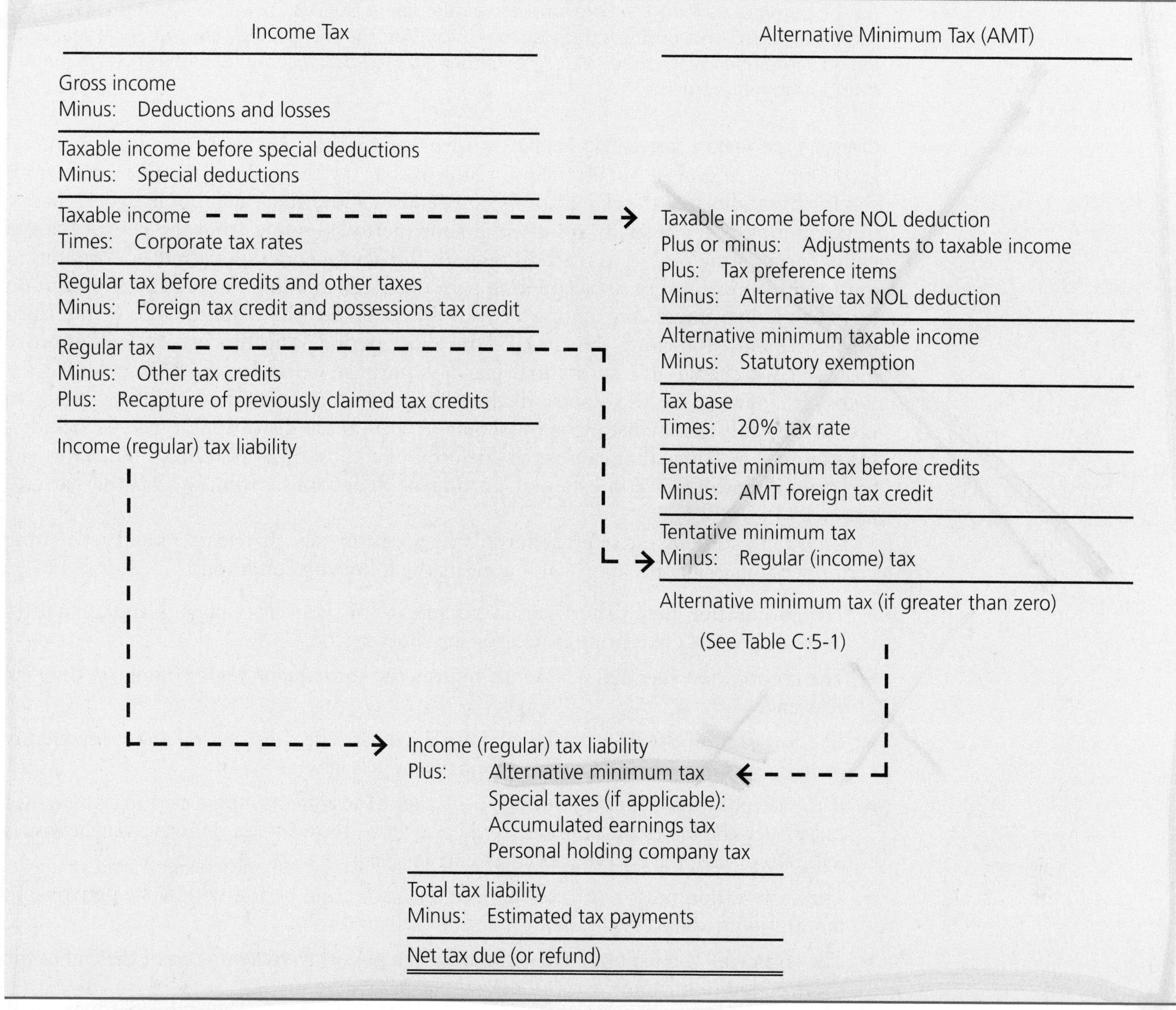

2018, thereby deferring income largely earned in 2017 to 2018. For this purpose, the IRC defines a PSC as a corporation whose principal activity is the performance of personal services by its employee-owners who own more than 10% of the stock (by value) on any day of the year.[4]

A PSC, however, may adopt a fiscal tax year if it can establish a business purpose for such a year. For example, it may be able to establish a natural business year and use that year as its tax year.[5] Deferral of income by shareholders is not an acceptable business purpose. Even when no business purpose exists, a new PSC may elect to use a September 30, October 31, or November 30 year-end if it meets minimum distribution requirements to employee-owners during the deferral period.[6] If it fails to meet these distribution requirements, the PSC may have to defer to its next fiscal year the deduction for amounts paid to employee-owners.[7]

[4] Sec. 441(i).

[5] The natural business year rule requires that the year-end used for tax purposes coincide with the end of the taxpayer's peak business period. (See the partnership and S corporation chapters and Rev. Proc. 2006-46, 2006-2 C.B. 859, for a further explanation of this exception.)

[6] Sec. 444.

[7] Sec. 280H.

EXAMPLE C:3-1 ▶ Alice and Bob form Cole Corporation with each shareholder owning 50% of its stock. Alice and Bob use the calendar year as their tax year. Alice and Bob are both active in the business and are the corporation's primary employees. The new corporation performs engineering services for the automotive industry. Cole must use a calendar year as its tax year unless it qualifies for a fiscal year based on a business purpose exception. Alternatively, it may adopt a fiscal year ending on September 30, October 31, or November 30, provided it complies with certain minimum distribution requirements. ◀

Changing the Annual Accounting Period. A corporation that desires to change its annual accounting period must obtain the prior approval of the IRS unless Treasury Regulations specifically authorized the change or IRS procedures allow an automatic change. A change in accounting period usually results in a short period running from the end of the old annual accounting period to the beginning of the new accounting period. A corporation must request approval of an accounting period change by filing Form 1128 (Application for Change in Annual Accounting Period) on or before the fifteenth day of the third calendar month following the close of the short period. The IRS usually will approve a request for change if a substantial business purpose exists for the change and if the taxpayer agrees to the IRS's prescribed terms, conditions, and adjustments necessary to prevent any substantial distortion of income. A substantial distortion of income includes, for example, a change that causes the "deferral of a substantial portion of the taxpayer's income, or shifting of a substantial portion of deductions, from one taxable year to another."[8]

Under IRS administrative procedures, a corporation may change its annual accounting period without prior IRS approval if it meets the following conditions:

- The corporation files a short-period tax return for the year of change and annualizes its income when computing its tax for the short period.
- The corporation files full 12-month returns for subsequent years ending on the new year-end.
- The corporation closes its books as of the last day of the short-period and subsequently computes its income and keeps its books using the new tax year.
- If the corporation generates an NOL or capital loss in the short period, it may not carry back the losses but must carry them over to future years. However, if the loss is $50,000 or less, the corporation may carry it back.
- The corporation must not have changed its accounting period within the previous 48 months (with some exceptions).
- The corporation must not have an interest in a pass-through entity as of the end of the short period (with some exceptions).
- The corporation is not an S corporation, personal service corporation, tax-exempt organization, or other specialized corporation.[9]

BOOK-TO-TAX ACCOUNTING COMPARISON

Treasury Regulations literally require taxpayers to use the same overall accounting method for book and tax purposes. However, the courts have allowed different methods if the taxpayer maintains adequate reconciling workpapers. The IRS has adopted the courts' position on this issue.

ACCOUNTING METHODS

A new corporation must select the overall **accounting method** it will use for tax purposes. The method chosen must be indicated on the corporation's initial return. The three possible accounting methods are: accrual, cash, and hybrid.[10]

Accrual Method. Under the accrual method, a corporation reports income in the year it earns the income and reports expenses in the year it incurs the expenses. A corporation must use the accrual method unless it qualifies under one of the following exceptions:

- It qualifies as a family farming corporation.[11]

[8] Reg. Sec. 1.442-1(b)(3). Also see Rev. Proc. 2002-39, 2002-1 C.B. 1046.
[9] Rev. Proc. 2006-45, 2006-2 C.B. 851. For automatic change procedures for S corporations and personal service corporations, see Rev. Proc. 2006-46, 2006-2 C.B. 859.
[10] Sec. 446.
[11] Sec. 448. Certain family farming corporations having gross receipts of less than $25 million may use the cash method of accounting. Section 447 requires farming corporations with gross receipts over $25 million to use the accrual method of accounting.

- It qualifies as a personal service corporation, which is a corporation substantially all of whose activities involve the performance of services in the fields of health, law, engineering, architecture, accounting, actuarial science, performing arts, or consulting; and substantially all of whose stock is held by current (or retired) employees performing the services listed above, their estates, or (for two years only) persons who inherited their stock from such employees.[12]
- It meets a $5 million gross receipts test for all prior tax years beginning after December 31, 1985. A corporation meets this test for any prior tax year if its average gross receipts for the three-year period ending with that prior tax year do not exceed $5 million. If the corporation was not in existence for the entire three-year period, the period during which the corporation *was* in existence may be used.
- It has elected S corporation status.

ADDITIONAL COMMENT

Whereas partnerships and S corporations are generally allowed to be cash method taxpayers, most C corporations must use the accrual method of accounting. This restriction can prove inconvenient for many small corporations (with more than $5 million of gross receipts) that would rather use the less complicated cash method of accounting.

If a corporation meets one of the exceptions listed above, it may use either the accrual method or one of the following two methods.

Cash Method. Under the cash method, a corporation reports income when it actually or constructively receives the income and reports expenses when it pays them. Corporations in service industries such as engineering, medicine, law, and accounting generally use this method because they prefer to defer recognition until they actually receive the income. This method may not be used if inventories are a material income-producing factor. In such case, the corporation must use either the *accrual* method or the *hybrid* method of accounting.

Hybrid Method. Under the hybrid method, a corporation uses the accrual method of accounting for sales, cost of goods sold, inventories, accounts receivable, and accounts payable, and uses the cash method of accounting for all other income and expense items. Small businesses with inventories (e.g., retail stores) often use this method. Although they must use the accrual method of accounting for sales-related income and expense items, they often find the cash method less burdensome to use for other income and expense items, such as utilities, rents, salaries, and taxes.

DETERMINING A CORPORATION'S TAXABLE INCOME

OBJECTIVE 2

Calculate deductions particular to corporations and arrive at corporate taxable income

Each year, C corporations must determine their corporate income (or regular) tax liability. In addition to the income tax, a C corporation may owe the corporate alternative minimum tax and possibly either the accumulated earnings tax or the personal holding company tax. A corporation's total tax liability equals the sum of its regular income tax liability plus any additional taxes that it owes.

This chapter explains how to compute a corporation's income (or regular) tax liability. Chapter C:5 explains the computation of the corporate alternative minimum tax, personal holding company tax, and accumulated earnings tax.

[12] The personal service corporation definition for the tax year election [Sec. 441(i)] is different from the personal service corporation definition for the cash accounting method election [Sec. 448].

Like an individual, a corporation is a taxpaying entity with gross income and deductions. However, a number of differences arise between individual and corporate taxation as summarized in Figure C:3-1. This section of the text expands on some of these items and discusses other tax aspects particular to corporations.

SALES AND EXCHANGES OF PROPERTY

Sales and exchanges of property generally are treated the same way for corporations as for an individual. However, special rules apply to capital gains and losses, and corporations are subject to an additional 20% depreciation recapture rule under Sec. 291 on sales of Sec. 1250 property.

1. **Gross income:** Generally, the same gross income definition applies to individuals and corporations. Certain exclusions are available to individuals but not to corporations (e.g., fringe benefits); other exclusions are available to corporations but not to individuals (e.g., capital contributions).
2. **Deductions:** Individuals have above-the-line deductions (for AGI), itemized deductions (from AGI), and personal exemptions. Corporations do not compute AGI, and their deductions are presumed to be ordinary and necessary business expenses.
3. **Charitable contributions:** Individuals are limited to 50% of AGI (30% for capital gain property). Corporations are limited to 10% of taxable income computed without regard to the dividends-received deductions, the U.S. production activities deduction, NOL and capital loss carrybacks, and the contribution deduction itself. Individuals deduct a contribution only in the year they pay it. Accrual basis corporations may deduct contributions in the year of accrual if the board of directors authorizes the contribution by year-end, and the corporation pays it by the fifteenth day of the fourth month of the next year (third month if the corporation has a June 30 year-end).
4. **Depreciation on Sec. 1250 property:** Individuals generally do not recapture depreciation under the MACRS rules because straight-line depreciation applies to real property. Corporations must recapture 20% of the amount that would be recaptured under Sec. 1245. Individuals are subject to a 25% (and possibly an incremental 3.8%) tax rate on unrecaptured Sec. 1250 gains. Corporations are not subject to this rate.
5. **Net capital gains:** The applicable capital gains tax rate for net capital gains and qualified dividends of noncorporate taxpayers is 0% for taxpayers in tax brackets of 15% and below, 15% for taxpayers in the 25% through 35% tax brackets, and 20% for taxpayers in the 39.6% tax bracket. Also, 25% and 28% rates apply for gains on certain types of property. In addition, an incremental 3.8% rate applies to net investment income for taxpayers whose modified AGI exceeds $200,000 ($250,000 for married filing jointly). Net investment income includes, among other things, interest, dividends, annuities, royalties, rents, and net gains from the disposition of property not used in a trade or business, all reduced by deductions allocable to such income or gains. Corporate capital gains are taxed at the regular corporate tax rates.
6. **Capital losses:** Individuals can deduct up to $3,000 of net capital losses to offset ordinary income. Individual capital losses carry over indefinitely. Corporations cannot offset any ordinary income with capital losses. However, capital losses carry back three years and forward five years and offset capital gains in those years.
7. **Dividends-received deduction:** This deduction is not available to individuals. Corporations receive a 70%, 80%, or 100% special deduction depending on the percentage of stock ownership.
8. **NOLs:** Individuals must make many adjustments to arrive at the NOL they are allowed to carry back or forward. A corporation's NOL is simply the excess of its deductions over its income for the year. The NOL carries back two years (or an extended period if applicable) and forward 20 years for individuals and corporations, or the taxpayer can elect to forgo the carryback and only carry the NOL forward.
9. For individuals, the U.S. production activities deduction is based on the lesser of qualified production activities income or AGI. For corporations, the deduction is based on the lesser of qualified production activities income or taxable income.
10. **Tax rates:** Individual's ordinary tax rates range from 10% to 39.6% (in 2017). Corporate tax rates range from 15% to 39%.
11. **AMT:** Individual AMT rates are 26% or 28%. The corporate AMT rate is 20%. Corporations are subject to a special AMTI adjustment, called adjusted current earnings (ACE), that does not apply to individuals.
12. **Passive losses:** Passive loss rules apply to individuals, partners, S corporation shareholders, closely held C corporations, and personal service corporations. They do not apply to widely held C corporations.
13. **Casualty losses:** Casualty losses are deductible in full by a corporation because all corporate casualty losses are considered to be business related. Moreover, they are not reduced by a $100 offset, nor are they restricted to losses exceeding 10% of AGI, as are an individual's nonbusiness casualty losses.

FIGURE C:3-1 ▶ DIFFERENCES BETWEEN INDIVIDUAL AND CORPORATE TAXATION

Capital Gains and Losses. A corporation has a capital gain or loss if it sells or exchanges a capital asset. As with individuals, a corporation must net all its capital gains and losses to obtain its net capital gain or loss position.

Net Capital Gain. A corporation includes all its net capital gains (net long-term capital gains in excess of net short-term capital losses) for the tax year in gross income. Unlike with individuals, a corporation's capital gains receive no special tax treatment and are taxed in the same manner as any other ordinary income item.

EXAMPLE C:3-2 ▶ Beta Corporation has a net capital gain of $40,000, gross profits on sales of $110,000, and deductible expenses of $28,000. Beta's gross income is $150,000 ($40,000 + $110,000). Its taxable income is $122,000 ($150,000 − $28,000). The $40,000 of net capital gain receives no special treatment and is taxed using the regular corporate tax rates described below. ◀

Net Capital Losses. If a corporation incurs a net capital loss, it cannot deduct the net loss in the current year. A corporation's capital losses can offset only capital gains. They never can offset the corporation's ordinary income.

A corporation must carry back a net capital loss as a short-term capital loss to the three previous tax years and offset capital gains in the earliest year possible (i.e., the losses carry back to the third previous year first). If the loss is not totally absorbed as a carryback, the remainder carries over as a short-term capital loss for five years. Any unused capital losses remaining at the end of the carryover period expire.

EXAMPLE C:3-3 ▶ In 2017, East Corporation reports gross profits of $150,000, deductible expenses of $28,000, and a net capital loss of $10,000. East reported the following capital gain net income (excess of gains from sales or exchanges of capital assets over losses from such sales or exchanges) during 2014 through 2016:

Year	*Capital Gain Net Income*
2014	$6,000
2015	–0–
2016	3,000

East has gross income of $150,000 and taxable income of $122,000 ($150,000 − $28,000) for 2017. East also has a $10,000 net capital loss that carries back to 2014 first and offsets the $6,000 capital gain net income reported in that year. East receives a refund for the taxes paid in 2014 on the $6,000 of capital gains. The $4,000 ($10,000 − $6,000) remainder of the loss carryback carries to 2016 and offsets East's $3,000 capital gain net income reported in that year. East still has a $1,000 net capital loss carryover to 2018. ◀

ADDITIONAL COMMENT

A corporation accomplishes the net capital loss carryback by filing either Form 1139, Corporation Application for Tentative Refund, or Form 1120X, Amended U.S. Corporation Income Tax Return. Form 1139 usually results in a quicker refund than does Form 1120X but must be filed within one year after the end of the year in which the net capital loss occurred.

Sec. 291: Tax Benefit Recapture Rule. If a taxpayer sells Sec. 1250 property at a gain, Sec. 1250 requires that the taxpayer report the recognized gain as ordinary income to the extent the depreciation taken exceeds the depreciation that would have been allowed had the taxpayer used the straight-line method. This ordinary income is known as Sec. 1250 depreciation recapture. For individuals, any remaining gain is characterized as a combination of unrecaptured Sec. 1250 gain and Sec. 1231 gain. Corporations, however, must recapture as ordinary income an amount equal to 20% of the ordinary income that would have been recognized had the property been Sec. 1245 property instead of Sec. 1250 property.

ADDITIONAL COMMENT

Under the modified accelerated cost recovery system (MACRS), Sec. 1250 depreciation recapture seldom, if ever, occurs for individuals because MACRS requires straight-line depreciation for Sec. 1250 property. Nevertheless, individuals would be subject to the 25% tax rate on unrecaptured Sec. 1250 gains.

EXAMPLE C:3-4 ▶ Texas Corporation purchased residential real estate several years ago for $125,000, of which $25,000 was allocated to the land and $100,000 to the building. Texas took straight-line MACRS depreciation deductions of $10,606 on the building during the period it held the building. In December of the current year, Texas sells the property for $155,000, of which $45,000 is allocated to the land and $110,000 to the building. Texas has a $20,000 ($45,000 − $25,000) gain on the land sale, all of which is Sec. 1231 gain. This gain is not affected by Sec. 291 because land is not Sec. 1250 property. Texas has a $20,606 [$110,000 sales price − ($100,000 original cost − $10,606 depreciation)] gain on the sale of the building. If Texas were an individual taxpayer, $10,606 would be an unrecaptured Sec. 1250 gain subject to a 25% tax rate, and the remaining

ADDITIONAL COMMENT

Section 291 results in the recapture, as ordinary income, of up to 20% of the gain on sales of Sec. 1250 property. This recapture requirement reduces the amount of net Sec.1231 gains that can be offset by corporate capital losses.

ADDITIONAL COMMENT

If an individual sold the same business property as in Example C:3-4, he or she would recognize $10,606 of nonrecaptured Sec. 1250 gain, $30,000 of Sec. 1231 gain, and no ordinary income.

$10,000 would be a Sec. 1231 gain. However, a corporate taxpayer reports $2,121 of gain as ordinary income. These amounts are summarized below:

	Land	Building	Total
Amount of gain:			
Sales price	$45,000	$110,000	$155,000
Minus: Adjusted basis	(25,000)	(89,394)	(114,394)
Recognized gain	$20,000	$ 20,606	$ 40,606
Character of gain:			
Ordinary income	$ -0-	$ 2,121[a]	$ 2,121
Sec. 1231 gain	20,000	18,485	38,485
Recognized gain	$20,000	$ 20,606	$ 40,606

[a]0.20 × lesser of $10,606 depreciation claimed or $20,606 recognized gain. ◀

BUSINESS EXPENSES

Corporations are allowed deductions for ordinary and necessary business expenses, including salaries paid to officers and other employees of the corporation, rent, repairs, insurance premiums, advertising, interest, taxes, losses on sales of inventory or other property, bad debts, and depreciation. No deductions are allowed, however, for interest on amounts borrowed to purchase tax-exempt securities, illegal bribes or kickbacks, fines or penalties imposed by a government, or insurance premiums incurred to insure the lives of officers and employees when the corporation is the beneficiary.

Organizational Expenditures. When formed, a corporation may incur some organizational expenditures such as legal fees and accounting fees incident to the incorporation process. These expenditures normally must be capitalized. Nevertheless, under Sec. 248, a corporation may elect to deduct the first $5,000 of organizational expenditures. However, the corporation must reduce the $5,000 by the amount by which cumulative organizational expenditures exceed $50,000 although the $5,000 cannot be reduced below zero. The corporation can amortize the remaining organizational expenditures over a 180-month period beginning in the month it begins business.

EXAMPLE C:3-5 ▶ Sigma Corporation incorporates on January 10 of the current year, and begins business on March 3. Sigma elects a September 30 year-end. Thus, it conducts business for seven months during its first tax year. During the period January 10 through September 30, Sigma incurs $52,000 of organizational expenditures. Because these expenditures exceed $50,000, Sigma must reduce the first $5,000 by $2,000 ($52,000 − $50,000), leaving a $3,000 deduction. Sigma amortizes the remaining $49,000 ($52,000 − $3,000) over 180 months beginning in March of its first year. This portion of the deduction equals $1,906 ($49,000/180 × 7 months). Accordingly, its total first-year deduction is $4,906 ($3,000 + $1,906). ◀

WHAT WOULD YOU DO IN THIS SITUATION?

You are a CPA with a medium-size accounting firm. One of your corporate clients is an electrical contractor in New York City. The client is successful and had $10 million of sales last year. The contracts involve private and government electrical work. Among the corporation's expenses are $400,000 of kickbacks paid to people working for general contractors who award electrical subcontracts to the corporation, and $100,000 of payments to individuals in the electricians' union. Technically, these payments are illegal. However, your client says that everyone in this business needs to pay kickbacks to obtain contracts and to have enough electricians to finish the projects in a timely manner. He maintains that it is impossible to stay in business without making these payments. In preparing its tax return, your client wants you to deduct these expenses. What is your opinion concerning the client's request?

BOOK-TO-TAX ACCOUNTING COMPARISON

Most corporations amortize organizational expenditures for tax purposes over the specified period. For financial accounting purposes, they are expensed currently under ASC 720-15. Thus, the differential treatment creates a deferred tax asset.

For organizational expenditures paid or incurred after August 16, 2011, a corporation is deemed to have made the Sec. 248 election for the tax year the corporation begins business.[13] If the corporation chooses to forgo the deemed election, it can elect to capitalize the expenditures (without amortization) on a timely filed tax return for the tax year the corporation begins business. Either election, to amortize or capitalize, is irrevocable and applies to all organizational expenditures of the corporation.

A corporation begins business when it starts the business operations for which it was organized. Merely coming into existence is not sufficient. For example, obtaining a corporate charter does not in itself establish the beginning of business. However, acquiring assets necessary for operating the business may be sufficient.

Organizational expenditures include expenditures (1) incident to the corporation's creation; (2) chargeable to the corporation's capital account; and (3) of a character that, if expended incident to the creation of a corporation having a limited life, would be amortizable over that life.

Specific organizational expenditures include

- Legal services incident to the corporation's organization (e.g., drafting the corporate charter and bylaws, minutes of organizational meetings, and terms of original stock certificates)
- Accounting services necessary to create the corporation
- Expenses of temporary directors and of organizational meetings of directors and stockholders
- Fees paid to the state of incorporation[14]

Organizational expenditures do not include expenditures connected with issuing or selling the corporation's stock or other securities (e.g., commissions, professional fees, and printing costs) and expenditures related to the transfer of assets to the corporation.

EXAMPLE C:3-6 ► Omega Corporation incorporates on July 12 of the current year, starts business operations on August 10, and elects a tax year ending on September 30. Omega incurs the following expenditures while organizing the corporation:

Date	*Type of Expenditure*	*Amount*
June 10	Legal expenses to draft charter	$ 2,000
July 17	Commission to stockbroker for issuing and selling stock	40,000
July 18	Accounting fees to set up corporate books	2,400
July 20	Temporary directors' fees	1,000
August 25	Directors' fees	1,500

Omega's first tax year begins July 12 and ends on September 30. Omega has organizational expenditures of $5,400 ($2,000 + $2,400 + $1,000). The commission for selling the Omega stock is treated as a reduction in the amount of Omega's paid-in capital. Omega deducts the directors' fees incurred in August as a trade or business expense under Sec. 162 because Omega had begun business operations by that date. Assuming a deemed election to amortize its organizational expenditures, Omega can deduct $5,000 in its first tax year and amortize the remaining $400 over 180 months. Thus, its first year deduction is $5,004 [$5,000 + ($400/180) × 2 months].

The following table summarizes the classification of expenditures:

			Type of Expenditure		
Date	*Expenditure*	*Amount*	*Organizational*	*Capital*	*Business*
June 10	Legal	$ 2,000	$2,000		
July 17	Commission	40,000		$40,000	
July 18	Accounting	2,400	2,400		
July 20	Temporary directors' fees	1,000	1,000		
August 25	Directors' fees	1,500			$1,500
	Total	$46,900	$5,400	$40,000	$1,500 ◄

[13] Reg. Sec. 1.248-1(c) and 1(f).

[14] Reg. Sec. 1.248-1(b)(2).

Start-Up Expenditures. A distinction must be made between a corporation's organizational expenditures and its start-up expenditures. Start-up expenditures are ordinary and necessary business expenses paid or incurred by an individual or corporate taxpayer

- ▶ To investigate the creation or acquisition of an active trade or business
- ▶ To create an active trade or business
- ▶ To conduct an activity engaged in for profit or the production of income before the time the activity becomes an active trade or business

BOOK-TO-TAX ACCOUNTING COMPARISON

For tax purposes, a corporation amortizes start-up expenditures over 180 months (after the initial deduction). ASC 915 holds that the financial accounting practices and reporting standards used for development stage businesses should be no different for an established business. The two different sets of rules can lead to different reporting for tax and book purposes.

Examples of start-up expenditures include the costs for a survey of potential markets; an analysis of available facilities; advertisements relating to opening the business; the training of employees; travel and other expenses for securing prospective distributors, suppliers, or customers; and the hiring of management personnel and outside consultants. The expenditures must be such that, if incurred in connection with the operation of an existing active trade or business, they would be allowable as a deduction in the year paid or incurred.

Under Sec. 195, a corporation may elect to deduct the first $5,000 of start-up expenditures. However, this amount is reduced (but not below zero) by the amount by which the cumulative start-up expenditures exceed $50,000. The corporation can amortize the remaining start-up expenditures over a 180-month period beginning in the month it begins business.

For start-up expenditures paid or incurred after August 16, 2011, a corporation is deemed to have made the Sec. 195 election for the tax year the business to which the expenditures relate begins.[15] If the corporation chooses to forgo the deemed election, it can elect to capitalize the expenditures (without amortization) on a timely filed tax return for the tax year the business to which the expenditures relate begins. Either election, to amortize or capitalize, is irrevocable and applies to all start-up expenditures related to the business.

STOP & THINK

Question: What is the difference between an organizational expenditure and a start-up expenditure?

Solution: Organizational expenditures are outlays made in forming a corporation, such as fees paid to the state of incorporation for the corporate chapter and fees paid to an attorney to draft the documents needed to form the corporation. Start-up expenditures are outlays that otherwise would be deductible as ordinary and necessary business expenses but that are capitalized because they were incurred prior to the start of the corporation's business activities.

A corporation may elect to deduct the first $5,000 of organizational expenditures and the first $5,000 of start-up expenditures. The corporation can amortize the remainder of each set of expenditures over 180 months. Like a corporation, a partnership can deduct and amortize its organizational and start-up expenditures. A sole proprietorship may incur start-up expenditures, but sole proprietorships do not incur organizational expenditures.

Limitation on Deductions for Accrued Compensation. If a corporation accrues an obligation to pay compensation, the corporation must make the payment within 2½ months after the close of its tax year. Otherwise, the deduction cannot be taken until the year of payment.[16] The reason is that, if a payment is delayed beyond 2½ months, the IRS treats it as a deferred compensation plan. Deferred compensation cannot be deducted until the year the corporation pays it and the recipient includes the payment in income.[17]

EXAMPLE C:3-7 ▶ On December 10 of the current year, Bell Corporation, a calendar year taxpayer, accrues an obligation for a $100,000 bonus to Marge, a sales representative who has had an outstanding year. Marge owns no Bell stock. Bell must make the payment by March 15 of next year. Otherwise, Bell Corporation cannot deduct the $100,000 in its current year tax return but must wait until the year it pays the bonus. ◀

[15] Reg. Sec. 1.195-1(b) and 1(d).
[16] Temp. Reg. Sec. 1.404(b)-1T.
[17] Sec. 404(b).

Charitable Contributions. The treatment of charitable contributions by individual and corporate taxpayers differs in three ways: the timing of the deduction, the amount of the deduction permitted for the contribution of certain noncash property, and the maximum deduction permitted in any given year.

Timing of the Deduction. Corporations may deduct contributions to qualified charitable organizations. Generally, the contribution must have been *paid* during the year (not just pledged) for a deduction to be allowed for a given year. A special rule, however, applies to corporations using the accrual method of accounting (corporations using the cash or hybrid methods of accounting are not eligible).[18] These corporations may elect to treat part or all of a charitable contribution as having been made in the year it accrued (instead of the year paid) if

- The board of directors authorizes the contribution in the year it accrued
- The corporation pays the contribution on or before the fifteenth day of the fourth month following the end of the accrual year (third month if the corporation has a June 30 year-end).

The corporation makes the election by deducting the contribution in its tax return for the accrual year and by attaching a copy of the board of director's resolution to the return. Any portion of the contribution for which the corporation does not make the election is deducted in the year paid.

EXAMPLE C:3-8 ▶ Echo Corporation is a calendar year taxpayer using the accrual method of accounting. In the current year, its board of directors authorizes a $10,000 contribution to the Girl Scouts. Echo pays the contribution on March 10 of next year. Echo may elect to treat part or all of the contribution as having been paid in the current year. If the corporation pays the contribution after March 15 of next year, it may not deduct the contribution in the current year but may deduct it next year. ◀

TAX STRATEGY TIP

The tax laws do not require a corporation to recognize a gain when it contributes appreciated property to a charitable organization. Thus, except for inventory and limited other properties, a corporation can deduct the FMV of its donation without having to recognize any appreciation in its gross income. On the other hand, a decline in the value of donated property is not deductible. Thus, the corporation should sell the loss property to recognize the loss and then donate the sales proceeds to the charitable organization.

Deducting Contributions of Nonmonetary Property. If a taxpayer donates money to a qualified charitable organization, the amount of the charitable contribution deduction equals the amount of money donated. If the taxpayer donates property, the amount of the charitable contribution deduction generally equals the property's fair market value (FMV). However, special rules apply to donations of appreciated nonmonetary property known as ordinary income property and capital gain property.[19]

In this context, **ordinary income property** is property whose sale would have resulted in a gain other than a long-term capital gain (i.e., ordinary income or short-term capital gain). Examples of ordinary income property include investment property held for one year or less, inventory property, and property subject to depreciation recapture under Secs. 1245 and 1250. The deduction allowed for a donation of such property is limited to the property's FMV minus the amount of ordinary income or short-term capital gain the corporation would have recognized had it sold the property.

In some cases, a corporation may deduct the donated property's adjusted basis plus one-half of the excess of the property's FMV over its adjusted basis (not to exceed twice the property's adjusted basis). This special rule applies to inventory if

1. The use of the property is related to the donee's exempt function, and it is used solely for the care of the ill, the needy, or infants;
2. The property is not transferred to the donee in exchange for money, other property, or services; and
3. The donor receives a statement from the charitable organization stating that conditions (1) and (2) will be complied with.

A similar rule applies to contributions of scientific research property if the corporation created the property and contributed it to a college, university, or tax-exempt scientific research organization for its use within two years of creating the property.

EXAMPLE C:3-9 ▶ King Corporation donates inventory having a $26,000 adjusted basis and a $40,000 FMV to a qualified public charity. A $33,000 [$26,000 + (0.50 × $14,000)] deduction is allowed for the

[18] Sec. 170(a).

[19] Sec. 170(e).

contribution of the inventory if the charitable organization will use the inventory for the care of the ill, needy, or infants, or if the donee is an educational institution or research organization that will use the scientific research property for research or experimentation. Otherwise, the deduction is limited to the property's $26,000 adjusted basis. If instead the inventory's FMV is $100,000 and the donation meets either of the two sets of requirements outlined above, the charitable contribution deduction is limited to $52,000, the lesser of the property's adjusted basis plus one-half of the appreciation [$63,000 = $26,000 + (0.50 × $74,000)] or twice the property's adjusted basis ($52,000 = $26,000 × 2). ◀

When a corporation donates appreciated property whose sale would result in long-term capital gain (also known as **capital gain property**) to a charitable organization, the amount of the contribution deduction generally equals the property's FMV. However, special restrictions apply if

- The corporation donates a patent, copyright, trademark, trade name, trade secret, know-how, certain software, or other similar property;
- A corporation donates tangible personal property to a charitable organization and the organization's use of the property is unrelated to its tax-exempt purpose; or
- A corporation donates appreciated property to certain private nonoperating foundations.[20]

In these cases, the amount of the corporation's contribution is limited to the property's FMV minus the long-term capital gain that would have resulted from the property's sale.

EXAMPLE C:3-10 ▶ Fox Corporation donates artwork to the MacNay Museum. The artwork, purchased two years earlier for $15,000, is worth $38,000 on the date Fox donates it. At the time of the donation, the museum's directors intend to sell the work to raise funds to conduct museum activities. Fox's deduction for the gift is limited to $15,000. If the museum plans to display the artwork to the public, the entire $38,000 deduction is permitted. Fox can avoid losing a portion of its charitable contribution deduction by, as a condition of the donation, placing restrictions on the sale or use of the property. ◀

Substantiation Requirements. Section 170(f)(11) imposes substantiation requirements for noncash charitable contributions. If the corporation does not comply, it will lose the charitable contribution deduction. The requirements are as follows:

ADDITIONAL COMMENT

The $500, $5,000, and $500,000 thresholds apply on an aggregate basis for similar property donated to one or more donees.

- If the contribution deduction exceeds $500, the corporation must include with its tax return a description of the property and any other information required by Treasury Regulations.
- If the contribution deduction exceeds $5,000, the corporation must obtain a qualified appraisal and include with its tax return any information and appraisal required by Treasury Regulations.
- If the contribution deduction exceeds $500,000, the corporation must attach a qualified appraisal to the tax return.

The second and third requirements, however, do not apply to contributions of cash; publicly traded securities; inventory; or certain motor vehicles, boats, or aircraft the donee organization sells without any intervening use or material improvement. With regard to these vehicles, the donor corporation's deduction is limited to the amount of gross proceeds the donee organization receives on the sale.

Maximum Deduction Permitted. A limit applies to the amount of charitable contributions a corporation can deduct in a given year. The limit is calculated differently for corporations than for individuals. Contribution deductions by corporations are limited to 10% of adjusted taxable income. Adjusted taxable income is the corporation's taxable income computed without regard to any of the following amounts:

[20] Sec. 170(e)(5). The restriction on contributions of appreciated property to private nonoperating foundations does not apply to contributions of stock for which market quotations are readily available.

BOOK-TO-TAX ACCOUNTING COMPARISON

For financial accounting purposes, all charitable contributions can be claimed as an expense without regard to the amount of profits reported. For tax purposes, however, the charitable contribution deduction may be limited. Thus, the charitable contribution carryover for tax purposes creates a deferred tax asset, possibly subject to a valuation allowance.

- The charitable contribution deduction
- An NOL carryback
- A capital loss carryback
- The dividends-received deduction[21]
- The U.S. production activities deduction

Contributions that exceed the 10% limit are not deductible in the current year. Instead, they carry forward to the next five tax years. Any excess contributions not deducted within those five years expire. The corporation may deduct excess contributions in the carryover year only after it deducts any contributions made in that year. The total charitable contribution deduction (including any deduction for contribution carryovers) is limited to 10% of the corporation's adjusted taxable income in the carryover year.[22]

EXAMPLE C:3-11 ▶ Golf Corporation reports the following results in Year 1 and Year 2:

	Year 1	*Year 2*
Adjusted taxable income	$200,000	$300,000
Charitable contributions	35,000	25,000

Golf's Year 1 contribution deduction is limited to $20,000 (0.10 × $200,000). Golf has a $15,000 ($35,000 − $20,000) contribution carryover to Year 2. The Year 2 contribution deduction is limited to $30,000 (0.10 × $300,000). Golf's deduction for Year 2 is composed of the $25,000 donated in Year 2 and $5,000 of the Year 1 carryover. The remaining $10,000 carryover from Year 1 carries over to the next four years. ◀

Topic Review C:3-1 summarizes the basic corporate charitable contribution deduction rules.

TOPIC REVIEW C:3-1

Corporate Charitable Contribution Rules

1. Timing of the contribution deduction
   a. General rule: A deduction is allowed for contributions paid during the year.
   b. Accrual method corporations can accrue contributions approved by their board of directors prior to the end of the accrual year and paid within 3½ months of that year-end (2½ months for corporations having a June 30 year-end).
2. Amount of the contribution deduction
   a. General rule: A deduction is allowed for the amount of money and the FMV of other property donated.
   b. Exceptions for ordinary income property:
      1. If donated property would result in ordinary income or short-term capital gain if sold, the deduction is limited to the property's FMV minus this potential ordinary income or short-term capital gain. Thus, for gain property the deduction equals the property's cost or adjusted basis.
      2. Special rule: For donations of (1) inventory used for the care of the ill, needy, or infants, or (2) scientific research property or computer technology and equipment to certain educational institutions, a corporate donor may deduct the property's basis plus one-half of the excess of the property's FMV over its adjusted basis. The deduction may not exceed twice the property's adjusted basis.
   c. Exceptions for capital gain property: If the corporation donates tangible personal property to a charitable organization for a use unrelated to its tax-exempt purpose, or the corporation donates appreciated property to a private nonoperating foundation, the corporation's contribution is limited to the property's FMV minus the long-term capital gain that would result if the corporation sold the property.
3. Limitation on contribution deduction
   a. The contribution deduction is limited to 10% of the corporation's taxable income computed without regard to the charitable contribution deduction, any NOL or capital loss carryback, the dividends-received deduction, and the U.S production activities deduction.
   b. Excess contributions carry forward for a five-year period.

[21] Sec. 170(b)(2).

[22] Sec. 170(d)(2).

SPECIAL DEDUCTIONS

C corporations are allowed three special deductions: the U.S. production activities deduction, the dividends-received deduction, and the NOL deduction.

ADDITIONAL COMMENT

While discussed in this text under special deductions, the U.S. production activities deduction actually appears before Line 28 on Form 1120. This deduction also is referred to as the domestic production activities deduction or the manufacturing deduction.

U.S. Production Activities Deduction. Section 199 allows a **U.S. production activities deduction** equal to 9% times the lesser of (1) qualified production activities income for the year or (2) taxable income before the U.S. production activities deduction. The deduction, however, cannot exceed 50% of the corporation's W-2 wages allocable to qualifying U.S. production activities for the year.

Qualified production activities income is the taxpayer's domestic production gross receipts less the following amounts:

- Cost of goods sold allocable to these receipts;
- Other deductions, expenses, and losses directly allocable to these receipts; and
- A ratable portion of other deductions, expenses, and losses not directly allocable to these receipts or to other classes of income.

BOOK-TO-TAX ACCOUNTING COMPARISON

The U.S. production activities deduction is not expensed for financial accounting purposes. Thus, it creates a permanent difference that affects the corporation's effective tax rate but not its deferred taxes.

Domestic production gross receipts include receipts from the following taxpayer activities:

- The lease, rental, license, sale, exchange, or other disposition of (1) qualified production property (tangible property, computer software, and sound recordings) manufactured, produced, grown, or extracted in whole or significant part within the United States; (2) qualified film production; or (3) electricity, natural gas, or potable water produced within the United States
- Construction performed in the United States
- Engineering or architectural services performed in the United States for construction projects in the United States

ADDITIONAL COMMENT

In addition to providing a benefit, the U.S. production activities deduction will increase a corporation's compliance costs because of the time necessary to determine what income and deductions pertain to U.S. production activities.

Domestic production gross receipts, however, do not include receipts from the sale of food and beverages the taxpayer prepares at a retail establishment and do not apply to the transmission of electricity, natural gas, or potable water.

The U.S. production activities deduction has the effect of reducing a corporation's marginal tax rate on qualifying taxable income. For example, a 9% deduction for a corporation in the 35% tax bracket decreases the corporation's marginal tax rate by about 3% (0.09 × 35% = 3.15%).

EXAMPLE C:3-12 ▶ Gamma Corporation earns domestic production gross receipts of $1 million and incurs allocable expenses of $400,000. Thus, its qualified production activities income is $600,000. In addition, Gamma has $200,000 of income from other sources, resulting in taxable income of $800,000 before the U.S. production activities deduction. Its U.S. production activities deduction, therefore, is $54,000 ($600,000 × 0.09), and its taxable income is $746,000 ($800,000 − $54,000). ◀

EXAMPLE C:3-13 ▶ Assume the same facts as in Example C:3-12 except Gamma has $100,000 of losses from other sources rather than $200,000 of other income, resulting in taxable income of $500,000 before the U.S. production activities deduction. In this case, its U.S. production activities deduction is $45,000 ($500,000 × 0.09), and its taxable income is $455,000 ($500,000 − $45,000). ◀

Dividends-Received Deduction. A corporation must include in its gross income any dividends received on stock it owns in another corporation. As described in Chapter C:2, the taxation of dividend payments to a shareholder generally results in double taxation. When a distributing corporation pays a dividend to a corporate shareholder and the recipient corporation subsequently distributes these earnings to its shareholders, potential triple taxation of the earnings can result.

EXAMPLE C:3-14 ▶ Adobe Corporation owns stock in Bell Corporation. Bell reports taxable income of $100,000 and pays federal income taxes on its income. Bell distributes its after-tax income to its shareholders. The dividend Adobe receives from Bell must be included in its gross income and, to the extent it reports a profit for the year, Adobe will pay taxes on the dividend. Adobe distributes its remaining after-tax income to its shareholders. The shareholders must include Adobe's dividends in their gross income and pay federal income taxes on the distribution. Thus, Bell's income in this example potentially is taxed three times. ◀

BOOK-TO-TAX ACCOUNTING COMPARISON

A corporation includes dividends in its financial accounting income but does not subtract a dividends-received deduction in determining its book net income. Thus, the dividends-received deduction creates a permanent difference that affects the corporation's effective tax rate but not its deferred taxes.

To partially mitigate the effects of multiple taxation, corporations are allowed a **dividends-received deduction** for dividends received from other domestic corporations and from certain foreign corporations.

General Rule for Dividends-Received Deduction. Corporations that own less than 20% of the distributing corporation's stock may deduct 70% of the dividends received. If the shareholder corporation owns 20% or more of the distributing corporation's stock (both voting power and value) but less than 80% of such stock, it may deduct 80% of the dividends received.[23]

EXAMPLE C:3-15 ▶ Hale Corporation reports the following results in the current year:

Gross income from operations	$300,000
Dividends from 15%-owned domestic corporation	100,000
Operating expenses	280,000

Gross income from operations and expenses both pertain to qualified production activities, so Hale's qualified production activities income is $20,000 ($300,000 − $280,000). Hale's dividends-received deduction is $70,000 (0.70 × $100,000). Thus, Hale's taxable income is computed as follows:

Gross income	$400,000
Minus: Operating expenses	(280,000)
Taxable income before special deductions	$120,000
Minus: Dividends-received deduction	(70,000)
Taxable income before the U.S. production activities deduction	$ 50,000
Minus: U.S. production activities deduction ($20,000 × 0.09)	(1,800)
Taxable income	$ 48,200

◀

Limitation on Dividends-Received Deduction. In the case of dividends received from corporations that are less than 20% owned, the deduction is limited to the lesser of 70% of dividends received or 70% of taxable income computed without regard to any NOL deduction, any capital loss carryback, the dividends-received deduction itself, or the U.S. production activities deduction.[24] In the case of dividends received from a 20% or more owned corporation, the dividends-received deduction is limited to the lesser of 80% of dividends received or 80% of taxable income computed without regard to the same deductions.

EXAMPLE C:3-16 ▶ Assume the same facts as in Example C:3-15 except Hale Corporation's operating expenses for the year are $310,000 and that qualified production activities income is zero (or negative). Thus, the corporation cannot claim the U.S. production activities deduction. Hale's taxable income before the dividends-received deduction is $90,000 ($300,000 + $100,000 − $310,000). The dividends-received deduction is limited to the lesser of 70% of dividends received ($70,000 = $100,000 × 0.70) or 70% of taxable income before the dividends-received deduction ($63,000 = $90,000 × 0.70). Thus, the dividends-received deduction is $63,000. Hale's taxable income is $27,000 ($90,000 − $63,000). ◀

A corporation that receives dividends eligible for both the 80% dividends-received deduction and the 70% dividends-received deduction must compute the 80% dividends-received deduction first and then reduce taxable income by the aggregate amount of dividends eligible for the 80% deduction before computing the 70% deduction.

[23] Secs. 243(a) and (c).

[24] Sec. 246(b).

EXAMPLE C:3-17 ▶ Assume the same facts as in Example C:3-16 except Hale Corporation receives $75,000 of the dividends from a 25%-owned corporation and the remaining $25,000 from a 15%-owned corporation. The tentative dividends-received deduction from the 25%-owned corporation is $60,000 ($75,000 × 0.80), which is less than the $72,000 ($90,000 × 0.80) limitation. Thus, Hale can deduct the entire $60,000. The tentative dividends-received deduction from the 15%-owned corporation is $17,500 ($25,000 × 0.70). The limitation, however, is $10,500 [($90,000 – $75,000) × 0.70]. Note that, in computing this limitation, Hale reduces its taxable income by the entire $75,000 dividend received from the 25%-owned corporation. Thus, Hale can deduct only $10,500 of the $17,500 amount. Hale's taxable income is $19,500 ($90,000 – $60,000 – $10,500). ◀

Exception to the Limitation. The taxable income limitation on the dividends-received deduction does not apply if the tentative dividends-received deduction creates or increases an NOL for the year.

EXAMPLE C:3-18 ▶ Assume the same facts as in Example C:3-16 except Hale Corporation's operating expenses for the year are $331,000. Hale's taxable income before the dividends-received deduction is $69,000 ($300,000 + $100,000 – $331,000). The tentative dividends-received deduction is $70,000 ($100,000 × 0.70). Hale's dividends-received deduction is not restricted by the limitation of 70% of taxable income before the dividends-received deduction because, after taking into account the tentative $70,000 dividends-received deduction, the corporation has a $1,000 ($69,000 – $70,000) NOL for the year. If Hale's operating expenses were $410,000 instead of $331,000, it would have a $10,000 NOL before the dividends-received deduction ($300,000 + $100,000 – $410,000). Again, the dividends-received deduction is not restricted by the limitation because it increases the NOL. In this case, the corporation has an $80,000 [$(10,000) – $70,000] NOL for the year. ◀

ADDITIONAL COMMENT

When the dividends-received deduction creates (or increases) an NOL, the corporation gets the full benefit of the deduction because it can carry back or carry forward the NOL.

TAX STRATEGY TIP

A corporation can avoid the dividends-received deduction limitation either by (1) increasing its taxable income before the dividends-received deduction so the limitation exceeds the tentative dividends-received deduction or (2) decreasing its taxable income before the dividends-received deduction so the tentative dividends-received deduction creates an NOL.

The following table compares the results of Examples C:3-15, C:3-16, and C:3-18:

	Example C:3-15	*Example C:3-16*	*Example C:3-18*	
Gross income	$400,000	$400,000	$400,000	$400,000
Minus: Operating expenses	(280,000)	(310,000)	(331,000)	(410,000)
Taxable income (NOL) before special deductions	$120,000	$ 90,000	$ 69,000	$(10,000)
Minus: Dividends-received deduction	(70,000)	(63,000)	(70,000)	(70,000)
U.S. production activities deduction	(1,800)	–0–	–0–	–0–
Taxable income (NOL)	$ 48,200	$ 27,000	$ (1,000)	$(80,000)

Of these three examples, the only case where the dividends-received deduction does not equal the full 70% of the $100,000 dividend is Example C:3-16. In that case, the deduction is limited to $63,000 because taxable income before special deductions is less than the $100,000 dividend *and* because the full $70,000 deduction would not create an NOL. The special exception to the dividends-received deduction can create interesting situations. For example, the additional $21,000 of deductions incurred in Example C:3-18 (as compared to Example C:3-16) resulted in a $28,000 reduction in taxable income. Corporate taxpayers should be aware of these rules and consider deferring income or recognizing expenses to ensure being able to deduct the full 70% or 80% dividends-received deduction. If the taxable income limitation applies, the corporation loses the unused dividends-received deduction.

ADDITIONAL COMMENT

If the affiliated group files a consolidated tax return, the recipient of the dividend does not claim the 100% dividends received deduction because the intercompany dividend gets eliminated in the consolidation. See Chapter C:8 for a more detailed definition of affiliated corporations and discussion of consolidated tax returns.

Members of an Affiliated Group. Members of an affiliated group of corporations can claim a 100% dividends-received deduction with respect to dividends received from other group members.[25] A group of corporations is affiliated if a parent corporation owns at least 80% of the stock (both voting power and value) of at least one subsidiary corporation, and at least 80% of the stock (both voting power and value) of each other corporation is owned by other group members. The 100% dividends-received deduction is not subject to a taxable income limitation and is taken before the 80% or 70% dividends-received deduction.[26]

---

[25] Sec. 243(a)(3).

[26] Secs. 243(b)(5) and 1504.

EXAMPLE C:3-19 ▶ Hardy Corporation reports the following results for the current year:

Gross income from operations	$520,000
Dividend received from an 80%-owned affiliated corporation	100,000
Dividend received from a 20%-owned corporation	250,000
Operating expenses	550,000

Hardy does not file a consolidated tax return with the 80%-owned affiliate. Because Hardy's qualified production activities income is negative, it cannot claim the U.S. production activities deduction. Hardy's taxable income before any dividends-received deduction is $320,000 ($520,000 + $100,000 + $250,000 − $550,000). Hardy can deduct the entire dividend received from the 80%-owned affiliate without limitation. The tentative dividends-received deduction from the 20%-owned corporation is $200,000 ($250,000 × 0.80). The limitation, however, is $176,000 [($320,000 − $100,000) × 0.80]. Note that, in computing this limitation, Hardy first reduces its taxable income by the $100,000 dividend received from the 80%-owned affiliate. Thus, Hardy can deduct only $176,000 of the $200,000 amount. Hardy's taxable income is $44,000 ($320,000 − $100,000 − $176,000). ◀

Dividends Received from Foreign Corporations. The dividends-received deduction applies primarily to dividends received from domestic corporations. The dividends-received deduction does not apply to dividends received from a foreign corporation because the U.S. Government does not tax its income. Thus, that income is not subject to the multiple taxation illustrated above.[27]

ADDITIONAL COMMENT

Stock purchased on which a dividend has been declared has an increased value. This value will drop when the corporation pays the dividend. If the dividend is eligible for a dividends-received deduction and the drop in value also creates a capital loss, corporate shareholders could use this event as a tax planning device. To avoid this result, no dividends-received deduction is available for stock held 45 days or less.

Stock Held 45 Days or Less. A corporation may not claim a dividends-received deduction if it holds the dividend paying stock for less than 46 days during the 91-day period that begins 45 days before the stock becomes ex-dividend with respect to the dividend.[28] This rule prevents a corporation from claiming a dividends-received deduction if it purchases stock shortly before an ex-dividend date and sells the stock shortly thereafter. (The ex-dividend date is the first day on which a purchaser of stock is not entitled to a previously declared dividend.) Absent this rule, such a purchase and sale would allow the corporation to receive dividends at a low tax rate—a maximum of a 10.5% [(100% − 70%) × 0.35] effective tax rate—and to recognize a capital loss on the sale of stock that could offset capital gains taxed at a 35% corporate tax rate.

EXAMPLE C:3-20 ▶ Theta Corporation purchases 100 shares of Maine Corporation's stock for $100,000 one day before Maine's ex-dividend date. Theta receives a $5,000 dividend on the stock and then sells the stock for $95,000 shortly after the dividend payment date. Because the stock is worth $100,000 immediately before the $5,000 dividend payment, its value drops to $95,000 ($100,000 − $5,000) immediately after the dividend. The sale results in a $5,000 ($100,000 − $95,000) capital loss that may offset a $5,000 capital gain. Assuming a 35% corporate tax rate, the following table summarizes the profit (loss) to Theta with and without the 45-day rule.

	If Deduction Is Allowed	*If Deduction Is Not Allowed*
Dividends	$5,000	$5,000
Minus: 35% tax on dividend	(525)[a]	(1,750)
Dividend (after taxes)	$4,475	$3,250
Capital loss	$5,000	$5,000
Minus: 35% tax savings on loss	(1,750)	(1,750)
Net loss on stock	$3,250	$3,250
Dividend (after taxes)	$4,475	$3,250
Minus: Net loss on stock[b]	(3,250)	(3,250)
Net profit (loss)	$1,225	$ -0-

[a] [$5,000 − (0.70 × $5,000)] × 0.35 = $525
[b] This example assumes the corporation has capital gains against which to deduct this capital loss.

[27] Sec. 245. A limited dividends-received deduction is allowed on dividends received from a foreign corporation that earns income by conducting a trade or business in the United States and, therefore, is subject to U.S. taxes.

[28] Sec. 246(c)(1).

ADDITIONAL COMMENT

Borrowing money with deductible interest to purchase a tax-advantaged asset, such as stock eligible for the dividends-received deduction, is an example of "tax arbitrage." Many provisions in the IRC, such as the limits on debt-financial stock, are aimed at curtailing tax arbitrage transactions.

The profit is not available if Theta sells the stock shortly after receiving the dividend because Theta must hold the Maine stock for at least 46 days to obtain the dividends-received deduction. ◀

Debt-Financed Stock. The dividends-received deduction is not allowed to the extent the corporation borrows money to acquire the dividend paying stock.[29] This rule prevents a corporation from deducting interest paid on money borrowed to purchase the stock, while paying little or no tax on the dividends received on the stock.

EXAMPLE C:3-21 ▶ Palmer Corporation, whose marginal tax rate is 35%, borrows $100,000 at a 10% interest rate to purchase 30% of Sun Corporation's stock. The Sun stock pays an $8,000 annual dividend. If a dividends-received deduction were allowed for this investment, Palmer would have a net profit of $940 annually on owning the Sun stock even though the dividend received is less than the interest paid. The following table summarizes the profit (loss) to Palmer with and without the debt-financing rule.

REAL-WORLD EXAMPLE

Although sound in theory, the debt-financed stock limitation may be difficult to apply in practice. This difficulty became particularly apparent in a district court case, *OBH, Inc. v. U.S.*, 96 AFTR 2d, 2005-6801, 2005-2 USTC ¶50,627 (DC NB, 2005), where the IRS failed to establish that a corporation's debt proceeds were directly traceable to the acquisition of dividend paying stock.

	If Deduction Is Allowed	*If Deduction Is Not Allowed*
Dividends	$ 8,000	$ 8,000
Minus: 35% tax on dividend	(560)[a]	(2,800)
Dividend (after taxes)	$ 7,440	$ 5,200
Interest paid	$10,000	$10,000
Minus: 35% tax savings on deduction	(3,500)	(3,500)
Net cost of borrowing	$ 6,500	$ 6,500
Dividend (after taxes)	$ 7,440	$ 5,200
Minus: Net cost of borrowing	(6,500)	(6,500)
Net profit (loss)	$ 940	$ (1,300)

[a] [$8,000 − ($8,000 × 0.80)] × 0.35 = $560

This example illustrates how the rule disallowing the dividends-received deduction on debt-financed stock prevents corporations from making an after-tax profit by borrowing funds to purchase stocks paying dividends that are less than the cost of the borrowing. ◀

Net Operating Losses (NOLs). If a corporation's deductions exceed its gross income for the year, the corporation has a **net operating loss** (NOL). The NOL is the amount by which the corporation's deductions (including any dividends-received deduction) exceed its gross income.[30] In computing an NOL for a given year, no deduction is permitted for a carryover or carryback of an NOL from a preceding or succeeding year. However, unlike an individual's NOL, no other adjustments are required to compute a corporation's NOL. If the corporation has an NOL, it also would not be allowed a U.S. production activities deduction because it has no positive taxable income.

A corporation's NOL carries back two years and carries over 20 years. It carries to the earliest of the two preceding years first and offsets taxable income reported in that year. If the loss cannot be used in that year, it carries to the immediately preceding year, and then to the next 20 years in chronological order. The corporation may elect to forgo the carryback period entirely and instead carry over the entire loss to the next 20 years.[31]

EXAMPLE C:3-22 ▶ In 2017, Gray Corporation, a calendar year taxpayer, has gross income of $150,000 (including $100,000 from operations and $50,000 in dividends from a 30%-owned domestic corporation) and $180,000 of expenses. Gray has a $70,000 [$150,000 − $180,000 − (0.80 × $50,000)] NOL. The NOL carries back to 2015 unless Gray elects to forego the carryback period. If Gray had

[29] Sec. 246A.
[30] Sec. 172(c).
[31] Various other carryback and carryover periods have applied in past years.

$20,000 of taxable income in 2015, $20,000 of Gray's 2017 NOL offsets that income. Gray receives a refund of all taxes paid in 2015. Gray carries the remaining $50,000 of the 2017 NOL to 2016. Any of the NOL not used in 2016 carries over to 2018. ◀

BOOK-TO-TAX ACCOUNTING COMPARISON

An NOL carryover for tax purposes creates a deferred tax asset, possibly subject to a valuation allowance.

A corporation might elect not to carry an NOL back because its income was taxed at a low marginal tax rate in the carryback period and the corporation anticipates income being taxed at a higher marginal tax rate in later years or because it used tax credit carryovers in the earlier year that were about to expire. The corporation must make this election for the entire carryback by the due date (including extensions) for filing the return for the year in which the corporation incurred the NOL. The corporation makes the election by checking a box on Form 1120 when it files the return. Once made for a tax year, the election is irrevocable.[32] However, if the corporation incurs an NOL in another year, the decision as to whether that NOL should be carried back is a separate decision. In other words, each year's NOL is treated separately and is subject to a separate election.

To obtain a refund due to carrying an NOL back to a preceding year, a corporation files Form 1139 (Corporation Application for a Tentative Refund) if one year or less has elapsed since the year in which the NOL occurred. If a longer period has elapsed, the corporation files Form 1120X (Amended U.S. Corporation Income Tax Return).

ADDITIONAL COMMENT

The U.S. production activities deduction is last in the ordering of deductions because it is limited to taxable income after all other deductions. However, on the corporate tax return, it appears after the charitable contributions deduction but before the dividends-received and NOL deductions. Specifically, it appears on Form 1120, Line 25, before Line 28.

The Sequencing of the Deduction Calculations. The rules for charitable contributions, dividends-received, NOL, and U.S. production activities deductions require that these deductions be calculated in the following sequence:

1. All deductions other than the charitable contributions deduction, the dividends-received deduction, the NOL deduction, and the U.S. production activities deduction
2. The charitable contributions deduction
3. The dividends-received deduction
4. The NOL deduction
5. The U.S. production activities deduction

As stated previously, the charitable contributions deduction is limited to 10% of taxable income before the charitable contributions deduction, any NOL or capital loss carryback, the dividends-received deduction, or the U.S. production activities deduction, but *after* any NOL carryover deduction. Once the corporation determines its charitable contributions deduction, it adds back any NOL carryover deduction and subtracts the charitable contributions deduction before computing the dividends-received deduction. The corporation then subtracts the NOL deduction, if any, before determining its U.S. production activities deduction.

EXAMPLE C:3-23 ▶ East Corporation reports the following results for the current year:

Gross income from operations	$150,000
Dividends from 30%-owned domestic corporation	100,000
Operating expenses	100,000
Charitable contributions	35,000

These results include $50,000 of qualified production activities income in the current year ($150,000 gross income from operations – $100,000 operating expenses). East also has a $40,000 NOL carryover from the previous year. East's charitable contributions deduction is computed as follows:

Gross income from operations	$150,000
Plus: Dividends	100,000
Gross income	$250,000
Minus: Operating expenses	(100,000)
NOL carryover	(40,000)
Base for charitable contributions limitation (adjusted taxable income)	$110,000

East's charitable contributions deduction is limited to $11,000 ($110,000 × 0.10). The $11,000 limitation means that East has a $24,000 ($35,000 − $11,000) excess contribution that carries over for five years. East Corporation computes its taxable income as follows:

[32] Sec. 172(b)(3)(C).

ADDITIONAL COMMENT

If the NOL carryover to the current year is not fully used in the current year such that some of the NOL carries over to the next year, both the NOL carryover and charitable deduction carryover to the next year must be adjusted [IRC Sec. 170(d)(2)(B)]. These adjustments are beyond the scope of this text.

Gross income	$250,000
Minus: Operating expenses	(100,000)
Charitable contributions deduction	(11,000)
Taxable income before special deductions	$139,000
Minus: Dividends-received deduction ($100,000 × 0.80)	(80,000)
NOL carryover deduction	(40,000)
Taxable income before the U.S. production activities deduction	$ 19,000
Minus: U.S. production activities deduction ($19,000 × 0.09)	(1,710)
Taxable income	$ 17,290 ◀

Note that, if an NOL carries *back* from a later year, it is *not* taken into account in computing a corporation's charitable contributions limitation. In other words, the contribution deduction remains the same as in the year of the original return.

EXAMPLE C:3-24 ▶ Assume the same facts as in Example C:3-23, except the facts pertain to a prior year, and East carries back a $40,000 NOL to that year. East's base for calculation of the charitable contributions limitation was computed as follows when it filed the original prior year return:

ADDITIONAL COMMENT

These computations in the carryback year are done on an amended return or an application for refund.

Gross income from operations	$150,000
Plus: Dividends	100,000
Gross income	$250,000
Minus: Operating expenses	(100,000)
Adjusted taxable income	$150,000

East's charitable contributions deduction was limited to $15,000 ($150,000 × 0.10). The $15,000 limitation means that East had a $20,000 ($35,000 − $15,000) contribution carryover from the prior year. East Corporation computes its taxable income after the NOL carryback as follows:

Gross income ($150,000 + $100,000)	$250,000
Minus: Operating expenses	(100,000)
Charitable contributions deduction	(15,000)
Taxable income before special deductions	$135,000
Minus: Dividends-received deduction ($100,000 × 0.80)	(80,000)
NOL carryback deduction	(40,000)
Taxable income before the U.S. production activities deduction	$ 15,000
Minus: U.S. production activities deduction ($15,000 × 0.09)	(1,350)
Taxable income as recomputed	$ 13,650

Thus, East's prior year charitable contributions deduction remains the same as originally claimed. ◀

Question: Why does a corporation's NOL or capital loss carryback not affect its charitable contributions deduction, but yet the corporation must take into account an NOL or capital loss carryover when calculating its charitable contribution limitation?

Solution: A carryback affects a tax return already filed in a prior year. If a carryback had to be taken into account when calculating the charitable contribution deduction limitation in the prior year, it might change the amount of the allowable charitable contribution. This change in turn might affect other items such as the carryback year's dividends-received deduction and some later years' deductions as well. For example, assume Alpha Corporation has a $10,000 NOL in 2017 that it carries back to 2015. If the NOL were permitted to reduce Alpha's allowable charitable contribution for 2015 by $1,000, Alpha's dividends-received deduction for 2015 and its charitable contribution deduction for 2016 as well might change.

To avoid these complications, the law states that carrybacks are not taken into account in calculating the charitable contribution deduction limitation. Also, in the prior year, management made its charitable contribution decisions without knowledge of future NOLs. Altering the result of those prior decisions with future events might be unfair.

EXCEPTIONS FOR CLOSELY HELD CORPORATIONS

Congress has placed limits on certain transactions to prevent abuse in situations where a corporation is closely held. Some of these restrictions are explained below.

Transactions Between a Corporation and Its Shareholders. Special rules apply to transactions between a corporation and a controlling shareholder. Section 1239 may convert a capital gain realized on the sale of depreciable property between a corporation and a controlling shareholder into ordinary income. Section 267(a)(1) denies a deduction for losses realized on property sales between a corporation and a controlling shareholder. Section 267(a)(2) defers a deduction for accrued expenses and interest on certain transactions involving a corporation and a controlling shareholder.

In all three of the preceding situations, a controlling shareholder is one who owns more than 50% (in value) of the corporation's stock.[33] In determining whether a shareholder owns more than 50% of a corporation's stock, certain constructive stock ownership rules apply.[34] Under these rules, a shareholder is considered to own not only his or her own stock, but stock owned by family members (e.g., brothers, sisters, spouse, ancestors, and lineal descendants) and entities in which the shareholder has an ownership or beneficial interest (e.g., corporations, partnerships, trusts, and estates).

Gains on Sale or Exchange Transactions. If a controlling shareholder sells depreciable property to a controlled corporation (or vice versa) and the property is depreciable in the purchaser's hands, any gain on the sale is treated as ordinary income under Sec. 1239(a).

EXAMPLE C:3-25 ▶ Ann owns all of Cape Corporation's stock. Ann sells a building to Cape and recognizes a $25,000 gain, which usually would be Sec. 1231 gain or unrecaptured Sec. 1250 gain taxed at the applicable capital gains rates. However, because Ann owns more than 50% of the Cape stock and the building is a depreciable property in Cape's hands, Sec. 1239 requires that Ann recognize the entire $25,000 gain as ordinary income. ◀

BOOK-TO-TAX ACCOUNTING COMPARISON

The denial of deductions for losses involving related party transactions is unique to the tax area. Financial accounting rules contain no such disallowance provision.

Losses on Sale or Exchange Transactions. Section 267(a)(1) denies a deduction for losses realized on a sale of property by a corporation to a controlling shareholder or on a sale of property by the controlling shareholder to the corporation. If the purchaser later sells the property to another party at a gain, that seller recognizes gain only to the extent it exceeds the previously disallowed loss.[35] Should the purchaser instead sell the property at a loss, the previously disallowed loss is never recognized.

EXAMPLE C:3-26 ▶ Quattros Corporation sells an automobile to Juan, its sole shareholder, for $6,500. The corporation's adjusted basis for the automobile is $8,000. Quattros realizes a $1,500 ($6,500 − $8,000) loss on the sale. Section 267(a)(1), however, disallows the loss to the corporation. If Juan later sells the auto for $8,500, he realizes a $2,000 ($8,500 − $6,500) gain. He recognizes only $500 of that gain, the amount by which his $2,000 gain exceeds the $1,500 loss previously disallowed to Quattros. If Juan instead sells the auto for $7,500, he realizes a $1,000 ($7,500 − $6,500) gain but recognizes no gain or loss. The previously disallowed loss reduces the gain to zero but may not create a loss. Finally, if Juan instead sells the auto for $4,000, he realizes and may be able to recognize a $2,500 ($4,000 − $6,500) loss. However, the $1,500 loss previously disallowed to Quattros is permanently lost. ◀

KEY POINT

Section 267(a)(2) is primarily aimed at the situation involving an accrual method corporation that accrues compensation to a cash method shareholder-employee. This provision forces a matching of the income and expense recognition by deferring the deduction to the year the shareholder recognizes the income.

Corporation and Controlling Shareholder Using Different Accounting Methods. Section 267(a)(2) defers a deduction for accrued expenses or interest owed by a corporation to a controlling shareholder or by a controlling shareholder to a corporation when the two parties use different accounting methods and the payee thereby includes the amount in gross income later than when the payer accrues the deduction. Under this rule, accrued expenses or interest owed by a corporation to a controlling shareholder may not be deducted until the shareholder includes the payment in gross income.

---

33 Sec. 267(b)(2).

34 Sec. 267(e)(3).

35 Sec. 267(d).

EXAMPLE C:3-27 ▶ Hill Corporation uses the accrual method of accounting. Hill's sole shareholder, Ruth, uses the cash method of accounting. Both taxpayers use the calendar year as their tax year. The corporation accrues a $25,000 interest payment to Ruth on December 20 of the current year. Hill makes the payment on March 20 of next year. Hill, however, cannot deduct the interest in the current year but must wait until Ruth reports the income next year. Thus, the expense and income are matched. ◀

Loss Limitation Rules

At-Risk Rules. If five or fewer shareholders own more than 50% (in value) of a C corporation's outstanding stock at any time during the last half of the corporation's tax year, the corporation is subject to the at-risk rules.[36] In such case, the corporation can deduct losses pertaining to an activity only to the extent the corporation is at risk for that activity at year-end. Any losses not deductible because of the at-risk rules must be carried over and deducted in a succeeding year when the corporation's risk with respect to the activity increases. (See Chapter C:9 for additional discussion of the at-risk rules.)

Passive Activity Limitation Rules. Personal service corporations (PSCs) and **closely held C corporations** (those subject to the at-risk rules described above) also may be subject to the **passive activity limitations.**[37] If a PSC does not meet the material participation requirements, its net **passive losses** and credits must be carried over to a year when it has **passive income.** In the case of closely held C corporations that do not meet material participation requirements, passive losses and credits are allowed to offset the corporation's net active income but not its portfolio income (i.e., interest, dividends, annuities, royalties, and capital gains on the sale of investment property).[38]

COMPUTING A CORPORATION'S INCOME TAX LIABILITY

OBJECTIVE 3

Compute a corporation's regular income tax liability

Once a corporation determines its taxable income, it then must compute its tax liability for the year. Table C:3-2 outlines the steps for computing a corporation's regular (income) tax liability. This section explains the steps involved in arriving at a corporation's income tax liability in detail.

▼ **TABLE C:3-2**
Computation of the Corporate Regular (Income) Tax Liability

Taxable income	
Times:	Income tax rates
Regular tax liability	
Minus:	Foreign tax credit (Sec. 27)
Regular tax	
Minus:	General business credit (Sec. 38)
	Minimum tax credit (Sec. 53)
	Other allowed credits
Plus:	Recapture of previously claimed tax credits
Income (regular) tax liability	

[36] Sec. 465(a).
[37] Secs. 469(a)(2)(B) and (C).
[38] Sec. 469(e)(2).

GENERAL RULES

REAL-WORLD EXAMPLE

In 2015, the IRS collected $390 billion from corporations, which was 11.8% of the $3.3 trillion collected by the IRS. This percentage is up from 11.5% in 2014.

All C corporations (other than members of controlled groups of corporations and personal service corporations) use the same tax rate schedule to compute their **regular tax** liability. The following table shows these rates, which also are reproduced on the inside back cover of this textbook.

Taxable Income Over	*But Not Over*	*The Tax Is*	*Of the Amount Over*
$ -0-	$ 50,000	15%	$ -0-
50,000	75,000	$ 7,500 + 25%	50,000
75,000	100,000	13,750 + 34%	75,000
100,000	335,000	22,250 + 39%	100,000
335,000	10,000,000	113,900 + 34%	335,000
10,000,000	15,000,000	3,400,000 + 35%	10,000,000
15,000,000	18,333,333	5,150,000 + 38%	15,000,000
18,333,333	—	6,416,667 + 35%	18,333,333

EXAMPLE C:3-28 ▶ Copper Corporation reports taxable income of $100,000. Copper's regular tax liability is computed as follows:

Tax on first $50,000:	0.15 × $50,000 =	$7,500
Tax on second $25,000:	0.25 × 25,000 =	6,250
Tax on remaining $25,000:	0.34 × 25,000 =	8,500
Regular tax liability		$22,250

This tax liability also can be determined from the above tax rate schedule. ◀

If taxable income exceeds $100,000, a 5% surcharge applies to the corporation's taxable income exceeding $100,000. The surcharge phases out the lower graduated tax rates that apply to the first $75,000 of taxable income for corporations earning between $100,000 and $335,000 of taxable income. The maximum surcharge is $11,750 [($335,000 − $100,000) × 0.05]. The above tax rate schedule incorporates the 5% surcharge by imposing a 39% (34% + 5%) rate on taxable income from $100,000 to $335,000.

EXAMPLE C:3-29 ▶ Delta Corporation reports taxable income of $200,000. Delta's regular tax liability is computed as follows:

Tax on first $50,000:	0.15 × $ 50,000 =	$ 7,500
Tax on next $25,000:	0.25 × 25,000 =	6,250
Tax on remaining $125,000:	0.34 × 125,000 =	42,500
Surcharge (income over $100,000):	0.05 × 100,000 =	5,000
Regular tax liability		$61,250

Alternatively, from the above tax rate schedule, the tax is $22,250 + [0.39 × ($200,000 − $100,000)] = $61,250. ◀

If taxable income is at least $335,000 but less than $10 million, the corporation pays a flat 34% tax rate on all of its taxable income. A corporation whose income is at least $10 million but less than $15 million pays $3.4 million plus 35% of the income above $10 million.

EXAMPLE C:3-30 ▶ Elgin Corporation reports taxable income of $350,000. Elgin's regular tax liability is $119,000 (0.34 × $350,000). If Elgin's taxable income is instead $12 million, its tax liability is $4.1 million [$3,400,000 + (0.35 × $2,000,000)]. ◀

If a corporation's taxable income exceeds $15 million, a 3% surcharge applies to the corporation's taxable income exceeding $15 million (but not exceeding $18,333,333). The surcharge phases out the one percentage point lower rate (34% vs. 35%) that applies to the first $10 million of taxable income. The maximum surcharge is $100,000 [($18,333,333 − $15,000,000) × 0.03]. The above tax rate schedule incorporates the 3%

surcharge by imposing a 38% (35% + 3%) rate on taxable income from $15 million to $18,333,333. A corporation whose taxable income exceeds $18,333,333 pays a flat 35% tax rate on all its taxable income.

STOP & THINK

Question: Planner Corporation has an opportunity to realize $50,000 of additional income in either the current year or next year. Planner has some discretion as to the timing of this additional income. Not counting the additional income, Planner's current year taxable income is $200,000, and it expects next year's taxable income to be $500,000. In what year should Planner recognize the additional $50,000?

Solution: Even though Planner's current year taxable income is lower than next year's expected taxable income, Planner will have a lower marginal tax rate next year. The current year's marginal tax rate is 39% because Planner's taxable income is in the 5% surtax range (or 39% "bubble"). Next year's taxable income is beyond the 39% bubble and is in the flat 34% range. Thus, Planner can save $2,500 (0.05 × $50,000) in taxes by deferring the $50,000 until next year.

PERSONAL SERVICE CORPORATIONS

Personal service corporations are denied the benefit of the graduated corporate tax rates. Thus, all the income of personal service corporations is taxed at a flat 35% rate.

Section 448(d) defines a personal service corporation as a corporation that meets the following two tests:

- Substantially all its activities involve the performance of services in the fields of health, law, engineering, architecture, accounting, actuarial science, performing arts, and consulting.
- Substantially all its stock (by value) is held directly or indirectly by employees performing the services or retired employees who performed the services in the past, their estates, or persons who hold stock in the corporation by reason of the death of an employee or retired employee within the past two years.

TAX STRATEGY TIP

If the employee-owners are in a personal tax bracket below 35%, they may want to withdraw earnings from the corporation in the form of deductible salaries. See Tax Planning Considerations later in this chapter for a detailed discussion of this strategy. The owners also may want to consider operating the business as an S corporation or limited liability company (LLC). See Chapters C:9–C:11.

CONTROLLED GROUPS OF CORPORATIONS

OBJECTIVE 4

Recognize what a controlled group is and determine the tax consequences of being a controlled group

Special tax rules apply to corporations under common control to prevent them from avoiding taxes that otherwise would be due. The rules apply to corporations that meet the definition of a controlled group. This section explains why special rules apply to controlled groups, how the IRC defines controlled groups, and what special rules apply to controlled groups.

WHY SPECIAL RULES ARE NEEDED

Special controlled group rules prevent shareholders from using multiple corporations to avoid having corporate income taxed at a 35% rate. If these rules were not in effect, the owners of a corporation could allocate the corporation's income among two or more corporations and take advantage of the lower 15%, 25%, and 34% rates on the first $10 million of corporate income for each corporation.

The following example demonstrates how a group of shareholders could obtain a significant tax advantage by dividing a business enterprise among several corporate entities. Each corporation then could take advantage of the graduated corporate tax rates. To prevent a group of shareholders from using multiple corporations to gain such tax advantages, Congress enacted laws that limit the tax benefits of multiple corporations.[39]

[39] Secs. 1561 and 1563.

EXAMPLE C:3-31 ▶ Axle Corporation reports taxable income of $450,000. Axle's regular tax liability on that income is $153,000 (0.34 × $450,000). If Axle could divide its taxable income equally among six corporations ($75,000 apiece), each corporation's federal income tax liability would be $13,750 [(0.15 × $50,000) + (0.25 × $25,000)], or an $82,500 total regular tax liability for all the corporations. Thus, Axle could save $70,500 ($153,000 − $82,500) in federal income taxes. ◀

The law governing controlled corporations requires special treatment for two or more corporations controlled by the same shareholder or group of shareholders. The most important restrictions on a controlled group of corporations are that the group must share the benefits of the progressive corporate tax rate schedule and pay a 5% surcharge on the group's taxable income exceeding $100,000, up to a maximum surcharge of $11,750, and also pay a 3% surcharge on the group's taxable income exceeding $15 million, up to a maximum surcharge of $100,000.

EXAMPLE C:3-32 ▶ White, Blue, Yellow, and Green Corporations belong to a controlled group. Each corporation reports $100,000 of taxable income (a total of $400,000). Only one $50,000 amount is taxed at 15% and only one $25,000 amount is taxed at 25%. Furthermore, the group is subject to the maximum $11,750 surcharge because its total taxable income exceeds $335,000. This surcharge is levied on the group member(s) that received the benefit of the 15% and 25% rates. Therefore, the group's total regular tax liability is $136,000 (0.34 × $400,000), as though one corporation earned the entire $400,000. Each corporation would be allocated $34,000 of this tax liability. ◀

WHAT IS A CONTROLLED GROUP?

A **controlled group** is comprised of two or more corporations owned directly or indirectly by the same shareholder or group of shareholders. Controlled groups fall into three categories: a parent-subsidiary controlled group, a brother-sister controlled group, and a combined controlled group. Each of these groups is subject to the limitations described above.

ADDITIONAL COMMENT

For purposes of the Sec. 179 expense dollar limitation, a more-than-50% threshold replaces the at-least-80% threshold in defining a parent-subsidiary controlled group.

Parent-Subsidiary Controlled Groups. In a **parent-subsidiary controlled group**, one corporation (the parent corporation) must directly own at least 80% of the voting power of all classes of voting stock, or 80% of the total value of all classes of stock, of a second corporation (the subsidiary corporation).[40] The group can contain more than one subsidiary corporation. If the parent corporation, the subsidiary corporation, or any other members of the controlled group in total own at least 80% of the voting power of all classes of voting stock, or 80% of the total value of all classes of stock, of another corporation, that other corporation also is included in the parent-subsidiary controlled group.

EXAMPLE C:3-33 ▶ Parent Corporation owns 80% of Axle Corporation's single class of stock and 40% of Wheel Corporation's single class of stock. Axle also owns 40% of Wheel's stock. (See Figure C:3-2.) Parent, Axle, and Wheel are members of the same parent-subsidiary controlled group because Parent directly owns 80% of Axle's stock and therefore is its parent corporation, and Wheel's stock is 80% owned by Parent (40%) and Axle (40%).

If Parent and Axle together owned only 70% of Wheel's stock and an unrelated shareholder owned the remaining 30%, Wheel would not be included in the parent-subsidiary group. The controlled group then would consist only of Parent and Axle. ◀

EXAMPLE C:3-34 ▶ Beta Corporation owns 70% of Spectrum Corporation's single class of stock and 60% of Red Corporation's single class of stock. Blue Corporation owns the remaining stock of Spectrum (30%) and Red (40%). No combination of these corporations forms a parent-subsidiary group because no corporation has direct stock ownership of at least 80% of any other corporation's stock. ◀

---

[40] Sec. 1563(a)(1). Section 1563(d)(1) requires that certain attribution rules apply to determine stock ownership for parent-subsidiary controlled groups. If any person has an option to acquire stock, such stock is considered owned by the person having the option. Section 1563(c) excludes certain types of stock from the controlled group definition of stock.

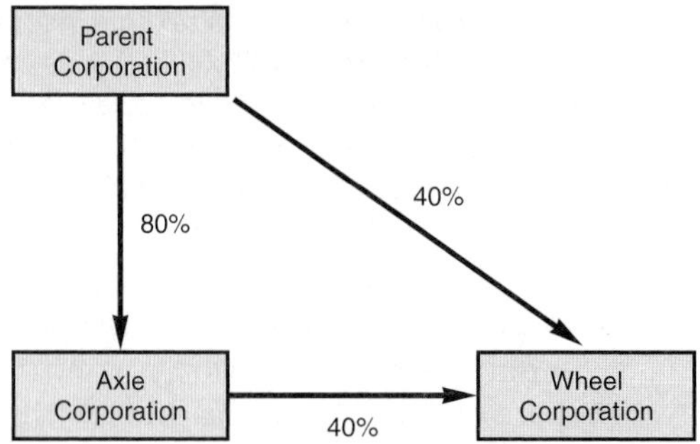

FIGURE C:3-2 ▶ PARENT-SUBSIDIARY CONTROLLED GROUP (EXAMPLE C:3-33)

Brother-Sister Controlled Groups. The IRC contains two definitions of a **brother-sister controlled group.** This textbook will refer to them as the 50%-80% definition and the 50%-only definition. Under the 50%-80% definition, a group of two or more corporations is a brother-sister controlled group if five or fewer individuals, trusts, or estates own stock that meets both of the following conditions:

- More than 50% of the voting power of all classes of stock (or more than 50% of the total value of the outstanding stock) of each corporation, taking into account only the stock ownership that is common with respect to each corporation.[41] A common ownership is the percentage of stock a shareholder owns that is common or identical in each of the corporations. For example, if a shareholder owns 30% of New Corporation and 70% of Old Corporation, his or her common ownership is 30%.
- At least 80% of the voting power of all classes of voting stock (or at least 80% of the total value of the outstanding stock) of each corporation.

Thus, under the 50%-80% definition, the five or fewer shareholders not only must have more than 50% common ownership in the corporations, they also must own at least 80% of the stock of each corporation in the brother-sister group. This definition is narrow because the shareholders must meet two tests.

The 50%-only definition, on the other hand, is broader than the 50%-80% definition in that the five or fewer shareholders must satisfy only the 50% common ownership test described above. Consequently, in situations where the 50%-only definition applies, more corporations may be pulled into the controlled group than under the 50%-80% definition. Table C:3-3 on page C:3-29 indicates which definition applies to specific situations.

EXAMPLE C:3-35 ▶ North and South Corporations have only one class of stock outstanding, owned by the following individuals:

	Stock Ownership Percentages		
Shareholder	*North Corp.*	*South Corp.*	*Common Ownership*
Walt	30%	70%	30%
Gail	70%	30%	30%
Total	100%	100%	60%

Five or fewer individuals (Walt and Gail) together own at least 80% (actually 100%) of each corporation's stock, and the same individuals own more than 50% (actually 60%) of the corporations' stock taking into account only their common ownership in each corporation. Because

[41] Sec. 1563(a)(2). Section 1563(d)(2) requires that certain attribution rules apply to determine stock ownership for brother-sister controlled groups. If any person has an option to acquire stock, such stock is considered to be owned by the person having the option. A proportionate amount of stock owned by a partnership, estate, or trust is attributed to partners having an interest of 5% or more in the capital or profits of the partnership or beneficiaries having a 5% or more actuarial interest in the estate or trust. A proportionate amount of stock owned by a corporation is attributed to shareholders owning 5% or more in value of the corporate stock. Family attribution rules also can cause an individual to be considered to own the stock of a spouse, child, grandchild, parent, or grandparent.

their ownership satisfies both tests, North and South are a brother-sister controlled group under the 50%-80% definition. (See Figure C:3-3.) ◀

EXAMPLE C:3-36 ▶ East and West Corporations have only one class of stock outstanding, owned by the following individuals:

	Stock Ownership Percentages		
Shareholder	*East Corp.*	*West Corp.*	*Common Ownership*
Javier	80%	25%	25%
Sara	20%	75%	20%
Total	100%	100%	45%

Five or fewer individuals (Javier and Sara) together own at least 80% (actually 100%) of each corporation's stock. However, those same individuals own only 45% of the corporations' stock taking into account only their common ownership. Because their ownership does not satisfy the more-than-50% test, East and West are not a brother-sister controlled group under either the 50%-80% or the 50%-only definition. Consequently, each corporation is taxed on its own income without regard to the earnings of the other. ◀

An individual's stock ownership can be counted for the 80% test only if that individual owns stock in each and every corporation in the controlled group.[42]

EXAMPLE C:3-37 ▶ Long and Short Corporations each have only a single class of stock outstanding, owned by the following individuals:

	Stock Ownership Percentages		
Shareholder	*Long Corp.*	*Short Corp.*	*Common Ownership*
Al	50%	40%	40%
Beth	20%	60%	20%
Carol	30%	—	—
Total	100%	100%	60%

Carol's stock does not count for purposes of Long's 80% stock ownership requirement because she owns no stock in Short. Only Al's and Beth's stock holdings count, and together they own only 70% of Long's stock. Thus, the 80% test fails. Consequently, Long and Short are not a brother-sister controlled group under the 50%-80% definition, but they are a brother-sister controlled group under the 50%-only definition. ◀

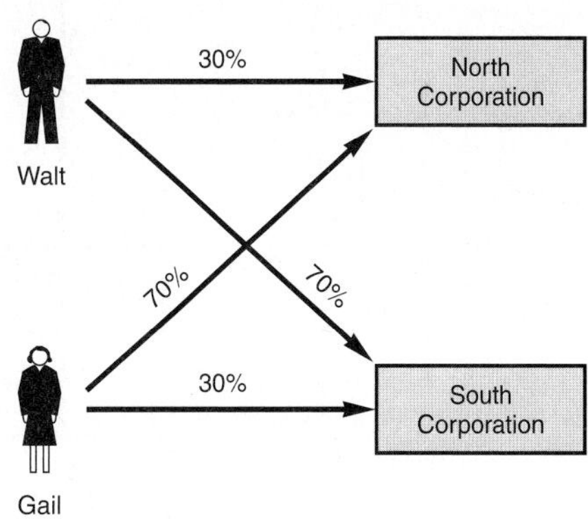

FIGURE C:3-3 ▶ BROTHER-SISTER CONTROLLED GROUP (EXAMPLE C:3-35)

[42] Reg. Sec. 1.1563-1(a)(3).

Combined Controlled Groups. A **combined controlled group** is comprised of three or more corporations meeting the following criteria:

- Each corporation is a member of a parent-subsidiary controlled group or a brother-sister controlled group.
- At least one of the corporations is both the parent corporation of a parent-subsidiary controlled group and a member of a brother-sister controlled group.[43]

KEY POINT

The combined controlled group definition does just what its name implies: It combines a parent-subsidiary controlled group and a brother-sister controlled group. Thus, instead of trying to apply the controlled group rules to two different groups, the combined group definition eliminates the issue by combining the groups into one controlled group.

EXAMPLE C:3-38 ▶ Able, Best, and Coast Corporations each have a single class of stock outstanding, owned by the following shareholders:

	Stock Ownership Percentages		
Shareholder	*Able Corp.*	*Coast Corp.*	*Best Corp.*
Art	50%	50%	—
Barbara	50%	50%	—
Able Corp.	—	—	100%

Able and Coast are a brother-sister controlled group under the 50%-80% definition because Art's and Barbara's ownership satisfy both the 80% and 50% tests. Able and Best are a parent-subsidiary controlled group because Able owns all of Best's stock. Each of the three corporations is a member of either the parent-subsidiary controlled group (Able and Best) or the brother-sister controlled group (Able and Coast), and the parent corporation (Able) of the parent-subsidiary controlled group also is a member of the brother-sister controlled group. Therefore, Able, Best, and Coast Corporations are members of a combined controlled group. (See Figure C:3-4.) ◀

APPLICATION OF THE CONTROLLED GROUP TEST

Controlled group status generally is tested on December 31. A corporation is included in a controlled group if it is a group member on December 31 and has been a group member on at least one-half of the days in its tax year that precede December 31. A corporation that is not a group member on December 31, nevertheless, is considered a member for the tax year if it has been a group member on at least one-half the days in its tax year that precede December 31. Corporations are excluded from the controlled group if they were members for less than one-half the days in their tax year that precede December 31 or if they retain certain special tax statuses such as being a tax-exempt corporation.

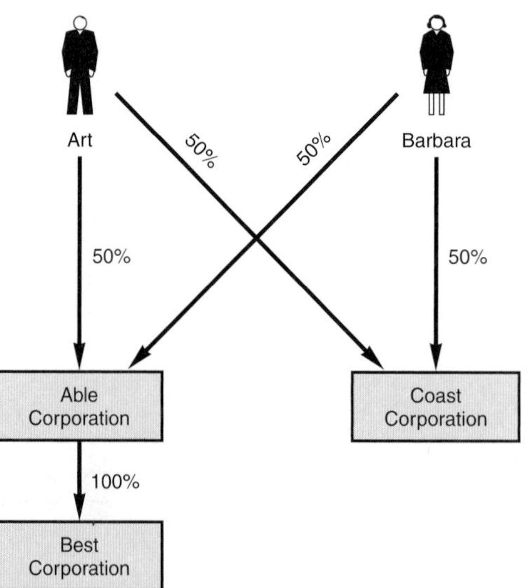

FIGURE C:3-4 ▶ COMBINED CONTROLLED GROUP (EXAMPLE C:3-38)

[43] Sec. 1563(a)(3).

▼ TABLE C:3-3
Items That Must Be Apportioned if a Controlled Group Exists

Item	Brother-Sister 50%-Only	Brother-Sister 50%–80%	Parent-Subsidiary ≥ 80%	Parent-Subsidiary > 50%
Low-bracket tax rates	X	X	X	
AMT exemption	X	X	X	
Minimum accumulated earnings tax credit	X	X	X	
Section 179 expense limitation		X	X	X
General business tax credit limitation		X	X	

EXAMPLE C:3-39 ▶ Ace and Copper Corporations are members of a parent-subsidiary controlled group of which Ace is the common parent. Both corporations are calendar year taxpayers and have been group members for the entire year. They do not file a consolidated return. Bell Corporation, which has a fiscal year ending on August 31, becomes a group member on December 1 of the current year. Although Bell is a group member on December 31 of the current year, it has been a group member for less than half the days in its tax year that precede December 31—only 30 of 121 days starting on September 1. Therefore, Bell is not a member of the Ace-Copper *controlled* group for its tax year beginning on September 1 of the current year. ◀

TAX STRATEGY TIP

A controlled group of corporations should elect to apportion the tax benefits in a manner that maximizes the tax savings from the tax benefits. See Tax Planning Considerations later in this chapter for details.

SPECIAL RULES APPLYING TO CONTROLLED GROUPS

As discussed earlier, if two or more corporations are members of a controlled group, the member corporations are limited to a total of $50,000 taxed at 15%, $25,000 being taxed at 25%, and $9,925,000 million being taxed at 34%. For brother-sister corporations, the broader 50%-only definition applies for limiting the reduced tax rates.

In addition, a controlled group must apportion certain other items among its group members, some of which are shown in Table C:3-3. For purposes of apportioning the Sec. 179 expense dollar limitation in a parent-subsidiary situation, the corporations are considered a controlled group if the ownership percentage is more than 50% rather than at least 80%.[44]

In addition to the above restrictions, Sec. 267(a)(1) allows no deduction for any loss on the sale or exchange of property between two members of the same controlled group, with control defined as more than 50% rather than as at least 80%. However, in contrast to losses between a corporation and controlling shareholder described earlier in this chapter, a loss realized on a transaction between members of a controlled group is deferred (instead of being disallowed). The original selling member recognizes the deferred loss when the property sold or exchanged in the intragroup transaction is sold outside the controlled group.

Section 267(a)(2) allows no deduction for certain accrued expenses or interest owed by one member of a controlled group to another member of the same controlled group when the two corporations use different accounting methods so that the payments would be reported in different tax years. (See page C:3-21 for a detailed discussion of Sec. 267.) The Sec. 1239 rules that convert capital gain into ordinary income on depreciable property sales between related parties also apply to sales or exchanges involving two members of the same controlled group. Sections 267 and 1239, however, provide special definitions of controlled groups that differ somewhat from those described above. These details are beyond the scope of this textbook.

TYPICAL MISCONCEPTION

The definitions of a parentsubsidiary controlled group and an affiliated group are similar, but not identical. For example, the 80% stock ownership test for controlled group purposes is satisfied if 80% of the voting power *or* 80% of the FMV of a corporation's stock is owned. For purposes of an affiliated group, 80% of both the voting power *and* the FMV of a corporation's stock must be owned.

CONSOLIDATED TAX RETURNS

Who Can File a Consolidated Return. Some groups of related corporations (i.e., affiliated groups) may elect to file a single income tax return called a **consolidated tax return.** An **affiliated group** is one or more chains of includible corporations connected through stock ownership with a common parent. In general, includible corporations are those other than foreign corporations, certain insurance companies, tax-exempt organizations,

[44] Secs. 179(d)(6) and (7).

BOOK-TO-TAX ACCOUNTING COMPARISON

The corporations included in a consolidated tax return may differ from those included in consolidated financial statements. Page 1 of Schedule M-3 reconciles financial statement worldwide consolidated net income to financial statement net income (loss) of corporations included in the consolidated tax return.

S corporations, and a few other specially defined corporations. The required ownership criteria are as follows:

- The common parent must directly own stock with at least 80% of the voting power *and* 80% of the value of at least one includible corporation.
- One or more group members must directly own stock with at least 80% of the voting power *and* 80% of the value of each other corporation included in the affiliated group.[45]

Many parent-subsidiary controlled groups also qualify as affiliated groups and thus are eligible to file a consolidated return in place of separate tax returns for each corporation. The parent-subsidiary portion of a combined group also can file a consolidated tax return if it also qualifies as an affiliated group. Brother-sister controlled groups, however, are not eligible to file consolidated returns because the requisite parent-subsidiary relationship does not exist.

An affiliated group elects to file a consolidated tax return by filing Form 1120, which includes all the income and expenses of each of its members. Each corporate member of the affiliated group must consent to the original election. Thereafter, any new member of the affiliated group must join in the consolidated return.

SELF-STUDY QUESTION

What is probably the most common reason for making a consolidated return election?

ANSWER

Filing consolidated returns allows the group to offset losses of one corporation against the profits of other members of the group.

Advantages of Filing a Consolidated Return. A consolidated return, in effect, is one tax return for the entire affiliated group of corporations. The main advantages of filing a consolidated return are

- Losses of one member of the group can offset profits of another member of the group.
- Capital losses of one member of the group can offset capital gains of another member of the group.
- Profits or gains realized on intercompany transactions are deferred until a sale outside the group occurs (i.e., if one member sells property to another member, the gain is postponed until the member sells the property to someone outside the affiliated group).

In contrast, if the group members file separate returns, members with NOLs or capital losses must either carry back these losses to earlier years or carry them over to future years rather than offset another member's profits or gains.

Although the losses of one group member can offset the profits of another group member when the group files a consolidated return, some important limitations apply to the use of a member corporation's NOL. These limitations prevent one corporation from purchasing another corporation's NOL carryovers to offset its own taxable income or purchasing a profitable corporation to facilitate the use of its own NOL carryovers. (See Chapters C:7 and C:8.)

The following example illustrates the advantage of a consolidated return election.

EXAMPLE C:3-40 ▶ Parent Corporation owns 100% of Subsidiary Corporation's stock. Parent reports $110,000 of taxable income, including a $10,000 capital gain. Subsidiary incurs a $100,000 NOL and a $10,000 capital loss. If Parent and Subsidiary file separate returns, Parent has a $26,150 [$22,250 + 0.39 × ($110,000 − $100,000)] tax liability. Subsidiary has no tax liability but may be able to use its $100,000 NOL and $10,000 capital loss to offset taxable income in other years. On the other hand, if Parent and Subsidiary file a consolidated return, the group's consolidated taxable income is zero and the group has no tax liability. By filing a consolidated return, the group saves $26,150 in taxes for the year. ◀

Disadvantages of Filing a Consolidated Return. The main disadvantages of a consolidated return election are

- The election is binding on all subsequent tax years unless the IRS grants permission to discontinue filing consolidated returns or the affiliated group terminates.
- Losses on intercompany transactions are deferred until a sale outside the group takes place.
- One member's Sec. 1231 loss offsets another member's Sec. 1231 gain instead of being reported as an ordinary loss.
- Losses of an unprofitable member of the group may reduce the deduction or credit limitations of the group below what would be available had the members filed separate tax returns.

ADDITIONAL COMMENT

Under Sec. 267 discussed earlier, intercompany losses may be deferred even if the corporations file separate tax returns.

---

[45] Sec. 1504(a).

- The group may incur additional administrative costs in maintaining the records needed to file a consolidated return.

Determining whether to make a consolidated tax return election is a complex decision because of the various advantages and disadvantages and because the election is so difficult to revoke once made. Chapter C:8 provides detailed coverage of the consolidated return rules.

TAX PLANNING CONSIDERATIONS

OBJECTIVE 5

Identify planning strategies to reduce taxes for corporations and their shareholders

COMPENSATION PLANNING FOR SHAREHOLDER-EMPLOYEES

Compensation paid to a shareholder-employee in the form of salary has the advantage of single taxation because, while taxable to the employee, salary is deductible by the corporation. Dividend payments, on the other hand, are taxed twice. The corporation is taxed on its income when earned, and the shareholder is taxed on profits distributed as dividends. Double taxation occurs because the corporation may not deduct dividend payments. The applicable capital gains tax rate on dividends, however, makes the difference between salary and dividends less substantial than it would be if dividends were taxed at ordinary rates.

EXAMPLE C:3-41 ▶ Delta Corporation earns $500,000 and wishes to distribute $100,000 or as much of the $100,000 as possible to Mary, its sole shareholder and CEO. Mary's ordinary tax rate is 39.6%, her capital gains rate is 23.8% (20% plus the 3.8% rate on net investment income), and the corporation's marginal tax rate is 34%. Ignoring payroll taxes, the following table compares salary and dividend payments to Mary with respect to the $100,000 of partial earnings:

	Salary	*Dividend at Capital Gains Tax Rate*
1. Corporate earnings (partial)	$100,000	$100,000
2. Minus: Salary deduction	(100,000)	-0-
3. Corporate taxable income (partial)	$ -0-	$100,000
4. Times: Corporate tax rate	0.34	0.34
5. Corporate income tax (on partial income)	$ -0-	$ 34,000
6. Dividend to Mary (Line 1 – Line 5)	$100,000	$ 66,000
7. Times: Mary's tax rate	0.396	0.238
8. Mary's tax	$ 39,600	$ 15,708
9. Total tax (Line 5 + Line 8)	$ 39,600	$ 49,708
10. Overall tax rate (Line 9 ÷ Line 1)	39.6%	49.7%

Thus, in this situation, the double taxation due to paying nondeductible dividends instead of deductible salary increases Mary's overall tax rate from 39.6% to 49.7%. ◀

To avoid double taxation, some owners of closely held corporations prefer to be taxed under the rules of Subchapter S (see Chapter C:11). Other owners of closely held corporations retain C corporation status to use the 15% and 25% marginal corporate tax rates and to benefit from nontaxable fringe benefits such as health and accident insurance. These fringe benefits are nontaxable to the employee and deductible by the corporation. For both tax and nontax reasons, closely held corporations must determine the appropriate level of earnings to be withdrawn from the business in the form of salary and fringe benefits and the amount of earnings to be retained in the business.

Advantage of Salary Payments. If a corporation distributes all its profits as deductible salary and fringe benefit payments, it will eliminate double taxation. However, the following considerations limit such tax planning opportunities:

ADDITIONAL COMMENT

Reasonableness of a salary payment is a question of fact to be determined in each case. No formula can be used to determine a reasonable amount.

- Regulation Sec. 1.162-7(a) requires salary or fringe benefit payments to be reasonable in amount and to be paid for services rendered by the employee. If the IRS deems compensation to be unreasonable, it may disallow the portion of the salary it deems unreasonable while still requiring the employee to include all compensation in gross income (see Chapter C:4). This disallowance will result in double taxation. The reasonable compensation restriction primarily affects closely held corporations.
- A corporation may not deduct compensation exceeding $1 million paid to certain executives of publicly traded corporations. This limitation, however, applies only to compensation paid to the chief executive officer (CEO) and the four top earning executives other than the CEO. In any case, the limitation does not apply to performance-based compensation.[46]
- A corporation is a taxpaying entity independent of its owners. The first $75,000 of a corporation's earnings is taxed at 15% and 25% corporate tax rates. These rates are lower than the marginal tax rate that may apply to an individual taxpayer and provides an incentive to retain some earnings in the corporation instead of paying them out as salaries.
- A combined employee–employer Social Security tax rate of 15.3% generally applies Employers and employees were each liable for 6.2% of old age security and disability insurance tax, or a total of 12.4% on wages up to the salary cap ($118,500 in 2016 and $127,200 in 2017). Employers and employees also are each liable for a 1.45% Medicare hospital insurance tax, for a total of 2.9% of all wages. An additional 0.9% for the Medicare hospital insurance tax applies to the employee's portion of wages exceeding $200,000 ($250,000 for married filing jointly). In addition to these taxes, state and federal unemployment taxes may be imposed on a portion of wages paid.

TAX STRATEGY TIP

A fringe benefit probably is the most cost effective form of compensation because the amount of the benefit is deductible by the employer and never taxed to the employee. Thus, where possible, fringe benefits are an excellent compensation planning tool. For closely held corporations, however, the tax savings to shareholder-employees are reduced because the fringe benefit must be offered to all employees without discrimination.

Advantage of Fringe Benefits. Fringe benefits provide two types of tax advantages: a tax deferral or an exclusion. Qualified pension, profit-sharing, and stock bonus plans provide a tax deferral; that is, the corporation's contribution to such a plan is not taxable to the employees when the corporation makes the contribution. Instead, employees are taxed on the benefits when they receive them. Other common fringe benefits, such as group term life insurance, accident and health insurance, and disability insurance, are exempt from tax altogether; that is, the employee never is taxed on the value of these fringe benefits.

Because the employee excludes the value of fringe benefits from gross income, the marginal individual tax rate applicable to these benefits is zero. Thus, conversion of salary into a fringe benefit provides tax savings for the shareholder-employee equal to the amount of the converted salary times the employee's marginal tax rate, assuming the shareholder-employee could not purchase the same fringe benefit and deduct its cost on his or her individual tax return.

SPECIAL ELECTION TO ALLOCATE REDUCED TAX RATE BENEFITS

A controlled group may elect to apportion the tax benefits of the 15%, 25%, and 34% tax rates to the member corporations in any manner it chooses. If the corporations elect no special apportionment plan, the $50,000, $25,000, and $9,925,000 amounts allocated to the three reduced tax rate brackets are divided equally among all the corporations in the group.[47] If a controlled group has one or more group members that report little or no taxable income, the group should elect special apportionment of the reduced tax benefits to obtain the full tax savings resulting from the reduced rates. The following steps outline a set of procedures for apportioning tax rates for taxable income levels at or below $10 million.[48]

1. If aggregate positive taxable income is $100,000 or less, apportion the 15%, 25%, and 34% rates to members that have positive taxable income so as to maximize their benefit.
   a. To avoid "wasting" low tax rates on loss members, elect special apportionment of tax benefits.

[46] Sec. 162(m).
[47] Sec. 1561(a).

[48] For the sake of simplicity, we do not extend the procedures to taxable income exceeding $10 million but similar procedures apply.

b. Summing the members' taxes results in the same total tax as would occur by applying the corporate tax rate schedule to the group's aggregate positive taxable income.

2. If aggregate positive taxable income is between $100,000 and $335,000, apportion the 15%, 25%, and 34% brackets as in Step 1 above. Follow the next steps to apportion the 5% surtax.

ADDITIONAL COMMENT

This apportionment method for the 5% surtax is one of two possible methods available. It apportions the surtax first to the corporation using the 15% bracket and then to the corporation using the 25% bracket. Hence, it is referred to as the FIFO method. The other method is called the proportionate method. See the Additional Comment next to Example C:3-43.

a. Calculate the surtax as 5% times (aggregate positive taxable income − $100,000).
b. If the calculated surtax is $9,500 or less, apportion the calculated surtax in proportion to the way the corporations apportioned the 15% bracket.
c. If the surtax is greater than $9,500 ($11,750 maximum), apportion the first $9,500 as in Step 2b, and apportion the excess in proportion to the way the corporations apportioned the 25% bracket in Step 1 above.
d. Summing the members' taxes results in the same total tax as would occur by applying the corporate tax rate schedule to the group's aggregate positive taxable income.

3. If aggregate positive taxable income is from $335,000 to $10,000,000, the 15% and 25% tax brackets are fully phased out, so each member's tax equals a flat 34% of its taxable income, and the group's total tax equals 34% of aggregate positive taxable income.

EXAMPLE C:3-42 ▶ North and South Corporations are members of a controlled group. The corporations file separate tax returns for the current year and report the following results:

Corporation	*Taxable Income (NOL)*
North	$(25,000)
South	100,000

If they elect no special apportionment plan, North and South are limited to $25,000 each taxed at a 15% rate and to $12,500 each taxed at a 25% rate. The tax liability for each corporation is determined as follows:

Corporation	*Calculation*	*Tax*
North		$ -0-
South	15% tax bracket: 0.15 × $25,000	$ 3,750
	25% tax bracket: 0.25 × $12,500	3,125
	34% tax bracket: 0.34 × $62,500	21,250
	Subtotal for South Corporation	$28,125
Total for North-South controlled group		$28,125

If the corporations elect a special apportionment plan, the group may apportion the full $50,000 and $25,000 amounts for each of the reduced tax rate brackets to South. The tax liability for each corporation is determined as follows:

Corporation	*Calculation*	*Tax*
North		$ -0-
South	15% tax bracket: 0.15 × $50,000	$ 7,500
	25% tax bracket: 0.25 × $25,000	6,250
	34% tax bracket: 0.34 × $25,000	8,500
	Subtotal for South Corporation	$22,250
Total for North-South controlled group		$22,250

By shifting the benefit of low tax brackets away from a corporation that cannot use it (North) to a corporation that can (South), the special apportionment election reduces the total tax liability for the North-South controlled group by $5,875 ($28,125 − $22,250). ◀

If a controlled group's total taxable income exceeds $100,000 ($15 million), a 5% (3%) surcharge recaptures the benefits of the reduced tax rates. The component member (or members) that took advantage of the lower tax rates pays this additional tax.

EXAMPLE C:3-43 ▶ Alpha, Beta, and Gamma Corporations are members of a controlled group and report the following results:

Corporation	*Taxable Income (Loss)*
Alpha	$ 80,000
Beta	(25,000)
Gamma	230,000

The group, which has aggregate taxable income of $310,000 ($80,00 + $230,000), elects special apportionment. They apportion the 15% tax bracket to Alpha with the balance of Alpha's income taxed at 34% (before the surtax apportionment), and they apportion the 25% tax bracket to Gamma with the balance of Gamma's income taxed at 34% (before the surtax apportionment). The surtax in this case is $10,500 (0.05 × ($310,000 − $100,000)). Using the procedures outlined above, the members apportion $9,500 of the surtax to Alpha because that corporation received the entire 15% tax bracket, and they apportion the remaining $1,000 surtax to Gamma because that corporation received the entire 25% tax bracket. Accordingly, the tax liability for each corporation is as follows:

ADDITIONAL COMMENT

If the group used the proportionate method, the surtax would be apportioned based on the relative tax benefit of the lower brackets. The tax benefit of the 15% bracket is $9,500 [$50,000 × (0.34 − 0.15)], and the tax benefit of the 25% bracket is $2,250 [$25,000 × (0.34 − 0.25)]. Thus, $8,489 of the surtax would be allocated to Alpha, calculated as $10,500 × ($9,500/$11,750), and $2,011 would be allocated to Gamma, calculated as $10,500 × ($2,250/$11,750).

Alpha:		
Tax on $50,000 at 15%	$ 7,500	
Tax on $30,000 at 34%	10,200	
Surtax	9,500	
Total for Alpha		$27,200
Beta		–0–
Gamma:		
Tax on $25,000 at 25%	$ 6,250	
Tax on $205,000 at 34%	69,700	
Surtax	1,000	
Total for Alpha		76,950
Total for the group		$104,150

The total tax for the group is the same as if they applied the corporate tax rate schedule to the $310,000 aggregate positive taxable income as follows: $22,250 + ($210,000 × 0.39) = $104,150. ◀

EXAMPLE C:3-44 ▶ Hill, Jet, and King Corporations are members of a controlled group and report the following results:

Corporation	*Taxable Income*
Hill	$300,000
Jet	(50,000)
King	100,000

The group's aggregate positive taxable income is $400,000 ($300,000 + $100,000), which exceeds $335,000. Therefore, with special apportionment, Hill's and King's tax equals 34% of each corporation's taxable income as follows:

Hill ($300,000 × 0.34)	$102,000
Jet	–0–
King ($100,000 × 0.34)	34,000
Total for the group ($400,000 × 0.34)	$136,000 ◀

TAX STRATEGY TIP

A corporation may want to elect to forgo the NOL carryback when tax credit carryovers are being used in the earlier years. If the NOLs are carried back, the tax credits may expire. Thus, before deciding to carry back NOLs, the prior tax returns should be carefully examined to ensure that expiring tax credits do not exist.

USING NOL CARRYOVERS AND CARRYBACKS

When a corporation incurs an NOL for the year, it has two choices:

- Carry the NOL back to the second and first preceding years in that order (assuming no extended carryback period), and then forward to the succeeding 20 years in chronological order until the NOL is exhausted.
- Forgo any carryback and just carry the NOL forward to the 20 succeeding years.

A corporation might elect to forgo an NOL carryback if it would offset income at a low tax rate, resulting in a small tax refund compared to a greater anticipated benefit if the NOL instead were carried over to a high tax rate year.

EXAMPLE C:3-45 ▶ Boyd Corporation, a calendar year taxpayer, incurs a $30,000 NOL in 2017. Boyd's 2015 taxable income was $50,000. If Boyd carries the NOL back to 2014, Boyd's tax refund is computed as follows:

Original tax on $50,000 (using 2015 rates)	$7,500
Minus: Recomputed tax on $20,000 [($50,000 − $30,000) × 0.15]	(3,000)
Tax refund	$4,500

If Boyd anticipates taxable income (after reduction for any NOL carryovers) of $75,000 or more in 2018, carrying over the NOL will result in the entire loss offsetting taxable income that otherwise would be taxed at a 34% or higher marginal tax rate. The tax savings is computed as follows:

Tax on $105,000 of expected taxable income	$24,200
Minus: Tax on $75,000 ($105,000 − $30,000)	(13,750)
Tax savings in 2018	$10,450

Thus, if Boyd expects taxable income to be $105,000 in 2018, it might elect to forgo the NOL carryback and obtain the additional $5,950 ($10,450 − $4,500) tax benefit. Of course, by carrying the NOL over to 2018, Boyd loses the value of having the funds immediately available. However, Boyd may use the NOL to reduce its estimated tax payments for 2018. If the corporation expects the NOL carryover benefit to occur at an appreciably distant point in the future, the corporation would have to determine the benefit's present value to make it comparable to a refund from an NOL carryback. This example ignores the effect the NOL carryover has on the U.S. production activities deduction in the carryover year. ◀

ETHICAL POINT

When tax practitioners take on a new client, they should review the client's prior year tax returns and tax elections for accuracy and completeness. Tax matters arising in the current year, such as an NOL, can affect prior year tax returns prepared by another tax practitioner. Positions taken or errors discovered in a prior year return may have ethical consequences for a practitioner who takes on a new client.

COMPLIANCE AND PROCEDURAL CONSIDERATIONS

OBJECTIVE 6

Comply with corporate tax filing requirements

ESTIMATED TAXES

Every corporation that expects to owe more than $500 in tax for the current year must pay four installments of estimated tax, each equal to 25% of its required annual payment.[49] For corporations that are not large corporations (defined below), the required annual payment is the lesser of 100% of the tax shown on the current year return or 100% of the tax shown on the preceding year return. A corporation may not base its required estimated tax amount on the tax shown on the preceding year return if the preceding year tax return showed a zero tax liability.[50] The estimated tax amount is the sum of the corporation's income tax and alternative minimum tax liabilities that exceeds its tax credits. The amount of estimated tax due may be computed on Schedule 1120-W (Estimated Tax for Corporations).

Estimated Tax Payment Dates. A calendar year corporation must deposit estimated tax payments in a Federal Reserve bank or authorized commercial bank on or before April 15, June 15, September 15, and December 15.[51] This schedule differs from that of an individual taxpayer. The final estimated tax installment for a calendar year corporation is due in December of the tax year rather than in January of the following tax year, as is the case for individual taxpayers. For a fiscal year corporation, the due dates are the fifteenth day of the fourth, sixth, ninth, and twelfth months of the tax year.

[49] Sec. 6655.

[50] Rev. Rul. 92-54, 1992-2 C.B. 320.

[51] Sec. 6655(c)(2). Fiscal year corporations must deposit their taxes on or before the fifteenth day of the fourth, sixth, ninth, and twelfth month of their tax year. If the fifteenth falls on a weekend or holiday, a payment made on the next business day is considered made on the fifteenth due date. Regarding an April 15 due date, the filer also must consider Emancipation Day, which is an observed holiday in Washington, D.C. on April 16. If April 16 falls on Saturday, the observed holiday is the preceding Friday. If it falls on Sunday, the observed holiday is the succeeding Monday.

EXAMPLE C:3-46 ▶ Garden Corporation, a calendar year taxpayer, expects to report the following results for the current year:

Regular tax	$119,000
Alternative minimum tax	25,000

Garden's current year estimated tax liability is $144,000 ($119,000 regular tax liability + $25,000 AMT liability). Garden's tax liability last year was $120,000. Assuming Garden is not a large corporation, its required annual payment for the current year is $120,000, the lesser of its prior year liability ($120,000) or its current year tax return liability ($144,000). Garden will not incur a penalty if it deposits four equal installments of $30,000 ($120,000 ÷ 4) on or before April 15, June 15, September 15, and December 15 of the current year. ◀

TYPICAL MISCONCEPTION

The easiest method of determining a corporation's estimated tax payments is to pay 100% of last year's tax liability. Unfortunately, for "large corporations," other than for its first quarterly payment, last year's tax liability is not an acceptable method of determining the required estimated tax payments. Also, last year's tax liability cannot be used if no tax liability existed in the prior year or if the corporation filed a short-year return for the prior year.

Different estimated tax payment rules apply to large corporations. A large corporation's required annual payment is 100% of the tax shown on the current year return. A large corporation's estimated tax payments cannot be based on the prior year's tax liability except the first installment. If a large corporation bases its first estimated tax installment on the prior year's liability, any shortfall between the required payment based on the current year's tax liability and the actual payment must be made up with the second installment.[52] A large corporation is one whose taxable income was $1 million or more in any of its three immediately preceding tax years. Controlled groups of corporations must allocate the $1 million amount among its group members.

EXAMPLE C:3-47 ▶ Assume the same facts as in Example C:3-46 except Garden is a large corporation (i.e., it had more than $1 million of taxable income in one of its prior three years). Garden can base its first estimated tax payment on either 25% of its current year tax liability or 25% of last year's tax liability. Garden should elect to use its prior year tax liability as the basis for its first installment because it can reduce the needed payment from $36,000 (0.25 × $144,000) to $30,000 (0.25 × $120,000). However, it must recapture the $6,000 ($36,000 − $30,000) shortfall when it pays its second installment. Therefore, the total second installment is $42,000 ($36,000 second installment + $6,000 recapture from first installment). The third and fourth installments are $36,000 each. ◀

KEY POINT

The amount of penalty depends on three factors: the applicable underpayment rate, the amount of the underpayment, and the amount of time that lapses until the corporation makes the payment.

Penalties for Underpayment of Estimated Tax. The IRS will assess a nondeductible penalty if a corporation does not deposit its required estimated tax installment on or before the due date for that installment. The penalty is the underpayment rate found in Sec. 6621 times the amount by which the installment due by a payment date exceeds the payment actually made.[53] The penalty accrues from the payment due date for the installment until the earlier of the actual date of the payment or the due date for the tax return (excluding extensions).

EXAMPLE C:3-48 ▶ Globe Corporation is a calendar year taxpayer that reported a $100,000 tax liability for 2016. Globe's tax liability for 2015 was $125,000. It should have made estimated tax payments of $25,000 ($100,000 ÷ 4) on or before April 15, June 15, September 15, and December 15, 2016. If any of these dates fall on a weekend or holiday, a payment made on the next business day is considered to have been made on the due date. No penalty is assessed if Globe deposited or is considered to have deposited the requisite amounts on or before each of those dates. However, if Globe deposited only $16,000 ($9,000 less than the required $25,000) on April 15, 2016, and did not deposit the remaining $9,000 before the due date for the 2016 return, the corporation must pay a penalty on the $9,000 underpayment for the period of time from April 16, 2016, through April 15, 2017. If Globe deposits, or is considered to have deposited, $34,000 on the second installment date (June 15, 2016), so that it has paid a total of $50,000 by the second installment due date, the penalty runs only from April 16, 2016, through June 15, 2016.

Now assume that Globe instead made, or is considered to have made, the following estimated tax payments in 2016:

ADDITIONAL COMMENT

This illustration pertains to 2016 because tax forms for that year are the latest available at the time this textbook was published.

[52] Sec. 6655(d)(2)(B). A revision to the required estimated tax payment amount also may be needed if the corporation is basing its quarterly payments on the current year's tax liability. Installments paid after the estimate of the current year's liability has been revised must take into account any shortage or excess in previous installment payments resulting from the change in the original estimate.

[53] Sec. 6621. This interest rate is the short-term federal rate as determined by the Secretary of the Treasury plus three percentage points. It is subject to change every three months. The interest rate for large corporations is the short-term federal rate plus five percentage points. This higher interest rate begins 30 days after the issuance of either a 30-day or 90-day deficiency notice.

Date	Amount
April 15	$16,000
June 15	16,000
September 15	21,000
December 15	35,000

Form 2220 in Appendix B calculates the underpayments and resultant penalty given this pattern of payments. ◀

Special Computation Methods. In lieu of the current year and prior year methods, corporations can use either of two special methods for calculating estimated tax installments:

- The annualized income method
- The adjusted seasonal income method

The Annualized Income Method. This method is useful if a corporation's income is likely to increase a great deal toward the end of the year. It allows a corporation to base its first and second quarterly estimated tax payments on its annualized taxable income for the first three months of the year. The corporation then bases its third payment on its annualized taxable income for the first six months of the year and its fourth payment on annualized taxable income for the first nine months of the year. (Two other options for the number of months used for each installment also are available.)

EXAMPLE C:3-49 ▶ Erratic Corporation, a calendar year taxpayer, reports taxable income of: $10,000 in each of January, February, and March; $20,000 in each of April, May, and June; and $50,000 in each of the last six months of the current year. Erratic's annualized taxable income and annualized tax are calculated as follows:

TAX STRATEGY TIP

Both the "annualized income exception" and the "adjusted seasonal income exception" are complicated computations. However, due to the large amounts of money involved in making corporate estimated tax payments along with the possible underpayment penalties, the time and effort spent in determining the least amount necessary for a required estimated tax payment are often worthwhile.

Through	*Cumulative Taxable Income*	*Annualization Factor*	*Annualized Taxable Income*	*Tax on Annualized Taxable Income*
Third month	$ 30,000	12/3	$120,000	$ 30,050
Sixth month	90,000	12/6	180,000	53,450
Ninth month	240,000	12/9	320,000	108,050

Assuming Erratic uses the annualized method for all four estimated tax payments, its installments will be as follows:

Installment Number	*Annualized Tax*	*Applicable Percentage*	*Installment Amount*	*Cumulative Installment*
One	$ 30,050	25%	$ 7,513[a]	$ 7,513
Two	30,050	50	7,512[b]	15,025
Three	53,450	75	25,063[c]	40,088
Four	108,050	100	67,962[d]	108,050

[a]$30,050 × 0.25
[b]($30,050 × 0.50) − $7,513
[c]($53,450 × 0.75) − $15,025
[d]($108,050 × 1.00) − $40,088
◀

A corporation may use the annualized income method for an installment payment only if it is less than the regular required installment (including the recapture described in the next sentence). It must recapture any reduction in an earlier required installment resulting from use of the annualized income method by increasing the amount of the next installment that does not qualify for the annualized income method.

For small corporations, the sure way to avoid a penalty for the underpayment of estimated tax is to base the current year's estimated tax payments on 100% of last year's tax. This approach is not possible, however, for large corporations or for corporations that owed no tax in the prior year or that filed a short period tax return for the prior year. This approach also is not advisable if the corporation had a high tax liability in the prior year and expects a low tax liability in the current year.

Adjusted Seasonal Income Method. A corporation may base its installments on its adjusted seasonal income. This method permits corporations that earn seasonal income to annualize their income by assuming income earned in the current year is earned in the same pattern as in preceding years. As in the case of the annualized income exception, a corporation can use the seasonal income exception only if the resulting installment payment is less than the regular required installment. Once the exception no longer applies, any savings resulting from its use for prior installments must be recaptured.

Reporting the Underpayment. A corporation reports its underpayment of estimated taxes and the amount of any penalty on Form 2220 (Underpayment of Estimated Tax by Corporations). A completed Form 2220 using the facts from Example C:3-48 appears in Appendix B.

Paying the Remaining Tax Liability. A corporation must pay its remaining tax liability for the year when it files its corporate tax return. An extension of time to file the tax return, however, does *not* extend the time to pay the tax liability. If any tax remains unpaid after the original due date for the tax return, the corporation must pay interest at the underpayment rate prescribed by Sec. 6621 from the due date until the corporation pays the tax. In addition to interest, the IRS assesses a penalty if the corporation does not pay the tax on time and cannot show reasonable cause for the failure to pay. The IRS presumes that reasonable cause exists if the corporation requests an extension of time to file its tax return and the amount of tax shown on the request for extension (Form 7004) or the amount of tax paid by the original due date of the return is at least 90% of the corporation's tax shown on its Form 1120.[54] A discussion of the failure-to-pay penalty and the interest calculation can be found in Chapter C:15.

STOP & THINK

Question: Why does the tax law permit a corporation to use special methods such as the annualized income method to calculate its required estimated tax installments?

Solution: A large corporation whose income varies widely may not be able to estimate its taxable income for the year until late in the year, and it is not allowed to base its estimates on last year's income. If, for example, a calendar year corporation earns income of $100,000 per month during the first six months of its year, it might estimate its first two installments on the assumption that it will earn a total taxable income of $1.2 million for the year. But if its income unexpectedly increases to $500,000 per month in the seventh month, it would need an annualized method to avoid an underpayment penalty for the first two installments. Were it not for the ability to use the annualized method, the corporation would have no way to avoid an underpayment penalty even though it could not predict its taxable income for the year when it made the first two installment payments.

REQUIREMENTS FOR FILING AND PAYING TAXES

A corporation must file a tax return, Form 1120 (U.S. Corporation Income Tax Return), even if it has no taxable income for the year.[55] If the corporation did not exist for its entire annual accounting period (either calendar year or fiscal year), it must file a short period return for the part of the year it did exist. For tax purposes, a corporation's existence ends when it ceases business and dissolves, retaining no assets, even if state law treats the corporation as continuing for purposes of winding up its affairs.[56]

A completed Form 1120 corporate income tax return appears in Appendix B. A spreadsheet that converts book income into taxable income for the Johns and Lawrence business enterprise (introduced in Chapter C:2) is presented with the C corporation tax return.

ADDITIONAL COMMENT

If a corporation has a June 30 year end, the filing deadline remains as the fifteenth day of the third month after the end of its taxable year (i.e., September 15) until tax years beginning after 2025. For corporations with taxable years ending on June 30, the extension for filing the tax return is seven months until 2026.

WHEN THE RETURN MUST BE FILED

For tax years beginning after 2015, the due date for a corporate tax return is the fifteenth day of the fourth month after the end of the corporation's tax year. For tax years beginning before

[54] Reg. Sec. 301.6651-1(c)(4).
[55] Sec. 6012(a)(2).
[56] Reg. Sec. 1.6012-2(a)(2).

2016, the due date for a corporate tax return is the fifteenth day of the third month after the end of the corporation's tax year.[57] The corporation can obtain a six-month extension for filing the tax return if the corporation files Form 7004 (Application for Automatic Extension of Time to File Certain Business Income Tax, Information, and Other Returns). Special rules apply for corporations having a June 30 year end. See the Additional Comment on the previous page for details.

EXAMPLE C:3-50 ▶ Palmer Corporation's fiscal tax year ends on September 30. Its corporate tax return for the year ending September 30, 2017, is due on or before January 15, 2018. If Palmer files Form 7004 by January 15, 2018, it can obtain an automatic extension of time to file until July 15, 2018. Palmer expects its tax liability for the year ending September 30, 2017 to be $72,000, and it has paid $68,000 in estimated tax during the year. Accordingly, Palmer pays $4,000 with its Form 7004. A completed Form 7004 appears in Appendix B. ◀

ADDITIONAL COMMENT

The IRS will not assess a late payment penalty if the corporation extends its due date and pays 90% of its total tax liability by the unextended due date and pays the balance by the extended due date.

Additional extensions beyond the automatic six-month period generally are not available. However, see the Additional Comment on the previous page regarding corporations with June 30 year-ends. The IRS can rescind the extension period by mailing a ten-day notice to the corporation before the end of the six-month period.[58]

BOOK-TO-TAX ACCOUNTING COMPARISON

Schedule L (of Form 1120) requires a financial accounting (book) balance sheet rather than a tax balance sheet.

TAX RETURN SCHEDULES

Schedule L (of Form 1120): The Balance Sheet. Schedule L of Form 1120 requires a balance sheet showing the financial accounting results at the beginning and end of the tax year.

Reconciliation Schedules. The IRS also requires the reconciliation of the corporation's financial accounting income (also known as book income) and its taxable income (before special deductions). Book income is calculated according to generally accepted accounting principles (GAAP) including rules promulgated by the Financial Accounting Standards Board (FASB). On the other hand, taxable income must be calculated using tax rules. Therefore, book income and taxable income usually differ.

Some small corporations that do not require audited statements keep their books on a tax basis. For example, they may calculate depreciation for book purposes the same way they do for tax purposes. Income tax expense for book purposes may simply reflect the federal income tax liability. Most corporations, however, must use GAAP to calculate net income per books. For such corporations, taxable income and book income may differ significantly. The reconciliation of book income and taxable income provides the IRS with information that helps it audit a corporation's tax return.

ADDITIONAL COMMENT

For examples of Schedules M-1, M-2, and M-3 (of Form 1120), see Figure C:3-5, Figure C:3-6, and tax forms in Appendix B.

For many corporations, the reconciliation must be provided on Schedule M-1 of Form 1120. Corporations with total assets of $10 million or more on the last day of the tax year, however, must complete Schedule M-3 instead of Schedule M-1. This schedule provides the IRS with much more detailed information on differences between book income and taxable income than does Schedule M-1. This additional transparency of corporate transactions will increase the IRS's ability to audit corporate tax returns. Form 1120 also requires an analysis of unappropriated retained earnings on Schedule M-2.

BOOK-TO-TAX ACCOUNTING COMPARISON

The Internal Revenue Code and related authorities determine the treatment of items in the tax return while Accounting Standards Codification (ASC) 740 (Income Taxes) dictates the treatment of tax items in the financial statements.

Book-Tax Differences. A corporation's book income usually differs from its taxable income for a large number of transactions. Some of these differences are permanent. **Permanent differences** arise because:

- Some book income is never taxed. Examples include:
  1. Tax-exempt interest received on state and municipal obligations
  2. Proceeds of life insurance carried by the corporation on the lives of key officers or employees
- Some book expenses are never deductible for tax purposes. Examples include:
  1. Expenses incurred in earning tax-exempt interest

[57] Sec. 6072(b). If the due date falls on a weekend or holiday, the return is due on the next business day. Regarding an April 15 due date, the filer also must consider Emancipation Day, which is an observed holiday in Washington, D.C. on April 16. If April 16 falls on Saturday, the observed holiday is the preceding Friday. If it falls on Sunday, the observed holiday is the succeeding Monday.

[58] Reg. Sec. 1.6081-3 and instructions to Form 7004.

SELF-STUDY QUESTION

Why might the IRS be interested in reviewing a corporation's Schedule M-1 or M-3?

ANSWER

Schedule M-1 or M-3 adjustments reconcile book income to taxable income. Thus, these schedules can prove illuminating to an IRS agent who is auditing a corporate return. Because Schedule M-1 or M-3 highlights each departure from the financial accounting rules, the schedules sometimes help the IRS identify tax issues it may want to examine further.

2. Premiums paid for life insurance carried by the corporation on the lives of key officers or employees
3. Fines and expenses resulting from a violation of law
4. Disallowed travel and entertainment costs
5. Political contributions
6. Federal income taxes per books, which is based on GAAP (ASC 740)

- Some tax deductions are never taken for book purposes. Examples include:
  1. The dividends-received deduction
  2. The U.S. production activities deduction
  3. Percentage depletion of natural resources in excess of their cost

Some of the differences are temporary. **Temporary differences** arise because:

- Some revenues or gains are recognized for book purposes in the current year but not reported for tax purposes until later years. Examples include:
  1. Installment sales reported in full for book purposes in the year of sale but reported over a period of years using the installment method for tax purposes
  2. Gains on involuntary conversions recognized currently for book purposes but deferred for tax purposes
- Some revenues or gains are taxable before they are reported for book purposes. These items are included in taxable income when received but are included in book income as they accrue. Examples include:
  1. Prepaid rent or interest income
  2. Advance subscription revenue
- Some expenses or losses are deductible for tax purposes after they are recognized for book purposes. Examples include:
  1. Excess of capital losses over capital gains, which are expensed for book purposes but carry back or over for tax purposes
  2. Book depreciation in excess of tax depreciation
  3. Charitable contributions exceeding the 10% of taxable income limitation, which are currently expensed for book purposes but carry over for tax purposes
  4. Bad debt accruals using the allowance method for book purposes and the direct write-off method for tax purposes
  5. Organizational and start-up expenditures, which are expensed currently for book purposes but partially deducted and amortized for tax purposes
  6. Product warranty liabilities expensed for book purposes when estimated but deducted for tax purposes when the liability becomes fixed
  7. Net operating losses (NOLs) that, for tax purposes, carry back two years (or extended period if applicable) and carry over 20 years
- Some expenses or losses are deductible for tax purposes before they are recognized for book purposes. Examples include:
  1. Tax depreciation in excess of book depreciation
  2. Prepaid expenses deducted on the tax return in the period paid but accrued over a period of years for book purposes

For book purposes, temporary differences listed under the first and fourth bullets create deferred tax liabilities while those listed under the second and third bullets create deferred tax assets. The Financial Statement Implications section later in this chapter discusses the financial accounting treatment of book-tax differences.

Schedule M-1 (of Form 1120). The Schedule M-1 reconciliation of book to taxable income begins with net income per books and ends with taxable income before special deductions, which corresponds with Line 28 of Form 1120. Thus, some book-tax differences enumerated above do not appear in the reconciliation, for example, the dividends-received deduction and the net operating loss deduction.

The left side of Schedule M-1 contains items the corporation adds back to book income. These items include the following categories:

- Federal income tax expense (per books)
- Excess of capital losses over capital gains

▶ Income subject to tax but not recorded on the books in the current year

▶ Expenses recorded on the books but not deductible for tax purposes in the current year

The right side of the schedule contains items the corporation deducts from book income. These items include the following categories:

▶ Income recorded on the books in the current year that is not taxable in the current year

▶ Deductions or losses claimed in the tax return that do not reduce book income in the current year

These categorizations, however, do not distinguish between permanent and temporary differences as does Schedule M-3 discussed below. The following example illustrates a Schedule M-1 reconciliation.

EXAMPLE C:3-51 ▶ Valley Corporation reports the following items for book and tax purposes in its first year of operations (Year 1):

	Book	Tax	Difference
Gross receipts	$1,500,000	$1,500,000	
Minus: Cost of goods sold	(550,000)	(550,000)	
Gross profit from operations	$ 950,000	$ 950,000	
Plus: Dividends from less than 20%-owned corporations	10,000	10,000	
Tax-exempt income	3,000	–0–	$ (3,000)
Prepaid rental income	–0–	8,000	8,000
Minus: Operating expenses	(300,000)	(300,000)	
Depreciation	(60,000)	(170,000)	(110,000)
Bad debt expense	(25,000)	(16,000)	9,000
Business interest expense	(75,000)	(75,000)	
Insurance premiums on life for key employee (Valley is the beneficiary)	(2,800)	–0–	2,800
Net capital loss disallowed for tax purposes	(12,000)	–0–	12,000
U.S. production activities deduction (rounded)	–0–	(35,000)	(35,000)
Net income before federal income taxes	$ 488,200		
Taxable income before special deductions		$ 372,000	
Minus: Federal income tax expense per books	(151,640)	–0–	151,640
Dividends-received deduction	–0–	(7,000)	(7,000)
Net income per books / Taxable income	$ 336,560	$ 365,000	
Federal tax liability ($365,000 × 0.34)		$ 124,100	
Effective tax rate ($151,640/$488,200)	31.06%		

Valley's Schedule M-1 reconciliation appears in Figure C:3-5.[59] ◀

BOOK-TO-TAX COMPARISON

Schedules M-1 and M-3 adjustments highlight the fact that financial accounting and tax accounting differ in many ways. A review of Schedule M-1 or M-3 is an excellent way to compare the financial accounting and tax accounting differences in a corporation.

Schedule M-3 (of Form 1120). Schedule M-3 requires extensive detail in its reconciliation. Moreover, the schedule has the corporation distinguish between its permanent and temporary differences. The schedule contains three parts. Part I adjusts worldwide income per books to worldwide book income for only includible corporations. As described in Chapter C:8, some corporations may be included in the financial statement consolidation that might be excluded from the tax consolidated tax return. This resulting figure is then reconciled to taxable income before special deductions (again Line 28 of Form 1120). Part II enumerates the corporation's income and loss items, and Part III enumerates the expense and deduction items. The total items from Part III carry over to Part II for the final reconciliation. Both Parts II and III contain the following four columns: (a) book items, (b) temporary differences, (c) permanent differences, and (d) tax items.

[59] A worksheet for converting book income to taxable income for a sample Form 1120 return is provided in Appendix B with that return.

1	Net income (loss) per books	336,560	7	Income recorded on books this year not included on this return (itemize):	
2	Federal income tax per books	151,640	a	Tax-exempt interest $ 3,000	
3	Excess of capital losses over capital gains	12,000	b	Other (itemize):	
4	Income subject to tax not recorded on books this year (itemize): Prepaid rent	8,000			3,000
5	Expenses recorded on books this year not deducted on this return (itemize):		8	Deductions on this return not charged against book income this year (itemize):	
a	Depreciation $		a	Depreciation $ 110,000	
b	Charitable contributions $		b	Charitable contributions $	
c	Travel and entertainment $		c	Other (itemize): U.S. prod. act. ded. 35,000	
d	Other (itemize): Bad debt expense 9,000 Premiums on life insurance 2,800	11,800			145,000
			9	Add lines 7 and 8	148,000
6	Add lines 1 through 5	520,000	10	Income—line 6 less line 9	372,000

FIGURE C:3-5 ▶ VALLEY CORPORATION'S FORM 1120 SCHEDULE M-1 (EXAMPLE C:3-51)

Appendix B provides an example of Schedule M-3 using the data from Example C:3-51. Valley Corporation in that example is too small to be required to use Schedule M-3 although it may elect to do so. Nevertheless, that data is used to allow for comparison of Schedules M-1 and M-3. Note that Lines 1 and 2 of Schedule M-3, Part III, break the $151,640 federal income tax expense into its current and deferred components. In this example, the current expense ties to the current tax liability ($124,100), and the deferred expense ties to the change in net deferred tax liabilities and assets arising from temporary differences, specifically, depreciation, net capital loss, prepaid rent, and bad debt expense [$27,540 = 0.34 × ($110,000 − $12,000 − $8,000 − $9,000)]. These temporary differences appear in Column b of Schedule M-3, Parts II and III.

BOOK-TO-TAX ACCOUNTING COMPARISON

Schedule M-2 requires an analysis of a corporation's retained earnings. Retained earnings is a financial accounting number that has little relevance to tax accounting. A more relevant analysis for tax purposes is one of current and accumulated earnings and profits (E&P). If a corporation distributes more than its E&P, the excess is a nondividend distribution. In this case, the corporation must file Form 5452, Corporate Report of Nondividend Distributions, which requires an analysis of E&P along with other supporting information.

Schedule M-2 (of Form 1120). Schedule M-2 of Form 1120 requires an analysis of changes in unappropriated retained earnings from the beginning of the year to the end of the year. The schedule supplies the IRS with information regarding dividends paid during the year and any special transactions that caused a change in retained earnings for the year.

Schedule M-2 starts with the balance in the unappropriated retained earnings account at the beginning of the year. The following items, which must be added to the beginning balance amount, are listed on the left side of the schedule:

- Net income per books
- Other increases (e.g., refund of federal income taxes paid in a prior year taken directly to the retained earnings account instead of used to reduce federal income tax expense)

The following items, which must be deducted from the beginning balance amount, are listed on the right side of the schedule:

- Dividends (e.g., cash or property)
- Other decreases (e.g., appropriation of retained earnings made during the tax year)

The result is the amount of unappropriated retained earnings at the end of the year.

EXAMPLE C:3-52 ▶ In the current year, Beta Corporation reports net income and other capital account items as follows:

Unappropriated retained earnings, January 1, current year	$400,000
Net income	350,000
Federal income tax refund for capital loss carryback	15,000
Cash dividends paid in the current year	250,000
Unappropriated retained earnings, December 31, current year	515,000

Beta Corporation's Schedule M-2 appears in Figure C:3-6. ◀

Topic Review C:3-2 summarizes the requirements for paying the taxes due and filing the corporate tax return.

Schedule M-2 **Analysis of Unappropriated Retained Earnings per Books**

1	Balance at beginning of year	400,000	5	Distributions: a Cash	250,000
2	Net income (loss) per books	350,000		b Stock	
3	Other increases (itemize):			c Property	
			6	Other decreases (itemize):	
	Federal tax refund	15,000	7	Add lines 5 and 6	250,000
4	Add lines 1, 2, and 3	765,000	8	Balance at end of year (line 4 less line 7)	515,000

FIGURE C:3-6 ► BETA CORPORATION'S FORM 1120 SCHEDULE M-2 (EXAMPLE C:3-52)

FINANCIAL STATEMENT IMPLICATIONS

OBJECTIVE 7

Determine the financial statement implications of corporate federal income taxes

The book-tax differences discussed on pages C:3-39 and C:3-40 have implications not only for preparing the reconciliation Schedules M-1 and M-3 but also affect how a firm's financial statements present income taxes. Income taxes impact both the income statement and balance sheet. For example, the tax section of the income statement might appear as follows:

Net income before federal income taxes
Minus: Federal income tax expense
Net income

Moreover, the **income tax expense** (also called the total tax provision) usually breaks down into a current component and a deferred component. The current component ties into the taxes payable for the current year, and the deferred component arises from book-tax temporary differences. The income tax expense also can contain state and foreign tax components. For this textbook, however, we focus primarily on federal income taxes. Financial statements usually publish details concerning its tax provision in a footnote to the financial statements. Temporary differences also create **deferred tax liabilities** and **deferred tax assets,** which appear on the balance sheet.

The primary standard that dictates financial statement treatment is Accounting Standards Codification (ASC) 740, issued by the Financial Accounting Standards Board (FASB). This section first describes the basic principles of ASC 740 and then presents a comprehensive example to demonstrate its application.

TOPIC REVIEW C:3-2

Requirements for Paying Taxes Due and Filing Tax Returns

1. Estimated Tax Requirement
   a. Corporations that expect to owe more than $500 in tax for the current year must pay four installments of estimated tax, each equal to 25% of its required annual payment.
   b. Taxes for which estimated payments are required of a C corporation include regular tax and alternative minimum tax, minus any tax credits.
   c. If a corporation is not a large corporation, its required annual payment is the lesser of 100% of the tax shown on the current year's return or 100% of the tax shown on the preceding year's return.
   d. If a corporation is a large corporation, its required annual payment is 100% of the tax shown on the current year's return. Its first estimated tax payment may be based on the preceding year's tax liability, but any shortfall must be made up when the second installment is due.
   e. Special rules apply if the corporation bases its estimated tax payments on the annualized income or adjusted seasonal income method.
2. Filing Requirements
   a. For tax years beginning after 2015, the corporate tax return is due by the fifteenth day of the fourth month after the end of the tax year (fifteenth day of the third month for corporations whose tax year ends on June 30, and begins before 2026).
   b. A corporate taxpayer may request an automatic six-month extension to file its tax return (but not to pay its tax due). For corporations with taxable years ending on June 30 (and beginning before 2026), the extension is seven months.

SCOPE, OBJECTIVES, AND PRINCIPLES OF ASC 740

ASC 740 establishes principles of accounting for current income taxes and for deferred taxes arising from temporary differences. Specifically, ASC 740 addresses the financial statement consequences of the following events:

- Revenues, expenses, gains, or losses recognized for tax purposes in an earlier or later year than recognized for financial statement purposes
- Other events that create differences between book and tax bases of assets and liabilities
- Operating loss and tax credit carrybacks or carryforwards

ASC 740 sets out two objectives: (1) to recognize current year taxes payable or refundable and (2) to recognize deferred tax liabilities and assets for the future tax consequences of events recognized in a firm's financial statements or tax return. To implement these objectives, ASC 740 applies the following principles:

- Recognize a current tax liability or asset for taxes payable or refundable on current year tax returns
- Recognize a deferred tax liability or asset for future tax effects attributable to temporary differences and carryforwards
- Measure current and deferred tax liabilities and assets using only enacted tax law, not anticipated future changes
- Reduce deferred tax assets by the amount of tax benefits the firm does not expect to realize, based on available evidence and adjusted via a valuation allowance
- Establish a liability for uncertain tax positions if necessary

Interestingly, the only comment ASC 740 makes about permanent differences is that "[s]ome events do not have tax consequences. Certain revenues are exempt from taxation and certain expenses are not deductible." In this context, ASC 740 does not mention certain events that do have tax consequences but, nevertheless, create permanent differences, for example, the dividends-received deduction and the U.S. production activities deduction. As we show later, permanent differences do not affect deferred taxes, but they do impact the firm's effective tax rate.

TEMPORARY DIFFERENCES

Similarly to the discussion on pages C:3-39 and C:3-40, the following lists describe events that generate (1) taxable temporary differences and thus deferred tax liabilities and (2) deductible temporary differences and thus deferred tax assets. Deferred tax liabilities and assets appear on a firm's balance sheet.

Taxable temporary differences and deferred tax liabilities occur when:

- Revenue or gains are recognized earlier for book purposes than for tax purposes
- Expenses or losses are deductible earlier for tax purposes than for book purposes
- Tax basis of an asset is less than its book basis
- Tax basis of a liability exceeds its book basis

Deductible temporary differences and deferred tax assets occur when:

- Revenue or gains are recognized earlier for tax purposes than for book purposes
- Expenses or losses are deductible earlier for book purposes than for tax purposes
- Tax basis of an asset exceeds its book basis
- Tax basis of a liability is less than its book basis
- Operating loss or tax credit carryforwards exist

DEFERRED TAX ASSETS AND THE VALUATION ALLOWANCE

A deferred tax asset indicates that a firm will realize the tax benefit of an event some time in the future. For example, if the firm generates a net operating loss in the current year and, for tax purposes carries the loss forward, the firm will realize a tax benefit only if it earns sufficient future income to use the carryover before it expires. If the firm likely will not realize the entire tax benefit, it must record a **valuation allowance** to reflect the unrealizable portion. The valuation allowance is a contra-type account that reduces the deferred tax asset.

EXAMPLE C:3-53 ▶ Delta Corporation's NOL carryover is $200,000, and it expects to realize (deduct) the entire carryover at a 34% tax rate. Thus, Delta's deferred tax asset is $68,000 ($200,000 × 0.34), and it makes the following book journal entry:

Deferred tax asset	68,000	
Deferred federal income tax expense (benefit)		68,000

Consequently, the deferred tax asset reduces the income tax expense or creates an income tax benefit.

If Delta determines that it likely will realize (deduct) only $150,000 of the NOL carryover, it must record a $17,000 ($50,000 × 0.34) valuation allowance. Accordingly, Delta makes the following book journal entry:

Deferred tax asset	68,000	
Valuation allowance		17,000
Deferred federal income tax expense (benefit)		51,000

◀

ASC 740 specifically states that a deferred tax asset must be reduced by a valuation allowance if, based on the weight of evidence available, the firm *more likely than not* will fail to realize the benefit of the deferred tax asset. For this purpose, the term *more likely than not* means a greater than 50% likelihood. In assessing this likelihood, a firm must consider both negative and positive evidence, where negative evidence leads toward establishing a valuation allowance while positive evidence helps avoid a valuation allowance. ASC 740 lists several examples of each type of evidence. Examples of negative evidence include the following items:

- Cumulative losses in recent years
- A history of expiring loss or credit carryforwards
- Expected losses in the near future
- Unfavorable contingencies with future adverse effects
- Short carryback or carryover periods that might limit realization of the deferred tax asset

Examples of positive evidence include the following items:

- Existing contracts or sales backlogs that will produce sufficient income to realize the deferred tax asset
- Excess of appreciated asset value over tax basis (i.e., built-in gain) sufficient to realize the deferred tax asset
- A strong earnings history aside from the event causing the deferred tax asset along with evidence that the event is an aberration

In essence, a firm can realize a deferred tax asset when it has sufficient taxable income to offset the reversal of the underlying deductible temporary differences. ASC 740 suggests the following potential sources of such income:

- Future reversals of taxable temporary differences (and deferred tax liabilities)
- Future taxable income other than reversing taxable temporary differences (and deferred tax liabilities)
- Taxable income in carryback years assuming the tax law allows a carryback
- Taxable income from prudent and feasible tax planning strategies that a firm ordinarily would not take but nevertheless would pursue to realize an otherwise expiring deferred tax asset

ACCOUNTING FOR UNCERTAIN TAX POSITIONS

ADDITIONAL COMMENT

This financial statement standard used to be referred to as FIN 48, a pre-codification designation. Many practitioners, however, still use the FIN 48 terminology.

ASC 740 also prescribes acceptable accounting for uncertain tax positions. This standard addresses the following basic situation: For tax purposes, a firm may take a position in claiming a tax benefit that might not be sustained under IRS scrutiny. The FASB, however, believes that, for determining the financial statement tax provision, such uncertain tax positions either should not be recognized or should be recognized only partially.

REAL-WORLD EXAMPLE

The IRS has developed Schedule UTP for inclusion in Form 1120. This schedule requires certain taxpayers to provide information about their uncertain tax positions. The required information will provide the IRS a road map for auditing the tax return.

In applying the tax position standard, a firm takes a two-step approach. First, the firm determines whether the tax position has a *more likely than not* (greater than 50%) probability of being sustained upon an IRS examination. This determination requires substantial judgment and necessitates careful documentation for the financial statement audit and any IRS examination. If the tax position does not exceed this threshold, the firm cannot recognize the tax benefit for financial reporting purposes until one of the following three events occur:

- ▶ The position subsequently meets the *more likely than not* threshold.
- ▶ The firm favorably settles the tax issue with the IRS or in court.
- ▶ The statute of limitations on the transaction expires.

If the firm determines that a tax position meets the *more like than not* threshold, it then must measure the amount of benefit it can recognize for financial reporting purposes. This measure is the largest amount of tax benefit that exceeds a 50% probability of realization upon settlement with the taxing authorities. Further details of this measurement process and other procedures under the tax position standard become quite complex and are beyond the scope of this textbook.

EXAMPLE C:3-54 ▶ Lambda Corporation claims a $1 million deduction on its tax return, which provides a $350,000 tax savings, assuming a 35% tax rate. After some analysis and judgment, management determines the deduction has only a 45% chance of being allowed should the IRS audit Lambda's tax return. Assume for simplicity that Lambda has no deferred tax assets or liabilities. Assume further that Lambda's pretax book income and taxable income equal $20 million after taking the $1 million deduction. Thus, Lambda's tax liability is $7 million. Under the tax position standard, Lambda makes the following journal entry (ignoring potential penalties and interest):

Current federal income tax expense	7,350,000	
Liability for unrecognized tax benefits		350,000
Federal income taxes payable		7,000,000

Suppose in a subsequent period Lambda negotiates a settlement with the IRS that allows $200,000 of the deduction, and Lambda pays $280,000 tax on the $800,000 disallowed portion. Ignoring penalties and interest, Lambda would make the following journal entry:

Liability for unrecognized tax benefits	350,000	
Cash		280,000
Current federal income tax expense (benefit)		70,000

◀

EXAMPLE C:3-55 ▶ Assume the same facts as in Example C:3-54 except Lambda meets the *more likely than not* threshold. Lambda then measures the benefit more than 50% likely to be realized as $600,000 of the $1 million deduction taken. Thus, Lambda may not recognize $400,000 in determining its federal income tax expense for financial reporting purposes and, accordingly, makes the following journal entry:

Current federal income tax expense	7,140,000	
Liability for unrecognized tax benefits		140,000
Federal income taxes payable		7,000,000

◀

BALANCE SHEET CLASSIFICATION

Prior to a recent FASB accounting standards update, deferred tax assets and liabilities had to be classified as current or noncurrent depending on the related asset, liability, or expected reversal date. The update simplifies the classification rules by requiring that all deferred tax assets and liabilities be presented in financial statements as noncurrent. The change is effective for annual periods beginning after December 15, 2016, for public entities and for annual periods beginning after December 15, 2017, for other entities. The update, however, allows entities to adopt the changes earlier than these dates. Accordingly, this textbook will conform to the updated rules and, for brevity, will refer only to deferred tax assets and deferred tax liabilities without the noncurrent designation attached to the terms. Nevertheless, the noncurrent status should be considered implied in the abbreviated terms. For financial statement presentation, the accounting standard also requires that deferred tax liabilities and assets (as well as any related valuation allowance) be netted and presented as a single (noncurrent) amount for each taxing jurisdiction.

TAX PROVISION PROCESS

The following steps outline the approach used in this chapter to provide for income taxes in the financial statements. This process addresses only federal income taxes.

ADDITIONAL COMMENT

Determining the valuation allowance and uncertain tax position adjustments requires a great deal of professional judgment.

1. Identify temporary differences by comparing the book and tax bases of assets and liabilities, and identify tax carryforwards.
2. Prepare "roll forward" schedules of temporary differences that tabulate cumulative differences and current-year changes.
3. In the roll forward schedules, apply the appropriate statutory tax rates to determine the ending balances of deferred tax assets and liabilities.
4. Adjust deferred tax assets by a valuation allowance if necessary.
5. Adjust the income tax expense for uncertain tax positions if necessary.
6. Determine current federal income taxes payable, which, in many cases, also is the current federal income tax expense for book purposes.
7. Determining the total federal income tax expense (benefit).
8. Prepare and record tax related journal entries.
9. Prepare a tax provision reconciliation.
10. Prepare the tax rate reconciliation.
11. Prepare financial statements.

In practice, various firms may use different approaches. For this chapter, however, the above steps provide a logical and systematic approach.

ADDITIONAL COMMENT

The format used in this example is a basic framework. Each firm preparing or reviewing the tax provision will have its own workpaper format for this process.

COMPREHENSIVE EXAMPLE – YEAR 1

To provide comprehensiveness, this example continues with the facts set forth in Example C:3-51. Thus, when completed, the two examples together provide the financial statement implications of federal income taxes as well as the tax return reporting in Schedules M-1 and M-3 for Year 1. We then continue the example with events occurring in Year 2.

In addition to the facts stated in Example C:3-51, Valley reports the following book and tax balance sheet items at the end of Year 1, prior to adjustment for tax related items. Step 11 below presents the completed book balance sheet after making tax related journal entries.

Assets:	*Book*	*Tax*	*Difference*
Cash	$ 230,200	$ 230,200	
Accounts receivable	300,000	300,000	
Minus: Allowance for bad debts	(9,000)	–0–	
Net accounts receivable	291,000	300,000	$ 9,000
Investment in corporate stock	90,000	90,000	
Investment in tax-exempt bonds	50,000	50,000	
Inventory	500,000	500,000	
Fixed assets	1,200,000	1,200,000	
Minus: Accumulated depreciation	(60,000)	(170,000)	
Net fixed assets	1,140,000	1,030,000	110,000
Liabilities and stock equity:			
Accounts payable	225,000	225,000	
Unearned rental income	8,000	–0–	8,000
Long-term liabilities	930,000	930,000	
Common stock	650,000	650,000	

Steps 1 through 3.
The book and tax balance sheets on the previous page indicate the items where the book and tax bases differ, thereby indicating temporary differences. In addition, the facts from Example C:3-51 indicates a nondeductible net capital loss, which creates a capital loss carryover.

The following two roll forward schedules calculate the deferred tax assets and deferred tax liability associated with these temporary differences. The beginning and ending balances for the balance sheet items reflect the differences between the book and tax bases for these assets and liabilities. The first schedule also reflects changes in the capital loss carryover.

Deferred tax asset:	*Beg. of Year 1*	*End of Year 1*	*Change*
Net accounts receivable	$ –0–	$ 9,000	$ 9,000
Unearned rental income	–0–	8,000	8,000
Capital loss carryover	–0–	12,000	12,000
Total	$ –0–	$ 29,000	$ 29,000
Times: Tax rate	0.34	0.34	
Deferred tax asset	$ –0–	$ 9,860	$ 9,860

Deferred tax liability:	*Beg. of Year 1*	*End of Year 1*	*Change*
Net fixed assets	$ –0–	$110,000	$110,000
Times: Tax rate	0.34	0.34	
Deferred tax liability	$ –0–	$ 37,400	$ 37,400

The amounts in the change column also appear as book-tax differences in the book and tax income schedules in Example C:3-51. In those schedules, the differences occur in the related income or expense accounts, specifically, bad debt expense, prepaid rental income, and depreciation.

One last aspect of these schedules needs mentioning. Specifically, the changes in the deferred tax assets and liabilities also represent the deferred federal tax expense or benefit for the current year. See Step 7 below.

Step 4.
Assuming evidence supports that Valley will realize the entire amount of its deferred tax assets, Valley need not establish a valuation allowance.

Step 5.
Assume that Valley requires no adjustments for uncertain tax positions.

Step 6.
As provided in Example C:3-51, current federal income taxes payable is $124,100. In this example, the current payable amount also is the current federal income tax expense for book purposes. (The equality of the current payable amount and the federal income tax expense may not occur, however, under some uncertain tax position situations and in other special circumstances.)

Step 7.
The net deferred federal tax expense from the roll forward schedules equals $27,540 ($37,400 – $5,780 – $4,080). Therefore, the total federal income tax expense for this year can be calculated as shown on the next page:

Current federal income tax expense	$124,100
Deferred income tax expense	27,540
Total federal income tax expense	$151,640

Step 8.
Given the amounts determined in previous steps, Valley makes the following book journal entry:

Current federal income tax expense	124,100	
Deferred federal income tax expense	27,540	
Deferred tax asset	9,860	
Deferred tax liability		37,400
Federal income taxes payable		124,100

Also, Valley could make the following combined book journal entry for financial statement presentation:

Total federal income tax expense	151,640	
Net deferred tax liability (37,400 − 9,860)		27,540
Federal income taxes payable		124,100

ADDITIONAL COMMENT

In practice, this reconciliation can be much more complex than the one shown here. For example, changes in the valuation allowance and in the liability for unrecognized tax benefits (both discussed later) can complicate the analysis, as can tax credits. Note also that the permanent difference part of the provision reconciliation ties into the tax rate reconciliation shown in Step 10 below.

Step 9.
As a cross check on the previous steps, Valley can prepare the following tax provision reconciliation:

Net income before federal income taxes (FIT)	$488,200
Permanent differences:	
Nondeductible insurance premiums	2,800
Tax-exempt income	(3,000)
U.S. production activities deduction	(35,000)
Dividends-received deduction	(7,000)
Net income after permanent differences	$446,000
Temporary differences:	
Unearned rental income	8,000
Net capital loss disallowed for tax	12,000
Net accounts receivable (bad debt expense)	9,000
Net fixed assets (depreciation)	(110,000)
Taxable income	$365,000

ADDITIONAL COMMENT

This approach and the balance sheet approach may not always lead to the same result when enacted tax rates change, in some situations involving uncertain tax positions, and in other special circumstances.

Assuming no enacted change in future tax rates, net income after permanent differences times the tax rate results in the total federal income tax expense. Specifically, $446,000 × 0.34 = $151,640. Similarly, taxable income times the tax rate results in current federal income taxes payable. Specifically, $365,000 × 0.34 = $124,100.

ADDITIONAL COMMENT

Remember that we are looking only at federal income taxes in these examples. Foreign, state, and local taxes also can affect a firm's total effective tax rate. For example, if the firm had a 5% effective state income tax rate and a 34% statutory federal income tax rate, the reconciling item would be 3.3% [5% × (1 − 0.34)].

Step 10.
A firm's effective tax rate is its income tax expense divided by its pretax book income. Because the income tax expense is based on net income after adjustment for permanent differences (see Step 9), these differences cause a firm's effective tax rate to differ from the statutory tax rate. In the footnotes to financial statements, firms reconcile the statutory tax rate to their effective tax rate. Accordingly, Valley's effective tax rate reconciliation is as follows:

Statutory tax rate	34.00%
Nondeductible insurance premiums ($2,800/$488,200 × 34%)	0.20%
Tax-exempt income [($3,000)/$488,200 × 34%]	(0.21)%
U.S. production activities deduction [($35,000)/$488,200 × 34%]	(2.44)%
Dividends-received deduction [($7,000)/$488,200 × 34%]	(0.49)%
Effective tax rate ($151,640/$488,200)	31.06%

In practice, a firm would not disclose the detail shown here but would aggregate small percentage amounts into an "other" category. Also, if the enacted future tax rate changes, that change also would be reflected in this schedule.

Step 11.
At this point, Valley can complete its financial statements. The income statement appears in Example C:3-51, but the tax portion is repeated here.

Partial income statement:	
Net income before federal income taxes	$488,200
Minus: Federal income tax expense	(151,640)
Net income	$336,560
Effective tax rate ($151,640/$488,200)	31.06%

As shown in Step 7, the total federal income tax expense has two components as follows:

Current federal income tax expense	$124,100
Deferred income tax expense	27,540
Total federal income tax expense	$151,640

The book balance sheet for Year 1 is as follows:

Assets:		
Cash		$ 230,200
Accounts receivable	$ 300,000	
Minus: Allowance for bad debts	(9,000)	291,000
Investment in corporate stock		90,000
Investment in tax-exempt bond		50,000
Inventory		500,000
Fixed assets	$1,200,000	
Minus: Accumulated depreciation	(60,000)	1,140,000
Total assets		$2,301,200
Liabilities and equity:		
Accounts payable		$ 225,000
Unearned rental income		8,000
Federal income taxes payable		124,100
Net deferred tax liability ($37,400 − $9,860)		27,540
Long-term liabilities		930,000
Common stock		650,000
Retained earnings		336,560
Total liabilities and equity		$2,301,200

ADDITIONAL COMMENT

This example ignores estimated tax payments, so that the entire amount of federal income taxes payable appears on the balance sheet.

COMPREHENSIVE EXAMPLE – YEAR 2

Valley reports the following book and tax balance sheet items at the end of Year 2, prior to adjustment for tax related items. Pertinent to the temporary differences, in Year 2 Valley earned the rental income that was prepaid in Year 1 and did not collect additional amounts. It also adjusted its allowance for bad debts and claimed additional depreciation on fixed assets. It did not recognize any capital gains to offset the capital loss carryover. Step 11 below presents the completed book balance sheet after making tax related journal entries.

Assets:	*Book*	*Tax*	*Difference*
Cash	$ 318,800	$ 318,800	
Accounts receivable	400,000	400,000	
Allowance for bad debts	(37,000)	–0–	
Net accounts receivable	363,000	400,000	$ 37,000
Investment in corporate stock	90,000	90,000	
Investment in tax-exempt bonds	50,000	50,000	
Inventory	600,000	600,000	
Fixed assets	1,200,000	1,200,000	
Accumulated depreciation	(180,000)	(465,000)	
Net fixed assets	1,020,000	735,000	285,000
Liabilities and stock equity:			
Accounts payable	295,000	295,000	
Unearned rental income	–0–	–0–	
Long-term liabilities	530,000	530,000	
Common stock	650,000	650,000	

Valley also reports the following book income statement through net income before federal income taxes and tax return schedule through taxable income. The tax portion of the book income statement appears in Step 11.

	Book	*Tax*	*Difference*
Gross receipts	$2,000,000	$2,000,000	
Minus: Cost of goods sold	(700,000)	(700,000)	
Gross profit from operations	$1,300,000	$1,300,000	
Plus: Dividends from less than 20%-owned corporations	15,000	15,000	
Tax-exempt income	3,200	–0–	$ (3,200)
Prepaid rental income	8,000	–0–	(8,000)
Minus: Operating expenses	(500,000)	(500,000)	
Depreciation	(120,000)	(295,000)	(175,000)
Bad debt expense	(40,000)	(12,000)	28,000
Business interest expense	(60,000)	(60,000)	
Insurance premiums on life insurance for key employee (Valley is the beneficiary)	(3,500)	–0–	3,500
U.S. production activities deduction (rounded)	–0–	(39,000)	(39,000)
Dividends-received deduction	–0–	(10,500)	(10,500)
Net income before federal income taxes	$ 602,700		
Taxable income		$ 398,500	

Steps 1 through 3.

The book and tax balance sheets above indicate the items where the book and tax bases differ, thereby indicating temporary differences. In addition, the net capital loss carryforward remains unused.

The following two roll forward schedules calculate the deferred tax assets and deferred tax liability associated with these temporary differences. The beginning and ending balances for the balance sheet items reflect the differences between the book and tax bases for these assets and liabilities. In the first schedule, the net accounts receivable temporary difference increases, and the unearned rental income item reverses. Also, in the first schedule, Valley has not realized the deferred tax asset related to the capital loss carryover because it recognized no capital gains in Year 2. Therefore, this deferred tax asset has not yet reversed. In the second schedule, the fixed asset temporary difference increases.

Deferred tax asset:	*Beg. of Year 2*	*End of Year 2*	*Change*
Net accounts receivable	$ 9,000	$ 37,000	$ 28,000
Unearned rental income	8,000	–0–	(8,000)
Capital loss carryover	12,000	12,000	–0–
Total	$ 29,000	$ 49,000	$ 20,000
Times: Tax rate	0.34	0.34	
Deferred tax asset	$ 9,860	$ 16,660	$ 6,800

Deferred tax liability:	*Beg. of Year 2*	*End of Year 2*	*Change*
Net fixed assets	$110,000	$285,000	$175,000
Times: Tax rate	0.34	0.34	
Deferred tax liability	$ 37,400	$ 96,900	$ 59,500

The amounts in the change column also appear as book-tax differences in the above book and tax income schedules. In those schedules, the differences occur in the related income or expense accounts, specifically, bad debt expense, prepaid rental income, and depreciation.

As before, the changes in the deferred tax assets and liabilities also represent the deferred federal tax expense or benefit for the current year. See Step 7 below.

ADDITIONAL COMMENT

If a firm has reversing taxable differences in an amount equal to or exceeding reversing deductible temporary differences, the firm can be fairly certain that it can realize the benefit of its deferred tax assets, which is the case in this example as indicated by the firm having a net deferred tax liability.

Step 4.
Assuming evidence supports that Valley still will realize the entire amount of its deferred tax assets, Valley need not establish a valuation allowance.

Step 5.
Assume again that Valley requires no adjustments for uncertain tax positions.

Step 6.
As provided in the schedule above, taxable income is $398,500. Therefore, current federal income taxes payable is $135,490 ($398,500 × 0.34). In this example, the current payable amount also is the current federal income tax expense for book purposes. (The equality of the current payable amount and the federal income tax expense may not occur, however, under some uncertain tax position situations and in other special circumstances.)

Step 7.
The net deferred federal tax expense from the roll forward schedules equals $52,700 ($59,500 − $6,800). Therefore, the total federal income tax expense for this year can be calculated as follows:

Current federal income tax expense	$135,490
Deferred income tax expense	52,700
Total federal income tax expense	$188,190

Step 8.
Given the amounts determined in previous steps, Valley makes the following book journal entry:

Current federal income tax expense	135,490	
Deferred federal income tax expense	52,700	
Deferred tax asset	6,800	
Deferred tax liability		59,500
Federal income taxes payable		135,490

Also, Valley could make the following combined book journal entry:

Total federal income tax expense	188,190	
Net deferred tax liability		52,700
Federal income taxes payable		135,490

ADDITIONAL COMMENT

In practice, this reconciliation can be much more complex than the one shown here. For example, changes in the valuation allowance and in the liability for unrecognized tax benefits (both discussed later) can complicate the analysis, as can tax credits. Note also that the permanent difference part of the provision reconciliation ties into the tax rate reconciliation shown in Step 10 below.

Step 9.

As a cross check on the previous steps, Valley can prepare the following tax provision reconciliation:

Net income before federal income taxes (FIT)	$602,700
Permanent differences:	
Nondeductible insurance premiums	3,500
Tax-exempt income	(3,200)
U.S. production activities deduction	(39,000)
Dividends-received deduction	(10,500)
Net income after permanent differences	$553,500
Temporary differences:	
Unearned rental income	(8,000)
Net accounts receivable (bad debt expense)	28,000
Net fixed assets (depreciation)	(175,000)
Taxable income	$398,500

ADDITIONAL COMMENT

This approach and the balance sheet approach may not always lead to the same result when enacted tax rates change, in some situations involving uncertain tax positions, and in other special circumstances.

Assuming no enacted change in future tax rates, net income after permanent differences times the tax rate results in the total federal income tax expense. Specifically, $553,500 × 0.34 = $188,190. Similarly, taxable income times the tax rate results in current federal income taxes payable. Specifically, $398,500 × 0.34 = $135,490.

Step 10.

Valley's Year 2 effective tax rate is its income tax expense divided by its pretax book income, or $188,190/$602,700 = 31.23% (rounded up). Accordingly, Valley's effective tax rate reconciliation is as follows:

Statutory tax rate	34.00%
Nondeductible insurance premiums ($3,500/$602,700 × 34%)	0.20%
Tax-exempt income [($3,200)/$602,700 × 34%]	(0.18)%
U.S. production activities deduction [($39,000)/$602,700 × 34%]	(2.20)%
Dividends-received deduction [($10,500)/$602,700 × 34%]	(0.59)%
Effective tax rate ($188,190/$602,700)	31.23%

Step 11.

At this point, Valley can complete its financial statements. The first part of the income statement appears in the schedule appearing before Steps 1 through 3, and the tax portion is as follows:

Partial income statement:	
Net income before federal income taxes	$602,700
Minus: Federal income tax expense	(188,190)
Net income	$414,510
Effective tax rate ($188,190/$602,700)	31.23%

As shown in Step 7, the federal income tax expense has two components as follows:

Current federal income tax expense	$135,490
Deferred income tax expense ($59,500 − $6,800)	52,700
Total federal income tax expense	$188,190

The book balance sheet for Year 2 is as follows:

Assets:		
Cash		$ 318,800
Accounts receivable	$ 400,000	
Minus: Allowance for bad debts	(37,000)	363,000
Investment in corporate stock		90,000
Investment in tax-exempt bond		50,000
Inventory		600,000
Fixed assets	$1,200,000	
Minus: Accumulated depreciation	(180,000)	1,020,000
Total assets		$2,441,800
Liabilities and equity:		
Accounts payable		$ 295,000
Unearned rental income		–0–
Federal income taxes payable		135,490
Net deferred tax liability ($96,900 – $16,660)		80,240
Long-term liabilities		530,000
Common stock		650,000
Retained earnings		751,070
Total liabilities and equity		$2,441,800

ADDITIONAL COMMENT

This example ignores estimated tax payments, so the entire amount of federal income taxes payable appears on the balance sheet.

OTHER TRANSACTIONS

Chapters C:5, C:7, C:8, and C:16 describe the financial statement implications of other transactions, for example, the alternative minimum tax (Chapter C:5), corporate acquisitions (Chapter C:7), intercompany transactions (Chapter C:8), and the foreign tax credit and deferred foreign earnings (Chapter C:16). Also, Problem C:3-64 provides a comprehensive tax return and financial accounting exercise.

PROBLEM MATERIALS

DISCUSSION QUESTIONS

C:3-1 High Corporation incorporates on May 1 and begins business on May 10 of the current year. What alternative tax years can High elect to report its initial year's income?

C:3-2 Port Corporation wants to change its tax year from a calendar year to a fiscal year ending June 30. Port is a C corporation owned by 100 shareholders, none of whom own more than 5% of the stock. Can Port change its tax year? If so, how can it accomplish the change?

C:3-3 Stan and Susan, two calendar year taxpayers, are starting a new business to manufacture and sell digital circuits. They intend to incorporate the business with $600,000 of their own capital and $2 million of equity capital obtained from other investors. The company expects to incur organizational and start-up expenditures of $100,000 in the first year. Inventories are a material income-producing factor. The company also expects to incur losses of $500,000 in the first two years of operations and substantial research and development expenses during the first three years. The company expects to break even in the third year and be profitable at the end of the fourth year, even though the nature of the digital circuit business will require continual research and development activities. What accounting methods and tax elections must Stan and Susan consider in their first year of operation? For each method and election, explain the possible alternatives and the advantages and disadvantages of each alternative.

C:3-4 Compare the tax treatment of capital gains and losses by a corporation and by an individual.

C:3-5 What are organizational expenditures? How are they treated for tax purposes?

C:3-6 What are start-up expenditures? How are they treated for tax purposes?

C:3-7 Describe three ways in which the treatment of charitable contributions by individual and corporate taxpayers differ.

C:3-8 Carver Corporation uses the accrual method of accounting and the calendar year as its tax year. Its board of directors authorizes a cash contribution on November 3 of Year 1, that the corporation pays on March 9 of Year 2. In what year(s) is it deductible? What happens if the corporation does not pay the contribution until April 20 of Year 2?

C:3-9 Zero Corporation contributes inventory (computers) to State University for use in its mathematics program. The computers have a $1,225 cost basis and a $2,800 FMV. How much is Zero's charitable contribution deduction for the computers? (Ignore the 10% limit.)

C:3-10 Why are corporations allowed a dividends-received deduction? What dividends qualify for this special deduction?

C:3-11 Why is a dividends-received deduction disallowed if the stock on which the corporation pays the dividend is debt-financed?

C:3-12 Crane Corporation incurs a $75,000 NOL in the current year. In which years can Crane use this NOL if it makes no special elections? When might a special election to forgo the carryback of the NOL be beneficial for Crane?

C:3-13 What special restrictions apply to the deduction of a loss realized on the sale of property between a corporation and a shareholder who owns 60% of the corporation's stock? What restrictions apply to the deduction of expenses accrued by a corporation at year-end and owed to a cash method shareholder who owns 60% of the corporation's stock?

C:3-14 Deer Corporation is a C corporation. Its taxable income for the current year is $200,000. What is Deer Corporation's income tax liability for the year?

C:3-15 Budget Corporation is a personal service corporation. Its taxable income for the current year is $75,000. What is Budget's income tax liability for the year?

C:3-16 Describe the three types of controlled groups.

C:3-17 Why do special restrictions on using the progressive corporate tax rates apply to controlled groups of corporations? List five restrictions on claiming multiple tax benefits that apply to controlled groups of corporations.

C:3-18 What are the major advantages and disadvantages of filing a consolidated tax return?

C:3-19 What are the tax advantages of substituting fringe benefits for salary paid to a shareholder-employee?

C:3-20 Explain the tax consequences to both the corporation and a shareholder-employee if an IRS agent determines that a portion of the compensation paid in a prior tax year exceeds a reasonable compensation level.

C:3-21 What is the advantage of a special apportionment plan for the benefits of the 15%, 25%, and 34% tax rates to members of a controlled group?

C:3-22 What corporations must pay estimated taxes? When are the estimated tax payments due?

C:3-23 What is a "large" corporation for purposes of the estimated tax rules? What special rules apply to such large corporations?

C:3-24 What penalties apply to the underpayment of estimated taxes? The late payment of the remaining tax liability?

C:3-25 Describe the situations in which a corporation must file a tax return.

C:3-26 When is a corporate tax return due for a calendar-year taxpayer? What extension(s) of time in which to file the return are available?

C:3-27 List four types of differences that can cause a corporation's book income to differ from its taxable income.

ISSUE IDENTIFICATION QUESTIONS

C:3-28 X-Ray Corporation received a $100,000 dividend from Yancey Corporation this year. X-Ray owns 10% of the Yancey's single class of stock. What tax issues should X-Ray consider with respect to its dividend income?

C:3-29 Williams Corporation sold a truck with an adjusted basis of $100,000 to Barbara for $80,000. Barbara owns 25% of the Williams stock. What tax issues should Williams and Barbara consider with respect to the sale/purchase?

C:3-30 You are the CPA who prepares the tax returns for Don, his wife, Mary, and their two corporations. Don owns 100% of Pencil Corporation's stock. Pencil's current year taxable income is $100,000. Mary owns 100% of Eraser Corporation's stock. Eraser's current year taxable income is $150,000. Don and Mary file a joint federal income tax return. What issues should Don and Mary consider with respect to the calculation of the three tax return liabilities?

C:3-31 Rugby Corporation has a $50,000 NOL in the current year. Rugby's taxable income in each of the previous two years was $25,000. Rugby expects its taxable income for next year to exceed $400,000. What issues should Rugby consider with respect to the use of the NOL?

PROBLEMS

C:3-32 *Depreciation Recapture.* Young Corporation purchased residential real estate several years ago for $225,000, of which $25,000 was allocated to the land and $200,000 was allocated to the building. Young took straight-line MACRS deductions of $30,000 during the years it held the property. In the current year, Young sells the property for $285,000, of which $60,000 is allocated to the land and $225,000 is allocated to the building. What are the amount and character of Young's recognized gain or loss on the sale?

C:3-33 *Depreciation Recapture, Sec. 1231, and Capital Gains and Losses.* Gamma Corporation sold the following property on March 3 of the current year:

	Securities	*Equipment*	*Building*	*Land*
Selling price	$ 65,000	$210,000	$385,000	$175,000
Cost	$100,000	$200,000	$400,000	$190,000
Accumulated depreciation	–0–	(125,000)	(120,000)	–0–
Adjusted basis	$100,000	$ 75,000	$280,000	$190,000
Gain (loss)	$ (35,000)	$135,000	$105,000	$(15,000)

The corporation used the equipment, building, and land in its business and has held all the property for more than one year. Aside from these transactions, Gamma had $720,000 of operating net income during the current year. Gamma has a $24,000 nonrecaptured Sec. 1231 loss from prior years. Determine the character of the gains and losses, and calculate the corporation's taxable income. Ignore the U.S. production activities deduction.

C:3-34 *Organizational and Start-Up Expenditures.* Delta Corporation incorporates on January 7, begins business on July 10, and elects to have its initial tax year end on October 31. Delta incurs the following expenses between January and October related to its organization during the current year:

Date	*Expenditure*	*Amount*
January 30	Travel to investigate potential business site	$2,000
May 15	Legal expenses to draft corporate charter	2,500
May 30	Commissions to stockbroker for issuing and selling stock	4,000
May 30	Temporary directors' fees	2,500
June 1	Expense of transferring building to Delta	3,000
June 5	Accounting fees to set up corporate books	1,500
June 10	Training expenses for employees	5,000
June 15	Rent expense for June	1,000
July 15	Rent expense for July	1,000

a. What alternative treatments are available for Delta's expenditures?
b. What amount of organizational expenditures can Delta Corporation deduct on its first tax return for the fiscal year ending October 31?
c. What amount of start-up costs can Delta Corporation deduct on its first tax return?

C:3-35 *Charitable Contribution of Property.* Yellow Corporation donates the following property to the State University:

- ABC Corporation stock purchased two years ago for $18,000. The stock, which trades on a regional stock exchange, has a $25,000 FMV on the contribution date.
- Inventory with a $17,000 adjusted basis and a $22,000 FMV. State will use the inventory for scientific research that qualifies under the special Sec. 170(e)(4) rules.
- An antique vase purchased two years ago for $10,000 and having an $18,000 FMV. State University plans to sell the vase to obtain funds for educational purposes.

Yellow Corporation's taxable income before any charitable contributions deduction, NOL or capital loss carryback, or dividends-received deduction is $300,000.
a. What is Yellow Corporation's charitable contributions deduction for the current year?
b. What is the amount of its charitable contributions carryover (if any)?

C:3-36 *Charitable Contributions of Property.* Blue Corporation donates the following property to Johnson Elementary School:

- XYZ Corporation stock purchased two years ago for $25,000. The stock has a $19,000 FMV on the contribution date.
- ABC Corporation stock purchased three years ago for $2,000. The stock has a $16,000 FMV on the contribution date.
- PQR Corporation stock purchased six months ago for $12,000. The stock has an $18,000 FMV on the contribution date.

The school will sell the stock and use the proceeds to renovate a classroom to be used as a computer laboratory. Blue's taxable income before any charitable contribution deduction, dividends-received deduction, or NOL or capital loss carryback is $400,000.

a. What is Blue's charitable contributions deduction for the current year?
b. What is Blue's charitable contribution carryback or carryover (if any)? In what years can it be used?
c. What would have been a better tax plan concerning the XYZ stock donation?

C:3-37 *Charitable Contribution Deduction Limitation.* Zeta Corporation reports the following results for Year 1 and Year 2:

	Year 1	*Year 2*
Adjusted taxable income	$180,000	$125,000
Charitable contributions (cash)	20,000	12,000

The adjusted taxable income is before Zeta claims any charitable contributions deduction, NOL or capital loss carryback, dividends-received deduction, or U.S. production activities deduction.

a. How much is Zeta's charitable contributions deduction in Year 1? In Year 2?
b. What is Zeta's contribution carryover to Year 3, if any?

C:3-38 *Taxable Income Computation.* Omega Corporation reports the following results for the current year:

Gross profits on sales	$120,000
Dividends from less-than-20%-owned domestic corporations	40,000
Operating expenses	100,000
Charitable contributions (cash)	11,000

a. What is Omega's charitable contributions deduction for the current year and its charitable contributions carryover to next year, if any?
b. What is Omega's taxable income for the current year, assuming qualified production activities income is $20,000?

C:3-39 *Dividends-Received Deduction.* Theta Corporation reports the following results for the current year:

Gross profits on sales	$220,000
Dividends from less-than-20%-owned domestic corporations	100,000
Operating expenses	218,000

a. What is Theta's taxable income for the current year, assuming qualified production activities income is $2,000?
b. How would your answer to Part a change if Theta's operating expenses are instead $234,000, assuming qualified production activities income is zero or negative?
c. How would your answer to Part a change if Theta's operating expenses are instead $252,000, assuming qualified production activities income is zero or negative?
d. How would your answers to Parts a, b, and c change if Theta received $75,000 of the dividends from a 20%-owned corporation and the remaining $25,000 from a less-than-20%-owned corporation?

C:3-40 *Stock Held 45 Days or Less.* Beta Corporation purchased 100 shares of Gamma Corporation common stock (less than 5% of the outstanding stock) two days before the ex-dividend date for $200,000. Beta receives a $10,000 cash dividend from Gamma. Beta sells the Gamma stock one week after purchasing it for $190,000. What are the tax consequences of these three events?

C:3-41 *Debt-Financed Stock.* Cheers Corporation purchased for $500,000 5,000 shares of Beer Corporation common stock (less than 5% of the outstanding Beer stock) at the beginning

of the current year. It used $400,000 of borrowed money and $100,000 of its own cash to make this purchase. Cheers paid $50,000 of interest on the debt this year. Cheers received a $40,000 cash dividend on the Beer stock on September 1 of the current year.
a. What amount can Cheers deduct for the interest paid on the loan?
b. What dividends-received deduction can Cheers claim with respect to the dividend?

C:3-42 *Net Operating Loss Carrybacks and Carryovers.* In 2017, Ace Corporation reports gross income of $200,000 (including $150,000 of profit from its operations and $50,000 in dividends from less-than-20%-owned domestic corporations) and $220,000 of operating expenses. Ace's 2015 taxable income (all ordinary income) was $75,000, on which it paid taxes of $13,750.
a. What is Ace's NOL for 2017?
b. What is the amount of Ace's tax refund if Ace carries back the 2017 NOL to 2015?
c. Assume that Ace expects 2018's taxable income to be $400,000. Ignore the U.S. production activities deduction. What election could Ace make to increase the tax benefit from its NOL? What is the dollar amount of the expected benefit (if any)? Assume a 10% discount rate as a measure of the time value of money.

C:3-43 *Ordering of Deductions.* Beta Corporation reports the following results for the current year:

Gross income from operations	$180,000
Dividends from less-than-20%-owned domestic corporations	100,000
Operating expenses	150,000
Charitable contributions	20,000

In addition, Beta has a $10,000 NOL carryover from the preceding tax year, and its qualified production activities income is $30,000.
a. What is Beta's taxable income for the current year?
b. What carrybacks or carryovers are available to other tax years?

C:3-44 *Sale to a Related Party.* Union Corporation sells a truck for $18,000 to Jane, who owns 70% of its stock. The truck has a $24,000 adjusted basis on the sale date. Jane sells the truck to an unrelated party, Mike, for $28,000 two years later after claiming $5,000 in depreciation.
a. What is Union's realized and recognized gain or loss on selling the truck?
b. What is Jane's realized and recognized gain or loss on selling the truck to Mike?
c. How would your answers to Part b change if Jane instead sold the truck for $10,000?

C:3-45 *Payment to a Cash Basis Employee-Shareholder.* Value Corporation is a calendar year taxpayer that uses the accrual method of accounting. On December 10 of the current year, Value accrues a bonus payment of $100,000 to Brett, its president and sole shareholder. Brett is a calendar year taxpayer who uses the cash method of accounting. When can Value deduct the bonus if it pays it to Brett early next year?

C:3-46 *Capital Gains and Losses.* Western Corporation reports the following results for the current year:

Gross profits on sales	$150,000
Long-term capital gain	8,000
Long-term capital loss	15,000
Short-term capital gain	10,000
Short-term capital loss	2,000
Operating expenses	61,000

a. What are Western's taxable income and income tax liability for the current year, assuming qualified production activities income is $89,000?
b. How would your answers to Part a change if Western's short-term capital loss is $5,000 instead of $2,000?

C:3-47 *Corporate Taxable Income and Tax Liability.* Alpha Corporation has been in business for two years. It incurred the following items last year (Year 1):

Gross profits on sales	$240,000
Operating expenses	100,000
Long-term capital gain	8,000
Short-term capital loss	12,000

Alpha reported the following items this year (Year 2):

Gross profits on sales	$600,000
Operating expenses	165,000
Long-term capital gain	10,000

Assume that qualified production activities income in each year equals gross profit minus operating expenses. Compute Alpha's taxable income and tax liability for Year 1 and Year 2.

C:3-48 *Computing the Corporate Income Tax Liability.* What is Beta Corporation's income tax liability assuming its taxable income is (a) $94,000, (b) $300,000, and (c) $600,000. How would your answers change if Beta were a personal service corporation?

C:3-49 *Computing the Corporate Income Tax Liability.* Fawn Corporation, a C corporation, paid no dividends and recognized no capital gains or losses in the current year. What is its income tax liability assuming its taxable income for the year is

a. $50,000
b. $14,000,000
c. $18,000,000
d. $34,000,000

C:3-50 *Computing Taxable Income and Income Tax Liability.* Pace Corporation reports the following results for the current year:

Gross profit on sales	$120,000
Long-term capital loss	10,000
Short-term capital loss	5,000
Dividends from 40%-owned domestic corporation	30,000
Operating expenses	65,000
Charitable contributions	10,000

a. What are Pace's taxable income and income tax liability, assuming qualified production activities income is $55,000?
b. What carrybacks and carryovers (if any) are available and to what years must they be carried?

C:3-51 *Computing Taxable Income and Income Tax Liability.* Roper Corporation reports the following results for the current year:

Gross profits on sales	$80,000
Short-term capital gain	40,000
Long-term capital gain	25,000
Dividends from 25%-owned domestic corporation	15,000
NOL carryover from the preceding tax year	9,000
Operating expenses	45,000

What are Roper's taxable income and income tax liability, assuming qualified production activities income is $35,000?

C:3-52 *Controlled Groups.* Which of the following groups constitute controlled groups? (Any stock not listed below is held by unrelated individuals each owning less than 1% of the outstanding stock.) For brother-sister corporations, which definition applies?

a. Judy owns 100% of the single classes of stock of Hot and Ice Corporations.
b. Jones and Kane Corporations each have only a single class of stock outstanding. The two controlling individual shareholders own the stock as follows:

	Stock Ownership Percentages	
Shareholder	*Jones Corp.*	*Kane Corp.*
Tom	60%	100%
Mary	40%	

c. Link, Model, and Name Corporations each have a single class of stock outstanding. The stock is owned as follows:

	Stock Ownership Percentages	
Shareholder	*Model Corp.*	*Name Corp.*
Link Corp.	80%	50%
Model Corp.		40%
Unrelated individuals	20%	10%

Link Corporation's stock is widely held by over 1,000 shareholders, none of whom owns directly or indirectly more than 1% of Link's stock.

d. Oat, Peach, Rye, and Seed Corporations each have a single class of stock outstanding. The stock is owned as follows:

	Stock Ownership Percentages			
Shareholder	*Oat Corp.*	*Peach Corp.*	*Rye Corp.*	*Seed Corp.*
Bob	100%	90%		
Oat Corp.			80%	30%
Rye Corp.				60%
Unrelated individuals		10%	20%	10%

C:3-53 ***Controlled Groups of Corporations.*** Sally owns 100% of the outstanding stock of Eta, Theta, Phi, and Gamma Corporations, each of which files a separate return for the current year. During the current year, the corporations report taxable income as follows:

Corporation	*Taxable Income*
Eta	$40,000
Theta	(25,000)
Phi	50,000
Gamma	10,000

a. What is each corporation's separate tax liability, assuming the corporations do not elect a special apportionment plan for allocating the corporate tax rates?

b. What is each corporation's separate tax liability, assuming the corporations make a special election to apportion the reduced corporate tax rates in such a way that minimizes the group's total tax liability? Note: More than one plan can satisfy this goal.

c. How does the result in Part b change if Gamma's income is $30,000 instead of $10,000?

C:3-54 ***Compensation Planning.*** Marilyn owns all of Bell Corporation's stock. Bell is a C corporation and employs 40 people. Marilyn is married, has two dependent children, and files a joint tax return with her husband. She projects that Bell will report $300,000 of pretax profits for the current year. Marilyn is considering four salary levels as shown below. Ignore the U.S. production activities deduction for this problem.

			Tax Liability		
Total Income	*Salary Paid to Marilyn*	*Earnings Retained by Bell Corporation*	*Marilyn*	*Bell Corporation*	*Total*
$300,000	$ –0–	$300,000			
300,000	$100,000	200,000			
300,000	200,000	100,000			
300,000	300,000	–0–			

a. Determine the total tax liability for Marilyn and Bell for each of the four proposed salary levels. Assume no other income for Marilyn's family, and assume that Marilyn and her husband claim a combined itemized deduction and personal exemption of $30,000. Ignore employment taxes.

b. What recommendations can you make about a salary level for Marilyn that will minimize the total tax liability? Assume salaries paid up to $300,000 are considered reasonable compensation.

c. What is the possible disadvantage to Marilyn if Bell retains funds in the business and distributes some of the accumulated earnings as a dividend in a later tax year?

C:3-55 ***Fringe Benefits.*** Refer to the facts in Problem C:3-54. Marilyn has read an article explaining the advantages of paying nontaxable fringe benefits (premiums on group term life insurance, accident and health insurance, etc.) and having deferred compensation plans (e.g., qualified pension and profit-sharing plans). Provide Marilyn with information on the tax savings associated with converting $3,000 of her salary into nontaxable fringe benefits. What additional costs might Bell Corporation incur if it adopts a fringe benefit plan?

C:3-56 ***Estimated Tax Requirement.*** Zeta Corporation's taxable income for 2016 was $1.5 million, on which Zeta paid federal income taxes of $510,000. Zeta estimates calendar year 2017's taxable income to be $2 million, on which it will owe $680,000 in federal income taxes.

a. What are Zeta's minimum quarterly estimated tax payments for 2017 to avoid an underpayment penalty?

b. When is Zeta's 2017 tax return due?
c. When are any remaining taxes due? What amount of taxes are due when Zeta files its return assuming Zeta timely pays estimated tax payments equal to the amount determined in Part a?
d. If Zeta obtains an extension to file, when is its tax return due? Will the extension permit Zeta to delay making its final tax payments?

C:3-57 ***Filing the Tax Return and Paying the Tax Liability.*** Wright Corporation's taxable income for calendar years 2014, 2015, and 2016 was $120,000, $150,000, and $100,000, respectively. Its total tax liability for 2016 was $22,250. Wright estimates that its 2017 taxable income will be $500,000, on which it will owe federal income taxes of $170,000. Assume Wright earns its 2017 taxable income evenly throughout the year.
a. What are Wright's minimum quarterly estimated tax payments for 2017 to avoid an underpayment penalty?
b. When is Wright's 2017 tax return due?
c. When are any remaining taxes due? What amount of taxes are due when Wright files its return assuming it timely paid estimated tax payments equal to the amount determined in Part a?
d. How would your answer to Part a change if Wright's tax liability for 2016 had been $200,000?

C:3-58 ***Converting Book Income to Taxable Income.*** The following income and expense accounts appeared in the book accounting records of Rocket Corporation, an accrual basis taxpayer, for the current calendar year.

	Book Income	
Account Title	*Debit*	*Credit*
Net sales		$3,230,000
Dividends		10,000 (1)
Interest		18,000 (2)
Gain on sale of stock		9,000 (3)
Key-person life insurance proceeds		100,000
Cost of goods sold	$2,000,000	
Salaries and wages	500,000	
Bad debts	13,000 (4)	
Payroll taxes	62,000	
Interest expense	12,000 (5)	
Charitable contributions	50,000 (6)	
Depreciation	70,000 (7)	
Other expenses	40,000 (8)	
Federal income taxes	165,920	
Net income	454,080	
Total	$3,367,000	$3,367,000

The following additional information applies.
1. Dividends were from Star Corporation, a 30%-owned domestic corporation.
2. Interest revenue consists of interest on corporate bonds, $15,000; and municipal bonds, $3,000.
3. The stock is a capital asset held for three years prior to sale.
4. Rocket uses the specific writeoff method of accounting for bad debts.
5. Interest expense consists of $11,000 interest incurred on funds borrowed for working capital and $1,000 interest on funds borrowed to purchase municipal bonds.
6. Rocket paid all contributions in cash during the current year to State University.
7. Rocket calculated depreciation per books using the straight-line method. For income tax purposes, depreciation amounted to $95,000.
8. Other expenses include premiums of $5,000 on the key-person life insurance policy covering Rocket's president, who died in December.
9. Qualified production activities income is $300,000.
10. Rocket has a $90,000 NOL carryover from prior years.

Required:
a. Prepare a worksheet reconciling Rocket's book income with its taxable income (before special deductions). Six columns should be used—two (one debit and one credit) for each of the following three major headings: book income, Schedule M-1 adjustments,

and taxable income. (See the sample worksheet with Form 1120 in Appendix B if you need assistance).

b. Prepare a tax provision reconciliation as in Step 9 of the Tax Provision Process. Assume a 34% corporate tax rate.

C:3-59 ***Reconciling Book Income and Taxable Income.*** Omega Corporation reports the following results for the current year:

Net income per books (before federal income taxes)	$738,000
Federal income tax expense per books	(231,540)
Net income per books (after federal income taxes)	$506,460
Tax-exempt interest income	10,000
Interest on loan to purchase tax-exempt bonds	7,000
MACRS depreciation exceeding book depreciation	40,000
Net capital loss	8,000
Insurance premium on life of corporate officer where Omega is the beneficiary	9,000
Excess charitable contributions carried over to next year	4,000
U.S. production activities deduction ($700.0000 × 0.09)*	63,000

* Assume that qualified production activities income is $700,000.

a. Prepare a reconciliation of Omega's taxable income before special deductions with its book income.

b. Prepare a tax provision reconciliation as in Step 9 of the Tax Provision Process.

C:3-60 ***Reconciling Unappropriated Retained Earnings.*** White Corporation's financial accounting records disclose the following results for the period ending December 31 of the current year:

Retained earnings balance on January 1	$246,500
Net income for year	259,574
Contingency reserve established on December 31	60,000
Cash dividend paid on July 23	23,000

What is White's unappropriated retained earnings balance on December 31 of the current year?

C:3-61 ***Tax Reconciliation Process.*** Omega Corporation, a regular C corporation, presents you with the following partial *book* income statement for the current year:

Sales	$1,900,000	
Cost of goods sold	(1,100,000)	
Gross profit		$800,000
Operating expenses:		
Depreciation	$ 80,000	
Interest expense	18,000	
Warranty expense	12,000	
Fines and penalties	10,000	
Other business expenses	220,000	(340,000)
Net operating income		$460,000
Other income (losses):		
Interest received on municipal bonds	$ 1,000	
Income on installment sale	9,000	
Net losses on stock sales	(20,000)	(10,000)
Net income before federal income taxes		$450,000

Omega also provides the following partial balance sheet information:

	Book		*Tax*	
	Beg. of Year	*End of Year*	*Beg. of Year*	*End of Year*
Installment note receivable	$ –0–	$ 30,000	$ –0–	$ 30,000
Minus: Unrecognized income on note	–0–	–0–	–0–	(9,000)
Net basis of note receivable	–0–	30,000	–0–	21,000
Tax-exempt bonds	18,000	18,000	18,000	18,000
Deferred tax asset	5,100	?	–0–	–0–
Investment stocks	100,000	40,000	100,000	40,000

Fixed assets	400,000	400,000	400,000	400,000
Minus: Accumulated depreciation	(40,000)	(120,000)	(80,000)	(208,000)
Net basis of fixed assets	360,000	280,000	320,000	192,000
Liability for warranties	–0–	12,000	–0–	–0–
Deferred tax liability	13,600	?	–0–	–0–

You have gathered the following additional information:

1. Depreciation for tax purposes is $128,000.
2. Of the $18,000 interest expense, $2,000 is allocable to a loan used to purchase the municipal bonds.
3. The warranty expense is an estimated amount for book purposes. Omega expects actual claims on these warranties to be filed and paid next year.
4. Your research determines that the fines and penalties are not deductible for tax purposes.
5. In the current year, Omega sold property using the installment method as follows:

Selling price	$30,000
Adjusted basis	(21,000)
Gain	$9,000

   Omega obtains a $30,000 installment note receivable this year and will receive the $30,000 sales proceeds next year. For book purposes, Omega recognizes the $9,000 gain in the current year. For tax purposes, Omega will recognize the $9,000 gain next year when it receives the $30,000 sales proceeds.
6. Omega sold a significant portion of its stock portfolio in the current year. The $20,000 net loss per books from these stock sales includes the following components:

Long-term capital gain	$15,000
Long-term capital loss	(38,000)
Short-term capital gain	3,000

   Omega had no capital gains in prior years, so it cannot carry the net capital losses back.
7. Omega does not expect to realize capital gains next year, but it does expect sufficient capital gains within the next five years so that it can use the capital loss carryover before it expires. Thus, Omega determines that it needs no valuation allowance.
8. Omega has a $15,000 net operating loss carryover from last year, which it then expected to use in the next year (now the current year).
9. Qualified production activities income for the current year equals $300,000, which is less than taxable income before the U.S. production activities deduction. The applicable percentage is 9%.
10. Omega's tax rate is 34% and will remain so in future years.
11. The beginning deferred tax asset pertains to the NOL carryover, and the beginning deferred tax liability pertains to fixed assets. Other deferred tax assets and deferred tax liabilities may arise in the current year.
12. Omega determines that it needs no adjustment for uncertain tax positions.

Required: Perform the tax provision process steps as outlined in the text. For Step 11, just present partial income statement and balance sheet disclosures as allowed by the given facts.

C:3-62 ***Valuation Allowance.*** In the current year, Alpha Corporation generated $500,000 of ordinary operating income and incurred a $20,000 capital loss on the sale of marketable securities from its investment portfolio. Alpha expects to generate $500,000 of ordinary operating income in each of the next five years. Alpha incurred no capital gains in its previous three years, so it must carry over the $20,000 capital loss for up to five years. Alpha estimates that its remaining marketable securities would produce a $12,000 capital gain if sold. Thus, Alpha determines that, more likely than not, the corporation will not realize (deduct) $8,000 of the current year capital loss. Alpha has no other book-tax differences and is subject to a 34% tax rate.

Required:

a. Determine Alpha's deferred tax asset and valuation allowance for the current year.
b. Determine Alpha's current federal income tax expense, deferred federal income tax expense (benefit), total federal income tax expense, and federal income taxes payable.

c. Prepare the journal entry necessary to record the above amounts.
d. Prepare a tax provision reconciliation and effective tax rate reconciliation for the current year.

C:3-63 *Uncertain Tax Positions.* In the current year, Kappa Corporation earned $1 million of net income before federal income taxes. This amount of book income includes a $100,000 expense for what the company considers an ordinary and necessary business expense. Kappa also deducted the entire $100,000 for tax purposes. In assessing the expense for its tax provision, Kappa determines that it has a more-likely-than-not probability of sustaining some portion of the deduction upon an IRS examination. However, some uncertainty remains as to whether the entire amount is deductible. Any amount ultimately disallowed by the IRS would be a permanent disallowance and not merely a temporary item that could be amortized over time. Upon further analysis, Kappa measures the benefit that is more than 50% likely to be realized as $70,000. Thus, Kappa may not recognize $30,000 of the expense in determining its federal income tax provision. In addition, Kappa has a $25,000 temporary difference that decreases its taxable income to $975,000 and increases its deferred tax liability.

Required:

a. Determine Kappa's liability for unrecognized tax benefits, total federal income tax expense, deferred federal income tax expense, current federal income tax expense, increase in deferred tax liability, and federal income taxes payable.
b. Prepare the journal entry necessary to record the current year tax provision.

COMPREHENSIVE PROBLEM

C:3-64 Jackson Corporation prepared the following *book* income statement for its year ended December 31, 2017:

Sales			$950,000
Minus:	Cost of goods sold		(450,000)
Gross profit			$500,000
Plus:	Dividends received on Invest Corporation stock	$ 3,000	
	Gain on sale of Invest Corporation stock	30,000	
	Total dividends and gain		33,000
Minus:	Depreciation ($7,500 + $52,000)	$ 59,500	
	Bad debt expense	22,000	
	Other operating expenses	105,500	
	Loss on sale of Equipment 1	70,000	
	Total expenses and loss		(257,000)
Net income per books before taxes			$276,000
Minus:	Federal income tax expense		(90,000)
Net income per books			$186,000

Information on equipment depreciation and sale:

Equipment 1:

- Acquired March 3, 2015 for $180,000
- For books: 12-year life; straight-line depreciation
- Sold February 17, 2017 for $80,000

Sales price				$ 80,000
Cost			$180,000	
Minus:	Depreciation for 2015 (½ year)	$ 7,500		
	Depreciation for 2016 ($180,000/12)	15,000		
	Depreciation for 2017 (½ year)	7,500		
	Total book depreciation		(30,000)	
Book value at time of sale				(150,000)
Book loss on sale of Equipment 1				$(70,000)

- For tax: Seven-year MACRS property for which the corporation made no Sec. 179 election in the acquisition year and elected out of bonus depreciation.

Equipment 2:

- Acquired February 16, 2016 for $624,000
- For books: 12-year life; straight-line depreciation
- Book depreciation in 2017: $624,000/12 = $52,000
- For tax: Seven-year MACRS property for which the corporation made the Sec. 179 election in 2016 but elected out of bonus depreciation.

Other information:

- Under the direct writeoff method, Jackson deducts $15,000 of bad debts for tax purposes.
- Jackson has a $40,000 NOL carryover and a $6,000 capital loss carryover from last year.
- Jackson purchased the Invest Corporation stock (less than 20% owned) on June 21, 2015, for $25,000 and sold the stock on December 22, 2017, for $55,000.
- Jackson Corporation has qualified production activities income of $120,000.

Required:

a. For 2017, calculate Jackson's tax depreciation deduction for Equipment 1 and Equipment 2, and determine the tax loss on the sale of Equipment 1.
b. For 2017, calculate Jackson's taxable income and tax liability.
c. Prepare a schedule reconciling net income per books to taxable income before special deductions (Form 1120, line 28).

TAX STRATEGY PROBLEM

C:3-65 Mike Barton owns Barton Products, Inc. The corporation has 30 employees. Barton Corporation expects $800,000 of net income before taxes in 2017. Mike is married and files a joint return with his wife, Elaine, who has no earnings of her own. They have one dependent son, Robert, who is 16 years old. Mike and Elaine have no other income and do not itemize. Mike's salary is $200,000 per year (already deducted in computing Barton Corporation's $800,000 net income). Assume that variations in salaries will not affect the U.S. production activities deduction already reflected in taxable income.

a. Should Mike increase his salary from Barton by $50,000 to reduce the overall tax burden to himself and Barton Products? Because of the Social Security cap, the corporation and Mike each would incur a 1.45% payroll tax with the corporate portion being deductible.
b. Should Barton employ Mike's wife Elaine for $50,000 rather than increase Mike's salary? Take into consideration employment taxes as well as federal income taxes. Note, that Elaine's salary would be well below the Social Security cap, so that she and the corporation each would incur the full amount of payroll taxes with the corporate portion being deductible. Both Elaine's and the corporation's portion is 7.65%.

TAX FORM/RETURN PREPARATION PROBLEMS

C:3-66 Melodic Musical Sales, Inc. is located at 5500 Fourth Avenue, City, ST 98765. The corporation uses the calendar year and accrual basis for both book and tax purposes. It is engaged in the sale of musical instruments with an employer identification number (EIN) of XX-2018016. The company incorporated on December 31, 2012, and began business on January 2, 2013. Table C:3-4 contains balance sheet information at January 1, 2016, and December 31, 2016. Table C:3-5 presents an unaudited GAAP income statement for 2016. These schedules are presented on a book basis. Other information follows the tables.

Estimated Tax Payments (Form 2220):
The corporation deposited estimated tax payments as follows:

April 15, 2016	$110,000
June 15, 2016	220,000
September 15, 2016	270,000
December 15, 2016	270,000
Total	$870,000

▼ **TABLE C:3-4**

Melodic Musical Sales, Inc.—Book Balance Sheet Information

Account	January 1, 2016 Debit	January 1, 2016 Credit	December 31, 2016 Debit	December 31, 2016 Credit
Cash	$ 216,673		$ 328,673	
Accounts receivable	380,000		475,000	
Allowance for doubtful accounts		$ 19,000		$ 23,750
Inventory	2,375,000		3,325,000	
Investment in corporate stock	285,000		50,000	
Investment in municipal bonds	60,000		60,000	
Cash surrender value of insurance policy	80,000		100,000	
Land	400,000		400,000	
Buildings	2,000,000		2,000,000	
Accumulated depreciation—Buildings		100,000		140,000
Equipment	1,200,000		2,300,000	
Accumulated depreciation—Equipment		300,000		355,000
Trucks	200,000		200,000	
Accumulated depreciation—Trucks		60,000		100,000
Accounts payable		400,000		360,000
Notes payable (short-term)		900,000		720,000
Accrued payroll taxes		14,136		17,670
Accrued state income taxes		4,275		7,125
Accrued federal income taxes		2,375		122,304
Bonds payable (long-term)		2,400,000		2,200,000
Net deferred tax liability		146,887		276,247
Capital stock—Common		950,000		950,000
Retain earnings—Unappropriated		1,900,000		3,966,577
Totals	$7,196,673	$7,196,673	$9,238,673	$9,238,673

Taxable income in 2015 was $1.6 million, and the 2015 tax was $544,000. The corporation earned its 2016 taxable income evenly throughout the year. Therefore, it does not use the annualization or seasonal methods.

Inventory and Cost of Goods Sold (Form 1125-A):
The corporation uses the periodic inventory method and prices its inventory using the lower of FIFO cost or market. Only beginning inventory, ending inventory, and purchases should be reflected on Form 1125-A. No other costs or expenses are allocated to cost of goods sold. Note: the corporation is exempt from the uniform capitalization (UNICAP) rules because average gross income for the previous three years was less than $10 million.

Line 9 (a)	Check (ii)
(b), (c) & (d)	Not applicable
(e) & (f)	No

Compensation of Officers (Form 1125-E):

(a)	*(b)*	*(c)*	*(d)*	*(f)*
Mary Travis	XXX-XX-XXXX	100%	50%	$275,500
John Willis	XXX-XX-XXXX	100%	25%	171,000
Chris Parker	XXX-XX-XXXX	100%	25%	171,000
Total				$617,500

Bad Debts:
For tax purposes, the corporation uses the direct writeoff method of deducting bad debts. For book purposes, the corporation uses an allowance for doubtful accounts. During 2016, the corporation charged $38,000 to the allowance account, such amount representing actual writeoffs for 2016.

▼ TABLE C:3-5
Melodic Musical Sales, Inc.—Book Income Statement 2016

Sales		$ 9,500,000
Returns		(237,500)
Net sales		$ 9,262,500
Beginning inventory	$2,375,000	
Purchases	5,225,000	
Ending inventory	(3,325,000)	
Cost of goods sold		(4,275,000)
Gross profit		$ 4,987,500
Expenses:		
Depreciation	$ 255,000	
Repairs	19,760	
General insurance	52,250	
Net premium-Officers' life insurance	28,500	
Officers' compensation	617,500	
Other salaries	380,000	
Utilities	68,400	
Advertising	45,600	
Legal and accounting fees	47,500	
Charitable contributions	28,500	
Payroll taxes	58,900	
Interest expense	199,500	
Bad debt expense	42,750	
Total expenses		(1,844,160)
Gain on sale of equipment		160,000
Interest on municipal bonds		4,750
Net gain on stock sales		35,000
Dividend income		11,400
Net income before income taxes		$ 3,354,490
Federal income tax expense		(1,121,663)
State income tax expense		(71,250)
Net income		$ 2,161,577

Additional Information (Schedule K):

1 b	Accrual	8	Do not check box
2 a	451140	9	Fill in the correct amount
b	Retail sales	10	3
c	Musical instruments	11	Do not check box
3	No	12	Not applicable
4 a	No	13-14	No
b	Yes; omit Schedule G		
5 a	No	15a	No
b	No	b	Do not check box
6-7	No	16-19	No

Organizational Expenditures:
The corporation incurred less than $5,000 of organizational expenditures in the year it began business. For book purposes, the corporation expensed the entire expenditure. For tax purposes, the corporation elected under Sec. 248 to deduct the entire amount of expenditures in the year it began business. Therefore, no amortization expenditures appear in the tax return or book financial statements for the current year.

Capital Gains and Losses:
The corporation sold 100 shares of PDQ Corp. common stock on October 7, 2016, for \$150,000. The corporation acquired the stock on December 15, 2015, for \$100,000. The corporation also sold 75 shares of JSB Corp. common stock on June 17, 2016, for \$120,000. The corporation acquired this stock on September 18, 2014, for \$135,000. The corporation has a \$20,000 capital loss carryover from 2015. These transactions were not reported to the corporation on Form 1099-B.

Fixed Assets and Depreciation:
For book purposes: The corporation uses straight-line depreciation over the useful lives of assets as follows: store building, 50 years; equipment, ten years; and trucks, five years. The corporation takes a half-year's depreciation in the year of acquisition and the year of disposition and assumes no salvage value. The book financial statements in Tables C:3-4 and C:3-5 reflect these calculations.

For tax purposes: All assets are MACRS property as follows: store building, 39-year nonresidential real property; equipment, seven-year property; and trucks, five-year property. The corporation acquired the store building for \$2 million and placed it in service on January 2, 2013. The corporation acquired two pieces of equipment for \$400,000 (Equipment 1) and \$800,000 (Equipment 2) and placed them in service on January 2, 2013. The corporation acquired the trucks for \$200,000 and placed them in service on July 18, 2014. The trucks are not listed property and are not subject to the limitation on luxury automobiles. The corporation did not make the expensing election under Sec. 179 or take bonus depreciation on any property acquired before 2016. Accumulated tax depreciation through December 31, 2015, on these properties is as follows:

Store building	\$151,780
Equipment 1	225,080
Equipment 2	450,160
Trucks	104,000

On October 16, 2016, the corporation sold for \$440,000 Equipment 1 that originally cost 400,000 on January 2, 2013. The corporation had no Sec. 1231 losses from prior years. In a separate transaction on October 17, 2016, the corporation acquired and placed in service a piece of equipment costing \$1,500,000. Assume these two transactions do not qualify as a like-kind exchange. The new equipment is seven-year property. The corporation made the Sec. 179 expensing election with regard to the new equipment but elected out of bonus depreciation. Where applicable, use published IRS depreciation tables to compute 2016 depreciation (reproduced in Appendix C of this text).

Other Information:

- The corporation's activities do not qualify for the U.S. production activities deduction.
- Ignore the AMT and accumulated earnings tax.
- The corporation received dividends (see Income Statement in Table C:3-5) from taxable, domestic corporations, the stock of which Melodic Musical Sales, Inc. owns less than 20%.
- The corporation paid \$95,000 in cash dividends to its shareholders during the year and charged the payment directly to retained earnings.
- The state income tax in Table C:3-5 is the exact amount of such taxes incurred during the year.
- The corporation is not entitled any credits.
- Ignore the financial statement impact of any underpayment penalties incurred on the tax return.

Required: Prepare the 2016 corporate tax return for Melodic Musical Sales, Inc. along with any necessary supporting schedules.

Optional: Prepare both Schedule M-3 (but omit Schedule B and Form 8916-A) and Schedule M-1 even though the IRS does not require both Schedule M-1 and Schedule M-3.

Note to Instructor: See solution in the Instructor's Resource Manual for other optional information to provide to students.

C:3-67 Permtemp Corporation formed in 2015 and, for that year, reported the following book income statement and balance sheet, excluding the federal income tax expense, deferred tax assets, and deferred tax liabilities:

Sales		$20,000,000
Cost of goods sold		(15,000,000)
Gross profit		$ 5,000,000
Dividend income		50,000
Tax-exempt interest income		15,000
Total income		$ 5,065,000
Expenses:		
Depreciation	$ 800,000	
Bad debts	400,000	
Charitable contributions	100,000	
Interest	475,000	
Meals and entertainment	45,000	
Other	3,855,000	
Total expenses		(5,675,000)
Net loss before federal income taxes		$ (610,000)

Cash		$ 500,000
Accounts receivable	$ 2,000,000	
Allowance for doubtful accounts	(250,000)	1,750,000
Inventory		4,000,000
Fixed assets	$10,000,000	
Accumulated depreciation	(800,000)	9,200,000
Investment in corporate stock		1,000,000
Investment in tax-exempt bonds		50,000
Total assets		$16,500,000
Accounts payable		$2,610,000
Long-term debt		8,500,000
Common stock		6,000,000
Retained earnings		(610,000)
Total liabilities and equity		$16,500,000

Additional information for 2015:

- The investment in corporate stock is comprised of less-than-20%-owned corporations.
- Depreciation for tax purposes is $1.4 million under MACRS.
- Bad debt expense for tax purposes is $150,000 under the direct writeoff method.
- Limitations to charitable contribution deductions and meals and entertainment expenses must be tested and applied if necessary.
- Qualified production activities income is zero.

Required for 2015:

a. Prepare page 1 of the 2015 Form 1120, computing the corporation's NOL.

b. Determine the corporation's deferred tax asset and deferred tax liability situation, and then complete the income statement and balance sheet to reflect proper GAAP accounting under ASC 740. Use the balance sheet information to prepare Schedule L of the 2015 Form 1120.

c. Prepare the 2015 Schedule M-3 for Form 1120.

d. Prepare a schedule that reconciles the corporation's effective tax rate to the statutory 34% tax rate.

Note: For 2015 forms, go to forms and publications, prior year, at the IRS website, *www.irs.gov*.

For 2016, Permtemp reported the following book income statement and balance sheet, excluding the federal income tax expense, deferred tax assets, and deferred tax liabilities:

Sales		$33,000,000
Cost of goods sold		(22,000,000)
Gross profit		$11,000,000
Dividend income		55,000
Tax-exempt interest income		15,000
Total income		$11,070,000
Expenses:		
Depreciation	$ 800,000	
Bad debts	625,000	
Charitable contributions	40,000	
Interest	455,000	
Meals and entertainment	60,000	
Other	4,675,000	
Total expenses		(6,655,000)
Net income before federal income taxes		$ 4,415,000

Cash		$ 2,125,000
Accounts receivable	$ 3,300,000	
Allowance for doubtful accounts	(450,000)	2,850,000
Inventory		6,000,000
Fixed assets	$10,000,000	
Accumulated depreciation	(1,600,000)	8,400,000
Investment in corporate stock		1,000,000
Investment in tax-exempt bonds		50,000
Total assets		$20,425,000
Accounts payable		$ 2,120,000
Long-term debt		8,500,000
Common stock		6,000,000
Retained earnings		3,805,000
		$20,425,000

Additional information for 2016:

- Depreciation for tax purposes is $2.45 million under MACRS.
- Bad debt expense for tax purposes is $425,000 under the direct writeoff method.
- Qualified production activities income is $3 million.

Required for 2016:

a. Prepare page 1 of the 2016 Form 1120, computing the corporation's taxable income and tax liability.

b. Determine the corporation's deferred tax asset and deferred tax liability situation, and then complete the income statement and balance sheet to reflect proper GAAP accounting ASC 740. Use the balance sheet information to prepare Schedule L of the 2016 Form 1120.

c. Prepare the 2016 Schedule M-3 for Form 1120.

d. Prepare a schedule that reconciles the corporation's effective tax rate to the statutory 34% tax rate.

CASE STUDY PROBLEMS

C:3-68 Marquette Corporation, a tax client since its creation three years ago, has requested that you prepare a memorandum explaining its estimated tax requirements for the current year. The corporation is in the fabricated steel business. Its earnings have been growing each year. Marquette's taxable income for the last three tax years has been $500,000, $1.5 million, and $2.5 million, respectively. The Chief Financial Officer expects its taxable income in the current year to be approximately $3 million.

Required: Prepare a one-page client memorandum explaining Marquette's estimated tax requirements for the current year, providing the necessary supporting authorities.

C:3-69 Susan Smith accepted a new corporate client, Winter Park Corporation. One of Susan's tax managers conducted a review of Winter Park's prior year tax returns. The review revealed that an NOL for a prior tax year was incorrectly computed, resulting in an overstatement of NOL carrybacks and carryovers to prior tax years. Apply the Statements on Standards for Tax Services (SSTSs) to the following situations. The SSTSs are in Appendix E of this text.

a. Assume the incorrect NOL calculation does not affect the current year's tax liability. What recommendations (if any) should Susan make to the new client? See SSTS No. 6.
b. Assume the IRS is currently auditing a prior year. What are Susan's responsibilities in this situation? See SSTS No. 6.
c. Assume the NOL carryover is being carried to the current year, and Winter Park does not want to file amended tax returns to correct the error. What should Susan do in this situation? See SSTS No. 1.

C:3-70 The Chief Executive Officer of a client of your public accounting firm saw the following advertisement in a financial newspaper:

> DONATIONS WANTED
> The Center for Restoration of Waters
> A Nonprofit Research and Educational Organization
> Needs Donations—Autos, Boats, Real Estate, Etc.
> ALL DONATIONS ARE TAX-DEDUCTIBLE

Prepare a memorandum to your client Phil Nickelson explaining how the federal income tax laws regarding donations of cash, automobiles, boats, and real estate apply to corporate taxpayers.

TAX RESEARCH PROBLEMS

C:3-71 Wicker Corporation made estimated tax payments of $6,000 in Year 1. On March 12 of Year 2, it filed its Year 1 tax return showing a $20,000 tax liability, and it paid the $14,000 balance at that time. On April 20 of Year 2, it discovers an error and files an amended return for Year 1 showing a reduced tax liability of $8,000. Prepare a memorandum for your tax manager explaining whether Wicker can base its estimated tax payments for Year 2 on the amended $8,000 tax liability for Year 1, or whether it must use the $20,000 tax liability reported on its original Year 1 return. Your manager has suggested that, at a minimum, you consult the following resources:

- IRC Sec. 6655(d)(1)
- Rev. Rul. 86-58, 1986-1 C.B. 365

C:3-72 Alice, Bill, and Charles each received an equal number of shares when they formed King Corporation a number of years ago. King has used the cash method of accounting since its inception. Alice, Bill, and Charles, the shareholder-employees, operate King as an environmental engineering firm with 57 additional employees. King had gross receipts of $4.3 million last year. Gross receipts have grown by about 15% in each of the last three years and were just under $5 million in the current year. The owners expect the 15% growth rate to continue for at least five more years. Outstanding accounts receivable average about $600,000 at the end of each month. Forty-four employees (including Alice, Bill, and Charles) actively engage in providing engineering services on a full-time basis. The remaining 16 employees serve in a clerical and support capacity (secretarial staff, accountants, etc.). Bill has read about special restrictions on the use of the cash method of accounting and requests information from you about the impact these rules might have on King's continued use of that method. Prepare a memorandum for your tax manager addressing whether King can continue using the cash method under the gross receipts or personal service corporation exceptions.

Your manager has suggested that, at a minimum, you should consult the following resources:

- IRC Secs. 446 and 448
- Temp. Reg. Sec. 1.448-1T
- H. Rept. No. 99-841, 99th Cong., 2d Sess., pp. 285–289 (1986)

TAX & FINANCIAL ACCOUNTING

C:3-73 James Bowen owns 100% of Bowen Corporation stock. Bowen is a calendar year, accrual method taxpayer. During the current year, Bowen made three charitable contributions:

Donee	*Property Donated*	*FMV of Property*
State University	Bates Corporation stock	$110,000
Red Cross	Cash	5,000
Girl Scouts	Pledge to pay cash	25,000

Bowen purchased the Bates stock three years ago for $30,000. Bowen holds a 28% interest, which it accounts for under GAAP using the equity method of accounting. The current carrying value for the Bates stock for book purposes is $47,300. Bowen will pay the pledge to the Girl Scouts by check on March 3 of next year. Bowen's taxable income for the current year before the charitable contributions deduction, dividends-received deduction, NOL deduction, and U.S. production activities deduction is $600,000. Your tax manager has asked you to prepare a memorandum explaining how these transactions are to be treated for tax purposes and for accounting purposes. Your manager has suggested that, at a minimum, you should consult the following resources:

- IRC Sec. 170
- Accounting Standards Codification (ASC) 720

C:3-74 Production Corporation owns 70% of Manufacturing Corporation's common stock and Rita Howard owns the remaining 30%. Each corporation operates and sells its product within the United States, and the corporations engaged in no intercompany transactions. Production's Chief Financial Officer (CFO) presents you with the following information pertaining to current year operations:

	Production Corporation	*Manufacturing Corporation*
Gross profit on sales	$500,000	$225,000
Minus: Operating expenses	(200,000)	(100,000)
Qualified production activities income	$300,000	$125,000
Plus: Dividends received from 20%-owned corporations	20,000	–0–
Minus: Dividends-received deduction	(16,000)	–0–
NOL carryover deduction	–0–	(15,000)
Taxable income before the U.S. production activities deduction	$304,000	$110,000

Operating expenses include W-2 wages allocable to U.S. production activities of $75,000 and $35,000 for Production and Manufacturing, respectively. Given this information, the CFO asks you to determine each corporation's qualified production activities deduction. The applicable deduction percentage is 9%. At a minimum, you should consult the following resources:

- IRC Sec. 199
- Reg. Sec. 1.199-7

CHAPTER

4

CORPORATE NONLIQUIDATING DISTRIBUTIONS

LEARNING OBJECTIVES

After studying this chapter, you should be able to

1. Ask the key questions pertaining to corporate liquidations
2. Calculate a corporation's earnings and profits (E&P)
3. Determine the tax consequences of nonliquidating distributions
4. Determine the tax consequences of stock dividends and the issuance of stock rights
5. Decide whether a stock redemption should be treated as a sale or a dividend
6. Explain the tax treatment of preferred stock bailouts
7. Assess the applicability and tax consequences of Sec. 304 to stock sales
8. Identify tax planning opportunities in nonliquidating distributions
9. Comply with procedural rules for nonliquidating distributions

CHAPTER OUTLINE

A corporation may distribute money, property, or stock to its shareholders. Shareholders who receive such distributions might have to recognize ordinary income, capital gain, or no taxable income at all. The distributing corporation might be required to recognize gain or loss when making the distribution. How the corporation and its shareholders treat distributions for tax purposes depends on not only what the corporation distributes but also on the circumstances surrounding the distribution. Was the corporation in the process of liquidating? Was the distribution made in exchange for some of the shareholder's stock?

This chapter addresses distributions made when a corporation is not in the process of liquidating. It discusses the tax consequences of the following types of distributions:

- Distributions of cash or other property where the shareholder does not surrender any stock
- Distributions of stock or rights to acquire stock of the distributing corporation
- Distributions of property in exchange for the corporation's own stock (i.e., stock redemptions)

Chapter C:6 discusses **liquidating distributions**, and Chapter C:7 discusses distributions associated with corporate reorganizations.

NONLIQUIDATING DISTRIBUTIONS IN GENERAL

OBJECTIVE 1

Ask the key questions pertaining to corporate liquidations

When a corporation makes a nonliquidating distribution to a shareholder, the shareholder must answer the following three questions:

- What is the amount of the distribution?
- To what extent is this amount treated as a dividend?
- What is the basis of the distributed property, and when does its holding period begin?

In addition, the distributing corporation must answer the following two questions:

- What are the amount and character of gain or loss the corporation must recognize?
- What effect does the distribution have on the distributing corporation's earnings and profits (E&P) account?

SELF-STUDY QUESTION

How does a shareholder classify a distribution for tax purposes?

ANSWER

Distributions are treated as follows: (1) dividends to the extent of corporate E&P, (2) return of capital to the extent of the shareholder's stock basis, and (3) gain from the sale of stock.

A brief summary of the rules for determining the taxability of a distribution follows, along with a simple example.

Section 301 requires a shareholder to include in gross income the amount of any corporate distribution to the extent it is treated as a dividend. Qualified dividends received by a noncorporate shareholder are subject to a maximum 20% tax rate. Section 316(a) defines a **dividend** as a distribution of property made by a corporation out of its earnings and profits (E&P), which are discussed in the next section of this chapter. Section 317(a) defines **property** broadly to include money, securities, and any other property except stock or stock rights of the distributing corporation. Distributed amounts that exceed a corporation's E&P are treated as a return of capital that reduces the shareholder's basis in his or her stock (but not below zero). Distributions exceeding the shareholder's basis are treated as gain from the sale of the stock. If the stock is a capital asset in the shareholder's hands, the gain is capital in character.

EXAMPLE C:4-1 ▶ On March 1, Gamma Corporation distributes $60,000 in cash to each of its two equal shareholders, Ellen and Bob. At the time of the distribution, Gamma's E&P is $80,000. Ellen's basis in her stock is $25,000, and Bob's basis in his stock is $10,000. Ellen and Bob each recognize $40,000 (0.50 × $80,000) of dividend income. This portion of the distribution reduces Gamma's E&P to zero. The additional $20,000 that each shareholder receives is treated first as a return of capital and then as a capital gain. The following table illustrates the relevant calculations:

	Ellen	*Bob*	*Total*
Distribution	$60,000	$60,000	$120,000
Dividend income[a]	(40,000)	(40,000)	(80,000)
Remaining distribution	$20,000	$20,000	$ 40,000
Return of capital[b]	(20,000)	(10,000)	(30,000)
Capital gain[c]	$ -0-	$10,000	$ 10,000

[a]Smaller of E&P allocable to the distribution or the distribution amount.
[b]Smaller of remaining distribution amount to the shareholder or his or her stock basis.
[c]Any amount that exceeds the shareholder's basis in his or her stock. ◀

EARNINGS AND PROFITS (E&P)

OBJECTIVE 2

Calculate a corporation's earnings and profits (E&P)

The term E&P is not defined in the IRC. Its meaning must be gleaned from judicial opinions, Treasury Regulations, and IRC provisions relating to how certain transactions affect E&P.

To some extent, E&P measures a corporation's economic ability to pay dividends to its shareholders. Distributions are presumed to be made out of the corporation's E&P, unless the corporation reports no E&P.

CURRENT EARNINGS AND PROFITS

TYPICAL MISCONCEPTION

Because E&P is such an important concept in many corporate transactions, one would assume that corporations know exactly what their E&P is. However, many corporations do not compute their E&P on a regular basis.

A corporation's E&P falls into two categories: current and accumulated. As explained below, **current E&P** is calculated annually. **Accumulated E&P** is the sum of undistributed current E&P balances for all previous years reduced by the sum of all previous current E&P deficits and any distributions the corporation made out of accumulated E&P. Distributions are deemed to have been made first out of current E&P and then out of accumulated E&P to the extent that current E&P is insufficient.

EXAMPLE C:4-2 ▶ Zeta Corporation was formed in Year 1. Its current E&P balance (or deficit) and distributions for each year through Year 4 are as follows:

Year	*Current E&P (Deficit)*	*Distributions*
1	$(10,000)	-0-
2	15,000	-0-
3	18,000	$9,000
4	8,000	-0-

The corporation is deemed to have made the $9,000 distribution out of its Year 3 current E&P balance. At the beginning of Year 4, Zeta's accumulated E&P balance is $14,000 (− $10,000 + $15,000 + $18,000 − $9,000). At the beginning of Year 5, Zeta's accumulated E&P balance is $22,000 ($14,000 + $8,000). ◀

Computing Current E&P. A corporation computes its current E&P on an annual basis at the end of each year. The starting point for computing current E&P is the corporation's taxable income or net operating loss (NOL) for the year. Taxable income or the NOL must be adjusted to derive the corporation's economic income or loss (current E&P) for the year. For example, federal income taxes must be deducted from taxable income to derive E&P. Because the corporation must pay these taxes to the U.S. government, they reduce the amount available to pay dividends to shareholders. On the other hand, tax-exempt income must be added to taxable income (or the NOL) because, even though not taxable, such income increases the corporation's ability to pay dividends.

Table C:4-1 lists some of the adjustments a corporation must make to taxable income (NOL) to derive current E&P. Some of these adjustments are explained below.[1]

[1] The adjustments are based on rules set forth in Sec. 312 and related Treasury Regulations.

▼ **TABLE C:4-1**
Computation of Current E&P

Taxable income	
Plus:	*Income excluded from taxable income but included in E&P*
	Tax-exempt interest
	Proceeds from a life insurance contract in which the corporation is named as the beneficiary
	Recoveries of bad debts and other deductions from which the corporation received no tax benefit
	Federal income tax refunds from prior years
Plus:	*Income deferred to a later year when computing taxable income but included in E&P in the current year*
	Deferred gain on installment sales. Such gain is included in E&P in the year of sale.
Plus or minus:	*Income and deduction items that must be recomputed for E&P purposes*
	Income on long-term contracts based on the percentage of completion rather than the completed contract method
	Depreciation on personal and real property based on:
	The straight-line method for other than MACRS property
	The alternative depreciation system for MACRS property
	Excess of percentage depletion over cost depletion
Plus:	*Deductions that are allowed for taxable income purposes but denied for E&P purposes*
	Dividends-received deduction
	NOL carryovers, charitable contribution carryovers, and capital loss carryovers applied in the current year
	U.S. production activities deduction
Minus:	*Expenses and losses that are denied for taxable income purposes but allowed for E&P purposes*
	Federal income taxes
	Premiums on life insurance contracts in which the corporation is named as the beneficiary
	Excess capital losses that are not currently deductible
	Excess charitable contributions that are not currently deductible
	Expenses related to the production of tax-exempt income
	Nondeductible losses on sales to related parties
	Nondeductible penalties and fines
	Nondeductible political contributions and lobbying expenses
Current E&P balance (or deficit)	

Income Excluded from Taxable Income but Included in E&P. Although certain items of income are excluded from taxable income, these items must be included in E&P if they increase the corporation's ability to pay dividends. For example, a corporation's current E&P includes both tax-exempt interest and life insurance proceeds. Current E&P also includes the recovery of an item deducted in a previous year if the deduction produced no tax benefit for the corporation and therefore was excluded from its taxable income.

EXAMPLE C:4-3 ▶ Ace Corporation deducted $10,000 of bad debts in Year 1. In the same year, Ace generated an NOL that it could not carry back. Consequently, it derived no tax benefit from the deduction. In Year 2, Ace recovers $8,000 of the debt owed to it. Ace excludes the $8,000 from its gross income for Year 2 because it derived no tax benefit from the bad debt deduction in Year 1. However, Ace must add the $8,000 to its taxable income when computing current E&P for Year 2 because the NOL reduced current E&P in Year 1. (Ace also reduces its NOL carryover by $8,000 because of the recovery.) ◀

Income Deferred to a Later Year When Computing Taxable Income but Included in E&P in the Current Year. Gains and losses on property transactions generally are included in E&P in the same year they are recognized for taxable income purposes.

EXAMPLE C:4-4 ▶ In a like-kind exchange, Stone Corporation exchanges investment property with a $12,000 basis and an $18,000 fair market value (FMV) for $1,000 cash and investment property worth $17,000. Stone recognizes a $1,000 gain—the amount of boot received—and defers the remaining $5,000 of realized gain. Stone includes the recognized gain in both taxable income and current E&P. It does not include the deferred gain in either taxable income or current E&P. ◀

In the case of an installment sale, the entire realized gain must be included in current E&P in the year of the sale. This rule applies to sales made by dealers and nondealers.

EXAMPLE C:4-5 ▶ In the current year, Tally Corporation sells land with a $12,000 basis and $20,000 FMV to Rick, an unrelated individual. Rick makes a $5,000 down payment this year and promises to pay Tally, in each of the next three years, an additional $5,000 plus interest at the prevailing market rate on the unpaid balance. Tally's realized gain is $8,000 ($20,000 − $12,000). For taxable income purposes, Tally currently recognizes $2,000 of gain [($8,000 ÷ $20,000) × $5,000] under the installment method for nondealers. For E&P purposes, Tally includes all $8,000 of its realized gain in current E&P. Thus, in computing current E&P, Tally increases taxable income by $6,000. As it receives the installments over the next three years, Tally will recognize the remaining $6,000 of gain ($2,000 per year) for taxable income purposes. It will reduce E&P by $2,000 in each of those years because it included in E&P all $8,000 in the current year. ◀

SELF-STUDY QUESTION

In computing taxable income and E&P, different depreciation methods are often used. What happens when the taxpayer sells such assets?

ANSWER

The taxpayer must calculate gain or loss for taxable income and E&P purposes separately. This difference is an added complexity in making E&P calculations.

Income and Deduction Items That Must Be Recomputed for E&P Purposes. Some deductions are computed differently for E&P purposes than for taxable income purposes, thereby requiring adjustments.

- E&P must be computed under the percentage of completion method even where the corporation uses the completed contract method for taxable income purposes.
- Depreciation must be recomputed under the alternative depreciation system of Sec. 168(g). Also, the cost of property expensed under Sec. 179 must be recovered ratably over a five-year period starting with the month in which it was expensed. Other personal property must be depreciated over the property's class life under the half-year convention. Real property must be depreciated over a 40-year period under the straight-line method and mid-month convention.

EXAMPLE C:4-6 ▶ In January of last year, Radon Corporation placed in service equipment costing $25,000. For regular tax purposes, the corporation expensed the $25,000 under Sec. 179. However, for E&P purposes, the corporation expensed only $5,000 ($25,000/5). Thus, in last year's E&P calculation, the corporation would have increased its taxable income amount by $20,000 ($25,000 − $5,000) to derive last year's current E&P (a positive adjustment). In the current year's E&P calculation (and for the next three years), the corporation reduces its taxable income amount by $5,000 to derive its current E&P balance (a negative adjustment). ◀

- Cost depletion must be used for E&P purposes even where percentage depletion is used for taxable income purposes.
- Intangible drilling costs must be capitalized and amortized over 60 months.

BOOK-TO-TAX ACCOUNTING COMPARISION

Many corporations use retained earnings to measure the taxability of their dividend payments. However, because retained earnings are based on financial accounting concepts, E&P may represent a different amount and may provide a different measure of the corporation's economic ability to pay dividends.

Deductions Allowed for Taxable Income Purposes but Denied for E&P Purposes. Some deductions allowed for taxable income purposes are not allowed for E&P purposes.

- The dividends-received deduction is denied for E&P purposes because it does not reduce the corporation's ability to pay dividends. In the computation of E&P, this deduction must be added back to taxable income.
- NOL, charitable contribution, and capital loss carryovers that reduce current taxable income cannot be deducted to derive E&P. These excess losses or deductions reduce E&P in the year they are incurred or taken.
- The U.S. production activities deduction is disallowed for E&P purposes because it does not reduce the corporation's ability to pay dividends. It must be added back to taxable income to derive E&P.
- Deduction and amortization of organizational expenses are disallowed for E&P purposes.

EXAMPLE C:4-7 ▶ Thames Corporation's taxable income is $500,000 after deductions for the following items: a $10,000 NOL carryover from two years ago, $20,000 for dividends received, and $8,000 for U.S. production activities. To compute current E&P, Thames must add these items (totaling $38,000) back to its taxable income. As a result, current E&P is $538,000. ◀

Expenses and Losses Denied for Taxable Income Purposes but Allowed for E&P Purposes. Some expenses and losses that are not deductible for taxable income purposes are deductible for E&P purposes.

- For taxable income purposes, federal income taxes are not deductible. For E&P purposes, however, federal income taxes are deductible in the year they accrue if the corporation uses the accrual method and in the year they are paid if the corporation uses the cash method.

EXAMPLE C:4-8 ▶ Perch Corporation, an accrual basis taxpayer, earns taxable income of $100,000 on which it owes $22,250 of federal income taxes. In computing current E&P, Perch reduces taxable income by the amount of these taxes, or $22,250. ◀

- For E&P purposes, charitable contributions are fully deductible. Thus, when current E&P is computed, taxable income must be reduced by any charitable contributions disallowed because of the 10% limitation.

EXAMPLE C:4-9 ▶ Dot Corporation computes $25,000 of taxable income before any charitable contribution deduction. Dot contributed $10,000 to the Red Cross. For taxable income purposes, Dot's charitable contribution deduction is limited to $2,500 because of the 10% limitation. However, Dot deducts the entire $10,000 in computing current E&P. In this computation, it must subtract the remaining $7,500 from taxable income of $22,500 ($25,000 − $2,500). In a later year, when the corporation deducts the $7,500 carryover to compute taxable income, it must add that amount back to taxable income to derive current E&P. ◀

- Premiums paid on insurance policies covering the lives of key corporate personnel (net of any increase in the cash surrender value) are not deductible when computing taxable income but are deductible when computing E&P.
- Capital losses exceeding capital gains cannot be deducted when computing taxable income but can be deducted when computing current E&P.
- Nondeductible expenses related to the production of tax-exempt income (e.g., interest charges to borrow money to purchase tax-exempt securities) are deductible when computing E&P.
- Losses on related party sales that are disallowed under Sec. 267 are allowed when computing E&P.
- Fines, penalties, and political contributions that are nondeductible for taxable income purposes are deductible for E&P purposes.

The foregoing items constitute only a partial list of adjustments that must be made to taxable income to compute current E&P. The basic rule is that an adjustment to taxable income must be made so that current E&P reflects the corporation's economic ability to pay dividends.

DISTINCTION BETWEEN CURRENT AND ACCUMULATED E&P

A distinction must be made between current and accumulated E&P. A nonliquidating distribution is taxed as a dividend if made out of either current or accumulated E&P. Corporate distributions are deemed to be made first out of current E&P and then out of accumulated E&P to the extent that current E&P is insufficient.[2] If current E&P is sufficient to cover all distributions during the year, each distribution is treated as a taxable

[2] The distinction between current and accumulated E&P is explained in Reg. Sec. 1.316-2.

dividend. This rule applies even where the corporation reports a deficit in its beginning accumulated E&P account. Current E&P is computed as of the last day of the tax year without reduction for distributions during the year.

EXAMPLE C:4-10 ▶ At the beginning of the current year, Water Corporation has a $30,000 accumulated E&P deficit. For the entire year, Water generates current E&P of $15,000. During the year, Water distributes $10,000 in cash to its shareholders. The $10,000 distribution is treated as a taxable dividend to the shareholders because it is deemed to be made entirely out of current E&P. At the beginning of the next tax year, Water's accumulated E&P deficit is $25,000 ($30,000 E&P deficit reduced by $5,000 of undistributed current E&P) computed as of the last day of the previous year. ◀

TAX STRATEGY TIP

A corporation with an accumulated E&P deficit and current E&P balance may want to postpone distributions to a later year to avoid dividend treatment in the current year. See Example C:4-53 later in this chapter.

If distributions during the year exceed current E&P, current E&P is allocated on a pro rata basis regardless of when during the year the distributions occurred. Distributions exceeding current E&P are deemed to be made in chronological order out of accumulated E&P (if any). Distributions exceeding current and accumulated E&P are treated as a return of capital and reduce the shareholder's stock basis. However, such distributions cannot create an E&P deficit, which results only from losses. These rules are particularly relevant if stock changes hands during the year and total E&P is insufficient to cover all distributions.

EXAMPLE C:4-11 ▶ At the beginning of the current year, Cole Corporation has $20,000 of accumulated E&P. For the entire year, Cole's current E&P is $30,000. On April 10, Cole distributes $20,000 in cash to Bob, its sole shareholder. On July 15, Cole distributes an additional $24,000 in cash to Bob. On August 1, Bob sells all of his Cole stock to Lynn. On September 15, Cole distributes $36,000 in cash to Lynn. Cole's current and accumulated E&P must be allocated among the three distributions as follows:

Date	*Distribution Amount*	*Current E&P*	*Accumulated E&P*	*Dividend Income*	*Return of Capital*
April 10	$20,000	$ 7,500	$12,500	$20,000	$ -0-
July 15	24,000	9,000	7,500	16,500	7,500
September 15	36,000	13,500	-0-	13,500	22,500
Total	$80,000	$30,000	$20,000	$50,000	$30,000

The current E&P allocated to the April 10 distribution is calculated as follows:

$$\$30{,}000\ (\text{Current E\&P}) \times \frac{\$20{,}000\ (\text{April 10 distribution})}{\$80{,}000\ (\text{Total distributions})}$$

Note that the total amount of dividends paid by Cole equals $50,000, the sum of $30,000 of current E&P and $20,000 of accumulated E&P. Current E&P is allocated among all three distributions on a pro rata basis, whereas accumulated E&P is reduced first by the April 10 distribution ($12,500), then by the July 15 distribution, so that no accumulated E&P is available for the September 15 distribution. Thus, Bob's dividend income from Cole is $36,500 ($20,000 + $16,500). He also receives a $7,500 return of capital that reduces his stock basis accordingly. Lynn's dividend income from Cole is $13,500. She also receives a $22,500 return of capital that reduces her stock basis accordingly. Bob cannot determine his gain on the stock sale until after the end of the year. He must wait until he knows the extent to which the April 10 and July 15 distributions reduce his stock basis. ◀

If the corporation generates both a current E&P deficit and an accumulated E&P deficit, none of the distributions is treated as a dividend. Instead, all distributions are treated as a return of capital to the extent of the shareholder's stock basis. Distributions exceeding this basis are taxed as a capital gain.

EXAMPLE C:4-12 ▶ At the beginning of the current year, Rose Corporation has a $15,000 accumulated E&P deficit. Rose's current E&P deficit is $20,000. Rose distributes $10,000 on July 1. The distribution is treated not as a dividend but rather as a return of capital to the extent of the shareholder's stock basis. Any amount exceeding stock basis is taxed as a capital gain. Rose's accumulated E&P deficit on January 1 of next year is $35,000 because the distribution was not made out of E&P and because the negative balance in the current E&P account is transferred to the accumulated E&P account at the end of the current year. ◀

SELF-STUDY QUESTION

When is E&P measured for purposes of determining whether a distribution is a dividend?

ANSWER

Usually at year-end. However, if a current deficit exists, the E&P available for measuring dividend income is determined at the distribution date.

If the corporation has a current E&P deficit and a positive accumulated E&P balance, it must net the two accounts at the time of the distribution to determine the dividend amount.[3] The deficit in current E&P that has accrued up through the day before the distribution reduces the accumulated E&P balance on that date. If the balance remaining after the reduction is positive, the distribution is treated as a dividend to the extent of the lesser of the distribution amount or the E&P balance. If the E&P balance is zero or negative, the distribution is treated as a return of capital to the extent of the shareholder's stock basis and capital gain to the extent the distribution exceeds stock basis. If the actual deficit in current E&P to the date of distribution cannot be determined, the current E&P deficit is prorated on a daily basis to the day before the distribution.

EXAMPLE C:4-13 ▶ Assume the same facts as in Example C:4-12 except that Rose Corporation has a $15,000 accumulated E&P balance. Unless information indicates otherwise, the current E&P deficit of $20,000 accrues on a daily basis. The amount of the July 1 distribution treated as a dividend is calculated as follows:

Date	*Distribution Amount*	*Accumulated E&P*	*Dividend Income*	*Return of Capital*
January 1	$ –0–	$15,000	–0–	–0–
July 1	10,000	(9,918)[a]	$5,082	$4,918
Total	$10,000	$ 5,082[b]	$5,082	$4,918

[a]181/365 × $(20,000) = $(9,918)—the current E&P deficit accrued up to the distribution date. (The denominator in the 181/365 fraction assumes that the current year is not a leap year.)

[b]$15,000 − $9,918 = $5,082—accumulated E&P at beginning of year minus the current E&P deficit accrued up to the distribution date. ◀

STOP & THINK

Question: Why is it necessary to keep separate balances for current and accumulated E&P, and why is it necessary to track E&P to individual distributions?

Solution: Separate balances are necessary because of the way dividends are accounted for. If total current and accumulated E&P is less than the total distributions to the shareholders, E&P must be allocated to all distributions during the year to determine the amount of each distribution that should be treated as a dividend. When no change in the shareholder's stock ownership occurs during the year and all distributions are proportional to stock ownership, an E&P allocation is needed only to track each shareholder's stock basis. Tracking E&P to individual distributions is necessary to determine the taxability of a particular distribution when a change in a shareholder's stock ownership occurs because current E&P is allocated on a pro rata basis and accumulated E&P is allocated chronologically. As a result of the chronological allocation, a greater portion of distributions early in a tax year may be taxed as a dividend relative to distributions later in the year. On the other hand, because accrued current E&P deficits offset accumulated E&P balances, a smaller portion of distributions later in a tax year may be taxed as a dividend relative to distributions earlier in the year.

NONLIQUIDATING PROPERTY DISTRIBUTIONS

OBJECTIVE 3

Determine the tax consequences of nonliquidating distributions

CONSEQUENCES OF NONLIQUIDATING PROPERTY DISTRIBUTIONS TO THE SHAREHOLDERS

Property includes cash, securities, and any other property except stock in the corporation making the distribution (or rights to acquire such stock).[4] When a corporation distributes property to its shareholders, the following three questions must be answered:

[3] Reg. Sec. 1.316-2(b).

[4] Sec. 317(a).

KEY POINT

The amount of the distribution is measured by the FMV of the property less liabilities assumed (but not below zero) because this net amount represents the real economic value received by the shareholder.

- What is the amount of the distribution?
- To what extent is this amount treated as a dividend?
- What is the basis of the property distributed to the shareholder, and when does its holding period begin?

For cash distributions, these questions are easy to answer. The distribution is the amount of cash distributed, which is treated as a dividend to the extent of the corporation's current and accumulated E&P. The E&P account is reduced by the amount distributed, and the shareholder's basis in the cash received is its face value. The distributing corporation recognizes no gain or loss on cash distributions.

When the corporation distributes property, such as land or inventory, the above questions are more difficult to answer. Neither the distribution amount nor the shareholder's basis in the property is immediately apparent. The corporation must recognize gain (but not loss) on the distribution, and the impact of the distribution on the corporation's E&P, as well as the taxability of the distribution, must be ascertained. The following sections set forth rules that address these issues.

When the corporation distributes property to a shareholder, the distribution amount is the property's FMV, determined as of the distribution date.[5] The amount of any liability assumed by the shareholder in the distribution, or to which the distributed property is subject, reduces the distribution amount, but never below zero. The distribution amount is treated as a dividend to the extent of the distributing corporation's E&P.

The shareholder takes a FMV basis in any property received. This basis is not reduced by any liabilities assumed by the shareholder or to which the property is subject.[6] The holding period for the property begins on the day after the distribution date and does not include the distributing corporation's holding period.

EXAMPLE C:4-14 ► Post Corporation has $100,000 of current and accumulated E&P. On March 1, Post distributes to Meg, its sole shareholder, land with a $60,000 FMV and a $35,000 adjusted basis. The land is subject to a $10,000 liability, which Meg assumes. The distribution amount is $50,000 ($60,000 − $10,000), all of which is treated as a dividend to Meg because it does not exceed Post's E&P balance. Meg's basis in the property is its $60,000 FMV, and her holding period for the property begins on March 2. ◄

STOP & THINK

Question: When a corporation distributes property, why do liabilities reduce the amount of income realized by the shareholder but not the shareholder's adjusted basis in the property?

Solution: The liabilities reduce the amount of income realized, but not the shareholder's adjusted basis, because the distribution is analogous to the corporation's transferring an asset that it has financed with debt. Recall that financing the purchase of an asset has no bearing on the asset's cost basis. On the other hand, assuming a liability is tantamount to the transferee's settling the liability with the transferee's own funds, and thus receiving less value from the transferor.

Topic Review C:4-1 summarizes the tax consequences of a nonliquidating distribution to the shareholders.

CONSEQUENCES OF PROPERTY DISTRIBUTIONS TO THE DISTRIBUTING CORPORATION

KEY POINT

Property distributions may trigger income at both the shareholder and the distributing corporation level. This result is another example of the double taxation that exists in our corporate tax system.

Two questions must be answered with respect to a corporation that distributes property:

- What amount and character of gain or loss must the distributing corporation recognize?
- What effect does the distribution have on the corporation's E&P?

[5] Sec. 301(b).

[6] Sec. 301(d).

TOPIC REVIEW C:4-1

Tax Consequences of a Nonliquidating Distribution to the Shareholders

1. The amount of a distribution equals cash received plus the FMV of any noncash property received reduced by any liabilities assumed or acquired by the shareholder.
2. The distribution is treated as a dividend to the extent of the distributing corporation's current and accumulated E&P. Any distribution amount exceeding E&P is treated as a return of capital that reduces the shareholder's stock basis (but not below zero). Any additional excess is treated as a capital gain.
3. The shareholder's basis in the property received is its FMV.
4. The shareholder's holding period for the property begins on the day after the distribution date.

Corporate Gain or Loss on Property Distributions. When a corporation distributes property that has appreciated in value, the corporation must recognize gain for both tax purposes and current E&P purposes as though the corporation had sold the property for its FMV. On the other hand, a corporation does not recognize a tax loss when it distributes property that has depreciated in value even though the corporation would have recognized a loss upon selling the property.[7]

EXAMPLE C:4-15 ▶ Silver Corporation distributes to Mark, a shareholder, land (a capital asset) worth $60,000. Silver's adjusted basis in the land is $20,000. Upon distributing the land, Silver recognizes a $40,000 ($60,000 − $20,000) capital gain, as if Silver had sold the property. If the land instead had a $12,000 FMV, Silver would not have recognized a loss. ◀

TAX STRATEGY TIP

Rather than distribute loss property, the corporation should consider selling it and distributing the proceeds. The sale will allow the corporation to deduct the loss.

If the distributed property is subject to a liability or the shareholder assumes a liability in the distribution, for the purpose of calculating gain, the property's FMV is deemed to be no less than the amount of the liability.[8]

EXAMPLE C:4-16 ▶ Assume the same facts as in Example C:4-15 except the land's FMV instead is $25,000, and the land is subject to a $35,000 mortgage. For the purpose of calculating gain, the land's FMV is deemed to be $35,000 because this value cannot be less than the liability amount. Thus, Silver Corporation's gain is $15,000 ($35,000 – $20,000), the extent to which the land's deemed FMV exceeds its adjusted basis.[9] ◀

TAX STRATEGY TIP

If possible, a corporation should avoid distributing property subject to a liability exceeding the property's FMV because of the potential gain recognition caused by the excess liability.

Effect of Property Distributions on the Distributing Corporation's E&P. Distributions have two effects on E&P:[10]

- ▶ When a corporation distributes appreciated property to its shareholders, it must increase E&P by the **E&P gain**, which is the excess of the property's FMV over its adjusted basis for E&P purposes. Because a property's **E&P adjusted basis** may differ from its tax basis (as discussed earlier in this chapter), this E&P gain may differ from the corporation's recognized gain for taxable income purposes.
- ▶ If the E&P adjusted basis of the noncash asset distributed equals or exceeds its FMV, E&P is reduced by the asset's E&P adjusted basis. If the FMV of the asset distributed exceeds its E&P adjusted basis, E&P is reduced by the asset's FMV. In either case, the E&P reduction is net of any liability to which the asset is subject or that the shareholder assumes in the distribution. E&P also is reduced by the income tax liability incurred on any gain recognized.[11]

[7] Sec. 311(a).
[8] Sec. 311(b)(2).
[9] The tax treatment of the shareholder is not entirely clear. Section 336(b), which Sec. 311(b)(2) makes applicable to nonliquidating distributions, specifically states that this liability rule applies only for determining the corporation's gain or loss. Thus, its applicability does not seem to extend to Sec. 301(d), which gives the shareholder a FMV basis in the distributed property. Some commentators have suggested that a strict interpretation of the statutory provision that gives the shareholder an actual FMV basis, rather than the greater liability basis, produces an illogical result. (See B. C. Randall and D. N. Stewart, "Corporate Distributions: Handling Liabilities in Excess of the Fair Market Value of Property Remains Unresolved," *The Journal of Corporate Taxation*, 1992, pp. 55–64.) Also, in principle, given that the liability exceeds the distributed property's FMV, the shareholder's amount distributed should be zero, resulting in no dividend.
[10] Secs. 312(a) and (b).
[11] Secs. 312(a) and (c).

EXAMPLE C:4-17 ▶ Brass Corporation distributes to its shareholder, Joan, property with a $25,000 adjusted basis for taxable income purposes, a $22,000 adjusted basis for E&P purposes, and a $40,000 FMV. The property is subject to a $12,000 mortgage, which Joan assumes. In the distribution, Brass recognizes a $15,000 ($40,000 FMV − $25,000 tax adjusted basis) gain for taxable income purposes. For E&P purposes, Brass's E&P is increased by an $18,000 ($40,000 FMV − $22,000 E&P adjusted basis) gain and reduced by the amount of income taxes paid or accrued by Brass on the $15,000 tax gain. E&P is further reduced by the $28,000 ($40,000 FMV − $12,000 liability) net value of the distribution. ◀

A special rule applies when a corporation distributes its own obligations (e.g., its notes, bonds, or debentures) to a shareholder. In such case, the distributing corporation's E&P is reduced by the principal amount, not the fair market value, of the obligations.[12]

Topic Review C:4-2 summarizes the tax consequences of a nonliquidating distribution to the distributing corporation.

BOOK-TO-TAX ACCOUNTING COMPARISON

The distributing corporation reports dividends-in-kind at their FMV for financial accounting (book) purposes. For book purposes, the distributing corporation recognizes the difference between the property's FMV and its carrying value as a gain or loss. For tax purposes, however, the corporation recognizes gains but not losses.

CONSTRUCTIVE DIVIDENDS

A **constructive dividend** (or deemed distribution) is the manner in which the IRS or the courts might recharacterize an excessive corporate payment to a shareholder to reflect the true economic benefit conferred upon the shareholder. As a result of the recharacterization, the IRS or courts usually recast a corporate-shareholder transaction as an E&P distribution, deny the corporation an offsetting deduction, and treat all or a portion of the income recognized by the shareholder as a dividend. Ordinarily, a corporate dividend involves a direct, pro rata distribution to all shareholders and is declared by the board of directors. By contrast, a constructive dividend need not be direct or pro rata, nor be declared by the board of directors.

Constructive dividends generally are deemed to be paid in the context of a closely held corporation where the shareholders (or relatives of shareholders) and management groups overlap. In such situations, the dealings between the corporation and its shareholders are likely to be less formal and subject to closer review than dealings between a publicly held corporation and its shareholders. Constructive dividends also may occur in the context of a publicly held corporation.

ADDITIONAL COMMENT

The incentive to disguise dividends as salary, however, is somewhat diminished with the reduced tax rate on dividends.

Intentional Efforts to Avoid Dividend Treatment. The IRS's recharacterization of a payment as a constructive dividend often is in response to a shareholder's attempt either to bail out E&P without subjecting the corporate income to taxation at the shareholder level or to obtain a deduction at the corporate level that otherwise would be disallowed. If a corporation generates sufficient E&P, dividend distributions are fully taxable to the shareholder but are not deductible by the distributing corporation. For this reason,

TOPIC REVIEW C:4-2

Tax Consequences of a Nonliquidating Property Distribution to the Distributing Corporation

1. When a corporation distributes appreciated property, it must recognize gain as if it sold the property for its FMV immediately before the distribution.
2. For gain recognition purposes, a property's FMV is deemed to be at least equal to any liability to which the property is subject or that the shareholder assumes in connection with the distribution.
3. A corporation recognizes no loss when it distributes to its shareholders property that has depreciated in value.
4. The corporation increases current E&P by any E&P gain (FMV – E&P basis) resulting from the distribution of appreciated property, and it decreases current E&P by the taxes incurred on the tax gain (FMV – tax basis) recognized on the distribution.
5. The corporation reduces its E&P by the amount of cash and FMV of any appreciated property distributed, and it reduces E&P by the adjusted basis of distributed property whose adjusted basis exceeds its FMV. In either case, the reduction amount is offset by any liabilities associated with the property.

---

[12] Sec. 312(a)(2).

shareholders may try to disguise a dividend as a salary payment. Without recharacterization, the payment would be taxable to the shareholder-employee and deductible by the distributing corporation as long as the payment is reasonable in amount. Shareholders also may try to disguise dividends as loans to themselves. Without recharacterization, a loan would be neither deductible by the corporation nor taxable to the shareholder. If the IRS recharacterizes either payment as a dividend, the payment is taxable to the shareholder and nondeductible by the corporation.

ETHICAL POINT

A CPA should always be an advocate for his or her client if the question of whether a constructive dividend has been paid is in doubt (i.e., when the facts and the law are sufficiently gray and the taxpayer's position has reasonable support).

Unintentional Constructive Dividends. Some constructive dividends are inadvertent. Shareholders may not realize that the benefits they receive from the corporation are effectively taxable dividends until a tax advisor or the IRS examines the transactions. If a payment in the form of a salary, loan, lease, etc. is recast as a dividend, corresponding adjustments must be made at the corporate and shareholder levels. These adjustments may increase the shareholder's taxable income (e.g., because the distribution has been recharacterized as a dividend rather than a loan) or increase the distributing corporation's taxable income (i.e., because dividends are not deductible). Transactions most likely to be recast and treated as dividends are described below.

ADDITIONAL COMMENT

The government requires that, when loans exist between a corporation and its shareholders, the loans must bear a reasonable interest rate. If a "below-market" interest rate loan exists, the IRS will impute a reasonable rate of interest (Sec. 7872).

Loans to Shareholders. Loans to shareholders may be viewed as disguised dividends unless the shareholders can prove that the loans are bona fide. Whether a loan is bona fide ordinarily depends on the shareholder's intent at the time he or she makes the loan. To prove that the loan is bona fide (and thus to avoid recharacterization of the loan as a dividend), the shareholder must show that he or she intends to repay the loan. Factors indicative of an intent to repay include

- Recording the loan on the corporate books
- Evidencing the loan with a written note
- Charging a reasonable rate of interest
- Scheduling regular payment of principal and interest

Factors that suggest the loan is *not* bona fide include

- Borrowing on "open account" (i.e., the shareholder borrows from the corporation with no fixed repayment schedule, whenever he or she needs cash)
- Failing to charge a market rate of interest
- Failing to enforce the regular payment of interest and principal
- Paying advances in proportion to stockholdings
- Paying advances to a controlling shareholder

If the corporation lends money to a shareholder and then, after a period of time, cancels the loan, the amount cancelled might be treated as a dividend to the extent of the corporation's E&P. If the corporation charges a below market interest rate, the IRS could impute interest on the loan. In such case, the corporation would be deemed to have earned interest income on the loan, and the shareholder would be allowed a deduction for interest deemed paid.

Excessive Compensation Paid to Shareholder-Employees. Shareholders may be compensated for services in the form of salary, bonus, or fringe benefits. Ordinarily, the corporate employer may deduct such compensation as long as it represents an ordinary and necessary business expense and is reasonable in amount. However, if the IRS finds the compensation to be excessive, the excess amount will not be deductible by the corporation but still will be taxable to the shareholder. Depending upon the circumstances, this amount may be treated as a dividend or simply be included in the gross income of the recipient. No hard and fast rules offer guidance for determining when compensation is excessive. As a result, the issue frequently is litigated.

Before 2003, the IRS's main focus was the corporation's deducting the excess amount of wages paid to a shareholder-employee. The shareholder-employee recognized ordinary income regardless of whether the excess was characterized as compensation or a dividend.

Because the tax rate on qualified dividends is now lower than the tax rate on salaries and wages, the corporation still will lose the deduction for excess compensation, but the IRS is unlikely to classify the excess as a dividend. Instead, the IRS probably will treat the excess as compensation to the shareholder-employee even though the corporation is not allowed to deduct it.[13]

Excessive Compensation Paid to Shareholders for the Use of Shareholder Property. As with compensation, corporate payments to shareholders for the use of property (i.e., rents, interest, and royalties) are deductible under Sec. 162(a) if they are ordinary, necessary, and reasonable in amount. The corporation may not deduct any amount exceeding what it would have paid to an unrelated party in an arm's-length transaction.

Corporate Payments for the Shareholder's Benefit. If a corporation pays the personal obligation of a shareholder, the corporate payment may result in gross income to the shareholder. Such a payment may cover the shareholder's personal debt, expenses in connection with the shareholder's personal residence, expenses incurred for the improvement of the shareholder's real property, or an obligation personally guaranteed by the shareholder.

In addition, if the IRS denies a corporate deduction, the disallowed deduction may result in gross income to the shareholder if the expenditure associated with the deduction conferred an economic benefit upon the shareholder. Examples of such expenditures are unsubstantiated travel and entertainment expenses; club dues; and automobile, airplane, and yacht expenses related to the shareholder-employee's personal use.

Bargain Purchase of Corporate Property. If a shareholder purchases corporate property at a discount relative to the property's FMV, the discount may be treated as a constructive dividend to the shareholder.

Shareholder Use of Corporate Property. If a shareholder uses corporate property (such as a hunting lodge, yacht, or airplane) without paying adequate consideration to the corporation, the fair rental value of such property (minus any amounts paid) may be treated as a constructive dividend to the shareholder.

Stock Dividends and Stock Rights

OBJECTIVE 4

Determine the tax consequences of stock dividends and the issuance of stock rights

In 1919, the Supreme Court held in *Eisner v. Macomber* that a stock dividend is not income to the shareholder because it takes no property from the corporation and adds no property to the shareholder.[14] Subsequently, Congress enacted the Revenue Act of 1921, which provides that stock dividends are nontaxable. Although this general rule still applies today, Congress has carved out several exceptions to prevent abuses.

Section 305(a) states, "Except as otherwise provided in this section, gross income does not include the amount of any distribution of the stock of a corporation made by such corporation to its shareholders with respect to its stock." Thus, a distribution of additional common stock with respect to a shareholder's pre-existing common stock holdings represents a nontaxable stock dividend. However, whenever a stock dividend changes or has the potential to change the shareholders' proportionate interest in the distributing corporation, the distribution will be taxable. Taxable stock distributions include those where

TYPICAL MISCONCEPTION

Stock dividends generally are nontaxable as long as a shareholder's proportionate interest in the corporation does not increase. If a shareholder's stock interest increases, Sec. 305(b) causes the dividend to be taxable.

- Any shareholder can elect to receive either stock of the distributing corporation or other property (e.g., cash).
- Some shareholders receive property and other shareholders receive an increase in their proportionate interest in the distributing corporation's assets or E&P.

[13] *Sterno Sales Corp. v. U.S.*, 15 AFTR 2d 979, 65-1 USTC ¶9419 (Ct. Cl., 1965).

[14] *Eisner v. Myrtle H. Macomber*, 3 AFTR 3020, 1 USTC ¶32 (USSC, 1919).

- Some holders of common stock receive preferred stock and others receive additional common stock.
- The underlying stock is preferred unless the distribution involves a change in the conversion ratio of convertible preferred stock to take into account a common stock dividend or a common stock split.
- The distributed stock is convertible preferred, unless it can be established that the distribution will have no disproportionate effect.

The following example illustrates one such exception.

EXAMPLE C:4-18 ▶ Two shareholders, Al and Beth, each own 100 of the 200 outstanding shares of Peach Corporation stock. Because Al's marginal tax rate is high, he does not want to recognize any additional income in the current year. Beth has a low marginal tax rate and needs additional cash. Peach, whose current E&P is $100,000, declares a dividend payable in stock or cash. Each taxpayer can receive one share of Peach stock (valued at $100) or $100 in cash for each share of Peach stock already owned. Al, who elects to receive stock, receives 100 additional Peach shares. Beth, who elects to receive cash, receives $10,000. Beth's distribution is taxable as a dividend. Absent any exceptions to Sec. 305, Al's dividend would be nontaxable because it was paid in Peach stock. After the distribution, however, Al owns two-thirds of the outstanding shares of Peach stock, whereas before the distribution he owned only one-half of Peach's outstanding shares. In this case, an exception to the general rule of Sec. 305(a) applies so that Al is deemed to have received a taxable dividend equal to the value of the additional shares he received. Even if both shareholders elected to receive a stock dividend, this dividend would be taxable because each shareholder had the option to receive cash. In this example, Al and Beth each recognize $10,000 of dividend income. Al's basis in his new shares is their $10,000 FMV. His basis in his original shares is unchanged. Peach reduces its E&P by $20,000, the amount of the taxable dividend to Al and Beth. ◀

NONTAXABLE STOCK DIVIDENDS

If a **stock dividend** is nontaxable, the basis of the stock with respect to which the distribution was made must be allocated between the old and new shares.[15] The holding period for the new shares includes the holding period for the old shares.[16]

If the old and new shares are identical, the basis of each share is determined by dividing the basis of the old shares by the total number of shares held by the shareholder after the distribution.

EXAMPLE C:4-19 ▶ Barbara owns 1,000 shares of Axle Corporation common stock having a $66,000 basis ($66 per share). Barbara receives a nontaxable 10% common stock dividend and now owns 1,100 Axle common shares. Her basis in each share becomes $60 ($66,000 ÷ 1,100). ◀

If the old and new shares are not identical, the basis of the old shares is allocated according to the relative FMVs of the old and new shares on the distribution date.

EXAMPLE C:4-20 ▶ Mark owns 1,000 shares of Axle Corporation common stock having a $60,000 basis. In a nontaxable distribution, Mark receives 50 shares of Axle preferred stock. At the time of the distribution, the FMV of the common stock is $90,000 ($90 × 1,000 shares), and the FMV of the preferred stock is $10,000 ($200 × 50 shares). After the distribution, $6,000 [($10,000 ÷ $100,000) × $60,000] of the common stock basis is allocated to the preferred stock, and the basis of the common stock is reduced from $60,000 to $54,000. ◀

REAL-WORLD EXAMPLE

Tracking the effects of nontaxable dividends, stock splits, stock dividends, and stock rights distributions on the basis of a stock investment can be difficult and time consuming. A number of publishers offer capital change reporters that provide a complete history of these four types of events for publicly traded companies. These reporters greatly simplify the stock basis calculations.

NONTAXABLE STOCK RIGHTS

Under Sec. 305, a distribution of **stock rights** is nontaxable unless it changes, or has the potential to change, the shareholders' proportionate interest in the distributing corporation. The same Sec. 305(b) exceptions to the nontaxability of stock dividends also apply to distributions of stock rights.

If the value of the stock rights is less than 15% of the value of the stock with respect to which the rights were distributed (i.e., the underlying stock), the basis of the rights is zero unless the shareholder elects to allocate stock basis to the rights.[17] If the taxpayer intends to sell the

[15] Sec. 307(a) and Reg. Secs. 1.307-1 and -2.
[16] Sec. 1223(5).
[17] Sec. 307(b)(1).

rights, an allocation of his or her stock basis to the rights might be advisable so as to minimize the amount of gain recognized on the sale. The election to allocate stock basis to the rights must be made in a statement attached to the shareholder's return for the year in which the rights are received. The allocation must be based on the relative FMVs of the stock and the stock rights. The holding period for the rights includes the holding period for the underlying stock.[18]

EXAMPLE C:4-21 ▶ Linda owns 100 shares of Yale Corporation common stock having a $27,000 basis and a $50,000 FMV. Linda receives 100 nontaxable stock rights with a $4,000 FMV. Because the FMV of the stock rights is less than 15% of the FMV of the underlying stock (0.15 × $50,000 = $7,500), the basis of the stock rights is zero unless Linda elects to allocate the $27,000 stock basis between the stock and the stock rights. If Linda makes the election, the basis of the rights is $2,000 [($4,000 ÷ $54,000) × $27,000], and the basis of the stock is $25,000 ($27,000 − $2,000). ◀

If the value of the stock rights is 15% or more of the value of the underlying stock, the shareholder must allocate the basis of the underlying stock between the stock and the stock rights. This provision is mandatory, not elective.

EXAMPLE C:4-22 ▶ Kay owns 100 shares of Minor Corporation common stock having a $14,000 basis and a $30,000 FMV. Kay receives 100 stock rights with a total FMV of $5,000. Because the FMV of the stock rights is at least 15% of the stock's FMV (0.15 × $30,000 = $4,500), the $14,000 basis must be allocated between the stock rights and the underlying stock based on their relative FMVs. The basis of the stock rights is $2,000 [($5,000 ÷ $35,000) × $14,000], and the basis of the underlying stock is $12,000 [($30,000 ÷ $35,000) × $14,000]. ◀

TYPICAL MISCONCEPTION

Taxpayers often get confused about what happens to a stock right. A stock right may be sold or exercised, which means the actual stock is acquired. If the rights are not sold or exercised, they eventually will lapse.

If the taxpayer sells the stock rights, he or she calculates gain or loss by subtracting the allocated basis of the rights (if any) from the sale price. A shareholder cannot claim a loss if the stock rights expire. If the stock rights do expire, the basis of the allocated rights is added back to the basis of the underlying stock. If the taxpayer exercises the rights before they expire, the basis of the allocated rights is added to the basis of the stock acquired through the exercise of the rights.[19] The holding period for the stock acquired begins on the exercise date.[20]

EXAMPLE C:4-23 ▶ In a nontaxable distribution, Jeff receives ten stock rights to which no stock basis is allocated. Each stock right entitles Jeff to acquire one share of Jackson stock for $20. If Jeff exercises all ten rights, the Jackson stock acquired will have a $200 (10 rights × $20) basis. If instead Jeff sells the ten rights for $30 each, he will recognize a gain of $300 [($30 × 10 rights) − 0 basis]. If the rights expire, Jeff may not claim a loss. ◀

EFFECT OF NONTAXABLE STOCK DIVIDENDS ON THE DISTRIBUTING CORPORATION

BOOK-TO-TAX ACCOUNTING COMPARISON

For financial accounting purposes, stock dividends reduce retained earnings. However, for tax purposes, nontaxable stock dividends have no effect on a corporation's E&P.

From a tax perspective, nontaxable distributions of stock and stock rights have no tax effect on the distributing corporation. The corporation recognizes no gain or loss and does not reduce its E&P balance.[21]

TAXABLE STOCK DIVIDENDS AND STOCK RIGHTS

If a distribution of stock or stock rights is taxable, the distribution amount equals the FMV of the stock or stock rights on the distribution date. The distribution is treated in the same way as any other property distribution. It is a dividend to the extent of the distributing corporation's E&P, and the recipient takes a FMV basis in the stock or stock rights received.[22] The holding period for the stock or stock rights begins on the day after the distribution date. No adjustment is made to the basis of the underlying stock. The distributing corporation recognizes no gain or loss on the distribution,[23] and the corporation reduces its E&P by the FMV of the stock or stock rights on the distribution date.

Topic Review C:4-3 summarizes the tax consequences of a stock dividend.

[18] Sec. 1223(5).
[19] Reg. Sec. 1.307-1(b).
[20] Sec. 1223(6).
[21] Secs. 311(a) and 312(d).
[22] Reg. Sec. 1.301-1(h)(2)(i).
[23] Sec. 311(a). Gain may be recognized when the shareholder can elect to receive either appreciated property or stock or stock rights of the distributing corporation.

TOPIC REVIEW C:4-3

Tax Consequences of a Stock Dividend

SHAREHOLDERS:

1. A stock dividend is nontaxable except where (1) a shareholder can elect to receive other property in lieu of the stock dividend; (2) some shareholders receive property and other shareholders increase their proportionate equity interest; (3) some common shareholders receive preferred and others receive common stock; (4) the underlying stock is preferred stock, unless the conversion ratio, if any, is adjusted to account for a common stock split or dividend; or (5) the distributed stock is convertible preferred, and the distribution has a disproportionate effect.
2. If the stock dividend meets one of the exceptions to nontaxable treatment, the stock dividend is treated as a property distribution under Sec. 301, where the FMV of the distribution is a taxable dividend to the extent of the distributing corporation's E&P.
3. If the stock dividend is nontaxable, (1) the basis of the underlying stock (old shares) is allocated among the old and new shares according to relative FMVs, and (2) the holding period for the new shares includes the holding period for the old shares.
4. If the stock dividend is taxable, (1) the distributed stock takes a basis equal to its FMV on the distribution date, and (2) the holding period begins the after the distribution date.

DISTRIBUTING CORPORATION:

1. The distributing corporation recognizes no gain or loss on the stock dividend, whether it is nontaxable or taxable.
2. If the stock dividend is nontaxable, the distributing corporation does not reduce its E&P.
3. If the stock dividend is taxable, the distributing corporation reduces its E&P to the extent the distribution is treated as a taxable dividend.

STOCK REDEMPTIONS

OBJECTIVE 5

Decide whether a stock redemption should be treated as a sale or a dividend

A **stock redemption** is a corporation's acquiring its own stock in exchange for corporate property. This property may be cash, securities of other corporations, or any other consideration the corporation uses to acquire its own stock.[24] The corporation may cancel the acquired stock, retire it, or hold it as treasury stock.

A stock redemption may be desirable for the following reasons:

- A shareholder may want to withdraw from the corporate business and sell his or her equity interest. In such a case, the shareholder may prefer that the corporation, rather than an outsider, purchase his or her stock so that the remaining shareholders (who may be family members) retain complete control and ownership of the corporation after his or her withdrawal from the business.
- A shareholder may be required to sell stock to the corporation under the terms of a stock purchase agreement with the issuing corporation.
- A shareholder may want to reduce his or her equity interest in a corporation but may be unwilling or unable to sell stock to outsiders. For example, no market may exist for the shares, or sales to outsiders may be restricted.
- A shareholder may want to withdraw assets from a corporation before a sale of the corporation's business. A potential purchaser may not be interested in acquiring all the assets or be able to pay full value for all outstanding shares. A withdrawal of some assets by the seller in exchange for some of his or her shares allows the purchaser to acquire the remaining shares and business assets at a lower total price.
- After the death of a major shareholder, a corporation may agree to purchase the decedent's stock from either the estate or a beneficiary to provide sufficient funds to pay estate and inheritance taxes and funeral and administrative expenses.
- Management may believe that the corporation's stock is selling at a low price and that, to increase share value, the corporation should acquire some of its stock in the open market.

[24] Sec. 317.

Whatever the reason for the redemption, the shareholder must answer the following questions:

- What is the amount of the income, gain, or loss recognized as a result of the redemption, and what is its character?
- What basis does the shareholder take in any property received in exchange for his or her stock?
- When does the holding period for the distributed property begin?
- What basis does the shareholder take in any distributing corporation stock held after the redemption?

The distributing corporation must answer the following questions:

- What amount and character of gain or loss, if any, must the corporation recognize when it redeems stock with noncash property?
- What effect does the redemption have on the corporation's E&P?[25]

TAX CONSEQUENCES OF THE REDEMPTION TO THE SHAREHOLDER

KEY POINT

As far as a shareholder is concerned, the basic issue in a stock redemption is whether the redemption is treated as a dividend or a sale.

As a general rule, when a shareholder sells or exchanges corporate stock, any gain or loss in the transaction is capital in character. In some cases, a redemption is treated as a stock sale. In other cases, it is treated as a dividend. The reason for this difference is that some redemptions resemble a stock sale to a third party, whereas others are essentially equivalent to a dividend. The following two examples illustrate the difference between a redemption resembling a dividend and a redemption resembling a sale. (The IRC refers to a "sale or exchange," but for simplicity in this chapter, we will use only the term "sale.")

EXAMPLE C:4-24 ▶ John owns all 100 outstanding shares of Tango Corporation stock. John's basis in his shares is $50,000, and Tango's E&P is $100,000. If Tango redeems 25 of John's shares for $85,000, John still owns 100% of Tango stock. Because John's proportionate ownership of Tango has not changed as a result of the redemption, the redemption resembles a dividend (i.e., a distribution of corporate earnings). Accordingly, for tax purposes, John is deemed to have received an $85,000 dividend. ◀

EXAMPLE C:4-25 ▶ Carol has owned three of the 1,000 outstanding shares of Water Corporation stock for two years. Her basis in the shares is $1,000, and Water's E&P is $100,000. If Water redeems all three of Carol's shares for $5,000, Carol is essentially in the same position as a seller of stock to a third party. She has received $5,000 for her stock and has no further ownership interest in the corporation. Thus, the redemption resembles a sale and is not essentially equivalent to a dividend. Accordingly, Carol recognizes a $4,000 ($5,000 − $1,000) capital gain. ◀

Example C:4-24 is an extreme case involving a redemption that clearly should be treated as a dividend to the shareholder. Example C:4-25 also is an extreme case involving a redemption that clearly should be treated as a sale of stock by the shareholder. Many cases, however, fall between the two extremes, and the way the redemption should be treated is not immediately apparent. The problem for Congress and the courts has been how to distinguish redemptions that should be treated as sales from those that should be treated as dividends. Under current law, a redemption qualifies for sale treatment if it satisfies one of the following conditions:

- The redemption is substantially disproportionate.
- The redemption is a complete termination of the shareholder's interest.
- The redemption is not essentially equivalent to a dividend.
- The redemption involves a partial liquidation of the corporation in conjunction with its redeeming stock from a noncorporate shareholder.
- The redemption provides funds for an estate to pay death taxes.

If a redemption qualifies as a sale, the transaction is treated as though the shareholder sold stock to a third party. The shareholder recognizes gain or loss equal to the FMV of

[25] This discussion concerns the redemption of C corporation stock. Different rules apply to the redemption of S corporation stock.

the property received less the shareholder's adjusted basis in the stock surrendered. The gain or loss is capital in character if the stock is a capital asset in the hands of the shareholder. The shareholder's basis in any property received is its FMV. The holding period for the property begins on the day following the exchange date.

A redemption that does not satisfy any of the five conditions necessary for sale treatment is regarded as a property distribution under Sec. 301. Accordingly, the entire amount of the distribution is treated as a dividend to the extent of the distributing corporation's E&P.[26] The shareholder's stock basis is not taken into account in determining the dividend amount. Generally, this basis is added to the basis of any remaining shares owned by the shareholder. If all the shareholder's stock has been redeemed, the basis of the redeemed shares is added to the basis of shares owned by those individuals whose ownership is attributed to the shareholder under attribution rules described below.[27]

EXAMPLE C:4-26 ▶ Amy and Rose each own 50 of the 100 outstanding shares of stock in York Corporation, which reports $100,000 of E&P. On May 10, York redeems 20 of Amy's shares with property worth $25,000. Amy's adjusted basis in those shares is $20,000. If the redemption satisfies one of the conditions necessary for sale treatment, Amy recognizes a capital gain of $5,000 ($25,000 − $20,000). Her basis in the property received is its $25,000 FMV, and its holding period begins on May 11. If the redemption does not satisfy any of the conditions necessary for sale treatment, Amy recognizes $25,000 of dividend income. Her $20,000 basis in the surrendered shares is added to the basis of her remaining 30 shares. ◀

ADDITIONAL COMMENT

Because capital gains and qualified dividends are taxed at the same rate, the difference in tax between exchange treatment and dividend treatment is primarily a function of the taxpayer's basis in the redeemed stock. Another difference is that dividends cannot offset capital losses.

Structuring a stock redemption as a sale offers two advantages. First, capital gains may be offset by capital losses. Second, in a sale, the basis of the shares redeemed reduces the amount of income recognized. By contrast, if a redemption is treated as a dividend, the basis of the shares redeemed does not reduce the dividend amount. Instead, the basis shifts to the shareholder's remaining stock, which reduces the gain (or increases the loss) recognized in a later sale of this stock.

Topic Review C:4-4 summarizes the tax consequences of stock redemptions to both the shareholder and the distributing corporation.

ATTRIBUTION RULES

Three of the five tests for determining how a redemption should be treated (i.e., as a sale or dividend) are based on stock ownership before and after the redemption. The tests measure the extent to which the shareholder's proportionate interest in the corporation has been reduced as a result of the exchange. In general, if the shareholder's proportionate interest has been substantially reduced, the redemption is treated as a sale. On the other hand, if this

TOPIC REVIEW C:4-4

Tax Consequences of Stock Redemptions

SHAREHOLDERS:

General Rule: The distribution amount received by a shareholder in exchange for his or her stock is treated as a dividend to the extent of the distributing corporation's E&P. The basis of the surrendered stock is added to the basis of the shareholder's remaining stock.

Sale Exception: If the redemption meets specific requirements, the distribution amount received by the shareholder is offset by the adjusted basis of the shares surrendered. The difference generally is treated as a capital gain or loss. No basis adjustment occurs.

DISTRIBUTING CORPORATION:

Gain/Loss Recognition: Under either the general rule or sale exception, the corporation recognizes gain (but not loss) as though it had sold distributed noncash property for its FMV immediately before the redemption.

Earnings and Profits Adjustment: For a redemption treated as a dividend, E&P is reduced in the same manner as for a regular dividend (e.g., by the amount of any money or the FMV of any property distributed). For a redemption treated as a sale, E&P is reduced by the portion of current and accumulated E&P attributable to the redeemed stock. Any distribution amount exceeding this portion reduces the corporation's paid-in capital.

---

[26] Sec. 302(d).

[27] Reg. Sec. 1.302-2(c).

interest remains essentially the same or increases, the redemption is treated as a dividend (assuming sufficient E&P).

For the purpose of applying these tests, stock ownership is determined under the constructive ownership or attribution rules of Sec. 318.[28] According to these rules, a shareholder owns not only the shares he or she directly owns but also shares owned by his or her spouse, other immediate family members, and related entities. In addition, corporations, partnerships, trusts, and estates are considered to constructively own shares owned by their shareholders, partners, and beneficiaries.

The attribution rules prevent shareholders from taking advantage of favorable tax rules or avoiding unfavorable tax rules by transferring to family members or related entities stock that the shareholder previously owned. The proportionate stock ownership tests would be subject to abuse if only direct ownership were considered.

Section 318(a) sets forth four types of attribution rules: attribution among family members, attribution from entities, attribution to entities, and option attribution. These rules are discussed below.

ADDITIONAL COMMENT

The family attribution rules of Sec. 318 are not as inclusive as the family attribution rules of Sec. 267 (covered in Chapter C:3). For example, siblings and grandparents are not considered family members by Sec. 318 but are included under Sec. 267.

Family Attribution. Under the first set of rules, an individual is considered to own constructively all stock owned by or for his or her spouse, children, grandchildren, and parents. An individual is not considered to own stock owned by his or her brothers, sisters, or grandparents.

Once attributed to an individual under one set of attribution rules, stock ownership may not be reattributed to another individual under the same set of rules. Thus, stock ownership attributed to one family member under the family attribution rules may not be reattributed to a second family member under the same set of rules. However, once attributed to an individual under one set of attribution rules, stock ownership may be reattributed to another individual under a different set of attribution rules. For example, stock ownership attributed from a corporation to its shareholder under the corporate attribution rules may be reattributed to the shareholder's spouse under the family attribution rules.

EXAMPLE C:4-27 ▶ Harry; his wife, Wilma; their son, Steve; and Harry's father, Frank, each own 25 of the 100 outstanding shares of Strong Corporation stock. Under the family attribution rules, Harry is considered to own all 100 Strong shares (25 directly plus constructively the shares owned by Wilma, Steve, and Frank). Wilma is considered to own 75 shares (25 directly plus constructively the 50 shares owned by Harry and Steve). Ownership of Frank's shares is neither directly attributed to Wilma nor reattributed to Wilma through Harry. Steve is considered to own 75 shares (25 directly plus constructively the 50 shares owned by his parents Harry and Wilma). Ownership of Frank's shares is neither directly attributed to Steve nor reattributed to Steve through Harry. Frank is considered to own 75 shares (25 directly plus constructively the shares owned by Harry and Steve (his grandson)). Ownership of Wilma's shares is neither directly attributed to Frank nor reattributed to Frank through Harry.

The diagram below illustrates the constructive stock ownership of the four shareholders. The arrows indicate the direction(s) of ownership attribution.

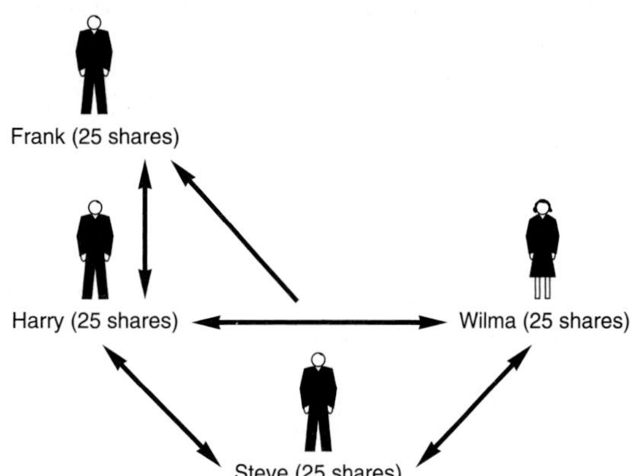

[28] Sec. 302(c).

The table below shows each shareholder's direct and constructive stock ownership. Note that the total number of shares owned directly and constructively by all shareholders may exceed the total number of actual shares issued and outstanding.

		Shares Constructively Owned From:				
Shareholder	*Direct Ownership*	*Spouse*	*Child*	*Grandchild*	*Parent(s)*	*Total*
Frank	25		25	25		75
Harry	25	25	25		25	100
Wilma	25	25	25			75
Steve	25				50	75
	100					

Attribution from Entities. Under the second set of attribution rules, stock owned by or for a partnership is considered to be owned proportionately by the partners. Stock owned by or for an estate is considered to be owned proportionately by the beneficiaries. Stock owned by or for a trust is considered to be owned by the beneficiaries in proportion to their actuarial interests. Stock owned by or for a C corporation is considered to be owned proportionately only by shareholders owning (directly or indirectly) 50% or more of the corporation's stock value.[29]

EXAMPLE C:4-28 ▶ Bill, who is married to Nancy, owns a 50% interest in Partnership A. Partnership A owns 40 of the 100 outstanding shares of Yellow Corporation stock, and Bill owns the remaining 60 shares. Under the entity attribution rules, Bill is considered to own 80 shares, 60 directly and 20 (0.50 × 40 shares) constructively. In addition, the stock ownership attributed to Bill under the entity attribution rules is reattributed to Nancy under the family attribution rules. ◀

Attribution to Entities. Under the third set of attribution rules, all stock owned by or for a partner is considered to be constructively owned by the partnership. All stock owned by or for a beneficiary of an estate or a trust is considered to be constructively owned by the estate or trust. All stock owned by or for a shareholder who owns (directly or indirectly) 50% or more of a C corporation's stock value is considered to be constructively owned by the corporation.

Stock ownership attributed to a partnership, estate, trust, or corporation from a partner, beneficiary, or shareholder is not reattributed from the entity to another partner, beneficiary, or shareholder.

EXAMPLE C:4-29 ▶ Assume the same facts as in Example C:4-28. The partnership in which Bill is a partner is considered to own all 100 shares of Yellow stock (40 directly and 60 constructively through Bill). Bill's stock ownership attributed to the partnership cannot be reattributed from the partnership to Bill's partners. ◀

Option Attribution. Under the last set of attribution rules, a person who holds an option to purchase stock is considered to own the underlying stock.

EXAMPLE C:4-30 ▶ John owns 25 of the 100 outstanding shares of Yard Corporation stock. He holds an option to acquire an additional 50 shares. John is considered to own 75 Yard shares (25 directly plus 50 constructively through the option). ◀

SUBSTANTIALLY DISPROPORTIONATE REDEMPTIONS

Under Sec. 302(b)(2), if a stock redemption is substantially disproportionate with respect to a shareholder, it is treated as a sale and thus qualifies for capital gain as opposed to dividend treatment. A redemption is substantially disproportionate with respect to a shareholder if all the following conditions are met:

- After the redemption, the shareholder owns less than 50% of the total combined voting power of all classes of voting stock.

[29] For purposes of the attribution rules, S corporations are treated as partnerships, not corporations. Thus, attribution occurs to and from shareholders owning less than 50% of the S corporation stock. Unless otherwise stated, all corporations in the examples are C corporations.

- After the redemption, the shareholder owns less than 80% of his or her percentage ownership of voting stock before the redemption.
- After the redemption, the shareholder owns less than 80% of his or her percentage ownership of common stock (whether voting or nonvoting) before the redemption.

TAX STRATEGY TIP

If possible, taxpayers should structure a redemption to meet the substantially disproportionate test rather than the subjective "not equivalent to a dividend" test (discussed on page C:4-23), thereby obtaining certainty of results.

These tests are applied mechanically to each shareholder's ownership interest. The 50% test precludes shareholders from qualifying for capital gains treatment if they own a controlling interest in the distributing corporation after the redemption. The 80% tests define a degree of change in the shareholder's proportionate interest that constitutes a substantial reduction in that interest. A redemption may be substantially disproportionate with respect to one shareholder but not another. If only one class of stock is outstanding, the second and third requirements are essentially the same.

EXAMPLE C:4-31 ▶

Long Corporation has issued 400 shares of common stock and plans to redeem 100 of these shares. Before the redemption, Ann, Bob, Carl, and Dana (all unrelated) own 100 shares each. Long redeems 55 shares from Ann, 25 shares from Bob, and 20 shares from Carl. The following table illustrates ownership before and after the redemption.

ADDITIONAL COMMENT

In calculating the percentage of stock owned *after* a redemption note that the denominator used is the number of shares outstanding *after* the redemption.

	Before Redemption			*After Redemption*	
Shareholder	*No. of Shares Owned*	*Percentage of Ownership*	*Shares Redeemed*	*No. of Shares Owned*	*Percentage of Ownership*
	(1)	(1) ÷ 400	(2)	(1) − (2)	[(1) − (2)] ÷ 300
Ann	100	25%	55	45	15.00%
Bob	100	25%	25	75	25.00%
Carl	100	25%	20	80	26.67%
Dana	100	25%	—	100	33.33%
Total	400	100%	100	300	100.00%

The redemption is substantially disproportionate with respect to Ann because, after the redemption, she owns less than 50% of Long's stock, and her stock ownership percentage (15%) is less than 80% of her stock ownership percentage before the redemption (0.80 × 25% = 20%). The redemption is not substantially disproportionate with respect to Bob because the percentage reduction in his stock ownership is not less than 80% of his pre-redemption ownership percentage. In fact, Bob owns the same percentage of stock (25%) after the redemption as he did before the redemption (25%). The redemption also is not substantially disproportionate with respect to Carl because his stock ownership percentage increases from 25% to 26.67%. Thus, only the redemption of Ann's shares is treated as a sale and qualifies for capital gains treatment. ◀

The constructive ownership rules of Sec. 318(a) apply in determining whether the shareholder has met the three conditions for a substantially disproportionate redemption.[30]

EXAMPLE C:4-32 ▶

Assume the same facts as in Example C:4-31 except that Ann is Bob's mother. In this case, the redemption is not substantially disproportionate with respect to either Ann or Bob because, before the redemption, each directly and constructively owns 200 shares, or 50% of the Long stock, and after the redemption each directly and constructively owns 120 shares, or 40% of the stock. Although the 50% test is met, neither Ann nor Bob satisfies the 80% test. After the redemption each directly and constructively owns *exactly* 80% of the percentage owned before the redemption (0.80 × 50% = 40%). ◀

COMPLETE TERMINATION OF THE SHAREHOLDER'S INTEREST

Under Sec. 302(b)(3), if a stock redemption completely terminates a shareholder's interest in the corporation, the redemption also is treated as a sale. At first glance, this rule does not offer a route to sale treatment that is not already provided by the other Sec. 302 rules. If a corporation redeems all of a shareholder's stock, in most cases the requirements for a substantially disproportionate redemption under Sec. 302(b)(2) would have been satisfied.

[30] Reg. Sec. 1.302-3(a).

However, the complete termination rule extends sale treatment to two redemptions not covered by the substantially disproportionate redemption rules:

- If a shareholder's interest in a corporation consists exclusively of nonvoting stock, a redemption of all the stock could not qualify as substantially disproportionate under Sec. 302(b)(2) because no reduction of voting power occurs. However, it could qualify as a complete termination of the shareholder's interest under Sec. 302(b)(3) because the interest need not consist of voting stock.
- If a shareholder owns some voting stock and the redemption terminates his or her entire interest in the corporation, the family attribution rules of Sec. 318(a)(1) may be waived. Consequently, the redemption could qualify for sale treatment even though other family members continue to own some or all of the corporation's stock.[31]

To have the family attribution rules waived, the shareholder must meet all of the following conditions:

- After the redemption, the shareholder must not retain any interest in the corporation except as a creditor. This restriction includes any interest as an officer, director, or employee.
- The shareholder must not acquire any such interest (other than by bequest or inheritance) for at least ten years from the date of the redemption.
- The shareholder must file a written agreement with the IRS that he or she will notify the IRS upon acquiring any prohibited interest.

The written agreement authorizes the IRS to assess additional taxes for the year of the redemption if the prohibited interest is acquired, even when the basic three-year limitations period has expired.

EXAMPLE C:4-33 ▶ Father and Son each own 50 of the 100 outstanding shares of Short Corporation stock. Short redeems all of Father's shares. Under the family attribution rules, Father is considered to own directly and constructively 100% of the Short stock both before and after the redemption. Thus, the redemption is not substantially disproportionate with respect to him. However, if Father agrees not to retain or acquire any interest in Short for ten years (except as a creditor, devisee, or heir), the family attribution rules may be waived. Consequently, the redemption could qualify as a complete termination of Father's interest and be treated as a sale. ◀

Waiver of the family attribution rules is not permitted in the following two situations involving related parties:

- Within the ten-year period ending on the distribution date, the distributee acquired, directly or indirectly, part or all of the redeemed stock from a person whose stock ownership would be attributable (at the time of the distribution) to the distributee under Sec. 318.
- Any person owns (at the time of the distribution) stock of the redeeming corporation the ownership of which is attributable to the distributee under Sec. 318, and such person acquired any stock in the redeeming corporation, directly or indirectly, from the distributee within the ten-year period ending on the distribution date.

The first restriction is aimed at an individual who transfers stock to a related party (e.g., family member or controlled entity) purportedly to enable the related party to invoke the complete termination provision so as to recognize a capital gain when the corporation redeems the transferred stock. The second restriction is aimed at an individual who transfers some of his or her stock to a related party purportedly to invoke the complete termination provision so as to recognize a capital gain when the corporation redeems his or her remaining stock. These prohibitions against waiving the family attribution rules do not apply if the shareholder transferred the stock more than ten years before the redemption or if the distributee can show that the acquisition or disposition of the stock did not have tax avoidance as one of its principal purposes. In the second situation above, the family attribution rules also can be waived if the corporation redeems as part of the same transaction stock previously transferred to the related party.

Note that only the family attribution rules can be waived. Entities may have the family attribution rules waived if both the entity and the individual whose stock is attributed to the entity agree not to acquire any prohibited interest in the corporation for at least ten years.

[31] Section 302(c)(2) provides for the waiver of family attribution rules.

EXAMPLE C:4-34 ▶ Andrew created the A Trust, which owns 30% of Willow Corporation stock. Andrew's wife, Wanda, is the sole beneficiary of the trust. Their son, Steve, owns the remaining 70% of Willow stock. Willow redeems all of its stock owned by the A Trust. At first glance, the redemption does not qualify for sale treatment because the trust is deemed to own all the stock owned by Wanda, and Wanda is deemed to own all the stock owned by Steve. However, if both A Trust and Wanda agree not to acquire any interest in the corporation for ten years, the family attribution rules may be waived. Consequently, the redemption will be treated as a complete termination of the trust's interest in Willow and will be eligible for sale treatment. ◀

REDEMPTIONS NOT ESSENTIALLY EQUIVALENT TO A DIVIDEND

KEY POINT

Section 302(b)(1) has generally been interpreted to require that a shareholder incur a "meaningful reduction" of its stock interest. What constitutes a "meaningful reduction" remains unsettled.

Section 302(b)(1) provides that a redemption will be treated as a sale if it is not essentially equivalent to a dividend. The tax law sets forth no mechanical test for determining when a redemption is not essentially equivalent to a dividend. Instead, it implies that a determination should be based on the facts and circumstances of each case.[32] Sec. 302(b)(1) does not provide a safe harbor similar to the rules for substantially disproportionate redemptions or redemptions that are a complete termination of a shareholder's interest. On the other hand, the provision prevents the redemption rules from being too restrictive, especially in the case of transactions involving preferred stock.

The Supreme Court's decision in *Maclin P. Davis* sets forth guidelines for determining when a redemption is not essentially equivalent to a dividend.[33] The Supreme Court held that (1) in this determination, a business purpose is irrelevant; (2) the Sec. 318 attribution rules must be applied to establish dividend equivalency; and (3) a redemption of part of a sole shareholder's stock is always essentially equivalent to a dividend. The Court further held that for Sec. 302(b)(1) purposes, there must be a "meaningful reduction" in the shareholder's proportionate interest in the corporation after taking into account the constructive ownership rules of Sec. 318(a). Despite this holding, the definition of "a meaningful reduction in interest" remains unclear.

Because of this lack of clarity, Sec. 302(b)(1) generally applies to a redemption of nonvoting preferred stock only where the shareholder does not own any common stock,[34] or to redemptions resulting in a substantial reduction in the shareholder's rights to vote and exercise control over the corporation, participate in earnings, and share in net assets upon liquidation. Generally, the IRS allows sale treatment if a controlling shareholder reduces his or her interest to a noncontrolling position,[35] or a noncontrolling shareholder further reduces his or her minority interest.[36] A shareholder does not qualify for sale treatment if he or she maintains control both before and after the redemption,[37] or if he or she assumes a controlling position.

EXAMPLE C:4-35 ▶ Four unrelated individuals own all of Thyme Corporation's single class of stock as follows: Alan, 27%; Betty, 24.33%; Clem, 24.33%; and David, 24.33%. Thyme redeems some of Alan's stock holdings, resulting in a reduction of Alan's interest to 22.27%. Betty, Clem, and David own equally the remaining 77.73% of Thyme stock. The redemption of Alan's stock does not qualify as substantially disproportionate because Alan's interest is not reduced below 21.6% (0.80 × 27% = 21.6%). Nor does the redemption qualify as a complete termination of Alan's interest because Alan still owns Thyme shares. However, the redemption might be treated as a sale under Sec. 302(b)(1) because the transaction results in a meaningful reduction of Alan's noncontrolling interest in Thyme. ◀

PARTIAL LIQUIDATIONS

Under Sec. 302(b)(4), a redemption of a noncorporate shareholder's stock qualifies for sale treatment if the redemption is in **partial liquidation** of the corporation. A partial liquidation occurs when a corporation discontinues one line of business, distributes assets used in that business to its shareholders, and continues at least one other line of business.[38] A distribution

[32] Reg. Sec. 1.302-2(b).

[33] *U.S. v. Maclin P. Davis,* 25 AFTR 2d 70-827, 70-1 USTC ¶9289 (USSC, 1970).

[34] Reg. Sec. 1.302-2(a).

[35] In Rev. Rul. 75-502, 1975-2 C.B. 111, a reduction in stock ownership from 57% to 50% where the shareholder no longer had control was considered a meaningful reduction in interest.

[36] In Rev. Rul. 76-364, 1976-2 C.B. 91, a reduction in stock ownership from 27% to 22% was considered a meaningful reduction in interest.

[37] See *Jack Paparo,* 71 T.C. 692 (1979), where reductions in stock ownership from 100% to 81.17% and from 100% to 74.15% were not considered meaningful reductions in interest.

[38] A partial liquidation also can occur when a corporation sells one line of business, distributes the sales proceeds (after paying taxes on any gain from the sale), and continues at least one other line of business. See Rev. Rul. 79-275, 1979-2 C.B. 137.

in partial liquidation qualifies for sale treatment if it is not essentially equivalent to a dividend. The distribution must be made within the tax year in which a plan of partial liquidation has been adopted or within the succeeding tax year.

Determination Made at the Corporate Level. For purposes of Sec. 302(b)(4), whether a distribution is not essentially equivalent to a dividend is determined at the corporate level.[39] The distribution must result from a bona fide contraction of the corporate business. In relevant Treasury Regulations and revenue rulings, the government provides guidance as to what constitutes a bona fide business contraction. Examples include

- The distribution of insurance proceeds received as a result of a fire that destroys part of a business.[40]
- Termination of a contract representing 95% of a domestic corporation's gross income.[41]
- Change in a corporation's business from a full-line department store to a discount apparel store, which results in the elimination of certain units; the elimination of most forms of credit; and a reduction in inventory, floor space, and employees.[42]

Safe Harbor Rule. Under Sec. 302(e)(2), a distribution satisfies the not-essentially-equivalent-to-a-dividend requirement and qualifies as a partial liquidation if

- The distribution is attributable to the distributing corporation's ceasing to conduct a qualified trade or business, or consists of the assets of a qualified trade or business; and
- Immediately after the distribution, the distributing corporation is engaged in the active conduct of at least one qualified trade or business.

  A qualified trade or business is any trade or business that

- Has been actively conducted throughout the five-year period ending on the date of the redemption, and
- Was not acquired by the corporation within such five-year period in a partially or wholly taxable transaction.

The definition of an active trade or business is the same as that used for Sec. 355 (corporate division) purposes, as discussed in Chapter C:7.

EXAMPLE C:4-36 ▶ Sage Corporation has manufactured hats and gloves for the past five years. In the current year, Sage discontinues hat manufacturing, sells all of its hat manufacturing machinery, and distributes the proceeds to its shareholders in redemption of some of their Sage shares. The corporation continues glove manufacturing. The distribution is pursuant to a partial liquidation and thus qualifies for sale treatment. ◀

Tax Consequences of a Partial Liquidation to the Shareholders. If a distribution is in partial liquidation of the corporation, a noncorporate shareholder treats the redemption of his or her stock as a sale, whether or not the distribution is pro rata. In contrast, a corporate shareholder treats the redemption distribution as a dividend unless the corporation meets one of the other tests for sale treatment (i.e., Sec. 302(b)(1)-(3) or Sec. 303). For a corporate shareholder, dividend treatment may be more advantageous than sale treatment because a corporation receives no preferential tax rate on capital gains, but may be eligible for a 70%, 80%, or 100% dividends-received deduction. In determining whether stock is owned by a corporate or noncorporate shareholder, stock held by a partnership, trust, or estate is considered to be held proportionately by its partners or beneficiaries.

EXAMPLE C:4-37 ▶ Assume the same facts as in Example C:4-36 except Sage Corporation is owned by Ted and Jolly Corporation. Each shareholder owns 50 shares of Sage stock with a $20,000 basis and has owned the stock since Sage's inception. Sage reports $100,000 of current and accumulated E&P. Sage distributes $18,000 to each shareholder in redemption of ten shares of stock worth $18,000. Because the redemption involves a partial liquidation, Ted treats

[39] Sec. 302(e)(1)(A).
[40] Reg. Sec. 1.346-1.
[41] Rev. Rul. 75-3, 1975-1 C.B. 108.
[42] Rev. Rul. 74-296, 1974-1 C.B. 80.

the transaction as a sale and recognizes a capital gain of $14,000 ($18,000 − $4,000). Jolly, however, cannot treat the transaction as a sale because Jolly is a corporate shareholder and thus must recognize $18,000 of dividend income. On the other hand, Jolly is eligible for a $14,400 (0.80 × $18,000) dividends-received deduction. Jolly's $4,000 basis in the ten redeemed shares is added to the basis of its 40 remaining shares, resulting in a $20,000 basis in those shares. ◀

STOP & THINK

Question: Why is a distribution in partial liquidation of a corporation treated as a sale by its noncorporate shareholders and as a dividend by its corporate shareholders?

Solution: The different tax treatment probably reflects different tax advantages. Noncorporate shareholders benefit most from sale treatment because they can offset their stock basis against any amount realized in the distribution. Corporate shareholders benefit most from dividend treatment because they can take the dividends-received deduction, thereby reducing the dividend tax burden. These disparate advantages stem from the different tax status of corporations, other entities, and individuals.

TAX STRATEGY TIP

An estate with liquidity problems owing to large holdings of a closely held business also may want to consider installment payment of the estate tax under Sec. 6166. See Chapter C:13 for further details.

REDEMPTIONS TO PAY DEATH TAXES

If corporate stock represents a substantial portion of a decedent's gross estate, a redemption of the stock from the estate or its beneficiaries may be eligible for sale treatment under Sec. 303. This IRC section helps shareholders who inherit stock in a closely held corporation pay estate and inheritance taxes and funeral and administrative expenses. If the stock is not readily marketable, a stock redemption may be the only way to provide the estate and its beneficiaries with sufficient liquidity to defray the costs of estate administration. Under the substantially disproportionate or complete termination rules, ownership attribution would disqualify the redemption from sale treatment. Consequently, the redemption would be treated as a dividend. Under Sec. 303, ownership attribution does not apply to the portion of a stock redemption that meets certain requirements.

Section 303 provides that a redemption of stock that was included in a decedent's gross estate is treated as a stock sale by the shareholder (i.e., either the estate or the beneficiary of the estate) if the following conditions are met:

1. The value of the redeeming corporation's stock included in the decedent's gross estate is more than 35% of the adjusted gross estate. The adjusted gross estate consists of the FMV of all property on the date of the decedent's death less allowable deductions for funeral and administrative expenses, claims against the estate, debts, and casualty and other losses.

EXAMPLE C:4-38 ▶ A decedent's gross estate, valued at $10 million, includes $3 million in cash and Pepper Corporation stock worth $7 million. Funeral and other deductible estate expenses amount to $1 million. Thus, the decedent's adjusted gross estate is $9 million ($10,000,000 − $1,000,000). Because the $7 million value of the Pepper stock included in the gross estate exceeds 35% of the adjusted gross estate ($3.15 million = 0.35 × $9,000,000), a redemption of this stock qualifies for sale treatment under Sec. 303. ◀

2. The maximum amount of the redemption distribution that can qualify for sale treatment is the sum of all federal and state estate and inheritance taxes, plus any interest due on those taxes, and all funeral and administrative expenses allowable as deductions in computing the federal estate tax. The redemption must be of stock held by the estate or by the decedent's heirs who are liable for estate taxes and other administrative expenses.

3. Section 303 applies to a redemption distribution only to the extent the shareholder's interest in the estate is reduced by the payment of death taxes and funeral and administration expenses. The maximum distribution eligible for sale treatment is the amount of estate taxes and expenses the shareholder is obligated to bear.

EXAMPLE C:4-39 ▶ Assume the same facts as in Example C:4-38 except that, before the decedent's death, all the stock was gifted to the decedent's son, Sam. The remaining assets were bequeathed to the decedent's wife, Wilma, who as beneficiary is indirectly liable for all estate taxes and administrative expenses. Section 303 sale treatment is not available to Sam because he is not liable for estate taxes or administrative expenses. If instead $2 million in nonstock assets had been gifted to Wilma before the decedent's death, and the remaining assets bequeathed to Sam, Sam as beneficiary would be indirectly liable for all estate taxes and administrative expenses. In such case, he could use Sec. 303 to obtain sale treatment for the redemption of enough of his stock to pay estate taxes and administrative expenses. ◀

4. Section 303 applies only to distributions within certain time limits.
   a. In general, the redemption must occur not later than 90 days after the expiration of the period for assessing the federal estate tax. Because the limitations period for the federal estate tax expires three years after the estate tax return is due and because the return is due nine months after the date of death, the redemption generally must occur within four years after the date of death.
   b. If a petition for redetermination of an estate tax deficiency is filed with the Tax Court, the distribution period is extended to 60 days after the Tax Court's decision becomes final.
   c. If the taxpayer made a valid election under Sec. 6166 to defer paying of federal estate taxes under an installment plan, the distribution period is extended to the time the installment payments are due.
5. The stock of two or more corporations may be aggregated to meet the 35% threshold, provided that 20% or more of the value of each corporation's outstanding stock is included in the gross estate.

EXAMPLE C:4-40 ▶ A decedent's gross estate, valued at $11.8 million, includes 80% of the stock in Curry Corporation, valued at $2.6 million, and 90% of the stock in Brodie Corporation, valued at $1.4 million. Deductible funeral and administrative expenses amount to $1.8 million. Thus, the decedent's adjusted gross estate is $10 million ($11,800,000 − $1,800,000). Although the value of neither the Curry stock nor the Brodie stock exceeds 35% of the $10 million adjusted gross estate, the $4 million ($2,600,000 + $1,400,000) total value of both corporations' stock does exceed 35% of the adjusted gross estate ($3.5 million = 0.35 × $10,000,000). Therefore, a redemption of sufficient Curry stock and/or Brodie stock to pay estate taxes and funeral and administrative expenses qualifies for sale treatment under Sec. 303. ◀

Although the legislative intent behind Sec. 303 is to provide liquidity for the payment of estate taxes and administrative expenses where a significant portion of the estate consists of stock in a closely held corporation, a redemption can qualify for Sec. 303 sale treatment even where the estate includes sufficient liquid assets to pay estate taxes and defray administrative costs. The redemption proceeds need not be used for these purposes.

The advantage of a Sec. 303 redemption is that the redeeming shareholder usually realizes little or no capital gain because his or her basis in the redeemed stock is the stock's FMV on date of the decedent's death (or an alternate valuation date, if applicable). If the redemption does *not* qualify as a sale, the redeeming shareholder recognizes dividend income equal to the distribution proceeds received in redemption of the stock.

EXAMPLE C:4-41 ▶ Chili Corporation pays $105,000 to redeem 100 shares of stock from Art, who inherited the stock from his father, Fred. The stock's FMV on Fred's date of death was $100,000. Chili reports an E&P balance of $500,000. If the redemption qualifies for sale treatment under Sec. 303, Art recognizes a $5,000 ($105,000 − $100,000) capital gain. On the other hand, if the redemption does not qualify for sale treatment under Sec. 303 or one of the other redemption provisions, Art recognizes $105,000 of dividend income. Although both the capital gain and the dividend income are subject to the applicable capital gains tax rate, the dividend amount significantly exceeds the capital gain amount. ◀

SELF-STUDY QUESTION

How much gain is the redeeming shareholder likely to recognize in a qualifying Sec. 303 redemption?

ANSWER

Probably little or none. The basis in the redeemed stock equals its FMV at the decedent's date of death (or an alternate valuation date). The recognized gain generally is only the post-death appreciation.

EFFECT OF REDEMPTIONS ON THE DISTRIBUTING CORPORATION

As in the case of property distributions that are not in redemption of stock, two questions relating to property distributions in redemption of stock must be answered:

- What amount and character of gain or loss must the distributing corporation recognize?
- What effect does the distribution have on the corporation's E&P?

Each of these questions is addressed below.

Corporate Gain or Loss on Property Distributions. The rules for gain or loss recognition for a corporation that distributes property in redemption of its stock are the same as the Sec. 311 rules pertaining to property distributions not in redemption of stock.

- The corporation recognizes gain when it redeems its stock by distributing property that has appreciated in value. The character of the gain depends on the character of the property distributed.
- The corporation recognizes no loss when it redeems its stock by distributing property that has declined in value.

Effect of Redemptions on E&P. A stock redemption affects a corporation's E&P in two ways. First, if the corporation distributes appreciated property, the excess of the property's FMV over its E&P adjusted basis increases the balance in the E&P account. Second, if the corporation distributes cash, or other property, the corporation's E&P balance is reduced accordingly. The extent of the reduction depends on whether the shareholder treats the redemption as a sale or a dividend.

If the redemption is treated as a dividend, the corporation reduces its E&P by the amount of any cash, the principal amount of any obligations, and the greater of the adjusted basis or FMV of any other property distributed, in the same way as it does for a property distribution not in redemption of stock.

If the redemption is treated as a sale, the corporation reduces its E&P by the portion of its current and accumulated E&P attributable to the redeemed stock. In other words, E&P is reduced by the percentage of the total outstanding shares redeemed, not to exceed the actual distribution amount. Any distribution amount exceeding this percentage reduces the corporation's tax basis paid-in capital.[43] Ordinary dividend amounts are subtracted from current E&P before the subtraction of stock redemption amounts. No such sequencing exists for accumulated E&P. Both ordinary dividend distributions and redemption distributions reduce accumulated E&P in chronological order.

EXAMPLE C:4-42 ▶ Apex Corporation has 100 shares of stock outstanding, 30 of which are owned by Mona. On December 31, Apex pays $36,000 to redeem all 30 of Mona's shares in a redemption qualifying as a sale. At the time of the redemption, Apex has $60,000 in paid-in capital and $40,000 of E&P. Because Apex redeemed 30% of its outstanding stock, the distribution reduces Apex's E&P by $12,000 (0.30 × $40,000). The remaining $24,000 ($36,000 − $12,000) reduces Apex's tax basis paid-in capital to $36,000 ($60,000 − $24,000).[44] ◀

Preferred Stock Bailouts

OBJECTIVE 6

Explain the tax treatment of preferred stock bailouts

The stock redemption rules permit sale treatment in certain situations and require dividend treatment in all others. Generally, taxpayers prefer sale treatment for two reasons. First, sale treatment allows taxpayers to offset their stock basis against the distribution proceeds. Second, gain on a stock sale generally is long-term and capital in character. This gain may be entirely offset by the taxpayer's capital losses and thus not be taxed at all. With these results in mind, taxpayers have attempted various schemes to obtain sale rather than dividend treatment.

[43] Sec. 312(n)(7). This adjustment to paid-in capital might be necessary for companies that maintain tax basis balance sheets, for example, to determine book-tax differences in complying with ASC 740, Income Taxes, which is the FASB Accounting Standards Codification for SFAS No. 109.

[44] Distributions during the year require a different calculation, which is beyond the scope of this text.

ADDITIONAL COMMENT

When the term *bailout* is used in the corporate context, it generally refers to a scheme that allows a corporation to make a dividend distribution that for tax purposes is treated as a sale of a capital asset.

One such method is a **preferred stock bailout**. Prior to Congress' enacting anti-tax avoidance measures, a preferred stock bailout typically proceeded as follows:

1. A corporation issued a nontaxable dividend of nonvoting preferred stock to its common shareholders. Under the rules relating to nontaxable stock dividends, a portion of the common stock basis was allocated to the preferred stock. Its holding period included the holding period for the common stock.

2. The recipient shareholder then sold the preferred stock at its FMV to an unrelated third party. As a result of the sale, the shareholder recognized a capital gain equal to the difference between the preferred stock's sale price and its allocated basis.

3. Next, the corporation redeemed the preferred stock from the third-party (usually at a small premium to reward the third party for his or her cooperation in the scheme).

4. As an alternative to steps 2 and 3, the corporation redeemed the preferred stock directly from the shareholder.

As a result of this preferred stock bailout, the shareholder extracted the corporation's E&P and converted what otherwise would have been a dividend into a long-term capital gain without changing his or her equity position. To deter such tax avoidance, Congress enacted Sec. 306, which "taints" certain stock (usually preferred stock) when distributed to a shareholder in a nontaxable stock dividend. Section 306 treats the distribution proceeds as a dividend if the corporation redeems the tainted stock directly from the shareholder and treats the amount realized as ordinary income if the shareholder sells the stock to a third party. Either way, Sec. 306 prevents shareholders from using a preferred stock bailout to convert ordinary income into capital gain.

Recent tax acts, however, have taken the "sting" out of Sec. 306 by taxing dividends at the same rate as capital gains. Thus, both the dividend recognized on a direct redemption of Sec. 306 stock and the "deemed" dividend recognized on a third-party sale of the stock are taxed at the applicable capital gains rate. Nevertheless, the Sec. 306 taint is still disadvantageous because, even though subject to the preferential capital gains tax rate, dividends cannot offset capital losses as can "real" capital gains. Also, if Sec. 306 recasts the redemption as a dividend, the shareholder is taxed on the entire amount of distribution proceeds rather than just the net gain.

SEC. 306 STOCK DEFINED

Section 306 stock is defined as follows:[45]

- Stock (other than common issued with respect to common) received in a nontaxable stock dividend
- Stock (other than common) received in a nontaxable corporate reorganization or corporate division if the effect of the transaction was substantially the same as the receipt of a stock dividend, or if the stock was received in exchange for Sec. 306 stock
- Stock that has a basis determined by reference to the basis of Sec. 306 stock (i.e., a substituted or transferred basis)
- Stock (other than common) acquired in an exchange to which Sec. 351 applies if the receipt of money (in lieu of the stock) would have been treated as a dividend

Preferred stock issued by a corporation with no current or accumulated E&P in the year the stock is issued is not Sec. 306 stock. Also, inherited stock is not Sec. 306 stock because the basis of such stock is its FMV on the date of the decedent's death (or alternate valuation date) and, therefore, is not determined by reference to the decedent's basis.[46]

TYPICAL MISCONCEPTION

Although the amount of deemed dividend income recognized on a sale of Sec. 306 stock is measured by the E&P existing in the year the Sec. 306 stock was distributed, the E&P of the distributing corporation is not reduced by the amount of the deemed dividend.

DISPOSITIONS OF SEC. 306 STOCK

If a shareholder sells or otherwise disposes of Sec. 306 stock (except in a redemption), the amount realized is treated as a deemed dividend to the extent the shareholder would have recognized a dividend at the time of the distribution had cash equal to the stock's FMV, instead of stock, been distributed. The shareholder's deemed dividend is measured by

[45] Sec. 306(c).

[46] Reg. Sec. 1.306-3(e).

reference to the corporation's E&P in the year the Sec. 306 stock was issued, although the corporation does not reduce its E&P upon the sale. Any additional amount received for the Sec. 306 stock generally is treated as a return of capital. If the additional amount exceeds the shareholder's basis in the Sec. 306 stock, the excess is treated as a capital gain. If the additional amount is less than the shareholder's basis, the unrecovered basis is not treated as a loss. Rather, it is added back to the shareholder's basis in his or her common shares.

EXAMPLE C:4-43 ▶ Carlos owns all 100 outstanding shares of Adobe Corporation common stock. His basis in the shares is $100,000. Adobe, which has $150,000 of E&P, distributes 50 shares of nonvoting preferred to Carlos in a nontaxable stock dividend. On the distribution date, the FMV of the preferred stock is $50,000, and the FMV of the common stock is $200,000. Carlos must allocate his $100,000 common stock basis between the common and preferred shares according to their relative FMVs as follows:

	FMV	*Basis*
Common stock	$200,000	$ 80,000[a]
Preferred stock	50,000	20,000[b]
Total	$250,000	$100,000

[a] $\frac{\$200{,}000}{\$250{,}000} \times \$100{,}000$ [b] $\frac{\$50{,}000}{\$250{,}000} \times \$100{,}000$

Carlos subsequently sells the preferred stock to Dillon for $50,000. The $50,000 sales proceeds are treated as a deemed dividend because Adobe's E&P in the year the corporation distributed the preferred stock exceeded the stock's FMV. Carlos's $20,000 basis in the preferred shares is added back to his basis in the common shares, thereby restoring his common stock basis to $100,000. If instead Carlos sells the preferred stock for $80,000, he recognizes a $50,000 deemed dividend, a $20,000 return of capital, and a $10,000 capital gain computed as follows:

Sales proceeds	$80,000
Minus: Deemed dividend income[a]	(50,000)
Remaining sales proceeds	$30,000
Minus: Return of capital[b]	(20,000)
Capital gain[c]	$10,000

[a]Smaller of E&P in year stock was issued or stock's FMV on the distribution date.
[b]Smaller of remaining sales proceeds or stock adjusted basis.
[c]Sales proceeds received in excess of stock adjusted basis. ◀

REDEMPTIONS OF SEC. 306 STOCK

KEY POINT

The amount realized in a redemption of Sec. 306 stock is a dividend to the extent of E&P existing in the year of redemption. Unlike a sale of Sec. 306 stock, E&P is reduced as a result of a redemption.

If the issuing corporation redeems Sec. 306 stock, the shareholder's total amount realized is treated as a distribution to which the Sec. 301 dividend rules apply. Specifically, it is treated as a dividend to the extent of the redeeming corporation's current and accumulated E&P measured *in the year of the redemption* and reduces corporate E&P accordingly. Amounts received in excess of the corporation's E&P are treated as a recovery of the shareholder's basis in his or her Sec. 306 stock, and then as a capital gain to the extent such amounts exceed basis. If all or a portion of the shareholder's basis in the redeemed stock is not recovered, the unrecovered amount increases the basis of the shareholder's common stock.

EXAMPLE C:4-44 ▶ Don owns all 100 shares of Brigham Corporation common stock having a $300,000 adjusted basis. Four years ago, Brigham issued 50 shares of preferred stock to Don. On the distribution date, the FMVs of the preferred stock and common stock were $100,000 and $400,000, respectively. Brigham's E&P in the distribution year was $200,000. Don's allocated basis in the preferred stock was $60,000 {[$100,000 ÷ ($100,000 + $400,000)] × $300,000}. The basis of Don's common stock was reduced to $240,000 ($300,000 − $60,000) as a result of this allocation. On January 2 of the current year, Brigham redeems the preferred shares for $250,000. In the redemption year, Brigham's total E&P is $400,000. Thus, Don recognizes dividend income of $250,000. If Brigham's total E&P instead had been $200,000 in the redemption year, Don would have recognized $200,000 of dividend income and a $50,000 nontaxable return of capital.

Because Don's basis in his preferred stock is $60,000, the $10,000 unrecovered basis would have increased his basis in the common stock to $250,000 ($240,000 + $10,000). ◀

EXCEPTIONS TO SEC. 306 TREATMENT

Section 306 does not apply in the following situations.

- A shareholder sells all of his or her common and preferred stock, thereby completely terminating his or her interest in the issuing corporation.
- The corporation redeems all the shareholder's common and preferred stock, completely terminating the shareholder's interest in the corporation.
- The corporation redeems an individual shareholder's stock in a partial liquidation qualifying for sale treatment under Sec. 302(b)(4).
- A shareholder disposes of Sec. 306 stock in a way that triggers no gain or loss recognition (e.g., a gift). Although the donor recognizes no income when he or she disposes of Sec. 306 stock by gift, the stock retains its taint and remains Sec. 306 stock in the donee's hands. On the other hand, because heirs and devisees take a FMV basis in estate assets, the taint disappears when they inherit the stock.
- Section 306 does not apply if the taxpayer demonstrates to the IRS's satisfaction that the distribution and subsequent disposition of Sec. 306 stock did not have tax avoidance as a principal purpose.

TAX STRATEGY TIP

A taxpayer owning a portfolio of stock that includes Sec. 306 stock may want to retain the Sec. 306 stock and pass it on to his or her heirs, thereby eliminating the Sec. 306 taint. Market conditions, however, will dictate whether retaining the stock is a good investment strategy.

STOCK REDEMPTIONS BY RELATED CORPORATIONS

OBJECTIVE 7

Assess the applicability and tax consequences of Sec. 304 to stock sales

If a shareholder sells stock in one corporation (the issuing corporation) to a second corporation (the acquiring corporation), the shareholder usually recognizes a capital gain or loss. However, if the shareholder controls both corporations, he or she may have to recognize dividend income because the net result may resemble a dividend more than a sale.

To prevent shareholders from using two corporations they commonly control to convert what is essentially a dividend into a capital gain, Sec. 304 requires that a sale of stock of one controlled corporation to a second controlled corporation be treated as a stock redemption. If the redemption meets the requirements for sale treatment (e.g., if the redemption is substantially disproportionate), the transaction will be treated as a sale. Otherwise, the redemption will be treated as a dividend to the extent of E&P. As in the case of Sec. 306 preferred stock bailouts, because individuals pay the applicable capital gains tax rate on qualified dividends and capital gains, Sec. 304 does not deliver a major "sting." Nevertheless, when it does apply, shareholders may have to recognize dividend income rather than capital gain and cannot offset either stock basis or capital losses against this dividend income.

Section 304 applies to two types of sales. The first is a sale of stock involving two brother-sister corporations. The second is a sale of a parent corporation's stock to one of its subsidiaries. The following sections define brother-sister and parent-subsidiary corporations and explain how Sec. 304 applies to each group.

BROTHER-SISTER CORPORATIONS

ADDITIONAL COMMENT

The definition of brother-sister corporations for Sec. 304 differs from the definition for controlled groups discussed in Chapter C:3.

Two corporations are called brother-sister corporations when one or more shareholders control each of the corporations and a parent-subsidiary relationship does not exist. Control means ownership of at least 50% of the voting power or 50% of the total value of all the corporation's stock. The shareholder(s) who acquired such ownership are called controlling shareholders. If a controlling shareholder (or shareholders) transfers stock in one corporation to the other corporation in exchange for property, the exchange must be recast as a redemption.

To determine whether the redemption is treated as a sale or a dividend, reference is made to the shareholder's stock ownership in the issuing corporation. For purposes of this determination, the attribution rules of Sec. 318(a) apply.[47]

Redemption Treated as a Distribution. If the redemption does not qualify for sale treatment, it is treated as a dividend paid first by the acquiring corporation to the extent of its E&P, and then by the issuing corporation to the extent of its E&P. The shareholder's basis in the issuing corporation's stock sold is added to his or her basis in the acquiring corporation's stock. The acquiring corporation takes the same basis in the issuing corporation's stock as the shareholder's.

EXAMPLE C:4-45 ▶ Bert owns 60 of the 100 outstanding shares of First Corporation stock and 60 of the 100 outstanding shares of Second Corporation stock (see Figure C:4-1). First and Second have $50,000 and $20,000 of E&P, respectively. Bert sells to Second for $20,000 20 shares of First stock with an adjusted basis of $10,000. Because Bert owns at least 50% of each corporation's stock, Bert is deemed to control both First and Second, and Sec. 304 governs the transaction. Accordingly, the sale is recast as a redemption. To determine whether the redemption qualifies for sale treatment, reference is made to Bert's percentage ownership of First stock. Before the redemption, Bert owned 60% of First stock. After the redemption, Bert owns 52% of First stock (40 shares directly and 12 [0.60 × 20] shares constructively through Second). Because the redempton satisfies none of the Sec. 302 tests for sale treatment, Sec. 301 governs the outcome. Under this provision, the entire distribution is treated as a dividend because it does not exceed First's and Second's total E&P of $70,000. All $20,000 of the distribution is deemed to have been made out of Second's E&P because it is sufficient to cover the distribution amount. Second's basis in the First stock is $10,000, the same as Bert's. Bert increases his basis in Second stock by $10,000, his basis in the First stock he is deemed to have contributed to Second. ◀

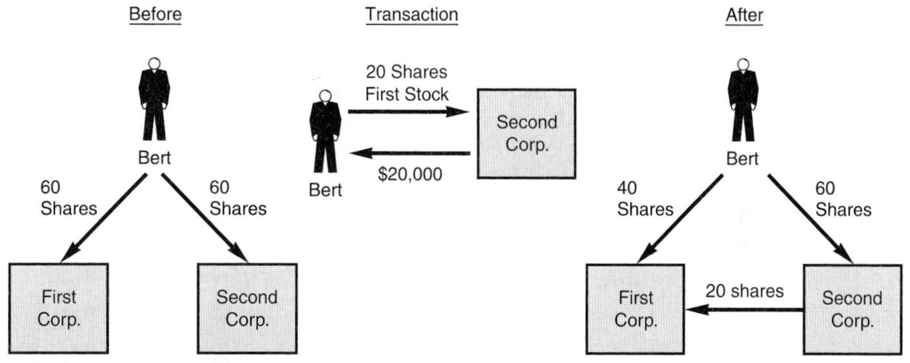

FIGURE C:4-1 ▶ ILLUSTRATION OF A BROTHER-SISTER REDEMPTION (EXAMPLE C:4-45)

Redemption Treated as a Sale. If the redemption qualifies for sale treatment, the shareholder's recognized gain or loss equals the difference between the amount received from the acquiring corporation and the shareholder's basis in the surrendered shares. The acquiring corporation is treated as having purchased the issuing corporation's shares and thus takes a cost basis in such shares.

EXAMPLE C:4-46 ▶ Assume the same facts as in Example C:4-45 except Bert sells to Second Corporation for $40,000 40 shares of First stock having an adjusted basis of $20,000. After the redemption, Bert owns

[47] For Sec. 304 purposes, the attribution rules of Sec. 318(a) are modified so that a shareholder is considered to own an amount of stock proportionate to that owned by any corporation of which he or she owns 5% or more (instead of 50% or more) of the value of the stock.

44 shares of First stock (20 shares directly and 24 [0.60 × 40] shares constructively through Second). Therefore, he meets both the 50% and the 80% tests for a substantially disproportionate redemption, treats the redemption as a sale, and recognizes a capital gain of $20,000 ($40,000 received from Second − $20,000 adjusted basis in the First shares). Second's basis in the First shares acquired from Bert equals the $40,000 stock purchase price. ◀

ADDITIONAL COMMENT

The definition of a parent-subsidiary relationship for Sec. 304 differs from the definition for controlled groups or affiliated corporations discussed in Chapter C:3.

PARENT-SUBSIDIARY CORPORATIONS

If a shareholder sells stock in a parent corporation to a subsidiary of the parent, the sale is treated as a distribution in redemption of part or all of the shareholder's parent stock. A parent-subsidiary relationship exists if one corporation owns at least 50% of the voting power or 50% of the total value of all stock in another corporation.

To determine whether the redemption is treated as a sale or a dividend, reference is made to the shareholder's ownership of parent stock before and after the redemption. In this determination, the constructive ownership rules of Sec. 318 apply.

Redemption Treated as a Dividend. If the redemption does not qualify for sale treatment, the distribution is treated as a dividend, first from the subsidiary to the extent of its E&P and then from the parent to the extent of its E&P. This rule effectively sets the combined E&P of both corporations as the standard for measuring the amount of the distribution that constitutes a dividend. The shareholder's basis in his or her remaining parent shares is increased by his or her basis in the shares transferred to the subsidiary. The subsidiary's basis in the parent stock is the amount the subsidiary paid for the stock.[48]

EXAMPLE C:4-47 ▶ Of the 100 shares of Parent Corporation stock, Brian owns 60 shares with a $15,000 basis. Parent owns 60 of the 100 shares of Subsidiary stock. Parent and Subsidiary have $10,000 and $30,000 of E&P, respectively. Brian sells ten of his Parent shares to Subsidiary for $12,000. (See Figure C:4-2 for an illustration.) Parent is deemed to have redeemed its stock from Brian, who owned 60% of Parent stock before the redemption and 53 shares (50 shares directly and 3 [0.60 × 0.50 × 10] shares constructively) after the redemption. Because the 50% and 80% tests of Sec. 302(b)(2) are not met, the redemption is not substantially disproportionate and thus does not qualify for sale treatment. Therefore, it is treated as a distribution subject to Sec. 301. Under this provision, Brian recognizes

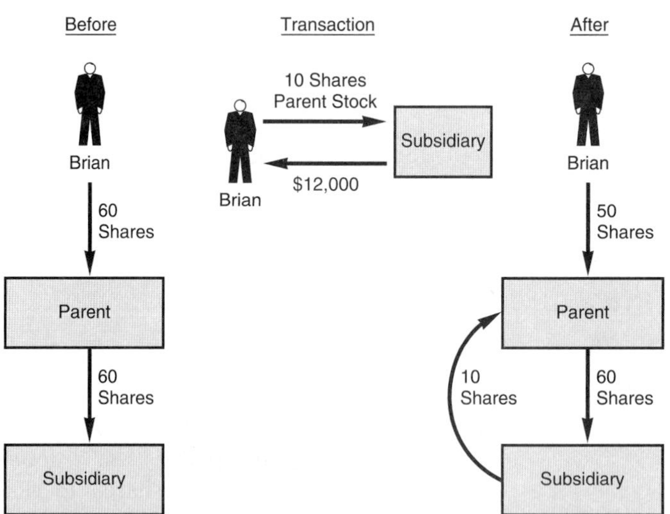

FIGURE C:4-2 ▶ ILLUSTRATION OF A PARENT-SUBSIDIARY REDEMPTION (EXAMPLE C:4-47)

[48] Rev. Rul. 80-189, 1980-2 C.B. 106.

a $12,000 dividend. This dividend is deemed to have been paid out of Subsidiary's E&P, which is sufficient to cover the entire distribution amount. Brian's $2,500 basis in the redeemed shares increases his $12,500 basis in his remaining Parent shares, so that his total basis in those shares remains $15,000. Subsidiary's basis in the ten Parent shares acquired from Brian is $12,000, the amount that Subsidiary paid for the shares. ◀

Redemption Treated as a Sale. If the redemption of the parent's stock qualifies for sale treatment, the basis of the stock transferred to the subsidiary is subtracted from the amount realized in the distribution to derive the shareholder's recognized gain or loss.

EXAMPLE C:4-48 ▶ Assume the same facts as in Example C:4-47 except Brian sells 40 shares of Parent stock to Subsidiary for $48,000. Because Brian owns 60% of Parent stock before the redemption and 24.8% (20 shares directly and 4.8 [0.60 × 0.20 × 40] shares constructively) after the redemption, the redemption meets the Sec. 302(b)(2) 50% and 80% tests for a substantially disproportionate redemption. Consequently, Brian recognizes a capital gain of $38,000 ($48,000 selling price − $10,000 adjusted basis in the 40 shares sold). Brian's adjusted basis in his remaining 20 shares of Parent stock is $5,000. Subsidiary's basis in the 40 Parent shares purchased from Brian is $48,000, the amount that Subsidiary paid for the shares. ◀

Topic Review C:4-5 summarizes the alternative treatments of stock redemptions.

TOPIC REVIEW C:4-5

Alternative Treatments of Stock Redemptions

General Rule: A distribution in redemption of stock generally is treated as a dividend (Secs. 302(d) and 301).
Exception: The following transactions qualify for sale (i.e., capital gains) treatment:

1. Redemptions that are not essentially equivalent to a dividend (Sec. 302(b)(1))
2. Substantially disproportionate redemptions (Sec. 302(b)(2))
3. Complete terminations of a shareholder's interest (Sec. 302(b)(3))
4. Partial liquidations in redemption of a noncorporate shareholder's stock (Sec. 302(b)(4))
5. Redemptions to pay death taxes (Sec. 303)

Special Redemption Rules

1. Redemptions of Sec. 306 preferred stock generally are taxed as dividends to the shareholder (Sec. 306).
2. A sale of stock in one controlled corporation to another controlled corporation is treated as a redemption (Sec. 304).

TAX PLANNING CONSIDERATIONS

OBJECTIVE 8

Identify tax planning opportunities in nonliquidating distributions

AVOIDING UNREASONABLE COMPENSATION

Chapter C:3 discussed the use of salary and fringe benefits to permit a shareholder of a closely held corporation to withdraw funds from the corporation and be subject to a single level of taxation. If a corporation pays too large a salary to a shareholder-employee, some of the salary may be disallowed as a corporate deduction while still taxed to the shareholder-employee as a constructive dividend. In such case, double taxation of the disallowed portion results.

Corporations can avoid this result by entering into a **hedge agreement** with a shareholder-employee. This agreement obligates the shareholder-employee to repay any portion of salary the IRS disallows as a corporate deduction. Under Sec. 162, the shareholder-employee may deduct this amount in the year he or she repays it, provided state law imposes a legal obligation to repay.[49] If a hedge agreement is not in effect, voluntary repayment of the salary is not deductible by the shareholder-employee.[50]

EXAMPLE C:4-49 ▶ Theresa owns one-half the stock in Marine Corporation and serves as its president. The remaining Marine stock is owned by eight investors, none of whom owns more than 10% of the outstanding shares. In Year 1, Theresa and Marine conclude a hedge agreement requiring Theresa to repay all compensation the IRS declares unreasonable. In Year 3, Marine pays Theresa a salary and bonus of $750,000. The IRS subsequently claims that $300,000 of the salary is unreasonable and thus nondeductible by Marine. After protracted negotiations, Marine and the IRS settle on $180,000 as unreasonable and nondeductible by Marine. Theresa repays the $180,000 in Year 6. The entire $750,000 is taxable to Theresa in Year 3. However, she can deduct the $180,000 as a trade or business expense in Year 6. ◀

Hedge agreements also have been used in connection with other payments between a corporation and its shareholders (e.g., travel and entertainment expenses). Some employers are averse to hedge agreements because the IRS might consider the very existence of such an agreement as evidence of unreasonable compensation.

BOOTSTRAP ACQUISITIONS

A prospective purchaser who wants to acquire stock in a corporation may not have sufficient cash to do so. To facilitate the purchase, corporate funds could be used in the following way: a shareholder sells part of his or her stock to the purchaser and then causes the corporation to redeem the shareholder's remaining shares. Such an arrangement is called a **bootstrap acquisition.**

EXAMPLE C:4-50 ▶ Ted owns all 100 shares of Dragon Corporation stock having a $100,000 FMV. Vickie wants to purchase the stock from Ted but has only $60,000 in cash. Dragon has a large cash balance, which it does not need for its operations. Ted sells Vickie 60 Dragon shares for $60,000 and then causes Dragon to redeem his remaining shares for $40,000. The redemption qualifies as a complete termination of Ted's interest under Sec. 302(b)(3) and, therefore, is eligible for sale treatment. ◀

Court cases have held that such redemptions qualify for sale treatment as long as the third-party sale and redemption are part of an integral plan to terminate the seller's entire corporate interest. Whether the redemption precedes the sale is immaterial.[51] The purchaser, however, must carefully avoid generating a dividend, actual or constructive. For example, a purchaser who contracts to acquire all the stock in a corporation on an installment basis and then causes the corporation to pay the installment obligations will recognize dividend income. The use of corporate funds results in a constructive dividend to the purchaser where the corporation discharges the purchaser's legal obligation. Even if the corporation uses its own funds to redeem the seller's shares, a purchaser who was legally obligated to purchase the shares is considered to have received a constructive dividend.[52]

EXAMPLE C:4-51 ▶ Assume the same facts as in Example C:4-50 except that, after Vickie purchases the 60 shares from Ted, she becomes legally obligated to purchase Ted's remaining 40 shares. After entering into the contract, Vickie causes Dragon Corporation to redeem the 40 shares. Because Dragon has extinguished Vickie's legal obligation, the corporation is deemed to have paid Vickie a $40,000 constructive dividend. No constructive dividend would have resulted had Vickie been legally obligated to purchase only 60 shares from Ted. ◀

Rev. Rul. 69-608 provides guidance to a bootstrap acquirer on how to avoid constructive dividend treatment.[53] According to this ruling, when the corporation redeems some of the seller's shares, the buyer will not be deemed to have received a constructive dividend as

---

[49] Rev. Rul. 69-115, 1969-1 C.B. 50, and *Vincent E. Oswald*, 49 T.C. 645 (1968), *acq*. 1968-2 C.B. 2.

[50] *Ernest H. Berger*, 37 T.C. 1026 (1962), and *John G. Pahl*, 67 T.C. 286 (1976).

[51] See, for example, *U.S. v. Gerald Carey*, 7 AFTR 2d 1301, 61-1 USTC ¶9428 (8th Cir., 1961).

[52] *H. F. Wall v. U.S.*, 36 AFTR 423, 47-2 USTC ¶9395 (4th Cir., 1947).

[53] Rev. Rul. 69-608, 1969-2 C.B. 42.

WHAT WOULD YOU DO IN THIS SITUATION?

One of the most cherished traditions observed by many professional firms centers around the year-end bonus. Legal, medical, business, and accounting administrators often use bonus compensation to clear the books at the end of the year. In partnerships, bonuses are characterized as distributive shares or a form of compensation. As such, they are taxed only once as income paid to professionals for services rendered, net of appropriate accounting adjustments.

With the advent of the professional corporation, an entity intended to limit personal liability, many professionals have opted to do business as shareholders. The continued use of the year-end bonus in the professional corporation has come under close IRS scrutiny. The position taken by the IRS is clear. If the payments to the shareholder-professional are in exchange for his or her services rendered to the firm, the corporation may deduct them as salaries (assuming they are reasonable in amount). On the other hand, if they are a disguised bailout of owners' profits, the corporation cannot deduct them. As a result, the corporation's taxable income will be increased by the amount of the disallowed deduction. The shareholder who receives the bonus must treat it as a dividend rather than salary. However, treating the bonus as a dividend generally results in less tax paid by the shareholder because dividends are taxed at a maximum rate of 23.8% (including the 3.8% net investment tax rate) as opposed to 39.6% for salary. The consequences are negative only to the corporation, which may not deduct the dividend payment.

This principle is illustrated in a case, *Rapco, Inc. v. CIR*, 77 AFTR 2d 2405, 96-1 USTC ¶50,297 (CA-2, 1996), decided by the Second Circuit. In *Rapco*, the court denied a deduction for bonus payments to the president of the company, even though he played a significant role in the company's rapid growth and had guaranteed third party loans to Rapco. Reasons cited by the court were that Rapco's compensation scheme was "bonus-heavy and salary light," suggesting dividend avoidance; Rapco had ignored its own bonus policy set forth in its preincorporation minutes; the corporation had a history of never paying dividends; the shareholder who determined the amount of his own salary owned 95% of the corporation's stock; and Rapco's own expert testified that $400,000 to $500,000 was fair compensation for the president's services. (The IRS allowed a salary deduction of $405,000.)

Assuming your CPA firm is acting as a tax advisor to several similarly situated professional corporations, what advice that complies with the IRC, Treasury Regulations, and the AICPA's *Statements on Standards for Tax Services* would you give?

long as he or she does not have a primary and unconditional obligation to purchase the shares, and the corporation pays no more for the redeemed shares than their FMV. Furthermore, a purchaser who has an option—not a legal obligation—to purchase the seller's remaining shares, and who assigns the option to the redeeming corporation, is unlikely to generate a constructive dividend.[54]

TIMING OF DISTRIBUTIONS

Dividends can be paid only out of a corporation's E&P. Therefore, if a distribution can be made when the corporation has little or no E&P, it will be treated as a return of capital rather than as a dividend.

If a corporation generates a current E&P deficit, the deficit reduces accumulated E&P evenly throughout the year unless the corporation can demonstrate that it incurred the deficits on particular dates. Thus, if a corporation with a current E&P deficit, but a positive accumulated E&P balance, makes a distribution in the current year, the timing of the distribution will be critical in determining whether the distribution should be treated as a dividend or as a return of capital.

EXAMPLE C:4-52 ▶ Major Corporation has a $30,000 accumulated E&P balance at the beginning of the year and incurs a $50,000 deficit during the year. Because of its poor operating performance, Major pays to its sole shareholder only two of its four $5,000 quarterly dividends, specifically those usually paid on March 31 and June 30. The tax treatment of the two distributions is determined as follows:

[54] *Joseph R. Holsey v. CIR*, 2 AFTR 2d 5660, 58-2 USTC ¶9816 (3rd Cir., 1958).

E&P balance, January 1	$30,000
Minus: Reduction for first quarter loss	(12,500)
Reduction for March 31 distribution	(5,000)
E&P balance, April 1	$12,500
Minus: Reduction for second quarter loss	(12,500)
E&P balance, June 30	$ -0-

The first and second quarter losses each are $12,500 [($50,000) × 0.25 = ($12,500)].

The operating loss reduces the accumulated E&P balance evenly throughout the year. All of the March 31 distribution is taxable because the corporation did not incur sufficient losses to offset the positive accumulated E&P balance at the beginning of the year. The second quarter loss results in return of capital treatment for the June 30 distribution and any other distributions before year-end (assuming that the shareholder's basis in his or her stock exceeds the distribution amount). Delaying all the distributions until late in the year could result in a nontaxable return of capital. ◀

The timing of a distribution also can be critical if the distributing corporation has an accumulated E&P deficit and a positive current E&P balance.

EXAMPLE C:4-53 ▶ At the beginning of Year 1, Yankee Corporation has an accumulated E&P deficit of $250,000. During Year 1 and Year 2, Yankee reports the following current E&P balances and makes the following distributions to Joe, its sole shareholder:

Year	*Current E&P*	*Distributions*	*Distribution Date*
1	$100,000	$75,000	December 31
2	-0-	-0-	None

The $75,000 distribution in Year 1 is taxable as a dividend. The $25,000 of current E&P that is not distributed reduces Yankee's accumulated E&P deficit to $225,000. Had Yankee delayed distributing the $75,000 until sometime in Year 2, the distribution would have been treated as a nontaxable return of Joe's capital. ◀

COMPLIANCE AND PROCEDURAL CONSIDERATIONS

OBJECTIVE 9

Comply with procedural rules for nonliquidating distributions

CORPORATE REPORTING OF NONDIVIDEND DISTRIBUTIONS

A corporation that makes a nondividend distribution to its shareholders must file with its income tax return Form 5452 (Corporate Report of Nondividend Distributions), along with supporting computations. Form 5452 reports the distributing corporation's E&P so as to enable the IRS to verify the tax treatment of the distribution. Form 5452 requires the following information: current and accumulated E&P, distribution amounts paid to shareholders during the tax year, the percentage of each payment that is taxable and nontaxable, and a detailed computation of E&P from the date of incorporation.

ADDITIONAL COMMENT

Information on basis adjustments for nontaxable dividends, stock splits, stock dividends, etc. for individual firms can be found in special tax services.

AGREEMENT TO TERMINATE INTEREST UNDER SEC. 302(b)(3)

As mentioned earlier, if a redemption completely terminates a shareholder's interest in a corporation, the family attribution rules of Sec. 318(a)(1) may be waived. To have the rules waived, the shareholder must agree in writing that he or she will notify the IRS upon acquiring any prohibited interest within the ten-year period following the redemption. A copy of this agreement (in the form of a signed statement in duplicate) must be attached to the first return filed by the shareholder for the tax year in which the redemption occurs. If the agreement cannot be filed on time, the IRS may grant an extension. Regulation Sec. 1.302-4(a) provides that an extension will be granted only if reasonable cause exists for

KEY POINT

The limitations period extends to one year beyond the date a shareholder notifies the IRS that a forbidden interest has been acquired. Otherwise, it would be almost impossible for the IRS to administer this provision.

failure to timely file the agreement and if the request for such an extension is filed within such time as the appropriate IRS official considers reasonable in the circumstances.

Treasury Regulations do not indicate what constitutes reasonable cause for failure to file or what constitutes a reasonable extension of time. In *Edward J. Fehrs* the U.S. Court of Claims held that late filing of a ten-year agreement was permissible where a taxpayer could not reasonably have expected that a filing would be necessary, where the taxpayer filed the agreement promptly after receiving notice that it was required, and where the agreement was filed before the issues in question were presented for trial.[55] However, in *Robin Haft Trust,* an agreement was filed *after* an adverse court ruling. In an appeal for a rehearing, the judge ruled that the filing of the agreement after the case was brought to trial was too late. Consequently, the judge denied the appeal for a rehearing.[56]

If the shareholder acquires a prohibited interest within the ten-year period following the redemption, the IRS may assess additional taxes. Such an acquisition ordinarily results in recasting the redemption as a dividend rather than a sale. The limitations period for assessing additional taxes extends to one year after the date the shareholder files with the IRS notice of acquiring the prohibited interest.[57]

PROBLEM MATERIALS

DISCUSSION QUESTIONS

C:4-1 Explain how a corporation computes its current and accumulated E&P balances.

C:4-2 Why is it necessary to distinguish between current and accumulated E&P?

C:4-3 Describe the effect of a $100,000 cash distribution paid on January 1 to the sole shareholder of a calendar year corporation whose stock basis is $25,000 when the corporation has

a. $100,000 of current E&P and $100,000 of accumulated E&P
b. A $50,000 accumulated E&P deficit and a $60,000 current E&P balance
c. A $60,000 accumulated E&P deficit and a $60,000 current E&P deficit
d. An $80,000 current E&P deficit and a $100,000 accumulated E&P balance

Answer Parts a through d again, assuming instead that the corporation makes the distribution on October 1 in a nonleap year.

C:4-4 Pecan Corporation distributes land to a noncorporate shareholder. Explain how the following items are determined:

a. The amount of the distribution
b. The amount of the dividend
c. The shareholder's basis in the land
d. When the holding period for the land begins.

How would your answers change if the distribution were made to a corporate shareholder?

C:4-5 What effect do the following transactions have on the calculation of Young Corporation's current E&P? Assume that the starting point for the calculation is Young's taxable income for the current year.

a. The corporation earns tax-exempt interest income of $10,000.
b. Taxable income includes a $10,000 dividend and is reduced by a $7,000 dividends-received deduction.
c. A $5,000 capital loss carryover from the preceding tax year offsets $5,000 of capital gains.
d. The corporation accrued federal income taxes of $25,280.
e. The corporation took a U.S. production activities deduction of $3,000.

C:4-6 Badger Corporation was incorporated in the current year. It reports an $8,000 NOL on its initial tax return. Badger distributes $2,500 to its shareholders. Is it possible for this distribution to be taxed as a dividend to Badger's shareholders? Explain.

C:4-7 Does the timing of a distribution matter as to whether it is taxed as a dividend or treated as a return of capital? Explain.

C:4-8 Hickory Corporation owns a building with a $160,000 adjusted basis and a $120,000 FMV. Hickory's E&P is $200,000. Should the

---

55 *Edward J. Fehrs v. U.S.,* 40 AFTR 2d 77-5040, 77-1 USTC ¶9423 (Ct. Cl., 1977).

56 *Robin Haft Trust,* 62 T.C. 145 (1974).

57 Sec. 302(c)(2)(A).

corporation sell the building and distribute the sales proceeds to its shareholders or distribute the property to its shareholders and let them sell it? Why?

C:4-9 Walnut Corporation owns a building with a $120,000 adjusted basis and a $160,000 FMV. Walnut's E&P is $200,000. Should the corporation sell the building and distribute the sales proceeds to its shareholders or distribute the building to its shareholders and let them sell it? Why?

C:4-10 What is a constructive dividend? Under what circumstances is the IRS likely to argue that a constructive dividend has been paid?

C:4-11 Why are stock dividends generally nontaxable? Under what circumstances are stock dividends taxable?

C:4-12 What is a stock redemption? What are some reasons for redeeming stock? Why are some redemptions treated as sales and others as dividends?

C:4-13 Field Corporation redeems 100 shares of its stock from Andrew for $10,000. Andrew's basis in the shares is $8,000. Explain possible alternative tax treatments of Andrew's receiving the $10,000.

C:4-14 What conditions must be met for a redemption to be treated as a sale by the redeeming shareholder?

C:4-15 Explain the purpose of the attribution rules in determining stock ownership in a redemption. Describe the four types of attribution rules that apply to redemptions.

C:4-16 Abel, the sole shareholder of Ace Corporation, has an opporunity to purchase the assets of a sole proprietorship for $50,000 in cash. Ace has a substantial E&P balance. Abel does not have sufficient cash to personally make the purchase. If Abel obtains the needed $50,000 from Ace via a nonliquidating distribution, Abel will have to recognize dividend income. Alternatively, would Ace's purchase of the assets of the sole proprietorship followed by their distribution to Abel in redemption of part of his stock holdings constitute a partial liquidation? Explain.

C:4-17 Why does a redemption that qualifies for sale treatment under Sec. 303 usually result in the shareholder's recognizing little or no gain or loss?

C:4-18 Under what circumstances does a corporation recognize gain or loss when it distributes noncash property in redemption of its stock? What effect does a redemption distribution have on the distributing corporation's E&P?

C:4-19 What is a preferred stock bailout? How does Sec. 306 operate to prevent a shareholder from realizing the otherwise available tax benefits of a preferred stock bailout?

C:4-20 Explain the tax consequences, to both the corporation and a shareholder-employee, of an IRS determination that a portion of the compensation paid in a prior tax year is unreasonable. What steps can the corporation and shareholder-employee take to avoid the double taxation usually associated with such a determination?

C:4-21 What is a bootstrap acquisition? What are the tax consequences of such a transaction?

ISSUE IDENTIFICATION QUESTIONS

C:4-22 Marsha receives a $10,000 cash distribution from Dye Corporation in April of the current year. At the beginning of the year, Dye has $4,000 of accumulated E&P and $8,000 of current E&P. Dye also distributed $10,000 in cash to Barbara, who purchased all 200 shares of Dye stock from Marsha in June of the current year. What tax issues should be considered with respect to the distributions to Marsha and Barbara?

C:4-23 Neil purchased land from Spring Harbor, his 100%-owned corporation, for $275,000. The corporation purchased the land three years ago for $300,000. Similar tracts of land located nearby have sold for $400,000 in recent months. What tax issues should be considered with respect to the corporation's sale of the land?

C:4-24 Price Corporation has 100 shares of common stock outstanding. Price repurchased all of Penny's 30 shares for $35,000 cash during the current year. Three years ago, Penny received the shares as a gift from her mother. Her basis in the shares is $16,000. Price has $100,000 of current and accumulated E&P. Penny's mother owns 40 of the remaining shares; unrelated individuals own the other 30 shares. What tax issues should be considered with respect to the corporation's purchase of Penny's shares?

C:4-25 George owns all 100 shares of Gumby's Pizza Corporation. The shares are worth $200,000, while George's basis is only $70,000. Mary and George have reached a tentative agreement under which George will sell all his shares to Mary. However, Mary is unwilling to pay more than $150,000 for the stock because the corporation currently has an excess cash balance. They have agreed that George can withdraw $50,000 in cash from Gumby's before the stock sale. What tax issues should be considered with respect to George and Mary's agreement?

PROBLEMS

C:4-26 ***Current E&P Calculation.*** Alabre Corporation has 150,000 shares of common stock outstanding and pays quarterly dividends of $0.15 per share. At the beginning of the current year, the balance in its accumulated E&P account is $23,000. Alabre would like to have sufficient E&P to pay its dividends in the current year. To do so, what minimum amount of E&P must the corporation generate in the current year?

C:4-27 ***Current E&P Calculation.*** Beach Corporation, an accrual basis taxpayer, reports the following results for the current year:

Income:	
Gross profit from manufacturing operations	$250,000
Dividends received from 25%-owned domestic corporation	20,000
Interest income: Corporate bonds	10,000
Municipal bonds	12,000
Proceeds from life insurance policy on key employee	100,000
Section 1231 gain on sale of land	8,000
Expenses:	
Administrative expenses	110,000
Bad debts	5,000
Depreciation:	
Financial accounting	68,000
Taxable income	86,000
Alternative depreciation system (for E&P)	42,000
NOL carryover	40,000
Charitable contributions: Current year	8,000
Carryover from last year	3,500
Capital loss on sale of stock	1,200
U.S. production activities deduction	1,500
Penalty on late payment of federal taxes	450

a. What is Beach's taxable income?
b. What is Beach's current E&P?

C:4-28 ***Current E&P Computation.*** Water Corporation reports $500,000 of taxable income for the current year. The following additional information is available:

- For the current year, Water reports an $80,000 long-term capital loss and no capital gains.
- Taxable income includes $80,000 of dividends from a 10%-owned domestic corporation.
- Water paid fines and penalties of $6,000 that were not deducted in computing taxable income.
- In computing this year's taxable income, Water deducted a $20,000 NOL carryover from a prior tax year.
- Water claimed a $10,000 U.S. production activities deduction.
- Taxable income includes a deduction for $40,000 of depreciation that exceeds the depreciation allowed for E&P purposes.

Assume a 34% corporate tax rate. What is Water's current E&P for this year?

C:4-29 ***Calculating Accumulated E&P.*** Investors formed Peach Corporation in Year 1. Its current E&P (or current E&P deficit) and distributions for Years 1 through 4 are as follows:

Year	*Current E&P (Deficit)*	*Distributions*
1	$ (8,000)	$ 2,000
2	(12,000)	–0–
3	10,000	5,000
4	14,000	17,000

What is Peach's accumulated E&P at the beginning of Years 1 through 4?

C:4-30 *Consequences of a Single Cash Distribution.* Clover Corporation is a calendar year taxpayer. Connie owns all of its stock. Her basis in the stock is $10,000. On April 1 of the current (non-leap) year Clover distributes $52,000 to Connie. Determine the tax consequences of the cash distribution in each of the following independent situations:
a. Current E&P of $15,000; accumulated E&P of $25,000.
b. Current E&P of $30,000; accumulated E&P deficit of ($20,000).
c. Current E&P deficit of ($73,000); accumulated E&P of $50,000.
d. Current E&P deficit of ($20,000); accumulated E&P deficit of ($15,000).

C:4-31 *Consequences of a Single Cash Distribution.* Pink Corporation is a calendar year taxpayer. Pete owns one-third (100 shares) of Pink stock. His basis in the stock is $25,000. Cheryl owns two-thirds (200 shares) of Pink stock. Her basis in the stock is $40,000. On June 10 of the current year, Pink distributes $40,000 to Pete and $80,000 to Cheryl. Determine the tax consequences of the cash distributions to Pete and Cheryl in each of the following independent situations:
a. Current E&P of $60,000; accumulated E&P of $100,000.
b. Current E&P of $36,000; accumulated E&P of $30,000.

C:4-32 *Consequences of Multiple Cash Distributions.* At the beginning of the current (non-leap) year, Charles owns all of Pearl Corporation's outstanding stock. His basis in the stock is $80,000. On July 1, he sells all his stock to Donald for $125,000. During the year, Pearl, a calendar year taxpayer, makes two cash distributions: $60,000 on March 1 to Charles and $90,000 on September 1 to Donald. How are these distributions treated in the following independent situations? What are the amount and character of Charles' gain on his sale of stock to Donald? What is Donald's basis in his Pearl stock at the end of the year?
a. Current E&P of $40,000; accumulated E&P of $30,000.
b. Current E&P of $100,000; accumulated E&P (deficit) of ($50,000).
c. Current E&P (deficit) of ($36,500); accumulated E&P of $120,000.

C:4-33 *Distribution of Appreciated Property.* In the current year, Sedgwick Corporation has $100,000 of current and accumulated E&P. On March 3, Sedgwick distributes to its shareholder Dina a parcel of land (a capital asset) having a $56,000 FMV. The land has a $40,000 adjusted basis (for both taxable income and E&P purposes) to Sedgwick and is subject to an $8,000 mortgage, which Dina assumes. Assume a 34% marginal corporate tax rate.
a. What are the amount and character of the income Dina recognizes as a result of the distribution?
b. What is Dina's basis in the land?
c. What are the amount and character of Sedgwick's gain or loss as a result of the distribution?
d. What effect does the distribution have on Sedgwick's E&P?

C:4-34 *Distribution of Property Subject to a Liability.* On May 10 of the current year, Stowe Corporation distributes to its shareholder Arlene $20,000 in cash and land (a capital asset) having a $50,000 FMV. The land has a $15,000 adjusted basis (for both taxable income and E&P purposes) and is subject to a $60,000 mortgage, which Arlene assumes. Stowe has an E&P balance exceeding the amount distributed and is subject to a 34% marginal corporate tax rate.
a. What are the amount and character of the income Arlene recognizes as a result of the distribution?
b. What is Arlene's basis in the land?
c. What are the amount and character of Stowe's gain or loss as a result of the distribution?

C:4-35 *Distribution of Depreciable Property.* On May 15 of the current year, Quick Corporation distributes to its shareholder Calvin a building having a $250,000 FMV and used in Quick's business. The building originally cost $180,000. Quick claimed $30,000 of straight-line depreciation, so that the adjusted basis of the building on the date of distribution for taxable income purposes is $150,000. The adjusted basis of the building for E&P purposes is $160,000. The building is subject to an $80,000 mortgage, which Calvin assumes. Quick has an E&P balance exceeding the amount distributed and is subject to a 34% marginal tax rate.
a. What are the amount and character of the income Calvin recognizes as a result of the distribution?
b. What is Calvin's basis in the building?

c. What are the amount and character of Quick's gain or loss as a result of the distribution?
d. What effect does the distribution have on Quick's E&P?

C:4-36 *Distribution of Various Types of Property.* During the current year, Zeta Corporation distributes the assets listed below to its sole shareholder, Susan. For each asset listed, determine the gross income recognized by Susan, her basis in the asset, the amount of gain or loss recognized by Zeta, and the effect of the distribution on Zeta's E&P. Assume that Zeta has an E&P balance exceeding the amount distributed and is subject to a 34% marginal tax rate. Unless stated otherwise, adjusted bases for taxable income and E&P purposes are the same.
a. A parcel of land used in Zeta's business that has a $200,000 FMV and a $125,000 adjusted basis.
b. Assume the same facts as in Part a except that the land is subject to a $140,000 mortgage.
c. FIFO inventory having a $25,000 FMV and an $18,000 adjusted basis.
d. A building used in Zeta's business having an original cost of $225,000, a $450,000 FMV, and a $150,000 adjusted basis for taxable income purposes. Zeta has claimed $75,000 of depreciation for taxable income purposes under the straight-line method. Depreciation for E&P purposes is $60,000.
e. An automobile used in Zeta's business having an original cost of $12,000, an $8,000 FMV, and a $5,760 adjusted basis. For taxable income purposes, Zeta has claimed $6,240 of MACRS depreciation on the automobile. For E&P purposes, depreciation is $5,200.
f. Installment obligations having a $35,000 face amount (and FMV) and a $24,500 adjusted basis. The obligations were created when Zeta sold a Sec. 1231 asset.

C:4-37 *Disguised Dividends.* King Corporation is a profitable manufacturing concern with $800,000 of E&P. It is owned in equal shares by Harry and Wilma, husband and wife. Both individuals are actively involved in the business. Determine the tax consequences of the following independent events:
a. In reviewing a prior year tax return for King, the IRS determines that the $500,000 of salary and bonuses paid to Wilma is unreasonable and that reasonable compensation is $280,000.
b. King loaned Harry $400,000 over the past three years. None of the money has been repaid. Harry does not pay interest on the loans.
c. King sells a building to Wilma for $150,000 in cash. The property has an adjusted basis of $90,000 and is subject to a $60,000 mortgage, which Wilma assumes. The FMV of the building is $350,000.
d. Harry leases a warehouse to King for $50,000 per year. According to an IRS auditor, similar warehouses can be leased for $35,000 per year.
e. Wilma sells to King for $250,000 land on which King intends to build a factory. According to a recent appraisal, the FMV of the land is $185,000.
f. The corporation owns an airplane that it uses to fly executives to business meetings. When the airplane is not being used for business, Harry and Wilma use it to travel to their ranch in Idaho for short vacations. The approximate cost of their trips to the ranch in the current year is $8,000.

C:4-38 *Unreasonable Compensation.* Forward Corporation is owned by a group of 15 shareholders. During the current year, Forward pays $550,000 in salary and bonuses to Alvin, its president and controlling shareholder. The corporation's marginal tax rate is 34%, and Alvin's marginal tax rate is 39.6%. The IRS audits Forward's tax return and determines that reasonable compensation for Alvin is $350,000. Forward agrees to the adjustment. What effect does the disallowance of part of the salary and bonus deduction have on Forward's and Alvin's respective tax positions? Ignore payroll taxes, such as FICA.

C:4-39 *Stock Dividend Distribution.* Wilton Corporation has a single class of common stock outstanding. Robert owns 100 shares, which he purchased six years ago for $100,000. In the current year, when the stock is worth $1,200 per share, Wilton declares a 10% dividend payable in common stock. On December 10 of the current year, Robert receives ten additional shares. On January 30 of the subsequent year, he sells five of the ten shares for $7,000.
a. How much income must Robert recognize when he receives the stock dividend?
b. How much gain or loss must Robert recognize when he sells the common stock?
c. What is Robert's basis in his remaining common shares? When does his holding period in the new common shares begin?

C:4-40 *Stock Dividend Distribution.* Moss Corporation has a single class of common stock outstanding. Tillie owns 1,000 shares, which she purchased five years ago for $100,000. Moss declares a stock dividend payable in 8% preferred stock having a $100 par value. Each shareholder receives one share of preferred stock for ten shares of common stock. On the distribution date—December 16 of the current year—the common stock was worth $180 per share, and the preferred stock was worth $100 per share. On April 1 of the current year, Tillie sells half of her preferred stock for $5,000.

a. How much income must Tillie recognize when she receives the stock dividend?
b. How much gain or loss must Tillie recognize when she sells the preferred stock? (Ignore the implications of Sec. 306.)
c. What is Tillie's basis in her remaining common and preferred shares after the sale? When does her holding period for the preferred shares begin?

C:4-41 *Stock Rights Distribution.* Trusty Corporation has a single class of common stock outstanding. Jim owns 200 shares, which he purchased for $50 per share two years ago. On April 10 of the current year, Trusty distributes to its common shareholders one right to purchase for $60 one common share for each common share owned. At the time of the distribution, each common share is worth $75, and each right is worth $15. On September 10, Jim sells 100 rights for $2,000 and exercises the remaining 100 rights. On November 10, he sells for $80 each 60 of the shares acquired through exercise of the rights.

a. What are the amount and character of income Jim recognizes upon receiving the rights?
b. What are the amount and character of gain or loss Jim recognizes upon selling the rights?
c. What are the amount and character of gain or loss Jim recognizes upon exercising the rights?
d. What are the amount and character of gain or loss Jim recognizes upon selling the newly acquired common shares?
e. What basis does Jim take in his remaining shares?

C:4-42 *Attribution Rules.* George owns 100 of the 1,000 outstanding shares of Polar Corporation common stock. Under the Sec. 318 family attribution rules, to which of the following individuals will ownership of George's stock be attributed? In other words, who is deemed to constructively own George's stock?

a. George's wife
b. George's father
c. George's brother
d. George's mother-in-law
e. George's daughter
f. George's son-in-law
g. George's grandfather
h. George's grandson
i. George's mother's brother (his uncle)

C:4-43 *Attribution Rules.* Moose Corporation's 400 shares of outstanding stock are owned as follows:

Name	*Shares*
Lara (an individual)	60
LMN Partnership (Lara is a 20% partner)	50
LST Partnership (Lara is a 70% partner)	100
Lemon Corporation (Lara is a 30% shareholder)	100
Lime Corporation (Lara is a 60% shareholder)	90
Total	400

How many shares is Lara deemed to own under the Sec. 318 attribution rules?

C:4-44 *Redemption from a Sole Shareholder.* Paul owns all 100 shares of Presto Corporation stock. His basis in the stock is $10,000. Presto has $100,000 of E&P. Presto redeems 25 of Paul's shares for $30,000. What are the tax consequences of the redemption to Paul and to Presto?

C:4-45 *Multiple Redemptions.* Four unrelated shareholders own Benton Corporation's 400 shares of outstanding stock. As indicated below, Benton redeems a total of 100 shares for $500 per share from three of its shareholders. Each shareholder has a $230 per share basis in his or her stock. Benton's current and accumulated E&P at the end of the tax year is $150,000.

Shareholder	*Shares Held Before the Redemption*	*Shares Redeemed*
Ethel	200	40
Fran	100	30
Georgia	50	30
Henry	50	–0–
Total	400	100

a. What are the tax consequences (e.g., basis of remaining shares and amount and character of recognized income, gain, or loss) of the redemptions to Ethel, Fran, and Georgia?
b. How would your answer to Part a change if Ethel were Georgia's mother?

C:4-46 *Redemption Requirements for Sale Treatment.* Of the 9,500 shares of Favor Corporation stock outstanding, Olsen owns 6,100 shares. Unrelated parties own the remaining shares. To bolster its stock price, Favor plans to reduce the total number of shares outstanding by redeeming some of the shares held by Olsen.
a. To qualify the redemption as "substantially disproportionate" and thereby make it eligible for sale treatment, how many of Olsen's shares must Favor redeem?
b. How would your answer change if Olsen owns only 5,800 out of 9,500 shares before the redemption?

C:4-47 *Partial Liquidation.* Unrelated parties Amy, Beth, Carla, and Delta Corporation each own 25 of the 100 outstanding shares of Axle Corporation stock. In a transaction that qualifies as a partial liquidation, Axle distributes $20,000 cash to each shareholder in exchange for five Axle shares. Each redeemed share has a $1,000 basis to the shareholder and a $4,000 FMV. How does each shareholder treat the distribution for tax purposes?

C:4-48 *Redemption to Pay Death Taxes.* John died on March 3, 2017. His gross estate of $8.25 million includes First Corporation stock (400 of the 1,000 outstanding shares) worth $5 million or $12,500 per share ($5,000,000/400). This FMV amount also is the estate's basis in the stock (see Chapter C:13). John's wife, Myra, owns the remaining 600 shares. Deductible funeral and administrative expenses total $250,000. John, Jr. is the sole beneficiary of John's estate. Estate taxes amount to $950,000.
a. Does a redemption of First Corporation stock from John's estate, John, Jr., or John's wife qualify for sale treatment under Sec. 303?
b. On September 10, 2017, First Corporation redeems 200 shares of its stock from John's estate for $3 million or $15,000 per share ($3,000,000/200). How does the estate treat this redemption for tax purposes?

C:4-49 *Effect of Redemption on E&P.* White Corporation has 100 shares of stock outstanding. Ann owns 40 of these shares, and unrelated individuals own the remaining 60 shares. White redeems 30 of Ann's shares for $30,000. In the year of the redemption, White has $30,000 of paid-in capital and $80,000 of E&P.
a. How does the redemption affect White's E&P balance if the redemption qualifies for sale treatment?
b. How does the redemption affect White's E&P balance if the redemption does *not* qualify for sale treatment?

C:4-50 *Various Redemption Issues.* Alan, Barbara, and Dave are unrelated. Each has owned 100 shares of Time Corporation stock for five years and each has a $60,000 basis in those shares. Time's E&P is $240,000. Time redeems all 100 of Alan's shares for their $100,000 FMV.
a. What are the amount and character of Alan's recognized gain or loss? What basis do Barbara and Dave take in their remaining shares? What effect does the redemption have on Time's E&P?
b. If Alan were Barbara's son, how would your answers to the questions in Part a change?
c. Assume the same facts as in Part b except Alan agrees with the IRS to waive the family attribution rules. Based on this assumption, how would your answers to the questions in Part a again change?

C:4-51 *Various Redemption Issues.* Andrew, Bea, Carl, and Carl, Jr. (Carl's son), and Tetra Corporation own all of the single class of Excel Corporation stock as follows:

Shareholder	*Shares Held*	*Adjusted Basis*
Andrew	20	$3,000
Bea	30	6,000
Carl	25	4,000
Carl, Jr.	15	3,000
Tetra Corporation	10	2,000
Total	100	

Andrew, Bea, and Carl are unrelated. Bea owns 75% of the Tetra stock, and Andrew owns the remaining 25%. Excel's E&P is $100,000. Determine the tax consequences of the following independent transactions to the shareholders and Excel:

a. Excel redeems 25 of Bea's shares for $30,000.
b. Excel redeems 10 of Bea's shares for $12,000.
c. Excel redeems all of Carl's shares for $30,000.
d. Assume the same facts as in Part c except the stock is redeemed from Carl's estate to pay death taxes, and the entire redemption qualifies for sale treatment under Sec. 303. The stock has a $28,000 FMV on the date of Carl's death. The alternate valuation date is not elected.
e. Excel redeems all of Andrew's shares for Excel land having a $6,000 basis for both taxable income and E&P purposes and a $24,000 FMV. Assume a 34% marginal corporate tax rate.
f. Assume that Carl owns 25 shares of Excel stock and that Carl, Jr. owns the remaining 75 shares. Determine the tax consequences to Carl and Excel if Excel redeems all 25 of Carl's shares for $30,000.

C:4-52 *Various Redemption Issues.* Alice, Bob, Carol, the ABC Partnership, Franklin Corporation, and the Gleason Family Trust own shares of Holston Corporation's single class of stock as follows:

Shareholder	*Shares Held*	*Adjusted Basis*
Alice	300	$ 75,000
Bob (Alice's brother)	500	125,000
Carol (Alice's daughter)	100	25,000
ABC Partnership	200	50,000
Franklin Corporation	600	150,000
Gleason Family Trust	300	75,000
Total	2,000	

The Holston shareholders have owned their shares for more than one year. The partners of the ABC Partnership have the following interests in the partnership: Alice 40%, Bob 30%, and Carol 30%. The shareholders of Franklin Corporation own shares as follows: Alice 10%, Bob 60%, and Carol 30%. The equal beneficiaries of the Gleason Family Trust are David (Alice's grandson) and Edgar (Bob's grandson). Alice is considering having Holston redeem some of her Holston shares in exchange for cash. On the day of the planned redemption, Holston will have $25,000 of current E&P and $75,000 of prior accumulated E&P. Determine the tax consequences of the following two independent transactions to Alice and Holston Corporation.

a. Holston redeems 100 shares of its stock from Alice in exchange for $80,000.
b. Holston redeems 200 shares of its stock from Alice in exchange for $160,000.

C:4-53 ***Comparison of Dividends and Redemptions.*** Bailey is one of four equal unrelated shareholders of Checker Corporation. Bailey has held Checker stock for four years and has a basis in her stock of $40,000. Checker has $280,000 of current and accumulated E&P and distributes $100,000 to Bailey.

a. What are the tax consequences to Checker and to Bailey if Bailey is an individual and the distribution is treated as a dividend?
b. In Part a, what would be the tax consequences if Bailey were a corporation?
c. What are the tax consequences to Checker and to Bailey (an individual) if Bailey surrenders all her stock in a redemption qualifying for sale treatment?
d. In Part c, what would be the tax consequences if Bailey were a corporation?

e. Which treatment would Bailey prefer if Bailey were an individual? Which treatment would Bailey Corporation prefer?

C:4-54 *Preferred Stock Bailout.* Fran owns all 100 shares of Star Corporation stock. Her stock basis is $60,000. On December 1 of the current year, Star distributes 50 shares of preferred stock to Fran in a nontaxable distribution. In the year of the distribution, Star's total E&P is $100,000, the preferred shares are worth $150,000, and the common shares are worth $300,000.

a. What are the tax consequences to Fran and to Star if Fran sells her preferred stock to Ken for $200,000 on January 10 of the following year? In that year, Star's current E&P is $75,000 (in addition to the $100,000 balance from the prior year).

b. How would your answer to Part a change if Fran sells her preferred stock to Ken for $110,000 instead of $200,000?

c. How would your answer to Part a change if Star redeems Fran's preferred stock for $200,000 on January 10 of the following year?

C:4-55 *Brother-Sister Redemptions.* Bob owns 60 of the 100 outstanding shares of Dazzle Corporation stock and 80 of the 100 outstanding shares of Razzle Corporation stock. Bob's basis in his Dazzle shares is $12,000, and his basis in his Razzle shares is $8,000. Bob sells 30 of his Dazzle shares to Razzle for $50,000. At the end of the year of sale, Dazzle and Razzle have E&P of $25,000 and $40,000, respectively.

a. What are the amount and character of Bob's recognized gain or loss on the sale?

b. What is Bob's basis in his remaining shares of the Dazzle and Razzle stock?

c. How does the sale affect the E&P of Dazzle and Razzle?

d. What basis does Razzle take in the Dazzle shares it purchases?

e. How would your answer to Part a change if Bob owns only 50 of the 100 outstanding shares of Razzle stock?

C:4-56 *Parent-Subsidiary Redemptions.* Jane owns 150 of the 200 outstanding shares of Parent Corporation stock. Parent owns 160 of the 200 outstanding shares of Subsidiary Corporation stock. Jane sells 50 shares of her Parent stock to Subsidiary for $40,000. Jane's basis in her Parent shares is $15,000 ($100 per share). At the end of the year of sale, Subsidiary and Parent have E&P of $60,000 and $25,000, respectively.

a. What are the amount and character of Jane's recognized gain or loss on the sale?

b. What is Jane's basis in her remaining shares of Parent stock?

c. How does the sale affect the E&P of Parent and Subsidiary?

d. What basis does Subsidiary take in the Parent shares it purchases?

e. How would your answer to Part a change if Jane instead sells 100 of her Parent shares to Subsidiary for $80,000?

C:4-57 *Bootstrap Acquisition.* Jana owns all 100 shares of Stone Corporation stock having a $1 million FMV. Her basis in the stock is $400,000. Stone's E&P balance is $600,000. Michael would like to purchase the stock but wants only the corporation's non-cash assets valued at $750,000. Michael is willing to pay $750,000 for these assets.

a. What are the tax consequences to Jana, Michael, and Stone if Michael purchases 75 shares of Stone stock for $750,000 and Stone redeems Jana's remaining 25 shares for $250,000 cash?

b. How would your answer to Part a change (if at all) if Stone first redeems 25 shares of Jana's stock for $250,000 and then Michael purchases the remaining 75 shares from Jana for $750,000?

COMPREHENSIVE PROBLEM

C:4-58 Several years ago, Brian formed Sigma Corporation, a retail company ineligible for the U.S. production activities deduction. Sigma uses the accrual method of accounting. In 2017, the corporation reported the following items:

Gross profit	$290,000
Long-term capital gain	20,000
Tax-exempt interest received	7,000
Salary paid to Brian	80,000
Payroll tax on Brian's salary (Sigma's share)	6,120
Depreciation	25,000 ($21,000 for E&P purposes)
Other operating expenses	89,000
Dividend distribution to Brian	60,000

In addition to owning 100% of Sigma's stock, Brian manages Sigma's business and earns the $80,000 salary listed above. This salary is an ordinary and necessary business expense of the corporation and is reasonable in amount. The payroll tax on Brian's $80,000 salary is $12,240, $6,120 of which Sigma pays and deducts, and the other $6,120 of which Brian pays through Social Security withholding. Brian is single with no dependents and claims the standard deduction.

a. Calculate Sigma's and Brian's 2017 taxable income and total tax liability, as well as their combined tax liability. Also, calculate the corporation's current E&P after the dividend distribution.
b. Assume instead that Brian operates Sigma as a sole proprietorship. In the current year, the business reports the same operating results as above, and Brian withdraws $140,000 in lieu of the salary and dividend. Brian's self-employment tax is $20,486. Compute Brian's total tax liability for 2017.
c. Assume a C corporation such as in Part a distributes all of its after-tax earnings. Compare the tax treatment of long-term capital gains, tax-exempt interest, and operating profits if earned by a C corporation with the tax treatment of these items if earned by a sole proprietorship.

TAX STRATEGY PROBLEM

C:4-59 John owns all 100 shares of stock in Jamaica Corporation, which has $100,000 of current E&P. John would like to receive a $50,000 distribution from the corporation. Jamaica owns several assets that it could distribute to John. What are the tax consequences of Jamaica's distributing each of the following assets? Assume Jamaica has a 34% marginal tax rate and, unless stated otherwise, its bases for E&P and taxable income purposes are the same.

a. $50,000 cash.
b. 100 shares of XYZ stock purchased two years ago for $10,000 and now worth $50,000.
c. 100 shares of ABC stock purchased one year ago for $72,000 and now worth $50,000.
d. Equipment purchased four years ago for $120,000 that now has a tax adjusted basis of $22,000 and an E&P adjusted basis of $40,000. John would assume a liability of $31,000 on the equipment. The equipment is now worth $81,000.
e. An installment obligation with a face value of $50,000 and a basis of $32,000. Jamaica acquired this obligation three years ago when it sold land held as an investment.
f. Would your answers in Parts a–e change if Jamaica redeems 50 of John's shares for each of the properties listed?
g. Based on the foregoing results, which distribution would you recommend? Which distribution(s) should be avoided?
h. Would your answers in Parts a–e change if John's 100 shares represented one third of Jamaica's outstanding shares, unrelated parties owned the remaining 200 shares, and Jamaica exchanged all of John's shares for each of the properties listed?
i. If John were an investor, would treating the distribution as a sale be preferable to treating the distribution as a dividend? Why or why not?

CASE STUDY PROBLEMS

C:4-60 Amy, Beth, and Meg each own 100 of the 300 outstanding shares of Theta Corporation stock. Amy wants to sell her shares, which have a $40,000 basis and a $100,000 FMV. Either Beth and/or Meg can purchase Amy's shares (50 shares each) or Theta can redeem all of them. Theta has a $150,000 E&P balance.

Required: Write a memorandum comparing the tax consequences of the two options to the three sisters, who actively manage Theta.

C:4-61 Maria Garcia is a CPA whose firm has prepared the tax returns of Stanley Corporation for many years. A review of Stanley's last three tax returns by a new staff accountant, who has been assigned to the client for the first time, reveals that the corporation may be paying excessive compensation to one of its key officers. The staff accountant feels that the firm should inform the IRS and/or report the excess amount as a nondeductible dividend. Although the facts are ambiguous, they tend to support the contention that the compensation paid in current and prior years is reasonable.

Required: In a client letter, discuss Maria's role as an advocate for Stanley, and discuss the possible tax consequences resulting from a subsequent audit.

TAX RESEARCH PROBLEMS

C:4-62 Fifteen years ago, husband and wife Stuart and Marsha Widell organized Widell Engineering Associates (WEA), a Delaware corporation that builds, repairs, and manages waste treatment plants throughout the Southwest. The Widells capitalized WEA with cash of $500,000 and industrial equipment having an adjusted basis of $4.5 million, each in exchange for 2,500 shares of WEA common stock. Three years later, Stuart and Marsha each gifted 500 shares of their WEA stock to their son Weymouth.

As a result of a sharp upswing in the economy, WEA's profits swelled under the joint management of Stuart and Weymouth. After ten years of joint control, however, and because of irreconcilable differences with his father, Weymouth decided to leave WEA and organize his own engineering firm, Fortunelle.

To keep WEA's business in the family and to give Stuart complete WEA management control, Stuart, Marsha, and Weymouth agreed that WEA would redeem all of Weymouth's 1,000 shares with waste treatment property worth $8.5 million. To ensure capital gains treatment, Weymouth obtained a waiver of the family attribution rules in return for an agreement with the IRS not to acquire an equity interest in WEA for ten years and to notify the IRS if he does so. Following the redemption, Weymouth transferred the property to Fortunelle in exchange for all 8,500 shares of Fortunelle common stock.

Last year, Stuart suffered a heart attack. He now has proceeded to reconcile his differences with Weymouth. To retain Widell family control of WEA's business, Stuart, Marsha, and Weymouth propose that WEA and Fortunelle conclude an "arms length" agreement under which Fortunelle would manage WEA's waste treatment plants in return annually for 20% of WEA's gross rental revenues, but no equity interest. The Widells are convinced that the proposed arrangement does not violate either the Sec. 302 waiver rules or Weymouth's agreement with the IRS. They have asked you to draft a letter that confirms this understanding. In researching the issue, consult at a minimum the following authorities:

- IRC Sec. 302(c)(2)
- Rev. Rul. 70-104, 1970 C.B. 66
- *Chertkof v. Commissioner*, 48 AFTR 2d 81-5194, 81-1 USTC ¶9462 (4th Cir, 1981)

C:4-63 When the IRS audited Winter Corporation's current year tax return, the IRS disallowed $10,000 of travel and entertainment expenses incurred by Charles, an officer-shareholder, because of inadequate documentation. The IRS asserted that the $10,000 expenditure was a constructive dividend to Charles, who maintained that the expense was business related. Charles argued that he derived no personal benefit from the expenditure and therefore received no constructive dividend. Prepare a memorandum for your tax manager explaining whether the IRS's assertion or Charles's assertion is correct. Your manager has suggested that, at a minimum, you consult the following resources:

- IRC Secs. 162 and 274
- Reg. Secs. 1.274-1 and -2

C:4-64 Scott and Lynn Brown each own 50% of Benson Corporation stock. During the current year, Benson made the following distributions to its shareholders:

Shareholder	*Property Distributed*	*Adjusted Basis to Corporation*	*Property's FMV*
Scott Brown	Land parcel A	$ 40,000	$75,000
Lynn Brown	Land parcel B	120,000	75,000

Benson had E&P of $250,000 immediately before the distributions. Prepare a memorandum for your tax manager explaining how Benson should treat these transactions for tax and financial accounting purposes. How will the two shareholders report the distributions? Assume Benson's marginal tax rate is 34%. Your manager has suggested that, at a minimum, you consult the following resources:

- IRC Sec. 301
- IRC Sec. 311
- IRC Sec. 312
- Accounting Standards Codification (ASC) 845, formerly APB No. 29

C:4-65 John and Jean own 80% and 20%, respectively, of Plum Corporation stock. Thanks to their hard work, Plum's software sales have sky rocketed. In its first year of operation Plum's earnings were minimal, but four years later, Plum grossed $10 million. Plum compensated John and Jean as follows: John received a bonus of 76% of net profits and Jean received a bonus of 19% of net profits at the end of each year. Plum never paid any dividends. Can Plum deduct any or all of the "salaries" paid to John and Jean?

C:4-66 Sara owns 60% of Mayfield Corporation's single class of stock. A group of five family members and three key employees own the remaining 40%. Mayfield is a calendar year taxpayer that uses the accrual method of accounting. Sara is a Mayfield officer and director and uses the cash method of accounting. During the period Year 1 through Year 3, Sara received the following amounts as salary and nontaxable fringe benefits from Mayfield: Year 1, $160,000; Year 2, $240,000; and Year 3, $290,000. She earned these amounts evenly throughout the tax years in question. In Year 4, upon auditing Mayfield's tax returns for Year 1 through Year 3, a revenue agent determined that reasonable compensation for Sara's services for the three years in question is $110,000, $165,000, and $175,000, respectively. The bylaws of Mayfield were amended on December 15, Year 2, to provide that:

> Any payments made to an officer of the corporation, including salary, commissions, bonuses, other forms of compensation, interest, rent, or travel and entertainment expenses incurred, and which shall be disallowed in whole or in part as a deductible expense by the Internal Revenue Service, shall be reimbursed by such officer to the corporation to the full extent of such disallowance.

Following the disallowance of $240,000 of the total salary expense, the board of directors met and requested that Sara reimburse Mayfield for the portion of her salary deemed to be excessive. Because of the large amount of money involved, the board of directors approved an installment plan whereby Sara would repay the $240,000 in five annual installments of $48,000 each over the period Year 5 through Year 9. The corporation would not charge Sara interest on the unpaid balance of $240,000. Prepare a memorandum for your tax manager explaining what salary and fringe benefits are taxable to Sara in the period Year 1 through Year 3 and what reimbursements Sara can deduct during the period Year 5 through Year 9.

CHAPTER

5

OTHER CORPORATE TAX LEVIES

LEARNING OBJECTIVES

After studying this chapter, you should be able to

1. Determine whether a corporation is subject to the alternative minimum tax (AMT) and, if so, calculate the AMT
2. Determine whether a corporation is a personal holding company (PHC) and, if so, calculate the PHC tax
3. Establish whether a corporation is subject to the accumulated earnings tax and, if so, calculate the tax
4. Identify tax planning opportunities to minimize the AMT and to avoid the PHC and accumulated earnings taxes
5. Comply with AMT, PHC tax, and accumulated earnings tax procedures
6. Describe the financial statement implications of the alternative minimum tax

Chapter C:3 examines a corporation's regular income tax and the procedures for calculating, reporting, and paying this tax. Chapter C:5 focuses on the following three additional taxes the tax law may impose on a C corporation: (1) the alternative minimum tax, (2) the personal holding company tax, and (3) the accumulated earnings tax. For a specific taxable year, a corporation could be liable for none, one, or two of these three taxes (as is discussed later in the chapter, a corporation cannot be liable for the personal holding company tax and accumulated earnings tax for the same taxable year). A corporation pays these additional taxes, if any, in addition to its regular tax liability. For each of these additional taxes, this chapter examines the requirements for the tax to be imposed, the calculation of the tax imposed, and the measures a corporation can take to avoid it.

THE ALTERNATIVE MINIMUM TAX

OBJECTIVE 1

Determine whether a corporation is subject to the alternative minimum tax (AMT) and, if so, calculate the AMT

THE GENERAL FORMULA

The **alternative minimum tax (AMT)** is Congress' attempt to ensure that taxpayers with substantial economic income cannot use exclusions, deductions, and credits to avoid a significant part of their tax liability.[1] Chapter I:14 discusses the AMT as it applies to individuals. Some aspects of the AMT apply to corporations and individuals in the same way, but other aspects of the AMT apply to these two types of taxpayers in different ways.

Table C:5-1 summarizes the calculation of a corporation's AMT. Starting with its regular taxable income, the corporation adds AMT preference items and adds and/or subtracts AMT adjustment items, all of which results in **alternative minimum taxable income (AMTI)**. AMT preferences and adjustments are income and deduction items that are treated differently for regular tax and AMT purposes and are discussed more fully later in this chapter. The tax base for the AMT equals AMTI minus an AMT exemption amount. The corporation multiplies this tax base by a 20% tax rate and subtracts an AMT foreign tax credit to determine its **tentative minimum tax (TMT)**. AMT, then, is the amount by which the TMT exceeds the corporation's regular tax.[2]

ADDITIONAL COMMENT

When AMTI exceeds $150,000 and is less than $310,000, the effective marginal AMT tax rate is 25% due to the AMT exemption amount phase-out [20% + (0.25 × 20%) = 25%].

The AMT exemption amount for corporations is $40,000 reduced by 25% of the amount by which AMTI exceeds $150,000. Thus, the AMT exemption amount is completely phased out if AMTI is $310,000 or more. If two or more corporations comprise a controlled group, they apportion among themselves one $40,000 AMT exemption amount (see Chapter C:3). In addition, the controlled group phases out its AMT exemption amount based on its members' combined AMTIs.

EXAMPLE C:5-1 ▶ Yellow Corporation's AMTI is $200,000. Because its AMTI is more than $150,000 but less than $310,000, Yellow's AMT exemption amount is less than $40,000 but more than $0. Specifically, its AMT exemption equals $27,500 {$40,000 – [0.25 × ($200,000 – $150,000)]}.[3] ◀

EXAMPLE C:5-2 ▶ Badger Corporation's regular taxable income is $400,000. It also has $350,000 of AMT preference items, $285,000 of positive AMT adjustment items, $35,000 of negative AMT adjustment items, and no tax credits. Badger's regular tax is $136,000 (0.34 × $400,000). Badger's AMTI is $1 million ($400,000 + $350,000 + $285,000 − $35,000). Its AMT exemption amount is zero, as its AMTI exceeds $310,000. Thus, Badger's AMT tax base is $1 million ($1,000,000 AMTI − $0 AMT exemption amount), and its TMT is $200,000 (0.20 × $1,000,000 AMT tax base). Badger's AMT is $64,000 ($200,000 − $136,000). In total, Badger pays $200,000 ($136,000 + $64,000) of total federal income tax. ◀

ADDITIONAL COMMENT

The AMT is a small part of corporate taxes. In 2013, the federal government collected $4.2 billion of AMT from corporations compared to $293 billion of regular income tax net of tax credits. Of the 1.6 million corporate tax returns (Form 1120) filed in 2013, only 10,202 reported any AMT.

A corporation is liable for any amount of positive AMT, no matter how small. Thus, a corporation needs to calculate its AMT every year (unless it is exempt from the AMT, a topic discussed later).

---

[1] S corporations are not subject to the AMT (Sec. 1363(a)). Instead, an S corporation's AMT preference and adjustment items pass through to their shareholders.

[2] The regular tax is the tax imposed on regular taxable income (see Chapter C:3), reduced by the regular foreign tax credit. The regular tax does not include any accumulated earnings tax or personal holding company tax, which are discussed later in the chapter, and it does not include any AMT.

[3] In the examples, assume that all corporations are C corporations not exempt from the AMT.

▼ **TABLE C:5-1**
Calculation of a Corporation's Alternative Minimum Tax Liability

Regular taxable income or loss before the NOL deduction
Plus: Tax preference items
Plus or minus: AMT adjustment items other than the ACE adjustment and the alternative tax NOL deduction

Preadjustment AMTI
Plus or minus: 75% of the difference between preadjustment AMTI and adjusted current earnings (ACE)
Minus: Alternative tax NOL deduction

Alternative minimum taxable income (AMTI)
Minus: AMT exemption amount

Tax base for the AMT (not less than zero)
Times: 0.20 tax rate

Tentative minimum tax before credits
Minus: AMT foreign tax credit

Tentative minimum tax (TMT)
Minus: Regular (income) tax

Alternative minimum tax (AMT, not less than zero)

STOP & THINK

Question: In Example C:5-2, Badger Corporation pays both the regular tax and the AMT because its TMT exceeds its regular tax. How is this result possible if the regular tax rate for corporations with \$335,000 to \$10 million of taxable income is 34% while the AMT rate is a flat 20%?

Solution: The result is possible because different tax bases are used to calculate the two taxes. The regular tax is based on regular taxable income while the TMT is based on AMTI minus the AMT exemption amount. The circumstances in which the TMT will exceed the regular tax can be expressed as follows (assuming the AMT exemption amount is completely phased out):

$$[\text{Regular taxable Income (RTI)} + \text{Preferences (P)} \pm \text{Adjustments (A)}] \times 0.20 > \text{RTI} \times 0.34$$

The inequality can be simplified as follows:

$$0.20 \times (P \pm A) > 0.14 \times \text{RTI}$$
$$(P \pm A) > 0.70 \times \text{RTI}$$

For Example C:5-2, the inequality indicates that Badger will incur an AMT if its total AMT preference and adjustment items exceed \$280,000 (0.70 × \$400,000 regular taxable income). Badger's \$600,000 (\$350,000 + \$285,000 − \$35,000) of total AMT preference and adjustment items exceed \$280,000, so the inequality correctly indicates that Badger incurs an AMT. If Badger's total AMT preference and adjustment items were \$280,000, its AMTI would be \$680,000 (\$400,000 + \$280,000), its TMT would be \$136,000 (0.20 × \$680,000), and its AMT would be zero because its TMT would not exceed its \$136,000 regular tax.[a]

[a] The inequality will be different if the corporation's marginal regular tax rate is different than 34% as used above (i.e., it is 15%, 25%, 35%, 38%, or 39%) or if the AMT exemption amount is more than zero.

EXEMPTION FROM THE AMT FOR SMALL CORPORATIONS AND FIRST-YEAR CORPORATIONS

A qualifying small corporation is exempt from the AMT. To qualify, the corporation's average gross receipts generally must be \$7.5 million or less for all three-taxable-year periods before the taxable year for which the corporation is determining qualification.[4] A corporation that did not exist for a full three-year period calculates its average gross receipts for the period it existed. For the corporation's second year of existence, it has only its first taxable year to use when applying the gross receipts test, and it applies the test using $5 million instead of $7.5 million as the threshold. At this point, the corporation will have tested its first three-year period (or, in this case, a portion thereof). For its third year, the corporation applies the gross receipts test using its first and second years, subject to the $7.5 million threshold. For its fourth and subsequent years, the corporation applies the $7.5 million threshold to the average gross receipts of the immediately preceding three years. A corporation generally is exempt from the AMT for its first year of existence, regardless of its gross receipts. If a corporation does not qualify for exemption from the AMT, it is subject to the AMT for the year it does not so qualify and all subsequent years.[5]

EXAMPLE C:5-3 ▶ Kiho Corporation forms on January 1 of Year 1 and has gross receipts as follows:

Year 1	$4,500,000	Year 4	8,400,000
Year 2	6,000,000	Year 5	7,650,000
Year 3	7,800,000	Year 6	6,300,000

Kiho is exempt from the AMT for Year 1 because it is the first year the corporation exists. For each subsequent year, Kiho calculates its average gross receipts and determines whether it is exempt from the AMT as follows:

Year 2: For its second year of existence, Kiho applies the test using only its Year 1 gross receipts and a $5 million threshold. The Year 1 gross receipts of $4.5 million is less than or equal to $5 million, so Kiho is exempt from the AMT for Year 2.

Year 3: For its third year of existence, Kiho applies the test using its average gross receipts for Years 1 and 2. This $5.25 million [($4,500,000 + $6,000,000) ÷ 2] average is less than or equal to the $7.5 million threshold that applies after the second year of existence, so Kiho is exempt from the AMT for Year 3.

Year 4: Kiho averages its gross receipts for Years 1 through 3. This $6.1 million [($4,500,000 + $6,000,000 + $7,800,000) ÷ 3] average is less than or equal to $7.5 million, so Kiho is exempt from the AMT for Year 4.

Year 5: Kiho averages its gross receipts for Years 2 through 4. This $7.4 million [($6,000,000 + $7,800,000 + $8,400,000) ÷ 3] average is less than or equal to $7.5 million, so Kiho is exempt from the AMT for Year 5.

Year 6: Kiho averages its gross receipts for Years 3 through 5. This $7.95 million [($7,800,000 + $8,400,000 + $7,650,000) ÷ 3] average is greater than $7.5 million, so Kiho is not exempt from the AMT for Year 6. However, Kiho's failure to qualify for exemption from the AMT does not necessarily mean it will pay any AMT for Year 6. Kiho would not pay any AMT if its TMT were less than its regular tax for Year 6.

Year 7: Kiho is not exempt from the AMT because it failed to so qualify in a prior year. It is irrelevant that Kiho's $7.45 million [($8,400,000 + $7,650,000 + $6,300,000) ÷ 3] average gross receipts for Years 4 through 6 is less than $7.5 million. ◀

A corporation also applies the following rules when determining whether it is exempt from the AMT:

- Gross receipts include total sales and amounts received for services. Gross receipts are not reduced for cost of goods sold and expenses. Gross receipts differ from gross income, gross profit, and taxable income. Thus, even though a corporation may have low gross profit or taxable income, it still may not qualify for exemption if it has high gross receipts.
- For any short taxable year (e.g., a corporation's initial year of existence), gross receipts are annualized.
- Gross receipts of a controlled group of corporations are aggregated. For example, if two corporations each have $4 million of average gross receipts and comprise a controlled group, the corporations will not be exempt from the AMT because their $8 million aggregate average gross receipts exceeds $7.5 million (or $5 million, if applicable).

ADDITIONAL COMMENT

Only a small fraction of corporations are subject to the AMT because most corporations' average gross receipts are less than $5 million.

[4] Sec. 55(e). To determine average gross receipts, the corporation takes into account only taxable years beginning after 1993.

[5] A corporation losing its exemption from the AMT applies the AMT on a prospective basis. For example, the AMT adjustment item for depreciation, discussed later, does not apply for property placed into service while the corporation is exempt from the AMT but whose recovery period includes years the corporation is subject to the AMT. This rule and similar rules for other AMT preference and adjustment items are beyond the scope of this chapter.

- A corporation that is a successor to another entity aggregates its gross receipts with those of its predecessor (e.g., a newly created subsidiary's gross receipts include those of its parent corporation).

TAX PREFERENCE ITEMS

A corporation adds **tax preference items** to its regular taxable income when calculating preadjustment AMTI. Tax preference items always increase a corporation's AMTI. Tax preference items include:[6]

- The depletion deduction allowable for the tax year in excess of the depletable property's adjusted basis at the end of the tax year (before reducing the adjusted basis for the current year's depletion deduction).[7]
- The amount by which excess intangible drilling and development costs (IDCs) incurred in connection with oil, gas, and geothermal wells exceeds 65% of the net income from such property.[8]
- Tax-exempt interest on private activity bonds. A private activity bond is a bond issued by a state or local government whose proceeds are used wholly or partially for private business activities (e.g., the bond proceeds are used to construct a stadium used by professional sports teams).

ADDITIONAL COMMENT

Tax-exempt interest on private activity bonds issued in 2009 or 2010 is not treated as a tax preference item, even if such interest is earned after 2010.

EXAMPLE C:5-4 ▶ Duffy Corporation mines iron ore. The adjusted basis for one of its properties is zero due to previous years' depletion deductions. Duffy earns $125,000 of gross income and $45,000 of taxable income from the sale of iron ore extracted from this property in the current year. The iron ore depletion percentage is 15%. Duffy's percentage deduction for regular taxable income before any reduction is $18,750 ($125,000 × 0.15), but Duffy reduces this deduction by $3,750 ($18,750 × 0.20) under Sec. 291(a)(2). Duffy's $15,000 ($18,750 − $3,750) deduction is less than the $22,500 ($45,000 × 0.50) maximum deduction. For AMT purposes, the $15,000 deduction for regular taxable income in excess of the property's zero adjusted basis is a tax preference item, which effectively disallows the $15,000 deduction for preadjustment AMTI. ◀

EXAMPLE C:5-5 ▶ Salek Corporation earns the following interest income in the current year:

Source	*Amount*
IBM Corporation bonds	$25,000
Madison County School District bonds	30,000
City of Franklin bonds	15,000

The interest on the IBM bonds is taxable because the bonds are not issued by a state or local government, so Salek includes the $25,000 in its regular taxable income. The Madison County School District issued its bonds to renovate school facilities. Thus, the bonds' proceeds were not used for private business activities and are not private activity bonds. Salek does not include the $30,000 in its regular taxable income, and it is not a tax preference item. The City of Franklin issued its bonds three years ago to finance a parking garage, where 35% of the space is leased exclusively to a nonexempt corporation. Thus, the bonds are private activity bonds. Salek does not include the $15,000 in its regular taxable income but adds the $15,000 to its regular taxable income when calculating preadjustment AMTI. ◀

AMT ADJUSTMENT ITEMS

Although tax preference items always *increase* AMTI, **AMT adjustment items** can either *increase* or *decrease* AMTI. Common AMT adjustment items are discussed below.[9]

Depreciation. Taxpayers calculate depreciation on some property differently for pread-justment AMTI than for regular taxable income (see Chapter I:10 for depreciation rules for regular tax

[6] Sec. 57(a).

[7] Independent producers and royalty owners are not required to treat the oil and gas depletion deduction in excess of the depletable property's adjusted basis as a tax preference item, so this tax preference item applies almost exclusively to integrated oil companies.

[8] Excess IDCs are the amount by which IDCs in the tax year exceed the deduction that would have been allowable if the IDCs had been capitalized and amortized over a ten-year period. The oil and gas excess IDC preference applies to a more limited extent for independent oil companies than it does for integrated oil companies.

[9] Sec. 56(a).

purposes). These AMT depreciation rules apply to individual and corporate taxpayers. For simplicity, this chapter discusses rules for property placed in service after 1998.[10]

Personal Property Placed in Service After 1998. For AMT purposes, the taxpayer uses the same recovery period (e.g., MACRS recovery period) and same convention (i.e., half-year or mid-quarter) for AMT purposes as it uses for regular tax purposes. However, the taxpayer generally uses the 150% declining balance method to calculate AMT depreciation but uses the 200% declining balance method to calculate regular tax depreciation.[11] The AMT adjustment equals the difference between AMT and regular tax depreciation, and the adjustment could be positive or negative. For property depreciated under the half-year convention, see Table 1 in Appendix C for the regular tax depreciation rates and Table 10 for the AMT depreciation rates. No AMT adjustment is required for property eligible for bonus depreciation placed in service after 2015 (see discussion below).

EXAMPLE C:5-6 ▶ In Year 1, Euclid Corporation places into service used office furniture costing $10,000. The property has a seven-year MACRS recovery period, and the half-year convention applies to it. Euclid does not elect Sec. 179 expensing for the property, and it does not qualify for bonus depreciation because it is not new property. In Year 1, regular tax depreciation is $1,429 ($10,000 × 0.1429), and AMT depreciation is $1,071 ($10,000 × 0.1071). Euclid adds the $358 ($1,429 – $1,071) difference in the depreciation amounts when calculating preadjustment AMTI. This AMT adjustment is positive because regular taxable income, which is the starting point for the preadjustment AMTI calculation, includes a larger depreciation deduction than is allowed for AMT purposes.

Toward the end of the recovery period, the depreciation adjustment becomes negative. For example, in Year 6, regular tax depreciation is $892 ($10,000 × 0.0892) while AMT depreciation is $1,225 ($10,000 × 0.1225). Thus, Euclid makes a negative $333 ($892 – $1,225) adjustment in Year 6. ◀

Any amount the taxpayer elects to expense under Sec. 179 for regular tax purposes also is allowed for AMT purposes.

EXAMPLE C:5-7 ▶ Assume the same facts as in Example C:5-6, except Euclid elects Sec. 179 expensing for $6,000 of the property's cost. In Year 1, Euclid's regular tax depreciation is $6,572 [$6,000 + (0.1429 × ($10,000 – $6,000))], and its AMT tax depreciation is $6,428 [$6,000 + (0.1071 × ($10,000 – $6,000))]. Euclid makes a $144 ($6,572 – $6,428) positive AMT adjustment in Year 1. ◀

Bonus Depreciation for Personal Property. For regular tax purposes, *new* personal property acquired and placed in service in 2012 through 2017 is generally eligible for 50% bonus depreciation, which allows the taxpayer to deduct 50% of the cost of qualified property in the year the taxpayer places the property in service.[12] Qualified property is primarily computer software and personal property with a MACRS recovery period of 20 years or less. Any Sec. 179 expensing the taxpayer elects with respect to qualified property applies before applying bonus depreciation. After taking the Sec. 179 expense, the taxpayer applies 50% bonus depreciation to the property's cost minus the amount expensed under Sec. 179. Finally, the MACRS depreciation percentages apply to the remaining cost, if any. Property for which the taxpayer claims bonus depreciation is depreciated the same way for AMT purposes as it is for regular tax purposes. Thus, no AMT depreciation adjustment is required. Property eligible for bonus depreciation for which the taxpayer elects out of bonus depreciation also is depreciated the same way for AMT and regular tax purposes if it is placed in service after

---

[10] AMT depreciation rules different than those discussed in the text apply to personal property and real property placed in service before 1999. For such property, the AMT adjustment usually differs from that which would apply to property placed in service after 1998.

[11] If a taxpayer elects to use the straight-line or 150% declining balance method of depreciation for personal property for regular tax purposes, AMT depreciation is the same as regular tax depreciation, so the taxpayer makes no AMT adjustment for depreciation.

[12] Sec. 168(k)(5). Bonus depreciation is scheduled to be 40% in 2018, 30% in 2019, and be unavailable for property acquired after 2019. Bonus depreciation was allowed for new personal property acquired and placed in service from September 11, 2001 through December 31, 2011 at rates of 30%, 50%, or 100%, depending on the date placed in service.

2015. However, if the taxpayer elects out of bonus depreciation for property placed into service before 2016, the taxpayer calculates AMT depreciation using the 150% declining balance method discussed above.[13]

EXAMPLE C:5-8 ▶

In 2017, Brighton Corporation purchases and places in service $710,000 of new MACRS five-year property. For 2017, Brighton expenses $510,000 under Sec. 179. In addition, it claims $100,000 [0.50 × ($710,000 − $510,000)] of bonus depreciation on the cost that remains after Sec. 179 expensing. The corporation also claims $20,000 [0.20 × ($710,000 − $510,000 − $100,000)] of regular MACRS depreciation on the cost that remains after subtracting Sec. 179 expensing and bonus depreciation. Thus, for regular tax purposes, total 2017 depreciation is $630,000 ($510,000 + $100,000 + $20,000). This $630,000 also is 2017 AMT depreciation for the property because it is eligible for bonus depreciation. Thus, Brighton has no AMT adjustment for depreciation on this property in 2017 or subsequent years. ◀

ADDITIONAL COMMENT

When a taxpayer claims Sec. 179 expensing and/or bonus depreciation, all subsequent cost recovery years are affected because, in the first year, these amounts reduce the basis of the property subject to MACRS depreciation in subsequent years.

Real Property Placed in Service After 1998. Depreciation on real property is the same for preadjustment AMTI as it is for regular taxable income. Thus, the taxpayer makes no AMT adjustment for it.

Basis Calculations. For regular tax purposes, a taxpayer reduces the adjusted basis of property for depreciation allowed for regular tax purposes. Similarly, a taxpayer reduces a property's AMT adjusted basis for allowable AMT depreciation. Thus, a property's adjusted basis for regular tax and AMT purposes will differ if these depreciation amounts differ. When selling such property, the taxpayer calculates separate amounts of gain or loss for regular tax and AMT purposes. Typically, a property's AMT adjusted basis will be more than its regular tax adjusted basis because regular tax depreciation is more accelerated than AMT depreciation, so the taxpayer has a smaller gain (or larger loss) for AMT purposes than it has for regular tax purposes. When calculating preadjustment AMTI, the taxpayer typically subtracts the regular tax gain in excess of the AMT gain (or subtracts the AMT loss in excess of the regular tax loss). These gain difference are a result of the differing regular tax and AMT bases.

EXAMPLE C:5-9 ▶

Assume the same facts as in Example C:5-6 except, on February 1 of Year 4, Euclid Corporation sells the property for $6,000. Euclid claims the following depreciation amounts each year for regular tax and AMT purposes.

Year	*Regular Tax Depreciation (1)*[a]		*AMT Depreciation (2)*[b]		*AMT Adj. (1) − (2)*
Year 1	$10,000 × 0.1429	$1,429	$10,000 × 0.1071	$1,071	$ 358
Year 2	$10,000 × 0.2449	2,449	$10,000 × 0.1913	1,913	536
Year 3	$10,000 × 0.1749	1,749	$10,000 × 0.1503	1,503	246
Year 4	$10,000 × 0.1249 × 0.5	625	$10,000 × 0.1225 × 0.5	613	12
Total		$6,252	Total	$5,100	$1,152

[a] See Table 1, Appendix C for depreciation percentages.
[b] See Table 10, Appendix C for depreciation percentages.

Because the mid-year convention applies to the property, Euclid claims a half-year of depreciation in Year 4, the year it sells the property. When Euclid sells the property, its adjusted basis for regular tax purposes is $3,748 ($10,000 – $6,252), and its adjusted basis for AMT purposes is $4,900 ($10,000 – $5,100). Thus, Euclid's gain when it sells the property is $2,252 ($6,000 – $3,748) for regular tax purposes and $1,100 ($6,000 – $4,900) for AMT purposes. Euclid makes a $1,152 ($2,252 – $1,100) negative AMT adjustment in Year 4 because the gain it includes in regular taxable income is $1,152 more than the gain it has for AMT purposes. This $1,152 difference is attributable to the regular tax depreciation in excess of the AMT depreciation for Years 1 through 4. For Year 4, Euclid's net AMT adjustment for the property is a negative $1,140 ($12 positive adjustment for depreciation minus $1,152 negative adjustment for the gain (basis) difference). ◀

ADDITIONAL COMMENT

In Example C:5-9, the $1,152 adjustment also can be calculated by subtracting the tax adjusted basis from the AMT adjusted basis ($4,900 − $3,748 = $1,152).

[13] Sec. 168(k)(2)(D)(iii) and Reg. Sec.1.168(k)-1(e)(6).

ADDITIONAL COMMENT

Because of the AMT small corporation exemption, many corporations that can use the completed contract method for regular tax purposes because their average gross receipts are $10 million or less do not have to make an AMT adjustment for long-term contracts.

Long-Term Contracts. For regular tax purposes, taxpayers generally use the percentage of completion method to account for long-term contracts (e.g., a contract to construct a building). However, a taxpayer may use the completed contract method for construction contracts it expects to complete within two years if its average gross receipts for the three preceding tax years is $10 million or less. A taxpayer also may use the completed contract method for home construction contracts (see Chapter I:11). For AMT purposes, the completed contract method is allowed for home construction contracts, but the percentage of completion method must be used for other long-term contracts.

U.S. Production Activities Deduction. A special rule applies for the U.S. production activities deduction. For regular tax purposes, the deduction is 9% of qualified production activities income but is limited to 9% of taxable income before this deduction (see Chapter C:3). For AMT purposes, the deduction is limited to 9% of AMTI before the deduction, but the taxpayer does not have to recompute qualified production activities income based on the AMT rules.[14] Thus, the taxpayer usually will have an AMT adjustment for this deduction if its qualified production activities income is more than its regular taxable income and/or AMTI (both before the deduction). However, if qualified production activities income is less than regular taxable income and also is less than AMTI (both before the deduction), the taxpayer usually will not have to make an AMT adjustment for this deduction because the deduction will be 9% of qualified production activities income for both purposes.

NOL Deduction. For AMT purposes, a taxpayer claims the alternative tax NOL deduction instead of the regular tax NOL deduction. Similar to the regular tax NOL, the alternative tax NOL is the excess of deductions over gross income, but it is based on deductions and gross income determined under the AMT rules. The alternative tax NOL deduction is limited to 90% of AMTI before this deduction and the U.S. production activities deduction. A taxpayer generally carries its alternative tax NOL back two years and forward 20 years, but it foregoes the two-year carryback period for AMT purposes if it elects to do so for regular tax purposes.[15]

The following example illustrates the computation of **preadjustment AMTI** (see Table C:5-1). Preadjustment AMTI is a component of the ACE and AMTI calculations presented later.

EXAMPLE C:5-10 ▶ In the current year, Marion Corporation reports $300,000 of regular taxable income. The $300,000 includes a $70,000 deduction for percentage depletion (the $70,000 is after the 20% reduction under Sec. 291(a)(2)). The depletable property's adjusted basis at the beginning of the year is $40,000. Regular taxable income also includes an $80,000 deduction for MACRS depreciation. For AMT purposes, depreciation for the depreciable property is $55,000.

Regular taxable income	$300,000
Plus: Percentage depletion in excess of basis ($70,000 − $40,000)	30,000
AMT depreciation adjustment ($80,000 − $55,000)	25,000
Preadjustment AMTI	$355,000

◀

Application of Other Regular Tax Rules. As discussed above, the IRC treats many income and deduction items differently for regular tax and AMT purposes. In addition, for AMT purposes, a corporation recomputes income and deduction items for which the regular tax and AMT rules do not differ, based on the regular tax rules and the AMT amounts.[16] For example, for regular tax purposes, the charitable contributions deduction is limited to 10% of taxable income before deducting certain items (see Chapter C:3). For AMT purposes, this limitation is 10% of AMTI before deducting those items. Similarly,

[14] Sec. 199(d)(6).

[15] Instructions for Form 4626, Alternative Minimum Tax—Corporations.

[16] Reg. Sec. 1.55-1(a). However, Reg. Sec. 1.56(g)-1(r) allows the taxpayer to elect to use a simplified inventory method for AMT purposes.

closely held corporations and personal service corporations recalculate their at-risk and passive activity losses, taking into account their AMT preference and adjustment items.

ADDITIONAL COMMENT

In 2013, corporations' ACE adjustments totaled $7.2 billion while other AMT preference and adjustment items were a net positive $8.1 billion.

ADJUSTED CURRENT EARNINGS (ACE) ADJUSTMENT

Congress added the ACE adjustment in an attempt to bring the AMT tax base closer to a corporation's economic income. The IRC requires C corporations, but not individuals and S corporations, to make the ACE adjustment when calculating the AMT.[17] The ACE adjustment generally equals 75% of ACE minus preadjustment AMTI. ACE is similar to the concept of earnings and profits (E&P) that determines whether a corporate distribution is a dividend (see Chapter C:4), but ACE is not exactly the same as E&P because the tax law treats some items differently for ACE purposes than for E&P purposes. ACE equals preadjustment AMTI plus and/or minus adjustments for items whose treatment differs for the two purposes. These differences are discussed below.

The ACE adjustment generally can be positive or negative. However, a corporation's negative ACE adjustment is limited to the cumulative net positive amount of its ACE adjustments in all prior years. A corporation cannot carry over to another year any negative ACE adjustment that exceeds this limitation.

EXAMPLE C:5-11 ▶ Kantro Corporation's ACE adjustments prior to Year 1 net to a positive $10,000. Kantro reports the following ACE and preadjustment AMTI amounts for Years 1 through 3:

	Year 1	*Year 2*	*Year 3*
ACE	$600,000	$535,000	$570,000
Preadjustment AMTI	500,000	575,000	650,000

Kantro makes a positive $75,000 [0.75 × ($600,000 – $500,000)] ACE adjustment in Year 1 and a negative $30,000 [0.75 × ($535,000 – $575,000)] ACE adjustment in Year 2. Kantro's Year 2 negative ACE adjustment is limited to $85,000 ($10,000 + $75,000), so Kantro is allowed all $30,000 of the negative ACE adjustment. Kantro's Year 3 ACE adjustment is negative $60,000 [0.75 × ($570,000 – $650,000)] before considering the limitation on it. This negative adjustment is limited to $55,000 ($10,000 + $75,000 – $30,000), so Kantro's Year 3 ACE adjustment is negative $55,000. In Year 4, Kantro will not be allowed any negative ACE adjustment because its limitation will be zero ($10,000 + $75,000 – $30,000 – $55,000). ◀

ADDITIONAL COMMENT

Under the American Recovery and Reinvestment Act of 2009, interest on tax-exempt bonds issued in 2009 or 2010 is not treated as an adjustment for ACE purposes, even if such interest is earned after 2010.

The following rules apply for determining ACE.[18]

- Any income or gains permanently excluded from gross income for preadjustment AMTI purposes but increase E&P are included in gross income for ACE purposes (e.g., interest on tax-exempt bonds that are not private activity bonds and life insurance proceeds).[19] A corporation adds these items to its preadjustment AMTI when calculating its ACE.
- Any expenses or losses deductible for preadjustment AMTI purposes but not deductible for E&P are not deductible for ACE purposes (e.g., 70% dividends-received deduction). A corporation adds these items to its preadjustment AMTI when calculating its ACE. The 80% and 100% dividends-received deductions and the U.S. production activities deduction are exceptions to this rule. These two deductions are allowed for ACE purposes even though they are not deductible for E&P.
- Any expenses or losses not deductible for preadjustment AMTI purposes but deductible for E&P are not deductible for ACE purposes (e.g., federal income taxes). A corporation does not adjust for these items when calculating ACE because they are not deductible for preadjustment AMTI or ACE.

[17] Sec. 56(c)(1) and (g)(6).

[18] Sec. 56(g)(4) and Reg. Sec. 1.56(g)-1.

[19] The items are reduced by any deduction that would be allowable in computing preadjustment AMTI if the income were includible in preadjustment AMTI. No adjustment is made for timing differences (e.g., income or gains that are included in preadjustment AMTI and E&P but in different taxable years).

- The installment method generally is not allowed for ACE purposes. A corporation with a sale to which the installment method applies makes a positive adjustment to preadjustment AMTI to calculate ACE in the year of sale, and it makes a negative adjustment in the year(s) it receives the sales proceeds.
- Organizational expenditures are not deductible for ACE purposes. A corporation adds such a deduction to its preadjustment AMTI when calculating its ACE. Any organizational expenditures deducted for regular tax purposes are also deductible for preadjustment AMTI purposes, so a corporation makes no adjustment when calculating preadjustment AMTI.
- The increase or decrease in the annual LIFO recapture amount increases or decreases ACE. The LIFO recapture amount is the amount by which ending inventory under the first-in, first-out (FIFO) method exceeds ending inventory under the last-in, first-out (LIFO) method. This adjustment effectively converts the corporation's inventory method from LIFO to FIFO for ACE purposes.
- Depletion is determined under the cost method. For ACE purposes, a corporation amortizes intangible drilling costs over 60 months beginning with the month in which it pays or incurs them.
- For ACE purposes, a corporation recomputes income and deductions for which the preadjustment AMTI and ACE rules do not differ, based on the preadjustment AMTI rules and the ACE amounts.[20] For example, a corporation recalculates the charitable contribution and percentage depletion deduction limitations. For many corporations, recalculating the charitable contribution deduction limitation results in no adjustment to preadjustment AMTI because their charitable contributions are less than the limit for both preadjustment AMTI and ACE purposes.

Topic Review C:5-1 summarizes the ACE calculation.

Comprehensive Example. Glidden Corporation does not qualify for the first year or small corporation exemption from the AMT. Glidden calculates its regular taxable income and regular tax as follows:

Gross profit from sales	$300,000
Dividends: From 30%-owned corporation	10,000
From 10%-owned corporation	20,000
Gain on sale of machine	12,778
Gain on installment sale of land	25,000
Gross income	$367,778
Operating expenses (other than depreciation)	(175,000)
Depreciation	(40,000)
Deduction for organizational expenditures	(500)
Dividends-received deduction	(22,000)
Total deductions	($237,500)
Taxable income	$130,278
Regular tax	$ 34,058

Assume the following additional facts:

- Glidden receives $15,000 of tax-exempt bond interest. The bonds are not private activity bonds and were not issued in 2009 or 2010.
- Glidden receives $100,000 of life insurance proceeds upon the death of one of its executives.
- Glidden sells land for a $77,000 gain, $25,000 of which it reports in the current year for regular tax purposes under the installment method.
- The gain on the machine sale for AMT purposes is $5,860.

[20] Reg. Sec. 1.56(g)-1(a)(5).

TOPIC REVIEW C:5-1

Summary of Common Alternative Minimum Tax Preference and Adjustment Items

Income/Expense Item	Typical Adjustment to: Regular Taxable Income to Calculate Preadjustment AMTI	Preadjustment AMTI to Calculate ACE
Tax-exempt interest:		
Private activity bonds	Increase[a]	None
Other bonds	None	Increase[a]
Life insurance proceeds	None	Increase
Deferred gain on installment method sale:		
Year of sale	None	Increase
Subsequent years' proceeds received	None	Decrease
LIFO inventory adjustment	None	Increase or decrease
Depreciation	Increase or decrease	None
"Basis adjustment" on asset sale	Decrease	None
Excess charitable contributions:		
Year of contribution	Decrease	Decrease
Carryover year	Increase	Increase
Excess capital losses	None	None
Dividends-received deduction:		
80% and 100% DRD	None	None
70% DRD	None	Increase
U.S. production activities deduction	Decrease or None	None
Organizational expenditure deduction	None	Increase
Federal income taxes	None	None
Penalties and fines	None	None
Disallowed travel and entertainment expenses and club dues	None	None

[a] Except for bonds issued in 2009 or 2010.

- ► Depreciation for AMT purposes is $32,500.
- ► Glidden incurred $12,500 of organizational expenditures three years ago. It expensed $5,000 of these expenditures in that year and is amortizing the remaining $7,500 over 180 months. The deduction for the current year is $500.
- ► Glidden's ACE adjustments for prior years are a net positive $311,296.

Based on the above facts, Glidden calculates its preadjustment AMTI as follows:

Taxable income	$130,278
Plus: Depreciation adjustment	7,500[a]
Minus: Basis adjustment on machine sale	(6,918)[b]
Preadjustment AMTI	$130,860

[a] $40,000 − $32,500 = $7,500.
[b] $5,860 − $12,778 = $(6,918).

Glidden makes the $7,500 depreciation adjustment because the depreciation method it uses for regular tax purposes differs from that for AMT purposes. Similarly, Glidden's gain on the machine sale differs for regular tax and AMT purposes because the different depreciation methods result in different adjusted bases for the property for these two purposes. Glidden makes no adjustment for preadjustment AMTI for the tax-exempt interest because it is not earned on private activity bonds, so Glidden treats the interest in the same manner for regular tax and preadjustment AMTI purposes. Likewise, Glidden makes no adjustment for the life insurance proceeds, the installment sale gain, or the organizational expenditures because it treats these items in the same manner to calculate regular taxable income and preadjustment AMTI.

Glidden calculates its ACE as follows:

Preadjustment AMTI	$130,860
Plus: Tax-exempt bond interest	15,000
Life insurance proceeds	100,000
Deferred gain on installment sale	52,000[a]
Deduction for organizational expenditures	500
Dividends-received deduction	14,000[b]
Adjusted current earnings	$312,360

[a] $77,000 − $25,000 = $52,000.
[b] $20,000 × 70% = $14,000.

The tax-exempt interest and life insurance proceeds are not included in regular taxable income and preadjustment AMTI but are included in ACE, so Glidden adds these items to preadjustment AMTI when calculating ACE. The portion of the installment sale gain whose taxation is deferred for regular tax and preadjustment AMTI purposes is not deferred for ACE purposes, so Glidden makes a positive adjustment for it. (Glidden will make negative adjustments in subsequent years as this deferred gain is recognized for regular tax and preadjustment AMTI purposes but not for ACE purposes.) Glidden adds the organizational expenditures and 70% dividends-received deductions because they are not allowed for ACE purposes.

Glidden calculates its AMT as follows:

Preadjustment AMTI		$130,860
ACE adjustment:		
ACE	$312,360	
Minus: Preadjustment AMTI	(130,860)	
Difference	$181,500	
Times: 75%	× 0.75	136,125
Alternative minimum taxable income (AMTI)		$266,985
Minus: AMT exemption amount		(10,754)[a]
AMT base		$256,231
Times: 20% tax rate		× 0.20
Tentative minimum tax (TMT)		$ 51,246
Minus: Regular tax		(34,058)[b]
Alternative minimum tax (AMT)		17,188

[a] $40,000 − [0.25 × ($266,985 − $150,000)] = $10,754.
[b] $22,250 + [0.39 × ($130,278 − $100,000)] = $34,058.

Glidden reduces its AMT exemption amount, but not to zero, because its AMTI is more than $150,000 and less than $310,000. Glidden's total federal income tax is $51,246 ($34,058 regular tax + $17,188 AMT), which equals its TMT. A completed Form 4626 for this comprehensive example appears in Appendix B.

MINIMUM TAX CREDIT

If applicable, a corporation incurs the AMT in addition to its regular tax. The AMT also creates a **minimum tax credit**, which the corporation may use to offset future regular taxes. The amount of unused minimum tax credits from prior years a corporation can use in a tax year is limited to the extent its regular tax (minus all credits other than refundable credits) exceeds its TMT. That is, a corporation's unused minimum tax credits can offset its regular tax but not its AMT. Also, the limitation prevents the minimum tax credit from reducing the regular tax below the TMT in a given year. A corporation's unused minimum tax credits carry forward indefinitely. Because of the minimum tax credit, the AMT generally accelerates a corporation's tax liability rather than permanently increasing it.[21] In effect, the AMT is a prepaid tax on corporate preferences and AMT adjustments.

[21] Sec. 53. Several of the differences between regular taxable income and AMTI are timing differences (e.g., depreciation). If no minimum tax credit were allowed, a corporation might incur AMT in one year when such a timing difference results in a positive AMT adjustment that causes its TMT to exceed its regular tax, but the corporation might not save AMT when the timing difference reverses and results in a negative AMT adjustment because its regular tax exceeds its TMT that year. Regular taxable income and AMTI can differ due to permanent differences that will never reverse (e.g., tax-exempt interest on private activity bonds or an ACE adjustment resulting from the 70% dividends-received deduction). A corporation generally is allowed a minimum tax credit for all of its AMT, whether it is due to timing or permanent differences. This treatment differs from that for individuals, who are allowed a minimum tax credit only for the AMT attributable to certain AMT preference and adjustment items (see Chapter I:14).

EXAMPLE C:5-12 ▶ For the current year, Woodford Corporation's regular tax is $59,300, and its TMT is $70,000. Thus, Woodford's AMT is $10,700 ($70,000 − $59,300). This $10,700 of AMT generates a $10,700 minimum tax credit for Woodford. Woodford's total tax is $70,000 ($59,300 + $10,700).

In the next year, Woodford's regular tax is $86,600, and its TMT is $75,000. Thus, Woodford's AMT is zero. Woodford claims all $10,700 of its unused minimum tax credit because its use is limited to $11,600 ($86,600 − $75,000). Woodford's net tax for the next year is $75,900 ($86,600 − $10,700). If Woodford's regular tax in the next year had been $83,000 instead of $86,600, it could have taken only $8,000 ($83,000 − $75,000) of the minimum tax credit that year with $2,700 carrying forward to a subsequent year. ◀

ADDITIONAL COMMENT

In Example C:5-12, the $145,900 ($70,000 + $75,900) total tax that Woodford pays in the current year and next year equals the $145,900 ($59,300 + $86,600) total regular tax that Woodford pays in those years. This equality illustrates that the AMT generally accelerates a corporation's tax liability rather than permanently increasing it. With discounting, the total present value of the $70,000 and $75,900 amounts exceeds the total present value of the $59,300 and $86,600 amounts, demonstrating the time value of money.

ADDITIONAL COMMENT

Because the general business credit limitation depends on the TMT, *every* corporation not exempt from the AMT needs to compute its TMT, even if it owes no AMT.

TAX CREDITS AND THE AMT

AMT and the General Business Credit. The general business credit is the sum of many business credits, such as the credit for research activities (see Chapter I:14). The IRC limits the general business credit a taxpayer may claim for regular tax purposes, which the following points describe:[22]

- A taxpayer's general business credit limitation is:
  - **a.** Net income tax in excess of
  - **b.** Greater of:
    - **i.** TMT, or
    - **ii.** 25% of its net regular tax in excess of $25,000.
- The net income tax is the sum of the regular tax and AMT, reduced by the foreign tax credit.
- The net regular tax is regular tax, reduced by the foreign tax credit.
- A small corporation exempt from the AMT is treated as having a zero TMT.
- The taxpayer can carry back one year and forward 20 years any general business credit that cannot be used in the current year because of the credit limitation.[23]

The effect of this limitation is that the general business credit can offset, at most, only the portion of the regular tax that exceeds the TMT, and it cannot offset any AMT.

EXAMPLE C:5-13 ▶ In the current year, Keene Corporation's regular tax before credits is $165,000, its TMT is $120,000, and the only available credit it has is a $55,000 general business credit. Keene's AMT is zero because its TMT does not exceed its regular tax. Keene calculates its general business credit limitation as follows:

Net income tax		$165,000
Minus: Greater of:		
(1) Tentative minimum tax, or	$120,000	
(2) 25% of regular tax (reduced by the foreign tax credit) in excess of $25,000 [0.25 × ($165,000 − $25,000)]	$ 35,000	(120,000)
General business credit limitation		$ 45,000

Keene may claim $45,000 of its general business credit in the current year, so its regular tax (net of credits) is $120,000 ($165,000 − $45,000). Keene's general business credit in excess of the limitation is $10,000 ($55,000 − $45,000), which it carries back one year and forward 20 years. ◀

AMT and the Foreign Tax Credit. A taxpayer may reduce its TMT by a modified version of the foreign tax credit. For regular tax purposes, the foreign tax credit is limited to the regular tax before credits multiplied by the ratio of foreign source regular taxable income to worldwide regular taxable income (see Chapter I:14). For AMT

[22] Sec. 38(c). Special rules apply for certain credits that comprise the general business credit, such as the empowerment zone employment credit.

[23] Sec. 39.

TOPIC REVIEW C:5-2

Alternative Minimum Tax (AMT) for Corporations

1. Qualifying small corporations are exempt from the AMT. To qualify, a corporation's average gross receipts generally must be $7.5 million or less. Also, first-year corporations generally are exempt from the AMT. S corporations are exempt from the AMT and, instead, pass through their AMT preference and adjustment items to their shareholders.
2. The starting point for calculating preadjustment alternative minimum taxable income (AMTI) is regular taxable income. A taxpayer increases this amount for tax preference items and increases and/or decreases it for AMT adjustment items (other than the adjusted current earnings (ACE) adjustment and the alternative tax net operating loss (NOL) deduction). The resulting amount is preadjustment AMTI.
3. The ACE adjustment generally equals 75% of ACE minus preadjustment AMTI. ACE is a modified version of preadjustment AMTI.
4. AMTI equals preadjustment AMTI, plus or minus the ACE adjustment, and minus the alternative tax NOL deduction.
5. The AMT tax base is AMTI minus a $40,000 AMT exemption amount. The $40,000 amount phases out as AMTI increases from $150,000 to $310,000.
6. A corporation's tentative minimum tax (TMT) equals 20% of its AMT tax base. It is reduced by the AMT foreign tax credit allowed. The TMT can limit the amount of general business credit allowed for regular tax purposes.
7. The AMT is the excess of the TMT over the regular tax, and it is levied in addition to the regular tax.
8. A corporation's AMT generates an equal amount of minimum tax credit, which the corporation can carry forward indefinitely to offset future regular taxes. Minimum tax credits can be used only to the extent the regular tax exceeds the TMT.
9. When determining its quarterly estimated tax payments, a taxpayer includes its regular tax and AMT.

purposes, a taxpayer calculates its credit limitation by substituting the TMT (before subtracting any AMT foreign tax credit) for the regular tax and by substituting AMTI for regular taxable income.[24]

Topic Review C:5-2 presents an overview of the AMT for corporations. Also see the financial statement implications of the AMT later in this chapter.

PERSONAL HOLDING COMPANY TAX

OBJECTIVE 2

Determine whether a corporation is a personal holding company (PHC) and, if so, calculate the PHC tax

A corporation that meets both a stock ownership test and a passive income test is classified as a **personal holding company (PHC)** for the tax year. Congress enacted the PHC tax to prevent taxpayers from using closely held corporations to shelter passive income from the higher individual tax rates. The PHC tax is 20% of the PHC tax base (called undistributed personal holding company income and discussed later in the chapter). A corporation subject to the PHC tax pays this tax in addition to the regular tax and the alternative minimum tax. Corporations, however, can escape the PHC tax by intentionally failing either the stock ownership test or passive income test or, as discussed later, through dividend distributions that reduce the PHC tax base to zero.

The significance of the PHC tax has been diminished since Congress reduced the PHC tax rate (20% in 2017) to match the top tax rate on qualified dividends. Prior to the reduction, the PHC tax rate was the same rate as the top individual tax rate (e.g., 39.6%).

[24] Sec. 59(a). A taxpayer may elect to use a simplified AMT foreign tax credit limitation, which uses the ratio of foreign source regular taxable income to worldwide AMTI rather than the ratio of foreign source AMTI to worldwide AMTI.

ADDITIONAL COMMENT

The Congressional intent behind enacting the personal holding company and accumulated earnings taxes was not to produce large amounts of tax revenues. However, the presence of these taxes in the IRS's arsenal prevents substantial revenue losses from certain tax-motivated transactions involving closely held corporations.

PERSONAL HOLDING COMPANY DEFINED

A personal holding company is any corporation that (1) has five or fewer individual shareholders who own more than 50% of the corporation's outstanding stock at any time during the last half of its tax year and (2) has personal holding company income that is at least 60% of its adjusted ordinary gross income for the tax year.[25]

Corporations with special tax status generally are excluded from the PHC definition. Among these are S corporations and tax-exempt organizations.

STOCK OWNERSHIP REQUIREMENT

Section 542(a)(2) provides that a corporation satisfies the PHC stock ownership requirement if more than 50% of the value of its outstanding stock is directly or indirectly owned by five or fewer individuals at any time during the last half of its tax year.[26] Any corporation with fewer than ten individual shareholders at any time during the last half of its tax year, which is not an excluded corporation, will meet the stock ownership requirement.[27]

For purposes of determining whether the 50% requirement is satisfied, stock owned directly or indirectly by or for an individual is considered to be owned by that individual. The Sec. 544 stock attribution rules provide that

ADDITIONAL COMMENT

The Sec. 544 stock attribution rules are similar to the Sec. 318 stock attribution rules discussed in Chapter C:4, but they are not identical. For example, family members include brothers and sisters for the Sec. 544 rules but not for the Sec. 318 rules.

- Stock owned by a family member is considered to be owned by the other members of his or her family. Family members include a spouse, brothers and sisters, ancestors, and lineal descendants.
- Stock owned directly or indirectly by or for a corporation, partnership, estate, or trust is considered to be owned proportionately by its shareholders, partners, or beneficiaries.
- A person who holds an option to acquire stock is considered to own such stock whether or not the individual intends to exercise the option.
- Stock owned by a partnership's partner is considered to be owned by his or her partners.
- The family, partnership, and option rules can be used only to make a corporation a PHC. They cannot be used to prevent a corporation from acquiring PHC status.[28]

PASSIVE INCOME REQUIREMENT

A corporation whose shareholders satisfy the stock ownership requirement is not a PHC unless the corporation also earns predominantly passive income. The passive income requirement is met if at least 60% of the corporation's **adjusted ordinary gross income (AOGI)** for the tax year is personal holding company income (PHCI). The following text sections define AOGI and PHCI and outline ways in which a corporation can sidestep the passive income requirements.

KEY POINT

To be deemed a PHC, a corporation must satisfy two tests: a stock ownership test and a passive income test. Because most closely held corporations satisfy the stock ownership test, the passive income test usually is decisive.

Adjusted Ordinary Gross Income Defined. The first step toward determining AOGI is calculating the corporation's gross income (see Figure C:5-1). Gross income is determined under the same accounting method used to compute taxable income. Thus, an income item excluded from gross income also is excluded from AOGI. Gross receipts from sales are reduced by the corporation's cost of goods sold.

The next step toward determining AOGI is calculating the corporation's **ordinary gross income (OGI)**. To do this, the corporation's gross income is reduced by the amount of its capital gains and Sec. 1231 gains.[29] These items are neutral in determining whether a corporation is a PHC; that is, the realization and recognition of a large Sec. 1231 or capital gain cannot make a corporation a PHC.

---

[25] Sec. 542(a).

[26] The PHC stock ownership test also is used to determine whether a closely held C corporation is subject to the at-risk rules (Sec. 465) or the passive activity loss and credit limitation rules (Sec. 469). Thus, a closely held corporation that is not a PHC may be subject to certain restrictions because of the PHC stock ownership rules.

[27] This statement may not be valid if entities own stock that might be attributed to the individual owners.

[28] Sec. 544(a)(4)(A).

[29] Sec. 543(b)(1).

▼ FIGURE C:5-1

Determining Adjusted Ordinary Gross Income

Gross income (GI) reported for taxable income and PHC purposes
Minus: Gross gains on the sale of capital assets
Gross gains on the sale of Sec. 1231 property

Ordinary gross income (OGI)
Minus: Certain expenses relating to gross income from rents; mineral, oil, and gas royalties; and working interests in oil or gas wells
Interest earned on certain U.S. obligations held for sale to customers by dealers
Interest on condemnation awards, judgments, or tax refunds
Certain expenses relating to rents from tangible personal property manufactured or produced by the corporation, provided it has engaged in substantial manufacturing or production of the same type of personal property in the current tax year

Adjusted ordinary gross income (AOGI)

Next, OGI is reduced by certain expenses. These expenses relate to the generation of rental income; mineral, oil, and gas (M, O, & G) royalties; and income from working interests in oil or gas wells.[30] The rental income adjustment is described below.

Reduction by Rental Income Expenses. Gross income from rents is reduced by deductions for depreciation or amortization, property taxes, interest, and rental payments. This net amount is known as **adjusted income from rents (AIR)**.[31] No other Sec. 162 expenses incurred in the generation of rental income reduce OGI. The expense adjustment cannot exceed total gross rental income.

EXAMPLE C:5-14 ▶ Ingrid owns all of Keno Corporation's stock. Keno reports the following results for the current year:

Rental income	$100,000
Depreciation	15,000
Interest expense	9,000
Real estate taxes	4,000
Maintenance expenses	8,000
Administrative expenses	12,000

Keno's AIR is $72,000 ($100,000 − $15,000 − $9,000 − $4,000). The maintenance and administrative expenses are deductible in determining taxable income and, as discussed later, undistributed PHC income, but these expenses do not reduce the AIR amount. ◀

ADDITIONAL COMMENT

Income not included in AOGI cannot be PHCI. In calculating the 60% passive income test, PHCI is the numerator and AOGI is the denominator. Because the passive income test is purely objective, both the numerator and denominator can be manipulated. When the ratio is close to 60%, one planning opportunity is to accelerate the recognition of income that is AOGI but not PHCI.

Personal Holding Company Income Defined. Personal holding company income includes dividends, interest, annuities, adjusted income from rents, royalties, produced film rents, income from personal service contracts involving a 25% or more shareholder, rental income from corporate property used by a 25% or more shareholder, and distributions from estates or trusts.

PHCI is determined according to the following general rules:

- *Dividends:* Includes only distributions out of E&P. Any amounts that are tax exempt (e.g., return of capital distributions) or eligible for capital gain treatment (e.g., liquidating distributions) are excluded from PHCI.[32]
- *Interest income:* Includes interest included in gross income. Interest excluded from gross income also is excluded from PHCI.[33]

[30] Sec. 543(b)(2).
[31] Sec. 543(b)(3).
[32] Reg. Sec. 1.543-1(b)(1).
[33] Reg. Sec. 1.543-1(b)(2).

- *Annuity proceeds:* Includes only annuity amounts included in gross income. Annuity amounts excluded from gross income (for example, as a return of capital) also are excluded from PHCI.[34]
- *Royalty income:* Includes amounts received for the use of intangible property (e.g., patents, copyrights, and trademarks). Special rules apply to copyright royalties, mineral, oil, and gas royalties, active business computer software royalties, and produced film rents. Each of these four types of income constitutes a separate PHCI category that may be excluded under one of the exceptions discussed below and set forth in Table C:5-2.[35]
- *Distributions from an estate or trust:* Included in PHCI.[36]

In the calculation of PHCI, special rules apply that could result in the exclusion of rents; mineral, oil, and gas royalties; copyright royalties; produced film rents; rental income from the use of property by a 25% or more shareholder; and active business computer software royalties from PHCI. These rules, summarized in Table C:5-2, reduce the likelihood that a corporation will be deemed a PHC. The two most frequently encountered exclusions, for rental income and personal service contract income, are explained in the next two sections.

ADDITIONAL COMMENT

Without the exception for royalties on computer software, many closely held computer software companies would qualify as PHCs.

SELF-STUDY QUESTION

What is the effect of the two-pronged test that allows the exclusion from PHCI of certain AIR?

ANSWER

This two-pronged test makes it difficult to use rents to shelter other passive income. For example, the 50% test would require at least $100 of AIR to shelter $100 of interest income. The 10% test is even more restrictive. To satisfy this test, it would be necessary to generate $900 of OGI (AIR and other items) to shelter the same $100 of interest income.

Exclusion for Rents. Adjusted income from rents (AIR) is included in PHCI unless a special exception applies for corporations earning predominantly rental income. PHCI does not include rents if (1) AIR is at least 50% of AOGI and (2) the dividends-paid deduction equals or exceeds the amount by which nonrental PHCI exceeds 10% of OGI.[37] The special exception permits corporations earning predominantly rental income and very little nonrental PHCI to avoid PHC status. The dividends-paid deduction generally is available for (1) dividends paid during the tax year, (2) dividends paid within 3½ months of the end of the tax year for which the PHC makes a special throwback election to treat the distribution as

TAX STRATEGY TIP

Taxpayers potentially liable for the PHC tax should carefully monitor the PHC exclusion requirements to avoid having to pay the tax or having to make a deficiency dividend payment.

▼ TABLE C:5-2

Tests to Determine Exclusions from Personal Holding Company Income

PHCI Category	A PHCI Category Is Excluded If: Income in the Category Is:	Other PHCI Is:	Business Expenses Are:
Rents	≥50% of AOGI[a]	≤10% of OGI (unless reduced by distributions)	—
Mineral, oil, and gas royalties	≥50% of AOGI[a]	≤10% of OGI	≥15% of AOGI
Copyright royalties	≥50% of OGI	≤10% of OGI	≥25% of OGI
Produced film rents	≥50% of OGI	—	—
Compensation for use of property by a shareholder owning at least 25% of the outstanding stock	—	≤10% of OGI	—
Active business computer software royalties	≥50% of OGI	≤10% of OGI (unless reduced by distributions)	≥25% of OGI[b]
Personal services contract income	—[c]	—	—

[a] Measured in terms of adjusted income from rents or mineral, oil, and gas royalties, respectively.
[b] The deduction test can apply to either the single tax year in question or the five-year period ending with the tax year in question.
[c] Personal services income is excluded from PHCI if the corporation has the right to designate the person who is to perform the services or if the person performing the services owns less than 25% of the corporation's outstanding stock.

[34] Reg. Sec. 1.543-1(b)(4).

[35] Reg. Sec. 1.543-1(b)(3). Royalties include mineral, oil, and gas royalties, royalties on working interests in oil or gas wells, computer software royalties, copyright royalties, and all other royalties.

[36] Sec. 543(a)(8).

[37] Sec. 543(a)(2). AIR excludes rental income earned from leasing property to a shareholder owning 25% or more of the corporation's stock. Such income is included in PHCI as a separate category.

having been paid on the last day of the preceding tax year, and (3) consent dividends (see page C:5-21). Nonrental PHCI includes all PHCI (determined without regard to the exclusions for copyright royalties and mineral, oil, and gas royalties) *other than* adjusted income from rents and rental income earned from leasing property to a shareholder owning 25% or more of the corporation's stock.

EXAMPLE C:5-15 ▶ Karen owns all of Texas Corporation's stock. Texas reports the following results for the current year:

Rental income	$100,000
Operating profit from sales	40,000
Dividend income	15,000
Interest income on corporate bonds	10,000
Rental expenses:	
Depreciation	15,000
Interest	9,000
Real estate taxes	4,000
Other expenses	20,000

Texas pays no dividends during the current year or during the 3½-month throwback period following year-end. Because one shareholder owns all the Texas stock, Texas satisfies the stock ownership requirement. Texas's AOGI is calculated as follows:

Rental income		$100,000
Operating profit from sales		40,000
Dividend income		15,000
Interest income		10,000
Gross income and OGI		$165,000
Minus: Depreciation	$15,000	
Interest expense	9,000	
Real estate taxes	4,000	(28,000)
AOGI		$137,000

The two AIR tests are illustrated as follows:

Test 1: Rental income	$100,000
Minus: Depreciation	(15,000)
Interest expense	(9,000)
Real estate taxes	(4,000)
AIR	$ 72,000
50% of AOGI (0.50 × $137,000 AOGI) [Test passed]	$ 68,500
Test 2: Dividend income	$ 15,000
Interest income	10,000
Nonrental income	$ 25,000
Minus: 10% of OGI (0.10 × $165,000)	(16,500)
Minimum amount of distributions	$8,500
Actual dividends paid [Test failed]	$ –0–

AIR exceeds the 50% threshold, so Texas passes Test 1. Because Texas pays no dividends, its dividends-paid deduction is less than the nonrental income ceiling, and Texas fails Test 2. AIR is included in PHCI because Texas passes only one of the two tests. Application of the 60% PHC income test is illustrated below:

AIR	$ 72,000
Dividend income	15,000
Interest income	10,000
PHCI	$ 97,000
AOGI	$137,000
Times: AOGI threshold	0.60
AOGI ceiling [Test passed]	$ 82,200

Texas is a PHC because PHCI exceeds 60% of AOGI and because it satisfies the stock ownership requirement.

Texas could have avoided PHC status by paying sufficient cash dividends during the current year or a consent dividend following year-end. The amount of dividends required to avoid PHC status is the excess of nonrental PHCI ($25,000) over 10% of OGI ($16,500), or $8,500. Thus, an $8,500 cash dividend paid during the current year or during the 3½-month throwback period in the next year or an $8,500 consent dividend would have permitted Texas to exclude the $72,000 of AIR from PHCI. PHCI then would have been $25,000 ($15,000 + $10,000), which is less than 60% of AOGI ($82,200). (Throwback dividends and consent dividends are discussed on page C:5-21.) ◀

ADDITIONAL COMMENT

Congress enacted the provision for personal service contracts to prevent entertainers, athletes, and other highly compensated professionals from incorporating their activities and, after paying themselves a below-normal salary, having the rest of the income taxed at the corporate rates. Even if it is apparent that a 25%-shareholder will perform the services, as long as no one other than the corporation has the right to designate who performs the services, the income is not PHCI. Thus, the careful drafting of contracts is important.

Exclusion for Personal Service Contracts. Income earned from contracts under which the corporation is obligated to perform personal services, as well as income earned on the sale of such contracts, is included in PHCI if the following two conditions are met:

- A person other than the corporation has the right to designate (by name or by description) the individual who is to perform the services, or the individual who is to perform the services is designated (by name or by description) in the contract.
- 25% or more of the value of the corporation's outstanding stock is directly or indirectly owned by the person who has performed, is to perform, or may be designated as the person to perform the services.[38]

The 25% or more requirement must be satisfied at some point during the tax year and is determined under the Sec. 544 constructive stock ownership rules. Congress enacted this provision to prevent professionals, entertainers, and sports figures from incorporating their activities, paying themselves a substandard salary, and sheltering at the lower corporate tax rates the difference between their actual earnings and their substandard salary.

EXAMPLE C:5-16 ▶

Dr. Kellner owns all the stock in a professional corporation that provides medical services. The professional corporation concludes with Dr. Kellner an exclusive employment contract that specifies the terms of his employment and that provides for the hiring of a qualified substitute when Dr. Kellner is off duty. The corporation provides office space for Dr. Kellner and employs office staff to enable Dr. Kellner to perform medical services. The income earned by Dr. Kellner does not constitute PHCI because (1) the normal patient–physician relationship generally does not involve a contract that designates a doctor who will perform the services, nor will the patient generally be permitted to designate a doctor who will perform the services, and (2) the professional corporation will be able to appoint a qualified substitute when Dr. Kellner is not on duty (for example, when he is on vacation or not on call).[39]

The income earned by the corporation in connection with Dr. Kellner's services would constitute PHCI if the contract with the patient specified that only Dr. Kellner would provide the services or if the services provided by Dr. Kellner were so unique that only he could provide them. Any portion of the corporation's income from the personal service contract attributable to "important and essential" services provided by persons other than Dr. Kellner is not included in PHCI.[40] ◀

CALCULATING THE PHC TAX

The PHC tax is calculated in two basic steps. First, the corporation determines the amount of its undistributed personal holding company income (UPHCI). It then applies the 20% PHC tax rate (for 2013 and later years) to UPHCI. If the corporation owes the PHC tax, it can avoid paying the tax by making a timely consent or deficiency dividend distribution.

Calculating UPHCI. The starting point for calculating UPHCI is the corporation's taxable income. A series of adjustments are made to taxable income to derive UPHCI. The most important of these adjustments are outlined in Figure C:5-2 and discussed in the following paragraphs.

---

[38] Sec. 543(a)(7).

[39] Rev. Rul. 75-67, 1975-1 C.B. 169. See also Rev. Ruls. 75-249, 1975-1 C.B. 171 (relating to a composer), and 75-250, 1975-1 C.B. 172 (relating to an accountant).

[40] Reg. Sec. 1.543-1(b)(8)(ii).

TYPICAL MISCONCEPTION

The PHC tax applies to any corporation deemed to be a personal holding company based on objective criteria. No improper intent is necessary. Thus, the PHC tax truly fits into the category of "a trap for the unwary."

KEY POINT

The PHC tax is in addition to the corporate income tax. Thus, the existence of both taxes reduces any advantage obtained by interposing a corporation between the taxpayer and his or her income-producing assets.

▼ FIGURE C:5-2

Calculating the Personal Holding Company Tax

Regular taxable income
Plus: Positive adjustments
1. Dividends-received deduction
2. NOL deduction
3. Excess charitable contributions carried over from a preceding tax year and deducted in current year in determining regular taxable income
4. Net loss attributable to the operation or maintenance of certain property owned or operated by the corporation
Minus: Negative adjustments
1. Accrued U.S. and foreign income taxes
2. Current year charitable contributions that exceed the 10% corporate limitation
3. NOL (computed without regard to the dividends-received deduction) incurred in the immediately preceding tax year
4. Net capital gain minus the amount of any income taxes attributed to it
Minus: Dividends-paid deduction

Undistributed personal holding company income (UPHCI)
Times: 0.20

Personal holding company tax

Positive Adjustments to Taxable Income. The dividends-received deduction is not allowed for UPHCI. Thus, a PHC adds any dividends-received deduction to its regular taxable income when calculating its UPHCI.[41] Rental expenses that exceed rental income also are added back to taxable income to derive UPHCI.

Because PHCs may deduct only the NOL for the immediately preceding tax year, two NOL compensating adjustments must be made. First, the amount of the NOL deduction claimed in determining taxable income must be added back to taxable income. Second, the entire amount of the corporation's NOL (computed without regard to the dividends-received deduction) for the immediately preceding tax year must be subtracted from taxable income.[42] The U.S. production activities deduction, however, is not added back to taxable income.

KEY POINT

The negative adjustments made to taxable income in deriving UPHCI (e.g., federal income taxes) represent items that do not reduce taxable income but reduce the earnings available for distribution to the shareholders. In contrast, positive adjustments made to taxable income (e.g., the dividends-received deduction) are not allowed in deriving UPHCI because they do not represent a reduction in earnings available for distribution to the shareholders.

TYPICAL MISCONCEPTION

A PHC does not adjust its taxable income for all items that affect taxable income differently than they affect the earnings available for distribution to its shareholders (e.g., no adjustment is required for tax-exempt interest and the U.S. production activities deduction).

Negative Adjustments to Taxable Income. Charitable contributions made by corporations are deductible for regular taxable income purposes up to 10% of taxable income without regard to the charitable contribution deduction, an NOL carryback, a capital loss carryback, the dividends-received deduction, and the U.S. production activities deduction. Charitable contributions made by individuals are deductible up to 20%, 30%, or 50% of adjusted gross income, depending on the type of contribution and type of donee. For purposes of a corporation's PHC tax, the deduction limitation is expanded from 10% to 20%, 30%, or 50% of taxable income (without regard to the same five items as for the 10% limitation), depending on the type of contribution and type of donee. Thus, a PHC has two adjustments for charitable contributions when calculating its UPHCI: (1) subtracting the amount of current year charitable contributions exceeding the 10% corporate limitation, but not exceeding the 20%, 30%, or 50% limitation, and (2) adding back charitable contribution carryovers deducted in the current year for regular tax purposes, but in an earlier year for PHC tax purposes.[43]

Income taxes (i.e., federal income taxes, the AMT, foreign income taxes, and U.S. possessions' income taxes) accrued by the corporation reduce UPHCI.[44]

---

41 Sec. 545(b)(3).
42 Sec. 545(b)(4) and Rev. Rul. 79-59, 1979-1 C.B. 209.
43 Sec. 545(b)(2).
44 Sec. 545(b)(1).

A PHC is allowed to deduct for UPHCI its net capital gain (i.e., net long-term capital gain over net short-term capital loss) minus income taxes attributable to the net capital gain.[45] The portion of federal income taxes attributable to the net capital gain equals the tax imposed on the corporation's taxable income minus the tax imposed on the corporation's taxable income excluding the net capital gain. The tax offset eliminates the possibility of a double benefit for federal income taxes, which are deductible in determining UPHCI.

The capital gains adjustment precludes a corporation from being classified as a PHC because of a large capital gain. Even where the corporation is classified as a PHC, the capital gains adjustment allows it to avoid the PHC tax on its long-term (but not short-term) capital gains.

ADDITIONAL COMMENT

The intent behind the PHC rules is not to collect taxes from a corporation. Instead, the rules are meant to compel the distribution of income by a closely held corporation so that such income will be taxed at the shareholders' individual tax rates. This purpose is evidenced by the flexibility of the dividends-paid deduction.

AVOIDING THE PHC DESIGNATION AND TAX LIABILITY BY MAKING DIVIDEND DISTRIBUTIONS

The PHC can claim a **dividends-paid deduction** for distributions made during the current year if they are made out of the corporation's current or accumulated E&P.[46] A property dividend can qualify for the dividends-paid deduction, but a nontaxable stock dividend cannot qualify. A dividends-paid deduction is not available for **preferential dividends.** A dividend is preferential when (1) the amount distributed to a shareholder exceeds his or her ratable share of the distribution as determined by the number of shares of stock owned or (2) the amount received by a class of stock is greater or less than its rightful amount.[47] In either case, the entire distribution (and not just any excess distributions) is considered to be a preferential dividend.

ADDITIONAL COMMENT

The timing for throwback dividends increased from 2½ months to 3½ months, effective for taxable years beginning after 2015. However, for corporations whose taxable year ends on June 30, the 2½-month rule continues to apply until tax years beginning after 2025.

Throwback dividends are distributions made in the first 3½ months after the close of the tax year. A dividend paid in the first 3½ months of the next tax year is treated as a throwback distribution in the preceding tax year only if the PHC makes the appropriate election.[48] Otherwise, the dividends-paid deduction is allowable only in the tax year in which the PHC actually makes the distribution. Throwback dividends paid by a PHC are limited to the lesser of the PHC's UPHCI or 20% of the amount of any dividends (other than consent dividends) paid during the tax year. Thus, a PHC that fails to make any dividend distributions during its tax year is precluded from paying a throwback dividend.

TAX STRATEGY TIP

If the corporation does not have the cash to pay a throwback dividend, it should consider a consent dividend. The consent dividend is not subject to the 20% limitation on throwback dividends and may be elected up to the extended due date for the corporation's tax return.

Consent dividends are hypothetical dividends deemed to have been paid to shareholders on the last day of the corporation's tax year. Consent dividends permit a corporation to reduce its PHC tax liability when it cannot make an actual dividend distribution because of a lack of cash, a restrictive loan covenant, or other financial or legal constraints. Any shareholder who owns stock on the last day of the corporation's tax year can elect to be treated as having received a consent dividend.[49] For PHC tax purposes, the election results in a hypothetical cash dividend on the last day of the PHC's tax year for which the dividends-paid deduction is claimed. The shareholder treats the consent dividend as received on the distribution date and then immediately contributed by the shareholder to the distributing corporation's capital account. The contribution increases the shareholder's stock basis. The shareholder can make the consent dividend election through the due date for the corporation's income tax return (including any permitted extensions).

TAX STRATEGY TIP

A deficiency dividend can be beneficial if a corporation fails to eliminate its UPHCI, either under the erroneous assumption that it was not a PHC or due to a miscalculation of its UPHCI. If certain requirements are satisfied, a deficiency dividend can be retroactively paid and thus be deductible from UPHCI earned in a previous year.

Dividend Carryovers. Dividends paid in the preceding two tax years may be used as a dividend carryover to reduce the amount of the current year's PHC tax liability.[50] Section 564 permits a PHC to deduct the amount by which its dividend distributions eligible for a dividends-paid deduction in each of the two preceding tax years exceed the corporation's UPHCI for such year.

Liquidating Dividends. Section 562 allows a dividends-paid deduction for liquidating distributions made by a PHC within 24 months of adopting a plan of liquidation.[51]

Deficiency Dividends. Under Sec. 547, a corporation liable for the PHC tax can avoid paying the tax by electing to pay a **deficiency dividend.** The deficiency dividend provisions

[45] Sec. 545(b)(5).
[46] Secs. 561(a) and 562(a).
[47] Sec. 562(c).
[48] Sec. 563(b).
[49] Sec. 565.
[50] Sec. 561(a)(3).
[51] Sec. 562(b).

substitute a tax on the dividend at the shareholder level for the PHC tax at the corporate level. The distributing corporation's shareholders must include the deficiency dividend in their gross income in the tax year in which it is received, not the tax year for which the PHC claims a dividends-paid deduction. Payment of a deficiency dividend does not relieve the PHC from liability for interest and penalties relating to the PHC tax.

To claim a dividends-paid deduction for a deficiency dividend, a PHC must meet the following requirements:

- Obtain a determination (e.g., judicial decision or IRS agreement) that establishes the amount of the PHC tax liability.
- Pay a dividend within 90 days after this determination.
- File a claim for a dividends-paid deduction within 120 days of the determination date.[52]

EXAMPLE C:5-17 ▶ On its current year return, Boston Corporation characterizes a $200,000 distribution received pursuant to a stock redemption as a capital gain. Upon audit, the IRS and Boston agree that the distribution should be recharacterized as a dividend and that Boston is liable for the PHC tax. Boston can extinguish its PHC tax liability if it pays a deficiency dividend that is large enough to reduce its UPHCI to zero within 90 days after signing the agreement and if Boston files a timely claim. ◀

PHC TAX CALCULATION

The following example illustrates how UPHCI is calculated and how a corporation's regular tax and PHC tax liabilities are determined.

EXAMPLE C:5-18 ▶ In the current year, Marlo Corporation qualifies as a PHC, contributes $60,000 to charities, and pays $50,000 in dividends in August. It reports $226,000 of taxable income as follows:

Operating profit	$100,000
Long-term capital gain	60,000
Short-term capital gain	30,000
Dividends (20%-owned corporation)	200,000
Interest	100,000
Gross income	$490,000
Salaries	(40,000)
General and administrative expenses	(20,000)
Charitable contributions	(43,000)[a]
Dividends-received deduction	(160,000)[b]
U.S. production activities deduction	(1,000)
Taxable income	$226,000

[a] $43,000 limit = 0.10 × ($490,000 − $40,000 − $20,000).
[b] $200,000 × 0.80

Marlo's regular income tax is $71,390 [$22,250 + 0.39 × ($226,000 − $100,000)]. Assuming its AMT is zero, Marlo's PHC tax is calculated as follows:

Taxable income			$226,000
Plus:	Dividends-received deduction		160,000
Minus:	Excess charitable contributions		(17,000)[c]
	Federal income taxes		(71,390)
	Dividends-paid deduction		(50,000)
	Net capital gain (NCG)	$60,000	
	Minus: Federal income taxes on the NCG	(23,400)[d]	
	NCG adjustment		(36,600)
Undistributed personal holding company income (UPHCI)			$211,010
Times:	Tax rate		0.20
Personal holding company tax			$ 42,202

[c] $60,000 total contributions − $43,000 deducted.
[d] Because Marlo is in the 39% tax bracket with and without the LTCG, it calculates the applicable federal income tax as 0.39 × $60,000 = $23,400.

ADDITIONAL COMMENT

Net capital gain is defined as the excess of net long-term capital gain over net short-term capital loss.

[52] Secs. 547(c) through (e).

WHAT WOULD YOU DO IN THIS SITUATION?

Shareholders formed Taylor Corporation on July 1 of the previous year, contributing $1 million of capital to the corporation. Because of delays in procuring manufacturing equipment, Taylor did not begin business until January of the current year. During the last six months of the previous year, the corporation earned $50,000 of taxable interest and incurred $20,000 of deductible expenses. A second-year accountant in a small accounting firm was assigned to prepare the Taylor corporate tax return. All of his previous assignments were for individual tax returns. The senior accountant responsible for the assignment told him that the return "would be simple and that all you need to do is input the interest and expense information into the Form 1120 software." Because of the rush to finish and deliver the return to the client by the return's due date, no one in the office noticed during the review process that Taylor might be a personal holding company (PHC) in the previous year. The corporation timely filed its return without paying any PHC tax. Another Taylor corporate issue arose later in the current year and was assigned to you. When you considered the issue, you asked yourself, "Does Taylor have a PHC tax problem?" If so, what can Taylor and/or you do to resolve the problem?

Marlo's total federal tax liability is $113,592 ($71,390 + $42,202). Marlo can avoid the $42,202 PHC tax by timely paying a deficiency dividend of $211,010, which equals the amount of UPHCI in the current year. ◀

Topic Review C:5-3 presents an overview of the personal holding company tax.

ACCUMULATED EARNINGS TAX

OBJECTIVE 3

Establish whether a corporation is subject to the accumulated earnings tax and, if so, calculate the tax

Corporations not subject to the personal holding company tax may be subject to the accumulated earnings tax. The **accumulated earnings tax** attempts "to compel the company to distribute any profits not needed for the conduct of its business so that, when so distributed, individual stockholders will become liable" for taxes on the dividends received.[53] Unlike its name, the tax is not levied on the corporation's total accumulated earnings balance but only on its current year addition to the balance. In other words, the tax is levied on current earnings that are not needed for a reasonable business purpose, such as excessive earnings invested by a corporation in speculative securities. Note, however, that the 23.8% (20% + 3.8% net investment tax rate) maximum tax rate on qualified dividends reduces somewhat the negative effect of double taxation, and the 0% and 15% tax rates applicable to qualified dividends of lower-bracket taxpayers eliminate or reduce the negative effect even further.

ADDITIONAL COMMENT

The accumulated earnings tax is a penalty tax imposed on corporations that accumulate unreasonable amounts of earnings for the purpose of avoiding shareholder-level taxes. When corporate tax rates are lower than individual rates, tax incentives exist for accumulating earnings inside a corporation. These opportunities should lead to the IRS imposing the accumulated earnings tax.

CORPORATIONS SUBJECT TO THE PENALTY TAX

Section 532(a) states that the accumulated earnings tax applies "to every corporation . . . formed or availed of for the purpose of avoiding the income tax with respect to its shareholders . . . by permitting earnings and profits to accumulate instead of being divided or distributed." Certain corporate forms are excluded from the accumulated earnings tax, including the following:

- Personal holding companies
- Corporations exempt from tax under Secs. 501 through 530
- S corporations[54]

[53] *Helvering v. Chicago Stock Yards Co.*, 30 AFTR 1091, 43-1 USTC ¶9379 (USSC, 1943).

[54] Secs. 532(b) and 1363(a).

TOPIC REVIEW C:5-3

Personal Holding Company (PHC) Tax

1. The PHC tax applies only to corporations deemed to be PHCs. A PHC has (1) five or fewer individual shareholders owning more than 50% in value of the corporation's stock at any time during the last half of the tax year and (2) PHCI that is at least 60% of its adjusted ordinary gross income for the tax year.
2. Two special exceptions to the PHC test may apply. First, certain types of corporations (e.g., S corporations) are excluded from the tax. Second, certain categories of income (e.g., rents and active business computer software royalties) are excluded if conditions relating to percentage of income, maximum level of other PHC income, and minimum level of business expenses are met. Table C:5-2 on page C:5-17 summarizes the excludable categories of income and related requirements.
3. The PHC tax equals 20% times UPHCI. UPHCI equals taxable income plus certain positive adjustments (e.g., dividends-received deduction) and minus certain negative adjustments (e.g., federal income taxes, excess charitable contributions, and net capital gain reduced by federal income taxes attributable to the gain).
4. UPHCI can be reduced by a deduction for cash and property dividends paid during the tax year, as well as consent and throwback dividends distributed after year-end.
5. A PHC tax liability (but not liability for related interest and penalties) can be extinguished through payment of a deficiency dividend. Deficiency dividend provisions effectively substitute an income tax levy at the shareholder level for the corporate-level PHC tax.

In principle, the accumulated earnings tax applies to both large and small corporations.[55] In practice, however, it applies primarily to closely held corporations where management can implement a corporate dividend policy to reduce the tax liability of the shareholder group.

PROVING A TAX-AVOIDANCE PURPOSE

Section 533(a) provides that the accumulation of E&P by a corporation beyond the reasonable needs of the business indicates a tax-avoidance purpose unless the corporation can prove that it is not accumulating the earnings merely to avoid taxes. In limited circumstances, this burden of proof may be shifted to the IRS under rules set forth in Sec. 534.

The existence of a tax-avoidance purpose may be inferred from all pertinent facts and circumstances. Regulation Sec. 1.533-1(a)(2) lists the following specific circumstances that suggest a tax-avoidance purpose:

- Dealings between the corporation and its shareholders (e.g., loans made by the corporation to its shareholders or funds expended by the corporation for the shareholders' personal benefit).
- Investments of undistributed earnings in assets having no reasonable connection to the corporation's business.
- The extent to which the corporation has distributed its E&P (e.g., a low dividend payout rate, low salaries, and substantial earnings accumulation may indicate a tax-avoidance purpose).

TAX STRATEGY TIP

When the IRS determines that the accumulation of earnings is unreasonable, it presumes that its determination is correct. To rebut this presumption, the taxpayer must show by a preponderance of the evidence that the IRS's determination is improper. Thus, periodic updating of the plans to use corporate earnings should be undertaken to reduce accumulated earnings tax problems.

Holding or investment companies are held to a standard different from that which applies to operating companies. Section 533(b) provides that holding or investment company status is prima facie evidence of a tax-avoidance purpose.[56] A holding company, like an operating company, can rebut this presumption by showing that it was neither formed nor availed of to avoid shareholder income taxes.

A tax-avoidance purpose may be only one of several reasons for the corporation's accumulation of earnings. In *U.S. v. The Donruss Company*, the Supreme Court held that tax avoidance does not have to be the dominant motive for the accumulation of earnings, which could lead to imposition of the accumulated earnings tax. According to the court,

---

[55] Sec. 532(c). See, however, *Technalysis Corporation v. CIR* [101 T.C. 397 (1993)] where the Tax Court held that the accumulated earnings tax can be imposed on a publicly held corporation regardless of the concentration of ownership or whether the shareholders are actively involved in corporate operations.

[56] Regulation Sec. 1.533-1(c) defines a holding or investment company for this purpose as "a corporation having practically no activities except holding property and collecting income therefrom or investing therein."

for a tax avoidance purpose to exist, the corporation must know about the tax consequences of accumulating earnings.[57] Such knowledge need not be the dominant motive or purpose for the accumulation of the earnings.

EVIDENCE CONCERNING THE REASONABLENESS OF AN EARNINGS ACCUMULATION

The courts have not specified any single factor that indicates an unreasonable level of accumulated earnings. Instead, they have alluded to several factors that suggest a tax-avoidance purpose. The IRS and the courts have cited other factors that indicate reasonable business needs for the legitimate accumulation of earnings and profits.

TYPICAL MISCONCEPTION

The IRC refers to the existence of a tax-avoidance purpose, which would appear to involve a subjective test. However, the existence of the tax-avoidance purpose really hinges on the objective determination of whether a corporation has accumulated earnings beyond the reasonable needs of the business.

Evidence of a Tax-Avoidance Purpose. A corporation that wants to avoid liability for the accumulated earnings tax should act defensively. It can minimize this liability by avoiding or restricting the following transactions:

- Loans to shareholders
- Corporate expenditures for the personal benefit of shareholders
- Loans having no reasonable relation to the conduct of business (e.g., loans to relatives or friends of shareholders)
- Loans to a corporation controlled by the same shareholders that control the lending corporation
- Investments in property or securities unrelated to the activities of the corporation
- Insuring against unrealistic hazards[58]

Loans to shareholders or corporate expenditures for the personal benefit of shareholders are viewed as substitutes for dividend payments to shareholders. Similarly, corporate loans made to relatives or friends of shareholders are viewed as substitutes for dividend payments to shareholders, who then make personal loans to their friends and relatives. All three measures suggest an unreasonable accumulation of corporate earnings, which should have been distributed as dividends.

Likewise, loans or corporate expenditures made for the benefit of a second corporation controlled by the shareholder (or the shareholder group) who also controls the first corporation may be considered to have a tax-avoidance purpose. Theoretically, the first corporation instead could have paid a dividend to the shareholder who in turn could have paid income taxes on the dividend and then contributed after-tax funds to the second corporation.

Another factor indicative of a tax-avoidance motive, but not mentioned in Treasury Regulations, is operating a corporation as a holding or investment company that pays little or no dividends.

Question: In the current year, an IRS auditor examines Baylor Corporation's C corporation tax return filed three years ago. What items might the auditor scrutinize to ascertain excess accumulated earnings?

Solution: The auditor might look first at the retained earnings accounts in the beginning and year-end balance sheets (Schedule L of Form 1120). Then, the auditor might review Schedule M-2 (Analysis of Unappropriated Retained Earnings per Books) for current year earnings, the amount of earnings distributed as dividends, and the manner in which the corporation used the undistributed earnings. Next, the auditor might examine the beginning and year-end balance sheets for evidence of transactions suggesting a tax-avoidance motive. Such transactions might include loans to shareholders (Schedule L, Line 7), loans to persons other than shareholders (Schedule L, Lines 6 and 14), and portfolio investments

[57] *U.S. v. The Donruss Company*, 23 AFTR 2d 69-418, 69-1 USTC ¶9167 (USSC, 1969).

[58] Reg. Sec. 1.537-2(c).

(Schedule L, Lines 4, 5, 6, and 9). Information about expenditures of corporate funds made for the personal benefit of shareholders might be found in the noncurrent asset section of the balance sheets (e.g., corporate ownership of a boat, airplane, or second home of a major shareholder).

Reasonable Needs of the Business. Section 537 identifies several needs as being among the reasonable needs of the business. Two of these are:

- The reasonably anticipated needs of the business, which are discussed in more detail below.
- The amount needed (or reasonably anticipated to be needed) for stock redemptions qualifying under Sec. 303. This IRC section treats certain redemptions to pay death taxes as a sale of stock rather than a Sec. 301 distribution (see Chapter C:4).[59]

The terms "reasonable" and "reasonably" appear frequently with respect to the accumulated earnings tax. Treasury Regulations specify a "prudent businessman" standard for determining reasonableness.[60] Applying this standard to a specific corporation requires much judgment and attention to its particular facts and circumstances, but the courts generally are reluctant to substitute their judgment for that of corporate management.

The Treasury Regulations and the courts have identified several circumstances for which accumulations of earnings are likely to be for reasonable needs:[61]

- Expansion of business or replacement of plant.
- Acquiring a business enterprise. This activity might involve extending the corporation's current business or expanding into a new business, and it could occur through purchasing the stock or the assets of the enterprise conducting the acquired business. The corporation should be careful to acquire a sufficient interest so it will be considered the corporation's business activity and not a passive investment.
- Debt retirement.
- Working capital build-up, such as for the purchase of inventories. This topic is discussed in more detail below.
- Loans to suppliers or customers.
- Business contingencies. The courts and the IRS have accepted earnings accumulations for business contingencies, such as actual or potential litigation, a likely decline in business activities following the loss of a major customer, insuring against a potential loss, providing for a threatened strike, and funding an employee retirement plan.[62]

Reasonably Anticipated Needs of the Business. Corporations operate in business settings that change over time, making their future business needs uncertain. As discussed, a prudent businessman standard is used to determine reasonableness. Treasury Regulations identify several other factors to be taken into account when determining a corporation's reasonably anticipated business needs.[63]

Need for Accumulation. Some evidence must indicate that the future needs of the business require the accumulation of earnings.

[59] Sec. 537(a)(3) also treats as a reasonable need of the business any excess business holdings redemption needs, meaning the amount needed (or reasonably anticipated to be needed) to redeem stock from a private foundation that meets certain conditions.

[60] Reg. Sec. 1.537-1(a). This standard is "the amount that a prudent businessman would consider appropriate for the present business purposes and for the reasonably anticipated future needs of the business." The Regulation's use of the term "businessman" also includes a businesswoman.

[61] Reg. Sec. 1.537-2(b).

[62] Sec. 537(b)(4) treats the accumulation of reasonable amounts for reasonably anticipated product liability losses as being accumulated for the reasonably anticipated needs of the business.

[63] Reg. Sec. 1.537-1(b).

Specific, Definite, and Feasible Plans. The corporation must have specific, definite, and feasible plans for using earnings accumulated for its reasonably anticipated business needs. The plans should not be uncertain or vague.[64] The plans need not be written, but written documentation helps to establish the plans' existence.

No Specific Time Limitations. The corporation need not use the accumulated earnings immediately nor within a short period after the close of the tax year. However, the plans must provide that the corporation will use the accumulated earnings within a reasonable period of time, which depends on the facts and circumstances relating to the future business needs.

Impact of Subsequent Events. The facts and circumstances at the close of the tax year should be used to determine the corporation's reasonably anticipated business needs. Subsequent events also may be used to determine such facts and circumstances but only for such purposes. For example, events in Year 2 may indicate that, as of the close of Year 1, the corporation did not intend to use the accumulated earnings within a reasonable period of time. In this case, the subsequent events should be taken into account. On the other hand, events in Year 2 may indicate the infeasibility of plans that appeared to be feasible as of the close of Year 1. In this case, the subsequent events should not be taken into account for Year 1.

Working Capital: The *Bardahl* Formula. Firms need to spend cash to generate sales. For example, some firms need to purchase raw materials or already-manufactured items to sell goods to their customers. In addition, a firm's sales may be on credit, so it does not receive cash immediately but instead has accounts receivable. The operating cycle is the amount of time from the corporation's acquisition of inventory to the collection of cash from its sale. The need for working capital for one operating cycle is a reasonable need of the business.

The *Bardahl* formula is an estimate of the working capital needed for an operating cycle.[65] The formula is comprised of three financial statement ratios:

- Inventory cycle: This ratio equals an inventory amount divided by annual cost of goods sold. It is the average time from the purchase of raw materials or merchandise inventory to the sale of goods to customers, expressed as a fraction of a year. This ratio is similar to the inverse of the inventory turnover ratio used in financial statement analysis.
- Accounts receivable cycle: This ratio equals an accounts receivable amount divided by annual sales. It is the average time from the sale of goods to customers to the collection of cash from those sales. This ratio is similar to the inverse of the receivables turnover ratio used in financial statement analysis.
- Credit cycle: This ratio equals a trade accounts payable amount divided by annual operating expenses and inventory purchases. It is the average time from the occurrence of these expenses and purchases to their payment. The annual operating expenses are reduced by noncash expenses, such as depreciation. The credit cycle reduces the operating cycle because the corporation can incur these expenses and purchases without paying them for the length of the credit cycle.

---

[64] See, for example, *Myron's Enterprises v. U.S.*, 39 AFTR 2d 77-693, 77-1 USTC ¶9253 (9th Cir., 1977) and *Atlas Tool Co., Inc. v. CIR*, 45 AFTR 2d 80-645, 80-1 USTC ¶9177 (3rd Cir., 1980).

[65] *Bardahl Manufacturing Corp.*, 1965 PH T.C. Memo ¶65,200, 24 TCM 1030 and *Bardahl International Corp.*, 1966 PH T.C. Memo ¶66,182, 25 TCM 935.

These ratios are used to determine the operating cycle, which equals the inventory cycle, plus the accounts receivable cycle, minus the credit cycle. The operating cycle, in turn, is used to estimate the corporation's working capital needs as follows:

$$\text{Operating cycle (as a fraction of a year)} \times \left[\text{Cost of goods sold} + \text{Operating expenses minus noncash expenses}\right] = \text{Estimated working capital needed}$$

Cost of goods sold takes into account both direct and indirect expenses. Operating expenses include federal income taxes, for example, quarterly estimated tax payments.[66]

Working capital typically is defined as the excess of current assets over current liabilities. Any estimated working capital needed in excess of actual working capital at year-end is deemed to be a reasonable need of the business. Any actual working capital at year-end in excess of estimated working capital needed is deemed not to be a reasonable need of the business unless the accumulation otherwise is reasonable (for example, for plant replacement).

EXAMPLE C:5-19 ▶ Austin Corporation's records contain the following information pertaining to the current year:

Average accounts receivable	$ 750,000
Average inventory	675,000
Average trade accounts payable	350,000
Cost of goods sold	2,700,000
Estimated federal income tax payments	100,000
Inventory purchases	3,000,000
Operating expenses (including $75,000 of depreciation)	875,000
Sales (all on account)	6,000,000
Working capital on December 31	825,000

Using the *Bardahl* formula, Austin's operating cycle is calculated as follows:

Inventory cycle:	$675,000 ÷ $2,700,000 = 0.2500
Accounts receivable cycle:	$750,000 ÷ $6,000,000 = 0.1250
Credit cycle:	$350,000 ÷ ($875,000 + $3,000,000 − $75,000) = 0.0921
Operating cycle:	0.2500 + 0.1250 − 0.0921 = 0.2829

Austin's estimated working capital needed is:

0.2829 × ($2,700,000 + $875,000 − $75,000 + $100,000) = $1,018,440

The $1,018,440 is $193,440 more than the $825,000 of actual working capital on December 31. Accordingly, Austin can justify accumulating $193,440 of its current earnings for reasonable needs of the business, plus the amount it can justify for other reasons (e.g., for plant replacement). ◀

The *Bardahl* formula can provide a false sense of mathematical precision. In practice, it often is modified to better fit a corporation's specific facts and circumstances. For instance, in Example C:5-19, the average inventory was used to determine the inventory cycle (and likewise for the accounts receivable and credit cycles). Some courts have used peak amounts instead of average amounts, reasoning that the corporation needs to accumulate earnings for its peak working capital needs and not its average needs.[67] Using

[66] *Doug-Long, Inc.*, 72 T.C. 158 (1979).
[67] *State Office Supply, Inc.*, 1982 PH T.C. Memo ¶82,292, 43 TCM 1481.

peak amounts usually results in a larger amount of estimated working capital needs than does using average amounts. Another modification sometimes applied is the use of estimates for the following year rather than actual amounts for the current year. For example, if a corporation has expanding operations, its working capital needs will tend to increase from the current to the following year. If the *Bardahl* formula is applied using current-year amounts, it may produce an estimate of working capital needs that is too low. As a result of factors such as these, disputes have arisen between the IRS and corporations over what constitutes working capital needs.

TYPICAL MISCONCEPTION

No exact method exists for determining a corporation's working capital needs. The *Bardahl* formula is merely a rule of thumb adopted by several courts. Modifications to the *Bardahl* formula, as well as other factors, may be used by a court as it deems appropriate.

The *Bardahl* formula can be applied to a corporation whose business activities involve services (e.g., engineering), but it is applied differently than for manufacturing or merchandising companies because a service company generally holds little or no inventory. Like nonservice companies, service companies often have accounts receivable, but salaries are an important working capital need for these types of businesses. Their principal asset is their workforce, and they need to retain employees when a below-normal level of business occurs. Some amount may be added to working capital to cover the cost of retaining personnel during such times.[68]

CALCULATING THE ACCUMULATED EARNINGS TAX

The accumulated earnings tax calculation is set forth in Figure C:5-3. As with the PHC tax, a corporation can reduce its tax liability by paying dividends. However, corporations generally do not avail themselves of this tax planning device because they often pay only a nominal dividend or no dividend at all. Also, IRS auditors generally do not raise the accumulated earnings tax issue until one or more years after the corporation has filed its tax return. Unlike the PHC tax liability, the accumulated earnings tax liability cannot be extinguished through the payment of deficiency dividends.

ADDITIONAL COMMENT

Accumulated taxable income should not be confused with current E&P. In fact, the accumulated earnings tax has been assessed in years where no increase in the corporation's E&P had occurred.

Accumulated Taxable Income. The starting point for calculating **accumulated taxable income** is the corporation's regular taxable income. A series of positive and negative adjustments to regular taxable income are made to derive accumulated taxable income.

ADDITIONAL COMMENT

The accumulated earnings tax adjustments derive an amount that more closely corresponds to the corporation's economic income and thus better measures the dividend-paying capability of the corporation than does taxable income.

Positive Adjustments to Regular Taxable Income. A corporation may not claim a dividends-received deduction. Thus, regular taxable income must be increased by the amount of this deduction in a manner similar to that under the PHC tax rules.[69] The U.S. production activities deduction, however, is not added back to regular taxable income to derive accumulated taxable income. Any NOL deduction claimed must be added back to regular taxable income. The IRC allows no special deduction for an NOL incurred in the immediately preceding year, as it does under the PHC tax rules.

[68] See, for example, *Simons-Eastern Co. v. U.S.*, 31 AFTR 2d 73-640, 73-1 USTC ¶9279 (D.C. GA, 1972).

[69] Sec. 535(b)(3).

▼ FIGURE C:5-3

Calculating the Accumulated Earnings Tax

Regular taxable income
Plus: Positive adjustments
1. Dividends-received deduction
2. NOL deduction
3. Excess charitable contributions carried over from a preceding tax year and deducted in determining current year regular taxable income
4. Excess capital losses carried over from another tax year and deducted when calculating current year regular taxable income

Minus: Negative adjustments
1. Accrued U.S. and foreign income taxes
2. Current year charitable contributions that exceed the 10% corporate limitation
3. Net capital losses (where capital losses for the year exceed capital gains)
4. Net capital gain minus the amount of any associated income taxes

Minus: Dividends-paid deduction
Minus: Accumulated earnings credit

Accumulated taxable income
Times: 0.20

Accumulated earnings tax

TYPICAL MISCONCEPTION

A corporation incurring the accumulated earnings tax does not adjust its taxable income for all items that affect its taxable income differently than they affect the earnings available for distribution to its shareholders (e.g., no adjustment is required for tax-exempt interest and the U.S. production activities deduction).

Negative Adjustments to Taxable Income. Charitable contributions are deductible without regard to any percentage limitation. Thus, two adjustments are required for charitable contributions when calculating accumulated taxable income: (1) subtracting the amount of current year charitable contributions exceeding the 10% limitation, and (2) adding back charitable contribution carryovers deducted in the current year for regular tax purposes but in an earlier tax year for accumulated earnings tax purposes.

U.S. and foreign income taxes accrued by the corporation reduce accumulated taxable income whether the corporation uses the accrual or cash method of accounting. A corporation may deduct the amount of its net capital gain (i.e., net long-term capital gain over net short-term capital loss), minus income taxes attributable to this gain. The capital gains adjustment prevents a corporation with substantial capital gains from paying the accumulated earnings tax on that portion of the gains retained in the business. Net capital losses (the excess of capital losses over capital gains for the year) represent a negative adjustment to regular taxable income.

WHAT WOULD YOU DO IN THIS SITUATION?

Magnum Corporation, your client, has manufactured handguns and rifles for years. Because of competition from foreign manufacturers, demand for U.S. manufactured guns has recently declined. The total historical cost of Magnum's operating assets at the end of its most recent fiscal year is $10 million. Total gross operating revenues are $18 million. Over the years, the company accumulated $2.5 million of earnings that Magnum's CEO Allen Blay invested in securities. The investment portfolio consists primarily of growth stocks, debt instruments, and Internet stocks. Along with his other duties as CEO, Allen manages this portfolio. With the recent surge in the stock market, the value of Magnum's investment securities have increased to more than $12 million. The portfolio took a small "hit" in the Fall of the previous year. The dividend and interest income earned on the portfolio represents only a small portion of Magnum's gross income. During a meeting with you, Allen brings to your attention this investment and its stellar performance. Is Magnum liable for the accumulated earnings tax? What action(s) do you recommend that the corporation take?

Dividends-Paid Deduction. A deduction is allowed for four types of dividends paid:

- Regular dividends
- Throwback dividends
- Consent dividends
- Liquidating distributions

ADDITIONAL COMMENT

The timing for throwback dividends increased from 2½ months to 3½ months, effective for taxable years beginning after 2015. However, for corporations whose taxable year ends on June 30, the 2½-month rule continues to apply until tax years beginning after 2025.

With minor exceptions, the rules for the dividends-paid deduction are the same in the accumulated earnings tax calculation as in the PHC tax calculation. Nonliquidating distributions paid during the tax year are eligible for the dividends-paid deduction only if paid out of the corporation's E&P. A dividends-paid deduction is not available for preferential dividends.[70]

Throwback dividends generally are distributions made out of E&P in the first 3½ months following the close of the tax year. The accumulated earnings tax rules require that any distribution made in the first 3½ months following the close of the tax year be treated as if paid on the last day of the preceding tax year without regard to the amount of dividends actually paid during the preceding tax year.[71] Because the IRS generally does not raise the accumulated earnings tax issue until after it has audited a corporation's tax return, throwback and consent dividends are of limited use in avoiding the accumulated earnings tax. Liquidating distributions eligible for the dividends-paid deduction include those made in connection with a complete liquidation, a partial liquidation, or a stock redemption.[72]

ADDITIONAL COMMENT

The minimum accumulated earnings credit is $250,000 ($150,000 for certain personal service corporations) reduced by accumulated E&P at the close of the preceding year. In many situations, corporations that have been in existence for some time have accumulated E&P exceeding $250,000. Thus, the minimum credit is of little practical significance for them.

Unlike the PHC tax, a corporation liable for the accumulated earnings tax cannot reduce the tax by electing to pay a deficiency dividend. Thus, if a determination (e.g., judicial decision or IRS agreement) establishes the amount of accumulated earnings tax, the corporation must pay the tax, as well as any related interest and penalties.

Accumulated Earnings Credit. The accumulated earnings credit permits a corporation to accumulate E&P up to either a minimum amount ($250,000 for most C corporations) or the level of its earnings accumulated for the reasonable needs of the business. Unlike other credits, the **accumulated earnings credit** does not offset the accumulated earnings tax liability on a dollar-for-dollar basis. Instead, it is like a deduction because it reduces accumulated taxable income. Different rules for the accumulated earnings credit exist for operating companies, service companies, and holding or investment companies.[73]

TYPICAL MISCONCEPTION

The maximum accumulated earnings credit is the amount of current E&P retained to meet the reasonable needs of the business minus an adjustment for net capital gains. This amount does not include the entire accumulation for business needs but only the accumulation in the current tax year. Thus, to calculate the maximum credit, it is necessary to determine how much of prior accumulations are retained for reasonable business needs.

- Operating companies can claim a credit equal to the greater of (1) $250,000 minus accumulated E&P at the end of the preceding tax year[74] or (2) current E&P retained to meet the reasonable needs of the business.
- The accumulated E&P balance mentioned in the previous bullet point is reduced by the amount of any current year throwback distributions treated as having been made out of the preceding year's E&P.
- Current E&P is reduced by the dividends-paid deduction. Any net capital gains (reduced by federal taxes attributable to the gains) reduce the amount of current E&P retained for business needs.
- Special rules apply to personal service companies operating primary in the fields of health, law, engineering, architecture, accounting, actuarial science, performing arts, and consulting. For these companies, the basic calculation set forth above applies, but the $250,000 minimum credit is reduced to $150,000.
- Holding and investment companies may claim a credit equal to $250,000 minus accumulated E&P at the end of the preceding tax year. An increased credit based on the reasonable needs of the business is not available to a holding or investment company.

EXAMPLE C:5-20 ▶ Midway Corporation reports accumulated E&P, current E&P, and current E&P retained for business needs as shown in the table below. The corporation paid no dividends during the current year. Midway is a C corporation that is not a personal service or investment company. Its minimum credit is $250,000.

---

[70] Sec. 562(c). See page C:5-21 for a more detailed discussion.

[71] Sec. 563(a). Personal holding companies, on the other hand, generally may elect throwback treatment for dividends paid in the 3½ month period following the end of the tax year, but a throwback dividend is limited to the lesser of the PHC's UPHCI or 20% of any dividends paid during the year (other than consent dividends).

[72] Sec. 562(b)(1)(B).

[73] Sec. 535(c).

[74] Section 1561(a)(2) limits a controlled group of corporations to a single $250,000 amount for the accumulated earnings credit.

TYPICAL MISCONCEPTION

Although called a *credit*, the accumulated earnings credit actually is a *deduction* in deriving accumulated taxable income.

Tax Items	*Scenario One*	*Scenario Two*
1. Accumulated E&P	$ 75,000	$ 75,000
2. Lifetime minimum credit	250,000	250,000
2a. Current year minimum credit (2a = 2 − 1)	175,000	175,000
3. Current E&P	400,000	400,000
3a. Current E&P retained for business needs	300,000	50,000
3b. Current E&P exceeding business needs (3b = 3 − 3a)	100,000	350,000
4. Accumulated earnings credit (Greater of 2a or 3a)	300,000	175,000

In both scenarios, $175,000 of the minimum credit is available. In Scenario One, because the available $175,000 minimum credit is less than $300,000 of E&P retained for business needs, the accumulated earnings credit is $300,000. In Scenario Two, because the available $175,000 minimum credit is greater than the $50,000 of E&P retained for business needs, the accumulated earnings credit is $175,000. In both scenarios, no minimum credit is available in future years. All future accumulated earnings credits are based on E&P retained for business needs. ◀

COMPREHENSIVE EXAMPLE

The following example illustrates the calculation of accumulated taxable income and the accumulated earnings tax liability.

EXAMPLE C:5-21 ▶ Pasadena is a closely held C corporation that is not a personal holding company. Pasadena has conducted a successful manufacturing business for several years. On January 1 of the current year, Pasadena reports a $750,000 accumulated E&P balance. The following information pertains to current year operations:

Operating profit	$650,000
Long-term capital gain	30,000
Dividends received from a 20%-owned corporation	150,000
Interest	70,000
Gross income	$900,000
Salaries	(100,000)
General and administrative expenses	(200,000)
Charitable contribution deduction	(60,000)[a]
Dividends-received deduction	(120,000)
U.S. production activities deduction	(10,000)
Regular taxable income	$410,000

[a] $60,000 = 0.10 × [$900,000 − ($100,000 + $200,000)].

Federal income taxes accrued by Pasadena are $139,400 ($410,000 × 0.34). Actual charitable contributions are $75,000. On June 30, the corporation pays cash dividends of $20,000. Pasadena's current E&P retained for the reasonable needs of the business (after the dividends-paid deduction) is $160,000.

If the IRS determines that Pasadena has accumulated earnings exceeding the reasonable needs of its business, Pasadena's accumulated earnings tax liability would be calculated as follows:

ADDITIONAL COMMENT

Net capital gain is defined as the excess of net long-term capital gain over net short-term capital loss.

Regular taxable income			$410,000
Plus:	Dividends-received deduction		120,000
Minus:	Excess charitable contributions		(15,000)[a]
	Federal income taxes		(139,400)
	Net capital gain (NCG)	$ 30,000	
	Minus: Federal income taxes on the NCG	(10,200)[b]	(19,800)
	Dividends-paid deduction		(20,000)
	Accumulated earnings credit:		
	Increase in current year reasonable needs	$160,000	
	Minus: Long-term capital gain (net of taxes)	(19,800)	(140,200)

Accumulated taxable income	$195,600
Times: Tax rate	0.20
Accumulated earnings tax liability	$ 39,120

[a] $75,000 total contributions − $60,000 limitation = $15,000 excess contributions.
[b] $10,200 = $30,000 × 0.34

Pasadena's accumulated earnings credit is based on its current E&P retained for reasonable business needs (minus its net capital gain, net of taxes) because its $750,000 accumulated E&P exceeds the $250,000 minimum credit.

Assuming the corporation owes no AMT, Pasadena's total federal tax liability for the current year would be $178,520 ($139,400 + $39,120). ◄

Topic Review C:5-4 presents an overview of the accumulated earnings tax.

TAX PLANNING CONSIDERATIONS

OBJECTIVE 4

Identify tax planning opportunities to minimize the AMT and to avoid the PHC and accumulated earnings taxes

This section examines five areas of tax planning: special accounting method elections for AMT purposes, eliminating the ACE adjustment, multiyear effects of the AMT, avoiding the PHC tax, and avoiding the accumulated earnings tax.

DEPRECIATION ELECTION

Personal property generally is depreciated using the 200% declining balance method for regular tax purposes but using the 150% declining balance method for AMT purposes. For regular tax purposes, a taxpayer can elect to use the same depreciation method used for AMT purposes.[75] Such an election can reduce a taxpayer's AMT compliance burden by eliminating the need to keep an additional set of depreciation records to determine the AMT depreciation adjustment, as well as the AMT adjustment that arises when the taxpayer sells depreciable property. This election usually will reduce a taxpayer's AMT but also increase its regular tax. The reduced AMT and increased regular tax often will exactly offset each other.

TOPIC REVIEW C:5-4

Accumulated Earnings Tax

1. The accumulated earnings tax rules apply to all but certain types of corporations. As a practical matter, the tax is assessed primarily on closely held corporations (other than S corporations and personal holding companies).
2. Certain transactions generally lead IRS auditors to believe that an accumulated earnings tax problem exists. These transactions include loans made by the corporation to its shareholders, the expenditure of corporate funds for the personal benefit of shareholders, and investments in property or securities unrelated to the corporation's principal activities.
3. Earnings accumulated for the reasonable needs of the business are exempt from the accumulated earnings tax. Among such needs are a business acquisition, debt retirement, and the build up of working capital. A $250,000 minimum credit is available to reduce accumulated taxable income. The credit amount declines to $150,000 for certain personal service corporations.
4. The accumulated earnings tax is 20% of accumulated taxable income. Accumulated taxable income is regular taxable income plus certain positive adjustments (e.g., dividends-received deduction) and minus certain negative adjustments (e.g., federal income taxes, excess charitable contributions, and a portion of net capital gains). An accumulated earnings credit equal to the greater of a fixed dollar amount or earnings accumulated during the year for the reasonable needs of the business also is available.
5. Accumulated taxable income can be reduced by cash and property dividends paid during the year as well as consent and throwback dividends paid after year-end. Deficiency dividends, available for PHC tax purposes, are not available for accumulated earnings tax purposes.

[75] Sec. 168(b)(2) and (5). The taxpayer generally depreciates certain bonus depreciation property using the 200% declining balance method for both regular tax and AMT purposes. Such property includes property eligible for bonus depreciation (if placed in service after 2015) or for which the taxpayer claims bonus depreciation (if placed in service before 2016).

For any tax year, a taxpayer may make this election with respect to one or more classes of property. The election applies to all property in such class(es) placed in service during the tax year. The taxpayer must make the election by the due date for that year's tax return (including permissible extensions). Depreciation for real property generally is the same for regular tax and AMT purposes, so the election is not relevant for such property.

ELIMINATING THE ACE ADJUSTMENT

C corporations make the ACE adjustment, which substantially increases AMTI for many C corporations. A C corporation can eliminate the ACE adjustment by electing to be taxed as an S corporation, assuming it qualifies to make the election (see Chapter C:11). S corporations are not subject to the AMT but pass through their tax preference and AMT adjustment items to their shareholders. On the other hand, a corporation that qualifies to make an S election also may have average gross receipts that qualify it to be exempt from the AMT. If such a corporation were taxed as a C corporation, it would incur no AMT and would not pass through any preference and adjustment items to its shareholders.

MULTIYEAR EFFECTS OF AMT

A corporation pays any AMT in addition to its regular tax, which increases its current tax liability. However, its AMT also generates the same amount of minimum tax credit, which can reduce its future regular tax liabilities. A corporation's tax planning with respect to the AMT should take into account the multiyear effects on its regular tax and AMT.

STOP & THINK

Question: Flair Corporation is considering investing in municipal bonds. Flair's Chief Financial Officer (CFO) thought that the interest earned on these bonds is tax-exempt, but she was surprised to learn that it could be taxed by the federal government at a rate of up to 20% if earned by a corporation. Can such tax-exempt interest be taxed at a rate of up to 20%?

Solution: If the bond is a private activity bond not issued in 2009 or 2010, the interest income is a tax preference item. Assuming its inclusion in AMTI does not affect the phase out of Flair's AMT exemption amount, each $1 of interest income on a private activity bond increases Flair's AMTI by $1 and its TMT by $0.20. The effect this $0.20 increase has on Flair's total income tax depends on its TMT versus its regular tax.

TMT < regular tax with and without the tax-exempt interest income: The tax-exempt interest income does not increase Flair's total income tax because it has zero AMT.

TMT > regular tax with and without the tax-exempt interest income: Each $1 of private activity bond interest income increases Flair's current year tax by $0.20 because it increases Flair's AMT by $0.20. However, this increased AMT also generates $0.20 of minimum tax credit that Flair can carry forward. Assuming Flair can use the credit in the subsequent year and it discounts cash flows at an 11% rate, the $0.20 of tax Flair saves has a $0.18 ($0.20 ÷ 1.11) present value. Thus, the net increase in the present value of Flair's taxes is $0.02 ($0.20 − $0.18). If Flair cannot use the $0.20 minimum tax credit until after the subsequent year, the net increase in the present value of Flair's taxes will be greater than $0.02 but less than $0.20, depending on the number of years until Flair can use the credit.

TMT < regular tax without tax-exempt interest income but TMT > regular tax with it: Each $1 of private activity bond interest income increases Flair's tax by less than $0.20 because part of the interest income merely increases its TMT up to its regular tax, but Flair's tax does increase because the rest of the interest income generates some AMT. This AMT creates an equal amount of minimum tax credit that Flair can carry forward. Thus, Flair should consider the present value of these future tax savings.

AVOIDING THE PERSONAL HOLDING COMPANY TAX

Five tax planning techniques can be used to avoid the PHC tax.

Changes in the Corporation's Stock Ownership. To circumvent the stock ownership rules, a potential PHC can issue additional stock to unrelated parties. The stock may be either common or preferred. The issuance of nonvoting preferred stock to unrelated parties permits the corporation to distribute stock ownership among a larger number of individuals without diluting the voting power of the current common shareholder group.

Changing the Amount and Type of Income Earned by the Corporation. A corporation can change the amount and type of its income in the following ways:

- Adding "operating" activities to its business to decrease the proportion of passive or investment earnings in its total income.
- Converting taxable interest or dividends earned on an investment portfolio into non-taxable interest or long-term capital gains. Nontaxable interest and long-term capital gains are excluded from PHCI.
- Generating passive income of a type that is excludible from PHCI or in an amount that diminishes the proportion of other items includible in PHCI. For example, a corporation might attempt to increase the proportion of its rental income to more than 50% of AOGI so as to exclude from PHCI adjusted income from rents.

KEY POINT

One of the easiest ways to avoid the PHC penalty tax is a dividend distribution. If a corporation lacks the funds to pay a cash dividend, its shareholders can elect a consent dividend (which is a hypothetical dividend). In addition, throwback and consent dividends can be declared after year-end in after-the-fact tax planning.

Dividend Distributions. Dividend payments reduce the PHC tax base. A corporation can exclude certain categories of income (e.g., adjusted income from rents) from PHCI through the payment of dividends sufficient to reduce the amount of other PHCI to 10% or less of OGI. Some of these dividends (e.g., throwback and consent) can be declared after year-end, thereby allowing last-minute tax planning.

Making an S Corporation Election. As mentioned earlier, an S corporation election eliminates liability for the PHC tax because S corporations are exempt from this tax. The election also eliminates the double taxation of corporate earnings distributed as dividends (see Chapter C:11). Such an election is advantageous where corporate tax rates exceed individual tax rates. The LLC form offers many of the same tax and nontax benefits offered by the S corporation form.

Liquidating the Corporation. A PHC could liquidate and distribute its assets to the shareholders. Liquidating distributions made out of E&P are eligible for the dividends-paid deduction and thus can reduce UPHCI. This alternative, however, may be unattractive where top individual tax rates exceed corporate tax rates.

AVOIDING THE ACCUMULATED EARNINGS TAX

The primary defense against an IRS argument that the corporation has accumulated an unreasonable amount of earnings is that the earnings accumulations are necessary to meet the future needs of the business. Business plans in support of this defense should be documented and revised periodically. The plans should describe completed, but not abandoned, projects in sufficient detail. In the event of an IRS challenge, a tentative timetable for the completion of current projects should be set forth. Such plans might be incorporated into the minutes of one or more board meetings.

Transactions suggesting an unreasonable earnings accumulation (e.g., loans to shareholders or large investment portfolios) should be avoided. The business purpose for major transactions should be thoroughly documented.

Corporations potentially liable for the accumulated earnings tax should consider making an S corporation election. S corporations avoid accumulated earnings tax liability on a prospective basis. By implication, an S corporation election will not eliminate potential exposure to the accumulated earnings tax for tax years prior to the year in which the election becomes effective.

Compliance and Procedural Considerations

OBJECTIVE 5

Comply with AMT, PHC tax, and accumulated earnings tax procedures

ALTERNATIVE MINIMUM TAX

A corporation reports its AMT calculation on Form 4626 (Alternative Minimum Tax—Corporations). A completed Form 4626, based on the facts in the comprehensive example on pages C:5-10 through C:5-12, appears in Appendix B. The instructions for Form 4626 include a worksheet for calculating ACE. A corporation uses Form 8827 (Credit for Prior Year Minimum Tax—Corporations) to calculate the minimum tax credit it claims, as well as the minimum tax credit it carries forward to the subsequent year.

Section 6655(g) provides that a corporation's required quarterly estimated tax payments take into account its regular tax and AMT. A corporation whose estimated tax payments are not large enough incurs an underpayment penalty, which is discussed in Chapter C:3.

ETHICAL POINT

A tax practitioner has a responsibility to advise his or her client early in the year about potential PHC problems and steps that can be taken to avoid the penalty tax. Because the PHC tax is self-assessed, a PHC must file Schedule PH even if it owes no PHC tax.

PERSONAL HOLDING COMPANY TAX

Filing Requirements for Tax Returns. A PHC must file a corporate income tax return (Form 1120). Schedule PH must accompany the return. Schedule PH incorporates the tests for determining whether a corporation is a PHC and includes the UPHCI and PHC tax calculations. Section 6501(f) extends from three to six years the limitations period for the PHC tax if a PHC fails to file Schedule PH, even if the corporation owes no additional tax.

Payment of the Tax, Interest, and Penalties. Corporations ordinarily pay the PHC tax when they file Form 1120 and Schedule PH, or when the IRS or the courts determine that the corporation owes the tax. Unlike the AMT, the PHC tax is not included in the corporation's required estimated tax payments. Corporations that pay the PHC tax after the due date for filing their return (without regard to extensions) generally will also owe interest and penalties on the unpaid PHC tax balance. Interest will accrue from the date the return is originally due (without regard to extensions) until the entire tax is paid.[76]

ETHICAL POINT

Notwithstanding the tax practitioner's responsibility to advise his or her client about potential accumulated earnings tax problems, because the tax is not self-assessed, the CPA or the client are under no duty to notify the IRS of the tax problem.

ACCUMULATED EARNINGS TAX

No schedule or return is required for reporting the accumulated earnings tax. Because of the ad hoc nature of this tax, a corporation generally will not pay it until some time after the IRS has audited its tax return. Sec. 6601(b) requires the charging of interest on the accumulated earnings tax balance from the original due date for the return (without regard to extensions) until the date the IRS receives full tax payment.[77] The IRS also may impose a penalty for negligent underpayment of an accumulated earnings tax.[78]

---

[76] *Hart Metal Products Corp. v. U.S.*, 38 AFTR 2d 76-6118, 76-2 USTC ¶9781 (Ct. Cls., 1976).

[77] Rev. Rul. 87-54, 1987-1 C.B. 349.

[78] Rev. Rul. 75-330, 1975-2 C.B. 496.

FINANCIAL STATEMENT IMPLICATIONS

OBJECTIVE 6

Describe the financial statement implications of the alternative minimum tax

ALTERNATIVE MINIMUM TAX

When a corporation pays AMT, it also obtains a minimum tax credit that it can carryforward indefinitely. Accounting Standards Codification (ASC) 740 prescribes the following rules for accounting for income taxes in financial statements when a firm pays AMT:

- For a firm's temporary differences and carryforwards, calculate its deferred tax assets and liabilities for regular tax temporary differences using the regular tax rate and the difference between the book basis and regular tax basis of its assets and liabilities.
- Include in a firm's deferred tax assets its minimum tax credit carryforwards, which may be comprised of minimum tax credits arising from AMT in the current year and unused minimum tax credits from prior years. As with other deferred tax assets, reduce the deferred tax asset for the minimum tax credit by a valuation allowance if, based on available evidence, it is more likely than not (i.e., greater than 50%) that all or some of the deferred asset will not be realized.

EXAMPLE C:5-22 ▶ In the current year, Alpha Corporation's regular tax is $40,000, and its tentative minimum tax is $50,000. Alpha's current year AMT of $10,000 ($50,000 − $40,000) generates a $10,000 minimum tax credit. Alpha assesses a more than 50% probability that it will realize (use) the entire credit in future years. Therefore, it need not establish a valuation allowance. Assuming Alpha has no book-tax differences, the minimum tax credit carryover is its only deferred tax asset or liability item. Accordingly, Alpha makes the following book journal entry:

Current federal income tax expense	50,000	
Deferred tax asset	10,000	
Deferred federal income tax expense		10,000
Federal income taxes payable		50,000

In the above entry, Alpha's taxes payable includes its $40,000 regular tax plus the $10,000 AMT. Alpha's $40,000 current year federal income tax expense for its financial statements equals its current year regular tax. This result occurs because Alpha pays $10,000 of AMT in the current year but expects to recover all $10,000 in subsequent years by using its minimum tax credit.

In the subsequent year, Alpha's regular tax is $90,000, and its tentative minimum tax is $70,000. Thus, its AMT is zero, and it can realize (use) the entire minimum tax credit because the regular tax exceeds its tentative minimum tax by more than $10,000. Alpha's net tax liability is $80,000 ($90,000 − $10,000). Accordingly, it makes the following book journal entry:

Current federal income tax expense	80,000	
Deferred federal income tax expense	10,000	
Deferred tax asset		10,000
Federal income taxes payable		80,000

◀

See Chapter C:3 for a general discussion of financial implications of federal income taxes.

Problem Materials

Discussion Questions

C:5-1 Explain Congress' intent for enacting the AMT.

C:5-2 Define the following terms relating to the AMT:
a. Tax preference item
b. AMT adjustment item
c. Adjusted current earnings
d. Alternative minimum taxable income
e. AMT exemption amount
f. Tentative minimum tax
g. Minimum tax credit

C:5-3 Dunn Corporation is not a small corporation exempt from the AMT. Dunn's CPA does not calculate the AMT because he knows that Dunn's taxable income is less than the $40,000 AMT exemption amount allowed to corporations. Is the CPA correct in his belief? Explain.

C:5-4 What special rules (if any) apply to the AMT calculation for the following entities:
a. Corporations, particularly small ones
b. Controlled groups
c. S corporations

C:5-5 Agnew Corporation operates a small manufacturing business. During Year 1 (its first tax year, which is 12 months long), Agnew sells goods for $3.8 million for which the cost of goods sold is $2.8 million. Agnew's owner estimates that future sales and cost of goods sold will grow by 25% each year. Agnew is not related to any other corporations. Is Agnew exempt from the AMT in Year 1? In any of the next five years? Explain.

C:5-6 Menifee Corporation has conducted business for several years, and its annual gross receipts never have been more than $4 million. Jackie, who has owned all of Menifee's stock since she incorporated it, purchases all of Estill Corporation's stock in the current year. Estill's annual gross receipts have been approximately $6 million in recent years. Explain to Jackie how her acquisition of Estill's stock will affect the AMT that Menifee pays.

C:5-7 Determine whether the following statements relating to the AMT for a corporation are true or false. If false, explain why.
a. Tax preference items only increase AMTI.
b. A corporation uses the same NOL carryover amount for regular tax and AMT purposes.
c. A corporation is allowed a tax credit for the excess of its AMT over its regular tax.
d. The general business credit can reduce a corporation's regular tax and also its AMT.
e. The ACE adjustment only increases AMTI.
f. An S corporation is exempt from the AMT, regardless of its gross receipts.

C:5-8 Identify each of the following as a tax preference item (PREF), an AMT adjustment item to calculate preadjustment AMTI (ADJ), an item to adjust from preadjustment AMTI to ACE (ACE), or none of these (NONE):
a. Percentage depletion in excess of a property's adjusted basis at the beginning of the tax year
b. MACRS depreciation deducted on a machine placed in service in the current year
c. Sec. 179 expense deducted on delivery trucks placed in service in the current year
d. Gain or loss realized on the sale of a machine placed in service four years ago
e. Tax-exempt interest earned on State of Michigan private activity bonds
f. Tax-exempt interest earned on State of Michigan general revenue bonds
g. Long-term contract for which the taxpayer uses the completed contract method

C:5-9 What adjustment does a corporation make if ACE is more than preadjustment AMTI? If ACE is less than preadjustment AMTI?

C:5-10 Florida Corporation incurs AMT for the first time in the current year. The main reason for incurring the AMT is a $2 million gain on a current year installment sale that Florida is recognizing over ten years for regular tax purposes. Explain to Florida's president how the installment sale can cause Florida to incur the AMT, how its treatment for ACE is similar to and different from the E&P treatment with which she is familiar, and whether its ACE treatment will partially or completely reverse in future years.

C:5-11 Some tax scholars say tax-exempt interest on state or local bonds that are not private activity bonds can, because of the ACE adjustment, produce three different effective tax rates depending on the corporation's tax situation: (1) a 0% effective tax rate, (2) a 15% effective tax rate, or (3) between a 0% and 15% effective tax rate. Explain what the tax scholars mean.

C:5-12 Indicate whether the following items are includible in regular taxable income, preadjustment AMTI, and/or ACE. Also indicate whether a corporation must make a positive, negative, or zero adjustment when calculating preadjustment AMTI and when calculating ACE.
a. Tax-exempt interest on private activity bonds (not issued in 2009 or 2010)
b. Tax-exempt interest on a state's general revenue bonds (not issued in 2009 or 2010)

c. Proceeds from a life insurance policy (with no cash surrender value) paid on account of a corporate officer's death
d. Gain on a current year sale of property for which a corporation uses the installment method
e. Gain on a previous year sale of property for which a corporation uses the installment method
f. Deduction of organizational expenditures made in the previous year
g. Deduction for a dividend received from a 25%-owned domestic corporation
h. Deduction for a dividend received from a 5%-owned domestic corporation

C:5-13 Discuss the regular tax and AMT depreciation rules applicable to the following types of property acquired in the current year.
a. Section 1250 property—a factory building
b. Section 1245 property—a drill press

C:5-14 In the current year, Burbank Corporation incurs an AMT for the first time. Its AMT is due to an ACE adjustment resulting from Burbank's receiving $4 million of life insurance proceeds upon the death of the corporation's chief executive officer. The policy had no cash surrender value. Explain to Burbank's chief financial officer whether Burbank can reduce its future regular taxes by the AMT paid in the current year.

C:5-15 The personal holding company tax and the accumulated earnings tax reflect efforts to prevent use of the corporate entity to avoid taxation. Explain the congressional intent behind these two tax measures.

C:5-16 Which of the following corporate forms are exempt from the PHC tax? The accumulated earnings tax?
a. Closely held corporations
b. S corporations
c. Professional corporations
d. Tax-exempt organizations
e. Publicly held corporations
f. Corporations filing a consolidated tax return
g. Limited liability companies

C:5-17 Because of its quality investments, Carolina Corporation has always generated 30% to 40% of its gross income from passive sources. In the current year, Carolina sold a block of stock in a company it acquired several years ago. As a result of the sale, the corporation realized a substantial long-term capital gain that will increase this year's investment income from 40% to 70% of gross income. Explain to Carolina's president why she should or should not be worried about the personal holding company tax.

C:5-18 Which of the following income items, when received by a corporation, are included in personal holding company income (PHCI)? Indicate whether any special circumstances would exclude an income item that is generally includible in PHCI.
a. Dividends
b. Interest on a corporate bond
c. Interest on a general revenue bond issued by a state government
d. Rental income from a warehouse leased to a third party
e. Rental income from a warehouse leased to the corporation's sole shareholder
f. Royalty income on a book whose copyright is owned by the corporation
g. Royalty income on a computer software copyright developed by the corporation and leased to a software marketing firm
h. Accounting fees earned by a professional corporation owned by three equal shareholders, which offers public accounting services to various clients
i. Long-term capital gain on the sale of a stock investment

C:5-19 Grayson Corporation is a calendar year taxpayer. In the following independent situations, which of the pro rata dividends paid by Grayson during the current year are eligible for the dividends-paid deduction when it calculates its PHC tax for the current year? Its accumulated earnings tax?
a. Cash dividends paid on June 30 of the current year to common shareholders.
b. Cash dividends paid on May 31 of the current year to preferred shareholders. Grayson pays no dividends to its common shareholders.
c. Dividends paid on April 30 of the current year using Butler Corporation stock from Grayson's investment portfolio. Grayson does not own enough Butler stock to be considered a related party.
d. Dividends paid on March 31 of the current year to common shareholders using Grayson's own common stock.
e. Cash dividends paid on February 28 of next year to common shareholders.

C:5-20 Define the term *consent dividend*. How can a consent dividend be used to avoid the PHC and accumulated earnings taxes? In each case, what requirements must be met by the distributing corporation and/or its shareholders to qualify a consent dividend for the dividends-paid deduction? What are the tax consequences of a consent dividend to the shareholders and the distributing corporation?

C:5-21 Explain the advantages of a deficiency dividend. What requirements must a PHC and its shareholders meet to use a deficiency dividend to reduce or eliminate the PHC tax liability? Can a deficiency dividend eliminate interest and penalties, in addition to the PHC tax liability?

C:5-22 Determine whether the following statements regarding the PHC tax are true or false:

a. In a given tax year, a corporation might not owe the PHC tax even though it is deemed to be a PHC.
b. A sale of a large tract of land held for investment can make a manufacturing corporation a PHC.
c. Federal income taxes (including the alternative minimum tax) accrued by the PHC reduce UPHCI for the tax year.
d. To reduce UPHCI, the corporation's shareholders can elect to be treated as having received consent dividends. They can make this election any time from the first day of the corporation's tax year through the due date for the corporation's tax return (including extensions).
e. The payment of a deficiency dividend permits a PHC to eliminate its PHC tax liability, as well as related interest and penalties.
f. A corporation deemed to be a PHC for a particular tax year also can be liable for the accumulated earnings tax for that year.
g. A PHC can be subject to the alternative minimum tax.

C:5-23 Explain the implication of the following statement: "Like many dogs, the threat (bark) of the PHC tax is much worse than the actual penalties assessed in connection with its (bite)."

C:5-24 Explain the following statement: "Although the accumulated earnings tax can be imposed on both publicly held and closely held corporations, the tax is likely to be imposed primarily on closely held corporations."

C:5-25 The accumulated earnings tax is imposed only when the corporation is "formed or availed of for the purpose of avoiding the income tax." Does tax avoidance have to occur at the corporate or the shareholder level for the accumulated earnings tax to be imposed? Does tax avoidance have to be the sole motive for earnings accumulation before such imposition?

C:5-26 How, in its first year of operation, can a newly formed corporation be subject to the PHC tax but not the AMT and the accumulated earnings tax?

C:5-27 Gamma Corporation has generated substantial cash flows from its manufacturing activities. It has only a moderate need to reinvest its earnings in existing facilities or for expansion. In recent years, the corporation has amassed a large investment portfolio due to management's unwillingness to pay dividends. The corporation is unlikely to be deemed a PHC but is concerned about its exposure to the accumulated earnings tax. Explain to Gamma's president what steps he can take to avoid liability for the accumulated earnings tax in the current year? In future tax years? Do these steps require the payment of a cash dividend?

C:5-28 Explain the *Bardahl* formula. Why have some tax authorities said that this formula implies a greater degree of mathematical precision than is actually the case? Does the *Bardahl* formula apply to service companies?

C:5-29 Different rules for calculating the accumulated earnings credit apply to operating companies, holding and investment companies, and service companies. Explain the differences.

C:5-30 Determine whether the following statements about the accumulated earnings tax are true or false:

a. Before the IRS can impose the accumulated earnings tax, it need only show that tax avoidance was one of the motives for the corporation's unreasonable accumulation of earnings.
b. Long-term capital gains are included in the accumulated earnings tax base.
c. Each corporate member of a controlled group can claim a separate $150,000 or $250,000 accumulated earnings credit.
d. A dividends-paid deduction can be claimed for both cash and property distributions (other than nontaxable stock dividends) made by a corporation. This deduction reduces both regular taxable income and accumulated taxable income.
e. The accumulated earnings tax liability cannot be eliminated by paying a deficiency dividend.
f. Interest and penalties on the accumulated earnings tax deficiency accrue only from the date the IRS or the courts determine that the tax is owed.
g. The accumulated earnings tax is self-reported on Form 1120-AET that is filed along with the corporate tax return.

C:5-31 For each of the following statements, indicate whether the statement is true for the PHC tax only, the accumulated earnings tax only, both taxes, or neither tax.

a. The tax is imposed only if the corporation satisfies certain stock ownership and income requirements.
b. The tax applies to both closely held and publicly traded corporations.
c. The tax is ad hoc in nature (i.e., assessed in the course of an audit).
d. Long-term capital gains are a neutral factor in determining the amount of the tax liability.
e. Tax-exempt interest income is excluded from the tax base.
f. A credit that reduces the tax liability on a dollar-for-dollar basis is available.
g. Throwback dividends may be paid without limit.
h. Consent dividends are eligible for a dividends-paid deduction.
i. Throwback and consent dividends are effective in reducing or eliminating the tax liability.
j. The tax can be avoided by paying a deficiency dividend.
k. The tax applies to S corporations.

ISSUE IDENTIFICATION QUESTIONS

C:5-32 Bird Corporation purchases machinery for $3 million and places it in service in June 2017. Installation costs are $75,000. The machine replaces an old machine that Bird purchased several years ago, which Bird sells at a $125,000 financial accounting profit. What issues must you, as Bird's director of taxes, address because of the sale of the old machine and purchase of the new machine?

C:5-33 Parrish is a closely held C corporation. Robert and Kim Parrish own all its stock. The corporation, now in its second month of operation, expects to earn $200,000 of gross income in the current tax year. This income is expected to consist of approximately 40% dividends, 30% corporate bond interest, and 30% net real estate rentals (after interest expense, property taxes, and depreciation). Administrative expenses are estimated to be $40,000. What special problems does Parrish Corporation's earning substantial passive income present to you as its CPA?

C:5-34 McHale is a C corporation owned by eight individuals, three of whom own 51% of the stock and comprise the board of directors. The corporation operates a successful automobile repair parts manufacturing business. It has accumulated $2 million of E&P and expects to accumulate another $300,000 annually. Annual dividends are $30,000. Because Americans retain their vehicles longer than they did 20 years ago, demand for McHale's repair parts has been strong for the past five years. However, little expansion or replacement of the current plant is projected for three to five years. Management has invested $200,000 annually in growth stocks. Its current investment portfolio, which is held primarily as protection against a business downturn, is valued at $1.2 million. Loans to shareholder-employees currently amount to $400,000. As McHale's tax return preparer, what tax issues should you have your client consider?

PROBLEMS

C:5-35 *General Formula for AMT.* In the current year, Whitaker Corporation has taxable income of $700,000 and tax preference items of $100,000. It also has $250,000 of positive AMT adjustment items and $80,000 of negative AMT adjustment items (neither of which includes the ACE adjustment). Whitaker's ACE amount is $1.3 million. Whitaker is not a small corporation exempt from the AMT. Determine the following for Whitaker:

a. AMTI
b. Tentative minimum tax (TMT)
c. AMT
d. Minimum tax credit
e. How much smaller would Whitaker's tax preference and AMT adjustment items have to be for its AMT to be zero?

C:5-36 *General Formula for AMT.* Westwood Corporation has $100,000 of taxable income and $20,000 of tax preference items in the current year. Westwood's positive and negative AMT adjustment items (other than the ACE adjustment) are $38,000 and $45,000, respectively, and its ACE amount is $175,000. Westwood is not a small corporation exempt from the AMT. Determine Westwood's AMT for the current year.

C:5-37 *Small Corporation Exemption from AMT.* Willis Corporation is a calendar year corporation that forms on April 1 of Year 1. Willis Corporation reports the following gross receipts:

Year	*Gross Receipts*
1	$ 3,000,000
2	5,400,000
3	7,400,000
4	8,800,000
5	10,500,000
6	12,400,000

Willis is not a member of a controlled group and is not a successor to another corporation. In which year(s) is Willis exempt from the AMT?

C:5-38 *AMT Depreciation.* On June 1 of Year 1, Water Corporation places into service a machine costing $10,000. The machine is seven-year property under the MACRS rules and has a 12-year class life. Water does not elect Sec. 179 expensing, and assume that bonus depreciation is not available for the property. Based on the half-year convention, calculate each year's depreciation deductions for regular tax and AMT purposes, and determine the amount of Water's AMT depreciation adjustment each year.

C:5-39 *AMT Gain or Loss.* Assume the same facts as in Problem C:5-38 except Water Corporation sells the machine for $9,000 on August 31 of Year 3. Determine the following:

a. Water's gain or loss on the machine's sale for regular tax and AMT purposes.
b. The amount of Water's AMT adjustments for Year 3.

C:5-40 *AMT Depreciation and Gain or Loss.* Wabash Corporation, a calendar year taxpayer, purchases and places into service $400,000 of equipment in Year 1. The equipment is seven-year MACRS property, and the half-year convention applies to it. Wabash sells the equipment for $245,000 in Year 3. Assume that 50% bonus depreciation is available in Year 1. For each of the following two independent cases, determine Wabash's gain or loss on the equipment's sale for regular tax and AMT purposes, and determine the amount of Wabash's AMT adjustments for Years 1, 2, and 3.

a. Wabash elects to expense $120,000 of the equipment's cost under Sec. 179 and does not elect out of bonus depreciation for Year 1.
b. Wabash does not elect to expense any of the equipment's cost under Sec. 179 and elects out of bonus depreciation for Year 1.

C:5-41 *ACE Adjustment.* Towne Corporation has the following amounts of ACE and preadjustment AMTI for Years 1 through 5:

	Year				
	1	*2*	*3*	*4*	*5*
ACE	$ 700	$ 700	$ 700	$700	$(700)
Preadjustment AMTI	(100)	1,300	1,000	–0–	(200)

Towne's net ACE adjustments prior to Year 1 are zero. Calculate Towne's ACE adjustment and AMTI for each year.

C:5-42 *Municipal Bond Interest and AMT.* Maple Corporation reports $500,000 of regular taxable income for the current year. Maple also reports the following amounts of interest income earned during the current year (reflected in regular taxable income, if applicable):

Franklin County bonds	$5,000
Omega Corporation bonds	4,400
Springfield School District bonds	3,700
U.S. Treasury bonds	2,100

The Springfield School District bonds are general obligation bonds and are not private activity bonds. The Franklin County bonds were issued to finance redevelopment activities and are private activity bonds. Maple's preference and adjustment items (other than those relating to interest income) are a net positive $100,000, and its items to adjust from preadjustment AMTI to adjusted current earnings (other than those relating to interest income) are a net positive $125,000.

a. Assuming none of the bonds were issued in 2009 or 2010, determine Maple's alternative minimum taxable income for the current year.
b. How would your answer to Part a change if the Franklin County bonds were issued in 2010?

C:5-43 *Regular Tax and AMT Calculations.* Bronze Corporation reports the following data for the current year:

Net profit from recurring operations	$278,000
Other income and expenses not included in the $278,000 amount:	
Dividend from 10%-owned corporation	40,000
Life insurance proceeds received upon death of a Bronze officer	500,000
Tax-exempt interest on private activity bonds	25,000
Tax-exempt interest on general revenue bonds	30,000
Installment sale in current year:	
Total realized gain	400,000
Portion of gain on installment collections in current year	32,000

Depreciation:	
For regular tax purposes	120,000
For AMT purposes	85,000
Sec. 1245 property sold in current year:	
Gain for regular tax purposes	30,000
Basis for regular tax purposes	54,000
Basis for AMT purposes	60,000

Bronze is not a small corporation exempt from the AMT and has no AMT adjustment for the U.S. production activities deduction. The tax-exempt bonds were not issued in 2009 or 2010.

a. What is Bronze's regular taxable income and regular tax?
b. What is Bronze's preadjustment AMTI?
c. What is Bronze's ACE?
d. What is Bronze's AMTI?
e. What is Bronze's AMT?
f. What minimum tax credit does Bronze obtain in the current year? In what year(s) can Bronze use it?
g. Does Bronze have to include the AMT when determining its estimated tax payments and any tax underpayment penalty for the current year?

C:5-44 *Regular Tax and AMT Calculations.* Campbell Corporation reports regular taxable income of $210,000 in the current year. Campbell takes into account the following facts when calculating the $210,000 amount.

- Campbell deducts $100,000 of MACRS depreciation for regular tax purposes. Depreciation for AMT purposes is $75,000.
- Campbell recognizes a $12,000 Sec. 1245 gain on the sale of an asset. The asset's regular tax basis at the time of sale is $9,000 less than its AMT basis.
- Campbell's ACE is $290,000.

Campbell is not a small corporation exempt from the AMT and has no AMT adjustment for the U.S. production activities deduction.

a. What is Campbell's AMTI?
b. What is Campbell's AMT?
c. What minimum tax credit does Campbell obtain in the current year? In what year(s) can Campbell use it?
d. Does Campbell have to include the AMT when determining its estimated tax payments and any tax underpayment penalty for the current year?

C:5-45 *Regular Tax and AMT Calculations.* Sheldon Corporation reports regular taxable income of $150,000 in the current year. Its regular tax is $41,750. Sheldon takes into account the following facts when calculating the $150,000 amount.

- Sheldon deducts $90,000 of MACRS depreciation for regular tax purposes. Depreciation for AMT purposes is $60,000.
- Sheldon sells equipment for $28,000. The equipment's regular tax basis at the time of sale is $16,000, and its AMT basis is $25,000.
- Sheldon's ACE is $340,000.

Sheldon is not a small corporation exempt from the AMT and has no AMT adjustment for the U.S. production activities deduction.

a. What is Sheldon's AMT?
b. What minimum tax credit does Sheldon obtain in the current year? In what year(s) can Sheldon use it?

C:5-46 *Regular Tax and AMT Calculations.* Subach Corporation reports $600,000 of regular taxable income for the current year. Subach also reports the following information (reflected in regular taxable income, if applicable):

Depreciation:	
For regular tax purposes	$440,000
For AMT purposes	410,000
Tax-exempt interest:	
On general revenue bonds	100,000
On private activity bonds	75,000

Current year installment sale:	
Total realized gain	150,000
Portion of gain on current year installment collections	25,000
Prior year installment sale:	
Total realized gain	140,000
Portion of gain on current year installment collections	35,000
Life insurance proceeds received upon the death of a Subach executive	500,000
Organizational expenditures deducted in current year	5,000
Dividend received from 25%-owned corporation	90,000

Subach is not a small corporation exempt from the AMT and has no AMT adjustment for the U.S. production activities deduction. The general revenue bonds and private activity bonds were not issued in 2009 or 2010. What is Subach's total current year federal income tax?

C:5-47 *Regular Tax and AMT Calculations.* Alabama Corporation conducts a copper mining business. During the current year, it reports regular taxable income of $400,000, which includes a $100,000 deduction for percentage depletion. The depletable property's adjusted basis at year-end (before reduction for current year depletion) is $40,000. Cost depletion, had Alabama deducted it, would have been $30,000. Depreciation for other property is $140,000 for regular tax purposes and $90,000 for AMT purposes. Alabama sells an asset for which it includes a $12,000 gain in regular taxable income. The asset's adjusted basis is $10,000 higher for AMT purposes than for regular tax purposes. Alabama's adjusted current earnings are $800,000. Alabama is not a small corporation exempt from the AMT and has no AMT adjustment for the U.S. production activities deduction.

a. What is Alabama's AMTI and AMT?

b. What minimum tax credit does Alabama obtain in the current year? In what year(s) can Alabama use it?

C:5-48 *Regular Tax and AMT Calculations.* What is Middle Corporation's regular tax, AMT, total federal income tax, and minimum tax credit generated in each of the following scenarios? Assume that Middle's ACE adjustments in prior years net to a positive $120,000 and that Middle is not a small corporation exempt from the AMT.

	Scenario 1	*Scenario 2*	*Scenario 3*
Regular taxable income	$200,000	$ 50,000	$300,000
AMT preference and adjustment items (other than the ACE adjustment)	100,000	25,000	160,000
Adjusted current earnings	500,000	150,000	400,000

C:5-49 *Regular Tax and AMT Calculations.* For the current year, Delta Corporation reports taxable income of $2 million, tax preference items of $100,000, net positive AMT adjustment items (other than the ACE adjustment) of $600,000, and adjusted current earnings of $4 million. Delta is not a small corporation exempt from the AMT and has no AMT adjustment for the U.S. production activities deduction.

a. What is Delta's regular tax?

b. What is Delta's AMT?

c. What is Delta's total tax?

d. What minimum tax credit does Delta obtain? In what year(s) can Delta use it?

e. Suppose Delta qualifies as a small corporation exempt from the AMT. How would your answers to Parts a, b, and c change?

C:5-50 *Regular Tax and AMT Calculations.* Jones Corporation has $550,000 of regular taxable income, $120,000 of tax preference items, $240,000 of net positive AMT adjustment items (other than the ACE adjustment), and $970,000 of adjusted current earnings. Jones is not a small corporation exempt from the AMT and has no AMT adjustment for the U.S. production activities deduction.

a. What is Jones' total federal income tax?

b. What minimum tax credit does Jones obtain? In what year(s) can Jones use it?

c. Suppose Jones qualifies as a small corporation that is exempt from the AMT. How would your answers to Parts a and b change?

C:5-51 *Installment Sale and AMT.* Duncan Corporation sells land in the current year (Year 1) for $900,000. The land is Sec. 1231 property having a $360,000 adjusted basis. The purchaser of the land pays Duncan $300,000 in the current year and in each of the next two years. Duncan charges the purchaser a market interest rate on the unpaid balance. Duncan's CEO asks you to prepare a year-by-year analysis of the impact of this land sale on the firm's tax position. By how much will the land sale affect Duncan's regular tax and AMT each year? In your calculation, you can ignore the interest Duncan charges the purchaser. Assume that Duncan is not a small corporation exempt from the AMT, has no AMT adjustment for the U.S. production activities deduction, and has a 34% regular tax rate. Also assume that Duncan has AMT in each year whether or not it takes the land sale into consideration.

C:5-52 *Minimum Tax Credit.* Gulf Corporation reports the following amounts for Years 1 through 4:

Type of Tax	*Year 1*	*Year 2*	*Year 3*	*Year 4*
Regular tax	$75,000	$100,000	$120,000	$144,000
Tentative minimum tax	40,000	150,000	105,000	95,000

Gulf is not a small corporation exempt from the AMT. In what year(s) does Gulf obtain a minimum tax credit? In what year(s) can Gulf use the minimum tax credit?

C:5-53 *General Business Credit.* In the current year, Edge Corporation's regular tax before credits is $165,000. Its tentative minimum tax is $100,000, and its only available tax credit is a $200,000 general business credit relating to research expenditures.

a. What amount of general business credit may Edge claim for the current year?
b. To what year(s) may Edge carry any unused general business credit from the current year?

C:5-54 *General Business Credit.* In the current year, Harden Corporation has $700,000 of regular taxable income, $60,000 of tax preference items, $140,000 of net positive AMT adjustment items (other than the ACE adjustment), and $1 million of adjusted current earnings. Harden's only available tax credit is a $45,000 general business credit relating to research expenditures.

a. What is Harden's AMT for the current year?
b. What amount of general business credit may Harden claim for the current year?
c. To what year(s) may Harden carry any unused general business credit from the current year?

C:5-55 *Estimated Tax Payments and AMT.* Ajax Corporation expects to have a $100,000 regular tax and a $70,000 AMT for the current year. Last year, it had a $200,000 regular tax and no AMT. What minimum quarterly estimated tax payment must Ajax make for the current year?

C:5-56 *Estimated Tax Payments and AMT.* Dallas Corporation reports the following amounts for Years 1 and 2:

Type of Tax	*Year 1*	*Year 2*
Regular tax	$100,000	$150,000
AMT	–0–	25,000

Each tax year is a 12-month period. Dallas qualifies as a small corporation for purposes of estimated tax payments, but it does not qualify as a small corporation exempt from the AMT. Dallas makes $23,000 of estimated tax payments for each quarter of Year 2.

a. How much tax will Dallas owe when it files its Year 2 tax return?
b. Is Dallas liable for any estimated tax underpayment penalty? If so, how much did Dallas underpay in each quarter?

C:5-57 *Stock Ownership and Passive Income Requirements.* Zhao (an individual) and nine other unrelated individuals own all of Duck Corporation's stock. The following information pertains to Duck for the current year:

Adjusted ordinary gross income	$390,000
Ordinary gross income	450,000
Personal holding company income	284,000
Taxable income	195,000

In each of the following independent cases, determine whether Duck qualifies as a personal holding company for the current year.

a. Zhao owns 19% of Duck's stock and each of the nine other individuals owns 9% of Duck's stock.
b. Zhao owns 10% of Duck's stock and each of the nine other individuals owns 10% of Duck's stock.
c. Zhao owns 9.1% of Duck's stock and each of the nine other individuals owns 10.1% of Duck's stock.

C:5-58 *PHC Definition.* In which of the following situations will Small Corporation be deemed to be a PHC? Assume that personal holding company income comprises more than 60% of Small's adjusted ordinary gross income.

a. Art owns 100% of Parent Corporation stock, and Parent owns 100% of Small's stock. Parent and Small file separate tax returns.
b. Art owns one-third of Small's stock. The PRS Partnership, of which Phil, Robert, and Sue each have a one-third capital and profits interest, also owns one-third of Small's stock. The remaining shares of Small's stock are owned by 50 individuals unrelated to Art, Phil, Robert, and Sue.
c. Art and his wife, Becky, each own 20% of Small's stock. The remaining shares of Small's stock are owned by the Whitaker Family Trust. Becky and her three sisters each have a one-fourth beneficial interest in the trust.

C:5-59 *Personal Holding Company Status.* In each of the following four scenarios, determine whether the corporation is a personal holding company. Assume the corporation's outstanding stock is owned equally by three individuals.

Item	*Scenario 1*	*Scenario 2*	*Scenario 3*	*Scenario 4*
Gross profit from sales	$40,000	$ 80,000	$40,000	$ 60,000
Capital gains	–0–	10,000	5,000	10,000
Taxable interest income	15,000	15,000	10,000	20,000
Dividends received	10,000	10,000	2,000	–0–
Rental income	80,000	150,000	–0–	–0–
Copyright royalties	–0–	5,000	80,000	–0–
Personal service income	–0–	–0–	–0–	100,000
Rent-related expenses	20,000	30,000	–0–	–0–
Copyright-related expenses	–0–	–0–	25,000	–0–
Dividends paid	8,000	10,000	5,000	10,000

C:5-60 *PHC Tax.* In the current year, Moore Corporation is deemed to be a PHC and reports the following results:

Taxable income	$200,000
Dividend received from an 18%-owned domestic corporation	50,000
Dividends paid in the sixth month of the current year	75,000

a. What is Moore's regular tax liability (ignoring any AMT implications)?
b. What is Moore's PHC tax liability?
c. What measures can Moore take to eliminate its PHC tax liability after year-end and before it files its tax return? After it files its tax return?

C:5-61 *PHC Tax.* In the current year, Kennedy Corporation is deemed to be a PHC and reports the following results:

Taxable income	$400,000
Federal income taxes	136,000
Dividends paid in the fifth month of the current year	75,000

The following information is available:

- The corporation received $100,000 of dividends from a 25%-owned domestic corporation.
- The corporation received $30,000 of tax-exempt interest income.
- The corporation recognized a $175,000 Sec. 1231 gain on the sale of land.

a. What is Kennedy's PHC tax liability?
b. What measures can Kennedy take to eliminate the PHC tax liability after year-end and before Kennedy files its tax return? After Kennedy files its tax return?

C:5-62 *PHC Tax.* Alice and Barry own all the shares of Alpha Corporation. For the current year, the corporation reports the following income and expenses:

Rental income		$ 750,000
Dividend income from less than 20%-owned corporations		200,000
Tax-exempt interest income		40,000
Gross profit on sale of merchandise		50,000
Long-term capital gain on the sale of stocks		200,000
Total income		$1,240,000
Minus: Rent related expenses:		
Interest expense	$140,000	
Depreciation expense	150,000	
Property taxes	175,000	
Other Sec. 162 expenses	165,000	(630,000)
Minus: Administrative expenses		(90,000)
Pre-tax profit		$ 520,000

During the eighth month of the current year, Alpha Corporation paid $50,000 in dividends to its shareholders. Assume Alpha is not eligible for the U.S. production activities deduction.

a. Is Alpha a personal holding company?
b. What is Alpha's regular tax liability?
c. What is Alpha's personal holding company tax liability (if any)?

C:5-63 *Unreasonable Accumulation of Earnings.* In each of the following scenarios, indicate why Adobe Corporation's accumulation of earnings might be unreasonable relative to its business needs. Provide one or more arguments the corporation might put forth to support its position that the accumulation is reasonable. Assume that Tess owns all the Adobe stock.

a. Ten years ago, Adobe established a sinking fund to retire its ten-year notes and has added cash to the fund annually. Six months ago, the corporation decided to refinance the notes at maturity at a lower interest rate through the issuance of a new series of bonds sold to an insurance company. The sinking fund balance is invested in stocks and commercial paper. A general plan exists to use the balance to purchase operating assets. No definite plans have been established by year-end.
b. Adobe regularly lends money to Tess at a rate slightly below the rate charged by a commercial bank. Tess has repaid about 20% of these loans. The current balance on the loans is $500,000, which approximates one year's net income for Adobe.
c. Adobe has heavily invested in stocks and bonds. The current market value of its investments is $2 million. The investment portfolio comprises approximately one-half of Adobe's assets.
d. Tess owns three other corporations, which, together with Adobe, form a brother-sister controlled group. Adobe regularly lends funds to Tess's three other corporations. Current loans amount to $500,000. The interest rate charged approximates the commercial rate for similar loans.

C:5-64 *Bardahl Formula.* Lion Corporation is concerned about a potential accumulated earnings tax liability. It accumulates E&P for working capital necessary to conduct its manufacturing business. The following data appear in its current year balance sheets.

Account	*Beginning Balance*	*Ending Balance*	*Peak Balance for the Year*
Accounts receivable	$300,000	$400,000	$400,000
Inventory	240,000	300,000	375,000
Accounts payable	150,000	200,000	220,000

Lion reports the following data in its current year income statement:

Sales	$3,200,000
Cost of goods sold	1,500,000
Purchases	1,200,000
Operating expenses (other than cost of goods sold)	1,000,000

Included in operating expenses are depreciation of $150,000 and federal income taxes of $100,000 (assume paid at one time rather than in installments).

a. What is Lion's operating cycle in days? As a decimal?
b. What is Lion's reasonable working capital amount as determined under the *Bardahl* formula?
c. What steps must Lion take to justify accumulating earnings that exceed the amount prescribed under the *Bardahl* formula?

C:5-65 *Accumulated Earnings Credit.* In each of the following scenarios, calculate the accumulated earnings credit. Assume the corporation uses a calendar year as its tax year. Also assume that it realizes no current year capital gains.

a. Frank Corporation, a manufacturer of plastic toys, started business last year and reported E&P of $50,000. In the current year, the corporation reports E&P of $150,000 and pays no dividends. Of the $150,000 current E&P, the corporation retains $130,000 to meet its business needs.
b. How would your answer to Part a change if Frank were a service company that provides accounting services?
c. Hall Corporation's accumulated E&P balance at January 1 of the current year is $200,000. During the year, Hall, a glass container manufacturer, reports $100,000 of current E&P, all of which is retained to meet the reasonable needs of the business. Hall pays no dividends.

C:5-66 *Accumulated Earnings Tax.* Century Cleaning, Inc. provides cleaning services in Atlanta, Georgia. It is not a member of a controlled or an affiliated group. Century reports the following results for the current year:

Taxable income	$500,000
Federal income taxes (at 34%)	170,000
Dividends paid in August of the current year	75,000

Included in taxable income are the following items that may require special treatment:

Long-term capital gains	$ 30,000
Short-term capital gains	10,000
Dividends from 21%-owned domestic corporation	100,000
Excess charitable contributions from last year that are deductible in the current year	25,000

Century's accumulated E&P balance and its reasonable business needs on January 1 of the current year, were $125,000. The firm can justify the retention of $90,000 of current E&P to meet its reasonable business needs. Assume the corporation is not eligible for the U.S. production activities deduction.

a. What is Century's accumulated taxable income?
b. What is Century's accumulated earnings tax liability?

C:5-67 *Accumulated Earnings Tax.* Howard Corporation conducts a manufacturing business and has a compelling need to accumulate earnings. Its January 1, E&P balance is $600,000. It reports the following operating results for the current year:

Taxable income		$700,000
Federal income taxes		238,000
Dividends paid:	July 15 of the current year	50,000
	February 10 of the following year	100,000

Other information relating to Howard's current year operations is as follows:

NOL carryover from last year deducted in the current year	$100,000
Net capital gain	100,000
Dividends received from 10%-owned domestic corporation	75,000

Current year E&P before dividend payments is $400,000. Howard can justify the retention of $120,000 of current E&P to meet the reasonable needs of its business.

a. What is Howard's accumulated taxable income?
b. What is Howard's accumulated earnings tax liability?

C:5-68 *Financial Statement Implications.* Woodland Corporation reports the following financial accounting results and other depreciation information for the current year:

Sales revenue	$ 2,000,000
Plus: Interest income on municipal bonds	300,000
Minus: Depreciation for financial accounting purposes	(92,000)
Other operating expenses	(1,500,000)
Financial accounting net income before federal income taxes	$ 708,000
Depreciation for:	
For regular tax purposes	$ 152,000
For AMT purposes	114,000

Woodland's sales revenue and other operating expenses are the same for financial accounting, regular tax, and AMT purposes. The municipal bonds are not private activity bonds and were not issued in 2009 or 2010. The depreciation pertains to $900,000 of property Woodland acquired and placed in service during the current year. Assume that Woodland is not exempt from the AMT and has zero deferred tax assets and liabilities at the beginning of the current year. Also assume that Woodland does not have to establish a valuation allowance for any of its deferred tax assets and that the enacted tax rate for all future years is 34%.

a. Determine Woodland's regular taxable income, preadjustment AMTI, and ACE.
b. Determine Woodland's regular tax and AMT.
c. Prepare the journal entry to record Woodland's federal income tax expense, and determine Woodland's financial accounting net income.

COMPREHENSIVE PROBLEM

C:5-69 Stock in Random Corporation is owned equally by two individual shareholders. During the current year, Random reports the following results:

Income:	Rentals	$200,000
	Dividend (from a 25%-owned domestic corporation)	30,000
	Taxable interest	15,000
	Short-term capital gains	3,000
	Long-term capital gains	17,000
Expenses related to rental income:		
	Interest	30,000
	Depreciation	32,000
	Property taxes	11,000
	Other Sec. 162 expenses	50,000
General and administrative expenses		10,000
Dividend paid on June 30		15,000

a. What is Random's gross income?
b. What is Random's ordinary gross income?
c. What is Random's adjusted income from rents?
d. What is Random's adjusted ordinary gross income?
e. What is Random's personal holding company income?
f. Is Random a PHC?
g. What is Random's regular taxable income and regular tax liability?
h. What is Random's undistributed PHC income (UPHCI) and PHC tax liability?
i. What measures can Random take before year-end to avoid the PHC tax? Alternatively, what can Random do after year-end but before the corporation files its tax return? If the corporation takes no action before or after filing its return, what remedy does it have after filing?
j. Assume that Random's income and expense items will be similar in future years unless management changes Random's asset mix. What changes can management make to reduce the corporation's PHC exposure in future years?
k. If Random is a PHC, can it also be subject to the accumulated earnings tax?

TAX STRATEGY PROBLEMS

C:5-70 Galadriel and John, married with no children, own all the stock in Marietta Horse Supplies. The couple's C corporation has been in business for ten years. The business has been successful, permitting both owners to pay themselves a reasonable salary from its revenues. Although the salaries cover life's necessities, a review of industry statistics shows that the salary of each owner is about one-half or two-thirds of salaries paid by similar-sized horse supply businesses. The reason for the low salaries is that, for a number of years, the owners felt continual pressure to retain as much of the profits in the business as possible to have sufficient working capital to finance inventories and other business needs. In the past two years, the firm has established lines of credit with two local banks that have alleviated much of this pressure. However, the couple has never had time to review the level of their compensation. Recently, an IRS agent asked the couple about items reported in a previously filed tax return. The agent reviewed all three open years and proposed a settlement for the items in question. While in the office, the IRS agent indicated to you as the couple's CPA that, in her opinion, the company had unreasonably accumulated earnings and that she would be investigating the issue before closing the audit. What advice can you give the couple about their salaries and potential liability for the accumulated earnings tax?

C:5-71 Steve and Andrew write music and lyrics for popular songs. Two years ago, they organized S&A Music Corporation, each brother owning one-half of its stock. Through the end of the current year, they contributed a total of $250,000 in capital to the business. The songs that Steve and Andrew write and promote have been successful. Annually, the firm earns $300,000 of royalties from the copyrights that it owns. With the aid of their aunt who operates a local bookkeeping service, Steve and Andrew organized their business as a C corporation. The brothers decide that, with the success of their music business, perhaps they should move their accounting services to an accounting firm that specializes in providing tax advice for small- and medium-sized businesses. As a staff member of this accounting firm, what advice can you provide the brothers about possible tax problems and potential tax strategies?

TAX FORM/RETURN PREPARATION PROBLEM

C:5-72 King Corporation, an accrual method taxpayer, reports the following results for 2016:

Regular taxable income before regular tax NOL deduction	$800,000
Minus: Regular tax NOL deduction	(200,000)
Regular taxable income	$600,000
Alternative tax NOL deduction	$175,000
AMT depreciation adjustment	148,000
Personal property acquired eight years ago and sold this year:	
Acquisition cost	50,000
Regular tax depreciation	38,845
AMT depreciation	26,845
Increase in LIFO recapture amount	75,000
Tax-exempt interest income:	
Private activity bonds (not issued in 2009 or 2010)	31,000
Other bonds (not issued in 2009 or 2010)	33,000
Dividends received (less than 1% ownership)	120,000
Dividends paid	110,000

King is not a small corporation exempt from the AMT, and it has no AMT adjustment for the U.S. production activities deduction. Regular taxable income includes $35,000 of Sec. 1231 gain from a prior year installment sale on which King's total realized gain was $350,000. Regular taxable income also includes $39,000 of Sec. 1231 gain from a 2016 installment sale on which King's total realized gain is $195,000. King's ACE adjustments for prior years are a net positive $500,000. Prepare Form 4626 for King Corporation to report its 2016 AMT liability (if any).

CASE STUDY PROBLEMS

C:5-73 Eagle Corporation operates a family business established by Edward Eagle, Sr. ten years ago. Edward Eagle, Sr. died, and the Eagle stock passed to his children. The corporation operates rental property and also invests in dividend paying stock and corporate bonds. Eagle's tax advisor made the following profit projection for the current year:

Rentals	$260,000
Dividend income (from a 40%-owned domestic corporation)	90,000
Interest income	20,000
Gross income	$370,000
Rental expenses:	
Depreciation expense	$ 70,000
Interest expense	100,000
Property taxes	10,000
Other Sec. 162 expenses	20,000
General and administrative expenses	15,000
Total expenses	$215,000
Net profit	$155,000

Eagle paid dividends of $40,000 in each of the past three years. Eagle was not a PHC in prior years.

Required: Prepare a memorandum to Edward Eagle, Jr. regarding potential liability for the PHC tax. In your memorandum, discuss the following two questions:

a. Is Eagle likely to be deemed a PHC for the current year?

b. If Eagle is likely to be deemed a PHC for the current year, what measures (if any) should be taken before year-end to eliminate the PHC tax liability? After year-end?

C:5-74 Goss Corporation is a leading manufacturer of hangers for the laundry and dry cleaning industry. The family-owned business has prospered for many years and has generated approximately $100 million of sales and $8 million in after-tax profits. Your accounting firm has performed the audit and tax work for Goss and its executives since the company was created many years ago. The advent of plastic hangers and improved fabrics has kept the company's market share constant, and the corporation plans no major plant expansions or additions. Salaries paid to corporate executives, most of whom are family members, are above the national averages for similar officers. Dividend payments in recent years have not exceeded 10% of the after-tax profits. On December 1 of the current year, you were assigned to oversee the preparation of the current year Goss tax return. In undertaking the assignment, you review Goss tax returns for the past three years. You note from Schedule L (the balance sheet) that, during this period, the corporation made about $1.5 million in loans to three executives and regularly increased the size of its stock portfolio. This increase leads you to believe that Goss may be liable for the accumulated earnings tax in the current year and prior years.

Required:

a. What responsibility do you have to make Goss or the partner in charge of the Goss account aware of the potential accumulated earnings tax liability?

b. Should you advise the IRS of the potential liability for prior years? Should you disclose the potential liability on the current year return?

c. Prepare a list of measures that can be taken to reduce or eliminate Goss' liability for the accumulated earnings tax.

TAX RESEARCH PROBLEMS

C:5-75 Broadway Corporation is a C corporation not exempt from the AMT. During the current year, Broadway contributed significant amounts of cash to various charitable organizations. Should Broadway make any adjustment for its charitable contributions when calculating its alternative minimum taxable income and/or adjusted current earnings?

A partial list of sources is:

- IRC Sec. 170(b)(1) and (2)
- Reg. Sec. 1.55-1(a)

- Reg. Sec. 1.56(g)-1(a)(5)
- Ltr. Rul. 9320003 (February 1, 1993)
- Ltr. Rul. 9321063 (March 2, 1993)

C:5-76 Camp Corporation is owned by Hal and Ruthie, who have owned their stock since the corporation was formed fourteen years ago. The corporation uses the calendar year as its tax year and the accrual method of accounting. In Year 1, Camp borrowed $4 million from a local bank. The loan is secured by a lien on its machinery. Camp loaned 90% of the borrowings to Vickers Corporation at the same annual rate as the rate on the bank loan. Vickers also is owned equally by Hal and Ruthie. Vickers sells to the automobile industry parts that are manufactured by Camp and unrelated companies. Camp's operating results suffered as a result of a slowdown in the automobile industry. The gross margin on its sales declined from $1 million in Year 1 to $200,000 in Year 2. Interest earned by Camp on the loan to Vickers is $432,000 in Year 2. Other passive income earned by Camp is $40,000. Camp's accountant believes that the corporation is not a PHC because the interest income Camp earns can be netted against the $432,000 interest expense paid to the bank for the loan to Vickers. Is he correct in his belief?

A partial list of sources is

- IRC Secs. 542(a) and 543(a)(1)
- Reg. Sec. 1.543-1(b)(2)
- *Bell Realty Trust,* 65 T.C. 766 (1976)
- *Blair Holding Co., Inc.,* 1980 PH T.C. Memo ¶80,079, 39 TCM 1255

C:5-77 William Queen owns all the stock in Able and Baker Corporations. Able, a successful enterprise, has generated excess working capital of $3 million. Baker is still in its developmental stages and has had substantial capital needs. To meet some of these needs, William had Able lend Baker $2 million during Year 1 and Year 2. These loans are secured by Baker notes, but not other Baker property. Able has charged Baker interest at a rate ordinarily charged by a commercial lender. Upon reviewing Able's books in the audit of its Year 1 tax return, an IRS agent indicates that Able is liable for the accumulated earnings tax because of its build up of excess working capital and its loans to Baker. Later this week, you will meet with the agent for a third time. Before this meeting, you must research whether loans to a related corporation to finance its working capital meet a reasonable need of the business. At a meeting to discuss this problem, William asks whether filing a consolidated tax return would eliminate this potential problem and, if so, how must the ownership structure change to accomplish this objective.

A partial list of research sources is

- IRC Secs. 532 and 537
- Reg. Secs. 1.537-2(c) and -3(b) and 1.1502-43
- *Latchis Theatres of Keene, Inc. v. CIR,* 45 AFTR 1836, 54-2 USTC ¶9544 (1st Cir., 1954)
- *Bremerton Sun Publishing Co.,* 44 T.C. 566 (1965)

CHAPTER

6

CORPORATE LIQUIDATING DISTRIBUTIONS

LEARNING OBJECTIVES

After studying this chapter, you should be able to

1. Discuss the issues involved in corporate liquidations
2. Determine the tax consequences to the shareholders and liquidating corporation when the general liquidation rules apply
3. Determine the tax consequences when a parent corporation liquidates a controlled subsidiary
4. Recognize special reporting issues pertaining to shareholders and the liquidating corporation
5. Assess when a liquidating corporation recognizes gains and losses on the retirement of debt
6. Identify tax planning opportunities in corporate liquidations
7. Comply with procedural rules for corporate liquidations

CHAPTER OUTLINE

As part of the corporate life cycle, management may decide to discontinue the operations of a profitable or unprofitable corporation by liquidating it. As a result of this decision, the shareholders may receive liquidating distributions of the corporation's assets. Preceding the formal liquidation of the corporation, management may sell part or all the corporation's assets, which the shareholders may not want to receive in a liquidating distribution. An asset sale also generates cash to pay the corporation's liabilities (including federal income taxes incurred on the liquidation).

Ordinarily, the liquidation is motivated by a combination of tax and business reasons. However, sometimes it is undertaken principally for tax reasons.

- If the corporation liquidates and its shareholders hold the assets in an unincorporated form (e.g., sole proprietorship or partnership), the marginal tax rate may be reduced from the 35% top corporate rate to a lower rate for individuals in tax brackets less than 35%. For example, even low amounts of taxable income are taxed at 35% in a personal service corporation and thus could be taxed at a lower rate in noncorporate form.
- If the assets are producing losses, the shareholders may prefer to hold them in an unincorporated form and deduct the losses on their personal tax returns.
- Corporate earnings are taxed once under the corporate income tax rules and a second time when the corporation distributes the earnings as dividends or when the shareholder sells or exchanges the corporate stock at a gain. Liquidation of the corporation permits the assets to be held in an unincorporated form, thereby avoiding double taxation of subsequent earnings.

ADDITIONAL COMMENT

The applicable capital gains tax rate for net capital gains and qualified dividends of noncorporate taxpayers is 0% for taxpayers in tax brackets of 15% and below, 15% for taxpayers in the 25% through 35% tax brackets, and 20% for taxpayers in the 39.6% tax bracket. Also, 25% and 28% rates apply for gains on certain types of property. In addition, an incremental 3.8% rate applies to net investment income for taxpayers whose modified AGI exceeds $200,000 ($250,000 for married filing jointly). Net investment income includes, among other things, interest, dividends, annuities, royalties, rents, and net gains from the disposition of property not used in a trade or business, all reduced by deductions allocable to such income or gains. Thus, dividends and capital gains receive comparable tax rate treatment except that capital gain taxation is deferred until sale of the stock or liquidation of the corporation.

Liquidating a corporation carries a tax cost, however. The liquidating corporation is taxed as though it sold its assets, and the shareholders receiving liquidating distributions are taxed as though they sold their stock. A C corporation cannot simply elect to be treated as a pass-through entity under the check-the-box regulations (see Chapter C:2). Thus, the only route to converting a C corporation into a sole proprietorship, partnership, limited liability company, or limited liability partnership is via a taxable corporate liquidation followed by formation of the desired entity. Alternatively, a C corporation could obtain pass-through status without liquidating if it elects S corporation status. Even with this approach, the S corporation faces potential taxation on its built-in gains (see Chapter C:11).

This chapter explains the tax consequences of corporate liquidations to both the liquidating corporation and its shareholders. In so doing, the chapter presents two sets of liquidation rules. The general liquidation rules apply to liquidations of corporations not controlled by a parent corporation. Special rules apply to the liquidation of a controlled subsidiary.

OVERVIEW OF CORPORATE LIQUIDATIONS

OBJECTIVE 1

Discuss the issues involved in corporate liquidations

This chapter initially presents an overview of the tax and nontax consequences of a corporate liquidation to both the shareholders and the distributing corporation.

THE SHAREHOLDER

Determining the tax consequences of the liquidation to each of the liquidating corporation's shareholders entails several questions:

- What are the amount, timing, and character of the shareholder's recognized gain or loss?
- What is the shareholder's adjusted basis of each property received?
- When does the holding period begin for each property received by the shareholder?

When a corporation liquidates under the general rules, a shareholder treats the liquidating distribution as an amount received in exchange for his or her stock. The shareholder recognizes a capital gain or loss equal to the excess of any money received plus the FMV of any noncash property received over the adjusted basis of his or her stock. The basis of each property received is stepped-up or stepped-down to the property's FMV on the liquidation date. The holding period for the asset begins the day after the liquidation date.

If a parent corporation liquidates a controlled subsidiary under special rules, however, the parent corporation (shareholder) recognizes no gain or loss. In addition, the bases and holding periods of the subsidiary's assets carry over to the parent.

TAX STRATEGY TIP

Although the shareholders and corporation usually incur no tax cost upon forming a corporation, the tax costs of liquidating a corporation (other than a controlled subsidiary) may be substantial. The tax consequences of liquidating a corporation should be a consideration in the initial decision to use the corporate form. For example, assuming a 34% corporate tax rate and a 15% capital gains rate at the shareholder level, the effective tax cost of a complete liquidation is approximately 43.9% {34% + [(1 − 0.34) × 15%]}. The effective tax increases accordingly for shareholders facing a capital gains tax rate higher than 15%.

THE CORPORATION

Two questions must be answered to determine the tax consequences of the liquidation transaction for the liquidating corporation:

- What are the amount and character of the corporation's recognized gain or loss?
- What happens to the corporation's tax attributes upon liquidation?

When a liquidation occurs under the general rules, the liquidating corporation recognizes gain or loss on the distribution of property to its shareholders. The recognized gain or loss is the same as what the corporation would recognize had it sold the distributed property to its shareholders. Some restrictions (discussed later in the chapter) limit loss recognition in certain potentially abusive situations. Also, tax attributions, such as net operating loss (NOL) carryovers and earnings and profits, disappear when the corporation liquidates under the general rules.

If the liquidating corporation is an 80%-controlled subsidiary of the parent corporation, the liquidating corporation recognizes no gain or loss under special rules. In this case, the subsidiary's tax attributes carry over to the parent corporation.

EXAMPLE C:6-1 ► Randy Jones owns Able Corporation, a C corporation. Randy's basis for his Able stock is $100,000. The corporation's assets are summarized below. In addition, Able Corporation owes $60,000 to its creditors.

Assets	*Adjusted Basis*	*Fair Market Value*
Cash	$ 50,000	$ 50,000
General stock	75,000	125,000
Machinery	115,000	200,000
Total	$240,000	$375,000

See Figure C:6-1 for an illustration of the corporate liquidation. In step 1, Able sells its machinery to an unrelated purchaser for $200,000 cash. The machinery originally cost $250,000, and Able has claimed $135,000 of depreciation on the machinery. Able recognizes a total gain on the machinery sale of $85,000 ($200,000 − $115,000). Because depreciation taken exceeds the amount of gain, the entire gain is Sec.1245 recapture (ordinary income). In step 2, Able uses $60,000 in cash to pay its creditors. In step 3, Able distributes remaining cash and the General stock, a capital asset, to Randy. Able recognizes a $50,000 ($125,000 − $75,000) capital gain on the General stock distribution. Assuming a 34% marginal tax rate, Able must pay $45,900 [($85,000 + $50,000) × 0.34] in federal income taxes on the distribution of the General stock and the sale of the machinery (step 4). The tax payment reduces Able's remaining cash to $144,100 ($50,000 + $200,000 sale proceeds − $60,000 paid to creditors − $45,900 paid in federal income taxes). Thus, Randy recognizes a $169,100 ($144,100 cash + $125,000 securities − $100,000 basis for stock) long-term capital gain on the liquidating distribution. The same federal income taxes would have occurred had Able sold both the General stock and machinery to unrelated purchasers, or had Able distributed both the stock and machinery to Randy because each of Able's noncash assets have FMVs exceeding their adjusted bases.[1] ◄

DEFINITION OF A COMPLETE LIQUIDATION

The term *complete liquidation* is not defined in the IRC, but Reg. Sec. 1.332-2(c) indicates that distributions made by a liquidating corporation must either completely cancel or redeem all its stock in accordance with a plan of liquidation or be one of a series of distributions that completely cancels or redeems all its stock in accordance with a plan of liquidation (see page C:6-20 for a discussion of plans of liquidation). When more than one distribution occurs, the corporation must be in a liquidation status when it makes the first

[1] The corporation's recognized gains and losses might be different if one or more of the properties had declined in value. Under some circumstances, the loss might be disallowed if the property were distributed to Randy Jones, where it would be recognized if the property had been sold to an unrelated purchaser.

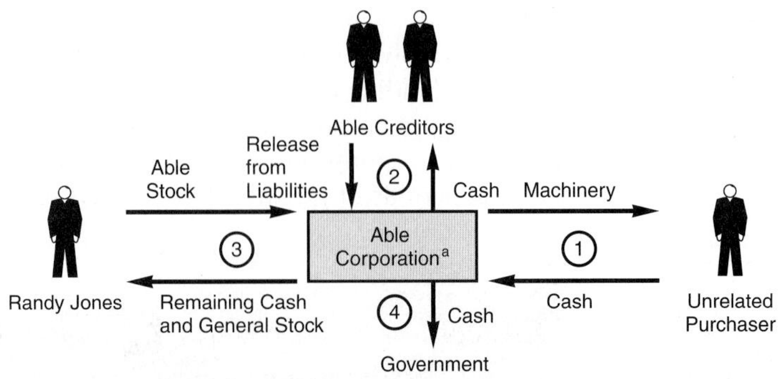

FIGURE C:6-1 ▶ ILLUSTRATION OF CORPORATE LIQUIDATION (EXAMPLE C:6-1)

liquidating distribution under the plan, and such status must continue until the liquidation is completed. A distribution made before the corporation adopts a plan of liquidation is taxed to the shareholders as a dividend distribution or stock redemption (see Chapter C:4).

Liquidation status exists when the corporation ceases to be a going concern and its activities are for the purpose of winding up its affairs, paying its debts, and distributing any remaining property to its shareholders. A liquidation is completed when the liquidating corporation has divested itself of substantially all property. Retention of a nominal amount of assets (e.g., to retain the corporation's name) does not prevent a liquidation from occurring under the tax rules.

The liquidation of a corporation does not mean the corporation has undergone dissolution. **Dissolution** is a legal term that implies the corporation has surrendered the charter it received from the state. A corporation may complete its liquidation before surrendering its charter to the state and undergoing dissolution. Dissolution may never occur if the corporation retains its charter to protect the corporate name from being acquired by another party.

EXAMPLE C:6-2 ▶ Thompson Corporation adopts a plan of liquidation in December of the current year. The corporation distributes all but a nominal amount of assets to its shareholders in January of the next year. The nominal assets retained are the minimum amount needed to preserve the corporation's existence under state law and to prevent others from acquiring its name. Despite the retention of a nominal amount of assets, Thompson Corporation has liquidated for tax purposes even though it has not dissolved. ◀

STOP & THINK

Question: Peter Jenkins, age 58, is considering forming a new business entity to operate the rental real estate activities that he and his wife have owned personally for a number of years. He has heard about corporations and limited liability companies from reading various real estate journals. Because of their level of personal wealth and the liability protection afforded by the corporate form of doing business, Peter wants to use a corporation to own and operate their real estate. The assets Peter and his wife plan to transfer to the corporation have a $600,000 FMV and a $420,000 adjusted basis. As Peter's CPA, why should you consider the tax cost of liquidating the corporation as part of the overall analysis of the business entity selection decision?

Solution: A transfer of real estate by Peter and his wife to a corporation is nontaxable. A subsequent liquidation of the corporation is taxable, however, because both the corporation and the shareholder may recognize gain or loss. Peter and his wife have $180,000 ($600,000 − $420,000) of appreciation in their real estate. Even if no change in value occurs, liquidation of the real estate corporation at a later date will cause gain to be taxed twice, once at the corporate level and again at the shareholder level. On the other hand, creation and liquidation of a limited liability company are not taxable events to the entity or its owners. Thus, the difference in liquidation treatment at a future date is one of many differences the owners must consider when forming an entity. More information on liquidating a limited liability company can be found in Chapter C:10.

GENERAL LIQUIDATION RULES

OBJECTIVE 2

Determine the tax consequences to the shareholders and liquidating corporation when the general liquidation rules apply

This chapter section presents the general liquidation rules. These rules are considered in two parts: the effects of liquidating on the shareholders and the effects of liquidating on the corporation.

EFFECTS OF LIQUIDATING ON THE SHAREHOLDERS

Three aspects of the general liquidation rules are discussed below: amount and timing of gain or loss recognition, character of the recognized gain or loss, and basis and holding period of property received in the liquidation. Table C:6-1 summarizes the liquidation rules applying to shareholders under both the general liquidation rules and the controlled subsidiary corporation exception.

Amount of Recognized Gain or Loss. Section 331(a) requires that liquidating distributions received by a shareholder be treated as full payment in exchange for his or her stock. The shareholder's recognized gain or loss equals the difference between the amount realized (the FMV of the assets received from the corporation plus any money) and his or her basis in the stock. If a shareholder assumes or acquires liabilities of the liquidating corporation, the amount of these liabilities reduces the shareholder's amount realized.

EXAMPLE C:6-3 ▶ Gamma Corporation liquidates, with Joseph receiving $10,000 in cash plus other property having a $12,000 FMV. Joseph's basis in his Gamma stock is $16,000. Joseph's amount realized is $22,000 ($12,000 + $10,000). Therefore, he recognizes a $6,000 ($22,000 − $16,000) gain on the liquidation. ◀

EXAMPLE C:6-4 ▶ Assume the same facts as in Example C:6-3 except Joseph also assumes a $2,000 mortgage attaching to the other property. The $2,000 liability assumed reduces Joseph's amount realized to $20,000 ($22,000 − $2,000). His recognized gain on the liquidation is $4,000 ($20,000 − $16,000). ◀

▼ **TABLE C:6-1**
Tax Consequences of a Liquidation to the Shareholders

	Amount of Gain or Loss Recognized	Character of Gain or Loss Recognized	Adjusted Basis of Property Received	Holding Period of Property Received
General rule	Shareholders recognize gain or loss (money + FMV of noncash property received − adjusted basis of stock) upon liquidation (Sec. 331).	Long-term or short-term capital gain or loss (Sec. 1222). Limited ordinary loss treatment available (Sec. 1244).	FMV of the property (Sec. 334(a)).	Begins on the day after the liquidation date (Sec. 1223(1)).
Controlled subsidiary corporation rule	Parent corporation recognizes no gain or loss when an 80% controlled subsidiary corporation liquidates into the parent corporation (Sec. 332).[a]	Not applicable.[a]	Carryover basis for property received from subsidiary corporation (Sec. 334(b)).[a]	Includes subsidiary corporation's holding period for the assets (Sec. 1223(2)).[a]

[a] Minority shareholders use the general rule.

Impact of Accounting Method. Shareholders who use the accrual method of accounting recognize gain or loss when all events have occurred that fix the amount of the liquidating distribution and the time the shareholders are entitled to receive the distribution upon surrender of their shares. Shareholders who use the cash method of accounting report the gain or loss when they have actual or constructive receipt of the liquidating distribution(s).[2]

ADDITIONAL COMMENT

Calculating the gain or loss separately on each block may result in (1) both gains and losses existing in the same liquidating distribution and (2) the character of the various gains or losses being different.

When Stock Is Acquired. A shareholder may have acquired his or her stock at different times or for different per-share amounts. In this case, the shareholder must compute the gain or loss separately for each share or block of stock owned.[3]

Character of the Recognized Gain or Loss. Generally, the liquidating corporation's stock is a capital asset in the shareholder's hands. The gain or loss recognized, therefore, is a capital gain or loss for most shareholders. Two exceptions to these rules are indicated below.

- Loss recognized by an individual shareholder on Sec. 1244 stock is an ordinary loss, within limits (see Chapter C:2).
- Loss recognized by a corporate shareholder on the worthlessness of the controlled subsidiary's stock is an ordinary loss under Sec. 165(g)(3) (see Chapter C:2).

Basis and Holding Period of Property Received in the Liquidation. Section 334(a) provides that the shareholder's basis of property received under the general liquidation rules is its FMV on the distribution date. The holding period for the property starts on the day after the distribution date.

EFFECTS OF LIQUIDATING ON THE LIQUIDATING CORPORATION

Two aspects of the general liquidation rules are discussed below: (1) the recognition of gain or loss by the liquidating corporation when it distributes property in redemption of its stock and (2) the special valuation rules used when the liabilities assumed or acquired by the shareholder exceed the property's adjusted basis in the liquidating corporation's hands. Table C:6-2 summarizes rules applying to the liquidating corporation.

Recognition of Gain or Loss When Corporation Distributes Property in Redemption of Stock. Section 336(a) provides that the liquidating corporation must recognize gain or loss when it distributes property in a complete liquidation. The amount and character of the gain or loss are determined as if the corporation sold the property to the shareholder at its FMV.

EXAMPLE C:6-5 ▶ Under a plan of liquidation, West Corporation distributes land to one of its shareholders, Arnie. Arnie's basis in his stock is $70,000. The land, which is used in West's trade or business, has a $40,000 adjusted basis and a $120,000 FMV on the distribution date. West recognizes an $80,000 ($120,000 − $40,000) Sec. 1231 gain when it makes the liquidating distribution. Arnie recognizes a $50,000 ($120,000 − $70,000) capital gain on the distribution, and his basis for the land is its $120,000 FMV. A nonliquidating distribution would have produced similar results for the corporation. However, for the shareholder, the entire FMV would have been a dividend instead of a capital gain assuming sufficient E&P. Thus, both liquidating and nonliquidating distributions produce double taxation although the amount and character of the shareholder's gain or income differ. (Also, see Example C:6-1 for another illustration.) ◀

With limited exceptions, the liquidating corporation can recognize a loss when it distributes property that has declined in value to its shareholders. This rule eliminates the need for a liquidating corporation to sell property that has declined in value to recognize its losses.

EXAMPLE C:6-6 ▶ Assume the same facts as in Example C:6-5 except the land's FMV is instead $10,000. West recognizes a $30,000 ($10,000 − $40,000) Sec. 1231 loss when it distributes the land to Arnie. Arnie recognizes a $60,000 ($10,000 − $70,000) capital loss, and his basis for the land is $10,000. ◀

---

[2] Rev. Rul. 80-177, 1980-2 C.B. 109.

[3] Reg. Sec. 1.331-1(e).

▼ **TABLE C:6-2**
Tax Consequences of a Liquidation to the Liquidating Corporation

	Amount and Character of Gain, Loss, or Income Recognized	Treatment of the Liquidating Corporation's Tax Attributes
General rule	The liquidating corporation recognizes gain or loss when it distributes property as part of a complete liquidation (Sec. 336(a)).	Tax attributes disappear when the liquidation is completed.
Controlled subsidiary corporation rules	1. The liquidating subsidiary corporation recognizes no gain or loss upon a distribution of property to its parent corporation when the Sec. 332 nonrecognition rules apply to the parent corporation (Sec. 337(a)). 2. The liquidating subsidiary corporation recognizes no loss upon a distribution of property to minority shareholders when the Sec. 332 nonrecognition rules apply to the parent corporation (Sec. 336(d)(3)). It does recognize gains, however.	Tax attributes of a subsidiary corporation carry over to the parent corporation when the Sec. 332 rules apply (Sec. 381(a)).
Related party rule	The liquidating subsidiary corporation recognizes no loss upon a distribution of property to a related person unless the corporation distributes such property ratably to all shareholders *and* the liquidating corporation did not acquire the property in a Sec. 351 transaction or as a capital contribution during the five years preceding the distribution (Sec. 336(d)(1)).	
Tax avoidance rule	The liquidating subsidiary corporation recognizes no loss when a sale, exchange, or distribution of property occurs and the liquidating corporation acquired such property in a Sec. 351 transaction or as a capital contribution having as a principal purpose the recognition of loss (Sec. 336(d)(2)).	

TAX STRATEGY TIP

If possible, a corporation should avoid distributing property subject to a mortgage that exceeds the property's FMV. Such distributions cause excessive corporate gain recognition and uncertainty of results at the shareholder level.

Liabilities Assumed or Acquired by the Shareholders. As described earlier, for purposes of determining the amount of gain or loss recognized under Sec. 336, property distributed by the liquidating corporation is treated as having been sold to the shareholder for its FMV on the distribution date. Section 336(b) contains a special restriction on valuing a liquidating property distribution when the shareholders assume or acquire liabilities. According to this rule, the FMV of the distributed property cannot be less than the amount of the liability assumed or acquired. Congress enacted Sec. 336(b) because the corporation realizes an economic gain or benefit equal to the amount of the liability the shareholder assumes or acquires (and not just the lower FMV of the property distributed) as part of the liquidation. Treatment at the shareholder level is not completely clear. Section 336(b) specifically states that this liability rule applies only for determining the corporation's gain or loss. Thus, it does not seem to extend to Sec. 334(a), which requires the shareholder to take a FMV basis in the distributed property. Some commentators have suggested that the strict statutory interpretation of giving the shareholders the actual FMV basis, rather than the greater liability basis, produces an illogical result.[4] Also, given that the liability exceeds the distributed property's FMV, the shareholder's amount realized should be zero, resulting in a capital loss equal to the shareholder's stock basis.

[4] For a detailed discussion, see B. C. Randall and D. N. Stewart, "Corporate Distributions: Handling Liabilities in Excess of the Fair Market Value of Property Remains Unresolved," *The Journal of Corporate Taxation*, Spring 1992, pp. 55–64.

EXAMPLE C:6-7 ▶ Jersey Corporation owns an apartment complex originally costing $3 million and, after depreciation, having a $2.4 million adjusted basis. The property is secured by a $2.7 million mortgage. Pursuant to a plan of liquidation, Jersey distributes the property and the mortgage to Rex, Jersey's sole shareholder, at a time when the property's FMV is $2.2 million. Rex's stock basis is $500,000. Jersey recognizes a $300,000 ($2,700,000 − $2,400,000) gain on distributing the property because its FMV cannot be less than the $2.7 million mortgage. The shareholder recognizes a $500,000 capital loss on the corporate stock and takes either a $2.2 million or $2.7 million basis in the property, depending on which interpretation applies. ◀

Exceptions to the General Gain or Loss Recognition Rule. The IRC provides four exceptions to the general recognition rule of Sec. 336(a). Two of these exceptions apply to liquidations of controlled subsidiary corporations and are covered later. The other two exceptions prevent certain abusive practices (e.g., the manufacturing of losses) from being accomplished and are examined below. Also, Sec 362(e)(2) may reduce a liquidating corporation's loss recognition. Specifically, for property contributed to a controlled corporation, the corporation must reduce the basis of loss property if the total adjusted basis of property contributed by a shareholder exceeds the total FMV of that property (see Chapter C:2 for details). Consequently, upon a later liquidating distribution, the corporation will realize a smaller loss or no loss at all.[5]

ADDITIONAL COMMENT

The disqualified property rule prohibits a shareholder from infusing loss property into the liquidating corporation and generating losses at both the corporate and shareholder levels by liquidating the corporation.

Distributions to Related Persons. Section 336(d)(1)(A) prevents loss recognition in connection with property distributions to a related person if (1) the distribution of loss property is other than pro rata to all shareholders based on their stock ownership or (2) the distributed property is disqualified property. Section 267(b) defines a related person as including, for example, an individual and a corporation whose stock is more than 50% owned (in terms of value) by such individual, as well as two corporations that are members of the same controlled group. Section 336(d)(1)(B) defines disqualified property as (1) any property acquired by the liquidating corporation in a transaction to which Sec. 351 applies, or as a contribution to capital, during the five-year period ending on the distribution date or (2) any property having an adjusted basis that carries over from disqualified property.

EXAMPLE C:6-8 ▶ Lei owns 60% and Betty owns 40% of Mesa Corporation's stock. Pursuant to a plan of liquidation, Mesa distributes Beta stock to Lei that Mesa purchased two years ago. The Beta stock, which is not disqualified property, has a $40,000 FMV and a $100,000 adjusted basis. Betty receives only cash in the liquidation. The non–pro rata distribution of the Beta stock (the loss property), however, prevents Mesa from claiming a $60,000 capital loss when it makes the distribution. If Mesa instead distributes the Beta stock 60% to Lei and 40% to Betty, Mesa deducts the entire capital loss, assuming Mesa has offsetting capital gains. ◀

EXAMPLE C:6-9 ▶ Assume the same facts as in Example C:6-8 except Mesa acquired the Beta stock two years ago as a capital contribution from Lei when the Beta stock basis was $100,000 and its FMV was $105,000. Thus, the stock was not subject to the Sec. 362(e)(2) basis reduction rule when contributed, and Mesa took a $100,000 carryover basis in the stock. The stock's FMV now is $40,000, and the corporation distributes it to Lei upon liquidation of the corporation. The Beta stock in this case is disqualified property. The $60,000 realized loss is disallowed because Lei is a related party under Sec. 267(b). If Mesa instead distributes the Beta stock 60% to Lei and 40% to Betty, Mesa still is prohibited from deducting the portion of the $60,000 capital loss attributable to the stock distributed to the related party even though Mesa distributed it ratably to Lei and Betty. Mesa can deduct only the $24,000 ($60,000 × 0.40) capital loss attributable to the Beta stock distributed to Betty because she is not a related party. Alternatively, a sale of the disqualified property to an unrelated purchaser permits Mesa to recognize the entire $60,000 loss, again assuming offsetting capital gains exist. ◀

EXAMPLE C:6-10 ▶ Assume the same facts as in Example C:6-9 except the Beta stock had an $85,000 FMV when contributed, and Mesa had to reduce its basis in the stock to $85,000 at that time. Upon

[5] For a detailed discussion, see B. C. Randall, B. C. Spilker, and J. M. Werlhof, "The Interaction of New Section 362(e)(2) With the Loss Disallowance Rules in Corporate Liquidations," *Corporate Taxation*, September/October 2005.

liquidation and distribution to Lei, Mesa realizes a $45,000 ($40,000 − $85,000) loss, which is disallowed under the related person, disqualified property rule. If instead Mesa distributes the Beta stock ratably to Lei and Betty, Mesa can deduct $18,000 ($45,000 × 0.40) of the loss attributable to the stock distributed to Betty, again assuming Mesa recognizes offsetting gains on other property. ◄

Sales Having a Tax-Avoidance Purpose. Section 336(d)(2) restricts loss recognition with respect to the sale, exchange, or distribution of property acquired in a Sec. 351 transaction, or as a contribution to capital, where the liquidating corporation acquired the property as part of a plan having the principal purpose of loss recognition by the corporation in connection with its liquidation. This loss limitation prevents a shareholder from transferring loss property into a corporation to reduce or eliminate the gain the liquidating corporation otherwise would have recognized from the distribution of other appreciated property.

TAX STRATEGY TIP

To avoid loss disallowance under Sec. 336(d)(2), a corporation should delay adopting a plan of liquidation until two years after receiving loss property in a Sec. 351 transaction.

TAX STRATEGY TIP

If the corporation made a basis reduction for contributed loss property under Sec. 362(e)(2), it might argue that no tax avoidance purpose existed, thereby making a Sec. 336(d) disallowance inapplicable. See article referenced in footnote 5.

Property acquired by the liquidating corporation in any Sec. 351 transaction or as a contribution to capital within two years of the date on which a plan of complete liquidation is adopted are treated as part of a plan having a tax-avoidance purpose unless exempted by forthcoming regulations. Treasury Regulations, when issued, should not prevent corporations from deducting losses associated with dispositions of assets that are contributed to the corporation and used in a trade or business (or a line of business), or dispositions occurring during the first two years of a corporation's existence.[6]

The basis of the contributed property for loss purposes equals its adjusted basis to the corporation at the time of liquidation reduced (but not below zero) by the excess (if any) of the property's adjusted basis over its FMV immediately after its contribution to the corporation. This adjusted basis already may include a reduction under Sec. 362(e)(2) for contributed loss property. No adjustment occurs to the contributed property's adjusted basis when determining the corporation's recognized gain.

EXAMPLE C:6-11 ► Terry contributed a widget maker having a $1,000 adjusted basis and a $100 FMV to Pirate Corporation in exchange for additional stock on January 10 of Year 2. At the same time, Terry contributed a second property having a $2,000 FMV and a $900 adjusted basis. Because the total FMV of Terry's contributed property ($2,100) exceeded the total adjusted basis of that property ($1,900), the corporation did not reduce the loss property's basis under Sec. 362(e)(2) at that time. On April 1 of Year 3, Pirate adopts a plan of liquidation. Between January 10 of Year 2, and April 1 of Year 3, Pirate does not use the widget maker in its trade or business. Liquidation occurs on July 1 of Year 3, and Pirate distributes the widget maker and a second property that has a $2,500 FMV and a $900 adjusted basis. Because Terry contributed the widget maker to Pirate after April 1 of Year 1 (two years before Pirate adopted its plan of liquidation), and the widget maker is not used in Pirate's trade or business, its acquisition and distribution are presumed to be motivated by a desire to recognize the $900 loss. Unless Pirate can establish otherwise (e.g., by arguing that Sec. 362(e)(2) precludes a tax avoidance purpose), Sec. 336(d)(2) will apply to the distribution of the widget maker. Pirate's basis for determining its loss will be $100 [$1,000 − ($1,000 − $100)]. Thus, Pirate cannot claim a loss upon distributing the widget maker. This rule prevents Pirate from offsetting the $1,600 ($2,500 − $900) gain recognized on distributing the second property by the $900 loss realized on distributing the widget maker. ◄

The basis adjustment also affects sales, exchanges, or distributions of property made before the adoption of the plan of liquidation or in connection with the liquidation. Thus, losses claimed in a tax return filed before the adoption of the plan of liquidation may be restricted by Sec. 336(d)(2). The liquidating corporation may recapture these losses in the tax return for the tax year in which the plan of liquidation is adopted, or it can file an amended tax return for the tax year in which it originally claimed the loss.

EXAMPLE C:6-12 ► Assume the same facts as in Example C:6-11 except Pirate sells the widget maker for $200 on July 10 of Year 2. Pirate reports an $800 loss ($200 − $1,000) on its Year 2 tax return. The adoption of the plan of liquidation on April 1 of Year 3 causes the loss on the sale of the widget maker to be

[6] H. Rept. No. 99-841, 99th Cong., 2d Sess., p. II-201 (1986). The Conference Committee Report for the 1986 Tax Act indicates that property transactions occurring more than two years in advance of the adoption of the plan of liquidation will be disregarded unless no clear and substantial relationship exists between the contributed property and the conduct of the corporation's current or future business enterprises.

covered by the Sec. 336(d)(2) rules, again assuming a tax avoidance purpose exists. Pirate can file an amended Year 2 tax return showing the $800 loss being disallowed, or it can file its Year 3 tax return reporting $800 of income under the loss recapture rules.[7] ◀

Topic Review C:6-1 summarizes the general corporate liquidation rules.

TOPIC REVIEW C:6-1

Tax Consequences of a Corporate Liquidation

GENERAL CORPORATE LIQUIDATION RULES

1. The shareholder's recognized gain or loss equals the amount of cash plus the FMV of the other property received minus the adjusted basis of stock surrendered. Corporate liabilities assumed or acquired by the shareholder reduce the amount realized.
2. The gain or loss is capital if the stock investment is a capital asset. If the shareholder recognizes a loss on the liquidation, Sec. 1244 permits ordinary loss treatment (within limits) for qualifying individual shareholders.
3. The adjusted basis of the property received is its FMV on the distribution date.
4. The shareholder's holding period for the property begins the day after the distribution date.
5. With certain limited exceptions, the distributing corporation recognizes gain or loss when making the distribution. The amount and character of the gain or loss are determined as if the corporation sold the property for its FMV immediately before the distribution. Special rules apply when the shareholders assume or acquire corporate liabilities and the amount of such liabilities exceeds the property's FMV.
6. The liquidated corporation's tax attributes disappear upon liquidation.

LIQUIDATION OF A CONTROLLED SUBSIDIARY

OBJECTIVE 3

Determine the tax consequences when a parent corporation liquidates a controlled subsidiary

After a brief overview, the discussion of the controlled subsidiary exception is divided into three parts: the requirements for using the exception, the effects of liquidating on the parent corporation, and the effects of liquidating on the subsidiary corporation.

OVERVIEW

Section 332(a) provides that the parent corporation recognizes no gain or loss when a controlled subsidiary corporation liquidates into its parent corporation. This liquidation rule permits a corporation to modify its corporate structure without incurring any adverse tax consequences. Section 332 applies only to the parent corporation. Other shareholders owning a minority interest are taxed under the general liquidation rules of Sec. 331. When Sec. 332 applies to the parent corporation, Sec. 337 permits the liquidating corporation to recognize no gains or losses on the assets distributed to the parent corporation. The liquidating corporation, however, recognizes gains (but not losses) on distributions made to shareholders holding a minority interest. The nonrecognition of gain or loss rule is logical for the distribution to the parent corporation because the assets remain within the corporate group following the distribution. Thus, the subsidiary corporation can be liquidated and operated as a division of its parent corporation without gain or loss recognition.

EXAMPLE C:6-13 ▶ Parent Corporation owns all of Subsidiary Corporation's stock. Subsidiary's assets have a $1 million FMV and a $400,000 adjusted basis. Parent's basis for its Subsidiary stock is $250,000. The liquidation of Subsidiary results in a $600,000 ($1,000,000 – $400,000) realized gain for Subsidiary on the distribution of its assets, none of which is recognized. Parent

[7] The property has a $1,000 basis when determining Pirate's gain on the sale and a $100 ($1,000 – $900) basis when determining its loss on the sale. Therefore, Pirate recognizes no gain or loss because the $200 sale price lies between the gain and loss basis amounts.

has a $750,000 ($1,000,000 − $250,000) realized gain on surrendering its Subsidiary stock, none of which is recognized. If Secs. 332 and 337 were not available, both Subsidiary and Parent would recognize their realized gains. In this case, Parent's gain would be reduced by the taxes paid by Subsidiary on its gain because Subsidiary's taxes reduce the amount available for distribution to Parent. ◀

REQUIREMENTS

TAX STRATEGY TIP

A parent corporation that does not own the requisite 80% should consider purchasing additional subsidiary stock from minority shareholders or consider having the subsidiary redeem shares from its minority shareholders. In either case, the strategy to attain 80% ownership must be applied before the corporations adopt a plan of liquidation. See Tax Planning Considerations for further details.

All the following requirements must be met for a liquidation to qualify for the Sec. 332 nonrecognition rules:

- The parent corporation must own at least 80% of the total combined voting power of all classes of stock entitled to vote and 80% of the total value of all classes of stock (other than certain nonvoting preferred stock) from the date on which the plan of liquidation is adopted until receipt of the subsidiary corporation's property.[8]
- The property distribution must be in complete cancellation or redemption of all the subsidiary corporation's stock.
- Distribution of the property must occur within a single tax year or be one of a series of distributions completed within three years of the close of the tax year during which the subsidiary makes the first of the series of liquidating distributions.

If the corporations meet all these requirements, the Sec. 332 nonrecognition rules are mandatory. If one or more of the conditions listed above are not met, the parent corporation is taxed under the previously discussed general liquidation rules.

TYPICAL MISCONCEPTION

The 80% stock ownership requirement of Sec. 332 is not the same stock ownership requirement for corporate formations in Chapter C:2. Instead, the Sec. 332 ownership requirement is the same one used for affiliated groups filing consolidated tax returns (see Chapter C:8).

Stock Ownership. For Sec. 332 to apply, the parent corporation must own the requisite amount of voting and nonvoting stock. In applying this requirement, the Sec. 318 attribution rules for stock ownership do not apply (see Chapter C:4).[9] The parent corporation must own the requisite 80% of voting and nonvoting stock from the date on which the plan of liquidation is adopted until the liquidation is completed. Failure to satisfy this requirement denies the transaction the benefits of Secs. 332 and 337.

Cancellation of the Stock. The subsidiary corporation must distribute its property in complete cancellation or redemption of all its stock in accordance with a plan of liquidation. When more than one liquidating distribution occurs, the subsidiary corporation must have adopted a plan of liquidation and be in a status of liquidation when it makes the first distribution. This status must continue until the liquidation is completed. Regulation Sec. 1.332-2(c) indicates that a liquidation is completed when the liquidating corporation has divested itself of all its property. The liquidating corporation, however, may retain a nominal amount of property to permit retention or sale of the corporate name.

Timing of the Distributions. The distribution of all the subsidiary corporation's assets within one subsidiary tax year in complete cancellation or redemption of all its stock is considered a complete liquidation.[10] Although a formal plan of liquidation can be adopted, the shareholders' adoption of a resolution authorizing the distribution of the corporation's assets in complete cancellation or redemption of its stock is considered to be the adoption of a plan of liquidation when the distribution occurs within a single tax year. The tax year in which the liquidating distribution occurs does not have to be the same as the one in which the plan of liquidation is adopted.[11]

The subsidiary corporation can carry out the plan of liquidation by making a series of distributions that extend over a period of more than one tax year to cancel or redeem its stock. In this case, however, a formal plan of liquidation must be adopted, and the liquidation must be completed within three years of the close of the tax year in which the subsidiary makes the first distribution under the plan.[12]

---

[8] The stock definition used for Sec. 332 purposes excludes any stock that is not entitled to vote, is limited and preferred as to dividends and does not participate in corporate growth to any significant extent, has redemption and liquidation rights that do not exceed its issue price (except for a reasonable redemption or liquidation premium), and is not convertible into another class of stock.

[9] Sec. 332(b)(1).

[10] Sec. 332(b)(2) and Reg. Sec. 1.332-3.

[11] Rev. Rul. 76-317, 1976-2 C.B. 98.

[12] Sec. 332(b)(3) and Reg. Sec. 1.332-4.

EFFECTS OF LIQUIDATING ON THE SHAREHOLDERS

Recognition of Gain or Loss to Parent Corporation. The Sec. 332(a) nonrecognition rules apply only to a parent corporation that receives a liquidating distribution from a solvent subsidiary. Section 332(a) does not apply to a parent corporation that receives a liquidating distribution from an insolvent subsidiary, to minority shareholders who receive liquidating distributions, or to a parent corporation that receives a payment to satisfy the subsidiary's indebtedness to the parent. All of these exceptions are discussed below.

SELF-STUDY QUESTION

What are the tax consequences if the liquidating subsidiary is insolvent?

ANSWER

The parent generally is entitled to an ordinary loss deduction under Sec. 165(g)(3) when it fails to receive any liquidation proceeds because the subsidiary is insolvent. The parent also may have a bad debt deduction under Sec. 166.

Section 332 does not apply if the subsidiary corporation is insolvent at the time of the liquidation because the parent corporation does not receive the distributions in exchange for its stock investment. An insolvent subsidiary is one whose liabilities exceed the FMV of its assets. Regulation Sec. 1.332-2(b) requires that the parent corporation receive at least partial payment for the stock it owns in the subsidiary corporation to qualify for nonrecognition under Sec. 332. If the subsidiary is insolvent, however, the special worthless security rules of Sec. 165(g)(3) for affiliated corporations and the bad debt rules of Sec. 166 permit the parent corporation to recognize an ordinary loss with respect to its investment in the subsidiary's stock or debt obligations (see Chapter C:2).

EXAMPLE C:6-14 ▶ Parent Corporation owns all of Subsidiary Corporation's stock. Parent established Subsidiary to produce and market a product that proved unsuccessful. Parent has a $1.5 million basis in its Subsidiary stock. In addition, it made a $1 million advance to Subsidiary that is not secured by a note. Under a plan of liquidation, Subsidiary distributes all its assets, having a $750,000 FMV, to Parent in partial satisfaction of the advance after having paid all third-party creditors. No assets remain to pay the remainder of the advance or to redeem the outstanding stock. Because Subsidiary is insolvent immediately before the liquidating distribution, it distributes none of its assets in redemption of the Subsidiary stock. Therefore, the liquidation cannot qualify under the Sec. 332 rules. Parent, therefore, claims a $250,000 business bad debt with respect to the unpaid portion of the advance and a $1.5 million ordinary loss for its stock investment. ◀

TYPICAL MISCONCEPTION

Section 332 applies only to the parent corporation. If a minority interest exists, the general liquidation rules of Sec. 331 apply to the minority shareholders.

STOP & THINK

Question: In Example C:6-14, assume Subsidiary Corporation had a $3 million net operating loss (NOL) carryover, which would disappear upon liquidation because Sec. 332 did not apply. To prevent this disappearance, Parent Corporation proposes to cancel the $1 million advance as a contribution to Subsidiary's capital. Thus, Parent would have a $2.5 million basis in its Subsidiary stock prior to the liquidation and no advances receivable. Now when Parent liquidates Subsidiary, all of Subsidiary's assets redeem Subsidiary's outstanding stock, and the transaction seems to qualify for Sec. 332 treatment. Under these circumstances, the $3 million NOL would carry over to Parent under Sec. 381, giving Parent $3 million worth of NOL deductions rather than $1.75 million worth of bad debt and worthless stock deductions under the original transaction. Do you think the IRS would condone this proposed transaction?

Solution: No. In Rev. Rul. 68-602, 1968-2 C.B. 135, the IRS held under similar circumstances that, because the cancellation "was an integral part of the liquidation and had no independent significance other than to secure the tax benefits of [Subsidiary's] net operating loss carryover, such step will be considered transitory and, therefore, disregarded." Thus, if Parent proceeded with the proposed transaction, the IRS would ignore it and treat the liquidation the same as originally done in Example C:6-14.

Treatment of Minority Shareholders. Liquidating distributions made to minority shareholders are taxed under the Sec. 331 general liquidation rules. These rules require the minority shareholders to recognize gain or loss—which generally is capital—upon the redemption of their stock in the subsidiary corporation.

EXAMPLE C:6-15 ▶ Parent Corporation and Jane own 80% and 20%, respectively, of Subsidiary Corporation's single class of stock. Parent and Jane have adjusted bases of $100,000 and $15,000, respectively, for their stock interests. Subsidiary adopts a plan of liquidation on May 30 and makes liquidating

SELF-STUDY QUESTION

What bases do both the parent and minority shareholders take in the assets received in a Sec. 332 liquidation?

ANSWER

Because the parent corporation recognizes no gain or loss in the transaction, the parent corporation takes a carryover basis in its assets. However, because the minority shareholders are involved in a taxable exchange, they take a FMV basis in their assets.

distributions of two parcels of land having $250,000 and $62,500 FMVs to Parent and Jane, respectively, on November 1 in exchange for their stock. Parent does not recognize its $150,000 ($250,000 − $100,000) gain because of Sec. 332. Jane recognizes a $47,500 ($62,500 − $15,000) capital gain under Sec. 331. (Subsidiary also faces gain recognition on the distribution of appreciated property to its minority shareholder as demonstrated in Example C:6-18.) ◀

Basis of Property Received. Under Sec. 334(b)(1), the parent corporation's basis for property received in the liquidating distribution is the same as the subsidiary corporation's basis prior to the distribution. This carryover basis rule reflects the principle that the liquidating corporation recognizes no gain or loss when it distributes the property and that the property's tax attributes (e.g., the depreciation recapture potential) carry over from the subsidiary corporation to the parent corporation. The parent corporation's basis for its stock investment in the subsidiary corporation is ignored in determining the basis for the distributed property and disappears once the parent surrenders its stock in the subsidiary. Property received by minority shareholders takes a basis equal to its FMV.

EXAMPLE C:6-16 ▶ Assume the same facts as in Example C:6-15 and that the two parcels of land received by Parent Corporation and Jane have adjusted bases of $175,000 and $40,000, respectively, to Subsidiary. Parent takes a $175,000 carryover basis for its land, and Jane takes a $62,500 FMV basis for her land. ◀

A special rule prevents the importation of built-in losses upon the liquidation of a foreign subsidiary. Specifically, the parent takes a FMV basis in each transferred property if the following three conditions prevail: (1) the parent is a U.S. corporation, (2) the liquidating subsidiary is a foreign corporation, and (3) the aggregate adjusted basis of the transferred property exceeds the aggregate FMV.

STOP & THINK

Question: Why should a corporation that is 100%-owned by another corporation be treated differently when it liquidates than a corporation that is 100%-owned by an individual?

Solution: A corporation that is 100%-owned by another corporation can file a consolidated tax return (see Chapters C:3 and C:8). As a result, the parent and its subsidiary corporations are treated as a single entity. This result is the same as if the subsidiary were one of a number of divisions of a single corporation. An extension of the single-entity concept is that a subsidiary corporation can be liquidated tax-free into its parent corporation. An individual and his or her corporation are treated as two separate tax entities when calculating their annual tax liabilities. As separate entities, nonliquidating distributions (e.g., ordinary distributions and stock redemptions) from the corporation to its shareholder(s) are taxable. The same principle applies to liquidating distributions.

EFFECTS OF LIQUIDATING ON THE SUBSIDIARY CORPORATION

Recognition of Gain or Loss. Section 337(a) provides that the liquidating corporation recognizes no gain or loss on the distribution of property to the 80% distributee in a complete liquidation to which Sec. 332 applies.[13] The term 80% distributee refers to a corporation that meets the 80% stock ownership requirement described on page C:6-11.

EXAMPLE C:6-17 ▶ Parent Corporation owns all the stock of Subsidiary Corporation. Pursuant to a plan of complete liquidation, Subsidiary distributes land having a $200,000 FMV and a $60,000 basis to Parent. Subsidiary recognizes no gain with respect to the distribution. Parent takes a $60,000 basis for the land. ◀

[13] Section 336(e) permits a corporation to sell, exchange, or distribute the stock of a subsidiary corporation and to elect to treat such a transaction as a disposition of all the subsidiary corporation's assets. The parent corporation recognizes no gain or loss on the sale, exchange, or distribution of the stock. The economic consequences of making this election for a stock sale are essentially the same as if the parent corporation instead liquidates the subsidiary in a transaction to which Sec. 332 applies and then immediately sells the properties to the purchaser.

TAX STRATEGY TIP

A corporation that sells, exchanges, or distributes the stock of a subsidiary may elect to treat the sale of the stock as a sale of the subsidiary's assets. This election could prove beneficial when a sale of the subsidiary stock occurs and the assets of the subsidiary corporation are substantially less appreciated than the subsidiary stock itself.

The depreciation recapture provisions in Secs. 1245, 1250, and 291 do not override the Sec. 337(a) nonrecognition rule if a controlled subsidiary corporation liquidates into its parent corporation. Instead, the parent corporation assumes the depreciation recapture potential associated with the distributed property, and recapture occurs when the parent corporation sells or exchanges the property.[14]

The Sec. 337(a) nonrecognition rule applies only to distributions to the parent corporation. Liquidating distributions to minority shareholders are not eligible for nonrecognition under Sec. 337(a). Consequently, the liquidating corporation must recognize gain under Sec. 336(a) when it distributes appreciated property to the minority shareholders. Section 336(d)(3), however, prevents the subsidiary corporation from recognizing loss on distributions made to minority shareholders. Thus, for the subsidiary, liquidating distributions made to minority shareholders are treated the same way as nonliquidating distributions.

EXAMPLE C:6-18 ▶ Assume the same facts as in Example C:6-17 except Parent owns 80% of the Subsidiary stock, Chuck owns the remaining 20% of such stock, and Subsidiary distributes two parcels of land to Parent and Chuck. The parcels have FMVs of $160,000 and $40,000, and adjusted bases of $50,000 and $10,000, respectively. Subsidiary does not recognize the $110,000 ($160,000 – $50,000) gain realized on the distribution to Parent. However, Subsidiary does recognize the $30,000 ($40,000 – $10,000) gain realized on the distribution to Chuck because the Sec. 337(a) nonrecognition rule applies only to distributions to the 80% distributee. Assume that the land distributed to Chuck instead has a $40,000 FMV and a $50,000 adjusted basis. Subsidiary can deduct none of the $10,000 loss because it distributed the land to a minority shareholder. ◀

Tax Attribute Carryovers. The **tax attributes** of the liquidating corporation disappear when the liquidation is completed under the general rules. They carry over, however, in the case of a controlled subsidiary corporation liquidated into its parent corporation under Sec. 332.[15] The following items are included among the carried-over attributes:

- ▶ NOL carryovers
- ▶ Earnings and profits
- ▶ Capital loss carryovers
- ▶ General business and other tax credit carryovers

The carryover amount is determined as of the close of the day on which the subsidiary corporation completes the distribution of all its property. Chapter C:7 contains further discussion of these rules.

Topic Review C:6-2 summarizes the special rules applicable to the liquidation of a controlled subsidiary corporation.

TOPIC REVIEW C:6-2

Tax Consequences of a Corporate Liquidation

TAX CONSEQUENCES OF LIQUIDATING A CONTROLLED SUBSIDIARY CORPORATION

1. Specific requirements must be met with respect to (a) stock ownership, (b) distribution of the property in complete cancellation or redemption of all the subsidiary's stock, and (c) distribution of all property within a single tax year or within a three-year period. To satisfy the stock ownership requirement, the parent corporation must own at least 80% of the total voting power of all voting stock and at least 80% of the total value of all stock.
2. The parent corporation recognizes no gain or loss when it receives distributed property from the liquidating subsidiary. Section 332 does not apply to liquidations of insolvent subsidiaries and distributions to minority shareholders.
3. The basis of the distributed property carries over from the subsidiary corporation to the parent corporation.
4. The parent corporation's holding period for the assets includes the subsidiary corporation's holding period.
5. The subsidiary corporation recognizes no gain or loss when making a distribution to an 80% distributee (parent). The liquidating subsidiary recognizes gain (but not loss) on distributions to minority shareholders. Also, the liquidating subsidiary recognizes no gain when it distributes appreciated property to satisfy certain subsidiary debts owed to the parent corporation.
6. The subsidiary corporation's tax attributes carry over to the parent corporation as part of the liquidation.

[14] Secs. 1245(b)(3) and 1250(d)(3).

[15] Sec. 381(a).

SPECIAL REPORTING ISSUES

PERTAINING TO SHAREHOLDERS

OBJECTIVE 4

Recognize special reporting issues pertaining to shareholders and the liquidating corporation

Four special shareholder reporting rules apply to liquidation transactions described below. These rules add different degrees of complexity to the general liquidation rules outlined above.

Partially Liquidating Distributions. Shareholders often receive a series of partially liquidating distributions that culminate in the redemption of all the corporation's stock. Section 346(a) treats this situation as a complete liquidation. Consequently, the distributions received are taxed under the Sec. 331 liquidation rules instead of under the Sec. 302 rules applying to redemptions in partial liquidation. The IRS permits the shareholder's basis to be recovered first and requires the recognition of gain once the shareholder fully recovers the basis of a particular share or block of stock. The shareholder cannot recognize a loss with respect to a share or block of stock until he or she receives the final liquidating distribution, or until it becomes clear that no more liquidating distributions will occur.[16]

EXAMPLE C:6-19 ▶ Diane owns 1,000 shares of Adobe Corporation stock, which she acquired five years ago. Her basis in the stock is $40,000. Recently, she initiated a series of liquidating distributions from Adobe to be received over a three-year period (Years 1–3) as follows: $25,000 on July 23 of Year 1, $17,000 on March 12 of Year 2, and $10,000 on April 5 of Year 3. Diane recognizes no gain in Year 1 because she has not fully recovered her $40,000 basis by year-end. The $15,000 ($40,000 − $25,000) unrecovered basis remaining after the first distribution is less than the $17,000 liquidating distribution received on March 12 of Year 2, so Diane recognizes a $2,000 gain in Year 2. She recognizes an additional $10,000 gain in Year 3 when she receives the final liquidating distribution. ◀

EXAMPLE C:6-20 ▶ Assume the same facts as in Example C:6-19 except Diane paid $60,000 for her Adobe stock. The receipt of each of the liquidating distributions is nontaxable because Diane's $60,000 basis exceeds the $52,000 ($25,000 + $17,000 + $10,000) total of the distributions. Diane recognizes an $8,000 ($52,000 − $60,000) loss in Year 3 when she receives the final liquidating distribution. ◀

SELF-STUDY QUESTION

If a cash method shareholder is subsequently obligated to pay a contingent liability of the liquidated corporation, what are the tax consequences of such a payment?

ANSWER

First, the prior tax year return is not amended. The additional payment results in a loss recognized in the year of payment. The character of the loss depends on the nature of the gain or loss recognized by the shareholder in the year of liquidation.

Subsequent Assessments. At some date after the liquidation, the shareholders may be required to pay a contingent liability of the corporation or a liability not anticipated at the time of the liquidating distribution (e.g., an income tax deficiency determined after the liquidation occurs or a judgment that is contingent when the corporation makes the final liquidating distribution). The additional payment does not affect the reporting of the initial liquidation. The tax treatment for the additional payment depends on the nature of the gain or loss originally reported by the shareholder and not on the type of loss or deduction the liquidating corporation would have reported had it paid the liability.[17] If the liquidation results in a recognized capital gain or loss, a cash method shareholder treats the additional payment as a capital loss in the year of payment (i.e., the shareholder does not file an amended tax return for the year in which he or she originally reported the gain or loss from the liquidation). An accrual method shareholder recognizes the capital loss when he or she incurs the liability.

EXAMPLE C:6-21 ▶ Coastal Corporation liquidated three years ago with Tammy, a cash method taxpayer, reporting a $30,000 long-term capital gain on the exchange of her Coastal stock. In the current year, Tammy pays $5,000 as her part of the settlement of a lawsuit against Coastal. All shareholders pay an additional amount because the settlement exceeds the amount of funds that Coastal placed into an escrow account as a result of the litigation. The amount placed into the escrow account was not included in the amount Tammy realized from the liquidating distribution

---

[16] Rev. Ruls. 68-348, 1968-2 C.B. 141, 79-10, 1979-1 C.B. 140, and 85-48, 1985-1 C.B. 126.

[17] *F. Donald Arrowsmith v. CIR*, 42 AFTR 649, 52-2 USTC ¶9527 (USSC, 1952).

three years ago. Because Tammy had not been taxed on the cash placed in the escrow account, she cannot deduct the amount of the payment made from the escrow account in the current year. Nevertheless, Tammy treats the $5,000 paid from her personal funds as a long-term capital loss in the current year. ◀

Open Versus Closed Transactions. Sometimes the value of property received in a corporate liquidation cannot be determined by the usual valuation techniques. Property that can be valued only on the basis of uncertain future payments falls into this category. In such a case, the shareholders may attempt to rely on the **open transaction doctrine** of *Burnet v. Logan* and treat the liquidation as an open transaction.[18] Under this doctrine, the shareholder's gain or loss from the liquidation is not determined until the assets that cannot be valued are subsequently sold, collected, or able to be valued. Any assets that cannot be valued are assigned a zero value. The IRS's position is that the FMV of almost any asset should be ascertainable. Thus, the IRS assumes that the open transaction method should be used only in extraordinary circumstances. For example, an open transaction cannot be used merely because a market valuation for an investment in a closely held corporation is not readily available through market quotations for the stock.

ETHICAL POINT

A tax practitioner needs to ensure that the client obtains appropriate appraisals to support the values assigned to property distributed to shareholders in a corporate liquidation. A 20% substantial underpayment penalty may be imposed on corporations and shareholders that substantially understate their income tax liabilities.

Installment Obligations. Shareholders who receive an installment obligation as part of their liquidating distribution ordinarily report the FMV of their obligation as part of the consideration received to calculate the amount of the recognized gain or loss. Shareholders who receive an installment obligation that was acquired by the liquidating corporation in connection with the sale or exchange of its property are eligible for special treatment in reporting their gain on the liquidating transaction if the sale or exchange takes place during the 12-month period beginning on the date a plan of complete liquidation is adopted and the liquidation is completed during such 12-month period. These shareholders may report their gain as they receive the installment payments.[19]

PERTAINING TO THE LIQUIDATING CORPORATION

Expenses of the Liquidation. The corporation can deduct the expenses incurred in connection with the liquidation. These expenses include attorneys' and accountants' fees, costs incurred in drafting the plan of liquidation and obtaining shareholder approval, and so on.[20] Such amounts ordinarily are deductible in the liquidating corporation's final tax return.

A liquidating corporation treats expenses associated with selling its property as an offset against the sales proceeds. When a corporation sells an asset pursuant to its liquidation, the selling expenses reduce the amount of gain or increase the amount of loss reported by the corporation.[21]

EXAMPLE C:6-22 ▶ Madison Corporation adopts a plan of liquidation on July 15 and shortly thereafter sells a parcel of land on which it realizes a $60,000 gain (excluding the effects of a $6,000 sales commission). Madison pays its legal counsel $1,500 to draft the plan of liquidation. Madison distributes all its remaining properties to its shareholders on December 15. The $1,500 paid to legal counsel is deductible as a liquidation expense in Madison's current year income tax return. The sales commission reduces the $60,000 gain realized on the land sale, so that Madison's recognized gain is $54,000 ($60,000 − $6,000). ◀

---

[18] *Burnet v. Edith A. Logan,* 9 AFTR 1453, 2 USTC ¶736 (USSC, 1931).

[19] Sec. 453(h)(1)(A). A tax deferral is available only with respect to the gain realized by the shareholder. The liquidating corporation must recognize the deferred gain when it distributes the installment obligation to the shareholder as if it had sold the obligation immediately before the distribution.

[20] *Pridemark, Inc. v. CIR,* 15 AFTR 2d 853, 65-1 USTC ¶9388 (4th Cir., 1965).

[21] See, for example, *J. T. Stewart III Trust,* 63 T.C. 682 (1975), *acq.* 1977-1 C.B. 1.

Any capitalized expenditures unamortized at the time of liquidation should be deducted if they have no further value to the corporation (e.g., unamortized organizational costs).[22] Capitalized expenditures that have value must be allocated to the shareholders receiving the benefit of such an outlay (e.g., prepaid insurance and prepaid rent).[23] Expenses related to issuing the corporation's stock are nondeductible, even at the time of liquidation, because they are treated as a reduction of paid-in capital. Unamortized bond premiums, however, are deductible at the time the corporation retires the bonds.

TAX STRATEGY TIP

If a liquidating corporation creates an NOL in the year of liquidation or already has NOL carryovers, these losses may disappear with the liquidated corporation. If the liquidation qualifies under Sec. 332, however, the parent corporation acquires the NOL. If the liquidation falls under the general liquidation rules, the liquidating corporation may want to consider an S election for the liquidation year so any NOLs created in that year can pass through to the shareholders.

Treatment of Net Operating Losses. If the liquidating corporation reports little or no income in its final income tax return, the corporation may create an NOL when it deducts its liquidating expenses and any remaining capitalized expenditures. The NOL carries back to reduce corporate taxes paid in prior years. The resultant federal income tax refund increases (decreases) the gain (loss) previously reported by the shareholder. Alternatively, the shareholders might consider having the corporation make an S election for the liquidation year and have the flow-through loss reported on the shareholders' tax returns. (See Chapter C:11 for the tax treatment of S corporations.)

The need for a liquidating corporation to recognize gains when distributing appreciated property can be partially or fully offset by expenses incurred in carrying out the liquidation or by any available NOL carryovers. Losses recognized by the liquidating corporation when distributing property that has declined in value can offset operating profits or capital gains earned in the liquidation year. Should such losses produce an NOL or net capital loss, the losses may be carried back to provide a refund of taxes paid in a prior year, or they may be passed through to the corporation's shareholders if the corporation makes an S corporation election for the tax year.

RECOGNITION OF GAIN OR LOSS WHEN PROPERTY IS DISTRIBUTED IN RETIREMENT OF DEBT

OBJECTIVE 5

Assess when a liquidating corporation recognizes gains and losses on the retirement of debt

GENERAL RULE

A shareholder recognizes no gain or loss when the liquidating corporation pays off an unsecured debt obligation it owes to the shareholder. However, when the corporation retires a security at an amount different from the shareholder's adjusted basis for the obligation, the shareholder recognizes gain or loss for the difference. These rules apply whether the debtor corporation pays or retires the debt as part of its operations or as part of its liquidation. The debtor corporation recognizes no gain or loss when it uses cash to satisfy its debt obligations. However, the debtor corporation recognizes gain when it uses appreciated noncash property to satisfy its debt obligations. Similarly, a debtor corporation recognizes a loss when it uses noncash property that has declined in value to satisfy its debt obligations.

SATISFACTION OF THE SUBSIDIARY'S DEBT OBLIGATIONS

The Sec. 332(a) nonrecognition rules apply only to amounts received by the parent corporation in its role as a shareholder. The parent corporation, however, does recognize gain or loss upon receipt of property in payment of a subsidiary corporation indebtedness if the payment differs from the parent's basis in the debt.[24]

As mentioned above, the use of property to satisfy an indebtedness generally results in the debtor recognizing gain or loss at the time it transfers the property.[25] Section 337(b), however, prevents a liquidating subsidiary corporation from recognizing gain or loss

[22] Reg. Sec. 1.248-1(b)(3).

[23] *Koppers Co., Inc. v. U.S.*, 5 AFTR 2d 1597, 60-2 USTC ¶9505 (Ct. Cls., 1960).

[24] Sec. 1001(c). This general IRC section requires realized gains or losses to be recognized unless otherwise excluded or disallowed.

[25] Ibid.

WHAT WOULD YOU DO IN THIS SITUATION?

Andrea has operated her trendy, upscale clothing store as a C corporation for a number of years. Annually, the corporation earns $200,000 in pre-tax profits. The corporation's assets have an $800,000 FMV and a $700,000 adjusted basis. Andrea's stock has a basis of $125,000. One of her good friends, Jenna, has opened a clothing store as a limited liability company (LLC) and has been telling Andrea about the advantage of not having to pay the corporate income tax. Andrea calls and asks you to advise her on making the change from being taxed as a C corporation to being treated as an LLC. What advice should you provide Andrea in this situation?

when it transfers noncash property to its parent corporation in satisfaction of an indebtedness. The IRC provides this exception because the property remains within the economic unit of the parent-subsidiary group.

Section 337(b) applies only to the subsidiary's indebtedness owed to the parent corporation on the date the plan of liquidation is adopted and that is satisfied by the transfer of property pursuant to a complete liquidation of the subsidiary corporation. It does not apply to liabilities owed to other shareholders or third-party creditors, or to liabilities incurred after the plan of liquidation is adopted. In addition, if the subsidiary corporation satisfies the indebtedness for less than its face amount, it may have to recognize income from the discharge of an indebtedness.

EXAMPLE C:6-23 ▶ Parent Corporation owns all of Subsidiary Corporation's single class of stock. When Parent acquired the Subsidiary stock, it also purchased $1 million of Subsidiary bonds at their face amount. Subsequently, Parent and Subsidiary adopt a plan of liquidation, and Subsidiary distributes to Parent property having a $1 million FMV and a $400,000 adjusted basis in cancellation of the bonds. Subsidiary also distributes its remaining property to Parent in exchange for all of its outstanding stock. Subsidiary recognizes no gain on the transfer of the property in cancellation of its bonds. Parent recognizes no gain on receipt of the property because the property's FMV equals Parent's adjusted basis of the bonds. Parent takes a $400,000 carryover basis for the noncash property it receives in cancellation of the bonds. ◀

TAX PLANNING CONSIDERATIONS

OBJECTIVE 6

Identify tax planning opportunities in corporate liquidations

TIMING THE LIQUIDATION TRANSACTION

Sometimes corporations adopt a plan of liquidation in one year but do not complete the liquidation until a subsequent year. Corporations planning to distribute properties that have both increased in value and decreased in value may find it advantageous to sell or distribute property that has declined in value in a tax year in which they also conducted business activities. As such, the loss recognized when selling or distributing the property can offset profits that are taxed at higher rates. Deferring the sale or distribution of property that has appreciated in value may delay the recognition of gain for one tax year and also place the gain in a year in which the marginal tax rate is lower.

EXAMPLE C:6-24 ▶ Miami Corporation adopts a plan of liquidation in November of the current year, a tax year in which it earns $150,000 in operating profits. Miami discontinues its operating activities before the end of the current year. Pursuant to the liquidation, it distributes assets, producing $40,000 of recognized ordinary losses. In January of next year, Miami distributes assets that have appreciated in value, producing $40,000 of recognized ordinary income. Distributing the loss property in the current year results in a $15,600 tax savings ($40,000 × 0.39). Only $6,000 ($40,000 × 0.15) in taxes result from distributing the appreciated property next year. The rate differential provides a $9,600 ($15,600 − $6,000) net savings to Miami. ◀

TAX STRATEGY TIP

Timing the distribution of loss property so that the losses may be used to offset high-bracket taxable income at the corporate level makes good tax sense if the general liquidation rules are applicable. However, this planning opportunity would not exist in a Sec. 332 parent-subsidiary liquidation because the liquidating subsidiary does not recognize losses.

Timing the liquidating distributions should not proceed without the planner also considering the tax position of the various shareholders. Taxpayers should be careful about timing the liquidating distributions to avoid creating a short-term capital gain taxed at ordinary rates rather than long-term capital gains taxed at the lower capital gains rate. If the liquidation results in a recognized loss, shareholders should take advantage of the opportunity to offset the loss against capital gains plus $3,000 of ordinary income, as well as attempt to increase the portion of the loss eligible for ordinary loss treatment under Sec. 1244 (see next section).

RECOGNITION OF ORDINARY LOSSES WHEN A LIQUIDATION OCCURS

Shareholders sometimes recognize losses when a liquidation occurs. Individual shareholders should be aware that, because a complete liquidation is treated as an exchange transaction, Sec. 1244 ordinary loss treatment is available when a small business corporation liquidates. This treatment permits the shareholder to claim $50,000 of ordinary loss when he or she surrenders the stock ($100,000 if the taxpayer is married and files a joint return).

Ordinary loss treatment also is available for a domestic corporation that owns stock or debt securities in a subsidiary corporation. Because the rules in Sec. 332 regarding nonrecognition of gain or loss do not apply when a subsidiary corporation is insolvent (see page C:6-12), the parent corporation can recognize a loss when the subsidiary corporation's stocks and debt securities are determined to be worthless. This loss is an ordinary loss (instead of a capital loss) if the domestic corporation owns at least 80% of the voting stock and 80% of each class of nonvoting stock, and more than 90% of the liquidating corporation's gross income for all tax years has been other than passive income.[26]

OBTAINING 80% OWNERSHIP TO ACHIEVE SEC. 332 BENEFITS

The 80% stock ownership requirement provides tax planning opportunities when a subsidiary corporation liquidates. A parent corporation seeking nonrecognition under Sec. 332 may acquire additional shares of the subsidiary corporation's stock *before* the adoption of the plan of liquidation. This acquisition helps the parent corporation meet the 80% minimum and avoids gain recognition on the liquidation. If the parent corporation purchases these additional shares of stock from other shareholders to satisfy the 80% minimum *after* adopting the plan of liquidation, Sec. 332 will not apply.[27]

EXAMPLE C:6-25 ▶ Parent Corporation owns 75% of Subsidiary Corporation's single class of stock. On March 12, Parent purchases for cash the remaining 25% of the Subsidiary stock from three individual shareholders pursuant to a tender offer. Parent and Subsidiary adopt a plan of liquidation on October 1, and Subsidiary distributes its assets to Parent on December 1 in exchange for all of Subsidiary's outstanding stock. Parent recognizes no gain or loss on the liquidation of Subsidiary because all the Sec. 332 requirements had been satisfied prior to adoption of the plan of liquidation. ◀

Alternatively, the parent corporation might cause the subsidiary corporation to redeem some of its shares held by minority shareholders before the plan of liquidation is adopted. The IRS originally held that the intention to liquidate is present once the subsidiary corporation agrees to redeem the shares of the minority shareholders. Thus, redemption of a 25% minority interest did not permit Sec. 332 to be used even though the parent corporation owned 100% of the outstanding stock after the redemption.[28]

In *George L. Riggs, Inc.,* however, the Tax Court held that a parent corporation's tender offer to minority shareholders and the calling of the subsidiary's preferred stock do not invalidate the Sec. 332 liquidation because "the formation of a conditional intention to liquidate in the future is not the adoption of a plan of liquidation."[29] The IRS has acquiesced to the *Riggs* decision.

[26] Sec. 165(g)(3).

[27] Rev. Rul. 75-521, 1975-2 C.B. 120.

[28] Rev. Rul. 70-106, 1970-1 C.B. 70.

[29] *George L. Riggs, Inc.,* 64 T.C. 474 (1975), *acq.* 1976-2 C.B. 2.

Thus, careful planning can help both the parent corporation and subsidiary corporation avoid gain recognition under Secs. 332 and 337. Nonrecognition, however, does not extend to minority shareholders as discussed earlier.

EXAMPLE C:6-26 ▶ Parent Corporation owns 80% of Subsidiary Corporation's stock. Anthony owns the remaining 20% of Subsidiary stock. Parent and Anthony have adjusted bases of $200,000 and $60,000, respectively, for their Subsidiary stock. Subsidiary distributes land having a $250,000 adjusted basis and a $400,000 FMV to Parent and $100,000 in cash to Anthony. Subsidiary recognizes no gain or loss on the distribution of the land or the cash. Parent recognizes no gain on the liquidation and takes a $250,000 basis for the land. Anthony recognizes a $40,000 ($100,000 − $60,000) capital gain on the receipt of the money. Alternatively, distribution of the land and cash ratably to Parent and Anthony would require Subsidiary to recognize as gain the appreciation on the portion of land distributed to Anthony. ◀

ADDITIONAL COMMENT

The parent corporation, however, would not acquire the subsidiary's tax attributes if a taxable liquidation occurs.

AVOIDING SEC. 332 TO RECOGNIZE LOSSES

A parent corporation may want to avoid the Sec. 332 nonrecognition rules to recognize a loss when a solvent subsidiary corporation liquidates. Because the stock ownership requirement must be met during the entire liquidation process, the parent corporation apparently can sell some of its stock in the subsidiary corporation to reduce its stock ownership below the 80% level at any time during the liquidation process and be able to recognize the loss.[30] Such a sale permits the parent corporation to recognize a capital loss when it surrenders its stock interest in the subsidiary corporation. The parent corporation may desire this capital loss if it has offsetting capital gains.

The sale of a portion of the subsidiary's stock after the plan of liquidation is adopted prevents Sec. 332 from applying to the parent corporation. The Sec. 337 rules, which prevent the subsidiary corporation from recognizing gain or loss when making a liquidating distribution to an 80% distributee, also do not apply because nonrecognition is contingent on Sec. 332 applying to the distributee. Thus, the subsidiary corporation also can recognize a loss when it distributes property that has declined in value.

COMPLIANCE AND PROCEDURAL CONSIDERATIONS

OBJECTIVE 7

Comply with procedural rules for corporate liquidations

GENERAL LIQUIDATION PROCEDURES

Section 6043(a) requires a liquidating corporation to file Form 966 (Corporate Dissolution or Liquidation) within 30 days after the adoption of any resolution or plan calling for the liquidation or dissolution of the corporation. The liquidating corporation files this form with the District Director of the IRS for the district in which it files its income tax return. Any amendment or supplement to the resolution or plan must be filed on an additional Form 966 within 30 days of making the amendment or supplement. The liquidating corporation must file Form 966 whether the shareholders' realized gain is recognized or not. The information included with Form 966 is described in Reg. Sec. 1.6043-1(b).

Regulation Sec. 1.6043-2(a) requires every corporation that makes a distribution of $600 or more during a calendar year to any shareholder in liquidation of part or all of its capital stock to file Form 1099-DIV (Dividends and Distributions). A separate Form 1099-DIV is required for each shareholder. The information that must be included with the Form 1099-DIV is described in Reg. Secs. 1.6043-2(a) and (b).

Regulation Sec. 1.6012-2(a)(2) requires a corporation that exists for part of a year to file a corporate tax return for the portion of the tax year that it existed. A corporation that ceases business and dissolves, while retaining no assets, is not considered to be in existence for federal tax purposes even though under state law it may be considered for certain purposes to be continuing its affairs (e.g., for purposes of suing or being sued).

[30] *CIR v. Day & Zimmerman, Inc.*, 34 AFTR 343, 45-2 USTC ¶9403 (3rd Cir., 1945).

ADDITIONAL COMMENT

As evidenced in this chapter, the compliance and procedural requirements of complete liquidations are formidable. Any taxpayer contemplating this type of corporate transactions should consult competent tax and legal advisors to ensure that the technical requirements of the proposed transaction are satisfied.

SECTION 332 LIQUIDATIONS

Regulation Sec. 1.332-6 requires every corporation receiving distributions in a Sec. 332 complete liquidation to maintain permanent records. A complete statement of all facts pertinent to the nonrecognition of gain or loss must be included in the corporate distributee's return for the tax year in which it receives a liquidating distribution. This statement includes the following: a certified copy of the plan of liquidation, a list of all property received upon the distribution, a statement of any indebtedness of the liquidating corporation to the recipient corporation, and a statement of stock ownership.

Treasury Regulations require a special waiver of the general three-year statute of limitations when the liquidation covers more than one tax year.[31] The distributee corporation must file a waiver of the limitations period on assessment for each of its tax years that falls partially or wholly within the liquidation period. The distributee corporation files this waiver at the time it files its income tax return. This waiver must extend the assessment period to a date at least one year after the last date of the period for assessment of such taxes for the last tax year in which the liquidation may be completed under Sec. 332.

PLAN OF LIQUIDATION

A **plan of liquidation** is a written document detailing the steps to be undertaken while carrying out the complete liquidation of the corporation. Although a formal plan of liquidation is not required, it may assist the corporation in determining when it enters a liquidation status and, therefore, when distributions to the shareholders qualify for exchange treatment under Sec. 331 (instead of possibly being treated as a dividend under Sec. 301). The adoption of a formal plan of liquidation can provide the liquidating corporation or its shareholders additional benefits under the tax laws. For example, the adoption of a plan of liquidation permits a parent corporation to have a three-year time period (instead of one tax year) to carry out the complete liquidation of a subsidiary corporation.

PROBLEM MATERIALS

DISCUSSION QUESTIONS

C:6-1 What is a complete liquidation? A partial liquidation? Explain the difference in the tax treatment accorded these two different events.

C:6-2 Summitt Corporation has manufactured and distributed basketball equipment for 20 years. Its owners would like to avoid the corporate income tax and are considering becoming a limited liability company (LLC). What tax savings may result from electing to be treated as an LLC? What federal tax costs will be incurred to make the change from a C corporation to an LLC? Would the same transaction costs be incurred if instead the corporation made an S election? Would the transaction costs be incurred had LLC status been adopted when the entity was initially organized?

C:6-3 Explain why tax advisors caution people who are starting a new business that the tax costs of incorporating a business may be low while the tax costs of liquidating a business may be high.

C:6-4 Explain the following statement: A corporation may be liquidated for tax purposes even though dissolution has not occurred under state corporation law.

C:6-5 Compare the tax consequences to the shareholder and the distributing corporation of the following three kinds of corporate distributions: ordinary dividends, stock redemptions, and complete liquidations.

C:6-6 What event or occurrence determines when a cash or accrual method of accounting taxpayer reports a liquidating distribution?

C:6-7 Explain why a shareholder receiving a liquidating distribution would prefer to receive either capital gain treatment or ordinary loss treatment.

C:6-8 A liquidating corporation could either (1) sell its assets and then distribute remaining cash to its shareholders or (2) distribute its assets directly to

[31] Reg. Sec. 1.332-4(a)(2).

the shareholders who then sell the distributed assets. Do the tax consequences of these alternatives differ?

C:6-9 Explain the circumstances in which a liquidating corporation does not recognize gain and/or loss when making a liquidating distribution.

C:6-10 Kelly Corporation makes a liquidating distribution. Among other property, it distributes land subject to a mortgage. The mortgage amount exceeds both the adjusted basis and FMV for the land. Explain to Kelly Corporation's president how the amount of its recognized gain or loss on the distribution and the shareholder's basis for the land are determined.

C:6-11 Explain the congressional intent behind the enactment of the Sec. 332 rules regarding the liquidation of a subsidiary corporation.

C:6-12 What requirements must be satisfied for the Sec. 332 rules to apply to a corporate shareholder?

C:6-13 Compare the general liquidation rules with the Sec. 332 rules for liquidation of a subsidiary corporation with respect to the following items:

a. Recognition of gain or loss by the distributee corporation
b. Recognition of gain or loss by the liquidating corporation
c. Basis of assets in the distributee corporation's hands
d. Treatment of the liquidating corporation's tax attributes

C:6-14 Parent Corporation owns 80% of the stock of Subsidiary Corporation, which is insolvent. Tracy owns the remaining 20% of the stock. The courts determine Subsidiary to be bankrupt. The shareholders receive nothing for their investment. How do they report their losses for tax purposes?

C:6-15 Parent Corporation owns all the stock of Subsidiary Corporation and a substantial amount of Subsidiary Corporation bonds. Subsidiary proposes to transfer appreciated property to Parent in redemption of its bonds pursuant to the liquidation of Subsidiary. Explain the tax consequences of the redemption of the stock and bonds to Parent and Subsidiary.

C:6-16 Explain the differences in the tax rules applying to distributions made to the parent corporation and a minority shareholder when a controlled subsidiary corporation liquidates.

C:6-17 Parent Corporation owns 80% of Subsidiary Corporation's stock. Sally owns the remaining 20% of the Subsidiary stock. Subsidiary plans to distribute cash and appreciated property pursuant to its liquidation. It has more than enough cash to redeem all of Sally's stock. What strategy for distributing the cash and appreciated property would minimize the gain recognized by Subsidiary on the distribution? Does the substitution of appreciated property for cash change the tax consequences of the liquidating distribution for Sally?

C:6-18 Parent Corporation owns 70% of Subsidiary Corporation's stock. The FMV of Subsidiary's assets is significantly greater than their basis to Subsidiary. The FMV of Parent's interest in the assets also substantially exceeds Parent's basis for the Subsidiary stock. Also, Parent's basis in its Subsidiary stock exceeds Subsidiary's basis in its assets. On January 30, Parent acquired an additional 15% of Subsidiary stock from one of Subsidiary's shareholders who owns none of the Parent stock. Subsidiary adopts a plan of liquidation on March 12. The liquidation is completed before year-end. What advantages accrue to Parent with respect to the liquidation by acquiring the additional Subsidiary stock?

C:6-19 Texas Corporation liquidates through a series of distributions to its shareholders after a plan of liquidation has been adopted. How are these distributions taxed?

C:6-20 Able Corporation adopts a plan of liquidation. Under the plan, Robert, who owns 60% of the Able stock, is to receive 2,000 acres of land in an area where a number of producing oil wells have been drilled. No wells have been drilled on Able's land. Discussions with two appraisers have produced widely differing market values for the land, both of which are above Able's basis for the land and Robert's basis for the Able stock. Explain the alternatives available to Able and Robert for reporting the liquidating distribution.

C:6-21 Explain the IRS's position regarding whether a liquidation transaction will be considered open or closed.

C:6-22 For a corporation that intends to liquidate, explain the tax advantages to the shareholders of having the corporation (1) adopt a plan of liquidation, (2) sell its assets in an installment sale, and then (3) distribute the installment obligations to its shareholders.

C:6-23 Cable Corporation is 60% owned by Anna and 40% owned by Jim, who are unrelated. It has noncash assets, which it sells to an unrelated purchaser for $100,000 in cash and $900,000 in installment obligations due 50% in the current year and 50% in the following year. Cable will distribute its remaining cash, after payment of the federal income taxes on the sale and other corporate obligations, to Jim and Anna along with the installment obligations. Explain to the two shareholders the alternatives for reporting the gain realized on their receipt of the installment obligations.

C:6-24 Describe the tax treatment accorded the following expenses associated with a liquidation:

a. Commissions paid on the sale of the liquidating corporation's assets
b. Accounting fees paid to prepare the corporation's final income tax return
c. Unamortized organizational expenditures
d. Prepaid rent for office space occupied by one of the shareholders following the liquidation (Assume the prepaid rent was deducted in the preceding year's corporate tax return.)

C:6-25 Yancy owns 70% of Andover Corporation stock. At the beginning of the current year, the corporation has $400,000 of NOLs. Yancy plans to liquidate the corporation and have it distribute assets having a $600,000 FMV and a $350,000 adjusted basis to its shareholders. Explain to Yancy the tax consequences of the liquidation to Andover Corporation.

C:6-26 Nils Corporation, a calendar year taxpayer, adopts a plan of liquidation on April 1 of the current year. The final liquidating distribution occurs on January 5 of next year. Must Nils Corporation file a tax return for the current year? For next year?

C:6-27 What is a plan of liquidation? Why is it advisable for a corporation to adopt a formal plan of liquidation?

C:6-28 Indicate whether each of the following statements about a liquidation is true or false. If the statement is false, explain why.

a. Liabilities assumed by a shareholder when a corporation liquidates reduce the amount realized by the shareholder on the surrender of his or her stock.
b. The loss recognized by a shareholder on a liquidation generally is characterized as an ordinary loss.
c. A shareholder's basis for property received in a liquidation is the same as the property's basis in the liquidating corporation's hands.
d. The holding period for property received in a liquidation includes the period of time it is held by the liquidating corporation.
e. The tax attributes of a liquidating corporation are assumed ratably by its shareholders.
f. A parent corporation can elect to recognize gain or loss when it liquidates a controlled subsidiary corporation.
g. A liquidating subsidiary recognizes no gain or loss when it distributes its property to its parent corporation.
h. A parent corporation's basis for the assets received in a liquidation where gain is not recognized remains the same as it was to the liquidating subsidiary corporation.

ISSUE IDENTIFICATION QUESTIONS

C:6-29 Cable Corporation, which operates a fleet of motorized trolley cars in a resort city, is undergoing a complete liquidation. John, who owns 80% of the Cable stock, plans to continue the business in another city, and will receive the cable cars, two support vehicles, the repair parts inventory, and other tools and equipment. Peter, who owns the remaining 20% of the Cable stock, will receive a cash distribution. The corporation will incur $15,000 of liquidation expenses to break its lease on its office and garage space and cancel other contracts. What tax issues should Cable, John, and Peter consider with respect to the liquidation?

C:6-30 Parent Corporation, which operates an electric utility, created a 100%-owned corporation, Subsidiary, that built and managed an office building. Assume the two corporations have filed separate tax returns for a number of years. The utility occupied two floors of the office building, and Subsidiary offered the other ten floors for lease. Only 25% of the total rental space was leased because of the high crime rate in the area surrounding the building. Rental income was insufficient to cover the mortgage payments, and Subsidiary filed for bankruptcy because of the poor prospects. Subsidiary's assets were taken over by the mortgage lender. Parent lost its entire $500,000 investment. Another $100,000 of debts remained unpaid for the general creditors, which included a $35,000 account payable to Parent, at the time Subsidiary was liquidated. What tax issues should Parent and Subsidiary consider with respect to the bankruptcy and liquidation of Subsidiary?

C:6-31 Alpha Corporation is a holding company owned equally by Harry and Rita. They acquired the Alpha stock many years ago when the corporation was formed. Alpha has its money invested almost entirely in stocks, bonds, rental real estate, and land. Market quotations are available for all of its stock and bond investments except for 10,000 shares of Mayfair Manufacturing Corporation stock. Mayfair is privately held with 40 individuals owning all 100,000 outstanding shares. Last year, Mayfair reported slightly more than $3 million in net income. In a discussion with Harry and Rita, you find that they plan to liquidate Alpha Corporation in the next six months to avoid the personal holding company tax. What tax issues should Harry and Rita consider with respect to this pending liquidation?

PROBLEMS

C:6-32 *Shareholder Gain or Loss Calculation.* For seven years, Monaco Corporation has been owned entirely by Stacy and Monique, who are husband and wife. Stacy and Monique have a $165,000 basis in their jointly owned Monaco stock. The Monaco stock is Sec. 1244 stock. They receive the following assets in liquidation of their corporation: accounts receivable, $25,000 FMV; a car, $16,000 FMV; office furniture, $6,000 FMV; and $5,000 cash.

a. What are the amount and character of their gain or loss?
b. How would your answer change if the accounts receivable instead had a $140,000 FMV?
c. What is the Monaco's basis for each property received in the liquidation in Parts a and b?

C:6-33 *Shareholder Gain or Loss Calculation.* For three years, Diamond Corporation has been owned equally by Arlene and Billy. Arlene and Billy have $40,000 and $20,000 adjusted bases, respectively, in their Diamond stock. Arlene receives a $30,000 cash liquidating distribution in exchange for her Diamond stock. Billy receives as a liquidating distribution a parcel of land having a $70,000 FMV and subject to a $45,000 mortgage, which he assumes, and $5,000 of cash in exchange for his Diamond stock.

a. What are the amount and character of each shareholder's gain or loss?
b. What is each shareholder's basis for the property received in the liquidation?

C:6-34 *Timing of Gain/Loss Recognition.* Peter owns 25% of Crosstown Corporation stock in which he has a $200,000 adjusted basis. In each of the following situations, what amount of gain/loss will Peter report in the current year? In the next year?

a. Peter is a cash method of accounting taxpayer. Crosstown determines on December 24 of the current year that it will make a $260,000 liquidating distribution to Peter. Crosstown pays the liquidating distribution on January 3 of the next year.
b. Assume the same facts as in Part a except that Peter is an accrual method of accounting taxpayer.

C:6-35 *Corporate Formation/Corporate Liquidation.* Len Wallace contributed assets with a $100,000 adjusted basis and a $400,000 FMV to Ace Corporation in exchange for all of its single class of stock. The corporation conducted operations for five years and was liquidated. Len received a liquidating distribution of $500,000 cash (less federal income taxes owed on the liquidation by the corporation) and the assets that he had contributed, which now have a $100,000 adjusted basis and a $500,000 FMV. Assume a 34% corporate tax rate.

a. What are the tax consequences of the corporate formation transaction?
b. What are the tax consequences of the corporate liquidation transaction?
c. Would your answers to Parts a and b remain the same if instead the assets had been contributed by Wallace Corporation to Ace Corporation? If not, explain how your answer(s) would change?

C:6-36 *Gain or Loss on Making a Liquidating Distribution.* What are the amount and character of the gain or loss recognized by the distributing corporation when making liquidating distributions in the following situations? What is the shareholder's basis for the property received? In any situation where a loss is disallowed, indicate what changes would be necessary to improve the tax consequences of the transaction.

a. Best Corporation distributes land having a $200,000 FMV and a $90,000 adjusted basis to Tanya, its sole shareholder. The land, a capital asset, is subject to a $40,000 mortgage, which Tanya assumes.
b. Wilkins Corporation distributes depreciable property to its two equal shareholders. Robert receives a milling machine having a $50,000 adjusted basis and a $75,000 FMV. The corporation claimed $30,000 depreciation on the machine. The corporation purchased the milling machine from an unrelated seller four years ago. Sharon receives an automobile that originally cost $40,000 two years earlier and has a $26,000 FMV. The corporation claimed $25,000 depreciation on the automobile.
c. Jordan Corporation distributes marketable securities having a $100,000 FMV and a $175,000 adjusted basis to Brad, a 66.67% shareholder. Jordan purchased the marketable securities three years ago. Jordan distributes $50,000 cash to Ann, a 33.33% shareholder.
d. Assume the same facts as in Part c except the securities and cash are instead each distributed two-thirds to Brad and one-third to Ann.

C:6-37 *Gain or Loss Recognition by a Distributing Corporation.* Melon Corporation, which is owned equally by four individual shareholders, adopts a plan of liquidation for distributing the following property:

- Land (a capital asset) having a $30,000 FMV and a $12,000 adjusted basis.
- Depreciable personal property having a $15,000 FMV and a $9,000 adjusted basis. Melon has claimed depreciation of $10,000 on the property during the three years since its acquisition.
- Installment obligations having a $30,000 FMV and face amount and a $21,000 adjusted basis, acquired when Melon sold a Sec. 1231 property.
- Supplies that cost $6,000 and were expensed in the preceding tax year. The supplies have a $7,500 FMV.
- Marketable securities having a $15,000 FMV and an $18,000 adjusted basis. Melon purchased the marketable securities from a broker 12 months ago.

a. Which property, when distributed by Melon Corporation to one of its shareholders, will require the distributing corporation to recognize gain or loss?
b. How will your answer to Part a change if the distribution instead is made to Melon's parent corporation as part of a complete liquidation meeting the Sec. 332 requirements?
c. How will your answer to Part b change if the distribution instead is made to a minority shareholder?

C:6-38 *Distribution of Property Subject to a Mortgage.* Titan Corporation adopts a plan of liquidation. It distributes an apartment building having a $3 million FMV and a $1.8 million adjusted basis, and land having a $1 million FMV and a $600,000 adjusted basis, to MNO Partnership in exchange for all the outstanding Titan stock. MNO Partnership has an $800,000 basis in its Titan stock. Titan has claimed $600,000 of MACRS depreciation on the building. MNO Partnership agrees to assume the $3 million mortgage on the land and building. All of Titan's assets other than the building and land are used to pay its federal income tax liability.
a. What are the amount and character of Titan's recognized gain or loss on the distribution?
b. What are the amount and character of MNO Partnership's gain or loss on the liquidation? What is its basis for the land and building?
c. How would your answer to Parts a and b change if the mortgage instead was $4.5 million?

C:6-39 *Sale of Loss Property by a Liquidating Corporation.* In March of Year 2, Mike contributed the following two properties, which he acquired in February of Year 1, to Kansas Corporation in exchange for additional Kansas stock: (1) land having a $50,000 FMV and a $75,000 basis and (2) another property having an $85,000 FMV and a $70,000 adjusted basis. Kansas' employees use the land as a parking lot until Kansas sells it in March of Year 3 for $45,000. One month after the sale, in April of Year 3, Kansas adopts a plan of liquidation.
a. What is Kansas' adjusted basis in the land immediately after its contribution in March of Year 2?
b. What is Kansas' recognized gain or loss on the subsequent land sale?
c. How would your answer to Part b change if the land were not used in Kansas' trade or business?
d. How would your answer to Part c change if Mike contributed the land and other property in March of Year 1 instead of March of Year 2?
e. How would your answer to Part c change if the corporation sold the land (contributed in March of Year 2) for $80,000 instead of $45,000?

C:6-40 *Tax Consequences of a Corporate Liquidation.* Marsha owns 100% of Gamma Corporation's common stock. Gamma is an accrual basis, calendar year corporation. Marsha formed the corporation six years ago by transferring $250,000 of cash in exchange for the Gamma stock. Thus, she has held the stock for six years and has a $250,000 adjusted basis in the stock. Gamma's balance sheet at January 1 of the current year is as follows:

Assets	*Basis*	*FMV*
Cash	$ 400,000	$ 400,000
Marketable securities	50,000	125,000
Inventory	300,000	350,000
Equipment	200,000	275,000
Building	500,000	750,000
Total	$1,450,000	$1,900,000

Liabilities and Equity		
Accounts payable	$ 175,000	$ 175,000
Common stock	250,000	1,725,000
Retained earnings (and E&P)	1,025,000	
Total	$1,450,000	$1,900,000

Gamma has held the marketable securities for two years. In addition, Gamma has claimed $60,000 of MACRS depreciation on the machinery and $90,000 of straight-line depreciation on the building. On January 2 of the current year, Gamma liquidates and distributes all property to Marsha except that Gamma retains cash to pay the accounts payable and any tax liability resulting from Gamma's liquidation. Assume that Gamma has no other taxable income or loss. Determine the tax consequences to Gamma and Marsha. Assume a 34% corporate tax rate.

C:6-41 ***Sale of Assets Followed by a Corporation Liquidation.*** Assume the same facts as in Problem C:6-40 except, on January 2 of the current year, Gamma Corporation sells all property other than cash to Acquiring Corporation for FMV. Gamma pays off the accounts payable and retains cash to pay any tax liability resulting from Gamma's liquidation. Gamma then liquidates and distributes all remaining cash to Marsha. Assume that Gamma has no other taxable income or loss. Determine the tax consequence to Gamma, Acquiring, and Marsha. How do these results compare to those in Problem C:6-40?

C:6-42 ***Tax Consequences of a Corporate Liquidation.*** Pamela owns 100% of Sigma Corporation's stock. She purchased her stock ten years ago, and her current basis for the stock is $300,000. On June 10, Pamela decided to liquidate Sigma. Sigma's balance sheet prior to the sale of the assets, payment of the liquidation expenses, and payment of federal income taxes is as follows:

Assets	*Basis*	*FMV*
Cash	$240,000	$ 240,000
Marketable securities	90,000	80,000
Equipment	150,000	200,000
Land	320,000	680,000
Total	$800,000	$1,200,000
Equity		
Common stock	$300,000	$1,200,000
Retained earnings (and E&P)	500,000	
Total	$800,000	$1,200,000

- The corporation has claimed depreciation of $150,000 on the equipment.
- The corporation received the marketable securities as a capital contribution from Pamela three years earlier at a time when their adjusted basis was $90,000 and their FMV was $70,000.
- Sigma incurred $20,000 in liquidation expenses in its final tax year.

a. What are the tax consequences of the liquidation to Pamela and Sigma Corporation? Assume a 34% corporate tax rate.
b. How would your answer change if Pamela contributed the marketable securities six years ago?

C:6-43 ***Liquidation of a Subsidiary Corporation.*** Parent Corporation owns 100% of Subsidiary Corporation's stock. The adjusted basis of its stock investment is $175,000. A plan of liquidation is adopted, and Subsidiary distributes to Parent assets having a $400,000 FMV and a $300,000 adjusted basis (to Subsidiary), and liabilities in the amount of $60,000. Subsidiary has a $150,000 E&P balance.

a. What are the amount and character of Subsidiary's recognized gain or loss on the distribution?
b. What are the amount and character of Parent's recognized gain or loss on the surrender of the Subsidiary stock?
c. What basis does Parent take in the assets?
d. What happens to Parent's basis in the Subsidiary stock and to Subsidiary's tax attributes?

C:6-44 *Liquidation of a Subsidiary Corporation.* Parent Corporation owns 100% of Subsidiary Corporation's single class of stock. Its adjusted basis for the stock is $175,000. After adopting a plan of liquidation, Subsidiary distributes the following property to Parent: money, $20,000; LIFO inventory, $200,000 FMV; and equipment, $150,000 FMV. The inventory has a $125,000 adjusted basis. The equipment originally cost $280,000. Subsidiary has claimed depreciation of $160,000 on the equipment. Subsidiary has a $150,000 E&P balance and a $40,000 NOL carryover on the liquidation date.

a. What are the amount and character of Subsidiary's recognized gain or loss when it makes the liquidating distributions?
b. What are the amount and character of Parent's recognized gain or loss on its surrender of the Subsidiary stock?
c. What is Parent's basis in each noncash property?
d. What happens to Subsidiary's E&P balance and NOL carryover following the liquidation?
e. What happens to Parent's $175,000 basis in the Subsidiary stock?

C:6-45 *Liquidation of a Subsidiary Corporation.* Parent Corporation owns 100% of Subsidiary Corporation's single class of stock and $2 million of Subsidiary debentures. Parent purchased the debentures in small blocks from various unrelated parties at a $100,000 discount from their face amount. Parent has a $1.3 million basis in the Subsidiary stock. Subsidiary adopts a plan of liquidation whereby it distributes property having a $4 million FMV and a $2.4 million adjusted basis in redemption of the Subsidiary stock. The debentures are redeemed for Subsidiary property having a $2 million FMV and a $2.2 million adjusted basis.

a. What income or gain does Subsidiary recognize as a result of making the liquidating distributions?
b. What gain or loss does Parent recognize on the surrender of the Subsidiary stock? The Subsidiary debentures?
c. What is Parent's basis for the property received from Subsidiary?

C:6-46 *Comparison of Liquidations.* Shareholder owns 100% of Lambda Corporation stock and has a $700,000 basis in that stock. Shareholder has owned the stock for several years. Prior to liquidating, Lambda had the following balance sheet:

Assets	*Basis*	*FMV*
Cash	$200,000	$ 200,000
Property	600,000	1,000,000
Total	$800,000	$1,200,000
Equity		
Common stock	$700,000	$1,200,000
Retained earnings (and E&P)	100,000	
Total	$800,000	$1,200,000

For Parts a and b below, determine the following results for the liquidating corporation (Lambda): Gain realized, gain recognized, corporate tax, and disposition of E&P. For Shareholder, determine the following results: Total distribution, gain realized, gain recognized, and basis of noncash property received. Assume a 34% corporate tax rate and that the liquidating corporation pays any necessary taxes resulting from the liquidation. Also, assume no other transactions for the year of liquidation.

a. Shareholder is an individual.
b. Shareholder is a parent corporation of Lambda.

C:6-47 *Liquidation of an Insolvent Subsidiary.* Subsidiary Corporation is a wholly owned subsidiary of Parent Corporation. The two corporations have the following balance sheets:

Assets	*Parent*	*Subsidiary*
General assets	$1,500,000	$ 750,000
Investment in Subsidiary stock	200,000	
Note receivable from Subsidiary	1,000,000	
Total	$2,700,000	$ 750,000

Liabilities & Equity		
General liabilities	$1,500,000	$ 150,000
Note payable to Parent		1,000,000
Common Stock	300,000	200,000
Retained earnings (deficit)	900,000	(600,000)
Total	$2,700,000	$ 750,000

Other Facts:

- Parent's basis in its Subsidiary stock is $200,000, which corresponds to the $200,000 common stock on Subsidiary's balance sheet.
- The $1 million note payable on Subsidiary's balance sheet is payable to Parent and corresponds to the note receivable on Parent's balance sheet.
- The corporations do not file consolidated tax returns.
- Subsidiary has $600,000 of net operating loss (NOL) carryovers.
- The FMV and adjusted basis of Subsidiary's assets are the same amount.
- Just prior to the liquidation, Subsidiary uses $150,000 of its assets to pay off its general liabilities.
- Subsidiary transfers all its assets and liabilities to Parent upon a complete liquidation.

Determine the tax consequences to Parent and Subsidiary upon Subsidiary's liquidation.

C:6-48 ***Liquidation of a Subsidiary Corporation.*** Majority Corporation owns 90% of Subsidiary Corporation's stock and has a $45,000 basis in that stock. Mindy owns the other 10% and has a $5,000 basis in her stock. Subsidiary holds $20,000 cash and other assets having a $110,000 FMV and a $40,000 adjusted basis. Pursuant to a plan of liquidation, Subsidiary (1) distributes to Mindy assets having an $11,000 FMV and a $4,000 adjusted basis prior to the liquidation, (2) distributes to Majority assets having a $99,000 FMV and a $36,000 adjusted basis prior to the liquidation, and (3) distributes ratably to the two shareholders any cash remaining after taxes. Assume a 34% corporate tax rate and a 15% capital gains tax rate.

a. What are the tax consequences of the liquidation to Majority Corporation, Subsidiary Corporation, and Mindy?

b. Can you recommend a different distribution of assets that will produce better tax results than in Part a?

C:6-49 ***Tax Consequences of a Corporate Liquidation.*** Gabriel Corporation is owned 90% by Zeier Corporation and 10% by Ray Goff, a Gabriel employee. A preliquidation balance sheet for Gabriel is presented below:

Assets	*Basis*	*FMV*
Cash	$ 100,000	$ 100,000
Inventory	420,000	700,000
Equipment	80,000	100,000
Land	400,000	300,000
Total	$1,000,000	$1,200,000
Liabilities & Equity		
Accounts payable	$ 100,000	$ 100,000
Bonds payable to Zeier	500,000	500,000
Common stock	100,000	600,000
Retained earnings (and E&P)	300,000	
Total	$1,000,000	$1,200,000

Gabriel has claimed $150,000 of MACRS depreciation on the equipment. Gabriel purchased the land three years ago as a potential plant site. Plans to build the plant never were consummated, and Gabriel has held the land since then as an investment. Zeier and Ray Goff have $90,000 and $10,000 bases, respectively, in their Gabriel stock. Both shareholders have held their stock since the corporation's inception ten years ago.

Gabriel adopts a plan of liquidation. Gabriel transfers $500,000 of inventory to Zeier to retire the bonds. The shareholders receive their share of Gabriel's remaining assets and assume their share of Gabriel's liabilities (other than federal income taxes). Gabriel pays federal income taxes owed on the liquidation. Assume a 34% corporate tax rate. What are the tax consequences of the liquidation to Ray Goff, Zeier Corporation, and Gabriel Corporation?

C:6-50 *Tax Consequences of a Corporate Liquidation.* Art owns 80% of Pueblo Corporation stock, and Peggy owns the remaining 20%. Art and Peggy have $320,000 and $80,000 adjusted bases, respectively, for their Pueblo stock. Pueblo owns the following assets: cash, $25,000; inventory, $150,000 FMV and $100,000 adjusted basis; marketable securities, $100,000 FMV and $125,000 adjusted basis; and equipment, $325,000 FMV and $185,000 adjusted basis. Pueblo purchased the equipment four years ago and subsequently claimed $215,000 of MACRS depreciation. The securities are not disqualified property. On July 1 of the current year, Pueblo adopts a plan of liquidation at a time when it has $250,000 of E&P and no liabilities. Pueblo distributes the equipment, $50,000 of inventory, the marketable securities, and $5,000 of money to Art before year-end as a liquidating distribution. Pueblo also distributes $20,000 of cash and $100,000 of inventory to Peggy before year-end as a liquidating distribution.

a. What are the gain and loss tax consequences of the liquidation to Pueblo Corporation and to Art and Peggy?

b. Can you offer any suggestions to Pueblo's management that could improve the tax consequences of the liquidation? Explain.

c. How would your answers to Parts a and b change if Art and Peggy instead were domestic corporations rather than individuals?

C:6-51 *Tax Attribute Carryovers.* Bell Corporation is 100% owned by George, who has a $400,000 basis in his Bell stock. Bell's operations have been unprofitable in recent years, and it has incurred small NOLs. Its operating assets currently have a $300,000 FMV and a $500,000 adjusted basis. George is approached by Time Corporation, which wants to purchase Bell's assets for $300,000. Bell expects to have approximately $200,000 in cash after the payment of its liabilities.

a. What are the tax consequences of the transaction if Bell adopts a plan of liquidation, sells the assets, and distributes the cash in redemption of the Bell stock within a 12-month period?

b. What advantages (if any) would accrue to Bell and George if the corporation remains in existence and uses the $200,000 of cash that remains after payment of the liabilities to conduct a new trade or business?

C:6-52 *Series of Liquidating Distributions.* Union Corporation is owned equally by Ron and Steve. Ron and Steve purchased their stock several years ago and have adjusted bases for their Union stock of $15,000 and $27,500, respectively. Each shareholder receives two liquidating distributions. The first liquidating distribution, made in the current year, results in each shareholder receiving a one-half interest in a parcel of land that has a $40,000 FMV and an $18,000 adjusted basis to Union Corporation. The second liquidating distribution, made in the next year, results in each shareholder receiving $20,000 in cash.

a. What are the amount and character of Ron and Steve's recognized gain or loss for the current year? For the next year?

b. What is the basis of the land in Ron and Steve's hands?

c. How would your answers to Parts a and b change if the land has a $12,000 FMV instead of a $40,000 FMV?

C:6-53 *Subsequent Assessment on the Shareholders.* Meridian Corporation originally was owned equally by five individual shareholders. Four years ago, Meridian adopted a plan of liquidation, and each shareholder received a liquidating distribution. Tina, a cash method taxpayer, reported a $30,000 long-term capital gain in the prior liquidation year on the redemption of her stock. Pending the outcome of a lawsuit in which Meridian is one of the defendents, $5,000 of Tina's liquidating distribution was held back and placed in escrow. Settlement of the lawsuit in the current year requires that the escrowed funds plus the interest earned on these funds be paid out to the plaintiff and that each shareholder pay an additional $2,500. Tina pays the amount due in the next year. How does Tina report the settlement of the lawsuit and the payment of the additional amount?

COMPREHENSIVE PROBLEM

C:6-54 The following facts pertain to Lifecycle Corporation:

- Able owns a parcel of land (Land A) having a $30,000 FMV and $16,000 adjusted basis. Baker owns an adjacent parcel of land (Land B) having a $20,000 FMV and $22,000 adjusted basis. On January 2, 2017, Able and Baker contribute their parcels of land to newly formed Lifecycle Corporation in exchange for 60% of the corporation's stock for Able and 40% of the corporation's stock for Baker. The corporation elects a calendar tax year and the accrual method of accounting.
- On January 2, 2017, the corporation borrows $2 million and uses the loan proceeds to build a factory ($1 million), purchase equipment ($500,000), produce inventory ($450,000), pay other operating expenses ($30,000), and retain working cash ($20,000). Assume the corporation sells all inventory produced and collects on all sales immediately so that, at the end of any year, the corporation has no accounts receivable or inventory balances.
- Operating results for 2017 are as follows:

Sales	$964,000	
Cost of goods sold	450,000	
Interest paid on loan	140,000	
Depreciation:		
Equipment	70,000	($25,000 for E&P)
Building	24,000	($24,000 for E&P)
Operating expenses	30,000	

Of these amounts, $250,000 is qualified production activities income. The deduction percentage is 9%.

- In 2018, Lifecycle Corporation invests $10,000 of excess cash in Macro Corporation stock (less than 20% owned) and $20,000 in tax-exempt bonds. In addition, the corporation pays Able a $12,000 salary and distributes an additional $42,000 to Able and $28,000 to Baker. The corporation also makes a $100,000 principal payment on the loan.
- Results for 2018 are as follows:

Sales	$990,000	
Cost of goods sold	500,000	
Interest paid on loan	130,000	
Depreciation:		
Equipment	125,000	($50,000 for E&P)
Building	25,000	($25,000 for E&P)
Operating expenses	40,000	
Salary paid to Able	12,000	
Dividend received on Macro Corporation stock	2,000	
Short-term capital gain on sale of portion of Macro Corporation stock holdings ($4,000 − $3,000)	1,000	
Tax-exempt interest received	1,500	
Charitable contributions	500	

Of these amounts, $158,000 is qualified production activities income. The deduction percentage is 9%.

- In 2019, the corporation did not pay a salary to Able and made no distributions to the shareholders. The corporation, however, made a $30,000 principal payment on the loan.
- Results for 2019 are as follows:

Sales	$500,000
Cost of goods sold	280,000
Interest paid on loan	125,000

Depreciation:		
Equipment	90,000	($50,000 for E&P)
Building	25,000	($25,000 for E&P)
Operating expenses	60,000	
Long-term capital gain on sale of remaining Macro Corporation stock ($9,000 – $7,000)	2,000	
Long-term capital gain on sale of tax-exempt bond ($21,000 – $20,000)	1,000	

Of these amounts, qualified production activities income is zero (because it is negative).

- On January 2, 2020, the corporation receives a refund for the 2019 NOL carried back to 2017. When carrying back the NOL, remember to recalculate the U.S. production activities deduction in the carryback year because of the reduced taxable income resulting from carryback. In addition, the corporation sells its assets, pays taxes on the gain, and pays off the $1.87 million remaining debt.

	Sales Price	*Tax Adj. Basis**	*E&P Adj. Basis*
Equipment	$ 250,000	$ 215,000	$ 375,000
Building	986,000	926,000	926,000
Land A	80,000	16,000	16,000
Land B	50,000	20,000	20,000
Total	$1,366,000	$1,177,000	$1,337,000

*Note: Technically, the equipment should be depreciated for 1/2 year in the year of disposition, and the building should be depreciated for 1/2 month (because of the January disposition). However, for simplicity, the above calculations ignore depreciation deductions in the disposition year, which creates an offsetting overstatement of adjusted basis. Section 362(e)(2) limits Land B basis to the FMV.

Immediately after these transactions, the corporation makes a liquidating distribution of the remaining cash to Able and Baker. The remaining cash is $348,639, which the corporation distributes in proportion to the shareholders' ownership (60% and 40%). Assume that the shareholder's long-term capital gains will be taxed in 2020 at 23.8% (the 20% maximum capital gains rate plus the 3.8% rate on net investment income).

Required:

a. Determine the tax consequences of the corporate formation to Able, Baker, and Lifecycle Corporation.
b. For 2017 through 2019, prepare schedules showing corporate taxable income, taxes, and E&P activity. Assume that Lifecycle pays its taxes in the same year they accrue.
c. For 2020, prepare a schedule showing the results of this year's transactions on Lifecycle Corporation, Able, and Baker.

Note: See Problem C:10-56 for a partnership variation of this problem.

TAX STRATEGY PROBLEMS

C:6-55 Sarah plans to invest $1 million in a business venture that will last five years. She is debating whether to operate the business as a C corporation or a sole proprietorship. If a C corporation, she will liquidate the corporation at the end of the five-year period. She expects the business to generate taxable income as follows:

Year	*Taxable Income*
1	$ 40,000
2	70,000
3	90,000
4	150,000
5	350,000

If incurred in corporate form, these taxable income amounts will be subject to the corporate tax rate schedule. If in proprietorship form, they will be subject to Sarah's 39.6% marginal tax rate because she has income from other sources that puts her in the top individual tax bracket. Any capital gain upon corporate liquidation will be taxed at 23.8% (the 20% maximum capital gain rate plus the 3.8% rate on net investment income). Assume that Sec. 1202 does not apply.

Required: Determine the after-tax amount Sarah will have at the end of five years under each alternative. Which alternative do you recommend?

C:6-56 One way to compare the accumulation of income by alternative business entity forms is to use mathematical models. The following models express the investment after-tax accumulation calculation for a particular entity form:

Flow-through entities and sole proprietorships: Contribution $\times [1 + R(1 - t_p)]^n$
C corporation: Contribution $\times \{[1 + R(1 - t_c)]^n(1 - t_g) + t_g\}$

Where: ATA = after-tax accumulation in n years
R = before-tax rate of return for the business entity
t_p = owner's marginal tax rate on ordinary income
t_c = corporation's marginal tax rate
t_g = owner's tax rate on capital gains
n = number of periods

In the C corporation model, the corporation operates for n years, paying taxes currently and distributing no dividends. At the end of its existence, the corporation liquidates, causing the shareholder to recognize a capital gain. In the flow-through model, the entity or sole proprietorship distributes just enough cash for the owner or owners to pay individual taxes, and the entity reinvests the remaining after-tax earnings in the business. (See Chapter I:18 of the *Individuals* volume for a detailed explanation of these models. The *Comprehensive* volume, however, does not contain Chapter I:18.)

Now consider the following facts. Twelve years ago, your client formed a C corporation with a $100,000 investment (contribution). The corporation's before-tax rate of return (R) has been and will continue to be 10%. The corporate tax rate (t_c) has been and will continue to be 35%. The corporation pays no dividends and reinvests all after-tax earnings in its business. Thus, the corporation's value grows at its after-tax rate of return. Your client's marginal ordinary tax rate (t_p) has been 33%, and her capital gains rate (t_g) has been 15%. Your client expects her ordinary tax rate to drop to 25% at the beginning of this year and stay at that level indefinitely. Her capital gains tax rate will remain at 15%. Assume the corporate stock does not qualify for the Sec. 1202 exclusion.

Your client wants you to consider two alternatives:

1. Continue the business in C corporation form for the next 20 years and liquidate at that time (32 years in total).
2. Liquidate the C corporation at the end of the 12-year period, invest the after-tax proceeds in a sole proprietorship, and operate as a sole proprietorship for the next 20 years.

The sole proprietorship's before-tax rate of return (R) also will be 10% for the next 20 years. Earnings from the sole proprietorship will be taxed currently at your client's ordinary tax rate, and your client will withdraw just enough earnings from the business to pay her taxes on the business's income. The remaining after-tax earnings will remain in the business until the end of the investment horizon (20 years from now).

Required: Show the results of each alternative along with supporting models and calculations. Ignore self employment taxes and the accumulated earnings tax. Which alternative should your client adopt?

Note: See Problem C:11-61 for a third alternative to consider.

CASE STUDY PROBLEMS

C:6-57 Paul, a long-time client of yours, has operated an automobile repair shop (as a C corporation) for most of his life. The shop has been fairly successful in recent years. His children are not interested in continuing the business. Paul is age 62 and has accumulated approximately $500,000 in assets outside of his business, most of which are in his personal residence and retirement plan. A recent balance sheet for the business shows the following amounts:

Assets	*Adjusted Basis*	*FMV*	*Liabilities & Equity*	*Amount*
Cash	$ 25,000	$ 25,000	Accounts payable	$ 30,000
Inventory	60,000	75,000	Mortgage payable	70,000
Equipment	200,000	350,000	Paid-in capital	120,000
Building	100,000	160,000	Retain earnings	205,000
Land	40,000	60,000		
Goodwill	–0–	100,000		
Total	$425,000	$770,000	Total	$425,000

The inventory is accounted for using the first-in, first-out inventory method. The corporation has claimed depreciation of $250,000 on the equipment. The corporation acquired the building 11 years ago and has claimed $25,000 of depreciation under the MACRS rules. The goodwill is an estimate that Paul feels reflects the value of his business over and above the other tangible assets.

Paul has received an offer of $775,000 from a competing automobile repair company for the noncash assets of his business, which will be used to establish a second location for the competing company. The corporation will sell the assets within 60 days and distribute remaining cash to Paul in liquidation of the corporation. The purchaser has obtained the necessary bank financing to make the acquisition. Paul's basis in his stock is $300,000.

Required: Prepare a memorandum for Paul outlining the tax consequences of the sale transaction and liquidation of the corporation.

C:6-58 Your accounting firm has done the audit and tax work for the Peerless family and their business entities for 20 years. Approximately 25% of your accounting and tax practice billings come from Peerless family work. Peerless Real Estate Corporation owns land and a building (MACRS property) having a $4.5 million FMV and a $1.0 million adjusted basis. The corporation owes a $1.3 million mortgage balance on the building. The corporation used substantial leverage to acquire the building so Myron Peerless and his brother Mark Peerless, who are equal shareholders in Peerless Real Estate, each have only $200,000 adjusted bases in their stock. Cash flows are good from the building, and only a small portion of the annual profits is needed for reinvestment in the building. Myron and Mark have decided to liquidate the corporation to avoid the federal and state corporate income taxes and continue to operate the business as a partnership. They want the MM Partnership, which has Mark and Myron equally sharing profits, losses, and liabilities, to purchase the building from the corporation for $400,000 cash plus their assumption of the $1.3 million mortgage. Mark knows a real estate appraiser who, for the right price, will provide a $1.7 million appraisal. Current corporate cash balances are sufficient to pay any federal and state income taxes owed on the sale of the building. Mark and Myron each would receive $200,000 from the corporation in cancellation of their stock.

Required: Prepare notes on the points you will want to cover with Myron and Mark Peerless about the corporate liquidation and the Peerless' desire to avoid federal and state corporate income taxes at your meeting tomorrow.

TAX RESEARCH PROBLEMS

C:6-59 Parent Corporation owns 85% of the common stock and 100% of the preferred stock of Subsidiary Corporation. The common stock and preferred stock have adjusted bases of $500,000 and $200,000, respectively, to Parent. Subsidiary adopts a plan of liquidation on July 3 of the current year, when its assets have a $1 million FMV. Liabilities on that date amount to $850,000. On November 9, Subsidiary pays off its creditors and distributes $150,000 to Parent with respect to its preferred stock. No cash remains to be paid to Parent with respect to the remaining $50,000 of its liquidation preference for the preferred stock, or with respect to any of the common stock. In each of Subsidiary's tax years, less than 10% of its gross income has been passive income. What are the amount and character of Parent's loss on the preferred stock? The common stock?

A partial list of research sources is

- IRC Secs. 165(g)(3) and 332(a)
- Reg. Sec. 1.332-2(b)
- *Spaulding Bakeries, Inc.*, 27 T.C. 684 (1957)
- *H. K. Porter Co., Inc.*, 87 T.C. 689 (1986)

C:6-60 Parent Corporation has owned 60% of Subsidiary Corporation's single class of stock for a number of years. Tyrone owns the remaining 40% of the Subsidiary stock. On August 10 of the current year, Parent purchases Tyrone's Subsidiary stock for cash. On September 15, Subsidiary adopts a plan of liquidation. Subsidiary then makes a single liquidating distribution on October 1. The activities of Subsidiary continue as a separate division of Parent. Does the liquidation of Subsidiary qualify for nonrecognition treatment under Secs. 332 and 337? Must Parent assume Subsidiary's E&P balance?

A partial list of research sources is

- IRC Secs. 332(b) and 381
- Reg. Sec. 1.332-2(a)

CHAPTER

7

CORPORATE ACQUISITIONS AND REORGANIZATIONS

LEARNING OBJECTIVES

After studying this chapter, you should be able to

1. Identify types of taxable acquisitions and determine the consequences of a Sec. 338 deemed sale election
2. Distinguish between taxable and nontaxable acquisitions
3. Recognize the types of nontaxable reorganizations and determine their tax consequences
4. Describe the structure and requirements of each type of acquisitive reorganization
5. Describe the structure and requirements of divisive reorganizations
6. Define other types of reorganizations
7. Explain judicial doctrines pertaining to corporate reorganizations
8. Determine the tax treatment of NOL carryovers and other tax attributes in a reorganization
9. Identify tax planning opportunities in taxable acquisitions and reorganizations
10. Comply with procedural rules for taxable acquisitions and reorganizations
11. Determine the financial statement implications of corporate acquisitions

CHAPTER OUTLINE

A corporation's directors or shareholders may decide to acquire another corporation either directly or indirectly. Alternatively, they may decide to divest the corporation of part or all of its assets, such as the assets of an operating division or stock in a subsidiary. Depending on the transactional structure, these acquisitions or divestitures can be either taxable or nontaxable. In a taxable transaction, the entire realized gain or loss is recognized. To qualify as nontaxable, the transaction must meet certain statutory and judicial requirements. If the transaction meets these requirements, part or all of the realized gain or loss generally goes unrecognized. This unrecognized gain or loss is deferred until the assets or stock exchanged are sold or disposed of in a taxable transaction. The nontaxable reorganization rules comply with the continuity of interest doctrine, which holds that no tax is imposed if the taxpayer retains a continuing interest in the acquired corporation via an equity interest in the acquiring corporation. A tax is imposed, however, where the taxpayer receives cash or property other than stock or securities.[1] On the other hand, taxpayers are likely to engage in a taxable transaction (instead of a nontaxable reorganization) where they prefer to recognize loss on an asset sale or stock disposition.

This chapter presents an overview of taxable and nontaxable acquisitions and divestitures. It also examines the statutory provisions and judicial doctrines that determine the tax consequences of these types of transactions.

TAXABLE ACQUISITION TRANSACTIONS

OBJECTIVE 1

Identify types of taxable acquisitions and determine the consequences of a Sec. 338 deemed sale election

In taxable acquisitions, corporations acquire a **target corporation** in two principal ways.[2] First, they purchase target assets directly from the target corporation. Second, they acquire target corporation stock directly from target shareholders or target's parent corporation. Two options exist once the acquiring corporation has purchased the target stock.

- The acquiring corporation and its new subsidiary can exist as separate entities.
- The acquiring corporation can liquidate its new subsidiary in a nontaxable transaction. Following the liquidation, the parent corporation retains a direct interest in target corporation assets.

Under the first option, the acquiring corporation can make a Sec. 338 election (discussed below), which adjusts the aggregate basis of subsidiary assets to the price the acquiring corporation paid for the subsidiary stock, plus the amount of any subsidiary liabilities.

The principal asset and stock acquisitions are examined below. Table C:7-1 summarizes the tax consequences of these transactions.

ASSET ACQUISITIONS

From a tax perspective, accounting for an asset purchase is straightforward. The selling corporation simply calculates the gain or loss recognized on the sale of each asset. Sales of depreciable assets (e.g., Sec. 1245 and 1250 property) may result in the recapture of previously claimed depreciation.

The purchaser's bases in the acquired assets equal their acquisition cost.[3] The purchaser eventually can claim depreciation deductions based on the acquisition cost of depreciable property.

A taxable asset acquisition provides the purchaser with two major advantages. First, a significant portion of the acquisition cost can be debt-financed. Interest accruing on the debt is deductible for federal income tax purposes. By contrast, in a nontaxable asset acquisition, the use of debt is either prohibited or restricted. Second, only assets and liabilities specified in the purchase-sale agreement are acquired. The purchaser need not acquire all or substantially all the target corporation's assets, as in the case of a taxable or

TAX STRATEGY TIP

Three types of state taxes may arise in an *asset* sale—transfer taxes, state income taxes, and sales taxes (some state sales tax laws allow certain bulk-sale exceptions). These taxes need to be taken into account by both the buyer and seller when drafting the sales agreement. When a *stock* sale occurs, these taxes can be avoided because the assets remain inside the same entity before and after the stock sale.

[1] The tax deferral can be permanent if the stock and securities are held until death. At death, the carryover or substituted basis is stepped up to its fair market value (FMV) without income tax consequences.

[2] The terms *target* and *acquired corporation* are used interchangeably here.

[3] Sec. 1012.

▼ TABLE C:7-1
Comparison of Taxable Acquisition Transactions

	Taxable Asset Acquisition	Taxable Stock Acquisition with: No Liquidation of Target	Nontaxable Liquidation of Target	Sec. 338 Election for Target
Acquiring corporation's basis in stock	N/A	Cost basis	Cost basis initially; disappears upon liquidation of target corporation	Cost basis
Parent-subsidiary relationship created	No	Yes	Yes, until liquidation occurs	Yes
Consolidated tax return election available	No	Yes	Yes, until liquidation occurs	Yes
Gain/loss recognized by target corporation on asset sale	Yes	No	No	Yes, on deemed sale of assets by target corporation
Gain/loss recognized by target corporation upon liquidating	Yes, if target elects to liquidate before or after the asset sale	N/A	No	No
Gain recognized by acquiring corporation in liquidating distribution	N/A	N/A	No	No
Acquiring corporation's basis in assets acquired	Cost basis to acquiring corporation	No change in basis of target corporation's assets	Carryover basis upon liquidation	Cost basis in target stock acquired plus amount of target liabilities
Transfer of tax attributes to acquiring corporation	Remain with target corporation	Remain with target corporation	Carryover to acquiring corporation upon liquidation	Disappear upon deemed sale of assets by old target corporation

N/A = Not applicable.

ADDITIONAL COMMENT

In specific examples and some problems, we will use Alpha Corporation to designate the acquiring corporation and Theta Corporation to designate the target corporation.

nontaxable stock acquisition or a nontaxable asset acquisition. Similarly, the purchaser assumes only liabilities specified in the purchase-sale agreement. Contingent or unknown liabilities generally remain the responsibility of the seller.

The target (acquired) corporation recognizes gain or loss on the sale of assets and may subsequently liquidate. If it liquidates, any property retained by the target corporation is distributed to the shareholders as part of the liquidation. The liquidating corporation recognizes gain or loss on the distribution as if such property had been sold. Upon receiving the liquidating distribution, the target corporation's shareholders each recognize capital gain or loss depending on his or her respective stock basis (see Chapter C:6).

EXAMPLE C:7-1 ► Six years ago, Ann, Bob, and Cathy each acquired one-third of Theta Corporation stock. Each shareholder has a $20,000 basis in his or her stock. Alpha Corporation purchases Theta's noncash assets for $100,000 in cash and $300,000 in Alpha debt obligations (three notes at $100,000 each). Theta retains its $50,400 of cash. On the sale date, Theta's noncash assets have a $280,000 adjusted basis and a $400,000 FMV. Its liabilities total $100,000 on the sale date. Theta recognizes a $120,000 aggregate gain [($100,000 + $300,000) − $280,000]. The character of its separate asset gains and losses depends on the type of properties sold. Based on a 34% corporate tax rate, Theta's tax liability on the sale is $40,800 ($120,000 × 0.34). Alpha takes a

$400,000 basis in the noncash assets acquired. After Theta pays its income tax and other liabilities, Theta has remaining cash of $9,600 ($50,400 retained cash + $100,000 cash received − $100,000 liabilities paid − $40,800 tax paid) and holds the three $100,000 notes received. Ann, Bob, and Cathy then decide to liquidate Theta with each receiving $3,200 cash ($9,600 ÷ 3) plus a $100,000 note. Thus, each shareholder recognizes a capital gain of $83,200 ($103,200 − $20,000 stock basis). ◀

Sometimes a target corporation liquidates before it sells its assets. In this case the target corporation distributes the assets to the shareholders who then sell them. The tax consequences of the liquidation are set forth in Chapter C:6. In general, the total tax liability of the corporation and its shareholders are the same whether the liquidation of the target corporation precedes or follows the asset sale.

STOCK ACQUISITIONS

KEY POINT

In a stock acquisition, only the shareholders of the target corporation recognize gain. In an asset acquisition, both the target corporation and its shareholders may recognize gain.

Stock Acquisition with No Liquidation. A stock purchase is the simplest of acquisition transactions. Gain recognized on the sale is capital in character if the stock is a capital asset in the seller's hands. If payment of part or all of the consideration is deferred to a later year, the seller can defer gain recognition under the installment method of accounting.[4] If part of the total amount received by the seller represents consideration for a promise not to compete with the purchaser, this portion is taxed as ordinary income.[5]

The purchaser's basis in the stock is its acquisition cost.[6] The target corporation's basis in its assets ordinarily does not change as a result of the stock sale. Any potential for depreciation recapture that exists on the transaction date remains with the target corporation's assets and, therefore, is assumed by the purchaser. If the target corporation has loss or credit carryovers, these carryovers can be subject to special limitations in the post-acquisition tax years (see pages C:7-43 through C:7-46).

ADDITIONAL COMMENT

A shareholder's basis in stock sometimes is referred to as "outside basis" as opposed to "inside basis," which is the corporation's basis in its assets.

Stock sales are popular with sellers because they often are less costly than asset sales due to a single level of taxation. No adjustment to the bases of the target corporation's assets is made after a stock sale even though the basis of the stock acquired may be substantially higher than the aggregate basis of these assets. Thus, one of the tax advantages of purchasing target corporation assets—a higher asset basis—is not available in a stock purchase unless the purchasing corporation makes a Sec. 338 deemed sale election (discussed later in this chapter).

EXAMPLE C:7-2 ▶

Assume the same facts as in Example C:7-1 except Alpha offers to purchase Theta stock for $50 per share. Ann, Bob, and Cathy tender their 7,000 Theta shares in response to Alpha's offer. Alpha's $350,000 (7,000 shares × $50/share) purchase price equals Theta's net asset value ($450,000 − $100,000 liabilities). Ann, Bob, and Cathy each recognize a long-term capital gain on the sale of their stock. Theta becomes a wholly-owned subsidiary of Alpha and, without a Sec. 338 election, does not adjust the bases of its assets. ◀

KEY POINT

In Example C:7-2, the built-in gain in Theta's assets is not recognized in a stock acquisition. Likewise, the bases of Theta's assets are not stepped-up even though Alpha pays their full $350,000 FMV for the Theta stock.

If the purchasing corporation is a member of an affiliated group that files a consolidated tax return, the new subsidiary must join in the consolidated return election if the purchasing corporation owns at least 80% of the subsidiary's stock and if the subsidiary is an includible corporation (see Chapter C:8). Otherwise, the parent and subsidiary may make an initial consolidated return election.

TYPICAL MISCONCEPTION

Taxpayers often do not understand that the parent's basis in its subsidiary's stock disappears in a Sec. 332 liquidation. Instead, the subsidiary's bases in the liquidated assets carry over to the parent.

Stock Acquisition Followed by a Liquidation. The type of stock acquisition discussed in the preceding section can be followed by a liquidation of the acquired (subsidiary) corporation into its acquiring (parent) corporation. If the parent owns at least 80% of subsidiary stock, the liquidation is nontaxable under the Sec. 332 and 337 rules outlined in Chapter C:6.[7] The bases of the subsidiary's assets carry over to the parent. If the parent paid a premium for the assets (i.e., an amount exceeding the aggregate

---

[4] Sec. 453(a).

[5] The purchaser can amortize over a 15-year period any amounts paid to the seller with respect to the agreement not to compete (Sec. 197).

[6] Sec. 1012.

[7] The liquidation may be taxable to any minority shareholders and to the subsidiary corporation upon distributions to the minority shareholders.

asset adjusted basis), this premium is lost upon liquidation because the parent's basis in the stock disappears. The stock basis "loss" cannot be deducted and provides no tax benefit. If the parent paid less than the aggregate asset adjusted basis, the "excess" asset basis is included in the asset carryover basis, which can provide additional tax benefits.

EXAMPLE C:7-3 ▶ Assume the same facts as in Example C:7-2 except that, following the stock acquisition, Alpha and Theta Corporations continue to file separate tax returns, and Theta liquidates into Alpha shortly after the acquisition. Theta's assets have the following adjusted bases and FMVs immediately before the sale:

Assets	*Adjusted Basis*	*FMV*
Cash	$ 50,000	$ 50,000
Marketable securities	49,000	55,000
Accounts receivable	60,000	60,000
Inventory	60,000	90,000
Building	27,000	44,000
Land	10,000	26,000
Machinery and equipment[a]	74,000	125,000
Total	$330,000	$450,000

[a]The machinery and equipment are Sec. 1245 property. Recapture potential of the machinery and equipment is $107,000.

Theta and Alpha recognize no gain or loss on the liquidation. Alpha assumes Theta's $100,000 in liabilities and takes a $330,000 total basis in Theta assets, the basis of each asset carrying over. In addition, Alpha inherits all of Theta's tax attributes, including any NOL carryovers, E&P, and the $107,000 depreciation recapture potential of the machinery and equipment. ◀

ADDITIONAL COMMENT

A Sec. 338 election triggers immediate taxation to the target corporation. Therefore, in most situations it makes little sense to pay an immediate tax to obtain a step-up in basis when such additional basis can be recovered only in future years. The election can be beneficial, however, if the target corporation has enough NOLs to offset most or all of the gain recognized on the deemed asset sale. The election also can be beneficial if Sec. 338(h)(10) applies (see footnote 9).

Section 338 Deemed Sale Election. The Sec. 338 **deemed sale election** operates as follows: First target corporation's shareholders sell their stock to the acquiring corporation. Then the acquiring corporation makes a Sec. 338 deemed sale election with respect to the purchased stock. This election results in a hypothetical sale of the "old" target corporation's assets to a "new" target corporation for their **aggregate deemed sale price (ADSP)** in a transaction that requires the seller ("old" target) to recognize gains and losses on its final tax return. The "old" target corporation goes out of existence for tax purposes only.[8] The "new" target corporation is treated as a new entity for tax purposes (i.e., it makes new accounting method and tax year elections). The bases of old target corporation assets are stepped-up or stepped-down to the price paid by the acquiring corporation for target corporation stock plus the amount of target corporation liabilities (including any federal income taxes owed on the hypothetical sale). Corporate purchasers generally do not find the Sec. 338[9] election appealing because, in the year of the election, the target corporation usually incurs a significant tax liability.

PRACTICAL APPLICATION

The purchasing corporation most likely would not make a Sec. 338 election if it resulted in the target corporation's asset tax bases being stepped-down, resulting in, among other things, smaller depreciation deductions.

Eligible Stock Acquisitions. Section 338 requires the acquiring corporation to purchase 80% or more of target corporation voting stock and 80% or more of the total value of all classes of target stock except certain nonvoting preferred stock during a continuous 12-month (or shorter) qualified stock acquisition period.[10] The acquisition period begins on the date the acquiring corporation first purchases target stock and ends on the date the qualified stock purchase is completed. If the acquiring corporation does not acquire the necessary 80% minimum within the 12-month acquisition period, it cannot make a Sec. 338 election.

[8] The target corporation's legal existence does not change under the applicable corporation laws. For federal income tax purposes only, the target corporation (commonly referred to as "old" target) goes out of existence. A "new" target corporation is created. For tax purposes, this new corporation acquires all the assets of the "old" corporation.

[9] An alternative Sec. 338 election is permitted under Sec. 338(h)(10) for members of an affiliated group. This election generally is used by affiliated groups that file consolidated tax returns. The Sec. 338(h)(10) election permits the target corporation (e.g., a subsidiary) to recognize gain or loss as if it had sold its assets in a single transaction. The corporation selling the stock (e.g., a parent corporation) does not recognize gain on the stock sale, thereby resulting in a single level of taxation. This special Sec. 338 election has become popular in recent years. In addition, the Treasury Department has issued Reg. Secs. 1.336-2–1.336-5, which would allow a parent corporation to elect under Sec. 336(e) to treat certain dispositions of a subsidiary corporation's stock as a taxable sale of the subsidiary's underlying assets. See page C:7-10.

[10] The basic definition of a controlled subsidiary used for Sec. 332 purposes also is used for Sec. 338 purposes (see Chapter C:6).

EXAMPLE C:7-4 ▶ Alpha Corporation purchases a 25% block of Theta Corporation's single class of stock on each of four dates: April 1, July 1, and December 1 of Year 1, and February 1 of Year 2. Because Alpha acquires at least 80% of Theta stock within a 12-month period (April 1 of Year 1 through February 1 of Year 2), it is eligible to make a Sec. 338 deemed sale election. ◀

EXAMPLE C:7-5 ▶ Assume the same facts as in Example C:7-4 except Alpha Corporation instead purchases the final 25% block on May 15 of Year 2. In this case, Alpha acquires only 75% of the Theta stock during a 12-month period. Two possible 12-month periods may occur—April 1 of Year 1 through March 31 of Year 2, and May 16 of Year 1 through May 15 of Year 2. The 80% stock ownership minimum is not achieved in either period. Thus, Alpha is not eligible to make a Sec. 338 election. ◀

For the purpose of the 80% requirement, the following stock acquisitions are not treated as purchases:

- Stock whose adjusted basis is determined in whole or part by its basis in the hands of the person from whom it was acquired (e.g., stock acquired as a capital contribution)
- Stock whose basis is determined under Sec. 1014(a) (i.e., FMV on the date of decedent's death or alternative valuation date)
- Stock acquired in a nontaxable transaction under Sec. 351, 354, 355, or 356 (e.g., corporate formations, divisions, or reorganizations)
- Stock acquired from a related party where stock ownership may be attributed to the purchaser under Secs. 318(a)(1) through (3)

The Election. A Sec. 338 election must be made no later than the fifteenth day of the ninth month beginning after the month in which the acquisition date falls. The acquisition date is the first date during the 12-month acquisition period on which the 80% stock ownership requirement is met.[11]

EXAMPLE C:7-6 ▶ On April 1 of Year 1, Alpha Corporation purchased 40% of Theta Corporation's single class of stock. On October 20 of Year 1, it purchases an additional 50% of Theta stock. The acquisition date is October 20 of Year 1. Alpha must make a Sec. 338 election on or before July 15 of Year 2. ◀

Deemed Sale Transaction. When the acquiring corporation makes a Sec. 338 election, the target corporation is treated as having sold all its assets at their aggregate deemed sale price (ADSP) in a single transaction at the close of the acquisition date. The asset sale is a taxable transaction, with gain or loss recognized by the target corporation. ADSP is calculated as follows:[12]

$$ADSP = \frac{G + L - (T_R \times B)}{(1 - T_R)}$$

Where: G = The acquiring corporation's grossed-up basis in recently purchased target corporation stock;
L = The target corporation's liabilities other than its tax liability for the deemed sale gain determined by reference to the ADSP;
T_R = The applicable federal income tax rate; and
B = The adjusted basis of the asset(s) deemed sold.

EXAMPLE C:7-7 ▶ Assume the same facts as in Examples C:7-2 and C:7-3 except Alpha makes a timely Sec. 338 election. Also assume that Theta's marginal tax rate is 34%. The aggregate deemed sale price is calculated as follows:

$$ADSP = \frac{G + L - (T_R \times B)}{(1 - T_R)}$$

[11] Secs. 338(g) and 338(h)(2).

[12] This equation is derived as follows:

$$ADSP = G + L + [T_R \times (ADSP - B)]$$
$$ADSP = G + L + (T_R \times ADSP) - (T_R \times B)$$
$$ADSP - (T_R \times ADSP) = G + L - (T_R \times B)$$
$$ADSP \times (1 - T_R) = G + L - (T_R \times B)$$
$$ADSP = \frac{G + L - (T_R \times B)}{(1 \times T_R)}$$

$$\text{ADSP} = \frac{\$350{,}000 + \$100{,}000 - (0.34 \times \$330{,}000)}{(1 - 0.34)}$$

$$0.66\ \text{ADSP} = \$337{,}800$$
$$\text{ADSP} = \$511{,}818$$

Thus, Theta recognizes a gain of $181,818 ($511,818 − $330,000) and pays a tax of $61,818 (0.34 × $181,818) on the gain. ◀

TAX STRATEGY TIP

Many taxpayers avoid Sec. 338 because it requires an advance payment of taxes to achieve a step-up in basis of target corporation's assets. A Sec. 338 election becomes more attractive, however, when the target corporation has NOLs that can offset its gain on the deemed sale of its assets, thereby reducing the cost of making the election.

The Sec. 338 election was intended for transactions in which the acquisition price of target stock exceeds the adjusted basis of target assets. In many of these transactions, the amount of gain recognized by the target corporation, as well as the associated tax liability, could be substantial. This potential tax cost might induce companies to forego the Sec. 338 election or lower the price they are willing to pay for target stock if they intend to make a Sec. 338 election.

Tax Basis of the Assets After the Deemed Sale. Similarly to the ADSP, the tax basis in the assets of the new target corporation is based on the amount paid by the acquiring corporation for target corporation stock. This amount is called the **adjusted grossed-up basis** in the target corporation stock. The adjusted grossed-up basis equals the sum of

- The purchasing corporation's grossed-up basis in recently purchased target corporation stock;
- The purchasing corporation's basis in nonrecently purchased target corporation stock;
- The liabilities of the new target corporation; and
- Other relevant items.[13]

The adjusted grossed-up basis is determined as of the beginning of the day following the acquisition date. Example C:7-10 illustrates the calculation of the adjusted grossed-up basis.

A target corporation's stock owned by the acquiring corporation falls into two categories: recently purchased stock and nonrecently purchased stock. This categorization is necessary because only the recently purchased stock is treated as consideration used in a deemed purchase of target corporation assets. Recently purchased stock includes any target corporation stock held on the acquisition date that the acquiring corporation purchased during the 12-month (or shorter) acquisition period. Nonrecently purchased stock includes all other target corporation stock acquired before the acquisition period and held by the acquiring corporation on the acquisition date.[14] The basis of the purchasing corporation's ownership interest equals the grossed-up basis of the recently purchased stock plus the basis of the nonrecently purchased stock.

EXAMPLE C:7-8 ▶ On July 23 of the current year, Alpha Corporation purchases all of Theta Corporation's single class of stock. All the Theta stock is considered to be recently purchased because it is purchased in a single transaction. The acquisition date is July 23 of the current year. ◀

EXAMPLE C:7-9 ▶ Assume the same facts as in Example C:7-8 except Alpha already owns 10% of Theta stock (purchased five years ago) and purchases the remaining 90% of Theta stock. The original block of Theta stock is not considered to be recently purchased because it was acquired more than 12 months before the acquisition date (July 23 of the current year). ◀

When the acquiring corporation does not own all of target corporation outstanding stock, the basis of the acquiring corporation's recently purchased stock must be increased or grossed-up to a hypothetical value that reflects ownership of all the stock.[15]

[13] Secs. 338(b)(1) and (2). The IRS has indicated that other relevant items include only items that arise from adjustment events that occur after the close of the new target's first tax year and items discovered as a result of an IRS examination of a tax return (e.g., the payment of contingent amounts for recently or nonrecently purchased stock).

[14] Sec. 338(b)(6). A special gain recognition election is available to adjust the basis of nonrecently purchased stock. This election, which is set forth in Sec. 338(b)(3), is beyond the scope of this text.

[15] Sec. 338(b)(4). The gross-up procedure involves taking the purchasing corporation's basis for the recently purchased target stock and dividing it by the percentage (by value) of recently purchased target stock owned (expressed as a decimal).

Specifically, the basis of the recently purchased stock must be increased by the face amount of any target liabilities outstanding on the day following the acquisition date, plus the tax liability incurred on any gain realized in the deemed sale.[16] This liability adjustment embodies the notion that, if the acquisition had been structured as an asset purchase, the assumption of liabilities would have been reflected in the total purchase price.

Allocation of Basis to Individual Assets. The adjusted grossed-up basis of the stock is allocated among seven classes of assets under the residual method.[17] The residual method requires that the adjusted grossed-up basis be allocated to the corporation's tangible and intangible property (other than goodwill and going concern value) on a sequential hierarchical basis. Any amount exceeding the aggregate FMVs of this property is assigned to target corporation goodwill and going concern value.

The seven classes of assets to which the adjusted grossed-up basis is allocated are as follows:

TAX STRATEGY TIP

Under Sec. 197, amounts allocated to goodwill are amortized for tax purposes over 15 years. This feature can be particularly beneficial if the target corporation has pre-Sec. 197 unamortizable goodwill on its tax balance sheet. If the Sec. 338 election creates goodwill, any of the pre-Sec. 197 goodwill included in the newly created goodwill effectively will be converted to amortizable goodwill under Sec. 197.

- Class I: cash and general deposit accounts, including demand deposit and similar accounts in banks, savings and loan associations, and other financial institutions.
- Class II: actively traded personal property (as defined in Sec. 1092(d)(1)), such as U.S. government obligations and publicly traded securities.
- Class III: accounts receivable, mortgages, and credit card receivables that arise in the ordinary course of business.
- Class IV: inventory or other property held primarily for sale to customers in the ordinary course of business.
- Class V: all assets other than Class I, II, III, IV, VI, and VII assets. Included in this category are tangible and intangible property without regard to whether such property is depreciable, depletable, or amortizable.
- Class VI: all amortizable Sec. 197 intangible assets except goodwill and going concern value.
- Class VII: Sec. 197 intangible assets in the nature of goodwill and going concern value.[18]

ADDITIONAL COMMENT

The residual method ensures that any premium paid for the target stock is reflected in goodwill. Because the residual method is the only acceptable allocation method, the only uncertainty that remains is to determine the FMVs of the assets listed in Classes II through VI.

Class VI and VII intangible assets are amortizable over a 15-year period if they are used in the active conduct of a trade or business. Among such assets are goodwill, going concern value, and covenants not to compete.

The adjusted grossed-up basis is first allocated to individual Class I assets based on their actual dollar amounts.[19] Any excess is allocated to Class II assets based on, and to the extent of, their relative gross FMVs. Similar allocations are made to Class III through VI assets based on, and to the extent of, the relative gross FMVs of individual assets within each class. The intra-class allocation is based on the asset's total gross FMV, not its net FMV (gross FMV minus liabilities secured by the property). Any remaining adjusted grossed-up basis is assigned to Class VII (goodwill).

EXAMPLE C:7-10 ▶ Assume the same facts as in Example C:7-7, with assets classified as follows:

Asset Class	*Assets*	*FMV*
I	Cash	$ 50,000
II	Marketable securities	55,000
III	Accounts receivable	60,000
IV	Inventory	90,000
V	Building	44,000
V	Land	26,000
V	Machinery and equipment	125,000
	Total	$450,000

16 Sec. 338(b)(2) and Reg. Secs. 1.338(b)-1(f)(1) and (2).
17 Reg. Sec. 1.338-6(a).
18 Reg. Sec. 1.338-6(b).
19 Ibid.

The adjusted grossed-up basis of Alpha's interest in Theta stock is calculated as follows:

Recently purchased stock	$350,000
Plus: Theta's nontax liabilities	100,000
Theta's tax liability [($511,818 − $330,000) × 0.34]	61,818
Adjusted grossed-up basis	$511,818

ADDITIONAL COMMENT

The effects of a Sec. 338 election include termination of the "old" target corporation, creation of a "new" target corporation with the option of a new tax year and different accounting methods, new depreciation elections without regard to anti-churning rules, and elimination of the old target's tax attributes (i.e., NOL carryforwards). Because it is a separate legal entity, the "new" target corporation files a tax return separate from that of the acquiring corporation (unless the group files a consolidated return).[20]

The adjusted grossed-up basis is allocated to Theta's seven asset classes in the following steps:

Step 1: Allocate $50,000 to cash (Class I asset).

Step 2: Allocate $55,000 to marketable securities (Class II asset).

Step 3: Allocate $60,000 to accounts receivable (Class III asset).

Step 4: Allocate $90,000 to inventory (Class IV asset).

Step 5: Allocate $195,000 to the building, land, machinery, and equipment (Class V assets). Because the total basis that remains after the Step 4 allocation ($256,818) exceeds the aggregate FMV of the Class V assets ($195,000), each asset will take a basis exactly equal to its FMV.

Step 6: No allocation to Class VI assets.

Step 7: Allocate the residual $61,818 [$511,818 − ($50,000 + $55,000 + $60,000 + $90,000 + $195,000)] to goodwill (Class VII asset). The $61,818 is amortizable under Sec. 197. ◀

Topic Review C:7-1 summarizes the requirements for, and tax consequences of, a Sec. 338 deemed sale election.

TOPIC REVIEW C:7-1

Section 338 Deemed Sale Election

ELECTION REQUIREMENTS

1. The acquiring corporation must make a qualified stock purchase (i.e., within a 12-month period purchase 80% or more of target corporation voting stock and 80% or more of the total value of all target corporation stock).
2. Stock received in transactions that result in a substituted basis (e.g., nontaxable reorganizations, corporate formations, and gifts), transfers at death, and related party exchanges do not count toward the 80% minimum threshold.
3. The acquiring corporation must make the election not later than the fifteenth day of the ninth month beginning after the month in which the acquisition date falls. The acquisition date is the first date on which the 80% stock ownership requirement is met.

TAX CONSEQUENCES OF A SEC. 338 ELECTION

1. The old target corporation is treated as having sold all its assets to the new target corporation at their aggregate deemed sales price in a single transaction at the close of the acquisition date. The old target corporation recognizes gain or loss on the deemed sale.
2. The new target corporation takes an aggregate asset basis equal to the acquiring corporation's adjusted grossed-up basis in the target stock, that is, the sum of the acquiring corporation's basis in the target corporation stock on the day following the acquisition date, the target corporation's liabilities on the day after the acquisition date, and other relevant items (e.g., contingent liabilities that become fixed).
3. The total adjusted grossed-up basis is allocated to individual assets under the residual method. This method requires allocation of basis first to cash and near-cash items, then to other tangible and intangible assets based on their relative FMVs, and finally to goodwill and going concern value.
4. After the Sec. 338 deemed asset sale, the tax attributes of the old target corporation disappear.
5. The new target corporation makes new tax year and accounting method elections.

[20] The "old" target also files a separate tax return that includes the gains from the Sec. 338 deemed sale. The "old" target may not file a consolidated tax return with the acquiring corporation.

Section 336(e) Deemed Sale Election. Another election similar in principle to the Sec. 338 election is available to shareholders who sell their target corporation stock. Under IRC Sec. 336(e) and associated Treasury Regulations, a domestic corporation (the seller) that sells, exchanges, or distributes stock in another domestic corporation (the target corporation) that it controls may, under certain circumstances, elect to have the transaction treated as if the target corporation disposed of its assets in a taxable transaction. As a result of the election, the seller recognizes no gain or loss on the sale, exchange, or distribution of the target corporation stock. On the other hand, the target corporation recognizes gain or loss, except in the case of certain distributions to shareholders.

To qualify for the election, the seller must dispose of at least 80% of the target stock by vote and value within a 12-month period. As a result of the election, the following events are deemed to occur:

- The old target corporation is deemed to sell all its assets in a single sale to an unrelated person at an aggregate deemed asset disposition price (ADADP), calculated and allocated to the assets in a manner similar to that of ADSP under Sec. 338. This deemed sale results in recognized taxable gain or loss to the target corporation.
- The new target is deemed to acquire the assets from an unrelated person for a value that is used to determine an aggregate grossed up basis (AGUB), allocated to the assets in a manner similar to the asset allocation under Sec. 338.
- The old target goes out of existence.

The Sec. 336(e) election is intended to provide relief to the parties in a stock sale where gain on the stock sale is subject to taxation, without a corresponding step up in the basis of the underlying assets. The election gives the parties an opportunity to adjust the bases of the target corporation's underlying assets via the AGUB allocation to a level that approximates the FMV of the assets. As a practical matter, the parties should negotiate the stock selling price to reflect the incidence of taxation on any recognized gain. Where a stock disposition under Sec. 336(e) also qualifies as a stock purchase under Sec. 338, the latter IRC provision controls. However, Sec. 336(e) can apply in situations where Sec. 338 cannot apply, for example, in stock sales to multiple parties, some of which can be entities other than a corporation.

Comparison of Taxable and Nontaxable Acquisitions

OBJECTIVE 2

Distinguish between taxable and nontaxable acquisitions

KEY POINT

Determining whether a transaction is taxable or nontaxable is doubly important to the target corporation because it is affected by two potentially taxable exchanges: the exchange between the target corporation and the acquiring corporation and the exchange between the acquiring corporation and its shareholders.

Taxable and Nontaxable Asset Acquisitions

One way to illustrate the difference between taxable and nontaxable asset acquisitions is to identify the type of consideration used to acquire the assets and to compare the tax consequences of the transactions. For this discussion, we assume that the acquiring corporation acquires all the target corporation's assets and liabilities and that the target corporation liquidates immediately after the acquisition. If the acquiring corporation uses cash and/or other property to purchase the assets, the target corporation is taxed on the sale, and its shareholders are taxed on the liquidation. On the other hand, if the acquiring corporation uses its own stock, the asset acquisition may qualify as a reorganization that is nontaxable to the target corporation and its shareholders. If the acquiring corporation supplements its stock with a limited amount of cash and/or other property, the transaction still may qualify as a reorganization but may be partially taxable.

Tax Consequences to the Target Corporation. Section 1001(c) requires that, with certain exceptions, the entire gain or loss realized on a sale or exchange of property be recognized. Thus, the target corporation recognizes all gains and losses realized on selling its assets.

A reorganization is one exception to the general rule. The target corporation generally recognizes no gain or loss when it exchanges its assets for acquiring corporation stock. It also recognizes no gain or loss when it distributes the acquiring corporation stock to its shareholders. The target corporation, however, could recognize gain if it receives boot and does not distribute the boot to its shareholders, or if it distributes boot or retained property whose FMV exceeds its adjusted basis. The term *retained property* refers to property not transferred to the acquiring corporation as part of the acquisition.

SELF-STUDY QUESTION

Why would an acquiring corporation want an acquisition to be nontaxable if it gets only a substituted basis rather than an FMV basis in the acquired assets?

ANSWER

Usually the motivation for an acquisition to be nontaxable comes from the target corporation and its shareholders. However, two reasons why the acquiring corporation may desire a nontaxable acquisition are (1) the acquiring corporation has no cash to acquire the assets, so it must use stock as the consideration for the purchase and (2) the target corporation may have favorable tax attributes (e.g., an NOL) that the acquiring corporation would like to use.

Tax Consequences to the Acquiring Corporation. The acquiring corporation recognizes no gain or loss when it issues its stock in exchange for property in either a taxable or nontaxable acquisition. In a taxable acquisition, the acquiring corporation takes a cost (FMV) basis in the assets received, and the holding period for the acquired assets begins the day after the acquisition date. In a reorganization, the acquiring corporation takes a carryover basis equal to target corporation's basis before the transfer. If the target corporation recognizes a gain because it does not distribute boot property to its shareholders, the carryover basis is adjusted upward to reflect this recognized gain. The acquiring corporation's holding period includes the target corporation's holding period.

In a taxable acquisition, all the target corporation's tax attributes (e.g., an NOL carryover) disappear when it liquidates, while in a nontaxable reorganization, the acquiring corporation inherits the target corporation's tax attributes.

Tax Consequences to the Target Corporation Shareholders. If the target corporation liquidates as part of a taxable acquisition, its shareholders recognize gain or loss on the surrender of their stock. The target corporation assets they receive take a basis equal to their FMV. A reorganization requires the shareholders to recognize gain only to the extent they receive boot. The gain generally is capital in character. In some circumstances, however, target corporation shareholders could recognize dividend income. The stock and securities they receive take a substituted basis that references the basis of target corporation stock and securities surrendered. Their basis in any boot property received is its FMV.

Accounting for the Acquisition. For financial reporting purposes, only the purchase method is available to account for acquisitions. Thus, the acquired assets must be recorded at their fair market values. Any goodwill created in the acquisition cannot be amortized, but rather must be periodically tested for impairment. Also, any impairment of an indefinite-life intangible asset must be reported in the acquiring corporation's financial statements as a loss from continuing operations. For other accounting issues, see Financial Statement Implications at the end of this chapter.

Topic Review C:7-2 compares various aspects of taxable and nontaxable asset acquisitions.

TAX STRATEGY TIP

Taxes can be important in determining the acquisition method used to acquire the target corporation's stock or assets. In addition, all parties need to consider nontax variables associated with the transaction. For example, a stock-for-stock acquisition may minimize taxes but leave the target corporation's shareholders controlling the acquiring corporation. Facing loss of control, the acquiring corporation's owners may prefer financing the transaction with borrowed funds (and taxing the acquisition to the seller) while retaining control of the acquiring corporation.

COMPARISON OF TAXABLE AND NONTAXABLE STOCK ACQUISITIONS

For purposes of this discussion, we assume that the acquiring corporation acquires all the stock of target corporation instead of its assets and that the target corporation becomes a controlled subsidiary of the acquiring corporation. If the acquiring corporation uses cash and/or other property alone or along with its own stock to acquire the target stock, the acquisition is taxable. If the acquiring corporation uses solely its voting stock or voting stock of its parent corporation to acquire the target corporation stock, the acquisition may qualify as a nontaxable reorganization.

Tax Consequences to the Target Corporation. The target corporation's basis in its assets does not change as a result of either a taxable or nontaxable stock acquisition (unless the acquiring corporation makes a Sec. 338 election after a taxable

TOPIC REVIEW C:7-2

Comparison of Taxable and Nontaxable Asset Acquisitions

Tax Feature	Taxable Acquisition	Nontaxable Reorganization
1. Consideration used in acquisition	Primarily cash and debt instruments; may involve some stock of the acquiring corporation or its parent corporation.	Primarily stock and limited amount of cash or debt of the acquiring corporation or its parent corporation.
2. The target corporation		
a. Amount of gain or loss	All gains and losses are recognized. Installment method available if payments are deferred.	Generally, no gain or loss recognized. Gain recognized on an asset transfer when the target corporation receives boot property and does not distribute the boot property to its shareholders. Gain also recognized on the distribution of appreciated boot or retained property.
b. Character of gain or loss	Depends on nature of each asset transferred or distributed.	Depends on nature of each asset transferred or distributed.
c. Depreciation recapture	Sec. 1245 or 1250 depreciation is recaptured.	Sec. 1245 or 1250 depreciation is not recaptured unless boot triggers the recognition of gain.
3. The acquiring corporation		
a. Gain or loss when stock is exchanged for property	None recognized.	None recognized.
b. Gain or loss when boot is exchanged for property	Gain or loss recognized if noncash boot property is transferred to the target corporation.	Gain or loss recognized if noncash boot property is transferred to the target corporation.
c. Basis of acquired assets	Cost.	Same as the target corporation's basis, increased by gain recognized.
d. Holding period of acquired assets	Begins the day after the transaction date.	Includes holding period of the target corporation.
e. Acquisition of target corporation tax attributes	No.	Yes.
4. The target corporation shareholders		
a. Amount of gain or loss	Realized gain or loss is recognized. Installment method available if payments are deferred.	Realized gain is recognized to the extent of boot received; realized losses are not recognized.
b. Character of gain or loss	Capital gain or loss; may be Sec. 1244 loss.	Capital gain and/or dividend income if boot is received.
c. Basis of stock and securities received	Cost; generally FMV of stock, securities, or other property received.	Substituted basis referenced to the stock and securities surrendered; FMV for boot property.
d. Holding period of stock and securities received	Begins the day after the transaction date.	Includes holding period for the stock and securities surrendered; day after the transaction date for boot property.

stock purchase). Any depreciation recapture potential on the transaction date stays with target corporation assets and, therefore, is inherited by the purchaser. Also, the target corporation retains any loss or credit carryovers, which may be subject to special limitations in the post-acquisition tax years.

If the acquiring corporation is a member of an affiliated group that files a consolidated tax return, the target corporation must join in the consolidated return election if the acquiring corporation owns at least 80% of the target corporation stock, and the target corporation is an includible corporation. Otherwise, the acquiring corporation and the target corporation can make an initial consolidated tax return election (see Chapter C:8).

Tax Consequences to the Acquiring Corporation. In either a taxable or nontaxable stock acquisition, the acquiring corporation recognizes no gain or loss when it exchanges its own stock for target corporation stock. In a taxable acquisition, the acquiring corporation's basis in the target corporation stock is its acquisition cost. A taxable acquisition may qualify for the Sec. 338 deemed sale election. In a reorganization, the acquiring corporation's basis in the target corporation stock is the same as that in the hands of target corporation shareholders, and a Sec. 338 election is not available. The acquiring corporation recognizes any realized gain or loss when it exchanges noncash boot property for target corporation stock.

Tax Consequences to the Target Corporation Shareholders. The gain recognized in a taxable stock sale is capital in character if the target corporation stock is a capital asset in the seller's hands. The seller can account for the gain under the installment method if payment of part or all of the consideration is deferred to a later tax year and if the stock is not traded on an established securities exchange. Consideration received by the seller that represents compensation for an agreement not to compete with the purchaser for a specified time period is taxable as ordinary income.

Because only voting stock may be used in a nontaxable stock acquisition, the target corporation's shareholders recognize no gain or loss. The shareholders take a substituted basis in the acquiring corporation stock, which is the same as their basis in the target corporation stock.

Topic Review C:7-3 compares various aspects of taxable and nontaxable stock acquisitions.

TOPIC REVIEW C:7-3

Comparison of Taxable and Nontaxable Stock Acquisitions

Tax Feature	Taxable Acquisition	Nontaxable Reorganization
1. Consideration used in acquisition	Primarily cash and debt instruments; may include some stock of the acquiring corporation or its parent corporation.	Solely voting stock of the acquiring corporation or its parent corporation.
2. The target corporation		
a. Parent-subsidiary relationship established	Yes.	Yes.
b. Consolidated tax return election available	Yes.	Yes.
c. Basis in assets	Unchanged by stock acquisition unless a Sec. 338 election is made.	Unchanged by stock acquisition. No Sec. 338 election available.
d. Tax attributes	Retained by the target corporation.	Retained by the target corporation.
3. The acquiring corporation		
a. Basis in stock acquired	Cost basis.	Carryover basis from the target corporation shareholders.
4. The target corporation shareholders		
a. Amount of gain or loss recognized	Realized gain or loss is recognized.	No boot is received; therefore, no gain is recognized.
b. Character of gain or loss	Capital gain or loss; may be Sec. 1244 loss.	Not applicable.
c. Basis of stock, securities, or other property received	Cost; generally FMV of stock, securities, or other property received.	Substituted basis from stock surrendered.
d. Holding period of stock, securities, or other property received	Begins the day after the transaction date.	Includes holding period of the stock surrendered.

Types of Reorganizations and Their Tax Consequences

OBJECTIVE 3

Recognize the types of nontaxable reorganizations and determine their tax consequences

Section 368(a)(1) authorizes seven types of nontaxable reorganizations that correspond to the principal forms of business acquisitions, divestitures, and restructurings. Generally, tax practitioners refer to the reorganization type by the subparagraph of Sec. 368(a)(1) that defines it. For example, a merger is referred to as a *Type A* reorganization because it is defined in Sec. 368(a)(1)(A). The seven types of reorganizations also can be classified according to the transactional form, with the most common forms being acquisitive and divisive. In an **acquisitive reorganization**, the acquiring corporation obtains part or all of a target (or transferor) corporation's assets or stock. Types A, B, and C reorganizations generally are acquisitive. In a **divisive reorganization**, some of a transferor corporation's assets are transferred to a second corporation that is controlled by either the transferor or its shareholders. As part of the reorganization, the controlled (or transferee) corporation's stock or securities exchanged for the transferor's assets are distributed to the transferor's shareholders. Subsequent to the transfer, the transferor corporation can either remain in existence or be liquidated. If the transferor corporation remains in existence, its assets usually are divided between at least two corporations. Types D and G reorganizations may be either acquisitive or divisive.

TYPICAL MISCONCEPTION

For an acquisition to be treated as nontaxable, the transaction must qualify as a reorganization. The term *reorganization* includes only transactions that comply with the provisions of Sec. 368. Other transactions that may constitute reorganizations in a more general context are not considered nontaxable reorganizations.

KEY POINT

A summary of the acquisitive reorganizations is presented below:

Type	*Description*
A	Merger or consolidation
B	Stock-for-stock
C	Asset-for-stock
D	Asset-for-stock
G	Bankruptcy

Two types of reorganizations are neither acquisitive or divisive. A Type E reorganization—a recapitalization—involves a change in a corporation's capital structure. A Type F reorganization—a change in identity, legal form, or state of incorporation—involves the transfer of an existing corporation's assets to a new corporation, in which the shareholders of the transferor corporation generally retain the same equity interest.

Not all reorganizations fit neatly into one of the seven categories. Some reorganizations satisfy the requirements of two or more reorganization provisions. In this situation, the IRC or the IRS generally determines which reorganization rules prevail. In other situations, a reorganization may satisfy the requirements of a reorganization provision, but for various reasons the IRS and courts prescribe an entirely different tax treatment (e.g., if the transaction lacks a business purpose, it may be treated as taxable). These issues are discussed further in the next section.

The remainder of this section examines the tax consequences of a reorganization to the target (or transferor) corporation, the acquiring (or transferee) corporation, and the shareholders and other security holders.[21]

The Target or Transferor Corporation

Recognition of Gain or Loss on Asset Transfer. Under Sec. 361(a), the target corporation recognizes no gain or loss on the exchange of property exclusively for stock in another corporation that is a party to the reorganization.[22] In addition, under Sec. 361(b), the target corporation recognizes no gain if it also receives cash or noncash boot property as part of the reorganization and distributes such property to its shareholders or

[21] The corporation that transfers its assets as part of a reorganization is referred to as either a **target** or **transferor corporation.** The term *target corporation* generally is used in the context of an acquisitive reorganization where substantially all of a corporation's assets are acquired by the acquiring corporation. The term *target corporation* also applies to a corporation whose stock is acquired from its shareholders. The term *transferor corporation* is used in the context of a divisive and other reorganizations where only part of a corporation's assets are transferred to a transferee corporation, and the transferor corporation may remain in existence. Tax law provisions generally apply equally to target or transferor corporations and acquiring or transferee corporations, so usually only a single reference to the target or acquiring corporation is provided in the text.

[22] Section 361(a) permits securities (e.g., long-term debt obligations) to be received tax-free when the target corporation surrenders the same or a larger face amount of securities. Generally, a securities exchange does not occur in an acquisitive reorganization, so all debt obligations received by the target corporation are treated as boot property.

creditors. On the other hand, the target corporation recognizes gain equal to the lesser of the realized gain or the amount of cash plus the FMV of any noncash boot property received unless it distributes the property to its shareholders. However, because most acquisitive and divisive reorganization provisions require the target corporation to be liquidated or distribute all its assets, the target corporation generally retains no boot and thus recognizes no gain on the exchange. (Note: the target corporation might recognize gain on the distribution of appreciated property to its shareholders, as discussed below.)

TYPICAL MISCONCEPTION

One perplexing aspect of the reorganization provisions is the overlap between the different statutory reorganizations. One transaction often can qualify as more than one type of reorganization.

EXAMPLE C:7-11 ▶ In a reorganization, Theta Corporation transfers assets having a $175,000 adjusted basis to Alpha Corporation in exchange for $400,000 of Alpha common stock. In the exchange, Theta realizes a $225,000 gain ($400,000 amount realized − $175,000 adjusted basis). Because Theta received no boot, however, it recognizes none of the gain. If Theta instead received $350,000 of Alpha common stock plus $50,000 of cash or other property, Theta would recognize gain unless it distributes the $50,000 of boot to its shareholders. ◀

TYPICAL MISCONCEPTION

Often, taxpayers do not realize that Sec. 361 applies to two exchanges. Section 361(a) applies to the exchange between the acquiring and target corporations (which already has been discussed). Section 361(c) deals with the exchange between the target corporation and its shareholders. Therefore, the target corporation is the only party to the reorganization that may recognize two separate gains.

Depreciation Recapture. The depreciation recapture rules of Secs. 1245 and 1250 do not override the gain or loss nonrecognition rules of Sec. 361.[23] The recapture potential that accumulates before the reorganization remains with the assets transferred to the acquiring corporation and is recognized when the acquiring corporation later sells or exchanges the assets in a taxable transaction.

Assumption of Liabilities. Neither the acquiring corporation's assuming the target corporation's liabilities nor its acquiring the target corporation's property subject to a liability triggers gain recognition on the asset transfer. Section 357(c), however, requires the target corporation to recognize gain if the sum of the liabilities assumed or acquired exceeds the total adjusted bases of the property transferred *and* the transaction is a divisive Type D reorganization.

SELF-STUDY QUESTION

How can the target corporation distribute appreciated boot property to its shareholders if it receives an FMV basis in all such property received from the acquiring corporation?

ANSWER

If the property appreciates in the hands of the target corporation before it is distributed, gain will result under Sec. 361(c). In addition, the target corporation may retain some of its own assets and distribute these assets to its shareholders, again causing the target corporation to recognize gain.

Recognition of Gain or Loss on Distribution of Stock and Securities. The target corporation recognizes no gain or loss when, pursuant to a plan of reorganization, it distributes to its shareholders or creditors either (1) its stock, stock rights, or obligations or (2) any stock, stock rights, or obligations of a party to a reorganization that it received in the reorganization (see page C:7-47 for an explanation of a plan of reorganization).[24] Distributions of noncash boot property (including property retained by the target corporation) pursuant to the reorganization plan result in the recognition of gain (but not loss) in the same manner as if the target corporation had sold such property at its FMV.[25] Normally the gain recognized upon the distribution of boot property is inconsequential because of the brief period of time between the receipt of the boot from the acquiring corporation (with a basis equal to its FMV) and its distribution to the shareholders.

EXAMPLE C:7-12 ▶ In a statutory merger (Type A reorganization), Theta Corporation transfers all its assets and liabilities to Alpha Corporation in exchange for $300,000 of Alpha common stock and $100,000 of cash. Theta's basis in the assets is $250,000. In the exchange, Theta realizes a $150,000 [($300,000 + $100,000) − $250,000] gain. Theta recognizes none of this gain, even though it receives boot, because Theta must liquidate as part of the reorganization. Upon distributing the Alpha stock to its shareholders, Theta recognizes no gain. However, depending on their Theta stock basis, Theta shareholders who receive cash may have to recognize gain. ◀

THE ACQUIRING OR TRANSFEREE CORPORATION

Amount of Gain or Loss Recognized. Under Sec. 1032, the acquiring corporation recognizes no gain or loss when it receives cash or other property in exchange for its stock. Similarly, a target corporation recognizes no gain or loss when in a reorganization it

---

[23] Secs. 1245(b)(3) and 1250(d)(3). Similar provisions are found in the other recapture rules.

[24] Secs. 361(c)(1)–(c)(3).

[25] Sec. 361(c).

SELF-STUDY QUESTION

Because the acquiring corporation is merely purchasing assets, can it ever recognize gain or loss on the transaction?

ANSWER

Yes. If the acquiring corporation uses noncash boot property, it recognizes gain or loss to the extent of the built-in gain or loss in the noncash boot property (Sec. 1001(a)).

receives cash or other property in exchange for its securities. Under Sec. 1001, however, the acquiring corporation recognizes gain or loss when it transfers appreciated or depreciated (in value) noncash boot property to the target corporation or its shareholders.[26]

Basis of Acquired Property. Under Sec. 362(b), property acquired from the target corporation in a reorganization takes a carryover basis, increased by the amount of gain recognized by the target corporation on the exchange. As a practical matter, however, because the target corporation generally recognizes no gain on the asset transfer, the carryover basis is not stepped up.

EXAMPLE C:7-13 ▶ Assume the same facts as in Example C:7-12. Alpha's basis in the acquired property is the same as Theta's basis, or $250,000. ◀

Holding Period of Acquired Property. The acquiring corporation's holding period for acquired property includes the target corporation's holding period.[27]

SHAREHOLDERS AND SECURITY HOLDERS

Amount of Gain or Loss Recognized. Under Sec. 354(a), shareholders recognize no gain or loss if, pursuant to a plan of reorganization, stock or securities in a corporate party to a reorganization are exchanged solely for stock or securities in the same corporation or another corporate party to the reorganization. The receipt of property other than stock or securities (nonqualifying property) does not necessarily disqualify the entire transaction from nontaxable treatment. Section 356(a) requires that a shareholder or security holder recognize gain to the extent of the lesser of the realized gain or the amount of cash received plus the FMV of any other property received. Thus, a shareholder recognizes gain to the extent he or she receives nonqualifying property that does not represent a continuity of equity interest.

EXAMPLE C:7-14 ▶ Upon the liquidation of Theta Corporation in a reorganization, Brian surrenders 1,000 Theta shares having a $13,000 basis in exchange for Alpha Corporation stock having a $28,000 FMV. Brian's realized gain is $15,000 ($28,000 − $13,000), none of which is recognized. If instead Brian had received $25,000 of Alpha stock and $3,000 of cash, he would have recognized $3,000 of the $15,000 realized gain. ◀

ADDITIONAL COMMENT

The acquiring corporation may increase its basis in assets received only to the extent of gain recognized by the target corporation on its exchange with the acquiring corporation. Any gain recognized by the target corporation on distributing stock or other property to its shareholders does not increase the basis of any assets.

With some limitations, the general rule of Sec. 354(a) permits a nontaxable exchange of stock for securities. The receipt of securities is completely nontaxable only if the principal amount of the securities surrendered equals or exceeds the principal amount of the securities received. If such is the case, the FMV of the "excess" constitutes boot.[28] If no securities are surrendered, the FMV of the entire principal amount received constitutes boot. Certain types of preferred stock (e.g., preferred stock that the issuer must redeem) also may constitute boot.

EXAMPLE C:7-15 ▶ Assume the same facts as in Example C:7-14 except Brian instead receives $25,000 of Alpha stock and Alpha debt securities having a $3,000 principal amount and a $2,850 FMV. Brian's realized gain is $14,850 [($25,000 + $2,850) − $13,000], of which $2,850 is recognized. If Brian had received $3,000 in Alpha securities and surrendered $2,000 of Theta securities, the FMV of the $1,000 "excess" principal amount, or $950 [$1,000 × ($2,850/$3,000)], would have been treated as boot. ◀

SELF-STUDY QUESTION

In addition to receiving stock in Alpha Corporation, shareholder Sue receives debt securities with an FMV of $120,000 and a principal amount of $100,000. In the exchange, Sue surrenders securities of Theta Corporation with an FMV and principal amount of $80,000. Is Sue treated as having received any boot?

Character of the Recognized Gain. Section 356(a)(2) requires that the recognized gain be taxed as a dividend if the receipt of the boot property has the same effect as the payment of a dividend. The amount of this dividend equals the lesser of the shareholder's recognized gain or the shareholder's ratable share of the transferor or target

[26] Rev. Rul. 72-327, 1972-2 C.B. 197.

[27] Sec. 1223(1).

[28] Secs. 354(a)(2) and 356(d)(2)(B). The FMV of the debt obligations surrendered is irrelevant when determining the amount of recognized gain.

corporation's current and accumulated earnings and profits (E&P). Any additional recognized gain generally is capital in character.

The Sec. 302(b) stock redemption rules determine whether the exchange has the effect of a dividend payment.[29] (See Chapter C:4 for a review of the Sec. 302(b) rules.) Reorganizations generally do not involve the actual redemption of target corporation stock. For purposes of Sec. 356 and the characterization of any gain, however, they involve the hypothetical redemption of a portion of acquiring corporation stock. When the distribution of boot meets the hypothetical Sec. 302 redemption requirements for sale treatment, the shareholder recognizes capital gain.

The following example applies the dividend equivalency test to the receipt of boot in a reorganization.

ANSWER

Yes. $100,000 − $80,000 = $20,000 of excess principal amount received. The boot received is $24,000. This amount represents the FMV of the excess principal amount [($20,000/$100,000) × $120,000].

EXAMPLE C:7-16 ▶

Betty owns all 80 outstanding shares of Theta Corporation stock having a total FMV of $600,000. In a reorganization, Theta merges with Alpha Corporation, with Betty receiving $250,000 in cash and 35 shares of Alpha stock worth $350,000 in exchange for her Theta stock. Four other individuals own the remaining 100 shares of Alpha stock. Betty's Theta stock has a $200,000 basis. Theta and Alpha have E&P balances of $300,000 and $500,000, respectively. Betty's realized gain is $400,000 [($350,000 stock + $250,000 cash) − $200,000 adjusted basis], of which $250,000 must be recognized because the cash is treated as boot property.

Based on equivalent Alpha per share values, the Theta stock initially is treated as having been exchanged exclusively for Alpha stock (and not for a combination of cash and Alpha stock). Thus, because the Theta stock is worth $600,000 and the Alpha stock is worth $10,000 ($350,000 ÷ 35) per share, Betty initially is treated as having exchanged her 80 shares of Theta stock for 60 shares of Alpha stock, resulting in 160 (100 + 60) shares of Alpha stock deemed outstanding. Next, the $250,000 cash Betty actually received is treated as having been used to redeem 25 ($250,000 ÷ $10,000 per share) of the 60 shares of Alpha stock that Betty hypothetically received in the initial exchange. Because Betty is deemed to have owned 37.5% (60 shares ÷ 160 shares) of Alpha stock before the hypothetical redemption and 25.93% (35 shares ÷ 135 shares) after the hypothetical redemption, the $250,000 gain is capital in character under the Sec. 302(b)(2) substantially disproportionate redemption rules (i.e., 25.93% is less than 80% × 37.5% = 30%). ◀

TYPICAL MISCONCEPTION

Before the *Clark* decision, the IRS referenced the target corporation's E&P to measure the amount of dividend income. Since the *Clark* decision, the IRS has not ruled definitively and generally whether the parties look only to the target corporation's E&P or to the combined E&P of the acquiring and target corporations. However, in CCA 201032035, the IRS's Chief Counsel concluded that the parties must use the combined E&P based on the facts set forth in that advice memorandum.

The Sec. 302(b) test would apply in the same manner where securities are received in the reorganization. In such a case, the boot portion of the transaction would equal the FMV of the "excess" principal amount received by the shareholder or security holder.

Whether capital gain treatment is available for boot received in a reorganization depends on the relative sizes of the target and acquiring corporations. If the acquiring corporation is larger in market value than the target corporation, the Sec. 302(b)(2) (substantially disproportionate redemption) or Sec. 302(b)(1) (not essentially equivalent to a dividend) rules generally will allow capital gain treatment. (See Chapter C:4 for an explanation of these rules.) If the acquiring corporation is smaller in market value than the target corporation, the target corporation's shareholder could be considered as having received dividend income or a combination of dividend income and capital gain (e.g., if the boot received exceeds the shareholder's ratable share of E&P).

Because dividends and capital gains are taxed at the same rate for noncorporate shareholders, the distinction between the two possible treatments in a reorganization may seem insignificant. Nevertheless, capital gains treatment can provide a benefit not available to dividend treatment in that the capital gains can be offset by (1) capital losses recognized in the current year or (2) capital loss carryovers from prior tax years. Dividend income, even though taxed at the capital gains rate, cannot be offset by capital losses.

Corporate shareholders may prefer dividend treatment because they can claim a 70%, 80%, or 100% dividends-received deduction to reduce their tax liability. On the other hand, capital gains recognized in the reorganization can be offset by capital losses

[29] *CIR v. Donald E. Clark*, 63 AFTR 2d 89-1437, 89-1 USTC ¶9230 (USSC, 1989). The IRS has agreed to follow the *Clark* decision in Rev. Rul. 93-61, 1993-2 C.B. 118.

recognized by corporate and noncorporate shareholders in other transactions. Finally, Sec. 453(f)(6)(C) permits a corporate or noncorporate shareholder who is a party to a reorganization to use the installment method to defer recognizing part of the gain realized, provided such gain is not characterized as a dividend.[30]

STOP & THINK

Question: The character of the shareholder's recognized gain is determined under the Sec. 302(b) stock redemption rules. Why are the relative sizes of the acquiring and target corporations in terms of market value important in determining the character of the gain recognized in a reorganization?

Solution: If the target corporation is smaller in market value than the acquiring corporation, the receipt of boot almost always will qualify for capital gains treatment under the redemption rules because generally no shareholder(s) will own more than 50% of the acquiring corporation's stock before and after the hypothetical redemption. If the boot is distributed proportionately to stock ownership, the pre- and post-redemption interests of the target corporation shareholder(s) are likely to be reduced. If the target corporation is larger in market value than the acquiring corporation, a shareholder could own more than 50% of the acquiring corporation stock before and after the hypothetical redemption, resulting in the characterization of boot as a dividend.

KEY POINT

In a nontaxable reorganization, shareholders defer recognition of their realized gain or loss. Consequently, they take a substituted basis in the new nonrecognition property received (i.e., any deferred gain or loss is reflected in the basis of the nonrecognition property received).

Basis of Stock and Securities Received. The basis of stock and securities (nonrecognition property) received by target corporation shareholders and security holders is determined according to the Sec. 358 rules, as discussed in Chapter C:2. Accordingly, the basis of nonrecognition property is calculated as follows:

Adjusted basis of stock and securities surrendered
Plus: Any gain recognized in the exchange
Minus: Cash received in the exchange
FMV of any noncash property received in the exchange
Basis of nonrecognition property received

If a shareholder or security holder receives no boot, the stock and securities take a substituted basis from the stock and securities surrendered. If the shareholder recognizes gain, the basis of stock and securities surrendered is increased by the amount of such gain and then reduced by the amount of cash plus the FMV of any other boot property received in the reorganization. The basis of any other boot property is its FMV.

EXAMPLE C:7-17 ▶ Keith owns Theta Corporation stock having a $10,000 adjusted basis. In a reorganization, Keith exchanges his Theta stock for $12,000 of Alpha stock and $4,000 of Alpha securities. Keith realizes a $6,000 gain [($12,000 + $4,000) − $10,000], of which he must recognize $4,000 because he received securities worth $4,000 but surrendered no securities. The basis of the Alpha securities that Keith received is $4,000. Keith's basis in the Alpha stock is $10,000 ($10,000 basis of Theta stock + $4,000 gain recognized − $4,000 FMV of Alpha securities). ◀

When the target corporation shareholders initially own a single class of stock (or a single class of securities) and exchange that stock for two or more classes of stock or securities in a reorganization, the total basis in the nonrecognition property as calculated under the above formula must be allocated among the stock and/or securities in proportion to the relative FMVs of each class.[31]

Holding Period. The holding period for the stock and securities that are nonrecognition property includes the holding period for the stock and securities surrendered. The holding period for boot property begins the day after the exchange date.[32]

[30] *King Enterprises, Inc. v. U.S.*, 24 AFTR 2d 69-5866, 69-2 USTC ¶9720 (Ct. Cls., 1969).

[31] Reg. Sec. 1.358-2(a)(2)-(4).

[32] Sec. 1223(1).

Topic Review C:7-4 summarizes the tax consequences of a reorganization to the target corporation, acquiring corporation, and target corporation shareholders and security holders.

TOPIC REVIEW C:7-4

Tax Consequences of a Reorganization

THE TARGET CORPORATION

1. The target corporation recognizes no gain or loss on the asset transfer except to the extent that it receives and retains cash or other boot property (Secs. 361(a)–(b)). Generally, boot is not retained because the reorganization provisions require the target corporation to liquidate or otherwise distribute all its assets.
2. The character of any recognized gain or loss depends on the nature of the assets transferred.
3. The acquiring corporation's assumption or acquisition of target corporation liabilities does not trigger recognition of gain on the asset transfer except where "excess" liabilities are assumed in divisive Type D reorganizations (Sec. 357(a)).
4. The target corporation recognizes no gain or loss when it distributes qualified stock and securities to its shareholders and security holders. The target corporation recognizes gain (but not loss) when it distributes to its shareholders or security holders noncash boot property or retained assets (Sec. 361(c)).

THE ACQUIRING CORPORATION

1. The acquiring corporation recognizes no gain or loss when it receives cash or other boot property in exchange for its stock or debt obligations (Sec. 1032).
2. On the other hand, the acquiring corporation recognizes gain or loss when it transfers appreciated or depreciated (in value) noncash boot property to the target corporation or its shareholders (Sec. 1001).
3. The basis of noncash property received by the acquiring corporation equals its basis in the transferor's hands increased by any gain recognized by the transferor (Sec. 362(b)).
4. The acquiring corporation's holding period for such property includes the transferor's holding period (Sec. 1223(1)).

SHAREHOLDERS AND SECURITY HOLDERS

1. Shareholders and security holders recognize no gain or loss if they receive only stock (Sec. 354(a)). They recognize gain (but not loss) when they receive cash, excess securities, or other boot property. The amount of recognized gain equals the lesser of the realized gain or the amount of cash plus the FMV of any other boot property received (Sec. 356(b)).
2. The character of recognized gain is based on the Sec. 302(b) redemption rules, as applied hypothetically to receipt of acquiring corporation stock. Dividend income cannot exceed the shareholder's ratable share of the transferor or target corporation's E&P (Sec. 356(a)(2)).
3. The total basis of stock and securities received equals the adjusted basis of stock and securities surrendered plus any gain recognized by the shareholders and security holders on the exchange minus the sum of cash and FMV of other boot property received. This basis is allocated among the stock and securities received according to their relative FMVs. The basis of boot property is its FMV (Sec. 358(a)).
4. The holding period for stock and securities received includes the holding period for stock and securities surrendered. The holding period for boot property received begins the day after the exchange date (Sec. 1223(1)).

ACQUISITIVE REORGANIZATIONS

OBJECTIVE 4

Describe the structure and requirements of each type of acquisitive reorganization

This section is devoted to Types A, B, C, D, and G acquisitive reorganizations. Each of these types is explained below. Topic Review C:7-5 summarizes the tax aspects of acquisitive reorganizations.

TYPE A REORGANIZATION

Type A reorganizations encompass four transactional structures: mergers, consolidations, triangular mergers, and reverse triangular mergers. Each of these structures is summarized in Topic Review C:7-5.

TOPIC REVIEW C:7-5

Summary of Major Acquisitive Reorganizations

Type of Reorganization	The Target (T) Corporation Property Acquired	Consideration That Can Be Used	What Happens to the Target (T) Corporation?	Shareholders' Recognized Gain	Other Requirements
A—Merger or consolidation	Assets and liabilities of T Corporation.[a]	Voting and nonvoting stock, securities, and other property of A Corporation.[b]	T Corporation liquidates as part of the merger.	Lesser of realized gain or FMV of boot received.	Transaction must have a business purpose and meet continuity of interest and business enterprise requirements.
B—Stock for stock	At least 80% of voting and 80% of nonvoting T Corporation stock.	Voting stock of A Corporation.	Becomes a subsidiary of A Corporation.	None	Boot paid by the transferor may render the entire transaction taxable.
C—Assets for stock	Substantially all T Corporation assets (and possibly some or all of its liabilities).	A Corporation stock, securities, and other property, provided at least 80% of the assets are acquired for voting stock.	Stock, securities, and boot received in the reorganization and all of T Corporation's remaining properties must be distributed to its shareholders and creditors; as a practical matter, T Corporation liquidates.	Lesser of realized gain or FMV of boot received.	For advance ruling purposes, "substantially all" is 70% of the gross assets and 90% of the net assets of T Corporation.
D—Acquisitive	Substantially all T Corporation assets (and possibly some or all of its liabilities) are acquired by a "controlled" transferee corporation (A Corporation[b]).	A Corporation stock, securities, and other property.	Stocks, securities, and boot received in the reorganization and all of T Corporation's remaining property must be distributed to its shareholders and creditors; as a practical matter, T Corporation liquidates.	Lesser of realized gain or FMV of boot received.	"Substantially all" definition is same as in a Type C reorganization; continuity of interest requirement applies; control is defined as 50% of the voting power or 50% of the value of A Corporation stock.

[a]T Corporation is the target or transferor corporation.
[b]A Corporation is the acquiring or controlled transferee corporation. In a Type D reorganization, A Corporation is 50% or more controlled by T Corporation shareholders.

KEY POINT

The Type A reorganization is unique in comparison to other statutory reorganizations because corporation law determines whether a transaction qualifies as a nontaxable merger.

Merger or Consolidation. In its broadest sense, a Type A reorganization is a **merger** or a **consolidation** that satisfies the corporation laws of the United States, a state, the District of Columbia, or a foreign country.[33] State law authorizes several different merger forms. Two common forms are discussed below. Other permitted forms, such as triangular mergers and reverse triangular mergers, are discussed later in this chapter. The first form involves the acquiring corporation's transferring its stock, securities, and other consideration (boot) directly to the target corporation in exchange for its assets and liabilities. The acquiring corporation stock, securities, and other consideration received by the target corporation are then distributed to its shareholders and security holders in exchange for their target corporation stock and securities. The target corporation then goes out of existence (i.e., it is legally "dissolved"). Figure C:7-1 illustrates this type of merger. The second form involves the acquiring corporation's exchanging its stock, securities, and other consideration directly for target corporation stock and securities held by target corporation shareholders and security holders. The acquiring corporation then liquidates the target corporation and acquires its assets and liabilities.

In a consolidation, a new corporation uses stock, securities, and other consideration to acquire the assets of two or more existing target corporations. Each target corporation distributes the stock, securities, and other consideration to its shareholders and security holders in exchange for target corporation stock and securities. It then liquidates. Figure C:7-2 illustrates this type of consolidation. In another type, the new acquiring corporation transfers its stock, securities, and other consideration directly to target corporation shareholders and security holders in exchange for their target corporation stock and securities. Each target corporation transfers its assets and liabilities to the acquiring corporation and then liquidates.

KEY POINT

An A reorganization is the most flexible type of reorganization in terms of the consideration that may be used. The only requirement that must be satisfied concerns continuity of interest, which is discussed later in the chapter.

Requirements for Mergers and Consolidations. In terms of consideration, a Type A reorganization gives the acquiring corporation the greatest flexibility. Section 368 places no restrictions on the kind of consideration that can be used. Under the continuity of

ADDITIONAL COMMENT

The actual exchange of acquiring corporation stock for target corporation stock may be different from the illustrations provided in this chapter. These illustrations represent how the IRC construes the steps in each reorganization. As a practical matter, the exchange of stock between the parties usually is performed through an independent stock transfer agent rather than flowing from the acquiring corporation to the target corporation and finally to the target corporation shareholders.

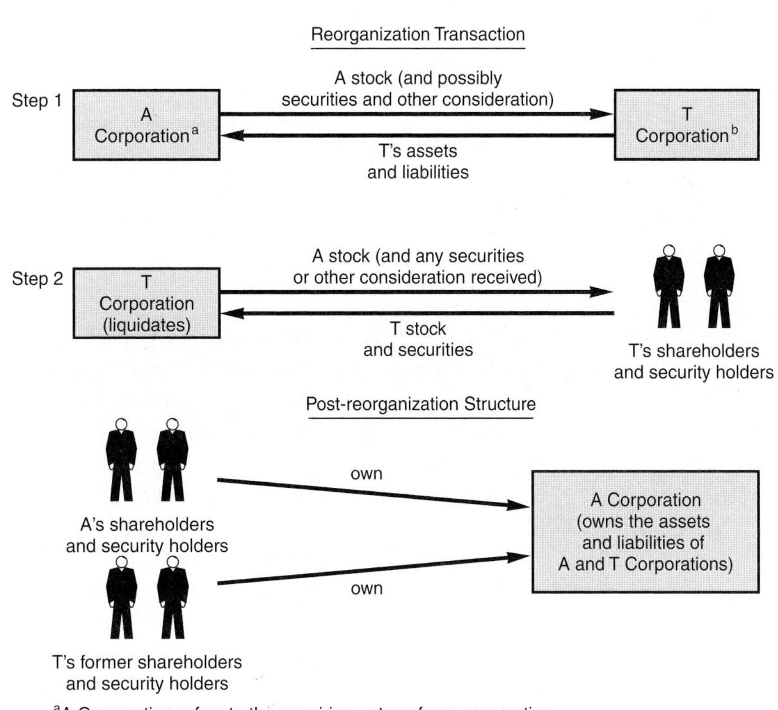

[a]A Corporation refers to the acquiring or transferee corporation.

[b]T Corporation refers to the target or transferor corporation.

FIGURE C:7-1 ▶ TYPE A REORGANIZATION—MERGER

[33] Sec. 368(a)(1)(A) and Reg. Sec. 1.368-2(b)(1).

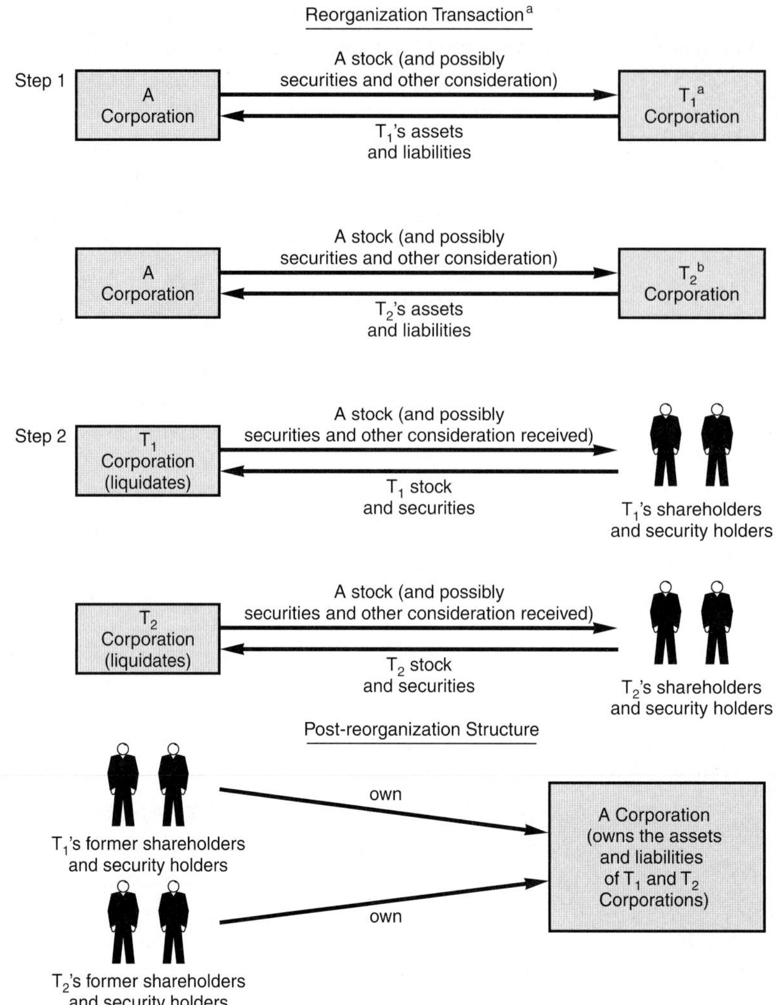

FIGURE C:7-2 ▶ TYPE A REORGANIZATION: CONSOLIDATION

interest doctrine, as interpreted by the IRS, stock of the acquiring corporation must be a significant part of the total consideration used. In the past, the IRS did not issue a private letter ruling regarding the tax-free nature of the transaction if the percentage of the acquiring corporation stock used as consideration was less than 50% of the total consideration.[34] The stock could be voting, nonvoting, or a combination of the two, and it could be common or preferred. More recent Treasury Regulations, however, allow continuity of interest with only 40% of the consideration consisting of the acquiring corporation stock.[35] Thus, these regulations appear to have superseded the IRS's previous ruling position.

The IRS requires that, to qualify as a Type A reorganization, the merger must satisfy the requirements of the applicable federal, state, or foreign corporate merger law. In addition, the target corporation must go out of existence or be dissolved.[36] An acquisition does not qualify as a Type A reorganization if the target corporation retains some assets and target corporation shareholders retain some target stock. Revenue Ruling 2000-5 holds that, if a target corporation merges under state law into two or more acquiring corporations and the target corporation does not go out of existence, the transaction does not qualify as a Type A reorganization.

[34] See Rev. Proc. 77-37, 1977-2 C.B. 568, Sec. 3.02. In recent years, tax opinions from tax counsel have largely replaced private letter rulings for most acquisitive reorganizations.

[35] Reg. Sec. 1.368-1(e)(2)(v), Example 1.

[36] Rev. Rul. 2000-5, 2000-1 C.B. 436.

ADDITIONAL COMMENT

Shareholder approval is time consuming, expensive, and difficult to obtain, particularly in the case of large public corporations having shareholders that are widely dispersed.

Because a merger or consolidation must comply with state, federal, or foreign corporation laws, transactions that qualify as mergers or consolidations, and the procedures that must be followed to effect them, vary according to the laws of the jurisdictions in which the acquiring and target corporations are incorporated. Generally, these laws require approval by a majority of shareholders of the corporate parties to the merger. Where the stock in one or both of the companies is publicly traded, holding a shareholder's meeting, soliciting proxies, and obtaining the necessary corporate approvals may be costly and time consuming.

The rights of any dissenting shareholders are defined in merger law. Among these rights are the right to dissent and have shares independently valued and purchased for cash. Liquidating the interests of a substantial number of dissenting shareholders may require a large cash outlay and could, in some circumstances, violate the continuity-of-interest doctrine.

A transaction that does not satisfy the requirements of the applicable corporation law does not qualify as a Type A reorganization.[37] Generally, this deficiency renders the entire transaction taxable.

Advantages and Disadvantages of a Type A Reorganization. A Type A reorganization offers a number of advantages and disadvantages.

Advantages:

- A Type A reorganization is more flexible than other types of reorganizations because the consideration need not be solely voting stock, as in the case of some other types. Cash, securities, other property, and the assumption of the target corporation's liabilities can constitute up to 60% of the total consideration used.[38]
- Substantially all the assets of the target corporation need not be acquired, as in the case of a Type C reorganization. Thus, dispositions of unwanted assets by the target corporation prior to, or as part of, the acquisition generally do not render the merger taxable.

Disadvantages:

- The parties to the merger must comply with applicable corporation laws. In most states, the shareholders of both the acquiring and target corporations must approve a plan of merger by a two-thirds majority. Such approvals can take time and be costly if stock in one or both of the corporations is publicly traded.
- Dissenting shareholders of both corporations generally have the right to have their shares independently appraised and purchased for cash, which may require a substantial cash outlay.
- All liabilities of the target corporation, including unknown and contingent liabilities, must be assumed.
- A merger requires the transfer of real estate titles, leases, and contracts. The target corporation may have licenses, rights, or other privileges that are nontransferable. This limitation may necessitate a reverse triangular merger or Type B reorganization discussed below.

Tax Consequences of a Merger. The following example illustrates the tax consequences of a merger.

EXAMPLE C:7-18 ▶ In a merger that qualifies as a Type A reorganization, Theta Corporation transfers to Alpha Corporation all its assets having a $2 million FMV and a $1.3 million adjusted basis, respectively, together with $400,000 in liabilities, in exchange for $1 million of Alpha common stock having a $16 per share market value and $600,000 of cash. At the time of the transfer, Alpha's E&P balance is $1 million, and Theta's is $750,000. Theta distributes the Acquiring stock and cash to its sole shareholder, Millie, in exchange for all her Theta stock, which has a $175,000 basis. If Millie had received only Alpha stock (instead of a combination of Alpha stock and cash), she would have held 6.25% of Alpha stock (100,000 out of 1.6 million shares deemed outstanding) immediately after the exchange.

---

[37] *Edward H. Russell v. CIR*, 15 AFTR 2d 1107, 65-2 USTC ¶9448 (5th Cir., 1965).

[38] Previous advance ruling requirements generally limited nonstock consideration to 50% of the total consideration. In certain circumstances, the courts have permitted the 50% ceiling to be exceeded. Treasury Regulations now allow up to 60% nonstock consideration. See footnote 35.

In the asset transfer, Theta realizes a $700,000 gain [($1,000,000 stock + $600,000 cash + $400,000 liabilities) − $1,300,000 adjusted basis] but recognizes none of this gain. Alpha takes a $1.3 million carryover basis in the assets it receives. Theta recognizes no gain when it distributes the stock and cash to Millie.

Upon Theta's liquidation, Millie realizes a $1,425,000 gain [($1,000,000 stock + $600,000 cash) − $175,000 adjusted basis], of which $600,000 must be recognized because of the cash (i.e., boot) received. The hypothetical redemption of Millie's Alpha stock required under the *Clark* case and Rev. Rul. 93-61 (see pages C:7-16 and C:7-17) qualifies for Sec. 302(b)(2) sale treatment because the deemed redemption of 37,500 ($600,000 cash ÷ $16) shares of Alpha stock reduces Millie's interest from 6.25% (100,000 shares ÷ 1,600,000 shares) to 4.00% (62,500 shares ÷ 1,562,500 shares). Millie's basis in her Alpha stock is $175,000 ($175,000 basis of Theta stock + $600,000 gain recognized − $600,000 cash received). Millie's holding period for the Alpha stock includes her holding period for the Theta stock. ◀

ADDITIONAL COMMENT

If the IRS applies Sec. 351 to the drop-down transaction, and if the total adjusted basis for all property transferred exceeds the total FMV of that property, the subsidiary's total basis will be limited to the total FMV (see Chapter C:2 for details).

Drop-Down Type A Reorganization. The reorganization rules permit the acquiring corporation to transfer (drop down) to a controlled subsidiary part or all the assets and liabilities acquired in the merger or consolidation.[39] The drop down does not affect the nontaxable nature of the transaction. Thus, neither the parent nor subsidiary recognize gain or loss. The subsidiary takes from its parent a carryover basis in the assets.

Triangular Mergers. Triangular mergers are authorized under Sec. 368(a)(2)(D). They are similar to straight mergers (previously discussed) except the parent corporation uses a controlled subsidiary to acquire target corporation stock or assets. The target corporation then merges into the subsidiary under one of the two merger structures described earlier (see Figure C:7-3).

Triangular mergers must satisfy the same legal requirements as straight mergers. In addition, the stock used as consideration in the transaction is restricted to that of the parent corporation. On the other hand, a limited amount of subsidiary cash and securities can be used, and the subsidiary can assume the target corporation's liabilities.

The "Substantially All" Requirement. To be nontaxable, the subsidiary must acquire substantially all of target corporation's assets pursuant to a plan of reorganization. For advance ruling purposes, the IRS has defined *substantially all* to be at least 70% of the FMV of the target corporation's gross assets and 90% of the FMV of its net assets.[40]

EXAMPLE C:7-19 ▶ In a triangular merger, Alpha Corporation's subsidiary, Alpha-Sub Corporation, plans to acquire $2.5 million (FMV) in assets and $1 million in liabilities of Theta Corporation. Under the IRS's advance ruling policy, Alpha must acquire at least 70% of Theta's gross assets ($1,750,000 = $2,500,000 FMV of assets × 0.70) and 90% of its net assets [$1,350,000 = ($2,500,000 FMV of assets − $1,000,000 liabilities) × 0.90], or $1.75 million in assets. Theta can sell or otherwise dispose of the remaining assets. ◀

Advantages of a Triangular Merger. The tax treatment of a triangular merger is the same as for a straight merger. A triangular merger, however, offers three advantages over a straight merger:

PRACTICAL APPLICATION

The triangular merger is a very popular form of acquisition because the type of consideration that may be used is still very flexible and yet the parent corporation does not have to assume the known or unknown liabilities of the target corporation. Rather, the controlled subsidiary assumes these liabilities.

- In a triangular merger, the target corporation's assets and liabilities become the responsibility of the subsidiary. Thus, the parent corporation generally cannot be held liable for any unknown or contingent liabilities. Potential claims against the parent corporation from the target corporation's creditors are thus minimized.
- Because the parent corporation is the principal shareholder in the acquiring subsidiary, obtaining shareholder approval for the transaction is relatively easy. Accordingly, the cost of obtaining shareholder approval may be less, especially if the parent corporation's stock is widely held.

[39] Sec. 368(a)(2)(C). As defined in Sec. 368(c), *control* requires the parent corporation to own at least 80% of the voting power and 80% of each class of nonvoting stock. The ability to "drop down" the assets acquired to a subsidiary corporation without recognizing any gain also applies to Type B, C, and G reorganizations.

[40] Rev. Proc. 77-37, 1977-2 C.B. 568, Sec. 3.01. Also see Rev. Rul. 2001-46, 2001-2 C.B. 321.

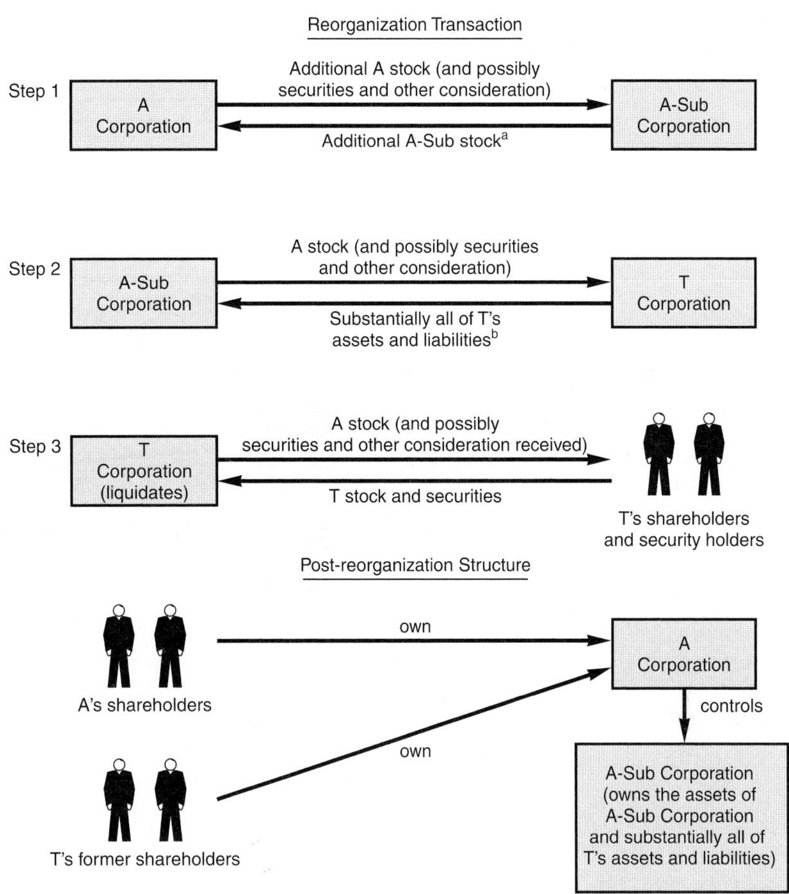

FIGURE C:7-3 ▶ TRIANGULAR TYPE A REORGANIZATION

- ▶ The target corporation shareholders may prefer to receive parent corporation stock, especially if such stock is publicly traded, because of its greater marketability. By selling shares of this stock over an extended period of time, target shareholders can recognize the gain as if they were using the installment method of accounting.

ADDITIONAL COMMENT

In addition to the Type B reorganization, which will be discussed later, the reverse triangular merger is an acquisitive reorganization in which the target corporation remains in existence. It is a popular reorganization form because, unlike the Type B reorganization, the acquiring corporation can use a limited amount of boot.

Reverse Triangular Mergers. A **reverse triangular merger** is similar to the triangular merger illustrated in Figure C:7-3 except the subsidiary (A-Sub Corporation) merges into the target corporation (T Corporation), the target corporation remains in existence as a subsidiary of the parent corporation (A Corporation), and A-Sub Corporation goes out of existence. Continuing the target corporation as a going concern may be desirable from a business standpoint where the corporation holds nontransferable rights, licenses, and contracts. Technical details of this type of acquisition are beyond the scope of this text.

TYPE C REORGANIZATION

A **Type C reorganization** is an asset-for-stock acquisition. This type of transaction, illustrated in Figure C:7-4, requires the acquiring corporation to obtain substantially all the target corporation's assets in exchange for acquiring corporation voting stock and possibly a limited amount of other consideration.[41]

[41] Sec. 368(a)(1)(C).

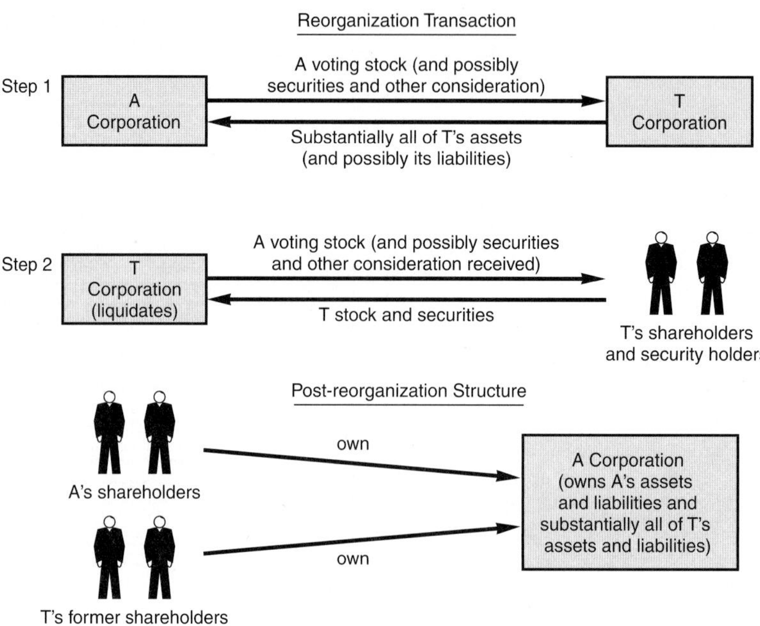

FIGURE C:7-4 ▶ TYPE C (ASSET-FOR-STOCK) REORGANIZATION

The term "substantially all" is not defined in the IRC or Treasury Regulations. For advance ruling purposes, however, the same minimum standard that applies to triangular Type A mergers (i.e., 70% of the FMV of gross assets and 90% of the FMV of net assets) applies to Type C reorganizations.[42]

ADDITIONAL COMMENT

The term "dissolution" means the corporation ceases to exist as a legal entity. The term "liquidation" means the corporation distributes all its assets without necessarily dissolving.

In a Type C reorganization the target corporation must distribute the stock, securities, and other property it receives, plus any other property it retains, to its shareholders as part of the reorganization. Although the corporation need not formally dissolve, as a practical matter it usually liquidates.[43] If it does dissolve, any liabilities not assumed by the acquiring corporation usually become the responsibility of the target corporation's directors by statute. Because the economic effect of a Type C reorganization is the same as that of a merger (i.e., the acquisition of target corporation assets) without dissolving the target corporation, many tax practitioners call it a practical merger.

In a Type C reorganization, the target corporation can retain its corporate charter to prevent others from using its corporate name or sell its corporate name to a third party. Assets other than the corporate charter can be retained to satisfy the minimum capital requirements of state law.[44]

ADDITIONAL COMMENT

Because of the solely-for-voting-stock requirement, a Type C reorganization is much less flexible than a Type A reorganization in terms of the type of consideration that can be used.

Consideration Used to Effect the Reorganization. Section 368(a)(1)(C) requires that the consideration used to effect the reorganization be solely voting stock of the acquiring corporation (or its parent corporation). Both the acquiring corporation's assumption of part or all of target corporation liabilities and its acquiring property subject to a liability are disregarded for purposes of the solely-for-voting-stock requirement.

Section 368(a)(2)(B) permits the acquiring corporation to use other consideration in the reorganization, provided it obtains at least 80% of target property solely for its voting stock. Effectively, this provision allows the acquiring corporation to use cash, securities, nonvoting stock, or other property to acquire up to 20% of target assets. Liabilities assumed or acquired reduce on a dollar-for-dollar basis the amount of cash or other property the acquiring corporation can use in the reorganization. If the liabilities assumed or acquired equal or exceed 20% of the FMV of target assets, the transaction will qualify as a Type C reorganization only if the acquiring corporation uses no cash, securities, nonvoting stock, or other property as consideration.

[42] Rev. Proc. 77-37, 1977-2 C.B. 568, Sec. 3.01.
[43] Sec. 368(a)(2)(G).
[44] Rev. Proc. 89-50, 1989-1 C.B. 631.

EXAMPLE C:7-20 ▶ Alpha Corporation wants to acquire all of Theta Corporation's assets and liabilities in a Type C reorganization. The following table illustrates how the solely-for-voting-stock test applies in four different situations:

	Situation 1	*Situation 2*	*Situation 3*	*Situation 4*
FMV of Theta assets	$200,000	$200,000	$200,000	$200,000
Theta liabilities assumed by Alpha	–0–	30,000	60,000	40,000
Consideration given by Alpha:				
FMV of Alpha voting stock	160,000	160,000	140,000	150,000
Cash	40,000	10,000	–0–	10,000

In Situation 1, because the FMV of the Alpha stock equals 80% of total assets, the transaction qualifies as a Type C reorganization. In Situation 2, although the liabilities assumed reduce the amount of cash Alpha can pay, the transaction is still a Type C reorganization because the amount of cash and liabilities, in total, do not exceed 20% of the FMV of Theta assets. In Situation 3, the high percentage of liabilities (30%) does not disqualify the transaction from Type C reorganization treatment because Alpha paid no cash.[45] In Situation 4, the transaction fails as a Type C reorganization because Alpha uses cash and stock, and the total amount of cash given plus liabilities assumed by Alpha exceed 20% of the total FMV of Theta assets. ◀

ADDITIONAL COMMENT

A target corporation's liabilities assumed by the acquiring corporation do not have tax consequences unless the target corporation receives boot as part of the consideration. In this case, when applying the 20% boot relaxation rule, liabilities are treated as cash. Situation 4 in Example C:7-20 illustrates that, if the target corporation has liabilities exceeding 20% of the FMV of its assets, the boot relaxation rule is of no benefit.

Advantages and Disadvantages of a Type C Reorganization. Relative to a statutory merger, a Type C reorganization offers the following advantages and disadvantages.

SELF-STUDY QUESTION

Must the acquiring corporation assume all liabilities of the target corporation in a Type C reorganization?

ANSWER

No. The acquiring corporation may leave liabilities with the target corporation. These liabilities would then have to be satisfied with assets retained by the target corporation or with assets acquired by the target corporation in the reorganization.

Advantages:

- A Type C reorganization does not have to comply with the merger laws of a state or the federal government as does a Type A reorganization (merger). However, it might have to comply with other laws (e.g., corporate and securities laws).
- In a Type C reorganization, the acquiring corporation assumes only those target corporation liabilities specified in the acquisition agreement. Unknown and contingent liabilities are not assumed, as they are in a merger.
- In a Type C reorganization, shareholders of the acquiring corporation generally need not approve the acquisition, thereby reducing the total transaction cost. In a merger, however, acquiring and target corporation shareholders must approve the transaction.

Disadvantages:

- In a Type C reorganization, the acquiring corporation must use voting stock in contrast to a Type A reorganization, in which the acquiring corporation may use nonvoting stock.
- A Type C reorganization has much tighter boot restrictions than does a Type A reorganization in which up to 60% of consideration other than stock can be used (see footnote 35).
- In many cases, target liabilities assumed by the acquiring corporation may be so substantial (i.e., equaling or exceeding 20% of total consideration) as to preclude the use of any consideration other than voting stock.
- The target corporation might want to sell, dispose of, or retain assets the acquiring corporation does not want. However, doing so shortly before an asset-for-stock acquisition might cause the transaction to fail the substantially all test and thereby disqualify it as a Type C reorganization. By contrast, the substantially all test does not apply to a merger, and dispositions of unwanted assets generally will not disqualify a merger as a Type A reorganization.

ADDITIONAL COMMENT

In either a Type A or Type C reorganization, dissenting shareholders of the target corporation may have the right under state law to have their shares independently appraised and purchased for cash.

[45] The IRS, however, may attempt to treat a transaction as a purchase under the continuity of interest doctrine (see page C:7-41) when the amount of liabilities assumed or acquired is high relative to the total FMV of the assets acquired.

Tax Consequences of a Type C Reorganization. The following example illustrates the tax consequences of a Type C reorganization.

EXAMPLE C:7-21 ▶ Alpha Corporation acquires all Theta Corporation's assets and liabilities in exchange for $1.2 million of Alpha voting stock. Theta distributes the Alpha stock to its sole shareholder, Andrew, in exchange for all his Theta stock. Theta's assets have a $1.4 million FMV and a $600,000 adjusted basis. Alpha assumes liabilities of $200,000. Theta has a $500,000 E&P balance. Andrew's basis in his Theta stock is $400,000. Theta realizes an $800,000 gain [($1,200,000 + $200,000) − $600,000], none of which is recognized. Alpha recognizes no gain when it exchanges its stock for the assets, in which it takes a $600,000 carryover basis. Upon surrendering his Theta shares, Andrew realizes an $800,000 ($1,200,000 − $400,000) gain, none of which is recognized. Andrew's substituted basis in the Alpha stock is $400,000. Andrew's holding period for the Alpha stock includes his holding period for the Theta stock. Alpha inherits all of Theta's tax attributes, including the $500,000 E&P balance. ◀

TYPICAL MISCONCEPTION

As with a Type A reorganization, a Type C reorganization can be structured as a triangular (but not reverse triangular) acquisition. Although this feature provides greater flexibility in tax planning, it makes the tax consequences more complicated because of the substantial overlap between the different types of reorganizations.

Drop-Down and Triangular Type C Reorganizations. In a Type C reorganization, the acquiring corporation can transfer (drop down) the acquired assets and liabilities to a controlled subsidiary without adversely affecting the nontaxable character of the Type C reorganization. Alternatively, an acquiring subsidiary can use parent corporation voting stock to acquire substantially all the target corporation's assets.[46] The triangular Type C reorganization requirements are the same as those for a basic Type C reorganization except the voting stock used by the acquiring subsidiary to acquire target corporation assets must consist solely of the parent's stock. The acquiring subsidiary, however, can provide additional consideration in the form of securities, cash, or other property.

KEY POINT

When a Type D reorganization is used as an acquisitive reorganization, it generally involves commonly controlled corporations. However, its most common usage is as part of a divisive reorganization under Sec. 355 (discussed later in this chapter).

TYPE D REORGANIZATION

Type D reorganizations can be either acquisitive or divisive. (Divisive Type D reorganizations are discussed on pages C:7-33 through C:7-38.) In an acquisitive Type D reorganization, a target (transferor) corporation transfers substantially all its assets to an acquiring (transferee) corporation in exchange for the transferee's stock and securities (and possibly other consideration) pursuant to a plan of reorganization. The exchange must be followed by a distribution of the stock, securities, and other consideration received in the reorganization, plus any other property retained by the transferor corporation, to the transferor's shareholders and security holders pursuant to a complete liquidation.[47] (See Figure C:7-5 for an illustration of an acquisitive Type D reorganization.)

What constitutes "substantially all" is based on the facts and circumstances. For advance ruling purposes, however, the 70% of the FMV of gross assets and 90% of the FMV of net assets tests used in the triangular Type A and Type C reorganizations also apply here.[48]

ADDITIONAL COMMENT

The 50% control requirement makes the Type D reorganization a useful tool for the IRS to recast certain tax avoidance transactions.

Control Requirements. The transferor (target) corporation or one or more of its shareholders must control the transferee (acquiring) corporation immediately after the asset transfer. Section 368(a)(2)(H) defines control as either 50% or more of the total combined voting power of all classes of voting stock, or 50% or more of the total value of all classes of stock.

In one version of an acquisitive Type D reorganization, an acquiring corporation acquires all the assets of a larger corporation (target corporation), and target corporation shareholders control the acquiring corporation after the reorganization. Type C reorganizations (in which the target corporation does not control the acquiring corporation) and Type A reorganizations (which must comply with state, federal, or foreign merger law) are more common than acquisitive Type D reorganizations.

Tax Consequences of a Type D Reorganization. Acquisitive Type D reorganization requirements are similar to those for a Type C reorganization. If the reorganization satisfies both the Type C and Type D reorganization requirements, Sec. 368(a)(2)(A) mandates that the

[46] Sec. 368(a)(2)(C) and Sec. 368(a)(1)(C).
[47] Secs. 368(a)(1)(D) and 354(b)(1).
[48] Rev. Proc. 77-37, 1977-2 C.B. 568, Sec. 3.01.

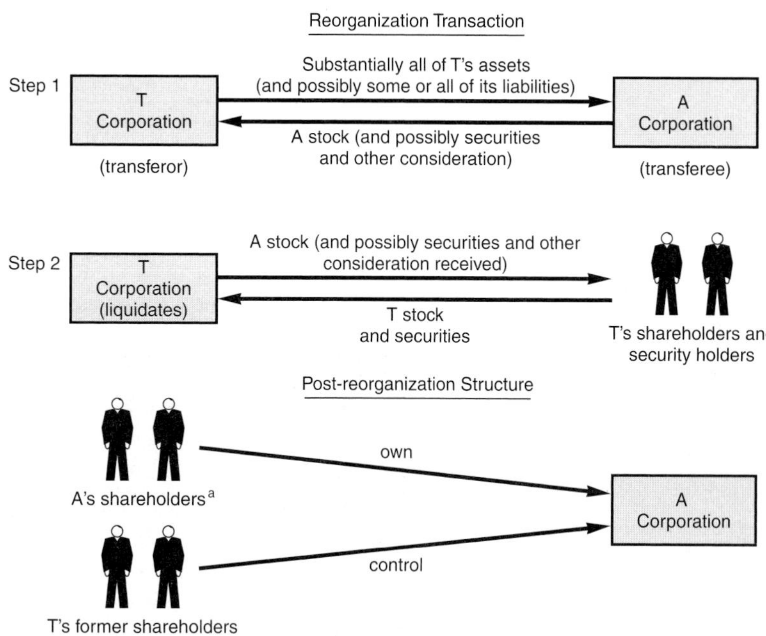

FIGURE C:7-5 ▶ ACQUISITIVE TYPE D REORGANIZATION

reorganization be treated as Type D. The basic tax consequences of a Type D reorganization to the target corporation, the acquiring corporation, and target corporation shareholders are the same as those in a Type C reorganization.

ADDITIONAL COMMENT

If the acquiring corporation wants the target corporation to remain in existence, the two transactional alternatives in Sec. 368 that can accomplish this objective are a Type B reorganization or a reverse triangular merger.

TYPE B REORGANIZATION

A **Type B reorganization** is the simplest of acquisitive reorganizations. In this type of reorganization, target corporation shareholders (or parent company) exchange their stock for acquiring corporation voting stock, and the target corporation remains in existence as the acquiring corporation's subsidiary (see Figure C:7-6). No Sec. 338 election is available because, in any reorganization, the stock is not considered "purchased" for purposes of this election.

A Type B reorganization generally preserves the target corporation as a going concern. The basis of the target's assets (inside basis) and its tax attributes generally remain unchanged. After the reorganization, the target corporation and its parent may elect to file a consolidated tax return (see Chapter C:8). If the target corporation liquidates into its parent shortly after the stock-for-stock exchange, the IRS may attempt to collapse the two-step transaction into a single transaction and treat it as a Type C asset-for-stock reorganization.[49]

KEY POINT

The IRC allows no relaxation of the solely-for-voting-stock requirement for the Type B reorganization. Thus, the Type B reorganization has the least flexible consideration requirement of any of the reorganizations.

Solely-for-Voting-Stock Requirement. Under Sec. 368(a)(1)(B), the acquiring corporation must acquire target corporation stock solely in exchange for acquiring corporation voting stock. The acquiring corporation must own sufficient stock to be in control of the target corporation immediately after the exchange.

The solely-for-voting-stock requirement generally precludes the use of other property as consideration in the transaction. However, the voting stock used can be either common or preferred. If the acquiring corporation uses consideration other than voting stock (e.g., nonvoting preferred stock), the transaction will not qualify as a Type B reorganization and thus will be taxable to target corporation shareholders.

In a Type B reorganization, acquiring corporation debt obligations can be exchanged for target corporation debt obligations held by target shareholders, who will not recognize gain or loss if the face amounts of the two obligations are the same.[50]

---

[49] Rev. Rul. 67-274, 1967-2 C.B. 141. If the transaction is "collapsed" into a Type C reorganization, the Type C reorganization requirements (and not the Type B) must be satisfied.

[50] Rev. Rul. 98-10, 1998-1 C.B. 643.

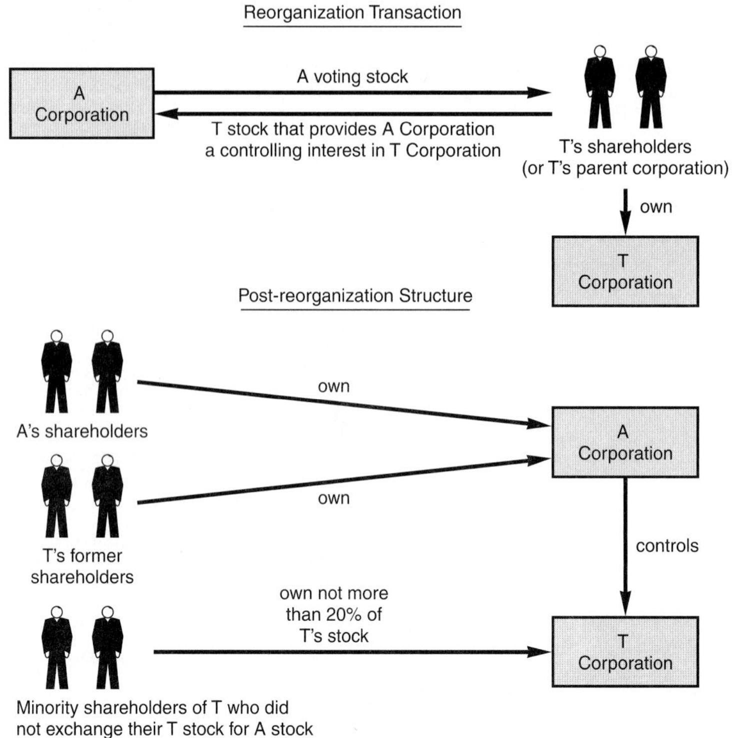

FIGURE C:7-6 ▶ TYPE B (STOCK-FOR-STOCK) REORGANIZATION

SELF-STUDY QUESTION

How can dissenters in a Type B reorganization be handled given the no-boot restriction?

ANSWER

The target corporation can redeem the dissenting shares before the reorganization. Also, the nondissenting shareholders could buy out the dissenters' stock.

ADDITIONAL COMMENT

"Creeping acquisitions" are allowed in a Type B reorganization because the requirement is merely that the acquiring corporation own 80% after the transaction. Transactions within 12 months generally are considered related transactions. This aggregation rule can be either an advantage or a disadvantage depending on what consideration the acquiring corporation used in the various acquisition steps.

Exceptions. The acquiring corporation can use cash in limited circumstances without violating the solely-for-voting-stock requirement. For example:

- ▶ The target corporation shareholders can receive cash in exchange for their right to receive a fractional share of acquiring corporation stock.[51]
- ▶ The acquiring corporation can pay reorganization expenses (such as legal expenses, accounting fees, and administrative costs) of the target corporation without violating the solely-for-voting-stock requirement.[52]

Control. For the purpose of a Type B reorganization, Section 368(c) defines control as 80% of the total combined voting power of all classes of voting stock and 80% of each class of nonvoting stock. Because the acquiring corporation need not acquire all the target corporation stock, a minority interest of up to 20% may remain. Under state law, minority shareholders can have their shares independently valued and acquired for cash without impairing the tax-free nature of the transaction. The target corporation can use its cash to redeem the minority shareholders' stock before or after the reorganization. The acquiring corporation, however, cannot use cash to purchase the dissenting minority shareholders' stock either before or as part of the reorganization. Doing so will render the entire transaction taxable.[53]

Timing of the Transaction. Some Type B reorganizations are conducted in a single transaction by exchanging stock of the acquiring corporation for 100% of target corporation shares. In other instances, the reorganization is accomplished through a series of transactions over an extended period of time. Regulation Sec. 1.368-2(c) provides that a cash purchase of stock may be disregarded for purposes of the solely-for-voting-stock requirement if it was independent of the stock-for-stock exchange. According to this regulation, stock acquisitions over a relatively short period of time—12 months or less—are to be aggregated for purposes of the solely-for-voting-stock requirement.

[51] Rev. Rul. 66-365, 1966-2 C.B. 116, as amplified by Rev. Rul. 81-81, 1981-1 C.B. 122.

[52] Rev. Rul. 73-54, 1973-1 C.B. 187.

[53] Rev. Rul. 68-285, 1968-1 C.B. 147.

EXAMPLE C:7-22 ▶ In July of last year, Alpha Corporation purchased for cash 12% of Theta Corporation's single class of stock. In January of the current year, Alpha acquires the remaining 88% in a stock-for-stock exchange. The IRS probably will aggregate the cash and stock-for-stock acquisitions because they occurred within a 12-month period. Even though Alpha achieves 80% control in a single stock-for-stock exchange, this transaction does not qualify as a Type B reorganization because, if the two stock purchases are aggregated, the solely-for-voting-stock requirement is not met. The transaction could qualify as a Type B reorganization if Alpha unconditionally sold its 12% interest in Theta and then acquired the requisite 80% interest in a single stock-for-stock exchange, or if Alpha postponed the stock-for-stock exchange until after July of the current year, when the exchange might be considered independent of the cash purchase.[54] ◀

EXAMPLE C:7-23 ▶ Seven years ago, Alpha Corporation acquired 85% of Theta Corporation's single class of stock in a transaction that qualified as a Type B reorganization. In December of the current year, Alpha acquires the remaining 15% of Theta stock in a stock-for-stock exchange. Even though Alpha already controls Theta, the second transaction qualifies for Type B reorganization treatment because Alpha owns at least 80% of Theta after the exchange. ◀

Tax Consequences of a Type B Reorganization. The tax consequences of a Type B reorganization are as follows:

- The target corporation shareholders (or parent company) recognize no gain or loss on the exchange unless their fractional shares are acquired for cash or the target corporation redeems some of their stock.
- The target corporation shareholders (or parent company) take a substituted basis in their acquiring corporation stock referenced to the basis of their target corporation stock surrendered. The holding period for the acquiring corporation stock includes the holding period for the target corporation stock.
- The acquiring corporation recognizes no gain or loss when it issues its voting stock for target corporation stock.
- The acquiring corporation's basis in the target corporation stock is the same as in the hands of target corporation shareholders (or parent company).

EXAMPLE C:7-24 ▶ Mark owns all of Theta Corporation's single class of stock, which has a $400,000 basis. Mark exchanges his Theta stock for $700,000 of Alpha Corporation voting stock. Mark realizes a $300,000 gain ($700,000 − $400,000), none of which is recognized. Mark's substituted basis in the Alpha stock is $400,000. Alpha recognizes no gain or loss when it issues its stock to Mark, and it takes a $400,000 carryover basis in the acquired Theta stock. ◀

Question: Assume that stock in both Alpha and Theta Corporations is publicly traded and each corporation has several thousand shareholders. Alpha acquires Theta stock in a Type B reorganization. What problems might arise in determining Alpha's basis in the Theta stock?

Solution: Under Sec. 358(a), Alpha's basis in the Theta stock is the same as that in the hands of Theta's shareholders. Many shareholders may not know their basis in stock purchased several years ago. The basis for these shares may have changed as a result of stock dividends, stock splits, or nonliquidating distributions. This lack of information may make it difficult to accurately determine Alpha's basis in the Theta stock acquired. To address the issue, the IRS allows sampling to extrapolate Alpha's basis from the stock holdings of a small number of Theta shareholders' aggregate stock basis.

ADDITIONAL COMMENT

The IRS has concluded that compliance with the sampling standards in Rev. Proc. 81-70, 1981-2 C.B. 729, may be "unduly burdensome or impossible." Thus, the IRS has sought comments from those who perform basis studies and other interested parties in an effort to revise the revenue procedure (see Rev. Proc. 2011-35, 2011-25 I.R.B. 890).

Advantages of a Type B Reorganization. A Type B reorganization has a number of advantages.

- The acquisition of target corporation stock usually can be accomplished in a single transaction without formal shareholder approval. Even if the target corporation's management does not approve the transaction, the acquiring corporation can acquire the requisite number of shares through a tender offer directly to target corporation shareholders including target's parent corporation, if applicable.

---

[54] See, for example, *Eldon S. Chapman et al. v. CIR*, 45 AFTR 2d 80-1290, 80-1 USTC ¶9330 (1st Cir., 1980).

WHAT WOULD YOU DO IN THIS SITUATION?

You have just joined Professional CPA, LLP as a new associate. Professional CPA's principal audit client is Intergalactic Enterprises, a public company that accounts for roughly a quarter of Professional CPA's revenues. Intergalactic wants to acquire the stock of Nebula Industries in a tender offer that qualifies as a Type B reorganization. In the proposed transaction, Intergalactic would offer three shares of Intergalactic stock for every two shares of Nebula stock. Currently, in the open market, Intergalactic stock trades at $15 a share while Nebula stock trades at $25 a share. Intergalactic would terminate the offer upon the tender of 55% of Nebula's outstanding shares.

Because Intergalactic's principal shareholder, Herman Islander, wants to retain control of the Intergalactic board of directors, he proposes to restrict the voting rights of Intergalactic stock issued to Nebula's shareholders. Under the proposed restriction, holders of the newly issued Intergalactic shares would have the right to vote for only two out of seven Intergalactic board members while holders of currently issued Intergalactic shares have the right to vote for all seven board members. Moreover, the voting rights inherent in all Nebula shares issued and outstanding are unrestricted.

Islander has requested from Professional CPA a written opinion to the effect that the exchange of Nebula shares with unrestricted voting rights, for Intergalactic shares with restricted voting rights, meets the continuity of interest requirement. Although your supervisor questions whether the exchange in fact does meet the requirement, she recognizes that Intergalactic is a key audit client that contributes substantially to the firm's revenues.

Your supervisor approaches you with a request that you draft the opinion. What should be your response?

- The target corporation remains in existence, and its assets, liabilities, and tax attributes need not be transferred to the acquiring corporation. However, the use of its NOLs may be limited under Sec. 382 (see pages C:7-43 through C:7-45).[55]
- The corporate name, goodwill, licenses, and rights of the target corporation may be preserved after the acquisition.
- The acquiring corporation does not directly assume the target corporation's liabilities, as is the case in some other reorganizations.
- The acquiring and target corporations can report their post-acquisition results on a consolidated basis (see Chapter C:8).

Disadvantages of a Type B Reorganization. Offsetting those advantages are a number of disadvantages.

- The acquiring corporation can use only voting stock as consideration in the transaction.
- Issuing additional stock for the acquisition can dilute the voting power and control of acquiring corporation shareholders.
- The acquiring corporation must obtain at least 80% of target corporation stock even though effective control can be achieved through ownership of less than 80%.
- The acquisition of less than 100% of target corporation stock may give rise to dissenting minority shareholders. Under state law, these shareholders have the right to have their shares appraised and purchased for cash.
- The bases of target corporation stock (outside basis) and assets (inside basis) are not stepped-up (or stepped-down) to their FMVs upon the change in ownership, as would be the case in a taxable asset acquisition or in a taxable stock purchase with a Sec. 338 election.

Drop-Down and Triangular Type B Reorganizations. As with Type A and C reorganizations, a triangular Type B reorganization, or a drop down of target corporation stock into a subsidiary before the stock-for-stock exchange, can be accomplished tax-free. In a triangular Type B reorganization, the acquiring subsidiary exchanges its parent stock for a controlling interest in the target corporation. As in a basic Type B reorganization,

[55] A Type B reorganization can result in an ownership change that, under Sec. 382, restricts the use of the target corporation's NOL carryovers but does not, in total, diminish the amount of its carryovers.

the target corporation remains in existence as a subsidiary of the acquiring subsidiary. In a triangular Type B reorganization, however, it becomes a second-tier subsidiary of the parent corporation.

TYPE G REORGANIZATION

Section 368(a)(1)(G) defines a **Type G reorganization** as "a transfer by a corporation of part or all of its assets to another corporation in a Title 11 [bankruptcy] or similar case, but only if, in pursuance of the plan, stock or securities of the corporation to which the assets are transferred are distributed in a transaction that qualifies under sections 354, 355, or 356." Type G reorganizations are infrequent because the reorganization must occur pursuant to a court-approved plan in a bankruptcy, receivership, or similar situation.

In an acquisitive Type G reorganization, an insolvent corporation might transfer substantially all its assets to an acquiring corporation under a court-approved plan (e.g., a bankruptcy reorganization plan). It then might distribute all the stock, securities, and other property received in the exchange, plus any property retained, to its shareholders and creditors in exchange for their stock and debt obligations.

DIVISIVE REORGANIZATIONS

OBJECTIVE 5

Describe the structure and requirements of divisive reorganizations

A divisive reorganization involves the transfer of some of a transferor corporation's assets to a controlled corporation in exchange for the controlled corporation's stock and securities (and possibly boot property).[56] The transferor then distributes the stock and securities (and possibly boot property) to its shareholders. A divisive reorganization generally is governed by the Type D reorganization rules, although a divisive reorganization involving an insolvent corporation could be governed by the Type G reorganization rules. Topic Review C:7-6 summarizes the requirements for divisive and other reorganizations.

ADDITIONAL COMMENT

In a divisive transaction governed by Sec. 355, the "transferor corporation" is referred to as the "distributing corporation." Accordingly, the discussion of divisive reorganizations in this text will use that terminology and thus refer to the transferor corporation as the distributing corporation.

TYPICAL MISCONCEPTION

The existence of a bona fide business purpose is necessary before the stock of a controlled subsidiary can be distributed tax-free to the shareholders of the distributing corporation. This requirement is much more difficult to satisfy in a Sec. 355 distribution than it is in an acquisitive reorganization.

DIVISIVE TYPE D REORGANIZATION

A divisive Type D reorganization must satisfy the requirements of Secs. 368(a)(1)(D) and 355, which are explained below.[57] Divisive Type D reorganizations can assume three forms: spin-offs, split-offs, and split-ups (see Figure C:7-7).

In the reorganization, a distribution of a controlled corporation's stock may be nontaxable under Sec. 355 even if the distributing corporation transfers no assets to the controlled corporation, in which case the division is not classified as a reorganization. To be a nontaxable Type D reorganization, however, both the asset transfer and the Sec. 355 distribution must be part of a single transaction governed by a plan of reorganization.

A divisive Type D reorganization can accomplish various business objectives, including

- Dividing an enterprise into two or more corporations to separate a high-risk business from a low-risk business
- Splitting up a single business to settle a dispute among two or more disputing shareholders
- Reorganizing an enterprise according to functions, profit centers, or geographical areas
- Divesting operations because of antitrust laws

Forms of Divisive Type D Reorganizations. Three types of divisive transactions are nontaxable under Sec. 368(a)(1)(D):

- **Split-off**—the distributing corporation transfers some of its assets to a controlled corporation in exchange for stock and possibly securities, cash, or other boot property. The distributing corporation then distributes stock in the controlled corporation to some or all of its shareholders in exchange for some of their stock. The context for such a transaction might be a management dispute between two distinct shareholder groups. To resolve the dispute, the parent corporation might redeem all the stock of one of the groups (see Figure C:7-7).

[56] In a divisive Type D reorganization, Sec. 368(c) defines the term control because Sec. 355 (not Sec. 354) governs the distribution. In such a reorganization, control requires ownership of at least 80% of the voting and nonvoting stock. In an acquisitive Type D reorganization, on the other hand, control requires ownership of only 50% of the voting and nonvoting stock.

[57] The requirements of a divisive Type D reorganization are contrasted with the acquisitive Type D reorganization (previously discussed), where substantially all the transferor's assets must be transferred to a controlled corporation.

TOPIC REVIEW C:7-6

Summary of Divisive and Other Reorganizations

Type of Reorganization	Distributing (D) or Transferor (T) Corporation Property Acquired	Consideration That Can Be Used	What Happens to the Distributing (D) or Transferor (T) Corporation?	Shareholders' Recognized Gain	Other Requirements
D—Divisive	D Corporation transfers part or all of its assets (and possibly some or all of its liabilities) to C Corporation.	Stock, securities, and other property of C Corporation.	D Corporation must distribute stock, securities, and boot received to its shareholders. D Corporation may liquidate or remain in existence.	Lesser of realized gain or FMV of boot received.	Transactions can assume three forms—spin-off, split-off, or split-up. Control is defined as 80% under Sec. 368(c).
E—Recapitalization	No increase or decrease in assets. The capital structure of T Corporation changes.	Stock, securities, and other property of T Corporation.	T Corporation remains in existence.	Lesser of realized gain or FMV of boot received.	May involve stock-for-stock, bond-for-bond, or bond-for-stock exchanges.
F—Change in form, identity, or place of organization	Old T Corporation transfers assets or stock to new T Corporation.	Stock, securities, and other property of new T Corporation.	Old T Corporation liquidates.	Lesser of realized gain or FMV of boot received.	Must involve only a single operating company.
G—Acquisitive or divisive	T Corporation transfers part or all of its assets (and possibly some or all of its liabilities) to A Corporation in bankruptcy.	Stock, securities, and other property of A Corporation.	T Corporation may liquidate, divide, or remain in existence.	Lesser of realized gain or FMV of boot received.	Stock and securities of A Corporation received by T Corporation must be distributed to its shareholders, security holders, or creditors.

Key:
D Corporation refers to the distributing corporation.
C Corporation refers to the controlled corporation.
T Corporation refers to the transferor corporation.
A Corporation refers to the transferee or acquiring corporation.

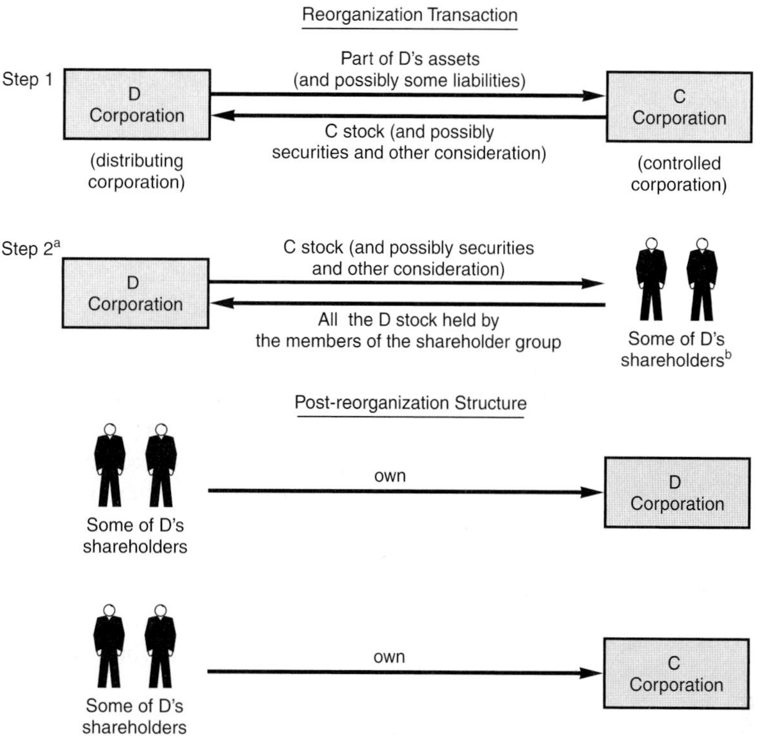

[a] Step 1 remains the same for a spin-off. In a spin-off, D's shareholders surrender no D stock. In a split-up, Step 1 involves the transfer of D Corporation's assets and liabilities to two controlled corporations. Step 2 involves the distribution of the stock of the two controlled corporations pursuant to the liquidation of D Corporation.

[b] This distribution also could be made on a pro rata basis to all of D's shareholders, in which case the shareholders surrender only a portion of their D shares.

FIGURE C:7-7 ▶ DIVISIVE TYPE D REORGANIZATION (SPLIT-OFF FORM)

- **Spin-off**—the distributing corporation transfers some of its assets to a controlled corporation in exchange for stock and possibly securities, cash, or other boot property. The distributing corporation then distributes the controlled corporation stock ratably to all its shareholders who do not surrender their distributing corporation stock. Such a transaction might be motivated by a desire to minimize the risk associated with distinct operations (e.g., automobile manufacturing and car financing) within a single corporation.
- **Split-up**—the distributing corporation transfers all its assets to two controlled corporations in exchange for controlled corporation stock and possibly securities, cash, or other boot property. The distributing corporation then distributes stock in the two controlled corporations to all its shareholders, in exchange for all its outstanding stock. Such a transaction might be motivated by a desire to separate and continue distinct operations of an old corporation having a weak brand or little goodwill.

If the Sec. 355 requirements discussed below are *not* met, a spin-off is taxed as a dividend to the shareholders; a split-off is taxed as a stock redemption to the shareholders; and a split-up is taxed to its shareholders as a liquidation of the distributing corporation.

ADDITIONAL COMMENT

If the IRS applies Sec. 351 to the asset transfer, and if the total adjusted basis for all property transferred exceeds the total FMV of that property, the subsidiary's total basis will be limited to the total FMV (see Chapter C:2 for details).

Asset Transfer. The distributing corporation recognizes no gain or loss on the asset transfer except where it receives and retains boot property or where the controlled corporation acquires or assumes distributing corporation liabilities, and total liabilities exceed the total adjusted bases of the assets transferred.[58] The controlled corporation recognizes no gain or loss when it exchanges its stock for the distributing corporation's property. The controlled corporation takes a carryover basis in the acquired assets, increased by any gain recognized by the distributing corporation on the asset transfer. Its holding period includes the distributing corporation's holding period for the assets.

TYPICAL MISCONCEPTION

Section 355 can apply to a distribution of stock of an existing subsidiary as well as the distribution of stock of a new subsidiary that is created as part of the transaction.

Distribution of Stock and Securities. In a Type D reorganization, the distributing corporation recognizes no gain or loss when it distributes controlled corporation stock (or securities) to its shareholders.[59] On the other hand, the distributing corporation recognizes gain (but not loss) when it distributes noncash boot property to its shareholders and when it makes a disqualified distribution of the controlled corporation's stock or securities.

The shareholders recognize no gain or loss on the receipt of the stock (and securities) except to the extent they receive boot property.[60] A shareholder's basis in the stock (or securities) equals his or her basis in the stock (or securities) held before the distribution, increased by any gain recognized and decreased by the sum of any cash and the FMV of any other boot property received. If the shareholder holds more than one class of stock or securities before or after the distribution, the total basis in the nonrecognition property is allocated to each class based on their relative FMVs. The basis in any noncash boot property is its FMV. The holding period for the stock and nonboot securities received includes the holding period for the stock and securities surrendered. The holding period for boot property begins on the day after the distribution date.

EXAMPLE C:7-25 ▶ Distributing Corporation is owned equally by Ruth and Pat, who cannot agree on how Distributing should be managed. Ruth and Pat agree to divide the business by organizing Controlled Corporation and by exchanging Pat's Distributing shares for Controlled shares while leaving Ruth's equity interest intact (i.e., a split-up). Pat's basis in her Distributing shares is $400,000. Pursuant to this plan, Distributing transfers assets having a $600,000 FMV and a $350,000 adjusted basis to Controlled in exchange for all of Controlled's single class of stock. In the asset transfer, Distributing realizes a $250,000 gain ($600,000 − $350,000), none of which is recognized. Distributing recognizes no gain on the distribution of the Controlled shares to Pat. Upon surrendering her Distributing shares, Pat realizes a $200,000 ($600,000 − $400,000) gain, none of which is recognized. Her basis in the Controlled stock is $400,000. The holding period for the Controlled shares includes Pat's holding period for the Distributing shares. Upon issuing its stock for Distributing assets, Controlled recognizes no gain and takes a $350,000 basis in the acquired assets. ◀

SELF-STUDY QUESTION

Does the receipt of boot make the entire Sec. 355 transaction taxable to the shareholders?

ANSWER

No. The shareholders may recognize part of the gain. The amount and type of gain recognized depends on whether the shareholders surrender stock of the distributing corporation in the transaction.

Under Sec. 355, boot consists of cash, short-term debt, property other than stock or securities of a controlled corporation, stock in the controlled corporation purchased within the previous five years in a taxable transaction, securities of the controlled corporation to the extent the principal amount of securities received exceeds the principal amount of securities surrendered, and stock or securities attributable to accrued interest.[61] When the shareholder receives boot, the amount and character of the recognized income or gain depend on whether he or she surrendered stock and securities in the distributing corporation (i.e., a split-off or split-up) or retained stock or securities (i.e., a spin-off).

When the shareholder receives boot in a spin-off, the FMV of the boot is treated as a dividend to the extent of the shareholder's ratable share of the distributing corporation's E&P. Any securities the shareholders receive in a spin-off are treated as boot because the

[58] Secs. 361(a) and 357(c)(1)(B).

[59] Sec. 361(c)(1). Two special rules may require the distributing corporation to recognize gain when it distributes stock and securities. A disqualifying distribution occurs if, immediately after the distribution, any person holds a 50% disqualified stock interest in either the distributing corporation or the controlled corporation. Disqualified stock generally is defined as any stock in the distributing or a controlled corporation purchased within the five-year period ending on the distribution date. The disqualifying distribution rules prevent a divisive transaction following a stock purchase to accomplish the disposition of a significant part of the historical shareholders' interests in one or more of the divided corporations. A second set of rules, the anti-Morris Trust rules, also requires the distributing corporation to recognize gain when a distribution of stock or securities is made and is preceded or followed by a disposition of the stock or securities.

[60] Sec. 355(a). As with an acquisitive reorganization, Sec. 361(a) permits securities (e.g., long-term debt obligations) to be received tax-free in a divisive transaction when the shareholders surrender the same face amount of securities, or a larger amount. The excess amount of securities received constitutes boot property.

[61] Secs. 355(a)(3) and 356(b).

shareholders do not surrender any securities in this type of transaction. Thus, the FMV of the securities constitutes a dividend to the extent of the shareholder's ratable share of the distributing corporation's E&P.

TYPICAL MISCONCEPTION

In a spin-off, the FMV of the boot received is treated as a Sec. 301 distribution to the shareholder. In a split-off or split-up, the shareholders recognize gain to the extent of the lesser of boot received or the gain realized. This gain may be a dividend or capital gain under Sec. 302.

In a split-off or split-up, in addition to the exchange of stock, a shareholder may receive boot property. If the shareholder realizes a loss on the exchange, the loss is not recognized, whether or not boot is received.[62] If the shareholder realizes a gain on the exchange, he or she recognizes the gain to the extent of the FMV of any boot received.

If the exchange is essentially equivalent to a dividend under Sec. 302 in a hypothetical redemption, the recognized gain is treated as a dividend to the extent of the shareholder's ratable share of the distributing corporation's E&P.[63] Otherwise it is treated as a capital gain. In either case, the income is taxed at the capital gains rate. Under the Sec. 302 rules, the shareholder is treated as though he or she continued to own stock in the distributing corporation and surrendered only the portion of his or her shares equal in value to the amount of boot received. This hypothetical redemption is then tested under the Sec. 302(b) rules to determine whether the shareholder is entitled to sale or dividend treatment.[64]

EXAMPLE C:7-26 ►

Distributing Corporation owns assets with a $60,000 FMV plus all the outstanding shares of Controlled Corporation stock valued at $40,000. Distributing formed Controlled by transferring some of its assets to Controlled as part of the reorganization. Distributing's E&P balance is $35,000. Carl and Diane each own 100 shares of Distributing stock. In a split-off, Distributing distributes all the Controlled stock to Carl in exchange for his 100 shares. Carl also receives $10,000 in cash. Carl's basis in the surrendered Distributing shares is $22,000. Carl has a $28,000 realized gain, calculated as follows:

FMV of Controlled stock	$40,000
Plus: Cash received	10,000
Amount realized	$50,000
Minus: Basis of Distributing stock	(22,000)
Realized gain	$28,000

Carl recognizes $10,000 of this gain (i.e., the lesser of the $28,000 realized gain or the $10,000 FMV of boot received). If Carl surrenders Distributing stock solely for the $10,000 cash, he would effectively be exchanging 20 Distributing shares ($10,000 boot ÷ $500 FMV for each share of Distributing stock) worth $10,000. Before this hypothetical redemption, he owns 50% of the outstanding Distributing shares (100 ÷ 200). Afterward, he owns 44% (80 ÷ 180). Thus, the hypothetical redemption is not substantially disproportionate under Sec. 302(b)(2) because the 44% post-redemption stock ownership exceeds 80% of the pre-redemption stock ownership (50% × 0.80 = 40%). If the exchange can meet one of the other tests for sale treatment (e.g., not essentially equivalent to a dividend), the $10,000 will be taxed as a capital gain. Otherwise it will be taxed as a dividend. ◄

TYPICAL MISCONCEPTION

Unlike Sec. 351, securities (long-term debt) can be exchanged in a Sec. 355 transaction without the recognition of gain as long as the principal amount surrendered is equal to or greater than the principal amount received.

In a split-off or split-up, a shareholder will receive securities of the controlled corporation tax-free only if the shareholder surrenders securities in the distributing corporation with an equal or larger principal amount. To the extent the principal amount of securities received exceeds the principal amount of securities surrendered, the excess will be taxable.

The Sec. 355 Requirements. Under Sec. 355, a distributing corporation's distribution of a controlled corporation's stock is nontaxable to the shareholders if all six of the following conditions are met:[65]

- The property distributed consists solely of stock or securities of a corporation controlled by the distributing corporation immediately before the distribution. The distributing corporation owns and distributes stock possessing at least 80% of the total

[62] Sec. 356(c).
[63] Sec. 356(a)(2).
[64] Rev. Rul. 93-62, 1993-2 C.B. 118.
[65] Sec. 355(a) and Reg. Secs. 1.355-2(b) and (c). Also, Rev. Proc. 2013-30, 2013-36 I.R.B. 173, provides a checklist questionnaire of the information that must be included in a ruling request under Sec. 355. Appendix A of this revenue procedure contains guidelines regarding the business purpose of Sec. 355 transactions including information submission requirements for nine specific situations where rulings may or may not be granted.

ADDITIONAL COMMENT

The control requirement of Sec. 355 is the same control requirement relating to the formation of a corporation under Sec. 351 (see Chapter C:2).

combined voting power of all classes of stock entitled to vote and at least 80% of the total number of shares of all other classes of stock.[66]

- The distribution has not been used principally as a device to distribute the E&P of the distributing corporation, the controlled corporation, or both. Whether the distribution has been used as such a device will depend on the facts and circumstances of each case. A sale or exchange of distributing or controlled corporation stock after the distribution is evidence that the distribution was used as such a device, especially if the sale was prearranged.[67]

TYPICAL MISCONCEPTION

The active trade or business requirement has two conditions: a pre-distribution five-year history must exist, and both the distributing and controlled corporations must be actively engaged in a trade or business immediately after the distribution.

- Immediately after the distribution, the distributing and controlled corporations each engage in a trade or business that was actively conducted for at least five years before the distribution. This requirement prevents a corporation from spinning off a newly formed subsidiary whose only assets are unneeded cash and other liquid assets. The shareholders then could sell or liquidate the subsidiary and extract the liquid assets in a transaction characterized as a sale rather than a dividend.[68]
- The distributing corporation distributes either all controlled corporation stock and securities held by it immediately before the distribution or an amount of controlled corporation stock constituting control. The distributing corporation may retain some stock if it can establish to the IRS's satisfaction that the stock was not retained as part of a tax avoidance plan.
- The distribution has a substantial corporate business purpose. Qualifying distributions include those made to comply with antitrust laws and those made to separate businesses where the shareholders have major disagreements.[69]
- Shareholders who directly or indirectly owned the controlled corporation(s) and a substantial number of shareholders who owned the distributing corporation's stock before the distribution maintain a continuing equity interest in one or more of the corporations following the division.[70] The distribution of stock and securities need not be pro rata. Disproportionate distributions may be used to eliminate the stock ownership of dissenting shareholders. In a split-off, some shareholders may exchange all their distributing corporation stock for all the controlled corporation stock.

DIVISIVE TYPE G REORGANIZATION

A divisive Type G reorganization involves the transfer of some of a corporation's assets to a second corporation under a court-approved plan. The transferor corporation then distributes the transferee corporation's stock and securities to its shareholders, security holders, and creditors. The transferor corporation may continue as a separate enterprise after restructuring its operations. Alternatively, the transferor corporation may liquidate under a court approved bankruptcy plan.

OTHER REORGANIZATIONS

OBJECTIVE 6

Define other types of reorganizations

Two types of transactions do not fit into the acquisitive or divisive reorganization categories: Type E reorganizations, which are recapitalizations, and Type F reorganizations, which are changes in identity, form, or state of incorporation. Topic Review C:7-6 presented earlier summarizes the requirements for Type E and Type F reorganizations.

TYPE E REORGANIZATION

Section 368(a)(1)(E) refers to a **Type E reorganization** simply as a "recapitalization." A 1942 Supreme Court opinion defined **recapitalization** as "the reshuffling of the corporate

[66] Sec. 368(c).
[67] Reg. Sec. 1.355-2(d).
[68] Sec. 355(b)(2). A corporation is engaged in the active conduct of a trade or business if it actively conducts all activities necessary to generate a profit and these activities encompass all steps in the process of earning income. Specifically excluded are passive investment activities such as merely holding stock, securities, and land.
[69] Reg. Sec. 1.355-2(b)(5), Exs. (1) and (2).
[70] Reg. Sec. 1.355-2(c).

KEY POINT

A Type E reorganization is neither acquisitive nor divisive in nature. Instead, it simply allows a single corporation to change its capital structure without creating a taxable exchange between the corporation and its shareholders or creditors.

structure within the framework of an existing corporation."[71] To qualify as a nontaxable reorganization, a recapitalization must have a bona fide business purpose. One reason for a recapitalization is to reduce a corporation's interest payments and debt-to-equity ratio by exchanging additional common or preferred stock for outstanding bonds. Alternatively, a family corporation might exchange newly issued preferred stock for part or all of the common stock held by a retiring, controlling shareholder so the shareholder can transfer management control to his or her children. This type of recapitalization facilitates estate planning (see discussion after Example C:7-28).

Three types of corporate capital structure adjustments can qualify as a Type E reorganization: a stock-for-stock exchange, a bond-for-stock exchange, and a bond-for-bond exchange.[72] Normally, these exchanges do not result in an increase or decrease in the corporation's assets except to the extent shareholders or creditors receive a distribution of cash or other property.

Stock-for-Stock Exchange. An exchange of common stock for common stock, or preferred stock for preferred stock, in the same corporation can qualify as a recapitalization if it is pursuant to a plan of reorganization. Section 1036 permits similar types of exchanges in a non-reorganization context. In either context, shareholders recognize no gain or loss on the exchange and take a substituted basis in the shares received that references the basis in the shares surrendered.

EXAMPLE C:7-27 ▶ The shareholders of Epsilon Corporation exchange all their nonvoting Class B common stock for additional shares of Epsilon voting Class A common stock. The exchange is nontaxable under Sec. 1036 even if not pursuant to a plan of reorganization. An exchange of some of Epsilon Class A preferred stock for Class B preferred stock also would be nontaxable under Sec. 1036. ◀

Section 1036 does not apply to an exchange of common stock for preferred stock, or preferred stock for common stock, in the same corporation, or an exchange of stock of two corporations. On the other hand, the reorganization rules apply to an exchange of two different classes of stock (e.g., common for preferred) in the same corporation if the exchange is pursuant to a plan of reorganization. Under the Sec. 354(a) nonrecognition rules, the exchange is nontaxable to the shareholders except to the extent they receive boot property. If the FMV of stock received differs from that of stock surrendered, the difference may be recharacterized as a gift, a contribution to capital, compensation for services, a dividend, or a payment to satisfy a debt obligation, depending on the facts and circumstances.[73] The tax consequences of that portion of the exchange will not be governed by the reorganization rules.

EXAMPLE C:7-28 ▶ John owns 60% of Eta Corporation's common stock and all its preferred stock. The remainder of Eta common stock is held by 80 unrelated individuals. John's basis in his preferred stock is $300,000. The preferred stock is valued at $500,000. John exchanges his preferred stock for $400,000 of additional common stock and $100,000 in cash. In the exchange, John realizes a $200,000 [($400,000 + $100,000) − $300,000] gain, of which he recognizes $100,000 as dividend income (assuming Boise has sufficient E&P). None of the Sec. 302(b) exceptions that permit capital gain treatment applies. John's basis in the additional common stock is $300,000 ($300,000 + $100,000 gain recognized − $100,000 cash received). ◀

A recapitalization often is used as an estate planning device through which a parent's controlling common stock interest is exchanged for both common and preferred stock. The common stock often is gifted to a child who, following the recapitalization, owns a controlling common stock interest in the corporation and manages its business. The parent derives a steady stream of income from preferred stock dividends. The preferred stock's

---

71 *Helvering v. Southwest Consolidated Corp.*, 28 AFTR 573, 42-1 USTC ¶9248 (USSC, 1942).

72 An exchange of stock for bonds has been held in *J. Robert Bazely v. CIR* (35 AFTR 1190, 47-2 USTC ¶9288 [USSC, 1947]) not to be a recapitalization. Even if it were a recapitalization, it generally would be taxable because receipt of the entire principal amount of the bonds represents boot under Sec. 356. Regulation Sec. 1.368-1(b) holds that continuity of interest and continuity of business enterprise are not necessary for a qualified Type E reorganization.

73 Rev. Ruls. 74-269, 1974-2 C.B. 87, and 83-120, 1983-2 C.B. 170.

value is less likely to increase significantly over time, thereby limiting the value of that portion of the parent's estate and minimizing the estate tax liability. Relatively more capital appreciation could accrue to the child who owns the common stock.

Substantial income, estate, and gift tax planning opportunities previously existed in the recapitalization of a closely held corporation. To prevent abuses, Congress added Secs. 2701–2704, which, for transfer tax purposes, set forth procedures for more accurately valuing interests transferred to, and retained in, corporations and partnerships. Additional coverage of this topic is presented in Chapter C:12.

Bond-for-Stock Exchange. A bond-for-stock exchange is nontaxable to the shareholder except to the extent the shareholder receives a portion of the stock in satisfaction of the corporation's liability to him or her for accrued interest.[74] The latter portion is taxed as ordinary income.

Bond-for-Bond Exchange. These exchanges are nontaxable only where the principal amount of the bonds received does not exceed the principal amount of the bonds surrendered. If such is the case, the FMV of the "excess" is taxed to the bondholder as boot.

TYPE F REORGANIZATION

Section 368(a)(1)(F) defines a **Type F reorganization** as a "mere change in identity, form, or place of organization of one corporation, however effected." Typically, Type F reorganizations are used to change either the jurisdiction in which the business is incorporated or the name of a corporation, without requiring the old corporation or its shareholders to recognize gain or loss. In a Type F reorganization, the assets and liabilities of the old corporation are transferred to a new corporation in exchange for stock and possibly debt obligations. The shareholders and creditors of the old corporation then exchange their stock and debt interests for similar interests in the new corporation.

EXAMPLE C:7-29 ▶ Phi Corporation is incorporated in Illinois. Its management decides to change its state of incorporation to Delaware because of that state's favorable securities and corporation laws. To effect the change, Old Phi exchanges its assets for all the stock in New Phi, incorporated in Delaware. The shareholders of Old Phi then exchange their stock for New Phi stock. Old Phi goes out of existence. Neither the shareholders nor the "two" corporations recognize gain or loss. Each shareholder takes a substituted basis in the New Phi stock that references their basis in the Old Phi stock. Their holding period for the New Phi stock includes their holding period for the Old Phi stock. New Phi's asset bases are the same as Old Phi's asset bases, and New Phi acquires Old Phi's tax attributes. Although the two corporations are legally distinct, they represent the same enterprise that merely has changed its state of incorporation. ◀

The reorganization illustrated in Example C:7-29 also could be accomplished if Old Phi's shareholders exchanged their Old Phi stock for New Phi stock. Old Phi then would liquidate into New Phi. The tax consequences would be the same for both transactions.

JUDICIAL RESTRICTIONS ON THE USE OF CORPORATE REORGANIZATIONS

OBJECTIVE 7

Explain judicial doctrines pertaining to corporate reorganizations

The U.S. Supreme Court has held that compliance with the letter of the law of reorganization provisions does not necessarily make a transaction nontaxable.[75] To be nontaxable, the transaction must comply with the following four judicial doctrines in addition to the IRC reorganization provisions. Some of these doctrines also have been written into Treasury Regulations.

[74] Sec. 354(a)(2)(B).

[75] *Evelyn F. Gregory v. Helvering*, 14 AFTR 1191, 35-1 USTC ¶9043 (USSC, 1935).

- Continuity of interest
- Continuity of business enterprise
- A bona fide business purpose
- The step transaction doctrine

All four doctrines elevate economic substance over legal form.

TYPICAL MISCONCEPTION

The continuity of interest requirement is unrelated to the relative sizes of the acquiring and target corporations. The target shareholders may end up with a minimal amount of the total outstanding stock of the acquiring corporation, and yet the merger will be a valid reorganization as long as 40% of the consideration received by the target shareholders is an equity interest in the acquiring corporation.

CONTINUITY OF INTEREST

The continuity of interest doctrine is based on the principle that the tax deferral associated with a reorganization is available because the shareholder merely has changed his or her investment from one form to another rather than liquidated that interest. According to Reg. Sec. 1.368-1(b), the requirements of this doctrine are met by a continuity of the business enterprise under a modified corporate form and a continuity of interest on the part of the shareholders who, directly or indirectly, own the enterprise before its reorganization. In a series of decisions, the courts have held that a continuing interest is ensured through ownership of common or preferred stock.[76] Thus, a transaction that involves the receipt of only cash or short-term debt obligations by the target corporation or its shareholders does not qualify as a nontaxable reorganization.

SELF-STUDY QUESTION

For which reorganizations is the continuity of interest requirement most important?

The IRC does not specify how much stock is necessary for continuity of interest. For advance ruling purposes, however, the IRS traditionally required that at least 50% of the total consideration received by target corporation shareholders consist of the acquiring corporation's stock. As previously mentioned, however, the courts have accepted lower percentages, and Treasury Regulations now accept 40% as the continuity of interest threshold.[77]

EXAMPLE C:7-30 ▶

In a Type C reorganization, Theta Corporation transfers all its assets to Alpha Corporation in exchange for $200,000 of Alpha stock and the assumption of $800,000 of Theta liabilities. Theta distributes the Alpha stock to its sole shareholder, Nancy, in exchange for all her Theta stock. Even though the transaction meets the statutory requirements for a Type C reorganization, the IRS probably will claim that the transaction does not qualify for nontaxable treatment because it lacks continuity of proprietary interest. Only 20% of the total consideration paid consists of an equity interest in Alpha. ◀

ANSWER

The only limitation on consideration used for both regular and triangular mergers is the continuity of interest requirement. The other reorganizations, including reverse triangular mergers, have statutory requirements more restrictive than the continuity of interest doctrine.

Recently, the IRS amended Reg. Sec. 1.368-1(b) to clarify that neither the continuity of interest nor the continuity of business enterprise doctrine applies to Type E and Type F reorganizations.

SELF-STUDY QUESTION

Does the acquiring corporation have to continue its own historic business?

ANSWER

No. Treasury Regulations hold that continuity of business enterprise can be satisfied if the acquiring corporation uses a significant portion of the target's historic business assets in any business, not necessarily the target's old business (Reg. Sec. 1.368-1(d)(1)).

CONTINUITY OF BUSINESS ENTERPRISE

Continuity of business enterprise implies that the acquiring corporation either continue the target corporation's business or use a significant portion of the target corporation's operating assets in a new business.[78] This doctrine limits nontaxable reorganizations to transactions involving *continuing interests* in the target's business or target property under a modified corporate form. The **continuity of business enterprise doctrine**, however, does not require that the target corporation's historic business be continued.

Whether the continuity of business enterprise requirement is met depends on the facts and circumstances of each case. The historic business requirement can be satisfied if the acquiring corporation continues one or more of the target corporation's significant lines of business.

EXAMPLE C:7-31 ▶

Historically, Theta Corporation has manufactured resins and chemicals and has distributed chemicals for the production of plastics. All three lines of business generate the same level of revenues. Theta merges into Alpha Corporation. Two months after the merger, Alpha sells the resin manufacturing and chemicals distribution lines to an unrelated party for cash. The transaction satisfies the continuity of business enterprise requirement because Alpha continues at least one of Theta's three significant lines of business.[79] ◀

---

[76] See, for example, *V. L. LeTulle v. Scofield*, 23 AFTR 789, 40-1 USTC ¶9150 (USSC, 1940).

[77] Reg. Sec. 1.368-1(e)(2)(v), Example 1. See also *John A. Nelson Co. v. Helvering*, 16 AFTR 1262, 36-1 USTC ¶9019 (USSC, 1935), in which the Supreme Court permitted a nontaxable reorganization where the stock exchanged constituted only 38% of the total consideration. See footnote 35.

[78] Reg. Sec. 1.368-1(d)(1).

[79] Reg. Secs. 1.368-1(d)(3) and −1(d)(5), Ex. (1).

The business (asset) continuity requirement is satisfied if the acquiring corporation uses in its business a significant portion of the assets used in the target corporation's business. Significance relates to the relative importance of the assets to target's historic business operations.

EXAMPLE C:7-32 ▶

Both Alpha and Theta Corporations manufacture computers. Theta merges into Alpha. Alpha terminates Theta's manufacturing activities and retains Theta's equipment as a source of supply for its components. Alpha satisfies the continuity of business enterprise requirement by continuing to use a significant portion of Theta's business assets. Thus, Alpha need not continue Theta's historic business to satisfy the continuity of business enterprise requirement.[80] If instead Alpha had sold Theta's assets for cash and placed the proceeds in an investment vehicle, the continuity of business enterprise requirement would not have been met. ◀

ADDITIONAL COMMENT

Because the target corporation and its shareholders have the most to lose, they should protect themselves from tax liability by stipulating that the acquiring corporation retain the historic assets. If not, the acquiring corporation can arbitrarily dispose of the historical assets and invalidate the nontaxable reorganization.

The acquiring corporation need not hold the target corporation's business assets for a prolonged period of time. The assets (business activities) may be held (conducted) by an 80%-or-more-owned subsidiary included in a chain of corporations that includes the acquiring corporation. In some cases, the acquired assets can be held by (or business conducted by) a partnership or LLC owned in full or in part by the acquiring corporation or one of its subsidiaries.

BUSINESS PURPOSE REQUIREMENT

To qualify for reorganization treatment, a transaction must serve a bona fide **business purpose.**[81] Regulation Sec. 1.368-1(c) states that a transactional scheme that uses "the form of a corporate reorganization as a disguise for concealing its real character, and the object and accomplishment of which is the consummation of a preconceived plan having no business or corporate purpose, is not a plan of reorganization."

EXAMPLE C:7-33 ▶

Distributing Corporation transfers appreciated stock from its investment portfolio to newly created Controlled Corporation in exchange for all its stock. It then distributes the Controlled stock to its sole shareholder, Kathy, in exchange for some of her Distributing stock. Shortly after the stock transfer, Controlled liquidates, and Kathy receives the appreciated stock held by Controlled. If the liquidation were treated as a separate event, Kathy would recognize a capital gain, which she could use to offset capital loss carryovers from other tax years. In addition, she could step up the basis in the appreciated stock to its FMV without incurring a tax liability. Even though the stock transfer to Controlled complies with the letter of Sec. 368(a)(1)(D) as a divisive Type D reorganization, the IRS probably will claim that the Sec. 355 trade or business requirement has not been met. It also will rely on the Supreme Court's decision in *Gregory v. Helvering* (see footnote 81) to rule that the series of transactions serves no business purpose. As a result, Kathy's receipt of the appreciated stock from Controlled most likely will be treated as a dividend. ◀

KEY POINT

Business purpose is much more difficult to establish in divisive (Sec. 355) transactions than it is in acquisitive (Sec. 354) transactions.

STEP TRANSACTION DOCTRINE

The IRS can invoke the **step transaction doctrine** to collapse a multistep reorganization into a single taxable transaction. Alternatively, the IRS can invoke the doctrine to collapse a series of steps, which the taxpayer claims as independent taxable events, into an integrated nontaxable reorganization. Both IRS actions prevent the taxpayer from elevating legal form over economic substance.

EXAMPLE C:7-34 ▶

Jody transfers business property from his sole proprietorship to wholly owned Theta Corporation. Three days after this transaction, purportedly in a Type C reorganization, Theta transfers all its assets to Alpha Corporation in exchange for Alpha stock. Subsequently, Theta liquidates and distributes the Alpha stock to Jody. After the liquidation, Jody owns 15% of the Alpha stock. The IRS might collapse the two steps (the Sec. 351 asset transfer to Theta and the Type C asset-for-stock reorganization) into a single transaction: an asset transfer by Jody to Alpha. It might claim that the Sec. 351 requirements have not been met because Jody does not own at least 80% of the Alpha stock immediately after the exchange. Furthermore, it might rule that, because Jody owns only 15% of Alpha stock, Jody must recognize gain or loss on the asset transfer.[82] ◀

---

[80] Reg. Secs. 1.368-1(d)(4) and −1(d)(5), Ex. (2).

[81] *Evelyn F. Gregory v. Helvering*, 14 AFTR 1191, 35-1 USTC ¶9043 (USSC, 1935). Other Sec. 355 requirements, such as not constituting a device for distributing of E&P, probably were not met in this case.

[82] Rev. Rul. 70-140, 1970-1 C.B. 73.

Tax attributes

OBJECTIVE 8

Determine the tax treatment of NOL carryovers and other tax attributes in a reorganization

Under Sec. 381(a), the acquiring or transferee corporation inherits the target or transferor corporation's tax attributes (e.g., loss or tax credit carryovers) in certain types of reorganizations. Sections 269, 382, 383, and 384, however, restrict the taxpayer's ability to use certain corporate tax attributes (e.g., NOL carryovers) following the acquisition of a loss corporation's stock or assets.

ASSUMPTION OF TAX ATTRIBUTES

In Type A, C, acquisitive D, F, and acquisitive G reorganizations, the acquiring corporation obtains both the target corporation's tax attributes and assets. The tax attributes do not change hands in either a Type B or Type E reorganization because assets are not transferred from one corporation to another. Even though assets are transferred in divisive Type D and G reorganizations, the only tax attribute allocated to the transferee corporation is a pro rata portion of the transferor corporation's E&P.[83]

KEY POINT

An often-cited advantage of a nontaxable asset reorganization over a taxable acquisition is that the tax attributes (e.g., NOLs and net capital losses) carry over to the acquiring corporation.

In acquisitive reorganizations, tax attributes carried over under Sec. 381(c) include

- Net operating losses
- Capital losses
- Earnings and profits (E&P)
- General business credits
- Inventory methods

KEY POINT

The thrust of Sec. 381, as it relates to NOLs, is to allow a target corporation's NOL carryovers to offset only the post-acquisition income of the acquiring corporation.

The target corporation's NOL carryover is determined as of the acquisition date and carries over to tax years ending after such date. Generally, the acquisition date for a reorganization is that on which the transferor or target corporation transfers the assets. When losses carryover from more than one tax year, the loss from the earliest tax year is used first. NOLs from the period following the acquisition date cannot be carried back by the acquiring corporation to offset target corporation profits earned in tax years preceding the acquisition date.[84]

EXAMPLE C:7-35 ▶ Theta Corporation merges into Alpha Corporation at the close of business on June 30 of the current year. Both corporations use the calendar year as their tax year. At the beginning of the year, Theta reports a $200,000 NOL carryover from the preceding year. Theta must file a final tax return for the period January 1 through June 30 of the current year. Theta reports $60,000 of taxable income (before any NOL deductions) on its tax return for the short period. Theta's taxable income for the January 1 through June 30 period reduces its NOL carryover to $140,000 ($200,000 − $60,000). Alpha succeeds to this carryover. ◀

Section 381(c) restricts the acquiring corporation's use of the NOL carryover in its first tax year ending after the acquisition date. The NOL deduction is limited to the portion of the acquiring corporation's taxable income allocable on a daily basis to the post-acquisition period.

EXAMPLE C:7-36 ▶ Assume the same facts as in Example C:7-35 except Alpha's accountants determine that its taxable income is $146,000, earned evenly throughout the current year. Alpha can use Theta's NOL carryover to offset $73,600 [(184 ÷ 365) × $146,000] of its taxable income attributable to the 184 days in the July 1 through December 31 current year post-acquisition period. The remaining NOL of $66,400 ($140,000 − $73,600) carries over to offset Alpha's taxable income in the following year. Both the pre- and post-acquisition periods in the current year are treated as full tax years for loss carryover purposes. ◀

LIMITATION ON USE OF TAX ATTRIBUTES

Sections 382 and 269 are intended to discourage taxpayers from purchasing the assets or stock of a corporation having loss carryovers (known as the **loss corporation**) primarily to acquire the corporation's tax attributes. Similarly, Secs. 382 and 269 are intended to discourage

[83] Reg. Sec. 1.312-10.

[84] Special rules apply to Type F reorganizations. Because this type of reorganization involves only a change in form or identity of a single corporation, NOLs generated after the acquisition date can be carried back to offset profits earned in pre-acquisition tax years.

a loss corporation from acquiring assets or stock of a profitable corporation primarily to use its carryovers. Section 383 imposes similar restrictions on acquisitions intended to facilitate the use of capital loss and tax credit carryovers. Additionally, Sec. 384 restricts the use of pre-acquisition losses to offset built-in gains.

Section 382. The Sec. 382 NOL restrictions are triggered when a substantial change in the stock ownership of the loss corporation occurs.

TYPICAL MISCONCEPTION

To effect an ownership change, the 5% shareholders must increase their stock ownership by more than 50 *percentage points.* For example, if a shareholder increases her stock ownership from 10% to 20%, this increase is not an ownership change even though it doubles her ownership.

Stock Ownership Change. A substantial change in stock ownership occurs where

- Stock ownership of any person(s) owning 5% or more of a corporation's stock has changed or a reorganization (other than a divisive Type D or G or a Type F reorganization) has occurred *and*
- The percentage of stock in the new loss corporation owned by one or more 5% shareholders has increased by more than 50% over the lowest percentage of stock in the old loss corporation owned by such shareholder(s) at any time during the preceding three-year (or shorter) "testing" period.[85]

The 5% shareholder test is based on the value of the loss corporation's stock. Nonvoting preferred stock is excluded from the calculation of ownership.

An **old loss corporation** is any corporation entitled to use an NOL carryover or that has an NOL for the tax year in which the ownership change occurs, and that undergoes the requisite stock ownership change. A **new loss corporation** is any corporation entitled to use an NOL carryover after the stock ownership change.[86] The old and new loss corporations are the same in most taxable acquisitions (e.g., the purchase of a loss corporation's stock by a new shareholder group). The identity of the old and new loss corporations differ, however, in many acquisitive reorganizations (e.g., a merger transaction where an unprofitable target [old loss] corporation merges into the acquiring [new loss] corporation).

KEY POINT

One of the burdensome aspects of Sec. 382 is that each time the stock ownership of a 5% shareholder changes, all 5% shareholders must be tested at that date to determine whether an ownership change has occurred.

Ownership changes are tested any time a transaction affects a person owning 5% or more of the stock either before or after the change. Such change may occur because a stock transaction involving a 5% shareholder or a person who does not own a 5% interest in the loss corporation affects the size of the stock interest owned by another 5% shareholder (i.e., a stock redemption). When applying the 5% test, all shareholders owning less than 5% of the loss corporation's stock are considered to be a single shareholder.

EXAMPLE C:7-37 ▶ Stock in Spencer Corporation is publicly traded with no single individual owning more than 5% of its outstanding shares. In recent years, Spencer has incurred a series of NOLs. On July 3, Barry acquires for cash 80% of Spencer's single class of stock. Barry owned none of the Spencer stock before the acquisition. A substantial stock ownership change has occurred because, as a result of a stock purchase, a 5% shareholder (Barry) now owns 80 percentage points more stock than the 0% he owned at any time during the three-year testing period. Because Spencer incurred the NOLs prior to the ownership change and can use the NOLs after the change, it is considered to be both the old and new loss corporation. Consequently, Spencer's NOLs are subject to the Sec. 382 limitations. ◀

In many acquisitive reorganizations, the Sec. 382 stock ownership test is applied first with respect to the old loss (or target) corporation and then with respect to the new loss (or acquiring) corporation.

EXAMPLE C:7-38 ▶ Theta Corporation has a single class of stock. None of its 300 shareholders owns more than 5% of the outstanding shares. Theta has incurred substantial NOLs in recent years. Pursuant to an agreement, Theta merges into Alpha Corporation. Alpha also has a single class of stock, and none of its 500 shareholders owns more than 5% of its outstanding shares, or any of the Theta shares before the merger. After the merger, Theta shareholders own 40% of the

[85] Sec. 382(g). For the purpose of determining the 50-percentage-point ownership change, special rules permit a testing period of less than three years. For example, where a recent previous change in stock ownership involving a 5% shareholder has occurred, the testing period begins on the date of the earlier ownership change.

[86] Secs. 382(k)(1)–(3).

Alpha stock. For purposes of applying the Sec. 382 stock ownership test, the stockholdings of all Alpha shareholders are aggregated. The Sec. 382 rules limit the use of Theta NOL carryovers because Alpha shareholders owned none of the old loss corporation (Theta) stock before the reorganization and own 60% of the new loss corporation (Alpha) stock immediately after the reorganization. ◀

Divisive Type D and G reorganizations or Type F reorganizations may be subject to the Sec. 382 limitations if the underlying transactions result in a more than 50% increase in the transferor corporation's stock ownership.

TYPICAL MISCONCEPTION

Section 382 does not necessarily disallow NOLs. It merely limits the amount of NOL carryovers the new loss corporation can use on an annual basis.

Loss Limitation. The Sec. 382 loss limitation for any tax year ending after the stock ownership change equals the value of the old loss corporation's stock (including nonvoting preferred) immediately before the ownership change multiplied by the long-term tax-exempt federal rate.[87] The IRS periodically publishes the long-term tax-exempt federal rate, which is the highest of the adjusted federal long-term tax-exempt rates applicable in any month during the three-calendar-month period ending with the month in which the stock ownership change occurs.[88]

ADDITIONAL COMMENT

The new loss corporation's use of the old loss corporation's NOLs is limited annually to the FMV of the old loss corporation multiplied by the long-term tax-exempt federal rate because this limitation approximates a reasonable rate of return on an equivalent investment.

A new loss corporation first claims its current year deductions. It then deducts any NOLs from the old loss corporation (pre-change tax years) not limited by Sec. 382. If the NOL carryovers from the old loss corporation exceed the Sec. 382 loss limitation, the unused portion is deferred until the following year, provided the 20-year NOL carryforward period has not expired. If the Sec. 382 loss limitation exceeds the new loss corporation's taxable income for the current year, the unused loss portion carries forward and increases the Sec. 382 loss limitation in the following year.[89] Finally, any of its NOL and other carryovers from post-change taxable years are deducted. A new loss corporation that discontinues the business of the old loss corporation throughout the two-year period beginning on the stock ownership change date must use a zero Sec. 382 limitation for any post-change year. This zero limitation, in effect, disallows the use of the NOL carryovers.[90]

EXAMPLE C:7-39 ▶

KEY POINT

If the old loss corporation is a very large corporation relative to its NOL carryovers, Sec. 382 will not be a real obstacle in the use of the NOLs by the new loss corporation. Only when the old loss corporation has a small FMV relative to its NOL carryovers does Sec. 382 become a major obstacle.

Peter purchased all the stock in Taylor Corporation (the old and new loss corporation) from Karl at the close of business on December 31 of last year. Taylor manufactures brooms and has a $1 million NOL carryover from last year. Taylor continues to manufacture brooms after Peter's acquisition and in the current year earns $300,000 of taxable income. The value of the Taylor stock immediately before the acquisition is $3.5 million. The requisite stock ownership change has occurred because Peter has increased his stock ownership from zero during the three-year testing period to 100% immediately after the acquisition. Assume the applicable long-term tax-exempt federal rate is 5%. Thus, the Sec. 382 loss limitation for the current year is $175,000 ($3,500,000 × 0.05). Taylor can claim a $175,000 NOL deduction in the current year, thereby reducing its taxable income to $125,000. The remaining $825,000 ($1,000,000 − $175,000) NOL carries over to subsequent years, subject to the Sec. 382 limitation in those years. ◀

ADDITIONAL COMMENT

Although the legislative intent of Sec. 382 has not been seriously questioned, the complexity of the statute with its accompanying Treasury Regulations is of concern to many tax practitioners.

Special rules apply to the loss corporation for the year in which the stock ownership change occurs. Taxable income earned before the change is not subject to the Sec. 382 limitation. Taxable income earned after the change, however, is subject to the limitation. Allocation of income earned during the tax year to the time periods before and after the stock ownership change is based on the number of days in each of the two time periods under procedures similar to those for allocating tax attributes under Sec. 381.

Old loss corporation NOLs incurred before the date of the stock ownership change are limited by Sec. 382. These include NOLs incurred in tax years ending before the date of change plus the pre-change portion of the NOL for the tax year that includes the date of change. Allocation of an NOL for the tax year that includes the date of change is based on the number of days before and after the change.[91]

[87] Sec. 382(b)(1).
[88] Sec. 382(f).
[89] Sec. 382(b)(2).
[90] Sec. 382(c). In addition, failure to continue the old loss corporation's business enterprise may change the transaction's status from a nontaxable reorganization to a taxable acquisition.
[91] Sec. 382(b)(3).

Section 383. Section 383 restricts the use of tax credit and capital loss carryovers when a stock ownership change occurs, within the meaning of Sec. 382. The same restrictions that apply to NOLs apply to the general business credit, the minimum tax credit, and the foreign tax credit.

Section 384. Section 384 restricts the use of pre-acquisition losses of either the acquiring or target corporation (the loss corporation) to offset built-in gains recognized by another corporation (the gain corporation) during the five-year post-acquisition recognition period. Such gains may be offset only by pre-acquisition losses of the gain corporation. This limitation applies if a corporation acquires either a controlling stock interest or the assets of another corporation and either corporation is a gain corporation.

ADDITIONAL COMMENT

Section 269 represents the IRS's oldest and broadest weapon in dealing with trafficking in NOLs. However, because of the subjectivity of their application, Secs. 382, 383, and 384 have turned out to be the IRS's main statutory weapons in this area.

Section 269. Section 269 applies where control of a corporation is obtained and the principal purpose of the transaction is "the evasion or avoidance of federal income tax by securing the benefit of a deduction" or credit that otherwise would not be available. The IRC defines control as 50% of the voting power or 50% of the value of the outstanding stock. The IRS can use this provision to disallow a loss or credit carryover in situations where Sec. 382 does not apply.

TAX PLANNING CONSIDERATIONS

OBJECTIVE 9

Identify tax planning opportunities in taxable acquisitions and reorganizations

WHY USE A REORGANIZATION INSTEAD OF A TAXABLE TRANSACTION?

Choosing between a taxable and nontaxable transaction can be difficult. The advantages and disadvantages of a nontaxable reorganization are important for both the buyer and the seller. Depending on their relative importance, they may serve as points of negotiation and compromise in the effort to structure the transaction.

From the target shareholders' perspective, several factors are relevant. First, a nontaxable reorganization affords shareholders a tax deferral except to the extent they receive boot. This tax deferral may permit a shareholder to preserve a higher percentage of his or her capital investment than otherwise would be possible in a taxable acquisition. Second, a taxable transaction permits target corporation shareholders to convert their former equity interests into liquid assets (e.g., when they receive cash or property other than stock or securities of the acquiring corporation). These liquid assets can be invested however the shareholder chooses.

ETHICAL POINT

The choice between structuring an acquisition as taxable or nontaxable involves a large number of considerations for both the buyer and the seller. All parties must examine the tax, financial, and legal aspects with the assistance of their own experts.

In a reorganization, the shareholder must obtain a proprietary interest in the acquiring corporation. The future success of the acquiring corporation is likely to enhance the value of this interest. Conversely, if the acquiring corporation encounters financial difficulties, the value of the shareholder's investment may diminish. Third, losses realized in a reorganization cannot be recognized. A taxable transaction permits the immediate recognition of realized losses. Fourth, gains recognized in a reorganization are taxed as dividends if the distribution of boot is substantially equivalent to a dividend. Taxable transactions generally result in the shareholder's recognizing capital gains. Finally, a taxable transaction permits the shareholder to step-up to FMV the basis of stock and securities received. A nontaxable transaction, on the other hand, results in a substituted basis.

SELF-STUDY QUESTION

Is a nontaxable reorganization always preferable to a taxable acquisition?

ANSWER

No. What form an acquisition should take involves a myriad of issues relating to the parties involved in the transaction. A number of these issues are discussed in this section.

From the transferor corporation's point of view, a reorganization permits the exchange of assets without gain recognition. In addition, depreciation is not recaptured in a reorganization. Instead, the recapture potential shifts to the acquiring corporation.

From the acquiring corporation's point of view, a reorganization permits an acquisition without the expenditure of substantial amounts of cash or securities. Because the target corporation shareholders do not recognize gain unless they receive boot, they may be

TYPICAL MISCONCEPTION

When an acquisition is structured, the tax consequences are only one of many factors the parties must consider. Often, the final acquisition structure will not be optimal from a tax perspective because other factors may be deemed more important.

willing to accept a lower sales price than would otherwise be the case in a taxable acquisition. In a reorganization, the transferee takes the same property basis as the transferor's. The inability to step up basis to cost or FMV reduces the attractiveness of a reorganization and could lower the price the acquirer is willing to pay.

In a reorganization, the acquirer obtains the benefits of NOL, tax credit, and other carryovers from the target corporation (subject to limitations). In a taxable transaction, such tax attributes are not inherited by the buyer although they can be used to reduce the seller's tax cost in the sale.

AVOIDING THE REORGANIZATION PROVISIONS

TYPICAL MISCONCEPTION

The reorganization provisions are not elective. If a transaction qualifies as a Sec. 368 reorganization, it must be treated as such. It usually is not difficult to disqualify a nontaxable reorganization if the parties desire a taxable acquisition.

An acquisition can be converted from a nontaxable reorganization into a taxable transaction if the restrictions on the use of consideration incidental to a particular type of reorganization are ignored. For example, the Type B reorganization rules can be skirted if the acquiring corporation obtains target corporation stock through a combination of acquiring corporation stock and cash. Because this structure does not meet the solely-for-voting-stock requirement, the transaction will be taxable to the selling shareholders. It also will be treated as a stock purchase, thereby permitting the acquiring corporation to make a Sec. 338 election and step-up the basis in target corporation assets.

EXAMPLE C:7-40 ▶ Alpha Corporation offers to exchange one share of its common stock (valued at $40) plus $20 cash for each share of Theta Corporation's single class of common stock. All of Theta's shareholders accept the offer and exchange a total of 2,000 Theta shares for 2,000 Alpha shares and $40,000 cash. At the time of the exchange, Theta's assets have a $35,000 adjusted basis and a $110,000 FMV. Theta recognizes no gain or loss in the exchange. The basis of its assets remains $35,000 unless Alpha makes a Sec. 338 election. Depending on their stock bases, Theta's shareholders recognize gain or loss in the exchange, whether or not Alpha makes a Sec. 338 election. ◀

COMPLIANCE AND PROCEDURAL CONSIDERATIONS

OBJECTIVE 10

Comply with procedural rules for taxable acquisitions and reorganizations

SECTION 338 ELECTION

The acquiring corporation makes a Sec. 338 election by filing Form 8023 (Elections Under Section 338 for Corporations Making Qualified Stock Purchases) with the IRS. This election must be made by the fifteenth day of the ninth month beginning after the month of the acquisition date. The required information about the acquiring corporation, the target corporation, and the election is set forth in Reg. Sec. 1.338-1(d).

PLAN OF REORGANIZATION

Nonrecognition of gain by a transferor corporation in an asset acquisition (Sec. 361) or a shareholder in a stock acquisition (Sec. 354) requires that the acquisition be pursuant to a plan of reorganization. A **plan of reorganization** is a plan for restructuring an enterprise that complies with the reorganization provisions of the Internal Revenue Code and associated Treasury Regulations. Nonrecognition of gain or loss is limited to exchanges or distributions that are a direct part of a reorganization undertaken to continue the business of a corporation that is a party to a reorganization.[92] Although a written plan is not required, it would be prudent for all parties to the reorganization to reduce the plan to writing, either as a communication to the shareholders, a document in the corporate records, a memorandum of understanding, or a written agreement between the parties. The transaction generally is taxable if a plan of reorganization does not exist or if a transfer or distribution is not pursuant to a plan.[93]

[92] Reg. Sec. 1.368-2(g).

[93] *A. T. Evans*, 30 B.T.A. 746 (1934), *acq*. XIII-2 C.B. 7; and *William Hewitt*, 19 B.T.A. 771 (1930).

PARTY TO A REORGANIZATION

For an asset or stock transfer to be nontaxable under Secs. 354 and 361, a shareholder or a transferor must be a party to a reorganization. Section 368(b) includes as a **party to a reorganization** "any corporation resulting from a reorganization, and both corporations involved in a reorganization where one corporation acquires the stock or assets of a second corporation." In a triangular reorganization, the corporation controlling the acquiring corporation, and whose stock is used to effect the reorganization, also is a party to the reorganization.

RULING REQUESTS

Before proceeding with an acquisition or disposition, some taxpayers request an advance ruling from the IRS on the tax consequences of the transaction. They generally do so because of the complexity of tax reorganization law and the substantial dollar amounts involved in the transaction. An after-the-fact determination by the IRS or the courts that a completed transaction is taxable could be costly to all parties. The IRS will issue an advance ruling only for reorganizations that conform to the guidelines of various IRS revenue procedures and other IRS pronouncements. It will not issue an advance ruling for a reorganization if the consequences are adequately addressed in the IRC, Treasury Regulations, Supreme Court decisions, tax treaties, revenue rulings, revenue procedures, notices, or other IRS pronouncements.[94] Because of IRS policy not to issue these so-called "comfort rulings," many taxpayers instead seek opinion letters from tax counsel.

FINANCIAL STATEMENT IMPLICATIONS

OBJECTIVE 11

Recognize the financial statement implications of corporate acquisitions

An acquiring corporation must use the acquisition method for financial statement purposes whether the business combination is a taxable purchase or a nontaxable reorganization.[95] However, differences occur in the recording of deferred tax accounts and the treatment of goodwill. Also, a stock acquisition has its own particularities because recording the transaction occurs in the process of consolidating the financial statements of the acquiring parent and the acquired subsidiary.

For subsequent illustrations, assume Theta Corporation (the target corporation) has the following balance sheet of identified assets and liabilities, where the tax basis and book basis are the same. Thus, prior to the acquisition, Theta has no temporary differences or deferred tax accounts.

	FMV	*Basis*	*Difference*
Accounts receivable	$ 12,000	$ 12,000	$ -0-
Inventory	30,000	25,000	5,000
Plant and equipment	100,000	75,000	25,000
Land	50,000	40,000	10,000
Total assets	$192,000	$152,000	$40,000
Liabilities	$ 20,000	$ 20,000	
Equity	172,000	132,000	
Total liabilities and equity	$192,000	$152,000	

TAXABLE ASSET ACQUISITION

In a taxable purchase, the acquiring corporation's tax basis in the purchased assets likely will be the same as the recorded book basis. If so, deferred tax liabilities and assets will not arise as a result of the business combination. Also, if tax goodwill and book goodwill

[94] Rev. Proc. 2017-1, 2017-1, I.R.B. 1, Rev. Proc. 2017-3, 2017-1 I.R.B. 130.

[95] Accounting Standards Codification (ASC) 805, Business Combinations, which codifies SFAS No. 141R.

are equal, future amortization of tax goodwill under Sec. 197 will create temporary differences because book goodwill can be expensed only if impaired.[96] (If tax and book goodwill differ in a taxable business combination, the financial statement treatment gets complicated, a topic beyond the scope of this textbook.)

EXAMPLE C:7-41 ▶ At the beginning of the current year, Alpha Corporation purchases all of Theta Corporation's assets for $207,000 cash and does not assume Theta's liabilities. For both book and tax purposes, each asset gets an FMV allocation of this purchase price with the remainder allocated to goodwill. Because the book and tax bases are equal, Alpha records no deferred tax accounts. Accordingly, Alpha makes the following book journal entry to record the purchase:

Accounts receivable	12,000	
Inventory	30,000	
Plant and equipment	100,000	
Land	50,000	
Goodwill	15,000	
Cash		207,000

In the acquisition year, Alpha deducts $1,000 of goodwill amortization for tax purposes but takes no impairment loss for book purposes. Assuming no other book-tax differences, $150,000 of pretax book income, and a 35% tax rate, Alpha realizes the following results for this year.

Net income before FIT expense	$150,000
Goodwill amortization (temporary difference)	(1,000)
Taxable income	$149,000

Thus, Alpha's federal income tax expense is $52,500 ($150,000 × 0.35), and its federal tax liability is $52,150 ($149,000 × 0.35). Also, Alpha records a deferred tax liability of $350 ($1,000 × 0.35). Accordingly, Alpha makes the following book journal entry:

Federal income tax expense	52,500	
Deferred tax liability		350
Federal income taxes payable		51,150

The deferred tax liability will increase by the same amount each year of the 15-year tax amortization period and will reverse if and when Alpha takes an impairment loss on the book goodwill. ◀

NONTAXABLE ASSET ACQUISITION

In a nontaxable business combination, such as a Type A or Type C reorganization, the bases recorded for financial statement purposes differ from the carryover tax bases of acquired assets. For business combinations, the acquiring corporation recognizes a deferred tax asset or liability for differences between the assigned financial statement values and the tax bases of the transferred assets and liabilities.[97] Goodwill for which the corporation is not allowed an amortization deduction for tax purposes, the usual situation in a nontaxable acquisition, does not give rise to a temporary difference.

EXAMPLE C:7-42 ▶ At the beginning of the current year, Alpha Corporation acquires all of Theta's assets and assumes Theta's liabilities in a Type A merger. In addition to assuming the liabilities, Alpha issues $187,000 worth of its preferred stock as consideration, for a total consideration of $207,000. For tax purposes, Alpha takes a carryover basis in each asset, but for financial statement purposes, Alpha records each asset at its FMV. Assuming a 35% corporate tax rate, the $40,000 difference between the total book value and total tax basis creates a $14,000 ($40,000 × 0.35) deferred tax liability. Thus, aside from $15,000 of goodwill from the excess of consideration paid ($207,000) over the FMV of identified assets ($192,000), Alpha records $14,000 of additional goodwill. Accordingly, Alpha makes the following book journal entry to record the acquisition:

Accounts receivable	12,000
Inventory	30,000
Plant and equipment	100,000

[96] Accounting Standards Codification (ASC) 350, Intangibles—Goodwill and Other, which codifies SFAS No. 142.

[97] Accounting Standards Codification (ASC) 740, Income Taxes, which codifies SFAS No. 109.

Land	50,000	
Goodwill	29,000	
Deferred tax liability		14,000
Liabilities		20,000
Preferred stock		187,000

In the acquisition year, Alpha's book net income before federal income tax (FIT) expense is $150,000, which includes $12,000 of book depreciation on the acquired plant and equipment and $2,800 of book goodwill impairment. For tax purposes, Alpha recognizes a $5,000 gain on the sale of the acquired inventory and takes $9,000 of depreciation on the acquired plant and equipment, but it amortizes no goodwill. The difference between the $2,800 book goodwill impairment and the zero tax goodwill amortization produces a permanent difference. The other book-tax differences are temporary, resulting in the following net income to taxable income reconciliation:

Net income before FIT expense	$150,000
Goodwill (permanent difference)	2,800
Net income after permanent differences	$152,800
Inventory sale (temporary difference)	5,000
Depreciation (temporary difference)	3,000
Taxable income	$160,800

Thus, assuming a 35% tax rate, Alpha's federal income tax expense is $53,480 ($152,800 × 0.35), and its federal tax liability is $56,280 ($160,800 × 0.35). Also, Alpha reduces its deferred tax liability by $2,800 ($8,000 × 0.35). Accordingly, Alpha makes the following book journal entry:

Federal income tax expense	53,480	
Deferred tax liability	2,800	
Federal income taxes payable		56,280

◀

STOCK ACQUISITION

In a stock acquisition, the target corporation remains intact as a subsidiary of the acquiring corporation. The adjustments necessary to implement income tax accounting rules occur when the corporations prepare their consolidated financial statements.

EXAMPLE C:7-43 ▶ At the beginning of the current year, Alpha Corporation acquires 100% of Theta's stock for $187,000 cash. As a result, Theta's shareholders recognize gain or loss on their sale of the stock. Alpha makes the following book journal entry to record the purchase:

Investment in Theta Corporation	187,000	
Cash		187,000

If Alpha instead acquired the Theta stock in a Type B reorganization using $187,000 of common voting stock, Alpha would have made a similar journal entry with the credit being to common stock rather than cash. In the consolidating journal entry for either type acquisition, Alpha eliminates the investment account, adjusts Theta's tax bases to book value, and records the necessary deferred accounts as follows:

Inventory	5,000	
Plant and equipment	25,000	
Land	10,000	
Goodwill	29,000	
Theta's equity	132,000	
Deferred tax liability		14,000
Investment in Theta Corporation		187,000

◀

PRICING THE ACQUISITION

In the above examples, the numerical amount of consideration is the same for the taxable and nontaxable asset acquisitions ($207,000). Economically, however, they are not comparable because, in the taxable purchase, the seller bears the tax burden. In the nontaxable asset acquisition, however, the acquiring corporation assumes the tax burden because it pays the same amount of consideration for assets having a low tax basis and a built-in gain. Consequently, it incurs the tax liability when it sells or depreciates the low basis assets. To shift the tax burden back to the seller in a nontaxable acquisition, the acquiring corporation might want to negotiate a reduced price for the assets. Similarly, in either a taxable or nontaxable stock acquisition, the acquiring corporation obtains a subsidiary with low basis assets. Hence, it might want to negotiate a stock price that reflects that built-in tax liability.

NET OPERATING LOSSES

If the target corporation has net operation loss carryovers (NOLs), the acquiring corporation must establish a deferred tax asset along with a valuation allowance if necessary. See Chapter C:3 for a discussion of the valuation allowance as well as a general discussion of the financial implications of federal income taxes.

PROBLEM MATERIALS

DISCUSSION QUESTIONS

C:7-1 From the standpoint of the target corporation shareholders, what is the advantage of a taxable stock acquisition by a purchaser corporation compared to the purchaser's acquiring all the target's assets in a taxable transaction followed by a liquidating distribution from the target to its shareholders?

C:7-2 What tax advantages exist for a corporate buyer when it acquires the assets of another corporation in a taxable transaction? For a seller when he or she exchanges stock in a taxable transaction? In a nontaxable transaction?

C:7-3 What tax and nontax advantages and disadvantages accrue when an acquiring corporation purchases all of a target corporation's stock for cash and subsequently liquidates the target corporation?

C:7-4 Why might a parent corporation make a Sec. 338 election after acquiring a target corporation's stock? When would such an election not be advisable?

C:7-5 a. Holt Corporation acquires all the stock of Star Corporation and makes a timely Sec. 338 election. The adjusted grossed-up basis of the Star stock is $2.5 million. The FMV of tangible assets on Star's balance sheet is $1.8 million. How are the new bases in Star's individual assets determined?
b. How would your answer change if instead the adjusted grossed-up basis were $1.4 million?

C:7-6 Compare the tax consequences of a taxable asset acquisition and a Type C asset-for-stock reorganization, based on the following factors:
a. Consideration used to effect the transaction.
b. Recognition of gain or loss by the target corporation on the asset transfer.
c. Basis of property to the acquiring corporation.
d. Recognition of gain or loss when the target corporation liquidates.
e. Use and/or carryover of the target corporation's tax attributes.

C:7-7 Which of the following events as part of an acquisitive reorganization require the target corporation to recognize gain? Assume in all cases that the target corporation liquidates in the reorganization.
a. Transfer of appreciated target corporation assets in exchange for acquiring corporation stock and short-term notes.
b. Transfer of appreciated target corporation assets in exchange for acquiring corporation stock and the assumption of the target corporation's liabilities.
c. Assume the same facts as in Part b except the amount of liabilities assumed by the acquiring corporation exceeds the adjusted basis of the target corporation assets transferred.
d. Transfer of appreciated target corporation assets in exchange for stock and cash. The target corporation distributes the cash to its shareholders.
e. Transfer of appreciated target corporation assets in exchange for stock and cash. The target uses the cash to pay off its liabilities.

C:7-8 A shareholder receives stock and cash in an acquisitive reorganization. The shareholder recognizes a gain because of the boot (cash) received. What rules determine whether the character of the shareholder's recognized gain is dividend income or capital gain?

C:7-9 Evaluate the following statement: Individual shareholders who recognize gain as the result of receiving boot in a corporate reorganization generally prefer to report capital gain, whereas corporate shareholders generally prefer to report dividend income.

C:7-10 How is the basis in nonboot stock and securities received by a shareholder determined? How is the basis in boot property determined?

C:7-11 Compare the types of consideration that can be used in Type A, B, and C reorganizations.

C:7-12 How does the IRS interpret the continuity of interest doctrine for a Type A reorganization?

C:7-13 How does the IRS interpret the continuity of business enterprise requirement for a Type A reorganization?

C:7-14 What are the advantages of a Type C asset-for-stock reorganization as opposed to a Type A merger reorganization? The disadvantages?

C:7-15 How does the IRS interpret the "substantially all" asset requirement for a Type C reorganization?

C:7-16 Explain why an acquiring corporation might be prohibited from using cash as part of the consideration paid in a Type C reorganization.

C:7-17 Some acquisitive transactions may be characterized as either a Type C or a Type D reorganization. Which reorganization provision controls if the two types overlap?

C:7-18 What is the difference between an acquisitive Type C reorganization and an acquisitive Type D reorganization?

C:7-19 Explain the circumstances in which cash and other property can be used in a Type B reorganization.

C:7-20 Alpha Corporation purchased for cash a 5% interest in Theta Corporation stock. After buying the stock and examining Theta's books, Alpha's management wants to make a tender offer to acquire the remaining Theta stock in exchange for Alpha voting stock. Can this tender offer be accomplished as a Type B reorganization? What problems might be encountered in structuring the acquisition as a nontaxable reorganization?

C:7-21 In a tender offer, Alpha Corporation wants to exchange its voting common stock for all of Theta Corporation's single class of stock. Only 85% of Theta's shareholders agree to tender their shares. After the tender, what options exist for Alpha to acquire the remaining shares as part of the reorganization? At a later date? How will a subsequent cash acquisition of the remaining outstanding shares affect the tax treatment of the tender offer?

C:7-22 Explain the structure of a triangular reorganization. What advantages would a triangular reorganization provide the acquiring corporation?

C:7-23 Compare and contrast the requirements for, and the tax treatment of, the spinoff, split-off, and split-up forms of divisive Type D reorganizations.

C:7-24 Stock in a controlled subsidiary corporation can be distributed tax-free to the distributing corporation's shareholders under Sec. 355. Explain the difference between such a distribution and a divisive Type D reorganization.

C:7-25 Under what circumstances is the distribution of a controlled corporation's stock or securities nontaxable to the distributing corporation's shareholders? What events trigger the recognition of gain or loss by the shareholders?

C:7-26 When does the distributing corporation recognize gain or loss on the distribution of stock or securities of a controlled corporation to its shareholders?

C:7-27 What is a recapitalization? What types of recapitalizations are nontaxable?

C:7-28 In a family corporation, how can a recapitalization be used to transfer voting control tax-free from a retiring senior generation to an upcoming junior generation?

C:7-29 Explain why a transaction might satisfy the letter of Sec. 368 for a reorganization yet fail to be treated as a reorganization.

C:7-30 Which types of reorganizations (acquisitive, divisive, and other) permit the carryover of tax attributes from a target or transferor corporation to an acquiring or transferee corporation?

C:7-31 What restrictions are placed on the acquisition and use of a loss corporation's tax attributes?

C:7-32 Explain why Sec. 382 will not be an obstacle to the use of NOL carryovers following an acquisition if the value of the old loss corporation is large relative to its NOL carryovers.

C:7-33 What is a plan of reorganization? Does such a plan need to be reduced to writing?

C:7-34 Why do some taxpayers secure an advance ruling for a proposed reorganization transaction?

C:7-35 Does the receipt of a favorable advance ruling provide the taxpayer with a guarantee that the IRS will follow the ruling if it audits the completed transaction?

ISSUE IDENTIFICATION QUESTIONS

C:7-36 Rodger Powell owns all the stock in Fireside Bar and Grill Corporation in Pittsburgh. Now that he has turned 65, Rodger wants to sell his business and retire to sunny Florida. Karin Godfrey, a long-time bartender at Fireside, offers to purchase all the corporation's noncash assets in exchange for a 25% down payment, with the remaining 75% paid in five equal annual installments. Interest will accrue at a market rate on the unpaid installments. Rodger plans to liquidate the corporation that has operated the Bar and Grill. He also plans to have Fireside Bar and Grill distribute the installment notes and any remaining assets. What tax issues should Fireside Bar and Grill, Rodger, and Karin consider with respect to the proposed purchase?

C:7-37 Adolph Coors Co. transferred part of its assets to ACX Technologies Corporation in exchange for all of ACX's stock. The transferred assets included its aluminum unit, which makes aluminum sheet; its paper packaging unit, which makes consumer-products packaging; and its ceramic unit, which makes high-technology ceramics used in computer boards and automotive parts. The ACX Technologies stock received for the assets was distributed to the Coors shareholders. What tax issues should the parties to the divisive reorganization consider?

C:7-38 Johnson & Johnson announced that it had entered into a merger agreement with Alza Corporation, a research-based pharmaceutical company and a leader in drug delivery technologies. In a nontaxable reorganization, Alza shareholders were offered a fixed exchange ratio of 0.49 shares of Johnson & Johnson common stock for each share of Alza stock. Alza had approximately 295 million shares outstanding at the time of the announcement. The boards of directors of both companies approved the merger. What tax issues might have been important to the two companies and to the two shareholder groups?

PROBLEMS

C:7-39 *Qualified Stock Purchase.* Alpha Corporation purchased 20% of Theta Corporation's stock on each of the following dates in the current year: January 2, April 1, June 1, October 1, and December 31.

a. Has a qualified stock purchase occurred? If it so desires, when must Alpha make the deemed sale election under Sec. 338?
b. How would your answer to Part a change if instead the purchase dates were January 1, April 1, and September 2 of the current year, and January 3, and April 15 of the following year?
c. If either Part a or b fails to be a qualified stock purchase and Alpha made its initial purchase on April 1 of the current year, what is the latest date on which Alpha can make the final stock purchase needed to qualify for a Sec. 338 election?

C:7-40 *Sec. 338 Election.* Alpha Corporation purchases 20% of Theta Corporation stock from Milt on August 10 of the current year. Alpha purchases an additional 30% of the stock from Nick on November 15 of the current year. Alpha purchases the remaining 50% of the Theta stock from Phil on April 10 of the following year. The total price paid for the stock is $1.9 million. Theta's balance sheet on April 10 of the following year shows assets with a $2.5 million FMV, a $1.6 million adjusted basis, and $500,000 in liabilities.

a. What is the acquisition date for the Theta stock for Sec. 338 purposes? By what date must Alpha make the Sec. 338 election?
b. If Alpha makes a Sec. 338 election, what is the aggregate deemed sale price for the assets?
c. What is the total basis of the assets following the deemed sale, assuming a 34% corporate tax rate?
d. How does the tax liability attributable to the deemed sale affect the price Alpha might be willing to pay for the Theta stock?
e. What happens to Theta's tax attributes following the deemed sale?

C:7-41 *Sec. 338 Election.* Gator Corporation is considering the acquisition of Bulldog Corporation's stock in exchange for cash. Two options are under review: (1) Gator purchases the assets from Bulldog for $1.4 million or (2) Gator purchases the Bulldog stock for $1 million and makes a Sec. 338 election shortly after the stock purchase. Bulldog has no NOL or capital loss carryovers. Bulldog's balance sheet is presented below.

Assets	*Adjusted Basis*	*FMV*	*Liabilities and Equity*	*Amount*
Cash	$100,000	$ 100,000	Short-term debt	$ 200,000
Marketable securities	140,000	200,000	Long-term debt	200,000
Accounts receivable	100,000	100,000	Paid-in capital	300,000
Inventory (FIFO)	100,000	150,000	Retained earnings	700,000
Plant and equipment	200,000	500,000		
Intangibles	–0–	350,000		
Total	$640,000	$1,400,000	Total	$1,400,000

a. What advantages would accrue to Gator if it purchases the assets directly? What disadvantages would accrue to Bulldog if it sells the assets and then liquidates?

b. What advantages would accrue to Gator if it purchases the Bulldog stock for cash and subsequently makes a Sec. 338 election? What advantages would accrue to Bulldog if its shareholders sell the Bulldog stock?
c. How would your answers change if Bulldog in the current year had incurred $250,000 of NOLs that it cannot carry back in full due to insufficient taxable income in the preceding two years?

C:7-42 *Sec. 338 Election.* J.S. Bachman owns 100% of Legato Corporation's stock, having a $350,000 basis. On December 31 of the current year, Legato Corporation reported the following balance sheet:

Assets	*Adjusted Basis*	*FMV*	*Liabilities and Equity*	*Amount*
Inventory	$200,000	250,000	Liabilities	$100,000
Land	250,000	600,000	Equity	750,000
Total	$450,000	$850,000	Total	$850,000

Staccato Corporation wishes to purchase, for cash, 80% of Legato's stock from Mr. Bachman and then make a Sec. 338 election. Determine the following amounts resulting from the transaction and Sec. 338 election: Grossed-up basis (G), aggregated deemed sale price (ADSP), total gain (loss) recognized, tax liability, adjusted grossed-up basis (AGUB), basis of each asset after allocating the AGUB, and gain recognized by Mr. Bachman. Assume a 34% corporate tax rate, and determine the required amounts in each of the following independent situations.
a. Staccato pays $491,200 for the Legato stock.
b. Staccato pays $600,000 for the Legato stock.
c. Staccato pays $470,000 for the Legato stock.
d. Staccato pays $670,000 for the Legato stock.

C:7-43 *Sec. 338 Basis Allocation.* Alpha Corporation purchases all of Theta Corporation's stock for $300,000 cash. Alpha makes a timely Sec. 338 election. Theta's balance sheet at the close of business on the acquisition date is as follows:

Assets	*Adjusted Basis*	*FMV*	*Liabilities and Equity*	*Amount*
Cash	$ 50,000	$ 50,000	Accounts payable	$ 40,000
Marketable securities	18,000	38,000	Note payable	60,000
Accounts receivable	66,000	65,000	Owner's equity	300,000
Inventory (FIFO)	21,000	43,000		
Equipment[a]	95,000	144,000		
Land	6,000	12,000		
Building[b]	24,000	48,000		
Total	$280,000	$400,000	Total	$400,000

[a]The equipment cost $200,000.
[b]The building is MACRS property on which Theta has claimed $10,000 of depreciation.

a. What is the aggregate deemed sale price for the Theta assets (assume a 34% corporate tax rate)?
b. What amount and character of gain or loss must Theta recognize on the deemed sale?
c. What is the adjusted grossed-up basis for the Theta stock? What basis is allocated to each of the individual properties?
d. What happens to "old" Theta's tax attributes? Do they carry over to "new" Theta?
e. What amount (if any) of goodwill can Theta amortize following the acquisition? Over what period and under what method may Theta amortize the goodwill?

C:7-44 *Amount of Corporate Gain or Loss.* In a merger in which it subsequently liquidates, Thomas Corporation transfers to Andrews Corporation all its assets and $100,000 of its liabilities in exchange for Andrews voting common stock, having a $600,000 FMV. Thomas's basis in its assets is $475,000.
a. What is the amount of Thomas's realized and recognized gain or loss on the asset transfer?
b. What is Andrews's basis in the assets received?
c. What is the amount of Thomas's realized and recognized gain or loss when it distributes the stock to its shareholders?
d. How would your answers to Parts a–c change if Thomas's basis in the assets instead had been $750,000?

e. How would your answers to Parts a–c change if Andrews instead had exchanged $600,000 cash for Thomas assets, and Thomas subsequently liquidated. Assume a 34% corporate tax rate.

C:7-45 *Amount of Shareholder Gain or Loss.* Silvia exchanges all her Theta Corporation stock (acquired August 1, 2013) for $300,000 of Alpha Corporation voting common stock pursuant to Theta's merger into Alpha. Immediately after the stock-for-stock exchange Silvia owns 25% of Alpha's 2,000 outstanding shares of stock. Silvia's adjusted basis in the Theta stock is $200,000 before the merger.

a. What are the amount and character of Silvia's recognized gain or loss?
b. What is Silvia's basis in the Alpha stock? When does her holding period begin?
c. How would your answers to Parts a and b change if instead Silvia received $60,000 cash and Alpha common stock worth $240,000?

C:7-46 *Amount and Character of Shareholder Gain or Loss.* Yong owns 100% of Theta Corporation stock having a $600,000 adjusted basis. As part of the merger of Theta into Alpha Corporation, Yong exchanges his Theta stock for $750,000 cash and Alpha common stock having a $3 million FMV. Yong retains a 60% interest in Alpha's 100,000 shares of outstanding stock immediately after the merger.

a. What are the amount and character of Yong's recognized gain?
b. What is Yong's basis in the Alpha stock?
c. How would your answers to Parts a and b change if instead Yong's 60,000 Alpha shares were one-third of Alpha's outstanding shares?

C:7-47 *Amount and Character of Gain Recognized.* Springs Corporation has developed a nature park at the site of Blue Springs. Because Newberry Corporation wants to develop several other springs in the area, Newberry wants to merge with Springs under Florida law. Newberry offers $650,000 of nonvoting preferred shares plus 1,000 shares of voting common (FMV of $50,000) to Springs in exchange for all of Springs' assets. As part of the merger, Springs' sole shareholder, Mr. High, exchanges all his shares in Springs for the shares in Newberry. Immediately before this transaction, Mr. High had a $240,000 basis in his Springs shares and owned no shares in Newberry. After the transaction he owns 20% of the value of the Newberry stock.

a. Does this transaction qualify as a Type A reorganization?
b. Does Springs recognize any gain or loss on the asset sale or the exchange of shares with Mr. High?
c. Does Mr. High recognize any gain or loss? What is his basis and holding period in his Newberry shares?

C:7-48 *Characterization of the Shareholder's Gain or Loss.* Turbo Corporation has one million shares of common stock and 200,000 shares of nonvoting preferred stock outstanding. Pursuant to a merger under state law, Ace Corporation exchanges its common stock worth $15 million for the Turbo common stock and pays $10 million in cash for the Turbo preferred stock. Some shareholders of Turbo received only Ace common stock for their common stock. Some shareholders received only cash for their preferred stock. Some shareholders received both cash and Ace common stock for their Turbo preferred and common stock, respectively. Shareholders owning approximately 10% of the Turbo common stock also owned Turbo preferred stock. The total cash received by these shareholders amounted to $1.5 million. The Turbo common stockholders end up with 15% of the Ace stock. What is the tax treatment of the common stock and/or cash received by each of the three groups of Turbo shareholders? Assume that some Turbo shareholders realize a gain on the transaction while other shareholders realize a loss.

C:7-49 *Requirements for a Type A Reorganization.* In a merger under state law, Anchor Corporation acquires all the assets of Tower Corporation. Tower's assets have a $5 million FMV and a $2.2 million adjusted basis. Assuming Tower liquidates, which of the following transactions qualify as a Type A reorganization?

a. The assets are exchanged for $5 million of Anchor common stock.
b. The assets are exchanged for $5 million of Anchor nonvoting preferred stock.
c. The assets are exchanged for $5 million of Anchor securities.
d. The assets are exchanged for $3.5 million of Anchor nonvoting preferred stock and $1.5 million in cash.
e. The assets are exchanged for $3 million of Anchor common stock and Anchor's assumption of $2 million of Tower liabilities.
f. The assets are exchanged for $5 million in cash provided by Anchor. An "all cash" merger transaction is permitted under state law.

C:7-50 *Tax Consequences of a Merger.* Armor Corporation exchanges $1 million of its common stock and $300,000 of Armor bonds for all of Trail Corporation's outstanding stock. As part of the same transaction, Trail then merges into Armor, which receives assets having a $1.3 million FMV and an $875,000 adjusted basis. In the merger, Antonello, a Trail shareholder, exchanges his 20% interest in Trail's single class of stock for $200,000 in Armor stock and $60,000 in Armor bonds. Antonello's 20% interest in Trail is comprised of 4,000 shares having a $100,000 adjusted basis. Following the reorganization, Antonello owns 5% (1,000 shares) of Armor's stock. Armor's E&P balance is $375,000.

a. What is the amount of Trail's recognized gain or loss in the asset transfer?
b. What is Armor's basis in the assets received in the exchange?
c. What are the amount and character of Antonello's recognized gain or loss?
d. What is Antonello's basis in the Armor stock? In the Armor bonds?

C:7-51 *Requirements for a Type C Reorganization.* Arnold Corporation plans to acquire all the assets of Turner Corporation in an asset-for-stock exchange. Turner's assets have a $600,000 adjusted basis and a $1 million FMV. Which of the following transactions qualify as a Type C reorganization (assuming Turner liquidates as part of the reorganization)?

a. The assets are exchanged for $800,000 of Arnold voting common stock and $200,000 of cash.
b. The assets are exchanged for $800,000 of Arnold voting common stock and $200,000 of Arnold bonds.
c. The assets are exchanged for $1 million of Arnold nonvoting preferred stock.
d. The assets are exchanged for $700,000 of Arnold voting common stock and Arnold's assumption of $300,000 of Turner's liabilities.
e. The assets are exchanged for $700,000 of Arnold voting common stock, Arnold's assumption of $200,000 of Turner's liabilities, and $100,000 in cash.

C:7-52 *Tax Consequences of a Type C Reorganization.* As part of a Type C reorganization, Ash Corporation exchanges $250,000 of its voting common stock and $50,000 of its bonds for all of Texas Corporation's assets. Texas liquidates, with each of its two shareholders receiving equal amounts of the Ash stock and bonds. Barbara has a $50,000 basis in her stock, and George has a $200,000 basis in his stock. George and Barbara, who are unrelated, each own 8% of Ash's stock (5,000 shares) immediately after the reorganization. At the time of the reorganization, Texas's E&P balance is $75,000, and its assets have an adjusted basis of $225,000.

a. What is the amount of Texas's recognized gain or loss in the asset transfer? On the distribution of the stock and bonds?
b. What is Ash's basis in the assets it acquired?
c. What are the amount and character of each shareholder's recognized gain or loss?
d. What is the basis of each shareholder's Ash stock? Ash bonds?

C:7-53 *Tax Consequences of a Type C Reorganization.* As part of a Type C reorganization, Tulsa Corporation exchanges assets having a $300,000 FMV and a $175,000 adjusted basis for $250,000 of Akron Corporation voting common stock and Akron's assumption of $50,000 of Tulsa's liabilities. Tulsa liquidates, with its sole shareholder, Michelle, receiving the Akron stock in exchange for her Tulsa stock having an adjusted basis of $100,000. Michelle owns 12% (2,500 shares) of Akron's stock immediately after the reorganization.

a. What is the amount of Tulsa's recognized gain or loss in the asset transfer? On the distribution of the stock?
b. What is Akron's basis in the assets it receives?
c. What effect would the transfer of Tulsa's assets to Subsidiary Corporation (controlled by Akron) have on the reorganization?
d. What are the amount and character of Michelle's recognized gain or loss?
e. What is Michelle's basis and holding period for her Akron stock?
f. What are the tax consequences of the transaction if Akron first transfers its stock to Akron-Sub Corporation, which then acquires Tulsa's assets?

C:7-54 *Requirements for a Type B Reorganization.* Allen Corporation plans to acquire all the stock in Taylor Corporation in a stock-for-stock exchange. Which of the following transactions will qualify as a Type B reorganization?

a. All of Taylor's common stock is exchanged for $1 million of Allen voting preferred stock.
b. All of Taylor's common stock is exchanged for $1 million of Allen voting common stock, and $500,000 face amount of Taylor bonds are exchanged for $500,000 face amount of Allen bonds. Both bonds are trading at their par values.

c. All of Taylor's stock is exchanged for $750,000 of Allen voting common stock and $250,000 of Allen bonds.
d. All of Taylor's stock is exchanged for $1 million of Allen voting common stock, and Taylor shareholders end up with less than 1% of Allen stock.
e. Ninety percent of Taylor's stock is exchanged for $900,000 of Allen voting common stock. One shareholder who owns 10% of the Taylor stock exercises his right under state law to have his shares independently appraised and redeemed for cash by Taylor. He receives $100,000.
f. Assume the same facts as in Part d except the Allen stock is contributed to Allen-Sub Corporation. The Allen stock is exchanged by Allen-Sub for all the Taylor stock.

C:7-55 *Tax Consequences of a Type B Reorganization.* Trent Corporation's single class of stock is owned equally by Juan and Miguel, who are unrelated. Juan has a $125,000 basis in his 1,000 Trent shares, and Miguel has a $300,000 basis in his 1,000 Trent shares. In a single transaction, Adams Corporation exchanges 2,500 shares of its voting common stock for each shareholder's Trent stock. Immediately after the reorganization, each shareholder owns 15% of the Adams stock, which has an FMV of $100 per share.
a. What are the amount and character of each shareholder's recognized gain or loss?
b. What is each shareholder's basis in his Adams stock?
c. What is Adams's basis in the Trent stock?
d. How would your answers to Parts a–c change if Adams instead exchanged 2,000 shares of Adams common stock and $50,000 in cash for each shareholder's Trent stock?

C:7-56 *Tax Consequences of a Type B Reorganization.* Austin Corporation exchanges $1.5 million of its voting common stock for all of Travis Corporation's single class of stock. Ingrid, who owns all the Travis stock, has a $375,000 stock basis. Immediately after the reorganization, Ingrid owns 25% of the 15,000 outstanding shares of Austin stock.
a. What are the amount and character of Ingrid's recognized gain or loss?
b. What is Ingrid's basis in her Austin stock?
c. What is Austin's basis in the Travis stock?
d. What are the tax consequences for all parties if Austin subsequently liquidates Travis as part of the plan of reorganization?
e. As part of the reorganization, Austin exchanges $1 million of its 7% bonds for $1 million Travis 7% bonds held equally by ten private investors.

C:7-57 *Tax Consequences of a Type B Reorganization.* On January 30 of the current year, Ashton Corporation purchased from Cathy 10% of Todd Corporation stock for $250,000 in cash. On May 30 of the following year, Andrea and Bill each exchange one-half of the remaining 90% of the Todd stock for $1.2 million of Ashton voting common stock. Andrea and Bill each have a $150,000 basis in their Todd stock, and each owns 15% of the Ashton stock (12,000 shares) immediately after the reorganization.
a. What are the amount and character of each shareholder's recognized gain or loss?
b. What is each shareholder's basis in his or her Ashton stock?
c. What is Ashton's basis in the Todd stock?
d. How would your answers to Parts a–c change if instead Ashton had acquired the remaining Todd stock on May 30 of the current year?
e. What effect would the stock acquisition have on the adjusted bases of individual assets and the tax attributes of Todd?
f. Can the Ashton-Todd corporate group file a consolidated tax return?
g. Can a Sec. 338 election be made with respect to Todd's assets?

C:7-58 *Tax Consequences of a Divisive Type D Reorganization.* Road Corporation is owned equally by four shareholders. It conducts activities through two operating divisions: the road construction division and the meat packing division. To segregate the two activities into distinct corporations, Road transfers the assets and liabilities of the meat packing division (60% of Road's total net assets) to Food Corporation in exchange for all of Food's single class of stock. The assets of the meat packing division have a $2.75 million FMV and a $1.1 million adjusted basis. Its liabilities total $500,000. Road distributes the $2.25 million of Food stock (90,000 shares) ratably to each of the four shareholders.
a. What is the amount of Road's recognized gain or loss on the asset transfer? On the distribution of the Food stock?
b. What are the amount and character of each shareholder's recognized gain or loss on the distribution? (Assume each shareholder's basis in Road stock is $200,000.)

c. What is the basis of each shareholder's Road and Food stock after the reorganization? (Assume the Road stock is worth $1.5 million immediately after the distribution.)

C:7-59 *Tax Consequences of a Divisive Type D Reorganization.* Light Corporation is owned equally by two individual shareholders, Bev and Tarek. The shareholders no longer agree on how to manage Light's operations. Tarek agrees to a plan whereby $500,000 of Light's assets (having an adjusted basis of $350,000) and $100,000 of Light's liabilities are transferred to Dark Corporation in exchange for all its single class of stock (5,000 shares). Tarek will exchange all his Light common stock, having a $150,000 adjusted basis, for the $400,000 of Dark stock. Bev will continue to operate Light.

a. What is the amount of Light's recognized gain or loss on the asset transfer? On the distribution of the Dark stock?
b. What are the amount and character of Tarek's recognized gain or loss?
c. What is Tarek's basis in his Dark stock?
d. What tax attributes of Light will be allocated to Dark?

C:7-60 *Distribution of Stock: Spin-Off.* Parent Corporation has been in the business of manufacturing and selling trucks for the past eight years. Its subsidiary, Diesel Corporation, has been in the business of manufacturing and selling diesel engines for the past seven years. Parent acquired control of Diesel six years ago when it purchased 100% of its single class of stock from Large Corporation at a price of $650 per share. A federal court has ordered Parent to divest itself of Diesel pursuant to an antitrust ruling. Consequently, Parent distributes all its Diesel stock pro rata to its shareholders. Alan owns less than 1% of Parent's outstanding stock having a $40,000 basis. As a result of Parent's distribution, he receives 25 shares of Diesel stock having a $25,000 FMV and a $16,250 ($650 × 25) basis to Parent immediately before the distribution. Parent distributes no cash or other assets. Parent's E&P at the end of the year in which the spinoff occurs is $2.5 million. The Parent stock held by Alan has a $75,000 FMV immediately after the distribution.

a. What are the amount and character of the gain, loss, or income Alan must recognize as a result of Parent's distributing the Diesel stock?
b. What basis does Alan have in the Diesel and Parent stock after the distribution?
c. When does Alan's holding period for the Diesel stock begin?
d. What amount and character of gain or loss does Parent recognize on the distribution?
e. How would your answer to Part a change if Parent had been in the truck business for only three years before the distribution, and it had acquired the Diesel stock in a taxable transaction only two years ago?

C:7-61 *Distribution of Stock: Split-Off.* Parent Corporation has owned all 100 shares of Subsidiary Corporation common stock since 2010. Parent has been in the business of manufacturing and selling light fixtures, and Subsidiary has been in the business of manufacturing and selling light bulbs. Amy and Bill are the two equal shareholders of the Parent stock and have owned their stock since 2010. Amy's basis in her 50 Parent shares is $80,000, and Bill's basis in his 50 Parent shares also is $80,000. On April 10, 2017, Parent distributes all 100 Subsidiary shares to Bill in exchange for all his Parent shares (which are cancelled). The distribution has a bona fide business purpose. The Subsidiary stock had a $30,000 basis to Parent on the distribution date. At the end of 2017, Parent has $150,000 of E&P. Immediately after the distribution, the FMVs of the Parent and Subsidiary stocks are $3,000 and $1,500 per share, respectively.

a. What are the amount and character of the gain, loss, or income Bill must recognize as a result of Parent's distributing the Subsidiary stock?
b. What basis does Bill take in the Subsidiary stock?
c. When does Bill's holding period for the Subsidiary stock begin?
d. Assume instead that Andrew formed Subsidiary in 2013 to manufacture and sell lightbulbs. Andrew sold the Subsidiary stock to Parent for cash in 2015. How would your answers to Parts a–c change?

C:7-62 *Distribution of Stock and Securities: Split-Off.* Ruby Corporation has 100 shares of common stock outstanding. Fred, a shareholder of Ruby, exchanges his 25% interest in the Ruby stock for Garnet Corporation stock and securities. Ruby purchased 80% of the Garnet stock ten years ago for $25,000. At the time of the exchange, Fred has a $50,000 basis in his Ruby stock, and the stock has an $80,000 FMV. Fred receives Garnet stock that has a $60,000 FMV and Garnet securities that have a $20,000 FMV. Ruby has $50,000 of E&P. Assume that all the requirements of Sec. 355 are met except with respect to the receipt of boot.

a. What are the amount and character of Fred's recognized gain or loss in the exchange?
b. What is Fred's basis in the Garnet stock and the Garnet securities?
c. What are the amount and character of Ruby's recognized gain or loss on the distribution?

d. When does Fred's holding period begin for the Garnet stock and the Garnet securities?
e. How would your answers to Part a change if the exchange did not meet the requirements of Sec. 355 or Sec. 356?

C:7-63 *Distribution of Stock and Securities: Split-Up.* Jean Corporation has two divisions—home cookware and electric home appliances. Bill and Bob Jean own all of Jean Corporation's single class of stock. Bill, the older brother, owns 70% of the Jean stock, and Bob owns the remaining 30%. Bill and Bob's adjusted bases in their Jean stock are $700,000 and $300,000, respectively. They have owned the stock for eight years. The divisions have the following assets:

Division	*FMV Assets*	*Adjusted Basis*
Cookware	$980,000	$600,000
Home appliances	420,000	300,000

To divide the business, Jean transfers the cookware assets to Cookware Corporation in exchange for all of Cookware stock. Jean transfers the home appliance assets to Home Appliance Corporation in exchange for all of Home Appliance stock. Jean transfers the Cookware stock to Bill in exchange for all of his Jean stock. Jean transfers the Home Appliance stock to Bob in exchange for all of his Jean stock. Finally, Jean liquidates with its remaining cash used to pay off its liabilities.

a. What gain or loss is recognized on the transfer of the Jean assets to Cookware and Home Appliance? What basis do the two corporations take in the assets transferred?
b. What gain or loss do Bill and Bob recognize when they exchange their Jean stock for the Cookware and Home Appliance stock? What basis does each shareholder take in his or her new stock?

C:7-64 *Requirements for a Type E Reorganization.* Master Corporation plans a recapitalization. Explain the tax consequences of each of the following unrelated transactions:

a. Holders of Class A nonvoting preferred stock exchange their stock for newly issued common stock. Master paid $300,000 of cash dividends on the preferred stock in the current year and each prior year.
b. Holders of Master bonds in the amount of $3 million exchange their bonds for the same dollar amount of preferred stock. In addition, $180,000 of unpaid interest will be paid by issuing additional Master preferred stock to the former bondholders.
c. Because of a decline in the prevailing rate of interest, Master 9% bonds in the amount of $3 million are called and exchanged by their holders before their maturity date for the same dollar amount of Master 6% bonds. In addition, Master will pay with cash $180,000 of unpaid interest.

C:7-65 *Tax Consequences of a Type E Reorganization.* Milan Corporation is owned by four shareholders. Andy and Bob each own 40% of the outstanding common and preferred stock. Chris and Doug each own 10% of the outstanding common and preferred stock. The shareholders want to retire the preferred stock that was issued five years ago when the corporation was in the midst of a major expansion. Retirement of the preferred stock will eliminate the need to pay annual preferred dividends. Explain the tax consequences of the following two alternatives to the shareholders:

- Milan redeems the $100 par preferred stock for its $120 call price. Each shareholder purchased his preferred stock at its par value five years ago.
- The shareholders exchange each share of the $100 par value preferred stock for $120 of additional common stock.

What nontax advantages might exist for selecting one alternative over the other?

C:7-66 *Types of Reorganizations.* Identify the type of each of the following reorganizations.

a. Briggs Corporation was originally incorporated in Georgia but now conducts most of its business in Florida. The firm transfers substantially all its Georgia assets to a new Florida corporation. The Georgia entity liquidates shortly after the transfer. All Georgia-based shareholders swap their "old" Briggs stock for "new" Briggs stock, thereby acquiring an ownership interest in the Florida entity.
b. Jones Corporation exchanges all $1 million of its $1,000 face amount, 6% bonds for the same amount of new convertible bonds bearing a lower interest rate.
c. Bill Smith owns 100% of Smith Corporation and James Jones owns 100% of Jones Corporation. The two corporations are combined into a single entity called Smith & Jones Corporation. Each shareholder in the two original corporations receives stock in the new combined entity in proportion to the value of his original stock holdings.

d. Dupree Corporation is in bankruptcy. The corporation works out an arrangement whereby bondholders and other creditors receive Dupree notes and stock in exchange for discharge of their original claims.

C:7-67 *Reorganization Requirements.* Discuss the tax consequences of the following corporate reorganizations to the parties to the reorganization:

a. Adobe Corporation and Tyler Corporation merge under Florida law. Tyler shareholders receive for their Tyler stock $300,000 of Adobe common stock and $700,000 of Adobe securities.
b. Alabama Corporation exchanges $1 million of its voting common stock for all the noncash assets of Texas Corporation. The transaction meets all requirements of a Type C reorganization. Alabama then splits the acquired business into two operating divisions: meat packing and meat distribution. Alabama retains the meat packing division's assets and continues its activities but sells for cash the assets of the meat distribution division. The meat distribution division's assets constitute 40% of Texas's noncash assets.
c. Parent Corporation transfers $500,000 of investment securities to Subsidiary Corporation in exchange for all its single class of stock. The Subsidiary stock is exchanged for one-third of the stock held by each of Parent's shareholders. Six months after the reorganization, Subsidiary distributes the investment securities to its shareholders pursuant to the liquidation of Subsidiary.

C:7-68 *Determining the Type of Reorganization Transaction.* For each of the following transactions, indicate the reorganization type (e.g., Type A, Type B, etc.). Assume all common stock is voting.

a. Anderson and Brown Corporations exchange their assets for all the single class of stock of newly created Computer Corporation. Following the exchange, Anderson and Brown liquidate. The transaction satisfies Michigan corporation law requirements.
b. Price Corporation (incorporated in Texas) exchanges all its assets for all the single class of stock in Price Corporation (incorporated in Delaware). Following the exchange, Price (Texas) liquidates.
c. All of Gates Corporation's noncumulative, 10% preferred stock is exchanged for Gates common stock.
d. Hobbs Corporation exchanges its common stock for 90% of the outstanding common stock and 80% of the outstanding nonvoting preferred stock in Calvin Corporation. The remaining Calvin stock is held by about 30 individual investors.
e. Scale Corporation transfers the assets of its two operating divisions to Major and Minor Corporations in exchange for all of each corporation's single class of stock. Scale then distributes the Major and Minor stock pursuant to the liquidation of Scale.
f. Tobias Corporation has $3 million of assets and $1 million of liabilities. Andrew Corporation exchanges $2 million of its voting common stock for all of Tobias' assets and liabilities. Tobias liquidates, and its shareholders end up with 11% of the Andrew stock.
g. How would your answer to Part f change (if at all) if Tobias' balance sheet indicates that liabilities constitute 90% of the corporation's capital structure and common stock, the remaining 10%?

C:7-69 *Tax Attribute Carryovers.* At the close of business on May 31, 2017, Alaska Corporation exchanges $2 million of its voting common stock for all the noncash assets of Tennessee Corporation. Tennessee uses its cash to pay off its liabilities and then liquidates. Tennessee and Alaska report the following taxable income (loss):

Tax Year Ending	*Alaska Corp.*	*Tennessee Corp.*
December 31, 2014	($100,000)	($95,000)
December 31, 2015	60,000	20,000
December 31, 2016	70,000	(90,000)
May 31, 2017	XXX	(40,000)
December 31, 2017	73,000	XXX

a. What tax returns must Alaska and Tennessee file for 2017?
b. What amount of the NOL carryover does Alaska acquire?
c. Ignoring any implications of Sec. 382, what amount of Tennessee's NOL can Alaska use in 2017?

C:7-70 *Sec. 382 Limitation: Purchase Transaction.* Murray Corporation's stock is owned by about 1,000 shareholders, none of whom own more than 1% of the outstanding shares. Pursuant to a tender offer, Said purchased all the Murray stock for $7.5 million cash at the close of business on December 31, 2016. Before the acquisition, Said owned no Murray stock. Murray had incurred substantial NOLs, which totaled $1 million at the end of 2016. Murray's taxable income is expected to be $200,000 and $600,000, respectively, for 2017 and 2018. Assuming the long-term tax-exempt federal rate is 5% and Murray continues in the same trade or business, what amount of NOLs can Murray use in 2017 and/or 2018? What amount of NOLs and Sec. 382 limitation carryover to 2019?

C:7-71 *Sec. 382 Limitation: Nontaxable Reorganization.* Albert Corporation is a profitable publicly traded corporation. None of its shareholders owns more than 1% of its outstanding shares. On December 31, 2016, Albert exchanged $8 million of its stock for all the stock of Turner Corporation as part of a merger. Turner is owned by Tara, who receives 15% of the Albert stock as part of the reorganization. Tara owned none of the Albert stock before the merger. Turner accumulated $2.5 million in NOL carryovers before merging into Albert. Albert expects to earn $1 million and $1.5 million in taxable income during 2017 and 2018, respectively. Assuming the long-term tax-exempt federal rate is 4.5%, what amount of NOLs can Albert use in 2017 and 2018?

C:7-72 *Sec. 338 Limitation: Value of NOLs.* At the beginning of the current year, Allegro Corporation acquires all of Tempo Corporation's stock in a Type B reorganization. At the time of the acquisition, Tempo's stock has a $900,000 FMV, and Tempo has a $115,000 net operating loss (NOL) carryover. Assuming a 3.25% long-term tax-exempt federal rate, a 34% corporate tax rate, and a 5% discount rate, determine the present value of the tax benefits that will result from the NOLs. Assume that any NOL benefit will occur at the end of each relevant tax year.

COMPREHENSIVE PROBLEM

C:7-73 Sid Kess, a long-time tax client of yours, has decided to acquire the snow blower manufacturing firm owned by Richard Smith, one of his closest friends. Richard has a $200,000 adjusted basis in his Richard Smith Snow Blowers (RSSB) stock. Sid Kess Enterprises (SKE), a C corporation 100%-owned by Sid Kess, will make the acquisition. RSSB operates as a C corporation and reports the following assets and liabilities as of November 1 of the current year.

Assets	*Adjusted Basis*	*FMV*
Cash	$ 200,000	$ 200,000
Inventory (LIFO)	470,000	600,000
Equipment	100,000	275,000
Building	200,000	295,000
Land	80,000	120,000
Goodwill	–0–	250,000
Total	$1,050,000	$1,740,000

Liabilities and Equity	*Amount*
Accounts payable	$ 60,000
Mortgage payable	120,000
Paid-in capital	220,000
Retained earnings	650,000
Total	$1,050,000

RSSB has claimed depreciation of $200,000 and $80,000 on the equipment and building, respectively, and has claimed no amortization on the goodwill. Retained earnings approximate RSSB's E&P. No NOL, capital loss, or credit carryovers exist at the time of the acquisition. What are the tax consequences of each alternative acquisition transaction to SKE and RSSB? Assume a 34% corporate tax rate.

a. SKE acquires all the single class of RSSB stock for $1.56 million in cash. RSSB is not liquidated.

b. SKE acquires all the noncash assets of RSSB for $1.54 million in cash. RSSB is liquidated.

c. SKE acquires all the RSSB stock for $1.56 million in cash. RSSB is liquidated into SKE shortly after the acquisition.
d. SKE acquires all the RSSB stock for $1.56 million in cash. SKE makes a timely Sec. 338 election. Assume that RSSB's corporate tax rate is 34%.
e. SKE exchanges $1.54 million of its common stock for all of RSSB's noncash assets ($1,540,000 = $1,740,000 total assets − $200,000 cash). SKE has 10,000 shares of stock outstanding with a $3 million FMV before the acquisition. RSSB liquidates as part of the transaction. RSSB uses part of the retained cash to pay off the corporation's liabilities. The remaining cash is distributed along with the SKE stock in the liquidation of RSSB.
f. SKE exchanges $1.56 million of its common stock for all of Richard Smith's RSSB stock. Assume that RSSB does not liquidate. Each share of SKE stock has a $300 FMV.
g. Assume the same facts as in Part d except SKE transfers $1.56 million of its common stock to SKE-Sub. In the transaction, SKE-Sub is the acquiring corporation and uses $1.56 million of the SKE stock to acquire RSSB's stock.
h. Assume the same facts as in Part e except SKE transfers $1.54 million of its common stock to SKE-Sub. In the transaction, SKE-Sub is the acquiring corporation and uses $1.54 million of the SKE stock to acquire RSSB's noncash assets.

TAX STRATEGY PROBLEMS

C:7-74 Angel Macias is considering selling his business (organized as Theta Corporation), which has the following assets and liabilities:

Assets	*Adjusted Basis*	*FMV*
Cash	$ 400,000	$ 400,000
Securities	400,000	300,000
Inventory (LIFO)	100,000	200,000
Equipment	200,000	400,000
Building	50,000	300,000
Goodwill	–0–	200,000
Total	$1,150,000	$1,800,000

Theta's balance sheet also shows $200,000 of accounts payable and $400,000 in bank loans. No NOL carryovers or carrybacks are available. Bill Jones and Sam Smith, each of whose net worth exceeds $1 million, are interested in acquiring the business by using S&J Corporation as the vehicle for making the acquisition. Theta's management and its owners are interested in selling the business. What advice would you give Bill and Sam about acquiring the assets directly from Theta, or by acquiring Theta stock from its shareholders and then liquidating Theta into S&J? Bill and Sam also have expressed concern about possible differences in the financial reporting of a nontaxable versus a taxable acquisition.

C:7-75 Pedernales, a cash-rich Texas company that produces petrochemicals, would like to expand its operations in the Southwest. It considers acquiring Dorado, a Nevada corporation that disposes chemical wastes. Dorado owns key licenses, facilities, and technological processes. Over the years, it has accumulated substantial business and foreign tax credits. Because waste disposal sites are scarce in the United States, the value of Dorado's assets has increased threefold, while the value of Dorado stock has increased fivefold. The Rodriguez family, which owns a 52% equity stake in Pedernales, wants to retain control of the Texas company. How might Pedernales structure an acquisition? What tax and other issues should it consider?

C:7-76 Tom Smith owns 100% of Alpha Corporation's single class of stock, and Alpha owns 100% of Beta Corporation's single class of stock. Alpha and Beta have filed separate tax returns for a number of years. Neither corporation has any NOL carryovers. Although in recent years Alpha and Beta have been profitable, Beta needs an infusion of additional capital from outside investors. The corporations have received a proposal from an investor, Karla Boroff, to invest $2 million in Beta to enable Beta to expand its operations and to eliminate a current working capital shortage. Karla has imposed one constraint on her capital contribution—that Alpha and Beta become two independent entities. Alpha would continue to be owned entirely by Tom, but Beta would be controlled by the two individuals, Tom and Karla, with each owning 50% of Beta's stock. What tax strategies can you offer for separating the two companies?

CASE STUDY PROBLEMS

TAX & FINANCIAL ACCOUNTING

C:7-77 *Comparative Acquisition Forms.* Bailey Corporation owns a number of automotive parts shops. Bill Smith owns an automotive parts shop that has been in existence for 40 years and has competed with one of Bailey's branches. Bill is considering retiring and would like to sell his business. He has his CPA prepare the following balance sheet, which he presents to John Bailey, president of Bailey Corporation and a long-time friend of Bill's.

Assets	*Adjusted Basis*	*FMV*
Cash	$ 250,000	$ 250,000
Accounts receivable	75,000	70,000
Inventories (LIFO)	600,000	1,750,000
Equipment	200,000	250,000
Building	30,000	285,000
Land	30,000	115,000
Total	$1,185,000	$2,720,000

If Bailey Corporation pursues the acquisition, it will operate the automotive parts shop under its own tradename in the location Bill has used for 40 years. Mr. Bailey has asked you to prepare a summary of the tax consequences of the following three transactions: (1) a cash purchase of the noncash assets, (2) a purchase of the stock of Bill's corporation with cash and Bailey notes, and (3) an asset-for-stock reorganization conducted exclusively with Bailey stock. Upon interviewing Bill, you obtain the following additional information: Bill's business is operated as a C corporation. Bill has a $160,000 adjusted basis in his stock. Accounts payable of $200,000 are outstanding. The corporation has depreciated the building under the straight-line method and to date has claimed $100,000 in depreciation. The equipment is Sec. 1245 property for which the corporation has claimed $150,000 in depreciation. The after-tax profits in each of the last three years have exceeded $300,000. Bill suspects that some goodwill value exists that is not shown on the balance sheet. No NOL carryovers are available from prior years.

Required: Prepare a memorandum that outlines the tax consequences of each of the three alternative acquisitions. Assume that the anticipated cash purchase price is $2.55 million for the noncash assets and $2.6 million for the stock. Furthermore, assume that the transaction takes place in the current year. How would the acquiring corporation report each of the three alternatives under GAAP?

C:7-78 The following advertisement appeared in a financial journal:

$17 MILLION CASH WITH
ADDITIONAL CASH AVAILABLE
$105 MM TAX LOSS GOOD THROUGH 2031
CAPITAL GROUP, INC.
NASDAQ listed w/300 shareholders
WANTS TO ACQUIRE COMPANY
with Net Before Tax Audited Earnings of $7MM to $10MM
Exceptional Opportunity and Participation for Sellers and
Existing Management. Contact: Albert M. Zlotnick or Ross P.
Lederer, Tel: (000)-000-0000 and Fax: (000)-000-0000.

Required: Prepare a memorandum explaining the tax advantages that would accrue to the Capital Group if it acquired the stock or assets of a profitable corporation in a nontaxable reorganization or a taxable transaction. Would the advantages be the same if a profitable corporation acquired Capital? In addition, explain any tax law provisions that might restrict the use of these loss carryovers.

TAX RESEARCH PROBLEMS

C:7-79 On January 10 of the current year, Austin Corporation acquires for cash 8% of Travis Corporation's single class of stock. On August 25 of the current year, Austin makes a tender offer to exchange Austin common stock for the remaining Travis shares. Travis shareholders tender an additional 75% of the outstanding Travis stock. The exchange is completed on September 25 of the current year. Austin ends up with slightly more than

83% of the Travis shares. The remaining 17% of the Travis stock is held by about 100 former shareholders of Travis who own small blocks of stock. Your tax manager has asked you to draft a memorandum explaining whether one or both of the two acquisition transactions qualify as a nontaxable reorganization. If part or all of either transaction is taxable to Travis' shareholders, suggest ways to restructure the acquisitions so as to maximize tax benefits of the transaction. Assume that Austin does not want to make a Sec. 338 election.

Matt Bonner, CEO of Travis, asked a question that might be relevant to reporting the transaction: To simplify the corporate structure, can Austin liquidate Travis into Austin without recognizing any gain or loss?

At a minimum you should consult:

- IRC Sec. 368(a)(1)(B)
- Reg. Sec. 1.368-2(c)
- *Eldon S. Chapman, et al. v. CIR,* 45 AFTR 2d 80-1290, 80-1 USTC ¶9330 (1st Cir., 1980)
- *Arden S. Heverly, et al. v. CIR,* 45 AFTR 2d 80-1122, 80-1 USTC ¶9322 (3rd Cir., 1980)

C:7-80 ABC Corporation is the object of a hostile takeover bid by XYZ Corporation. ABC incurs a total of $400,000 in attorneys' fees, accounting fees, and printing costs for information mailed to ABC shareholders in its effort to defeat the XYZ takeover bid. XYZ finally concedes, and ABC remains a separate corporation. What is the appropriate tax treatment of the $400,000 in fees? Would that treatment be different if XYZ succeeds in acquiring ABC? Tax authorities you should consult include the following:

- IRC Sec. 162
- IRC Sec. 165
- *INDOPCO, Inc. v. Comm.,* 69 AFTR 2d 92-694, 92-1 USTC ¶50,113 (USSC, 1992)
- *U.S. v. Federated Department Stores, Inc.,* 74 AFTR 2d 94-5519, 94-2 USTC ¶50,418 (S.D. Ohio, 1994)
- *A.E. Staley Manufacturing Co. v. Comm.,* 80 AFTR 2d 97-5060, 97-2 USTC ¶50,521 (7th Cir., 1997)
- Reg. Sec. 1.263(a)-5

C:7-81 Diversified Corporation operates a successful bank with ten branches. Al, Bob, and Cathy created Diversified six years ago and own all the Diversified stock in equal shares. Diversified has constructed in downtown Metropolis a new building that houses a banking facility on the first floor, offices for its employees on the second and third floors, and office space to be leased out to third party lessees on the fourth through twelfth floors. Since the building was completed six months ago, approximately 75% of the floor space on the upper floors has been occupied. Under a plan of reorganization, Diversified proposes to transfer the building to Metropolis Real Estate (MRE) Corporation in exchange for all the MRE common stock. A team of commercial real estate experts has been hired to manage MRE. Following the reorganization, the building will be the only property owned by MRE. Diversified owns no other real estate because it currently leases from third parties the facilities for its ten retail banking branches. Diversified will distribute the MRE common stock ratably to Al, Bob, and Cathy, who will end up with all the Diversified and MRE common stock. Your tax manager has asked you to draft a memorandum explaining whether or not the proposed transaction will satisfy the requirements of a nontaxable divisive reorganization. At a minimum you should consult:

- IRC Sec. 368(a)(1)(D)
- Reg. Sec. 1.355-3(b), (c)
- *Appleby v. Comm.,* 9 AFTR 2d 372, 62-1 USTC ¶9178 (3rd Cir., 1962)

CHAPTER

8

CONSOLIDATED TAX RETURNS

LEARNING OBJECTIVES

After studying this chapter, you should be able to

1. Determine whether a group of corporations is an affiliated group
2. Describe how an affiliated group makes a consolidated return election and how it discontinues the election
3. Calculate consolidated taxable income for a consolidated group
4. Apply the rules for reporting intercompany transactions
5. Compute on a consolidated basis deductions and credits subject to limitations
6. Determine a consolidated group's NOL, calculate the carryback or carryover of a consolidated NOL, and apply the SRLY restrictions on NOL usage
7. Adjust the parent's basis in stock of a consolidated subsidiary
8. Compare the advantages and disadvantages of filing a consolidated tax return
9. Comply with the procedures for making a consolidated return election
10. Explain the financial statement implications of various consolidated transactions

CHAPTER OUTLINE

Many corporations have complex entity structures. For example, a corporation may have one or more subsidiaries, and some of these subsidiaries may have their own subsidiaries. A group of corporations form into complex entity structures for many reasons. For example, a parent corporation may want to insulate itself from liabilities related to its subsidiaries, or it may want to make it easier to implement a plan that links the compensation of the subsidiary's managers to the subsidiary's performance.

An **affiliated group** of corporations generally is a parent corporation and all its subsidiaries that are at least 80%-owned by the parent and other subsidiaries in the group (this topic will be discussed later in the chapter). The affiliated group has two options for filing its federal income tax returns:

- Each member of the group can file a separate tax return that reports its own income, deductions, credits, and other items.[1]
- The affiliated group can file a single, consolidated tax return that reports a combined result for all its group members.

If the affiliated group elects to file a **consolidated tax return**, it does not merely add up the members' incomes, deductions, and other items. Instead, the group must make adjustments so that it generally is treated as if it were a single corporation, as discussed in more detail later in the chapter. For example, the capital gains and losses for all group members are netted to determine the deductibility of capital losses against capital gains rather than netting these items separately for each group member. The group also must make adjustments for transactions among themselves, called *intercompany transactions*, so the consolidated tax return reflects the correct amount of consolidated taxable income.

Some consolidated tax returns include as few as two corporations. Other consolidated tax returns include hundreds of corporations. Most of the nation's largest corporate groups file consolidated tax returns. In 2013, only 35,185 consolidated tax returns were filed, which was less than 3% of all Form 1120s filed. However, these tax returns reported more than 97% of total taxable income and paid more than 97% of total income taxes of all corporations filing Form 1120.[2]

This chapter discusses the requirements for a group of corporations to qualify as an affiliated group that can elect to file a consolidated tax return. It also explains several rules that pertain to computing consolidated taxable income and the consolidated tax liability. The discussion then turns to some issues that arise when corporations enter or leave an affiliated group that is filing a consolidated tax return, such as when subsidiaries are bought and sold. The chapter also considers the advantages and disadvantages of filing a consolidated tax return instead of separate tax returns and discusses some financial statement implications.

DEFINITION OF AN AFFILIATED GROUP

OBJECTIVE 1

Determine whether a group of corporations is an affiliated group

REQUIREMENTS

Stock Ownership Requirements. Only an affiliated group of corporations can elect to file a consolidated tax return. A group of corporations must satisfy the following stock ownership requirements to qualify as an affiliated group:

- The parent corporation must own directly at least 80% of the stock in one or more includible corporations (defined below).
- At least 80% of the stock of *each* corporation in the group (other than the parent corporation) must be owned directly by the parent corporation and other group members.

[1] If the affiliated group members file separate tax returns, some special tax rules apply because group members are related taxpayers under Sec. 267. These rules include, but are not limited to, matching of income and deductions (Sec. 267(a)(2)), deferral of loss on intragroup sales (Sec. 267(f)(2)), and ordinary income recognition on intragroup sales of depreciable property (Sec. 1239). The members also may constitute a controlled group subject to the restrictions of Sec. 1563. See Chapter C:3 for details.

[2] Internal Revenue Service, Statistics of Income Division (*www.irs.gov*).

- Both 80% stock ownership requirements must be satisfied in two ways for each includible corporation (other than the parent): the stock owned directly must be at least 80% of the total voting power of all the includible corporation's outstanding stock entitled to vote, and it must be at least 80% of the total value of all the includible corporation's outstanding stock.[3]

EXAMPLE C:8-1 ▶ P Corporation owns 95% of S1 Corporation's stock, and S1 owns 100% of S2 Corporation's stock. Unrelated individuals own the remainder of S1's stock. P, S1, and S2 comprise an affiliated group because P owns at least 80% of S1's stock, and S1 owns at least 80% of S2's stock. The P-S1-S2 affiliated group can elect to file a consolidated tax return with P as the common parent.[4] ◀

EXAMPLE C:8-2 ▶ P Corporation owns 90% of S1 Corporation's stock and 35% of S2 Corporation's stock. S1 owns 50% of S2's stock. Unrelated individuals own the remainder of S1's and S2's stock. P, S1, and S2 comprise an affiliated group because P owns at least 80% of S1's stock, and P and S1 together own 85% (50% + 35%) of S2's stock. ◀

EXAMPLE C:8-3 ▶ Ted (an individual) owns all the stock of Alpha and Beta Corporations. Alpha and Beta are not an affiliated group because a parent-subsidiary relationship is not present even though the same individual owns 100% of each corporation. Alpha and Beta cannot elect to file a consolidated tax return. The Tax Strategy Tip on page C:8-4 suggests ways to restructure the corporations so they qualify as an affiliated group. ◀

EXAMPLE C:8-4 ▶ S Corporation has 1,000 shares of common stock and 600 shares of preferred stock outstanding. Each share of common stock has two votes and is worth $45. Each share of preferred stock has one vote and is worth $75. P Corporation owns all 1,000 shares of S's common stock and 150 shares of S's preferred stock. Unrelated individuals own the remaining preferred stock.

The total voting power of S's stock is 2,600 [(1,000 × 2) + (600 × 1)] votes, and the total value of S's stock is $90,000 [(1,000 × $45) + (600 × $75)]. P's ownership of S's stock possesses 2,150 [(1,000 × 2) + (150 × 1)] votes and is worth $56,250 [(1,000 × $45) + (150 × $75)]. This ownership is 82.69% (2,150 ÷ 2,600) of S's total voting power and 62.50% ($56,250 ÷ $90,000) of the value of S's stock. Because both 80% stock ownership requirements are not met, P and S are not an affiliated group. ◀

BOOK-TO-TAX ACCOUNTING COMPARISON

The group of corporations included in a consolidated tax return may be quite different from the group of corporations included in a set of consolidated financial statements because of different stock ownership requirements and the different types of corporations that are included in or excluded from the groups. Page 1 of Schedule M-3 reconciles these differences (see Appendix B).

Includible Corporation Requirement. All corporations are includible except certain specified corporations having special tax statuses. Important types of corporations that are not includible are:

- Corporations exempt from tax under Sec. 501
- Life insurance companies subject to tax under Sec. 801[5]
- Foreign corporations[6]
- Regulated investment companies
- Real estate investment trusts
- S corporations

Most of the nation's largest corporations have a great number of subsidiaries, many of which are not part of an affiliated group because they are not includible corporations. Consequently, they cannot be included in a consolidated tax return, and they usually file their own separate corporate tax returns (if required to do so). Moreover, their stock ownership of other group members cannot be counted toward satisfying the 80% stock ownership requirement for an affiliated group.

[3] When determining whether these stock ownership requirements are met, nonvoting preferred stock is ignored if it is limited and preferred as to dividends (and does not participate in corporate growth to any significant extent), has redemption and liquidation rights limited to its issue price (plus a reasonable redemption or liquidation premium), and is not convertible into another class of stock (Sec. 1504(a)(4)).

[4] All corporations in this chapter are includible corporations and have a single class of stock unless otherwise indicated.

[5] Two or more Sec. 801 life insurance companies may elect to file a consolidated tax return. If an affiliated group contains one or more Sec. 801 domestic life insurance companies, Sec. 1504(c)(2)(A) permits the parent corporation to elect to treat as includible corporations all such companies that have met the affiliated group stock ownership tests for the five immediately preceding tax years.

[6] Section 1504(d) allows a domestic corporation to elect to treat a 100%-owned Canadian or Mexican corporation as a domestic corporation if such foreign corporation is maintained solely for the purpose of complying with local law regarding title and operation of property.

EXAMPLE C:8-5 ▶ P Corporation owns all the stock of S1 and S2 Corporations. S1 owns all of S3 Corporation's stock, and S2 (a foreign corporation) owns all of S4 Corporation's stock. S2 is not a member of the affiliated group because, as a foreign corporation, it is not an includible corporation. P, S1, S3, and S4 are includible corporations, but only P, S1, and S3 qualify as an affiliated group. Although S4 is an includible corporation, it is not a member of the affiliated group because the group's members (P, S1, and S3) do not own at least 80% of S4's stock. S2's ownership of S4's stock is disregarded because S2 is not an includible corporation even though S2 is wholly-owned by a group member. ◀

ADDITIONAL COMMENT

In Example C:8-5, P, S1, S3, and S4 (but not S2, generally) comprise a parent-subsidiary controlled group. P constructively owns all of S4's stock for controlled group purposes but not for affiliated group purposes. Thus, S4 is in the same controlled group as P, S1, and S3 even though it is not in their affiliated group.

Under the check-the-box regulations discussed in Chapter C:2, noncorporate entities can elect to be treated as a corporation. A partnership or LLC that makes this election (and that does not elect to be treated as an S corporation) is an affiliated group member and is eligible to participate in a consolidated tax return provided it is an includible corporation and satisfies the stock ownership requirements. If a partnership or LLC does not elect to be treated as a corporation, it cannot be a member of the affiliated group and cannot participate in a consolidated tax return. Instead, the partnership's or LLC's income and losses pass through to each affiliated group member having an ownership interest in it.

TYPICAL MISCONCEPTION

The terms *controlled group, affiliated group,* and *consolidated group* are easily confused. These terms have different definitions and applications.

COMPARISON WITH CONTROLLED GROUP DEFINITIONS

Chapter C:3 discusses the three types of controlled groups: parent-subsidiary, brother-sister, and combined controlled groups. Special tax rules apply to controlled groups of corporations to prevent them from avoiding taxes. For example, a controlled group's members are limited to a total of $50,000 of taxable income being taxed at 15%, $25,000 being taxed at 25%, and $9,925,000 being taxed at 34%. A brother-sister controlled group cannot elect to file a consolidated tax return because it does not qualify as an affiliated group, as illustrated in Example C:8-3. However, a parent-subsidiary controlled group and the parent-subsidiary portion of a combined controlled group often also qualify as an affiliated group and can elect to file a consolidated tax return if they so qualify.

TAX STRATEGY TIP

A brother-sister controlled group cannot file a consolidated tax return. One way to convert it into an affiliated group is for the owner(s) of one of the group's corporations to transfer 80% or more of the corporation's stock to one of its sibling corporations in a nontaxable transaction meeting the Sec. 351 requirements (see Chapter C:2). The two corporations, being in a parent-subsidiary relationship, then can make the consolidated return election and begin filing on a consolidated basis. Alternatively, the owner(s) could transfer the stock of all the sibling corporations to a new corporation, e.g., a holding company that would be the common parent.

The criteria for a parent-subsidiary controlled group and those for an affiliated group are similar but not identical. Differences in the criteria include:

- The stock ownership requirement for a parent-subsidiary controlled group is at least 80% of voting power *or* value. For an affiliated group, it is at least 80% of voting power *and* value.
- Through stock attribution rules, stock owned by certain related persons is taken into account in determining whether a controlled group exists. They are not used to determine whether an affiliated group exists.
- The types of corporations excluded from a controlled group differ from those excluded from an affiliated group.
- The controlled group definition is tested only on December 31, but the affiliated group definition is tested on each day of the year.

Because of these differences, a corporation could be a member of a controlled group but not be a member of an affiliated group.

CONSOLIDATED TAX RETURN ELECTION

OBJECTIVE 2

Describe how an affiliated group makes a consolidated return election and how it discontinues the election

CONSOLIDATED RETURN REGULATIONS

A consolidated group is an affiliated group of corporations that files a consolidated tax return. The IRC contains very few rules pertaining to consolidated tax returns, and these few rules primarily address the composition of affiliated groups. Instead of enacting voluminous IRC rules, Congress gave the Treasury Department the authority to issue regulations addressing the determination of the consolidated tax liability and the filing of consolidated tax returns. Thus, the IRC allows an affiliated group to elect to file a consolidated

TYPICAL MISCONCEPTION

A corporation's tax year can be both a consolidated return year and a separate return year. For example, P1 Corporation sells all of S Corporation's stock to P2 Corporation at the end of Year 1. If P1 and S file a consolidated tax return for Year 1, Year 1 is a consolidated return year for S with respect to the P1-S consolidated group, but it is a separate return year with respect to the P2-S consolidated group.

ADDITIONAL COMMENT

Filing a consolidated income tax return does not affect the reporting of other taxes, such as payroll, sales, or property taxes. Also, some states do not allow the filing of consolidated tax returns for state income tax purposes.

tax return, but it does so on the condition that all the group's members abide by the consolidated return regulations.

Terminology. A **consolidated return year** is a corporation's tax year for which it files a consolidated tax return with the other members of its affiliated group. A **separate return year** is a corporation's tax year for which it files a separate tax return or files a consolidated tax return with another affiliated group. A corporation could have a separate return year because it was not a member of the affiliated group or because the group did not file a consolidated tax return.[7]

An affiliated group elects to file its tax return on a consolidated basis by filing a corporate tax return (Form 1120) that includes the income, expenses, etc. of all its members. The group must make the election no later than the due date for the common parent's tax return including any permitted extensions. Each corporation that is a member of the affiliated group during the initial consolidated return year must consent to the election. The Compliance and Procedural Considerations section later in this chapter provides further details about the election process.

TERMINATION OF CONSOLIDATED TAX RETURN FILING

Termination of the Affiliated Group. Once an affiliated group has elected to file a consolidated tax return, it must continue to file on a consolidated basis as long as the affiliated group exists unless the IRS permits it to file separate tax returns. An affiliated group "remains in existence for a tax year if the common parent remains as the common parent and at least one subsidiary that was affiliated with it at the end of the prior year remains affiliated with it at the beginning of the year."[8] The parent corporation need not own the *same* subsidiary throughout the entire tax year nor own any subsidiary throughout the entire tax year as long as the parent owns a subsidiary at the beginning of the current tax year that it owned at the end of the prior tax year.

EXAMPLE C:8-6 ▶ P and S1 Corporations have filed a consolidated tax return for several calendar years. At the close of business on August 31 of the current year, P purchases all of S2 Corporation's stock. At the close of business on September 30, P sells all its S1 stock. The affiliated group, P-S1-S2, must file a consolidated tax return for the current year because P remained the common parent and at least one subsidiary that was affiliated with it at the end of the prior year remained affiliated with it at the beginning of the current year (i.e., S1).

Alternatively, assume the order of the purchase and sale transactions are reversed, i.e., P sells the S1 stock on August 31 and purchases the S2 stock on September 30. In this case, the affiliated group still must file a consolidated tax return for the current year. Even though P did not have a subsidiary from September 1 through September 30, it nevertheless remained as the common parent, and S1 was affiliated with it at the end of the prior year and at the beginning of the current year. In both cases, the consolidated tax return will include S1's and S2's income only for the portion of the year S1 and S2 were in the group. In addition, P and S2 generally will be required to file a consolidated tax return for the next year because their affiliated group has not terminated. ◀

EXAMPLE C:8-7 ▶ P and S Corporations have filed a consolidated tax return for several calendar years. At the close of business on December 31 of the current year, P sells all its S stock to an unrelated individual. On January 1 of the next year, P purchases all of T Corporation's stock. P and S must file a consolidated tax return for the current year. However, the P-S affiliated group terminates at the end of the current year and a new affiliated group, P-T, forms in the next year. P and T may elect to file a consolidated tax return in the next year but are not required to do so. ◀

ADDITIONAL COMMENT

The IRS seldom grants permission to discontinue the filing of consolidated tax returns when the request relates to a change in the tax situation of the affiliated group that is not related to a tax law change.

Good Cause Request to Discontinue Consolidation. The IRS may give an affiliated group permission to discontinue filing a consolidated tax return, even though the group remains in existence, if it makes a "good cause" request. The IRS ordinarily will grant the request if changes to the IRC or Treasury Regulations having effective dates in

[7] Reg. Sec. 1.1502-1.

[8] Reg. Sec. 1.1502-75(d)(1).

that tax year create a substantial adverse effect on the consolidated tax liability for the tax year (relative to what the aggregate tax liability would be if the group members filed separate tax returns).[9]

Effects on Former Members. The termination of a consolidated group affects its former members in several ways, two of which are examined later in this chapter.

- Any gains and losses that have been deferred on intercompany transactions (e.g., profits on inventory sales between group members) may have to be recognized under the acceleration rule.
- Consolidated tax attributes (e.g., NOLs, capital losses, tax credits, and charitable contribution carryovers) may have to be allocated among the former group members.

If a corporation departs an affiliated group and had been included in the group's consolidated tax return, it cannot be included again in the group's consolidated tax return (or that of another affiliated group with the same common parent corporation) until after the 60-month period beginning with the first tax year in which the corporation ceased to be a group member.[10] The IRS can waive this five-year rule.

Consolidated Taxable Income

OBJECTIVE 3

Calculate consolidated taxable income for a consolidated group

ACCOUNTING PERIODS AND METHODS

Accounting Periods. Beginning with the first year the affiliated group files a consolidated tax return, each subsidiary corporation in the group must adopt the parent corporation's tax year, and the group must file its return using the parent's tax year. The requirement for a common tax year also applies when a new member joins the affiliated group, such as when its stock is acquired.[11] Unless the IRS grants permission otherwise, a subsidiary that leaves a consolidated group must retain its former group's tax year (or adopt the tax year of the acquiring consolidated group, if applicable).

Accounting Methods. Each group member determines the accounting methods it uses by applying the same rules as if it were filing a separate tax return unless the IRS grants it permission to change its accounting method.[12] This requirement applies when the group makes a consolidated tax return election and when a new corporation joins an existing consolidated group. Thus, one group member may use the cash method and another group member may use the accrual method with respect to the same consolidated tax return. The possibility of finding a mixture of cash and accrual basis corporations in an affiliated group is limited because of the Sec. 448 restrictions on the use of the cash method by C corporations (see Chapter C:3).

KEY POINT

Even though members of a consolidated group must use the same tax year-end, members are not required to use the same tax accounting methods. For example, different inventory methods (e.g., LIFO and FIFO) can occur within the same consolidated group.

INCOME INCLUDED IN THE CONSOLIDATED TAX RETURN

An affiliated group includes in its consolidated tax return the parent corporation's income for its entire tax year except for any part of the year it was a member of another affiliated group that filed a consolidated tax return. The group includes a subsidiary corporation's income in the consolidated tax return only for the part of the year that it was a group member. The subsidiary's income for any part of the year it was not a group member is included in its own separate tax return or the consolidated tax return of another affiliated group.[13]

EXAMPLE C:8-8 ▶ P and S Corporations were unaffiliated prior to 2017 and filed separate tax returns. P uses a fiscal year ending May 31 as its tax year, and S uses a calendar year. At the close of business on February 12, 2017, P acquires all of S's stock, and the P-S affiliated group elects to file a

[9] Reg. Sec. 1.1502-75(c).
[10] Sec. 1504(a)(3).
[11] Reg. Sec. 1.1502-76(a).
[12] Reg. Sec. 1.1502-17(a).
[13] Sec. 1501 and Reg. Sec. 1.1502-76(b)(1)(i).

consolidated tax return. S must change its tax year to a fiscal year ending May 31. The group's first consolidated tax return will include P's income for June 1, 2016, through May 31, 2017, and S's income for February 13, 2017, through May 31, 2017. S must file a separate, short-period tax return for January 1, 2017, through February 12, 2017. ◀

EXAMPLE C:8-9 ▶ P1 Corporation owns all of S Corporation's stock, and the two corporations have filed consolidated tax returns for several years on a calendar year basis. At the close of business on August 8 of the current year, P1 sells all of S's stock to P2 Corporation, which has a September 30 tax year. P2 has filed consolidated tax returns for several years with its other subsidiaries. S must change its tax year from a calendar year to a fiscal year ending September 30 when it leaves the P1 consolidated group and enters the P2 consolidated group. ◀

EXAMPLE C:8-10 ▶ P and S1 Corporations have filed consolidated tax returns for several calendar years. At the close of business on August 31 of the current year, P sells all its S1 stock to an unrelated individual. At the close of business on September 30 of the current year, P purchases all of S2 Corporation's stock from an unrelated individual. S2 had been using a fiscal year ending March 31 as its tax year. As discussed in Example C:8-6, the affiliated group, with P as the parent corporation, does not terminate. The current year's consolidated tax return includes P's income for the entire year, S1's income for January 1 through August 31 of the current year, and S2's income for October 1 through December 31 of the current year. S1 must file a short-period, separate tax return for September 1 through December 31 of the current year (unless the IRS grants it permission to change its tax year), and S2 must file a short-period, separate tax return for April 1 through September 30 of the current year. ◀

KEY POINT

Two basic rules determine what income must be included in a consolidated tax return: the common parent's income for the entire tax year and each subsidiary's income for the part of the tax year it is a member of the consolidated group.

A corporation that becomes or ceases to be a member of an affiliated group filing a consolidated tax return generally does so at the end of the day its status changes.[14] A corporation entering the consolidated group will have to file a separate tax return (or participate in the consolidated tax return of the affiliated group in which it previously was a member), and this tax return often will be a short-period return, which is a return for less than one year. However, the separate tax return does not require annualization of the corporation's taxable income.[15]

A corporation entering a consolidated group does not have to change its tax year if it already is using the same tax year as the group. In this case, the group can elect to ratably allocate the entering member's income, except for extraordinary items, between the separate return and consolidated return portions of the year. The group also can make this election for a departing group member that does not have to change its tax year.[16]

WHAT WOULD YOU DO IN THIS SITUATION?

The P-S-T affiliated group has filed consolidated tax returns for many years using the calendar year as its tax year. On October 1, P Corporation created a new subsidiary, X Corporation, with a $10,000 initial capital contribution, and X issued its stock to P. X opened a bank account and obtained a federal tax identification number. X did not conduct any business activities before year-end. Its only income was $125 in interest earned from the bank account. Due to a lack of communication or oversight, P's tax department did not include X's income in the current year's consolidated tax return.

Your CPA firm has provided tax advice to P for several years, but P's tax department has handled the federal tax return filings. Most of your work for P has been in the state and local tax area and on special federal tax assignments. You were aware of the affiliated group's future business plans for creating X. Will the oversight with respect to X disqualify the group from filing a consolidated tax return for the current year and future years? Can you avoid having to file a federal income tax return for X because of the small amount of its income? Does the failure to include X in this year's consolidated tax return prevent it from being included in future years? What advice can you give your client about needing to include X in the consolidated tax return?

14 Reg. Sec. 1.1502-76(b)(1)(ii)(A).

15 Reg. Sec. 1.1502-76(b)(2)(i).

16 Reg. Sec. 1.1502-76(b)(2)(ii). The group can make this election only if the entering corporation does not have to change its accounting method (e.g., entering the group allows the corporation to retain the cash method because the group's gross receipts do not exceed the $5 million limit under Sec. 448(c)).

EXAMPLE C:8-11 ▶ P Corporation acquires all the stock of S Corporation on February 26 of the current year (the 57th day of the year, which is not a leap year). P has been filing consolidated tax returns on a calendar year basis for several years with its other subsidiaries. S previously was unaffiliated and had been filing separate tax returns using a calendar year. S's income for the current year is $730,000 and includes no extraordinary items. The consolidated group can elect to ratably allocate the $730,000 because S does not have to change its tax year when entering the group. If it so elects, $114,000 ($730,000 × (57 days ÷ 365 days)) will be allocated to S's separate tax return for January 1 through February 26, and the other $616,000 ($730,000 × (308 days ÷ 365 days)) will be allocated to the consolidated tax return for the current year. ◀

If the consolidated group does not elect to ratably allocate an entering or departing group member's income, the group must allocate the member's income according to its accounting method, i.e., a closing of its books. This treatment also applies to extraordinary items, even if a ratable allocation is elected, and to an entering or departing member that must change its tax year. Extraordinary items include capital gains and losses, Sec. 1231 gains and losses, NOL carrybacks and carryovers, and several other items that are beyond the scope of this textbook.

CALCULATION OF CONSOLIDATED TAXABLE INCOME AND TAX

To arrive at its consolidated federal income tax liability, the group first must calculate **consolidated taxable income.** The process is more complicated than merely adding the consolidated group members' taxable incomes and losses. Instead, the group must make adjustments so that it generally is treated as if it were a single corporation. The calculation of consolidated taxable income involves the five steps presented in Table C:8-1. Later in the chapter, after discussing the various components of consolidated taxable income, we will discuss the consolidated tax calculation.

INTERCOMPANY TRANSACTIONS

OBJECTIVE 4

Apply the rules for reporting intercompany transactions

Corporations in an affiliated group filing a consolidated tax return may engage in transactions with each other. The discussion here usually will designate the two consolidated group members involved in the intercompany transaction as S and B Corporations instead of the usual P and S Corporations. This designation makes it easier to remember which group member is the seller (S) or provider of services and which group member is the buyer (B) or recipient of services.

BASIC CONCEPTS

An **intercompany transaction** is a transaction between two corporations that are in the same consolidated group immediately after the transaction.[17] Intercompany transactions include:

- S's sale, exchange, contribution, or other transfer of property to B whether or not S recognizes gain or loss
- S's performance of services for B, and B's payment or accrual of its expense for the services
- S's licensing of technology, renting of property, or lending of money to B, and B's payment or accrual of its expense for these items
- A distribution by a subsidiary to its parent corporation in connection with the parent's investment in the subsidiary's stock, such as a dividend or a redemption

In general, S and B are treated as separate entities. S and B each report on their own books any income, gains, deductions, and losses related to intercompany transactions using the same basic rules that would apply if they were unaffiliated corporations. For

[17] Reg. Sec. 1.1502-13(b)(1)(i).

▼ **TABLE C:8-1**
Consolidated Taxable Income Calculation

Step 1: Compute each group member's taxable income (or loss) based on the member's own accounting methods as if it were filing its own separate tax return.

Step 2: Adjust each group member's taxable income as follows:
1. Income, gains, and losses on intercompany transactions occurring in the current year may be deferred until a later year.
2. Income, gains, and losses on intercompany transactions occurring in prior years may be taken into account in the current year.
3. Dividends received by one group member from another group member are excluded from the recipient's gross income.

Step 3: Remove certain items from each member's taxable income because they must be computed on a consolidated basis (see Step 5):
1. Section 1231 gains and losses
2. Capital gains and losses
3. Charitable contributions deduction
4. Dividends-received deduction
5. Net operating loss (NOL) deduction
6. U.S. production activities deduction

The result of making the adjustments to a member's taxable income in Steps 2 and 3 is the member's **separate taxable income (loss)**.

Step 4: Combine the members' separate taxable incomes and losses. This amount is called the group's **combined taxable income**.

Step 5: Adjust the group's combined taxable income for the following items computed on a consolidated basis (see Step 3):
1. Determine the consolidated net Sec. 1231 gain or loss. Add any net Sec. 1231 gain treated as ordinary income due to the five-year lookback rule, or deduct any net Sec. 1231 loss as an ordinary loss.
2. Determine the consolidated net capital gain or loss (taking into account any capital loss carrybacks and carryovers and any net Sec. 1231 gain not treated as ordinary income). Add the consolidated net capital gain to combined taxable income.
3. Determine and deduct the consolidated charitable contribution deduction (taking into account any charitable contribution carryovers).
4. Determine and deduct the consolidated dividends-received deduction.
5. Determine and deduct the consolidated NOL deduction (taking into account any allowable NOL carryovers and carrybacks).
6. Determine and deduct the consolidated U.S. production activities deduction.

Consolidated taxable income (or consolidated NOL)[18]

ADDITIONAL COMMENT

These adjustments are listed in the same computational order as shown on page C:3-19, but they appear in a different order on Form 1120.

example, if B purchases some property from S for cash, B's adjusted basis in the property would be B's cost to acquire it, and B's holding period for it would begin the day after B purchases the property.

To determine consolidated taxable income, S and B give special treatment to income, gains, deductions, and losses related to intercompany transactions. Specifically, the consolidated return regulations usually require that S's income, gains, deductions, or losses be deferred, and therefore excluded, in determining consolidated taxable income until a subsequent event occurs for B. These subsequent events include the following situations:

- B sells property it acquired in an intercompany transaction to a party outside the consolidated group.
- S or B leaves the consolidated group while B still owns property it acquired from S in an intercompany transaction.
- B claims a depreciation, depletion, or amortization deduction on property it acquired in an intercompany transaction.

[18] Reg. Sec. 1.1502-11.

- The corporations in an affiliated group discontinue filing a consolidated tax return and begin filing separate tax returns.

The intercompany transaction rules, in effect, have the members calculate consolidated taxable income as though S and B were a single entity. That is, if S and B were two divisions of a single corporation, any transactions between them would not affect the single corporation's taxable income. Likewise, consolidated taxable income should reflect only the consolidated group's income, gains, deductions, and losses from transactions with parties outside the group. The intercompany transaction rules adjust the consolidated group members' income, gains, deductions, and losses related to intercompany transactions, which the members reported on their separate books. Thus, the intercompany adjustments transform separate entity treatment into single entity treatment for calculating consolidated taxable income. This coexistence of separate entity treatment and single entity treatment is a challenging aspect of consolidated tax returns.

EXAMPLE C:8-12 ▶ S and B Corporations are members of a consolidated group. S owns marketable securities having a $120,000 basis. S sells the securities to B in the current year for $200,000 cash. S's $80,000 ($200,000 − $120,000) gain is determined and reported on its books on a separate entity basis in the current year. However, the $80,000 gain is not included in the current year's consolidated taxable income. On a single entity basis, the consolidated group did not sell the securities to an outside party, so it makes an adjustment to remove the gain from consolidated taxable income in the current year. B's basis in the securities is its $200,000 cost, and B's holding period begins the day after it purchases the securities from S. The group will take the $80,000 gain into account for consolidated taxable income at a later time, in accordance with the matching and acceleration rules discussed below. ◀

MATCHING AND ACCELERATION RULES

Treasury Regulations have two principal rules regarding intercompany transactions: the matching rule and the acceleration rule. Unlike many tax rules, the matching and acceleration rules are not detailed and mechanical. Instead, they are broad and conceptual, thereby allowing enough flexibility to apply to the wide variety of intercompany transactions that arise in practice.[19] The purpose of the intercompany transaction rules is to clearly reflect a consolidated group's taxable income by preventing intercompany transactions from creating, accelerating, avoiding, or deferring consolidated taxable income.[20] The following three terms will be used in the discussion of the intercompany transaction rules:[21]

- **Intercompany item:** S's income, gain, deduction, and loss from an intercompany transaction
- **Corresponding item:** B's income, gain, deduction, and loss from an intercompany transaction or from property acquired in an intercompany transaction
- **Recomputed corresponding item:** The corresponding item B would take into account if S and B were divisions of a single corporation and the transaction occurred between those divisions

EXAMPLE C:8-13 ▶ S and B Corporations are members of a consolidated group. S owns property having a $70 basis. S sells this property to B for $100. A few years later, B sells the property to a third party for $110. The sale from S to B is an intercompany transaction. The intercompany item is S's $30 ($100 − $70) gain on its sale of the property to B. The corresponding item is B's $10 ($110 − $100) gain on its sale of the property to the third party. The recomputed corresponding item is the $40 ($110 − $70) gain that B would realize on the sale to the third party had S and B been divisions of a single corporation. ◀

ADDITIONAL COMMENT

The intercompany transaction rules are an excellent example of the additional recordkeeping necessary to file consolidated tax returns.

Matching Rule. To determine consolidated taxable income, the matching rule requires a consolidated group to take into account an intercompany item in a manner that produces the same result as if the transaction were between two divisions of a single

[19] Preamble to T.D. 8597.
[20] Reg. Sec. 1.1502-13(a)(1).
[21] Reg. Secs. 1.1502-13(b)(2), (3), and (4).

corporation.[22] That is, the amount of S's intercompany item taken into account for consolidated taxable income is such that, when combined (i.e., matched) with B's corresponding item, the result is the same as if the consolidated group were a single corporation. The amount of S's intercompany item taken into account for consolidated taxable income can be calculated as follows:

Amount of recomputed corresponding item
Minus: Amount of B's corresponding item

Amount of S's intercompany item taken into account for consolidated taxable income

Working backwards from the desired outcome for consolidated taxable income, the starting point of the calculation is the amount of the recomputed corresponding item. The portion of the desired outcome comprised of B's corresponding item is subtracted out, leaving the amount of S's intercompany item that needs to be taken into account.[23]

EXAMPLE C:8-14 ► S and B Corporations are members of a consolidated group. S owns property having a $150 basis. S sells this property to B for $200 in Year 1. In Year 3, B sells the property to an unrelated corporation, X, for $215.

S's intercompany item is the $50 ($200 − $150) gain on its sale of the property to B. B's corresponding item is the $15 ($215 − $200) gain in Year 3 on its sale of the property to X. The recomputed corresponding item is the $65 ($215 − $150) gain in Year 3 that B would realize on the sale to X had S and B been divisions of a single corporation.

Year 1: If S and B were two divisions of a single corporation, the single corporation would realize no gain or loss, so the recomputed corresponding item for Year 1 is zero. B has no gain or loss in Year 1, so its corresponding item is zero. Thus, none of S's gain is taken into account for consolidated taxable income.

Year 3: If S and B were two divisions of a single corporation, it would realize a $65 gain. Subtracting B's $15 corresponding item from this $65 recomputed corresponding item yields the $50 amount of S's intercompany item taken into account for Year 3. Thus, recognition of S's $50 gain in Year 1 is deferred for consolidated taxable income until Year 3. In Year 3, S's $50 gain is matched with B's $15 gain to produce the $65 gain that accrued while the group held the property. ◄

EXAMPLE C:8-15 ► Assume the same facts as in Example C:8-14 except B sells the property to X for $180. The intercompany item again is S's $50 gain. However, B's corresponding item now is a $20 ($180 − $200) loss, and the recomputed corresponding item is a $30 ($180 − $150) gain.

Year 1: The property has not yet been sold outside the group, and B has not yet sold the property, so the recomputed corresponding item and B's corresponding item are both zero. None of S's gain is taken into account for consolidated taxable income.

Year 3: The property now has been sold to a person outside the consolidated group. Subtracting B's corresponding item ($20 loss) from the recomputed corresponding item ($30 gain) results in all of S's $50 intercompany item being taken into account for consolidated taxable income ($30 − (− $20) = $50). Note that a negative number is being subtracted because B's corresponding item is a loss. In summary, S's $50 gain is matched with B's $20 loss to produce the net $30 gain that accrued while the group held the property. ◄

TAX STRATEGY TIP

A member of a consolidated group should consider selling property with a built-in loss to a party outside the group rather than to another group member. For example, S Corporation owns Sec. 1231 property with a $15,000 adjusted basis and a $9,000 FMV. If S sells the property to another group member, the $6,000 loss will not be deducted for consolidated taxable income until a later time. If S sells the property to an unrelated third party, the $6,000 loss will be deductible immediately for consolidated taxable income. Thus, the income tax savings from the $6,000 loss is accelerated.

Acceleration Rule. In some situations, it may not be possible to match S's intercompany item with B's corresponding item to produce the same outcome as if S and B were two divisions of a single corporation. For example, S may sell property to B while they are members of the same consolidated group, but B then departs the group before it has sold the property. In this situation, B's corresponding item will occur when B is outside the consolidated group, so it cannot be matched with S's intercompany item. The acceleration rule requires that the consolidated group take into account S's intercompany item immediately before the time it first becomes impossible to apply the matching rule.[24]

[22] Reg. Sec. 1.1502-13(c).

[23] In addition to the timing of income, gain, deduction, or loss, the matching rule requires that various other attributes be redetermined, such as the character and source of such amounts.

[24] Rec. Sec. 1.1502-13(d).

EXAMPLE C:8-16 ▶ Assume the same facts as in Examples C:8-14 and C:8-15 except P, the common parent of S and B, sells all of its B stock to an unrelated corporation, Y, on June 4 of Year 2, which is before B sells the property to X. On that date, B departs the consolidated group, so it becomes impossible to match B's subsequent corresponding item in Year 3 with S's intercompany item. This situation triggers the acceleration rule, and the portion of S's intercompany item that has not yet been taken into account, which is all $50, is taken into account in Year 2, immediately before the stock sale on June 4. ◀

APPLICATIONS OF MATCHING AND ACCELERATION RULES

The matching and acceleration rules are two principles used to implement the single entity approach to reporting intercompany transactions. The discussion below provides several examples to illustrate the two rules. Unless otherwise stated, S Corporation and B Corporation are in the same affiliated group, with P Corporation as their common parent. Also, the group has filed consolidated tax returns for several years on a calendar year basis.

EXAMPLE C:8-17 ▶ S purchased 1,000 shares of publicly traded stock as an investment several years ago for $175,000. In the current year (Year 1), S sells all the stock to B for $200,000. B sells 400 shares of the stock (40%) to a third party for $78,000 in Year 3, and B sells the other 600 shares (60%) to another third party for $134,000 in Year 5. S's intercompany item is its $25,000 ($200,000 − $175,000) gain on the sale to B. The timing of and extent to which S's intercompany item is taken into account for consolidated taxable income is as follows:

Year 1: No corresponding item or recomputed corresponding item occurs this year because B has not yet sold the stock. Therefore, none of S's $25,000 gain is taken into account.

Year 3: B's corresponding item is its $2,000 ($78,000 − (40% × $200,000)) loss on the sale of 400 shares to the third party. From the perspective of a single entity, the consolidated group acquired the 400 shares for $70,000 (40% × $175,000) and sold them for $78,000, producing an $8,000 gain (the recomputed corresponding item). To achieve this result in consolidated taxable income, $10,000 of S's intercompany item is taken into account. The $10,000 gain, when matched with B's $2,000 loss, results in the $8,000 gain.

Year 5: B's corresponding item is its $14,000 ($134,000 − (60% × $200,000)) gain on the sale of the 600 shares. The recomputed corresponding item, from a single-entity perspective, is a $29,000 gain ($134,000 − (60% × $175,000)). The remaining $15,000 ($25,000 − $10,000) of S's gain is taken into account. The matching of this $15,000 with B's $14,000 corresponding item produces a $29,000 gain in consolidated taxable income, which is the outcome that would occur if S and B were two divisions of a single corporation. ◀

The timing and extent to which S's $25,000 gain in Example C:8-17 is taken into account for consolidated taxable income can be determined by applying the formula for the matching rule.

ADDITIONAL COMMENT

Note that, for Year 3, a negative $2,000 is subtracted, which is equivalent to adding $2,000. Subsequent examples of this type use similar notation.

	Year 1	*Year 3*	*Year 5*
Recomputed corresponding item	$-0-	$ 8,000	$29,000
Minus: B's corresponding item	-0-	(−2,000)	(14,000)
S's intercompany item taken into account	$-0-	$10,000	$15,000

The consolidated group can report the three sales made by S and B in Example C:8-17 by using a worksheet format such as that illustrated in the consolidated tax return example in Appendix B (see partial worksheet below). Each transaction initially is reported in the selling corporation's separate tax return column. The adjustments for the deferred gain on S's sale of the stock to B appear as negative and positive entries in the adjustments and eliminations column of the worksheet. The Year 1 negative adjustment removes the $25,000 gain realized on the intercompany transaction from Year 1 consolidated taxable income. The Year 3 and Year 5 positive adjustments restore the deferred gain when B sells the stock outside the consolidated group.

Transaction	Consolidated Taxable Income	Adjustments & Eliminations	S Corporation's Separate Reporting	B Corporation's Separate Reporting
S's sale to B in Year 1	$ -0-	$(25,000)	$25,000	
B's sale to third party in Year 3	8,000	10,000		$(2,000)
B's sale to third party in Year 5	29,000	15,000		14,000
Total	$37,000	$ -0-	$25,000	$12,000

EXAMPLE C:8-18 ▶ Assume the same facts as in Example C:8-17 except S's and B's common parent corporation, P, sells all its B stock to a third party in Year 4. B's departure from the consolidated group triggers the acceleration rule in Year 4 because it is not possible to match B's subsequent corresponding item with the $15,000 portion of S's intercompany item that has not yet been taken into account. Thus, the $15,000 is included in Year 4 consolidated taxable income rather than Year 5 consolidated taxable income. The results would be the same if the common parent sold all of S's stock in Year 4 rather than all of B's stock. B still has a $14,000 gain in Year 5, but B includes the gain in its separate tax return (or the consolidated tax return of the affiliated group to which B belongs at that time). ◀

Installment Sale of Property from Buyer to Third Party. Under the installment method, if some or all of the proceeds from the sale of property are to be received after the taxable year of sale, the seller spreads recognition of any gain on the sale over the years it collects the proceeds (see Chapter I:11). The installment method does not apply if the seller realizes a loss. Also, in a gain situation, the seller can elect to not use the installment method. Applying the matching rule to an installment sale requires an understanding of how the installment method operates on both a separate and single entity basis.

EXAMPLE C:8-19 ▶ S owns land having a $64,000 basis. In Year 1, S sells the land to B for $90,000. In Year 3, B sells the land to a third party for $100,000. The third party is to pay B $60,000 of the $100,000 in Year 4 and the remaining $40,000 in Year 5. B charges the third party an interest rate acceptable to the IRS on the unpaid balance.

Because S's sale of the land to B is an intercompany transaction, S's $26,000 ($90,000 − $64,000) gain on the sale will not be taken into account until a later time. When B sells the property in Year 3, it realizes a $10,000 ($100,000 − $90,000) gain. Under the installment method, B's gross profit percentage on the sale is 10% ($10,000 ÷ $100,000), so B has a $6,000 (10% × $60,000) corresponding item in Year 4 and a $4,000 (10% × $40,000) corresponding item in Year 5. From the perspective of a single entity, the consolidated group acquired the land for $64,000 and sold it for $100,000, which produces a $36,000 gain. The group's gross profit percentage is 36% ($36,000 ÷ $100,000), so the recomputed corresponding items are $21,600 (36% × $60,000) in Year 4 and $14,400 (36% × $40,000) in Year 5.

S's $26,000 gain on the intercompany transaction is taken into account for consolidated taxable income such that, when matched with B's corresponding items, they combine to be the same as the recomputed corresponding items as follows:

	Year 1	Year 3	Year 4	Year 5
Recomputed corresponding item	$-0-	$-0-	$21,600	$14,400
Minus: B's corresponding item	-0-	-0-	(6,000)	(4,000)
S's intercompany item taken into account	$-0-	$-0-	$15,600	$10,400 ◀

In Example C:8-19, all of S's $26,000 gain is removed in the calculation of Year 1 consolidated taxable income, $15,600 of it is restored in the calculation of Year 4 consolidated taxable income, and the other $10,400 of it is restored in Year 5.[25]

[25] Reg. Sec. 1.1502-13(c)(7) Example 5.

Transaction	*Consolidated Taxable Income*	*Adjustments & Eliminations*	*S Corporation's Separate Reporting*	*B Corporation's Separate Reporting*
S's sale to B in Year 1	$ –0–	$(26,000)	$26,000	
B's sale to third party in Year 3	–0–			
B's collection of first installment in Year 4	21,600	15,600		$ 6,000
B's collection of second installment in Year 5	14,400	10,400		4,000
Total	$36,000	$ –0–	$26,000	$10,000

EXAMPLE C:8-20 ▶ Assume the same facts as in Example C:8-19 except B sells the land to a third party for $80,000 in Year 3. The third party is to pay B $48,000 of the $80,000 in Year 4 and the remaining $32,000 in Year 5. B's corresponding item is now its $10,000 ($80,000 − $90,000) loss in Year 3. The installment method does not apply to losses, so B reports the entire loss in the year of sale. From a single entity perspective, the consolidated group realizes a $16,000 ($80,000 − $64,000) gain, which produces a 20% ($16,000 ÷ $80,000) gross profit percentage. The group's recomputed corresponding items are $9,600 (20% × $48,000) in Year 4 and $6,400 (20% × $32,000) in Year 5. S's $26,000 gain on the intercompany transaction taken into account for consolidated taxable income is determined as follows:

	Year 1	*Year 3*	*Year 4*	*Year 5*
Recomputed corresponding item	$–0–	$ –0–	$9,600	$6,400
Minus: B's corresponding item	–0–	(–10,000)	–0–	–0–
S's intercompany item taken into account	$–0–	$10,000	$9,600	$6,400 ◀

Example C:8-20 illustrates the process underlying the matching rule. It requires an understanding of how the transactions affect each of the group members on a separate entity basis and how the transactions would affect the corporations in the consolidated group if they were a single entity. Applying the same worksheet format used above, Example C:8-20 is presented as:

Transaction	*Consolidated Taxable Income*	*Adjustments & Eliminations*	*S Corporation's Separate Reporting*	*B Corporation's Separate Reporting*
S's sale to B in Year 1	$ –0–	$(26,000)	$26,000	
B's sale to third party in Year 3	–0–	10,000		$(10,000)
B's collection of first installment in Year 4	9,600	9,600		
B's collection of second installment in Year 5	6,400	6,400		
Total	$16,000	$ –0–	$26,000	$(10,000)

BOOK-TO-TAX ACCOUNTING COMPARISON
The intercompany rental income and expense in Example C:8-21 are eliminated in preparing the consolidated financial statements.

Performance of Services. Some intercompany transactions involve one consolidated group member performing services for another group member. For example, one group member may rent property or lend money to another group member. The matching rule generally applies in a manner similar to that for intercompany property transactions, matching S's intercompany item to B's corresponding item so their net effect results in the recomputed corresponding item.

EXAMPLE C:8-21 ▶ S rents land to B for $25,000 per year. S and B both use the accrual method of accounting. S's rental income is its intercompany item, and B's rental expense is its corresponding item. The recomputed corresponding item is zero because, from the perspective of a single corporation with divisions S and B, the single entity would have no rental income or expense. The group will take into account $25,000 ($0 – (–$25,000)) of S's annual rental income as B reports the $25,000 annual rental expense. Note that B's corresponding item is negative because it is an expense. S's rental income and B's rental expense are recognized simultaneously for consolidated taxable income and thus offset each other. ◀

EXAMPLE C:8-22 ▶ On March 1 of Year 1, S lends B $100,000 for one year. B pays the $100,000 debt, plus 12% annual interest, to S on March 1 of Year 2. S and B each use the accrual method of accounting. In determining their separate taxable incomes, S reports interest income of $10,000 ($100,000 × 12% × 10/12) in Year 1 and $2,000 ($100,000 × 12% × 2/12) in Year 2, and B reports interest expense of $10,000 in Year 1 and $2,000 in Year 2. The recomputed corresponding item is zero in Year 1 and in Year 2. Application of the matching rule results in S's intercompany items being reported in consolidated taxable income at the same time S reports them in its separate taxable income.

	Year 1	*Year 2*
Recomputed corresponding item	$ –0–	$ –0–
Minus: B's corresponding item	(–10,000)	(–2,000)
S's intercompany item taken into account	$ 10,000	$ 2,000

◀

Applying the worksheet format used for the earlier intercompany transactions, S and B report the interest income and expense as follows:

Year	*Consolidated Taxable Income*	*Adjustments & Eliminations*	*S Corporation's Separate Reporting*	*B Corporation's Separate Reporting*
Year 1	$–0–		$10,000	$(10,000)
Year 2	–0–		2,000	(2,000)
Total	$–0–		$12,000	$(12,000)

If S and B use different accounting methods, they might not report their respective sides of the intercompany transaction at the same time in determining their separate taxable incomes. The principle of the matching rule still applies, with S's intercompany item being matched with B's corresponding item.

EXAMPLE C:8-23 ▶ Assume the same facts as in Example C:8-22 except B uses the cash method of accounting. For separate taxable income, S reports interest income of $10,000 in Year 1 and $2,000 in Year 2, and B reports interest expense of $0 in Year 1 and $12,000 in Year 2. For consolidated taxable income, all $12,000 of S's interest income is reported in Year 2 under the matching rule.

	Year 1	*Year 2*
Recomputed corresponding item	$–0–	$ –0–
Minus: B's corresponding item	–0–	(–12,000)
S's intercompany item taken into account	$–0–	$ 12,000

◀

ADDITIONAL COMMENT

Corporations filing a consolidated tax return are related parties under Sec. 267 because they also are members of the same controlled group. One consequence of their related status is that B cannot deduct its expense from an intercompany transaction with S before S reports its income from the transaction. This rule also can apply to transactions with corporations that are in the same controlled group but not the same consolidated group, such as brother-sister corporations.

Applying the worksheet format used previously, S and B report the interest income and expense as follows:

Year	Consolidated Taxable Income	Adjustments & Eliminations	S Corporation's Separate Reporting	B Corporation's Separate Reporting
Year 1	$–0–	$(10,000)	$10,000	$ –0–
Year 2	–0–	10,000	2,000	(12,000)
Total	$–0–	$ –0–	$12,000	$(12,000)

In some circumstances, B might capitalize its expenditure for the services S provides. B's corresponding item still would be its income, gain, deduction, and loss from an intercompany transaction or from property in an intercompany transaction. However, the corresponding item might occur at a time later than S's intercompany item, requiring that some or all of S's intercompany item be deferred under the matching rule.

EXAMPLE C:8-24 ▶ S operates a drilling business, and B operates a farming business. S and B both use the accrual method of accounting. In Year 1, S drills a water well and charges B $9,000 for the service. S incurs $8,000 of expenses in drilling the well, realizing a $1,000 profit. B capitalizes the $9,000 cost of its well and amortizes it over the four-year period Years 2 through 5.

From a single entity perspective, the group's cost of the well is $8,000, so its recomputed corresponding item is $2,000 ($8,000 ÷ 4 years) for each of Years 2 through 5. B's annual corresponding item is its $2,250 ($9,000 ÷ 4 years) amortization deduction. S's $1,000 intercompany item is reported for consolidated taxable income as follows:

	Year 1	Year 2	Year 3	Year 4	Year 5
Recomputed corresponding item	$–0–	$(2,000)	$(2,000)	$(2,000)	$(2,000)
Minus: B's corresponding item	–0–	(–2,250)	(–2,250)	(–2,250)	(–2,250)
S's intercompany item taken into account	$–0–	$ 250	$ 250	$ 250	$ 250

Transaction	Consolidated Taxable Income	Adjustments & Eliminations	S Corporation's Separate Reporting	B Corporation's Separate Reporting
Drilling of well in Year 1	$ –0–	$(1,000)	$1,000	
Amortization deductions:				
Year 2	(2,000)	250		$(2,250)
Year 3	(2,000)	250		(2,250)
Year 4	(2,000)	250		(2,250)
Year 5	(2,000)	250		(2,250)
Total	$(8,000)	$ –0–	$1,000	$(9,000)

◀

Intercompany Sale of Inventory. Many consolidated groups have sales of inventory within the group. For example, one group member (S) may manufacture goods and sell them to another group member (B). B subsequently resells the goods to third-party customers. The matching rule applies in this situation and allows the consolidated group to defer taxation of profit from the intercompany transaction until B sells the inventory to a third party.[26]

EXAMPLE C:8-25 ▶ P, S, and B Corporations comprise a consolidated group with P being the common parent of subsidiaries S and B. S begins selling inventory items to B in Year 1, and both subsidiaries use the first-in, first-out (FIFO) inventory method. Information and treatment regarding S's inventory sales to B during Years 1 and 2 follow:

---

[26] Reg. Sec. 1.1502-13(e)(1) provides simplifying rules for intercompany inventory sales when S or B uses a dollar-value LIFO method to account for intercompany transactions.

Year 1: S sells inventory to B for $400,000. The cost of this inventory to S was $300,000. Thus, S realizes a profit of $100,000 ($400,000 − $300,000) on the sale, which is S's intercompany item. During the year, B sells 88% of this inventory to third parties for $414,000. B's cost for this inventory is $352,000 ($400,000 × 0.88). Thus, B realizes a profit of $62,000 ($414,000 − $352,000) on the sale to third parties, which is B's corresponding item. S's cost for this same inventory had been $264,000 ($300,000 × 0.88). Thus, S realized a profit of $88,000 ($352,000 − $264,000) when it sold this portion of the inventory to B, which is S's intercompany item taken into account. From the perspective of a single entity, the consolidated group realizes a profit of $150,000 ($414,000 − $264,000) on the sale to third parties, which is the recomputed corresponding item. At year-end, B's inventory includes the remaining 12% of inventory it purchased from S in Year 1. B's cost in this remaining inventory is $48,000 ($400,000 × 0.12), and S's cost for this same inventory was $36,000 ($300,000 × 0.12). Thus, the remaining inventory contains a deferred profit of $12,000 ($48,000 − $36,000). Applying the matching rule, these transactions are summarized as follows:

Recomputed corresponding item	$150,000
Minus: B's corresponding item	(62,000)
S's intercompany item taken into account	$88,000

Year 2: B sells to third parties the remaining inventory it purchased from S in Year 1. The selling price is $55,000 and is deemed sold first in Year 2 under FIFO. Thus, B realizes a profit of $7,000 ($55,000 − $48,000) on this sale. From the perspective of a single entity, the consolidated group realizes a profit of $19,000 ($55,000 − $36,000) on this sale to third parties.

Also in Year 2, S sells additional inventory to B for $550,000. The cost of this inventory to S was $420,000. Thus, S realizes a profit of $130,000 ($550,000 − $420,000) on the sale. During the year, B sells 80% of this inventory to third parties for $515,000. B's cost for this inventory is $440,000 ($550,000 × 0.80). Thus, B realizes a profit of $75,000 ($515,000 − $440,000) on the sale to third parties. S's cost for this same inventory had been $336,000 ($420,000 × 0.80). Thus, S realized a profit of $104,000 ($440,000 − $336,000) when it sold this portion of the inventory to B. From the perspective of a single entity, the consolidated group realizes a profit of $179,000 ($515,000 − $336,000) on this sale to third parties. At year-end, B's inventory includes the remaining 20% of inventory it purchased from S in Year 2. B's cost in this remaining inventory is $110,000 ($550,000 × 0.20), and S's cost for this same inventory was $84,000 ($420,000 × 0.20). Thus, the remaining inventory contains a deferred profit of $26,000 ($110,000 − $84,000). Applying the matching rule, these transactions are summarized as follows:

Recomputed corresponding item ($19,000 + $179,000)	$198,000
Minus: B's corresponding item ($7,000 + $75,000)	(82,000)
S's intercompany item taken into account ($12,000 + $104,000)	$116,000

Applying the worksheet format for the intercompany transactions in Years 1 and 2, S and B report their inventory profits as follows:

Year	*Consolidated Taxable Income*	*Adjustments & Eliminations*	*S Corporation's Separate Reporting*	*B Corporation's Separate Reporting*
Year 1	$150,000	$(12,000)	$100,000	$ 62,000
Year 2	198,000	(14,000)*	130,000	82,000
Total	$348,000	$(26,000)	$230,000	$144,000

* Positive $12,000 adjustment for inventory S sold to B in Year 1 that B sells to third parties in Year 2, minus $26,000 adjustment for inventory S sells to B in Year 2 that B has not sold to third parties by the end of Year 2. ◀

EXAMPLE C:8-26 ▶ Assume the same facts as in Example C:8-25 except P sells all of B's stock on December 31 of Year 2. Because B no longer is a member of the consolidated group after that date, the remaining group cannot match S's intercompany items with B's corresponding items. Thus, the acceleration rule is triggered, and the $26,000 ($110,000 − $84,000) of S's intercompany inventory profits that otherwise would be included in Year 3 consolidated taxable income is now included in Year 2 consolidated taxable income. ◀

ADDITIONAL COMMENT

The matching and acceleration rules also apply to intercompany sales of depreciable property and involve complex depreciation adjustments that are beyond the scope of this textbook.

RELEVANCE OF MATCHING AND ACCELERATION RULES

The matching and acceleration rules are broad and conceptual, thereby allowing enough flexibility to apply to a wide variety of intercompany transactions that arise in practice. Applying the rules can seem tedious and irrelevant, possibly causing one to wonder why it is necessary to determine the intercompany items and corresponding items if the consolidated group's taxable income ultimately reflects the recomputed corresponding items. In response, we can cite the following reasons why the rules are important (some of which receive further discussion later in this chapter). The rules affect:

- ▶ The time for recognizing intercompany transactions, i.e., how much gain or loss to recognize currently or in the future.
- ▶ The amount by which a parent corporation adjusts the basis of stock it owns in its subsidiary corporations.
- ▶ The amount of consolidated net operating losses attributed to a particular consolidated group member.
- ▶ The amount of a member's separate return net operating losses that the group may use.
- ▶ The amount of each member's earning and profits (E&P).

Topic Review C:8-1 summarizes the intercompany transaction rules.

ITEMS COMPUTED ON A CONSOLIDATED BASIS

OBJECTIVE 5

Compute on a consolidated basis deductions and credits subject to limitations

An affiliated group filing a consolidated tax return generally is treated as if it were a single corporation. To accomplish this treatment, the group calculates on a consolidated basis its deductions and credits that are subject to limitations. The computation of these items for a consolidated tax return is similar to their computation for an unaffiliated corporation. The group also must calculate its regular tax and its alternative minimum tax on a consolidated basis.

TOPIC REVIEW C:8-1

Reporting Intercompany Transactions

INTERCOMPANY TRANSACTIONS

1. **Intercompany transaction:** A transaction between two corporations that are in the same consolidated group immediately after the transaction.
2. **Three concepts of reporting intercompany transactions:**
   a. **Intercompany item:** The selling corporation's income, gain, deduction, and loss from an intercompany transaction.
   b. **Corresponding item:** The buying corporation's income, gain, deduction, and loss from an intercompany transaction or from property acquired in an intercompany transaction.
   c. **Recomputed corresponding item:** The corresponding item the buying corporation would have if it and the selling corporation were two divisions of a single corporation and the transaction occurred between those divisions.
3. **Separate entity concept:** The selling and buying corporations involved in the intercompany transaction generally are treated as separate entities in determining the amount of income, gain, deduction, and loss that each one incurs.
4. **Matching rule:** The selling corporation's intercompany item is taken into account for consolidated taxable income so that, when it is combined with the buying corporation's corresponding item, the result is the same as if the consolidated group were a single corporation (i.e., the recomputed corresponding item).
5. **Acceleration rule:** If it is not possible to apply the matching rule to match the selling corporation's intercompany item with the buying corporation's corresponding item, the consolidated group takes into account the selling corporation's intercompany item immediately before the time it first becomes impossible to apply the matching rule.
6. **Examples of events that can trigger recognition of an intercompany item:**
   a. The buying corporation sells to a third party property acquired in an intercompany transaction (matching rule).
   b. The selling corporation or buying corporation leaves the consolidated group (acceleration rule).
   c. The buying corporation claims depreciation, amortization, or depletion deductions for property acquired in an intercompany transaction (matching rule).
   d. The corporations in the affiliated group discontinue filing a consolidated tax return and begin filing separate tax returns (acceleration rule).

KEY POINT

The consolidated charitable contribution deduction could be equal to, greater than, or less than the total of the charitable contribution deductions if the group filed separate tax returns. The outcome depends on each individual situation.

CHARITABLE CONTRIBUTION DEDUCTION

Chapter C:3 discusses the charitable contribution deduction for an unaffiliated C corporation. Recall that the deduction is limited to 10% of adjusted taxable income. Adjusted taxable income is the corporation's taxable income computed without regard to its charitable contribution deduction, NOL carryback, capital loss carryback, dividends-received deduction, and U.S. production activities deduction. The corporation can carry forward to the five succeeding tax years its charitable contributions that exceed the 10% limitation. Any unused contributions remaining at the end of the five-year carryover period expire.

The consolidated charitable contribution deduction is calculated by first aggregating the consolidated group members' charitable contributions. The deductibility of the aggregate charitable contributions is limited to 10% of consolidated adjusted taxable income, and any aggregate contributions exceeding the 10% limitation carry forward for five years.[27] Consolidated adjusted taxable income is determined similarly to an unaffiliated corporation's adjusted taxable income except the group uses consolidated amounts.[28]

EXAMPLE C:8-27 ▶ P, S1, and S2 Corporations comprise a consolidated group. The group members have the following charitable contributions and adjusted taxable incomes for the current year:

Group Member	*Charitable Contributions*	*Adjusted Taxable Income*
P	$12,500	$150,000
S1	5,000	(40,000)
S2	2,000	10,000
Total	$19,500	$120,000

SELF-STUDY QUESTION

In Example C:8-27, what would be each corporation's current year charitable contribution deduction if the group filed separate tax returns?

ANSWER

$12,500 for P, $0 for S1, and $1,000 for S2. The total of these three deductions is $1,500 more than the $12,000 consolidated charitable contribution deduction. However, the total of the charitable contribution carryovers is $1,500 less than the consolidated charitable contribution carryover.

The consolidated group's charitable contribution deduction is limited to $12,000 (10% × $120,000). Because its aggregate charitable contributions exceed this limitation, it can deduct only $12,000 in the current year. The $7,500 ($19,500 − $12,000) excess charitable contribution carries over to the next five tax years in successive order until used. If not used, they expire at the end of the five-year carryover period. ◀

NET SEC. 1231 GAIN OR LOSS

An unaffiliated corporation determines its net Sec. 1231 gain or loss by netting its recognized gains and losses from the sale or exchange of Sec. 1231 property (see Chapter I:13). The corporation treats any net Sec. 1231 loss as an ordinary loss. A net Sec. 1231 gain generally is treated as a long-term capital gain, although some or all of it may be converted to ordinary income if the corporation has any unrecaptured net Sec. 1231 losses from the prior five years (the lookback rule). A consolidated group determines its net Sec. 1231 gain or loss by netting the members' Sec. 1231 gains and losses on a consolidated basis rather than for each member separately.[29]

ADDITIONAL COMMENT

An affiliated group's ordinary gain or loss and capital gain or loss often will be different when it nets its various gains and losses on a consolidated basis rather than on a separate basis.

CAPITAL GAINS AND LOSSES

Chapter C:3 discusses the treatment of capital gains and losses for an unaffiliated corporation. The corporation's capital gain net income or net capital loss is determined by netting its capital gains, capital losses, and net Sec. 1231 gains (to the extent they are not recaptured as ordinary income under the five-year lookback rule). Unlike with individuals, a corporation's net capital gain receives no preferential tax treatment. Also, a corporation cannot deduct a net capital loss. Instead, it must carry back the net capital loss to the three previous tax years and five following tax years, using the net capital loss in the earliest year(s) possible.

In a similar manner, the consolidated group determines its capital gain net income or net capital loss by netting the group members' capital gains and capital losses, as well as

---

[27] If a member leaves the consolidated group before the group fully uses its charitable contribution carryovers, the departing member takes with it its allocable share of the unused carryover. The allocation is based on the relative amount of the member's charitable contributions (when compared to the group's total charitable contributions) for the consolidated return year in which they were made. The allocation is similar to that for unused NOL carryovers discussed later in the chapter.

[28] Reg. Sec. 1.1502-24.

[29] Reg. Sec. 1.1502-23.

any consolidated net Sec. 1231 gain not recaptured under the lookback rule. If the group has a net capital loss for a tax year, it cannot deduct it in that year but must carry it back to the three preceding and forward to the five succeeding tax years. The consolidated net capital loss can offset any consolidated net capital gain in those eight carryback and carryover years.[30]

EXAMPLE C:8-28 ▶ P and S Corporations comprise a consolidated group. The group has no capital loss carryovers, and it has recognized no net Sec. 1231 losses in the previous five years. During the current year, the group reports $200,000 of ordinary income before taking into account the following gains and losses:

Group Member	Capital Gains and Losses: Short-Term Gains	Short-Term Losses	Long-Term Gains	Long-Term Losses	Net Sec. 1231 Gain (Loss)
P	$ -0-	$ -0-	$ 500	$1,500	$(3,100)
S	2,000	7,500	6,000	-0-	8,000
	$2,000	$7,500	$6,500	$1,500	$ 4,900

The P-S group's $4,900 consolidated net Sec. 1231 gain is treated as a long-term capital gain and is combined with the group's $5,000 ($6,500 − $1,500) net long-term capital gain and its $5,500 ($2,000 − $7,500) net short-term capital loss. Thus, the current year consolidated capital gain net income is $4,400 ($4,900 + $5,000 − $5,500). This amount is taxed at the regular corporate tax rates. ◀

KEY POINT

One member of the consolidated group may have a gain or loss from the sale of Sec. 1231 property or a capital asset to another group member. This sale is an example of an *intercompany transaction*, discussed earlier in the chapter. The consolidated group defers recognition of the gain or loss until a later time, and it does not include the gain or loss in the consolidated Sec. 1231 netting process or in the consolidated capital gain and loss netting process until that time.

Departing Group Members' Capital Losses. A particular issue arises with consolidated groups of corporations that does not arise with unconsolidated corporations. This issue pertains to the carryback and carryover of unused capital losses when the composition of the consolidated group changes. For example, suppose a consolidated group has capital loss carryovers when the parent corporation sells the stock in one of its subsidiaries. To what extent are the unused capital losses available to the departed group member on its separate tax return versus the remaining group members on their consolidated tax return? The group must determine the portion of the net capital loss attributable to the departing group member, and this portion is available to the departing group member and is not available to the remaining consolidated group members. The apportionment procedure is similar to that for NOLs for departing group members, which will be discussed later in the chapter.

ADDITIONAL COMMENT

In Example C:8-28, if P and S had filed separate tax returns, P's $3,100 net Sec. 1231 loss would have been treated as an ordinary loss, and P would have had a $1,000 ($500 − $1,500) net capital loss that would not have been deductible in the current year. S's $8,000 net Sec. 1231 gain would have been treated as a long-term capital gain, making S's capital gain net income $8,500 ($8,000 + $6,000 + $2,000 − $7,500).

SRLY Limitation. A consolidated group member may have net capital losses available from another tax year in which it was not member of the group. The consolidated group can use the net capital loss from this *separate return limitation year*, but the group's use of a member's SRLY net capital loss is limited to the member's cumulative contribution to consolidated capital gain net income. This restriction on the use of net capital losses is similar to the SRLY limitation on the use of NOLs, which will be discussed later in the chapter.

DIVIDENDS-RECEIVED DEDUCTION

Chapter C:3 discusses the dividends-received deduction for an unaffiliated corporation. Corporations that own less than 20% of the distributing corporation's stock may deduct 70% of the dividends received. If the shareholder (distributee) corporation owns 20% or more of the distributing corporation's stock but less than 80% of such stock, it may deduct 80% of the dividends received. The dividends-received deduction is limited to 70% of taxable income computed without regard to any NOL deduction, any capital loss carryback, the dividends-received deduction itself, or the U.S. production activities deduction. The limitation is 80% of such taxable income for dividends received qualifying

ADDITIONAL COMMENT

The IRC does not allow corporations to forego the three-year carryback period for net capital losses. This restriction can complicate matters when some of the current year consolidated group members filed separate tax returns during any of the three prior years because they were not group members then.

[30] Reg. Sec. 1.1502-22.

for the 80% deduction. The limitation does not apply if, after taking into account the full dividends-received deduction, the corporation has an NOL for the year.

Dividends Received from Non-Group Members. The calculation of the consolidated dividends-received deduction for dividends received from corporations that are not members of the consolidated group is similar to the calculation for an unaffiliated corporation. The group members' dividends-received deductions, calculated without regard to the limitation on them, are added. The sum of these dividends-received deductions is limited to 70% (or 80%) of consolidated taxable income computed without regard to any NOL deduction, any capital loss carryback, the dividends-received deduction itself, or the U.S. production activities deduction. Similar to an unaffiliated corporation, the limitation does not apply if the consolidated group would have an NOL for the year after taking the full dividends-received deduction.

EXAMPLE C:8-29 ▶ P and S Corporations comprise a consolidated group. Taxable income (without considering any dividends-received deductions, NOLs, capital loss carrybacks, or U.S. production activities deductions) is $16,000 for P and $18,000 for S. P received $20,000 of dividends from unaffiliated corporations that are less than 20%-owned; S received $15,000 of such dividends. The consolidated dividends-received deduction is $23,800, computed as follows:

Dividends-received deduction before limitation ((\$20,000 × 70%) + (\$15,000 × 70%))	\$24,500
Limitation ((\$16,000 + \$18,000) × 70%)	\$23,800
Dividends-received deduction (lesser of \$24,500 or \$23,800)	\$23,800 ◀

ADDITIONAL COMMENT

In Example C:8-29, if P and S did not file a consolidated tax return, P would report an $11,200 dividends-received deduction on its separate tax return, which is the lesser of $14,000 (70% × $20,000) or $11,200 (70% × $16,000). S would report a $10,500 dividends-received deduction, which is the lesser of $10,500 (70% × $15,000) or $12,600 (70% × $18,000). The total dividends-received deductions of $21,700 ($11,200 + $10,500) would be less than the $23,800 dividends-received deduction allowed when P and S file a consolidated tax return.

Dividends Received from Group Members. The deduction for dividends received by one affiliated group member from another member is determined differently than the deduction for dividends received from a non-group member. If the corporations in the affiliated group do not file a consolidated tax return, the distributee corporation may claim a 100% dividends-received deduction on its separate tax return. Also qualifying for the 100% dividends-received deduction are dividends from a corporation that would be a member of the distributee's consolidated group but is not an includible corporation because it is a life insurance company. The 100% dividends-received deduction is not subject to the taxable income limitation and is taken before the 80% or 70% dividends received deduction.

If the affiliated group members file a consolidated tax return, the distribution of a dividend from one group member to another group member (e.g., from subsidiary to parent) qualifies as an intercompany transaction. An intercompany dividend distribution is not included in the distributee member's gross income if it produces a corresponding negative adjustment to that member's basis of its stock in the distributing member (this basis adjustment is discussed later in the chapter).[31] This exclusion eliminates the intercompany dividend from consolidated taxable income, but the consolidated group cannot also claim a 100% dividends-received deduction for the excluded dividend. If the intercompany distribution is in the form of property, the excess of the property's FMV over the distributing member's adjusted basis in it is reported by that member as a gain in its separate taxable income calculation under Sec. 311(b). However, the reporting of this gain for consolidated taxable income is deferred because it is an intercompany transaction. The consolidated group determines the timing of the gain's inclusion in consolidated taxable income by the matching and acceleration rules.[32]

SELF-STUDY QUESTION

Are dividends received from members of the same affiliated group entitled to a dividends-received deduction?

ANSWER

Not if the affiliated group files a consolidated tax return because intercompany dividends are excluded; hence, no dividends-received deduction is necessary.

EXAMPLE C:8-30 ▶ P, S1, and S2 Corporations comprise a consolidated group. Consolidated taxable income (without considering any dividends-received deduction, NOLs, capital loss carrybacks, or U.S. production activities deduction) is $200,000. The group members receive the following dividend income from unaffiliated corporations that are less than 20%-owned: P, $6,000; S1, $10,000; and S2, $34,000. In addition, P receives a $40,000 dividend from S1, and the distribution reduces P's basis in its S1 investment.

---

[31] Reg. Sec. 1.1502-13(f)(2)(ii).

[32] Reg. Sec. 1.1502-13(f)(2)(iii).

REAL-WORLD EXAMPLE

When each corporation in an affiliated group prepares (but does not file) its own separate tax return, intercompany dividends might be included in gross income. In such a situation, the group needs to make a worksheet adjustment during the consolidation process to remove the dividend amount from consolidated taxable income.

- P excludes from its gross income the $40,000 dividend received from S1 because the distribution reduces P's basis in its S1 investment.
- The 70% dividends-received deductions included in the separate taxable income calculations are P, $4,200 (70% × $6,000); S1, $7,000 (70% × $10,000); and S2, $23,800 (70% × $34,000). The total 70% dividends-received deduction of $35,000 ($4,200 + $7,000 + $23,800) is not restricted by the $140,000 dividends-received deduction limitation (70% × $200,000 consolidated taxable income given in the facts).

Thus, the consolidated dividends-received deduction is $35,000. ◀

STOP & THINK

Question: Alpha Corporation has owned the stock of a 100%-owned subsidiary for many years. The CPA who has prepared both corporations' tax returns since their creation has been trying to persuade Alpha's Director of Federal Taxes to begin filing a consolidated tax return based on the tax exemption for intragroup dividends. Is the CPA right or wrong in this approach?

Solution: The CPA is wrong. If Alpha and its subsidiary file separate tax returns, Alpha can claim a 100% deduction for dividends received from its subsidiary, which will offset the dividend received. If the corporations file a consolidated tax return, Alpha can exclude the dividends from its gross income. Typically, these two alternatives result in the same outcome. The outcomes for these two alternatives may differ, however, when preparing state tax returns. The CPA should focus on other factors, such as deferring profits on intercompany transactions and offsetting profits and losses between the two corporations.

SELF-STUDY QUESTION

What is the dividends-received deduction in Example C:8-30 if the group has consolidated taxable income before special deductions of (a) $35,000? (b) $34,999? Should a $1 difference in consolidated taxable income make a $10,500 difference in the dividends-received deduction?

ANSWER

(a) $24,500 (70% × $35,000) due to the consolidated taxable income limitation. (b) All $35,000 is allowed because the full dividends-received deduction creates an NOL. Maybe a $1 difference should not have such a radical effect, but it does. Therefore, as a tax strategy, the corporation should plan its taxable income level to avoid losing a portion of the dividends-received deduction.

U.S. PRODUCTION ACTIVITIES DEDUCTION

If an affiliated group files a consolidated tax return, the group calculates the U.S. production activities deduction on a consolidated basis (see Chapter C:3 for a discussion of this deduction). Accordingly, the deduction for the consolidated group is the least of (1) 9% of the group's consolidated qualified production activities income, (2) 9% of the group's consolidated taxable income before this deduction, or (3) 50% of the group's consolidated W-2 wages allocable to U.S. production activities.

EXAMPLE C:8-31 ▶ P and S Corporations file consolidated tax returns and compute their consolidated taxable income for the current year as follows:

	Consolidated Taxable Income	Adjustments & Eliminations	P's Separate Reporting	S's Separate Reporting
Gross profit on outside sales	$725,000		$500,000	$225,000
Operating expenses	(300,000)		(200,000)	(100,000)
Interest from corporate bonds	9,000		9,000	-0-
Charitable contributions	–0–	$23,000[b]	(7,000)[a]	(16,000)[a]
Consol. taxable income before the charitable contribution and U.S. production activities deductions	$434,000	$23,000	$ 302,000	$ 109,000
Consolidated charit. contrib. ded.	(23,000)			
Consol. taxable income before the U.S. production activities deduction	$411,000			
Consolidated U.S. prod. act. ded.	(36,990)			
Consolidated taxable income	$ 374,010			

[a]Amount of charitable contributions before applying the charitable contribution limitation.
[b]Removes amounts for later calculation on a consolidated basis.
[c]Consolidated taxable income before the deduction ($411,000) is less than consolidated qualified production activities income ($425,000 = $725,000 − $300,000). Therefore, the deduction equals $411,000 × 0.09. This example assumes that all gross profit and operating expenses are related to qualified production activities. It also assumes that the 50% of W-2 wages limitation is not limiting. ◀

For purposes of the U.S. production activities deduction, the tax law expands the definition of an affiliated group by reducing the stock ownership threshold from at least 80% to more than 50% and by including in the definition insurance companies. An **expanded affiliated group** includes corporations that are eligible to file a consolidated tax return because they are in the same affiliated group, but it also may include other corporations (e.g., 51%-owned subsidiaries).

For purposes of calculating the U.S. production activities deduction, the expanded affiliated group is treated as one combined corporation, and the deduction is the least of (1) 9% of the group's combined qualified production activities income, (2) 9% of the group's combined taxable income before this deduction, or (3) 50% of the group's combined W-2 wages allocable to U.S. production activities. Each of the three combined amounts is the aggregate across the separate members. The expanded affiliated group then allocates the resultant deduction to each separate member with positive qualified production activities income based on the relative amounts of such income. If the expanded affiliated group includes a consolidated group in addition to corporations filing separate tax returns, the consolidated group is treated as one separate member of the expanded affiliated group.[33]

EXAMPLE C:8-32 ▶ Assume the same facts as in the previous example except P and S file separate tax returns.

	P's Separate Tax Return	*S's Separate Tax Return*
Gross profit on outside sales	$500,000	$225,000
Operating expenses	(200,000)	(100,000)
Interest from corporate bonds	9,000	-0-
Taxable income before the charit. contrib. ded.	$309,000	$125,000
Charitable contribution deduction[a]	(7,000)	(12,500)
Taxable income before the U.S. prod. act. ded.	$302,000	$112,500
U.S. production activities deduction[b]	(26,333)	(10,972)
Taxable income	$275,667	$101,528

[a]P's deduction is limited to $30,900 ($309,000 × 0.10), and S's deduction is limited to $12,500 ($125,000 × 0.10).
[b]Combined qualified production activities income ($300,000 + $125,000) $ 425,000

Combined taxable income before the U.S. prod. act. ded. ($302,000 + $112,500)	$ 414,500
Lesser of the two amounts	$ 414,500
Times: Percentage	0.09
Combined U.S. production activities deduction	$ 37,305

Combined deduction is allocated in proportion to each expanded affiliated group member's qualified production activities income as follows:

To P: 300/425 × $37,305 = $26,333
To S: 125/425 × $37,305 = $10,972

[33] Reg. Sec. 1.199-7.

REGULAR TAX LIABILITY

A consolidated group determines its consolidated regular income tax liability similarly to an unaffiliated corporation by applying the Sec. 11 corporate tax rates to its consolidated taxable income. These rates appear inside the back cover of this textbook.

The regular tax liability for a consolidated tax return resembles the total tax liability for a controlled group but is not exactly the same. As discussed in Chapter C:3, Sec. 1561 limits to an aggregate of $50,000 the taxable incomes of a controlled group's members to which the 15% tax rate applies, and it allows only an aggregate of $25,000 of the group's members' taxable incomes to be taxed at 25%. For a controlled group, however, each corporation computes its tax liability separately, with the benefits of the 15% and 25% tax brackets allocated among the group's members. In contrast, a consolidated group simply applies the normal corporate tax rate schedule to its consolidated taxable income.

CORPORATE ALTERNATIVE MINIMUM TAX

A consolidated group determines its corporate alternative minimum tax (AMT) on a consolidated basis.[34] In so doing the group calculates its AMT using an approach similar in many ways to the AMT calculation for an unaffiliated corporation except the amounts involved are determined on a consolidated basis (see Chapter C:5 for a detailed discussion of the corporate AMT for an unaffiliated corporation). The group increases or decreases its regular taxable income for each of its AMT preference and adjustment items (e.g., the difference between MACRS and AMT depreciation and the adjusted current earnings (ACE) adjustment) to arrive at alternative minimum taxable income (AMTI). The consolidated group reduces its AMTI by a $40,000 AMT exemption, but this amount phases out from $150,000 to $310,000 of AMTI.

EXAMPLE C:8-33 ▶ P and S Corporations comprise a consolidated group whose consolidated regular tax is $50,000. P's separate alternative minimum taxable income (AMTI) is $145,000, and S's separate AMTI is $140,000. The group's $40,000 exemption must be reduced by $33,750, calculated as follows: ($145,000 + $140,000 − $150,000) × 0.25 = $33,750. Thus, the reduced consolidated exemption is $6,250 ($40,000 − $33,750).

Even if P and S file separate returns instead of a consolidated tax return, the group is allowed only one $40,000 exemption under the controlled group rules discussed in Chapter C:3. In addition, the group members would have to limit that exemption in the same manner as does the consolidated group. The controlled group then apportions the reduced exemption between the two corporations. ◀

ADDITIONAL COMMENT

In Example C:8-33, the group's tentative minimum tax is $55,750 [($145,000 + $140,000 − $6,250) × 0.20], and its AMT is $5,750 ($55,750 − $50,000).

The group's tentative minimum tax (TMT) is 20% of its AMTI in excess of its AMT exemption, and this amount is reduced by the group's AMT foreign tax credit to arrive at its TMT. The AMT is the excess of the TMT over the regular tax liability for the tax year. The consolidated group must pay any consolidated AMT in addition to its regular tax liability, but this amount is available in future years as a consolidated minimum tax credit. The consolidated group is eligible for the small corporation exemption from the AMT, but the $5 million and $7.5 million tests are based on the entire group's gross receipts.

The consolidated group determines its preadjustment AMTI, ACE, and AMTI using an approach that generally parallels the determination of consolidated regular taxable income. For example, the group may defer recognition of income, gains, deductions, or losses from intercompany transactions, much like it would for consolidated regular taxable income. However, the intercompany items, corresponding items, and recomputed corresponding items may differ in amount for AMT and regular tax purposes, such as when the intercompany transaction involves depreciable property.

[34] Prop. Reg. Sec. 1.1502-55.

KEY POINT

Determining the AMT is complex for an unconsolidated corporation. Determining it on a consolidated basis adds greatly to the complexity of this computation.

Many complex issues arise for a consolidated group's AMT that do not arise for an unconsolidated corporation's AMT. For example, recall from Chapter C:5 that the negative ACE adjustment is limited to the cumulative net amount of positive and negative ACE adjustments. Applying this limitation on a consolidated basis requires the tracking of separate return and consolidated return positive and negative ACE adjustments in prior years if corporations enter or leave the consolidated group. Further discussion of these issues is beyond the scope of this textbook.

TAX CREDITS

A consolidated group can claim all tax credits available to corporate taxpayers. The group calculates these credits in much the same way as would an unaffiliated corporation. The discussion that follows examines the two major credits claimed by most consolidated groups—the general business credit and the foreign tax credit.

General Business Credit. A consolidated group determines its general business credit on a consolidated basis, combining its members' separate credit amounts into a single amount.[35] (See Chapter I:14 for more detailed coverage of the general business credit.) The extent to which this combined amount can be claimed as a credit is limited to the excess of the group's consolidated net income tax over the greater of (1) its consolidated tentative minimum tax or (2) 25% of its consolidated net regular tax liability exceeding $25,000. Any credit exceeding this limitation carries back one year and forward 20 years.[36]

The corporations in a consolidated group may find that the general business credit allowed in the current year is smaller on a consolidated basis than it would be on a separate return basis. For example, if the credit is attributable to a profitable group member and another group member has a loss, consolidation may result in that member's loss reducing the group's credit limitation. However, if the credit is attributable to an unprofitable group member, consolidation may allow the members to claim a greater amount of credit on a consolidated basis than on a separate return basis because the credit limitation is higher on a consolidated basis due to other group members' profits.

EXAMPLE C:8-34 ▶ P and S Corporations comprise a consolidated group. For the current year, P and S have separate taxable income and losses of $300,000 and ($100,000), respectively. P has a $40,000 research credit, and S has a $10,000 employer provided child care credit. P and S have $125,000 of AMT preference and adjustment items.

The group has a $50,000 ($40,000 + $10,000) tentative general business credit. The group's consolidated regular taxable income is $200,000 ($300,000 − $100,000), assuming no intercompany transactions or other items that would cause consolidated taxable income to differ from the sum of the separate taxable income and loss. The group's regular tax is $61,250 [$22,250 + (0.39 × ($200,000 − $100,000))]. The group's tentative minimum tax is $65,000 [20% × ($200,000 + $125,000)]; the AMT exemption is fully phased-out, so the consolidated AMT is $3,750 ($65,000 − $61,250). The group's general business credit limitation is calculated as follows:

Regular tax		$61,250
Plus: Alternative minimum tax		3,750
Minus: Credits allowed under Secs. 21-30C		-0-
Net income tax		$65,000
Minus: Greater of:		
(1) 25% of group's net regular tax liability exceeding $25,000 [0.25 × ($61,250 − $25,000)]	$ 9,062	
(2) Group's tentative minimum tax for the year	65,000	(65,000)
General business credit limitation		$ -0-

The $50,000 ($50,000 tentative credit − $0 credit limitation) of unused general business credits carries back one year and forward 20 years. ◀

BOOK-TO-TAX ACCOUNTING COMPARISON

A general business credit carryover creates a deferred tax asset on the group's consolidated financial statements. The group also establishes a valuation allowance for any part of the deferred tax asset that does not have a more likely than not probability of being realized, and it should record a liability for unrecognized tax benefit for the portion of it that is not more likely than not to be realized upon effective settlement with the IRS (see Chapter C:3 regarding uncertain tax positions under ASC 740).

35 Reg. Sec. 1.1502-3.

36 Sec. 39(a).

Foreign Tax Credit. A consolidated group determines its foreign tax credit on a consolidated basis.[37] The parent corporation makes the election to claim either a deduction or a credit for the group's foreign income taxes. If the parent chooses to claim a credit, the consolidated group computes its foreign tax credit limitation by taking into account its consolidated foreign-source income, consolidated taxable income, and consolidated regular tax in the manner described in Chapter C:16.

ESTIMATED TAX PAYMENTS

For the first two years for which an affiliated group files consolidated tax returns, it may elect to make estimated tax payments on either a consolidated or separate basis. Once an affiliated group has filed consolidated tax returns for two consecutive years, it must pay estimated taxes on a consolidated basis and continue doing so until the group's members again file separate tax returns.[38] The group's estimated tax payments and any underpayment exceptions or penalties are based on its consolidated tax liability for the current and preceding tax years without regard to the number of corporations comprising the group. If new, profitable corporations join the group, this treatment can be advantageous due to the time value of money.

EXAMPLE C:8-35 ▶ The P-S1 affiliated group has filed consolidated tax returns for several years. In the preceding year, the group reported a $100,000 consolidated tax liability. The P-S1 group acquires all of S2 Corporation's stock during the current year. S2 is profitable and causes the P-S1-S2 group to report a $300,000 consolidated tax liability in the current year. Assuming the P-S1-S2 group does not fall under the large corporation rules discussed below, it can base its current year estimated tax payments on its $100,000 consolidated tax liability from the prior tax year. The group will not incur an underpayment penalty if it makes $25,000 ($100,000 ÷ 4) of estimated tax payments by the fifteenth day of the fourth, sixth, ninth, and twelfth months of its tax year. The group must pay the balance of its consolidated tax liability by the due date of its consolidated tax return (without regard to any extensions) to avoid a penalty. ◀

Large Corporation Rule. Chapter C:3 discusses the special underpayment rules for large corporations imposed by Sec. 6655(d)(2)(B). A large corporation's estimated tax payments cannot be based on its prior year's tax liability except for the first installment. A large corporation is one whose taxable income was $1 million or more in any of its three preceding tax years. A controlled group of corporations must allocate the $1 million amount among its group members. An affiliated group that files a consolidated tax return is treated as a single corporation for this purpose. An affiliated group that files separate tax returns generally must allocate this $1 million amount because it also qualifies as a parent-subsidiary controlled group.

Consolidated or Separate Basis. During the first two tax years of filing consolidated tax returns, a consolidated group sometimes can reduce its quarterly tax payments by making estimated tax payments on a separate basis in the first year and on a consolidated basis in the second year or vice versa. These reduced quarterly estimated tax payments will cause the group to pay a larger balance of tax by the due date of its tax return (without extensions). The group can apply different exceptions for the underpayment penalty (e.g., prior year's liability or annualization of current year's income) on a consolidated or separate basis the first two years. Determination of the actual required estimated tax payments on a consolidated or separate basis, however, is beyond the scope of this textbook.

Short-Period Return. If a corporation joins a consolidated group after the beginning of its tax year or leaves a consolidated group before its tax year ends, it generally must file a separate, short-period tax return covering the time period it was unaffiliated with the group (however, it would not file a separate tax return if it left one consolidated

[37] Reg. Sec. 1.1502-4.

[38] Reg. Sec. 1.1502-5.

group to enter another consolidated group). Treasury Regulations provide rules covering estimated tax payments for short tax years.[39] No estimated tax payment is required for a short tax year that is less than four months.

NET OPERATING LOSSES (NOLs)

OBJECTIVE 6

Determine a consolidated group's NOL, calculate the carryback or carryover of a consolidated NOL, and apply the SRLY restrictions on NOL usage

One advantage of filing a consolidated tax return is the ability of the consolidated group to offset one member's NOLs against the taxable income of other group members. However, the profitable group members' taxable income may not be sufficient to fully offset the other members' NOLs, resulting in a consolidated NOL. The consolidated NOL carries back two years and forward 20 years unless the parent elects out of the carryback. If corporations enter or depart the consolidated group between the year the NOL arose and the carryback or carryover year, the group must determine the portion of the NOL that carries to the entering or departing corporation's separate return year. In addition, if a corporation entering the consolidated group has unused NOLs from years prior to its entry into the group (or a departing corporation has unused NOLs from years after its departure), the group may be able to use the NOLs. Because of the potential for abuse, the tax law limits the group's ability to use a separate return NOL in a consolidated return year. In addition, NOL, capital loss, and tax credit carryovers can be subject to the consolidated limitations under Secs. 382-384. The rules that apply to carrybacks and carryovers are discussed below.

CURRENT YEAR NOL

KEY POINT

Generally, the most significant benefit of filing a consolidated tax return is the group's ability to offset one member's losses against the income of other members.

A consolidated group's NOL equals the excess of its deductions over its gross income (i.e., its negative taxable income).[40] The group combines each member's separate taxable income or loss to determine a combined taxable income before adjusting for NOL carryovers (see Table C:8-1). The combining process allows one group member's losses to offset the taxable income of other group members. The group determines its consolidated NOL after applying the intercompany transaction rules and after calculating on a consolidated basis the various items discussed earlier, such as Sec. 1231 and capital gains and losses. The group must use a member's current year loss to first offset other members' current-year profits. A group member cannot elect separately to carry back its own losses from a consolidated return year to one of its earlier or later profitable separate return years. Only the consolidated group's NOL (if any) may carry back or over.

EXAMPLE C:8-36 ▶ P and S Corporations comprise an affiliated group. During Year 1, their initial year of operation, P and S file calendar year separate tax returns. Beginning in Year 2, the group elects to file a consolidated tax return. P and S report the following results for Years 1 and 2:

	Taxable Income	
Group Member	*Year 1*	*Year 2*
P	($15,000)	$40,000
S	250,000	(27,000)
Consolidated taxable income	N/A	$13,000

N/A = Not applicable

P may not use its Year 1 NOL to offset S's Year 1 profits because they file separate returns. In its Year 2 consolidated tax return, the group must first offset S's $27,000 separate loss against P's separate taxable income. S cannot carry back the $27,000 to its Year 1 separate tax return. (Note that the tax savings from deducting the $27,000 would be greater if S could carry it back

[39] Reg. Sec. 1.6655-5.

[40] Reg. Sec. 1.1502-21(e).

to Year 1.) Because P did not exist before Year 1, P carries its Year 1 NOL forward to offset all $13,000 of Year 2 consolidated taxable income that the P-S group reports prior to deducting any of the NOL carryover. The group's Year 2 consolidated taxable income is zero. P carries over to Year 3 its remaining NOL of $2,000 ($15,000 NOL from Year 1 − $13,000 used in Year 2). ◀

CARRYBACKS AND CARRYOVERS OF CONSOLIDATED NOLS

A consolidated NOL carries back to the two preceding tax years and carries over to the 20 succeeding tax years. The parent corporation may elect for the consolidated group to relinquish the carryback period for a consolidated NOL and use the NOL only as a carryforward to succeeding years.[41] (Chapter C:3 discusses reasons for making this election.)

If the same corporations comprise the consolidated group during the carryback and carryover periods as during the year in which the NOL occurs, the treatment of the consolidated NOL is much like the treatment of an unaffiliated corporation's NOL. However, if the group's composition changes, the treatment of a consolidated NOL becomes complicated.

General Rule. The consolidated group apportions a fraction of its consolidated NOL to each member that incurred a separate loss during the year the NOL arose as follows:[42]

$$\frac{\text{Separate NOL of the particular group member}}{\text{Sum of the separate NOLs of all group members having such losses}} \times \text{Consolidated NOL} = \text{Portion of consolidated NOL attributable to the particular group member}$$

KEY POINT

In Example C:8-37, because the P-S1-S2 affiliated group did not file a consolidated tax return prior to Year 3, P must either forgo the NOL carryback or allow $22,700 ($11,000 + $4,000 + $7,700) of the consolidated NOL to be carried back to S1's and S2's Years 1 and 2 separate tax returns.

EXAMPLE C:8-37 ▶ P, S1, and S2 Corporations comprise an affiliated group. The group filed separate tax returns in Years 1 and 2 but elected to file a consolidated tax return in Year 3. The members report the following amounts of income and loss (before any NOL deduction):

	Year 1	*Year 2*	*Year 3*
P	$80,000	$90,000	$ 75,000
S1	11,000	7,000	(60,000)
S2	4,400	3,300	(40,000)
Consolidated taxable income	N/A	N/A	$(25,000)

N/A = Not applicable

Of the $25,000 Year 3 consolidated NOL, the group apportions $15,000 [$25,000 × ($60,000 ÷ ($60,000 + $40,000))] to S1 and $10,000 [$25,000 × ($40,000 ÷ ($60,000 + $40,000))] to S2. Assuming P does not elect to forego the NOL carryback period, S1 carries back $11,000 of its apportioned NOL to offset all its Year 1 separate return taxable income and the remaining $4,000 ($15,000 − $11,000) to offset part of its Year 2 separate return taxable income. S2 carries back $7,700 of its $10,000 apportioned NOL to offset its Years 1 and 2 separate return taxable incomes. The remaining $2,300 ($10,000 − $4,400 − $3,300) of consolidated NOL attributable to S2 carries forward to Year 4. ◀

If a corporation ceases to be a member of a consolidated group, any consolidated NOL carryover apportioned to it first must be used to offset consolidated taxable income in the year of departure. This requirement applies even when the entire NOL carryover is attributable to the departing member. Any NOL carryover apportioned to the departing member not absorbed by departure year consolidated taxable income becomes the member's separate carryover and may be used in its subsequent separate return years.[43]

---

41 Reg. Sec. 1.1502-21(b)(3)(i).

42 Reg. Sec. 1.1502-21(b)(2)(iv). The member's separate NOL is determined in a manner similar to the calculation of separate taxable income except for a series of adjustments to take into account the member's charitable contributions, dividends-received deductions, and Sec. 1231 and capital gains and losses. The consolidated NOL apportioned to a member might be reduced under the unified loss rules of Reg. Sec. 1.1502-36, which are beyond the scope of this text.

43 Reg. Sec. 1.1502-21(b)(2)(ii)(A).

EXAMPLE C:8-38 ▶

P, S1, and S2 Corporations comprise an affiliated group that has filed consolidated tax returns on a calendar year basis for several years. At the close of business on September 30 of Year 2, P sells all its S1 stock. Therefore, S1 must file a separate tax return for the period October 1 through December 31 of Year 2. The members report the following amounts of income and loss (before any NOL deduction):

TAX STRATEGY TIP

In Example C:8-38, the group is entitled to use the consolidated NOL before S1 determines its NOL carryover. This privilege can affect the negotiated purchase price for S1.

	Year 1	*Year 2*
P	$ 48,000	$20,000
S1	(50,000)	43,000*
S2	(100,000)	10,000
Total	$(102,000)	$73,000

*S1 earns $30,000 from January 1 through September 30 and $13,000 from October 1 through December 31.

Assuming P elects to forego the NOL carryback period, the consolidated NOL carryover of $102,000 from Year 1 offsets the $60,000 ($20,000 + $30,000 + $10,000) of taxable income reported by P, S1, and S2 in their Year 2 consolidated tax return. Of the remaining $42,000 ($102,000 − $60,000), the group apportions $14,000 [$42,000 × ($50,000 ÷ ($50,000 + $100,000))] to S1 and $28,000 [$42,000 × ($100,000 ÷ ($50,000 + $100,000))] to S2. Of S1's carryover, $13,000 can be used in its separate tax return for October 1 through December 31 of Year 2. The remaining $1,000 ($14,000 − $13,000) carries over to S1's Year 3 separate tax return. The consolidated group carries over S2's $28,000 apportioned share of the Year 1 NOL to Year 3 and subsequent years. ◀

Offspring Rule. The offspring rule pertains to the consolidated NOL apportioned to a loss corporation that was newly formed by one or more of the affiliated group's members. The rule permits the NOL apportioned to the loss corporation to be carried back to a consolidated return year before it was a group member or to a separate return year of the parent corporation. Normally, the NOL apportioned to a loss member cannot be carried back in this way. The offspring rule applies if:[44]

- The loss corporation did not exist in the carryback year, and
- The loss corporation has been a member of the affiliated group continually since its organization.

If these two requirements are met, the part of the consolidated NOL apportioned to the loss member carries back to the two preceding consolidated return years (or separate return year of the common parent). The offspring rule does not apply if the common parent was a member of a different consolidated group or affiliated group filing separate returns for the year to which the loss carries.

EXAMPLE C:8-39 ▶

P and S1 Corporations were affiliated during Years 1 and 2 and filed consolidated tax returns in those years. On January 1 of Year 3, P creates S2 Corporation and acquires all its stock. S2 becomes a member of the affiliated group on that date. P, S1, and S2 report the following results for Years 1 through 3 (before any NOL deduction):

SELF-STUDY QUESTION

In Examples C:8-39 and C:8-40, what is the reason for allowing S2's portion of the consolidated NOL to carry back to Years 1 and 2?

	Year 1	*Year 2*	*Year 3*
P	$ 9,000	$11,000	$ 16,000
S1	8,000	7,000	4,000
S2			(30,000)
Consolidated taxable income	$17,000	$18,000	$(10,000)

ANSWER

The assets that make up S2 really were P's assets in Years 1 and 2, so it makes sense to allow the NOL to carry back to whatever tax return P filed in Years 1 and 2.

The entire Year 3 consolidated NOL is apportioned to S2. As discussed earlier, S2's $30,000 separate NOL is first used to offset the Year 3 taxable income of P and S1, leaving only a $10,000 consolidated NOL. If P does not elect to forego the NOL carryback period, the offspring rule allows the $10,000 NOL to carry back and offset $10,000 of the $17,000 Year 1 consolidated taxable income. The requirements for the offspring rule are met because S2 did not exist in Year 1 (the carryback year) and has been a group member continually since its organization in Year 3.

[44] Reg. Sec. 1.1502-21(b)(2)(ii)(B).

If P elects to forego the NOL carryback period, the $10,000 consolidated NOL offsets consolidated taxable income in Year 4 and up to 19 subsequent years assuming S2 does not depart the consolidated group before the $10,000 NOL is used. ◀

EXAMPLE C:8-40 ▶ Assume the same facts as in Example C:8-39 except P and S1 Corporations did not begin filing consolidated tax returns until Year 2. The offspring rule's requirements are still met, so the $10,000 consolidated NOL apportioned to S2 can carry back to P's Year 1 separate tax return, offsetting its $9,000 of taxable income (assuming P does not elect to forego the NOL carryback period). The remaining $1,000 offsets $1,000 of the $18,000 Year 2 consolidated taxable income. ◀

If the loss corporation is not a member of the affiliated group immediately after its organization, that member's portion of the consolidated NOL carries back only to its prior separate return years.

EXAMPLE C:8-41 ▶ Assume the same facts as in Example C:8-40 except a third party created S2 in Year 2, and P acquired all of S2's stock from the third party on January 1 of Year 3. P, S1, and S2 report the following results for Years 1 through 3 (before any NOL deduction):

TAX STRATEGY TIP

In deciding whether to elect out of the NOL carryback, a parent corporation should consider whether its subsidiaries have minority shareholders who might benefit if the subsidiaries receive a refund.

Group Member		*Taxable Income*	
	Year 1	*Year 2*	*Year 3*
P	$ 9,000	$11,000	$16,000
S1	8,000	7,000	4,000
S2		8,000	(30,000)
Consolidated taxable income	N/A	$18,000[a]	($10,000)

N/A = Not applicable
[a] Includes only the results of P and S1.

The offspring rule does not apply because S2 was not affiliated with the P-S1 group in Year 2. Because the entire $10,000 consolidated NOL is attributable to S2, S2 can carry it back to Year 2 and offset all $8,000 of its taxable income on its Year 2 separate return. S2 cannot carry back the loss to Year 1 because S2 did not exist then. The remaining NOL of $2,000 ($10,000 − $8,000) carries over to offset the consolidated group's Year 4 and later taxable income. Alternatively, the P-S1-S2 affiliated group could elect to carry over the entire $10,000 loss to offset taxable income in Year 4 and later years. ◀

SPECIAL LOSS LIMITATIONS

The term NOL trafficking refers to attempts by one tax entity to acquire NOL deductions from another entity. For example, a profitable corporation might consider acquiring an unprofitable corporation merely to obtain a tax benefit from the acquired corporation's unused NOLs. To inhibit NOL trafficking, the tax law imposes special limitations on the use of NOLs. The **Sec. 382 loss limitation rules**, which were discussed in Chapter C:7 on a separate return basis, also could apply to affiliated groups filing consolidated tax returns. The **separate return limitation year (SRLY) rules** apply only to consolidated groups and limit the use in a consolidated return year of a member's NOL that arose in a separate return year. Specifically, the SRLY rules limit use of the NOL to the loss member's subsequent contribution to consolidated taxable income. The SRLY rules are explained in detail below, as well as special aspects of the Sec. 382 rules with respect to consolidated tax returns.

BOOK-TO TAX ACCOUNTING COMPARISON

An NOL creates a deferred tax asset on an acquiring corporation's consolidated balance sheet, thereby highlighting the economic benefit the unprofitable corporation's NOLs provides for the acquiring corporation's consolidated group. However, a valuation allowance for this deferred tax asset may be needed because of the Sec. 382 and SRLY loss limitation rules.

Separate Return Limitation Year Rules. A SRLY generally is any separate return year (i.e., a year in which a corporation filed a separate tax return or joined in a consolidated tax return of another consolidated group). However, a SRLY does not include the following:[45]

- A separate return year of the group's parent corporation. The SRLY limitation thus does not apply to the parent corporation's NOLs, even if they arise in a separate return year.

[45] Reg. Sec. 1.1502-1(f).

KEY POINT

The SRLY rules limit a consolidated group's ability to acquire another corporation and use its already existing NOLs to offset the group's income.

- A separate return year of a corporation that was a member of the affiliated group for every day of the loss year (e.g., the group did not elect to file a consolidated tax return in the loss year). The SRLY limitation does not apply in this circumstance because the loss year would not have been a SRLY had the group elected to file a consolidated tax return.

An NOL incurred in a SRLY carries back two years and forward 20 years unless the corporation elects to carry forward the NOL only for 20 years. If the year to which the NOL carries is a consolidated return year, the NOL's deductibility is limited to the SRLY limitation for that group member:[46]

ADDITIONAL COMMENT

These two exceptions to the SRLY rules exist because, in both cases, the group has not acquired already existing NOLs.

Aggregate of consolidated taxable income for all consolidated return years of the group determined by taking into account only the loss member's items of income, gain, deduction, and loss	
Minus: Any of the loss member's NOLs previously absorbed by the consolidated group	
SRLY limitation (not less than zero)	

The SRLY rules limit the consolidated group's use of the loss member's NOL to that member's aggregate contribution to consolidated taxable income in excess of zero. As a result, an NOL incurred in a SRLY that is deductible on a consolidated tax return equals the lesser of (1) the SRLY limitation, (2) consolidated taxable income, or (3) the amount of the NOL carryover or carryback. Any NOL carryover or carryback exceeding the lesser of these three amounts carries over to subsequent tax years.

EXAMPLE C:8-42 ▶ P and S Corporations are calendar year corporations that formed in Year 1. P acquires 100% of S's stock at the close of business on December 31 of Year 1.[47] P and S file separate tax returns for Year 1 and begin filing a consolidated tax return for Year 2. Assume the U.S. production activities deduction does not apply. The corporations report the following taxable incomes (losses), before any NOL deductions, for Years 1 through 5:

SELF-STUDY QUESTION

What is the consequence of having NOLs subject to the SRLY limitations?

ANSWER

The effect of having a member's NOLs tainted as SRLY NOLs is that they can be used only to offset taxable income of the loss member. This restriction could delay deduction of the NOLs and increases the likelihood that they will expire unused.

	Taxable Income				
Group Member	*Year 1*	*Year 2*	*Year 3*	*Year 4*	*Year 5*
P	$(9,000)	$17,000	$ 6,000	$(6,000)	$ 2,000
S	(20,000)	(2,000)	5,000	5,000	16,000
Consolidated taxable income	N/A	$15,000	$11,000	$(1,000)	$18,000

N/A = Not applicable

Under the SRLY rules, the P-S consolidated group uses the NOLs as follows:

- *Year 2:* P's Year 1 NOL offsets the group's consolidated taxable income (CTI). For P, Year 1 is not a SRLY because P is the group's parent corporation. S's only contribution to CTI by the end of Year 2 is its $2,000 loss in Year 2. Therefore, S's SRLY limitation for Year 2 is zero because S makes no positive aggregate contribution to CTI. The group's resulting CTI is $6,000 ($15,000 − $9,000).
- *Year 3:* S's SRLY limitation for Year 3 is $3,000 [($2,000) + $5,000]. S's $20,000 unused NOLs and the group's $11,000 CTI are both more than $3,000, so the group can deduct $3,000 of S's Year 1 NOL. The group's resulting CTI is $8,000 ($11,000 − $3,000), and S's remaining NOL of $17,000 ($20,000 − $3,000) carries forward.
- *Year 4:* S's SRLY limitation is $5,000 [($2,000) + $5,000 + $5,000 − $3,000]. However, none of S's Year 1 NOL can be used because the group has no positive CTI for the NOL to offset. Assuming the group carries back the Year 4 consolidated NOL to Year 2, CTI in Year 2 is reduced from $6,000 to $5,000 ($15,000 − $9,000 carryover from Year 1 − $1,000 carryback from Year 4).

[46] Reg. Sec. 1.1502-21(c). If multiple group members have unexpired NOLs or a loss member has unexpired NOLs from multiple SRLYs, the group uses the NOLs on a first-in, first-out (FIFO) basis. The group uses NOLs from tax years ending on the same date on a pro rata basis.

[47] P's acquisition of S stock might trigger both the SRLY rules and the Sec. 382 rules. To simplify the example, assume that the acquisition does not trigger the Sec. 382 rules. The SRLY-Sec. 382 overlap rules are discussed later in this chapter.

▶ *Year 5:* S's SRLY limitation is $21,000 [($2,000) + $5,000 + $5,000 − $3,000 + $16,000]. However, S has only $17,000 of NOLs remaining, so the group deducts this amount. The group's resulting CTI is $1,000 ($18,000 − $17,000), and no NOLs remain to carry forward to Year 6. ◀

The SRLY rules generally apply separately to each corporation that has a loss carryover from a SRLY.

EXAMPLE C:8-43 ▶ At the close of business on December 31 of Year 1, P Corporation purchases 100% of S Corporation's stock and 100% of T Corporation's stock. S and T were unaffiliated prior to these purchases. From Year 1, S has a $12,000 NOL carryover, and T has an $11,000 NOL carryover. Assume the Sec. 382 limitation does not apply to these stock purchases. The P-S-T affiliated group elects to file a consolidated tax return for Year 2, and the members report the following separate taxable income for that year:

P Corporation	$100,000
S Corporation	$ 14,000
T Corporation	$ 10,000

The Year 2 SRLY limitation for S's NOL is $14,000, and the limitation for T's NOL is $10,000. The P-S-T consolidated group can deduct all $12,000 of S's Year 1 NOL, but it can deduct only $10,000 of T's Year 1 NOL. As a result, the group's Year 2 consolidated taxable income is $102,000 ($100,000 + $14,000 + $10,000 − $12,000 − $10,000). The remaining $1,000 ($11,000 − $10,000) of T's Year 1 NOL carries forward to Year 3. ◀

The SRLY limitation applies to a SRLY subgroup on a joint basis rather than to each corporation separately. For NOL carryovers, a SRLY subgroup is the loss corporation and each other group member that (1) became a member of the current affiliated group at the same time as the loss corporation, (2) was affiliated with the loss corporation in another affiliated group before becoming a member of the current affiliated group, and (3) has been continuously affiliated with the loss corporation after ceasing to be a member of the former affiliated group.

EXAMPLE C:8-44 ▶ Assume the same facts as in Example C:8-43 except S owns 100% of T's stock, and P purchased 100% of S's stock at the close of business on December 31 of Year 1. S and T are a SRLY subgroup. The S-T subgroup SRLY limitation for Year 2 is $24,000 ($14,000 + $10,000), so the P-S-T consolidated group can deduct on its Year 2 tax return all $23,000 ($12,000 + $11,000) of S's and T's NOL carryovers from Year 1. ◀

KEY POINT

The SRLY rules apply to both carryovers and carrybacks. Remember that SRLYs stem from a year in which a member files a separate tax return or joins in the filing of a consolidated return with a different affiliated group.

In addition to NOL carryovers, the SRLY rules apply to NOL carrybacks. For example, suppose P Corporation owns 100% of S Corporation's stock, and they have filed consolidated tax returns for many years. P sells all its stock in S at the end of Year 2, and S incurs an NOL in Year 3. If S does not elect to forego the NOL carryback period, the Year 3 NOL first carries to the P-S Year 1 consolidated tax return, and any remaining NOL then carries to the P-S Year 2 consolidated tax return. In Years 1 and 2, the SRLY rules restrict the consolidated group's use of S's Year 3 NOL to S's contribution to consolidated taxable income for all consolidated return years.

The SRLY rules also limit the use of built-in losses. A built-in loss is a loss that accrues in a separate return year but is realized in a consolidated return year. For example, S Corporation purchases land in a separate return year for $100,000. The land's fair market value declines to $85,000 before P purchases all of S's stock, when they start filing tax returns on a consolidated basis. If S sells the land during the five-year period beginning on the date P purchases S's stock, the SRLY rules limit the extent to which the P-S consolidated group can use the realized loss. As with NOLs, the group must compute S's SRLY limitation in determining how much of the loss it can use.[48]

In a reverse acquisition, the acquired corporation's shareholders own more than 50% of the fair market value of the acquiring corporation's stock immediately after the

[48] Reg. Sec. 1.1502-15(a).

acquisition. In such an acquisition, the SRLY limitation applies to the acquiring corporation's NOLs and does not apply to the acquired corporation's NOLs.[49] For example, suppose P Corporation acquires all of S Corporation's stock in exchange for P stock. Because P is smaller than S, persons who were S shareholders immediately before the purchase own more than 50% of the fair market value of P's stock immediately after the purchase. The form of the transaction is that P acquires S, but its substance is that S acquires P. The transaction qualifies as a reverse acquisition, so the SRLY limitation applies to P's NOLs but not to S's NOLs. That is, S is treated as if it were the parent corporation for purposes of applying the SRLY limitation. The details of this rule and other aspects of the reverse acquisition rules are beyond the scope of this textbook.

A discussion of the financial statement implications of SRLY losses appears at the end of this chapter.

Consolidated Sec. 382 Rules. The Sec. 382 rules may apply when a consolidated group acquires a corporation with an unused NOL. Section 382 inhibits NOL trafficking by limiting the acquiring corporation's use of a loss corporation's NOL to the Sec. 382 limitation, which is the value of the old loss corporation's stock multiplied by the long-term tax-exempt federal interest rate.[50] The 50 percentage point stock ownership change needed to trigger the Sec. 382 rules can occur in acquisitive transactions involving a single corporation or a group of corporations that file separate or consolidated returns. (See Chapter C:7 for a discussion of Sec. 382.) The consolidated Sec. 382 rules generally provide that the ownership change and Sec. 382 limitation are determined with respect to the entire consolidated group (or a subgroup of a consolidated group) and not separately for each corporation.[51] The details of these rules are beyond the scope of this textbook.

SRLY-Sec. 382 Overlap. A SRLY-Sec. 382 overlap occurs when an acquisition of a corporation falls under both the SRLY rules and the Sec. 382 rules (for example, a corporation in a consolidated group purchases 100% of the stock of a target corporation having an NOL carryover). Because both sets of rules inhibit NOL trafficking by restricting the use of NOLs, Treasury Regulations alleviate the burden of applying them by waiving the application of the SRLY rules in many SRLY-Sec. 382 overlap situations.[52]

To qualify for the overlap rule, a corporation must become a member of a consolidated group (the SRLY event) within six months of the date of an ownership change that triggers a Sec. 382 limitation (the Sec. 382 event). Often, the SRLY event and the Sec. 382 event are simultaneous.

EXAMPLE C:8-45 ▶ P Corporation purchases 60% of S Corporation's stock on February 28 of the current year. On June 30 of the current year, P purchases the other 40% of S's stock. P has filed consolidated tax returns with its other subsidiaries for several years. The Sec. 382 event occurs on February 28, when the 50 percentage-point ownership change takes place. The SRLY event occurs on June 30, when P's ownership of S reaches the 80% threshold needed to include S in the consolidated tax return. The overlap rule applies because the Sec. 382 event occurred within six months of the SRLY event, so the SRLY rules are waived beginning with the tax year that includes June 30. Instead, only the Sec. 382 rules apply. ◀

ADDITIONAL COMMENT

In some cases, the overlap rule will not apply. In Example C:8-45, if the 40% purchase had taken place on September 30, the SRLY event would have occurred more than six months after the Sec. 382 event. Consequently, the SRLY rules and the Sec. 382 rules both would apply.

If the SRLY event precedes the Sec. 382 event by six months or less, the overlap rule applies for the first tax year beginning after the Sec. 382 event (and the SRLY rules apply for the interim period). This situation could occur, for example, if the acquiring corporation had owned 45% of the target corporation's stock for many years, purchased 40% of the target's stock in the current year, and purchased the remaining 15% of the target's stock less than six months after the 40% purchase.

Topic Review C:8-2 summarizes the rules applying to carrybacks and carryovers of consolidated return and separate return NOLs.

---

[49] Reg. Sec. 1.1502-1(f)(3).

[50] The Sec. 382 limitation rules apply to the tax attributes limited by Secs. 382–384 (e.g., NOLs, capital losses, foreign tax credits, general business credits, minimum tax credit, built-in gains, and built-in losses).

[51] Reg. Sec. 1.1502-91(a)(1).

[52] Reg. Sec. 1.1502-21(g).

TOPIC REVIEW C:8-2

Rules Addressing NOL Carrybacks and Carryovers To or From Consolidated Tax Return Years

LOSS YEAR	CARRYOVER/ CARRYBACK YEAR	RULE AND SPECIAL LIMITATIONS
CRY[a]	CRY	1. Consolidated NOLs carry back two years and forward 20 years. The group's parent corporation can elect to forgo the carryback period. No special problems arise if the group members are the same in the loss year and the year to which the loss carries. 2. The Sec. 382 limitation applies to the loss carryover if a Sec. 382 ownership change occurs.
CRY	SRY[b]	1. Carryback to a member's prior separate return year is possible only if part or all of the NOL is apportioned to the member. Offspring rule permits carryback of an offspring member's allocable share of the consolidated NOL to a separate or consolidated return year of the group's parent corporation. 2. The departing member is allocated part of the consolidated NOL carryover. The consolidated NOL carryover is used first in the consolidated return year in which the member departs. The allocated share of the remaining consolidated NOL carryover is then available to be used in the departing member's first separate return year. The Sec. 382 loss limitation may apply to the loss carryover.
SRY	CRY	1. A separate return year NOL carries over to a consolidated return year, but the SRLY rules may limit the NOL's usage. The SRLY rules do not apply to the NOLs of the parent corporation or to a corporation that is a member of the affiliated group on each day of the loss year unless a reverse acquisition occurs. Section 382 loss limitation rules may apply to the loss carryover, but the SRLY rules may be waived under the overlap rule. 2. Carryback of a loss of a departed group member to a consolidated return year is a SRLY loss.

[a]Consolidated return year.
[b]Separate return year.

STOCK BASIS ADJUSTMENTS

OBJECTIVE 7

Adjust the parent's basis in stock of a consolidated subsidiary

A consolidated group member must annually adjust the basis of stock it owns in a subsidiary for the subsidiary's profits and losses, for distributions from the subsidiary, and for other items. These rules are similar to those that apply to partners of partnerships and shareholders of S corporations (see Chapters C:9 and C:11) and are intended to prevent the duplication of income or loss in consolidated taxable income.[53]

EXAMPLE C:8-46 ▶

KEY POINT

Positive stock basis adjustments reduce the amount of gain or increase the amount of loss reported when a sale of the stock of a consolidated group member (other than the parent) occurs.

P Corporation purchases all of S Corporation's stock on January 1 of the current year for $100,000. The corporations elect to file a consolidated tax return. S recognizes a $25,000 profit during the current year and pays no dividends to P. P sells all its S stock on December 31 of the current year for $125,000. P increases the basis of its S stock by $25,000. As a result, P realizes no gain or loss on the sale of its S stock [$125,000 amount realized − $125,000 basis ($100,000 + $25,000)].

Had P not adjusted its basis for S's profit, it would have realized a $25,000 gain on the stock sale ($125,000 − $100,000), and this gain would have been taxed on the current year's consolidated tax return. However, the increase in the S stock's value that led to this $25,000 gain is attributable to the $25,000 profit that S earned. Without the basis adjustment to the S stock, the consolidated group would have been taxed twice on the $25,000 gain. ◀

A consolidated group may be comprised of many tiers of corporations. For example, a parent corporation may have a subsidiary corporation (a first-tier subsidiary), and the subsidiary, in turn, may have its own subsidiary (a second-tier subsidiary). The stock basis

[53] Losses realized on the sale by one consolidated group member of another member's stock involve complicated rules and calculations that are beyond the scope of this text.

adjustments itemized below are discussed with respect to a parent corporation that owns stock of a subsidiary, but they also apply to a higher-tier subsidiary that owns stock of a lower-tier subsidiary.

The starting point for the calculation is the parent corporation's original basis in its subsidiary stock, which depends on the method used to acquire it (e.g., purchase, nontaxable corporate formation, or nontaxable reorganization). The parent makes the following adjustments to the original basis:[54]

- Increase basis for the subsidiary's income and gain items and decrease it for the subsidiary's deduction and loss items taken into account in determining consolidated taxable income. Items whose recognition is deferred under the intercompany transaction rules do not increase or decrease basis until they are taken into account for consolidated taxable income.
- Increase basis for the subsidiary's income permanently excluded from taxation (e.g., tax-exempt bond interest and federal income tax refunds).
- Increase basis for the subsidiary's deductions that do not represent a recovery of basis or an expenditure of money as if they were tax-exempt income (for example, the dividends-received and U.S. production activities deductions). However, the parent also decreases basis for the deductions themselves, so these two adjustments usually net to zero and thus have no net effect on the parent's basis in the subsidiary.[55]
- Decrease basis for the subsidiary's expenses that are not deductible and are not capital expenditures (e.g., federal income taxes, the nondeductible 50% of meals and entertainment expenses, expenses related to tax-exempt income, and losses disallowed under Sec. 267).
- Decrease basis for distributions received from the subsidiary (without regard to the subsidiary's E&P or whether the E&P accumulated before or after the subsidiary became a member of the consolidated group).
- Decrease basis for the subsidiary's NOLs that arise and are used in the current year against other group members' taxable income. NOLs that carry forward reduce basis in the year used. NOLs that carry back reduce basis in the year they arise. Expiring NOLs reduce basis in the year they expire. However, basis is not decreased when the subsidiary's pre-acquisition NOLs expire unused if the group waives the use of part or all of such losses. Similar rules apply to capital losses.

EXAMPLE C:8-47 ▶ On January 1 of the current year, P Corporation purchases all of S Corporation's stock for $1 million. P and S elect to file a consolidated tax return. During the current year, S reports taxable income of $300,000 and tax-exempt bond interest of $25,000, and S pays P a $40,000 dividend. On January 1 of the next year, P sells the S stock for $1.2 million. Assume that the portion of the consolidated tax liability allocable to S is $102,000 ($300,000 × 0.34) and that S pays it. P's basis in its S stock on the sale date is $1,183,000 ($1,000,000 + $300,000 + $25,000 − $102,000 − $40,000). Thus, P realizes a $17,000 gain on the stock sale ($1,200,000 − $1,183,000).[56] ◀

ADDITIONAL COMMENT

Determining the federal income tax allocable to each group member often is more complex than in Example C:8-47 because members' losses, credits, and other items affect the consolidated tax liability. The regulations specify methods for allocating the tax liability among a group's members, but the details are beyond the scope of this textbook.

TIERING UP OF STOCK BASIS ADJUSTMENTS

In adjusting the basis of its first-tier subsidiary's stock, the parent corporation also takes into account the adjustments the first-tier subsidiary makes to its basis in second-tier subsidiary stock. The adjustments are applied in order of the tiers, from the lowest to the highest.

EXAMPLE C:8-48 ▶ P Corporation owns all of S Corporation's stock, and S owns all of T Corporation's stock. The three corporations have filed on a consolidated basis for several years. At the beginning of the current year, P's basis in its S stock was $800,000, and S's basis in its T stock was $500,000. During the current year, S reports $100,000 of taxable income, and T reports $50,000 of taxable

[54] Reg. Sec. 1.1502-32. If the parent owns less than 100% of the subsidiary's stock, it adjusts the stock basis by its ownership percentage multiplied by the various adjustment items.

[55] Reg. Sec. 1502-32(b)(3)(ii)(B).

[56] Separate basis calculations are required for regular tax and AMT purposes. The AMT basis calculations parallel those made for regular tax purposes but use the appropriate numbers from the AMT calculation. Because the stock basis adjustments for regular tax and AMT purposes may differ (e.g., different amounts of expenses), the sale of subsidiary stock may result in different gain or loss amounts for the two purposes.

income. Assume that the portions of the consolidated tax liability allocable to S and T are \$34,000 (\$100,000 × 0.34) and \$17,000 (\$50,000 × 0.34), respectively, and that each pays its allocable portion. S increases the basis in its T stock to \$533,000 (\$500,000 + \$50,000 − \$17,000). P increases the basis in its S stock to \$899,000 (\$800,000 + \$100,000 − \$34,000 + \$50,000 − \$17,000), reflecting adjustments for both tiers below P. ◀

EXCESS LOSS ACCOUNT

If the negative basis adjustments (e.g., for losses and distributions) are sufficiently large, the parent reduces its basis in the subsidiary stock to zero. Additional negative basis adjustments create or increase an excess loss account. Creation of or change in the balance of an excess loss account does not trigger recognition of income or gain. Instead, it is treated as negative basis. Subsequent profits or other positive basis adjustments first reduce or eliminate the excess loss account before producing a positive basis in the subsidiary stock. A corporation disposing of a subsidiary's stock recognizes its excess loss account in the disposed shares as income or gain from the disposition.[57]

EXAMPLE C:8-49 ▶ P Corporation owns all of S Corporation's stock, and the two corporations have filed on a consolidated basis for several years. P's basis in its S stock was \$900,000 at the beginning of the current year. During the current year, S incurs a \$950,000 NOL, which offsets part of P's \$2.5 million of taxable income. On January 1 of the next year, P sells its S stock for \$80,000. P first reduces its basis in the S stock to zero, and the remaining \$50,000 (\$950,000 − \$900,000) of the negative adjustment creates an excess loss account. When P sells the S stock, it recognizes a \$130,000 gain (\$80,000 amount realized − \$0 basis + \$50,000 excess loss account). ◀

TAX PLANNING CONSIDERATIONS

OBJECTIVE 8

Compare the advantages and disadvantages of filing a consolidated tax return

Filing a consolidated tax return has several advantages and disadvantages as discussed below. Thus, the decision whether or not to file a consolidated tax return is one of an affiliated group's tax planning considerations.

ADVANTAGES OF FILING A CONSOLIDATED TAX RETURN

- The consolidated group can offset one member's operating losses against another member's operating profits. This offset usually is beneficial because it allows the losses to immediately reduce taxes. If the group members filed separate returns, the losses carry back or forward as an NOL. However, discounting decreases the present value of the tax savings from an NOL that carries forward.
- The group can offset one member's net capital loss against another member's net capital gain. Again, this offset allows the net loss to immediately reduce taxes, and it reduces the chance that the losses will expire unused.
- The group computes various credit and deduction limitations on a consolidated basis (e.g., charitable contributions). If the group members filed separate tax returns, some members' credits or deductions might be only partially used due to the limitations, while other members' credits or deductions fall short of the limitations. By filing a consolidated tax return, group members with "excess" credits or deductions can take advantage of other members' "excess" limitations.
- In the consolidated tax return, the group eliminates dividends paid from one group member to another group member. However, the recipient member would be eligible for a 100% dividends-received deduction if they filed separate tax returns.
- The group defers gains and profits on intercompany transactions, which reduces the present value of the taxes on these items (assuming tax rates do not increase).

[57] Reg. Sec. 1.1502-19.

- The parent corporation (and upper tier corporations) increase their bases in subsidiary (and lower tier corporation) stock investments for the subsidiary's (and lower tier corporations') taxable income, much like pass-through entities, thereby eliminating multiple taxation at the higher tier levels.
- The group calculates its alternative minimum tax (AMT) on a consolidated basis. If the group members filed separate tax returns, some group members might incur an AMT because they have large amounts of AMT preference and adjustment items, while other group members have no AMT because they have relatively few preference and adjustment items. If the group files a consolidated tax return, members with "excess" tentative minimum taxes can use them to take advantage of other members' "excess" regular taxes.

DISADVANTAGES OF FILING A CONSOLIDATED TAX RETURN

- The group must continue to file consolidated tax returns for all subsequent tax years until the affiliated group terminates or the IRS grants permission for the group to discontinue filing on a consolidated basis. By filing a consolidated tax return, the group forfeits the flexibility to choose between filing on a separate or consolidated basis in future years.
- Offsetting one member's losses against other members' profits or gains reduces the limitations on various deductions and credits (e.g., charitable contributions), which may reduce the amounts of such items currently allowed on a consolidated basis compared to those allowed on a separate return basis.
- All group members must use the same taxable year.
- The group defers losses and deductions on intercompany transactions, which reduces the present value of the tax savings on these items (assuming tax rates do not increase).
- The group may incur additional administrative costs to maintain the records necessary to account for intercompany transactions and the special loss limitations although it may realize some savings by filing a single tax return.

No general rule can be applied to determine whether an affiliated group should elect to file a consolidated tax return. Each group should examine the long- and short-term advantages and disadvantages of filing a consolidated tax return instead of separate tax returns before making this decision.

COMPLIANCE AND PROCEDURAL CONSIDERATIONS

OBJECTIVE 9

Comply with the procedures for making a consolidated return election

THE BASIC ELECTION AND RETURN

As discussed earlier in this chapter, an affiliated group elects to file its tax return on a consolidated basis by filing a corporate tax return (Form 1120) that includes the income, expenses, etc. of all its members. The group must make the election no later than the due date for the common parent's tax return including any permitted extensions.[58] Each corporation that is a member of the affiliated group during the initial consolidated return year must consent to the election. The parent corporation consents by joining in the consolidated tax return. Each subsidiary corporation consents to the election by filing Form 1122 (Authorization and Consent of Subsidiary Corporation to Be Included in a Consolidated Income Tax Return) as part of the initial consolidated tax return. Only newly acquired subsidiary corporations file Form 1122 with subsequent consolidated tax returns.

Each year's consolidated tax return also must include Form 851 (Affiliations Schedule). This form includes names, addresses, and identification numbers of the

[58] Reg. Sec. 1.1502-75(a)(1).

corporations in the consolidated group; the corporations' tax prepayments; the ownership of their stock at the beginning of the tax year; and all stock ownership changes occurring during the tax year. Treasury Regulations require the group to file supporting statements with its consolidated tax return. These statements show in columnar form a reconciliation of the members' taxable incomes with consolidated taxable income, and they also show the details of each member's gross income and deductions so the IRS can readily audit them.[59] An example of such a reconciliation appears in the consolidated tax return included in Appendix B.

ADDITIONAL COMMENT

If a corporation or consolidated group has a June 30 year end, the filing deadline is the fifteenth day of the third month after the end of its taxable year (i.e., September 15) until tax years beginning after 2025. For corporations and consolidated groups with taxable years ending on June 30, the extension for filing the tax return is seven months, until 2026.

For tax years beginning after 2015, the due date for a consolidated tax return is the fifteenth day of the fourth month after the end of the consolidated group's tax year. The group can obtain a six-month extension for filing the tax return if the parent corporation files Form 7004 (Application for Automatic Extension of Time To File Certain Business Income Tax, Information, and Other Returns). The IRS will not assess a late payment penalty if the group pays at least 90% of its total tax liability by the unextended due date and pays the balance by the extended due date. Special rules apply for corporations having a June 30 year end. See the adjoining Additional Comment for details. If a subsidiary corporation enters or departs the consolidated group, the due date for its separate tax return for the part of the year it was not affiliated with the group depends on the date the group files its consolidated tax return.[60]

Appendix B presents a sample Form 1120 for reporting the current year's results for the Alpha affiliated group described in Example C:8-50. The Form 1120 involves the three intercompany transactions mentioned in the example, and a worksheet that summarizes the income and expense items for the five corporations illustrates the reporting of the intercompany transactions and presents the details of the consolidated taxable income calculation.

EXAMPLE C:8-50 ▶

Alpha Manufacturing Corporation owns 100% of Beta, Charlie, Delta, and Echo Corporations' stock. The affiliated group has filed consolidated tax returns for several years using the calendar year as its tax year. The five corporations' separate taxable income components are reported on the supporting schedule of the group's consolidated tax return contained in Appendix B. This return illustrates the following three common transactions involving members of a consolidated group:

- ▶ The sale of inventory from Alpha to Beta, the profit from which is deferred for consolidated taxable income. Beta sells additional inventory to outsiders.
- ▶ Intragroup dividends paid from Beta and Echo to Alpha
- ▶ Payment of interest from Delta to Alpha ◀

ADDITIONAL COMMENT

If an affiliated group is considering making a consolidated return election, a properly executed Form 1122 should be obtained before any corporation is sold during the election year. After the sale, the consent form may be difficult to obtain.

ADDITIONAL COMMENT

The treatment for state income tax purposes of corporations affiliated for federal income tax purposes varies. Many states allow such corporations to file on a separate or consolidated basis, but several other states require combined unitary reporting, which is somewhat similar to consolidated reporting. The corporations comprising a consolidated or unitary reporting group for state income tax purposes often differs from those comprising an affiliated group for federal income tax purposes (e.g., 50% rather than 80% minimum ownership).

Students should review this sample return to see how the group reports the transactions and how it transfers the numbers from the consolidated taxable income schedule to the consolidated group's Form 1120. Although not displayed in Appendix B, the consolidated return should include a Schedule M-3 if applicable (see Chapter C:3).

PARENT CORPORATION AS AGENT FOR THE CONSOLIDATED GROUP

A consolidated group's parent corporation generally acts as the sole agent for all matters relating to the group's consolidated tax liability.[61] This agency role means that a subsidiary corporation cannot act in its own behalf with respect to a consolidated return year except to the extent that Treasury Regulations prohibit the parent from acting in the subsidiary's behalf. For example, the parent, not the subsidiary, makes or changes any election used in computing the subsidiary's separate taxable income, corresponds with the IRS regarding a tax liability determination, files any requests for extensions of time in which to file a tax return, files a claim for a refund or credit relating to a consolidated return year, or elects to deduct or credit foreign tax payments.

---

[59] Reg. Sec. 1.1502-75(j).

[60] Reg. Sec. 1.1502-76(c). The details of these rules are beyond the scope of this text.

[61] Reg. Sec. 1.1502-77(a).

SEPARATE ENTITY TREATMENT OF INTERCOMPANY TRANSACTIONS

The consolidated group's common parent can request consent from the IRS to treat the group's intercompany transactions on a separate entity basis, where the transactions are treated as if the group members involved were not members of the same consolidated group. When deciding whether to grant such consent, the IRS considers whether such treatment reduces the group's tax compliance burden and whether it has more than a 5% effect on the group's consolidated taxable income or consolidated tax liability. The group can make the request for all its intercompany transactions (other than those involving group members' stock or obligations) or only one or more classes of intercompany transactions. The group applies such separate entity treatment for the consolidated return year for which the IRS grants consent and subsequent tax years. The group's common parent can revoke such separate entity treatment if the IRS consents to it, and the IRS can revoke the group's use of such treatment.[62]

TAX STRATEGY TIP

Because of the several liability rule, the purchaser of a consolidated group's subsidiary should consider obtaining an agreement under which the purchaser will be reimbursed for any additional taxes, interest, and penalties the IRS assesses the subsidiary that are attributable to other group members.

LIABILITY FOR TAXES DUE

The parent corporation and every other corporation that was a group member for any part of the consolidated return year are liable for that year's consolidated tax liability.[63] Thus, the IRS may collect the entire consolidated tax liability from one group member if the other group members are unable to pay their allocable portion of the tax. The IRS can ignore any agreements among the group members to limit their share of the tax liability. A corporation that is a member of a consolidated group for even a few days during a tax year can be liable for the entire year's consolidated tax liability and related deficiencies.

An exception to this several liability rule occurs when a subsidiary corporation departs the consolidated group because its stock is sold or exchanged before the IRS assesses a deficiency against the group. The IRS can opt to assess a former subsidiary for only its allocable portion of the total deficiency if the IRS believes that the assessment and collection of the balance of the deficiency from the other group members will not be jeopardized.

FINANCIAL STATEMENT IMPLICATIONS

OBJECTIVE 10

Explain the financial statement implications of various consolidated transactions

INTERCOMPANY TRANSACTIONS

Intercompany transactions can raise deferred tax issues depending on the type of transaction and whether the affiliated group files consolidated tax returns or separate tax returns. The following discussion assumes a 100%-owned domestic subsidiary to avoid the complications of accounting for noncontrolling interests and for foreign subsidiaries. It also addresses just two types of intercompany transactions: (1) distributed and undistributed subsidiary profits and (2) intercompany sales of property.

For a parent with a 100%-owned domestic subsidiary, intercompany dividends and undistributed subsidiary earnings cause no temporary differences. If the group files a consolidated tax return, the intercompany dividend is eliminated for both tax and consolidated financial statement purposes. If the group files separate tax returns, the parent takes a 100% dividends-received deduction because it owns at least 80% of the subsidiary's stock. Therefore, in either case, no book-tax difference occurs that would create a temporary difference. Undistributed subsidiary earnings are included in consolidated financial statements, but a parent filing a separate tax return would not include these earnings in its income until the subsidiary distributes them as dividends. However, when ultimately distributed, the parent can take the 100% dividends-received deduction, thereby offsetting the dividend income. Consequently, undistributed subsidiary earnings also present no deferred tax issues (within the assumed parameters of this discussion).

[62] Reg. Sec. 1.1502-13(e)(3) and Rev. Proc. 2009-31, 2009-27 I.R.B. 107.

[63] Reg. Sec. 1.1502-6(a).

ADDITIONAL COMMENT

Although a consolidated group defers income or loss on intercompany sales for both tax and financial statement purposes, the amount of income or loss deferred may differ.

ADDITIONAL COMMENT

The prohibition on recognizing a deferred tax asset applies only to intra-entity inventory transfers. See the text after Example C:8-51 for a discussion of non-inventory assets.

Intercompany sales, however, do raise deferred tax issues in certain cases. If the group files a consolidated tax return, the group defers income or loss on intercompany sales of inventory and other property for both tax and consolidated financial statement purposes. Thus, temporary differences and deferred tax issues do not arise. On the other hand, if the group members each file a separate tax return, the selling member recognizes income or loss for tax purposes but not for consolidated financial statement purposes, thereby creating a temporary difference. Accounting Standards Codification (ASC) 810 requires the group to defer recognizing income taxes on intercompany profits on assets remaining within the group,[64] but ASC 740 prohibits "recognition of a deferred tax asset for the difference between the tax basis of inventory in the buyer's tax jurisdiction and the carrying value as reported in the consolidated financial statements as a result of an intra-entity transfer of inventory from one tax-paying component to another tax-paying component of the same consolidated group."[65] Thus, even though the buyer's tax basis (the intercompany purchase price) may exceed the financial statement basis (e.g., the original cost), the group does not recognize a deferred tax asset. Instead, the group recognizes a prepaid asset for the seller's tax on the intercompany profit.

EXAMPLE C:8-51 ▶ P Corporation forms S Corporation on January 2 of the current year as a 100%-owned subsidiary. P and S have no temporary or permanent differences aside from those that might arise on intercompany transactions. For the current year, P and S report the following transactions:

	P Corp.	*S Corp.*
Net income before intercompany transactions and income taxes	$900,000	$360,000
Profit on sale of inventory from P to S	150,000	
Profit on partial sale of same inventory from S to third parties		18,000
Dividend from S to P	120,000	

The $150,000 profit to P is the difference between the inventory's $180,000 cost to P and its $330,000 selling price to S. S, in turn, sells 30% of this inventory to third parties for $117,000. This portion of the inventory had a $99,000 ($330,000 × 0.30) tax basis to S, thereby generating the $18,000 profit.

If P and S file a consolidated tax return for the current year, the $120,000 intercompany dividend and the $105,000 ($150,000 × 0.70) profit in the remaining inventory will be eliminated in both the consolidated financial statements and the consolidated tax return, leaving no temporary differences. Thus, consolidated taxable income (as well as net income before federal income taxes) will equal $1,323,000 ($900,000 + $360,000 + ($150,000 − $105,000) + $18,000), and the federal income tax liability will be $449,820 ($1,323,000 × 0.34). Accordingly, the group makes the following book journal entry:

Federal income tax expense	449,820	
Federal income taxes payable		449,820

If instead, P and S file separate tax returns, P will claim a $120,000 dividends-received deduction. P, however, will eliminate the $105,000 inventory profit deferred for consolidated financial statement purposes but not for tax purposes. Thus, P's separate taxable income will be $1,050,000 ($900,000 + $150,000 + $120,000 − $120,000), and S's separate taxable income will be $378,000 ($360,000 + $18,000). The tax liabilities will be $357,000 ($1,050,000 × 0.34) for P and $128,520 ($378,000 × 0.34) for S, resulting in a total of $485,520. At the same time, the group's consolidated net income before federal income taxes remains at $1,323,000, which is $105,000 ($1,050,000 + $378,000 − $1,323,000) less than the group's total taxable income. The group records as prepaid taxes the $35,700 ($105,000 × 0.34) tax that P pays on the eliminated intercompany inventory profit, so the group's federal income tax expense is $449,820 ($485,520 − $35,700). This $449,820 also equals 34% of the group's $1,323,000 consolidated net income before federal income taxes. Accordingly, the group makes the following book journal entry:

Federal income tax expense	449,820	
Prepaid taxes	35,700	
Federal income taxes payable		485,520

[64] Accounting Standards Codification (ASC) 810-10-45-8.

[65] Accounting Standards Codification (ASC) 740-10-25-3 and 740-10-25-20.

Next year, P and S earn the same income before intercompany transactions ($900,000 and $360,000, respectively) and file separate tax returns. However, they have no intercompany transactions next year, and S sells the remaining inventory to third parties for a $42,000 profit. Thus, P's taxable income is $900,000, and S's taxable income is $402,000 ($360,000 + $42,000). In addition, P's tax liability is $306,000 ($900,000 × 0.34), and S's tax liability is $136,680 ($402,000 × 0.34), for a total of $442,680. At the same time, the group's consolidated net income after recognizing the $105,000 deferred profit but before federal income taxes is $1,407,000 ($900,000 + $402,000 + $105,000). The group now charges to federal income tax expense the $35,700 it previously recorded as prepaid taxes in the year the intercompany sale occurred, so the group's federal income tax expense is $478,380 ($442,680 + $35,700). This $478,380 also equals 34% of the group's $1,407,000 consolidated net income before federal income taxes. Accordingly, the group makes the following book journal entry:

Federal income tax expense	478,380	
Prepaid taxes		35,700
Federal income taxes payable		442,680

◀

The financial accounting treatment discussed above applies to intercompany sales of *inventory*, but a recent change in GAAP makes this treatment inapplicable to intercompany sales of other property.[66] For such a transaction, the group recognizes current and deferred income taxes on the sale's intercompany profit or loss, even though the group defers recognizing the profit or loss for consolidated financial statement purposes.

EXAMPLE C:8-52 ▶ Assume the same facts as in Example C:8-51, except the property is marketable securities. Because the property is not inventory, the group recognizes current and deferred income taxes on the intercompany profit. If P and S file separate tax returns, the federal income taxes payable for the current and next years are $485,520 and $442,680, respectively, for the same reasons as in Example C:8-51. S's $231,000 ($330,000 × 0.70) adjusted basis exceeds its $126,000 ($180,000 × 0.70) book value, so the group debits deferred tax assets rather than prepaid taxes for $35,700 (($231,000 − $126,000) × 0.34). Similarly, the group credits deferred tax assets rather than prepaid taxes for $35,700 for the next year. Federal income tax expense is $449,820 and $478,380 for current and next years, respectively.[67]

SRLY LOSSES

A net operating loss (NOL) from a separate return limitation year (SRLY) will create a deferred tax asset, possibly subject to a valuation allowance.

EXAMPLE C:8-53 ▶ Parent Corporation acquires 100% of Subsidiary Corporation at the beginning of the current year, when Subsidiary has a $200,000 NOL. Parent and Subsidiary elect to file a consolidated tax return for the current year. Assuming Parent's acquisition of Subsidiary is not a Sec. 382 ownership change, the SRLY limitation restricts the Parent-Subsidiary group's use of Subsidiary's NOL. Accordingly, management estimates that the group will be able to use only $150,000 of the NOL before it expires. The group's tax rate is 34%. The deferred tax asset is $68,000 ($200,000 × 0.34), and the valuation allowance is $17,000 ($50,000 × 0.34).

If Parent's acquisition of Subsidiary qualifies as a Sec. 382 ownership change, the SRLY limitation does not apply because of the overlap rule. However, the Sec. 382 limitation applies to restrict the group's use of Subsidiary's NOL. Assuming management estimates that the group will be able to use only $140,000 of the NOL before it expires, the deferred tax asset is $68,000 ($200,000 × 0.34), and the valuation allowance is $20,400 ($60,000 × 0.34).

If Parent and Subsidiary file separate tax returns, Subsidiary's use of its own NOL is restricted. If Parent's acquisition of Subsidiary does not qualify as a Sec. 382 ownership change, Subsidiary can use the $200,000 NOL only to offset the taxable income on its separate tax return, which restricts Subsidiary's use of its own NOL in much the same was as the SRLY limitation restricts it on a consolidated tax return. If the acquisition qualifies as a Sec. 382 ownership change, Subsidiary's use of its own NOL is limited to the same Sec. 382 limitation that applies had the corporations file a consolidated tax return. ◀

See Chapter C:3 for a general discussion of financial implications of federal income taxes.

[66] Accounting Standards Update 2016-16. This change generally is applicable to annual reporting periods beginning after December 15, 2017, but earlier adoption is allowed.

[67] Federal income tax expense is the same in Examples C:8-51 and C:8-52 because P and S are in the same taxing jurisdiction, i.e., federal government. If P and S were in different taxing jurisdictions, e.g., different countries, income tax expense could differ when the intercompany transaction involves inventory versus other property.

PROBLEM MATERIALS

DISCUSSION QUESTIONS

C:8-1 What minimum level of stock ownership does the IRC require for a corporation to be included in an affiliated group?

C:8-2 Which of the following entities are includible in an affiliated group (if the 80% stock ownership requirements are met)?
a. Domestic C corporation.
b. Foreign corporation.
c. Life insurance company taxed under Sec. 801.
d. Limited liability company.

C:8-3 Pamela (an individual) owns 100% of P Corporation's stock and 100% of R Corporation's stock. P owns 100% of S Corporation's stock and 49% of T Corporation's stock. S owns the remaining 51% of T's stock. All the corporations are includible corporations and have only one class of stock.
a. Which entities comprise an affiliated group?
b. Which entities comprise a controlled group?
c. How would your answer to Part a change if S were instead a foreign corporation?

C:8-4 P Corporation purchases all of S Corporation's stock in the current year. Both corporations are includible corporations. S is P's only subsidiary. Explain their federal income tax return filing alternatives.

C:8-5 How do the stock ownership requirements for an affiliated group of corporations differ from those for a controlled group?

C:8-6 P Corporation owns 100% of the stock of S1 and S2 Corporations. S1 owns 51% of S3 Corporation's stock, and unrelated persons own the remaining 49%. S2 is a foreign corporation. Explain why the corporations included in a consolidated tax return can differ from the corporations included in a set of consolidated financial statements.

C:8-7 Explain why the consolidated return Treasury Regulations are legislative regulations.

C:8-8 P Corporation has owned all the stock of S and T Corporations for several years. P sells all of T's stock to Z Corporation during the current year.
a. Does P's sale of T's stock cause the affiliated group to cease to exist?
b. Is T required to file a consolidated tax return with Z?
c. If P purchases all of T's stock from Z three years after it sells T's stock to Z, is T required to file a consolidated tax return with P and S?
d. How would your answers change if P did not own any of S's stock?

C:8-9 P Corporation owns all the stock of S and T Corporations, and the three corporations elected to file a consolidated tax return for the prior year. What circumstances would allow the corporations to file separate tax returns for the current year?

C:8-10 Define the following terms:
a. Intercompany transaction.
b. Intercompany item.
c. Corresponding item.
d. Recomputed corresponding item.
e. Matching rule.
f. Acceleration rule.

C:8-11 P and S1 Corporations have filed consolidated tax returns for several years. S1 acquires all of S2 Corporation's stock at the close of business on June 15 of the current year. Which of the following current year transactions are intercompany transactions?
a. S1 sells machinery (Sec. 1245 property) to S2 on September 1.
b. P sells inventory to S1 throughout the year.
c. S2 performs services for S1 throughout the year.
d. P sells inventory to the S1-S2 Partnership on July 23. S1 and S2 are equal partners in the partnership.

C:8-12 P, S1, and S2 Corporations comprise a consolidated group. The group members use the accrual method of accounting. For each of the following intercompany transactions that occur during the current year, determine the intercompany item and corresponding item.
a. P lends S1 money, and P charges interest at a 10% annual rate. The money and interest remain unpaid at the end of the tax year.
b. S1 sells inventory to P. At year end, P holds the entire inventory purchased from S1.
c. P sells land (Sec. 1231 property) to S2. S2 holds the land (Sec. 1231 property) at year-end.
d. S1 provides engineering services that are capitalized as part of the cost of S2's new factory building.

C:8-13 One consolidated group member lends money to another member of its group. Both corporations use the accrual method of accounting. Explain how the lending group member reports its interest income and how the borrowing group member reports its interest expense for consolidated tax return purposes. Discuss how this treatment compares to the consolidated financial accounting treatment of the transaction.

C:8-14 Brooklyn and Bronx Corporations become an affiliated group at the beginning of the current year. Will the corporations obtain a greater charitable contribution deduction for the current year by filing a consolidated tax return or separate tax returns?

C:8-15 An affiliated group elects to file a consolidated tax return. Explain why the group's consolidated capital gain net income or net capital loss is not merely the sum of the members' separate capital gain net incomes and net capital losses if they were to file separate tax returns.

C:8-16 Indicate the tax treatment for each of the following dividends received by a corporation that is a member of an affiliated group filing a consolidated tax return:

a. Dividend received from a corporation that is 5%-owned by the group member.
b. Dividend received from a corporation that is 100%-owned by the group member.
c. Dividend received from a foreign corporation that is 80%-owned by the group's parent corporation.
d. Dividend received from a life insurance company that is 100%-owned by the group's parent corporation.
e. Dividend received from a corporation that is 50%-owned by the group member and 50%-owned by the group's parent corporation.

C:8-17 P, S, and T Corporations comprise a consolidated group. In the current year, P has a profit, while S and T both incur a loss. The net of P's profit with S's and T's losses result in a consolidated NOL. In what years can P, S, and/or T deduct the consolidated NOL?

C:8-18 An affiliated group has a consolidated NOL for the current year. What factors could determine whether it would be advantageous or disadvantageous for the group to elect to forgo the carryback of the consolidated NOL?

C:8-19 Define the term SRLY and explain its significance and application to a consolidated tax return.

C:8-20 What is the SRLY-Sec. 382 overlap rule? Explain its significance and application to a consolidated tax return.

C:8-21 P Corporation owns 100% of S Corporation's stock, and the corporations file a consolidated tax return.

a. Explain why P must increase the basis in its S stock by S's taxable income and decrease the basis by the dividends S pays to P.
b. Suppose S owns 100% of T Corporation's stock. Explain the basis adjustments that P and S must make.

C:8-22 P Corporation owns 100% of the stock of S1 and S2 Corporations. The corporations currently are filing separate tax returns. P and S1 are profitable. S2 is a start-up company that has reported losses for its first two years of operations. S1 eventually will be purchasing cosmetics from S2 and reselling them to retailers. What are the advantages and disadvantages of the three corporations filing a consolidated tax return?

C:8-23 The president of your CPA firm's largest client, a medium-size manufacturing company, advises you that the firm is about to acquire its largest supplier. Both companies have been profitable for the past ten years. The president wants to know what tax return filing options are available for the two companies and the advantages and disadvantages of the options. What factors are likely to be most important for this decision? What additional information do you need to give the president an informed answer?

C:8-24 During what time period can an affiliated group elect to file a consolidated tax return? How does it make the election? During what time period can it request to terminate its consolidation?

C:8-25 For which of the following tax-related matters can an affiliated group's parent corporation act as the group's agent?

a. Consent by a subsidiary corporation to the filing of a consolidated tax return.
b. Changing a subsidiary corporation's accounting method.
c. Corresponding with the IRS during its audit regarding a subsidiary corporation's transaction that affects the group's consolidated taxable income.
d. Requesting an extension of time to file a consolidated tax return.

ISSUE IDENTIFICATION QUESTIONS

C:8-26 Mark owns all the stock of Red and Green Corporations. In each of the past five years, Red has reported approximately $125,000 of taxable income, and Green has reported NOLs of about $30,000. One-third of Red's profits come from sales to Green, and their intercompany sales have been increasing in recent years. What tax issues should Mark consider with respect to Red and Green?

C:8-27 Alpha and Baker Corporations, accrual method of accounting corporations that use the calendar year as their tax year, have filed consolidated tax returns for several years. Baker, a 100%-owned subsidiary of Alpha, transfers a patent, equipment, and working capital to newly created Charter Corporation in exchange for 100% of its stock. In the current year, Charter will begin to produce parts for the automotive industry. Charter incurs organizational expenditures of $12,000 and start-up expenditures of $60,000. What tax issues should Charter consider with respect to the selection of its overall accounting method, inventory method, and tax year, deducting its organizational and start-up expenditures, and the type of income tax return to file?

C:8-28 Wildcat Corporation is the parent company of a three-member affiliated group. Wildcat and Badger Corporations have filed consolidated tax returns for several years. Early in the current year, Wildcat purchases Hawkeye Corporation, a start-up business that incurred net operating losses in each of its first three years prior to the purchase. Hawkeye's losses total $260,000. Can the Wildcat-Badger-Hawkeye group deduct the losses on its consolidated tax return? The group expects annual profits to be $300,000, with Hawkeye's contribution to the total being $50,000. What tax issues should the three corporations consider when determining how they can deduct the NOLs?

PROBLEMS

C:8-29 *Affiliated Group Definition.* In each of the following cases, determine the corporations that comprise an affiliated group. All corporations are includible corporations and have one class of stock.

a. B Corporation owns 100% of C Corporation's stock and 90% of D Corporation's stock. Unrelated persons own 10% of D's stock.
b. B Corporation owns 100% of C Corporation's stock and 90% of D Corporation's stock. C owns 80% of E Corporation's stock, and D owns 75% of F Corporation's stock. Unrelated persons own the remainder of D's, E's, and F's stock.
c. B Corporation owns 80% of C Corporation's stock and 40% of D Corporation's stock. C owns 41% of D's stock. Unrelated individuals own the remainder of C's and D's stock.
d. Luciano, an individual, owns all the stock of M and N Corporations.
e. Viviana, an individual, owns all the stock of W and X Corporations. W owns all of Y Corporation's stock, and X owns all of Z Corporation's stock.

C:8-30 *Affiliated Group Definition* In each of the following cases, determine the corporations that comprise an affiliated group. All corporations are includible corporations and have one class of stock unless otherwise indicated.

a. P Corporation owns all the stock of S and T Corporations. T owns all of U Corporation's stock. T and U are Belgian corporations.
b. Assume the same facts as in Part a except U is a domestic corporation.
c. Omar, an individual, owns 100% of P Corporation's stock and 30% of S Corporation's stock. P owns 70% of S's stock.
d. G is a German corporation. G owns all of P Corporation's stock. P owns all of S Corporation's stock.
e. P Corporation owns all of S Corporation's stock. P and S each own 50% of T, a domestic limited liability company.

C:8-31 *Stock Ownership Requirement.* Pierre Corporation's management is negotiating with Salem Corporation's management to purchase some of Salem's stock. Salem's outstanding shares are as follows:

Type of Stock	*Votes per Share*	*Shares Outstanding*	*FMV per Share*
Common stock	4	60,000	$40
Preferred stock	1	10,000	75

Pierre's management wants to acquire enough Salem stock to allow Pierre and Salem to file a consolidated tax return. Pierre and Salem are includible corporations.

a. If Pierre acquires all of Salem's common stock and none of Salem's preferred stock, will they be eligible to file a consolidated tax return?
b. What minimum amount of Salem's common stock and/or preferred stock must Pierre acquire for the two corporations to be eligible to file a consolidated tax return?
c. Suppose that Salem also has 10,000 shares of nonvoting preferred stock outstanding. Each share's FMV is $90. The stock is nonparticipating, has redemption and liquidation rights limited to its issue price, and is not convertible. If Pierre acquires all of Salem's common and voting preferred stock, what minimum amount of Salem nonvoting preferred stock must Pierre acquire for the two corporations to be eligible to file a consolidated tax return?

C:8-32 *Affiliated Group Termination.* P Corporation owns all of S Corporation's stock. P and S have filed consolidated tax returns for several years. Determine whether the affiliated group terminates in each of the following circumstances. Assume that all corporations use the calendar year as their tax year.

a. On February 1 of the current year, P purchases all of T Corporation's stock.
b. On March 1 of the current year, P purchases all of T Corporation's stock. On October 1 of the current year, P sells all of S's stock.
c. On April 1 of the current year, P sells all of S's stock. On September 1 of the current year, P purchases all of T Corporation's stock.
d. On May 1 of the current year, P sells all of S's stock. On January 1 of the next year, P purchases all of T Corporation's stock.
e. On June 1, R Corporation purchases all of P's stock. R had no subsidiaries prior to June 1.
f. On July 1, R Corporation purchases all of P's stock. On July 1, R has several wholly owned subsidiaries with which it has filed consolidated tax returns for several years.

C:8-33 *Consolidated Taxable Income.* Assume the same facts as in Problem C:8-32. What tax returns must the corporations file for the current year?

C:8-34 *Consolidated Taxable Income.* P Corporation owns all the stock of S1 and S2 Corporations. The corporations have filed calendar year, consolidated tax returns for several years. On September 15 of the current year, P sells all of S1's stock to Michelle, an unrelated individual. What effect does P's sale of S1's stock have on the P-S1-S2 group's current year consolidated taxable income?

C:8-35 *Consolidated Return Election.* P Corporation uses the calendar year as its tax year and the accrual method as its overall accounting method. S Corporation uses a fiscal year ending June 30 as its tax year and the cash method as its overall accounting method. On July 31, 2018, P acquires all of S's stock, and the P-S affiliated group elects to file a consolidated tax return for 2018.

a. What tax year must the group use in filing its consolidated tax return?
b. What overall accounting method(s) can P and S Corporations use?
c. What tax returns must the corporations file?

C:8-36 *Consolidated Taxable Income.* P Corporation acquires all the stock of S Corporation on October 15 of the current year, which is the 288th day of the year (and not a leap year). Neither corporation is affiliated with another corporation prior to the acquisition. P and S use the accrual method of accounting, and each uses the calendar year as its taxable year. P's and S's income for the current year, which includes no extraordinary items, are \$876,000 and \$292,000, respectively. For each of the following circumstances, what tax returns must the corporations file for the current year, and what amount of income must each of those returns include?

a. P and S elect to file a consolidated tax return and also elect to ratably allocate the entering subsidiary's income.
b. P and S do not elect to file a consolidated tax return.

C:8-37 *Intercompany Transactions.* P, S1, and S2 Corporations have filed consolidated tax returns for several years. In the current year (Year 1), S1 sells land to S2 for \$275,000. S1 purchased the land for \$120,000 several years ago and has held it for possible expansion. S2 constructs a new plant facility on the land. In Year 3, S2 sells the land and the plant facility to a third party for cash, with \$400,000 of the sales price attributable to the land.

a. What are the intercompany item, the corresponding item, and the recomputed corresponding item for this intercompany transaction?
b. In what year(s) are S1's gain or loss and S2's gain or loss included in consolidated taxable income?

C:8-38 *Intercompany Transactions.* P Corporation owns all the stock of S and B Corporations. The three corporations have filed consolidated tax returns on a calendar year basis for several years. S owns property it had purchased for \$40,000 several years ago. On August 1 of Year 1, S sells the property to B for \$55,000. On February 1 of Year 3, B sells the property to an unrelated third party for \$60,000.

a. What are the intercompany item, the corresponding item, and the recomputed corresponding item for this intercompany transaction?
b. In what year(s) are S's and B's gains or losses included in consolidated taxable income?

c. Suppose B sells the property to the third party for $53,000 instead of $60,000. How would your answers to Part b change?
d. Suppose P sells all of its B stock to an unrelated third party on October 1 of Year 2. How would your answers to Part b change?

C:8-39 *Intercompany Transactions.* P Corporation owns all the stock of S1 and S2 Corporations, and the three corporations have filed consolidated tax returns on a calendar year basis for several years. P owns 2,400 shares of publicly traded stock it purchased several years ago for $30 per share. P sells all the stock to S1 for $45 per share on January 25 of the current year (Year 1). S1 sells 1,400 shares of the stock to a third party for $48 per share on December 6 of Year 1, and S1 sells the other 1,000 shares to another third party for $52 per share on March 18 of Year 2.
a. What are the intercompany item, the corresponding items, and the recomputed corresponding items for this intercompany transaction?
b. In what year(s) are P's gain or loss and S1's gain or loss included in consolidated taxable income?
c. Suppose P sells all of S1's stock to a third party on December 30 of Year 1. How would your answer to Part b change?
d. Suppose S1 sells the 1,000 shares on March 18 of Year 2, for $44 per share instead of $52 per share. How would your answers to Parts a and b change?

C:8-40 *Intercompany Transactions.* P and S Corporations have filed consolidated tax returns for several years. In Year 1, P purchased land as an investment for $20,000. In Year 3, P sold the land to S for $60,000. S used the land for four years as additional parking space for its employees and made no improvements to the land. In Year 7, S sells the land to Z Corporation, an unrelated party, for $180,000. The sale's terms require Z to pay S $36,000 in each of Years 7 through 11. The terms also require Z to pay S interest at a rate acceptable to the IRS. Z pays all the required amounts.
a. What are the intercompany item, the corresponding items, and the recomputed corresponding items?
b. In what year(s) does the consolidated group include P's gain or loss and S's gain or loss in its taxable income?
c. How does the consolidated group report the interest income?

C:8-41 *Intercompany Transactions.* P owns all the stock of S1 and S2 Corporations. The corporations have filed consolidated tax returns for several years. In the current year (Year 1), S1 sells land to P for $100,000. S1 purchased the land several years earlier for $35,000. P sells the land to an unrelated third party in Year 3 for $115,000. The sale's terms require the third party to pay P $50,000 in Year 3, $40,000 in Year 4, and $25,000 in Year 5, plus interest at a rate acceptable to the IRS. The third party pays all the required amounts.
a. In what year(s) does the consolidated group include S1's gain or loss and P's gain or loss in its taxable income?
b. Suppose P sells all of S1's stock on December 31 of Year 4. How would this sale change your answer to Part a?
c. Suppose S1 sold the land to P in Year 1 for $120,000 instead of $100,000. How would this sale change your answer to Part a?

C:8-42 *Intercompany Transactions.* P Corporation owns all of S Corporation's stock. Both corporations use the accrual method of accounting, and they file a consolidated tax return. S provides cleaning services to P. In so doing, S charges P $6,000 for the services and incurs $5,000 of expenses to provide them. How does this transaction affect the group's consolidated taxable income?

C:8-43 *Intercompany Transactions.* P and S Corporations have filed consolidated tax returns on a calendar year basis for several years. Both corporations use the accrual method of accounting. On August 1 of the current year (Year 1), P loans S $250,000 on a one-year note. P charges interest at a 12% simple rate. S repays the loan plus interest on July 31 of Year 2. How does this intercompany transaction affect the group's consolidated taxable income?

C:8-44 *Intercompany Transactions.* P and S Corporations have filed consolidated tax returns on a calendar year basis for several years. Both corporations use the accrual method of accounting. On January 1 of the current year, S begins renting a warehouse to P for $10,000 per month. P pays S $10,000 on the first day of each month of the current year. How does this transaction affect the group's consolidated taxable income?

C:8-45 *Intercompany Transactions.* S and B corporations are members of an affiliated group that has filed consolidated tax returns for several years. S drills a water well for B in Year

1 and charges B $5,000 for the service. S incurs $4,400 of expenses when drilling the well. B capitalizes the $5,000 cost of its well and amortizes it over the five-year period Years 2 through 6. S and B both use the accrual method of accounting.

a. What are the intercompany item, the corresponding items, and the recomputed corresponding items for this intercompany transaction?
b. In what year(s) are S's profit or loss and B's deductions taken into account for consolidated taxable income?

C:8-46 *Intercompany Transactions.* P and S Corporations have filed consolidated tax returns for several years. In the current year (Year 1), P began selling inventory items to S. P and S use the first-in, first-out (FIFO) inventory method. P's profits on its Year 1 inventory sales to S are $75,000. S's sales to third parties during Year 1 include inventory items that P sells to S during Year 1 for a $40,000 profit; S sells these inventory items to third parties for a $25,000 profit. S's inventory at the end of Year 1 includes items that P sells to S for a $35,000 profit. S is deemed to sell these to third parties during Year 2 due to its use of the FIFO method and realizes a $22,000 profit on their sale. P's profits on its Year 2 inventory sales to S are $240,000. S's sales to third parties during Year 2 include items that P sells to S during Year 2 for a $160,000 profit. S sells these inventory items to third parties for a $105,000 profit. S's inventory at the end of Year 2 includes items that P sells to S for an $80,000 profit. The group's consolidated taxable income (before taking into account any adjustments for profits on intercompany inventory sales) is $100,000 in Year 1 and $367,000 in Year 2. For simplicity, assume P and S have no other transactions in these two years. Also, ignore the U.S. production activities deduction. What is the group's consolidated taxable income for Years 1 and 2?

C:8-47 *Intercompany Transactions.* P and S Corporations have filed consolidated tax returns for several years. The group had no intercompany inventory sales before the current year (Year 1). P and S use the first-in, first-out (FIFO) inventory method. During Year 1, S sells 50,000 widgets to P, earning $8 per unit profit on the sale. Also during Year 1, P sells 37,500 of these widgets to third parties for an additional $6 per unit profit. Thus, P's inventory at the end of Year 1 includes 12,500 of unsold widgets. During Year 2, S sells 80,000 widgets to P, earning $9 per unit profit on the sale. Also during Year 2, P sells to third parties 65,000 of these widgets and also sells the 12,500 widgets from beginning inventory, all for an additional $6 per unit profit. Thus, P's inventory at the end of Year 2 includes 15,000 widgets P purchased from S in Year 2. No intercompany inventory sales occur in Year 3. However, during Year 3, P sells all widgets in beginning inventory for an additional $7 per unit profit. In addition to these intercompany transactions, P incurs a $40,000 loss and S earns $500,000 of profit in each year from other business activities. What is the group's consolidated taxable income for each of Years 1, 2, and 3? Ignore the U.S. production activities deduction.

C:8-48 *Charitable Contribution Deduction.* Topeka and Wichita Corporations have filed consolidated tax returns for several years. Topeka and Wichita report current year taxable incomes (without regard to any dividend income received, charitable contribution deduction, or dividends-received deduction) of $200,000 and $150,000, respectively. The $200,000 includes $30,000 profit on inventory that Topeka sold to Wichita on December 29 of the current year. Wichita sold none of the inventory before the end of the year. Topeka and Wichita received dividends of $10,000 and $4,000, respectively, during the current year that qualify for the 70% dividends-received deduction. Wichita's and Topeka's cash contributions to public charities during the current year are $45,000 and $5,000, respectively. Ignore the U.S. production activities deduction.

a. What is the Topeka-Wichita group's consolidated taxable income?
b. What is the amount of the charitable contribution carryover? How long can it be carried back and/or forward?
c. What is the Topeka-Wichita group's regular tax liability?

C:8-49 *Sec. 1231 Gains and Losses and Capital Gains and Losses.* Mobile, Newark, and Omaha Corporations comprise an affiliated group that has filed separate tax returns prior to the current year. The corporations report the following amounts for the current year:

Transaction	*Mobile*	*Newark*	*Omaha*	*Total*
Sec. 1231 gains	$ 18,000	$ 9,000	$ –0–	$ 27,000
Sec. 1231 losses	12,000	14,000	–0–	26,000
Short-term capital gains	3,500	–0–	–0–	3,500
Short-term capital losses	(2,000)	–0–	(6,200)	(8,200)
Long-term capital gains	–0–	8,100	5,500	13,600
Long-term capital losses	(2,400)	(7,300)	–0–	(9,700)
Other separate taxable income	300,000	200,000	100,000	600,000

The corporations have no intercompany transactions, no capital loss carryovers, and no nonrecaptured net Sec. 1231 losses. Ignore the U.S. production activities deduction.

a. Determine each corporation's current year taxable income if they file separate tax returns for the current year.

b. Determine the group's current year taxable income if the corporations elect to file a consolidated tax return.

C:8-50 *Capital Gains and Losses.* Alpha and Beta Corporations comprise an affiliated group that has filed separate tax returns prior to the current year. The corporations report the following amounts for the current year:

Transaction	*Alpha*	*Beta*	*Total*
Long-term capital gains	$ 20,000	$ 15,000	$ 35,000
Long-term capital losses	(11,900)	(17,000)	(28,900)
Other separate taxable income	80,000	70,000	150,000

Alpha's long-term capital gains include a $4,400 gain on land it sold to Beta during the current year. Beta had not sold the land by the end of the current year. The corporations have no other intercompany transactions and no capital loss carryovers. Ignore the U.S. production activities deduction.

a. Determine each corporation's current year taxable income if they file separate tax returns for the current year.

b. Determine the group's current year taxable income if the corporations elect to file a consolidated tax return.

C:8-51 ***Dividends-Received Deduction.*** P, S, and T Corporations have filed consolidated tax returns for several years. P, S, and T report taxable incomes or losses (without regard to any dividends received and dividends-received deductions) of $200,000, $(70,000), and $175,000, respectively, for the current year. P and S received cash dividends this year as follows:

Shareholder	*Distributing Corporation*	*Amount*
P Corporation	T Corporation	$125,000
P Corporation	100%-owned nonconsolidated U.S.-based life insurance company	15,000
S Corporation	25%-owned domestic corporation	40,000
P Corporation	51%-owned foreign corporation	10,000

a. What amount of dividend income does the group include in its consolidated taxable income?

b. What is the amount of the consolidated dividends-received deduction?

c. What is the amount of consolidated taxable income and consolidated regular tax liability? Ignore the U.S. production activities deduction.

C:8-52 *Regular Tax Liability.* Miami and Tampa Corporations comprise a parent-subsidiary controlled group. The corporations also comprise an affiliated group that has filed separate tax returns prior to the current year. In each case for the current year, determine each corporation's regular tax liability if they file separate tax returns, and determine the group's consolidated regular tax liability if they elect to file a consolidated tax return. Ignore the U.S. production activities deduction. Assume that, if they file separate tax returns, Miami and Tampa do not elect a special apportionment plan for allocating the corporate tax rates. Assume also that, if the group elects to file a consolidated tax return, its consolidated taxable income equals the sum of Miami's and Tampa's separate taxable incomes.

a. Miami's separate taxable income is $50,000, and Tampa's separate taxable income is $30,000.

b. Miami's separate taxable income is $70,000, and Tampa's separate taxable income is $(15,000), i.e., a loss.

c. Miami's separate taxable income is $45,000, and Tampa's separate taxable income is $40,000.

C:8-53 *Alternative Minimum Tax.* Dallas and Houston Corporations comprise an affiliated group that formed at the beginning of the current year. The following items pertain to Dallas and Houston for the current year:

Transaction	*Dallas*	*Houston*	*Total*
Taxable income	$500,000	$400,000	$ 900,000
AMT preference & adjustment items	175,000	210,000	385,000
Adjusted current earnings	740,000	720,000	1,460,000

Determine each corporation's AMT liability if they file separate tax returns, and determine the group's consolidated AMT liability if they elect to file a consolidated tax return. Assume that, if the group elects to file a consolidated tax return, its consolidated taxable income, consolidated AMT preference and adjustment items, and consolidated adjusted current earnings equal the sum of the corporations' separate amounts. Assume also that the corporations do not qualify for the small corporation and first-year exemptions from the AMT. Ignore the U.S. production activities deduction.

C:8-54 *General Business Credit.* Peoria and Salem Corporations have filed consolidated tax returns for several years. For the current year, consolidated adjusted current earnings are $750,000. Consolidated preadjustment alternative minimum taxable income is $400,000. Consolidated taxable income is $300,000. The consolidated general business credit amount (computed without regard to the overall limitation) is $15,000. Assume the Peoria-Salem group is not eligible for the small corporation exemption from the AMT. Ignore the U.S. production activities deduction.

a. What is the group's federal tax liability?

b. Are any credit carryovers created in the current year? How are they used?

C:8-55 *Consolidated NOL Carrybacks and Carryovers.* P and S Corporations form in Year 1, with S as P's wholly-owned subsidiary. The corporations immediately elect to file consolidated tax returns. The group reports the following results:

	Taxable Income				
Group Member	*Year 1*	*Year 2*	*Year 3*	*Year 4*	*Year 5*
P	$9,000	$10,000	$(6,000)	$ 20,000	$15,000
S	(7,800)	2,000	2,000	(30,000)	10,000
Consolidated taxable income (before NOL deduction)	$1,200	$12,000	$(4,000)	$(10,000)	$25,000

The group does not elect to forego any NOL carrybacks. Ignore the U.S. production activities deduction. In what years can the group deduct the Years 3 and 4 consolidated NOLs?

C:8-56 *Consolidated NOL Carryover.* P Corporation owns all the stock of S1 and S2 Corporations. The corporations have filed consolidated tax returns since their creation in Year 1. At the close of business on July 10 of Year 3, P sells all of its S2 stock. The group reports the following results:

	Taxable Income		
Group Member	*Year 1*	*Year 2*	*Year 3*
P	$ 8,000	$(18,000)	$16,000
S1	9,000	(24,000)	(4,000)
S2	10,000	(28,000)	15,000[a]
Consolidated taxable income (before NOL deduction)	$27,000	$(70,000)	$19,000[b]

[a] $7,000 is attributable to January 1 through July 10 of Year 3, and $8,000 is attributable to July 11 through December 31 of Year 3.

[b] $16,000 − $4,000 + $7,000.

Ignore the U.S. production activities deduction.

a. In what year(s) can the corporations deduct the Year 2 consolidated NOL if the group does not elect to forego the carryback period?

b. In what year(s) can the corporations deduct the Year 2 consolidated NOL if the group elects to forego the carryback period?

C:8-57 *Consolidated NOL Carrybacks and Carryovers.* P Corporation owns all the stock of S Corporation, and P and S file a consolidated tax return. On January 1 of Year 2, P creates T Corporation and acquires all of its stock. P, S, and T report the following results for Years 1 through 3 (before any NOL deduction):

		Taxable Income	
Group Member	*Year 1*	*Year 2*	*Year 3*
P	$21,000	$22,000	$23,000
S	11,000	12,000	13,000
T		10,000	(50,000)
Consolidated taxable income	$32,000	$44,000	$(14,000)

The group does not elect to forego any NOL carrybacks. Ignore the U.S. production activities deduction.

a. In what year(s) can the group deduct the Year 3 NOL?

b. Assume the same facts as in Part a except a third party created T in Year 2 and P acquires all of T's stock from the third party on January 1 of Year 3. Thus, Year 2 consolidated taxable income is $34,000 ($22,000 + $12,000). In what year(s) can the group deduct the Year 3 NOL?

c. Assume the same facts as in Part a except the group does not begin filing consolidated tax returns until Year 3. In what year(s) can the group deduct the Year 3 NOL?

C:8-58 *Separate Return and Consolidated NOL Carryovers and Carrybacks.* P Corporation acquires all of S Corporation's stock on January 1 of Year 2. In Year 1, the corporations were unrelated entities that filed separate returns. P and S report the following results:

		Taxable Income	
Group Member	*Year 1*	*Year 2*	*Year 3*
P	$40,000	$(30,000)	$21,000
S	(29,000)	20,000	6,000
Consolidated taxable income (before NOL deduction)	N/A	$(10,000)	$ 27,000

N/A = Not applicable

Ignore the Sec. 382 loss limitation that might apply to P's acquisition of S, and ignore the U.S. production activities deduction.

a. What are the Year 2 tax consequences if P and S file a consolidated tax return? What are the Year 2 tax consequences if P and S instead file separate tax returns?

b. What are the Year 3 tax consequences if P and S file consolidated returns for Years 2 and 3?

C:8-59 *Consolidated NOL Carryovers and Intercompany Transactions.* P Corporation owns all the stock of S1 and S2 Corporations, and the group has filed consolidated tax returns on a calendar year basis for several years. In the current year (Year 1), S2 sells to S1 for $90,000 land S2 had purchased for $75,000. On December 31 of Year 2, S1 sells the land to a third party for $91,000. On January 18 of Year 3, P sells all of its S2 stock to a third party for a sales price equal to P's basis in the S2 stock. The consolidated group members report the following amounts of taxable income and loss (before deducting any NOLs or applying the matching and acceleration rules):

	Taxable Income (Loss)	
Group Member	*Year 2*	*Year 3*
P	$165,000	$(30,000)
S1	(120,000)	(20,000)
S2	(140,000)	7,000[a]
Consolidated taxable income or loss before deducting any NOLs or applying the matching and acceleration rules	$ (95,000)	$(43,000)

[a] Pertains to January 1 through January 18 of Year 3.

Assume that the group elects to forego the carryback period for the Year 2 consolidated NOL.

a. Determine the amount of NOL available for S2's Year 3 separate tax return.
b. Assume the same facts as in Part a except S1's land sale to a third party for $91,000 occurred on January 1 of Year 3. Determine the amount of NOL available for S2's Year 3 separate tax return.

C:8-60 *SRLY Limitation.* P Corporation acquires all of S Corporation's stock at the close of business on December 31 of Year 1. The corporations, which file on the calendar year, begin filing a consolidated tax return for Year 2. The corporations report the following taxable incomes (losses), before any NOL deduction, for Years 1 through 5:

	Taxable Income Before NOL deduction				
Group Member	*Year 1*	*Year 2*	*Year 3*	*Year 4*	*Year 5*
P	$100,000	$125,000	$70,000	$(8,000)	$100,000
S	(63,000)	(15,000)	18,000	25,000	40,000
Consolidated taxable income (before NOL deduction)	N/A	$110,000	$ 88,000	$ 17,000	$140,000

N/A = Not applicable

P and S have no NOLs before Year 1, and S elects to forego the two-year carryback period for its Year 1 NOL. Ignore the Sec. 382 loss limitation that might apply to P's acquisition of S, assume that the acquisition does not qualify as a reverse acquisition, and ignore the U.S. production activities deduction. What is consolidated taxable income for each of Years 2 through 5?

C:8-61 *SRLY Limitation.* Bart, P's sole shareholder, creates P on January 1 of Year 1. P purchases all of S1's and S2's stock on September 1 of Year 1, after both corporations are in operation for about six months. P, S1, and S2 Corporations comprise the P-S1-S2 affiliated group and file separate tax returns for Year 1. The P-S1-S2 affiliated group then elects to file consolidated tax returns starting in Year 2. The group reports the following results:

	Taxable Income		
Group Member	*Year 1*	*Year 2*	*Year 3*
P	$(8,000)	$50,000	$10,000
S1	(24,000)	20,000	(18,000)
S2	(16,000)	(10,000)	15,000
Consolidated taxable income (before NOL deduction)	N/A	$60,000	$ 7,000

Ignore the Sec. 382 loss limitation that might apply to the acquisitions of S1 and S2, assume that P's purchase of S1 and S2 does not qualify as a reverse acquisition, and ignore the U.S. production activities deduction.

a. What is Year 2 consolidated taxable income?
b. What is Year 3 consolidated taxable income?
c. What NOL carryovers are available in Year 4?
d. How would your answer to Parts a through c change if Bart instead created P, S1, and S2 as an affiliated group on January 1 of Year 1?

C:8-62 *SRLY and Sec. 382 Loss Limitations.* P Corporation owns 100% of S Corporation's stock, and they have filed consolidated tax returns for several years. P also has owned 49% of T Corporation's stock for 10 years. On December 31 of the current year (Year 1), P purchases the other 51% of T's stock for $510,000 cash. T has $160,000 of NOLs it is carrying over on that date. In Year 2, the corporations report taxable profits as follows: P, $400,000; S, $250,000; and T, $90,000. Assume that the long-term tax-exempt federal interest rate is 5%.

a. Determine the amount of T's NOLs the group can deduct for its Year 2 consolidated taxable income.
b. Assume the same facts as in Part a except P purchases 45% of T's stock for $450,000 on December 31 of Year 1. Determine the amount of T's NOLs the group can deduct for its Year 2 consolidated taxable income.

C:8-63 *Stock Basis Adjustments.* P Corporation purchases 100% of S Corporation's stock for $2 million on January 1 of the current year. The corporations elect to file a consolidated tax return. During the current year, S reports $350,000 of taxable income and $30,000 of tax-exempt interest income, and it distributes a $100,000 dividend to P. Each corporation pays its portion of the consolidated tax liability. Assume a 34% corporate tax rate. What is P's basis for its S stock at the end of the current year?

C:8-64 *Stock Basis Adjustments.* P Corporation owns 100% of S Corporation's stock, and S owns 100% of T Corporation's stock. The three corporations have filed consolidated tax returns for several years. On January 1 of the current year, P's basis for its S stock is $5 million, and S's basis for its T stock is $3 million. The corporations' taxable incomes for the current year are $500,000 for P, $350,000 for S, and $250,000 for T. S and T pay no dividends during the year. Each corporation pays its portion of the consolidated tax liability. Assume a 34% corporate tax rate.

a. Determine P's basis for its S stock and S's basis for its T stock at the end of the current year.

b. Assume the same facts as in Part a except S pays an $80,000 dividend to P and T pays a $90,000 dividend to S. Determine P's basis for its S stock and S's basis for its T stock at the end of the current year.

C:8-65 *Financial Statement Implications.* P and S Corporations comprise an affiliated group that files separate tax returns. P and S had no intercompany inventory sales before the current year (Year 1). P and S use the first-in, first-out (FIFO) inventory method. During Year 1, S sells 40,000 widgets to P, earning $7 per unit profit on the sale. P's inventory at the end of Year 1 includes 10,000 of these widgets. During Year 2, S sells 75,000 widgets to P, earning $7.50 per unit profit on the sale. P's inventory at the end of Year 2 includes 12,000 of these widgets. During Year 3, no intercompany inventory sales occur, and P sells all widgets in beginning inventory. P's and S's taxable income each year (including any profits from intercompany inventory sales) is $380,000 and $300,000, respectively. Assume a 34% corporate tax rate.

a. Prepare the journal entries to record federal income tax expense for each of Years 1, 2, and 3.

b. Assume that, instead of units of inventory, S sells to P shares of marketable securities, with the same profits as in Part a. Again, prepare the journal entries to record federal income tax expense for each of Years 1, 2, and 3.

C:8-66 *Financial Statement Implications.* P Corporation acquires all of S Corporation's stock at the beginning of the current year in a transaction that qualifies as a Sec. 382 ownership change. P and S elect to file a consolidated tax return for the current year. At the time of the acquisition, S has $900,000 of NOLs it has not deducted. Management estimates that, because of the Sec. 382 limitation, the group will be able to use only $300,000 of the NOLs before they expire. The group's tax rate is 35%. Determine the amount of deferred tax asset and valuation allowance the group records for S's NOL.

COMPREHENSIVE PROBLEMS

C:8-67 P and S Corporations have filed consolidated tax returns for ten years. P and S use the accrual method of accounting, and they use the calendar year as their tax year. P and S report separate return taxable income (before any consolidation adjustments and eliminations, the NOL deduction, the charitable contributions deduction, and the dividends-received deduction) for the current year of $200,000 and $250,000, respectively. These amounts include the following current year transactions and events:

- P sells land to a third party for $80,000. P purchased the land from S two years ago for $70,000. S had purchased the land five years ago for $48,000.
- P's separate taxable income includes a $12,000 dividend S paid to P.
- P sold inventory to S in the previous year for which the deferred profit at the beginning of the current year is $5,000. S sells this inventory outside the consolidated group in the current year. P sells additional inventory to S in the current year, realizing a $100,000 profit. The intercompany profit on this unsold inventory is $8,000.
- The P-S group has a $20,000 consolidated NOL carryover available from the previous year. The NOL is wholly attributable to S.
- P receives $10,000 of dividends from corporations in which it owns less than 1% of the stock.
- P and S contribute cash to charities of $17,000 and $11,000, respectively.

- P lends S $150,000 early in the current year. S repays the loan later in the year. In addition, S pays P $6,000 interest at the time of repayment.
- S earns $1,600 of tax-exempt interest income, which is not included in S's $250,000 separate return taxable income.
- P and S have no qualified production activities income.

Determine the P-S group's consolidated taxable income and consolidated tax liability for the current year. What is P's basis for the S stock at the end of the current year? Assume that P's basis for the S stock was $1.4 million at the beginning of the current year.

C:8-68 Using the facts from Problem C:8-70 below, calculate the tax liabilities of Flying Gator and T Corporations for 2016. How much larger (or smaller) would be the total of the two separate return tax liabilities if they were to file separate tax returns than the affiliated group's consolidated return tax liability? What taxes are due (or refund available) if Flying Gator made $125,000 of estimated tax payments and T Corporation made $25,000 of estimated tax payments?

TAX STRATEGY PROBLEM

C:8-69 Sandra and John, who are unrelated, each own 50% of Alpha Corporation's stock and 50% of Beta Corporation's stock. For five years, Alpha has conducted manufacturing activities and sold machine parts primarily in the eastern United States. Alpha has reported $75,000 of operating profits in each of the last two years. Alpha's annual operating profits are expected to grow to $150,000 during the next five years. Alpha has $100,000 of NOLs it is carrying forward. Alpha sells 25% of its product to Beta. Beta has been working to establish a market niche for reselling Alpha products in the southwestern United States. In the start-up phase of establishing the market, Beta incurred $200,000 of NOLs. Under the sales arrangement with Alpha, probably the best that Beta can hope to achieve in the short-run is reach a break-even point.

Required: What suggestions can you offer Sandra and John about the short-term possibility of using Alpha's and Beta's NOLs against the profits that Alpha expects to earn and about minimizing their overall tax liabilities if both businesses become profitable? Sandra has specifically asked about merging the two companies into a single entity so the losses of one entity can offset the profits of the other and delay the need to pay income taxes to the federal government. Sandra indicates that the two companies were created for business reasons and not tax avoidance reasons. The operating situation has changed and, according to Sandra, now may be the time to combine the entities into one. However, John is not sure that bringing the two businesses together is a good idea.

TAX FORM/RETURN PREPARATION PROBLEM

C:8-70 Flying Gator Corporation and its 100%-owned subsidiary, T Corporation, have filed consolidated tax returns for many years. Both corporations use the hybrid method of accounting and the calendar year as their tax year. During 2016 (which is the current year for this problem), they report the operating results as listed in Table C:8-2. Note the following additional information:

- Flying Gator and T Corporations are the only members of their controlled group.
- Flying Gator's address is 2101 W. University Ave., Gainesburg, FL 32611. Its employer identification number is 38-2345678. Flying Gator was incorporated on June 11, 2004. Its total assets are $430,000.
- A $50,000 consolidated NOL carryover from the preceding year is available. The NOL is wholly attributable to Flying Gator.
- Flying Gator and T use the first-in, first-out (FIFO) inventory method. T began selling inventory to Flying Gator in the preceding year, which resulted in a $40,700 deferred intercompany profit at the end of the preceding year. Flying Gator is deemed to realize this profit in the current year because it uses the FIFO method. During the current year, T sells additional inventory to Flying Gator, realizing a $300,000 profit. At the end of the current year, Flying Gator holds inventory responsible for $45,100 of this profit.
- Flying Gator receives all its dividends from T. T receives all its dividends from a 60%-owned domestic corporation. All distributions are from E&P.
- Flying Gator receives all its interest income from T. T pays Flying Gator the interest on March 31 of the current year on a loan that was outstanding from October 1 of the

▼ TABLE C:8-2

Current Year Operating Results for Flying Gator and T Corporations (Problem C:8-67)

Income or Deductions	Flying Gator	T	Total
Gross receipts	$2,500,000	$1,250,000	$3,750,000
Cost of goods sold	(1,500,000)	(700,000)	(2,200,000)
Gross profit	$1,000,000	$ 550,000	$1,550,000
Dividends	100,000	50,000	150,000
Interest	15,000		15,000
Sec. 1231 gain		20,000	20,000
Sec. 1245 gain		25,000	25,000
Long-term capital gain (loss)	(5,000)	6,000	1,000
Short-term capital gain (loss)		(3,000)	(3,000)
Total income	$1,110,000	$ 648,000	$1,758,000
Salaries and wages	175,000	200,000	375,000
Repairs	25,000	40,000	65,000
Bad debts	10,000	5,000	15,000
Taxes	18,000	24,000	42,000
Interest	30,000	20,000	50,000
Charitable contributions	22,000	48,000	70,000
Depreciation (other than that included in cost of goods sold)	85,000	40,000	125,000
Other expenses	160,000	260,000	420,000
Total deductions	$ 525,000	$ 637,000	$1,162,000
Separate return taxable income (before the USPAD, NOL ded., and DRD)	$ 585,000	$ 11,000	$ 596,000

preceding year through March 31 of the current year. Flying Gator and T did not accrue any interest at the end of the preceding year because they use the hybrid method of accounting. T pays $5,000 of its interest expense to a third party.

- Officer's salaries are $80,000 for Flying Gator and $65,000 for T. These amounts are included in salaries and wages in Table C:8-2.
- Flying Gator's capital losses include a $9,000 long-term loss on a sale of land to T in the current year. T holds the land at year-end.
- The corporations have no nonrecaptured net Sec. 1231 losses from prior tax years.
- Qualified production activities income for Flying Gator is $340,000 and for T is $(35,000).
- Estimated tax payments for the current year are $150,000.

Determine the consolidated group's 2016 tax liability. Prepare the first page of the consolidated group's current year corporate income tax return (Form 1120). Hint: Prepare a spreadsheet similar to the one included in Appendix B to arrive at consolidated taxable income.

CASE STUDY PROBLEM

C:8-71 Carol owns all the stock of P Corporation and J Corporation. P operates six automotive service franchises in a metropolitan area. The service franchises have been a huge success in their first three years of operation, and P's annual taxable income exceeds $600,000. J owns the real estate associated with the six service franchises and leases it to P. J reports large interest and MACRS depreciation deductions because of a highly leveraged, capital intensive operation. As a result, J has reported NOLs in its first three years of operation. P and J file separate tax returns.

Carol sees the idea for the automotive service franchise chain starting to really develop and expects to add six more locations in each of the next two years. Because of the rapid expansion that is planned, she feels that she has outgrown her father's accountant and needs to have new ideas to help her save tax dollars so she can reinvest more money in the business.

Required: The tax partner that you are assigned to requests that you prepare a memorandum outlining your thoughts about Carol's tax problems and suggested solutions to those problems in preparation for his meeting next week with Carol.

TAX RESEARCH PROBLEMS

C:8-72 Angela owns all the stock of A, B, and P Corporations. P has owned all the stock of S1 Corporation for six years. The P-S1 affiliated group has filed a consolidated tax return in each of these six years using the calendar year as its tax year. On July 10 of the current year (a nonleap year). Angela sells her entire stock investment in A, which uses the calendar year as its tax year. No change takes place in Angela's ownership of B's and P's stock during the tax year. At the close of business on November 25 of this year, S1 purchases 90% of the common stock and 80% of the nonconvertible, nonvoting preferred stock (measured by value) of S2 Corporation. All the corporations are includible corporations. Which corporations are included in the affiliated group? In the controlled group? What income is included in the various tax returns? How is the allocation of the income between tax years made if the books are not closed on the sale or acquisition dates? If no special allocations are made, what portion of the reduced tax rate benefits of Sec. 11(b) can be claimed in the current year by the affiliated group? In future years?

A partial list of resources includes:

- IRC Sec. 1504
- IRC Sec. 1563
- Reg. Sec. 1.1502-76
- Reg. Sec. 1.1561-2

C:8-73 P, R, and T Corporations have filed a consolidated tax return for a number of years using the calendar year as its tax year. Current plans call for P to purchase all of X Corporation's stock at the close of business on June 30 of the current year from three individuals. X was created seven years ago and always has been an S corporation using the calendar year as its tax year. The chief financial officer of P comes to your office and makes a number of inquiries about the tax consequences of the acquisition including: Can X retain its S election? If so, does it file a federal income tax return separate from the consolidated group? Does X have to be included in the P-R-T group's consolidated tax return? Assuming the acquisition takes place as planned, what tax returns are required of the consolidated group and X? What income is included in the pre-affiliation tax return of X (if required) and the consolidated group's post-acquisition consolidated tax return? Prepare a brief memo for the chief financial officer outlining the answers to these questions and any other questions you feel are relevant.

A partial list of resources includes:

- IRC Sec. 1361(b)
- IRC Sec. 1362(d)(2)
- Reg. Sec. 1.1502-76

C:8-74 Anna, one of your firm's clients, is a physician who owns and operates her practice through a professional service corporation (PSC). She sees opportunities to grow the PSC, allowing her to serve more patients and generate more profits. Anna, however, cannot invest more funds in her practice because she is still paying off her medical school loans. She also is concerned that this growth would require her to spend more time managing her practice's business aspects and less time with patients.

Anna was discussing her situation with a friend, whose medical practice is in the same city. He told Anna that she should look into a practice management company (PMCo). He explained that the PSC would continue to perform the medical activities, but the PMCo would charge the PSC a fee for overseeing the practice's business aspects. The fee would be based on the practice's profits. This structure would allow the PMCo to invest funds to grow the business and would satisfy a state law requiring all PSC shareholders to be physicians. He mentioned that, although Anna would remain as the legal owner of the PSC's stock, the PMCo probably would prohibit her from using that ownership to exercise control over the PSC, thereby prohibiting her from selling the PSC's stock without the PMCo's consent and prohibiting the PSC from paying her a dividend without the PMCo's consent.

Anna wants to explore this opportunity and has asked a tax partner in your firm what the tax ramifications would be. The partner has asked you to determine whether Anna's PSC and the PMCo would have to file a consolidated federal income tax return. Prepare a brief memo for the partner answering this question.

A partial list of resources includes:

- IRC Sec. 1504
- Rev. Rul. 84-79
- PLR 201451009

CHAPTER

9

PARTNERSHIP FORMATION AND OPERATION

LEARNING OBJECTIVES

After studying this chapter, you should be able to

1. Compare and contrast the various partnership forms
2. Describe the basic concepts of partnership taxation
3. Explain the tax results of a contribution of property or services in exchange for a partnership interest
4. Establish the permitted tax year for a partnership
5. Distinguish between items included in partnership ordinary income or loss and those that must be separately stated
6. Determine a partner's distributive share of partnership income, gain, loss, deduction, or credit items
7. Calculate a partner's basis in a partnership interest and its effect on losses allowed
8. Discuss the at-risk and passive activity loss limitations
9. Determine the tax consequences of property sales between a partner and the partnership and of guaranteed payments to a partner
10. Recognize the special tax issues associated with family partnerships
11. Identify planning techniques to get the best tax advantages from partnership losses
12. Comply with the requirements for filing a partnership tax return

CHAPTER OUTLINE

Partnerships have long been one of the major entities for conducting business activities. Partnerships vary in complexity from the corner gas station owned and operated by two brothers to syndicated tax partnerships with their partnership interests traded on major security markets. Two different sets of rules apply to partnerships depending on their size. The rules discussed in Chapter C:9 and most of Chapter C:10 apply to the majority of partnerships. A different set of rules, discussed at the end of Chapter C:10, apply to electing large partnerships. The partnership rules are found in Subchapter K of the IRC, which includes Secs. 701–777.

Chapters C:9 and C:10 discuss the income tax rules applying to partnership business operations. The first part of this chapter defines a partnership, describes the types of partnerships, and discusses the formation of a partnership. The remainder of the chapter deals with the ongoing operations of a partnership, such as the annual taxation of partnership earnings, transactions between partners and the partnership, and a partner's basis in a partnership interest. This chapter also considers procedural matters, such as reporting the annual partnership income and IRS audit procedures for partnerships and their partners. Chapter C:10 continues by discussing distributions to the partners and the tax implications of transactions used to terminate a partner's interest in a partnership. Chapter C:10 also discusses the unique problems of limited partnerships and the taxation of publicly traded partnerships and electing large partnerships.

Definition of a Partnership

OBJECTIVE 1

Compare and contrast the various partnership forms

For tax purposes, the definition of a partnership includes "a syndicate, group, pool, joint venture, or other unincorporated organization" that carries on a business or financial operation or venture. However, a trust, estate, or corporation cannot be treated as a partnership. Unlike a corporation, which can exist only after incorporation documents are finalized, formation of a partnership requires no legal documentation. If two people (or business entities) work together to carry on any business or financial operation with the intention of making a profit and sharing that profit as co-owners, a partnership exists for federal income tax purposes.[1]

The IRC and Treasury Regulations define a **partner** simply as a member of a partnership. Years of case law and common business practice, however, have made clear that a partner can be an individual, trust, estate, or corporation. The only restriction on the number of partners is that a partnership must have at least two partners, but a large syndicated partnership may have hundreds or even thousands of partners.

GENERAL AND LIMITED PARTNERSHIPS

ADDITIONAL COMMENT

Even though the formation of a partnership requires no legal documentation, the partners should draft a formal written partnership agreement to prevent subsequent disagreements and arguments.

Each state has laws and statutes governing the rights and restrictions of partnerships, many of which are modeled on the Uniform Partnership Act (UPA), Uniform Limited Partnership Act (ULPA), or Revised Limited Partnership Act. A partnership can take two basic legal forms: a general partnership or a limited partnership. The differences between the two forms are substantial and extend to the partners' legal rights and liabilities as well as the tax consequences of operations to the partners. Because these differences are so important, we examine the two partnership forms before proceeding with further discussion of the partnership tax rules.

General Partnerships. A **general partnership** exists any time two or more partners join together and do not specifically provide that one or more of the partners is a limited partner (as defined below). In a general partnership, each partner has the right to

[1] Section 761(a) allows an election to avoid the Subchapter K rules for a very limited group of business owners.

participate in the management of the partnership. However, a general partnership is flexible enough to allow its business affairs to be managed by a single partner chosen by the general partners.

REAL-WORLD EXAMPLE

For 2014, 3.61 million domestic partnerships filed returns. Of these, 575,000 were general partnerships, 414,000 were limited partnerships, 140,000 were limited liability partnerships, and 2.43 million were limited liability companies. The average general partnership had 4.3 partners, the average limited partnership had 29.6 partners, the average limited liability partnership had 4.7 partners, and the average limited liability company had 4.2 members.

Although only one (or a few) of the general partners may exercise management duties, each **general partner** has the ability to make commitments for the partnership.[2] In a general partnership, each partner has unlimited liability for all partnership debts. If the partnership fails to pay its debts, each partner may have to pay far more than the amount he or she has invested in the venture. Thus, each partner faces the risk of losing personal assets if the partnership incurs business losses. This exposure is the single biggest drawback to the general partnership form of doing business.

Limited Partnerships. A **limited partnership** has two classes of partners. It must have at least one general partner, who essentially has the same rights and liabilities as any general partner in a general partnership,[3] and at least one **limited partner**. Even if a partnership becomes bankrupt, a limited partner can lose no more than his or her original investment plus any additional amount he or she has committed to contribute. However, a limited partner has no right to be active in the partnership's management.

The broad rights and obligations of general partners could make a general partnership an unwieldy form for operating a business with a large number of owners. On the other hand, a limited partnership having one (or a small number of) general partners can be useful for a business operation that needs to attract a large amount of capital. In fact, one common form for a tax shelter investment is a limited partnership having a corporation with a small amount of capital as its sole general partner. Such an arrangement allows the tax advantages of the partnership form while retaining the limited liability feature for virtually every investor.

Many of these limited partnerships are so large and widely held that in many ways they appear more like corporations than partnerships. As discussed in Chapter C:10, the tax laws provide that publicly traded partnerships may be reclassified for tax purposes as corporations.

Limited Liability Limited Partnerships (LLLPs). A variation on the limited partnership is the LLLP. As discussed above, a limited partnership, in addition to having limited partners, has one or more general partners whose personal liability exposure is unlimited. The LLLP is a partnership formed under a state's limited partnership laws but that can elect under the state's laws to provide the general partners with limited liability. Thus, the LLLP is similar to an LLC and becomes potentially useful in states that do not extend LLC status to personal service firms but allow such firms to operate as an LLLP.[4]

REAL-WORLD EXAMPLE

The number of limited liability companies has increased from 48,000 in 1994 to 2.43 million in 2014. Moreover, LLCs represented 67.3% of all domestic partnerships in 2014.

Limited Liability Companies (LLCs). With the advent of LLCs, businesses have the opportunity to be treated as a partnership for tax purposes while having limited liability protection for every owner. State law provides this limited liability. Unique tax rules for LLCs have not been developed. Instead, the check-the-box regulations (discussed in Chapter C:2) permit each LLC to choose whether to be treated as a partnership or taxed as a corporation. If an LLC is considered a partnership for tax purposes, the same tax rules apply to the LLC that apply to a traditional partnership. Chapter C:10 further discusses the tax treatment of LLCs.

TAX STRATEGY TIP

A business that expects losses in its early years may wish to form an LLC initially so that losses pass through to the owners. Later, if the business expects to grow, it can consider incorporating as a C corporation and retaining its earnings to fund this expansion.

Limited Liability Partnerships (LLPs). Initially, professional organizations in certain fields (e.g., public accounting and law) were not permitted to operate as LLCs and therefore remained general partnerships. Subsequently, many states have added LLPs to the list of permissible business forms. The primary difference between a general partnership and an LLP is that, in an LLP, a partner is not liable for damages resulting from failures in the

[2] Uniform Partnership Act.
[3] Uniform Limited Partnership Act.
[4] For a detailed discussion, see Shop Talk, "Service Firms Practicing as LLLPs: What Are the Tax Consequences?" *Journal of Taxation,* August 2005.

work of other partners or of people supervised by other partners. Under the check-the-box regulations, an LLP can be treated as a partnership or as a corporation. Like an LLC, the default tax classification of an LLP is a partnership. The same tax rules apply to an LLP that apply to a traditional partnership. Chapter C:10 further discusses the tax treatment of LLPs.

ADDITIONAL COMMENT

Section 775 for electing large partnerships is repealed for tax years beginning after 2017. Thus, the rules discussed in this paragraph and in Chapter C:10 are applicable only for tax years beginning before 2018.

Electing Large Partnerships. Partnerships that qualify as "large partnerships" may elect to have a simplified set of reporting rules apply. To qualify as a large partnership, the partnership must not be a service partnership and must not be engaged in commodity trading. Further, to qualify to make this election, the partnership must have at least 100 partners throughout the tax year (excluding partners who provide substantial services in connection with the partnership's business activities). Once the partnership makes the election, it reports its income under a simplified reporting scheme, is subject to different rules about when the partnership terminates, and is subject to a different system of audits. The election is irrevocable without IRS permission. Chapter C:10 presents details about the tax treatment of electing large partnerships.

Overview of Taxation of Partnership Income

OBJECTIVE 2

Describe the basic concepts of partnership taxation

The following overview gives a broad perspective of the taxation of partnership income other than income earned by electing large partnerships. (Appendix F compares the tax characteristics of a partnership, a C corporation, and an S corporation.) More detailed descriptions follow this overview.

PARTNERSHIP PROFITS AND LOSSES

A partnership is not a taxpaying entity, and income earned by a partnership is not subject to two layers of federal income taxes. Instead, each partner reports a share of the partnership's income, gain, loss, deduction, and credit items in his or her income tax return. The partnership, however, must file Form 1065 (U.S. Partnership Return of Income), an information return that provides the IRS with information about partnership earnings as well as how the earnings are allocated among the partners. The partnership must elect a tax year and accounting methods to calculate its earnings. (Appendix B includes a completed partnership tax return that shows a Form 1065 and Schedule K-1 for a partner along with a set of supporting facts.)

ADDITIONAL COMMENT

For tax years beginning after 2015, a partnership's tax return and related K-1 schedules are due on March 15, which gives partners who file their own tax returns on April 15 a month to process the information provided on the K-1s.

Each partner receives a Schedule K-1 from the partnership, which informs the partner of the amount and character of his or her share of partnership items. The partner then combines his or her partnership earnings and losses with all other items of income or loss for the tax year, computes the amount of taxable income, and calculates the tax liability. Partnership income is taxed at the applicable tax rate for its partners, which can range from 10% to 39.6% (in 2017) for partners who are individuals, trusts, or estates. Corporate partners pay tax on partnership income at rates ranging from 15% to 39%.

One of the major advantages of the partnership form of doing business is that partnership losses are allocated among the partners. If the loss limitation rules (explained later in this chapter) do not apply, these losses offset the partners' other income, resulting in immediate tax savings for the partners. The immediate tax saving available to the partner contrasts sharply with the net operating loss (NOL) carrybacks or carryforwards that may result from a C corporation's operations.

SELF-STUDY QUESTION

Why does a partner need to know his or her basis in his or her partnership interest?

ANSWER

Three important reasons are (1) to determine the gain or loss on a sale of the partnership interest, (2) to determine the amount of partnership losses a partner can deduct, and (3) to determine the amount of distributions that are nontaxable to the partner.

THE PARTNER'S BASIS

A partner's basis in his or her partnership interest is a crucial element in partnership taxation. When a partner makes a contribution to a partnership or purchases a partnership interest, he or she establishes a beginning basis. Because partners can be personally liable for partnership debts, a partner's basis in his or her partnership interest is increased by his or her share of any partnership liabilities. Accordingly, the partner's basis fluctuates as the partnership borrows and repays loans or increases and decreases its accounts payable. In addition, a partner's basis in his or her partnership interest increases by the partner's share of partnership income and decreases by his or her share of partnership losses. Because a partner's basis in his or her partnership interest can never be negative, the basis serves as one limit on the amount of deductible partnership losses. (See the discussion on pages C:9-26 and C:9-27 about the various loss limitations.)

EXAMPLE C:9-1 ► Tom purchases a 20% interest in the XY Partnership for $8,000 on January 1 of Year 1 and begins to materially participate in the partnership's business. The XY Partnership uses the calendar year as its tax year. At the time of the purchase, the XY Partnership has $2,000 in liabilities, of which Tom's share is 20%. Tom's basis in his partnership interest on January 1 is $8,400 [$8,000 + (0.20 × $2,000)]. ◄

EXAMPLE C:9-2 ► Assume the same facts as in Example C:9-1 except, during Year 1, the XY Partnership incurs $10,000 in losses, and its liabilities increase by $4,000. Tom's basis on December 31 of Year 1 is calculated as follows:

January 1, Year 1, basis	$8,400
Plus: Share of liability increase ($4,000 × 0.20)	800
Minus: Share of partnership losses ($10,000 × 0.20)	(2,000)
December 31, Year 1, basis	$7,200

◄

EXAMPLE C:9-3 ► Assume the same facts as in Example C:9-2, and further assume that, during Year 2, the XY Partnership incurs $60,000 in losses and its liabilities increase by $10,000. Tom's share of the losses is $12,000 ($60,000 × 0.20). The maximum amount Tom can deduct in Year 2 is calculated as follows:

January 1, Year 2, basis	$7,200
Plus: Share of liability increase	2,000
December 31, Year 2, basis before losses	$9,200
Minus: Maximum loss deduction allowed	(9,200)
December 31, Year 2, basis	$ -0-

Tom's remaining $2,800 in losses carry over to subsequent years, and he can deduct them when he regains sufficient basis in his partnership interest. ◄

ADDITIONAL COMMENT

The increase in a partner's basis for earnings prevents double taxation of those earnings upon a subsequent distribution, sale of the partnership interest, or liquidation of the partnership.

PARTNERSHIP DISTRIBUTIONS

When a partnership makes current (nonliquidating) distributions, the distributions generally are nontaxable to the partners because they represent the receipt of earnings that already have been taxed to the partners and that have increased the partners' bases in their partnership interests. Because they are a return of capital, these distributions reduce a partner's basis in his or her partnership interest. If a cash distribution is so large, however, that it exceeds a partner's basis in his or her partnership interest, the partner recognizes gain equal to the amount of the excess. When the partnership goes out of business or when a partner withdraws from the partnership, the partnership makes liquidating distributions to the partner. Like current distributions, these distributions cause the partner to recognize gain only if the cash received exceeds the partner's basis in his or her partnership interest. A partner may recognize a loss if he or she receives only cash, inventory, and unrealized receivables in complete liquidation of his or her partnership interest. Chapter C:10 presents detailed coverage of current and liquidating distributions.

TAX IMPLICATIONS OF FORMATION OF A PARTNERSHIP

OBJECTIVE 3

Explain the tax results of a contribution of property or services in exchange for a partnership interest

When two or more individuals or entities decide to operate an unincorporated business together, they form a partnership. The following sections examine the tax implications of property contributions, service contributions, and organization and syndication expenditures.

CONTRIBUTION OF PROPERTY

Nonrecognition of Gain or Loss. Section 721 governs the formation of a partnership. In most cases, a partner who contributes property in exchange for a partnership interest recognizes no gain or loss on the transaction. Likewise, the partnership recognizes no gain or loss on the contribution of property. The partner's basis for his or her partnership interest and the partnership's basis for the property are both the same as basis of the property transferred.[5]

Nonrecognition treatment is limited to transactions in which a partner receives a partnership interest in exchange for a contribution of property. As in the corporate formation area, the term *property* includes cash, tangible property (e.g., buildings and land), and intangible property (e.g., franchise rights, trademarks, and leases).[6] Services are specifically excluded from the definition of property, so a contribution of services for a partnership interest is a taxable transaction.

ADDITIONAL COMMENT

For contributions to a corporation to be nontaxable, the contributing shareholders must control (own at least 80%) the corporation immediately after the transaction. No such control requirement exists for contributions to a partnership to be nontaxable.

Recognition of Gain or Loss. The general rule of Sec. 721(a) provides that neither the partnership nor any partner recognizes gain or loss when partners contribute property in exchange for a partnership interest. Three exceptions to this general rule may require a partner to recognize a gain upon the contribution of property to a partnership in exchange for a partnership interest:

- Contribution of property to a partnership that would be treated as an investment company if it were incorporated
- Contribution of property followed by a distribution in an arrangement that may be considered a sale rather than a contribution
- Contribution of property to a partnership along with the partnership's assumption of the partner's liabilities if, as a result, the partner's share of partnership liabilities exceeds his or her basis in the partnership.

The investment company exception of Sec. 721(b) requires recognition of gain only if the exchange results in diversification of the transferor's property interest.[7] If the contribution of property is to an investment partnership, the contributing partner must recognize any gain (but not loss) realized on the property transfer as if he or she sold the stock or securities.

Sections 707(a)(2)(A) and (B) set out the second exception, which holds that a property contribution followed by a distribution (or an allocation of income or gain) may be treated as a property sale by the partner to the partnership rather than as a contribution by the partner to the partnership. For example, Treasury Regulations may require sale treatment (and the recognition of gain or loss) if the distribution would not have occurred except for the contribution.

EXAMPLE C:9-4 ▶ In return for a 40% interest in the CD Partnership, Cara contributed land with a $100,000 fair market value (FMV). The partners agreed that the partnership would distribute $100,000 in cash to Cara immediately after the contribution. Because the cash distribution would not have occurred had Cara not first contributed the land and become a partner, the transaction is likely to be treated as a sale of the land by Cara to the partnership. ◀

If the distribution does not occur simultaneously with the contribution, the transaction is treated as a sale if the later distribution is not dependent on the normal business risk of the enterprise.

EXAMPLE C:9-5 ▶ Elena received a 30% interest in the DEF Partnership in return for her contribution of land having a $60,000 FMV. The partnership waits six months and then distributes $60,000 in cash to Elena. If the $60,000 distribution is not contingent on the partnership's earnings or ability to borrow funds or other normal risks of doing business, the distribution and contribution will be treated as a sale of land by Elena to the partnership. ◀

---

[5] Secs. 722 and 723.

[6] For an excellent discussion of the definition of the term *property*, see footnote 6 of *D.N. Stafford v. U.S.*, 45 AFTR 2d 80-785, 80-1 USTC ¶9218 (5th Cir., 1980).

[7] Reg. Sec. 1.351-1(c)(1). This investment is taxed only when immediately after the exchange more than 80% of the value of the partnership's assets (excluding cash and nonconvertible debt obligations) is held for investment or is readily marketable stocks, securities, or interests in regulated investment companies or real estate investment trusts.

KEY POINT

A partner's relief of debt is treated as if the partner receives a cash distribution. A partner's assumption of debt is treated as if the partner makes a cash contribution. These two simple rules are critical to understanding transactions such as formations of partnerships, distributions from partnerships, and sales or liquidations of partnership interests.

Effects of Liabilities. The third condition that may cause a partner to recognize gain (but not loss) on the formation of a partnership is the contribution of property to a partnership along with the partnership's assumption of liabilities previously owed by the partner. Because each partner is liable for his or her share of partnership liabilities, increases and decreases in the partnership liabilities are reflected in each partner's basis. Specifically, Sec. 752 provides that two effects result from a partner's contribution of property to a partnership if the partnership also assumes the partner's liabilities.

- Each partner's basis is increased by his or her share of the partnership's liabilities as if he or she had contributed cash to the partnership in the amount of his or her share of partnership liabilities.
- The partner whose personal liabilities are assumed by the partnership has a reduction in the basis of his or her partnership interest as if the partnership distributed cash to him or her in the amount of the assumed liability. A cash distribution first reduces the partner's basis in the partnership interest. If the cash distribution exceeds the partner's predistribution basis in the partnership interest, the partner recognizes gain.

The net effect of these two basis adjustments, however, is seldom large enough to cause a transferor partner to recognize gain when he or she contributes property to the partnership. The transferor partner is deemed first to have made a contribution of property plus a contribution of cash equal to the partner's share of any partnership liabilities existing prior to his or her entrance into the partnership (or contributed by other partners concurrently with this transaction). The partner then is deemed to have received a cash distribution equal to the total amount of his or her own liability assumed by the *other* partners. Also, see the Additional Comment next to Example C:9-6 for an alternate way to view the transaction.

EXAMPLE C:9-6 ▶

In return for a 20% partnership interest, Mary contributes land having a $60,000 FMV and a $30,000 basis to the XY Partnership. The partnership assumes Mary's $15,000 liability arising from her purchase of the land, and Mary's share of partnership liabilities is 20%. The XY Partnership has $4,000 in liabilities immediately before her contribution. Mary's basis in her partnership interest is calculated as follows:

Basis of contributed property	$30,000
Plus: Mary's share of existing partnership liabilities ($4,000 × 0.20)	800
Minus: Mary's liabilities assumed by the other partners ($15,000 × 0.80)	(12,000)
Mary's basis in her partnership interest	$18,800

Mary recognizes no gain on the partnership's assumption of her liability because the deemed cash distribution from the assumption of her $12,000 in liabilities by the partnership does not exceed her $30,800 basis in the partnership interest immediately preceding the deemed distribution. ◀

ADDITIONAL COMMENT

In Example C:9-6, the $12,000 reduction in basis also can be viewed as the net of $3,000, which is Mary's 20% share of the $15,000 increase in partnership liabilities, and $15,000, which is Mary's liability assumed by the partnership.

EXAMPLE C:9-7 ▶

Assume the same facts as in Example C:9-6 except the amount of the liability assumed by the XY Partnership is $50,000. Mary's basis in her partnership interest is calculated as follows:

Basis of contributed property	$30,000
Plus: Mary's share of existing partnership liabilities ($4,000 × 0.20)	800
Predistribution basis	$30,800
Minus: Mary's liabilities assumed by the other partners ($50,000 × 0.80)	(40,000)
Basis in partnership interest (cannot be negative)	$ -0-

The cash deemed distributed in excess of Mary's predistribution basis causes her to recognize a $9,200 ($40,000 − $30,800) gain. Mary reduces her basis to zero by the distribution because a partner's basis in the partnership interest can never be less than zero. ◀

ADDITIONAL COMMENT

In contrast to partnership formations, had Example C:9-7 involved a formation of the XY Corporation, Mary would have recognized a $20,000 gain under Sec. 357(c) for the excess of the liability over basis ($50,000 − $30,000).

Question: Assume the land Mary contributed in Example C:9-6 has a $60,000 FMV and an $85,000 adjusted basis. Should Mary contribute it to the partnership?

Solution: If Mary contributes the land, she cannot recognize her $25,000 ($60,000 FMV − $85,000 adjusted basis) loss until the partnership disposes of the property. Accordingly, Mary might prefer to sell the property and recognize her loss now. If the partnership

ADDITIONAL COMMENT

If Mary's interest in the partnership exceeded 50%, she could not deduct the loss on the sale of property to the partnership. See page C:9-27.

can afford the $60,000 price and needs this property, Mary could sell the land to the partnership, recognize her loss on the sale, and then contribute the cash she receives from the partnership in exchange for her partnership interest. If the partnership does not need the property, Mary could sell the land to a third party, recognize her loss, and contribute the sales proceeds to the partnership in exchange for her partnership interest. However, a problem arises if the partnership needs this property and cannot afford to buy it from Mary. In that case, contributing the property to the partnership may be the only alternative despite the less-than-optimal tax results.

TYPICAL MISCONCEPTION

Example C:9-7 illustrates another difference between partnership and corporate formations. In the example, XY Partnership does not increase its basis in the property for the gain recognized by Mary, but if XY were a corporation, XY would increase its basis in the property by Mary's recognized gain.

Because the partnership's assumption of a partner's liabilities is treated as a cash distribution, the character of any gain recognized by the partner is controlled by the partnership distribution rules. Cash distributions exceeding predistribution basis always result in gain recognition, and that gain is deemed to be gain from the sale of the partnership interest.[8] Because a partnership interest is usually a capital asset, any gain arising from assumption of a partner's liabilities normally is a capital gain.

Partner's Basis in the Partnership Interest (Commonly Called Outside Basis). In general, the transferor partner's beginning basis in the partnership interest equals the sum of money contributed plus his or her basis in contributed property. If the partner recognizes any gain on the contribution because the partnership is an investment company, the amount of recognized gain increases his or her basis in the partnership interest.[9] Beginning basis also includes the partner's share of partnership liabilities at the time of contribution. Any gain recognized because of the effects of liabilities on the partner's basis does not increase the basis for the partnership interest because, in this situation, the basis is zero.

In some instances, a partner may contribute valuable property having little or no basis. For example, accounts receivable or notes receivable of a partner using the cash method of accounting can be a valued contribution to a partnership, but if the receivables' bases are zero, the beginning basis of the partnership interest also is zero.

TYPICAL MISCONCEPTION

If a partner contributes both ordinary income property and capital gain property to a partnership, the partner apparently has two different holding periods for his or her partnership interest, i.e., a split holding period.

Holding Period for Partnership Interest. The holding period for the partnership interest includes the transferor's holding period for the contributed property if that property is a capital asset or Sec. 1231 property in the transferor's hands.[10] If the contributed property is an ordinary income asset (e.g., inventory) to the partner, the holding period for the partnership interest begins the day after the contribution date.[11]

EXAMPLE C:9-8 ▶ On April 1, Sue contributes a building (Sec. 1231 property) to the ST Partnership in exchange for a 20% interest. Sue purchased the building three years ago. Her holding period for her partnership interest includes the three years she held the contributed building. ◀

EXAMPLE C:9-9 ▶ On April 1, Ted contributes inventory to the ST Partnership in exchange for a 20% interest. No matter when Ted acquired the inventory, his holding period for his partnership interest begins on April 2, the day after his contribution. ◀

BOOK-TO-TAX ACCOUNTING COMPARISON

Although the partnership takes a carryover tax basis in property, the partnership also records the property at FMV for book purposes. Thus, the partnership essentially maintains two sets of books.

Partnership's Basis in Property. Under Sec. 723, the partnership's basis for contributed property is the same as the property's basis in the hands of the contributing partner. If, however, the contributing partner recognizes gain because the partnership is an investment company, such gain increases the partnership's basis in the contributed property. Gain recognized by the contributing partner because of the assumption of a partner's liability does not increase the partnership's basis in the property.[12]

Not only does the property's basis carry over to the partnership from the contributing partner, but for some property the character of gain or loss on a subsequent disposition of the property by the partnership also references the character of the property in the contributing

---

[8] Sec. 731(a).
[9] Sec. 722.
[10] Sec. 1223(1).
[11] Reg. Sec. 1.1223-1(a).
[12] Rev. Rul. 84-15, 1984-1 C.B. 158.

partner's hands. Section 724 prevents the transformation of ordinary income into capital gains (or capital losses into ordinary losses) when a partner contributes property to a partnership. Properties that were (1) unrealized receivables, inventory, or capital loss property in the hands of the contributing partner and (2) contributed to a partnership retain their character for some subsequent partnership dispositions.[13]

Unrealized Receivables. The concept of unrealized receivables plays a key role for tax purposes in many different partnership transactions. An **unrealized receivable** is any right to payment for goods or services the holder has not included in income because of the accounting method used.[14] The most common occurrence of unrealized receivables is a cash basis taxpayer's accounts receivable.

If a partner contributes an unrealized receivable to his or her partnership, any gain or loss recognized on the partnership's later disposition or collection of the receivable is treated as ordinary income or loss. This rule mandates ordinary income or loss treatment regardless of how long the partnership holds the receivable or its character in the partnership's hands.

Inventory. If property was inventory to the contributing partner, its character remains ordinary for five years. Consequently, any gain or loss recognized by the partnership on the disposition of such property during the five-year period beginning on the date of contribution is ordinary gain or loss. Ordinary gain or loss treatment occurs even if the property is a capital asset or Sec. 1231 asset in the partnership's hands.

EXAMPLE C:9-10 ▶ On June 1, Jose, a real estate developer, contributes ten acres of land in an industrial park he developed to the Hi-Tech Partnership in exchange for a 30% interest in the partnership. Although Jose held the acreage in inventory, the land serves as the site for Hi-Tech's new research facility. Four years later Hi-Tech sells its research facility and the land. Although gain on the sale of the land usually would be taxed as Sec. 1231 gain, Hi-Tech must report it as ordinary income. ◀

ADDITIONAL COMMENT

Congress enacted Sec. 724 to eliminate the ability to transform the character of gain or loss on property by contributing the property to a partnership and having the partnership subsequently sell it.

Capital Loss Property. The final type of property whose character is fixed at the time of the contribution is property that would generate a capital loss if sold by the contributing partner rather than contributed to the partnership. A loss recognized by the partnership on the disposition of the property within five years of its contribution to the partnership is a capital loss. However, the amount of loss characterized as capital may not exceed the capital loss the contributing partner would have recognized had the partner sold the property on the contribution date. The character of any loss exceeding the difference between the property's FMV and its adjusted basis on the contribution date is determined by the property's character in the hands of the partnership.

EXAMPLE C:9-11 ▶ Pam holds investment land that she purchased six years ago for $50,000. The FMV of the land was only $40,000 two years ago when she contributed it to the PK Partnership, which is in the business of developing and selling lots. PK develops the contributed land and sells it in the current year for $28,000, or at a $22,000 loss. The $10,000 loss that accrued while Pam held the land as a capital asset retains its character as a capital loss. The remaining $12,000 of loss that accrues while the land is part of the partnership's inventory is an ordinary loss. ◀

Partnership's Holding Period. Under Sec. 1223(2), the partnership's holding period for its contributed assets includes the holding period of the contributing partner. This rule applies without regard to the character the property has in the contributing partner's hands or the partnership's hands.

Section 1245 and 1250 Property Rules. Although the Sec. 1245 and Sec. 1250 depreciation recapture rules override many gain nonrecognition provisions in the IRC, the partner incurs no depreciation recapture unless he or she recognizes gain upon contributing

[13] Sec. 724. The determination of whether property is an unrealized receivable, inventory, or a capital loss property in the contributing partner's hands occurs immediately before the contribution.

[14] Section 724(d)(1) references the unrealized receivables definition found in Sec. 751(c). For distributions and sale transactions, the unrealized receivables definition is broadened to include certain recapture items. This difference is discussed more fully in Chapter C:10.

property in exchange for a partnership interest.[15] Instead, both the adjusted basis and depreciation recapture potential carry over to the partnership. If the partnership later sells the property at a gain, the Sec. 1245 and 1250 provisions affect the character of the gain. In addition, any unrecaptured Sec. 1250 gain potential carries over to the partnership to affect gain characterization upon a future sale. Unrecaptured Sec. 1250 gain is taxed to individuals at a 25% capital gains rate (and possibly an additional 3.8% tax on net investment income).

Contribution of Property After Formation. Any time a partner contributes property in exchange for a partnership interest, the rules outlined above apply whether the contribution occurs during the formation of the partnership or at a later date. This treatment contrasts sharply with corporate contributions, where a nontaxable contribution after formation is rare because of the 80% control requirement. Most contributions of property in exchange for a partnership interest are nontaxable even if they occur years after forming the partnership.

CONTRIBUTION OF SERVICES

A partner who receives a partnership interest in exchange for services has been compensated as if he or she receives cash and thus must recognize ordinary income. The amount and timing of the income to be recognized are determined under Sec. 83. Consequently, receipt of an unrestricted interest in a partnership requires the service partner to immediately recognize income equal to the FMV of the partnership interest less any cash or property contributed by the partner. Generally, the service partner recognizes no income upon receiving a restricted interest in a partnership until the restriction lapses or the interest can be freely transferred.

Although a partnership interest seems to be a unified interest, it really is made up of two components: a capital interest and a profits interest. A partner may receive both components or only a profits interest in exchange for his or her services. (A capital interest without a profits interest rarely occurs.) Treasury Regulations indicate that a **capital interest** can be valued by determining the amount the partner would receive if the partnership liquidated on the day the partner receives the partnership interest.[16] If the partner would receive proceeds from the sale of the partnership's assets or receive the assets themselves, he or she is considered to own a capital interest. Alternatively, if the partner's only interest is in the future earnings of the partnership (with no interest in the current partnership assets), the partner owns a **profits interest** (but not a capital interest).

ADDITIONAL COMMENT

The Treasury Department has issued proposed regulations, and the IRS will issue a new revenue procedure that will alter the landscape of taxing partnership interests transferred for services. The new rules also will make Rev. Proc. 93-27, discussed on the next page, obsolete. However, taxpayers may not rely on the proposed rules until they are finalized and may continue to rely on existing rules and procedures. See Notice 2005-43, 2005-24 I.R.B. 1221.

Tax law has long been settled that receipt of a capital interest in a partnership in exchange for services is taxable under the rules outlined above. A profits interest, however, is no more than a right to future income taxable to the partners as the partnership earns it. To the extent the profits interest itself has a value, one might expect that value to be taxed when the partner receives the profits interest, as any other property received for services would be taxed.

EXAMPLE C:9-12 ▶ Carl arranges favorable financing for the purchase of an office building and receives a 30% profits interest in a partnership formed to own and operate the building. Less than three weeks later, Carl sells his profits interest to his partner for $40,000. Carl must recognize $40,000 as ordinary income from the receipt of a partnership profits interest in exchange for services. ◀

The facts in Example C:9-12 approximate those of *Sol Diamond*, a landmark partnership taxation case, which was the first case to tax the partner upon receipt of a profits interest.[17] The Tax Court pointed out that Sec. 61 included all compensation for services, and no other provision contained in the IRC or Treasury Regulations removed this transaction from taxation. The Seventh Circuit Court of Appeals seemed to limit the inclusion of a profits interest to situations in which the market value of the profits interest could

[15] Secs. 1245(b)(3) and 1250(d)(3). Property acquired as a capital contribution where gain is not recognized under Sec. 721 is subject to the MACRS anti-churning rules of Sec. 168(i)(7)(A). In general, the anti-churning rules require the partnership to use the same depreciation method as the partner who contributed the property. See Chapter C:2 for a discussion of these rules in connection with a corporate formation transaction.

[16] Reg. Sec. 1.704-1(e)(1)(v). The capital interest definition in this regulation relates to family partnerships, but such definition should apply generally in the partnership area. Rev. Proc. 93-27, 1993-2 C.B. 343, contains a similar definition.

[17] 33 AFTR 2d 74-852, 74-1 USTC ¶9306 (7th Cir., 1974), *aff'g*. 56 T.C. 530 (1971).

TAX STRATEGY TIP

A prospective profits interest partner should seek legal counsel to confirm that the partnership agreement clearly documents the arrangement. This review should ensure that the agreement conforms to the requirements of various IRS pronouncements setting out the parameters of a profits interest arrangement. See citations in footnotes 18 and 19.

be determined. The IRS resolved much of the uncertainty in this area of tax law when it issued Rev. Proc. 93-27, which provides that the IRS generally will tax a profits interest received for services only in three specified instances in which a FMV is readily ascertainable.[18] In the general case, therefore, an income tax is not levied on the profits interest separately, nor does the partnership take a deduction for the FMV of the profits interest at the time it is granted.[19] Instead, all partnership profits that pass through to the partner are treated under the normal rules of partnership taxation.

Consequences to the Partnership. Payments by the partnership for services are either deductible as an expense or capitalized, including those paid for services with an interest in the partnership. If the payment constitutes a deductible expense, the partnership takes the deduction in the same year the partner includes the value of his or her partnership interest in income.[20] This rule matches the timing of the partnership's deduction to the partner's income recognition.

Allocating the Expense Deduction. The partnership allocates the expense deduction or the amortization of the capital expenditure among the partners other than the service partner. This allocation occurs because these partners make the outlay by relinquishing part of their interest in the partnership.

EXAMPLE C:9-13 ▶ In June of the current year Jay, a lawyer, receives a 1% capital and profits interest (valued at $4,000) in the JLK Partnership in return for providing legal services to JLK's employees during the first five months of the current year. The legal services were a fringe benefit for JLK's employees and were deductible by JLK. Jay must include $4,000 in his current year gross income, and JLK can deduct the expense in the current year. JLK allocates the $4,000 expense to all partners other than Jay. Partnership gain or loss effects are discussed below. ◀

If the service performed is of a nature that should be capitalized, the partnership capitalizes the amount and amortizes it as appropriate. The related asset's basis is increased at the same time and in the same amount as the partner's gross income inclusion.[21]

EXAMPLE C:9-14 ▶ In June of the current year, Rob, an architect, receives a 10% capital and profits interest in the KLB Partnership for his services in designing a new building to house the partnership's operations. The June value of the partnership interest is $24,000. Rob must recognize $24,000 of ordinary income in the current year as a result of receiving the partnership interest. The KLB Partnership must capitalize the $24,000 as part of the building's cost and depreciate that amount (along with the building's other costs) over its recovery period. Partnership gain or loss effects are discussed below. ◀

The timing of the partner's recognition of income is the same in the preceding two examples even though the partnership could deduct one payment but had to capitalize the other.

Partnership Gain or Loss. By exchanging an interest in the partnership for services, the partnership, in effect, pays for services by transferring an interest in the underlying partnership property. Generally, when a debtor uses property to pay a debt, the debtor must recognize gain or loss equal to the difference between the property's FMV and adjusted basis. Likewise, the partnership must recognize the gain or loss existing in the proportionate share of its assets deemed to be transferred to the service partner.[22] Furthermore, because the partnership recognizes gain or loss, it must adjust the bases of the assets.

EXAMPLE C:9-15 ▶ On January 1 of the current year, Maria is admitted as a 25% partner in the already existing XYZ Partnership in exchange for services valued at $16,500. The partnership has no liabilities at the time but has assets with a basis of $50,000 and FMV of $66,000. The transaction is treated as if Maria received an undivided one-fourth interest in each asset. She is taxed on the $16,500 FMV

[18] 1993-2 C.B. 343. The three exceptions involve receipt of a profits interest having a substantially certain and predictable income stream, the partner disposes of the profits interest within two years of receipt, or the profits interest is a limited interest in a publicly traded partnership.

[19] Rev Proc. 2001-43, 2001 C.B. 191.

[20] Reg. Sec. 1.83-6(a)(1).

[21] Reg. Sec. 1.83-6(a)(4).

[22] Reg. Sec. 1.83-6(b).

of the assets and takes a $16,500 basis in her partnership interest. The partnership recognizes $4,000 of gain [0.25 × ($66,000 FMV − $50,000 adjusted basis)] on the assets deemed paid to Maria. The partnership calculates gain or loss for each asset XYZ holds, and the character of each asset determines the character of the gain or loss recognized. The recognized gain is allocated to the partners other than Maria. Also, the partnership's original basis in its assets ($50,000) is increased by the $4,000 recognized gain. ◀

SELF-STUDY QUESTION

What is the importance of the distinction between organizational expenditures and syndication expenditures?

ANSWER

Organizational expenditures can be deducted up to $5,000 and then amortized over a period of 180 months, but syndication expenditures are *not* deductible or amortizable.

ORGANIZATIONAL AND SYNDICATION EXPENDITURES

The costs of organizing a partnership are capital expenditures. However, under Sec. 709, the partnership can elect to deduct the first $5,000 of these expenditures in the tax year it begins business. As a limit, the partnership must reduce the $5,000 by the amount by which cumulative organizational expenditures exceed $50,000, although the $5,000 cannot be reduced below zero. The partnership can amortize the remaining organizational expenditures over an 180-month period beginning in the month it begins business.

For organizational expenditures paid or incurred after September 8, 2008, a partnership is deemed to have made the Sec. 709 election for the tax year the partnership begins business.[23] If the partnership chooses to forgo the deemed election, it can elect to capitalize the expenditures (without amortization) on a timely filed tax return for the tax year the partnership begins business. Either election, to amortize or capitalize, is irrevocable and applies to all organizational expenditures of the partnership.

Organizational expenditures that can be capitalized and amortized must meet the same requirements as the costs incurred by a corporation making the Sec. 248 election to amortize organizational expenditures (see Chapter C:3). The organizational expenditures must be incident to the creation of the partnership, chargeable to a capital account, and of a character that would be amortizable over the life of the partnership if the partnership had a limited life. Eligible expenditures include legal fees for negotiating and preparing partnership agreements, accounting fees for establishing the initial accounting system, and filing fees. Syndication expenditures for the issuing and marketing of interests in the partnership are not organizational expenditures and cannot be included in this election.[24] The partnership deducts unamortized organizational expenditures (but not capitalized syndication expenditures) when it terminates or liquidates.

Topic Review C:9-1 summarizes the tax consequences of forming a partnership.

PARTNERSHIP ELECTIONS

OBJECTIVE 4

Establish the permitted tax year for a partnership

Once formed, the partnership must make a number of elections. For example, a partnership must select a tax year and elect accounting methods for all but a few items affecting the computation of partnership taxable income or loss.

PARTNERSHIP TAX YEAR

The partnership's selection of a tax year is critical because it determines when each partner reports his or her share of partnership income or loss. Under Sec. 706(a), each partner's tax return includes his or her share of partnership income, gain, loss, deduction, or credit items for any taxable year of the partnership ending within or with the partner's tax year.

EXAMPLE C:9-16 ▶ Vicki is a member of a partnership having a November 30 year-end. In her tax return for calendar Year 1, she must include her share of partnership items from the partnership tax year that ends November 30 of Year 1. Results of partnership operations in December of Year 1 are reported in Vicki's Year 2 tax return along with her share of other partnership items from the partnership year that ends on November 30 of Year 2. She receives, in essence, a one-year deferral of the taxes due on December's partnership income. ◀

[23] Reg. Sec. 1.709-1.

[24] Reg. Sec. 1.709-2(b).

TOPIC REVIEW C:9-1

Formation of a Partnership

	Contribution to a Partnership	
	Property	Services
Recognition of gain, loss, or income by partner	Nontaxable unless (1) liabilities assumed by the partnership exceed partner's predistribution basis in partnership interest (gain recognized is amount by which liabilities assumed by partnership exceed predistribution basis), (2) the partnership formed is an investment partnership (gain recognized is excess of FMV of partnership interest over basis of assets contributed), or (3) a contribution is followed by a distribution that is treated as a sale (gain or loss recognized on sale transaction).	Taxable to partner equal to FMV of partnership interest received in exchange for the services.
Basis of partnership interest	Substituted basis from property contributed plus share of partnership liabilities assumed minus the partner's liabilities assumed by the partnership. Gain recognized because of the investment company rules increases the basis of the partnership interest.	Amount of income recognized plus share of partnership liabilities assumed by the partner minus partner's liabilities assumed by the partnership.
Gain or loss recognized by the partnership	No gain or loss recognized by the partnership.	1. Deduction or capitalized expense is created depending on the type of service rendered. 2. Gain or loss recognized equals difference between FMV of portion of assets used to pay service partner and the basis of such portion of the assets.
Basis of assets to the partnership	Carryover basis is increased by a partner's gain recognized only if gain results from the formation of an investment partnership. No basis adjustment occurs when assumption of partner's liabilities results in a partner's gain recognition. In a sale transaction, assets take a cost basis.	Increased or decreased to reflect the FMV of the assets paid to the service partner.

Section 706 Restrictions. Because of a substantial opportunity for tax deferral, Congress enacted Sec. 706 to restrict the available choices for a partnership's tax year. The partnership must use the same tax year as the one or more **majority partners** who have an aggregate interest in partnership profits and capital exceeding 50%. This rule must be used only if these majority partners have a common tax year and have had this tax year for the shorter of the three preceding years or the partnership's period of existence. If the tax year of the partner(s) owning a majority interest cannot be used, the partnership must use the tax year of all its principal partners (or the tax year to which all of its principal partners are concurrently changing). A **principal partner** is defined as one who owns a 5% or more interest in capital or profits. If the principal partners do not have a common tax year, the partnership must use the tax year that allows the least aggregate deferral. The least aggregate deferral test provided in Treasury Regulations[25] requires that, for each possible tax year-end, each partner's ownership percentage be multiplied by the number of months the partner would defer income (number of months from partnership year-end to partner year-end). The number arrived at for each partner is totaled across all partners. The same procedure is followed for each alternative tax year, and the partnership must use the tax year that produces the smallest total.

EXAMPLE C:9-17 ▶ Jane, Kerry Corporation, and Lanier Corporation form the JKL Partnership. The three partners use tax years ending on December 31, June 30, and September 30, respectively. Jane, Kerry

[25] Reg. Sec. 1.706-1.

WHAT WOULD YOU DO IN THIS SITUATION?

Bob Krause and his large family corporation have been longtime clients of your accounting firm. During the current year, Bob and his adult son, Tom, formed the BT Partnership to develop and sell vacation homes on the Suwanee River. Bob contributed a 1,000-acre tract of land in exchange for a 50% interest in BT Partnership's profits and losses. The land had a $300,000 FMV and a $30,000 adjusted basis. Tom contributed $150,000 in cash for the remaining 50% interest in the partnership. Two months after being formed, BT Partnership used the land as security for a $200,000 loan from a local bank. Of the $200,000 loan proceeds, the partnership used $50,000 to subdivide and plot the land. The partnership then distributed the other $150,000 of the loan proceeds to Bob. Bob plans not to report these transactions because property contributions in exchange for a partnership interest and distributions of money by a partnership that do not exceed the partner's basis are nontaxable transactions. What would you advise your client to do in this situation?

Corporation, and Lanier Corporation own 40%, 40%, and 20%, respectively, of the partnership. Neither the majority partner rule nor the principal partner rule can be applied to determine JKL's tax year because each partner has a different year-end. To determine the least aggregate deferral, all three possible year-ends must be analyzed as follows:

			Possible Tax Year-Ends					
			6/30		*9/30*		*12/31*	
Partner	*Partnership Interest*	*Partner Tax Year*	*Months Deferred*[a]	*Total*[b]	*Months Deferred*	*Total*	*Months Deferred*	*Total*
Jane	40%	12/31	6	2.4	3	1.2	0	0
Kerry	40%	6/30	0	0	9	3.6	6	2.4
Lanier	20%	9/30	3	0.6	0	0	9	1.8
				3.0		4.8		4.2

[a] Months from possible partnership tax year-end to partner tax year-end.
[b] Partnership interest × months deferred = Total.

The partnership must use a June 30 year-end because, with a total score of 3.0, that tax year-end produces the least aggregate deferral. ◀

If the partnership has a business purpose for using some tax year other than the year prescribed by these rules, the IRS may approve use of another tax year. Revenue Procedure 2002-39[26] states that an acceptable business purpose for using a different tax year is to end the partnership's tax year at the end of the partnership's natural business year. This revenue procedure explains that a business having a peak period and a nonpeak period completes its natural business year at the end of its peak season (or shortly thereafter). For example, a ski lodge has a natural business year that ends in early spring. Partnerships that do not have a peak period cannot use the natural business year exception.

EXAMPLE C:9-18 ▶ Amy, Brad, and Chris are equal partners in the ABC Partnership. Each partner uses a December 31 tax year-end. ABC earns 30% of its gross receipts in July and August each year and has experienced this pattern of earnings for more than three years. This two-month period is the peak season for their business each year. The IRS probably would grant approval for the partnership to use an August 31 tax year-end. ◀

KEY POINT

Because of the Sec. 706 requirements, most partnerships are required to adopt a calendar year. As a compromise, a Sec. 444 election permits a fiscal tax year as long as no more than a three-month deferral exists and as long as the deferral is not increased from any deferral already approved.

Section 444 provides an election that permits a partnership to use a year-end that results in a deferral of the lesser of the current deferral period or three months. The deferral period is the time from the beginning of the partnership's fiscal year to the close of the

[26] 2002-1 C.B. 1046. The IRS in Rev. Rul. 87-57, 1987-2 C.B. 117, has provided a series of situations illustrating the business purpose requirement. In addition, Rev. Proc. 2006-46, 2006-2 C.B. 859, provides expeditious IRS approval if the natural business year satisfies a 25% test. This test requires that 25% of the partnership's gross receipts be earned in the last two months of the requested year and in the last two months of the two preceding similar 12-month periods.

first required tax year ending within such year (i.e., usually December 31). The **Sec. 444 election** is available to both new partnerships making an initial tax year election or existing partnerships that are changing tax years. A partnership that satisfies the Sec. 706 requirements described above or has established a business purpose for its choice of a year-end (i.e., natural business year) does not need a Sec. 444 election.

STOP & THINK

Question: Suppose the ABC Partnership has had a December 31 year-end for many years. All its partners are individuals with calendar tax year-ends. Using Sec. 444, what tax year-ends are available for ABC?

Solution: Only December 31 can be used for a tax year-end for ABC even with Sec. 444. Section 444 allows a minimum deferral of the shorter of three months or the existing deferral. Because the existing deferral is zero months (the required tax year-end and the existing tax year-end are both December 31), no deferral is allowed under Sec. 444. The section allows a deferral only for new partnerships or for partnerships that already have a deferral.

HISTORICAL NOTE

Congress enacted Sec. 444, in part, as a concession to tax return preparers who already have the majority of their clients with calendar year-ends.

A partnership that makes a Sec. 444 election must make a required payment under Sec. 7519. (See the Compliance and Procedural Considerations section of this chapter for a discussion of the Sec. 444 election and Sec. 7519 required payment.) The required payment has the effect of assessing a tax on the partnership's deferred income at the highest individual marginal tax rate plus one percentage point.

Topic Review C:9-2 summarizes the allowable partnership tax year elections.

OTHER PARTNERSHIP ELECTIONS

With the exception of three specific elections reserved to the partners, Sec. 703(b) requires that the partnership make all elections that can affect the computation of taxable income derived from the partnership.[27] The three elections reserved to the individual partners relate to income from the discharge of indebtedness, deduction and recapture of certain mining exploration expenditures, and the choice between deducting or crediting foreign income taxes. Other than these elections, the partnership makes all elections at the entity level. Accordingly, the partnership elects its overall accounting method, which can differ from the methods used by its partners. The partnership also elects its inventory and depreciation methods.

TOPIC REVIEW C:9-2

Allowable Tax Year for a Partnership

Section 706 requires that a partnership select the highest ranked tax year-end from the ranking that follows:

1. The tax year-end used by the partners who own a majority interest in the partnership capital and profits.
2. The tax year-end used by all principal partners (i.e., partners who each owns an interest in at least 5% of the partnership capital or profits).
3. The tax year-end determined by the least aggregate deferral test.

The IRS may grant permission for the partnership to use a fiscal year-end if the partnership has a natural business year. If the partnership does not have a natural business year, it must either

- Use the tax year-end required by Sec. 706 or
- Elect a fiscal year-end under Sec. 444 and make a required payment that approximates the tax due on the deferred income.

[27] The partnership does not include depletion from oil or gas wells in its computation of income (Sec. 703(a)(2)(F)). Instead each partner elects cost or percentage depletion (Sec. 613A(c)(7)(D)).

Partnership Reporting of Income

OBJECTIVE 5

Distinguish between items included in partnership ordinary income or loss and those that must be separately stated

PARTNERSHIP TAXABLE INCOME

Although the partnership is not a taxable entity, the IRC requires that the partnership calculate **partnership taxable income** for various computational reasons, such as adjusting the partners' basis in their partnership interests. Partnership taxable income for partnerships that are not electing large partnerships is calculated in much the same way as the taxable income of individuals, with a few differences mandated by the IRC. First, taxable income is divided into separately stated items and ordinary income or loss. Section 703(a) specifies a list of deductions available to individuals but that cannot be claimed by a partnership. The forbidden deductions include income taxes paid or accrued to a foreign country or U.S. possession, charitable contributions, oil and gas depletion, and net operating loss (NOL) carrybacks or carryovers. The first three items must be separately stated and may or may not be deductible by the partner. Because all losses are allocated to the partners for deduction on their tax returns, the partnership itself never has an NOL carryover or carryback. Instead, a partner may have an NOL if his or her deductible share of partnership losses exceeds his or her other business income. These NOLs are used at the partner level without any further regard for the partnership entity.

ADDITIONAL COMMENT

The applicable capital gains tax rate for net capital gains and qualified dividends of noncorporate taxpayers is 0% for taxpayers in tax brackets of 15% and below, 15% for taxpayers in the 25% through 35% tax brackets, and 20% for taxpayers in the 39.6% tax bracket. Also, 25% and 28% rates apply for gains on certain types of property. In addition, an incremental 3.8% rate applies to net investment income for taxpayers whose modified AGI exceeds $200,000 ($250,000 for married filing jointly). Net investment income includes, among other things, interest, dividends, annuities, royalties, rents, and net gains from the disposition of property not used in a trade or business, all reduced by deductions allocable to such income or gains.

SEPARATELY STATED ITEMS

Each partner must report his or her distributive share of partnership income. However, Sec. 702, related Treasury Regulations, and tax return instructions require that certain items be separately stated at the partnership level so their character can remain intact at the partner reporting level. For example, the following items must be separately stated:

- Net short-term capital gains and losses
- Net long-term capital gains and losses
- Sec. 1231 gains and losses
- Unrecaptured Sec. 1250 gains
- Sec. 179 expense
- Charitable contributions
- Dividends and interest income
- Taxes paid or accrued to a foreign country or to a U.S. possession
- Tax-exempt or partially tax-exempt interest
- Investment income and expenses
- Any items subject to special allocations (discussed below)
- Any other item provided by Treasury Regulations and tax form instructions

As a general rule, an item must be separately stated if the income tax liability of any partner that would result from treating the item separately is different from the liability that would result if that item were included in partnership ordinary income.[28] For a comprehensive list of separately stated items, see Form 1065, Schedule K included in Appendix B.

ADDITIONAL COMMENT

The pass-through aspect of partnerships reflects the aggregate theory of partnerships, which holds that the partnership is merely an aggregate of its partners. In other ways, however, partnerships conform to the entity theory, for example, they report income and make elections at the entity level.

Once the partnership separately states each item and allocates a distributive share to each partner, the partners report the separately stated items on their tax returns as if the partnership entity did not exist. A partner's share of partnership net long-term capital gains or losses is combined with the partner's personal long-term capital gains and losses to calculate the partner's net long-term capital gain or loss. Likewise, a partner's share of partnership charitable contributions is combined with the partner's own charitable contributions with the total subject to the partner's charitable contribution limitations. In summary, Sec. 702(b) requires that the character of each separately stated item be determined at the partnership level. The amount then passes through to the partners and is reported in each partner's return as if the partner directly realized the amount.

[28] Reg. Sec. 1.702-1(a)(8)(ii).

TYPICAL MISCONCEPTION

Partnership ordinary income or loss is the sum of all taxable income or loss items not separately stated. The partnership reports this amount as a residual number on line 22 of Form 1065. Partnership taxable income includes both the taxable separately stated items and the partnership ordinary income or loss. These two terms are not interchangeable.

PARTNERSHIP ORDINARY INCOME

All taxable items of income, gain, loss, or deduction that do not have to be separately stated are combined into a total called **partnership ordinary income** or **loss**. This ordinary income amount sometimes is incorrectly referred to as partnership taxable income. Partnership taxable income is the sum of all taxable items among the separately stated items plus the partnership ordinary income or loss. Therefore, partnership taxable income often is substantially greater than partnership ordinary income.

Included in the partnership's ordinary income are items such as gross profit on sales, administrative expenses, and employee salaries. Such items are always ordinary income or expenses not subject to special limitations. Partnership ordinary income also includes Sec. 1245 depreciation recapture because such ordinary income is not eligible for preferential treatment.

The partnership allocates a share of partnership ordinary income or loss to each partner. Such an allocation is reported on Schedules K and K-1 of the partnership's Form 1065 (see the completed partnership tax return in Appendix B). An individual partner reports his or her distributive share of ordinary income, or the deductible portion of his or her distributive share of ordinary loss, on Schedule E of Form 1040. Schedule E includes rental and royalty income and income or losses from estates, trusts, S corporations, and partnerships. A corporate partner reports partnership ordinary income or loss in the Other Income category of Form 1120.

EXAMPLE C:9-19 ▶ Harry and Rita have been operating the HR Partnership for several years. Each partner has a 50% interest in the partnership. In the current year, the partnership incurred the following items:

Sales	$450,000
Cost of goods sold	250,000
Dividend income	6,000
Gain on sale of stock held for three years	7,000
Loss on sale of stock held for seven months	1,000
Gain on sale of equipment ($10,000 total depreciation taken)	14,000
Salaries paid to employees	45,000
Depreciation	15,000

The partnership will report these items as follows:

Partnership ordinary income items:		
Sales		$450,000
Minus: Cost of goods sold		(250,000)
Gross profit		200,000
Plus: Sec. 1245 depreciation recapture		10,000
Minus: Ordinary expenses:		
Salaries	$45,000	
Depreciation	15,000	(60,000)
Partnership ordinary income		$ 150,000
Separately stated items:		
Dividends		6,000
Net short-term capital loss		(1,000)
Net long-term capital gain		7,000
Sec. 1231 gain ($14,000 - $10,000)		4,000

As discussed in the next section of this chapter, each partner will report a 50% distributive share of partnership ordinary income and each separately stated item. ◀

U.S. PRODUCTION ACTIVITIES DEDUCTION

Chapter C:3 describes the corporate version of the U.S. production activities deduction, whereby the deduction equals 9% times the lesser of (1) qualified production activities income for the year or (2) taxable income before the U.S. production activities deduction. Individuals use a modified form of AGI instead of taxable income for this computation. The deduction, however, cannot exceed 50% of the employer's W-2 wages allocable to production activities for the year. In the case of a partnership, the deduction applies at the partner level, so the partnership must report each partner's share of qualified production activities income on the partner's Schedule K-1. For the 50% salary limitation, each partner is allocated a share of the partnership's W-2 wages.

Partner Reporting of Income

OBJECTIVE 6

Determine a partner's distributive share of partnership income, gain, loss, deduction, or credit items

PARTNER'S DISTRIBUTIVE SHARE

Once the partnership determines separately stated income, gain, loss, deduction, or credit items, and partnership ordinary income or loss, the partnership must allocate the totals among the partners. Each partner must report and pay taxes on his or her distributive share. Under Sec. 704(b), the partner's distributive share normally is determined by the terms of the partnership agreement or, if the partnership agreement is silent, by the partner's overall interest in the partnership as determined by taking into account all facts and circumstances.

Note that the term **distributive share** is misleading because it has nothing to do with the amount actually distributed to a partner. A partner's distributive share is the portion of partnership taxable and nontaxable income that the partner has agreed to report for tax purposes. Actual distributions in a given year may be more or less than the partner's distributive share.

Partnership Agreement. The **partnership agreement** may describe a partner's distributive share by indicating the partner's profits and loss interest, or it may indicate separate profits and loss interests. For example, the partnership agreement may state that a partner has a 10% interest in both partnership profits and losses or a partner has only a 10% interest in partnership profits (i.e., profits interest) but has a 30% interest in partnership losses (i.e., loss interest).

If the partnership agreement states only one interest percentage, it is used to allocate both partnership profit and loss. If the partnership agreement states profit and loss percentages separately, the partnership's taxable income for the year is first totaled to determine whether a net profit or net loss has occurred. Then the appropriate percentage (either profit or loss) applies to each class of income for the year.

EXAMPLE C:9-20 ▶ The ABC Partnership reports the following income and loss items for the current year:

Net long-term capital loss	$100,000
Net Sec. 1231 gain	90,000
Ordinary income	220,000

Carmelia has a 20% profits interest and a 30% loss interest in the ABC Partnership. Because the partnership earns a $210,000 ($90,000 + $220,000 − $100,000) net profit, Carmelia's distributive share is calculated using her 20% profits interest and is reported as follows:

Net long-term capital loss	$ 20,000
Net Sec. 1231 gain	18,000
Ordinary income	44,000

Her loss percentage is used only in years in which the partnership has a net loss. ◀

ADDITIONAL COMMENT

Under the varying interest regulations, extraordinary items include, among other things, the sale of capital assets or Sec. 1231 property not in the ordinary course of business. These items are allocated based on the partners' interest in the partnership on the date of the transaction. Cash basis items include, among other things, taxes, interest, and payments for services or use of property for which the partnership uses the cash basis method of accounting. These items must be prorated even if the partnership uses the interim closing method.

Varying Interest Rule. If a partner's ownership interest changes during the partnership tax year, the income or loss allocation takes into account the partner's varying interest.[29] This varying interest rule applies for changes occurring to a partner's interest as a result of buying an additional interest in the partnership, selling part (but not all) of a partnership interest, giving or being given a partnership interest, or admitting a new partner. Treasury Regulations prescribe two basic methods for applying the varying interest rule: (1) the interim closing method, whereby the partnership closes its books at the time of the variation and allocates items accordingly or (2) an elective proration method, whereby the partnership prorates items on either a calendar day, semi-monthly, or monthly convention.[30] Special rules apply to extraordinary items and so-called cash basis items.

EXAMPLE C:9-21 ▶ Jack and Kathy are equal partners in the Vargos Partnership, which uses the calendar year as its tax year. On December 1 of the current year, Larry contributes $50,000 cash for a

[29] Sec. 706(d)(1).

[30] Reg. Sec. 1.706-4.

ADDITIONAL COMMENT

Under the *calendar day convention*, the variation is deemed to occur at the end of the day on which the variation occurs. Under the *semi-monthly convention*, if the variation occurs on the first through fifteenth day of the current month, the variation is deemed to occur at the end of the last day of the previous month, and if the variation occurs on the sixteenth through the last day of the current month, the variation is deemed to occur at the end of the fifteenth day of the current month. Under the *monthly convention*, if the variation occurs on the first through fifteenth day of the current month, the variation is deemed to occur at the end of the last day of the previous month, and if the variation occurs on the sixteenth through the last day of the current month, the variation is deemed to occur at the end of the last day of the current month.

one-third interest in the partnership. The partnership reports $21,900 of ordinary income for the current tax year ending on December 31. The partners agree to the proration method with a calendar day convention. Thus, the variation is deemed to occur at the end of the day on December 1. Accordingly, the partners report their shares of the partnership income as follows (assuming a non-leap year).

Partner		*Income Allocation*
Jack	1/2 × $21,900 × 335/365	$10,050
	1/3 × $21,900 × 30/365	600
	Jack's share of income	$10,650
Kathy	Same as Jack	10,650
Larry	1/3 × $21,900 × 30/365	600
	Total allocation of income	$21,900

◄

SPECIAL ALLOCATIONS

Special allocations are unique to partnerships (and LLCs treated as partnerships). They allow tremendous flexibility in sharing specific items of income and loss among the partners. Special allocations can provide a specified partner with more or less of an item of income, gain, loss, or deduction than would be available using the partner's regular distributive share. Special allocations fall into two categories. First, Sec. 704 requires certain special allocations with respect to contributed property. Second, other special allocations are allowed as long as they meet the tests set forth in Treasury Regulations for having substantial economic effect. If the special allocation fails the substantial economic effect test, it is disregarded, and the income, gain, loss, or deduction is allocated according to the partner's interest in the partnership as expressed in the actual operations and activities.

BOOK-TO-TAX ACCOUNTING COMPARISON

For tax purposes, the partnership takes a carryover basis in contributed property. For book purposes, however, the partnership records the contributed property at its FMV.

Allocations Related to Contributed Property. As previously discussed, when a partner contributes property to a partnership, the property takes a carryover basis that references the contributing partner's basis. With no special allocations, this carryover basis rule would require the partnership (and each partner) to accept the tax burden of any gain or loss that accrued to the property before its contribution.

EXAMPLE C:9-22 ► In the current year, Elizabeth contributes land having a $4,000 basis and a $10,000 FMV to the DEF Partnership. Assuming the property continues to increase in value, or at least does not decline in value, DEF's gain on the ultimate sale of this property is $6,000 greater than the gain that accrues while the partnership owns the property. Without a special allocation, this $6,000 precontribution gain would be allocated among all partners. ◄

Section 704(c), however, requires precontribution gains or losses to be allocated to the contributing partner. Thus, the precontribution gain of $6,000 in Example C:9-22 would be allocated to Elizabeth. In addition, income and deductions reported with respect to contributed property must be allocated to take into account the difference between the property's basis and FMV at the time of contribution.

EXAMPLE C:9-23 ► Kay and Sam form an equal partnership when Sam contributes cash of $10,000 and Kay contributes land having a $6,000 basis and a $10,000 FMV. If the partnership sells the land two years later for $12,000, the $4,000 precontribution gain ($10,000 FMV − $6,000 basis) is allocated only to Kay. The $2,000 gain that accrued while the partnership held the land ($12,000 sales price − $10,000 FMV at contribution) is allocated to Kay and Sam equally. Kay reports a total gain of $5,000 ($4,000 + $1,000), and Sam reports a $1,000 gain on the sale of the land. ◄

BOOK-TO-TAX ACCOUNTING COMPARISON

The capital accounts for meeting the substantial economic effect requirements are maintained using book value accounting rather than tax accounting.

The allocation of depreciation is another common example of the special deduction allocation related to contributed property that is necessary under these rules. Tax Research Problem C:9-61 addresses the depreciation allocation issue.

Substantial Economic Effect. Special allocations not related to contributed property must meet several specific criteria established by Treasury Regulations. These criteria ensure that the allocations affect the partner's economic consequences and not just their tax consequences.

To distinguish transactions affecting only taxes from those affecting the partner's economic position, Treasury Regulations look at whether the allocation has an economic effect and whether the economic effect is substantial. Under the Sec. 704 regulations, the allocation has economic effect if it meets all three of the following conditions:

- The allocation results in the appropriate increase or decrease in the partner's capital account.
- The proceeds of any liquidation occurring at any time in the partnership's life cycle are distributed in accordance with positive capital account balances.
- Partners must make up negative balances in their capital accounts upon the liquidation of the partnership, and these contributions are used to pay partnership debts or are allocated to partners having positive capital account balances.[31]

BOOK-TO-TAX ACCOUNTING COMPARISON

In Example C:9-23, the partnership records a $6,000 tax gain and a $2,000 book gain, which provides another example of the difference between partnership tax and book accounting.

EXAMPLE C:9-24 ▶ Arnie and Bonnie each contribute $100,000 to form the AB Partnership on January 1 of Year 1. The partnership uses these contributions plus a $1.8 million mortgage to purchase a $2 million office building. To simplify the calculations, assume the partnership depreciates the building using the straight-line method over a 40-year life and that in each year income and expenses are equal before considering depreciation. AB makes a special allocation of depreciation to Arnie. The allocation reduces Arnie's capital account, and the partnership makes any liquidating distributions in accordance with the capital account balances. Allocations through Year 3 are as follows:

	Capital Account Balance	
	Arnie	*Bonnie*
January 1, Year 1, balance	$100,000	$100,000
Year 1 loss (from depreciation deduction)	(50,000)	–0–
Year 2 loss (from depreciation deduction)	(50,000)	–0–
Year 3 loss (from depreciation deduction)	(50,000)	–0–
December 31, Year 3, balance	$ (50,000)	$100,000

If we assume that the property has declined in value in an amount equal to the depreciation claimed and that the partnership now liquidates, the need for the requirement to restore negative capital account balances becomes apparent.

Sales price of property on December 31, Year 3	$1,850,000
Minus: Mortgage principal	(1,800,000)
Partnership cash to be distributed to partners	$ 50,000

If Arnie does not have to restore his negative capital account balance, Bonnie can receive only $50,000 in cash even though her capital account balance is $100,000. In effect, Bonnie has borne the economic burden of the Year 3 depreciation. Without a requirement to restore the negative capital account balance, the special allocation to Arnie would be ignored for Year 3, and Bonnie would receive the depreciation deduction. However, if Arnie must restore any negative capital account balance, he will contribute $50,000 when the partnership liquidates at the end of Year 3, and Bonnie will receive her full $100,000 capital account balance. The Year 3 special allocation to Arnie will then have economic effect. Note that Arnie's allocations for Years 1 and 2 are acceptable even without an agreement to restore negative capital account balances. This result occurs in each of these two years because Arnie has sufficient capital to absorb the economic loss if the property declines in value in an amount equal to the depreciation allocated to him.[32] ◀

ADDITIONAL COMMENT

Under the traditional application of economic effect rules, a partnership would allocate income, gain, deduction, and loss items pursuant to the partners' profit and loss sharing arrangement in the partnership agreement. Subsequently, when the partnership liquidates, the partnership distributes the liquidation proceeds in accordance with the capital account balances that resulted from the previously allocated items. In recent years, many partnerships have taken a targeted capital account approach to allocating partnership items. Under this approach, the partners agree on what distributions they should get upon a partnership liquidation (the targeted amount) and then allocate items to ensure that the targeted capital account balances are met.

The second requirement for a special allocation to be accepted under Treasury Regulations is that the economic effect must be substantial, which requires that a reasonable possibility exists that the allocation will substantially affect the dollar amounts to be received by the partners independent of tax consequences.[33] Moreover, allocations that involve shifting of tax benefits will not pass the substantiality test. Shifting occurs when the following two conditions are present:

- The net change in the partner's capital accounts will be the same for a normal allocation and the special allocation.

[31] Reg. Sec. 1.704-1(b)(2)(ii). Treasury Regulations provide other alternatives for meeting this portion of the requirements.

[32] Such allocations do not literally meet the three requirements outlined above for special allocations. However, allocations that meet the alternate standard—having sufficient capital to absorb the economic loss—are considered to have economic effect and will be allowed. See Reg. Sec. 1.704-1(b)(2)(ii)(d).

[33] Reg. Sec. 1.704-1(b)(2)(iii)(a). It should be noted that the substantial economic effect regulations go far beyond the rules covered in this text.

[34] Reg. Sec. 1.704-1(b)(2)(iii)(b). An allocation also can fail the substantiality test by being transitory, which is something like shifting except an allocation in one year is offset by another allocation in a future year (Reg. Sec. 1.704-1(b)(2)(iii)(c)).

► The total tax liability of the partners will be less with the special allocation than with a normal allocation.[34]

EXAMPLE C:9-25 ► The AB Partnership earns $10,000 in tax-exempt interest income and $10,000 in taxable interest income each year. Andy and Becky each have 50% capital and profit interests in the partnership. An allocation of the tax-exempt interest income to Andy, a 33% tax bracket partner, and the taxable interest income to Becky, a 15% tax bracket partner, does not have substantial economic effect. In particular, the allocation lacks substantiality because of shifting. The allocation increases each partner's capital account by $10,000 as would an equal allocation, and it reduces the partner's overall tax liability (see Problem C:9-36 at the end of this chapter). ◄

STOP & THINK

Question: The special allocation rules require that a partner who receives a special allocation of loss or expense receive less cash or property when the partnership liquidates. As we will see later in this chapter, losses reduce the partner's basis in the partnership interest, so a sale or liquidation of the partnership interest will cause the partner to recognize a larger gain (or a smaller loss) than would have resulted without this loss allocation. Because the basis is reduced, the partner also is more likely to recognize taxable gain on a distribution from the partnership. With these negative consequences, why would anyone want to be given a special allocation of partnership loss or expense?

Solution: The answer is a matter of timing. The specially allocated loss reduces taxable income now and saves more taxes now for the partner than would a "normal" loss allocation. The negative consequences occur when the partner incurs a larger gain (or smaller loss) upon a future sale or liquidation of his or her partnership interest. The special allocation scenario may have a greater after-tax present value to the partner than would the after-tax present value of receiving a normal share of losses and an increased liquidating distribution.

BASIS FOR PARTNERSHIP INTEREST

OBJECTIVE 7

Calculate a partner's basis in a partnership interest and its effect on losses allowed

The calculation of a partner's beginning basis in a partnership interest depends on the method used to acquire the interest, with different valuation techniques for a purchased interest, a gifted interest, and an inherited interest. The results of the partnership's operations and liabilities both cause adjustments to the beginning amount. Additional contributions to the partnership and distributions from the partnership further alter the partner's basis.

BEGINNING BASIS

ADDITIONAL COMMENT

A partner's basis in a partnership interest commonly is referred to as "outside basis" as opposed to "inside basis," which is the partnership's basis in its assets.

SELF-STUDY QUESTION

What are some of the common methods of acquiring a partnership interest, and what is the beginning basis?

ANSWER

1. Contribution—substituted basis from contributed property
2. Purchase—cost basis
3. Inheritance—FMV
4. Gift—usually donor's basis with a possible gift tax adjustment

A partner's beginning basis for a partnership interest received for a contribution of property or services has been discussed. However, a partner also can acquire a partnership interest by methods other than contributing property or services to the partnership. If a person purchases the partnership interest from an existing partner, the new partner's basis is the price paid for the partnership interest, including assumption of partnership liabilities. If a person inherits the partnership interest, the heir's basis is the FMV of the partnership interest on the decedent's date of death or, if elected by the executor, the alternate valuation date but not less than liabilities assumed. If a person receives the partnership interest as a gift, the donee's basis generally equals the donor's basis (including the donor's ratable share of partnership liabilities) plus the portion of any gift tax paid by the donor that relates to appreciation attaching to the gift property. In summary, the usual rules for the method of acquisition dictate the beginning basis for a partnership interest.

EFFECTS OF LIABILITIES

The early part of this chapter briefly discussed the effect of partnership liabilities on the basis of a partnership interest in connection with the contribution of property subject to a liability. However, further explanation is necessary to fully convey the pervasive impact of liabilities on partnership taxation.

Increases and Decreases in Liabilities. Two changes in a partner's liabilities are considered contributions of cash by the partner to the partnership.[35] The first is an increase in the partner's share of partnership liabilities. This increase can arise from either an increase in the partner's profit or loss interests or from an increase in total partnership liabilities. Accordingly, if a partnership incurs a large debt, the partners' bases in their partnership interests increase. The second way to increase a partner's basis is to have the partner assume partnership liabilities in his or her individual capacity.

Conversely, two liability changes are treated as distributions of cash from the partnership to the partner. These changes are a decrease in a partner's share of partnership liabilities and a decrease in the partner's individual liabilities resulting from the partnership's assumption of the partner's liability. Often, both an increase and a decrease in a partner's basis for his or her interest can result from a single transaction. The framework below illustrates the steps used to calculate the partner's basis in his or her partnership interest.

	Partner's basis before changes in liabilities
Plus:	Increases in share of partnership liabilities
Minus:	Decreases in share of partnership liabilities
Plus:	Partnership liabilities assumed by this partner
Minus:	This partner's liabilities assumed by the partnership
	Partner's basis in the partnership interest

EXAMPLE C:9-26 ▶ Juan, a 40% partner in the ABC Partnership, has a $30,000 basis in his partnership interest before receiving a partnership distribution of land. As part of the transaction, Juan agrees to assume a $10,000 mortgage on the land. First, Juan's basis in his partnership interest will decrease by $4,000 for the decline in Juan's share of partnership liabilities resulting from the partnership no longer owing the $10,000 mortgage. Second, his basis in the partnership interest will increase by $10,000, which is the partnership liability he assumes in his individual capacity. The net change in basis in his partnership resulting from the liabilities is $6,000 (−$4,000 + $10,000). His basis in his partnership interest also must be decreased for the land distribution he receives. Distributions will be discussed further in Chapter C:10. ◀

A Partner's Share of Liabilities. Having explained the general impact of liabilities on a partner's basis for his or her partnership interest, we now turn to how the specific amount of the partner's share of a partnership's liabilities is determined. All examples so far have considered only general partners who have the same interest in profits and losses. Partnerships, however, commonly have one or more limited partners, and thus partners can have differing profit and loss ratios. Moreover, the type of liability affects how it is allocated. Treasury Regulations provide guidelines for allocating partnership liabilities to the individual partners.

ADDITIONAL COMMENT

That a partner gets basis for his or her share of recourse debt is not controversial. That a partner gets basis for debt on which the partner is not personally liable seems questionable, yet other rules, such as the at-risk provisions, limit the benefit of the basis created by the nonrecourse debt.

Recourse and Nonrecourse Loans. A **recourse loan** is the usual kind of loan for which the borrower remains liable until the loan is paid. If the recourse loan is secured and the borrower fails to make payments as scheduled, the lender can sell the property used as security. If the sales proceeds are insufficient to repay a recourse loan, the borrower must make up the difference. Under Treasury Regulations, a recourse loan is one for which any partner or a related party will bear an economic loss if the partnership cannot pay the debt.[36] In contrast, a **nonrecourse loan** is one in which the lender may sell property used as security if the loan is not paid, but no partner is liable for any deficiency. In short, the lender has no recourse against the borrower for additional amounts. Nonrecourse debts most commonly occur in connection with the financing of real property that is expected to substantially increase in value over the life of the loan.

General and Limited Partners. A limited partner normally is not liable to pay partnership debts beyond the original contribution (which already is reflected in his or her basis in the partnership interest) and any additional amount the partner has pledged to contribute.[37]

[35] Sec. 752.

[36] Reg. Sec. 1.752-1(a).

[37] This rule may be modified by the limited partner agreeing to assume some of the risk of economic loss despite his or her limited partner status. For example, a limited partner may guarantee the debt or may agree to reimburse the general partner some amount if the general partner has to pay the debt. These arrangements mean that the limited partner shares the risk of loss.

Therefore, recourse debt increases a limited partner's basis only to the extent the partner has a risk of economic loss. Nonrecourse debts increase a limited partner's basis based primarily on the profit ratio.[38]

A general partner's share of nonrecourse liabilities also is determined primarily by his or her profit ratio. On the other hand, because limited partners seldom receive an allocated share of the recourse liabilities, the general partners share all recourse liabilities beyond any amounts the limited partners can claim according to their economic loss potential.

The Sec. 752 Treasury Regulations require that recourse liabilities be allocated to the partner who will bear the economic loss if the partnership cannot pay the debt. The regulations provide a complex procedure using a hypothetical liquidation to determine who would bear the loss. In this text, we generally assume that the hypothetical liquidation analysis has been completed and that the appropriate shares of economic loss as determined by the hypothetical liquidation procedure are stated as part of the problem or example information. However, Example C:9-28 below provides a simple example of this procedure.

EXAMPLE C:9-27 ▶ The ABC Partnership has one general partner (Anna) and a limited partner (Clay) with the following partnership interests:

	Anna (General)	*Clay (Limited)*
Loss interest	75%	25%
Profits interest	60%	40%
Basis before liabilities	$100,000	$100,000

Clay has an obligation to make an additional $5,000 contribution. He has made no other agreements or guarantees. The partnership has two liabilities at year-end: a $300,000 nonrecourse liability and a $400,000 recourse liability. Clay has an economic risk of loss only to the extent he has agreed to make additional contributions. The partners' year-end bases are calculated as follows:

	Anna (General)	*Clay (Limited)*
Year-end basis (excluding liabilities)	$100,000	$100,000
Share of:		
Recourse liability	395,000	5,000
Nonrecourse liability	180,000[a]	120,000[b]
Year-end basis	$675,000	$225,000

[a] 60% × $300,000 = $180,000
[b] 40% × $300,000 = $120,000 ◀

If the partnership has more than one general partner, the economic risk of loss computation entails computing a hypothetical loss and allocating that loss to the general partners. The hypothetical loss computation assumes the partnership sells all its assets (including cash) for the amount of nonrecourse liabilities. If the partnership does not have nonrecourse liabilities, the assets are deemed sold for zero dollars. The hypothetical loss then is subtracted from the partners' capital accounts to determine the economic risk of loss.

EXAMPLE C:9-28 ▶ Assume the same facts as in Example C:9-27 except that Clay is a general partner. In addition, the partnership has $900,000 of assets, and each partner's capital account is $100,000. If the partnership sold its assets for the amount of the nonrecourse liability, it would realize a $600,000 loss ($300,000 – $900,000). The economic risk of loss is calculated as follows:

	Anna (General)	*Clay (General)*
Capital accounts	$100,000	$100,000
Minus: Hypothetical loss (allocated according to loss percentages)	(450,000)	(150,000)
Economic risk of loss	($350,000)	($ 50,000)

[38] Some nonrecourse debt allocations involve two steps before an allocation according to profits interests. These two steps of the allocation process are beyond the scope of this explanation.

The partners' year-end bases are calculated as follows:

	Anna (General)	*Clay (General)*
Year-end basis (excluding liabilities)	$100,000	$100,000
Share of:		
Recourse liability	350,000	50,000
Nonrecourse liability	180,000	120,000
Year-end basis	$630,000	$270,000 ◀

Determining the partners' share of recourse liabilities can be simplified if the partners have the same interest in losses as they do for profits and if their capital accounts are in accordance with those percentages. In this situation, the recourse liability allocation also will be in accordance with the profit/loss percentages.

EFFECTS OF OPERATIONS

A partner's basis is a summary of his or her contributions and the partner's share of partnership liabilities, earnings, losses, and distributions. Basis prevents a second tax levy on a distribution of income that was taxed previously as a partner's distributive share. Section 705 mandates a basis increase for additional contributions made by the partner to the partnership plus the partner's distributive share for the current and prior tax years of the following items:[39]

- Partnership taxable income (both separately stated items and partnership ordinary income)
- Tax-exempt income of the partnership

Basis is decreased (but not below zero) by distributions from the partnership to the partner plus the partner's distributive share for the current and prior tax years of the following items:

- Partnership losses (both separately stated items and partnership ordinary loss)
- Expenditures that are not deductible for tax purposes and that are not capital expenditures

BOOK-TO-TAX ACCOUNTING COMPARISON

Although a partner's basis in the partnership cannot go below zero, a partner's book capital account (equity) may be negative.

The positive basis adjustment for tax-exempt income and the negative basis adjustment for nondeductible expenses preserve that tax treatment for the partner. If these adjustments were not made, tax-exempt income would be taxable to the partner upon a subsequent distribution or upon the sale or other disposition of the partnership interest.

EXAMPLE C:9-29 ▶ LMN Partnership has only one asset—a $100,000 municipal bond. Marta has a $20,000 basis in her 20% partnership interest. In the current year, the partnership collects $4,000 tax-exempt interest from the bond. Marta's basis at year-end is calculated as follows:

Beginning basis	$20,000
Share of tax-exempt income	800
Basis at year end	$20,800

On the first day of the next year, the partnership sells the bond for $100,000 cash. At this point, the partnership has $104,000 in cash and no other assets. The partnership liquidates and distributes her 20% share of the cash ($20,800) to Marta. Marta has no gain or loss because her $20,800 basis exactly equals her distribution. If the tax-exempt income had not increased her basis, she would have recognized an $800 gain on the distribution ($20,800 cash distribution – $20,000 basis if no increase were made for the tax-exempt income). Thus, her basis must be increased by tax-exempt income to prevent a taxable gain upon its distribution. ◀

Loss Limitations. Each partner is allocated his or her distributive share of ordinary income or loss and separately stated income, gain, loss, or deduction items each year. The partner always reports income and gain items in his or her current tax year, and these items increase the partner's basis in the partnership interest. However, the partner may not be able to use his or her full distributive share of losses because Sec. 704(d) limits a partner's loss deduction to the amount of his or her basis in the partnership interest before the loss. All positive basis adjustments for the year and all reductions for actual or deemed distributions must be made before determining the amount of the deductible loss.[40]

[39] Section 705 also contains adjustments pertaining to depletion.

[40] Reg. Sec. 1.704-1(d)(2).

EXAMPLE C:9-30 ▶ On January 1 of the current year, Miguel has a $32,000 basis for his general interest in the MT Partnership. He materially participates in the partnership's business activities. On December 1, Miguel receives a $1,000 cash distribution. His distributive share of MT's current items are a $4,000 net long-term capital gain and a $43,000 ordinary loss. Miguel's deductible loss is calculated as follows:

January 1 basis	$32,000
Plus: Long-term capital gain	4,000
Minus: Distribution	(1,000)
Limit for loss deduction	$35,000

Miguel can deduct $35,000 of the ordinary loss in the current year, which reduces his basis to zero. He cannot deduct the remaining $8,000 of ordinary loss currently but can deduct it in the following year if he regains sufficient basis in his partnership interest. ◀

SELF-STUDY QUESTION

What happens to losses that are disallowed due to lack of basis in a partnership interest?

ANSWER

The losses are suspended until that partner obtains additional basis.

Any distributive share of loss that a partner cannot deduct because of the basis limit is simply noted in the partner's financial records. It is not reported on the partner's tax return, nor does it reduce the partner's basis. However, the losses carry forward until the partner again has positive basis from capital contributions, additional partnership borrowings, or partnership earnings.

EXAMPLE C:9-31 ▶ Assume the same facts as in Example C:9-30. Miguel makes no additional contributions in the following year, and the MT Partnership's liabilities remain unchanged. Miguel's distributive share of MT's partnership items in the following year is $2,500 of net short-term capital gain and $14,000 of ordinary income. These items restore his basis to $16,500 ($0 + $2,500 + $14,000), and he can deduct the $8,000 loss carryover. After taking these transactions into account, Miguel's basis is $8,500 ($16,500 − $8,000). ◀

Topic Review C:9-3 summarizes the rules for determining the initial basis for a partnership interest and the annual basis adjustments required to determine the adjusted basis of a partnership interest.

TOPIC REVIEW C:9-3

Basis of a Partnership Interest

METHOD OF ACQUISITION	**BEGINNING BASIS IS**
Property contributed	Substituted basis from property contributed plus gain recognized for contributions to an investment partnership
Services contributed	Amount of income recognized for services rendered (plus any additional amount contributed)
Purchase	Cost
Gift	Donor's basis plus gift tax on appreciation
Inheritance	Fair market value at date of death or alternative valuation date

LIABILITY IMPACT ON BASIS	
Increase basis for	Increases in the partner's share of partnership liabilities Liabilities of the partnership assumed by the partner in his or her individual capacity
Decrease basis for	Decreases in the partner's share of partnership liabilities Liabilities of the partner assumed by the partnership

OPERATIONS IMPACT ON BASIS	
Increase basis for	Partner's share of ordinary income and separately stated income and gain items (including tax-exempt items) Additional contributions to the partnership Precontribution gain recognized
Decrease basis for	Distributions from the partnership to the partner Partner's share of ordinary loss and separately stated loss and deduction items (including items that are not deductible for tax purposes and are not capital expenditures) Precontribution loss recognized

Special Loss Limitations

OBJECTIVE 8

Discuss the at-risk and passive activity loss limitations

Three sets of rules limit the loss from a partnership interest that a partner may deduct. The Sec. 704(d) rules explained above limit losses to the partner's basis in the partnership interest. Two other rules establish more stringent limits. The at-risk rules limit losses to an amount called *at-risk basis*. The passive activity loss or credit limitation rules disallow most net passive activity losses.

AT-RISK LOSS LIMITATION

The Sec. 704(d) loss limitation rules were the only loss limits for many years. However, Congress became increasingly uncomfortable with allowing partners to increase their basis by a portion of the partnership's nonrecourse liabilities and then offset this basis with partnership losses. Accordingly, Congress established the **at-risk rules**, which limit loss deductions to the partner's at-risk basis. The **at-risk basis** is essentially the same amount as the regular partnership basis with the exception that liabilities increase the at-risk basis only if the partner is at risk for such an amount. The at-risk rules apply to individuals and closely held C corporations. Partners that are widely held C corporations are not subject to these rules.

REAL-WORLD EXAMPLE

In 2014, 44.4% of all domestic partnerships and LLCs reported net losses. These losses would have passed through to the partners and LLC members to offset income or gains from other sources.

Although much of the complexity of the *at-risk* term is beyond the scope of this text, a simplified working definition is possible. A partner is at risk for an amount if he or she would lose that amount should the partnership suddenly become worthless. Because a partner would not have to pay a partnership's nonrecourse liabilities even if the partnership became worthless, the usual nonrecourse liabilities cannot be included in any partner's at-risk basis. Under the at-risk rules, a partner's loss deduction may be substantially less than the amount deductible under the Sec. 704(d) rules.[41]

EXAMPLE C:9-32 ▶ Keesha is a limited partner in the KM Manufacturing Partnership. At the end of the partnership's tax year, her basis in the partnership interest is $30,000 ($10,000 investment plus a $20,000 share of nonrecourse financing). Keesha's distributive share of partnership losses for the tax year is $18,000. Although she has sufficient basis in the partnership interest, the at-risk rules limit her deduction to $10,000 because she is not at risk for the nonrecourse financing. ◀

The IRC allows one significant exception to the application of the at-risk rules. At-risk rules do not apply to nonrecourse debt if it is qualified real estate financing. The partner is considered at risk for his or her share of nonrecourse real estate financing if all of the following requirements are met:

TYPICAL MISCONCEPTION

The at-risk rules severely limit the use of nonrecourse debt to obtain loss deductions except for certain qualified real estate financing, yet this real estate exception is more apparent than real because of the final set of rules that must be satisfied: the passive activity limitations.

- ▶ The financing is secured by real estate used in the partnership's real estate activity.
- ▶ The debt is not convertible to any kind of equity interest in the partnership.
- ▶ The financing is from a qualified person or from any federal, state, or local government, or is guaranteed by any federal, state, or local government.[42] A qualified person is an unrelated party who is in the trade or business of lending money (e.g., bank, financial institution, or mortgage broker).

PASSIVE ACTIVITY LIMITATIONS

Subsequent to enacting the at-risk rules, Congress added still a third set of limitations to losses a partner may deduct: the passive activity loss and credit limitations of Sec. 469. Under these rules, income falls into one of three categories: (1) amounts derived from passive activities; (2) active income such as salary, bonuses, and income from businesses in which the taxpayer materially participates; and (3) portfolio income such as dividends, interest, and capital gains from investments other than passive activities. Generally, losses of an individual partner from a passive activity cannot be used to offset either active income or portfolio income. However, passive losses carry over to future years where they can offset passive income in those years. Moreover, passive losses are allowed in full when a taxpayer disposes of the entire interest in the passive activity. Passive losses generated by

[41] Sec. 465(a).

[42] Sec. 465(b)(6).

a passive rental activity in which an individual partner is an active participant can be deducted up to a maximum of $25,000 per year. This deduction phases out by 50% of the amount of the partner's adjusted gross income (AGI) that exceeds $100,000, so that no deduction is allowed if the partner has AGI of $150,000 or more. (The phase-out begins at $200,000 for low-income housing or rehabilitation credits.) Losses disallowed under the phase-out are deductible to the extent of passive income.

TAX STRATEGY TIP

If a partner is unable to use all of his or her share of partnership losses due to a lack of basis, contributions to capital or increasing partnership liabilities may provide the additional needed tax basis. If the passive activity limitation rules are the reason the partnership losses cannot be used, the possibility of investing in passive activities that generate passive income may be the best planning alternative. See Tax Planning Considerations for further discussion.

A passive activity is any trade or business in which the taxpayer does not materially participate. A taxpayer who owns a limited partnership interest in any activity generally fails the material participation test. Accordingly, losses from most limited partnership interests can be used only to offset income from passive activities even if the limited partner has sufficient Sec. 704(d) and at-risk basis.[43]

Although passive activity limitations may greatly affect the taxable income or loss reported by a partner, they have no unusual effect on basis. Basis is reduced (but not below zero) by the partner's distributive share of losses whether or not the losses are limited under the passive loss rules.[44] When the suspended passive losses later become deductible, the partner's basis in the partnership interest is not affected.

EXAMPLE C:9-33 ▶ Chris purchases a 20% capital and profits interest in the CJ Partnership in the current year, but he does not participate in CJ's business. Chris owns no other passive investments. His Sec. 704(d) basis in CJ is $80,000, and his at-risk basis is $70,000. Chris's distributive share of the CJ Partnership's loss for the current year is $60,000. After the results of this year's operations are taken into account, Chris's Sec. 704(d) basis is $20,000 ($80,000 − $60,000), and his at-risk basis is $10,000 ($70,000 − $60,000). However, Chris cannot deduct any of the CJ loss in the current year because it is a passive activity loss. The $60,000 loss, however, can be used in a subsequent year if the partner generates passive income. Because the $60,000 loss already has reduced basis for purposes of both Sec. 704(d) and the at-risk rules, the disallowed loss need not be tested against those rules a second time. ◀

TRANSACTIONS BETWEEN A PARTNER AND THE PARTNERSHIP

OBJECTIVE 9

Determine the tax consequences of property sales between a partner and the partnership and of guaranteed payments to a partner

The partner and the partnership are treated as separate entities for many transactions. Section 707(b) restricts sales of property between the partner and partnership by disallowing certain losses and converting certain capital gains into ordinary income. Section 707(c) permits a partnership to make guaranteed payments for capital and services to a partner that are separate from the partner's distributive share. Each of these rules is explored below.

SALES OF PROPERTY

Loss Sales. Without restrictions, a controlling partner could sell property to the partnership to recognize a loss for tax purposes while retaining a substantial interest in the property through ownership of a partnership interest. Congress closed the door to such loss recognition with the Sec. 707(b) rules.

KEY POINT

The IRC disallows losses on sales between persons and certain related partnerships, similar to the related party rules of Sec. 267. The concern is that tax losses can be artificially recognized without the property being disposed of outside the economic group.

The rules for partnership loss transactions are quite similar to the Sec. 267 related party rules discussed in Chapter C:3. Under Sec. 707(b)(1), no loss can be deducted on the sale or exchange of property between a partnership and a person who directly or indirectly owns more than 50% of the partnership's capital or profits interests. (Indirect ownership includes ownership by related parties such as members of the partner's family.[45]) Similarly, losses are disallowed on sales or exchanges of property between two partnerships in which the same persons own, directly or indirectly, more than 50% of the capital

[43] Sec. 469(h)(2).

[44] S. Rept. No. 99-313, 99th Cong., 2d Sess., p. 723, footnote 4 (1986).

[45] For purposes of Sec. 707, related parties include an individual and members of his or her family (spouse, brothers, sisters, lineal descendants, and ancestors), an individual and a more-than-50%-owned corporation, and two corporations that are members of the same controlled group.

or profits interests. If the seller is disallowed a loss under Sec. 707(b)(1), the purchaser can reduce any subsequent gain realized on a sale of the property by the previously disallowed loss.

EXAMPLE C:9-34 ▶ James, Karen, and Thelma own equal interests in the JKT Partnership. Karen and Thelma are siblings, but James is unrelated to the others. For purposes of Sec. 707, Karen owns two-thirds of the partnership (one-third directly and one-third indirectly from Thelma). Likewise, Thelma also owns two-thirds, but James has only a direct ownership interest of one-third. ◀

EXAMPLE C:9-35 ▶ Pat sold land having a $45,000 basis to the PTA Partnership for $35,000, its FMV. If Pat has a 60% capital and profits interest in the partnership, Pat realizes but cannot recognize a $10,000 loss on the sale. If Pat owns only a 49% interest, directly and indirectly, he can recognize the loss. ◀

EXAMPLE C:9-36 ▶ Assume the same facts as in Example C:9-35 except the partnership later sells the land for $47,000. The partnership's realized gain is $12,000 ($47,000 – $35,000 basis). If Pat has a 60% capital and profits interest, his previously disallowed loss of $10,000 reduces the partnership's recognized gain to $2,000. This $2,000 gain is then allocated to the partners according to the partnership agreement. ◀

Gain Sales. When gain is recognized on the sale of a capital asset between a partnership and a related partner, Sec. 707(b)(2) requires that the gain be ordinary (and not capital gain) if the property will not be a capital asset to its new owner. Sales or exchanges resulting in the application of Sec. 707(b)(2) include transfers between (1) a partnership and a person who owns, directly or indirectly, more than 50% of the partnership's capital or profits interests, or (2) two partnerships in which the same persons own, directly or indirectly, more than 50% of the capital or profits interests.[46] This provision prevents related parties from increasing the depreciable basis of assets (and thereby reducing future ordinary income) at the cost of recognizing only a current capital gain.

EXAMPLE C:9-37 ▶ Sharon and Tony have the following capital and profits interests in two partnerships:

Partner	*ST Partnership (%)*	*QRS Partnership (%)*
Sharon	42	58
Tony	42	30
Other unrelated partners	16	12
Total	100	100

The ST Partnership sells land having a $150,000 basis to the QRS Partnership for $180,000. The land was a capital asset for the ST Partnership, but QRS intends to subdivide and sell the land. Because the land is ordinary income property to the QRS Partnership and because Sharon and Tony control both partnerships, the ST Partnership must recognize $30,000 of ordinary income on the land sale. ◀

GUARANTEED PAYMENTS

A corporate shareholder can be an employee of the corporation. However, a partner generally is not an employee of the partnership, and most fringe benefits are disallowed for a partner who is "employed" by his or her partnership.[47]

A partner who provides services to the partnership in an ongoing relationship might be compensated like any other employee. Section 707(c) provides for this kind of payment and labels it a **guaranteed payment**. The term *guaranteed payment* also includes certain payments made to a partner for the use of invested capital. These payments are similar to interest. Both types of guaranteed payments must be determined without regard to the partnership's income.[48] Conceptually, this requirement separates guaranteed payments from distributive shares. As indicated below, however, such a distinction may not be so clear in practice.

Determining the Guaranteed Payment. Sometimes the determination of the guaranteed payment is quite simple. For example, some guaranteed payments are expressed as

[46] Sec. 707(b)(2).

[47] Rev. Rul. 91-26, 1991-1 C.B. 184, holds that accident and health insurance premiums paid for a partner by the partnership are guaranteed payments.

[48] Sec. 707(c).

TYPICAL MISCONCEPTION

If a partner, acting in his or her capacity as a partner, receives payments from the partnership determined without regard to the partnership's income, the partner has received a guaranteed payment. If the partner is acting as a nonpartner, the partner is treated as any other outside contractor.

specific amounts (e.g., $20,000 per year), with the partner also receiving his or her normal distributive share. In this case, the partnership deducts the guaranteed payment in arriving at partnership ordinary income and then allocates the resulting ordinary income based on the partners' profit sharing percentages. Other times, the guaranteed payment is expressed as a **guaranteed minimum.** However, these guaranteed minimum arrangements make it difficult to distinguish the partner's distributive share and guaranteed payments because no guaranteed payment occurs under this arrangement unless the partner's distributive share is less than his or her guaranteed minimum. If the distributive share is less than the guaranteed minimum, the guaranteed payment is the difference between the distributive share and the guaranteed minimum.

EXAMPLE C:9-38 ▶ Tina manages the real estate owned by the TAV Partnership, in which she also is a partner. She receives 30% of all partnership income before guaranteed payments, but no less than $60,000 per year. In the current year, the TAV Partnership reports $300,000 in ordinary income. Tina's 30% distributive share is $90,000 (0.30 × $300,000), which exceeds her $60,000 guaranteed minimum. Therefore, she has no guaranteed payment. The other partners are allocated $210,000 (0.70 × $300,000) of the ordinary income. ◀

EXAMPLE C:9-39 ▶ Assume the same facts as in Example C:9-38 except the TAV Partnership reports $150,000 of ordinary income. Tina has a guaranteed payment of $15,000, which represents the difference between her $45,000 distributive share (0.30 × $150,000) and her $60,000 guaranteed minimum.[49] As a result, Tina is allocated $60,000, and the other partners are allocated $90,000 ($150,000 - $60,000) of the ordinary income. ◀

Tax Impact of Guaranteed Payments. Like salary or interest income, guaranteed payments are ordinary income to the recipient. The guaranteed payment must be included in income for the recipient partner's tax year during which the partnership year ends and the partnership deducts or capitalizes the payments.[50]

EXAMPLE C:9-40 ▶ In January of Year 2, a calendar year taxpayer, Will, receives a $10,000 guaranteed payment from the WRS Partnership, which uses the accrual method of accounting. WRS accrues and deducts the payment during its tax year ending December 31 of Year 1. Will must report the guaranteed payment in his Year 1 tax return because that return includes the Year 1 partnership income that reflects the partnership's deduction of the guaranteed payment. ◀

The partnership treats the guaranteed payment as if it is made to an outsider. If the payment is for a service that is a capital expenditure (e.g., architectural services for designing a building for the partnership), the guaranteed payment must be capitalized and, if allowable, amortized. If the payment is for services deductible under Sec. 162, the partnership deducts the payment from ordinary income. Thus, deductible guaranteed payments offset the partnership's ordinary income but never its capital gains. If the guaranteed payment exceeds the partnership's ordinary income, the payment creates an ordinary loss that is allocated among the partners.[51]

EXAMPLE C:9-41 ▶ Theresa is a partner in the STU Partnership. She is to receive a guaranteed payment for deductible services of $60,000 and 30% of partnership income computed after the partnership deducts the guaranteed payment. The partnership reports $40,000 of ordinary income and a $120,000 long-term capital gain before deducting the guaranteed payment. Theresa's income from the partnership is determined as follows:

		Theresa's Share	
	STU Partnership	*Ratable Share*	*Amount*
Ordinary income (before guaranteed payment)	$ 40,000		
Minus: Guaranteed payment	(60,000)	100%	$60,000
Ordinary loss	($ 20,000)	30%	(6,000)
Long-term capital gain	$120,000	30%	36,000 ◀

[49] Reg. Sec. 1.707-1(c), Exs. (1) and (2).
[50] Reg. Secs. 1.707-1(c) and 1.706-1(a).
[51] Reg. Sec. 1.707-1(c), Ex. (4).

Family Partnerships

OBJECTIVE 10

Recognize the special tax issues associated with family partnerships

Capital Ownership

Because each partner reports and pays taxes on a distributive share of partnership income, a family partnership is an excellent way to spread income among family members and minimize the family's tax bill. However, to accomplish this tax minimization goal, the IRS must accept the family members as real partners. The question of whether someone is a partner in a family partnership is often litigated, but safe-harbor rules under Sec. 704(e) provide a clear answer if three tests are met: the partnership interest must be a capital interest, capital must be a material income-producing factor in the partnership's business activity, and the family member must be the true owner of the interest.

A capital interest gives the partner the right to receive assets if the partnership liquidates immediately upon the partner's acquisition of the interest. Capital is a material income-producing factor if the partnership derives substantial portions of gross income from the use of capital. For example, capital is a material income-producing factor if the business has substantial inventory or significant investment in plant or equipment. Capital is seldom considered a material income-producing factor in a service business.[52]

TAX STRATEGY TIP

In certain situations, family partnerships provide an excellent tax-planning tool, but the family members must be real partners. The rules that determine who is a real partner in a family partnership are guided by the assignment-of-income principle.

The remaining question is whether the family member is the true owner of the interest. Ownership is seldom questioned if one family member purchases the interest at a market price from another family member. However, when one family member gifts the interest to another, the major question is whether the donor retains so much control over the partnership interest that the donor is still the owner of the interest. If the donor still controls the interest, the donor is taxed on the distributive share.

Donor Retained Control. No mechanical test exists to determine whether the donor has retained too much control, but several factors may indicate a problem:[53]

- Retention of control over distributions of income can be a problem unless the retention occurs with the agreement of all partners or the retention is for the reasonable needs of the business.
- Retention of control over assets that are essential to the partnership's business can indicate too much control by the donor.
- Limitation of the donee partner's right to sell or liquidate his or her interest may indicate that the donor has not relinquished full control over the interest.
- Retention of management control that is inconsistent with normal partnership arrangements can be another sign that the donor retains control. This situation is not considered a fatal problem unless it occurs in conjunction with a significant limit on the donee's ability to sell or liquidate his or her interest.

If the donor has not directly or indirectly retained too much control, the donee is a full partner. As a partner, the donee must report his or her distributive share of income.

Minor Donees. When income splitting is the goal of a family, the appropriate donee for the partnership interest is often a minor. With the problem of donor-retained controls in mind, gifts to minors should be made with great attention to detail. Further, net unearned income of a child under age 18 is taxed to the child at the parents' marginal tax rate under the "kiddie tax" rules. This provision removes much of the incentive to transfer family partnership interests to young children, but gifting partnership interests to minors age 18 or older still can reap significant tax advantages, although in some situations the kiddie tax also applies to children ages 18 through 23.

Donor-Donee Allocations of Income

Partnership income must be properly allocated between a donor and a donee to be accepted by the IRS. Note that only the allocation between the donor and donee is questioned, with no impact on the distributive shares of any other partners.

[52] Reg. Sec. 1.704-1(e)(1)(iv).

[53] Reg. Sec. 1.704-1(e)(2)(ii).

Two requirements apply to donor-donee allocations. First, the donor must be allocated reasonable compensation for services rendered to the partnership. Then, after reasonable compensation is allocated to the donor, any remaining partnership income must be allocated based on relative capital interests.[54] This allocation scheme apparently overrides the partnership's ability to make special allocations of income.

EXAMPLE C:9-42 ▶

ETHICAL POINT

CPAs have a responsibility to review an entity's conduct of its activities to be sure it is operating as a partnership. If a donee receives a partnership interest as a gift and the donee is not the true owner of the interest (e.g., the donor retains too much control over the donee's interest), the partnership return must be filed without a distributive share of income or loss being allocated to the donee.

Andrew, a 40% partner in the ABC Partnership, gives one-half of his interest to his brother, John. During the current year, Andrew performs services for the partnership for which reasonable compensation is $65,000 but for which he accepts no pay. Andrew and John are each credited with a $100,000 distributive share, all of which is ordinary income. Reallocation between Andrew and John is necessary to reflect the value of Andrew's services.

Total distributive shares for the brothers	$200,000
Minus: Reasonable compensation for Andrew	(65,000)
Income to allocate	$135,000

John's distributive share: $\frac{20\%}{40\%} \times \$135{,}000 = \$67{,}500$

Andrew's distributive share: $\left(\frac{20\%}{40\%} \times \$135{,}000\right) + \$65{,}000 = \$132{,}500$ ◀

TAX PLANNING CONSIDERATIONS

OBJECTIVE 11

Identify planning techniques to get the best tax advantages from partnership losses

TIMING OF LOSS RECOGNITION

The loss limitation rules provide a unique opportunity for tax planning. For example, if a partner knows that his or her distributive share of active losses from a partnership for a tax year will exceed the Sec. 704 basis limitation for deducting losses, he or she should carefully examine the tax situation for the current and upcoming tax years. Substantial current personal income may make immediate use of the loss desirable. Current income may be taxed at a higher marginal tax rate than will future income because of, for example, an extraordinarily good current year, an expected retirement, or a decrease in future years' tax rates. If the partner chooses to use the loss in the current year, he or she can make additional contributions just before year-end (perhaps even from funds the partner borrows, as long as the additional benefit exceeds the cost of the funds). Alternatively, one partner may convince the other partners to have the partnership incur additional liabilities so that each partner's basis increases. This last strategy should be exercised with caution unless a business reason (rather than solely a tax reason) exists for the borrowing.

EXAMPLE C:9-43 ▶

Ted, a 60% general partner in the ST Partnership, expects to be allocated partnership losses of $120,000 for the current year from a partnership in which he materially participates but where his partnership basis is only $90,000. Because he has a marginal tax rate of 33% for the current year (and anticipates only a 25% marginal tax rate for next year), Ted wants to use the ST Partnership losses to offset his current year income. He could make a capital contribution to raise his basis by $30,000. Alternatively, he could get the partnership to incur $50,000 in additional liabilities, which would increase his basis by his $30,000 ($50,000 × 0.60) share of the liability. The partnership's $50,000 borrowing must serve a business purpose for the ST Partnership. ◀

Alternatively, if a partner has little current year income and expects substantial income in the following year, the partner may prefer to delay the deduction of partnership losses that exceed the current year's loss limitation. Similarly, if a partner has loss, deduction, or credit carryovers that expire in the current year, deferral of the distributive share of

[54] Sec. 704(e)(2).

partnership losses to the following year again may be desirable. Should the partner opt to deduct the loss in a later year, he or she needs only to leave things alone so that the distributive share of losses exceeds the loss limitation for the current year.

Compliance and Procedural Considerations

OBJECTIVE 12

Comply with the requirements for filing a partnership tax return

REPORTING TO THE IRS AND THE PARTNERS

Forms. For tax years beginning after 2015, the partnership must file a Form 1065 (U.S. Return of Partnership Income) with the IRS by the fifteenth day of the third month after the end of the partnership tax year. (See Appendix B for a completed Form 1065.) The IRS, however, allows an automatic six-month extension of time to file Form 1065. To obtain the extension, the partnership must file Form 7004 (Application for Automatic Extension of Time to File Certain Business Income Tax, Information, and Other Returns) on or before the partnership's normal filing date.[55] The IRS imposes penalties for failure to file a timely or complete partnership return. Because the partnership is only a conduit, Form 1065 is an information return and is not accompanied by any tax payment.[56] Included on the front page of Form 1065 are the ordinary items of income, gain, loss, and deduction that are not separately stated. Schedule K of Form 1065 reports both a summary of the ordinary income items and all the partnership's separately stated items. Schedule K-1, which the partnership must prepare for each partner, reflects a particular partner's distributive share of partnership ordinary income or loss, separately state items, and his or her special allocations. The partner's Schedule K-1 is notification of his or her share of partnership items for use in calculating income taxes and self-employment taxes.

ADDITIONAL COMMENT

The partnership Schedule K in Appendix B of this text makes apparent that the large number of items now having to be separately stated has substantially complicated the preparation of Form 1065.

Schedule M-3. A partnership must file Schedule M-3 in lieu of Schedule M-1 if any one of the following conditions holds:

- The amount of total assets reported in Schedule L of Form 1065 (Balance Sheet per Books) equals or exceeds $10 million.
- The amount of adjusted total assets equals or exceeds $10 million, where adjusted total assets equal the Schedule L amount plus the following items that appear in Schedule M-2 of Form 1065: (1) capital distributions made during the year, (2) net book loss for the year, and (3) other adjustments.
- Total receipts equal or exceed $35 million.
- A reportable entity partner owns at least a 50% interest in the partnership on any day of the tax year, where a reportable entity partner is one that had to file its own Schedule M-3.

Section 444 Election and Required Payments. A partnership can elect to use a tax year other than a required year by filing an election under Sec. 444. This election is made by filing Form 8716 (Election to Have a Tax Year Other Than a Required Tax Year) by the earlier of the fifteenth day of the fifth month following the month that includes the first day of the tax year for which the election is effective or the due date (without regard to extension) of the income tax return resulting from the Sec. 444 election. In addition, a copy of Form 8716 must be attached to the partnership's Form 1065 for the first tax year for which the Sec. 444 election is made.

A partnership making a Sec. 444 election must make a required payment annually under Sec. 7519. The required payment has the effect of remitting a deposit equal to the

[55] Reg. 1.6081-2.

[56] Reg. Sec. 301.6031-1(e)(2). Although the partnership pays no income tax, it still must pay the employer's share of social security taxes and any unemployment taxes as well as withhold income taxes from its employees' salaries. Remember, however, that the partners are not considered to be employees. In addition, some publicly traded partnerships may pay a tax as explained in Chapter C:10.

tax (at the highest individual tax rate plus one percentage point) on the partnership's deferred income.

A partnership can obtain a refund if past payments exceed the tentative payment due on the deferred income for the current year. Similar refunds are available if the partnership terminates a Sec. 444 election or liquidates. The required payments are not deductible by the partnership and are not passed through to a partner. The required payments are in the nature of a refundable deposit.

The Sec. 7519 required payment is due on or before May 15 of the calendar year following the calendar year in which the election year begins. The partnership remits the required payment with Form 8752 (Required Payment or Refund Under Section 7519) along with a computational worksheet, which is illustrated in the instructions to Form 1065. Refunds of excess required payments also are obtained by filing Form 8752.

Estimated Taxes. If the partnership is not an electing large partnership, it pays no income taxes and makes no estimated tax payments. However, the partners must make estimated tax payments based on their separate tax positions including their distributive shares of partnership income or loss for the current year. Thus, the partners are not making separate estimated tax payments for their partnership income but rather are including the effects of the partnership's results in the calculation of their normal estimated tax payments.

Self-Employment Income. Every partnership must report the net earnings (or loss) for the partnership that constitute self-employment income to the partners. The instructions to Form 1065 contain a worksheet to make such a calculation. The partnership's self-employment income includes both guaranteed payments, partnership ordinary income and loss, and some separately stated items, but generally excludes capital gains and losses, Sec. 1231 gains and losses, interest, dividends, and rentals. The distributive share of self-employment income for each partner is shown on a Schedule K-1 and is included with the partner's other self-employment income in determining his or her self-employment tax liability (Schedule SE, Form 1040). The distributive share of partnership income allocable to a limited partner is not self-employment income.

EXAMPLE C:9-44 ▶ Adam is a general partner in the AB Partnership. His distributive share of partnership income and his guaranteed payment for the year are as follows:

Ordinary income	$15,000
Short-term capital gain	9,000
Guaranteed payment	18,000

Adam's self-employment income is $33,000 ($15,000 + $18,000). ◀

EXAMPLE C:9-45 ▶ Assume the same facts as in Example C:9-44 except that Adam is a limited partner. His self-employment income includes only the $18,000 guaranteed payment. ◀

ADDITIONAL COMMENT

New streamlined partnership audit procedures go into effect for years beginning after 2017. Under the new procedures, adjustments are made at the partnership level, and the partnership generally pays any resulting taxes.

IRS AUDIT PROCEDURES

Any questions arising during an IRS audit about a partnership item must be determined at the partnership level (instead of at the partner level).[57] Section 6231(a)(3) defines **partnership items** as virtually all items reported by the partnership for the tax year including tax preference items, credit recapture items, guaranteed payments, and the at-risk amount. In fact, almost every item that can appear on the partnership return is treated as a partnership item. Each partner must either report partnership items in a manner consistent with the Schedule K-1 received from the partnership or notify the IRS of the inconsistent treatment.[58]

The IRS can bring a single proceeding at the partnership level to determine the characterization or tax impact of any partnership item. All partners have the right to participate in the administrative proceedings, and the IRS must offer a consistent settlement to all partners.

[57] Sec. 6221.

[58] Sec. 6222.

The partnership generally assigns a **tax matters partner** to facilitate communication between the IRS and the partners of a large partnership and to serve as the primary representative of the partnership.[59] If the partnership fails to assign the tax matters partner, the designation goes to the general partner having the largest profits interest at the close of the partnership's tax year.

ADDITIONAL COMMENT

Under the new procedures, partnerships issuing 100 or fewer Forms K-1 can elect out of the new procedures.

These audit procedures, however, do not apply to small partnerships. For this purpose, a small partnership is defined as one having no more than ten partners who must be natural persons (but excluding nonresident aliens), C corporations, or estates. In counting partners, a husband and wife (or their estates) count as a single partner. Further, the IRS has announced that a partnership can be excluded from the audit procedures only if it can be established that all partners fully reported their shares of partnership items on timely filed tax returns.[60]

PROBLEM MATERIALS

DISCUSSION QUESTIONS

C:9-1 Yvonne and Larry plan to begin a business that will grow plants for sale to retail nurseries. They expect to have substantial losses for the first three years of operations while they develop their plants and their sales operations. Both Yvonne and Larry have substantial interest income, and both expect to work full-time in this new business. List three advantages for operating this business as a partnership instead of a C corporation.

C:9-2 Bob and Carol want to open a bed and breakfast inn as soon as they buy and renovate a turn-of-the-century home. What would be the major disadvantage of using a general partnership rather than a corporation for this business? Should they consider any other form for structuring their business?

C:9-3 Sam wants to help his brother, Lou, start a new business. Lou is a capable auto mechanic but has little business sense, so he needs Sam to help him make business decisions. Should this partnership be arranged as a general partnership or a limited partnership? Why? Should they consider any other form for structuring their business?

C:9-4 Doug contributes services but no property to the CD Partnership upon its formation. What are the tax implications of his receiving only a profits interest versus his receiving a capital and profits interest?

C:9-5 An existing partner wants to contribute property having a basis less than its FMV for an additional interest in a partnership.

a. Should he contribute the property to the partnership?
b. What are his other options?
c. Explain the tax implications for the partner of these other options.

C:9-6 Jane contributes valuable property to a partnership in exchange for a general partnership interest. The partnership also assumes the recourse mortgage Jane incurred when she purchased the property two years ago.

a. How will the liability affect the amount of gain that Jane must recognize?
b. How will it affect her basis in the partnership interest?

C:9-7 Which of the following items can be deducted (up to $5,000) and amortized as part of a partnership's organizational expenditures?

a. Legal fees for drawing up the partnership agreement
b. Accounting fees for establishing an accounting system
c. Fees for securing an initial working capital loan
d. Filing fees required under state law in initial year to conduct business in the state
e. Accounting fees for preparation of initial short-period tax return
f. Transportation costs for acquiring machinery essential to the partnership's business
g. Syndication expenses

C:9-8 The BW Partnership reported the following current year earnings: $30,000 interest from tax-exempt bonds, $50,000 long-term capital gain, and $100,000 net income from operations. Bob saw these numbers and told his partner, Wendy, that the partnership had $100,000 of taxable income. Is he correct? Explain your answer.

C:9-9 How will a partner's distributive share be determined if the partner sells one-half of his or her beginning-of-the-year partnership interest at the beginning of the tenth month of the partnership's tax year?

---

[59] Sec. 6231(a)(7).

[60] Rev. Proc. 84-35, 1984-1 C.B. 509.

C:9-10 Can a recourse debt of a partnership increase the basis of a limited partner's partnership interest? Explain.

C:9-11 The ABC Partnership has a nonrecourse liability that it incurred by borrowing from an unrelated bank. It is secured by an apartment building owned and managed by the partnership. The liability is not convertible into an equity interest. How does this liability affect the at-risk basis of general partner Anna and limited partner Bob?

C:9-12 Is the Sec. 704(d) loss limitation rule more or less restrictive than the at-risk rules? Explain.

C:9-13 Jeff, a 10% limited partner in the recently formed JRS Partnership, expects to have losses from the partnership for several more years. He is considering purchasing an interest in a profitable general partnership in which he will materially participate. Will the purchase allow him to use his losses from the JRS Partnership?

C:9-14 Helen, a 55% partner in the ABC Partnership, owns land (a capital asset) having a $20,000 basis and a $25,000 FMV. She plans to transfer the land to the ABC Partnership, which will subdivide the land and sell the lots. Discuss whether Helen should sell or contribute the land to the partnership.

C:9-15 The TUV Partnership is considering two compensation schemes for Tracy, the partner who runs the business on a daily basis. Tracy can be given a $10,000 guaranteed payment, or she can be given a comparably larger distributive share (and distribution) so that she receives about $10,000 more each year. From the standpoint of when the income must be reported in Tracy's tax return, are these two compensation alternatives the same?

C:9-16 Roy's father gives him a capital interest in the Family Partnership. Discuss whether the Sec. 704(e) family partnership rules apply to this interest.

C:9-17 Andrew gives his brother Steve a 20% interest in the AS Partnership, and he retains a 30% interest. Andrew works for the partnership but is not paid. How will this arrangement affect the income from the AS Partnership that Andrew and Steve report?

ISSUE IDENTIFICATION QUESTIONS

C:9-18 Bob and Kate form the BK Partnership, a general partnership, as equal partners. Bob contributes an office building with a $130,000 FMV and a $95,000 adjusted basis to the partnership along with a $60,000 mortgage, which the partnership assumes. Kate contributes the land on which the building sits with a $50,000 FMV and a $75,000 adjusted basis. Kate will manage the partnership for the first five years of operations but will not receive a guaranteed payment for her work in the first year of partnership operations. Starting with the second year of partnership operations, Kate will receive a $10,000 guaranteed payment for each year she manages the partnership. What tax issues should Bob, Kate, and the BK Partnership consider with respect to the formation and operation of the partnership?

C:9-19 Suzanne and Laura form a partnership to market local crafts. In April, the two women spent $1,600 searching for a retail outlet, $1,200 to have a partnership agreement drawn up, and $2,000 to have an accounting system established. During April, they signed contracts with a number of local crafters to feature their products in the retail outlet. The outlet was fitted and merchandise organized during May. In June, the store opened and sold its first crafts. The partnership paid $500 to an accountant to prepare an income statement for the month of June. What tax issues should the partnership consider with regard to beginning this business?

C:9-20 Cara, a CPA, established an accounting system for the ABC Partnership and, in return for her services, received a 10% profits interest (but no capital interest) in the partnership. Her usual fee for the services would be approximately $20,000. No sales of profits interests in the ABC Partnership occurred during the current year. What tax issues should Cara and the ABC Partnership consider with respect to the payment made for the services?

C:9-21 George, a limited partner in the EFG Partnership, has a 20% interest in partnership capital, profits, and losses. His basis in the partnership interest is $15,000 before accounting for events of the current year. In December of the current year, the EFG Partnership repaid a $100,000 nonrecourse liability. The partnership earned $20,000 of ordinary income this year. What tax issues should George consider with respect to reporting the results of this year's activities for the EFG Partnership on his personal return?

C:9-22 Katie works 40 hours a week as a clerk in the mall and earns $20,000. In addition, she works five hours each week in the JKL Partnership's office. Katie, a 10% limited partner in the JKL Partnership, has been allocated a $2,100 loss from the partnership for the current year. The basis for her interest in JKL before accounting for current operations is $5,000. What tax issues should Katie consider with respect to her interest in, and employment by, the JKL Partnership?

C:9-23 Daniel has no family to inherit his 80% capital and profits interest in the CD Partnership. To ensure the continuation of the business, he gives a 20% capital and profits interest in the partnership to David, his best friend's son, on the condition that David work in the partnership for at least five years. David receives guaranteed payments for his work. Daniel takes no salary from the partnership, but he devotes all his time to the business operations of the partnership. What tax issues should Daniel and David consider with respect to the gift of the partnership interest and Daniel's employment arrangement with the partnership?

PROBLEMS

C:9-24 *Formation of a Partnership.* Suzanne and Bob form the SB General Partnership as equal partners. They make the following contributions:

Individual	*Asset*	*Basis to Partner*	*FMV*
Suzanne	Cash	$45,000	$ 45,000
	Inventory (securities)	14,000	15,000
Bob	Land	45,000	40,000
	Building	50,000	100,000

The SB Partnership assumes the $80,000 recourse mortgage on the building that Bob contributes, and the partners share the economic risk of loss on the mortgage equally. Bob has claimed $40,000 in straight-line depreciation under the MACRS rules on the building. Suzanne is a stockbroker and contributed securities from her inventory. The partnership will hold them as an investment.

a. What amount and character of gain or loss must each partner recognize on the formation of the partnership?
b. What is each partner's basis in his or her partnership interest?
c. What is the partnership's basis in each asset?
d. What is the partnership's initial book value of each asset?
e. The partnership holds the securities for two years and then sells them for $20,000. What amount and character of gain must the partnership and each partner report?

C:9-25 *Formation of a Partnership Compared to Formation of a Corporation.* At the beginning of the current year, Able and Baker formed the AB Partnership by transferring cash and property to the partnership in exchange for a partnership interest, with each having a 50% interest. Specifically, Able transferred property having a $50,000 FMV, a $30,000 adjusted basis, and subject to a $10,000 liability, which the partnership assumed. Baker contributed $40,000 cash to the partnership. The partnership also borrowed $28,000 from the bank to use in its operations. All liabilities are recourse for which the partners have an equal economic risk of loss. During the current year, the partnership earned $24,000 of net ordinary income and reinvested this amount in new property.

a. What is the partnership's and each partner's gain or loss recognized on the formation of the partnership?
b. What is each partner's basis in his or her partnership interest at the end of the current year?
c. For the partnership, prepare a tax and book balance sheet at the end of the current year.
d. Assume instead that Able and Baker formed a corporation rather than a partnership. What is the corporation's and each shareholder's gain or loss recognized on the formation of the corporation? What is each shareholder's basis in his or her stock at the end of the current year?

C:9-26 *Formation of a Partnership.* On May 31, six brothers decided to form the Grimm Brothers Partnership to publish and print children's stories. The contributions of the brothers and their partnership interests are listed below. They share the economic risk of loss from liabilities according to their partnership interests.

Individual	*Asset*	*Basis to Partner*	*FMV*	*Partnership Interest*
Al	Cash	$15,000	$ 15,000	15%
Bob	Accounts receivable	–0–	20,000	20%
Clay	Office equipment	13,000	15,000	15%
Dave	Land	50,000	15,000	15%
Ed	Building	15,000	150,000	20%
Fred	Services	?	15,000	15%

The following other information about the contributions may be of interest:

- Bob contributes accounts receivable from his proprietorship, which uses the cash method of accounting.
- Clay uses the office equipment in a small business he owns. When he joins the partnership, he sells the remaining business assets to an outsider. He has claimed $8,000 of MACRS depreciation on the office equipment.
- The partnership assumes a $130,000 mortgage on the building Ed contributes. Ed claimed $100,000 of straight-line MACRS depreciation on the commercial property.
- Fred, an attorney, drew up all the partnership agreements and filed the necessary paperwork. He receives a full 15% capital and profits interest for his services.

a. How much gain, loss, or income must each partner recognize as a result of the formation?
b. How much gain, loss, or income must the partnership recognize as a result of the formation?
c. What is each partner's basis in his partnership interest?
d. What is the partnership's basis in its assets?
e. What is the partnership's initial book value of each asset?
f. What effects do the depreciation recapture provisions have on the property contributions?
g. How would your answer to Part a change if Fred received only a profits interest?
h. What are the tax consequences to the partners and the partnership when the partnership sells for $9,000 the land contributed by Dave? Prior to the sale, the partnership held the land as an investment for two years.

C:9-27 *Formation of a Partnership.* On January 1, Julie, Kay, and Susan formed a partnership. The contributions of the three individuals are listed below. Julie received a 30% partnership interest, Kay received a 60% partnership interest, and Susan received a 10% partnership interest. They share the economic risk of loss from recourse liabilities according to their partnership interests.

Individual	*Asset*	*Basis to Partner*	*FMV*
Julie	Accounts receivable	$ –0–	$ 60,000
Kay	Land	30,000	58,000
	Building	45,000	116,000
Susan	Services	?	20,000

Kay has claimed $15,000 of straight-line MACRS depreciation on the building. The land and building are subject to a $54,000 mortgage, of which $18,000 is allocable to the land and $36,000 is allocable to the building. The partnership assumes the mortgage. Susan is an attorney, and the services she contributes are the drawing-up of all partnership agreements.

a. What amount and character of gain, loss, or income must each partner recognize on the formation of the partnership?
b. What is each partner's basis in her partnership interest?
c. What is the partnership's basis in each of its assets?
d. What is the partnership's initial book value of each asset?

e. To raise some immediate cash after the formation, the partnership decides to sell the land and building to a third party and lease it back. The buyer pays $40,000 cash for the land and $80,000 cash for the building in addition to assuming the $54,000 mortgage. Assume the partnership claimed no additional depreciation on the building before the sale. What is each partner's distributive share of the gains, and what is the character of the gains?

C:9-28 ***Contribution of Services.*** Sean is admitted to the calendar year XYZ Partnership on December 1 of the current year in return for his services managing the partnership's business during the year. The partnership reports ordinary income of $100,000 for the current year without considering this transaction. Assume a nonleap year and that the partners agree to the proration method with a calendar day convention.

a. What are the tax consequences to Sean and the calendar year XYZ Partnership if Sean receives a 20% capital and profits interest in the partnership with a $75,000 FMV?
b. What are the tax consequences to Sean and the XYZ Partnership if Sean receives only a 20% profits interest with no determinable FMV?

C:9-29 ***Contribution of Services and Property.*** Marjorie works for a large firm whose business is to find suitable real estate, establish a limited partnership to purchase the property, and then sell the limited partnership interests. In the current year, Marjorie received a 5% limited partnership interest in the Eldorado Limited Partnership. Marjorie received this interest partially in payment for her services in selling partnership interests to others, but she also was required to contribute $5,000 in cash to the partnership. Similar limited partnership interests sold for $20,000 at approximately the same time that Marjorie received her interest. What are the tax consequences for Marjorie and the Eldorado Limited Partnership of Marjorie's receipt of the partnership interest?

C:9-30 ***Partnership Tax Year.*** The BCD Partnership is being formed by three equal partners, Beta Corporation, Chi Corporation, and Delta Corporation. The partners' tax year-ends are June 30 for Beta, September 30 for Chi, and October 31 for Delta. The BCD Partnership's natural business year ends on January 31.

a. What tax year(s) can the partnership elect without IRS permission?
b. What tax year(s) can the partnership elect with IRS permission?
c. How would your answers to Parts a and b change if Beta, Chi, and Delta own 4%, 4%, and 92%, respectively, of the partnership?

C:9-31 ***Partnership Tax Year.*** The BCD Partnership is formed in April of the current year. The three equal partners, Boris, Carlton Corporation, and Damien have had tax years ending on December 31, August 30, and December 31, respectively, for the last three years. The BCD Partnership has no natural business year.

a. What tax year is required for the BCD Partnership under Sec. 706?
b. Can the BCD Partnership make a Sec. 444 election? If so, what are the alternative tax years BCD could select?

C:9-32 ***Partnership Income and Basis Adjustments.*** Mark and Pamela are equal partners in MP Partnership. The partnership, Mark, and Pamela are calendar year taxpayers. The partnership incurred the following items in the current year:

Sales	$450,000
Cost of goods sold	210,000
Dividends on corporate investments	15,000
Tax-exempt interest income	4,000
Sec. 1245 gain (recapture) on equipment sale	33,000
Sec. 1231 gain on equipment sale	18,000
Long-term capital gain on stock sale	12,000
Long-term capital loss on stock sale	10,000
Short-term capital loss on stock sale	9,000
Depreciation (no Sec. 179 or bonus depreciation components)	27,000
Guaranteed payment to Pamela	30,000
Meals and entertainment expenses	11,600
Interest expense on loans allocable to:	
Business debt	42,000
Stock investments	9,200
Tax-exempt bonds	2,800
Principal payment on business loan	14,000
Charitable contributions	5,000
Distributions to partners ($40,000 each)	80,000

a. Compute the partnership's ordinary income and separately stated items.
b. Show Mark's and Pamela's shares of the items in Part a.
c. Compute Mark's and Pamela's ending basis in their partnership interests assuming their beginning balances are $150,000 each.

C:9-33 ***Financial Accounting and Partnership Income.*** Jim, Liz, and Keith are equal partners in the JLK Partnership, which uses the accrual method of accounting. All three materially participate in the business. JLK reports financial accounting income of $186,000 for the current year. The partnership used the following information to determine financial accounting income.

Operating profit (excluding the items listed below)	$94,000
Rental income	30,000
Interest income:	
Municipal bonds (tax-exempt)	15,000
Corporate bonds	3,000
Dividend income (all from less-than-20%-owned domestic corporations)	20,000
Gains and losses on property sales:	
Gain on sale of land held as an investment (contributed by Jim six years ago when its basis was $9,000 and its FMV was $15,000)	60,000
Long-term capital gains	10,000
Short-term capital losses	7,000
Sec. 1231 gain	9,000
Unrecaptured Sec. 1250 gain	44,000
Depreciation:	
Rental real estate	12,000
Machinery and equipment	27,000
Interest expense related to:	
Mortgages on rental property	18,000
Loans to acquire municipal bonds	5,000
Guaranteed payments to Jim	30,000
Low-income housing expenditures qualifying for credit	21,000

The following additional information is available about the current year's activities.

- The partnership received a $1,000 prepayment of rent for next year but has not recorded it as income for financial accounting purposes.
- The partnership recorded the land for financial accounting purposes at $15,000.
- MACRS depreciation on the rental real estate and machinery and equipment were $12,000 and $29,000, respectively, in the current year.
- MACRS depreciation for the rental real estate includes depreciation on the low-income housing expenditures.

a. What is JLK's financial accounting income?
b. What is JLK's partnership taxable income? (See Appendix B for an example of a financial accounting-to-tax reconciliation.)
c. What is JLK's ordinary income (loss)?
d. What are JLK's separately stated items?

C:9-34 ***Partner's Distributive Shares.*** On January of the current year, Becky (20%), Chuck (30%), and Dawn (50%) are partners in the BCD Partnership. During the current year, BCD reports the following results. All items occur evenly throughout the year unless otherwise indicated. Assume the current year is not a leap year and that the partners agree to the proration method with a calendar day convention.

Ordinary income	$120,000
Long-term capital gain (recognized September 1)	18,000
Short-term capital loss (recognized March 2)	6,000
Charitable contribution (made October 1)	20,000

a. What are the distributive shares for each partner, assuming they all continue to hold their interests at the end of the year?
b. Assume that Becky purchases a 5% partnership interest from Chuck on June 30 so that Becky and Chuck each own 25% from that date through the end of the year. What are Becky and Chuck's distributive shares for the current year?

C:9-35 *Allocation of Precontribution Gain.* Last year, Patty contributed land with a $4,000 basis and a $10,000 FMV in exchange for a 40% profits, loss, and capital interest in the PD Partnership. Dave contributed land with an $8,000 basis and a $15,000 FMV for the remaining 60% interest in the partnership. During the current year, PD Partnership reported $8,000 of ordinary income and sold the land that Patty contributed for $14,000, thereby producing a taxable long-term capital gain of $10,000 ($14,000 – $4,000). What income or gain must Patty and Dave report from the PD Partnership in the current year?

C:9-36 *Special Allocations.* Refer to Example C:9-25 in the text. Provide computations showing that the partners' total tax liability under the special allocation is less than their total liability under an equal allocation of the two types of interest income.

C:9-37 *Special Allocations.* Clark sold securities for a $50,000 short-term capital loss during the current year, but he has no personal capital gains to recognize. The C&L General Partnership, in which Clark has a 50% capital, profits, and loss interest, reported a $60,000 short-term capital gain this year. In addition, the partnership earned $140,000 of ordinary income. Clark's only partner, Lois, agrees to divide the year's income as follows:

Type of Income	*Total*	*Clark*	*Lois*
Short-term capital gain	$ 60,000	$50,000	$10,000
Ordinary income	140,000	50,000	90,000

Both partners and the partnership use a calendar year-end, and both partners have a 33% marginal tax rate.

a. Have the partners made a special allocation of income that has substantial economic effect?

b. What amount and character of income must each partner report on his or her tax return?

C:9-38 *Special Allocations.* Diane and Ed have equal capital and profits interests in the DE Partnership, and they share the economic risk of loss from recourse liabilities according to their partnership interests. In addition, Diane has a special allocation of all depreciation on buildings owned by the partnership. The buildings are financed with recourse liabilities. The depreciation reduces Diane's capital account, and liquidation is in accordance with the capital account balances. Depreciation for the DE Partnership is $50,000 annually. Diane and Ed each have $50,000 capital account balances on January 1 of Year 1. Will the special allocation be acceptable for Year 1, Year 2, and Year 3 in the following independent situations?

a. The partners have no obligation to repay negative capital account balances, and the partnership's operations (other than depreciation) each year have no net effect on the capital accounts.

b. The partners have an obligation to repay negative capital account balances.

c. The partners have no obligation to repay negative capital account balances. The partnership operates at its break-even point (excluding any depreciation claimed) and borrows $200,000 on a full recourse basis on December 31 of Year 2.

C:9-39 *Basis in Partnership Interest.* What is Kelly's basis for her partnership interest in each of the following independent situations? The partners share the economic risk of loss from recourse liabilities according to their partnership interests.

a. Kelly receives her 20% partnership interest for a contribution of property having a $14,000 basis and a $17,000 FMV. The partnership assumes her $10,000 recourse liability but has no other debts.

b. Kelly receives her 20% partnership interest as a gift from a friend. The friend's basis (without considering partnership liabilities) is $34,000. The FMV of the interest at the time of the gift is $36,000. The partnership has liabilities of $100,000 when Kelly receives her interest. No gift tax was paid with respect to the transfer.

c. Kelly inherits her 20% interest from her mother. Her mother's basis was $140,000. The FMV of the interest is $120,000 on the date of death and $160,000 on the alternate valuation date. The executor chooses the date of death for valuing the estate. The partnership has no liabilities.

C:9-40 *Basis in Partnership Interest.* Yong received a 40% general partnership interest in the XYZ Partnership in each of the independent situations below. In each situation, assume the general partners share the economic risk of loss related to recourse liabilities according to their partnership interests. What is Yong's basis in his partnership interest?

a. Yong designs the building the partnership will use for its offices. Yong normally would charge a $20,000 fee for a similar building design. Based on the other partner's contributions, the 40% interest has a FMV of $25,000. The partnership has no liabilities.

b. Yong contributes land with a $6,000 basis and an $18,000 FMV, a car (which he has used in his business since he purchased it) with a $15,000 adjusted basis and a $6,000 FMV, and $2,000 cash. The partnership has recourse liabilities of $100,000.

C:9-41 *Basis in Partnership Interest.* Tina purchases an interest in the TP Partnership on January 1 of the current year for $50,000. The partnership uses the calendar year as its tax year and has $200,000 in recourse liabilities when Tina acquires her interest. The partners share economic risk of loss associated with recourse debt according to their loss percentage. Her distributive share of partnership items for the year is as follows:

Ordinary income (excluding items listed below)	$30,000
Long-term capital gains	10,000
Municipal bond interest income	8,000
Charitable contributions	1,000
Interest expense related to municipal bond investment	2,000

TP reports the following liabilities on December 31:

Recourse debt	$100,000
Nonrecourse debt (not qualified real estate financing)	80,000

a. What is Tina's basis on December 31 if she has a 40% interest in profits and losses? TP is a general partnership. Tina has not guaranteed partnership debt, nor has she made any other special agreements about partnership debt.
b. How would your answer to Part a change if Tina instead had a 40% interest in profits and a 30% interest in losses? Assume TP is a general partnership, and all other agreements continue in place. Also assume the partners share recourse liabilities in accordance with their loss interest percentages.
c. How would your answer to Part a change if Tina were instead a limited partner having a 40% interest in profits and 30% interest in losses? The partnership agreement contains no guarantees or other special arrangements.

C:9-42 *At-Risk Loss Limitation.* The KC Partnership is a general partnership that manufactures widgets. The partnership uses a calendar year as its tax year and has two equal partners, Kerry and City Corporation, a widely held corporation. On January 1 of the current year, Kerry and City Corporation each has a $200,000 basis in the partnership interest. Operations during the year produce the following results:

Ordinary loss	$900,000
Long-term capital loss	100,000
Short-term capital gain	300,000

The only change in KC's liabilities during the year is KC's borrowing $100,000 as a nonrecourse loan (not qualified real estate financing) that remains outstanding at year-end.
a. What is each partner's deductible loss from the partnership's activities before any passive loss limitation?
b. What is each partner's basis in the partnership interest after the year's operations?
c. How would your answers to Parts a and b change if the KC Partnership's business were totally in real estate but not a rental activity? Assume the loan is qualified real estate financing.

C:9-43 *At-Risk Loss Limitation.* Mary and Gary are partners in the MG Partnership. Mary owns a 40% capital, profits, and loss interest. Gary owns the remaining interest. Both materially participate in partnership activities. At the beginning of the current year, MG's only liabilities are $30,000 in accounts payable, which remain outstanding at year-end. In November, MG borrows $100,000 on a nonrecourse basis from First Bank. The loan is secured by property with a $200,000 FMV. These are MG's only liabilities at year-end. Bases for the partnership interests are $80,000 for Mary and $120,000 for Gary after considering the impact of liabilities but before considering operations. MG has a $200,000 ordinary loss from operations during the current year. How much loss can Mary and Gary recognize?

C:9-44 *Passive Loss Limitation.* Eve and Tom own 40% and 60%, respectively, of the ET Partnership, which manufactures clocks. The partnership is a limited partnership, and Eve is the only general partner. She works full-time in the business. Tom essentially is an investor in the firm and works full-time at another job. Tom has no other income except his salary from his full-time employer. During the current year, the partnership reports the following gain and loss:

Ordinary loss	$140,000
Long-term capital gain	20,000

Before including the current year's gain and loss, Eve and Tom had $46,000 and $75,000 bases for their partnership interests, respectively. The partnership has no nonrecourse liabilities. Tom has no further obligation to make any additional investment in the partnership.

a. What gain or loss should each partner report on his or her individual tax return?

b. If the partnership borrowed an additional $100,000 of recourse liabilities, how would your answer to Part a change?

C:9-45 ***Passive Loss Limitation.*** Kate, Chad, and Stan are partners in the KCS Partnership, which operates a manufacturing business. The partners formed the partnership ten years ago with Kate and Chad each as general partners having a 40% capital and profits interest. Kate materially participates; Chad does not. Stan has a 20% interest as a limited partner. At the end of the current year, the following information was available:

	Kate	*Chad*	*Stan*
Basis in partnership (before gains and losses)	$100,000	$100,000	$50,000
Distributive share of:			
Nonrecourse liability (already included in basis and not qualified real estate financing)	50,000	50,000	25,000
Operating loss	(80,000)	(80,000)	(40,000)
Capital gain	20,000	20,000	10,000

a. How much operating loss can each partner deduct in the current year?

b. Assuming each partner's individual AGI is less than $100,000, how much loss could each partner deduct if the KCS Partnership were engaged in rental activities? Assume Kate and Chad both actively participate, but Stan does not.

C:9-46 ***At-Risk and Passive Loss Limitations.*** At the beginning of year 1, Ed and Fran each contributed $1,000 cash to EF Partnership as equal partners. The partnership immediately borrowed $98,000 on a nonrecourse basis and used the contributed cash and loan proceeds to purchase equipment costing $100,000. The partnership leases out the equipment on a five-year lease for $10,000 per year. Over the five-year period, the partnership makes the following principal and interest payments on the loan:

Year	*Principal*	*Interest*
1	$3,000	$7,000
2	3,500	6,500
3	3,500	6,500
4	4,000	6,000
5	4,000	6,000

Assume the partnership depreciates the equipment according to the following hypothetical schedule:

Year	*Depreciation*
1	$40,000
2	25,000
3	15,000
4	8,000
5	8,000
6	4,000

At the beginning of Year 6, the partnership sells the equipment for $82,000. The partnership claims the last $4,000 of depreciation at the beginning of Year 6 as an expense, so the equipment has a zero basis when sold. At the beginning of Year 6, the partnership also pays off the $80,000 loan balance and distributes any remaining cash to Ed and Fran. Assume that each partner has a 33% ordinary tax rate and an 18.8% capital gains tax rate (including the 3.8% tax on net investment income).

a. Determine the partnership's gain (loss) for each of the five years and the beginning of the sixth year.

b. Assume that depreciation recapture applies but that the at-risk and passive activity loss rules do not apply. Using the results from Part a and a 7% discount rate, determine the present value of tax savings for both partners combined over the five-year period including the beginning of the sixth year. Why do these tax savings occur?

c. Now assume the at-risk and passive activity loss rules do apply. Determine what the partners recognize over the five-year period including the beginning of the sixth year. Do the partners have any tax savings in this situation? Why or why not?

d. Provide a schedule analyzing each partner's outside basis over the five-year period including the sixth year.

C:9-47 *Related Party Transactions.* Susan, Steve, and Sandy own 15%, 35%, and 50%, respectively, in the SSS Partnership. Susan sells securities for their $40,000 FMV to the partnership. What are the tax implications of the following independent situations?

a. Susan's basis in the securities is $60,000. The three partners are siblings.

b. Susan's basis in the securities is $50,000. Susan is unrelated to the other partners.

c. Susan's basis in the securities is $30,000. Susan and Sandy are sisters. The partnership will hold the securities as an investment.

d. What are the tax consequences in Part a if the partnership subsequently sells the securities to an unrelated third party for $70,000? For $55,000? For $35,000?

C:9-48 *Related Party Transactions.* Kara owns 35% of the KLM Partnership and 45% of the KTV Partnership. Lynn owns 20% of KLM and 3% of KTV. Maura, Kara's daughter, owns 15% of KTV. No other partners own an interest in both partnerships or are related to other partners. The KTV Partnership sells to the KLM Partnership 1,000 shares of stock, which KTV has held for investment purposes, for its $50,000 FMV. What are the tax consequences of the sale in each of the following independent situations?

a. KTV's basis for the stock is $80,000.

b. KTV's basis for the stock is $23,000 and KLM holds the stock as an investment.

c. KTV's basis for the stock is $35,000 and KLM holds the stock as inventory.

d. What are the tax consequences in Part a if the KLM Partnership subsequently sells the stock to an unrelated third party for $130,000? For $70,000? For $40,000?

C:9-49 *Guaranteed Payments.* Scott and Dave each invested $100,000 cash when they formed the SD Partnership and became equal partners. They agreed that the partnership would pay each partner a 5% guaranteed payment on his $100,000 capital account. Before the two guaranteed payments, current year results were $23,000 of ordinary income and $14,000 of long-term capital gain. What amount and character of income will Scott and Dave report for the current year from their partnership?

C:9-50 *Guaranteed Payments.* Allen and Bob are equal partners in the AB Partnership. Bob manages the business and receives a guaranteed payment. What amount and character of income will Allen and Bob report in each of the following independent situations?

a. The AB Partnership earns $160,000 of ordinary income before considering Bob's guaranteed payment. Bob is guaranteed a $90,000 payment plus 50% of all income remaining after the guaranteed payment.

b. Assume the same facts as Part a except Bob's distributive share is 50% with a guaranteed minimum of $90,000.

c. The AB Partnership earns a $140,000 long-term capital gain and no ordinary income. Bob is guaranteed $80,000 plus 50% of all amounts remaining after the guaranteed payment.

C:9-51 *Guaranteed Payments.* Pam and Susan own the PS Partnership. Pam takes care of daily operations and receives a guaranteed payment for her efforts. What amount and character of income will each partner report in each of the following independent situations?

a. The PS Partnership reports a $10,000 long-term capital gain and no ordinary income. Pam receives a $40,000 guaranteed payment plus a 30% distributive share of all partnership income after deducting the guaranteed payment.

b. The PS Partnership reports $80,000 of ordinary income, before considering any guaranteed payment, and a $60,000 Sec. 1231 gain. Pam receives a $35,000 guaranteed payment plus a 20% distributive share of all partnership income after deducting the guaranteed payment.

c. The PS Partnership reports $120,000 of ordinary income before considering any guaranteed payment. Pam receives 40% of partnership income but no less than $60,000.

C:9-52 *Family Partnership.* Dad gives Son a 20% capital and profits interest in the Family Partnership. Dad holds a 70% interest, and Fred, an unrelated individual, holds a 10% interest. Dad and Fred work in the partnership, but Son does not. Dad and Fred receive reasonable compensation for their work. The partnership earns $100,000 ordinary income, and the partners agree to divide this amount based on their relative ownership interests. What income must Father, Son, and Fred report if Family Partnership is a manufacturing firm with substantial inventories?

C:9-53 *Family Partnership.* Steve wishes to pass his business on to his children, Tracy and Vicki, and gives each daughter a 20% partnership interest to begin getting them involved. Steve retains the remaining 60% interest. Neither daughter is employed by the partnership, which buys and manages real estate. Steve draws only a $40,000 guaranteed payment for his work for the partnership. Reasonable compensation for his services would be $70,000. The partnership reports ordinary income of $120,000 after deducting the guaranteed payment. Distributive shares for the three partners are tentatively reported as: Steve, $72,000; Tracy, $24,000; and Vicki, $24,000. What is the proper distributive share of income for each partner?

COMPREHENSIVE PROBLEMS

C:9-54 Rick has a $50,000 basis in the RKS General Partnership on January 1 of the current year, and he owns no other investments. He has a 20% capital interest, a 30% profits interest, and a 40% loss interest in the partnership. Rick does not work in the partnership. The partnership's only liability is a $100,000 nonrecourse debt borrowed several years ago, which remains outstanding at year-end. Rick's share of the liability is based on his profits interest and is included in his $50,000 partnership basis. Rick and the partnership each report on a calendar year basis. Income for the entire partnership during the current year is:

Ordinary loss	$440,000
Long-term capital gain	100,000
Sec. 1231 gain	150,000

a. What is Rick's distributive share of income, gain, and loss for the current year?
b. What partnership income, gain, and loss should Rick report on his tax return for the current year?
c. What is Rick's basis in his partnership interest on the first day of next year?

C:9-55 Charles and Mary formed CM Partnership on January 1 of the current year. Charles contributed Inventory A with a $100,000 FMV and a $70,000 adjusted basis for a 40% interest, and Mary contributed $150,000 cash for a 60% interest. The partnership operates on a calendar year. The partnership used the cash to purchase equipment for $50,000, Inventory B for $80,000, and stock in ST Corporation for $5,000. The partnership used the remaining $15,000 for operating expenses and borrowed another $5,000 for operating expenses. During the year, the partnership sold one-half of Inventory A for $60,000 (tax basis, $35,000), one-half of Inventory B for $58,000 (tax basis, $40,000), and the ST stock for $6,000. The partnership claimed $7,000 of depreciation on the equipment for both tax and book purposes. Thus, for the year, the partnership incurred the following items:

Sales—Inventory A	$60,000
Sales—Inventory B	58,000
COGS—Inventory A	35,000
COGS—Inventory B	40,000
Operating expenses	20,000
Depreciation	7,000
Short-term capital gain	1,000
Interest on business loan	500

On December 31 of the current year, the partnership made a $1,000 principal payment on the loan and distributed $2,000 cash to Charles and $3,000 cash to Mary.

a. Determine partnership ordinary income for the year and each partner's distributive share.
b. Determine the separately stated items and each partner's distributive share.
c. Determine each partner's basis in the partnership at the end of the current year.
d. Determine each partner's book capital account at the end of the current year.
e. Provide an analysis of the ending cash balance.
f. Provide beginning and ending balance sheets using tax numbers.
g. Provide beginning and ending balance sheets using book values.

TAX STRATEGY PROBLEM

C:9-56 Sarah and Rex formed SR Entity on December 28 of last year. The entity operates on a calendar tax year. Each individual contributed $800,000 cash in exchange for a 50% ownership interest in the entity (common stock if a corporation; partnership interest if a partnership). In addition, the entity borrowed $400,000 from the bank. The entity operates on a calendar year. On December 28 of last year, the entity used the $2 million cash (contributions and loan) to purchase assets as indicated in the following balance sheet as of December 28 of last year:

Cash	$ 100,000
Inventory	1,770,000
Investment in tax-exempt bonds	50,000
Investment in corporate stock (less than 20%-owned)	80,000
Total	$2,000,000
Liability	$ 400,000
Equity*	1,600,000
Total	$2,000,000

*If a partnership, each partner's beginning capital account is $800,000.

The balance sheet did not change between December 28 of last year and the beginning of the current year. Thus, the above balance sheet also represents the balance sheet at January 1 of the current year.

The following data apply to the entity for the current year:

Sales	$3,000,000
Purchase of additional inventory	2,100,000
Ending inventory at December 31 of the current year	1,650,000
Gain on sale of corporate stock on December 31 of the current year	20,000
Dividends received on stock prior to its sale	4,000
Tax-exempt interest received	2,200
Operating expenses	500,000
Interest paid on loan (no principal paid)*	30,000
Distribution on December 31 of the current year:	
Sarah	60,000
Rex	60,000

*For simplicity, assume all the $30,000 interest expense pertains to business (and not to investments).

Sarah and Rex actively manage the entity's business, and the business does not qualify for the U.S. production activities deduction. At the individual level, Sarah and Rex are each single with no dependents. Each individual claims a standard deduction and one personal exemption (if applicable). Neither individual has income from sources other than listed above.

a. First, assume the entity is a regular C corporation and the distributions are dividends to Sarah and Rex. For the current year, determine the following:
   (1) The corporation's taxable income and tax liability.
   (2) Sarah's and Rex's individual AGI, taxable income, and tax liability.
   (3) The total tax liability for the corporation and its owners.
b. Next, assume the entity is a partnership. For the current year, determine the following:
   (1) Partnership ordinary income and each partner's share of partnership ordinary income.
   (2) Partnership separately stated items and each partner's share of each item.
   (3) Sarah's and Rex's AGI, taxable income, and total tax liability. Assume each partner will incur a $17,660 self-employment tax on his or her share of partnership ordinary income.
   (4) Each partner's basis in the partnership (outside basis) at the end of the current year.
c. Based on your analysis for the current year, which entity is better from an overall tax perspective? What are the shortcomings of examining only one year?
d. Given the corporate form, explain how the corporation can restructure the $60,000 distribution to each individual to reduce the overall tax liability. Assume the corporation and each individual pay a 7.65% payroll tax.

TAX FORM/RETURN PREPARATION PROBLEMS

C:9-57 The Dapper-Dons Partnership was formed ten years ago as a general partnership to custom tailor men's clothing. Dapper-Dons is located at 123 Flamingo Drive in City, ST, 54321. Bob Dapper manages the business and has a 40% capital and profits interest. His address is 709 Brumby Way, City, ST, 54321. Jeremy Dons owns the remaining 60% interest but is not active in the business. His address is 807 Ninth Avenue, City, ST, 54321. The partnership values its inventory using the cost method and did not change the method used during the current year. The partnership uses the accrual method of accounting. Because of its simplicity, the partnership is not subject to the partnership audit procedures. The partnership has no foreign partners, no foreign transactions, no interests in foreign trusts, and no foreign financial accounts. This partnership is neither a tax shelter nor a publicly traded partnership. No changes in ownership of partnership interests occurred during the current year. The partnership made cash distributions of $155,050 and $232,576 to Dapper and Dons, respectively, on December 30 of the current year. It made no other property distributions. Financial statements for the current year are presented in Tables C:9-1 and C:9-2. Assume that Dapper-Dons' business qualifies as a U.S. production activity and that its qualified production activities income is $600,000. Dapper-Dons, being an eligible small pass-through partnership, uses the small business simplified overall method for reporting these activities (see discussion for Line 13d of Schedules K and K-1 in the Form 1065 instructions).

Prepare a current year (2016 for this problem) partnership tax return for Dapper-Dons Partnership.

C:9-58 Healthwise Medical Supplies Company is located at 2400 Second Street, City, ST 12345. The company is a general partnership that uses the calendar year and accrual basis for both book and tax purposes. It engages in the development and sale of specialized surgical tools to hospitals. The employer identification number (EIN) is XX-2018016. The company formed and began business on January 1, 2015. It has no foreign partners or other foreign dealings. The company is neither a tax shelter nor a publicly traded partnership. The company has made no distributions other than cash, and no changes in ownership have occurred during the current year. Dr. Bailey is the Tax Matters Partner. The partnership makes no special elections. Table C:9-3 contains book balance sheet information at the beginning and end of the current year, and Table C:9-4 presents a book income statement for the current year. Other information follows:

Information on Partnership Formation:
Two individuals formed the partnership on January 1, 2015: Dr. Leisa H. Bailey (1200 First Pike, City, ST 12345) and Dr. Thomas J. Firth (3600 Third Blvd., City, ST 54321). For a 30% interest, Dr. Bailey contributed $600,000 cash. She is an active general partner who manages the company. For a 70% interest, Dr. Firth contributed $1.16 million cash and 1,000 shares of Fastgrowth, Inc. stock having, at the time of contribution, a $240,000 fair market value (FMV) and a $48,000 adjusted basis. Dr. Firth is an active general partner who designs and develops new products. For book purposes, the company recorded the contribution of stock at fair market value.

Inventory and Cost of Goods Sold (Form 1125-A):
The company uses the periodic inventory method and prices its inventory using the lower of FIFO cost or market. Only beginning inventory, ending inventory, and purchases should be reflected in Schedule A. No other costs or expenses are allocated to cost of goods sold. Note: the company is exempt from the uniform capitalization (UNICAP) rules because average gross income for the previous year was less than $10 million [Sec. 263A(b)(2)(B)].

Line 9 (a)	Check (ii)
(b)–(d)	Not applicable
(e) & (f)	No

Capital Gains and Losses (Schedule D):
The company sold all 1,000 shares of the Fastgrowth, Inc. common stock on July 2, 2016, for $720,000. Dr. Firth acquired the stock on January 2, 2013, for $48,000 and contributed the stock to the company on January 1, 2015, when its FMV was $240,000.

▼ TABLE C:9-1

Dapper-Dons Partnership Income Statement for the 12 Months Ending December 31 of the Current Year (Problem C:9-57)

Sales		$2,357,000
Returns and allowances		(20,000)
		$2,337,000
Beginning inventory (FIFO method)	$ 200,050	
Purchases	624,000	
Labor	600,000	
Supplies	42,000	
Other costs[a]	12,000	
Goods available for sale	$1,478,050	
Ending inventory[b]	(146,000)	(1,332,050)
Gross profit		$ 1,004,950
Salaries for employees other than partners (W-2 wages)	$51,000	
Guaranteed payment for Dapper	85,000	
Utilities expense	46,428	
Depreciation (MACRS depreciation is $74,311)[c]	49,782	
Automobile expense	12,085	
Office supplies expense	4,420	
Advertising expense	85,000	
Bad debt expense	2,100	
Interest expense (all trade- or business-related)	45,000	
Rent expense	7,400	
Travel expense (meals cost $4,050 of this amount)	11,020	
Repairs and maintenance expense	68,300	
Accounting and legal expense	3,600	
Charitable contributions[d]	16,400	
Payroll taxes	5,180	
Other taxes (all trade- or business-related)	1,400	
Total expenses		494,115
Operating profit		$ 510,835
Other income and losses:		
Gain on sale of AB stock[e]	$ 18,000	
Loss on sale of CD stock[f]	(26,075)	
Sec. 1231 gain on sale of land[g]	5,050	
Interest on U.S. Treasury bills for entire year ($80,000 face amount)	2,000	
Dividends from 15%-owned domestic corporation	11,000	9,975
Net income		$ 520,810

[a] Additional Sec. 263A costs of $7,000 for the current year are included in other costs.
[b] Ending inventory includes the appropriate Sec. 263A costs, and no further adjustment is needed to properly state cost of sales and inventories for tax purposes.
[c] The partnership reports a $10,000 positive AMT adjustment for property placed in service after 1986. Dapper-Dons acquired and placed in service $40,000 of rehabilitation expenditures for a certified historical property this year. The appropriate MACRS depreciation on the rehabilitation expenditures already is included in the MACRS depreciation total.
[d] The partnership made all contributions in cash to qualifying charities.
[e] The partnership purchased the AB stock as an investment two years ago on December 1 for $40,000 and sold it on June 14 of the current year for $58,000.
[f] The partnership purchased the CD stock as an investment on February 15 of the current year for $100,000 and sold it on August 1 for $73,925.
[g] The partnership used the land as a parking lot for the business. The partnership purchased the land four years ago on March 17 for $30,000 and sold it on August 15 of the current year for $35,050.

▼ TABLE C:9-2

Dapper-Dons Partnership Balance Sheet for January 1 and December 31 of the Current Year (Problem C:9-57)

	Balance January 1	Balance December 31
Assets:		
Cash	$ 10,000	$ 40,000
Accounts receivable	72,600	150,100
Inventories	200,050	146,000
Marketable securities[a]	220,000	260,000
Building and equipment	374,600	465,000
Minus: Accumulated depreciation	(160,484)	(173,100)
Land	185,000	240,000
Total assets	$901,766	$1,128,000
Liabilities and equities:		
Accounts payable	$ 35,000	$ 46,000
Accrued salaries payable	14,000	18,000
Payroll taxes payable	3,416	7,106
Sales taxes payable	5,200	6,560
Mortgage and notes payable (current maturities)	44,000	52,000
Long-term debt	210,000	275,000
Capital:		
Dapper	236,060	289,334
Dons	354,090	434,000
Total liabilities and equities	$901,766	$1,128,000

[a] Short-term investment.

▼ TABLE C:9-3

Healthwise Medical Supplies Company—Book Balance Sheet Information

Account	January 1, 2016 Debit	January 1, 2016 Credit	December 31, 2016 Debit	December 31, 2016 Credit
Cash	$ 233,500		$ 143,450	
Accounts receivable	540,000		600,000	
Inventory	1,000,000		1,200,000	
Investment in municipal bonds	40,000		40,000	
Investment in corporate stock	240,000		–0–	
Equipment	1,000,000		1,400,000	
Accumulated depreciation—Equipment		$ 142,900		$ 787,800
Accounts payable		100,000		130,000
Notes payable (short-term)		750,000		150,000
Accrued payroll expenses		3,500		5,250
Capital account balances:				
Dr. Leisa H. Bailey (30%)		617,130		693,120
Dr. Thomas J. Firth (70%)		1,439,970		1,617,280
Totals	$3,053,500	$3,053,500	$3,383,450	$3,383,450

▼ **TABLE C:9-4**
Healthwise Medical Supplies Company—Book Income Statement 2016

Sales		$5,000,000
Returns and allowances		(250,000)
Net sales		$4,750,000
Beginning inventory	$1,000,000	
Purchases	2,000,000	
Ending inventory	(1,200,000)	
Cost of goods sold		(1,800,000)
Gross profit		$2,950,000
Expenses:		
Depreciation (including Sec. 179)	$ 644,900	
Repairs	32,500	
General insurance	35,000	
Guaranteed payment (to Dr. Bailey)	100,000	
Other salaries	700,000	
Travel	20,000	
Utilities	60,000	
Rent expense	150,000	
Advertising expense	30,000	
Professional fees	50,000	
Employment taxes	70,000	
Business interest expense	36,000	
Investment expenses	3,600	
Investment interest expense	4,500	
Meals and entertainment	15,000	
Charitable contributions (cash)	40,000	
Total expenses		(1,991,500)
Other income:		
Interest on municipal bonds		1,600
Dividend income		13,200
Gain on stock sale:		
Selling price	$720,000	
Book value	(240,000)	
Book gain		480,000
Net income per books		$1,453,300

ADDITIONAL COMMENT

The AMT applies to this equipment because it was placed in service in 2015, and the corporation elected out of bonus depreciation.

Fixed Assets and Depreciation (Form 4562):
The company acquired the equipment on January 2, 2015, and placed it in service on that date. The equipment, which originally cost $1 million, is MACRS seven-year property. The company did not elect Sec. 179 expensing in the acquisition year and elected out of bonus depreciation. The company claimed the following depreciation on this property:

Year	*Book and Regular Tax Depreciation*	*AMT Depreciation*
2015	$142,900	$107,100
2016	244,900	191,300

On March 1, 2016, the company acquired and placed in service additional equipment costing $400,000. The company made the Sec. 179 expensing election for the entire cost of this new equipment. No depreciation or expensing is reported on Schedule A.

Other Information:

- The company paid Dr. Bailey a $100,000 guaranteed payment for her management services.
- The company made a $40,000 cash contribution to Fort Sanders Hospital System on December 1 of the current year.
- During the current year, the company made a $360,000 cash distribution to Dr. Bailey and a $840,000 cash distribution to Dr. Firth.
- The municipal bonds, acquired in 2015, are general revenue bonds, not private-activity bonds. Assume that no expenses of the company are allocable to the tax-exempt interest generated from the municipal bonds.
- Assume qualified production activities income (QPAI) equals $1.6 million. Employer's W-2 wages allocable to U.S. production activities equal $700,000. The company, being an eligible small pass-through partnership, uses the small business simplification overall method for reporting these activities (see discussion for Line 13d of Schedule K and Line 13 of Schedule K-1 in the Form 1065 instructions).
- Use book numbers for Schedule L, Schedule M-2, and Line 1 of Schedule M-1. Also use book numbers for Item L of Schedule K-1, and check the box for Sec. 704(b) book.
- The partners share liabilities, which are recourse, in the same proportion as their ownership percentages.

Required: Prepare the 2016 partnership tax return (Form 1065), including the following additional schedules and forms: Schedule D, Form 4562, and Schedule K-1.

Optional: Prepare a schedule for each partner's basis in his or her partnership interest. At January 1, 2016, Bailey's basis was $873,180, and Firth's was $1,845,420.

CASE STUDY PROBLEMS

C:9-59 Abe and Brenda formed the AB Partnership ten years ago as a general partnership and have been very successful with the business. However, in the current year, economic conditions caused them to lose significant amounts, but they expect the economy and their business to return to profitable operations by next year or the year after. Abe manages the partnership business and works in it full-time. Brenda has a full-time job as an accountant for a $39,000 annual salary, but she also works in the partnership occasionally. She estimates that she spent about 120 hours working in the partnership this year. Abe has a 40% profits interest, a 50% loss interest, and a basis in his partnership interest on December 31 (before considering this year's operations) of $81,000. Brenda has a 60% profits interest, a 50% loss interest, and a basis of $104,000 on December 31 (before considering this year's operations). The partnership has no liabilities at December 31. Neither Abe nor Brenda currently has other investments. The AB Partnership incurs the following amounts during the year.

Ordinary loss	$100,000
Sec. 1231 gain	10,000
Tax-exempt municipal bond income	14,000
Long-term capital loss	14,000
Short-term capital loss	136,000

Early next year, the AB Partnership is considering borrowing $100,000 from a local bank to be secured by a mortgage on a building owned by the partnership with $150,000 FMV.

Required: Prepare a presentation to be made to Abe and Brenda discussing this matter. Points that should be discussed include: What amounts should Abe and Brenda report on their income tax return for the current year from the AB Partnership? What are their bases in their partnership interests after taking all transactions into effect? What happens to any losses they cannot deduct in the current year? What planning opportunities are presented by the need to borrow money early next year? What planning ideas would you suggest for Brenda?

C:9-60 On the advice of his attorney, Dr. Andres, a local pediatrician, contributed several office buildings, which he had previously owned as sole proprietor, to a new Andres Partnership in which he became a one-third general partner. He gave the remaining limited partnership interests to his two sons, Miguel and Esteban. Last year, when the partnership was formed, the boys were 14 and 16. The real estate is well managed and extremely profitable. Dr. Andres regularly consults with a full-time hired manager about the business, but neither of his sons has any dealings with the partnership. Under the terms of the partnership agreement, the boys can sell their partnership interest to no one but their father. Distributions from the partnership have been large, and Dr. Andres has insisted that the boys put all their distributions into savings accounts to pay for their college education.

Last year's return (the partnership's first) was filed by Mr. Jones, a partner in the local CPA firm of Wise and Johnson. Mr. Jones, who was Dr. Andres's accountant for a decade, retired last summer. Dr. Andres's business is extremely profitable and is an important part of the client base of this small-town CPA firm. Ms. Watson, the young partner who has taken over Dr. Andres's account, asked John, a second-year staff accountant, to prepare the current year's partnership return.

John has done considerable research and is positive that the Andres Partnership does not qualify as a partnership at all because the father has retained too much control over the sons' interests. John has briefly talked to Mr. Jones about his concerns. Mr. Jones said he was really rushed in the prior year when he filed the partnership return and admitted he never looked into the question of whether the arrangement met the requirements for being taxed as a partnership. After hearing more of the details, Mr. Jones stated that John was probably correct in his conclusion. Dr. Andres's tax bill will be significantly larger if he has to pay tax on all the partnership's income. When John approached Ms. Watson with his conclusions, her response was, "Oh, no! Dr. Andres already is unhappy because Mr. Jones is no longer preparing his returns. He'll really be unhappy if we give him a big tax increase, too." She paused thoughtfully, and then went on. "My first thought is just to leave well enough alone and file the partnership return. Are you positive, John, that this won't qualify as a partnership? Think about it and let me know tomorrow."

Required: Prepare a list of points you want to go over with the tax partner that would support finding that the business activity is a partnership. Prepare a second list of points that would support finding that the business activity is not a partnership.

TAX RESEARCH PROBLEMS

C:9-61 Caitlin and Wally formed the C & W Partnership on September 20, 2017. Caitlin contributed cash of $195,000, and Wally contributed office furniture with a FMV of $66,000. He bought the furniture for $60,000 on January 5, 2017, and placed it in service on that date. Wally did not elect Sec. 179 expensing on the furniture, nor did he take bonus depreciation. He also contributed an office building and land with a combined FMV of $129,000. The land's FMV is $9,000. Wally bought the land in 2010 for $8,000 and had the building constructed for $100,000. The building was placed in service in June 2013.

Required: Your tax manager has asked you to prepare a schedule for the file indicating the basis of property at the time of contribution that Wally contributed, the depreciation for each piece of property that the partnership can claim, and the allocation of the depreciation to the two partners. Also indicate the amount and type of any recapture to which the contributed property may be subject at the time of the contribution and at a later time when the partnership sells the property. Your tax manager knows that, under Reg. Sec. 1.704-3, several alternatives exist for allocating depreciation relating to contributed property. He remembers that the Treasury Regulations describe a traditional method and a couple of others, but he's not sure what method applies in this situation. He wants you to check the alternatives and indicate which method should be used. Be certain to clearly label your schedule so that anyone who looks at the file later can determine where your numbers came from and the authority for your calculations. The manager has suggested that, at a minimum, you consult the following authorities:

- IRC Secs. 1(h), 168, 704, 1231, 1245
- Prop. Reg. Sec. 1.168-5(b)
- Reg. Sec. 1.704-1(b)(2)(iv)(g)(3)
- Reg. Sec. 1.704-3

C:9-62 Your clients, Lisa and Matthew, plan to form Lima General Partnership. Lisa will contribute $50,000 cash to Lima for a 50% interest in capital and profits. Matthew will contribute land having a $35,000 adjusted basis and a $50,000 FMV to Lima for the remaining 50% interest in capital and profits. Lima will borrow additional funds of $100,000 from a bank on a recourse basis and then will subdivide and sell the land. Prepare a draft memorandum for your tax manager's signature outlining the tax treatment for the partnership formation transaction. As part of your memorandum, compare the reporting of this transaction on the tax and financial accounting books. References:

- IRC Sec. 721
- Accounting Standards Codification (ASC) 845 (Nonmonetary Transactions)

C:9-63 Almost two years ago, the DEF Partnership was formed when Demetrius, Ebony, and Farouk each contributed $100,000 in cash. They are equal general partners in the real estate partnership, which has a December 31 year-end. The partnership uses the accrual method of accounting for financial accounting purposes but uses the cash method of accounting for tax purposes. The first year of operations resulted in a $50,000 loss. Because the real estate market plummeted, the second year of operations will result in an even larger ordinary loss. On November 30, calculations reveal that the year's loss is likely to be $100,000 for financial accounting purposes. Financial accounting results for the year are as follows:

	Quarter			
	First	*Second*	*Third*	*Fourth**
Revenue	$40,000	$60,000	$80,000	$100,000
Maintenance expense	(30,000)	(58,000)	(70,000)	(85,000)
Interest expense	(10,000)	(30,000)	(35,000)	(50,000)
Utilities expense	(3,000)	(3,000)	(3,000)	(3,000)
Projected loss	($ 3,000)	($31,000)	($28,000)	($38,000)

* Fourth quarter results are the sum of actual October and November results along with estimates for December results. December estimates are revenue, $33,000; maintenance, $60,000; interest, $20,000; and utilities, $1,000.

Cash has been short throughout the second year of operations, so more than $65,000 of expenses for second year operations have resulted in bills that are currently due or overdue. The unpaid bills are for July 1 through November 30 interest on a loan from the bank. In addition, all but essential maintenance has been postponed during the fourth quarter so that most of the fourth quarter maintenance is scheduled to be completed during December.

The DEF partners wants to attract a new partner to obtain additional capital. Raj is interested in investing $100,000 as a limited partner in the DEF Partnership if a good deal can be arranged. Raj would have a 25% profits and loss interest in the partnership but would expect something extra for the current year. In the current tax year, Raj has passive income of more than $200,000 from other sources, so he would like to have large passive losses allocated to him from DEF.

Required: Your tax partner has asked you to prepare a memorandum suggesting a plan to maximize the amount of current year loss that can be allocated to Raj. Assume none of the partners performs more than one-half of his or her personal service time in connection with real estate trades or businesses in which he or she materially participates. She reminded you to consider the varying interest rules for allocating losses to new partners found in Sec. 706 and to look into the possibilities of somehow capitalizing on the cash method of accounting or of using a special allocation. She wants you to be sure to check all the relevant case law for the plan you suggest.

C:9-64 Alice, Beth, and Carl formed the ABC Partnership early in Year 1. Alice and Beth each contributed $100,000 for their partnership interests, and Carl contributed land having a $100,000 FMV and $160,000 adjusted basis. The land remained a capital asset to the partnership. Late in Year 2, Carl sold his interest in the partnership to Dan for $100,000. Shortly after that transaction, the partnership sold the land to an outside party for $100,000. The partnership has no Sec. 754 election in effect (discussed in Chapter C:10). The partners have asked that you explain the consequences these transactions have to the partnership and the partners, especially Carl and Dan. At a minimum, you should consult the following resources:

- IRC Sec. 704
- Reg. Sec. 1.704-3(a)

CHAPTER 10

SPECIAL PARTNERSHIP ISSUES

LEARNING OBJECTIVES

After studying this chapter, you should be able to

1. Determine the gain, loss, and basis consequences of a nonliquidating partnership distribution
2. Identify a partnership's Sec. 751 assets and assess the tax consequences of a nonliquidating distribution when these assets are involved
3. Determine the gain, loss, and basis consequences of liquidating or selling a partnership interest
4. Recognize other means of terminating a partnership interest and related issues
5. Analyze the effects of optional and mandatory basis adjustments
6. Compare and contrast the various special forms a partnership might take
7. Identify tax planning opportunities in liquidating or selling a partnership interest

CHAPTER OUTLINE

Chapter C:10 continues the discussion of partnership taxation. The chapter first explains simple nonliquidating distributions and then discusses more complex nonliquidating and liquidating distributions. The chapter also explains methods of disposing of a partnership interest, including sales of the partnership interest and the retirement or death of a partner as well as transactions that terminate the entire partnership.

Finally, the chapter examines special partnership forms. These forms include publicly traded partnerships, limited liability companies, limited liability partnerships, and electing large partnerships.

NONLIQUIDATING DISTRIBUTIONS

OBJECTIVE 1

Determine the gain, loss, and basis consequences of a nonliquidating partnership distribution

Distributions from a partnership fall into two categories: liquidating distributions and nonliquidating (or current) distributions. A **liquidating distribution** is a single distribution, or one of a planned series of distributions, that terminates a partner's entire interest in the partnership. All other distributions, including those that substantially reduce a partner's interest in the partnership, are governed by the **nonliquidating (current) distribution** rules.

Although the tax consequences of the two types of distributions are similar in many respects, they are sufficiently different to require separate study. The chapter first discusses simple current distributions. It then covers complex current distributions involving Sec. 751 property and liquidating distributions.

RECOGNITION OF GAIN

A current distribution that does not bring Sec. 751 into play cannot result in the recognition of a loss by either the partnership or the partner who receives the distribution. Moreover, the partnership usually recognizes no gain on a current distribution (except for Sec. 751 property, defined later in this chapter). Under Sec. 731, partners who receive distributions recognize a gain if they receive money distributions that exceed their basis in the partnership. For distribution purposes, money includes cash, deemed cash from reductions in a partner's share of liabilities, and the fair market value (FMV) of marketable securities.

EXAMPLE C:10-1 ▶ Melissa is a 30% partner in the ABC Real Estate Partnership until Josh is admitted as a partner in exchange for a cash contribution. After Josh's admission, Melissa holds a 20% interest. Because of large loss deductions, Melissa's basis (before Josh's admission) is $20,000 including her 30% interest in the partnership liabilities of $250,000. She is deemed to receive a cash distribution equal to the $25,000 [(0.30 − 0.20) × $250,000] reduction in her share of partnership liabilities. Because the cash distribution exceeds her basis, Melissa recognizes a $5,000 ($25,000 distribution − $20,000 basis) gain. ◀

KEY POINT

Reductions in a partner's share of liabilities are treated as cash distributions.

SELF-STUDY QUESTION

Can gain or loss be recognized in a current distribution?

ANSWER

Current distributions with no Sec. 751 implications do not create losses to either the partner or partnership. Ignoring Sec. 751, the partnership recognizes no gains. However, a partner recognizes a gain if the partner receives a money distribution exceeding his or her basis in his or her partnership interest. A distribution also may trigger recognition of precontribution gain or loss for a partner.

Precontribution Gain Recognition. Although a current distribution usually causes gain recognition only if money distributions exceed a partner's basis, a distribution also may trigger recognition of previously unrecognized precontribution gain or loss. A precontribution gain or loss is the difference between the FMV and adjusted basis of property when contributed to the partnership. Two different distribution events may trigger recognition of precontribution gain or loss.

First, if a partner contributes property with a precontribution gain or loss, the contributing partner must recognize the precontribution gain or loss when the partnership distributes the property to any other partner within seven years of the contribution. The amount of precontribution gain or loss recognized by the contributing partner equals the amount of precontribution gain or loss remaining that would have been allocated to the contributing partner had the property instead been sold for its FMV on the distribution date. The partnership's basis in the property immediately before the distribution and the contributing partner's basis in his or her partnership interest are both increased by any gain recognized or decreased by any loss recognized.[1]

EXAMPLE C:10-2 ▶ Several years ago, Michael contributed land with a $3,000 basis and a $7,000 FMV to the AB Partnership. In the current year, the partnership distributed the land to Stephen, another partner in the partnership. At the time of the distribution, the land had a $9,000 FMV. Stephen recognizes no gain on the distribution. Michael, however, recognizes his $4,000 precontribution gain when the partnership distributes the property to Stephen. Michael increases the basis in his partnership interest by $4,000, and the partnership's basis in the land immediately before the distribution increases by $4,000. This increase in the partnership's basis for the land also increases the land's basis to the distributee partner (Stephen). ◀

KEY POINT

Note the differences in the two distributions that cause a contributing partner to recognize remaining precontribution gains. In the first distribution, the *contributed property* is distributed to *another partner.* In the second distribution, *property other than the contributed property* is distributed to the *contributing partner.*

Second, under Sec. 737, property distributions to a partner may cause the partner to recognize his or her remaining precontribution gain if the FMV of the distributed property exceeds the partner's basis in his or her partnership interest before the distribution. The gain recognized under Sec. 737 is the lesser of the remaining precontribution net gain or the excess of the FMV of the distributed property over the adjusted basis of the partnership interest immediately before the property distribution (but after reduction for any money distributed at the same time).[2] The remaining precontribution gain is the net of all precontribution gains and losses for property contributed to the partnership in the seven years immediately preceding the distribution to the extent that such precontribution gains and losses have not already been recognized. The character of the recognized gain is determined by referencing the type of property that had precontribution gains or losses. The gain recognized under Sec. 737 is in addition to any gain recognized on the same distribution because of distributed cash exceeding the partner's basis in his or her partnership interest.

EXAMPLE C:10-3 ▶ Several years ago, Sergio contributed land, a capital asset, with a $20,000 FMV and a $15,000 basis to the STU Partnership in exchange for a 30% general interest in the partnership. The partnership still holds the land on January 31 of the current year, and none of the $5,000 precontribution gain has been recognized. On January 31 of the current year, Sergio has a $40,000 basis in his partnership interest when he receives an $8,000 cash distribution plus property purchased by the partnership with a $45,000 FMV and a $30,000 basis. Under the Sec. 731 distribution rules Sergio recognizes no gain because the cash distribution ($8,000) does not exceed Sergio's predistribution basis in his partnership interest ($40,000). However, under Sec. 737 he recognizes gain equal to the lesser of the $5,000 remaining precontribution gain or the $13,000 difference between the FMV of the property distributed ($45,000) and the basis of the partnership interest after the cash distribution but before any property distributions ($32,000 = $40,000 adjusted basis − $8,000 cash distributed). Thus, Sergio recognizes a $5,000 capital gain. ◀

EXAMPLE C:10-4 ▶ Assume the same facts as in Example C:10-3 except the distribution was $20,000 in cash and $23,000 (FMV) in marketable securities, which are treated like money, plus the property. Sergio recognizes a $3,000 gain under Sec. 731 because he received a money distribution exceeding his basis in the partnership interest ($43,000 money distribution − $40,000 adjusted basis before distributions). Under Sec. 737 he also recognizes gain equal to the lesser of the remaining precontribution gain ($5,000) or the $45,000 excess of the FMV of the property distributed ($45,000) over the zero basis of the partnership interest after money distributions but before property distributions ($0 = $40,000 adjusted basis − $43,000 money distributed). Sergio, therefore, recognizes both a $5,000 capital gain under Sec. 737 and a $3,000 capital gain under Sec. 731. ◀

If a partner recognizes gain under Sec. 737, that gain increases the partner's basis in his or her partnership interest (illustrated in the next section). Further, the recognized gain also increases the partnership's basis in the property that was the source of the precontribution gain.

[1] Sec. 704(c). See Chapter C:9 for a discussion of precontribution gains and losses.

[2] Section 737 does not apply if the property distributed was contributed by this same partner. Only the provisions of Sec. 731 would be considered in such a situation.

EXAMPLE C:10-5 ▶ Assume the same facts as in Example C:10-3. At the time Sergio contributed the land, the partnership assumed Sergio's $15,000 basis in the land. Now, Sergio's $5,000 Sec. 737 gain increases the partnership's basis in the land to $20,000. ◀

BASIS EFFECTS OF DISTRIBUTIONS

In general, the partner's basis for property distributed by the partnership carries over from the partnership. The partner's basis in the partnership interest is reduced by the amount of money received and by the partner's basis in the distributed property.

EXAMPLE C:10-6 ▶ Jack has a $35,000 basis for his interest in the MLV Partnership before receiving a current distribution consisting of $7,000 in money, accounts receivable having a zero basis to the partnership, and land having an $18,000 basis to the partnership. Jack takes a carryover basis in the land and receivables. Following the distribution, his basis in the partnership interest is calculated as follows:

Predistribution basis in partnership interest	$35,000
Minus: Money received	(7,000)
Carryover basis in receivables	(–0–)
Carryover basis in land	(18,000)
Postdistribution basis in partnership interest	$10,000

◀

The total bases of all distributed property in the partner's hands is limited to the partner's predistribution basis in his or her partnership interest plus any gain recognized on the distribution under Sec. 737.[3] If the partner's predistribution basis plus Sec. 737 gain is less than the sum of the money received plus the carryover basis of any noncash property received, the order in which the basis is allocated becomes crucial. First, cash and deemed cash distributions reduce the partner's basis in his or her partnership interest. Next, the remaining basis is allocated to provide a carryover of the partnership's basis for receivables and inventory. If the partner's predistribution basis is not large enough to allow a carryover of the partnership's basis for these two property categories, the partner's remaining basis is allocated among the receivables and inventory items based on both the partnership's basis in the assets and their FMV.[4] First, each asset is given its basis to the partnership. Then, the difference between the carryover basis from the partnership and the partner's basis in the partnership interest is

WHAT WOULD YOU DO IN THIS SITUATION?

You have done the personal and business tax work for Betty and Thelma for a number of years. Betty and Thelma are partners in a retail shop. In addition, the two have decided they want to exchange some property that is not associated with their partnership. Betty wants to exchange undeveloped land she personally holds as an investment, having a $40,000 FMV and a $10,000 adjusted basis, for machinery and office equipment that Thelma owns but no longer uses. Thelma's machinery and office equipment in total have a $40,000 FMV and a $28,000 adjusted basis. Recently, a friend told Betty that several years ago he and an associate did a similar swap tax-free by contributing both pieces of property to be exchanged to a partnership, having the partnership hold the property for a few months, and then having the partnership distribute the property to the partner who wanted to receive it. The friend said the arrangement was nontaxable because the initial transfer qualified as a nontaxable contribution of property to the partnership in exchange for a partnership interest, and the distribution was nontaxable because it was simply a pro rata property distribution made by the partnership. Thelma and Betty have come to you asking that you structure their exchange using their retail shop partnership so that the transfer will be tax-free also. How should you respond to their request?

[3] Secs. 732(a)(2) and 737(c). Marketable securities have a basis equal to their Sec. 732 basis plus any gain recognized under Sec. 731(c).

[4] Sec. 732(c).

calculated. A decrease must be allocated if the partner's basis in the partnership interest (after any money distribution) is less than the carryover basis from the partnership. The decrease is first allocated to any asset that has declined in value in an amount equal to the smaller of the decline in value for the asset or the asset's share of the decrease. If the decrease is not fully used at this point in the calculation, the remaining decrease is allocated to the assets based on their relative adjusted bases at this point in the calculation.

EXAMPLE C:10-7 ▶ Tracy has a $15,000 basis in her interest in the TP Partnership and no remaining precontribution gain immediately before receiving a current distribution that consists of $6,000 in money, power tools held as inventory with a $4,000 basis to the partnership and FMV of $3,500, and steel rod held as inventory with an $8,000 basis to the partnership and FMV of $9,200. The basis of the distributed property in Tracy's hands is determined as follows:

KEY POINT

If different types of property are distributed, the partnership distribution rules assume that the property is distributed in the following order: (1) cash, (2) receivables and inventory, and (3) other property. This ordering can affect both the recognition of gain to the partner and the basis the partner takes in the distributed property.

Predistribution basis in partnership interest	$15,000
Minus: Money received	(6,000)
Plus: Sec. 737 gain	–0–
Basis to be allocated	$ 9,000

The calculation of bases for the steel rod and power tools is as follows:

	Steel Rods	*Power Tools*	*Total*
FMV of asset	$9,200	$3,500	$12,700
Minus: Partnership's basis for asset	(8,000)	(4,000)	(12,000)
Difference	$1,200	($ 500)	$ 700
Step 1: Give each asset the partnership's basis for the asset	$8,000	$4,000	$12,000
Minus: Tracy's basis to be allocated			(9,000)
Decrease to allocate			$ 3,000
Step 2: Asset basis after Step 1	$8,000	$4,000	$12,000
Allocate the decrease first to assets that have declined in value	–0–	(500)	(500)
Adjusted bases at this point in the calculation	$8,000	$3,500	$11,500
Step 3: Allocate $2,500 remaining decrease based on relative adjusted bases at this point in the calculation	(1,739)[a]	(761)[b]	(2,500)
Tracy's bases in the assets	$6,261	$2,739	$ 9,000

[a][$8,000 ÷ ($8,000 + $3,500)] × $2,500 = $1,739
[b][$3,500 ÷ ($8,000 + $3,500)] × $2,500 = $ 761

This process results in Tracy's total basis in the two assets she receives being exactly equal to the $9,000 amount to be allocated. Moreover, Tracy's basis in her partnership interest is zero after the property distributions. ◀

EXAMPLE C:10-8 ▶ Assume the same facts as in Example C:10-7 except Tracy recognizes $1,000 of remaining precontribution gain under Sec. 737 as a result of the distribution. The basis of the distributed property in Tracy's hands is determined as follows:

Predistribution basis in partnership interest	$15,000
Minus: Money received	(6,000)
Plus: Sec. 737 gain	1,000
Amount to be allocated	$10,000

The calculation of the basis for the steel rods and power tools are as follows:

	Steel Rods	*Power Tools*	*Total*
FMV of asset	$9,200	$3,500	$12,700
Minus: Partnership's basis for asset	(8,000)	(4,000)	(12,000)
Difference	$1,200	($ 500)	$ 700

Step 1: Give each asset the partnership's basis for the asset	$8,000	$4,000	$12,000
Minus: Tracy's basis to be allocated			(10,000)
Decrease to allocate			$ 2,000
Step 2: Adjusted basis after Step 1	$8,000	$4,000	$12,000
Allocate the decrease first to assets that have declined in value	–0–	(500)	(500)
Adjusted basis at this point in the calculation	$8,000	$3,500	$11,500
Step 3: Allocate $1,500 remaining decrease based on relative adjusted bases at this point in the calculation	(1,043)[a]	(457)[b]	(1,500)
Tracy's bases in the assets	$6,957	$3,043	$10,000

[a][$8,000 ÷ ($8,000 + $3,500)] × $1,500 = $1,043
[b][$3,500 ÷ ($8,000 + $3,500)] × $1,500 = $ 457

Again, Tracy's basis in her partnership interest is zero after the distributions. ◀

If a partner's predistribution basis plus Sec. 737 gain recognized exceeds the sum of his or her money distribution plus the carryover basis for any receivables and inventory, a carryover basis is allocated to the other property received. If the partner has an insufficient basis in the partnership interest to provide a carryover basis for all the distributed property, the remaining basis for the partnership interest is allocated to the other property first to any decrease in FMV below basis and then based on the relative bases of such property in the partnership's hands just as was calculated above.

EXAMPLE C:10-9 ▶ John has a $15,000 basis in his partnership interest and no remaining precontribution gain before receiving the following property as a current distribution:

SELF-STUDY QUESTION

Assume the same facts as in Example C:10-9 except the basis in the two parcels of land is only $4,000 in total. What are the tax consequences of the distribution?

ANSWER

If the basis in the two parcels of land were only $4,000 in total, the partner would take a $4,000 carryover basis in the land and retain a $2,000 basis in his partnership interest.

Property	*Basis to the Partnership*	*FMV*
Money	$5,000	$5,000
Inventory	4,000	4,500
Land parcel 1	4,500	6,000
Land parcel 2	3,000	4,000

John's basis in his distributed property is calculated as follows:

Predistribution basis	$15,000
Minus: Money received	(5,000)
Plus: Sec. 737 gain	–0–
Basis for noncash property	$10,000
Minus: Carryover basis for inventory	(4,000)
Remaining basis to be allocated	$ 6,000

The calculation of the basis for the two parcels of land is as follows:

	Parcel One	*Parcel Two*	*Total*
FMV of asset	$6,000	$4,000	$10,000
Minus: Partnership's basis for asset	(4,500)	(3,000)	(7,500)
Difference	$1,500	$1,000	$ 2,500
Step 1: Give each asset the partnership's basis for the asset	$4,500	$3,000	$ 7,500
Minus: John's basis to be allocated			(6,000)
Decrease to allocate			$ 1,500
Step 2: Adjusted basis after Step 1	$4,500	$3,000	$ 7,500
Allocate the decrease first to assets that have declined in value	–0–	–0–	–0–
Adjusted basis at this point in the calculation	$4,500	$3,000	$ 7,500

Step 3: Allocate $1,500 remaining decrease based on relative adjusted bases at this point in the calculation	(900)[a]	(600)[b]	(1,500)
John's bases in the assets	$3,600	$2,400	$ 6,000

[a][$4,500 ÷ ($4,500 + $3,000)] × $1,500 = $900
[b][$3,000 ÷ ($4,500 + $3,000)] × $1,500 = $600

John's basis in his partnership interest is zero after the distribution because all its basis is allocated to the money and other property received. ◀

TYPICAL MISCONCEPTION

The partner's basis in his or her partnership interest cannot be less than zero. However, a partner's capital account can be less than zero. One must distinguish between references to a partner's basis in his or her partnership interest (his outside basis) and the balance in a partner's capital account.

Two other points should be noted. First, even when a partner's basis in the partnership interest is reduced to zero by a current distribution, he or she retains an interest in the partnership. If the partner has no remaining interest in the partnership (as opposed to a zero basis), the distribution would have been a liquidating distribution. Second, the distributee's basis in property distributed as a current distribution is always equal to or less than the carryover basis. Basis for distributed property cannot be increased above the carryover basis amount when received as a nonliquidating distribution.

HOLDING PERIOD AND CHARACTER OF DISTRIBUTED PROPERTY

The partner's holding period for property distributed as a current distribution includes the partnership's holding period for such property.[5] The length of time the partner owns the partnership interest is irrelevant when determining the holding period for the distributed property. Thus, if a new partner receives a distribution of property the partnership held for two years before he or she became a partner, the new partner's holding period for the distributed property is deemed to begin when the partnership purchased the property (i.e., two years ago) rather than on the more recent date when the partner purchases the partnership interest.

KEY POINT

Consistent with the discussion in Chapter C:9, certain rules ensure that neither contributions to nor distributions from a partnership can be used to alter the character of certain gains and losses on property held by the partnership or by the individual partners.

Special rules determine the character of gain or loss recognized when a partner subsequently sells or exchanges unrealized receivables or inventory distributed to the partner. These properties are defined in the next section of this chapter.

If the partnership distributes property that is an unrealized receivable in its hands, the distributee partner recognizes ordinary income or loss on a subsequent sale of that property. This ordinary income or loss treatment occurs without regard to the character of the property in the distributee partner's hands or the length of time the partner holds the property before its disposition.[6]

If the partnership distributes property that is inventory in its hands, the distributee partner recognizes ordinary income or loss on a subsequent sale that occurs within five years of the distribution date.[7] The inventory rule mandates the ordinary income or loss result only for the five-year period beginning on the distribution date. After five years, the character of the gain or loss recognized on the sale of such property is determined by its character in the hands of the distributee partner.

NONLIQUIDATING DISTRIBUTIONS WITH SEC. 751

OBJECTIVE 2

Identify a partnership's Sec. 751 assets and assess the tax consequences of a nonliquidating distribution when these assets are involved

So far, the discussion of current distributions has ignored the existence of the Sec. 751 property rules. Now, we must expand our discussion to include them.

SECTION 751 ASSETS DEFINED

Section 751 assets include unrealized receivables and inventory. These two categories encompass all property likely to produce ordinary income when sold or collected. Each of these categories must be carefully defined before further discussion of Sec. 751.

[5] Sec. 735(b).
[6] Sec. 735(a)(1).
[7] Sec. 735(a)(2).

KEY POINT

Section 751 property represents property in a partnership that is likely to produce ordinary income or loss. The application of Sec. 751 in conjunction with partnership distributions or sales of a partnership interest is of concern to individual partners because the rules may trigger ordinary income recognition rather than capital gains.

Unrealized Receivables. **Unrealized receivables** includes a much broader spectrum of property than the name implies. Unrealized receivables are certain rights to payments to be received by a partnership to the extent they are not already included in income under the partnership's accounting methods. They include rights to payments for services performed or to be performed as well as rights to payment for goods delivered or to be delivered (other than capital assets). A common example of unrealized receivables is the accounts receivable of a cash method partnership.

In addition to rights to receive payments for goods and services, the term *unrealized receivables* includes most potential ordinary income recapture items. A primary example of this type of unrealized receivable is the potential Sec. 1245 or 1250 recapture on the partnership's depreciable property, which is the amount of depreciation that would be recaptured as ordinary income under Sec. 1245 or 1250 if the partnership sold property at its FMV.[8]

EXAMPLE C:10-10 ▶ The LK Partnership has two assets: $10,000 cash and a machine having a $14,000 basis and a $20,000 FMV. The partnership has claimed $8,000 of depreciation on the machine since its purchase. If the partnership sells the machine for its FMV, all $6,000 of the gain would be recaptured as ordinary income under Sec. 1245. Therefore, the LK Partnership has a $6,000 unrealized receivable. ◀

SELF-STUDY QUESTION

What is included in the definition of unrealized receivables?

ANSWER

Unrealized receivables include not only the obvious cash method accounts receivable that have yet to be recognized but also most of the potential ordinary income recapture provisions. Therefore, the term *unrealized receivables* is broader than it may appear.

The definition of unrealized receivables is not limited to Sec. 1245 and 1250 depreciation recapture. Among the other recapture provisions creating unrealized receivables are Sec. 617(d) (mining property), Sec. 1252 (farmland), and Sec. 1254 (oil, gas, and geothermal property). Assets covered by Sec. 1278 (market discount bonds) and Sec. 1283 (short-term obligations) generate unrealized receivables to the extent the partnership would recognize ordinary income if it sold the asset. This type of unrealized receivable is deemed to have a zero basis.

Inventory. Inventory is equally surprising in its breadth. Inventory for purposes of Sec. 751 includes three major types of property:

- ▶ Items held for sale in the normal course of partnership business
- ▶ Any other property that, if sold by the partnership, would not be considered a capital asset or Sec. 1231 property
- ▶ Any other property held by the partnership that, if held by the selling or distributee partner, would be property of the two types listed above[9]

In short, cash, capital assets, and Sec. 1231 assets are the only properties that are not inventory.

TYPICAL MISCONCEPTION

The definition of inventory is broadly construed by Sec. 751. In fact, for purposes of determining whether inventory is substantially appreciated, even unrealized receivables are treated as inventory items.

For purposes of calculating the impact of Sec. 751 on distributions, inventory is considered a Sec. 751 asset only if the inventory is **substantially appreciated.** (This substantially appreciated rule does not apply to sales of partnership interests, discussed later in this chapter.) The test to determine whether inventory is substantially appreciated (and therefore falling under Sec. 751) is purely mechanical. Inventory is substantially appreciated if its FMV exceeds 120% of its adjusted basis to the partnership. For purposes of testing whether the inventory is substantially appreciated (but *only* for that purpose), inventory also includes unrealized receivables. The inclusion of unrealized receivables in the definition of inventory increases the likelihood that the inventory will be substantially appreciated.

EXAMPLE C:10-11 ▶ The ABC Partnership owns the following assets on December 31:

Assets	*Basis*	*FMV*
Cash	$10,000	$ 10,000
Unrealized receivables	–0–	40,000
Inventory	30,000	34,000
Land (Sec. 1231 property)	40,000	70,000
Total	$80,000	$154,000

[8] Sec. 751(c). Unrealized receivables may have basis if costs or expenses have been incurred but not taken into account under the partnership's method of accounting (e.g., the basis of property sold in a nondealer installment sale).

[9] Sec. 751(d)(2).

For purposes of the substantially appreciated inventory test, both ABC's unrealized receivables and inventory are included. The inventory's $74,000 FMV exceeds 120% of its adjusted basis [($30,000 + $0) × 1.20 = $36,000]. Therefore, the ABC Partnership has substantially appreciated inventory. ◀

EXCHANGE OF SEC. 751 ASSETS AND OTHER PROPERTY

A current distribution receives treatment under Sec. 751 only if the partnership has Sec. 751 assets and an exchange of Sec. 751 property for non-Sec. 751 property occurs. Accordingly, if a partnership does not have *both* Sec. 751 property and other property, the rules discussed above for simple current distributions control the taxation of the distribution. Similarly, a distribution that is proportionate to all partners or (1) consists of only the partner's share of either Sec. 751 property or non-Sec. 751 property and (2) does not reduce the partner's interest in other property is not affected by the Sec. 751 rules.

ADDITIONAL COMMENT

The discussion in this chapter pertaining to disproportionate distributions conforms to existing Treasury Regulation under Sec. 751(b). The Treasury Department has issued proposed regulations that would alter the method for calculating disproportionate distributions and their tax consequences. When this textbook went to press, those regulations were still only proposed. Therefore, this textbook continues to apply the methods contained in existing Treasury Regulations.

However, any portion of the distribution that represents an exchange of Sec. 751 property for non-Sec. 751 property must be isolated and is not treated as a distribution at all. Instead, it is treated as a sale between the partnership and the partner, and any gain or loss realized on the sale transaction is fully recognized.[10] The character of the recognized gain or loss depends on the character of the property deemed sold. For the party deemed the seller of the Sec. 751 assets, the gain or loss is ordinary income or loss.

Analyzing the transaction to determine what property was involved in the Sec. 751 transaction is best accomplished by using an orderly, step-by-step approach.

STEP 1: DIVIDE THE ASSETS INTO SEC. 751 ASSETS AND NON-SEC. 751 ASSETS. Inventory must be tested at this time to see whether it is substantially appreciated to know whether it is a Sec. 751 asset for distribution purposes.

STEP 2: DEVELOP A SCHEDULE, SUCH AS THE ONE IN TABLE C:10-1, TO DETERMINE WHETHER THE PARTNER EXCHANGED SEC. 751 ASSETS FOR NON-SEC. 751 ASSETS OR VICE VERSA. This schedule must be based on the FMV of all the partnership's assets. To make the determination, compare the partner's interest in the partnership's assets before the distribution with his or her interest in the assets after the distribution. This part of the analysis assumes a hypothetical nontaxable pro rata distribution equal to the partner's decreased interest in the assets. We can see whether the partner exchanged Sec. 751 assets for non-Sec. 751 assets by comparing the hypothetical distribution with the actual distribution. Thus, in Table C:10-1,

KEY POINT

Steps 2 and 3 try to identify whether a disproportionate distribution of Sec. 751 assets has taken place. In Table C:10-1, if the column 5 total for Sec. 751 assets is zero, Sec. 751 is not applicable. But as the table illustrates, Anne received $10,000 more than her share of the partnership cash without receiving any of her $10,000 share of Sec. 751 assets.

- Column 1 represents the partner's interest (valued at FMV) in each asset before the distribution.
- Column 2 represents the partner's interest (valued at FMV) in each asset after the distribution.
- Column 3 shows a hypothetical proportionate distribution that would have occurred had the partner's ownership interest been reduced by the partner taking a pro rata share of each asset. (As such, the proportionate distribution would be nontaxable.)
- Column 4 shows the amounts actually distributed.
- Column 5 shows the difference between the hypothetical and actual distributions. This column indicates whether a Sec. 751 exchange has occurred (see Step 3).

STEP 3: ANALYZE COLUMN 5 TO DETERMINE WHETHER SEC. 751 ASSETS WERE EXCHANGED FOR NON-SEC. 751 ASSETS. If the column 5 total for the Sec. 751 assets section of Table C:10-1 is zero, no Sec. 751 exchange has occurred. The partner simply received an additional amount of one type of Sec. 751 asset in exchange for relinquishing an interest in some other type of Sec. 751 asset. For example, no Sec. 751 exchange occurs if a partner exchanges an interest in substantially appreciated inventory for an interest in unrealized receivables. However, if the column 5 total for the Sec. 751

[10] Sec. 751(b).

▼ **TABLE C:10-1**
Analysis of Sec. 751 Nonliquidating Distribution (Example C:10-12)

	Beginning Partnership Amount[a]	(1) Anne's Interest Before Distribution[a] (1/3)	(2) Anne's Interest After Distribution[a] (1/5)	(3) Hypothetical Proportionate Distribution (3) = (1) − (2)[a]	(4) Actual Distribution[a]	(5) Difference[b] (5) = (4) − (3)
Sec. 751 assets:						
Unrealized receivables	$15,000	$ 5,000	$ 3,000	$ 2,000	$ -0-	$ (2,000)
Inventory	60,000	20,000	12,000	8,000	-0-	(8,000)
Total Sec. 751 assets	$75,000	$25,000	$15,000	$10,000	$ -0-	$ (10,000)
Non-Sec. 751 assets:						
Cash	$75,000	$25,000	$10,000[c]	$15,000	$25,000	$ 10,000
Total non-Sec. 751 assets	$75,000	$25,000	$10,000	$15,000	$25,000	$ 10,000

[a]Valued at fair market value.
[b]A negative amount means that Anne gave up her interest in a particular property. A positive amount means that she received more than her proportionate interest.
[c]One-fifth interest in remaining cash of $50,000.

assets is an amount other than zero, a Sec. 751 exchange has occurred. One (or more) Sec. 751 properties has been exchanged for one (or more) non-Sec. 751 properties.

EXAMPLE C:10-12 ▶ On January 1, the ABC Partnership holds the assets listed below before making a $25,000 cash distribution to Anne that reduces her interest in the partnership from one-third to one-fifth.

Assets	*Basis*	*FMV*
Cash	$ 75,000	$ 75,000
Unrealized receivables	-0-	15,000
Inventory	30,000	60,000
Total	$105,000	$150,000

ABC owes no liabilities on January 1. Before the distribution, Anne has a $35,000 basis in her partnership interest. The following three steps indicate that a Sec. 751 exchange has occurred:

STEP 1. Determine ABC's Sec. 751 and non-Sec. 751 assets. ABC's Sec. 751 assets include the unrealized receivables and the substantially appreciated inventory. The cash is ABC's only non-Sec. 751 property.

STEP 2. Complete the table used to analyze the Sec. 751 distribution (see Table C:10-1).

STEP 3. Analyze column 5 of Table C:10-1 to see whether a Sec. 751 exchange has occurred. Because Anne's Sec. 751 asset total declined by $10,000, we know she gave up $10,000 of her proportionate interest in ABC's Sec. 751 assets in exchange for cash. ◀

ADDITIONAL COMMENT

Step 4 is crucial if a student is to understand the deemed sale that Sec. 751 creates. In Example C:10-13, Anne is treated as if she had exchanged her $10,000 interest in the unrealized receivables and inventory for $10,000 of cash. Thus, Anne has a taxable gain or loss on the deemed sale. To determine Anne's gain or loss on the deemed sale, the adjusted basis of the unrealized receivables and inventory equals whatever her basis would have been had the partnership actually distributed those assets to her.

STEP 4: DETERMINE THE GAIN OR LOSS ON THE SEC. 751 DEEMED SALE. We must assume that the exchange occurring in Step 3 above was a sale of the exchanged property between the partnership and the partner. This step follows logically from the premise that the partner "bargained" to receive the amounts actually distributed rather than a proportionate distribution. She sold her interest in some assets to receive more than her proportionate interest in other assets. As with any sale, the gain (or loss) equals the difference between the FMV of the property received and the adjusted basis of the property given up. Note that, up to this point, we have been dealing only in terms of the FMV, so the adjusted basis of property given up must be determined as if the hypothetical distribution actually had occurred.

EXAMPLE C:10-13 ▶ Assume the same facts as in Example C:10-12. The Sec. 751 sale portion of the distribution is analyzed as Anne receiving $10,000 more cash than her proportionate share and giving up a $2,000 (FMV) interest in the unrealized receivables and an $8,000 (FMV) interest in the inventory. By examining the balance sheet, we can see that the partnership's bases for the unrealized receivables and inventory are $0 and $4,000 [$8,000 × ($30,000 ÷ $60,000)]. If Anne received these properties in a current distribution, her basis would be the same as the property's basis in the partnership's hands, or $0 and $4,000, respectively. Therefore, Anne's deemed sale of the Sec. 751 assets is analyzed as follows:

Amount realized (cash)	$10,000
Minus: Adjusted basis of property deemed sold	(4,000)
Realized and recognized gain	$ 6,000

The character of the recognized gain depends on the character of the property deemed sold (in this case, the unrealized receivables and inventory). Therefore, Anne's $6,000 gain is ordinary income. ◀

STEP 5: DETERMINE THE IMPACT OF THE CURRENT DISTRIBUTION. The last step in analyzing the distribution's effect on the partner is to determine the impact of the portion of the distribution that is not a Sec. 751 exchange. This distribution is treated exactly like any other nonliquidating distribution.

EXAMPLE C:10-14 ▶ Assume the same facts as in Examples C:10-12 and C:10-13. Examining the distribution, we see in column 4 of Table C:10-1 that, as part of the Sec. 751 exchange, Anne received only $10,000 of the $25,000 cash actually distributed. The remaining $15,000 represents a current distribution. As described earlier in this chapter, a partner recognizes gain on a current distribution only if the money distributed exceeds his or her basis in the partnership interest. Thus, Anne recognizes no gain because she has a $16,000 basis in the partnership interest immediately after the current distribution. This basis is calculated as follows:

Predistribution basis for partnership interest	$35,000
Minus: Basis of property deemed distributed in Sec. 751 exchange ($0 unrealized receivables + $4,000 inventory)	(4,000)
Basis before current distribution	$31,000
Minus: Money distributed	(15,000)
Postdistribution basis of partnership interest	$16,000

After the entire distribution is complete, Anne owns a one-fifth partnership interest with a basis of $16,000 and has $25,000 in cash. In addition, she has recognized $6,000 of ordinary income. ◀

STOP & THINK

Question: Do most current distributions made by a partnership require a Sec. 751 calculation?

Solution: No. A partnership makes many current distributions pro rata to all partners, so Sec. 751 is not involved. Even if the distribution is not pro rata, the distribution often does not create an exchange of an interest in Sec. 751 assets for an interest in other assets. This exchange happens only when (1) the partner is reducing his or her overall interest in the partnership, (e.g., from a 15% to a 5% general partner) or (2) an explicit agreement provides that the distribution results in a partner giving up all or part of his or her interest in some asset(s) maintained by the partnership. Most current distributions do not involve Sec. 751.

Liquidating or Selling a Partnership Interest

A partner can terminate or dispose of an interest in a partnership in a number of ways. The two most common are receiving a liquidating distribution and selling the interest. Other possibilities include giving the interest away, exchanging the interest for corporate

OBJECTIVE 3

Determine the gain, loss, and basis consequences of liquidating or selling a partnership interest

stock, and transferring the interest at death. This part of the chapter considers each of these methods.

LIQUIDATING DISTRIBUTIONS

The IRC defines a liquidating distribution as a distribution, or one of a series of distributions, that terminates a partner's interest in the partnership.[11] If the partner's interest is drastically reduced but not terminated, the distribution is treated as a current distribution. A liquidating distribution can occur when only one member of a partnership terminates his or her interest, several partners terminate their interests but the partnership continues, or the entire partnership terminates and each partner receives a liquidating distribution. Rules for taxation of a liquidating distribution are the same whether one partner terminates his or her interest or the entire partnership liquidates.

Gain or Loss Recognition by the Partner. The rule for recognizing gain on a liquidating distribution is exactly the same rule used for a current distribution. A partner recognizes gain only if any money distributed exceeds the partner's predistribution basis in his or her partnership interest.[12] Distributed money includes money deemed distributed to the partner from a liability reduction or the FMV of marketable securities treated as money.

Although a partner can never recognize a loss from a current distribution, he or she can recognize a loss from a liquidating distribution. A partner recognizes a loss only if (1) the liquidating distribution consists of money (including money deemed distributed), unrealized receivables, and inventory, but no other property and (2) the partner's basis in the partnership interest exceeds the total basis of these distributed properties (including cash).[13] The amount of the loss is the difference between the partner's basis in the partnership interest before the distribution and the sum of money plus the bases of the receivables and inventory (to the partnership immediately before the distribution) that the partner receives.

EXAMPLE C:10-15 ▶ Maria terminates her interest in the ABC Partnership when her basis in the partnership is $35,000. She receives a liquidating distribution of $10,000 cash and inventory with a $12,000 basis to the partnership. Her recognized loss is $13,000 [$35,000 − ($10,000 + $12,000)]. The inventory has a $12,000 basis to Maria. ◀

Basis in Assets Received. A partner's basis of an asset received in a liquidating distribution is determined using rules similar to those used to determine the basis of an asset received in a current distribution. For both kinds of distributions, the basis in unrealized receivables and inventory is generally the same as the property's basis in the partnership's hands. Under no condition is the basis of these two types of assets increased. Occasionally, however, the partner's basis in his or her partnership interest is so small that after making the necessary reduction for money (and deemed money) distributions, the basis in the partnership interest is smaller than the partnership's bases for the unrealized receivables and inventory distributed. In such cases, the remaining basis in the partnership interest must be allocated among the unrealized receivables and inventory items based first on their decline in value and then on their relative bases as adjusted to reflect the decline in value.[14] As a result, the bases for the unrealized receivables and inventory are reduced, and the amount of ordinary income a partner recognizes on their ultimate sale, exchange, or collection increases.

TYPICAL MISCONCEPTION

The basis to a partner of distributed unrealized receivables or inventory can never be greater than the partnership's basis in those assets. Also, if the partner's basis in his or her partnership interest is not sufficient, the partner's basis in the distributed unrealized receivables and inventory is less than the partnership's basis in those assets.

Remember that a liquidating distribution of money, unrealized receivables, and inventory having a total basis to the partnership less than the partner's basis in his or her partnership interest results in the recognition of a loss. However, the partner recognizes no loss if the distribution includes any property other than money, unrealized receivables, and inventory. Instead, all the remaining basis in the partnership interest must be allocated

[11] Sec. 761(d).
[12] Sec. 731(a)(1).
[13] Sec. 731(a)(2).
[14] Sec. 732(c).

to the other property received regardless of that property's basis to the partnership or its FMV. Application of this rule can create strange results.

EXAMPLE C:10-16 ► Assume the same facts as in Example C:10-15 except Maria's distribution also includes an office typewriter having a $50 basis to the partnership and a $100 FMV. The allocation of basis proceeds as follows:

Predistribution basis for partnership interest	$35,000
Minus: Money received	(10,000)
Basis after money distribution	$25,000
Minus: Basis of inventory to partnership	(12,000)
Remaining basis of partnership interest	$13,000

The entire $13,000 remaining basis of the partnership interest is allocated to the typewriter. ◄

TAX STRATEGY TIP

The partnership in Example C:10-16 should avoid distributing low basis property along with cash, unrealized receivables, and inventory so that the partner can obtain an immediate loss deduction.

The basis allocation procedure illustrated in Example C:10-16 delays loss recognition until Maria either depreciates or sells the typewriter. The allocation procedure also may change the character of the loss because Maria would recognize a capital loss when she receives the liquidating distribution in Example C:10-15. In Example C:10-16, however, the character of Maria's loss is determined by the character of the typewriter in her hands (or in some cases by a series of specific rules that are discussed below). Worst of all, if she converts the typewriter into personal-use property, the loss on its sale or exchange is nondeductible.

If the partnership distributes two or more assets other than unrealized receivables or inventory in the same distribution, the remaining basis in the partnership interest is allocated among them based on both their relative FMVs and bases in the partnership's hands. Such an allocation process can lead to either a decrease or increase in the total basis of these assets. This potential for increasing the assets' bases is unique to liquidating distributions.

The allocation that results in a decrease in the basis of a distributed asset is identical to the allocation process described for current distributions. However, if the amount to be allocated is greater than the carryover bases of the distributed assets, the basis is first allocated among the distributed assets in an amount equal to their carryover basis from the partnership. Then, allocations are made based on relative appreciation of the assets up to the amount of appreciation, and further allocations are made to the assets based on their relative FMVs.

EXAMPLE C:10-17 ► Before receiving a liquidating distribution, Craig's basis in his interest in the BCD Partnership is $62,000. The distribution consists of $10,000 in cash, inventory having a $2,000 basis to the partnership and a $4,000 FMV, and two parcels of undeveloped land (not held as inventory) having bases of $6,000 and $18,000 to the partnership and having FMVs of $10,000 and $24,000, respectively. Assume that Sec. 751 does not apply. His bases in the assets received are calculated as follows:

Predistribution basis for partnership interest	$62,000
Minus: Money received	(10,000)
Basis of inventory to the partnership	(2,000)
Basis allocated to two parcels of land	$50,000

The calculation of the basis for the two parcels of land are as follows:

	Parcel One	*Parcel Two*	*Total*
FMV of asset	$10,000	$24,000	$34,000
Minus: Partnership's basis for asset	(6,000)	(18,000)	(24,000)
Difference	$ 4,000	$ 6,000	$10,000
Step 1: Give each asset the partnership's basis for the asset	$ 6,000	$18,000	$24,000
Minus: Craig's basis to be allocated			(50,000)
Increase to allocate			$26,000

Step 2: Adjusted basis after Step 1	$ 6,000	$18,000	$24,000
Allocate the increase first to assets that have increased in value	4,000	6,000	10,000
Adjusted basis at this point in the calculation	$10,000	$24,000	$34,000
Step 3: Allocate $16,000 remaining increase based on relative FMVs	4,706[a]	11,294[b]	16,000
Craig's bases in the assets	$14,706	$35,294	$50,000

[a]$10,000 ÷ ($10,000 + $24,000) × $16,000 = $ 4,706
[b]$24,000 ÷ ($10,000 + $24,000) × $16,000 = $11,294

KEY POINT

If the partner recognizes neither gain nor loss in a liquidating distribution, the partner's total basis in the distributed assets always equals the partner's predistribution basis in his or her partnership interest.

In a liquidating distribution, the amount of money received plus the distributee partner's total basis of the noncash property received normally equals the partner's predistribution basis in the partnership interest. The only two exceptions to this rule apply when the money received exceeds the partner's basis in his or her partnership interest, causing the partner to recognize a gain, or when money, unrealized receivables, and inventory are the only assets distributed and the partner recognizes a loss. In all other liquidating distributions, the distributee partner recognizes no gain or loss. Instead, that partner's predistribution basis in his or her partnership interest is transferred to the cash and other property received.

Holding Period in Distributed Assets. The distributee partner's holding period for any assets received in a liquidating distribution includes the partnership's holding period for such property.[15] If the partnership received the property as a contribution from a partner, the partnership's holding period also may include the period of time the contributing partner held the property prior to making the contribution (see Chapter C:9). The distributee partner's holding period for his or her partnership interest is irrelevant in determining the holding period of the assets received.

EXAMPLE C:10-18 ▶ George purchased an interest in the DEF Partnership on June 1, 2013, but he cannot get along with the other partners. Therefore, on July 1, 2015, he receives a liquidating distribution that terminates his interest in the partnership. George's distribution includes land that the partnership has owned since August 1, 2007. George's holding period for the land begins on August 1, 2007, even though his holding period for the partnership interest begins much later. ◀

The character of the gain or loss recognized on a subsequent sale of distributed property is determined using the same rules as for a current distribution.

KEY POINT

The main difference in how the Sec. 751 rules apply to current versus liquidating distributions is that, after a liquidating distribution, the partner always has a zero interest in the partnership assets because he or she is no longer a partner in the partnership.

Effects of Sec. 751. Section 751 has essentially the same impact on both liquidating and current distributions. To the extent the partner exchanges an interest in Sec. 751 assets for an interest in other assets (or vice versa), that portion of the transaction bypasses the distribution rules. Instead, this portion of the transaction is treated as a sale occurring between the partnership and the partner. One notable difference occurs between liquidating distributions and current distributions having Sec. 751 implications: the postdistribution interest in partnership assets is zero for the liquidating distribution because it terminates the partner's interest in the partnership.

EXAMPLE C:10-19 ▶ The ABC Partnership holds the assets listed below on December 31 before making a $50,000 cash distribution that reduces Al's one-third interest in the partnership to zero.

Assets	*Basis*	*FMV*
Cash	$75,000	$ 75,000
Unrealized receivables	–0–	15,000
Inventory	15,000	60,000
Total	$90,000	$150,000

[15] Sec. 735(b).

The partnership has no liabilities, and Al's predistribution basis in his partnership interest is $30,000. The following steps lead to the tax effects of the liquidating distribution:

STEP 1. Determine ABC's Sec. 751 and non-Sec. 751 assets. The Sec. 751 assets include the unrealized receivables and the substantially appreciated inventory. The cash is ABC's only non-Sec. 751 asset.

STEP 2. Complete the table used to analyze the Sec. 751 distributions (see Table C:10-2).

STEP 3. Analyze column 5 of Table C:10-2 to see whether a Sec. 751 exchange has occurred. Table C:10-2 shows that Al exchanges $5,000 of unrealized receivables and $20,000 of inventory for $25,000 cash.

SELF-STUDY QUESTION

What is the deemed Sec. 751 exchange shown in Table C:10-2?

ANSWER

Column 5 shows that Al received $25,000 of excess cash in lieu of $25,000 of Sec. 751 assets. Thus, the Sec. 751 exchange is a deemed sale by Al of $25,000 of unrealized receivables and inventory to the partnership in exchange for $25,000 of cash. With a table similar to Table C:10-2, the Sec. 751 computations are much easier to understand.

STEP 4. Determine the gain or loss on the Sec. 751 deemed sale. Al is deemed to have sold unrealized receivables and inventory for cash. Assume Al first got the receivables and inventory in a current distribution. He obtains the partnership's bases for the assets of $0 and $5,000, respectively. The subsequent deemed sale results in Al recognizing a $20,000 gain.

Amount realized (cash)	$25,000
Minus: Adjusted basis of property deemed sold	(5,000)
Realized and recognized gain	$20,000

Al's gain is ordinary income because it results from his deemed sale of receivables and inventory to the partnership.

STEP 5. Determine the impact of the non-Sec. 751 portion of the distribution. The liquidating distribution is only the $25,000 cash he receives that was *not* a part of the Sec. 751 transaction. To determine its impact, we first must find Al's basis in his partnership interest after the Sec. 751 transaction but before the $25,000 liquidating distribution.

Predistribution basis in the partnership interest	$30,000
Minus: Basis of receivables and inventory deemed distributed in Sec. 751 exchange	(5,000)
Basis before money distribution	$25,000
Minus: Money distribution	(25,000)
Gain recognized on liquidating distribution	$ -0-

Al recognizes no further gain or loss from the liquidating distribution portion of the transaction. ◀

▼ **TABLE C:10-2**

Analysis of Sec. 751 Liquidating Distribution (Example C:10-19)

	Beginning Partnership Amount[a]	(1) Al's Interest Before Distribution[a] (1/3)	(2) Al's Interest After Distribution[a] (-0-)	(3) Hypothetical Proportionate Distribution[a] (3) = (1) − (2)	(4) Actual Distribution[a]	(5) Difference[b] (5) = (4) − (3)
Sec. 751 assets:						
Unrealized receivables	$15,000	$ 5,000	$ -0-	$ 5,000	$ -0-	$ (5,000)
Inventory	60,000	20,000	-0-	20,000	-0-	(20,000)
Total Sec. 751 assets	$75,000	$25,000	$ -0-	$25,000	$ -0-	$ (25,000)
Non-Sec. 751 assets:						
Cash	$75,000	$25,000	$ -0-	$25,000	$50,000	$ 25,000
Total non-Sec. 751 assets	$75,000	$25,000	$ -0-	$25,000	$50,000	$ 25,000

[a]Valued at fair market value.

[b]A negative amount means that Al gave up his interest in a particular property. A positive amount means that Al received more than his proportionate interest.

SELF-STUDY QUESTION

What is the character of gain or loss on the sale of a partnership interest?

ANSWER

Because a partnership interest is generally a capital asset, the sale of a partnership interest results in the partner recognizing a capital gain or loss. However, if a partnership has Sec. 751 assets, the partner is deemed to sell his or her share of the underlying Sec. 751 assets, thereby causing a corresponding ordinary gain or loss to be recognized.

Effects of Distribution on the Partnership. A partnership generally recognizes no gain or loss on liquidating distributions made to its partners.[16] If a Sec. 751 deemed sale occurs, however, the partnership may recognize gain or loss on assets deemed sold to its partner. Although a liquidating distribution normally does not itself terminate the partnership, the partnership terminates if none of the remaining partners continue to operate the business of the partnership in a partnership form. In this case, all partners will receive liquidating distributions. Finally, the partnership's assets may be subject to optional or mandatory basis adjustments (discussed later in this chapter).

Topic Review C:10-1 summarizes the tax consequences of current and liquidating distributions.

SALE OF A PARTNERSHIP INTEREST

Absence any contrary rules, a partner's sale or exchange of a partnership interest would generate a capital gain or loss under Sec. 741 because a partnership interest is usually a capital asset. Section 751, however, modifies this result by requiring the partner to recognize ordinary

TOPIC REVIEW C:10-1

Current and Liquidating Distributions

Tax Consequences	Current Distributions	Liquidating Distributions
Impact on Partner:		
Money (or deemed money from liability changes or marketable securities) distributed	Gain recognized only if money distributed exceeds basis in partnership interest before distribution.	Gain recognized only if money distributed exceeds basis in partnership interest before distribution.
Unrealized receivables and/or inventory distributed	Carryover basis (limited to basis in partnership interest before distribution reduced by money distributed).	Carryover basis (limited to basis in partnership interest before distribution reduced by money distributed).
	No gain or loss recognized.[a]	Loss recognized if partnership distributes money, inventory, and receivables with basis less than partner's basis in partnership interest before distribution and partnership distributes no other property.[a]
Other property distributed	Carryover basis (limited to basis in partnership interest before distribution reduced by money and carryover basis in inventory and receivables).	Basis equal to basis in partnership interest before distribution reduced by money and carryover basis in inventory and receivables.
	No gain or loss recognized.[a]	No gain or loss recognized.[a]
Impact on Partnership:		
General rule	No gain or loss recognized.	No gain or loss recognized.
Partnership assets	May be subject to optional basis adjustments.	May be subject to optional or mandatory basis adjustments.
Other Tax Consequences:	If a Sec. 751 deemed sale or exchange occurs, the partner and/or the partnership may recognize gain or loss on the deemed sale.	If a Sec. 751 deemed sale or exchange occurs, the partner and/or the partnership may recognize gain or loss on the deemed sale.

[a]A partner may recognize precontribution gain (but not loss) under Sec. 737 if a precontribution net gain remains and the FMV of the property distributed exceeds the adjusted basis of the partnership interest immediately before the property distribution (but after any money distribution). The contributing partner also may recognize precontribution gain or loss if the partnership distributes the contributed property to another partner within seven years of the contribution (Sec. 704(c)).

[16] Sec. 731(b).

income or loss (and possibly unrecaptured Sec. 1250 gain) on the sale or exchange of a partnership interest to the extent the consideration received is attributable to the partner's share of unrealized receivables and inventory items. The sale of a partnership interest also may have two other effects: the purchaser acquires the partner's share of the partnership's liabilities, and the partnership may be terminated. Each of these situations related to the sale of a partnership interest is examined below.

Section 751 Property. The definition of Sec. 751 property is slightly different for sales or exchanges than for distributions because inventory does not have to be substantially appreciated to be included as Sec. 751 property. Thus, all inventory and all unrealized receivables are Sec. 751 assets in a sale or exchange situation.[17]

Treasury Regulations under Sec. 751 take a hypothetical asset sale approach to determine the amount of ordinary income or loss the partner recognizes on the sale or exchange of a partnership interest.[18] Under the regulations, the partnership is deemed to sell all its assets for their FMV immediately before the partner sells his or her interest in the partnership. The partner then is allocated his or her share of ordinary gain or loss (and possibly unrecaptured Sec. 1250 gain) attributable to the Sec. 751 assets. With this approach, the results of the sale or exchange can be determined using the following three steps:

STEP 1. Determine the total gain or loss on the sale or exchange of the partnership interest.

STEP 2. Determine the ordinary gain or loss component and the unrecaptured Sec. 1250 gain component, if applicable, using the hypothetical asset sale approach.[19]

STEP 3. Determine the capital gain component by calculating the residual gain or loss after assigning the ordinary gain or loss and the unrecaptured Sec. 1250 gain components.

EXAMPLE C:10-20 ▶ Troy sells his one-fourth interest in the TV Partnership to Steve for $50,000 cash when the partnership's assets are as follows:

Assets	*Basis*	*FMV*
Cash	$ 20,000	$ 20,000
Unrealized receivables	–0–	24,000
Inventory	20,000	68,000
Building	40,000	56,000
Land	40,000	32,000
Total	$120,000	$200,000

The partnership has no liabilities on the sale date and has claimed $19,000 of straight-line depreciation on the building. Troy's basis in his partnership interest is $30,000 on such date. Both the receivables and inventory are Sec. 751 assets, and the building is Sec. 1250 property. Application of Step 1 yields the following gain on Troy's sale of his partnership interest:

Amount realized on sale	$50,000
Minus: Adjusted basis of partnership interest	(30,000)
Total gain realized	$20,000

Application of Step 2 yields the following allocation to Sec. 751 and Sec. 1250 property:

Deemed Sale of Assets	*Partnership Gain (Loss)*	*Troy's Share (25%)*
Unrealized receivables	$24,000	$ 6,000
Inventory	48,000	12,000
Building	16,000	4,000
Land	(8,000)	(2,000)

[17] Regulation Sec. 1.751-1(a)(1) is outdated to some extent and still speaks in terms of substantially appreciated inventory. However, Sec. 751(a) in the IRC, which deals with the sale or exchange of a partnership interest, includes all inventory items, not just those that are substantially appreciated.

[18] Reg. Sec. 1.751-1(a)(2). This hypothetical sale approach allows for easy incorporation of special allocations under Sec. 704 into the Sec. 751 calculation.

[19] The unrecaptured Sec. 1250 gain is the lesser of the hypothetical gain on Sec. 1250 property (e.g., buildings) or the amount of depreciation claimed on the Sec. 1250 property (assuming straight-line depreciation). This gain applies to non-corporate taxpayers and is subject to the 25% capital gains tax rate. A similar rule applies to a collectibles gain subject to the 28% capital gains tax rate. See Reg. Sec. 1.1(h)-1.

Thus, on the sale of his partnership interest, Troy recognizes ordinary income of $18,000 ($6,000 + $12,000). Because the $19,000 of depreciation exceeds the hypothetical gain on the building, the entire $16,000 gain is unrecaptured Sec. 1250 gain, $4,000 of which is Troy's share.

Application of Step 3 yields the following residual allocation to capital gain or loss:

Total gain realized	$ 20,000
Minus: Allocation to ordinary income and unrecaptured Sec. 1250 gain	(22,000)
Capital loss recognized	$ (2,000)

In summary, on the sale of his partnership interest, Troy recognizes $18,000 of ordinary income, $4,000 of unrecaptured Sec. 1250 gain, and a $2,000 capital loss. Without Sec. 751, these three components would have been netted together as a $20,000 capital gain. ◀

STOP & THINK

Question: Bill owns 20% of Kraco and plans to sell his ownership interest for a $40,000 gain. Kraco has both unrealized receivables and inventory. If Kraco is a corporation, Bill will report a $40,000 capital gain. If Kraco is a partnership, part of the $40,000 gain (the gain on his 20% share of the Sec. 751 assets) will be ordinary income, and the remainder will be capital gain. Why did Congress decide to tax the gain on the sale of corporate stock differently from the gain on the sale of a partnership interest?

Solution: The corporation itself will pay tax on the ordinary income realized when it collects unrealized receivables or sells inventory, and the corporation's tax is unaffected by the identity of the shareholder. Under no conditions will the shareholder have to report any of the corporation's ordinary income. Accordingly, the sale of the corporate stock does not provide an opportunity to avoid ordinary income for the owner, nor can the owner convert ordinary income into capital gain by selling the corporate stock.[20]

Because the partners report and pay taxes on the ordinary income earned by the partnership, a sale of a partnership interest that produces only capital gains would represent an opportunity for a partner to avoid recognizing ordinary income and recognize capital gains instead. Imagine, for example, that Kraco is a cash basis service business whose only asset is a large account receivable where all work has been completed. If Bill stays in the partnership, he will recognize ordinary income when the partnership collects the receivable. If he were allowed to sell his partnership interest in this setting for a capital gain, he could convert his ordinary income into capital gain. However, Sec. 751 prevents this conversion from happening by requiring him to recognize ordinary income on the sale of the partnership interest to the extent the sales proceeds are attributable to Sec. 751 assets.

ADDITIONAL COMMENT

Section 751 treatment is another application of the aggregate theory of partnership taxation as opposed to the entity theory.

Liabilities. When a partnership has liabilities, each partner's distributive share of any liabilities is always part of the basis for the partnership interest. When a partner sells his or her partnership interest, the partner is relieved of the liabilities. Accordingly, the amount realized on the sale of a partnership interest is made up of money plus the FMV of noncash property received plus the seller's share of partnership liabilities assumed or acquired by the purchaser.

EXAMPLE C:10-21 ▶ Andrew is a 30% partner in the ABC Partnership when he sells his entire interest to Miguel for $40,000 cash. At the time of the sale, Andrew's basis is $27,000 (which includes his $7,000 share of partnership liabilities). The partnership has no Sec. 751 assets. Andrew's $20,000 gain on the sale is calculated as follows:

Amount realized:		
Cash	$40,000	
Liabilities assumed by purchaser	7,000	$47,000
Minus: Adjusted basis		(27,000)
Gain recognized on sale		$20,000

◀

[20] An exception used to exist under Sec. 341 for a so-called collapsible corporation. However, Congress has permanently repealed this provision.

Impact on the Partnership. When one partner sells his or her partnership interest, the sale usually has no more impact on the partnership than the sale of corporate stock by one shareholder has on the corporation. Only the partner and the purchaser of the interest are affected. However, the partnership itself is affected if the partnership interest sold is sufficiently large that, under Sec. 708, its sale terminates the partnership for tax purposes. This effect is discussed later in this chapter. Also, the partnership may have to make optional or mandatory basis adjustments to its assets (discussed later in this chapter).

OTHER PARTNERSHIP TERMINATION ISSUES

OBJECTIVE 4

Recognize other means of terminating a partnership interest and related issues

RETIREMENT OR DEATH OF A PARTNER

If a partner dies or retires from a partnership, that partner's interest can be sold either to an outsider or to one or more existing partners.[21] The results of such a sale are outlined above. Often, however, a partner or a deceased partner's successor-in-interest departs from the partnership in return for payments made by the partnership itself. When the partnership buys out the partner's interest, the analysis of the tax results focuses on two types of payments: payments made in exchange for the partner's interest in partnership property and other payments.

Payments for Partnership Property. Generally, the IRS accepts the valuation placed on the retiring partner's interest in the partnership property by the partners in an arm's-length transaction. Payments made for the property interest are taxed under the liquidating distribution rules. Like any liquidating distribution made to a partner, payments made to a retiring partner or a deceased partner's successor-in-interest[22] in exchange for his or her property interest are not deductible by the partnership.[23]

If the retiring or deceased partner was a general partner and the partnership is a service partnership (i.e., capital is not a material income producing factor), payments made to a general partner for unrealized receivables and goodwill (when the partnership agreement does not provide for a goodwill payment on retirement or death) are not considered payments for property. Instead, any such payments are treated as other payments. The other payment treatment permits the partnership to deduct the amounts paid to the retiring or deceased partner or to reduce the distributive share allocable to the other partners.

TYPICAL MISCONCEPTION

The significance of the two different kinds of payments is not readily apparent to some taxpayers. The payments for partnership property are not deductible by the partnership and often are not income to the retiring partner. However, payments considered in the second category are deductible by the partnership (or they reduce the distributive shares that other partners must recognize) and usually are income to the retiring partner.

Other Payments. Payments made to a retiring partner or to a deceased partner's successor-in-interest that exceed the value of that partner's share of partnership property have a different tax result for both the retiring partner and for the partnership. A few payments that do represent payments for property (e.g., payments to a general partner retiring from a service partnership for his or her interest in unrealized receivables and for his or her interest in partnership goodwill) also are taxed under these rules.

Under these rules, a payment is treated as either a distributive share or a guaranteed payment. If the excess payment is a function of partnership income (e.g., 10% of the partnership's net income), the income is considered a distributive share of partnership income.[24] Accordingly, the character of the income flows through to the partner, and each of the remaining partners is taxed on a smaller amount of partnership income. The income must be reported in the partner's tax year that includes the partnership year-end from which the distributive share arises, regardless of when the partner actually receives the distribution.

If the amount of the excess payment is determined without regard to the partnership income, the payment is treated as a guaranteed payment.[25] If the payment is a guaranteed

TYPICAL MISCONCEPTION

The main difference between a payment being taxed as a distributive share or as a guaranteed payment is the character of the income recognized by the recipient partner. If the payment is taxed as a distributive share, the character of the income is determined by the type of income earned by the partnership. In contrast, the payment is always ordinary income if it is treated as a guaranteed payment.

[21] Retirement from the partnership in this context has nothing to do with reaching a specific age and leaving the employ of the partnership but instead refers to the partner's withdrawal at any age from a continuing partnership.

[22] A deceased partner's successor-in-interest is the party that succeeds to the rights of the deceased partner's partnership interest (e.g., the decedent's estate or an heir or legatee of the deceased partner). A deceased partner's successor-in-interest is treated as a partner by the tax laws until his or her interest in the partnership has been completely liquidated.

[23] Sec. 736(b).

[24] Sec. 736(a)(1).

[25] Sec. 736(a)(2).

payment, the retiring partner recognizes ordinary income, and the partnership generally has an ordinary deduction. Like all guaranteed payments, the income is includible in the recipient's income for his or her tax year within which ends the partnership tax year in which the partnership claims its deduction (see Chapter C:9).

EXAMPLE C:10-22 ▶ When Sam retires from the STU Partnership, he receives a cash payment of $30,000. At the time of his retirement, his basis for his one-fourth limited partnership interest is $25,000. The partnership has no liabilities and the following assets:

Assets	*Basis*	*FMV*	*Sam's 1/4 FMV*
Cash	$ 40,000	$ 40,000	$10,000
Marketable securities	25,000	32,000	8,000
Land	35,000	48,000	12,000
Total	$100,000	$120,000	$30,000

In the absence of a valuation agreement, the partnership presumably pays Sam a ratable share of the FMV of each asset (and he receives no payment for any partnership goodwill). The $30,000 amount paid to Sam equals the FMV of his one-fourth interest in the partnership assets. The $30,000 Sam receives in exchange for his interest in partnership property is analyzed as a liquidating distribution in the following manner:

Cash distribution received	$30,000
Minus: Basis in partnership interest	(25,000)
Gain recognized on liquidating distribution	$ 5,000

Because the partnership holds no Sec. 751 assets, the entire gain is a capital gain. The partnership gets no deduction for the distribution. ◀

EXAMPLE C:10-23 ▶ Assume the same facts as in Example C:10-22 except Sam receives $34,000 instead of $30,000. This amount represents payment for Sam's one-fourth interest in partnership assets plus an excess payment of $4,000. Accordingly, this excess payment must be either a distributive share or a guaranteed payment. Because the $4,000 payment is not contingent on partnership earnings, it is taxed as a guaranteed payment. The partnership deducts the $4,000 payment, and Sam recognizes $4,000 of ordinary income.

In summary, Sam receives $34,000 as a payment on his retirement from the STU Partnership, $4,000 of which is considered a guaranteed payment taxed as ordinary income to Sam and deductible by the partnership. The remaining $30,000 Sam receives is in exchange for his interest in partnership property. Because the $30,000 cash payment exceeds his $25,000 basis in his partnership interest, he recognizes a $5,000 gain on the liquidating distribution. The partnership gets no deduction for the $30,000, which is considered a distribution. ◀

If the partnership has Sec. 751 assets, the calculations for a retiring partner are slightly more difficult. First, payments for substantially appreciated inventory and unrealized receivables are payments for property and must be analyzed using the liquidating distribution rules along with Sec. 751. The remainder of the transaction is analyzed as indicated above. (For partnership retirements only, unrealized receivables do not include recapture items.)

A retiring partner who receives payments from the partnership is considered to be a partner in that partnership for tax purposes until he or she receives the last payment. Likewise, a deceased partner's successor-in-interest is a member of the partnership until receiving the last payment.[26]

EXCHANGE OF A PARTNERSHIP INTEREST

Exchange for Another Partnership Interest. A partner also may terminate a partnership interest by exchanging it for either an interest in another partnership or a different interest in the same partnership. Exchanges involving interests in different partnerships do not qualify for like-kind exchange treatment.[27] Nevertheless, the IRS allows exchanges of interests within a single partnership.[28]

26 Reg. Sec. 1.736-1(a)(1)(ii).
27 Sec. 1031(a)(2)(D).
28 Rev. Rul. 84-52, 1984-1 C.B. 157, and Rev. Rul. 95-37, 1995-1 C.B. 130.

EXAMPLE C:10-24 ▶ Pam and Dean are equal partners in the PD General Partnership, which owns and operates a farm. The two partners agree to convert PD into a limited partnership, with Pam becoming a limited partner and Dean having both a general and a limited partnership interest in PD. Even though the partners exchange a general partnership interest for a limited partnership interest (plus an exchange of a general partnership interest for a general partnership interest for Dean), they recognize no gain or loss on the exchange. If, however, a partner's interest in the partnership's liabilities is changed, that partner's basis must be adjusted. If liabilities are reduced and a deemed distribution exceeding the basis for the partnership interest occurs, the partner must recognize gain on the excess. ◀

Exchange for Corporate Stock. A partnership interest may be exchanged for corporate stock in a transaction that qualifies under the Sec. 351 nonrecognition rules (see Chapter C:2). For Sec. 351 purposes, a partnership interest is property. If the other Sec. 351 requirements are met, a single partner's partnership interest can be transferred for stock in a new or an existing corporation in a nontaxable exchange. The partner treats this as if he or she had transferred any other property under the Sec. 351 rules. The basis in the corporate stock is determined by the partner's basis in the partnership interest. The holding period for the stock received in the exchange includes the holding period for the partnership interest. As a result of the exchange, one of the corporation's assets is an interest in a partnership, and the corporation (not the transferor) is now the partner of record. Thus, the corporation must report its distributive share of partnership income along with its other earnings.

Incorporation. When limited liability is important, the entire partnership may choose to incorporate. Normally such an incorporation can be structured to fall within the Sec. 351 provisions and can be partially or totally tax exempt. When a partnership chooses to incorporate, three possible alternatives are available:

- The partnership contributes its assets and liabilities to the corporation in exchange for the corporation's stock. The partnership then distributes the stock to the partners in a liquidating distribution of the partnership.
- The partnership liquidates by distributing its assets to the partners. The partners then contribute the property to the new corporation in exchange for its stock.
- The partners contribute their partnership interests directly to the new corporation in exchange for its stock. The partnership liquidates, with the corporation receiving all the partnership's assets and liabilities.

The tax implications of the incorporation and the impact of partnership liabilities, gain to be recognized, basis in the corporate assets, and the new shareholders' bases in their stock and securities may differ depending on the form chosen for the transaction.[29]

Formation of an LLC, LLP, or LLLP. A second option for obtaining limited liability protection for all owners is for the partnership to become an LLC. Under Rev. Rul. 95-37,[30] the conversion is viewed as a partnership-to-partnership transfer. The property transfer does not cause the partners to recognize gain or loss nor does the transfer terminate the tax year for the partnership or any partner. The basis for the partners' interest in the partnership will be changed only if the liability shares for the partners change. Under the check-the-box regulations, an LLC with more than one member is treated as a partnership unless it elects to be taxed as a corporation (see Chapter C:2). If the LLC elects to be taxed as a C or an S corporation, the transfer of the property to the LLC falls under the incorporation rules discussed above.

If a partnership chooses LLP status to reduce some of the liability risks facing the partners, the change from partnership to LLP status also falls under the partnership-to-partnership transfer rules described above. The transfer does not cause the partners to recognize

---

[29] Rev. Rul. 84-111, 1984-2 C.B. 88. In addition, Reg. Secs. 301.7701-1, 2, and 3 describe the tax consequences of a partnership electing to be taxed as a corporation under the check-the-box regulations.

[30] 1995-1 C.B. 130.

gain or loss nor does the property transfer terminate the tax year for the partnership or any partner. Basis for the partners' interest in the partnership will be changed only if the liability shares for the partners change.[31] Finally, in some states, partners can achieve limited liability through a limited liability limited partnership (LLLP) (see page C:10-31).

Topic Review C:10-2 summarizes the tax consequences of a number of alternative methods for terminating an investment in a partnership.

INCOME RECOGNITION AND TRANSFERS OF A PARTNERSHIP INTEREST

The partnership tax year closes with respect to any partner who sells or exchanges his or her entire interest in a partnership or any partner whose interest in the partnership is liquidated. The partnership tax year closes on the sale or exchange date or the date of final payment on a liquidation. As a result, that partner's share of all items earned by the partnership must be reported in the partner's tax year that includes the transaction date.[32]

A partner's tax year also closes on the date of death. The partner's final return will include all partnership income up to the date of death.

TERMINATION OF A PARTNERSHIP

Events Causing a Termination to Occur. Because of the complex relationships among partners and their liability for partnership debts, state partnership laws provide for the termination of a partnership under a wide variety of conditions. Section 708(b), however, avoids the tax complexity created by the wide variety of state laws and the numerous termination conditions. This IRC section provides that a partnership terminates for tax purposes only if

TOPIC REVIEW C:10-2

Terminating an Investment in a Partnership

Method	Tax Consequences to Partner
Death or retirement:	
Amounts paid for property[a]	Liquidating distribution tax consequences apply to the amount paid.
Amounts paid in excess of property values:	
Amounts not determined by reference to partnership income	Ordinary income.
Amounts determined by reference to partnership income	Distributive share of partnership income.
Sale of partnership interest to outsider	Capital gain (loss) except for ordinary income (loss) reported on Sec. 751 assets and unrecaptured Sec. 1250 gain on depreciable real property.
Exchange for partnership interest:	
In same partnership	No tax consequences
In different partnership	Capital gain (loss) except for ordinary income (loss) on Sec. 751 assets and unrecaptured Sec. 1250 gain on depreciable real property.
Exchange for corporate stock	No gain or loss generally recognized if it qualifies for Sec. 351 tax-free treatment. If the exchange does not qualify for Sec. 351 treatment, capital gain (loss) except for ordinary income (loss) on Sec. 751 assets and unrecaptured Sec. 1250 gain on depreciable real property.
Incorporation of partnership	Tax consequences depend on form of transaction used for incorporation.
Formation of LLC or LLP	No tax consequences except for distributions or contributions deemed to occur if liability shares change.

[a]Only for a general partner departing from a service partnership, property excludes unrealized receivables and goodwill if it is not mentioned in the partnership agreement.

[31] Ibid.

[32] Sec. 706(c)(2).

- No part of any business, financial operation, or venture of the partnership continues to be carried on by any of its partners in a partnership or
- Within a 12-month period a sale or exchange of at least 50% of the total interest in partnership capital and profits occurs.

TYPICAL MISCONCEPTION

Taxpayers often do not understand the difference between a partnership tax year closing for a specific partner versus a partnership tax year closing for all partners due to a termination of the partnership itself. The tax consequences of these two events are drastically different.

No Business Operated as a Partnership. If no partner continues to operate any business of the partnership through the same or another partnership, the original partnership terminates. To avoid termination, the partnership must maintain partners and business activity. For example, if one partner retires from a two-person partnership and the second partner continues the business alone, the partnership terminates. However, if one partner in a two-member partnership dies, the partnership does not terminate as long as the deceased's estate or successor-in-interest continues to share in the profits and losses of the partnership business.[33]

Likewise, a partnership terminates if it ceases to carry on any business or financial venture. The courts, however, have allowed a partnership to continue under this rule even though the partnership sold all its assets and retained only a few installment notes.[34] Despite the courts' flexibility in these circumstances, a partnership should maintain more than a nominal level of assets if continuation of the partnership is desired.

KEY POINT

For the 50% rule to terminate a partnership, a *sale* or *exchange* of 50% or more of the capital *and* profits interests must occur. Sales or exchanges occurring within a 12-month period are aggregated. However, if the same interest is sold twice within 12 months, it is only counted once.

Sale or Exchange of at Least a 50% Interest. The second condition that terminates a partnership is the sale or exchange of at least a 50% interest in both partnership capital and profits within a 12-month period.[35] The relevant 12-month period is determined without reference to the tax year of either the partnership or any partner but rather is any 12 consecutive months. To cause termination, the partner must transfer the partnership interest by sale or exchange. Transactions or occurrences that do not constitute a sale or exchange (e.g., the gifting of a partnership interest or the transferring of a partnership interest at death) do not cause a partnership to terminate as long as partners continue the partnership business. Likewise, as long as at least two partners remain, the removal of a partner who owns more than 50% of the total partnership capital and profits interests can be accomplished without terminating the partnership by making a liquidating distribution.[36]

Measuring the portion of the total partnership capital and profits interest transferred often presents difficulties. Multiple exchanges of the same partnership interest are counted only once for purposes of determining whether the 50% maximum is exceeded. When several different small interests are transferred within a 12-month period, the partnership's termination occurs on the date of the transfer that first crosses the 50% threshold.[37]

EXAMPLE C:10-25 ▶ On August 1 of Year 1, Miguel sells his 30% capital and profits interest in the LMN Partnership to Steve. On June 1 of Year 2, Steve sells the 30% interest acquired from Miguel to Andrew. For purposes of Sec. 708, the two sales are considered to be the transfer of a single partnership interest. Thus, the LMN Partnership does not terminate unless other sales of partnership interests occur totaling at least 20% of LMN's capital and profits interests during any 12-month period that includes either August 1 of Year 1, or June 1 of Year 2. ◀

EXAMPLE C:10-26 ▶ On July 15 of Year 1, Kelly sells Carlos a 37% capital and profits interest in the KRS Partnership. On November 14 of Year 1, Rick sells Diana a 10% capital and profits interest in the KRS Partnership. On January 18 of Year 2, Sherrie sells Evan a 5% capital and profits interest in the KRS Partnership. The KRS Partnership terminates on January 18 of Year 2 because the cumulative interest sold within the 12-month period that includes January 18 of Year 2, first exceeds 50% on that date. ◀

Effects of Termination.

Importance of Timing. When a partnership terminates, its tax year closes, requiring the partners to include their share of partnership earnings for the short-period partnership tax

---

33 Reg. Sec. 1.708-1(b)(1)(i)(A).

34 For example, see *Max R. Ginsburg v. U.S.*, 21 AFTR 2d 1489, 68-1 USTC ¶9429 (Ct. Cls., 1968).

35 Under Sec. 774(c), an electing large partnership does *not* terminate solely because 50% or more of its interests are sold within a 12-month period.

36 Reg. Sec. 1.708-1(b)(1)(ii).

37 Ibid.

year in their tax returns. If the termination is not properly timed, partnership income for a regular 12-month tax year already may be included in the same return that must include the short tax year, resulting in more than 12 months of partnership income or loss being reported in some partners' tax returns. As partners and partnerships are increasingly forced to adopt the same tax year, this problem will lessen.

EXAMPLE C:10-27 ▶ Joy is a calendar year taxpayer who owns a 40% capital and profits interest in the ATV Partnership. ATV has a natural business year-end of March 31 and with IRS permission uses that date as its tax year-end. For the partnership tax year ending March 31, 2017, Joy has an $80,000 distributive share of ordinary income. Pat, who owns the remaining 60% capital and profits interests, sells his interest to Collin on November 30, 2017. Because more than 50% of the capital and profits interests have changed hands, the ATV Partnership terminates on November 30, 2017, and the partnership's tax year ends on that date.

Joy's tax return for the tax year ending December 31, 2017, must include the $80,000 distributive share from the partnership tax year for the period April 1, 2016, through March 31, 2017, and the distributive share of partnership income for the short tax year including the period April 1, 2017, through November 30, 2017. ◀

Liquidating Distributions and Contributions. When a termination occurs for tax purposes, the partnership is deemed to have made a pro rata liquidating distribution to all partners. Accordingly, the partners must recognize gain or loss under the liquidating distribution rules. An actual liquidating distribution may occur if the termination occurs because of the cessation of business. However, if the termination occurs because of a 50% or greater change in ownership of the capital and profits interests, an actual distribution usually does not occur. In this case, the new group of partners continue the business, and Treasury Regulations provide for the termination of the old partnership and the formation of a new partnership. Specifically, the old partnership is deemed to contribute all its property and liabilities to a new partnership in exchange for the interests in the new partnership. The old partnership then is deemed to liquidate by distributing its only remaining asset (the interests in the new partnership) to its partners.[38]

EXAMPLE C:10-28 ▶ The AB Partnership terminates for tax purposes on July 15 when Anna sells her 60% capital and profits interest to Diane for $123,000. The partnership has no liabilities, and its assets at the time of termination are as follows:

Assets	*Basis*	*FMV*
Cash	$ 20,000	$ 20,000
Receivables	30,000	32,000
Inventory	22,000	28,000
Building	90,000	95,000
Land	40,000	30,000
Total	$202,000	$205,000

Beth, a 40% partner in the AB Partnership, has an $80,800 basis in her partnership interest at the time of the termination. She has held her AB Partnership interest for three years at the time of the termination.

The old AB Partnership is deemed to transfer all its assets to a new partnership (NewAB) on July 15 in exchange for all the interests in NewAB. The old partnership then is deemed to transfer all the NewAB interests to the partners of the old partnership (Diane and Beth). At this point, the old AB Partnership ceases to exist because it no longer has partners, nor does it carry on any business.

The basis and holding period of the assets held by NewAB are identical to the basis and holding period of the old AB Partnership assets.[39] The basis of Beth's interest in NewAB is identical to her basis in her interest in the AB Partnership ($80,800).[40] Her holding period for the NewAB partnership interest begins when she acquired the old AB Partnership interest. Diane's basis in her partnership interest is its $123,000 cost, and her holding period begins when she purchases the interest. ◀

---

38 Reg. Sec. 1.708-1(b)(1)(iv).

39 Secs. 723 and 1223(2).

40 Sec. 722.

Changes in Accounting Methods. The termination ends all partnership elections. Thus, the new partnership must make all elections concerning its tax year and accounting methods in its first new tax year.

KEY POINT

The principal concern when two or more partnerships combine is which partnership's tax year, accounting methods, and elections will survive the merger. This determination is made by examining the capital and profits interests of the partners of the old partnerships.

MERGERS AND CONSOLIDATIONS

When two or more partnerships join together to form a new partnership, the parties to the transaction must determine which, if any, of the old partnerships are continued and which are terminated. An old partnership whose partner(s) own more than 50% of the profits and capital interests of the new partnership is considered to be continued as the new partnership.[41] Accordingly, the new partnership must continue with the tax year and accounting methods and elections of the old partnership that is considered to continue. All the other old partnerships are considered to have been terminated.

EXAMPLE C:10-29 ▶ The AB and CD Partnerships merge to form the ABCD Partnership. April and Ben each own 30% of ABCD, and Carol and David each own 20% of ABCD. The ABCD Partnership is considered a continuation of the AB Partnership because April and Ben, the former partners of AB, own 60% of ABCD. ABCD is bound by the tax year, accounting method, and other elections made by AB. CD, formerly owned by Carol and David, is considered to terminate on the merger date. ◀

In some combinations, the partners of two or more of the old partnerships might hold the requisite profits and capital interest in the new partnership. When two or more old partnerships satisfy this requirement, the old partnership credited with contributing the greatest dollar value of assets to the new partnership is considered the continuing partnership, and all other partnerships terminate. Sometimes, none of the old partnerships account for more than 50% of the capital and profits of the new partnership. In that case, all the old partnerships terminate, and the merged partnership is a new entity that can make its own tax year and accounting method elections.

EXAMPLE C:10-30 ▶ Three partnerships merge to form the ABCD Partnership. The AB Partnership (owned by Andy and Bill) contributes assets valued at $140,000 to ABCD. BC Partnership (owned by Bill and Cathy) and CD Partnership (owned by Cathy and Drew) contribute assets valued at $180,000 and $120,000, respectively. The capital and profits interests of the partners in the new partnership are Andy, 20%; Bill, 35%; Cathy, 19%; and Drew, 26%. Both the AB and BC Partnerships had partners who now own more than 50% of the new partnership (Andy and Bill own 55%, and Bill and Cathy own 54%). The BC Partnership contributed more assets ($180,000) to the new partnership than did the AB Partnership ($140,000). Therefore, the ABCD Partnership is a continuation of the BC Partnership. Both the AB and CD Partnerships terminate on the merger date. ◀

KEY POINT

The principal concern of a partnership division is to determine which of the new partnerships is the continuation of the prior partnership.

DIVISION OF A PARTNERSHIP

When a partnership divides into two or more new partnerships, all the new partnerships whose partners own collectively more than 50% of the profits and capital interests in the old partnerships are considered a continuation of the old partnership.[42] All partnerships that are continuations of the old partnership are bound by the old partnership's tax year and accounting method elections. Any other partnership created by the division is considered a new partnership eligible to make its own tax year and accounting method elections. If no new partnership meets the criteria for continuation of the divided partnership, the divided partnership terminates on the division date. The interest of any partner of the divided partnership who does not own an interest in a continuing partnership is considered to be liquidated on the division date.

EXAMPLE C:10-31 ▶ The RSTV Partnership is in the real estate and insurance business. Randy owns a 40% interest and Sam, Thomas, and Vicki each own 20% of RSTV. The partners agree to split the partnership, with the RS Partnership receiving the real estate operations and the TV Partnership receiving the insurance business. Because Randy and Sam own more than 50% of the RSTV Partnership (40% + 20% = 60%), the RS Partnership is a continuation of the RSTV Partnership and must report its results using the same tax year and accounting method elections that RSTV

[41] Sec. 708(b)(2)(A).

[42] Sec. 708(b)(2)(B).

used. Thomas and Vicki are considered to have terminated their interests in RSTV and to have received a liquidating distribution of the insurance business property. The TV Partnership makes its tax year and accounting method elections following the rules for a new partnership. ◀

Optional and Mandatory Basis Adjustments

OBJECTIVE 5

Analyze the effects of optional and mandatory basis adjustments

In general, a partnership makes no adjustment to the basis of its property when a partner sells or exchanges his or her interest in the partnership, when a partner's interest transfers upon the partner's death, or when the partnership makes a property distribution to a partner. A partnership, however, may adjust basis of its assets if the partnership makes an **optional basis adjustment** election under Sec. 754. The following paragraphs compare the consequences of having no election to having such an election. The discussion focuses primarily on sale transactions but also briefly mentions distributions. Once made, the Sec. 754 election applies to all subsequent transfers of partnership interests (e.g., sales, exchanges, and transfers upon death) and all subsequent distributions. In addition, the partnership may have to make a **mandatory basis adjustment** in certain circumstances even if a Sec. 754 election is not in effect.

Adjustments on Transfers

Optional Adjustment. If a new incoming partner purchases his or her partnership interest from an existing partner, the new partner's basis in the partnership interest equals the purchase price plus the new partner's share of partnership liabilities. The new partner's basis in the partnership is likely to be different from his or her share of basis of the underlying assets in the partnership. This difference could lead to inequitable results as demonstrated by the following example.

EXAMPLE C:10-32 ▶ Amy, Bill, and Corey each own a one-third interest in ABC partnership, which has the following simple balance sheet:

	Basis	*FMV*
Assets:		
Cash	$30,000	$ 30,000
Inventory	60,000	90,000
Total	$90,000	$120,000
Liabilities and capital:		
Liabilities	$15,000	$ 15,000
Capital—Amy	25,000	35,000
—Bill	25,000	35,000
—Corey	25,000	35,000
Total	$90,000	$120,000

Eric purchases Amy's one-third interest for $35,000 cash and assumes her $5,000 share of partnerships liabilities. Eric pays this amount because one-third the FMV of the underlying partnership assets is $40,000 (1/3 × $120,000). In addition, the cash paid plus Eric's share of partnership liabilities gives him a $40,000 basis in his new partnership interest. Amy's basis at the time of sale is $30,000. Therefore, Amy recognizes a $10,000 gain ($40,000 amount realized − $30,000 basis). Amy's $10,000 gain also reflects her share of the difference between the inventory's FMV and basis at the partnership level. Thus, her gain will be ordinary income under Sec. 751.

Now suppose the partnership later sells the inventory for $90,000. The partnership recognizes $30,000 of ordinary income. Therefore, each partner, Bill, Corey, and Eric, recognizes a $10,000 distributive share of ordinary income from that sale, and each partner increases the basis of his partnership interest by the same amount. Accordingly, Eric increases his basis in the partnership from $40,000 to $50,000. In this situation, Eric appears to be taxed on the same gain as was Amy even though he paid a FMV price for his partnership interest (and the underlying partnership assets).

However, this result primarily is an issue of timing and possibly character of income and loss. For example, suppose further that, sometime after selling the inventory, the partnership distributes the $120,000 cash to the partners in liquidation. Eric would receive $40,000 and recognize a $10,000 ($40,000 distribution – $50,000 basis) capital loss.

In short, with no optional basis adjustment election in effect, Eric recognizes $10,000 of ordinary income when the partnership sells the inventory and a $10,000 capital loss when the partnership liquidates. This timing difference could be substantial if the partnership remains in existence for a long time. Also, the capital loss may offset only capital gains and up to $3,000 of ordinary income in the partner's personal tax return. ◀

ADDITIONAL COMMENT

The situation of a new partner purchasing an interest in a partnership is a good example of where a partner's outside basis can differ significantly from his or her share of the partnership's inside basis. The Sec. 754 election mitigates this difference.

Amount of the Adjustment. An incoming partner might view the situation in Example C:10-32 as unacceptable and wish the partnership to make a Sec. 754 election. If the partnership makes such an election or has a Sec. 754 election already in effect, Sec. 743 mandates a special basis adjustment equal to the difference between the transferee (purchasing) partner's basis in the partnership interest and the transferee partner's share of basis of partnership assets. This basis adjustment, arising from a transfer, belongs only to the transferee partner (and not to the other partners), and it eliminates the inequities noted in Example C:10-32.

EXAMPLE C:10-33 ▶ Assume the same facts as in Example C:10-32 except the partnership makes a Sec. 754 election. Eric's optional basis adjustment is calculated as follows:

Cash purchase price	$35,000
Share of partnership liabilities	5,000
Initial basis in partnership	$40,000
Minus: Eric's share of partnership's basis in assets (1/3 × $90,000)[43]	(30,000)
Optional basis adjustment	$10,000

Now when the partnership sells the inventory, Eric has an additional $10,000 basis in his share of the inventory that offsets the $10,000 income he otherwise would recognize. The other partners, however, still recognize their $10,000 distributive shares of income. Because Eric recognizes no income, he does not increase his partnership basis. Suppose the partnership liquidates sometime after selling the inventory. Again, Eric receives a $40,000 distribution, but he recognizes no capital gain or loss ($40,000 distribution – $40,000 basis). Thus, the optional basis adjustment eliminated both the timing and character differences that occurred in Example C:10-32. ◀

Mandatory Adjustment. The IRC imposes a mandatory basis adjustment for a sale or exchange of a partnership interest if the partnership has a substantial built-in loss and has no Sec. 754 optional basis adjustment election in effect. A substantial built-in loss exists if the partnership's adjusted basis in its property exceeds the FMV of the property by more than $250,000. This provision prevents the doubling of losses. Exceptions to the rule apply to certain specialized partnerships, discussion of which is beyond the scope of this textbook.

EXAMPLE C:10-34 ▶ David, Ellen, and Frank each own a one-third interest in DEF partnership, which has the following simple balance sheet:

	Basis	*FMV*
Assets:		
Cash	$ 100,000	$100,000
Land	1,100,000	800,000
Total	$1,200,000	$900,000

43 In some cases, the calculation of the transferee's share of the partnership's basis in assets can be more complicated than shown in this example. See Reg. Sec. 1.743-1(d).

Capital:		
David	$ 400,000	$300,000
Ellen	400,000	300,000
Frank	400,000	300,000
Total	$1,200,000	$900,000

Gwen purchases David's one-third interest for $300,000 cash, which gives Gwen a $300,000 initial basis in her new partnership interest. David's partnership interest basis at the time of sale is $400,000. Therefore, he recognizes a $100,000 loss. David's $100,000 loss also reflects his share of the difference between the land's FMV and basis at the partnership level.

Now suppose the partnership has no optional basis adjustment election in effect and later sells the land for $800,000. The partnership recognizes a $300,000 loss. As a result, each partner, Ellen, Frank, and Gwen, recognizes a $100,000 distributive share of that loss, and each partner decreases the basis of his or her partnership interest by the same amount. As a result, both David and Gwen recognize a $100,000 loss. To prevent this doubling of losses, the partnership must make a $100,000 mandatory downward basis adjustment with respect to Gwen's share of the land, thereby nullifying her distributive share of loss on the land sale. The adjustment is mandatory because the partnership has a substantial built-in loss (i.e., its $300,00 built-in loss exceeds $250,000). Note that, without this mandatory adjustment, Gwen's $100,000 loss would be temporary because her partnership basis would be reduced to $200,000, causing her to recognize a $100,000 gain should the partnership liquidate and distribute $300,000 to her. Nevertheless, Congress chose to eliminate the initial doubling of losses by requiring the mandatory basis adjustment. ◀

Other Issues. Examples C:10-32 through C:10-34 assume inventory or land is the only asset other than cash. If the assets instead had been depreciable property, the basis adjustments would give the transferee partner additional depreciation deductions in Examples C:10-32 and C:10-33 or reduced depreciation deductions in example C:10-34. Also, if a partnership has more than one asset other than cash, the optional or mandatory basis adjustment must be allocated to the assets under special rules found in Sec. 755 and related Treasury Regulations. These allocation rules are beyond the scope of this text.

ADJUSTMENTS ON DISTRIBUTIONS

Optional Adjustment. As mentioned earlier, if a partnership distributes property to a partner, the partnership makes no adjustment to the basis of its remaining property unless an optional basis adjustment election is in place or unless the mandatory basis adjustment rule discussed later applies. If the partnership has made a Sec. 754 election, the partnership makes the following adjustments upon the distribution to a partner:

- Increases the basis of *partnership* property by:
  1. Any gain recognized by the distributee partner on the distribution (e.g., cash distribution exceeding the partner's basis in his or her partnership interest)
  2. The amount by which the distributee partner decreases the basis of property received in a property distribution from the basis of the property in the partnership's hands
- Decreases the basis of *partnership* property by:
  1. Any loss recognized by the distributee partner on a liquidating distribution
  2. The amount by which the distributee partner increases the basis of property received in a property distribution from the basis of the property in the partnership's hands

Unlike the optional basis adjustments arising from a transfer of partnership interest, the basis adjustments arising from a distribution belong to the partnership as a whole. These adjustments eliminate many (but not all) basis and timing disparities resulting from distributions.

A partnership should take care in making a Sec. 754 election because, once made, the election affects many transactions in complicated ways. Moreover, the election can cause downward as well as upward adjustments. Finally, the election has long-range implications because it can be revoked only with IRS approval. The IRS will not grant such approval if the primary purpose of the revocation is to avoid reducing the basis of partnership assets.

Mandatory Adjustment. The discussion of the optional basis adjustment for distributions included increases and decreases to partnership property. The IRC makes the decreasing basis adjustment for distributions mandatory if it exceeds $250,000. As with exchange transactions, this provision prevents the doubling of losses. In effect, the mandatory adjustment rule applies only to liquidating distributions because such decreasing adjustments cannot occur in nonliquidating distribution situations.

SPECIAL FORMS OF PARTNERSHIPS

OBJECTIVE 6

Compare and contrast the various special forms a partnership might take

Here, we examine a series of special partnership forms, including tax shelters organized as limited partnerships, publicly traded partnerships, limited liability companies, limited liability partnerships, and electing large partnerships.

TAX SHELTERS AND LIMITED PARTNERSHIPS

Tax shelters at their best are good investments that reduce and/or defer the amount of an investor's tax bill. Traditionally, shelter benefits arise from leverage, income deferral, deduction acceleration, and tax credits.

ADDITIONAL COMMENT

The passive activity loss limitations eliminate the deferral benefit of tax shelters.

Many years ago, limited partnerships were the primary vehicle for tax shelter investments. However, subsequent tax law greatly reduced the benefits of limited partnerships as tax shelters by invoking the passive activity loss limitations for activity conducted in a limited partnership form. The limited partnership, however, still allows an investor to limit liability while receiving the benefits of the shelter's tax attributes to save taxes on other passive income. Moreover, limited partnerships that generate passive income rather than losses have become popular investments for investors who already hold loss-generating limited partnership interests. (See Problem C:9-46 in the previous chapter for an example of tax deferred benefits and their elimination by the at-risk and passive activity loss limitations.)

PUBLICLY TRADED PARTNERSHIPS

The IRC restricts still further the benefits of tax shelter ownership by imposing special rules on **publicly traded partnerships** (PTPs). A PTP is a partnership whose interests are traded either on an established securities exchange or in a secondary market or the equivalent thereof. A partnership that meets the requirements is taxed as a C corporation under Sec. 7704.

Two exceptions apply to partnerships that otherwise would be classified as PTPs:

- ▶ Partnerships that have 90% or more of their gross income being "qualifying income" continue to be taxed under the partnership rules.
- ▶ Partnerships that were in existence on December 17, 1987 and have not added a substantial new line of business since that date are grandfathered. In general, application of the PTP rules for these partnerships was delayed until tax years beginning after December 31, 1997.

REAL-WORLD EXAMPLE

Many PTPs are traded on major stock exchanges such as the New York Stock Exchange.

The Taxpayer Relief Act of 1997 added an election that allows the grandfathered partnerships to continue to be treated as partnerships after the original ten-year window and until the election is revoked. To elect to continue to be treated as a partnership, the publicly traded partnership (which must have been taxed as a partnership under the grandfather provision) must agree to pay a 3.5% annual tax on gross income from the active conduct of any trade or business.[44] The election may be revoked by the partnership, but once revoked, it cannot be reinstated.

[44] Sec. 7704(g)(3).

For the 90% of gross income test, Sec. 7704(d) defines qualifying income to include certain interest, dividends, real property rents (but not personal property rents), income and gains from the sale or disposition of a capital asset or Sec. 1231(b) trade or business property held for the production of passive income, and gain from the sale or disposition of real property. It also includes gains from certain commodity trading and natural resource activities. Any PTP not taxed as a corporation because of this 90% exception is subject to separate and more restrictive Sec. 469 passive loss rules than are partnerships that are not publicly traded.

If a partnership is first classified as a PTP taxed as a corporation during a tax year, the PTP incurs a deemed contribution of all partnership assets and all partnership liabilities to a corporation in exchange for all the corporation's stock. The stock is then deemed distributed to the partners in complete liquidation of the partnership. This transaction is taxed exactly as if it had physically occurred.

LIMITED LIABILITY COMPANIES

In recent years, the limited liability company (LLC) has emerged as a popular form of business entity in the United States. The LLC combines the legal and tax benefits of partnerships and S corporations. Currently, all 50 states have adopted LLC laws. The LLC business form combines the advantage of limited liability for all its owners with the ability of achieving the conduit treatment and the flexibility of being taxed as a partnership.

In the past, whether an LLC was characterized as a corporation or a partnership for federal tax purposes depended on the number of corporate characteristics the entity possessed, such as limited liability, free transferability of interests, centralized management, and continuity of life. The process of determining tax treatment was complex and time consuming. To alleviate this complexity, the Treasury Department issued regulations that allow entities (other than corporations and trusts) to choose whether to be taxed as a partnership or as an association. (An association is an unincorporated entity taxed as a corporation.) According to these check-the-box regulations, an LLC with two or more members can choose either partnership or association tax treatment. With a written and properly filed election, any LLC can choose to be taxed as an association. If the LLC makes no such election, an LLC with two or more members is treated as a partnership for tax purposes, while a single member LLC is treated as a sole proprietorship.

As already mentioned, an LLC with two or more members that does not elect association status is a partnership for tax purposes and is subject to all the rules applicable to other partnerships. Thus, the formation of the LLC; income, gain, loss, and deductions that flow through to the LLC members; current and liquidating distributions; and sale, gift, or exchange of an interest in the LLC all fall under the partnership rules. An LLC treated as a partnership is subject to the Sec. 704 rules for special allocations and allocations of precontribution gain or loss, to the Sec. 736 rules for retirement distributions, and to the Sec. 751 rules pertaining to unrealized receivables and inventory.

TAX STRATEGY TIP

The list of advantages of an LLC over an S corporation is substantial and suggests that an LLC should always be seriously considered as an option for a pass-through entity. However, one current, important advantage of an S corporation is that the shareholders are not subject to self-employment taxes on their share of the entity's earnings.

Using the LLC form for a business with publicly traded ownership interests is likely to result in taxation as a corporation. Even if the LLC does not elect association status, the public trading of the ownership interest brings the LLC under the publicly traded partnership rules. As discussed above, these rules result in the business being taxed as a corporation unless 90% or more of the income is qualifying income or unless the LLC is covered under the grandfather rules. However, given the recency of LLCs as a form for conducting business, the grandfather provisions are unlikely to apply.

If an LLC is treated as a partnership, it offers greater flexibility than does an S corporation because it is not subject to the restrictions that apply to S corporations as to the number of shareholders, the number of classes of stock, or the types of investments in related entities that the entity can make. Moreover, unlike S corporations, LLCs can use the special allocation rules of Sec. 704 to allocate income, gain, loss, or deductions to their members. Finally, each member's basis in the LLC interest includes that member's share of the organization's debts (and not just shareholder debt as with an S corporation).

LIMITED LIABILITY PARTNERSHIPS

REAL-WORLD EXAMPLE

All the Big 4 accounting firms and a number of other national, regional, and local accounting firms operate as LLPs. Even though the non-responsible partners in an LLP are not liable for the responsible partner's negligence, all partners and employees can suffer if the partnership itself is deemed guilty, as demonstrated by the demise of a former national accounting firm several years ago.

Many states have added limited liability partnerships (LLPs) to the list of business forms that can be formed. Under the current state laws, the primary difference between a general partnership and an LLP is that in a limited liability partnership, a partner is not liable for damages resulting from failures in the work of other partners or of people supervised by other partners. For example, assume that a limited liability accounting partnership is assessed damages in a lawsuit that resulted from an audit partner in New York being negligent in an audit. The tax partner for the same firm, who is based in San Diego and who had no involvement with the audit or the auditor, should not be liable to pay damages resulting from the suit.

Like a general or limited partnership, this business form is a partnership for tax purposes. All the partnership tax rules and regulations apply to this business form just as they do to any other partnership.

Question: What issues do you expect the check-the-box regulations to raise for new businesses making their initial choice of entity decision? What effect do you expect these regulations to have on existing corporations?

Solution: Consider the options facing a new business. The business can be formed as a C corporation, which provides limited liability protection to owners but subjects the corporate income to double taxation. A business formed as a C corporation can make an S election for tax purposes, which keeps the limited liability protection for the owners and eliminates the double taxation by taxing all income directly to the owners. However, as you will see in Chapter C:11, a number of restrictions prevent many corporations from electing S status. In addition, all income and loss of an S corporation must be allocated among the shareholders on a pro rata basis. A partnership offers the most flexible tax treatment with no double taxation of income, but the traditional partnership must have at least one general partner whose liability for partnership debts is not limited. An LLC, which is treated as a partnership, provides limited liability protection to its owners while avoiding both the double taxation of income found in a regular C corporation as well as the restrictions placed on S corporations. Because an LLC is treated as a partnership, the income and loss shares reported by each partner is flexible, and the partner's basis for his partnership interest includes his or her share of the LLC's liabilities. Thus, in some ways, the LLC has the best attributes of both the corporation and the partnership.

These are strong reasons why a new entity would choose to form as an LLC and be treated as a partnership. However, because the LLC is a relatively new business form, statutes, case law, and regulations are still being developed, and thus many areas of uncertainty remain to be resolved over time.

The check-the-box regulations are not helpful to existing C corporations and S corporations because an existing corporation cannot elect to be treated as a partnership. Instead, it must liquidate (with all the tax consequences of a liquidation, as described in Chapter C:6) before it can form as a partnership or an LLC. Potentially, the change in entity form has a high tax cost for an existing corporation.

LIMITED LIABILITY LIMITED PARTNERSHIP

Another recent innovation in some states (but not all) is the limited liability limited partnership (LLLP). Remember that a limited partnership, in addition to having limited partners, has one or more general partners whose personal liability exposure is unlimited. The LLLP is a partnership formed under a state's limited partnership laws but that can elect under the state's laws to provide the general partners with limited liability. Thus, the LLLP is similar to an LLC and becomes potentially useful in states that do not extend LLC status to personal service firms but allow such firms to operate as an LLLP.[45]

[45] For a detailed discussion, see Shop Talk, "Service Firms Practicing as LLLPs: What Are the Tax Consequences?" *Journal of Taxation*, August 2005.

ADDITIONAL COMMENT

Section 775 for electing large partnerships is repealed for tax years beginning after 2017. Thus, the rules discussed in this section are applicable only for tax years beginning before 2018.

ELECTING LARGE PARTNERSHIPS

Partnerships that qualify as "large partnerships" may elect to be taxed under a simplified reporting arrangement.[46] The partnership must meet the following four qualifications to be treated as an electing large partnership:

- It must not be a service partnership.
- It must not be engaged in commodity trading.
- It must have at least 100 partners.
- It must file an election to be taxed as an electing large partnership.

Section 775 defines a service partnership as one in which substantially all the partners perform substantial services in connection with the partnership's activities or the partners are retired but in the past performed substantial services in connection with the partnership's activities. One example of a partnership that could not make this election is a partnership that provides accounting services. An electing large partnership also cannot be engaged in commodity trading. Further, to qualify to make this election, the partnership must have at least 100 partners (excluding those partners who do provide substantial services in connection with the partnership's business activities) throughout the tax year.

Once it makes the election, the partnership reports its income under a simplified reporting scheme, is subject to different rules about when the partnership terminates, and is subject to a different system of audits. The election is irrevocable without IRS permission.

Electing Large Partnership Taxable Income. Much like other partnerships, the calculation of electing large partnership taxable income includes separately stated income and other income. However, the items that must be separately stated are very different for the electing large partnership. Likewise, the items included in other income differ significantly. The main reason that Congress added electing large partnerships to the IRC was to provide a form of flow-through entity that does not require so much separate reporting to each partner of many different income, loss, and deduction items. Simpler reporting from the partnership to the partners was the goal, so fewer items are separately stated and many more items are combined at the partnership level.

Like a regular partnership, calculation of an electing large partnership's taxable income is similar to the calculation for an individual. For an electing large partnership (just like for other partnerships), the deductions for personal exemptions and net operating losses are disallowed as well as most additional itemized deductions, such as medical expenses and alimony. However, calculation of the items that would qualify as miscellaneous itemized deductions for an individual differs from the calculation for either individuals or other partnerships. For an electing large partnership, miscellaneous itemized deductions are combined at the partnership level and subject to a 70% deduction at the partnership level. After the 70% deduction, the remaining miscellaneous itemized deductions are combined with other income and passed through to the partners. Because they are combined with other income at the partnership level, they are not subject to the 2% nondeductible floor at the individual partner level.[47]

Instead of flowing through as a separately stated item as they do with a regular partnership, charitable contributions made by an electing large partnership are subject to the 10% of taxable income limit similar to the limit that normally applies to corporations. Once the limit is applied, the partnership deducts allowable charitable contribution from its ordinary income, and the partners do not report the charitable contributions as a separate item.[48]

For a regular partnership, the first-year expensing deduction allowed under Sec. 179 is both limited at the partnership level and is separately stated and limited at the partner level. For an electing large partnership, the only limit is at the partnership level. The

[46] Sec. 775.

[47] Sec. 773(b).

[48] Sec. 773(b)(2).

allowable deduction is calculated at the partnership level, and the deduction amount offsets the partnership's ordinary income. For an electing large partnership, the Sec. 179 deduction is not separately stated and the impact of the Sec. 179 deduction is buried in the ordinary income amount reported by the partnership to the partners.

Separately Stated Large Partnership Items. An electing large partnership nevertheless is a pass-through entity, so some items still must be separately stated at the partnership level, and these items maintain their character when reported in the partners' tax returns. Section 772 lists the following items the electing large partnership must report separately:

- Taxable income or loss from passive loss limitation activities
- Taxable income or loss from other partnership activities
- Net capital gain or loss from passive loss limitation activities
- Net capital gain or loss from other partnership activities
- Tax-exempt interest
- Applicable net alternative minimum tax adjustment separately computed for passive loss limitation activities and other activities
- General credits
- Low income housing credit
- Rehabilitation credit
- Foreign income taxes
- Credit for producing fuel from a nonconventional source
- Any other item the IRS determines should be separately stated

The differences between the treatment of other partnerships versus electing large partnerships is significant. The most interesting aspect of this list is what items are combined for reporting by an electing large partnership. For example, Sec. 1231 gains and losses are netted at the partnership level, net 1231 losses are included in ordinary income or loss, and net 1231 gains are reported with capital gains and losses. The capital gains and losses also are combined at the partnership level with only a single, net number reported to the partners. The capital gain or loss is treated as long-term at the partner level. However, if the net is a short-term capital gain, that gain is treated as ordinary income and combined at the partnership level with other ordinary income items. All the partnership's credits are combined at the partnership level with the exceptions of the low income housing credit and the rehabilitation credit.

Both ordinary income and capital gains attributed to passive loss activities are reported separately from the results of other partnership activities. In addition, the taxable income or loss from activities other than passive activities generally are treated as items of income or expense with respect to property held for investment rather than as active trade or business income. Dividend income, for example, would fall into this category.

For the electing large partnership, all limits, such as the charitable contributions limit and the Sec. 179 expensing deduction limit, are applied at the partnership level rather than at the individual partner level with three exceptions. The three limits applied at the partner level are the Sec. 68 limit on itemized deductions, the limit on at-risk losses, and the limit on passive activity losses.[49] For the limitation to be applied at the partner level, these items must be separately stated.

For separately stated items, the character of amounts flowing through the partnership retain their character when reported on the partners' tax returns. However, because many more items are combined at the partnership level and not separately stated, the character of many fewer kinds of income is retained to flow through with the electing large partnership form.

---

[49] Sec. 773(a)

EXAMPLE C:10-35 ▶ The ABC Partnership is an electing large partnership that reports the following transactions for the current year. ABC has no passive activities.

Net long-term capital loss	$100,000
Sec. 1231 gain	120,000
Ordinary income	40,000
Dividend income	10,000
Charitable contributions	30,000
Tax-exempt income	4,000

ABC will report these earnings to its partners as follows:

Long-term capital gain	$20,000
Ordinary income	33,000
Dividend income	10,000
Tax-exempt income	4,000

Because the partnership has a net Sec. 1231 gain, it is treated as a long-term capital gain ($120,000) and combined at the partnership level with the long-term capital loss ($100,000) to result in a net long-term capital gain of $20,000. At the partnership level, the charitable contribution deduction is limited to 10% of taxable income, or $7,000 [0.10 × ($20,000 capital gain + $10,000 dividend income + $40,000 ordinary income)] and is subtracted from ordinary income of $40,000 before ordinary income is reported to the partners. The character of the long-term capital gain, dividend income, tax-exempt income, and ordinary income pass through to the partner. ◀

Reporting Requirement. An electing large partnership files Form 1065-B and must provide a Schedule K-1 to each of its partners on or before March 15 following the close of the partnership tax year without regard to when the partnership tax return is due.[50] Partnerships that are not electing large partnerships are only required to provide the information return by the due date of the partnership tax return—which, for a calendar year partnership, is April 15. The March 15 provision will help reduce the number of partners who must file an extension of their individual tax returns because they do not receive the Schedule K-1 from a regular partnership early enough to file a timely individual return.

Termination of the Partnership. Because electing large partnerships are quite large and often may be widely traded, Congress decided to change the conditions under which these partnership will be considered to terminate. An electing large partnership terminates only if its partners cease to conduct any business, financial operation, or venture in a partnership form. Unlike other partnerships, an electing large partnership will not terminate because of the sale or exchange of partnership interests involving at least a 50% interest in partnership capital or profits during a 12-month period.[51]

Electing Large Partnership Audits. An electing large partnership is not subject to the partnership audit rules but is subject to a much more restrictive set of partnership audit procedures.[52] First, all electing large partnership partners must report all items of partnership income, gain, loss, or deduction in the way the partnership reports the item. Deviations from that partnership reporting will be "corrected" by the IRS just as a math mistake is corrected.[53]

Because all partners are required to use identical reporting for partnership items, it becomes somewhat easier to audit partnership results only at the partnership level. Notice of audit proceedings, determination of errors, settlement offers, appeals proceedings, and court cases are all handled at the partnership level, and no individual partner can request separate treatment or refuse to participate in the partnership level result. In general, any adjustments determined at the partnership level by an audit agreement or court decision will be considered to be income or deduction that occurs in the year of the agreement or

[50] Sec. 6031.
[51] Sec. 774(c).
[52] Sec. 6240.
[53] Sec. 6241.

decision.[54] Accordingly, the effect of adjustments is borne by the partners who own interests in the year of the agreement or decision and not by the partners who originally reported the contested transaction results.

Tax planning considerations

OBJECTIVE 7

Identify tax planning opportunities in liquidating or selling a partnership interest

LIQUIDATING DISTRIBUTION OR SALE TO PARTNERS

An unusual tax planning opportunity exists when one partner withdraws from a partnership and the remaining partners proportionately increase their ownership of the partnership. The partners can structure the ownership change as either a liquidating distribution made by the partnership or as a sale of the partnership interest to the remaining partners. In fact, the substance of the two transactions is the same, only the form is different. However, this difference in form can make a substantial difference in the tax consequences in a number of areas.

- If the transferor partner receives payment for his or her interest in the partnership's Sec. 751 assets, he or she must recognize ordinary income no matter how the transaction is structured. The partnership's basis in Sec. 751 assets is increased in the case of a liquidating distribution. When a sale transaction takes place, the partnership's basis in Sec. 751 assets is increased only if the partnership has an optional basis adjustment election in effect.
- If the partnership has an optional basis adjustment election in effect, the allocation of the adjustment to the individual partnership assets can be different depending on whether the transaction is structured as a sale or as a liquidating distribution.
- If the interest being transferred equals or exceeds 50% of the profits and capital interests, a sale to the remaining partners terminates the partnership. A liquidating distribution does not cause a termination to occur.

Because the tax implications of the sale transaction and liquidating distribution alternatives are both numerous and complex, the partners should make their choice only after careful consideration. (See the Tax Strategy Problem later in the Problem Material.)

Problem materials

DISCUSSION QUESTIONS

C:10-1 Javier is retiring from the JKL Partnership. In January of the current year, he has a $100,000 basis in his partnership interest when he receives a $10,000 cash distribution. The partnership plans to distribute $10,000 each month this year, and Javier will cease to be a partner after the December payment. Is the January payment to Javier a current distribution or a liquidating distribution?

C:10-2 Mariel has a $60,000 basis in her partnership interest just before receiving a parcel of land as a liquidating distribution. She has no remaining precontribution gain and will receive no other distributions. Under what conditions will Mariel's basis in the land be $60,000?

C:10-3 Cindy has a $4,000 basis in her partnership interest before receiving a nonliquidating (current) distribution of property having a $4,500 basis and a $6,000 FMV from the CDE Partnership. Cindy has a choice of receiving either inventory or a capital asset. She will hold the distributed property as an investment for no more than two years before she sells it. What tax difference (if any) will occur as a result of Cindy's selection of one property or the other to be distributed by the partnership?

---

[54] Sec. 6242.

C:10-4 The AB Partnership purchases plastic components and assembles children's toys. The assembly operation requires a number of special machines that are housed in a building the partnership owns. The partnership has depreciated all its property under MACRS. The partnership sells the toys on account to a number of retail establishments and uses the accrual method of accounting. Identify any items you think might be classified as unrealized receivables.

C:10-5 Which of the following items are considered to be inventory for purposes of Sec. 751?

a. Supplies
b. Inventory
c. Notes receivable
d. Land held for investment purposes
e. Lots held for resale

C:10-6 Explain the conditions under which Sec. 751 has an impact on nonliquidating (current) distributions.

C:10-7 What conditions are required for a partner to recognize a loss upon receipt of a distribution from a partnership?

C:10-8 Can a partner recognize both a gain and a loss on the sale of a partnership interest? If so, under what conditions?

C:10-9 Tyra has a zero basis in her partnership interest and a share in partnership liabilities, which are quite large. Explain how these facts will affect the taxation of her departure from the partnership using the following methods of terminating her interest in the partnership.

a. A liquidating distribution of property
b. A sale of the partnership interest to a current partner for cash

C:10-10 Tom is a 55% general partner in the RST Partnership. Tom wants to retire, and the other two partners, Stacy and Rich, want to continue the partnership business. They agree that the partnership will liquidate Tom's interest in the partnership by paying him 20% of partnership profits for each of the next ten years. Explain why Sec. 736 does (or does not) apply to the partnership's payments to Tom.

C:10-11 Lucia has a $20,000 basis in her limited partnership interest before her retirement from the partnership. Her share of partnership assets have a $23,000 FMV, and the partnership has no Sec. 751 assets. In addition to being paid cash for her full share of partnership assets, Lucia will receive a share of partnership income for the next three years. Explain Lucia's tax treatment for the payments she receives.

C:10-12 What are the advantages and disadvantages to the partnership and its partners when a partnership termination is caused by a sale of at least a 50% capital and profits interest?

C:10-13 What is a publicly traded partnership? Are all publicly traded partnerships taxed as corporations?

C:10-14 What are the advantages of a firm being formed as a limited liability company (LLC) instead of as a limited partnership?

C:10-15 What is an electing large partnership? What are the advantages to the partnership of electing to be taxed under the electing large partnership rules?

ISSUE IDENTIFICATION QUESTIONS

C:10-16 When Kayla's basis in her interest in the JKL Partnership is $30,000, she receives a current distribution of office equipment. The equipment has an FMV of $40,000 and basis of $35,000. Kayla will not use the office equipment in a business activity. What tax issues should Kayla consider with respect to the distribution?

C:10-17 Joel receives a $40,000 cash distribution from the JM Partnership, which reduces his partnership interest from one-third to one-fourth. The JM Partnership is a general partnership that uses the cash method of accounting and has substantial liabilities. JM's inventory has appreciated substantially since it was purchased. What issues should Joel consider with regard to the distribution?

C:10-18 Scott sells his one-third partnership interest to Sally for $43,000 when his basis in the partnership interest is $33,000. On the date of sale, the partnership has no liabilities and the following assets:

Assets	*Basis*	*FMV*
Cash	$30,000	$30,000
Inventory	12,000	21,000
Building	45,000	60,000
Land	12,000	18,000

The partnership has claimed $5,400 of straight-line depreciation on the building. What tax issues should Scott and Sally consider with respect to the sale transaction?

C:10-19 David owns a 60% interest in the DDD Partnership, a general partnership, which he sells to the two remaining partners—Drew and Dana. The three partners have agreed that David will receive $150,000 in cash from the sale. David's basis in the partnership interest before the sale is $120,000, which includes his $30,000 share of partnership recourse liabilities. The partnership has assets with a $300,000 FMV and a $200,000 adjusted basis. What issues should David, Drew, and Dana consider before this sale takes place?

C:10-20 Andrew and Beth are equal partners in the AB Partnership. On December 30 of the current year, the AB Partnership agrees to liquidate Andrew's partnership interest for a cash payment on December 30 of each of the next five years. What tax issues should Andrew and Beth consider with respect to the liquidation of Andrew's partnership interest?

C:10-21 Alex owns 60% of the Hot Wheels LLC, which is treated as a partnership. He plans to give 15% of the LLC (one-fourth of his interest) to his daughter Haley for her high school graduation. He plans to put her interest in a trust, and he will serve as the trustee until Haley is 21. The trust will receive any distributions from the LLC, but Haley is unlikely to be given any of the cash until she is age 21. Alex's 60% interest has a $120,000 FMV and an $80,000 adjusted basis including his $48,000 share of the LLC's liabilities. Alex works full time for the LLC for a small salary and his share of LLC income. Alex also has a special allocation of income from rental property he manages for the LLC. What issues should Alex consider before he completes the gift?

C:10-22 Three individuals recently formed Krypton Company as a limited liability company (LLC). The three individuals—Jeff, Susan, and Richard—own equal interests in the company, and they all have substantial income from other sources. Krypton is a manufacturing firm and expects to earn approximately $130,000 of ordinary income and $30,000 of long-term capital gain each year for the next several years. Jeff will be a full time manager and will receive a salary of $60,000 each year. What tax issues should the owners consider regarding the LLC's initial year of operations?

C:10-23 XYZ Limited Partnership has more than 300 partners and is publicly traded. XYZ was grandfathered under the 1987 Tax Act and has consistently been treated as a partnership. In the current year, XYZ will continue to be very profitable and will continue to pay out about 30% of its income to its owners each year. The managing partners of XYZ want to consider the firm's options for taxation in the current and later years.

PROBLEMS

C:10-24 *Current Distributions.* Lisa has a $25,000 basis in her partnership interest before receiving a current distribution of $4,000 cash and land with a $30,000 FMV and a $14,000 basis to the partnership. Assume that any distribution involving Sec. 751 property is pro rata, that any precontribution gains have been recognized before the distribution, and that no Sec. 754 election is in effect.

a. Determine Lisa's recognized gain or loss, Lisa's basis in distributed property, and Lisa's ending basis in her partnership interest.
b. How does your answer to Part a change if the partnership's basis in the land is $24,000 instead of $14,000?
c. How does your answer to Part a change if Lisa receives $28,000 cash instead of $4,000 (along with the land)?
d. How does your answer to Part a change if, in addition to the cash and land, Lisa receives inventory with a $25,000 FMV and a $10,000 basis and receivables with a $3,000 FMV and a zero basis?
e. Suppose instead that Lisa receives the distribution in Part a from a C corporation instead of a partnership. The corporation has $100,000 of E&P before the distribution, and Lisa's stock basis before the distribution is $25,000. What are the tax consequences to Lisa and the C corporation?
f. Note: This part can be answered only after the student studies Chapter C:11 but is placed here to allow comparison with Parts a and e. Suppose instead that Lisa receives the distribution in Part a from an S corporation instead of a partnership. Lisa is a 50% owner in the corporation, and her stock basis before the distribution is $25,000. What are the tax consequences to Lisa and the S corporation?

C:10-25 ***Current Distributions.*** Complete the chart for each of the following independent distributions. Assume that all distributions are nonliquidating and pro rata to the partners, that no contributed property was distributed, that all precontribution gain has been recognized before these distributions, and that no Sec. 754 election is in effect.

	Partner's Basis and Gain/Loss	*Property Distributed*	*Property's Basis to Partnership*	*Property's FMV*	*Property's Basis to Partner*
a. Basis:					
Predistribution	$20,000	Cash	$ 6,000	$ 6,000	
Postdistribution	$_____	Land	4,000	15,000	$_____
Gain or loss	$_____	Machinery	3,000	2,000	$_____
b. Basis:					
Predistribution	$20,000	Cash	$ 3,000	$ 3,000	
Postdistribution	$_____	Land	6,000	4,000	$_____
Gain or loss	$_____	Inventory	7,000	7,500	$_____
c. Basis					
Predistribution	$26,000	Cash	$35,000	$35,000	
Postdistribution	$_____	Land—Parcel 1	6,000	10,000	$_____
Gain or loss	$_____	Land—Parcel 2	18,000	18,000	$_____
d. Basis:					
Predistribution	$28,000	Land—Parcel 1	$ 4,000	$ 6,000	$_____
Postdistribution	$_____	Land—Parcel 2	6,000	10,000	$_____
Gain or loss	$_____	Land—Parcel 3	4,000	10,000	$_____

C:10-26 ***Current Distribution with Precontribution Gain.*** Three years ago, Mario joined the MN Partnership by contributing land with a $10,000 basis and an $18,000 FMV. On January 15 of the current year, Mario has a basis in his partnership interest of $20,000, and none of his precontribution gain has been recognized. On January 15, Mario receives a current distribution of a property other than the contributed land with a $15,000 basis and a $23,000 FMV.

a. Does Mario recognize any gain or loss on the distribution?
b. What is Mario's basis in his partnership interest after the distribution?
c. What is the partnership's basis in the land Mario contributed after Mario receives this distribution?

C:10-27 ***Current Distribution of Contributed Property.*** Andrew contributed investment land having an $18,000 basis and a $22,000 FMV along with $4,000 in money to the ABC Partnership when it was formed. Two years later, the partnership distributed the investment land Andrew had contributed to Bob, another partner. At the time of the distribution, the land had a $21,000 FMV, and Andrew and Bob's bases in their partnership interests were $21,000 and $30,000, respectively.

a. What gain or loss must be recognized on the distribution, and who must recognize it?
b. What are the bases for Andrew and Bob's interests in the partnership after the distribution?
c. What is Bob's basis in the distributed land?

C:10-28 ***Current Distribution of Contributed Property.*** The ABC Partnership made the following current distributions in the current year. The dollar amounts listed are the amounts before considering any implications of the distribution.

	Property Received			
Partner	*Type of Property*	*Basis*	*FMV*	*Partner's Basis in Partnership Interest*
Alonzo	Land	$ 4,000	$10,000	$19,000
Beth	Inventory	1,000	10,000	15,000
Cathy	Cash	10,000	10,000	18,000

The land Alonzo received had been contributed by Beth two years ago when its basis was $4,000 and its FMV was $8,000. The inventory Beth received had been contributed by Cathy two years ago when its basis was $1,000 and its FMV was $4,000. For each independent situation, what gain or loss must be recognized? What is the basis of the distributed property after the distribution? What are the bases of the partnership interests after the distribution? Assume the distribution has no Sec. 751 implications.

C:10-29 *Current Distribution with Sec. 751.* The KLM Partnership owns the following assets on March 1 of the current year:

Assets	*Partnership's Basis*	*FMV*
Cash	$ 30,000	$ 30,000
Receivables	–0–	16,000
Inventory	50,000	52,000
Supplies	6,000	6,500
Equipment[a]	9,000	10,500
Land (investment)	40,000	65,000
Total	$135,000	$180,000

[a]The partnership has claimed depreciation of $4,000 on the equipment.

a. Which partnership items are unrealized receivables?
b. Is the partnership's inventory substantially appreciated?
c. Assume the KLM Partnership has no liabilities and that Kay's basis for her partnership interest is $33,750. On March 1 of the current year, Kay receives a $20,000 current distribution in cash, which reduces her partnership interest from one-third to one-fourth. What are the tax results of the distribution (i.e., the amount and character of any gain, loss, or income recognized and Kay's basis in her partnership interest)?

C:10-30 *Current Distribution with Sec. 751.* The JKLM Partnership owns the following assets on October 1 of the current year:

Assets	*Partnership's Basis*	*FMV*
Cash	$ 48,000	$ 48,000
Receivables	12,000	12,000
Inventory	21,000	24,000
Machinery[a]	190,000	240,000
Land	36,500	76,000
Total	$307,500	$400,000

[a]Sale of the machinery for its FMV would result in $50,000 of Sec. 1245 depreciation recapture. Thus, the machinery's FMV and original cost are the same numerical value, $240,000.

a. Which partnership items are unrealized receivables?
b. Is the partnership's inventory substantially appreciated?
c. Assume the JKLM Partnership has no liabilities and Jack's basis in his partnership interest is $76,875. On October 1 of the current year, Jack receives a $25,000 current distribution in cash, which reduces his partnership interest from one-fourth to one-fifth. What are the tax results of the distribution (i.e., the amount and character of any gain, loss, or income recognized and Jack's basis in his partnership interest)?

C:10-31 *Current Distribution with Sec. 751.* The PQRS Partnership owns the following assets on December 30 of the current year:

Assets	*Partnership's Basis*	*FMV*
Cash	$ 20,000	$ 20,000
Receivables	–0–	40,000
Inventory	80,000	100,000
Total	$100,000	$160,000

The partnership has no liabilities, and each partner's basis in his or her partnership interest is $25,000. On December 30 of the current year, Paula receives a current distribution of inventory having a $10,000 FMV, which reduces her partnership interest from one-fourth to one-fifth. What are the tax consequences of the distribution to the partnership, Paula, and the other partners?

C:10-32 *Current and Liquidating Distributions.* The CL Partnership has two partners, Cleo and Leo. Each partner's basis in his or her partnership interest is $10,000 before any distribution. The partnership distributes $12,000 cash to Cleo and $8,000 cash to Leo.

a. Assuming a current distribution, determine for each partner (1) gain on loss recognized and (2) basis in the partnership interest after the distribution.
b. Assuming a liquidating distribution, determine each partner's gain or loss recognized.

C:10-33 *Liquidating Distributions.* Assume the same four independent distributions as in Problem C:10-25. Fill in the blanks in that problem assuming the only change in the facts is that the distributions are now liquidating distributions instead of nonliquidating distributions.

C:10-34 *Liquidating Distribution.* Marinda is a one-third partner in the MWH Partnership before she receives $100,000 cash as a liquidating distribution. Immediately before Marinda receives the distribution, the partnership has the following assets:

Assets	*Partnership's Basis*	*FMV*
Cash	$100,000	$100,000
Marketable securities	50,000	90,000
Investment land	90,000	140,000
Total	$240,000	$330,000

At the time of the distribution, the partnership has $30,000 of outstanding liabilities, which the three partners share equally. Marinda's basis in her partnership interest before the distribution was $80,000, which includes her share of liabilities. What are the amount and character of the gain or loss recognized by Marinda and the MWH Partnership on the liquidating distribution? Assume that no Sec. 754 election is in effect.

C:10-35 *Liquidating Distributions.* The AB Partnership pays its only liability (a $100,000 mortgage) on April 1 of the current year and terminates that same day. Alison and Bob were equal partners in the partnership but have partnership bases immediately preceding these transactions of $110,000 and $180,000, respectively, including his or her share of liabilities. The two partners receive identical distributions with each receiving the following assets:

Assets	*Partnership's Basis*	*FMV*
Cash	$ 20,000	$ 20,000
Inventory	33,000	35,000
Receivables	10,000	8,000
Building	40,000	60,000
Land	15,000	10,000
Total	$118,000	$133,000

The building has no depreciation recapture potential. What are the tax implications to Alison, Bob, and the AB Partnership of the April 1 transactions (i.e., basis of assets to Alison and Bob, amount and character of gain or loss recognized, etc.)? Assume that no Sec. 754 election is in effect.

C:10-36 *Liquidating Distribution.* The LQD Partnership distributes the following property to Larry in a distribution that liquidates Larry's interest in the partnership. Assume that no Sec. 754 election is in effect. Larry's basis in his partnership interest before the distribution is $40,000. The adjusted bases and FMVs of the distributed property to the partnership before the distribution are as follows:

Assets	*Partnership's Basis*	*FMV*
Cash	$ 2,500	$ 2,500
Inventory	8,000	9,000
Capital asset 1	10,000	15,000
Capital asset 2	15,000	17,500
Total	$35,500	$44,000

Note that Sec. 751 does not apply because the inventory is not substantially appreciated.

a. Determine Larry's basis in each distributed asset.
b. Same as Part a except Larry's partnership basis before the distribution is $46,500.
c. Same as Part b except the basis of capital asset 2 is $20,000 instead of $15,000.
d. Same as Part c except Larry's partnership basis before the distribution is $34,500.

C:10-37 *Sale of a Partnership Interest.* Pat, Kelly, and Yvette are equal partners in the PKY Partnership before Kelly sells her partnership interest. On January 1 of the current year, Kelly's basis in her partnership interest, including her share of liabilities, was $35,000. During January, the calendar year partnership earned $15,000 ordinary income and $6,000 of tax-exempt income. The partnership has a $60,000 recourse liability on January 1, and this amount remains constant throughout the tax year. Kelly's share of that liability is $20,000. The partnership has no other liabilities. Kelly sells her interest on February 1 to Margaret for a cash payment of $45,000. On the sale date the partnership had the following assets:

Assets	*Partnership's Basis*	*FMV*
Cash	$ 20,000	$ 20,000
Inventory	60,000	120,000
Building	36,000	40,000
Land	10,000	15,000
Total	$126,000	$195,000

The partnership has claimed $5,000 of depreciation on the building using the straight-line method.

a. What is Kelly's basis in her partnership interest on February 1 just before the sale?
b. What are the amount and character of Kelly's gain or loss on the sale?
c. What is Margaret's basis in her partnership interest?
d. What is the partnership's basis in its assets after the sale?

C:10-38 *Sale of Partnership Interest and Termination.* Clay owned 60% of the CAP Partnership and sold one-half of his interest (30%) to Steve for $75,000 cash. Before the sale, Clay's basis in his entire partnership interest was $168,000 including his $30,000 share of partnership liabilities and his share of income up to the sale date. Partnership assets on the sale date were

Assets	*Partnership's Basis*	*FMV*
Cash	$ 50,000	$ 50,000
Inventory	30,000	60,000
Land	200,000	190,000
Total	$280,000	$300,000

a. What are the amount and character of Clay's recognized gain or loss on the sale? What is his remaining basis in his partnership interest?
b. What is Steve's basis in his partnership interest?
c. How will the partnership's basis in its assets be affected?
d. How would your answers to Parts a and c change if Clay sold his entire interest to Steve for $150,000 cash?

C:10-39 *Sale of a Partnership Interest.* Alice, Bob, and Charles are one-third partners in the ABC Partnership. The partners originally formed the partnership with cash contributions, so no partner has precontribution gains or losses. Prior to Alice's sale of her partnership interest, the partnership has the following balance sheet:

	Partnership's Basis	*FMV*
Assets:		
Cash	$ 12,000	$ 12,000
Receivable	–0–	21,000
Inventory	57,000	72,000
Machinery[a]	90,000	132,000
Building[b]	120,000	165,000
Land	36,000	30,000
Investments[c]	15,000	48,000
Total	$330,000	$480,000

Liabilities and capital:		
Liabilities	$105,000	$105,000
Partners' capital:		
Alice	75,000	125,000
Bob	75,000	125,000
Charles	75,000	125,000
Total	$330,000	$480,000

[a]The machinery cost $126,000, and the partnership has claimed $36,000 of depreciation.
[b]The building cost $150,000, and the partnership has claimed $30,000 of straight-line depreciation.
[c]The partnership has held the investments for more than one year.

Alice has a $110,000 basis in her partnership interest including her share of partnership liabilities, and she sells her partnership interest to Darla for $125,000 cash.
a. What are the amount and character of Alice's recognized gain or loss on the sale?
b. What is Darla's basis in her partnership interest?

C:10-40 ***Retirement of a Partner.*** Suzanne retires from the BRS Partnership when the basis of her one-third interest is $105,000, which includes her share of liabilities. At the time of her retirement, the partnership had the following assets:

Assets	*Partnership's Basis*	*FMV*
Cash	$145,000	$145,000
Receivables	40,000	40,000
Land	130,000	220,000
Total	$315,000	$405,000

The partnership has $60,000 of liabilities when Suzanne retires. The partnership will pay Suzanne cash of $130,000 to retire her partnership interest.
a. What are the amount and character of the gain or loss Suzanne must recognize?
b. What is the impact of the retirement on the partnership and the remaining partners?

C:10-41 ***Retirement of a Partner.*** Brian owns 40% of the ABC Partnership before his retirement on April 15 of the current year. On that date, his basis in the partnership interest is $40,000 including his share of liabilities. The partnership's balance sheet on that date is as follows:

	Partnership's Basis	*FMV*
Assets:		
Cash	$ 60,000	$ 60,000
Receivables	24,000	24,000
Land	16,000	40,000
Total	$100,000	$124,000
Liabilities and capital:		
Liabilities	$ 20,000	$ 20,000
Capital—Abner	16,000	20,800
—Brian	32,000	41,600
—Charles	32,000	41,600
Total	$100,000	$124,000

What are the amount and character of gain or loss that Brian and the ABC Partnership recognize for the following independent retirement payments?
a. Brian receives $41,600 cash on April 15.
b. Brian receives $50,000 cash on April 15.

C:10-42 ***Retirement of a Partner.*** Kim retires from the KLM Partnership on January 1 of the current year. At that time, her basis in the partnership is $75,000, which includes her share of liabilities. The partnership reports the following balance sheet:

	Partnership's Basis	FMV
Assets:		
Cash	$100,000	$100,000
Receivables	30,000	30,000
Inventory	40,000	40,000
Land	55,000	100,000
Total	$225,000	$270,000
Liabilities and capital:		
Liabilities	$ 75,000	$ 75,000
Capital—Kim	50,000	65,000
—Larry	50,000	65,000
—Michael	50,000	65,000
Total	$225,000	$270,000

Explain the tax consequences (i.e., amount and character of gain or loss recognized and Kim's basis for any assets received) of the partnership making the retirement payments described in the following independent situations. Kim's share of liabilities is $25,000.

a. Kim receives $65,000 cash on January 1.
b. Kim receives $75,000 cash on January 1.

C:10-43 *Death of a Partner.* When Jerry died on April 16 of the current year, he owned a 40% interest in the JM Partnership, and Michael owns the remaining 60% interest. All his assets are held in his estate for a two-year period while the estate is being settled. Jerry's estate is his successor-in-interest for the partnership interest. Under a formula contained in the partnership agreement, the partnership must pay Jerry's successor-in-interest $40,000 cash shortly after his death plus $90,000 for each of the two years immediately following a partner's death. The partnership agreement provides that all payments to a retiring partner will first be payments for the partner's share of assets, and then any additional payments will be Sec. 736(a) payments. When Jerry died, the partnership had the following balance sheet:

	Partnership's Basis	FMV
Assets:		
Cash	$100,000	$100,000
Land	200,000	300,000
Total	$300,000	$400,000
Liabilities and capital:		
Liabilities	$ 75,000	$ 75,000
Capital—Jerry	90,000	130,000
—Michael	135,000	195,000
Total	$300,000	$400,000

Jerry's basis for the partnership interest on the date of his death was $120,000 including his $30,000 share of partnership liabilities.

a. How will the payments be taxed to Jerry's successor-in-interest?
b. What are the tax implications of the payments for the partnership?

C:10-44 *Death of a Partner.* Bruce died on June 1 of the current year. On the date of his death, he held a one-third interest in the ABC Partnership, which had a $100,000 basis including his share of liabilities. Under the partnership agreement, Bruce's successor-in-interest, his wife, is to receive the following amounts from the partnership: $130,000 cash, the partnership's assumption of Bruce's $20,000 share of partnership liabilities, plus 10% of partnership net income for the next three years. The partnership's balance sheet immediately before Bruce's death is as follows:

	Partnership's Basis	FMV
Assets:		
Cash	$100,000	$100,000
Receivables	90,000	90,000
Inventory	40,000	40,000
Land	70,000	220,000
Total	$300,000	$450,000
Liabilities and capital:		
Liabilities	$ 60,000	$ 60,000
Capital—Bruce	80,000	130,000
—Others	160,000	260,000
Total	$300,000	$450,000

a. What are the amount and character of the gain or loss that Bruce's wife must recognize when she receives the first year's payment?
b. What is the character of the gain recognized from the partnership interest when she receives the payments in each of the following three years?
c. When does Bruce's successor-in-interest cease to be a member of the partnership?

C:10-45 ***Liquidation or Sale of a Partnership Interest.*** John has a 60% capital and profits interest in the JAS Partnership with a basis of $333,600, which includes his share of liabilities, when he decides to retire. Andrew and Stephen want to continue the partnership's business. On the date John retires, the partnership's balance sheet is as follows:

	Partnership's Basis	FMV
Assets:		
Cash	$160,000	$160,000
Receivables	100,000	100,000
Building[a]	200,000	300,000
Land	96,000	180,000
Total	$556,000	$740,000
Liabilities and capital:		
Liabilities	$120,000	$120,000
Capital—John	261,600	372,000
—Andrew	87,200	124,000
—Stephen	87,200	124,000
Total	$556,000	$740,000

[a]The partnership has claimed $60,000 of straight-line depreciation on the building.

a. What are the tax implications for John, Andrew, Stephen, and the JAS Partnership if Andrew and Stephen each purchase one-half of John's partnership interest for a cash price of $186,000 each? Include in your answer the amount and character of the recognized gain or loss, basis of the partnership assets, and any other relevant tax implications.
b. What are the tax implications for John, Andrew, Stephen, and the JAS Partnership if the partnership pays John a liquidating distribution equal to 60% of each partnership asset other than cash plus $24,000 of cash? Assume the assets are easily divisible.

C:10-46 ***Liquidation or Sale of a Partnership Interest.*** Amy, a one-third partner, retires from the AJS Partnership on January 1 of the current year. Her basis in her partnership interest is $120,000 including her share of liabilities. Amy receives $160,000 in cash from the partnership for her interest. On that date, the partnership balance sheet is as follows:

	Partnership's Basis	FMV
Assets:		
Cash	$180,000	$180,000
Receivables	60,000	60,000
Land	120,000	300,000
Total	$360,000	$540,000

Liabilities and capital:		
Liabilities	$ 60,000	$ 60,000
Capital—Amy	100,000	160,000
—Joan	100,000	160,000
—Stephanie	100,000	160,000
Total	$360,000	$540,000

a. What are the amount and character of Amy's recognized gain or loss?
b. How would your answers to Part a change if Joan and Stephanie each purchased one-half of Amy's partnership interest for $80,000 cash instead of having the partnership distribute the $160,000 in cash to Amy?

C:10-47 *Exchange of Partnership Interests.* Josh holds a general partnership interest in the JLK Partnership having a $40,000 basis and a $60,000 FMV. The JLK Partnership is a limited partnership that engages in real estate activities. Diana has an interest in the CDE Partnership having a $20,000 basis and a $60,000 FMV. The CDE Partnership is a general partnership that also engages in real estate activities. Neither partnership has any Sec. 751 assets or any liabilities.
a. What are the tax implications if Josh and Diana simply exchange their partnership interests?
b. What are the tax implications if instead Diana exchanges her general partnership interest in the CDE Partnership for a limited partnership interest in the same partnership (and Josh retains his general partnership interest in the JLK Partnership)?

C:10-48 *Termination of a Partnership.* Wendy, Xenia, and Yancy own 40%, 8%, and 52%, respectively, of the WXY Partnership. For each of the following independent situations occurring in the current year, determine whether the WXY Partnership terminates and, if so, the date on which the termination occurs.
a. Wendy sells her entire interest to Alan on June 1. Alan sells one-half of the interest to Beth on November 15.
b. Yancy receives a series of liquidating distributions totaling $100,000. He receives four equal annual payments on January 1 of the current year and the three subsequent years.
c. Wendy and Xenia each receive a liquidating distribution on September 14.
d. Yancy sells his interest to Karen on June 1 for $10,000 cash and a $90,000 installment note. The note will be paid in monthly installments of $10,000 principal plus interest (at a rate acceptable to the IRS) beginning on July 1.
e. The WXY and ABC Partnerships combine their businesses on December 30. Ownership of the new, combined partnership is as follows: Wendy, 20%; Xenia, 4%; Yancy, 26.5%; Albert, 20%; Beth, 19.5%; and Carl, 10%.
f. On January 1, the WXY Partnership divides its business into two new businesses. The WX Partnership is owned equally by Wendy and Xenia. Yancy continues his share of the business as a sole proprietorship.

C:10-49 *Termination of a Partnership.* For each of the following independent situations, determine which partnership(s) (if any) terminate and which partnership(s) (if any) continue.
a. The KLMN Partnership is created when the KL Partnership merges with the MN Partnership. The ownership of the new partnership is held 25% by Katie, 30% by Laura, 25% by Michael, and 20% by Neal.
b. The ABC Partnership, with $150,000 in assets, is owned equally by Amy, Beth, and Chuck. The CD Partnership, with $100,000 in assets, is owned equally by Chuck and Drew. The two partnerships merge, and the resulting ABCD Partnership is owned as follows: Amy, 20%; Beth, 20%; Chuck, 40%; and Drew, 20%.
c. The WXYZ Partnership results when the WX and YZ Partnerships merge. Ownership of WXYZ is held equally by the four partners. WX contributes $140,000 in assets, and YZ contributes $160,000 in assets to the new partnership.
d. The DEFG Partnership is owned 20% by Dawn, 40% by Eve, 30% by Frank, and 10% by Greg. Two new partnerships are formed by the division of DEFG. The two new partnerships, the DE and FG Partnerships, are owned in proportion to their relative interests in the DEFG Partnership by the individuals for whom they are named.
e. The HIJK Partnership is owned equally by its four partners, Hal, Isaac, Juan, and Katherine, before its division. Two new partnerships, the HI and JK Partnerships, are formed out of the division with the new partnerships owned equally by the partners for whom they are named.

C:10-50 *Disposal of a Tax Shelter.* Maria purchased an interest in a real estate tax shelter many years ago and deducted losses from its operation for several years. The real property owned by the tax shelter when Maria made her investment has been fully depreciated on a straight-line basis. Her basis in her limited partnership interest is zero, but her share of partnership liabilities is $100,000. Explain the tax results if Maria sells her partnership interest for $5 cash.

C:10-51 *Optional Basis Adjustment.* Patty pays $100,000 cash for Stan's one-third interest in the STU Partnership. The partnership has a Sec. 754 election in effect. Just before the sale of Stan's interest, STU's balance sheet appears as follows:

	Partnership's Basis	*FMV*
Assets:		
Cash	$ 80,000	$ 80,000
Land	160,000	220,000
Total	$240,000	$300,000
Partners' capital:		
Stan	$ 80,000	$100,000
Traffic Corporation	80,000	100,000
Union Corporation	80,000	100,000
Total	$240,000	$300,000

a. What is Patty's total optional basis adjustment?
b. If STU Partnership sells the land for its $220,000 FMV immediately after Patty purchases her interest, how much gain or loss will the partnership recognize?
c. How much gain will Patty report as a result of the sale?

C:10-52 *Mandatory Basis Adjustment.* The JKL Partnership has three equal partners, Jingjing, Kevin, and Latisha. Latisha sells her interest to Larry for $690,000. The partnership does not have a Sec. 754 election in effect. Just before the sale of Latisha's interest, the partnership's balance sheet appears as follows:

	Partnership's Basis	*FMV*
Assets:		
Inventory	$ 800,000	$1,070,000
Land	1,600,000	1,000,000
Total	$2,400,000	$2,070,000
Partners' capital:		
Jingjing	$ 800,000	$ 690,000
Kevin	800,000	690,000
Latisha	800,000	690,000
Total	$2,400,000	$2,070,000

a. What is Latisha's recognized net loss on the sale, and what is the character of its components?
b. What is Larry's mandatory basis adjustment?

C:10-53 *Taxation of LLC Income.* ABC Company, a limited liability company (LLC) organized in the state of Florida, reports using a calendar tax year-end. The LLC chooses to be taxed as a partnership. Alex, Bob, and Carrie (all calendar year taxpayers) own ABC equally, and each has a basis of $40,000 in his or her ABC interest on the first day of the current tax year. ABC has the following results for the current year's operation:

Operating income	$30,000
Short-term capital gain	12,000
Long-term capital loss	6,000

Each owner received a $12,000 cash distribution during the current year.
a. What are the amount and character of the income, gain, and loss Alex must report on his tax return as a result of ABC's operations?
b. What is Alex's basis in his ownership interest in ABC after the current year's operations?

C:10-54 *Electing Large Partnership.* Austin & Becker is an electing large partnership. During the current year, the partnership has the following income, loss, and deduction items:

Ordinary income	$5,200,000
Rental loss	(2,000,000)
Long-term capital loss from investments	(437,100)
Short-term capital gain from investments	827,400
Charitable contributions	164,000

a. What ordinary income will Austin & Becker report?
b. What are the separately stated items for Austin & Becker?

C:10-55 *Electing Large Partnership.* Happy Times Film Distributions is an electing large partnership. During the current year, the partnership has the following income, loss, and deduction items:

Ordinary income	$ 700,000
Passive income	3,000,000
Sec. 1231 gains	27,000
Sec. 1231 losses	(134,800)
Long-term capital gains from investments	437,600
General business tax credits	43,000

a. What ordinary income will Happy Times report?
b. What are the separately stated items reported by Happy Times?

COMPREHENSIVE PROBLEMS

C:10-56 Refer to the facts in Comprehensive Problem C:6-54. Now assume the entity is a partnership named Lifecycle Partnership. Additional facts are as follows:

- Except for precontribution gains and losses, the partners agree to share profits and losses in a 60% (Able)—40% (Baker) ratio.
- The partners actively and materially participate in the partnership's business. Thus, the partnership is not a passive activity.
- Partnership debt is recourse debt.
- The salary to Able is a guaranteed payment.
- The refund for the NOL is not relevant to the partnership, nor are the E&P numbers.
- In addition to the numbers provided for the assets on January 2, 2020, the following partnership book values apply:

Equipment	$ 215,000
Building	926,000
Land A	30,000
Land B	20,000
Total	$1,191,000

- On January 2, 2020, the partnership sells its assets and pays off the $1.87 million debt. The partnership then makes liquidating distributions of the $490,000 remaining cash to Able and Baker in accordance with their book capital account balances.

Required:

a. Determine the tax consequences of the partnership formation to Able, Baker, and Lifecycle Partnership.
b. For 2017 through 2019, prepare a schedule showing:
   (1) Partnership ordinary income and other separately stated items
   (2) Able's and Baker's book capital accounts at the end of 2017, 2018, and 2019
   (3) Able's and Baker's bases in their partnership interests at the end of 2017, 2018, and 2019

c. For 2020, determine:
   (1) The results of the asset sales
   (2) Able's and Baker's book capital accounts after the asset sales but before the final liquidating distribution
   (3) Able's and Baker's bases in their partnership interests after the asset sales but before the final liquidating distribution
   (4) The results of the liquidating distributions, assuming a 23.8% tax rate (the 20% maximum capital gain rate plus the 3.8% rate on net investment income)

C:10-57 Anne decides to leave the ABC Partnership after owning the interest for many years. She owns a 52% capital, profits, and loss interest in the general partnership (which is not a service partnership). Anne's basis in her partnership interest is $120,000 just before she leaves the partnership. The partnership agreement does not mention payments to partners who leave the partnership. The partnership has not made an optional basis adjustment election (Sec. 754). All partnership liabilities are recourse liabilities, and Anne's share is equal to her loss interest. When Anne leaves the partnership, the assets and liabilities for the partnership are as follows:

	Partnership's Basis	*FMV*
Assets:		
Cash	$240,000	$240,000
Receivables	–0–	64,000
Inventory	24,000	24,000
Land	60,000	100,000
Total	$324,000	$428,000
Liabilities	$ 60,000	$ 60,000

Analyze the following two alternatives, and answer the associated questions for each alternative.

a. Anne could receive a cash payment of $220,000 from the partnership to terminate her interest in the partnership. Does Anne or the partnership have any income, deduction, gain, or loss? Determine both the amount and character of any items.
b. Carrie already owns a 30% general interest in the ABC partnership prior to Anne's departure. Carrie is willing to buy Anne's partnership interest for a cash payment of $220,000. What income, gain, loss, or deduction will Anne recognize on the sale? What are the tax implications for the partnership if Carrie buys Anne's interest?

TAX STRATEGY PROBLEM

C:10-58 Consider the following balance sheet for DEF Partnership:

	Partnership's Basis	*FMV*
Assets:		
Cash	$60,000	$ 60,000
Receivables	–0–	60,000
Land A	10,000	20,000
Land B	10,000	20,000
Land C	10,000	20,000
Total	$90,000	$180,000
Partners' capital:		
Daniel	$30,000	$ 60,000
Edward	30,000	60,000
Frances	30,000	60,000
Total	$90,000	$180,000

Note: Land A, B, and C are Sec. 1231 property, and each partner's outside basis is $30,000.

Suppose Daniel wishes to exit the partnership completely. After discussions with Edward and Frances, the partners agree to let Daniel choose one of three options:

1. Daniel takes a liquidating distribution of $60,000 cash.
2. Daniel takes a pro rata liquidating distribution of $20,000 cash, $20,000 receivables, and Land A (FMV $20,000).

3. Daniel sells his entire partnership interest to Doris for $60,000 cash.
   Required:
a. Determine the tax consequences to Daniel of each option including gains (losses) realized, recognized, and deferred; character of gains (losses); and bases of assets.
b. Discuss the relative merits of each option to Daniel, that is, what are the advantages and disadvantages of each option? What factors could sway your recommendation one way or the other?

Note: See Case Study Problem C:10-59 for another situation involving various exit strategies.

CASE STUDY PROBLEM

C:10-59 Mark Green and his brother Michael purchased land in Orlando, Florida many years ago. At that time, they began their investing as Green Brothers Partnership with capital they obtained from placing second mortgages on their homes. Their investments have flourished both because of the prosperity and growth of the area and because they have shown an ability to select prime real estate for others to develop. Over the years, they have acquired a great amount of land and have sold some to developers.

Their current tax year has just closed, and the partnership has the following balance sheet:

	Partnership's Basis	*FMV*
Assets:		
Cash	$200,000	$ 200,000
Accounts receivable	90,000	90,000
Land held for investment	310,000	1,010,000
Total	$600,000	$1,300,000
Liabilities and capital:		
Mortgages	$400,000	$ 400,000
Capital—Mark	100,000	450,000
—Michael	100,000	450,000
Total	$600,000	$1,300,000

Mark and Michael each have a basis in their partnership interest of $300,000 including their share of liabilities. They share the economic risk of loss from the liabilities equally. Last spring, Mark had a serious heart attack. On his doctor's advice, Mark wants to retire from all business activity and terminate his interest in the partnership. He is interested in receiving some cash now but is not averse to receiving part of his payment over time.

You have been asked to provide the brothers with information on how to terminate Mark's interest in the partnership. Several possibilities have occurred to Mark and Michael, and they want your advice as to which is best for Mark from a tax standpoint. Michael understands that the resulting choice may not be the best option for him. The possibilities they have considered include the following:

- Michael has substantial amounts of personal cash and could purchase Mark's interest directly. However, the brothers think that option probably would take almost all the cash Michael could raise, and they are concerned about any future cash needs Michael might have. They would prefer to have Mark receive $120,000 now plus $110,000 per year for each of the next three years. Mark also would receive interest at a market rate on the outstanding debt. This alternative would qualify for installment reporting. However, the installment sale rules for related parties would apply.
- The partnership could retire Mark's interest. They have considered the option of paying Mark $150,000 now plus 50% of partnership profits for the next three years. Alternatively, they could arrange for Mark to have a $150,000 payment now and a guaranteed payment of $100,000 per year for the next three years. They expect that the dollar amounts to be received by Mark would be approximately the same for the next three years under these two options. Mark also would receive interest at a market rate on any deferred payments.
- John Watson, a long-time friend of the family, has expressed an interest in buying Mark's interest for $450,000 cash immediately. Michael and John are comfortable that they could work well together.

Mark has substantial amounts of money in savings accounts and in stocks and bonds that have a ready market. He has invested in no other business directly. Assume that, for each year, Mark's ordinary tax rate is 33% and his capital gains tax rate is 18.8% (the 15% capital gain rate for his tax bracket plus the 3.8% rate on net investment income).

Required: Prepare a memorandum summarizing the advice you would give the two brothers on the options that they have considered.

TAX RESEARCH PROBLEMS

C:10-60 Arnie, Becky, and Clay are equal partners in the ABC General Partnership. The three individuals each have a $120,000 tax basis in their partnership interest. For business reasons, the partnership needs to be changed into the ABC Corporation, and all three owners agree to the change. The partnership is expected to have the following assets on the date that the change is to occur:

Assets	*Partnership's Tax Basis & Book Value*	*FMV*
Cash	$ 50,000	$ 50,000
Accounts receivable	60,000	55,000
Inventory	150,000	200,000
Land	100,000	295,000
Total	$360,000	$600,000

Liabilities of $75,000 are currently outstanding. The liabilities are shared equally and are already included in the $120,000 bases of the partnership interests. The structure being considered for making the change is as follows:

- ABC Partnership transfers all its assets and liabilities to the new ABC Corporation in exchange for all the corporation's stock.
- ABC Partnership then liquidates by distributing the ABC stock to Arnie, Becky, and Clay.

Required: The tax manager you work for has asked you to determine the tax and financial accounting consequences. Describe the financial and tax treatments in a short memorandum to the partnership. Be sure to mention any relevant IRC sections, Treasury Regulations, revenue rulings, and accounting standards. Assume a 35% corporate tax rate.

C:10-61 Della retires from the BCD General Partnership when her basis in her partnership interest is $70,000 including her $10,000 share of liabilities. The partnership is in the business of providing house cleaning services for local residences. At the date of Della's retirement, the partnership's balance sheet is as follows:

	Partnership's Basis	*FMV*
Assets:		
Cash	$ 50,000	$ 50,000
Receivables	–0–	30,000
Equipment[a]	40,000	50,000
Building[b]	90,000	100,000
Land	30,000	40,000
Total	$210,000	$270,000
Liabilities and capital:		
Liabilities	$ 30,000	$ 30,000
Capital—Bruce	60,000	80,000
—Celia	60,000	80,000
—Della	60,000	80,000
Total	$210,000	$270,000

[a]If the equipment were sold for $50,000, the entire gain would be recaptured as Sec. 1245 ordinary income.
[b]The building has been depreciated using the straight-line method.

Della will receive payments of $20,000 cash plus 5% of partnership ordinary income for each of the next five years. The partnership agreement specifies that goodwill will be paid for when a partner retires. Bruce, Celia, and Della agree that the partnership has $21,000 in goodwill when Della retires and that she will be paid for her one-third share.

Required: A tax manager in your firm has asked you to determine the amount and character of the income Della must report for each of the next five years. In addition, he wants you to research the tax consequences of the retirement on the partnership for the next five years. (Assume the partnership earns $100,000 of ordinary income each year for the next five years.) Prepare an oral presentation to be made to Della explaining the tax consequences of the payments she will receive.

C:10-62 Pedro owns a 60% interest in the PD General Partnership having a $40,000 basis and $200,000 FMV. His share of partnership liabilities is $100,000. Because he is nearing retirement age, he has decided to give away his partnership interest on June 15 of the current year. The partnership's tax year ends on December 31. Pedro's tax year ends on June 30. He intends to give a 30% interest to his son, Juan, and the remaining 30% interest to the American Red Cross.

Required: A tax manager in your firm has asked you to prepare a letter to Pedro explaining fully the tax consequences of this gift to him, the partnership, and the donees. She reminds you to be sure to include information about the allocation of the current year's partnership income.

C:10-63 Frank, Greta, and Helen each have a one-third interest in the FGH Partnership. On December 31, 2016, the partnership reported the following balance sheet:

	Partnership's Basis	*FMV*
Assets:		
Cash	$120,000	$120,000
Asset 1	262,380	360,000
Asset 2	115,200	90,000
Total	$497,580	$570,000
Partners' Capital:		
Frank	$165,860	$190,000
Greta	165,860	190,000
Helen	165,860	190,000
Total	$497,580	$570,000

The partnership placed Asset 1 (seven-year property) in service in 2014 and Asset 2 (five-year property) in service in 2015. The partnership did not elect Sec. 179 expensing and elected out of bonus depreciation in both years. Accordingly, it computed the assets' adjusted bases at December 31, 2016 as follows:

		Asset 1		*Asset 2*
Cost		$600,000		$240,000
Depreciation:				
2014	$85,740			
2015	146,940		$48,000	
2016	104,940	(337,620)	76,800	(124,800)
Adjusted basis		$262,380		$115,200

At the end of business on December 31, 2016, Helen sold her partnership interest to Hank for $190,000. At the time of sale, the partnership had a Sec. 754 optional basis election in effect but has not elected to use the remedial method for allocating partnership items.

Required: The partners have asked you to determine (1) the amount and character of Helen's gain or loss; (2) Hank's optional basis adjustment and its allocation to Asset 1 and Asset 2; and (3) the amount of depreciation allocated to Hank in 2017, including the effects of the optional basis adjustment. At a minimum, you should consult the following resources:

- IRC Secs. 743 and 751
- Reg. Sec. 1.743-1(j)
- Reg. Sec. 1.755-1

CHAPTER 11

S CORPORATIONS

LEARNING OBJECTIVES

After studying this chapter, you should be able to

1. Discuss the advantages and disadvantages of making the S election
2. List the requirements for being eligible to elect S corporation status
3. Explain how a corporation elects, revokes, or terminates S corporation status
4. Classify an S corporation's ordinary and separately stated items, and calculate special S corporation taxes
5. Allocate an S corporation's ordinary and separately stated items to its shareholders and apply loss limitation rules
6. Calculate a shareholder's basis in his or her S corporation stock and debt
7. Determine the taxability of an S corporation's distributions to its shareholders
8. Explain other rules that pertain to S corporations
9. Identify tax planning opportunities for an S corporation and its shareholders
10. Comply with S corporation procedural and filing requirements

CHAPTER OUTLINE

This chapter discusses a special type of corporate entity known as an S corporation. The S corporation rules, located in Subchapter S of the Internal Revenue Code, permit small corporations to enjoy the nontax advantages of the corporate form of organization without being subject to the possible tax disadvantages of the corporate form (e.g., double taxation when the corporation pays a dividend to its shareholders). When enacting these rules, Congress stated three purposes:

- To permit businesses to select a particular form of business organization without being influenced by tax considerations
- To provide aid for small businesses by allowing the income of the business to be taxed to shareholders rather than being taxed at the corporate level
- To permit corporations realizing losses to obtain a tax benefit of offsetting the losses against income at the shareholder level[1]

As discussed in Chapter C:2, S corporations are treated as corporations for legal and business purposes. For federal income tax purposes, however, they are treated much like partnerships.[2] As in a partnership, the profits and losses of the S corporation pass through to the owners, and the S corporation can make nontaxable distributions of earnings previously taxed to its shareholders. Although generally taxed like a partnership, the S corporation still follows many of the basic Subchapter C tax provisions (e.g., S corporations use the corporate tax rules regarding formations, liquidations, and nontaxable reorganizations instead of the partnership rules). A tabular comparison of the S corporation, partnership, and C corporation rules appears in Appendix F.

ADDITIONAL COMMENT

An LLC (or partnership) that wishes to be treated as an S corporation can file the S election (Form 2553) and automatically be classified as an association (corporation) under the check-the-box regulations without having to file the entity classification election (Form 8832).

Changes over the past several years have caused many businesses to reexamine the implications of an S election. First, the restrictive nature of the S corporation requirements has caused many new businesses that were potential S corporations to look at alternative business forms. All 50 states have adopted limited liability company (LLC) legislation. LLCs offer many of the same tax advantages of S corporations because they are treated as partnerships. LLCs, however, are not subject to the same requirements that an S corporation and its shareholders must satisfy to make and retain an S election. Partially because of the S corporation restrictions, some new businesses have organized as LLCs to take advantage of the greater operational flexibility the LLC form provides the entity and its owners, as well as its liability protection. A number of small businesses, however, elected to be S corporations because of the greater certainty available within the legal system for corporate entities.

Over the last several years, tax legislation has relaxed restrictions and increased the S corporation's popularity. For example, the shareholder limit was increased to 100, and the prohibitions against certain entities and trusts becoming S corporation shareholders were lessened. Moreover, current law now treats family members as one shareholder for the 100-shareholder limit. In effect, these changes have reduced some of the differences between S corporations and LLCs and have renewed interest in the S corporation form of doing business.

For many existing C corporations, the tax cost of liquidating the corporate entity and creating an LLC may be a prohibitively expensive way to avoid the corporate level income tax (see Chapter C:6). However, many of these C corporations have taken the next best alternative, that is, making an S election.

This chapter examines the requirements for making an S election and the tax rules that apply to S corporations and their shareholders.

[1] S. Rept. No. 1983, 85th Cong., 2d Sess., p. 87 (1958).

[2] Some states do not recognize an S corporation as a conduit for state income tax purposes. Instead, they are taxed under the state income tax laws in the same manner as a C corporation.

Should an S Election Be Made?

OBJECTIVE 1

Discuss the advantages and disadvantages of making the S election

Advantages of S Corporation Treatment

A number of advantages are available to a corporation that makes an S election.

- The corporation's income is exempt from the corporate income tax. An S corporation's income is taxed only to its shareholders, whose tax bracket may be lower than a C corporation's tax bracket.
- The corporation's losses pass through to its shareholders and can be used to reduce the taxes owed on other types of income. This feature can be especially important for new businesses. The corporation can make an S election, pass through the start-up losses to the owners, and terminate the election once a C corporation becomes advantageous.
- Undistributed income taxed to the shareholder is not taxed again when subsequently distributed unless the distribution exceeds the shareholder's basis for his or her stock.
- Capital gains, dividends, and tax-exempt income are separately stated and retain their character when passed through to the shareholders. Such amounts become commingled with other corporate earnings and are taxed as dividends when distributed by a C corporation. However, the applicable capital gains tax rate on qualified dividends may alleviate the detrimental tax effect of C corporation dividends.
- Deductions, losses, and tax credits are separately stated and retain their character when passed through to the shareholders. These amounts may be subject to the various limitations at the shareholder level. This treatment can permit the shareholder to claim a tax benefit when it otherwise would be denied to the corporation (e.g., a shareholder can claim the general business credit benefit even though the S corporation reports a substantial loss for the year).
- Splitting the S corporation's income among family members is possible. However, income splitting is restricted by the requirement that reasonable compensation be provided to family members who provide capital and services to the S corporation.
- An S corporation's earnings that pass through to the individual shareholders are not subject to the self-employment tax. In contrast, a partnership must determine what portion of each general partner's net earnings constitutes self-employment income.
- An S corporation is not subject to the personal holding company tax or the accumulated earnings tax (although, as discussed later, passive income can trigger a corporate-level tax in special circumstances).

ADDITIONAL COMMENT

The applicable capital gains tax rate for net capital gains and qualified dividends of noncorporate taxpayers is 0% for taxpayers in tax brackets of 15% and below, 15% for taxpayers in the 25% through 35% tax brackets, and 20% for taxpayers in the 39.6% tax bracket. Also, 25% and 28% rates apply for gains on certain types of property. In addition, an incremental 3.8% rate applies to net investment income for taxpayers whose modified AGI exceeds $200,000 ($250,000 for married filing jointly). Net investment income includes, among other things, interest, dividends, annuities, royalties, rents, and net gains from the disposition of property not used in a trade or business, all reduced by deductions allocable to such income or gains.

REAL-WORLD EXAMPLE

The number of S corporations has grown from 725,000 in 1985 to 4.7 million in 2015.

Disadvantages of S Corporation Treatment

A number of tax disadvantages also exist for a corporation that makes an S election.

- A C corporation is treated as a separate tax entity from its shareholders, thereby permitting its first $50,000 of income to be taxed at a 15% marginal rate instead of the shareholder's marginal rate.
- The S corporation's earnings are taxed to the shareholders even though they are not distributed. This treatment may require the corporation to make distributions or salary payments so the shareholder can pay taxes owed on the S corporation's earnings.
- S corporations are subject to an excess net passive income tax and a built-in gains tax. Partnerships are not subject to either of these taxes.
- Dividends received by the S corporation are not eligible for the dividends-received deduction, as is the case for a C corporation.
- Allocation of ordinary income or loss and the separately stated items is based on the stock owned on each day of the tax year. Special allocations of particular items are not permitted, as they are in a partnership.

KEY POINT

The structure of an S corporation can create a real hardship for a shareholder if large amounts of income pass through without any compensation payments or distributions of cash to help pay the tax on the income.

- The loss limitation for an S corporation shareholder is smaller than for a partner in a partnership because of the treatment of liabilities. Shareholders can increase their loss limitations by the basis of any debt they loan to the S corporation. Partners, on the other hand, can increase their loss limitation by their ratable share of all partnership liabilities.
- S corporations and their shareholders are subject to the at-risk, passive activity limitation, and hobby loss rules. C corporations generally are not subject to these rules.
- An S corporation is somewhat restricted in the type and number of shareholders it can have and the capital structure it can use. Partnerships and C corporations are not so restricted.
- S corporations must use a calendar year as their tax year unless they can establish a business purpose for a fiscal year or unless they make a special election to use an otherwise nonpermitted tax year. Similar restrictions also apply to partnerships.

TAX STRATEGY TIP

With the top 39.6 % individual marginal tax rate now above the top 35% corporate marginal tax rate (ignoring the 39% and 38% bubble ranges), S corporations with positive income may be less attractive to high-bracket individuals than would C corporations, but S corporations with losses may be more attractive than would C corporations. Assuming an S corporation shareholder has sufficient offsetting income (and loss limitations do not apply), he or she could use the loss pass-through immediately at a high tax savings whereas a C corporation might have to carry over the loss to offset income in later years at perhaps a low tax savings.

Once the owners decide to incorporate, no general rule determines whether the corporation should make an S election. Before making a decision, management and the shareholders should examine the long- and short-run tax and nontax advantages and disadvantages of filing as a C corporation versus filing as an S corporation. Unlike a consolidated return election, the S election can be revoked or terminated at any time with minimal effort.

S CORPORATION REQUIREMENTS

OBJECTIVE 2

List the requirements for being eligible to elect S corporation status

The S corporation requirements are divided into two categories: shareholder-related and corporation-related requirements. A corporation that satisfies all the requirements is known as a small business corporation. Only small business corporations can make an S election. Each set of requirements is outlined below.

SHAREHOLDER-RELATED REQUIREMENTS

Three shareholder-related requirements must be satisfied on each day of the tax year.[3]

- The corporation must not have more than 100 shareholders.
- All shareholders must be individuals, estates, certain tax-exempt organizations, or certain kinds of trusts.
- None of the individual shareholders can be classified as a nonresident **alien.**

ADDITIONAL COMMENT

The Sec. 1244 stock rules (Chapter C:2) and the S corporation rules both use the term *small business corporations.* The definitions have different requirements, although most S corporation stock can qualify as Sec. 1244 stock.

100-Shareholder Rule. For purposes of applying the 100-shareholder limit, members of a family (and their estates) count as one shareholder. Members of a family include the common ancestor, lineal descendants of the common ancestor, spouses (or former spouses) of the common ancestor or lineal descendents, and estates of family members. An individual will not be considered a common ancestor if he or she is more than six generations removed from the youngest generation of family member shareholders. When two unmarried or nonfamily individuals own stock jointly (e.g., as tenants in common or as joint tenants), each owner is considered a separate shareholder.

REAL-WORLD EXAMPLE

In 2013, 63.4% of all S corporations had one owner. Only 0.11% of the 4.3 million S corporations that filed in 2013 had more than 30 owners.

Eligible Shareholders. C corporations and partnerships cannot own S corporation stock. This restriction prevents a corporation or a partnership having a large number of owners from avoiding the 100-shareholder limitation by purchasing S corporation stock and being treated as a single shareholder. Organizations exempt from the federal

[3] Sec. 1361.

income tax under Sec. 501(a) (e.g., a tax-exempt public charity or private foundation) can hold S corporation stock, and each such organization counts as one shareholder when calculating the 100-shareholder limit.

Seven types of trusts can own S corporation stock: grantor trusts, voting trusts,[4] testamentary trusts, **qualified Subchapter S trusts** (QSSTs),[5] qualified retirement plan trusts, small business trusts, and beneficiary-controlled trusts (i.e., trusts that distribute all their income to a single income beneficiary who is treated as the owner of the trust). Grantor trusts, QSSTs, and beneficiary-controlled trusts can own S corporation stock only if the grantor or the beneficiary is a qualified shareholder. Each beneficiary of a voting trust also must be an eligible shareholder. A qualified retirement plan trust is one formed as part of a qualified stock bonus, pension, or profit sharing plan or employee stock ownership plan (ESOP) that is exempt from the federal income tax under Sec. 501(a).

ETHICAL POINT

Tax professionals must assist their clients in monitoring that the S corporation requirements are met on each day of the tax year. Failing to meet one of the requirements for even one day terminates the election. Ignoring a terminating event until the IRS discovers it upon an audit probably will cause the corporation to be taxed as a C corporation and prevent it from having the termination treated as being inadvertent.

Small business trusts can own S corporation stock. These trusts can be complex trusts and primarily are used as estate planning devices. No interest in a small business trust can be acquired in a purchase transaction, that is, a transaction where the holder's interest takes a cost basis under Sec. 1012. Interests in small business trusts generally are acquired as a result of a gift or bequest. All current beneficiaries of a small business trust must be individuals, estates, or charitable organizations. Current beneficiaries are parties that can receive an income distribution for the period in question. Each beneficiary counts separately for purposes of the 100-shareholder limit. QSSTs and tax-exempt trusts are ineligible to elect to be a small business trust. The trustee must make an election to obtain small business trust status.

A testamentary trust (i.e., a trust created under the terms of a will) that receives S corporation stock can hold the stock and continue to be an eligible shareholder for a two-year period, beginning on the date the stock transfers to the trust. A grantor trust that held S corporation stock immediately before the death of the deemed owner, and which continues in existence after the death of the deemed owner, can continue to hold the stock and be an eligible shareholder for the two-year period beginning on the date of the deemed owner's death. Charitable remainder unitrusts and charitable remainder annuity trusts do not qualify as small business trusts.

EXAMPLE C:11-1 ▶ Joan, a U.S. citizen, owns 25% of Walden Corporation's stock. Walden is an S corporation. At the time of Joan's death in the current year, the Walden stock passes to her estate. The estate is a qualifying shareholder, and the transfer does not affect the S election. If the stock subsequently transfers to a trust provided for in Joan's will, the testamentary trust can hold the Walden stock for a two-year period before the S election terminates. ◀

The trust in Example C:11-1 can hold the S corporation stock for an indefinite period only if the trust's income beneficiary makes an election to have it treated as a QSST or small business trust. Otherwise, the S election terminates at the end of the two-year period.

Alien Individuals. Individuals who are not U.S. citizens (i.e., alien individuals) can own S corporation stock only if they are U.S. residents or are married to a U.S. citizen or resident alien and make an election to be taxed as a resident alien. The S election terminates if an alien individual purchases S corporation stock and does not reside in the United States or has not made the appropriate election.

CORPORATION-RELATED REQUIREMENTS

The corporation must satisfy the following three requirements on each day of the tax year:

---

[4] A **voting trust** is an arrangement whereby the stock owned by a number of shareholders is placed under the control of a trustee, who exercises the voting rights possessed by the stock. One reason for creating a voting trust is to increase the voting power of a group of minority shareholders in the selection of corporate directors or the establishment of corporate policies.

[5] A QSST is a domestic trust that owns stock in one or more S corporations and distributes (or is required to distribute) all its income to its sole income beneficiary. The income beneficiary must make an irrevocable election to have the QSST rules of Sec. 1361(d) apply. The beneficiary is treated as the owner (and, therefore, the shareholder) of the portion of the trust consisting of the S corporation stock. A separate election is made for each S corporation's stock owned by the trust.

ADDITIONAL COMMENT

An unincorporated eligible entity that makes a valid S election is automatically treated as making an election to be treated as a corporation under the check-the-box regulations. Thus, the entity does not have to make two separate elections.

- The corporation must be a domestic corporation or an unincorporated entity that elects to be treated as a corporation under the check-the-box regulations.
- The corporation must not be an "ineligible" corporation.
- The corporation must have only one class of stock.[6]

The first requirement precludes a foreign corporation from making an S election.

A corporation may be an ineligible corporation and thereby violate the second requirement in one of two ways:

- Corporations that maintain a special federal income tax status are not eligible to make an S election. For example, financial institutions (e.g., banks) that use the reserve method to account for bad debts and insurance companies are not eligible.
- Corporations that have elected the special Puerto Rico and U.S. possessions tax credit (Sec. 936) or that had elected the special Domestic International Sales Corporation tax exemption are ineligible to make the S election.

ADDITIONAL COMMENT

Current S corporation stock ownership rules and the approval of the check-the-box regulations permit great flexibility in creating groups of entities that fit the business needs of their owners.

S corporations can own the stock of a C corporation without any limitation on the percentage of voting power or value held. However, as mentioned earlier, a C corporation cannot own the stock of an S corporation. An S corporation that owns the stock of a C corporation cannot participate in the filing of a consolidated tax return. An S corporation also can own the stock of a **Qualified Subchapter S Subsidiary (QSub)**. A QSub is a domestic corporation that qualifies as an S corporation, is 100% owned by an S corporation, and for which the parent S corporation elects to treat the subsidiary as a QSub. The assets, liabilities, income, deductions, losses, etc. of the QSub are treated as those of its S corporation parent and reported on the parent's tax return.[7]

A corporation that has two classes of stock issued and outstanding has violated the third requirement and cannot be an S corporation. The single class of stock determination is more difficult than it appears at first glance because of the many different financial arrangements that are possible between an S corporation and its shareholders. A corporation is treated as having only one class of stock if all of its outstanding shares of stock possess identical rights to distribution and liquidation proceeds and the corporation has not issued any instrument or obligation, or entered into any arrangement, that is treated as a second class of stock.[8] A second class of stock is not created if the only difference between the two classes of stock pertains to voting rights.[9]

EXAMPLE C:11-2 ▶ Kelly Corporation has two classes of common stock outstanding. The Class A and Class B common stock give the shareholders identical rights and interests in the profits and assets of the corporation. Class A stock has one vote per share. Class B stock is nonvoting. Kelly Corporation is treated as having only one class of stock outstanding and can make an S election. ◀

General Rules. The determination of whether all outstanding shares of stock confer identical rights to distribution and liquidation proceeds is based on the corporate charter, articles of incorporation, bylaws, applicable state law, and binding agreements relating to distribution and liquidation proceeds (i.e., the governing agreements).[10] Treasury Regulations permit certain types of state laws, agreements, distributions, etc., to be disregarded in determining whether all of a corporation's outstanding shares confer identical rights to distribution and liquidation proceeds. These include

- Agreements to purchase stock at the time of death, divorce, disability, or termination of employment
- Distributions made on the basis of the shareholder's varying stock interests during the year
- Distributions that differ in timing (e.g., one shareholder receives a distribution in the current year and a second shareholder receives a similar dollar amount distribution shortly after the beginning of the next tax year)

---

[6] Sec. 1361(b)(1).
[7] Sec. 1361(b)(3).
[8] Reg. Sec. 1.1361-1(l).
[9] Sec. 1361(c)(4).
[10] Reg. Sec. 1.1361-1(l)(2).

Agreements to increase cash or property distributions to shareholders who bear heavier state income tax burdens so as to provide equal after-tax distributions provide unequal distribution and liquidation rights. The unequal distributions probably will cause a second class of stock to be created. However, state laws that require a corporation to pay or withhold state income taxes on behalf of some or all of a corporation's shareholders are disregarded.

Debt Instruments. Debt instruments, corporate obligations, and deferred compensation arrangements, in general, are not treated as a second class of stock. A number of safe harbors exist for characterizing corporate obligations as debt (and not as a second class of stock):[11]

- Unwritten advances from a shareholder that do not exceed $10,000 during the tax year, are treated as debt by the two parties, and are expected to be repaid within a reasonable time
- Obligations that are considered equity under the general tax laws but are owned solely by the shareholders in the same proportion as the corporations's outstanding stock

KEY POINT

If debt instruments satisfy the safe harbor rules, such instruments cannot be construed as equity. However, such debt must have been issued in an S corporation tax year.

In addition, Sec. 1361(c)(5) provides a safe harbor for straight debt instruments so that the debt is not treated as a second class of stock. For debt to qualify under the safe harbor, it must meet the following requirements if issued while an S election is in effect:

- The debt must represent an unconditional promise to pay a certain sum of money on a specified date or on demand.
- The interest rate and interest payment dates must not be contingent on profits, the borrower's discretion, or similar factors.[12]
- The debt must not be convertible directly or indirectly into stock.
- The creditor must be an individual, estate, or trust eligible to be an S corporation shareholder, or a nonindividual creditor actively and regularly engaged in the business of lending money.[13]

The safe harbor rules can apply to debt even if the debt otherwise would be considered a second class of stock under case law or other IRC provisions. An obligation that originally qualifies as straight debt may no longer qualify if it is materially modified so that it no longer satisfies the safe harbor or is transferred to a third party who is not an eligible shareholder.[14]

Election of S Corporation Status

OBJECTIVE 3

Explain how a corporation elects, revokes, or terminates S corporation status

The S election exempts a corporation from all taxes imposed by Chapter 1 of the Internal Revenue Code (Secs. 1-1399) except for the following:

- Sec. 1374 built-in gains tax
- Sec. 1375 excess net passive income tax
- Sec. 1363(d) LIFO recapture tax

This rule exempts the S corporation from the regular income tax, accumulated earnings tax, the personal holding company tax, and the corporate alternative minimum tax for all tax years the election remains in effect.

[11] Reg. Sec. 1.1361-1(l)(4). An exception applies to debt instruments, corporate obligations, and deferred compensation arrangements that are treated as stock under the general principles of the federal tax law where the principal purpose for the debt instrument, etc., is to circumvent the distribution or liquidation proceeds rights provided for by the outstanding stock or to circumvent the 100-shareholder limit.

[12] That the interest rate depends on the prime rate or a similar factor not related to the debtor corporation will not disqualify the instrument from coming under the safe harbor rules. If the interest being paid is unreasonably high, an appropriate portion may be treated as a payment of something other than interest.

[13] Sec. 1361(c)(5).

[14] Reg. Sec. 1.1361-1(l)(5)(ii) and (iii).

The S election affects the shareholders in three ways:

- Shareholders report their pro rata share of the S corporation's ordinary income or loss as well as any separately stated items.
- Shareholders treat most distributions as a nontaxable recovery of their stock investments.
- Shareholders' stock bases are adjusted for the shareholders' ratable share of ordinary income or loss and any separately stated items.

MAKING THE ELECTION

Only small business corporations can make the S election.[15] For a small business corporation to make a valid S election, the corporation must file a timely election (Form 2553), and all the corporation's shareholders must consent to the election. Existing corporations can make a timely S election at any time during the tax year preceding the year for which the election is to be effective or on or before the fifteenth day of the third month of the year for which the election is to be effective.

For a new corporation, the S election can be made at any time on or before the fifteenth day of the third month of its initial tax year. A new corporation's initial tax year begins with the first day the corporation has shareholders, acquires assets, or begins business.

If the corporation makes the S election during the first 2½ months of the tax year for which the election is first to be effective, the corporation also must meet all the small business corporation requirements on each day of the tax year preceding and including the election date. If the corporation fails to satisfy this requirement, the election becomes effective in the corporation's next tax year.

The tax law, however, provides some relief for improper elections. First, if the corporation misses the deadline for making the S corporation election, the IRS can treat the election as timely made if the IRS determines that the corporation had reasonable cause for making the late election. Second, if the election was ineffective because the corporation inadvertently failed to qualify as a small business corporation or because it inadvertently failed to obtain shareholder consents (see below), the IRS nevertheless can honor the election if the corporation and shareholders take steps to correct the deficiency within a reasonable period of time.[16]

EXAMPLE C:11-3 ▶ Wilco Corporation, a calendar year taxpayer, has been in existence for several years. Wilco wants to be treated as an S corporation for 2018 and subsequent years. The corporation can make the election any time during 2017 or from January 1 through March 15, 2018. If the corporation makes the election after March 15, 2018, it becomes effective in 2019. However, if Wilco can show reasonable cause for making the late election, the IRS may allow the election to be effective for 2018. ◀

SELF-STUDY QUESTION

Would the answer to Example C:11-3 change if Wilco is a member of an affiliated group through January 15, 2018?

ANSWER

Yes. Because Wilco is an ineligible corporation for a portion of the 2½-month period of 2018, an S election would not be effective until January 1, 2019.

Consent of Shareholders. Each person who is a shareholder on the election date must consent to the election. The consent is binding on the current tax year and all future tax years. No additional consents are required of shareholders who acquire the stock between the election date and its effective date or at any subsequent date.

Section 1362(b)(2) imposes a special rule on the shareholders when the corporation makes an election after the beginning of the tax year for which it is to be effective. Each shareholder who owned stock during any portion of the year preceding the election date, and who is not a shareholder on the election date, also must consent to the election.

EXAMPLE C:11-4 ▶ Sara and Harry own all of Kraft Corporation's stock. Sara sells all her Kraft stock to Lisa on February 10. The next day Kraft makes an S election. For the election to apply in the current year, Sara, Harry, and Lisa must consent to the election. If Sara refuses to consent, the election will not be effective until next year. ◀

---

15 Election rules are in Sec. 1362.

16 IRS spells out detailed procedures for relief in Rev. Proc. 97-48, 1997-2 C.B. 521, Rev. Proc. 2003-43, 2003-23 C.B. 998, Rev. Proc. 2004-48, 2004-2 C.B. 172, Rev. Proc. 2007-62, 2007-41, C.B. 786, and Rev. Proc. 2013-30, 2013-36 I.R.B. 173.

Each tenant (whether or not husband and wife) must consent to the S election if the shareholders own the stock as tenants in common, joint tenants, or tenants in the entirety. If the shareholders own the S corporation stock as community property, each person having a community property interest must consent to the election. If the shareholder is a minor, either the minor or the minor's legal representative (e.g., a natural parent or legal guardian) can make the consent.

Topic Review C:11-1 summarizes the S corporation requirements and procedures for making the S election.

TERMINATION OF THE ELECTION

Once made, the S election remains in effect until the corporation either revokes the election or terminates the election because it ceases to meet the small business corporation requirements. The following discussion examines each action and outlines the requirements for making a new S election following a termination.[17]

Revocation of the Election. A corporation can revoke its S election in any tax year as long as it meets the requirements regarding shareholder consent and timeliness. Shareholders owning more than one-half the corporation's stock (including nonvoting stock) on the day the corporation makes the revocation must consent to the revocation. A revocation made on or before the fifteenth day of the third month of the tax year is effective on the first day of that tax year. A revocation made after the first 2½ months of the tax year takes effect on the first day of the next tax year. An exception permits the S corporation to select a prospective date for the revocation to be effective. The prospective date can be the date the corporation makes the revocation or any subsequent date.

TOPIC REVIEW C:11-1

S Corporation Requirements and Election Procedures

REQUIREMENTS

Shareholder-related:

1. The corporation may have no more than 100 shareholders. Family members and their estates count as one shareholder.
2. All shareholders must be individuals, estates, certain kinds of trusts, or certain kinds of tax-exempt organizations. Eligible trusts include grantor trusts, voting trusts, testamentary trusts, beneficiary-controlled trusts, qualified Subchapter S trusts, qualified retirement plan trusts, and small business trusts.
3. All the individual shareholders must be U.S. citizens or resident aliens.

Corporation-related:

1. The corporation must be a domestic corporation or an unincorporated entity. An unincorporated entity that makes an S election is automatically treated as having elected to be taxed as a domestic corporation under the check-the-box regulations.
2. The corporation must not be an ineligible corporation (e.g., an ineligible bank or other financial institution, an insurance company, or a foreign corporation).
3. The corporation must have only one class of stock issued and outstanding. Differences in voting rights are ignored.

MAKING THE ELECTION

1. The corporation can make the S election any time during the tax year preceding the year for which the election is effective or on or before the fifteenth day of the third month of the tax year for which the election is effective. Late elections are effective with the next tax year unless the corporation obtains IRS relief for reasonable cause.
2. Each shareholder who owns stock on the date the corporation makes the election must consent to the election. If the corporation makes the election after the beginning of the tax year, each person who was a shareholder during the portion of the tax year preceding the election also must consent to the election.

[17] Termination and revocation rules are in Sec. 1362.

EXAMPLE C:11-5 ▶ Adobe Corporation, a calendar year taxpayer, has been an S corporation for several years. However, the corporation has become quite profitable, and management feels that it would be advantageous to make a public stock offering to obtain additional capital during 2018. Adobe can revoke its S election any time on or before March 15, 2018, making the revocation effective on January 1, 2018. If the corporation revokes the election after March 15, 2018, it takes effect January 1, 2019. In either case, the corporation may specify a prospective 2018 effective date as long as the date occurs on or after the date it makes the revocation. ◀

TAX STRATEGY TIP

When it is difficult to obtain the majority shareholder vote necessary for revocation, consideration should be given to purposely triggering a termination event.

Termination of the Election. The S election terminates if the corporation fails one or more of the small business corporation requirements any time after the election's effective date. The termination generally occurs on the day of the terminating event. Events that can terminate the election include

- Exceeding the 100-shareholder limit
- Having an ineligible shareholder own some of the stock
- Creating a second class of stock
- Attaining a prohibited tax status
- Selecting an improper tax year
- Failing the passive investment income test for three consecutive years

The passive investment income test applies annually. It terminates the S election if more than 25% of the corporation's gross receipts are passive investment income for each of three consecutive tax years *and* the corporation has Subchapter C earnings and profits (E&P) at the end of each of the three consecutive tax years. If the corporation meets these conditions for three consecutive tax years, the election terminates on the first day of the next (fourth) tax year.

Passive investment income includes royalties, rents,[18] dividends, interest, annuities, and gains from the sale or exchange of stocks and securities. Treasury Regulations hold that passive investment income excludes income derived from the active conduct of a trade or business. Subchapter C E&P includes only earnings that accrued in tax years in which an S election was not in effect (i.e., the corporation was taxed under the C corporation rules).

EXAMPLE C:11-6 ▶ Shareholders formed Silver Corporation in the current year, and the corporation promptly made an S election. Silver can earn an unlimited amount of passive income during a tax year without any fear of losing its S corporation status or being subject to the Sec. 1375 tax on excess net passive income because it has never been a C corporation and thus has no Subchapter C E&P. However, if a C corporation containing E&P merged into Silver, Silver would then have potential exposure to the passive income rules. (See page C:11-16 for a discussion of the Sec. 1375 tax.) ◀

HISTORICAL NOTE

Previously, a termination was deemed effective on the first day of the tax year in which the terminating event occurred. To stop potential abuse, Congress changed the rule so that an S election terminates on the day of the terminating event.

Allocation of Income. A terminating event occurring at some time other than the first day of the tax year creates an S termination year. The **S termination year** is divided into an S short year and C short year. The **S short year** begins on the first day of the tax year and ends on the day preceding the termination date. The **C short year** begins on the termination date and continues through the last day of the corporation's tax year.

EXAMPLE C:11-7 ▶ Dixon Corporation has been an S corporation for several years. Paula and Frank each own one-half of Dixon's stock. Paula sells one-half of her Dixon stock to Eagle Corporation on July 1. The sale terminates the S election on July 1 because Eagle is an ineligible shareholder. Assuming Dixon is a calendar year taxpayer, the S short year runs from January 1 through June 30. The C short year runs from July 1 through December 31. ◀

---

[18] Regulation Sec. 1.1362-2(c)(5)(ii)(B)(2) excludes from rents payments received for the use or occupancy of property if the corporation provides significant services or incurs substantial costs in the rental business. See page C:11-37 for additional explanations of the significant services and substantial costs definitions.

TAX STRATEGY TIP

Income or loss can be allocated in the termination year under either of two methods. Careful consideration should be given to the possible tax advantages of a daily allocation versus an actual closing of the books. See Tax Planning Considerations for further details.

ADDITIONAL COMMENT

To use an actual closing of the books to allocate Dixon's income or loss in Example C:11-7, Eagle must consent. Due to the consequences of such an election, the method of allocation should be considered in negotiating the Dixon stock sale.

The S corporation's shareholders report the S short year income according to the normal reporting rules described below. The C corporation reports the income earned during the C short year and calculates its C short year income tax liability on an annualized basis (see Chapter C:3). The S short year and C short year returns are due on the due date for the corporation's tax return for the tax year had the termination not occurred (including any extensions).

An S corporation can use either of two rules to allocate the termination year's income between the S short year and the C short year. The general rule of Sec. 1362(e)(2) allocates the ordinary income or loss and the separately stated items between the S short year and C short year based on the number of days in each year. A special election under Sec. 1362(e)(3) permits an allocation that accords with the corporation's normal tax accounting rules if all persons who were shareholders at any time during the S short year and all persons who are shareholders on the first day of the C short year consent to the election. The corporation cannot use a daily allocation when an S termination year occurs and, during such year, sales or exchanges of 50% or more of the corporation's outstanding stock occur. In such a case, the corporation must use its normal accounting rules to make the allocation.

Inadvertent Termination. Special rules permit the corporation to continue its S election if an inadvertent termination occurs by its ceasing to be a small business corporation or by its failing the passive investment income test for three consecutive years. If such a termination occurs, the S corporation or its shareholders must take the necessary steps, within a reasonable time period after discovering the event creating the termination, to restore the corporation's small business status. If the IRS determines that the termination was inadvertent, the corporation and all persons owning stock during the termination period must agree to make the adjustments necessary to report the income for this period as if the S election had been in effect continuously.[19]

EXAMPLE C:11-8 ▶ Shareholders formed Frye Corporation in 2014 and operated it as a C corporation during that year. Frye made an S election in 2015. During 2014, the corporation incorrectly computed its E&P and believed that no Subchapter C E&P existed for its only pre–S corporation tax year. From 2015 through 2017, Frye earned large amounts of passive income but did not pay the Sec. 1375 excess net passive income tax or worry about terminating its election because it thought it had no accumulated E&P from 2014. Upon auditing Frye's tax returns, the IRS finds that Subchapter C E&P, in fact, did exist from 2014 and terminates the S election effective on January 1, 2018. If the corporation distributes the E&P and the shareholders report the dividend income, the IRS probably will treat the occurrence as an inadvertent termination and not revoke the election. ◀

The IRS also can grant relief for inadvertent terminations of the election to treat a subsidiary as a Qualified Subchapter S Subsidiary (QSub). For example, a parent S corporation might inadvertently transfer shares of a QSub to another person, thereby violating the 100% ownership requirement. If the S corporation takes the necessary steps to correct the inadvertent transfer, the IRS can grant relief, thereby allowing the election to remain in effect.

Other IRS Waivers. The IRS not only can waive a termination it deems to be inadvertent, it also can validate certain invalid elections. Validation of an invalid election can occur when the election failed to meet the basic S corporation requirements of Sec. 1361 or failed to provide the necessary shareholder consents. The IRS also can exercise this authority in situations where a corporation never filed an election. In addition, the IRS can treat a late S election as being timely filed if the IRS determines that reasonable cause

[19] Regulation Sec. 1.1362-4(b) holds that a termination will be inadvertent if the terminating event was not reasonably within the control of the corporation and was not part of a plan to terminate the election or if it took place without the corporation's knowledge and reasonable safeguards were in place to prevent the event from occurring.

existed for failing to make a timely election and the corporation meets certain other requirements.[20]

New Election Following a Termination. A corporation that revokes or terminates its S election must wait five tax years before making a new election.[21] This delay applies unless the IRS consents to an earlier reelection. Regulation Sec. 1.1362-5(a) indicates that permission for an early reelection can occur (1) when more than 50% of the corporation's stock is owned by persons who did not own stock on the termination date or (2) when the event causing the termination was not reasonably within the control of the corporation or the shareholders having a substantial interest in the corporation *and* was not part of a plan to terminate the election involving the corporation or such shareholders.

EXAMPLE C:11-9 ▶ Terri owned Vector Corporation, a calendar year taxpayer that has been an S corporation for ten years. In January of last year, Terri sold all the Vector stock to Michelle with payments to be made over a five-year period. Two years after the sale, Michelle fails to make the necessary payments, and Terri repossesses the stock. During the time Michelle held the stock, Vector revoked its S election. Vector should immediately apply for reelection of S status because a more than 50% ownership change occurred since the revocation date. ◀

Avoiding Termination of an S Election. Termination of an S election potentially can increase corporate or shareholder taxes. The S corporation's owners, management, and tax advisor need to understand the various events that can cause the termination of the S election. Some steps shareholders can take to prevent an untimely termination include the following:

- Monitor all transfers of S corporation stock. Make certain the purchaser or transferee of the stock is not an ineligible shareholder (e.g., corporation, partnership, or nonresident alien) or that the total number of shareholders does not exceed 100 (e.g., an excess shareholder resulting from creation of a joint interest).
- Establish procedures for the S corporation to purchase the stock of deceased shareholders to avoid the stock being acquired by a trust that is ineligible to be a shareholder.
- Establish restrictions on the transferability of the S corporation stock by having shareholders enter into a stock purchase agreement. Such an agreement could provide that the stock cannot be transferred without the prior consent of all other shareholders

WHAT WOULD YOU DO IN THIS SITUATION?

Harry Baker formed Xeno Corporation on January 4, 2015. The corporation filed a valid S corporation election on January 19, 2015, to be in effect for 2015. Harry, the corporation's sole shareholder, consented to the election. The corporation had business ties to Mexico, and to strengthen these ties, Harry sold 25% of his Xeno shares to Pedro Gonzales on February 10, 2016. Pedro is one of Harry's business associates and is a citizen and resident of Mexico. Harry continued to operate Xeno as an S corporation throughout 2016. Early in March 2017, Harry became aware that, by selling stock to an ineligible shareholder, he may have jeopardized the corporation's S election. Thus, Harry immediately contacted Pedro and persuaded Pedro to sell his Xeno shares back to him (Harry). Harry hires you as his tax advisor on December 17, 2017, at which time you learn about the sale and repurchase of the Xeno shares. However, Harry tells you not to worry because, by buying back the shares, he already has rectified the situation, and thus the IRS need not be told about the transfers. How do you advise Harry on this matter?

---

[20] See footnote 16.

[21] *Termination* includes both revocation of the S election and loss of the election because one or more of the small business corporation requirements were not met.

and, if the necessary consent cannot be obtained, the corporation will repurchase the stock at a specified price (e.g., at book value).

- Monitor the passive income earned by an S corporation that previously had been a C corporation for one or more years. Make certain the passive income requirement is not failed for three consecutive years by reducing the level of passive income or by distributing the Subchapter C E&P.

S CORPORATION OPERATIONS

OBJECTIVE 4

Classify an S corporation's ordinary and separately stated items, and calculate special S corporation taxes

S corporations make the same accounting period and accounting method elections that a C corporation makes. Each year, the S corporation must compute and report to the IRS and to its shareholders its ordinary income or loss and its separately stated items. The special S corporation rules are explained below.

TAXABLE YEAR

Section 1378(a) requires that the S corporation's taxable year be a permitted year, defined as

- A tax year ending on December 31 (including a 52–53 week year)
- Any fiscal year for which the corporation establishes a business purpose[22]

Section 1378(b) specifically notes that income deferral for the shareholders is not a necessary business purpose. An S corporation that adopts a fiscal year coinciding with its natural business year has satisfied the business purpose requirement. The natural business year for an S corporation depends on the type of business conducted. When a trade or business has nonpeak and peak periods of business, the natural business year is considered to end at, or soon after, the close of the peak business period. A business whose income is steady throughout the year, does not have a natural business year.[23]

EXAMPLE C:11-10 ► Sable Corporation, an S corporation, operates a ski resort and reports $1 million of gross receipts for each of its last three tax years. If at least $250,000 (25% of gross receipts) of the receipts occurred in February and March for each of the three consecutive years, Sable can adopt, or change to, or continue to use a natural business year ending March 31.[24] ◄

An S corporation's adoption of, or a change to, a fiscal year that is an ownership tax year also is permitted. An ownership tax year is the same tax year used by shareholders owning more than 50% of the corporation's outstanding stock. The 50% requirement must be met on the first day of the tax year to which the change relates. Failure to meet the 50% ownership requirement on the first day of any later tax year requires a change to a calendar year or other approved fiscal year. S corporations also can adopt or change to a fiscal year for which it obtains IRS approval, based on the facts and circumstances of the situation.[25]

ADDITIONAL COMMENT

The requirement that all S corporations adopt calendar years (with March 15 return due dates) caused a hardship for tax return preparers. Section 444 is a compromise provision that allows a fiscal year for filing purposes, but it mandates a special payment of the deferred taxes.

Section 444 permits an S corporation to elect a fiscal year other than a permitted year. The fiscal year elected under Sec. 444 must have a deferral period of three months or less (e.g., a September 30 or later fiscal year-end for an S corporation otherwise required to use a calendar year). An S corporation that changes its tax year can elect to use a new fiscal year under Sec. 444 only if the deferral period is no longer than the shorter of three months or the deferral period of the tax year being changed.[26] A Sec. 444 election is not required of an S corporation that satisfies the business purpose exception.

---

[22] Some S corporations use a "grandfathered" fiscal year, which is a fiscal year for which IRS approval was obtained after June 30, 1974. Excluded are fiscal years that result in an income deferral of three months or less.

[23] Rev. Procs. 2002-39, 2002-1 C.B. 1046, and 2006-46, 2006-2 C.B. 859.

[24] See Rev. Proc. 2006-46, 2006-2 C.B. 859, for an explanation of the 25% test.

[25] Regulation Sec. 1.1378-1 and Rev. Proc. 2006-46, 2006-2 C.B. 859, explain the procedures for an S corporation adopting a fiscal year or changing the tax year of a new or existing S corporation. Rev. Rul. 87-57, 1987-2 C.B. 117, examines eight situations concerning whether the tax year is a permitted year.

[26] Special Sec. 444 transitional rules for 1986 permitted many S corporations to retain a previously adopted fiscal year (e.g., January 31) even though the deferral period is longer than three months.

S corporations that elect a fiscal year under Sec. 444 must make required payments under Sec. 7519, which approximate the deferral benefit of the fiscal year. Revocation or termination of the S election also terminates the Sec. 444 election unless the corporation becomes a personal service corporation. Termination of the Sec. 444 election permits the S corporation to obtain a refund of prior Sec. 7519 payments.

Topic Review C:11-2 summarizes the alternative tax years available to an S corporation.

ACCOUNTING METHOD ELECTIONS

As with a partnership, an S corporation makes accounting method elections independent of accounting method elections made by its shareholders. Three elections generally reserved for the S corporation's shareholders are as follows:

- Section 617 election relating to deduction and recapture of mining exploration expenditures
- Section 901 election to take a credit for foreign income taxes[27]

ORDINARY INCOME OR LOSS AND SEPARATELY STATED ITEMS

S corporations are treated much like partnerships and thus report both an ordinary income or loss amount and a series of separately stated items. Ordinary income or loss is the net of income and deductions other than the separately stated items described in the next paragraph.

KEY POINT

S corporations are much like partnerships in their method of reporting income and losses. Both are pass-through entities that provide K-1s to their owners with their respective shares of income and loss items.

The S corporation's separately stated items are the same ones that apply in partnership taxation under Sec. 702(a), related Treasury Regulations, and tax return instructions.[28] For example, the following items must be separately stated:

- Net short-term capital gains and losses
- Net long-term capital gains and losses
- Sec. 1231 gains and losses
- Unrecaptured Sec. 1250 gains
- Sec. 179 expense
- Charitable contributions

TOPIC REVIEW C:11-2

Alternative S Corporation Tax Years

Tax Year	Requirements
Calendar year (including certain 52–53 week years)	The permitted tax year unless an exception applies.
Permitted fiscal year:	IRS will grant approval if:
a. Ownership year	The tax year requested is the same as that used by shareholders owing more than 50% of the corporation's outstanding stock. This test must be met on the first day of the year for which approval is requested as well as for each succeeding year.
b. Natural business year	25% or more of the gross receipts for each of the three most recent 12-month periods are in the last two months of the requested tax year.
c. Facts and circumstances year	The corporation establishes a business purpose (other than an ownership year or natural business year) using the facts and circumstances of the situation.
Nonpermitted fiscal year	A Sec. 444 election permits the S corporation to use an otherwise nonpermitted tax year if the deferral period is three months or less and the corporation makes the necessary required payments.

[27] Secs. 1363(c).

[28] Sec. 1366(a).

- Dividends and interest income[29]
- Taxes paid or accrued to a foreign country or to a U.S. possession
- Tax-exempt or partially tax-exempt interest
- Investment income and expenses
- Any other item provided by Treasury Regulations and tax form instructions

For a comprehensive list of separately stated items, see Form 1120S, Schedule K included in Appendix B.

Section 1366(b) requires that the character of any separately stated item be determined as if the item were (1) realized directly by the shareholder from the same source from which it was realized by the corporation or (2) incurred by the shareholder in the same manner as it was incurred by the corporation. Thus, the character of an income, gain, deduction, loss, or credit item does not change merely because the item passes through to the shareholders.

Deductions That Cannot Be Claimed. S corporations also have several deductions that it cannot claim, including

- The 70%, 80%, or 100% dividends-received deduction (because dividends pass through to the S corporation's shareholders)
- The U.S. production activities deduction (because that deduction passes through to the S corporation's shareholders)
- The same deductions disallowed to a partnership under Sec. 703(a)(2) (e.g., personal and dependency exemptions, additional itemized deductions for individuals, taxes paid or accrued to a foreign country or to a U.S. possession, charitable contributions, oil and gas depletion, and NOL carrybacks and carryforwards).[30]

Similarity to C Corporation Treatment. S corporations are treated as corporations for certain tax matters. For example, an S corporation can elect to amortize its organizational expenditures under Sec. 248 (after deducting up to $5,000). Also, the 20% reduction in certain tax preference benefits under Sec. 291 applies to an S corporation if the corporation was a C corporation in any of its three preceding tax years.[31]

ADDITIONAL COMMENT

The 20-year carryover period continues to run on C corporation NOLS even during subsequent S corporation years.

Carryovers and Carrybacks When Status Changes. Some S corporations may operate as C corporations during a period of years that either precede the making of an S election or follow the termination of an S election. No carryovers or carrybacks that originate in a C corporation tax year can carry to an S corporation tax year other than carryovers that can be used to offset the built-in gains tax (see pages C:11-16 through C:11-18). Similarly, no carryovers or carrybacks created in an S corporation tax year can carry to a C corporation tax year.[32] Losses from an S corporation tax year pass through to the shareholder and, if greater than the shareholder's income for the year, can create an NOL carryover or carryback for the shareholder.

---

[29] Partnerships are permitted to have C corporations as owners of partnership interests. Thus, dividends eligible for the dividends-received deduction also are separately stated. Such is not the case with an S corporation, which cannot have a corporate shareholder.

[30] Sec. 1363(b)(2).

[31] Secs. 1363(b)(3) and (4).

[32] Sec. 1371(b).

U.S. PRODUCTION ACTIVITIES DEDUCTION

Chapter C:3 describes the C corporation version of the U.S. production activities deduction, whereby the deduction equals 9% times the lesser of (1) qualified production activities income for the year or (2) taxable income before the U.S. production activities deduction. Individuals use a modified form of AGI instead of taxable income for this computation. The deduction, however, cannot exceed 50% of the employer's W-2 wages allocable to U.S. production activities for the year. In the case of an S corporation, the deduction applies at the shareholder level, so the S corporation must report each shareholder's share of qualified production activities income on the shareholder's Schedule K-1. For the 50% salary limitation, each shareholder is allocated his or her share of the S corporation's W-2 wages.

SPECIAL S CORPORATION TAXES

The S corporation is subject to three special taxes: the excess net passive income tax, the built-in gains tax, and the LIFO recapture tax. Each of these taxes is explained below.

Excess Net Passive Income Tax. The **excess net passive income (or Sec. 1375) tax** applies when an S corporation has passive investment income for the tax year that exceeds 25% of its gross receipts and, at the close of the tax year, the S corporation has Subchapter C E&P. The excess net passive income tax equals the S corporation's excess net passive income times the highest corporate tax rate (35% in 2017).[33]

The **excess net passive income** is determined as follows:

$$\text{Excess net passive income} = \text{Net passive income} \times \frac{\text{Passive investment income} - 25\% \text{ of gross receipts}}{\text{Passive investment income}}$$

The excess net passive income is limited to the corporation's taxable income, which is defined as a C corporation's taxable income except with no reduction for the NOL deduction or the dividends-received deduction. Net passive income equals passive investment income minus any deductions directly related to its production. Passive investment income excludes income derived from the active conduct of a trade or business.[34]

KEY POINT

The excess net passive income tax is of concern to a former C corporation that has accumulated E&P. A corporation that always has been an S corporation will not have a passive income problem.

EXAMPLE C:11-11 ▶ Paoli Corporation, an S corporation, reports the following results for the current year:

Service (nonpassive) income	$35,000
Dividend income	37,000
Interest income	28,000
Passive income-related expenses	10,000
Other expenses	25,000

At the end of this year, Paoli's E&P from its prior C corporation tax years amounts to $60,000. Paoli's excess net passive income is determined as follows:

$$\$33,846 = (\$65,000 - \$10,000) \times \frac{\$65,000 - (0.25 \times \$100,000)}{\$65,000}$$

The excess net passive income tax is $11,846 ($33,846 × 0.35). The special tax reduces (on a pro rata basis) the dividend income and interest income items that pass through to the shareholders. The S election is not terminated at the end of the current year unless Paoli also was subject to the tax in the prior two tax years. ◀

TAX STRATEGY TIP

A former C corporation can avoid the Sec. 1375 tax (and the possibility of having its S election terminated) by electing to distribute its Subchapter C E&P. See Tax Planning Considerations for further details.

Built-in Gains Tax. A second corporate level tax may apply to gains recognized by an S corporation that formerly was a C corporation. This tax, called the **built-in gains (or Sec. 1374) tax**, applies to any income or gain the corporation would have included in

---

[33] Passive investment income and Subchapter C E&P for this purpose have the same definition here as given on page C:11-10.

[34] Reg. Sec. 1.1362-2(c)(5). Also, Reg. Sec. 1.1375-1(f), Ex. (2) indicates that passive income subject to the Sec. 1375 tax includes municipal bond interest that otherwise is exempt from the federal income tax.

ADDITIONAL COMMENT

For tax years beginning in 2009 and 2010, a seven-year recognition period applied. For tax years beginning before 2009, a ten-year recognition period applied.

gross income while a C corporation had the corporation used the accrual method of accounting (known as a **built-in gain**) and that the corporation reports during the five-year period beginning on the date the S election took effect (known as the recognition period). **Built-in losses** are any deductions or losses the corporation would have deducted while a C corporation had the corporation used the accrual method of accounting and that the corporation reports during the five-year period beginning on the date the S election took effect. Built-in gains and losses also include the differences between the FMVs and adjusted bases of assets held at the time the S election takes effect. Built-in losses reduce the amount of recognized built-in gains in determining the built-in gains tax liability.

Congress enacted this tax to prevent taxpayers from avoiding the corporate level tax by making an S election before distributing or selling its assets. The built-in gains tax applies to S corporation tax years beginning after December 31, 1986, where the S corporation was formerly a C corporation and made the current S election after December 31, 1986.

EXAMPLE C:11-12 ▶ Theta Corporation, a calendar year taxpayer, incorporated 12 years ago and operated as a C corporation through the end of last year. On February 4 of the current year, Theta filed an S election that was effective for the current year and later tax years. Theta is subject to the built-in gains tax for five years starting with January 1 of the current year. ◀

The Sec. 1374 tax is determined by using the following four-step calculation:

STEP 1: Determine the corporation's net recognized built-in gain for the tax year.

STEP 2: Reduce the net recognized built-in gain from Step 1 (but not below zero) by any NOL or capital loss carryovers from prior C corporation tax years.

STEP 3: Compute a tentative tax by multiplying the amount determined in Step 2 by the highest corporate tax rate (35% in 2017).

STEP 4: Reduce the tax determined in Step 3 (but not below zero) by the general business credit and minimum tax credit carryovers from any prior C corporation tax years and by the nonhighway use of gasoline and other fuels credit.

TAX STRATEGY TIP

An S corporation with NOL, capital loss, general business credit, and minimum tax credit carryovers from C corporation years can use these carryovers to reduce the effect of the built-in gains tax. Both NOL and capital loss carryforwards reduce the amount of recognized built-in gain taxed under Sec. 1374. The general business and minimum tax credit carryforwards reduce the actual built-in gains tax.

A recognized built-in gain or loss is any gain or loss recognized on an asset disposition during the five-year recognition period unless the S corporation can establish that it did not hold the asset on the first day of the first tax year to which the S election applies. A recognized built-in gain cannot exceed the excess of a property's FMV over its adjusted basis on the first day of the five-year recognition period. Dispositions include sales or exchanges and other events, including the collection of accounts receivable by a cash basis taxpayer, collection of an installment sale obligation, and the completion of a long-term contract by a taxpayer using the completed contract method.[35]

Built-in losses include not only losses originating from a disposition of property, but also any deductions claimed during the five-year recognition period that are attributable to periods before the first S corporation tax year. A recognized built-in loss cannot exceed the excess of a property's adjusted basis over its FMV on the first day of the five-year recognition period. Built-in losses, however, do not include any loss, deduction, or carryover originating from the disposition of an asset acquired before or during the recognition period where the principal purpose of such acquisition was avoiding the Sec. 1374 tax.

PRACTICAL APPLICATION

The application of the Sec. 1374 tax requires detailed records, which enable the taxpayer to track the built-in gain assets and determine when the corporation recognizes these gains.

The net recognized built-in gain for a tax year is limited to the smaller of:

- The excess of (1) the net unrealized built-in gain (i.e., excess of the FMV of the S corporation's assets at the beginning of its first tax year for which the S election is in effect over their total adjusted basis on such date) over (2) the total net recognized built-in gain for prior tax years beginning in the five-year recognition period.[36]

---

[35] Income and gains potentially can be taxed under both the excess net passive income (Sec. 1375) and built-in gains (Sec. 1374) taxes. Any such income or gain is fully taxed under the Sec. 1374 rules. The portion of the income or gain taxed under the Sec. 1374 tax is exempt from the Sec. 1375 tax.

[36] The recognition period can be extended beyond five years if property having a carryover basis is acquired in a tax-free transaction (e.g., a tax-free reorganization) from a C corporation. For such property, the five-year recognition period begins on the date the S corporation acquired the property.

- The S corporation's taxable income as if it were a C corporation but with no dividends-received deduction or NOL deduction allowed.

If the net of the recognized built-in gains and losses exceeds the corporation's taxable income and the corporation made the S election after March 30, 1988, the excess built-in gain carries over to the next tax year, where it may be subject to the Sec. 1374 built-in gains tax in the carryover year. The built-in gain carryover consists of a ratable share of each of the income categories (e.g., ordinary income or capital gains) making up the net recognized built-in gain for the tax year.

The built-in gains tax passes through to the shareholders as if it were a loss. The loss must be allocated proportionately among the net recognized built-in gains that resulted in the tax being imposed.

EXAMPLE C:11-13 ▶ Assume the same facts as in Example C:11-12 and that Theta Corporation uses the accrual method of accounting. Theta owns the following assets on January 1 of the current year:

Assets	*Adjusted Basis*	*FMV*
Cash	$ 10,000	$ 10,000
Marketable securities	39,000	45,000
Accounts receivable	60,000	60,000
Inventory (FIFO)	60,000	75,000
Building	27,000	44,000
Land	10,000	26,000
Machinery and equipment[a]	74,000	140,000
Total	$280,000	$400,000

[a] $50,000 of the gain is subject to recapture under Sec. 1245.

ETHICAL POINT

A C corporation that has substantially appreciated assets and wants to make an S election should obtain an appraisal of its assets on or about the first day of the S election period. The S corporation's tax accountant must make sure the appraiser does not assign an artificially low value to these assets to minimize the potential built-in gains tax burden.

During the current year, Theta collects $58,000 of accounts receivable and declares $2,000 uncollectible. It sells the FIFO inventory at a $25,000 profit in the first quarter, replacing the sold inventory with new inventory. It also sells two machines during the current year. One machine, having an $18,000 FMV and an $11,000 adjusted basis on January 1, produced a $7,000 gain (Sec. 1245 recapture income) on September 2. A second machine, having a $15,000 FMV and a $19,000 adjusted basis on January 1, produced a $4,000 loss on March 16.

- Theta recognizes no built-in gain or loss on collecting the receivables because it is an accrual method taxpayer. The $2,000 uncollectible debt is not a built-in loss because the loss arose after January 1. It is deductible as part of the ordinary income or loss calculation.
- Of the $25,000 inventory profit, $15,000 ($75,000 − $60,000) is a built-in gain taxed under Sec. 1374. Theta includes the entire $25,000 profit in ordinary income or loss.
- Theta recognizes a $7,000 built-in gain ($18,000 − $11,000) and a $4,000 ($15,000 − $19,000) built-in loss on the sale of the two machines. The $7,000 gain is ordinary income due to Sec. 1245 recapture and becomes part of Theta's S corporation ordinary income or loss. The $4,000 Sec. 1231 loss passes through separately to the shareholders.

REAL-WORLD EXAMPLE

The special S corporation taxes account for only a small amount of federal revenues. For example, collections on the built-in gains and excess net passive income taxes are less than 0.5% of total C corporation tax revenues.

In total, an $18,000 ($15,000 + $7,000 − $4,000) net recognized built-in gain is taxed under Sec. 1374, subject to the taxable income ceiling. Assuming C corporation taxable income (with no NOL deduction or dividends-received deduction) is at least $18,000, the built-in gains tax is $6,300 ($18,000 × 0.35). The entire tax amount reduces the shareholder's ordinary income from the inventory and machinery sales. ◀

LIFO Recapture Tax. If a C corporation using the LIFO inventory method makes an S election, Sec. 1363(d)(3) requires the corporation to include its LIFO recapture amount in gross income for its last C corporation tax year. The LIFO recapture amount is the excess of the inventory's basis for tax purposes under the FIFO method over its basis under the LIFO method at the close of the final C corporation tax year. Any tax increase incurred in the final C corporation tax year is payable in four annual installments, on or before the due date for the final C corporation tax return and on or before the due date for the first three S corporation tax returns. The S corporation's inventory basis is increased by the LIFO recapture amount included in gross income.

EXAMPLE C:11-14 ▶ Taylor Corporation, a calendar year C corporation since its inception in 2005, made an S election on December 21, 2017, effective for its 2018 tax year. Taylor has used the LIFO inventory method for a number of years. Its LIFO inventory has a $400,000 adjusted basis, a $650,000 FIFO inventory value, and an $800,000 FMV. Taylor's LIFO recapture amount is $250,000 ($650,000 − $400,000). Taylor includes this amount in gross income reported on its 2017 C corporation tax return. Assuming a 34% corporate tax, Taylor's increased tax liability is $85,000 (0.34 × $250,000), of which $21,250 (0.25 × $85,000) is due with Taylor's 2017 C corporation tax return. An additional $21,250 is due with the 2018 through 2020 S corporation tax returns. Taylor increases the basis of its inventory by the $250,000 LIFO recapture amount. ◀

STOP & THINK

Question: Former C corporations that are now treated as S corporations are subject to three corporate level taxes—the **LIFO recapture tax**, the built-in gains tax, and the excess net passive income tax. Why did Congress enact these three taxes?

Solution: Prior to enacting the LIFO recapture tax, Congress debated making the conversion of a C corporation into an S corporation a taxable event subject to the corporate liquidation rules. The corporation would have recognized all gains and losses at the time of conversion. As a compromise, only LIFO users are subject to an "automatic" tax when conversion occurs, and this tax applies only to the LIFO recapture amount and not all inventory appreciation. The built-in gains tax applies only when the corporation sells or exchanges assets during its first ten years after the S election. Assets not sold or exchanged during this time period escape the tax. The excess net passive income tax encourages S corporations to distribute their accumulated E&P. No tax is imposed, however, if the corporation keeps its passive income below the 25% of gross receipts threshold. Thus, former C corporations and their shareholders generally are better off under the current system than had Congress mandated corporate liquidation treatment.

TAXATION OF THE SHAREHOLDER

OBJECTIVE 5

Allocate an S corporation's ordinary and separately stated items to its shareholders and apply loss limitation rules

INCOME ALLOCATION PROCEDURES

An S corporation's shareholders must report their pro rata share of the ordinary income or loss and separately stated items for the S corporation's tax year that ends with or within the shareholder's tax year.[37] Each shareholder's pro rata share of these items is determined by

1. Allocating an equal portion to each day in the tax year (by dividing the amount of the item by the number of days in the S corporation's tax year)
2. Allocating an equal portion of the daily amount to each share of stock outstanding on each day (by dividing the daily amount for the item by the number of shares of stock outstanding on a particular day)
3. Totaling the daily allocations for each share of stock
4. Totaling the amounts allocated for each share of stock held by the shareholder

TYPICAL MISCONCEPTION

An S corporation's income or loss is allocated basically the same as a partnership's except that a partnership may have the added flexibility of making certain special allocations under Sec. 704(b).

These allocation rules are known as the "per day/per share" method. Special allocations (such as those possible under the partnership tax rules) of the ordinary income or loss and separately stated items are not permitted.

If a sale of the S corporation stock occurs during the year, the transferor reports the earnings allocated to the transferred shares through the day of the transfer.[38] The transferee reports his or her share of the earnings from the day after the transfer date through the end of the tax year.

[37] Sec. 1366(a). If the shareholder dies during the S corporation's tax year, the income earned during the portion of the tax year preceding death is reported on the shareholder's tax return. Income for the period the estate holds the S corporation stock is reported on the estate's fiduciary tax return.

[38] Reg. Sec. 1.1377-1(a)(2)(ii). Also see examples under Reg. Sec. 1.1377-1(c).

EXAMPLE C:11-15 ▶ Fox Corporation is an S corporation owned equally by Arnie and Bonnie during all of the current year (assume not a leap year). During this year, Fox reports ordinary income of $146,000 and a long-term capital gain of $36,500. Arnie and Bonnie each report $73,000 (0.50 × $146,000) of ordinary income and $18,250 (0.50 × $36,500) of long-term capital gain. ◀

EXAMPLE C:11-16 ▶ Assume the same facts as in Example C:11-15, except Bonnie sells one-half of her shares to Clay on March 31 of the current year (the 90th day of Fox's tax year). Arnie reports the same ordinary income and long-term capital gain from his investment. Bonnie and Clay report ordinary income and long-term capital gain as follows:

Ordinary Income

Bonnie: $\left(\$146{,}000 \times \frac{1}{2} \times \frac{90}{365}\right) + \left(\$146{,}000 \times \frac{1}{4} \times \frac{275}{365}\right) = \$45{,}500$

Clay: $\$146{,}000 \times \frac{1}{4} \times \frac{275}{365} = 27{,}500$

Total $73,000

Long-Term Capital Gain

Bonnie: $\left(\$36{,}500 \times \frac{1}{2} \times \frac{90}{365}\right) + \left(\$36{,}500 \times \frac{1}{4} \times \frac{275}{365}\right) = \$11{,}375$

Clay: $\$36{,}500 \times \frac{1}{4} \times \frac{275}{365} = 6{,}875$

Total $18,250 ◀

KEY POINT

Shareholders of an S corporation need to be aware that when they dispose of their stock, they have the option of having income or loss determined by an actual closing of the books rather than an allocation on a daily basis.

A special election is available for allocating the ordinary income or loss and separately stated items when the shareholder's interest in the S corporation terminates or is substantially reduced during the tax year. Under this election, the income is allocated according to the accounting methods used by the S corporation (instead of on a daily basis). The election divides the S corporation's tax year into two parts ending on

- The day the shareholder's interest in the corporation terminates
- The last day of the S corporation's tax year

The corporation can make this election only if all affected shareholders agree to the election.[39] Affected shareholders include the shareholder whose interest terminated and all shareholders who received S corporation shares during the year. The Tax Planning Considerations section of this chapter explores this election in greater detail.

LOSS AND DEDUCTION PASS-THROUGH TO SHAREHOLDERS

The S corporation's ordinary loss and separately stated loss and deduction items pass through to the shareholders at the end of the corporation's tax year. The shareholders report these items in their tax year in which the S corporation's tax year ends.

Allocation of the Loss. Under the rules outlined above, allocation of the loss also occurs on a daily basis. Thus, shareholders receive an allocation of ordinary loss and separately stated items even if they own the stock for only a portion of the year. If ordinary loss and other separately stated loss and deduction pass-through items exceed the shareholder's income, the excess may create an NOL for the shareholder and result in a carryback or carryover at the shareholder level.

EXAMPLE C:11-17 ▶ Kauai Corporation, an S corporation, reports a $73,000 ordinary loss during the current year (not a leap year). At the beginning of the current year, Edward and Frank own equally all of Kauai's stock. On June 30 of the current year (the 181st day of Kauai's tax year), Frank gives

[39] Sec. 1377(a)(2).

one-fourth of his stock to his son George. Edward is allocated \$36,500 (\$73,000 × 0.50) of ordinary loss. Frank and George are allocated ordinary losses as follows:

$$\text{Frank:}\quad \left(\$73{,}000 \times \frac{1}{2} \times \frac{181}{365}\right) + \left(\$73{,}000 \times \frac{3}{8} \times \frac{184}{365}\right) = \$31{,}900$$

$$\text{George:}\quad \$73{,}000 \times \frac{1}{8} \times \frac{184}{365} = \underline{4{,}600}$$

$$\text{Total} \quad \underline{\underline{\$36{,}500}}$$

All three shareholders can deduct these losses on their individual tax returns subject to the loss limitations described below. ◀

REAL-WORLD EXAMPLE

A U.S. Supreme Court case held that discharge of indebtedness income excluded from gross income under Sec. 108 nevertheless is a pass-through item that increases the shareholders' stock bases, thereby allowing loss pass-through items to be deducted by the shareholders. *Gitlitz et al. v. Comm.* 87 AFTR 2d 2001-417, 2001-1 USTC ¶50,147 (USSC, 2001). A subsequent tax act, however, disallowed the pass-through and stock basis increase for debt cancellations. This situation is a good example of Congress "overruling" the Supreme Court with its legislative power.

Shareholder Loss Limitations. Each shareholder's deduction for his or her share of the ordinary loss and the separately stated loss and deduction items is limited to the sum of the adjusted basis for his or her S corporation stock plus the adjusted basis of any indebtedness owed *directly* by the S corporation to the shareholder. Thus, a shareholder must account for stock basis and debt basis. Unlike the partnership taxation rules, however, a shareholder cannot increase his or her stock basis by a ratable share of the general S corporation liabilities.[40]

In determining the stock basis limitation for losses, the shareholder makes the following positive and negative adjustments:[41]

- Increase stock basis for any capital contributions during the year
- Increase stock basis for ordinary income and separately stated income or gain items
- Decrease stock basis for distributions not included in the shareholder's income
- Decrease stock basis for nondeductible, noncapital expenditures (unless the shareholder elects to determine the loss limitation without this decrease)

Sequencing the basis reduction for distributions ahead of losses means that distributions reduce the deductibility of S corporation loss and deduction pass-throughs, but losses do not affect the treatment of S corporation distributions.

TAX STRATEGY TIP

Rather than having the corporation borrow money, an S corporation shareholder might consider borrowing money directly from the bank and then lending the loan proceeds to the corporation with the corporation guaranteeing the bank loan. In this way, the shareholder obtains debt basis.

Many S corporations are nothing more than incorporated forms of sole proprietorships or partnerships. As a result, banks and other lending institutions often require one or more shareholders to personally guarantee loans the institutions make to the S corporation. The IRS and courts, however, have held that these guaranteed loans do not create corporate indebtedness to the shareholder. As a result, the shareholder's loss limitation does not increase until the shareholder pays part or all of the corporation's liability or the shareholder executes a note at the bank in full satisfaction of the corporation's liability. Such action by the shareholder converts the guarantee into an indebtedness of the corporation to the shareholder, which increases the shareholder's debt basis and loss limitation.[42]

The adjusted basis of S corporation stock and debt generally is determined as of the last day of the S corporation's tax year. If the shareholder disposes of the S corporation stock before that date, the stock and debt bases are instead determined immediately prior to the disposition.

Loss and deduction pass-through items are allocated to each share of stock and reduce each share's basis. Once the losses and deductions have reduced stock basis to zero, they then reduce the basis of any debt owed by the S corporation to the shareholder.

EXAMPLE C:11-18 ▶ Pat and Bill equally own Tillis Corporation, an S corporation. During the current year, Tillis reports an ordinary loss of \$104,000. Tillis's liabilities at the end of the current year include \$110,000 of accounts payable, \$150,000 of mortgage payable, and a \$20,000 note owed to Bill.

---

40 Sec. 1366(d)(1). Amounts owed by an S corporation to a conduit entity that has the shareholder as an owner or beneficiary will not increase the shareholder's loss limitation.

41 Sec. 1366(d) and Reg. Sec. 1.1366-2(a)(3). Special basis adjustment rules apply to oil and gas depletion.

42 Rev. Ruls. 70-50, 1970-1 C.B. 178; 71-288, 1971-2 C.B. 319; and 75-144, 1975-1 C.B. 277. See also *Estate of Daniel Leavitt v. CIR*, 63 AFTR 2d 89-1437, 89-1 USTC ¶9332 (4th Cir., 1989) among a series of decisions that uphold the IRS's position. However, see *Edward M. Selfe v. U.S.*, 57 AFTR 2d 86-464, 86-1 USTC ¶9115 (11th Cir., 1986) for a transaction where a guarantee was held to increase the shareholder's loss limitation because the transaction was structured so the bank looked primarily to the shareholder instead of the corporation for repayment.

Thus, Bill has a $20,000 debt basis for the amount he loaned to the corporation. Pat and Bill each had a $40,000 adjusted basis in their Tillis stock on January 1. The ordinary loss is allocated equally to Pat and Bill. Pat's $52,000 loss allocation is only partially deductible this year (i.e., up to $40,000) because the loss exceeds his $40,000 stock basis. Bill's $52,000 loss allocation is fully deductible this year because his loss limitation is $60,000 ($40,000 stock basis + $20,000 debt basis). After the loss pass-through, Pat and Bill each have a zero stock basis and Bill has an $8,000 debt basis.[43] ◀

Any loss or deduction pass-through not currently deductible is suspended until the shareholder regains basis in his stock or debt. The carryover period for the loss or deduction item is unlimited.[44] The additional adjusted basis amount can originate from a number of sources, including subsequent profits earned by the S corporation, additional capital contributions or loans made by the shareholder to the corporation, or purchases of additional stock from other shareholders.

EXAMPLE C:11-19 ▶ Assume the same facts as in Example C:11-18 and that Tillis Corporation reports ordinary income of $24,000 next year. Pat and Bill each are allocated $12,000 of ordinary income. This income provides Pat with the necessary $12,000 stock basis to deduct the $12,000 loss carryover. The $12,000 income allocated to Bill restores his debt basis to $20,000 (see footnote 43). ◀

If a limited loss is made up of more than one type of income, the loss limitation is prorated between the different types of losses. For example, if a shareholder has a $6,000 stock basis, a $9,000 ordinary loss pass-through, and a $3,000 long-term capital loss pass-through, $4,500 ($6,000 × $9,000/$12,000) of the allowed loss is ordinary, and $1,500 ($6,000 × $3,000/$12,000) of the allowed loss is a long-term capital loss.

If a shareholder sells his or her S corporation stock still having unused losses due to lack of stock or debt basis, these losses do not transfer to the new shareholder. Instead, the unused losses lapse when the shareholder sells the stock. If the shareholder transfers the S corporation stock to a spouse or former spouse incident to a divorce, however, the suspended losses transfer to the spouse or former spouse. Thus, the spouse or former spouse can deduct the losses when he or she obtains sufficient basis.

Special Shareholder Loss and Deduction Limitations. S corporation shareholders are subject to three special loss and deduction limitations. These limitations may prevent an S corporation's shareholder from using losses or deductions even though the general loss limitation described above does not otherwise apply. Application of the special loss limitations occurs as follows:

KEY POINT

An advantage of an S election is that losses pass through to the shareholders. This advantage, however, is significantly limited by the at-risk and passive activity rules.

- *At-Risk Rules:* The Sec. 465 at-risk rules apply at the shareholder level. Thus, a shareholder can deduct a loss from a particular S corporation activity only to the extent the shareholder is at risk in the S corporation's activity at year-end.
- *Passive Activity Limitation Rules:* Losses and credits from a passive activity offset income earned from that passive activity or other passive activities in the same or subsequent tax year. An S corporation shareholder personally must meet the material participation standard for an activity to avoid the passive activity limitation. The S corporation's material participation in an activity does not allow a passive investor to deduct S corporation losses against his or her salary and other "active" income.
- *Hobby Loss Rules:* S corporation losses are subject to the Sec. 183 hobby loss rules, which limit deductions to the activity's gross income unless the S corporation can establish that it is engaged in the activity for profit.

In addition, various separately stated loss and deduction items are subject to shareholder limitations (e.g., charitable contributions, capital losses, and investment interest expenses), but they are not subject to corporate limitations. Conversely, some separately stated items are subject to corporate limitations but not shareholder limitations (e.g., the 50% nondeductible portion of meal and entertainment expenses).

Post-Termination Loss Carryovers. Loss and deduction carryovers incurred in S corporation tax years can carry over at the shareholder level even though the

[43] See pages C:11-24 through C:11-27 for a detailed discussion of basis adjustments.

[44] Sec. 1366(d)(2). If more than one type of loss or deduction item passes through to the shareholder, the carryover amount is allocated to each of the pass-through items based on their relative amounts.

SELF-STUDY QUESTION

If losses are suspended due to the lack of basis in S corporation stock, do the losses expire when the S election terminates?

ANSWER

No. These loss carryovers may be deducted in the post-termination transition period (usually one year) if the shareholder creates additional stock basis in that period of time.

S election has terminated. Shareholders can deduct these carryovers only in the **post-termination transition period.**[45] The length of the post-termination transition period depends on the event causing the termination. In general, the period begins on the day after the last day of the corporation's final S corporation tax year and ends on the later of one year after the last day or the due date for the final S corporation tax return (including any extensions).

If the S election terminates for a prior tax year as a result of a determination, the period runs for 120 days beginning on the determination date. Section 1377(b)(2) defines a determination as a court decision that becomes final, a closing agreement entered into, a final disposition of a refund claim by the IRS, or an agreement between the corporation and the IRS that the corporation failed to qualify as an S corporation.

The shareholder can deduct the loss carryovers only up to his or her adjusted basis of the stock at the end of the post-termination transition period.[46] Losses that cannot be deducted because of the basis limitation are lost forever. Deducted losses reduce the shareholder's stock basis.

EXAMPLE C:11-20 ▶ Sigma Corporation has been a calendar year S corporation for several years. Helen's stock basis is $45,000. On July 1, 2017, its S election terminates when an ineligible shareholder acquires part of its stock. For the period ended June 30, 2017, Helen is allocated $60,000 of Sigma's ordinary loss. Helen can deduct only $45,000 of this loss because of her Sigma stock basis, which the loss reduces to zero. The $15,000 unused loss carries over to the post-termination transition period, which ends on June 30, 2018, assuming Sigma does not extend the March 15, 2018, due date for the S short-year tax return. Helen must have an adjusted basis for the Sigma stock of at least $15,000 at the close of business on June 30, 2018, to use the loss. Helen should consider making additional capital contributions of at least $15,000 between July 1, 2017, and June 30, 2018, to use the loss. ◄

Topic Review C:11-3 summarizes the rules governing deductibility of S corporation losses and deductions that pass through to the shareholders.

TOPIC REVIEW C:11-3

Deductibility of S Corporation Losses and Deductions

ALLOCATION PROCESS

1. Losses and deductions are allocated based on the number of shares of stock owned by each shareholder on each day of the tax year. Special allocations of losses and deductions are not permitted.
2. Termination of the S election requires the tax year to be divided into two parts. The corporation can elect (with the shareholders' consent) to allocate the loss or deduction according to the corporation's accounting methods. This election also is available when a shareholder's interest in the S corporation terminates.

LOSS LIMITATIONS

1. Losses and deductions pass through on a per-share basis and are limited to the shareholder's basis in stock and debt. Once the basis for all the shareholder's stock is reduced to zero, the losses reduce the basis of any S corporation indebtedness to the shareholder.
2. Losses and deductions that are not deducted carry over to a tax year in which the shareholder regains stock or debt basis. The time period for the carryover is unlimited. The unused losses lapse if the shareholder transfers the stock to anyone other than a spouse or former spouse incident to a divorce.
3. S corporation shareholders are subject to three special loss limitations:
   - ▶ At-risk rules
   - ▶ Passive activity limitations
   - ▶ Hobby loss rules

   Some separately stated loss and deduction items also are subject to shareholder limitations (e.g., investment interest expense). Other separately stated items are subject to corporate limitations but not shareholder limitations (e.g., the 50% nondeductible portion of meal and entertainment expenses).

---

[45] Sec. 1366(d)(3). The loss carryovers that carry over include those disallowed by the at-risk rules.

[46] Sec. 1366(d)(3)(B).

FAMILY S CORPORATIONS

Family S corporations have been an important tax planning device. This type of tax planning often involves a high-tax-bracket taxpayer gifting stock to a minor child who generally has little other income. The transfer results in income splitting among family members. The IRS has enjoyed success in litigating cases dealing with intrafamily transfers of S corporation stock when the transferor (usually a parent) retains the economic benefits and control over the stock transferred to the transferee (usually a child).[47] The IRS has attained less success when one family member purchases the stock from another family member at its market value.

ADDITIONAL COMMENT

The advantages of family S corporations have been somewhat curtailed. For example, income from stock of an S corporation gifted to a child under age 18 (and, in some cases, age 18 through 23) is subject to the "kiddie tax," where unearned income exceeding $2,100 (in 2017) is taxed at the parents' marginal tax rate.

The IRS also has the statutory authority to adjust the income, loss, deduction, or credit items allocated to a family member to reflect the value of services rendered or capital provided to the corporation. Section 1366(e) defines family as including spouse, ancestors, lineal descendants, and trusts created for such individuals. This provision permits the reallocation of income to provide for full compensation of a shareholder or nonshareholder for services and capital provided to the corporation. It also reduces the residual income reported by the S corporation and allocated to the shareholders according to their stock ownership. Such a reallocation prevents not only the shifting of income from the family member providing the services or capital to other family members, but also the avoidance of employment taxes. Alternatively, the IRS can determine that the corporation paid too much compensation to a shareholder and reduce that shareholder's salary and increase the residual income allocated based on stock ownership.

EXAMPLE C:11-21 ▶ Harvest Corporation, an S corporation, reports ordinary income of $200,000 after it claims a $20,000 deduction for Sid's salary. Sid and his three children own the Harvest stock equally. Harvest employs none of Sid's three children. The IRS subsequently determines that reasonable compensation for Sid is $80,000. This adjustment increases Sid's salary income and Harvest's compensation deduction by $60,000 ($80,000 − $20,000) and reduces Harvest's ordinary income to $140,000 ($200,000 − $60,000). Each shareholder's ratable share of ordinary income is reduced from $50,000 ($200,000 ÷ 4) to $35,000 ($140,000 ÷ 4). These adjustments have a twofold effect. First, they increase the amount of income allocable to Sid ($80,000 + $35,000 vs. $20,000 + $50,000), where Sid may be in a higher tax bracket than his children. Second, the increased salary increases Sid's employment taxes. Alternatively, if the IRS can prove that the stock transfer to the three children is not a bona fide transfer, all $220,000 of Harvest's income is taxed to Sid—$80,000 as salary and $140,000 as an allocation of ordinary income. ◀

BASIS ADJUSTMENTS

OBJECTIVE 6

Calculate a shareholder's basis in his or her S corporation stock and debt

Shareholder's must adjust their S corporation stock basis annually. In addition, if the S corporation is indebted to the shareholder, he or she may have to adjust the debt basis downward for loss or deduction pass-throughs and upward to reflect restoration of the debt basis when the corporation earns subsequent profits. Each of these adjustments is described below.

BASIS ADJUSTMENTS TO S CORPORATION STOCK

Basis adjustments to the shareholder's stock are made in the following order:[48]

Initial investment (or basis at beginning of tax year)
Plus: Additional capital contributions made during the year
 Allocable share of ordinary income
 Allocable share of separately stated income and gain items

---

[47] See, for example, *Gino A. Speca v. CIR*, 47 AFTR 2d 81-468, 80-2 USTC ¶9692 (7th Cir., 1980) and *Henry D. Duarte*, 44 T.C. 193 (1965), where the IRS's position prevailed. See also *Gavin S. Millar*, 1975 PH T.C. Memo ¶75,113, 34 TCM 554, and *Donald O. Kirkpatrick*, 1977 PH T.C. Memo ¶77, 281, 36 TCM 1122, where the taxpayers prevailed.

[48] Sec. 1367(a) and Reg. Sec. 1.1367-1(f).

SELF-STUDY QUESTION

Why is the determination of stock basis in an S corporation important?

ANSWER

To determine gain or loss on the sale of the stock, to determine the amount of losses that can be deducted, and to determine the amount of distributions to shareholders that are nontaxable.

Minus: Distributions excluded from the shareholder's gross income
Allocable share of any expense not deductible in determining ordinary income (loss) and not chargeable to the capital account (A shareholder, however, can elect to make this adjustment *after* the two following adjustments.)
Allocable share of ordinary loss
Allocable share of separately stated loss and deduction items

Adjusted basis for stock (but not less than zero)

A shareholder's initial basis for S corporation stock depends on how he or she acquires it. Stock purchased from the corporation or another shareholder takes a cost basis. Stock received as part of a corporate formation takes a substituted basis from the assets transferred. Stock acquired by gift takes the donor's basis (adjusted for gift taxes paid) or FMV (if lower). Stock acquired at death takes its FMV on the decedent's date of death or the alternate valuation date (if elected). The basis of S corporation stock inherited from a deceased shareholder is its FMV minus any corporate income that would have been income in respect of a decedent (see Chapter C:14) if the income had been acquired from the decedent. No basis adjustment occurs when the corporation makes the initial S election.

The basis adjustments to the S corporation stock parallel those made to a partnership interest. The ordinary income and separately stated income and gain items increase the shareholder's basis whether they are taxable, tax-exempt, or receive preferential tax treatment.

EXAMPLE C:11-22 ▶ Cathy owns Marlo Corporation, an S corporation. At the beginning of the current year, Cathy's adjusted basis in her Marlo stock is $105,000. Marlo reports the following operating results this year:

Ordinary income	$70,000
Municipal bond interest income	15,000
Dividends from domestic corporations	6,000
Long-term capital gain	8,000
Short-term capital loss	17,000

Cathy's adjusted basis in her Marlo stock at year-end is $187,000 ($105,000 + $70,000 + $15,000 + $6,000 + $8,000 − $17,000). ◀

Cathy makes the basis adjustment at the end of the S corporation's tax year, when the results for the entire period are known. Because profits and losses are allocated ratably on a daily basis to all shares held on each day of the tax year, a shareholder's gain or loss realized on the sale of S corporation stock during the tax year is not determinable until the ordinary income or loss and separately stated items allocable to the shares sold are known. Similarly, when S corporation stock becomes worthless during a tax year, the shareholder must make the necessary positive and negative basis adjustments before determining the amount of the worthless security loss.

EXAMPLE C:11-23 ▶ Mike, Carlos, and Juan equally own Diaz Corporation, an S corporation. Mike's 100 shares of Diaz stock have a $25,000 adjusted basis at the beginning of the current year (not a leap year). Diaz reports ordinary income of $36,500 and municipal bond interest income of $14,600 in the current year. On February 14 of the current year (the 45th day of Diaz's tax year), Mike sells all his Diaz stock for $30,000. Assuming the corporation uses the daily method to allocate the income items, Mike's basis for the Diaz stock is $27,100, determined as follows:

$$\$27{,}100 = \$25{,}000 + \left(\$36{,}500 \times \frac{45}{365} \times \frac{1}{3}\right) + \left(\$14{,}600 \times \frac{45}{365} \times \frac{1}{3}\right)$$

Mike reports a $2,900 ($30,000 − $27,100) gain on the sale. ◀

KEY POINT

Losses first reduce basis in stock and then any amount of debt owed to the shareholder by the S corporation. Subsequent *net* increases in basis are added first to debt and then to stock.

BASIS ADJUSTMENTS TO SHAREHOLDER DEBT

After the shareholder's basis in S corporation stock is reduced to zero, basis in any S corporation indebtedness to the shareholder is reduced (but not below zero) by the remainder of the available loss and deduction items.[49] If a shareholder has more than one loan outstanding at year-end, the basis reduction applies to all the indebtednesses based on the relative adjusted basis of each loan. Ordinary income and separately stated gain or income items allocated to the shareholder in subsequent tax years (net of distributions and losses to the shareholders) first restore debt basis. Once all previous decreases to debt basis are restored, any additional positive basis adjustments increase the shareholder's stock basis.[50]

Repayment of a shareholder indebtedness results in gain recognition to the shareholder if the payment amount exceeds the debt's adjusted basis. If the indebtedness is secured by a note, the difference is a capital gain. If the indebtedness is not secured by a note or other evidence of the indebtedness, the repayment is ordinary income.[51]

EXAMPLE C:11-24 ▶ At the beginning of Year 1, Betty owns one-half the stock of Trailer Corporation, an S corporation. Betty's basis in the Trailer stock is $40,000. Trailer owes Betty $20,000 on January 1, Year 1, evidenced by a note. Thus, Betty has a $20,000 debt basis. During Year 1, Trailer reports an ordinary loss of $100,000 and during Year 2 reports ordinary income of $10,000. Betty's $50,000 loss pass-through from Year 1 first reduces her stock basis from $40,000 to zero. Next, the $10,000 remainder of the loss pass-through reduces Betty's debt basis from $20,000 to $10,000. Betty's $5,000 allocation of Year 2's ordinary income increases her debt basis from $10,000 to $15,000. If the corporation repays the note before the end of Year 2, Betty reports a $5,000 ($20,000 − $15,000) long-term capital gain resulting from the repayment plus $5,000 of ordinary income from Trailer's Year 2 operations. If the debt instead were unsecured (i.e., an advance from the shareholder not secured by a note), the gain would be ordinary income. ◀

? STOP & THINK

Question: The text preceding Example C:11-24 says that ordinary income and separately stated gain or income items (net of losses and distributions) restore debt basis before increasing stock basis; that is, debt is restored first by any net increase. The following rule also applies: total basis for the loss limitation equals (1) stock basis *after* all current year adjustments other than for losses plus (2) debt basis *before* any current year adjustments.

Consider the following situation: Omega Corporation is an S corporation with one shareholder. At the beginning of last year, the shareholder's stock basis was $15,000, and her debt basis was $20,000. Last year, Omega incurred a $45,000 ordinary loss, $35,000 of which the shareholder could deduct and $10,000 of which carries over. The loss affected basis as follows:

	Stock Basis	*Debt Basis*
Basis at beginning of last year	$15,000	$20,000
Ordinary loss last year ($45,000)	(15,000)	(20,000)
Basis at beginning of current year	$ -0-	$ -0-

In the current year, Omega earns $18,000 of ordinary income. What does the shareholder recognize in the current year, and what is the effect on her stock and debt bases? Why is the net increase rule for debt basis restoration beneficial to the shareholder?

Solution: The shareholder recognizes $18,000 of ordinary income and deducts the entire $10,000 loss carryover. Current year basis adjustments are as follows:

	Stock Basis	*Debt Basis*
Balance at beginning of current year	$ -0-	$ -0-
Ordinary income	10,000	8,000
Loss carryover allowed	(10,000)	-0-
Basis at end of current year	$ -0-	$8,000

The net increase approach benefits the shareholder because it allows her to deduct the $10,000 loss carryover in the current year rather than next year. The net increase for debt

[49] The shareholder makes no basis reductions to debt repaid before the end of the tax year. Regulation Sec. 1.1367-2(d)(1) holds that restoration occurs immediately before a shareholder repays or disposes of indebtedness during the tax year.

[50] Sec. 1367(b)(2)(B).

[51] Rev. Ruls. 64-162, 1964-1 (Part I) C.B. 304 and 68-537, 1968-2 C.B. 372.

restoration is $8,000 ($18,000 − $10,000), which leaves $10,000 of the $18,000 ordinary income to increase stock basis. This net increase approach to debt restoration allows a stock basis increase sufficient to use the loss carryover. Alternatively, if debt were restored by ordinary income without netting, the debt basis would increase by the entire $18,000, leaving no positive adjustment to the stock basis. This increase to debt basis would not help the shareholder in the current year because debt basis for the loss limitation is the balance before any current year adjustments. Under this hypothetical alternative approach, the shareholder could deduct the loss next year because next year's beginning debt basis would be $18,000. However, the net increase approach is better than the alternative because it allows the shareholder to deduct the loss in the current year.

S CORPORATION DISTRIBUTIONS

OBJECTIVE 7

Determine the taxability of an S corporation's distributions to its shareholders

Two sets of rules apply to S corporation distributions. One applies to S corporations having accumulated E&P. Accumulated E&P may exist if an S corporation was a C corporation in a pre–S election tax year. Another set of distribution rules applies to S corporations that do not have E&P (e.g., a corporation formed after 1982 that makes a timely S election in its initial tax year). These rules are explained below.

CORPORATIONS HAVING NO EARNINGS AND PROFITS

For S corporations with no accumulated E&P, a two-tier rule applies. Distributions are initially nontaxable and reduce the shareholder's stock basis (but not below zero). If the distribution exceeds the shareholder's stock basis, the shareholder treats the excess as a gain from the sale or exchange of the stock. Stock basis for determining excess distributions is that after positive adjustments for ordinary income and separately stated income and gain items but before negative adjustments.[52]

EXAMPLE C:11-25 ▶ Sandy owns 100% of Liberty Corporation, an S corporation. At the beginning of the current year, Sandy's adjusted basis in her Liberty stock (a capital asset) is $20,000, and she has no debt basis. In the current year, Liberty reports ordinary income of $30,000 and a long-term capital loss of $7,000. Liberty makes a $35,000 cash distribution to Sandy on June 15. Sandy's basis for the stock must be adjusted for the ordinary income before determining the taxability of the distribution. Because Sandy's $50,000 ($20,000 + $30,000) adjusted stock basis exceeds the $35,000 distribution, she excludes the entire distribution from her gross income. The distribution reduces her stock basis to $15,000 ($50,000 − $35,000). Because Sandy still has sufficient stock basis, she can deduct the $7,000 capital loss, which further reduces her stock basis to $8,000.

If Liberty instead reports only $5,000 of ordinary income and a $7,000 capital loss, $10,000 of the distribution is taxable. The ordinary income increases the stock's basis to $25,000 ($20,000 + $5,000). Because the distribution exceeds the stock's adjusted basis by $10,000 ($35,000 − $25,000), Sandy recognizes a capital gain on the excess distribution. The distribution not included in Sandy's income ($25,000) reduces her stock basis to zero at year-end. Because the stock basis after the distribution is zero, Sandy cannot deduct the $7,000 capital loss in the current year. She must wait until she regains a positive stock basis (or obtains debt basis by lending money to the corporation). ◀

SELF-STUDY QUESTION

Can distributions that exceed stock basis be nontaxable to the extent of shareholder loans?

ANSWER

No. Although the amount of deductible losses can be increased by the amount of shareholder loans, nontaxable distributions are strictly limited to stock basis. Also, distributions never reduce debt basis.

If an S corporation distributes appreciated property to its shareholders, the S corporation recognizes gain as if it sold the property.[53] The corporation recognizes no loss, however, when it distributes property that has declined in value. The gain recognized on the distribution may be taxed at the corporate level as part of the S corporation's built-in gains or excess net passive income. The gain also becomes part of the S corporation's ordinary income or loss, or is passed through as a separately stated item, depending on the type of

[52] Secs. 1368(b)and (d).

[53] Sec. 311(b).

property distributed and the character of the gain recognized. After this recognition occurs, the distributed property causes no further taxation provided the sum of the money plus the FMV of the noncash property distributed does not exceed the shareholder's stock basis. The shareholder's stock basis is reduced by the FMV of the distribution, and the shareholder takes a FMV basis in the distributed property.

EXAMPLE C:11-26 ▶ Tad owns 100% of Echo Corporation, which always has been an S corporation. Tad's stock basis at the beginning of the current year is $50,000. Echo reports $30,000 of ordinary income for this year (exclusive of the effects of a property distribution to Tad). On December 1, Echo distributes some Cable Corporation stock to Tad. The stock cost $40,000 and has a $100,000 FMV, and Echo has held it as an investment for three years. Echo reports $60,000 ($100,000 – $40,000) of capital gain from distributing the stock. Tad reports $30,000 of ordinary income and $60,000 of long-term capital gain from Echo's current year activities. Tad's stock basis increases to $140,000 ($50,000 + $30,000 + $60,000). The distribution is free of further taxation because the $140,000 stock basis exceeds the $100,000 distribution. The stock basis is $40,000 ($140,000 – $100,000) at year-end. Tad takes a $100,000 FMV basis in the Cable stock. ◀

ADDITIONAL COMMENT

The distribution of appreciated stock in Example C:11-26 produced income to Echo, which passed through to Tad. A similar distribution by a C corporation would result in a double tax by causing income recognition to both Echo and Tad.

CORPORATIONS HAVING ACCUMULATED EARNINGS AND PROFITS

Prior Rules. Under pre-1983 rules, a corporation's undistributed taxable income was taxed to its shareholders as a deemed distribution at year-end. This income accumulated in a **previously taxed income (PTI)** account, which can be a source of S corporation distributions. For simplicity in this text, however, the following discussion assumes that S corporation status occurs after 1982 and thus ignores the implications of PTI.

KEY POINT

The AAA represents the cumulative income and loss recognized in post-1982 S corporation years. To the extent the AAA is positive and sufficient basis exists in the stock, distributions from an S corporation are nontaxable and reduce stock basis.

Current Rules. Under current (post-1982) rules, some S corporations have a post-1982 accumulated E&P balance earned while a C corporation. Part or all of a distribution may be treated as made from this balance. The current rules, however, also require S corporations that have accumulated E&P balances to maintain an **accumulated adjustments account (AAA)** from which they make most of their distributions. The existence of accumulated E&P and AAA balances makes the tax treatment of cash and property distributions somewhat more complicated than do the rules explained in the preceding section.

Money Distributions. For corporations making a post-1982 S election and having an accumulated E&P balance, money distributions come from the two tiers of earnings illustrated in Table C:11-1. The corporation makes distributions from the first tier until it is exhausted. The corporation then makes distributions from the second tier until that tier is used up. Amounts distributed after the two tiers of earnings are exhausted reduce the shareholder's remaining basis in his or her S corporation stock. Any additional amounts distributed once stock basis has been reduced to zero are taxed to the shareholder as a capital gain. The corporation usually maintains these tiers as working paper accounts and not as general ledger accounts.

The AAA is the cumulative total of the ordinary income or loss and separately stated items accumulated for the S period but excluding tax-exempt income and expenses related to its production. The S period is the most recent continuous period during which the corporation has been an S corporation. No tax years beginning before 1983 are included in this period.[54]

The year-end AAA balance is determined as follows:

AAA balance at the beginning of the year
Plus: Ordinary income
Separately stated income and gain items (except for tax-exempt income)

[54] Sec. 1368(e). An S corporation without accumulated E&P need not maintain the AAA to determine the tax effect of its distributions. If an S corporation having no E&P subsequently acquires E&P in a transaction where it assumes tax attributes under Sec. 381(a) (e.g., a merger), the corporation must calculate its AAA at the merger date to determine the tax effects of post-merger distributions. To accomplish this calculation, a firm may need to make calculations back to the original S election date. To reduce this hardship, the IRS, in the Form 1120S instructions, recommends that all S corporations maintain AAA information.

▼ **TABLE C:11-1**
Source of Money or Property Distributions Made by S Corporations Having Accumulated Earnings and Profits

Tier	Classification	Treatment of Distributions
1	Accumulated adjustments account	Nontaxable[a]
2	Accumulated E&P	Taxable (dividend)
3	Basis of S corporation stock	Nontaxable[a]
4	Excess over stock basis	Taxable (capital gain)

[a] These distributions reduce the basis of the S corporation stock. Although generally nontaxable, gain can be recognized if the amount of money plus the FMV of the noncash property distributed exceeds the shareholder's adjusted basis in the S corporation stock as indicated in Tier 4.

Minus:	Distributions made from AAA (see first bullet item below)
	Ordinary loss
	Separately stated loss and deduction items (except for expenses or losses related to the production of tax-exempt income)
	Expenses not deductible in determining ordinary income (loss) and not chargeable to the capital account
AAA balance at the end of the year	

Four differences exist between the positive and negative adjustments required for the AAA and the basis calculation for S corporation stock:

- Distributions not included in gross income reduce *stock* basis *before* other negative adjustments. Distributions reduce the AAA *after* other negative adjustments unless the other negative adjustments, when netted against positive adjustments, produce a "net negative adjustment." In this case, positive adjustments increase the AAA and negative adjustments other than distributions reduce the AAA to the extent of the positive adjustments. Then, distributions reduce the AAA before the net negative adjustment, and the net negative adjustment reduces the AAA after the distribution.[55]
- Tax-exempt income does not increase the AAA but increases the basis of S corporation stock.
- Nondeductible expenses that reduce stock basis also reduce the AAA except for expenses related to the production of tax-exempt income and federal income taxes related to a C corporation tax year.
- The AAA balance can be negative (e.g., when the cumulative losses exceed the cumulative profits), but a shareholder's stock basis cannot be less than zero.

TYPICAL MISCONCEPTION

Even though stock basis cannot be less than zero, the AAA can be negative if cumulative losses exceed cumulative profits.

Allocation of the AAA balance to individual distributions occurs at year-end after taking into account current year income and loss items. In general, the AAA balance is allocated ratably to individual distributions within a tax year (other than distributions coming from E&P) based on the amount of money or FMV of noncash property distributed.

[55] Reg. Secs. 1.1367-1(f) and 1.1368-2(a)(5). This ordering for AAA preserves nontaxable treatment for S corporation earnings from prior years distributed in the loss year.

Corporations also maintain an Other Adjustments Account (OAA) if they have accumulated E&P at year-end. The corporation increases this account for tax-exempt income earned and decreases it by expenses incurred in earning the tax-exempt income, distributions out of the OAA, and federal taxes paid by the S corporation that are attributable to C corporation tax years. The effect of creating a separate account for tax-exempt income earned by companies having accumulated E&P is that the AAA is determined by taking into account only the taxable portion of the S corporation's income and any expenses and losses other than those related to the production of the tax-exempt income. Although the corporation reports the OAA balance on page 4 of the Form 1120S, it is not an accumulated earnings account. Municipal bond interest and other forms of tax-exempt income (net of related deductions) become part of the stock basis and thus appear after accumulated E&P in the distribution order. A corporation having an accumulated E&P balance might consider having the tax-exempt income-producing property owned at the shareholder level rather than at the corporate level.

EXAMPLE C:11-27 ▶ Omega Corporation is an S corporation with one shareholder, George. George's stock basis at the beginning of the current year is $22,000. Omega reports the following results for the current year:

Ordinary loss	$10,000
Dividend income	2,000

In addition, at the beginning of the current year, the corporation has a $12,000 AAA balance and a $4,000 accumulated E&P balance. In December of the current year, Omega distributes $7,500 cash to George. Because the ordinary loss and dividend income produce an $8,000 ($2,000 − $10,000) net negative adjustment, the predistribution AAA remains at $12,000 while the $2,000 dividend increases predistribution stock basis. Accordingly, the predistribution balances are as follows:

	Stock Basis	*AAA*	*E&P*
Beginning balances	$22,000	$12,000	$4,000
Dividend income	2,000	2,000	
Partial ordinary loss		(2,000)	
Predistribution balance	$24,000	$12,000	$4,000

Given these predistribution balances, the distribution has the following effects:

	Stock Basis	*AAA*	*E&P*
Predistribution balance	$24,000	$12,000	$4,000
AAA distribution	(7,500)	(7,500)	
Ordinary loss	(10,000)		
Net negative adjustment		(8,000)	
Ending balance	$ 6,500	($3,500)	$4,000

Because the net negative adjustment to the AAA occurs after the distribution, the entire distribution comes out of the AAA, and none comes out of accumulated E&P. Also, the distribution does not exceed the predistribution stock basis. Thus, the entire distribution is nontaxable. ◀

EXAMPLE C:11-28 ▶ Sigma Corporation, an S corporation, reports the following results during the current year:

Ordinary income	$30,000
Long-term capital gain	15,000
Municipal bond interest income	5,000
Dividend from domestic corporation	3,000
Charitable contribution	8,000

Sigma's sole shareholder, Silvia, has a $60,000 stock basis on January 1. On January 1, Sigma has a $40,000 AAA balance, a $27,000 accumulated E&P balance, and a zero OAA balance. Sigma makes $50,000 cash distributions to Silvia, its sole shareholder, on June 1 and December 1. The stock basis, AAA, OAA, and accumulated E&P activity for the year (before any distributions) is summarized as follows:

TYPICAL MISCONCEPTION

If shareholders sell their S corporation stock, the AAA account remains with the S corporation. But if an S election terminates, other than for the post-termination transition period, the AAA disappears.

	Stock Basis	*AAA*	*E&P*	*OAA*
Beginning balance	$ 60,000	$40,000	$27,000	$ -0-
Ordinary income	30,000	30,000		
Long-term capital gain	15,000	15,000		
Municipal bond interest	5,000			5,000
Dividend income	3,000	3,000		
Charitable contribution		(8,000)		
Predistribution balance	$113,000	$80,000	$27,000	$5,000

The $80,000 AAA balance is allocated ratably to each of the distributions as follows:

$$\$40,000 = \$50,000 \times \frac{\$80,000}{\$50,000 + \$50,000}$$

The charitable contribution does not reduce the predistribution stock basis but does reduce the predistribution AAA because the reduction does not produce a net negative adjustment. Accordingly, $40,000 of each distribution comes out of AAA. This portion of the distribution is nontaxable because the AAA distributions in total are less than the stock's $113,000 predistribution basis. The remaining $10,000 ($50,000 − $40,000) of each distribution comes out of accumulated E&P and is taxable as dividend income. Accumulated E&P is reduced to $7,000 ($27,000 − $20,000) at year-end. The OAA balance reported on Form 1120S is not affected by the distribution because the accumulated E&P has not been exhausted. The stock's basis is $25,000 ($113,000 − $80,000 − $8,000) at year-end because a dividend distribution from accumulated E&P does not reduce its basis, but the charitable contribution does. After adjustment for the distribution, the AAA is zero. The effects of the distribution are summarized below:

	Stock Basis	*AAA*	*E&P*	*OAA*
Predistribution balance	$113,000	$80,000	$27,000	$5,000
AAA distribution	(80,000)	(80,000)		
E&P distribution			(20,000)	
Charitable contribution	(8,000)			
Ending balance	$ 25,000	$ -0-	$ 7,000	$5,000

◄

Property Distributions. Property distributions (other than money) made by an S corporation having accumulated E&P trigger gain recognition according to the general rules described on pages C:11-27 and C:11-28. The FMV of the noncash property distributed reduces AAA.

TAX STRATEGY TIP

If a shareholder has NOL carryforwards that are about to expire, the election to treat distributions as dividend income to the extent of E&P (as opposed to AAA distributions) may make sense.

Distribution Ordering Elections. An S corporation can elect to change the distribution order of E&P and the AAA. Specifically, the S corporation can elect to skip over the AAA in determining the source of a cash or property distribution, in which case distributions will come from accumulated E&P and then AAA. This election permits the S corporation to distribute Subchapter C E&P so as to avoid the excess net passive income tax and termination of the S election. The Tax Planning Considerations section of this chapter contains further discussion of this election.

Post-Termination Transition Period. Nontaxable distributions of money made during the S corporation's post-termination transition period can be made to those shareholders who owned S corporation stock on the termination date. These distributions come first from the former S corporation's AAA balance and then from current and accumulated E&P. The amounts from the AAA are nontaxable and reduce the shareholder's stock basis.[56] The AAA balance disappears when the post-termination period ends. Even though the profits earned during the S election period no longer can be distributed tax-free from the AAA after the post-termination period ends, they still can be distributed tax-free to the extent of the shareholder's stock basis once the corporation

[56] Sec. 1371(e).

TOPIC REVIEW C:11-4

Taxation of S Corporation Income and Distributions

Taxation of Income to the Corporation

1. Unlike with a partnership, special entity level taxes apply to an S corporation.
   a. Built-in gains tax: applicable to the net recognized built-in gain of an S corporation that formerly was a C corporation and that made its S election after December 31, 1986.
   b. Excess net passive income tax: applicable to S corporations that have Subchapter C E&P at year-end and that earn passive investment income exceeding 25% of gross receipts during the tax year.
   c. LIFO recapture tax: imposed when a C corporation that uses the LIFO inventory method in its final C corporation tax year makes an S election.

Allocation of Income to the Shareholders

1. Income and gains are allocated based on the number of shares of stock owned by each shareholder on each day of the tax year.
2. Termination of the S election or termination of the shareholder's interest in the S corporation during the tax year requires the tax year to be divided into two parts. The S corporation can elect to allocate the income or gain according to the general rule in (1) or the accounting methods used by the corporation.

Shareholder Distributions

1. Income and gain allocated to the shareholder increase the basis of the S corporation stock. For any S corporation that does not have an E&P balance, the amount of money plus the FMV of any noncash property distributed is nontaxable provided it does not exceed the shareholder's stock basis, determined before negative adjustments. The corporation recognizes gain (but not loss) when it distributes noncash property. The gain passes through to the shareholders.
2. If the S corporation made the S election after 1982 and has accumulated E&P, two earnings tiers must be maintained: the AAA and accumulated E&P. Distributions come from each tier in succeeding order until the tier is exhausted. Distributions out of accumulated E&P are taxable to the shareholder as dividends. Other distributions are nontaxable unless stock basis is reduced to zero, in which case the shareholder recognizes capital gain on the excess distribution.

distributes its current and accumulated E&P. Any distributions made from current or accumulated E&P and noncash distributions made during the post-termination transition period are taxable.

Topic Review C:11-4 summarizes the taxation of S corporation income and gains that pass through to the shareholders and the treatment of S corporation distributions.

? STOP & THINK

Question: Special earnings tracking rules apply to S corporations that formerly were C corporations. Why do we need to have these special rules, which add complexity to the distribution topic?

Solution: Former C corporations that were profitable usually have an accumulated E&P balance when they become an S corporation. These earnings have never been taxed as a dividend to the corporation's shareholders. If separate tracking of the S corporation earnings (AAA) and C corporation earnings (accumulated E&P) did not occur, it would be impossible to determine which cash and property distributions came from S corporation earnings and which ones came from C corporation earnings, thereby frustrating the government's ability to collect taxes on distributed E&P.

Other Rules

OBJECTIVE 8

Explain other rules that pertain to S corporations

In addition to the differences discussed above, S corporations differ from C corporations in a number of other ways. As discussed below, these differences include tax preference items and other alternative minimum tax (AMT) adjustments, expenses owed by the S corporation to a shareholder, related party sales and exchanges, and fringe benefits paid by the S corporation to a shareholder-employee.

TAX PREFERENCE ITEMS AND OTHER AMT ADJUSTMENTS

The S corporation is not subject to the corporate AMT. Instead, the S corporation computes and passes through tax preference items contained in Sec. 57(a) to its shareholders. The shareholders then include these tax preference items in their individual AMT calculations. Allocation of the tax preference items occurs on a daily basis unless the corporation makes one of the two special elections to allocate the items based on the corporation's tax accounting methods.

Section 56(a) prescribes a number of adjustments to the tax reporting of certain transactions and occurrences for AMT purposes from that used for income tax purposes. As with tax preference items, these special AMT adjustments pass through to the S corporation's shareholders to be included in their individual AMT calculations.

S corporations do not have to make an adjustment for the difference between adjusted current earnings and preadjustment alternative minimum taxable income that a C corporation makes in calculating its AMT liability. For certain corporations, this difference may make an S election attractive.[57]

TRANSACTIONS INVOLVING SHAREHOLDERS AND OTHER RELATED PARTIES

The Sec. 267(a)(2) related party transaction rules deny a payor a deduction for an expense paid to a related payee when a mismatching of the expense and income items occurs because of differences in accounting methods. A number of related party situations directly involve S corporations. Some of these transactions involve two S corporations or an S corporation and a C corporation where the same shareholders directly or indirectly own more than 50% of the value of each corporation's stock. Section 267(a)(2), for example, prevents an S corporation using the accrual method from currently deducting a year-end expense accrued for an item owed to a second S corporation that uses the cash method when the same shareholders own both corporations. The first S corporation can deduct the expense on the day the second S corporation includes the income in its gross income.

The S corporation, being a pass-through entity, is subject to Sec. 267(e), which extends the Sec. 267(a)(2) related party transaction rules described above to any payment made by the S corporation to *any* person who directly or indirectly owns S corporation stock. This rule prevents the S corporation from deducting a payment to be made to one of its shareholders or to someone who indirectly owns such stock until the payee reports the income. Payments made to the S corporation by a person who directly or indirectly owns S corporation stock are similarly restricted.

EXAMPLE C:11-29 ▶ Vassar Corporation, an S corporation, uses the accrual method of accounting and a calendar tax year. On September 1, Year 1, Vassar borrows $50,000 from Joan, a cash basis taxpayer who owns 10% of the Vassar stock. Joan charges interest at an 8% annual rate. At year-end, Vassar accrues $1,000 of interest expense on the loan. The corporation pays six months of interest (including the $1,000 of accrued interest) to Joan on April 1, Year 2. Vassar cannot deduct the Year 1 accrued interest until it pays the interest in Year 2. ◀

Section 267(a)(1) denies a deduction for losses incurred on the sale or exchange of property directly or indirectly between related parties. The same definition of a related party applies for this purpose as in applying Sec. 267(a)(2) to expense transactions involving an S corporation. Any loss disallowed to the seller on the related party sale or exchange can offset gains realized by the purchaser on a subsequent sale or exchange.

FRINGE BENEFITS PAID TO A SHAREHOLDER-EMPLOYEE

The S corporation is not treated as a corporate taxpayer with respect to many fringe benefits paid to 2% shareholders.[58] Instead, the S corporation is treated the same as a partnership,

---

[57] Sec. 56(g)(6).

[58] Section 1372(b) defines a 2% shareholder as any person who directly or indirectly owns on any day of the S corporation's tax year more than 2% of its outstanding stock or stock possessing more than 2% of its voting power. The Sec. 318 stock attribution rules apply to determine whether the 2% threshold has been exceeded.

TYPICAL MISCONCEPTION

Most fringe benefits provided by a C corporation are deductible to the corporation and nontaxable to the employee. However, fringe benefits paid to a more-than-2% shareholder-employee of an S corporation are in many cases nondeductible unless taxable to the shareholder-employee as compensation.

and a 2% shareholder is treated as a partner of such partnership.[59] Because of this restriction, many fringe benefits paid to a 2% shareholder-employee of an S corporation are deductible by the corporation and taxable to the shareholder unless the benefit is specifically excludible from the shareholder's gross income under the particular fringe benefit provision. Shareholders owning 2% or less of the S corporation stock are treated as ordinary employees.

The special fringe benefit rules apply only to statutory fringe benefits. They do not apply to stock options, qualified retirement plans, and nonqualified deferred compensation. The fringe benefits limited by the more-than-2%-shareholder rule include group term life insurance premiums (Sec. 79), accident and health benefit plan insurance premiums and payments (Secs. 105 and 106), meals and lodging furnished by the employer (Sec. 119), and cafeteria plan benefits (Sec. 125). Fringe benefits that may be excluded by more-than-2%-shareholders include compensation for injuries and sickness (Sec. 104), educational assistance program benefits (Sec. 127), dependent care assistance program benefits (Sec. 129), and certain other fringe benefits (Sec. 132). For purposes of the Sec. 162(l) above-the-line deduction for self-employed taxpayer's health insurance premiums, a more-than-2%-shareholder is deemed to be self-employed.

EXAMPLE C:11-30 ▶ Bill and his wife Cathy each own 50% of Edison Corporation, an S corporation. Edison employs Bill and ten other individuals. All employees receive group term life insurance benefits based on their annual salaries. All employees except Bill can qualify for the Sec. 79 group term life insurance premium exclusion. Bill is treated as a partner and, therefore, does not qualify as an employee. Bill's premiums are taxable to Bill. Nevertheless, Edison can deduct the premiums paid to all its employees, including Bill. Because Bill is treated as self-employed under the 2% shareholder rules, he can deduct a portion of the premiums paid on the health insurance as a "for" AGI deduction under the Sec.162(l) rules applicable to health insurance payments made by all self-employed individuals. ◀

TAX PLANNING CONSIDERATIONS

OBJECTIVE 9

Identify tax planning opportunities for an S corporation and its shareholders

ELECTION TO ALLOCATE INCOME BASED ON THE S CORPORATION'S ACCOUNTING METHODS

As a general rule, the S corporation's ordinary income or loss and separately stated items are allocated based on the amount of stock owned by each shareholder on each day of the S corporation's tax year. A special "closing of books" election allows the income to be allocated based on the S corporation's accounting methods when the S election terminates or when a shareholder terminates or substantially reduces his or her entire interest in the S corporation.[60] The use of the S corporation's tax accounting method to allocate the year's profit or loss can permit income shifting among shareholders.

EXAMPLE C:11-31 ▶ At the beginning of the current year (assume not a leap year), Rod and Dana equally own Apex Corporation, an S corporation. During the current year, Apex reports ordinary income of \$146,000. On March 31 of the current year (the 90th day of Apex's tax year), Dana sells all his Apex stock to Randy. Apex earns \$125,000 of its ordinary income after March 31 of the current year. Rod is allocated \$73,000 (\$146,000 × 0.50) of ordinary income. His income allocation is the same whether the corporation uses the daily allocation method or the special allocation election. In total, Dana and Randy are allocated \$73,000 of ordinary income. Dana and Randy can allocate the ordinary income amount in the following ways:

[59] Sec. 1372(a).

[60] The shareholder, however, still can be a creditor, director, or employee of the corporation. Sections 1362(e) and 1377(a) prevent the daily allocation method from applying to any items resulting from a sale or exchange of 50% or more of the S corporation's stock during an S termination year.

	Daily Allocation	*Closing of Books Election*
Dana:	$\$146{,}000 \times \frac{1}{2} \times \frac{90}{365} = \$18{,}000$	$(\$146{,}000 - \$125{,}000) \times \frac{1}{2} = \$10{,}500$
Randy:	$\$146{,}000 \times \frac{1}{2} \times \frac{275}{365} = \$55{,}000$	$\$125{,}000 \times \frac{1}{2} = \$62{,}500$

The shifting of the $7,500 in income from Dana ($18,000 – $10,500) to Randy ($62,500 – $55,000) under the special election also reduces Dana's adjusted basis for his Apex stock when determining his gain or loss on the sale. The $7,500 difference between the income allocations under the two methods may be a point for negotiation between Dana and Randy, particularly if their marginal tax rates differ. ◄

By electing to use the S corporation's tax accounting method to allocate profits or losses between the C short year and S short year in the termination year, the corporation can shift losses into an S short year where the shareholders obtain an immediate benefit at a marginal tax rate of up to 39.6%, or it can shift profits into a C short year to take advantage of the 15% and 25% marginal corporate tax rates. The C corporation, however, must annualize its short-year income in determining its tax liability.

EXAMPLE C:11-32 ► Delta Corporation has been an S corporation for several years using a calendar year as its tax year. The corporation has one shareholder whose marginal tax rate is 33%. Delta's S election terminates on July 1. The S short year includes January 1 through June 30, and the C short year includes July 1 through December 31. Total ordinary income this year is $10,000. If the corporation closes its books on June 30, $40,000 of ordinary loss is allocable to the S short year, and $50,000 of ordinary income is allocable to the C short year. Assuming each month has 30 days, the following income allocations are possible:

Period	*Daily Allocation*	*Closing of Books Election*
S short year	$ 5,000	($40,000)
C short year	5,000	50,000
Total	$10,000	$10,000

With the daily allocation, one-half the income is taxed to the shareholder, and the other half is taxed to the C corporation.[61] The daily allocation method causes the shareholder's tax to be $1,650 ($5,000 × 0.33) on the pass-through income and the C corporation's tax to be $750 ($5,000 × 2 × 0.15 × 0.5) on its annualized income, for a total tax of $2,500. By closing the books, the corporation passes the $40,000 S short year loss through to its shareholder and is taxed on the $50,000 C short year income as a C corporation. This method provides the shareholder with a $13,200 ($40,000 pass-through loss × 0.33) tax savings and causes the C corporation's tax to be $11,125 ($22,250 tax on $100,000 of annualized income × 0.5), for a net tax savings of $2,075 ($13,200 – $11,125). Thus, in this situation, the closing of books method provides the greater overall tax advantage ($2,075 vs. $2,500). ◄

INCREASING THE BENEFITS FROM S CORPORATION LOSSES

At the shareholder level, the deduction for S corporation pass-through losses is limited to the S corporation stock basis plus the basis of debt owed by the S corporation to the shareholder. Pass-through losses exceeding this limitation carry over to a subsequent tax year when the shareholder regains stock or debt basis. If the shareholder expects his or her marginal tax rate to be the same or lower in a carryover tax year, the shareholder should consider either increasing his or her stock basis or loaning additional funds to the corporation before the end of the current tax year. Conversely, if the shareholder never expects the loans to be repaid, he or she should not lend the S corporation additional amounts just to secure an additional tax deduction, which is worth at most 39.6 cents (at 2015 rates) for

[61] Section 1362(e)(5)(A) requires calculation of the tax liability for the C short year to be based on the annualized income of the former S corporation (see Chapter C:3 for a discussion of annualization).

each dollar loaned. If the shareholder expects his or her marginal tax rate to be higher in future tax years, the shareholder should consider deferring additional capital contributions or loans until after the end of the current tax year.

EXAMPLE C:11-33 ▶ Nancy owns 100% of Bailey Corporation, an S corporation. Bailey expects a $100,000 ordinary loss in the current year. Nancy's stock basis (before adjustment for the current loss) is $35,000. Bailey also owes Nancy $25,000. Nancy's current marginal tax rate is 33%, but she expects her marginal tax rate to decline to 15% next year. Nancy should consider making $40,000 [$100,000 loss − ($35,000 stock basis + $25,000 debt basis)] of additional capital contributions or loans before the end of the current year to obtain an additional $7,200 [(0.33 − 0.15) × $40,000] of tax benefits from deducting the loss in the current year rather than next year. If Nancy instead expects her marginal tax rates to be 15% in the current year and 33% next year, she can defer $7,200 [(0.33 − 0.15) × $40,000] of tax benefits (less the time value of money for one year) by postponing her capital contributions or loans until next year. Alternatively, Nancy could use the loss carryover to offset profits reported next year. These profits would restore part or all of her debt basis (and possibly increase her stock basis). The stock basis then would be partially or fully offset by the $40,000 loss carryover. ◀

KEY POINT

If an S corporation shareholder has losses that have been suspended due to lack of basis, either contributions to capital or bona fide loans to the corporation will create the necessary basis to use the losses.

The S corporation loss carryover is available only to the shareholder who held the stock when the loss occurred. A shareholder should consider increasing the stock basis to take advantage of the carryover before selling the stock. The purchasing shareholder does not acquire the carryover.

PASSIVE INCOME REQUIREMENTS

The S corporation can earn an unlimited amount of passive income each year without incurring any penalty provided it has no E&P accumulated in a C corporation tax year (known as Subchapter C E&P) at the end of its tax year. Thus, a corporation can make an S election to avoid the personal holding company tax that otherwise might apply to a C corporation's passive income.

S corporations that have operated as C corporations and have accumulated Subchapter C E&P are potentially liable for the excess net passive income tax. In addition, their S election may terminate if the passive investment income exceeds 25% of gross receipts for three consecutive tax years. The S corporation can avoid both of these possible problems by making a special election under Sec. 1368(e)(3) to distribute its entire Subchapter C E&P balance to its shareholders. A corporation that elects to distribute Subchapter C E&P before distributing from its accumulated adjustments account (AAA) can make a second special election to treat part or all of this "distribution" as a deemed dividend, which is deemed distributed to the shareholders and immediately contributed by the shareholders to the corporation on the last day of the corporation's tax year.[62] Such an election requires no cash outlay. The distribution, however, results in a tax cost for the shareholders who pay tax on the resulting deemed dividend income. To the shareholders, the cost of the election can be small if the accumulated E&P balance is insignificant or if the shareholder has a current year NOL (excluding the distribution) or an NOL carryover. The tax cost also could be low given the shareholder's applicable tax rate on dividends. The ultimate long-run benefit, however, may be great because it permits the S corporation to earn an unlimited amount of passive investment income free from corporate taxes in subsequent tax years.

EXAMPLE C:11-34 ▶ Hawaii Corporation incorporated 12 years ago and operated for a number of years as a C corporation, during which time it accumulated $30,000 of E&P. Most of Hawaii's gross income now comes from rentals and interest, constituting passive investment income. Hawaii makes an S election starting in the current year. The excess net passive income tax will apply in the current year if Hawaii's rentals and interest exceed 25% of its gross receipts for the year unless the corporation elects to distribute the accumulated E&P and then distributes the earnings by the end of the current year. ◀

---

[62] Reg. Sec. 1.1368-1(f)(3).

S corporations that earn rental income also can avoid the passive income tax and the possibility of having its election terminated if the corporation renders significant services to the occupant of the space or if the corporation incurs significant costs in the rental business.[63] Whether the corporation performs significant services or incurs substantial costs in the rental business depends on the facts and circumstances including, but not limited to, the number of persons employed to provide the services and the types and amounts of costs and expenses incurred (other than depreciation).

EXAMPLE C:11-35 ▶ Assume the same facts as in Example C:11-34 except Hawaii Corporation provides significant services to its tenants in connection with its rental activities. Because the services are significant, Hawaii has a passive income problem only if its interest income exceeds 25% of its gross receipts. If the 25% threshold is not exceeded, Hawaii can avoid having to distribute its Subchapter C E&P in the current year. ◀

S corporations that experience a passive income problem in two consecutive tax years should carefully monitor their passive income in the next year. If they see that their passive income for the third year will exceed the 25% threshold, they should elect to distribute their accumulated Subchapter C E&P before year-end. This strategy not only will prevent loss of the S election but also will avoid having to pay the Sec. 1375 tax.

COMPLIANCE AND PROCEDURAL CONSIDERATIONS

OBJECTIVE 10

Comply with S corporation procedural and filing requirements

MAKING THE ELECTION

A corporation makes the S election by filing Form 2553 (Election by a Small Business Corporation). Any person authorized to sign the S corporation's tax return under Sec. 6037 can sign the election form. The corporation files Form 2553 with the IRS Service Center designated in the instructions. The IRS can treat a late election as timely made if the corporation can show reasonable cause.[64]

A shareholder can consent to the S election either on Form 2553 or on a separate consent statement signed by the shareholder and attached to the corporation's election form. Regulation Sec. 1.1362-6(b) outlines other information that must be provided with a separate consent. The IRS can grant extensions of time for filing shareholder consents to the S election.[65]

A corporation makes a Sec. 444 election to use a fiscal year on Form 8716, which the corporation must file by the earlier of (1) the fifteenth day of the fifth month following the month that includes the first day of the tax year for which the election will first be effective or (2) the due date for the income tax return resulting from the election.[66] The corporation must attach a copy of Form 8716 to Form 1120S for the first tax year for which the Sec. 444 election is effective. A corporation desiring to make a Sec. 444 election also must state its intention in a statement attached to its S election form (Form 2553).[67]

FILING THE CORPORATE TAX RETURN

All S corporations, whether or not they owe taxes under Secs. 1374 or 1375, must file a tax return if they exist for part or all of the tax year. An S corporation must file its corporate tax return not later than the fifteenth day of the third month following the end of the tax year.[68] The S corporation reports its results on Form 1120S (U.S. Income Tax Return for an S Corporation). A completed S corporation tax return and the facts supporting the return appear in Appendix B. An S corporation is allowed an automatic six-month extension of

63 According to Reg. Sec. 1.1362-2(c)(5)(ii)(B)(2), however, significant services are not rendered and substantial costs are not incurred in connection with net leases.

64 Sec. 1362(b)(5). Also see footnote 16.

65 Reg. Sec. 1.1362-6(b)(3)(iii).

66 Temp. Reg. Sec. 1.444-3T(b)(1).

67 Temp. Reg. Sec. 1.444-3T(b)(3).

68 Sec. 6072(b).

time for filing its tax return by filing Form 7004 (Application for Automatic Extension of Time to File Certain Business Income Tax, Information, and Other Returns), also illustrated in Appendix B.[69]

EXAMPLE C:11-36 ▶ Simpson Corporation, an S corporation, uses the calendar year as its tax year. Its tax return generally is due on March 15. Simpson can file Form 7004 and obtain an automatic six-month extension for the return, thereby extending its due date until September 15. ◀

All S corporations that file a tax return must furnish each person who is a shareholder at any time during the tax year with pertinent information from the tax return, usually via Form 1120S, Schedule K-1. The corporation must make the Schedule K-1 available to the shareholder not later than the day on which it files its tax return.[70] An individual shareholder reports the S corporation's pass-through ordinary income or loss and certain passive income or loss items on his or her Form 1040, Schedule E. The shareholder reports most separately stated items on other supporting schedules to Form 1040, as illustrated on the Form 1120S, Schedule K-1 presented in Appendix B.

An S corporation is subject to the same basic three-year statute of limitations that applies to other taxpayers. This three-year limitations period applies for purposes of determining the time period during which

- The corporation remains liable for assessments of the excess net passive income and built-in gains taxes
- The IRS can question the correctness of an S election made for a particular tax year

The limitation period for assessing the income tax liability of an S corporation shareholder (e.g., for an erroneous S corporation loss deduction claimed), however, runs from the date on which the shareholder files his or her return and not from the date the S corporation files its tax return.[71]

If the corporation elects a fiscal year under Sec. 444, it determines the Sec. 7519 required payment on a computation worksheet provided in the instructions for the Form 1120S. The corporation need not make a required payment if the total of such payments for the current year and all preceding years is $500 or less. Amounts equal to or less than the $500 threshold carry over to succeeding years. The required payment is due on or before May 15 regardless of the fiscal year used. The required payment and the computation worksheet must accompany a Form 8752, which also is used to secure a refund of prior Sec. 7519 payments.[72]

ESTIMATED TAX PAYMENTS

S corporations must make estimated tax payments if their estimated tax liability is reasonably expected to be $500 or more.[73] Estimated tax payments are required for the corporate liability attributable to the built-in gains tax (Sec. 1374) and the excess net passive income tax (Sec. 1375). In addition, the S corporation's shareholders must include their income, gain, loss, deduction, and credit pass-through items in their own estimated tax calculations.

The corporate estimated tax payment requirements described for a C corporation in Chapter C:3 also apply to an S corporation's tax liabilities. The required quarterly installment is 25% of the lesser of (1) 100% of the tax shown on the return for the tax year or (2) the sum of 100% of the built-in gains tax shown on the return for the tax year plus 100% of the excess net passive income tax shown on the return for the preceding tax year.

An S corporation cannot use the prior year tax liability exception when determining the required payment to be made with respect to the built-in gains tax. This exception, however, is available with respect to the excess net passive income tax portion of the

[69] Reg. Sec. 1.6081-3.
[70] Sec. 6037(b).
[71] *Sheldon B. Bufferd v. CIR*, 71 AFTR 2d 93-573, 93-1 USTC ¶50,038 (USSC, 1993).
[72] Temp. Reg. Sec. 1.7519-2T.
[73] Estimate tax rules appear in Sec. 6655.

required payment without regard to whether the corporation owed any tax in the prior year. All corporations can use the prior year tax liability exception for the excess net passive income tax whether or not they are "large" corporations under Sec. 6655(d)(2). The annualization election of Sec. 6655(e) also is available when determining the quarterly estimated tax payment amounts. An S corporation's failure to make timely estimated tax payments, or a timely final payment when it files the tax return, will trigger interest and penalties.

SELF-STUDY QUESTION

Is an S corporation required to make estimated tax payments?

ANSWER

Yes. An S corporation is required to pay estimated taxes if the corporation is subject to built-in gains or excess net passive income taxes. Also, shareholders are required to include their S corporation income, loss, and credit pass-through items in determining their estimated tax payments.

The S corporation's shareholders must include their ratable share of ordinary income or loss and separately stated items in determining their estimated tax liability. Such amounts are treated as having been received concurrently by the shareholders throughout the S corporation's tax year. Thus, ordinary income or loss and separately stated items for an S corporation tax year that ends with or within the shareholder's tax year are included in the estimated tax calculation to the extent they are attributable to months in the S corporation tax year that precede the month in which the installment is due.[74]

CONSISTENCY RULES

ADDITIONAL COMMENT

When examining an S corporation, the IRS conducts the audit in a unified proceeding at the corporate level rather than in separate audits of each S corporation shareholder.

Section 6037(c) requires an S corporation shareholder to report on his or her return a Subchapter S item in a manner consistent with the treatment accorded the item on the S corporation's return. A Subchapter S item is any item (e.g., income, gain, deduction, loss, credit, accounting method, or tax year) of an S corporation where the reporting of the item is more appropriately determined at the corporation level than at the shareholder level. A shareholder must notify the IRS of any inconsistency when the corporation has filed a return but the shareholder's treatment on his return is (or may be) inconsistent with the treatment of the item on the corporation return. Failure to do so may result in the imposition of a negligence penalty under Sec. 6662. Any adjustment required to produce consistency with the corporate return is treated as a mathematical or clerical error for penalty calculation purposes. A similar notification also is required when the corporation has not filed a return. If a shareholder receives incorrect information from the S corporation regarding a Subchapter S item, the shareholder's consistent reporting of the item consistently with the information provided by the corporation generally will eliminate the imposition of any penalty.

SAMPLE S CORPORATION TAX RETURN

REAL-WORLD EXAMPLE

In 2015, of the 6.9 million corporate tax returns filed, 68% were S corporations.

A sample S corporation Form 1120S and supporting Schedule K-1 appear in Appendix B, along with the facts supporting the return. Two differences should be noted between the S corporation tax return and a partnership tax return. First, the S corporation tax return provides for the determination of a corporate tax liability and the payment of the special taxes that can be levied on the S corporation. No such items appear in the partnership return. Second, the S corporation return does not require a reconciliation of the shareholders' basis adjustments as occurs on a partnership tax return. Schedule M-1, M-2, and M-3 reconciliations similar to those required of a C corporation are required of an S corporation. Schedule M-1 requires a reconciliation of book income with the income or loss reported on line 23 of Schedule K, which includes not only the ordinary income (loss) amount but also separately stated income and deduction items. For tax years ending on or after December 31, 2006, an S corporation must file Schedule M-3 in lieu of Schedule M-1 if the amount of total assets reported in Schedule L of Form 1120S (Balance Sheet per Books) equals or exceeds $10 million. The S corporation also may file Schedule M-3 voluntarily even if not required to do so. If the corporation files Schedule M-3, in either case, it checks the appropriate box on page 1 of Form 1120S and does not file Schedule M-1. (The sample tax return in Appendix B does not include Schedule M-3.) Schedule M-2 requires a reconciliation of the AAA, OAA, and PTI accounts. (The PTI account pertains to pre-1983 S corporations.) Only S corporations that have an accumulated E&P balance must provide the AAA reconciliation and OAA balance although the IRS recommends that all S corporations maintain AAA and OAA balances.

[74] For example, see Ltr. Rul. 8639008 (June 23, 1986).

Problem Materials

Discussion Questions

C:11-1 List five advantages and five disadvantages of making an S election. Briefly explain each item.

C:11-2 Julio, age 50, is a U.S. citizen who has a 28% marginal tax rate. He has operated the A&B Automotive Parts Company for a number of years as a C corporation. Last year, A&B reported $200,000 of pre-tax profits, from which it paid $50,000 in salary and $25,000 in dividends to Julio. The corporation expects this year's pre-tax profits to be $300,000. To date, the corporation has created no fringe benefits or pension plans for Julio. Julio asks you to explain whether an S corporation election would reduce his taxes. How do you respond to Julio's inquiry?

C:11-3 Celia, age 30, is leaving a major systems development firm to establish her own firm. She will design computer-based systems for small- and medium-sized businesses. Celia will invest $100,000 in the business. She hopes to operate near her breakeven point during her first year, although a small loss is possible. Profits will build up slowly over the next four years until she is earning $150,000 a year in her fifth year. Celia has heard about S corporations and asks you whether the S corporation form would be advisable for her new business. How do you respond to Celia's inquiry?

C:11-4 Lance and Rodney are contemplating starting a new business to manufacture computer software games. They expect to encounter losses in the initial years. Lance's CPA has talked to them about using an S corporation. Rodney, while reading a business publication, encounters a discussion on limited liability companies (LLCs). The article talks about the advantages of using an LLC instead of an S corporation. How would you respond to their inquiry?

C:11-5 Which of the following classifications make a shareholder ineligible to own stock in an S corporation?

a. U.S. citizen
b. Domestic corporation
c. Partnership where all the partners are U.S. citizens
d. Estate of a deceased U.S. citizen
e. Grantor trust created by a U.S. citizen
f. Nonresident alien individual

C:11-6 Will the following events cause an S election to terminate?

a. The S corporation earning 100% of its gross receipts in its first tax year from passive sources
b. The S corporation issuing nonvoting stock that has a dividend preference
c. The S corporation purchasing 100% of the single class of stock of a second domestic corporation that has conducted business activities for four years
d. An individual shareholder donating 100 shares of S corporation stock to a charity that is exempt from tax under Sec. 501(c)(3)
e. The S corporation earning tax-exempt interest income

C:11-7 What is an inadvertent termination? What actions must the S corporation and its shareholders take to correct an inadvertent termination?

C:11-8 After an S corporation revokes or terminates its S election, how long must the corporation wait to make a new election? What circumstances permit an early reelection?

C:11-9 What tax years can a newly created corporation that makes an S election adopt for its first tax year? If a fiscal year is permitted, does it require IRS approval?

C:11-10 At the time Cable Corporation makes its S election, it elects to use a fiscal year based on a Sec. 444 election. What other requirements must Cable satisfy to continue to use its fiscal year election for future tax years?

C:11-11 What are Subchapter C earnings and profits (E&P)? How does the existence of such E&P affect the S corporation's ability to earn passive income?

C:11-12 Explain the procedures for allocating an S corporation's ordinary income or loss to each of the shareholders. What special allocation elections are available?

C:11-13 What limitations apply to the amount of loss pass-through an S corporation shareholder can deduct? What happens to any losses exceeding this limitation? What happens to losses if the shareholder transfers his or her stock?

C:11-14 What actions can an S corporation shareholder take before year-end to increase the amount of the S corporation's losses he or she can deduct in the year they are incurred?

C:11-15 What is a post-termination transition period? What loss carryovers can an S corporation shareholder deduct during this period?

C:11-16 Explain the positive and negative adjustments to the basis of an S corporation shareholder's stock investment and the basis of an S corporation debt owed to the shareholder.

C:11-17 Explain the differences between the tax treatment accorded nonliquidating property distributions made by S corporations and partnerships.

C:11-18 What nonliquidating distributions made by an S corporation are taxable to its shareholders? Tax-free to its shareholders?

C:11-19 What is an accumulated adjustments account (AAA)? What income, gain, loss, and deduction items *do not* affect this account assuming the S corporation has an accumulated E&P balance?

C:11-20 Explain the differences between the way the following items are reported by a C corporation and an S corporation:

a. Ordinary income or loss
b. Dividend income
c. Capital gains and losses
d. Tax-exempt interest income
e. Charitable contributions
f. Nonliquidating property distributions
g. Fringe benefits paid to a shareholder-employee

C:11-21 When is the S corporation's tax return due? What extensions are available for filing the return?

C:11-22 What taxes must an S corporation prepay by making quarterly estimated tax payments? Can a shareholder owning S corporation stock use the corporation's estimated tax payments to reduce the amount of his or her individual estimated tax payments? Explain.

C:11-23 Review the completed C corporation, partnership, and S corporation tax returns presented in Appendix B. List three major tax reporting similarities and three major tax reporting differences in either content or format among the three tax returns.

ISSUE IDENTIFICATION QUESTIONS

C:11-24 Jennelle and Paula are equal partners in the J&P Manufacturing Partnership. The partnership will form J&P Corporation by exchanging the assets and liabilities of the J&P Manufacturing Partnership for all the corporation's stock on September 1 of the current year. The partnership then will liquidate by distributing the J&P Corporation stock equally to Jennelle and Paula. Both shareholders use the calendar year as their tax year and desire that the corporation make an S election. What tax issues should Jennelle and Paula consider with respect to the incorporation?

C:11-25 Williams Corporation has operated as a C corporation for the last seven years. The corporation has assets with a $450,000 adjusted basis and an $800,000 FMV. Liabilities amount to $100,000. Dan Williams, who uses a calendar year as his tax year, owns all the Williams Corporation stock. The corporation uses the accrual method of accounting and a June 30 year-end. Dan's CPA has suggested that he convert the corporation to S corporation status to reduce his total corporate/personal federal income tax liability. Dan would like to complete the conversion on the last day of the corporation's tax year. What tax issues should Dan and his CPA consider with respect to the S election?

C:11-26 Peter owns 50% of Air South Corporation, an air charter service. His S corporation stock basis at beginning of the year is $100,000. Air South has not done well this year and will report an ordinary loss of $375,000. What tax issues should Peter consider with respect to the loss?

C:11-27 Glacier Smokeries has been an S corporation since its inception six years ago. On January 1 of the current year, the corporation's two equal shareholders, Adam and Rodney, had adjusted bases of $175,000 and $225,000, respectively, for their S corporation's stock. The shareholders plan to have the corporation distribute land with a $75,000 adjusted basis and a $300,000 FMV in the current year. The shareholders also expect ordinary income to be $125,000 in the current year. What tax issues should Adam and Rodney consider with respect to the distribution?

PROBLEMS

C:11-28 *Comparison of Entity Forms.* Carl Carson, a single taxpayer, owns 100% of Delta Corporation. During 2017, Delta reports $150,000 of taxable income. Carl reports no income other than that earned from Delta, and Carl claims the standard deduction.

a. What is Delta's income tax liability assuming Carl withdraws none of the earnings from the C corporation? What is Carl's income tax liability? What is the total tax liability for the corporation and its shareholder?
b. Assume that Delta instead distributes $80,000 of its after-tax earnings to Carl as a dividend in the current year. What is the total income tax liability for the C corporation and its shareholder?
c. How would your answer to Part a change if Carl withdrew $80,000 from the business in salary? Assume the corporation pays $6,120 of Social Security taxes on the salary,

which it can deduct from the $150,000 taxable income amount in Part a. Carl also pays $6,120 of Social Security taxes on the salary, which he cannot deduct.

d. How would your answers to Parts a–c change if Delta were instead an S corporation?

C:11-29 *Making the Election.* Voyles Corporation, a calendar year taxpayer formed five years ago, desires to make an S election beginning in 2017. Sue and Andrea each own one-half of the Voyles stock.

a. How does Voyles make the S election?

b. When can Voyles file its election form?

c. If in Part b the corporation does not file the election in a timely manner, when will the election take effect?

C:11-30 *Termination of the Election.* Orlando Corporation, a calendar year taxpayer, has been an S corporation for several years. On July 9, 2017, Orlando authorizes a second class of nonvoting preferred stock that pays a 10% annual dividend. The corporation issues the stock to Sid on September 11, 2017, to raise additional equity capital. Sid owns no other Orlando stock.

a. Does Orlando's S election terminate? If so, when is the termination effective?

b. What tax returns must Orlando file for 2017? When are they due?

c. How would your answer to Parts a and b change if instead the second class of stock were nonvoting Class B common stock?

C:11-31 *Revocation of the Election.* Tango Corporation, a calendar year taxpayer, has been an S corporation for several years. Tango's business activities have become very profitable in recent years. On June 16, 2017, its sole shareholder desires to revoke the S election.

a. How does Tango revoke its S election? When does the revocation take effect?

b. Assume Tango files a prospective revocation effective July 1, 2017. What tax returns are required of Tango for 2017? For 2018? When are these returns due?

c. If the corporation makes a new S election after the revocation, when does it take effect?

C:11-32 *Sale of S Corporation Interest.* Peter and his wife, Alice, own all the stock of Galleon Corporation. Galleon made its S election 12 years ago. Peter and Alice sold one-half their Galleon stock to a partnership owned by Rob and Susan (not husband and wife) at the close of business on December 31 of the current year for a $75,000 profit. What are the tax consequences of the sale transaction for Peter and Alice? For the corporation? As Peter and Alice's CPA, do you have any advice for them if all parties would like the S election to continue?

C:11-33 *Selecting a Tax Year.* Indicate in each of the following independent situations whether the taxpayer can accomplish what is proposed. Provide adequate authority for your answer including any special elections that are needed or requirements that must be satisfied. Assume all individuals use the calendar year as their tax year unless otherwise indicated.

a. Will and Carol form Classic Corporation. They want the corporation to adopt a fiscal year ending January 31 as its tax year to provide a maximum deferral for their income. The corporation makes an S election for its initial tax year ending January 31, 2018.

b. Mark and Dennis have owned and operated the Plastic Corporation for several years. Plastic has used a fiscal year ending June 30 since its organization as a C corporation because it conforms to the corporation's natural business year. The corporation makes an S election for its tax year beginning July 1, 2017.

C:11-34 *Passive Income Tax.* Oliver organized North Corporation 15 years ago. The corporation made an S election last year after it accumulated $60,000 of E&P as a C corporation. As of December 31 of the current year, the corporation has distributed none of its accumulated E&P. In the current year, North reports the following results:

Dividends from domestic corporations	$ 60,000
Rental income	100,000
Services income	50,000
Expenses related to rental income	30,000
Expenses related to services income	15,000
Other expenses	5,000

The corporation has not provided significant services nor incurred substantial costs in connection with earning the rental income. The services income is derived from the active conduct of a trade or business.

a. Is North subject to the excess net passive income tax? If so, what is its tax liability?

b. What is the effect of the excess net passive income tax liability on North's pass-throughs of ordinary income and separately stated items?

c. What advice would you give North regarding its activities?

C:11-35 *Built-in Gains Tax.* Theta Corporation formed 15 years ago. In its first year, it elected to use the cash method of accounting and adopted a calendar year as its tax year. It made an S election on August 15 of last year, effective for Theta's current tax year. At the beginning of the current year, Theta had assets with a $600,000 FMV and a $180,000 adjusted basis. During the current year, Theta reports taxable income of $400,000.

- In the current year, Theta collects all $200,000 of accounts receivables outstanding on January 1 of the current year. The receivables had a zero adjusted basis.
- On February 1, Theta sells an automobile for $3,500. The automobile had a $2,000 adjusted basis and a $3,000 FMV on January 1 of the current year. Theta claimed $800 of MACRS depreciation on the automobile in the current year.
- On March 1, Theta sells land (a Sec. 1231 asset) that it held three years in anticipation of building its own office building for a $35,000 gain. The land had a $45,000 FMV and a $25,000 adjusted basis on January 1 of the current year.
- In the current year, Theta paid $125,000 of accounts payable outstanding on January 1 of the current year. All the payables are deductible expenses.

What is the amount of Theta's built-in gains tax liability?

C:11-36 *Determination of Pass-Throughs and Stock Basis Adjustments.* Mike and Nancy are equal shareholders in MN Corporation, an S corporation. The corporation, Mike, and Nancy are calendar year taxpayers. The corporation has been an S corporation during its entire existence and thus has no accumulated E&P. The shareholders have no loans to the corporation. The corporation incurred the following items in the current year:

Sales	$300,000
Cost of goods sold	140,000
Dividends on corporate investments	10,000
Tax-exempt interest income	3,000
Sec. 1245 gain (recapture) on equipment sale	22,000
Sec. 1231 gain on equipment sale	12,000
Long-term capital gain on stock sale	8,000
Long-term capital loss on stock sale	7,000
Short-term capital loss on stock sale	6,000
Depreciation	18,000
Salary to Nancy	20,000
Meals and entertainment expenses	7,800
Interest expense on loans allocable to:	
Business debt	32,000
Stock investments	6,400
Tax-exempt bonds	1,800
Principal payment on business loan	9,000
Charitable contributions	2,000
Distributions to shareholders ($15,000 each)	30,000

a. Compute the S corporation's ordinary income and separately stated items.
b. Show Mike's and Nancy's shares of the items in Part a.
c. Compute Mike's and Nancy's ending stock bases assuming their beginning balances are $100,000 each. When making basis adjustments, apply the adjustments in the order outlined on pages C:11-24 and C:11-25 of the text.

C:11-37 *Allocation of Income to Shareholders.* John owns all the stock of Lucas Corporation, an S corporation. John's basis for the 1,000 shares is $130,000. On June 11 of the current year (assume a non-leap year), John gifts 100 shares of stock to his younger brother Michael, who has been working in the business for one year. Lucas Corporation reports $125,000 of ordinary income for the current year. What amount of income is allocated to John? To Michael?

C:11-38 *Sale of S Corporation Interest.* Al and Ruth each own one-half the stock of Chemical Corporation, an S corporation. During the current year (assume a non-leap year), Chemical earns $15,000 per month of ordinary income. On April 5, Ruth sells her entire stock interest to Patty. The corporation sells a business asset on August 18 and realizes a $75,000 Sec. 1231 gain. What alternatives (if any) exist for allocating Chemical's current year income?

C:11-39 *Allocation of Income to Shareholders.* Toyland Corporation, an S corporation, uses the calendar year as its tax year. Bob, Alice, and Carter own 60, 30, and 10 shares, respectively, of the Toyland stock. Carter's basis for his stock is $26,000 on January 1 of the current year (assume a non-leap year). On June 30, Alice gifted one-half of her stock to Mike. On November 30, Carter sold his stock to Mike for $45,000. Toyland reports the following results for the current year:

Ordinary income	$120,000
Long-term capital loss	10,000
Charitable contributions	6,000

a. What amount of income, loss, or deduction do the four shareholders report (assuming the corporation makes no special allocation election)?
b. What gain or loss does Carter recognize when he sells the Toyland stock?

C:11-40 *Allocation of Income to Shareholders.* Redfern Corporation, a calendar year taxpayer, has been an S corporation for several years. Rod and Kurt each own 50% of Redfern's stock. On July 1 of the current year (assume a non-leap year), Redfern issues additional common stock to Blackfoot Corporation for cash. Rod, Kurt, and Blackfoot each end up owning one-third of Redfern's stock. Redfern reports ordinary income of $125,000 and a short-term capital loss of $15,000 in the current year. Eighty percent of the ordinary income and all the capital loss accrue after Blackfoot purchases its stock. Redfern makes no distributions to its shareholders in the current year. What income and losses do Redfern, Blackfoot, Rod, and Kurt report as a result of the current year's activities?

C:11-41 *Allocation of Income Between Family Members.* Bright Corporation, an S corporation, has been 100% owned by Betty since its creation 12 years ago. The corporation has been profitable in recent years and, in the current year (assume a non-leap year), reports ordinary income of $240,000 after paying Betty a $60,000 salary. On January 1, Betty gifts 15% of her Bright stock to each of her three sons, John, Andrew, and Stephen, hoping they will work in the family business. Betty pays gift taxes on the transfers. The sons are ages 24, 17, and 15 at present and are not currently active in the business. Bright distributes $7,500 in cash to each son and $27,500 in cash to Betty in the current year.
a. What income does Betty, John, Andrew, and Stephen report for the current year as a result of Bright's activities assuming the sons are considered bona fide owners of the stock? How will the income be taxed to the children?
b. Assuming the IRS determines a reasonable salary for Betty to be $120,000, how would your answer to Part a change?
c. How would your answer to Part a change if the sons were not considered bona fide owners of the stock?

C:11-42 *Use of Losses by Shareholders.* Monte and Allie each own 50% of Raider Corporation, an S corporation. Both individuals actively participate in Raider's business. On January 1, Monte and Allie have adjusted bases for their Raider stock of $80,000 and $90,000, respectively. During the current year, Raider reports the following results:

Ordinary loss	$175,000
Tax-exempt interest income	20,000
Long-term capital loss	32,000

Raider's balance sheet at year-end shows the following liabilities: accounts payable, $90,000; mortgage payable, $30,000; and note payable to Allie, $10,000.
a. What income and deductions will Monte and Allie report from Raider's current year activities?
b. What is Monte's stock basis on December 31?
c. What are Allie's stock basis and debt basis on December 31?
d. What loss carryovers are available for Monte and Allie?
e. Explain how the use of the losses in Part a would change if instead Raider were a partnership and Monte and Allie were partners who shared profits, losses, and liabilities equally.

C:11-43 *Use of Loss Carryovers.* Assume the same facts as in Problem C:11-42. Assume further that Raider Corporation reports $75,000 of ordinary income, $20,000 of tax-exempt income, and a $25,000 long-term capital gain in the next year.
a. What income and deductions will Monte and Allie report from next year's activities?
b. What is Monte's stock basis on December 31 of next year?
c. What are Allie's stock basis and note basis on December 31 of next year?
d. What loss carryovers (if any) are available to Monte and Allie?

C:11-44 *Use of Losses by Shareholders.* Tom owns 100% of Hammer Corporation, an S corporation. Tom has a $100,000 stock basis on January 1. Tom actively participates in Hammer's business. Hammer's operating results were not good in the current year, with the corporation reporting an ordinary loss of $175,000. The size of the loss required Tom to lend Hammer $50,000 on August 10 of the current year to provide funds needed for operations. The loan is secured by a Hammer Corporation note. Hammer rebounds during the next year and reports ordinary income of $60,000. Hammer repays the $50,000 note on December 15.

a. What amount of Hammer's current year loss can Tom deduct on his income tax return?
b. What is Tom's basis for the Hammer stock and note at the end of the loss year?
c. What income and deductions will Tom report next year from Hammer's activities and the loan repayment?

C:11-45 *S Corporation and Partnership Losses.* In the current year, Harold and Faye form Entity Company by each contributing $50,000 to the company in exchange for a 50% ownership interest. In addition, the company borrows $40,000 from First Bank. In the current year, the company incurs a $110,000 loss from operations.

a. How much of the loss can each shareholder deduct in the current year if Entity is an S Corporation, and what is each shareholder's basis in his or her stock at the end of the year?
b. How much of the loss can each partner deduct in the current year if Entity is a partnership, and what is each partner's basis in his or her partnership interest at the end of the year?

C:11-46 *Allocation of Losses to Shareholders.* Harry and Rita formed Alpha Corporation as an S corporation, with each shareholder contributing $10,000 in exchange for stock. In addition, Rita loaned the corporation $7,000, and the corporation borrowed another $8,000 from the bank. In the current year, the corporation incurred a $26,000 operating loss. In the next year, the corporation will earn $16,000 of operating income.

a. For the current year and next year, determine the pass-through items for each shareholder and each shareholder's stock basis at the end of each year. Also, determine Rita's debt basis at the end of each year.
b. Same as Part a except the corporation also distributes $6,000 cash to each shareholder at the end of next year.
c. Assume the same facts as in Part b and that Alpha is a partnership instead of an S corporation. For the current year and next year, determine the pass-through items for each partner and each partner's basis in his or her partnership interest at the end of each year.

C:11-47 *Post-Termination Loss Use.* Stein Corporation, an S corporation, has 400 shares of stock outstanding. Chuck and Linda own an equal number of these shares, and both actively participate in Stein's business. Chuck and Linda each contributed $60,000 when they organized Stein on September 9 of Year 1. Start-up losses during Year 1 resulted in Stein reporting a $210,000 ordinary loss. Stein's activities have since become profitable, and the corporation voluntarily revokes the S election on March 1 of Year 2, with no prospective revocation date being specified. In Year 2, Stein reports $360,000 of taxable income ($30,000 per month). Stein makes no distributions to its shareholders in either year.

a. What amount of loss can Chuck and Linda deduct in Year 1?
b. What amount of loss do Chuck and Linda carry over to Year 2?
c. If Chuck reported only $5,000 of other business income in Year 1, what happens to the "excess" deductible S corporation losses?
d. What portion of the loss carryover from Part b can Chuck and Linda deduct in Year 2? What happens to any unused portion of the loss?
e. What advice can you offer to Chuck and Linda to enhance their use of the Stein loss?

C:11-48 *Use of Losses by Shareholders.* Tina, a single taxpayer, owns 100% of Rocket Corporation, an S corporation. She has an $80,000 stock basis for her investment on January 1 of the current year (Year 1). During the first 11 months of Year 1, Rocket reports an ordinary loss of $100,000. The corporation expects an additional $20,000 loss for December. Tina earns $295,000 of ordinary income from her other activities in Year 1. She expects her other income to decline to $125,000 in Year 2 and continue at that level in future years. The corporation expects Year 2 losses to be only $20,000. Rocket projects a $35,000 profit for Year 3 and each of the subsequent four years. What advice can you offer Tina about using her Rocket losses and retaining S corporation status in future years? How would your answer change if Tina expected her income from other activities to be $75,000 in Year 1 and $295,000 in Year 2?

C:11-49 *Stock Basis Adjustment.* For each of the following items, indicate whether the item will increase, decrease, or cause no change in the S corporation's ordinary income (loss), AAA, and in the shareholder's stock basis. The corporation was formed four years ago and made its S election two years ago. During the time it was a C corporation, it accumulated $30,000 of E&P. The corporation has not distributed any of this accumulated E&P.

a. Operating profit
b. Dividend income received from domestic corporation
c. Interest income earned on corporate bond held as an investment
d. Life insurance proceeds paid on death of corporate officer
e. Long-term capital gain
f. Sec. 1231 loss
g. Sec. 1245 gain (depreciation recapture)
h. Charitable contributions
i. Fines paid for having overweight trucks
j. Depreciation
k. Pension plan contributions for employees
l. Salary paid to owner
m. Premiums paid on life insurance policy in Part d
n. Distribution of money (but not exceeding current year's earnings)

C:11-50 ***Taxability of Distributions.*** Tammy organized Sweets Corporation in January of the current year, and the corporation immediately elected to be an S corporation. Tammy, who contributed $40,000 in cash to start the business, owns 100% of the corporation's stock. Sweets' current year results are reported below:

Ordinary income	$36,000
Short-term capital loss	5,000

On July 10, Sweets makes a $10,000 cash distribution to Tammy.

a. What income (if any) do Sweets and Tammy recognize as a result of the distribution?
b. What is Tammy's basis for the Sweets stock on December 31?
c. How would your answers to Parts a and b change if Sweets' distribution were instead $80,000?

C:11-51 ***Property Distributions.*** George and Martha formed Washington Corporation as an S corporation several years ago. George and Martha each have a 50% interest in the corporation. At the beginning of the current year, their stock bases are $45,000 each. In the current year, the corporation earns $40,000 of ordinary income. In addition, the corporation distributes property to George having a $26,000 FMV and a $40,000 adjusted basis and distributes property to Martha having a $26,000 FMV and a $16,000 adjusted basis.

a. Determine what George and Martha recognize in the current year, and determine their ending stock bases. What bases do George and Martha have in the distributed property?
b. What tax planning disadvantages do you see with these property distributions?
c. How would you answer to Part a change if George and Martha form the Washington Partnership instead of an S corporation?

C:11-52 ***Taxability of Distributions.*** Curt incorporates Vogel Corporation on January 15 of the current year. Curt makes a $70,000 capital contribution including land having a $12,000 FMV, and Vogel makes a timely S election for this year. Vogel reports $60,000 of ordinary income, $40,000 of Sec. 1231 gain, $5,000 of tax-exempt interest income, and $3,000 of charitable contributions this year. On December 1, Vogel distributes $5,000 cash plus the land contributed by Curt because the corporation no longer needs it in the business. The land, which had a $10,000 basis and a $12,000 FMV when contributed to the corporation in January, has an $18,000 FMV when distributed.

a. What income do Vogel Corporation and Curt report as a result of the distribution?
b. What is Curt's basis in the Vogel stock on December 31?
c. What is Vogel's accumulated adjustments account (AAA) balance on December 31?

C:11-53 ***Taxability of Distributions.*** Hal organized Stable Corporation five years ago and has continued to own all its stock. The corporation made an S election one year after its incorporation. At the beginning of the current year, Stable reports the following earnings accumulations:

Accumulated adjustments account (AAA)	$85,000
Accumulated E&P	22,000

Hal's basis in his Stable stock on January 1 of the current year is $120,000. During the current year, Stable reports the following results from its operations:

Ordinary income	$30,000
Tax-exempt interest income	15,000
Long-term capital loss	20,000

Stable makes a $65,000 cash distribution to Hal on August 8.

a. What income, gain, or loss (if any) do Stable and Hal recognize as a result of the distribution?

b. What is Hal's basis in the Stable stock on December 31?

c. What are Stable's AAA, E&P, and OAA balances on December 31?

d. How would your answers to Parts a–c change if Stable instead distributed $120,000?

C:11-54 *Taxability of Distributions.* Sigma Corporation, an S corporation with one shareholder, incurred the following items Year 1 and Year 2:

Year 1	
Tax-exempt income	$ 5,000
Ordinary income	30,000
Year 2	
Ordinary loss	($40,000)
Cash distribution	15,000

At the beginning of Year 1, the corporation had AAA and OAA balances of zero and accumulated E&P of $6,000. At the beginning of Year 1, the shareholder had a $10,000 basis in stock and a $12,000 basis in debt he loaned to the corporation.

a. Determine items reported by the shareholder in Year 1 and Year 2.

b. Determine the balances in each corporate account and the shareholder's stock and debt bases at the end of each year.

c. Determine the results if the distribution in Year 2 is $35,000 instead of $15,000.

d. How does the answer to Part c change if, in Year 2, the corporation has an $18,000 long-term capital gain in addition to the $40,000 ordinary loss?

C:11-55 *Taxability of Distributions.* Beta Corporation, an S corporation with one shareholder, incurred the following items:

Year 1	
Ordinary loss	($40,000)
Year 2	
Ordinary income	$27,000
Cash distribution	10,000
Year 3	
Ordinary income	$22,000
Cash distribution	17,000

At the beginning of Year 1, the shareholder's stock basis was $20,000, and her debt basis was $16,000.

a. Assuming the corporation has no accumulated E&P, show items reported by the shareholder in each year, show all basis adjustments to stock and debt, and show the stock and debt bases at the end of each year.

b. Redo Part a for Year 2 and Year 3 assuming ordinary income in Year 2 is $8,000 instead of $27,000.

c. Go back to the original facts and again redo Part a for all years assuming that, at the beginning of Year 1, the corporation had a AAA balance of zero and accumulated E&P of $12,000.

COMPREHENSIVE PROBLEMS

C:11-56 *Comparison of Entity Formations.* Cara, Bob, and Steve want to begin a business on January 1, 2018. The individuals are considering three business forms—C corporation, partnership, and S corporation.

- Cara has investment land with a $36,000 adjusted basis and a $50,000 FMV that she is willing to contribute. The land has a rundown building on it having a $27,000 basis and a $15,000 FMV. Cara has never used the building nor rented it. She would like to get rid of the building. Because she needs cash, Cara will take out a $25,000 mortgage on the property before the formation of the new business and have the new business assume the debt. Cara obtains a 40% interest in the entity.

- Bob will contribute machinery and equipment, which he purchased for his sole proprietorship in January 2012. He paid $100,000 for the equipment and has used the MACRS rules with a half-year convention on this seven-year recovery period property. He did not make a Sec. 179 expensing election for this property, and he elected out of bonus depreciation. The FMV of the machinery and equipment is $39,000. Bob obtains a 39% interest in the entity.
- Steve will contribute cash of $600 and services worth $20,400 for his interest in the business. The services he will contribute include drawing up the necessary legal documentation for the new business and setting up the initial books. Steve obtains a 21% interest in the entity.

To begin operations, the new business plans to borrow $50,000 on a recourse basis from a local bank. Each owner will guarantee his or her ownership share of the debt.

What are the tax and nontax consequences for the new business and its owners under each alternative? Assume that any corporation will have 200 shares of common stock authorized and issued. For the partnership alternative, each partner receives a capital, profits, and loss interest. How would your answer to the basic facts change if instead Steve contributes $2,600 in cash and $18,400 in services?

C:11-57 *Comparison of Operating Activities.* RST business entity reported the following items during the current year:

Dividends from 25%-owned domestic corporation	$ 19,000
Municipal bond interest received	18,000
Corporate bond interest received	29,000
Gain on land contributed by Karen[a]	40,000
Operating profit (excluding depreciation)[b]	120,000
MACRS depreciation	36,000
Sec. 1245 gain (depreciation recapture)	5,000
Sec. 1231 loss	28,000
Long-term capital losses	4,000
Short-term capital losses	5,000
Charitable contributions	23,000
Investment interest expense (related to General Electric bonds)	16,000
Salary (guaranteed payment)	37,000

[a] Karen held the land as an investment prior to contributing it to RST business entity three years ago in exchange for her ownership interest. When Karen contributed the land, it had a basis of $15,000 and a FMV of $40,000. RST sold the land in the current year for $55,000. RST business entity held the land as an investment. Assume that Sec. 351 applied to any corporate formation transaction.

[b] Assume that qualified production activities income is $47,000 and that operating profit includes sufficient W-2 wages so as not to be a limiting factor.

a. What is the corporate taxable income and income tax liability for the current year if RST is taxed as a C corporation?

b. What is the ordinary income and separately stated items for the current year if RST elects to be an S corporation? Assume that RST has never operated as a C corporation.

c. What are the ordinary income and separately stated items if RST is treated as a general partnership?

C:11-58 *Comparison of Nonliquidating Distributions.* Jeff and John organized Tampa Corporation 18 years ago and have each owned 50% of the corporation since its inception. In the current year, Tampa reports ordinary income/taxable income of $40,000. Assume the business does not qualify for the U.S. production activities deduction. On April 5, Tampa distributes $100,000 cash to Jeff and distributes land with a $100,000 FMV and a $70,000 adjusted basis to John. Tampa had purchased the land as an investment two years ago. What are the tax implications to Tampa, Jeff, and John of the land distribution in each of the four situations that follow?

a. Tampa has been a C corporation since its formation. On January 1 of the current year, Jeff's basis in his stock is $50,000, and John's stock basis is $45,000. Tampa has accumulated E&P of $155,000 on January 1 of the current year.

b. Tampa was formed as a C corporation but made an S election three years after its formation. On January 1 of the current year, Jeff's basis in his stock is $100,000, and John's stock basis is $80,000. Tampa had the following earnings balances on January 1 of the current year:

Accumulated Adjustments Account	$125,000
Accumulated E&P	30,000

c. Tampa was formed as a partnership and continues to operate in that form. On January 1 of the current year, Jeff's basis in his partnership interest is $100,000, and John's partnership basis is $80,000. The partnership has no liabilities and no unrecognized precontribution gains.

d. How would your answers to Parts a–c change if the land held as an investment and then distributed to John had been contributed to Tampa by Jeff two years ago? At the time of Jeff's contribution, the land had a FMV of $95,000 and a $70,000 basis.

TAX STRATEGY PROBLEMS

C:11-59 Alice, a single taxpayer, will form Morning Corporation in the current year. Alice plans to acquire all of Morning's common stock for a $100,000 contribution to the corporation. Morning will obtain additional capital by borrowing $75,000 from a local bank. Morning will conduct a variety of service activities with little need to retain its capital in the business. Alice expects start-up losses of $90,000 during Morning's first year of operation. She expects the corporation to earn pre-tax operating profits of $250,000 (before reduction for Alice's salary) starting next year. Alice plans to withdraw $100,000 of Morning's profits as salary. Her other income consists primarily of ordinary income (no dividends) from other sources, and she expects these amounts to total $120,000 annually. What advice can you provide Alice about the advisability of making an S election in the initial tax year? In the next tax year? In answering these questions, compare the following alternatives: (1) S corporation in both the current year and the next year, (2) S corporation in the current year and C corporation in the next year (i.e., by revoking the S election next year), (3) C corporation in both the current year and the next year, and (4) C corporation in the current year and S corporation in the next year. When analyzing these alternatives, consider the total taxes associated with each alternative, specifically, at the corporate and shareholder levels and across both years. Ignore payroll taxes, however. Also, assume the following facts: (1) for both years, Alice's combined standard deduction and exemption is $10,400; (2) 2017 tax rate schedules remain the same for both years; and (3) a 7% discount rate applies for present value calculations. Although this problem asks for only a two-year analysis, discuss some shortcomings of such a short time frame. Ignore the U.S. production activities deduction for this problem.

C:11-60 One way to compare the accumulation of income by alterative business entity forms is to use mathematical models. The following models express the investment after-tax accumulation calculation for a particular entity form:

Flow-through entities (S corporations, partnerships, and LLCs): $ATA = [1 + R(1 - t_p)]^n$

C corporation: $ATA = [1 + R(1 - t_c)]^n(1 - t_g) + t_g$

where: ATA = after-tax accumulation in n years

R = before-tax rate of return;

t_p = owner's marginal tax rate on ordinary income

t_c = corporation's marginal tax rate

t_g = owner's tax rate on capital gains

n = number of periods

For each alternative business form, the owner makes an initial investment of $1. The following operating assumptions apply:

Before-tax rate of return (R) = 0.18

Marginal tax rate for owner (t_p) = 0.396

Corporate tax rate (t_c) = 0.35

Capital gains rate (t_g) = 0.238 for regular capital gains, including the 3.8% tax on net investment income (assume the Sec. 1202 100% exclusion for small business corporations does not apply)

Investment horizon (n) = 2, 4, 20, 50, or 101 years

A flow-through entity distributes only enough cash each year for the owners to pay their taxes. The corporation pays no dividends. The shareholders sell their stock at the end of the investment horizon, and their gains are taxed at capital gains rates. (See Chapter I:18 of the *Individuals* volume for a detailed explanation of these models.)

Required: What is the after-tax accumulation if each business form is operated for the investment horizon and then sold for the amount of the accumulation? Which entity form is best for each investment horizon? How would your calculations and conclusions change if the C corporation's tax rate is 25%?

C:11-61 Problem C:6-56 considered two alternative forms for doing business. Now consider a third alternative. The C corporation could make an S election effective at the beginning of the current year (the 13th year), operate as an S corporation for the next 20 years, and liquidate the S corporation at that time (32 years in total). Compare this alternative to the other two alternatives in Problem C:6-56.

C:11-62 Assume the corporation in Problem C:11-61 (and C:6-56) had been an S corporation for its first 12 years, during which it distributed just enough cash for the shareholder to pay taxes on the pass-through income. Thus, the S corporation reinvested after-tax income. Now the corporation is considering revoking its S election and operating as a C corporation for the remaining 20 years with no dividend distributions. Show the results of remaining an S corporation versus revoking the election. Also show supporting models and calculations. Which alternative should the corporation adopt? Ignore the accumulated earnings tax for C corporations. How does your answer change if the C corporation's tax rate is 15% instead of 35%?

TAX FORM/RETURN PREPARATION PROBLEMS

C:11-63 Bottle-Up, Inc., was organized on January 8, 2007, and made its S election on January 24, 2007. The necessary consents to the election were filed in a timely manner. Its address is 1234 Hill Street, City, ST 33333. Bottle-Up uses the calendar year as its tax year, the accrual method of accounting, and the first-in, first-out (FIFO) inventory method. Bottle-Up manufactures ornamental glass bottles. It made no changes to its inventory costing methods this year. It uses the specific identification method for bad debts for book and tax purposes. Herman Hiebert and Melvin Jones own 500 shares each. Both individuals materially participate in Bottle-Up's single activity. Herman Hiebert is the tax matters person. Financial statements for Bottle-Up for the current year are shown in Tables C:11-2 through C:11-4. Assume that Bottle-Up's business qualifies as a U.S. production activity and that its qualified production activities income is $90,000. The S corporation uses the small business simplified overall method for reporting these activities (see discussion for Line 12d of Schedules K and K-1 in the Form 1120S instructions). Prepare a 2016 S corporation tax return for Bottle-Up, showing yourself as the paid preparer.

C:11-64 Refer to the facts in Tax Form/Return Preparation Problem C:9-58. Now assume the company is an S corporation rather than a partnership. Additional facts are as follows:

- Drs. Bailey and Firth formed the corporation on January 1, 2015, and the corporation immediately elected S corporation status effective at the beginning of 2015.
- Upon formation of the corporation, Dr. Bailey received common stock worth $600,000, and Dr. Firth received common stock worth $1.4 million.
- The balance sheet information is the same as in Table C:9-3 except the equity section is as follows:

	January 1, 2016	*December 31, 2016*
Common stock	$2,000,000	$2,000,000
Retained earnings	57,100	310,400

- The $100,000 paid to Dr. Bailey is salary constituting W-2 wages (instead of a guaranteed payment). Ignore employment taxes (Social Security, etc.) on Dr. Bailey's salary.
- Qualified production activities income (QPAI) still equals $1.6 million, but employer's W-2 wages allocable to U.S. production activities equal $800,000 (because of Dr. Bailey's salary). The company, being an eligible small pass-through S corporation, uses the small business simplification overall method for reporting these activities (see discussion for Line 12d of Schedule K and Line 12 of Schedule K-1 in the Form 1120S instructions).
- Use book numbers for Schedule L and Schedule M-1 in Form 1120S.

▼ TABLE C:11-2
Bottle-Up, Inc. Income Statement for the Year Ended December 31 of the Current Year (Problem C:11-63)

Sales		$2,500,000
Returns and allowances		(15,000)
Net sales		$2,485,000
Beginning inventory	$ 102,000	
Purchases	900,000	
Labor	200,000	
Supplies	80,000	
Utilities	100,000	
Other manufacturing costs	188,000[a]	
Goods available for sale	$1,570,000	
Ending inventory	(96,000)	1,474,000[b]
Gross profit		$1,011,000
Salaries[c]	$ 451,020	
Utilities expense	54,000	
Depreciation (MACRS depreciation is $36,311)	11,782	
Automobile and truck expense	26,000	
Office supplies expense	9,602	
Advertising expense	105,000	
Bad debts expense	620	
Rent expense	30,000	
Interest expense[d]	1,500	
Meals and entertainment expense	21,000	
Selling expenses	100,000	
Repairs and maintenance expense	38,000	
Accounting and legal expense	4,500	
Charitable contributions[e]	9,000	
Insurance expense[f]	24,500	
Hourly employees' fringe benefits	11,000	
Payroll taxes	36,980	
Other taxes	2,500	
Penalties (fines for overweight trucks)	1,000	(938,004)
Operating profit		$ 72,996
Other income and losses:		
Long-term gain on sale of capital assets	$ 48,666[g]	
Sec. 1231 loss	(1,100)[h]	
Interest on U.S. Treasury bills	1,200	
Interest on State of Florida bonds	600	
Dividends from domestic corporations	11,600	
Investment expenses	(600)	60,366
Net income		$ 133,362

[a] Total MACRS depreciation is $74,311. Assume that $38,000 of depreciation has been allocated to cost of sales for both book and tax purposes so that the book and tax inventory and cost of sales amounts are the same. The AMT depreciation adjustment on personal property is $9,000.

[b] The cost of goods sold amount reflects the Uniform Capitalization Rules of Sec. 263A. The appropriate restatements have been made in prior years.

[c] Officer salaries of $120,000 are included in the total. All are employer's W-2 wages.

[d] Investment interest expense is $500. All other interest expense is trade- or business-related. None of the interest expense relates to the production of tax-exempt income.

[e] The corporation made all contributions in cash to qualifying charities.

[f] Includes $3,000 of premiums paid for policies on lives of corporate officers. Bottle-Up is the beneficiary for both policies.

[g] The corporation acquired the capital assets on March 3, 2014 for $100,000 and sold them on September 15, 2016, for $148,666.

[h] The corporation acquired the Sec. 1231 property on June 5, 2015 for $10,000 and sold it on December 21, 2016, for $8,900.

▼ TABLE C:11-3

Bottle-Up, Inc. Balance Sheet for January 1 and December 31 of the Current Year (Problem C:11-63)

	January 1	December 31
Assets:		
Cash	$ 15,000	$116,948
Accounts receivable	41,500	45,180
Inventories	102,000	96,000
Stocks	103,000	74,000
Treasury bills	15,000	16,000
State of Florida bonds	10,000	10,000
Building and equipment	374,600	375,000
Minus: Accumulated depreciation	(160,484)	(173,100)
Land	160,000	190,000
Total	$660,616	$750,028
Liabilities and equities:		
Accounts payable	$ 36,000	$ 10,000
Accrued salaries payable	12,000	6,000
Payroll taxes payable	3,416	7,106
Sales taxes payable	5,200	6,560
Due to Mr. Hiebert	10,000	5,000
Mortgage and notes payable (current maturities)	44,000	52,000
Long-term debt	210,000	260,000
Capital stock	10,000	10,000
Retained earnings	330,000	393,362
Total	$660,616	$750,028

▼ TABLE C:11-4

Bottle-Up, Inc. Statement of Change in Retained Earnings, for the Current Year Ended December 31 (Problem C:11-63)

Balance, January 1		$330,000[a]
Plus: Net income	$133,362	
Minus: Dividends	(70,000)	63,362
Balance, December 31		$393,362

[a] The January 1 accumulated adjustments account balance is $274,300.

Required: Prepare the 2016 S corporation tax return (Form 1120S), including the following additional schedules and forms: Schedule D, Form 4562, and Schedule K-1.

Optional: (1) Complete Schedule M-2 in Form 1120S even though the company has never been a C corporation. For this purpose, the accumulated adjustments account at the beginning of 2016 is $57,100. (2) Prepare a schedule for each shareholder's basis in his or her S corporation stock. For this purpose, Bailey's stock basis at the beginning of 2016 is $617,130 and Firth's is $1,247,970.

CASE STUDY PROBLEM

C:11-65 Debra has operated a family counseling practice for a number of years as a sole proprietor. She owns the condominium office space that she occupies in addition to her professional library and office furniture. She has a limited amount of working capital and little need to accumulate additional business assets. Her total business assets are about $150,000, with an $80,000 mortgage on the office space being her only liability. Typically, she has withdrawn any unneeded assets at the end of the year. Debra has used her personal car for business travel and charged the business for the mileage at the appropriate mileage rate provided by the IRS. Over the last three years, Debra's practice has grown so that she now forecasts $80,000 of income being earned this year. Debra has contributed small amounts to an Individual Retirement Account (IRA) each year, but her contributions have never reached the annual limits. Although she has never been sued, Debra recently has become concerned about legal liability. An attorney friend of hers has suggested that she incorporate her business to protect herself against being sued and to save taxes.

Required: You are a good friend of Debra's and a CPA; she asks your opinion on incorporating her business. You are to meet with Debra tomorrow for lunch. Prepare a draft of the points you feel should be discussed over lunch about incorporating the family counseling practice.

TAX RESEARCH PROBLEMS

C:11-66 Cato Corporation incorporated six years ago in California, with Tim and Elesa, husband and wife, owning all the Cato stock. Immediately thereafter, Cato made an S election effective for that year. Tim and Elesa filed the necessary consents to the election. On March 10 of last year, Tim and Elesa transferred 15% of the Cato stock to the Reid and Susan Trust, an irrevocable trust created three years earlier for the benefit of their two minor children. Early in the current year, Tim and Elesa's tax accountant learns about the transfer and advises the couple that the transfer of the stock to the trust may have terminated Cato's S election. Prepare a memorandum for your tax manager indicating any action Tim and Elesa can take that will permit Cato to retain its S election. Research sources suggested by the tax manager include Secs. 1361(c)(2), 1362(d)(2), and 1362(f).

C:11-67 One of your wealthy clients, Cecile, invests $100,000 for sole ownership of an electing S corporation's stock. The corporation is in the process of developing a new food product. Cecile anticipates that the new business will need approximately $200,000 in capital (other than trade payables) during the first two years of its operations before it starts to earn sufficient profits to pay a return on the shareholder's investment. The first $100,000 of this total is to come from Cecile's contributed capital. The remaining $100,000 of funds will come from one of the following three sources:

- Have the corporation borrow the $100,000 from a local bank. Cecile is required to act as a guarantor for the loan.
- Have the corporation borrow $100,000 from the estate of Cecile's late husband. Cecile is the sole beneficiary of the estate.
- Have Cecile lend $100,000 to the corporation from her personal funds.

The S corporation will pay interest at a rate acceptable to the IRS. During the first two years of operations, the corporation anticipates losing $125,000 before it begins to earn a profit. Your tax manager has asked you to evaluate the tax ramifications of each of the three financing alternatives. Prepare a memorandum to the tax manager outlining the information you found in your research.

C:11-68 Joe Stephens formed Sigma Corporation on January 4 of Year 1, and the corporation immediately made an S election effective for that year. In forming the corporation, Joe contributed $50,000 cash in exchange for 100% of Sigma's stock. Shortly thereafter, the corporation obtained a $75,000 bank loan to assist with operations. Sigma's first two years did not go as well as expected, with Sigma incurring a $60,000 ordinary loss in Year 1 and a $12,000 ordinary loss in Year 2. Moreover, in Year 2, Joe and his wife Marsha divorced. As part of the divorce settlement, on March 31 of Year 2, Joe gave Marsha 50% of the Sigma stock. In Year 3, Sigma's performance improved, with the corporation earning $40,000 of ordinary income. Joe asks your help in determining the tax consequences of these events, particularly the usage of the S corporation losses. At a minimum, you should consider the following resources:

- IRC Sec. 1366
- Reg. Sec. 1.1366-2

CHAPTER

12

THE GIFT TAX

LEARNING OBJECTIVES

After studying this chapter, you should be able to

1. Explain the basic concepts of the unified transfer tax system
2. Apply the gift tax formula
3. Recognize a number of transactions subject to the gift tax
4. Determine whether an annual gift tax exclusion is available
5. Identify the deductions available for gift tax purposes
6. Apply the gift-splitting rules
7. Calculate the gift tax liability
8. Recognize how basis affects the overall tax consequences
9. Determine the tax consequences of below-market loans
10. Identify tax planning opportunities in gift situations
11. Comply with the filing requirements for gift tax returns

CHAPTER OUTLINE

The **gift tax** is a **wealth transfer tax** that applies if a person transfers property while alive. It is similar to the estate tax, which applies to transfers associated with death. Both the gift tax and the estate tax (discussed in Chapter C:13) are part of the unified transfer tax system that subjects gratuitous transfers of property between persons to taxation. Most property transfers are exempt from these transfer taxes because of the annual exclusion and the various deductions and credits.[1] However, planning for reducing these transfer taxes is a significant matter for wealthy individuals.

Various tax acts over the years have modified the unified transfer tax system in terms of (1) the threshold (called the exemption equivalent or basic exclusion amount) above which the tax becomes effective, (2) the tax rates applicable to estates and gifts, and (3) a number of other aspects of the unified transfer tax system. For 2016, the amount that could be transferred tax free was $5 million indexed to $5.45 million. For 2017, the threshold is indexed to $5.49 million. For both years, the top tax rate is 40%. The unified credit amounts (and basic exclusion amounts), and the unified transfer tax rates for all years, appear inside the back cover of this textbook. These amounts also are discussed within this chapter and Chapter C:13 where appropriate.

ADDITIONAL COMMENT

In this chapter and Chapter C:13, the terms *basic exclusion amount* and *exemption equivalent* are used interchangeably.

This chapter discusses both the structure of the gift tax (including the exclusion, deduction, and credit provisions) and exactly which property transfers fall within its purview. It reviews the income tax basis rules in the context of their implications for selecting properties to transfer by gift instead of at death.

THE UNIFIED TRANSFER TAX SYSTEM

OBJECTIVE 1

Explain the basic concepts of the unified transfer tax system

The recipient of a gift incurs no income tax liability because Sec. 102 explicitly excludes gifts and inheritances from the recipient's gross income.[2] The gift tax, a type of excise tax, is levied on the donor, the person who transferred the property. The gift tax applies to the act of transferring property to a recipient who pays either no consideration or consideration smaller than the value of the property received.

HISTORY AND PURPOSE OF TRANSFER TAXES

ADDITIONAL COMMENT

The continuity of the estate tax was interrupted for 2010 for estates whose executors elected to have a modified carryover basis rule apply instead of the estate tax applying.

The United States has had an estate tax since 1916 and a gift tax continuously since 1932. The structure of the gift and estate taxes has remained fairly constant, but details such as the amount of the exclusion and the rate schedules have changed numerous times. The Tax Reform Act of 1976 (the 1976 Act) made a very significant change by enacting a unified rate schedule for gift and estate tax purposes.

The gift tax has had several purposes, one of the most important of which was to raise revenue. However, because of the fairly generous annual exclusion and unified credit legislated by Congress, the gift tax yields only a small fraction of the federal government's total revenues. Only donors making relatively large gifts owe any gift taxes. Another purpose of the gift tax is to serve as a backstop to the estate tax and to prevent individuals from avoiding a significant amount of—or all—estate taxes by disposing of property before death. For example, without the gift tax, persons who know they are terminally ill could dispose of property "on their deathbed" and escape the transfer tax. In addition, the gift tax provides revenue to offset some of the reduction in income tax revenue resulting from the fact that income from gifted property sometimes is shifted to persons in lower income tax brackets. Another purpose for levying gift and estate taxes is to redistribute wealth.

No one knows what the distribution of wealth would have been had Congress not enacted transfer taxes. However, one study estimated that the top 0.1% of the population held 22% of this nation's personal wealth in 2012, compared with about 7% in the late 1970s.[3]

---

[1] For example, in 2015, of 11,917 estate tax returns filed, 4,918 paid an estate tax. Of these 4,918 returns, all but 665 reported a gross estate over $5 million.

[2] The income earned from property received as a gift or an inheritance, however, is not exempt from the income tax.

[3] Chris Matthews, "Wealth inequality in America: It's worse than you think," *Fortune* (online), October 31, 2014.

In 1976, Congress greatly revamped the transfer tax system by combining the separate estate and gift tax systems into one unified transfer tax system. Although Chapters C:12 and C:13 use the terms *gift tax* and *estate tax*, these taxes actually are components of the same unified transfer tax system. The system also includes the generation-skipping transfer tax, a topic discussed in Chapter C:13. The unification of the transfer tax system removed the previous law's bias favoring the tax treatment of lifetime gifts in comparison with transfers at death. The three most significant elements of the unified system—the unified rate schedule, the inclusion of taxable gifts in the death tax base, and the unified credit—are discussed below.

SELF-STUDY QUESTION

Use the rate schedule inside the back cover of this text to determine the amount of gift tax (before credits) on 2017 taxable gifts of $6 million.

ANSWER

The tax is $2,345,800 [$345,800 + 0.40 × ($6,000,000 − $1,000,000)].

UNIFIED RATE SCHEDULE

Before the 1976 Act mandated a **unified rate schedule**, effective both for gifts made after 1976 and deaths occurring after 1976, the gift tax rates were only 75% of the estate tax rates on a transfer of the same size. The progressive rates have varied over the years. The 2001 Act reduced the unified transfer tax rates beginning in 2002 by replacing the former top two brackets (on amounts exceeding $2.5 million) with a 50% maximum tax rate in 2002. The top rate declined each year for 2003 through 2006. In those years, the top rate applied to tax bases above $2 million. In 2007 through 2009, for both estate and gift tax purposes, a maximum tax rate of 45% applied to tax bases exceeding $1.5 million.

For 2010 through 2012, the top estate and gift tax rate was 35%, applicable to tax bases exceeding $500,000. For 2013 and after, a top rate of 40% applies to tax bases above $1 million. The estate and gift tax unified transfer tax rates for various years appear inside the back cover of this textbook.

IMPACT OF TAXABLE GIFTS ON DEATH TAX BASE

Before 1977, a separate system applied to lifetime gifts compared with dispositions at death. By making gifts, an individual could shift the taxation of property from the top of the estate tax rate schedule to the bottom of the gift tax rate schedule. Few taxpayers could take advantage of this shifting, however, because only people with a relatively large amount of property could afford to part with sizable amounts of their assets while alive.

ADDITIONAL COMMENT

At the taxpayer's death, the unified tax is computed on the sum of the taxable estate plus the adjusted taxable gifts. The tax on this sum is reduced by the tax that would have been payable (at current rates) on the taxable gifts made after December 31, 1976.

Under today's unified system, taxable gifts affect the size of the tax base at death. Any post-1976 taxable gifts (other than gifts included in the gross estate) are called **adjusted taxable gifts**, and such gifts are included in the donor's death tax base. Although they are valued at their fair market value (FMV) on the date of the gift, the addition of such taxable gifts to the tax base at death can cause the donor-decedent's estate to be taxed at a higher marginal tax rate. However, such gifts are not taxed for a second time upon the donor's death because gift taxes (computed at current rates) on these gifts are subtracted in determining the estate tax liability.

EXAMPLE C:12-1 ▶ In 1994, Dan made taxable gifts totaling $500,000. When Dan died the value of the gifted property had tripled. Dan's death tax base includes the $500,000 of post-1976 taxable gifts. They are valued for estate tax purposes at their FMV on the date of the gift; the post-gift appreciation escapes the transfer tax system. Thus, the transfer tax value is fixed or frozen at the date-of-gift value. ◀

Note that unification (including taxable gifts that become part of the tax base at death) extends only to gifts made after 1976. Congress exempted gifts made before 1977 from unification because it did not want to retroactively change the two separate transfer tax systems of the prior tax regime.

UNIFIED CREDIT

The **unified credit** reduces dollar for dollar a certain amount of the tax computed on the taxable gifts or the taxable estate. The amount of the credit has varied depending on the year of the transfer (see discussion on page C:12-6). In the gift and estate tax formulas, the full credit is available for lifetime transfers and again in determining the tax payable at death. In concept, however, an individual's estate does not receive the benefit of this unified credit amount at death to the extent the decedent had used the credit against lifetime transfers (as explained in Chapter C:13). The gift tax formula, including the unified credit, is discussed below.

GIFT TAX FORMULA

OBJECTIVE 2

Apply the gift tax formula

The formula described in this section is used to calculate a donor's gift tax liability for the year of the transfer. Gift tax reporting is done on an annual basis, always on a calendar year. Figure C:12-1 illustrates the formula for determining the donor's annual gift tax liability. This formula is discussed in detail later in the chapter.

ADDITIONAL COMMENT

The gift tax applies to cumulative lifetime gifts made since the enactment of the gift tax in 1932. The unified gift and estate tax, enacted in 1976, applies only to cumulative lifetime taxable gifts made after 1976. Thus, a taxable gift of $75,000 made in 1970 would not be included in a decedent's unified tax base for calculating the estate tax but would affect the gift tax payable by that person.

DETERMINATION OF GIFTS

The starting point in the process is to determine which, if any, of the taxpayer's transfers constitute gifts. The next section discusses the various types of transfers that the statute views as gifts. All gifts are valued at their FMVs on the date of the gift, and the aggregate amount of gifts for the period is determined. The aggregate gifts are then reduced by any exclusions and deductions. Finally, the tax is computed according to the formula illustrated in Figure C:12-1.

EXCLUSIONS AND DEDUCTIONS

For many years the maximum amount excludible annually was $10,000 per donee, but Congress amended the IRC to allow indexation beginning with gifts made after 1998. Inflation adjustments are rounded to the next *lowest* multiple of $1,000.[4] Accordingly, the annual exclusion rose to $11,000 for 2002 through 2005, to $12,000 for 2006 through 2008, to $13,000 for 2009 through 2012, and to $14,000 beginning in 2013. If the gifts made to a donee are less than the annual exclusion amount, the amount excludible is limited to the amount of the gift made to that donee. A donor may claim exclusions for transfers to an unlimited number of donees.

Two types of deductions (marital and charitable) reduce the amount of the taxable gifts. Most transfers to one's spouse generate a marital deduction; there is no ceiling on the amount of this deduction. Similarly, most transfers to charitable organizations are cancelled out by the charitable contribution deduction, which also is unlimited.

KEY POINT

The annual exclusion applies to each *donee* per year; therefore, the total amount of tax-free gifts in a given year can be much greater than the annual exclusion amount. Also, gift-splitting can double the tax-free amount per donee.

GIFT-SPLITTING ELECTION

Congress authorized gift-splitting provisions to achieve more comparable tax consequences between taxpayers of community property and noncommunity property (common law) states.[5] Under **community property law**, assets acquired after marriage are community property unless they are acquired by gift or inheritance. Typically, in a **community property state**, a large portion of the spouses' assets is community property, property in which each spouse has a one-half interest. One-half of a community property gift is automatically considered to be given by each spouse. By contrast, in a **common law state**, all assets acquired during the marriage are the property of the acquiring spouse. The other spouse does not automatically acquire an interest in the property. Thus, sometimes only one spouse owns enough assets to consider making large gifts.

Section 2513 authorizes spouses to elect gift splitting, which treats gifts made by one spouse to third parties as if each spouse made one-half of the gift. As a result, spouses in common law states can achieve the same benefits that apply automatically for gifts of community property. Thus, both spouses can claim a $14,000 per donee exclusion although only one spouse actually makes the gift, and the spouses can give each donee a total of $28,000 before either spouse's gift becomes taxable.

---

[4] Sec. 2503(b).

[5] The eight traditional community property states are Louisiana, Texas, New Mexico, Arizona, California, Washington, Idaho, and Nevada. Wisconsin's marital property law, though not providing for community property, is basically the same as community property.

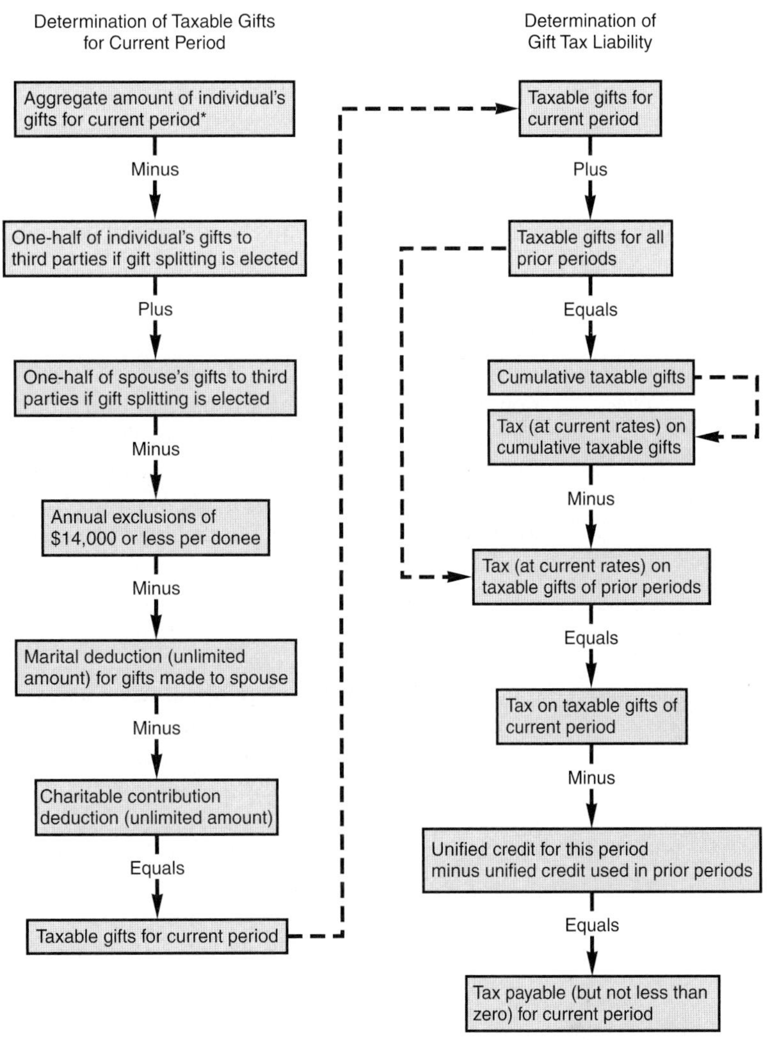

FIGURE C:12-1 ▶ THE GIFT TAX FORMULA

As a result of the Supreme Court's 2013 decision in *U.S. v. Windsor*,[6] same-sex spouses are eligible for the gift-splitting election. The Court ruled unconstitutional the section of the Defense of Marriage Act (DOMA) that recognized only marriages between a man and a woman as a marriage for purposes of federal law. In *Obergefell v. Hodges et al.*,[7] the Supreme Court concluded that all states must allow same-sex couples to marry and must recognize same-sex marriages lawfully performed in another state.

EXAMPLE C:12-2 ▶

ADDITIONAL COMMENT

Because the gift tax is a tax on *cumulative* lifetime gifts, taxpayers must keep track of all taxable gifts. All previous taxable gifts are part of the calculation for current gift tax due, and post-1976 taxable gifts affect the estate tax liability.

Andy and Bonnie, residents of a common law state, are married throughout 2017. In that year, Andy gives his brother $100,000 cash. Andy and Bonnie may elect gift splitting and thereby treat the $100,000 gift as if each spouse gave $50,000. As a result, the excludible portion of the gift totals $28,000 ($14,000 per donee for each of the two deemed donors). If they elect gift splitting, each donor's $36,000 taxable gift may be taxed at a lower marginal tax rate. In addition, Bonnie can use a unified credit amount that she might not otherwise be able to use. As a result of gift splitting, the tax consequences are the same as if Andy and Bonnie were residents of a community property state and each gave $50,000 of community property to Andy's brother. ◀

[6] 111 AFTR2d 2013-2385, 2013-2 USTC ¶50,400 (USSC, 2013).

[7] 15 AFTR2d 2015-2309, 2015-1 USTC ¶50,357 (USSC, 2015).

CUMULATIVE NATURE OF GIFT TAX

Unlike the income tax, computations of gift tax liabilities are cumulative in nature. The marginal tax rate applicable to the current period's taxable gifts is a function of both the taxable gifts for the current period and the aggregate taxable gifts for all earlier periods.

EXAMPLE C:12-3 ▶ Sandy and Jack each made taxable gifts in 2017 totaling $200,000. However, for previous periods, Sandy's taxable gifts totaled $100,000 and Jack's totaled $1.5 million. Because Jack's cumulative total taxable gifts were larger than Sandy's, Jack's marginal tax rate exceeds Sandy's. Specifically Jack's $200,000 gift is taxed at a 40% rate, while Sandy's $200,000 gift is taxed at the following rates: $50,000 at 30%, $100,000 at 32%, and $50,000 at 34%. ◀

SELF-STUDY QUESTION

Al and Beth, husband and wife, live in a common law state. Al gives $4 million to one child and $2 million to the other. Al and Beth agree to split the gifts. Neither Al nor Beth has made taxable gifts in any prior year. Explain their gift tax liability.

ANSWER

Each taxpayer reports $3 million on his or her gift tax return. Neither Al nor Beth has any gift tax liability for the current year due to the annual exclusions and the unified credit. Al has effectively used some of Beth's unified credit without Beth ever having ownership or control over Al's property.

ADDITIONAL COMMENT

The unified credit amounts after 2011 are $5 million adjusted for inflation.

UNIFIED CREDIT

Before 1977, the Internal Revenue Code (IRC) allowed donors a $30,000 specific exemption deductible by donors whenever they desired. The 1976 Act repealed this exemption and replaced it with the unified credit beginning in 1977.[8] Consequently, the gift tax computed for gifts made in 1977 and later is reduced dollar for dollar by the unified credit. The unified credit allows donors to make a certain amount of taxable gifts (known originally as the **exemption equivalent** and now referred to in the IRC as the **basic exclusion amount**) without needing to pay any gift tax. The unified credit has varied over the years, and a listing of the amounts year-by-year appears on the inside back cover of this textbook. The credit increased from $34,000 in 1978 to $345,800 (the tax on $1 million) in 2009 but decreased to $330,800 in 2010 because of a reduction in the top gift tax rate. In 2004 through 2010, the gift tax and estate tax credits were different because the exempt amounts for each tax differed. In 2011, the unified credit again became uniform at $1,730,800, the tax on $5 million at a top rate of 35%. The $5 million amount is adjusted each year for inflation. In 2014, the top rate rose from 35% to 40%. For 2015, the unified credit was $2,117,800, the tax on $5.43 million, for 2016 it was $2,125,800, the tax on $5.45 million, and for 2017 it is $2,141,800, the tax on $5.49 million. In each situation, the top rate of 40% begins at amounts above $1 million.

The amount creditable for a particular year is the credit amount for that year minus the credit that could have been claimed for the taxable gifts made by the individual in earlier years. Prior to 2010, top tax rates ranged from 45% to 55% depending on the particular tax year. However, because the top rate was 35% in 2010 through 2012 and 40% beginning in 2013, the credit is reduced not by the credit actually claimed in earlier years but by what the unified credit would have been, if lower, had the credit been calculated using the rates for the current year. Recall that no credit was allowed for gifts made before 1977.[9]

EXAMPLE C:12-4 ▶ Zheng made her first taxable gift ($325,000) in 1984. She used the $96,300 unified credit available for 1984 (as shown on the inside back cover) to reduce her $96,300 gift tax liability to zero. Zheng made her next taxable gift ($100,000) in 1985. Zheng's 1985 gift tax is computed as follows:

Tax on cumulative gifts [$70,800 + 0.34 × ($425,000 − $250,000)]	$130,300
Minus: Tax on 1984 taxable gift	(96,300)
Tax on 1985 gift	$ 34,000
Minus: Unified credit available in 1985 ($121,800 − $96,300)	(25,500)
Tax in 1985	$ 8,500

Thus, by 1985, Zheng has claimed credits totaling $121,800. If she makes taxable gifts in 2017, the maximum credit she can claim against her 2017 tax is $2,020,000 ($2,141,800 – $121,800 already used). In this situation, the credit actually claimed and the amount of the credit calculated using the 2017 rate are the same because the earlier gifts were not taxed at rates above 40%. ◀

ADDITIONAL COMMENT

Taxpayers must keep a record of how much of the specific exemption they used between September 9 and December 31, 1976, to determine how much of the unified credit is available to them.

After passage of the 1976 Act, prospective donors quickly realized they could make gifts before the end of 1976 and avoid the unification provisions, but Congress adopted a special rule that affects donors who used any portion of their specific exemption between September 9, 1976, and December 31, 1976.[10] The rule reduced the amount of unified

---

[8] Sec. 2505.

[9] Also, no credit is used for a gift that is completely nontaxable.

[10] Sec. 2505(b). Congress repealed this exemption for post-1976 years.

credit otherwise available to such donors by 20% of the amount of the specific exemption they claimed against gifts made between September 9 and December 31, 1976. The maximum reduction in the unified credit as a result of this provision is $6,000 (0.20 × $30,000 maximum specific exemption).

EXAMPLE C:12-5 ▶ In November 1976, to avoid unification, Maria made her first gift and used her $30,000 specific exemption. As a result, the unified credit that Maria could otherwise claim after 1976 is reduced by $6,000 (0.20 × $30,000). Her 1976 taxable gifts are not includible in her death tax base. ◀

TRANSFERS SUBJECT TO THE GIFT TAX

OBJECTIVE 3

Recognize a number of transactions subject to the gift tax

In general, property transferred for less than adequate consideration in money or money's worth is deemed to be a gift in the gift tax context. The gift occurs when the donor gives up control over the transferred property. Congress has legislated several provisions that exempt various property transfers that otherwise might be viewed as gifts from the scope of the gift tax. These exemptions include direct payments of medical expenses and tuition, transfers to political organizations, property settlements in conjunction with a divorce, and qualified disclaimers.

TRANSFERS FOR INADEQUATE CONSIDERATION

As mentioned earlier, the initial step in determining the donor's gift tax liability is deciding which transactions constitute gifts for gift tax purposes. Section 2501(a) states that a gift tax is imposed on "the transfer of property by gift." Thus, if *property* is transferred *by gift*, the transferor potentially incurs a gift tax liability. Perhaps surprisingly, the IRC does not define the term *gift*. Section 2511(a), however, elaborates on the gift concept by indicating that the tax is applicable "whether the transfer is in trust or otherwise, whether the gift is direct or indirect, and whether the property is real or personal, tangible or intangible."

A transaction is subject to the gift tax even though not entirely gratuitous if "the value of the property transferred by the donor exceeds the value in money or money's worth of the consideration given therefor."[11] In such circumstances, the amount of the gift is the difference between the value of the property the donor gave up and the value of the consideration in money or money's worth received. The following discussion examines in more depth the scope of the rule regarding transfers for less than adequate consideration.

ADDITIONAL COMMENT

At times, a transferor can inadvertently make a gift by selling property for an amount determined in an IRS audit to be less than its fair market value.

Bargain Sales. At times, an individual wants to sell an asset to a prospective buyer (perhaps a family member) who cannot afford to pay the full FMV of the property. If the buyer pays consideration of less than the FMV of the transferred property, the seller makes a gift to the buyer equal to the bargain element of the transaction, which is the excess of the property's FMV over its sales price.

EXAMPLE C:12-6 ▶ Martha sells her ranch, having a $1 million FMV, to her son Stan, who can afford to pay only $300,000 of consideration. In the year of the sale, Martha makes a gift to Stan of $700,000, the excess of the ranch's FMV over the consideration received. ◀

Transfers in Normal Course of Business. Treasury Regulations provide an exception to the general rule that a transfer for inadequate consideration triggers a gift. Specifically, a transaction arising "in the ordinary course of business (a transaction which is bona fide, at arm's length, and free from any donative intent)" is considered to have been made for adequate consideration.[12] Thus, no gift arises when a buyer acquires property for less than its FMV *if* the acquisition is in the ordinary course of business.

EXAMPLE C:12-7 ▶ John, a merchant, has a clearance sale and sells a diamond bracelet valued at $30,000 to Bess who pays $14,000, the clearance sale price. Because the clearance sale arose in the ordinary course of John's business, the bargain element ($16,000) does not constitute a gift to Bess. ◀

[11] Reg. Sec. 25.2512-8.

[12] Ibid.

STATUTORY EXEMPTIONS FROM THE GIFT TAX

For various reasons, including simplifying the administration of the gift tax, Congress enacted several provisions that exempt certain transactions from the purview of the gift tax. In the absence of these statutory rules, some of these transactions could constitute gifts.

Payment of Medical Expenses or Tuition. Section 2503(e) states that a qualified transfer is not treated as a transfer of property by gift. The IRC defines *qualified transfer* as an amount paid on behalf of an individual to an educational organization for tuition or to any person who provides medical care as payment for such medical care. Such payments are exempt from gift treatment only if made *directly* to the educational organization or to the person or entity providing the medical care. *Educational organization* has the same definition as for charitable contribution purposes,[13] and *medical care* has the same definition as for medical expense deduction purposes.[14] Note that the rule addresses only tuition, not room, board, and books. Moreover, the identity of the person whose expenses are paid is not important. The special exemption applies even if an individual makes payments on behalf of a non-relative.

SELF-STUDY QUESTION

Ben's adult son Clarence, who is not Ben's dependent, needs a liver transplant. Because Clarence cannot afford the surgical procedure, Ben pays the medical fee directly to the hospital. Is Ben's payment for Clarence's benefit a taxable gift?

ANSWER

The payment is not a taxable gift because of Sec. 2503(e).

If a taxpayer pays amounts benefitting someone else and the expenditures constitute support that the payor must furnish under state law, such payments are support, not gifts. State law determines the definition of support. Generally, payments of medical expenses for one's minor child would be categorized as support and not a gift, even in the absence of Sec. 2503(e). On the other hand, state law generally does not require parents to pay medical expenses or tuition for an adult child. Thus, the enactment of Sec. 2503(e) removed such payments from the gift tax.

According to the Staff of the Joint Committee on Taxation, special rules concerning tuition and medical expense payments were enacted because

> Congress was concerned that certain payments of tuition made on behalf of children who have attained their majority, and of special medical expenses on behalf of elderly relatives, technically could be considered gifts under prior law. The Congress believed such payments should be exempt from gift taxes.[15]

EXAMPLE C:12-8 ▶ Sergio (a widower) pays $20,000 for his adult grandson's tuition at medical school and $15,000 for the grandson's room and board in the medical school's dormitory. Sergio makes all payments directly to the educational organization. Section 2503(e) exempts the direct payment of the tuition to the medical school (but not the room and board) from being treated as a gift. Because Sergio is not required under state law to pay room and board for a grandson, such payments are not support. Sergio has made a $15,000 gift to the grandson. ◀

EXAMPLE C:12-9 ▶ Assume the same facts as in Example C:12-8 except that Sergio writes a $35,000 check to his grandson, who in turn pays the medical school. Sergio has made a $35,000 gift. Because Sergio does not pay the tuition directly to the school, Sergio does not meet all the conditions for exempting the tuition payments from gift tax treatment. Here, and in Example C:12-8, Sergio receives a $14,000 annual exclusion. ◀

Transfers to Political Organizations. Congress adopted a provision specifically exempting transfers to political organizations from being deemed to be a transfer of property by gift.[16] Without this special rule, these transfers generally would be subjected to gift tax treatment.

EXAMPLE C:12-10 ▶ Ann transfers $2,000 to a political organization founded to promote Thomas's campaign for governor. Ann's $2,000 transfer does not fall within the statutory definition of a gift. ◀

Property Settlements in Conjunction with Divorce. To reduce litigation, Congress enacted special rules addressing property transfers in the context of a divorce. Section 2516 and underlying Treasury Regulations specify the circumstances in which it automatically exempts property settlements in connection with a divorce from being treated as gifts.

For Sec. 2516 to be applicable, the spouses must adopt a written agreement concerning their marital and property rights and the divorce must occur during a three-year

---

[13] Section 170(b)(1)(A)(ii) defines *educational organization* in the context of the charitable contribution deduction.

[14] Section 213(d) defines *medical care* in the context of the medical expense deduction.

[15] U.S. Congress, Staff of the Joint Committee on Taxation, *General Explanation of the Economic Recovery Tax Act of 1981* (Washington, DC: U.S. Government Printing Office, 1981), p. 273.

[16] Sec. 2501(a)(4).

What Would You Do in This Situation?

You are a CPA with a very wealthy client, Ms. Atsushi Trong, who is a model of the U.S. success story. She immigrated to the United States as a teenager and studied clothing trends in both high school and college. She started her own clothing company, which has been very successful. She has a net worth of over $100 million and no immediate family.

She decided to plow some of her good fortune back into the educational system, which provided the intellectual foundation for her success. She selected the current class of her old high school, and in 2015 gave each of 100 graduating students $100,000 to be used to pay tuition costs for four years at her college alma mater. Each of the 100 student donees used the $100,000 to prepay the four-year tuition costs in 2015.

You have been asked to determine the tax consequences of these transactions. What position would you take after considering the requirements of the IRC and *Statements on Standards for Tax Services* (reproduced in Appendix E)?

period beginning one year before they make the agreement. No gift arises from any transfer made in accordance with such agreement if a spouse transfers property to settle the other spouse's marital or property rights or to provide reasonable support for the children while they are minors. In addition, Sec. 1041 provides for no gain or loss recognition and a carryover basis for the transferred property.

EXAMPLE C:12-11 ▶ In June 2016, Hal and Wanda signed a property agreement whereby Hal is to transfer $750,000 to Wanda in settlement of her property rights. Hal makes the transfer in May 2017. Hal and Wanda receive a divorce decree in July 2017. Hal is not deemed to have made a gift to Wanda when he transferred property to her. ◀

Qualified Disclaimers. Sometimes a person named to receive property under a decedent's will prefers not to receive such property and would like to disclaim (not accept) it. Typically, the person is quite ill and/or elderly or very wealthy. State disclaimer statutes allow individuals to say "no thank you" to the property willed to them. State law or another provision in the will addresses how to determine who will receive the property after the original beneficiary (the disclaimant) declines to accept it.

ADDITIONAL COMMENT

Individuals who execute disclaimers, in a sense, participate in shifting wealth to another.

Section 2518(a) states that individuals making a qualified disclaimer are treated as if the disclaimed property were never transferred to them. Thus, the person making the disclaimer is not deemed to have made a gift to the person who receives the disclaimed property.

A **qualified disclaimer** must meet the following four tests:

- It must be an irrevocable, unqualified, written refusal to accept property.
- The transferor or his or her legal representative must receive the refusal no later than nine months after the later of the day the transfer is made or the day the person named to receive the property becomes age 21.
- The disclaiming person must not have accepted the property interest or any of its benefits.
- As a result of the disclaimer, the property must pass to the decedent's spouse or a person other than the one disclaiming it. In addition, the person disclaiming the property cannot direct who is to receive the property.[17]

EXAMPLE C:12-12 ▶ Doug dies on February 1, 2017, and wills 500 acres of land to Joan. If Joan disclaims the property in a manner that meets all four of the tests for a qualified disclaimer, Joan will not be treated as making a gift to the person who receives the property as a result of her disclaimer. ◀

[17] Sec. 2518(b).

EXAMPLE C:12-13 ▶ Assume the same facts as in Example C:12-12 except Joan instead disclaims the property on January 2, 2018. Joan's action arose too late to meet the second qualified disclaimer test above. Thus, Joan makes a gift to the person who receives the property she disclaims. ◀

CESSATION OF DONOR'S DOMINION AND CONTROL

A gift occurs when a transfer becomes complete and is valued as of the date the transfer becomes complete. Thus, the concept of a completed transfer is important in two contexts: determination of whether a gift has arisen and, if so, the value of the gift. According to Treasury Regulations, a gift becomes complete—and is thus deemed made and valued—when the donor "has so parted with dominion and control as to leave in him no power to change its disposition, whether for his own benefit or for the benefit of another."[18] A gift is not necessarily complete just because the transferor cannot receive any further personal benefits, such as income, from the property. If the transferor still can influence the benefits others may receive from the transferred property, the transfer is incomplete with respect to the portion of the property over which the transferor retained control.

Revocable Trusts. A transferor who conveys property to a revocable trust makes an incomplete transfer because the creator of a revocable trust can change the trust provisions, including the identity of the beneficiaries. Moreover, the creator may demand the return of the trust property. Because the transferor does not give up any control over property conveyed to a revocable trust, the individual does not make a gift upon funding the trust. Once the trustee distributes trust income to a beneficiary, however, the creator of the trust loses control over the distributed funds and then makes a completed gift of the income the trustee pays out.

EXAMPLE C:12-14 ▶ On May 1, Ted transfers $500,000 to a revocable trust with First National Bank as trustee. The trustee must pay out all the income to Ed during Ed's lifetime and at Ed's death distribute the property to Ed, Jr. On December 31, the trustee distributes $35,000 of income to Ed. The May 1 transfer is incomplete because Ted may revoke the trust; thus, no gift arises upon the funding of the trust. A $35,000 gift to Ed occurs on December 31 because Ted no longer has control over the income distributed to Ed. The gift is eligible for the annual exclusion. ◀

EXAMPLE C:12-15 ▶ Assume the same facts as in Example C:12-14 and that Ted amends the trust instrument on July 7 of the next year to make the trust irrevocable. By this date, the trust property has appreciated to $612,000. Ted makes a completed gift of $612,000 on July 7 of the next year because he gives up his powers over the trust. The gift is eligible for the annual exclusion. ◀

KEY POINT

If the donor retains control over any portion of the property, no gift is considered to have been made of the portion of the property the donor still controls.

Other Retained Powers. Transfers to an irrevocable trust can be deemed incomplete for the portion of the trust over which the creator kept control. Treasury Regulations state that if "the donor reserves any power over its [the property's] disposition, the gift may be wholly incomplete, or may be partially complete and partially incomplete, depending upon all the facts in the particular case."[19] One must examine the trust agreement language to determine the scope of the donor's retention of control. The regulations elaborate by indicating that "[a] gift is . . . incomplete if and to the extent that a reserved power gives the donor the power to name new beneficiaries or to change the interests of the beneficiaries."[20]

EXAMPLE C:12-16 ▶ On May 3, Art transfers $300,000 of property in trust with a bank as trustee. Art names his friends Bob and/or Sue to receive the trust income for 15 years and Karl to receive the trust property at the end of 15 years. Art reserves the power to determine how the income is to be divided between Bob and Sue each year, but the trustee must distribute all of the income each year. Because Art reserves the power over payment of the income for the 15-year period, this portion of the transfer is incomplete on May 3. Actuarial tables discussed in the next section of the chapter address the valuation of the completed gift to Karl. As discussed in Chapter C:14, the grantor trust rules tax Art (the donor) on the trust income. ◀

---

[18] Reg. Sec. 25.2511-2(b).
[19] Ibid.
[20] Reg. Sec. 25.2511-2(c).

EXAMPLE C:12-17 ▶ Assume the same facts as in Example C:12-16 and that on December 31 Art instructs the trustee to distribute the trust's $34,000 of income as follows: $18,000 to Bob and $16,000 to Sue. Once the trustee pays out income, Art loses control over it. Thus, Art makes an $18,000 gift to Bob and a $16,000 gift to Sue on December 31. Each gift qualifies for the annual exclusion. ◀

EXAMPLE C:12-18 ▶ Assume the same facts as in Example C:12-16 and that on May 3 of the next year, when the trust assets are valued at $360,000, Art relinquishes his powers over payment of income and gives this power to the trustee. Art's transfer of the income interest (with a remaining term of 14 years) becomes complete on May 3 of the next year. The valuation of the gift of a 14-year income interest in the $360,000 trust assets is determined from actuarial tables in Appendix H. ◀

Topic Review C:12-1 provides examples of various complete, incomplete, and partially complete transfers.

VALUATION OF GIFTS

ADDITIONAL COMMENT

Because the determination of value is such a subjective issue, a large number of gift tax controversies involve valuation disagreements.

General Rules. All gifts are valued at their FMV as of the date of the gift (i.e., the date the transfer becomes complete). Treasury Regulations state that a property's value is "the price at which such property would change hands between a willing buyer and a willing seller, neither being under any compulsion to buy or to sell, and both having reasonable knowledge of relevant facts."[21] According to the regulations, stocks and bonds traded on a stock exchange or over the counter are valued at the mean of the highest and lowest selling price on the date of the gift.[22] In general, the guidelines for valuing properties are the same, regardless of whether the property is conveyed during life or at death. An exception is life insurance policies, which are less valuable while the insured is alive. Valuation of life insurance policies is discussed in a later section of this chapter, as well as in Chapter C:13's coverage of the estate tax.

KEY POINT

The value of the life estate plus the value of the remainder interest equals the total FMV of the property.

Life Estates and Remainder Interests. Often a donor transfers less than his or her entire interest in an asset. For example, an individual may transfer property in trust and reserve the right to the trust's income for life and name another individual to receive the property upon the transferor's death. In such a situation, the transferor retains a **life estate** and gives a **remainder interest**. In general, only the remainder interest is subject to the gift tax. An exception applies if the gift is to a family member, as discussed in the estate freeze section below. If the transferor keeps an annuity (a fixed amount) for life and names another person to receive the remainder at the transferor's death, in all situations the gift is of just the remainder interest.

A grantor also may transfer property in trust with the promise that another person will receive the income for a certain number of years and at the end of that time period the

TOPIC REVIEW C:12-1

Examples of Complete and Incomplete Transfers

1. Complete Transfers, Subject to Gift Tax:
   a. Property transferred outright to donee
   b. Property transferred to an irrevocable trust over which the donor retains no powers
2. Incomplete Transfers, Not Subject to Gift Tax:
   a. Property transferred to a revocable trust
   b. Property transferred to an irrevocable trust for which the donor retains discretionary powers over both income and the remainder interest
3. Partially Complete Transfers, Only a Portion Subject to Gift Tax:
   a. Property transferred to an irrevocable trust for which the donor retains discretionary powers over who receives the income but not the remainder interest[a]

[a]The gift of the remainder interest constitutes a completed transfer.

[21] Reg. Sec. 25.2512-1.

[22] Reg. Sec. 25.2512-2.

property will revert to the grantor. In this case, the donor retains a reversionary interest, whereas the other party receives a **term certain interest.**[23] As explained later in the discussion of estate freezes, unless the donee is a family member, only the term certain interest is subject to the gift tax. Trusts in which the grantor retains a reversionary interest have disadvantageous income tax consequences to the grantor if they were created after March 1, 1986. Chapter C:14 discusses the income tax treatment of such trusts.

Life estates, annuity interests, remainders, and term certain interests are valued from actuarial tables that incorporate the Sec. 7520 interest rate. In general, these tables must be used regardless of the actual earnings rate of the transferred assets. Excerpts from the tables appear in Appendix H. Table S is used for valuing life estates and remainders and Table B for term certain interests. The factor for a life estate or term certain interest is 1.0 minus the remainder factor. The remainder factor simply represents the present value of the right to receive a property at the end of someone's life (in the case of Table S) or at the end of a specified time (in the case of Table B). The value of the income interest plus the remainder interest is 1.0, the entire value of the property. The factor for an annuity is the life estate or the term factor divided by the Sec. 7520 interest rate. Section 7520 calls for the interest rate to be revised every month to the rate, rounded to the nearest 0.2%, that is 120% of the federal midterm rate applicable for the month of the transfer.[24] Congress mandated that at least once every ten years the tables be revised to reflect mortality experience. The most recent revised life tables became effective for transfers beginning on May 1, 2009.

TAX STRATEGY TIP

When gifting a remainder interest, the donor should consider giving property with an anticipated appreciation rate greater than the Sec. 7520 interest rate.

EXAMPLE C:12-19 ▶ On May 3 Art transfers $300,000 of property in trust with a bank as trustee. Art names his friends Bob and Sue to receive the trust income for 15 years but reserves the power to determine how the income is to be divided between them each year. However, the trustee must distribute all the income. Art specifies that Karl is to receive the trust property at the end of the fifteenth year. Because Art keeps power over the income, only the gift of the remainder interest is a completed transfer on May 3. The gift is valued from Table B. If the interest rate is 4%, the amount of the gift is $166,580 (0.555265 × $300,000), the present value of the property to be received by Karl at the end of 15 years. ◀

EXAMPLE C:12-20 ▶ Assume the same facts as in Example C:12-19 and that three years later, when the trust assets are valued at $360,000, Art relinquishes to the trustee his power over the payment of trust income. The income interest has a remaining term of 12 years. The gift is the present value of the 12-year income interest, which is valued from Table B by subtracting the factor for a remainder interest (0.624597 if the interest rate is 4%) from 1.0. Thus, the amount of the gift is $135,145 [(1.0 − 0.624597) × $360,000]. ◀

EXAMPLE C:12-21 ▶ On July 5 of the current year, Don transfers $100,000 of property in trust with a bank trustee and names his friends Larry (age 60) to receive all of the income for the rest of Larry's life and Ruth (age 25) to receive the assets upon Larry's death. The amount of each donee's gift is reported on the gift tax return and is determined from Table S. If the interest rate is 4% and Larry is age 60, the value of the remainder interest gift to Ruth, as calculated from the single life remainder factors column of Table S, is $46,310 (0.46310 × $100,000). This amount represents the present value of the property Ruth will receive after the death of Larry, age 60. The remaining portion of the $100,000 of property, $53,690 ($100,000 − $46,310), is the value of Larry's life estate. The total value of the income plus remainder interests is 1.0. ◀

EXAMPLE C:12-22 ▶ In July of the current year, Amy (age 62) transferred $1 million of stock to a trust from which she retained the right to receive $120,000 per year for five years. She provided that the remainder will pass to her son, Arthur, at the end of the fifth year. Assume that 4% was the Sec. 7520 rate at the time of her transfer. She anticipated that the stock would continue to appreciate at its recent appreciation rate of 6% a year. The factor for a five-year annuity, assuming a 4%

[23] *Term certain interest* means that a particular person has an interest in the property held in trust for a specified time period. The person having such interest does not own or hold title to the property but has a right to receive the income from such property for a specified time period. At the end of the time period, the property reverts to the grantor (or passes to another person, the remainderman).

[24] The IRS regularly issues revenue rulings with applicable rate information.

rate, is 4.451825 [(1.0 − 0.821927, the factor for a remainder interest)/(0.04, the Sec. 7520 rate)]. Thus, Amy is deemed to have retained $534,219 (4.451825 × $120,000) and is deemed to have gifted the difference of $465,781 ($1,000,000 − $534,219) to Arthur. ◀

Question: In which scenario would the amount of the gift be larger: (1) a gift of a remainder interest to a friend if a 68-year-old donor retained the income for life or (2) a gift of a remainder interest to a friend if an 86-year-old donor retained the income for life? Assume that each donor makes the gift on the same day so that the applicable interest rates are the same for each scenario.

Solution: The gift of the remainder interest would be larger if the donor is 86, instead of 68, because the actuarial value of the income interest the donor retains would be smaller if the donor is older. Under actuarial assumptions, older donors have shorter life expectancies.

ADDITIONAL COMMENT

In estate freeze transfers, Congress provided rules that generally increase the amount classified as a gift.

Special Valuation Rules: Estate Freezes. A number of years ago, Congress became concerned that individuals were able to shift wealth to other individuals, usually in a younger generation, without paying their "fair share" of the transfer taxes. An approach donors commonly used was to recapitalize a corporation (by exchanging common stock for both common and preferred shares) and then give the common stock to individuals in the younger generation. This technique was one of a variety of transactions known as estate freezes.

In 1990, Congress decided to address the perceived problem of estate freezes by writing new valuation rules that apply for certain gifts. The thrust of these rules—current IRC Chapter 14 (Secs. 2701 through 2704)—is to ensure that gifts are not undervalued. A couple of the more common situations governed by the new rules are described below, but the rules are too complicated to warrant a complete discussion. If a parent owns 100% of a corporation's stock and then gives the common stock to his or her children and retains the preferred stock, the value of the right to the preferred dividends is treated as zero unless the stock is cumulative preferred. Consequently, unless the preferred stock retained by the donor is *cumulative*, the value assigned to the common stock given away is relatively high. If the donor creates a trust in which he or she retains an interest and in which he or she gives an interest to a family member, the value of the transferor's retained interest is treated as zero unless the interest is an annuity interest (fixed payments) or a unitrust interest (calling for distributions equal to a specified percentage of the current FMV of the trust). Thus, the donor who retains an income interest is treated as having kept nothing. The effect of these rules increases the amount classified as a gift, compared with the result under prior law, unless the transferor structures the transaction to avoid having a zero value assigned to his or her retained interest.[25]

GIFT TAX CONSEQUENCES OF CERTAIN TRANSFERS

Some transactions that cause the transferor to make a gift are straightforward. It is easy to understand that a gift arises if, for example, an individual places the title to stock or real estate solely in another person's name and receives less than adequate consideration in return. Treasury Regulations include the following examples of transactions that may be subject to the gift tax: forgiving of a debt; assignment of the benefits of a life insurance policy; transfer of cash; and transfer of federal, state, or municipal bonds.[26] The gratuitous transfer of state and local bonds falls within the scope of the gift tax, even though interest on such bonds is exempt from federal income taxation. The following discussion concerns the gift tax rules for several transfers that are more complicated than, for example, transferring the title to real property or stock to another person.

[25] See Reg. Secs. 25.2701-1 through -6 and 25.2702-1 through -6 for guidance concerning the estate freeze provisions.

[26] Reg. Sec. 25.2511-1(a).

Creation of Joint Bank Accounts. Parties depositing money to a jointly owned bank account potentially face gift tax consequences. Funding a joint bank account is an incomplete transfer because the depositor is free to withdraw the amount deposited into the account. A gift occurs when one party withdraws an amount exceeding the amount he or she deposited.[27] The transfer is complete at that time because only the person who withdrew funds can control those funds.

EXAMPLE C:12-23 ▶ On May 1, Connie deposits $100,000 into a joint bank account in the names of Connie and Ben. Her friend Ben makes no deposits. On December 1, Ben withdraws $30,000 from the joint account. No gift arises upon the creation of the bank account. However, on December 1, Connie makes a gift to Ben of $30,000, the excess of Ben's withdrawal over Ben's deposit. ◀

Creation of Other Joint Tenancies. **Joint tenancy** is a popular form of property ownership from a convenience standpoint because, when one joint owner dies, the property is automatically owned by the survivor(s). Each joint tenant is deemed to have an equal interest in the property. A completed gift arises when the transferor titles real estate or other property in the names of himself or herself and another (e.g., a spouse, a sibling, or a child) as joint tenants. The person furnishing the consideration to acquire the property is deemed to have made a gift to the other joint tenant in an amount equal to the value of the donee's pro rata interest in the property.[28]

EXAMPLE C:12-24 ▶ Kwame purchases land for $250,000 and immediately has it titled in the names of Kwame and Kesha, as joint tenants with right of survivorship. Kwame and Kesha are not husband and wife. Kwame makes a gift to Kesha of $125,000, which is one-half the value of the property. ◀

TAX STRATEGY TIP

An owner of a life insurance policy who wishes to gift the ownership to someone else, such as the beneficiary, can use the following strategies to avoid the gift tax:

(1) Before making the gift, borrow enough against the policy to reduce its net value to the amount of the annual exclusion ($14,000 in 2017). The former owner (borrower) then can pay premiums and make loan repayments, not to exceed the annual exclusion in any given year.

(2) Have the insurance company rewrite the policy into separate policies, each having a value that does not exceed the annual exclusion. Then, gift one policy each year for several years.

Transfer of Life Insurance Policies. The mere naming of another as the beneficiary of a life insurance policy is an incomplete transfer because the owner of the policy can change the beneficiary designation at any time. However, if an individual irrevocably assigns all ownership rights in an insurance policy to another party, this event constitutes a gift of the policy to the new owner.[29] Ownership rights include the ability to change the beneficiary, borrow against the policy, and cash the policy in for its cash surrender value.

The payment of a premium on an insurance policy owned by another person is considered a gift to the policy's owner. The amount of the gift is the amount of the premium paid. The tax result is the same as if the donor transferred cash to the policy owner and the owner used the cash to pay the premium.

According to Reg. Sec. 25.2512-6, the value of the gift of a life insurance policy is the amount it would cost to purchase a comparable policy on the date of the gift. The regulations point out, however, that if the policy is several years old, the cost of a comparable policy is not readily ascertainable. In such a situation, the policy is valued at its interpolated terminal reserve (i.e., an amount similar to the policy's cash surrender value) plus the amount of any unexpired premiums. The insurance company will furnish information concerning the interpolated terminal reserve.

EXAMPLE C:12-25 ▶ On September 1, Bill transfers his entire ownership rights in a $300,000 life insurance policy on his own life to his sister Susan. The policy's interpolated terminal reserve is $24,000 as of September 1. On July 1, Bill had paid the policy's $4,800 annual premium. Bill makes a gift to Susan on September 1 of $28,000 [$24,000 + (10/12 × $4,800)] because he transferred ownership to Susan. If, however, the policy had been a term insurance policy, which has no interpolated terminal reserve, the gift would have been $4,000 (10/12 × $4,800), the amount of the unexpired premium.

On July 1 of the next year, Bill pays the $4,800 annual premium on the policy now owned by Susan. As a result of the premium payment, Bill makes a $4,800 gift to Susan that year, the same result as if he had given her $4,800 of cash to pay the premium. ◀

[27] Reg. Sec. 25.2511-1(h)(4).

[28] Reg. Sec. 25.2511-1(h)(5). If the two joint tenants are husband and wife, no taxable gift will arise because of the unlimited marital deduction.

[29] Reg. Sec. 25.2511-1(h)(8).

EXAMPLE C:12-26 ► Assume the same facts as in Example C:12-25 and that later Susan, who now owns the policy, changes the beneficiary of the policy from Frank to John. Susan does not make a gift because she has not given up control; she can change the beneficiary again in the future. ◄

Exercise of a General Power of Appointment. Section 2514 provides the rules concerning powers of appointment. A **power of appointment** exists when a person transfers property (perhaps in trust) and grants someone else the power to specify who eventually will receive the property. Thus, possession of a power of appointment over property has some of the same benefits as ownership of the property. Powers can be general or special. *Potential* gift tax consequences are associated with the powerholder's exercise of a **general power of appointment**. A person possesses a general power of appointment if he or she has the power to appoint the property (have the property distributed) to him- or herself, his or her creditors or estate, or the creditors of his or her estate. The words *his or her estate* mean that there are no restrictions concerning to whom the individual may bequeath the property. By default, a power that is not general is a special power.

A gift occurs when a powerholder exercises a general power of appointment and names some other person to receive the property.[30] The donee is the person named to receive the property. A person who exercises a general power of appointment in favor of himself or herself does not make a gift (i.e., one cannot make a gift to him- or herself).

EXAMPLE C:12-27 ► In 2017, Tina funds an irrevocable trust with $600,000 and names Van to receive the income for life. In addition, Tina grants Van a general power of appointment exercisable during his life as well as at his death. Tina made a gift to Van of $600,000 at the time she transferred the property to the trust in 2017. In 2018, Van instructs the bank trustee to distribute $50,000 of trust property to Kay. Through the exercise of his general power of appointment in favor of Kay, Van makes a $50,000 gift to Kay in 2018 because he diverted property to her. ◄

Net Gifts. A **net gift** occurs when an individual makes a gift to a donee who agrees to pay the gift tax as a condition of receiving the gift. The donee's payment of the gift tax is treated as consideration paid to the donor. The amount of the gift is the excess of the FMV of the transferred property over the amount of the gift tax paid by the donee. Because the amount of the gift depends on the amount of gift tax payable, which in turn depends on the amount of the gift, the calculations require the use of simultaneous equations.[31]

The net gift strategy is especially attractive for people who would like to remove a rapidly appreciating asset from their estate but are unable to pay the gift tax because of liquidity problems. However, a net gift has one potential disadvantage: the Supreme Court has ruled that the donor must recognize as a gain the excess of the gift tax payable over his or her adjusted basis in the property.[32] The Court's rationale is that the donee's payment of the donor's gift tax liability constitutes an "amount realized" for purposes of determining the gain or loss realized on a sale, exchange, or other disposition. From a practical standpoint, this decision affects only donors who transfer property so highly appreciated that the property's adjusted basis is less than the gift tax liability.

TAX STRATEGY TIP

As a general rule, substantially appreciated property should be transferred at death to take advantage of the step-up in basis to the estate tax value.

EXAMPLE C:12-28 ► Mary, who previously had made sizable taxable gifts, transferred land with a $3 million FMV to her son, Sam, who agreed to pay the gift tax liability. Mary's adjusted basis in the land was $15,000. Earlier in 2017, she gave him $14,000, which was covered by the annual exclusion. The taxable gift was $3 million, less the gift tax paid by Sam. Simultaneous equations are necessary to calculate the amount of the gift and the gift tax liability. Mary must recognize gain equal to the excess of the gift tax liability paid by Sam minus Mary's $15,000 basis in the property.

---

[30] In general, the exercise of a special power of appointment is free of gift tax consequences. In the case of special powers of appointment, the holder of the power does not have an unrestricted ability to name the persons to receive the property. For example, he or she may be able to appoint to only his or her descendants.

[31] In Rev. Rul. 75-72 (1975-1 C.B. 310), the IRS explained how to calculate the amount of the net gift and the gift tax. In Ltr. Rul. 7842068 (July 20, 1978), the IRS stated that the donor's available unified credit, not the donee's, is used to calculate the gift tax payable.

[32] *Victor P. Diedrich v. CIR*, 50 AFTR 2d 82-5054, 82-1 USTC ¶9419 (USSC, 1982).

Assume that, because of sizable previous taxable gifts, any additional gifts Mary made were subject to the 40% maximum gift tax rate for 2017. Assume Mary had used all of her unified credit. If G represents the amount of the gift and T is the amount of the tax, then

$$G = \$3{,}000{,}000 - T$$
$$T = 0.40G$$

Substituting 0.40G for T in the first equation and solving for G yields G = $3,000,000 ÷ 1.40 = $2,142,857, the amount of the gift. The tax is 40% of this amount, or $857,143. Mary's gain equals the $857,143 gift tax paid by Sam minus her $15,000 basis in the property, or $842,143. ◀

Exclusions

OBJECTIVE 4

Determine whether an annual gift tax exclusion is available

In many instances, a portion or all of a transfer by gift is tax-free because of the annual exclusion authorized by Sec. 2503(b). In 1932, the Senate Finance Committee explained the purpose of the **annual exclusion** as follows:

> Such exemption . . . is to obviate the necessity of keeping an account of and reporting numerous small gifts, and . . . to fix the amount sufficiently large to cover in most cases wedding and Christmas gifts and occasional gifts of relatively small amount.[33]

In most gift transactions, the donor makes no taxable gift because of the annual exclusion. Consequently, administration of the gift tax provisions is a much simpler task than it otherwise would be.

AMOUNT OF THE EXCLUSION

The amount of this exclusion, which is analogous to an exclusion from gross income for income tax purposes, is $14,000.[34] It is available each year for an unlimited number of donees. For transfers made in trust, each beneficiary is deemed to be a separate donee. Any number of donors may make a gift to the same donee, and each is eligible to claim the exclusion. The only limitations on the annual exclusion are the donor's wealth, generosity, and imagination in identifying donees.

EXAMPLE C:12-29 ▶ In 2016, Ann and Bob each gave $14,000 cash to Tad and also to Liz. Ann and Bob again make $14,000 cash gifts to Tad and Liz in 2017. For both 2016 and 2017, Ann receives $28,000 of exclusions ($14,000 for the gift to Tad and $14,000 for the gift to Liz). The same result applies to Bob. ◀

TAX STRATEGY TIP

Gifts up to the amount of the annual exclusion not only remove the gifted amounts from the donor's estate with no gift tax cost but also remove the property's future income from the donor's estate. In addition, the property's income can be shifted to someone whose tax bracket might be lower than the donor's, thereby reducing income taxes.

The annual exclusion is a significant tax planning device that has no estate tax counterpart. So long as a donor's gifts to a particular donee do not exceed the excludable amount, the donor will never make any taxable gifts or incur any gift tax liability. Because taxable gifts will be zero, the donor's estate tax base will not include any adjusted taxable gifts. A donor, for example, who each year for ten years gave $10,000 per donee to each of ten donees, removed $1 million (10 × $10,000 × 10) from being taxed in his or her estate. The donor accomplished these transfers without making any taxable gifts or paying any gift tax. If retained, the $1 million would have been taxed in the donor's estate unless the property was willed to the donor's surviving spouse or a charitable organization.

PRESENT INTEREST REQUIREMENT

Although we generally speak of the annual exclusion as if it were available automatically for all gifts, in actuality it is not. A donor receives an exclusion only for gifts that constitute a present interest.

---

[33] S. Rept. No. 665, 72nd Cong., 1st Sess. (1932), reprinted in 1939-1 C.B. (Part 2), pp. 525–526.

[34] On January 1, 1982, Congress increased the annual exclusion from $3,000 to $10,000. Later, Congress provided that the exclusion would be indexed after 1998, with inflation adjustments rounded to the next lowest multiple of $1,000. In 2002, the exclusion rose to $11,000 and remained there through 2005. It rose to $12,000 in 2006, to $13,000 in 2009, and to $14,000 in 2013.

Definition of Present Interest. A **present interest** is "an unrestricted right to the immediate use, possession, or enjoyment of property or the income from property (such as a life estate or term certain)."[35] Only present interests qualify for the annual exclusion. If only a portion of a transfer constitutes a present interest, the excluded portion of the gift may not exceed the value of the present interest.

Definition of Future Interest. A future interest is the opposite of a present interest. A **future interest** "is a legal term, and includes reversions, remainders, and other interests . . . which are limited to commence in use, possession, or enjoyment at some future date or time."[36] Gifts of future interests are ineligible for the annual exclusion. The following examples help demonstrate the attributes of present and future interests.

EXAMPLE C:12-30 ▶ Nancy transfers $500,000 of property to an irrevocable trust with a bank serving as trustee. Nancy names Norm (age 55) to receive all the trust income quarterly for the rest of Norm's life. At Norm's death, the property is to pass to Ellen (age 25) or Ellen's estate. Norm receives an unrestricted right to immediate enjoyment of the income. Thus, Norm has a present interest. Ellen, however, has a future interest because Ellen cannot enjoy the property or any of the income until Norm dies. The taxable gift is $486,000 ($500,000 − $14,000). ◀

EXAMPLE C:12-31 ▶ Greg transfers $800,000 of property to an irrevocable trust with a bank serving as trustee and instructs the trustee to distribute all the trust income semiannually to Greg's three adult children, Joe, Katy, and/or Laura. The trustee is to use its discretion in deciding how much to distribute to each beneficiary. Moreover, the trustee is authorized to distribute nothing to a particular beneficiary if it deems such action to be in the beneficiary's best interest. Although all the income must be paid out, the trustee has complete discretion to determine how much to pay to each particular beneficiary. No beneficiary has the assurance that he or she will receive a trust distribution. Thus, Greg created no present interests, and the annual exclusion does not apply. The taxable gift, therefore, is $800,000. ◀

Special Rule for Trusts for Minors. Congress realized that many donors would not want to require trusts for minor children to distribute all their income to the young children. Accordingly, Congress enacted Sec. 2503(c), which authorizes special trusts for minors, to address donors' concerns about the distribution of trust income to minors. Section 2503(c) authorizes an annual exclusion for gifts to trusts for beneficiaries under age 21 even though the trusts need not distribute all their income annually. Such trusts, known as **Sec. 2503(c) trusts**, allow donors to claim the annual exclusion if the following two conditions are met:

- Until the beneficiary becomes age 21, the trustee may pay the income and/or the underlying assets to the beneficiary.
- Any income and underlying assets not paid to the beneficiary will pass to that beneficiary when he or she reaches age 21. If the beneficiary dies before becoming age 21, the income and underlying assets are payable to either the beneficiary's estate or to any person the minor may appoint if the minor possesses a general power of appointment over the property.

ADDITIONAL COMMENT

The donor may serve as trustee of a Sec. 2503(c) trust, but this approach generally is not advisable. If the donor's powers are not sufficiently limited, the trust property will be included in the donor's estate if the donor's death occurs before the trust terminates.

If the trust instrument contains both the provisions listed above, no part of the trust is considered to be a gift of a future interest. Therefore, the entire transfer is treated as a present interest and is eligible for the annual exclusion.

As a result of Sec. 2503(c), donors creating trusts for donees under age 21 receive an exclusion even though the trustee has discretion over paying out the trust income. However, the IRC requires the trustee to distribute the assets and accumulated income at age 21.

***Crummey* Trust.** The ***Crummey* trust** is yet another technique that allows the donor to obtain an annual exclusion upon funding a discretionary trust. The trust can terminate at whatever age the donor specifies and can be created for a beneficiary of any age. Thus, the *Crummey* trust is a much more flexible arrangement than the Sec. 2503(c) trust.

---

[35] Reg. Sec. 25.2503-3(b).

[36] Reg. Sec. 25.2503-3(a).

ADDITIONAL COMMENT

The holder of a *Crummey* power must be given notice of a contribution to the trust to which the power relates and must be given a reasonable time period within which to exercise the power. The donor receives the annual exclusion regardless of whether the donee exercises the power.

The *Crummey* trust is named for a Ninth Circuit Court of Appeals decision holding that the trust beneficiaries received a present interest as a result of certain language in the trust instrument.[37] That language, which is referred to interchangeably as a *Crummey* power, *Crummey* demand power, or *Crummey* withdrawal power, entitled each beneficiary to demand a distribution of the lesser of $4,000 (the amount in the case) or the amount transferred to the trust that year. If the beneficiary did not exercise the power by a specified date, it expired. The trust instrument included the "lesser of" language for the demand power because the donor did not want to create a present interest larger than the annual exclusion amount. In years in which the gift is smaller than the annual exclusion amount, the donor simply wants to be able to exclude the amount of that year's gift. In addition, the donor wants to restrict the amount to which the beneficiary can have access. Because of potential changes in the annual exclusion amount, the trust instrument often states that the maximum amount the beneficiary can withdraw is "an amount equal to the annual exclusion for federal gift tax purposes" or twice that amount if gift splitting is anticipated.

The court held that the demand power provided each beneficiary with a present interest equal to the maximum amount the beneficiary could require the trustee to pay over to him or her that year. Use of the *Crummey* trust technique entitles the donor to receive the annual exclusion while creating a discretionary trust that terminates at whatever age the donor deems appropriate. The donor thereby avoids the restrictive rules of Sec. 2503(c). Generally, the donor hopes the beneficiary will not exercise the demand right.

EXAMPLE C:12-32 ▶ Al funds two $100,000 irrevocable trusts and names First Bank the trustee. The first trust is for the benefit of Kay, his 15-year-old daughter. The trustee has discretion to distribute income and/or principal to Kay until she reaches age 21. If she dies before age 21, the trust assets are payable to whomever she appoints in her will or to her estate if she dies without a will. The second trust is for the benefit of Bob, Al's 25-year-old son. Income and/or principal are payable to Bob in the trustee's discretion until Bob reaches age 35, whereupon Bob will receive the trust assets. Bob may demand by December 31 of each year that the trustee pay him the lesser of the amount of the gift tax annual exclusion or the amount transferred to the trust that calendar year. The trust for Kay is a Sec. 2503(c) trust, and the one for Bob is a *Crummey* trust. An annual exclusion is available for each trust. ◀

Question: For which of the following gifts would the donor receive an annual exclusion:

- A gift of a remainder interest in land if the donor retains the income interest for life
- A gift outright of a life insurance policy that has a cash surrender value
- A gift to a discretionary trust that is classified as a Sec. 2503(c) trust
- A gift to a *Crummey* trust?

Solution: All the transfers except the gift of the remainder interest in land (a future interest) are eligible for the annual exclusion. Even though the gift to the Sec. 2503(c) trust does not literally involve a gift of a present interest (the right to current income or enjoyment), the IRC explicitly allows this kind of transfer to qualify for the annual exclusion.

GIFT TAX DEDUCTIONS

OBJECTIVE 5

Identify the deductions available for gift tax purposes

The formula for determining taxable gifts allows both an unlimited marital deduction and an unlimited charitable contribution deduction. The **marital deduction** is for transfers to one's spouse. The **charitable contribution deduction** is for gifts to charitable organizations. Section 2524 states that the deductible amount in either case may not exceed the amount of the "includible gift"—that is, the amount of the gift exceeding the annual exclusion. Thus, the lowest possible taxable gift is zero, not a negative number, as could be the case if the deduction equaled the total amount of the gift.

[37] *D. Clifford Crummey v. CIR*, 22 AFTR 2d 6023, 68-2 USTC ¶12,541 (9th Cir., 1968).

MARITAL DEDUCTION

ADDITIONAL COMMENT

Congress allowed a marital deduction because a taxpayer who transfers property to his or her spouse has not made a transfer outside the economic (husband/wife) unit. For similar reasons, the interspousal gift has no *income* tax consequences. The donor spouse recognizes no gain or loss, and the donee spouse takes a carryover basis.

Generally, the marital deduction results in tax-free interspousal transfers, but an exception discussed below applies to gifts of certain terminable interests. Congress enacted the marital deduction in 1948 to provide more uniform treatment of community property and noncommunity property donors. To recap, in community property states, most property acquired after marriage is owned equally by each spouse. In noncommunity property states, however, the spouses' wealth often is divided unequally, and such spouses can equalize each individual's share of the wealth only by engaging in a gift-giving program. As a result of the marital deduction, spouses, including those in same sex marriages, can shift wealth between themselves completely free of any gift tax consequences.

Unlimited Amount. Over the years, the maximum marital deduction has varied, but since 1981 a spouse has been able to deduct up to 100% of the amount of gifts made to the other spouse. The amount of the marital deduction, however, is limited to the portion of the gift that exceeds the annual exclusion.[38] After 1981, transfers of community property became eligible for the marital deduction.

EXAMPLE C:12-33 ▶ Jane gives her husband stock valued at $450,000. She excludes $14,000 because of the annual exclusion and claims a $436,000 marital deduction. Thus, no taxable gift arises. ◀

Gifts of Terminable Interests: General Rule.

Nondeductible Terminable Interests. A **terminable interest** is an interest that ends or is terminated when some event occurs (or fails to occur) or a specified amount of time passes. Some, but not all, terminable interests are ineligible for the marital deduction.[39] A marital deduction is denied only when the transfer is of a *nondeductible* terminable interest. A nondeductible terminable interest has one of the following characteristics:

- The donee-spouse's interest ceases at a set time (such as at death) and the property then either passes back to the donor or passes to a third party who does not pay adequate consideration.
- Immediately after making the gift, the donor has the power to name someone else to receive an interest in the property, and the person named may possess the property upon the termination of the donee-spouse's interest.[40]

The next three examples illustrate some of the subtleties of the definition of nondeductible terminable interests. In Example C:12-34, a marital deduction is available because the transfer involves neither characteristic of a nondeductible terminable interest.

EXAMPLE C:12-34 ▶ A donor gives a patent to a spouse. A patent is a terminable interest because the property interest terminates at the end of the patent's legal life. Nevertheless, the patent does not constitute a nondeductible terminable interest. When the patent's legal life expires, a third party will not possess an interest in the patent. Thus, a donor will receive a marital deduction. ◀

In Example C:12-35, a marital deduction is denied because the first of the two alternative characteristics of a nondeductible terminable interest exists.

EXAMPLE C:12-35 ▶ A donor transfers property in trust and (1) names his wife to receive trust income, at the trustee's discretion, annually for the next 15 years and (2) states that at the end of the 15-year period the trust's assets are to be distributed to their child. The donor gave his wife a nondeductible terminable interest. When the spouse's interest ceases, the property passes to their child, who did not pay adequate consideration. Thus, the donor receives no marital deduction. ◀

In Example C:12-36, a marital deduction is available. In addition to having a lifetime income interest, the donee-spouse has a general power of appointment over the trust's assets and can specify who eventually receives the property.

[38] Sec. 2524.
[39] Sec. 2523(b).
[40] Ibid.

EXAMPLE C:12-36 ▶ The donor gives his wife the right to all the income from a trust annually for life plus a general power of appointment over the trust's assets. He has transferred an interest eligible for the marital deduction. The general power of appointment may be exercisable during life, at death, or at both times. In addition, the donee-spouse is entitled to receive the income annually. ◀

TAX STRATEGY TIP

Granting the spouse a general power of appointment can qualify a transfer for the marital deduction. For example, Brad transferred property to a trust, income to be distributed annually to his wife Sonia until her death, with a general power of appointment in Sonia over the remainder. Sonia's general power of appointment qualified the transfer for the marital deduction.

The rationale behind the nondeductible terminable interest rule is that a donor should obtain a marital deduction only if he or she conveys an interest that will have transfer tax significance to the donee-spouse. In other words, when a donee spouse later gives away property received as a result of an interspousal transfer, a transfer subject to the gift tax occurs. If the donee-spouse retains such property until death, the asset is included in the donee-spouse's gross estate.

TAX STRATEGY TIP

By using a QTIP, a donor can achieve a marital deduction while exercising some control over the property. For example, assume that Brad in the previous annotation has been married twice. He had two children by his first wife and three children with Sonia. Brad could not be sure his first two children would receive any assets from the trust if Sonia received a general power of appointment. If Brad funded a QTIP, the trust instrument could specify that the remainder, on Sonia's death, would go equally to all five children. Brad could thus control the ultimate disposition of the remainder and still receive a marital deduction.

QTIP Provisions. Beginning in 1982, Congress made a major change to the nondeductible terminable interest rule and allowed transfers known as qualified terminable interest property to be eligible for the marital deduction.[41] Such transfers are commonly referred to as *QTIP transfers*. **Qualified terminable interest property** is property

- That is transferred by the donor-spouse,
- In which the donee has a "qualifying income interest for life," and
- For which a special election has been made.

A spouse has the necessary "qualifying income interest for life" if

- The spouse is entitled to all the income from the property annually or more often, and
- No person has a power to appoint any part of the property to any person other than the donee-spouse unless the power cannot be exercised until after the spouse dies.

The QTIP rule enhances the attractiveness of making transfers to one's spouse because a donor can receive a marital deduction—and thereby make a nontaxable transfer—without having to grant the spouse full control over the gifted property. The QTIP rule is especially attractive for a donor who wants to ensure that the children by a previous marriage will receive the property upon the donee-spouse's death.

The donor does not have to claim a marital deduction even though the transfer otherwise qualifies as a QTIP transfer. Claiming the deduction on such transfers is elective.[42] If the donor elects to claim a marital deduction, the donee-spouse must include the QTIP trust property in his or her estate at its value as of the donee-spouse's date of death. Thus, as with other transfers qualifying for the marital deduction, the interspousal transfer is tax-free, and the taxable event is postponed until the donee-spouse transfers the property.

EXAMPLE C:12-37 ▶ Jo transfers $1 million of property in trust with a bank acting as trustee. All the trust income is payable to Jo's husband, Ed (age 64), quarterly for the rest of his life. Upon Ed's death, the property will pass to Jo's nieces. This gift is eligible for a marital deduction. If Jo elects to claim the marital deduction, she will receive a $986,000 ($1,000,000 − $14,000) marital deduction. The deduction is limited to the amount of the includible gift, i.e., the gift exceeding the annual exclusion. Jo's taxable gift will be zero. ◀

Note that Jo's marital deduction in the preceding example is for $986,000 and not for the value of Ed's life estate. If Jo elects to claim the marital deduction, Ed's gross estate will include the value of the entire trust, valued as of the date of Ed's death. The QTIP provision permits Jo to receive a marital deduction while still being able to specify who will receive the property upon her husband's death.

Topic Review C:12-2 summarizes the eligibility of a transfer for the marital deduction and the amount of the marital deduction that can be claimed.

---

41 Sec. 2523(f).

42 The donor might decide not to claim the marital deduction if the donee-spouse has substantial assets already or a short life expectancy, especially if the gifted property's value is expected to appreciate at a high annual rate.

TOPIC REVIEW C:12-2

Eligibility for and Amount of the Marital Deduction

Examples of Transfers Eligible for the Marital Deduction

Property transferred to spouse as sole owner

Property transferred in trust with all the income payable to the spouse for life and over which the donee-spouse receives a general power of appointment

Property transferred in trust with all the income payable annually or more often to the spouse for life and for which the donor-spouse designated the remainderman—marital deduction available if elected under QTIP rule

Examples of Transfers Ineligible for the Marital Deduction

Property transferred in trust with the income payable in the trustee's discretion to the spouse for life, and for which the donor-spouse designated the remainderman

Property transferred in trust with all the income payable to the spouse for a specified number of years and for which the donor-spouse designated the remainderman

Amount of the Marital Deduction, if Available

The amount of the transfer minus the portion eligible for the annual exclusion

CHARITABLE CONTRIBUTION DEDUCTION

A donor who makes no noncharitable gifts in excess of the excludible amount does not have to report gifts to charitable organizations on a gift tax return, provided a charitable contribution deduction is available and the charitable organization receives the donor's entire interest in the property. Claiming an income tax deduction for a charitable contribution does not preclude the donor from also obtaining a gift tax deduction. In contrast with the income tax provisions, the gift tax charitable contribution deduction has no percentage limitation. The only ceiling is imposed by Sec. 2524, which limits the deduction to the amount of the gift that exceeds the excluded portion.

EXAMPLE C:12-38 ► Julio gives stock valued at $76,000 to State University. Julio receives a $14,000 annual exclusion and a $62,000 charitable contribution deduction for *gift* tax purposes. However, he need not report the gift on a gift tax return if he does not have to file a return to report gifts to noncharitable donees. On his *income* tax return, he receives a $76,000 charitable contribution deduction, subject to AGI limitations. ◄

TAX STRATEGY TIP

A charitably minded taxpayer could avoid the gift (and the estate) tax entirely by giving all his or her property to a qualified charitable organization. Actually, in 2017 the taxpayer could give $5.49 million plus the amount shielded by the annual exclusion to noncharitable donees and still pay no gift tax, assuming the taxpayer had not earlier made any taxable gifts.

Transfers Eligible for the Deduction. To be deductible, the gift must be made to a charitable organization. The rules defining charitable organizations are quite similar for income, gift, and estate tax purposes.[43] According to Sec. 2522, a gift tax deduction is available for contributions to the following:

- The United States or any subordinate level of government within the United States as long as the transfer is solely for public purposes
- A corporation, trust fund, etc., organized exclusively for religious, charitable, scientific, literary, or educational purposes, or to foster amateur sports competition, including the encouragement of art and the prevention of cruelty to children or animals
- A fraternal society or similar organization operating under the lodge system if the gifts are to be used in the United States only for religious, charitable, scientific, literary, or educational purposes
- A war veterans' post or organization organized in the United States or one of its possessions if no part of its net earnings accrues to the benefit of private shareholders or individuals

[43] In contrast to the income tax rules, a charitable contribution deduction is available under the gift tax rules for transfers made to foreign charitable organizations. No deduction is available, however, for gifts made to foreign governments.

Split-Interest Transfers. Specialized rules apply when a donor makes a transfer for both private (i.e., an individual) and public (i.e., a charitable organization) purposes. Such arrangements are known as **split-interest transfers**. An example of a split-interest transfer is the gift of a residence to one's sister for life with the remainder interest to a university. If a donor gives a charitable organization a remainder interest, the donor forfeits the charitable contribution deduction unless the remainder interest is in either a personal residence (not necessarily the donor's principal residence), a farm, a charitable remainder annuity trust or unitrust, or a pooled income fund.[44] A split-interest gift of a present interest to a charity qualifies for a charitable contribution deduction only if the charity receives a guaranteed annuity interest or a unitrust interest. Actuarial tables are used to value split-interest transfers (see Appendix H).

EXAMPLE C:12-39 ▶ Al transfers $800,000 of property to a charitable remainder annuity trust. He reserves an annuity of $52,000 per year for his remaining life and specifies that upon his death the trust property will pass to the American Red Cross. Al must report this transaction on a gift tax return because the Red Cross did not receive his entire interest in the property. In the same year, Al gives a museum a remainder interest in his antique furniture collection and reserves a life estate for himself.

Each of these is a split-interest transfer. Unfortunately for the donor, only the remainder interest in the charitable remainder annuity trust is eligible for a charitable contribution deduction. Consequently, Al makes a taxable gift equal to the value of the remainder interest in the antique furniture. (If Al had given a remainder interest in a personal residence or farm, he would have received a charitable contribution deduction for this gift.) Even though the furniture is not an income-producing property, the value of the remainder interest is determined from the actuarial tables found in Appendix H.

Assume that Al was age 60 at the time of the gifts and that the Sec. 7520 interest rate was 4%. What is the amount of Al's charitable contribution deduction?

Answer: The portion of the annuity trust retained by Al is $697,970 {[(1.0 − 0.46310)/0.04] × $52,000 annuity}. The charitable deduction on the gift tax return is $102,030 ($800,000 − $697,970), the value of the remainder interest, a future interest. The $102,030 amount also is allowable—subject to the ceiling rules—as a charitable contribution deduction on Al's income tax return for that year. ◀

SELF-STUDY QUESTION

In Example C:12-39, does Al receive an annual exclusion for the gift of the furniture?

ANSWER

No. The remainder interest is a future interest, as is the remainder in the trust.

THE GIFT-SPLITTING ELECTION

OBJECTIVE 6

Apply the gift-splitting rules

The gift-splitting provisions of Sec. 2513 allow spouses to treat a gift actually made by just one of them as if each spouse made one-half of the gift. This election offers several advantages, as follows:

- If only one spouse makes a gift to a particular donee, the election enables a spouse to give $28,000 (instead of $14,000) to the donee before a taxable gift arises.
- If per-donee annual transfers exceed $28,000 and taxable gifts occur, the election may reduce the applicable marginal gift tax rate.
- Each spouse may use a unified credit to reduce the gift tax payable.

To take advantage of the gift-splitting election, the spouses must meet the following requirements at the time of the transfer:

- They must be U.S. citizens or residents.
- At the time of the gift(s) for which the spouses make an election, the donor-spouse must be married to the person who consents to gift splitting. In addition, the donor-spouse must not remarry before the end of the year.

TAX STRATEGY TIP

Donors can magnify the benefits of the annual exclusion by using gift splitting techniques.

[44] In a **charitable remainder annuity trust**, an individual receives trust distributions for a certain time period or for life. The annual distributions are a uniform percentage (5% or higher) of the value of the trust property, valued on the date of the transfer. For a **charitable remainder unitrust**, the distributions are similar, except that they are a uniform percentage (5% or higher) of the value of the trust property, revalued at least annually. Thus, the annual distributions from a unitrust, but not an annuity trust, vary from one year to the next. Both unitrusts and annuity trusts must meet the requirements that the payout rate does not exceed 50% of the value of the property and the value of the remainder interest is at least 10% of the initial FMV. A **pooled income fund** is similar in concept to a mutual fund. The various individual beneficiaries receive annual distributions of their proportionate shares of the pooled income fund's total income.

ADDITIONAL COMMENT

A wife makes a gift of $40,000 to a child in March and a gift of $60,000 to another child in November of the same year. The gift-splitting election, if made, will apply to both gifts because the election to gift split applies to all gifts made during the year. With gift splitting, her husband will be treated as making one-half of each gift.

The gift-splitting election is effective for all transfers to third parties made during the portion of the year that the spouses were married to each other.

A spouse living in a community property state who makes a gift of separate property (e.g., an asset received by inheritance) may desire to use gift splitting. In this case, the election automatically extends to gifts of community property even though splitting each spouse's gifts of community property has no impact on the "bottom-line" amount of taxable gifts.

Note that gift splitting is an all-or-nothing proposition. Spouses wanting to elect it for one gift must elect it for all gifts to third parties for that year. Each year's election stands alone, however, and is not binding on future years.[45] The procedural aspects of the gift-splitting election are discussed in the Compliance and Procedural Considerations section of this chapter.

EXAMPLE C:12-40 ▶ Eli married Joy on April 1 of the current year. They are still married to each other at the end of the year. In March, Eli gave Amy $60,000. In July, Eli gave Barb $52,000, and Joy gave Claire $28,000. If the couple elects gift splitting, the election is effective only for the July gifts. Each spouse is treated as giving $26,000 and $14,000 to Barb and Claire, respectively. Because they may not elect gift splitting for the gift Eli made before their marriage, Eli is treated as giving $60,000—the amount he actually transfers—to Amy. Under gift splitting, Eli and Joy each exclude $14,000 of gifts to both Barb and Claire, or a total of $56,000. Eli also excludes $14,000 of his gift to Amy. ◀

ADDITIONAL COMMENT

The gift-splitting election is a year-by-year election. For example, a husband and wife could elect to gift split in 2012, 2014, and 2016, but not elect to gift split in 2013, 2015, and 2017.

Upon the death of the actual donor or the spouse who consented to gift splitting, such decedent's estate tax base includes that decedent's post-1976 taxable gifts, known as adjusted taxable gifts. By electing gift splitting, a couple can reduce the amount of the taxable gifts the donor-decedent is deemed to have made. Under gift splitting, the adjusted taxable gifts include only the portions of the gifts that are taxable on the gift tax returns filed by the donor-decedent. Of course, the nondonor-spouse's estate reports his or her post-1976 taxable gifts.

STOP & THINK

Question: Bob made taxable gifts of $5.5 million in 2016, and Betty, his spouse, has not made any taxable gifts. Betty inherited a large fortune and is contemplating gifting $500,000 in 2017 to each of her two children. Bob does not anticipate making any taxable gifts in 2017. Should they elect gift splitting for Betty's gifts?

Solution: They should not necessarily elect gift splitting because the main advantage of the election will be that the aggregate annual exclusions will be $56,000 instead of $28,000. An adverse effect will be that Bob, who has exhausted his unified credit (except for the small increase to the current year amount) and whose rate is 40%, will be the deemed donor of $472,000 [(0.50 × $1,000,000) − $28,000] of taxable gifts.

Computation of the Gift Tax Liability

OBJECTIVE 7

Calculate the gift tax liability

EFFECT OF PREVIOUS TAXABLE GIFTS

The gift tax computation involves a cumulative process. All the donor's previous taxable gifts (i.e., those made in 1932 or later years) plus the donor's taxable gifts for the current year affect the marginal tax rate for current taxable gifts. Thus, two donors who make the same taxable gifts in the current period may incur different gift tax liabilities because one donor may have made substantially larger taxable gifts in earlier periods than did the other donor. The process outlined below must be used to compute the gross tax levied on the current period's taxable gifts.

1. Determine the gift tax liability (at current rates) on the donor's cumulative taxable gifts (taxable gifts of current period plus aggregate taxable gifts of previous periods).

[45] If the nondonor-spouse has made substantial taxable gifts relative to those made by the donor-spouse, the gift tax liability for the period in question may be lower if the spouses do not elect gift splitting because the nondonor-spouse may have little or no unified credit left and may have reached the highest marginal transfer tax rate.

2. Determine the gift tax liability (at current rates) on the donor's cumulative taxable gifts made through the end of the preceding period.
3. Subtract the gift tax determined in Step 2 from that in Step 1. The difference equals the gross gift tax on the current period's taxable gifts.

This calculation process results in taxing the gifts on a progressive basis over the donor's lifetime.

Note that, although the gift tax rates have varied over the years, the current rate schedule is used in the calculation even when the donor made some or all the earlier gifts when different rates were in effect. This process ensures that current taxable gifts are taxed at the appropriate rate, given the donor's earlier gift history.

EXAMPLE C:12-41 ▶ In 1975, Tony made $2 million in taxable gifts. These gifts were the first Tony ever made. The tax imposed under the 1975 rate schedule was $564,900. Tony made his next taxable gifts in 2017. The taxable amount of these gifts was $400,000. The tax on Tony's 2017 taxable gifts before applying the unified credit is calculated as follows:

Tax at current rates on $2.4 million of cumulative taxable gifts	$905,800
Minus: Tax at current rates on $2 million of prior period taxable gifts	(745,800)
Tax on $400,000 of taxable gifts made in the current period	$160,000 ◀

This cumulative process results in the $400,000 gift in Example C:12-41 being taxed at the maximum 40% gift tax rate for 2017, which applied to taxable transfers exceeding $1 million. If the gift tax computations were not cumulative, the tax on the $400,000 of gifts would be determined by using the lowest marginal rates and would have been only $121,800. Because the tax on taxable transfers made in previous periods is determined by reference to the current rate schedule, Tony's actual 1975 gift tax liability, incurred when the gift tax rates were lower, is not relevant to the determination of his current gift tax. As discussed below, the unified credit will reduce the tax liability.

UNIFIED CREDIT AVAILABLE

Congress enacted a unified credit for both gift and estate tax purposes beginning in 1977. The unified credit reduces the amount of the gross gift tax owed on current period gifts. The size of the tax base for which the unified credit exactly offsets the tax liability is referred to as the exemption equivalent (or basic exclusion amount). The amount of the credit has increased over the years (see inside back cover). For 2012, the $5 million amount became indexed. Beginning in 2013, the top tax rate rose to 40%. The amount for 2017 is $5 million indexed to $5.49 million. Thus, for 2017 the credit is $2,141,800. Donors who made taxable gifts in the post-1976 period have used some of their credit. Thus, the credit available for the current year is reduced by the aggregate amount allowable as a credit in all preceding years. Because of the reduction of the top rate beginning in 2010 the credit for the current year is reduced by what the credit would have been, if lower than the credit actually claimed, calculated using the rates for the current year.

EXAMPLE C:12-42 ▶ Hu made her first taxable gift in 1985. The taxable amount of the 1985 gift was $100,000, which resulted in a gross gift tax of $23,800. Hu claimed $23,800 (of the $121,800 credit then available) on her 1985 return to reduce her net gift tax liability to zero. Hu made her next taxable gift ($400,000) in 1994. The tax on the $400,000 gift equaled (1) the tax on $500,000 of total gifts (at 1994 gift tax rates) of $155,800 minus (2) the tax on $100,000 of previous gifts (at 1994 gift tax rates) of $23,800, or $132,000. The credit amount for 1994 was $192,800. Hu's gift tax was reduced to zero by a credit of $132,000 because for 1994 she had a remaining credit of $169,000 ($192,800 − $23,800). If in 2017 Hu makes additional taxable gifts, $1,986,000 [$2,141,800 − ($23,800 + $132,000)] of unified credit is available to reduce Hu's gift tax liability in 2017. Note that none of Hu's earlier gifts were taxed at rates above 40%. Thus, the credit available for the current year is reduced by the total amount of the credits actually claimed earlier. ◀

Question: In the process of preparing a current year gift tax return, you reviewed a 2014 gift tax return a different CPA prepared for your new client, George Winston. The tax return reported 2014 taxable gifts of $6 million and $500,000 of taxable gifts made in 1999. You note that the return showed tax of $2,345,800, claimed a unified credit of $2,081,800, and thus reported a $264,000 gift tax payable. What should you discuss with your new client?

Solution: You should explain that the 2014 unified credit of $2,081,800 (which equaled the tax on the first $5.34 million of taxable gifts) was not an annual credit maximum but rather the credit available during a donor's lifetime. Because in 1999 the client made $500,000 of taxable gifts, he used $155,800 of his $211,300 unified credit then available. In addition, you should explain the cumulative nature of the gift tax calculations. The tax calculated on $6 million of taxable gifts was $2,345,800. If the other CPA claimed a $2,081,800 unified credit and showed a $264,000 tax payable, he or she did not calculate the tax on the $6 million 2014 taxable gift by performing the cumulative calculations that take into effect the $500,000 of earlier taxable gifts. The tax *before* the credit was calculated incorrectly. The credit actually available was $1,926,000 ($2,081,800 − $155,800), the 2014 credit less the credit already used. In this situation you subtract the credit actually used in 1999 because that credit was calculated at a top rate of 34%. You should advise the client to file an amended return and pay the correct gift tax.

COMPREHENSIVE ILLUSTRATION

The following comprehensive illustration demonstrates the computation of one donor's gift tax liability for the situation where the spouses elect gift splitting. It demonstrates the computation of the wife's gift tax liability.

ADDITIONAL COMMENT

This illustration pertains to 2016 because tax forms for that year are the latest available at the time this textbook was published.

Background Data. Hugh and Wilma Brown are married to each other throughout 2016. Hugh made no taxable gifts in earlier periods. Wilma's previous taxable gifts were $300,000 in 1975 and $200,000 in 1988. In August 2016, Wilma makes the following gratuitous transfers:

- $80,000 in cash to son Billy
- $30,000 in jewelry to daughter Betsy (basis to donor, $18,000)
- $34,000 in medical expense payments to Downtown Infirmary for medical care of grandson Tim
- Remainder interest in vacation cabin to friend Ruth Cain. Wilma (age 60) retains a life estate. The vacation cabin is valued at $100,000 (basis to donor, $15,000).
- $600,000 of stocks (basis to donor, $480,000) to a bank in trust with all of the income payable semiannually to husband Hugh (age 72) for life and remainder payable at Hugh's death to Jeff Bass, Wilma's younger brother, or Jeff's estate. Wilma wants to elect the marital deduction.

In 2016, Hugh's only gifts were

- $100,000 of stock to State University (basis to donor, $32,000)
- $600,000 of land to daughter Betsy (basis to donor, $112,000)

Assume the applicable interest rate for valuing life estates and remainders is 4%.

Calculation of Tax Liability. Section 2503(e) exempts the medical expense payments from the gift tax. The Browns need to report the gift made to State University even though the university received Hugh's entire interest in the property, and even though the transfer is nontaxable, because they must file a gift tax return to report gifts to noncharitable donees. The vacation cabin is valued at $100,000, and the remainder interest therein at $46,310 (0.46310 × $100,000) (see Table S, age 60, 4%, in Appendix H). The stock is transferred to a QTIP trust, and the marital deduction election treats the entire interest (not just the life estate) as having been given to Hugh Brown.

Table C:12-1 shows the computation of Wilma's gift tax liability for 2016. These same facts are used for the sample United States Gift Tax Return, Form 709, in Appendix B. The form's format for reporting the gift-splitting aspects differs slightly from the format in the table. On the form, Part 1 of Schedule A splits the gifts earlier than Table C:12-1 does. Wilma does not have a predeceased spouse.

▼ TABLE C:12-1
Comprehensive Gift Tax Illustration

Wilma's actual 2016 gifts:		
Billy, cash		$ 80,000
Betsy, jewelry		30,000
Ruth, remainder interest in vacation cabin (future interest)		46,310
Husband Hugh and brother Jeff, transfer to QTIP trust		600,000
Total gifts made by Wilma		$756,310
Minus: One-half of Wilma's gifts made to third parties that are deemed made by Hugh [0.50 × ($80,000 + $30,000 + $46,310)]		(78,155)
Plus: One-half of Hugh's gifts made to third parties (Betsy and State University) that are deemed made by Wilma [0.50 × ($100,000 + $600,000)]		350,000
Minus: Annual exclusions for gifts of present interests ($14,000 each for gifts made to Billy, Betsy, Hugh, and State University)		(56,000)
Minus: Marital deduction ($600,000 − $14,000 exclusion)		(586,000)
Minus: Charitable contribution deduction ($50,000 deemed gift by Wilma − $14,000 exclusion)		(36,000)
Taxable gifts for current period		$350,155
Tax on cumulative taxable gifts of $850,155[a]		$287,360
Minus: Tax on previous taxable gifts of $500,000 (current rate schedule)		(155,800)
Tax on taxable gifts of $350,155 for the current period		$131,560
Minus: Unified credit:		
Credit for 2016	$2,125,800	
Minus: Credit allowable for prior periods	(68,000)[b]	
Remaining credit; credit actually used	$2,057,800	$131,560
Tax payable for 2016		$ -0-

[a]$300,000 (in 1975) + $200,000 (in 1988) + $350,155 (in 2016).
[b]$0 (for 1975) + $68,000 (for 1988). The $68,000, which is smaller than the maximum credit of $192,800 for 1988, is the excess of the $155,800 tax on cumulative taxable gifts less the $87,800 tax on the $300,000 previous taxable gifts. Taxpayer subtracts the same amount as the credit actually used because the credit was calculated at rates below 37%, the top tax rate applicable to the 1988 $600,000 exemption equivalent.

BASIS CONSIDERATIONS FOR A LIFETIME GIVING PLAN

OBJECTIVE 8

Recognize how basis affects the overall tax consequences

Prospective donors should consider the tax-saving features of making a series of lifetime gifts (discussed in the Tax Planning Considerations section of this chapter). Lifetime giving plans can remove income from the donor's income tax return and transfer it to the donee's income tax return, where it may be taxed at a lower marginal tax rate. A series of gifts may permit property to be transferred to a donee without incurring a gift tax liability and thus enable the donor to eliminate part or all of his or her estate tax liability. These two advantages must be weighed against the unattractive basis rules (discussed below) applicable for such transfers.

PROPERTY RECEIVED BY GIFT

The carryover basis rules apply to property received by gift. Provided the property's FMV on the date of the gift exceeds its adjusted basis, the donor's basis in the property carries over as the donee's basis. In addition, the donee's basis may be increased by some or all of the gift tax paid by the donor. For pre-1977 gifts, all the gift taxes paid by the donor may be added to the donor's adjusted basis. For post-1976 transfers, however, the donee may add only the portion of the gift taxes represented by the following fraction:

SELF-STUDY QUESTION

Barkley purchased land in 1965 for $90,000. In 1974, when the FMV of the land was $300,000, he gave the land to his son Tracy, claimed a $3,000 annual exclusion, and paid gift taxes of $23,000. What is Tracy's basis in the land? What if the gift had been made in 2017? For simplicity, assume the 2017 tax was $23,000.

ANSWER

If the gift were made in 1974, Tracy's basis is $90,000 plus the $23,000 gift tax, or $113,000. Had Barkley made the gift in 2017, Tracy's basis would be $90,000 plus [($210,000/$286,000) × $23,000], or $106,888.

$$\frac{\text{Amount of property's appreciation from acquisition date through date of gift}}{\text{FMV of property on the date of the gift minus exclusions and deductions}}$$

In no event, however, can the gift tax adjustment increase the donee's basis above the property's FMV on the date of the gift.[46]

If the gifted property's FMV on the date of the gift is less than the donor's adjusted basis, the basis rules are more complicated. For purposes of determining gain, the donee's basis is the same as the donor's adjusted basis. In determining loss, the donee's basis is the property's FMV on the date of the gift. If the donee sells the property for an amount between its FMV as of the date of the gift and the donor's adjusted basis, the donee recognizes no gain or loss. The property's basis cannot be increased by any gift taxes paid if the donor's adjusted basis exceeds the property's FMV as of the date of the gift. In general, prospective donors should dispose of property that has declined in value by selling it instead of gifting it.

PROPERTY RECEIVED AT DEATH

ADDITIONAL COMMENT

Phil owns investment property worth $350,000 in which his adjusted basis is $500,000. Unless there are reasons why the property should be kept in the family, Phil should sell the property and recognize an income tax loss. If he gifts the property to his child, the loss basis in the child's hands is $350,000 (and the gain basis is $500,000). Thus, if the value does not increase, a loss deduction for the $150,000 decline in market value can never be taken. If Phil dies holding the loss property, his heirs will take the estate tax return value (FMV) as their basis, and the potential income tax loss will not be recognized.

In general, the basis rules that apply to property received as a result of another's death call for a step up or step down to the property's FMV as of the decedent's date of death. The recipient's basis is the same as the amount at which the property is valued on the estate tax return, which is its FMV on either the decedent's date of death or the alternate valuation date. Generally, the alternate valuation date is six months after the date of death. Although these rules are usually thought of as providing for a step-up in basis, if the property has declined in value as of the transferor's death, the basis is stepped-down to its FMV at the date of death or alternate valuation date.

In certain circumstances, no step-up in basis occurs for appreciated property transferred at death.[47] This exception applies if both of the following conditions are present:

- The decedent receives the appreciated property as a gift during the one-year period preceding his or her death, and
- The property passes to the donor or to the donor's spouse as a result of the donee-decedent's death.

Before the enactment of this rule, a widely publicized planning technique involved transferring appreciated property to one's ill spouse who, in turn, could will the property back to the donor-spouse, who would receive the property at a stepped-up basis. Interspousal transfers by gift and at death are tax-free because of the unlimited marital deduction for both gift tax and estate tax purposes. Consequently, before the rule change, the property received a step-up in basis at no transfer tax cost.

EXAMPLE C:12-43 ►

In June 2016, Sarah gave property valued at $700,000 to Tom, her husband. Sarah's adjusted basis in the property was $120,000. Tom died in March 2017. At this time, the property was worth $740,000. If the property passed back to Sarah under Tom's will upon Tom's death, Sarah's basis would be $120,000. However, if the property passed to someone other than Sarah at Tom's death, its basis would be stepped-up to $740,000. If Tom lived for more than one year after receiving the gift, the basis would be stepped-up to its FMV as of Tom's date of death regardless of whether the property passed at Tom's death to Sarah or someone else. If Tom (the donee) sold the property a few months before his death in March 2017, Tom's basis would be the same as Sarah's was, or $120,000. ◄

For estates of decedents dying in 2010, the executor could elect to exempt the estate from the estate tax and forego the basis step-up and use instead a modified carryover basis rule. Under this rule, a person receiving property from a decedent obtained a basis equal to the lesser of (1) the decedent's adjusted basis in the property or (2) the property's fair market value at the date of the decedent's death. A special rule, however, allowed a total basis increase of

[46] See Reg. Sec. 1.1015-5(c) for examples of how to calculate the gift tax that can increase the property's basis.

[47] Sec. 1014(e).

$1.3 million to all assets (and an additional $3 million basis increase for property transferred to a surviving spouse) not to exceed the property's fair market value. Assume a decedent's estate consisted of $10 million cash and land the decedent purchased for $2 million. He died in 2010, when the land was worth $12 million and willed the land to his spouse and the cash to his children. The executor elected to be exempt from the estate tax. The spouse's basis in the land is $6.3 million ($2,000,000 + $1,300,000 + $3,000,000), compared with $12 million under the fair market value basis rule. Some additional special rules apply to the basis of property received from a decedent but are not detailed in this text.

BELOW-MARKET LOANS: GIFT AND INCOME TAX CONSEQUENCES

OBJECTIVE 9

Determine the tax consequences of below-market loans

GENERAL RULES

Section 7872 addresses the gift and income tax consequences of below-market loans. In general, it treats the lender as both making a gift to the borrower and receiving interest income. The borrower is treated as receiving a gift and paying interest expense.

In the case of a demand loan, the lender is treated as having made a gift in each year in which the loan is outstanding. The amount of the gift equals the forgone interest income for the portion of the year the loan is outstanding. The forgone interest income is calculated by referring to the excess of the federal short-term rate of Sec. 1274(d), for the period in question, over the interest rate the lender charged.

For income tax purposes, the forgone interest is treated as being retransferred from the borrower to the lender on the last day of each calendar year in which the loan is outstanding. The amount of the forgone interest is the same as for gift tax purposes and is reported by the lender as income for the year in question. The borrower can deduct interest expense for the same amount unless one of the rules limiting the interest deduction applies (e.g., personal interest or investment interest limitations).

EXAMPLE C:12-44 ▶ On July 1, Frank lends $500,000 to Susan, who signs an interest-free demand note. The loan is still outstanding on December 31. Assume that 10% is the applicable annual interest rate. Frank is deemed to have made a gift to Susan on December 31 of $25,000 (0.10 × $500,000 × 6/12). Frank must report $25,000 of interest income. Susan deducts $25,000 of interest expense provided the interest expense deduction rules do not otherwise limit or disallow her deduction. ◀

DE MINIMIS RULES

Under one of the *de minimis* rules, neither the income nor the gift tax rules apply to any gift loan made directly between individuals for any day on which the aggregate loans outstanding between the borrower and the lender are $10,000 or less. The *de minimis* exception does not apply to any loan directly attributable to the purchase or carrying of income-producing assets.

A second *de minimis* exception potentially permits loans of $100,000 or less to receive more favorable income tax (but not gift tax) treatment by limiting the lender's imputed income to the borrower's net investment income (as defined in Sec. 163(d)(3)) for the year. Moreover, if the borrower's net investment income for the year is $1,000 or less, such amount is treated as being zero.

The *de minimis* provisions do not apply to transactions having tax avoidance as a principal purpose and do not apply to any day on which the total outstanding loans between the borrower and the lender exceed $100,000. For purposes of the $100,000 or $10,000 loan limitations, a husband and wife are treated as one person.

EXAMPLE C:12-45 ▶ On August 1, Mike lends $100,000 to Don. No other loans are outstanding between the parties. Avoidance of federal taxes is not a principal purpose of the loan. Don signs an interest-free demand note when 10% is the applicable interest rate. The loan is still outstanding on December 31. Mike is treated as having made a present interest gift to Don on December 31 of $4,167 [$100,000 × 0.10 × 5/12]. Mike need not report this gift on a gift tax return unless his aggregate gifts to Don exceed the $14,000 gift tax annual exclusion.

The income tax consequences depend on Don's (the borrower's) net investment income. If Don's net investment income for the year exceeds $4,167, Mike reports $4,167 of imputed interest income under Sec. 7872. Subject to rules that may disallow some or all of the interest expense deduction, Don deducts the $4,167 interest expense imputed under Sec. 7872 . If Don's net investment income is between $1,001 and $4,167, each party reports imputed interest income or expense equal to Don's net investment income. Mike and Don report no interest income or expense under Sec. 7872 if Don's net investment income is $1,000 or less. ◀

Tax planning considerations

OBJECTIVE 10

Identify tax planning opportunities in gift situations

ADDITIONAL COMMENT

For 2017, the credit for the gift tax is $2,141,800.

The 1976 Act, which introduced the unification concept, reduced the tax law's bias favoring lifetime transfers. The 2001 Act, on the other hand, was more favorable toward transfers at death because the unified credit for gift tax purposes peaked at $345,800 beginning in 2004 whereas the credit against the estate tax continued to increase. Beginning in 2011, the unified credit again became the same amount for gift and estate tax purposes. Nevertheless, lifetime gifts provide more advantages than disadvantages. Many factors, including the expected appreciation rate, should affect the decision of whether to make gifts. Thus, the optimal result is not always clear. The pros and cons of lifetime gifts from an estate planning perspective are discussed below.

TAX-SAVING FEATURES OF *INTER VIVOS* GIFTS

Use of Annual Exclusion. The annual exclusion offers donors the opportunity to start making gifts to several donees per year relatively early in their lifetime and keep substantial amounts of property off the transfer tax rolls. The tax-free amount doubles if a husband and wife use the gift-splitting election.

The law provides no estate tax counterpart to the annual gift tax exclusion. Consequently, a terminally ill person whose will includes bequests of approximately $14,000 to numerous individuals would realize substantial transfer tax savings if gifts—instead of bequests—were made to these individuals.

Removal of Post-Gift Appreciation from Tax Base. Another important advantage of lifetime gifts is that their value is frozen at their date-of-gift value. That is, any post-gift appreciation escapes the transfer tax rolls. Consequently, transfer tax savings are maximized if the donor gives away the assets that appreciate the most.

Removal of Gift Tax Amount from Transfer Tax Base. With one exception, gift taxes paid by the donor are removed from the transfer tax base. The lone exception applies to gift taxes paid on gifts the donor makes within three years of dying. Under the gross-up rule (discussed in Chapter C:13), the donor's gross estate includes only gift taxes paid on gifts made within three years of the donor's death.

Income Shifting. Originally, one of the most favorable consequences of lifetime gifts was income shifting, but the compression of the income tax rate schedules beginning in 1987 has lessened these benefits. The 2003 Act, which lowered the tax rate on dividends, further reduced income shifting benefits from giving stock. The income produced by the gifted property is taxed to the donee, whose marginal income tax rate may be lower than the donor's. In addition, a high-income donor may be subject to the incremental 3.8% rate on net investment income, but the donee will not be subject to this rate if his or her income is sufficiently low. If income tax savings do arise, they accrue each year during the post-gift period. Thus, the income tax savings can be quite sizable over a span of several years. This tax saving aspect of gifts is a major reason Congress retained the gift tax in the 2001 Act.

Gift in Contemplation of Donee-Spouse's Death. At times, a terminally ill spouse may have very few assets. If such a spouse died, a sizable portion of his or her unified credit could be wasted in general because the decedent's estate would be well below the amount of the exemption equivalent provided by the unified credit. If the healthier spouse is relatively wealthy, he or she could give the ill spouse a gift in an amount equal to the estate tax exemption equivalent. Because of the unlimited marital deduction, the gift would be tax-free. Upon the death of the donee-spouse, no estate tax would be payable because the estate tax liability would not exceed the unified credit. The donee-spouse should not transfer his or her property back to the donor-spouse at death because the retransferred property would be included in the surviving spouse's estate.

A gift of appreciated property in contemplation of the donee-spouse's death provides an additional advantage. If the property does not pass back to the donor-spouse, its basis is increased to its value on the donee's date of death. In the event the property is willed to the donor-spouse, a step-up in basis still occurs if the date of the gift precedes the donee-spouse's date of death by more than one year.

TAX STRATEGY TIP

Trying to be sure that the first spouse to die uses the exemption equivalent is no longer as important an issue because the unused exemption equivalent of the first spouse to die is portable to the surviving spouse. The "portability" rule is discussed in Chapter C:13.

Lessening State Transfer Tax Costs. Currently about 16 states levy an estate or inheritance tax, but only one state imposes a gift tax.[48] State death taxes are deductible in calculating the taxable estate, but they still add to death-associated costs. Therefore, in some states, the state tax cost of lifetime transfers is lower than that for transfers at death.

Income Tax Savings from Charitable Gifts. Some individuals desire to donate a portion of their property to charitable organizations. Assuming the donation is eligible for a charitable contribution deduction, the transfer tax implications are the same—no taxable transfer—irrespective of whether the transfer occurs *inter vivos* or at death. From an income tax standpoint, however, a lifetime transfer is preferable because only lifetime transfers produce an income tax deduction for charitable contributions.

NEGATIVE ASPECTS OF GIFTS

Loss of Step-Up in Basis. Taxpayers deliberating about whether to make gifts or which property to give should keep in mind that the donee receives no step-up in basis for property acquired by gift. From a practical standpoint, sacrifice of the step-up in basis is insignificant if the donee does not plan to sell the property or if the property is not subject to an allowance for depreciation. Also, keep in mind that gain on the sale is likely to be taxed at the applicable long-term capital gain rate, and property in the estate may be taxed at 40%.

Prepayment of Estate Tax. A donor who makes taxable gifts that exceed the exemption equivalent (basic exclusion amount) must pay a gift tax. Upon the donor's death, the taxable gift is included in his or her estate tax base as an adjusted taxable gift. Because the gift tax paid during the donor's lifetime reduces the donor's estate tax liability, in a sense, the donor's payment of the gift tax results in prepayment of a portion of the estate tax.

COMPLIANCE AND PROCEDURAL CONSIDERATIONS

OBJECTIVE 11

Comply with the filing requirements for gift tax returns

FILING REQUIREMENTS

Section 6019 specifies the circumstances in which a donor should file a gift tax return. In general, the donor will file Form 709 (United States Gift Tax Return). A completed Form 709 appears in Appendix B. The facts used in the preparation of the completed Form 709 are the same as the facts in the comprehensive illustration, which uses a format for the gift-splitting aspects that differs slightly from that used in the form.

[48] Only one state imposes a gift tax—Connecticut. Beginning with 2011, the Connecticut gift tax applies only if cumulative gifts exceed $2 million. Minnesota enacted a tax applicable to gifts made after June 30, 2013, but subsequently repealed the tax. Louisiana repealed its gift tax effective July 1, 2008, and North Carolina its gift tax effective January 2009. Tennessee repealed its gift tax in May 2012 retroactive to the beginning of 2012.

As is the case for income tax returns, a return can be necessary even though the taxable amount and the tax payable are both zero. A donor must file a gift tax return for any calendar year in which the donor makes gifts other than

- Gifts to the spouse that qualify for the marital deduction
- Gifts that are fully shielded from taxation because they fall within the annual exclusion amount or are exempted from classification as a gift under the exception for educational or medical expenses
- Gifts to charitable organizations if the gift is deductible and the organization receives the donor's entire interest in the property

In addition, if the gift to the spouse is of qualified terminable interest property (QTIP), the donor must report the gift on the gift tax return. The marital deduction is not available for these transfers unless the donor makes the election, which is done by claiming a marital deduction on the gift tax return.

United States persons who receive aggregate gifts from foreign corporations or foreign partnerships exceeding $15,797 (in 2017) or aggregate gifts or bequests from nonresident aliens or foreign estates exceeding $100,000 (in 2017) must report such amounts as prescribed in Treasury Regulations.[49]

DUE DATE

All gift tax returns must be filed on a calendar-year basis. Under the general rule, gift tax returns are due no later than April 15 following the close of the year of the gift.[50] An extension of time granted for filing an individual income tax return is deemed to automatically extend the filing date for the individual's gift tax return for that year. The automatic extension period is until October 15.

If the donor dies early in the year in which a gift is made, the due date for the donor's final gift tax return may be earlier than April 15. Because information concerning the decedent's taxable gifts is necessary to complete the estate tax return, the gift tax return for the year of death is due no later than the due date (including extensions) for the donor's estate tax return.[51] Estate tax returns are due nine months after the date of death.

Receipt of an extension for filing a gift tax return does not postpone the due date for payment of the tax. Interest is imposed on any gift tax not paid by April 15. Donors should submit Form 8892 if they anticipate owing gift tax and/or if they need an extension for only their gift tax return. Unlike with the income tax, a donor does not have to make estimated payments of gift taxes.

GIFT-SPLITTING ELECTION

For taxable gifts to be computed under the gift-splitting technique, both spouses must indicate their consent to gift splitting in one of the following ways:[52]

- Each spouse signifies his or her consent on the other spouse's gift tax return.
- Each spouse signifies his or her consent on his or her own gift tax return.
- Both spouses signify their consent on one of the gift tax returns.

Treasury Regulations state that the first approach listed above is the preferred manner for designating consent.

KEY POINT

Similarly to a husband and wife filing a joint income tax return, if gift splitting is elected, the husband and wife have joint and several liability for the entire gift tax liability regardless of who actually made the gifts.

LIABILITY FOR TAX

The donor is responsible for paying the gift tax,[53] and if the spouses consent to gift splitting, the entire gift tax liability is a joint and several liability of the spouses.[54] Thus, if spouses do not pay the tax voluntarily, the IRS may attempt to collect whatever amount it deems appropriate from either spouse, irrespective of the size of the gift each spouse actually made.

In the rare event that the donor does not pay the gift tax, the donee becomes personally liable for the gift tax.[55] However, a donee's liability is limited to the value of the gift.

---

49 Sec. 6039F.

50 Sec. 6075(b).

51 The decedent's post-1976 taxable gifts affect the size of his or her estate tax base, as discussed in the next chapter.

52 Reg. Sec. 25.2513-2(a)(1).

53 Sec. 2502(c).

54 Sec. 2513(d).

55 Reg. Sec. 301.6324-1.

DETERMINATION OF VALUE

One of the most difficult problems encountered by donors and their tax advisors is determining the gifted property's FMV. This task is especially difficult if the gifted property is stock in a closely held business, an oil and gas property, or land in an area where few sales occur.

If a transaction involves a sale, the IRS can argue that the asset's value exceeds its sales price and, thus, there is a gift to the extent of the bargain element. This problem is especially common with sales to family members. If the donor gives or sells property whose value is not readily determinable, the donor should obtain an appraisal of the property before filing the gift tax return.

ETHICAL POINT

A CPA who advises a client about the tax consequences of making a gift also has a responsibility to make sure the property is correctly valued. Otherwise, if the valuation claimed is too low, the IRS can levy a penalty on the donor. For example, a gift of noncash property (e.g., land) may require that an appraisal be obtained. Failure to obtain an appraisal, or failure to investigate an appraisal that seems too low, may result in an undervaluation of the gift property, which may lead to the IRS imposing additional gift taxes, interest, and penalties.

Penalty for Undervaluation. Section 6662 imposes a penalty, at one of two rates, on underpayments of gift or estate taxes resulting from too low a valuation of property. The amount on which the penalty is imposed is the underpayment of the transfer tax attributable to the valuation understatement.

No penalty applies if the valuation shown on the return exceeds 65% of the amount determined during an audit or court trial to be the correct value. If the value reported on the return is 65% or less of the correct value, the penalty rate is as shown below.

Ratio of Value per Return to Correct Value	*Penalty Rate*
More than 40% but 65% or less	20%
40% or less	40%

Section 6662(g)(2) exempts a taxpayer from the penalty if the underpayment is less than $5,000.

EXAMPLE C:12-46 ▶ Assume Donna already had used her available unified credit when she gave land to her son and reported its value at $400,000 on her 2016 gift tax return. The IRS audited Donna's return late in 2017, and she agreed that $900,000 was the correct value of the property. Because the value stated on the return was 44.44% [($400,000 ÷ $900,000) × 100] of the correct value, the IRS levied a 20% penalty on the underpayment attributable to the valuation understatement. If Donna was in the 40% marginal gift tax bracket, the gift tax underpayment was $200,000 [0.40 × ($900,000 − $400,000)]. Thus, the penalty is $40,000 (0.20 × $200,000) unless Donna can demonstrate reasonable cause and good faith for the valuation. ◀

STATUTE OF LIMITATIONS

ADDITIONAL COMMENT

If a taxpayer is unsure whether a taxable gift has been made, it is a good idea to file a gift tax return and at least disclose the transaction. The filing of the return with adequate disclosure of the transaction causes the statute of limitations to begin and limits the time during which the IRS may question the valuation and the amount of the gift, if any.

In general, the statute of limitations for gift tax purposes is three years after the later of the date the return was filed or the return's due date.[56] The statute of limitations increases from three to six years if the donor omits from the gift tax return gifts whose total value exceeds 25% of the gifts reported on the return. If the donor files no return because, for example, he or she is unaware that he or she made any gifts, the IRS may assess the tax at any time.

The cumulative nature of the gift tax causes the taxable gifts of earlier years to affect the gift tax owed in subsequent periods. After the statute of limitations has expired for pre-1997 gifts, the IRS cannot argue that taxable gifts of prior periods were undervalued (and thus that the current period's gifts should be taxed at a higher rate than that used by the donor) as long as the donor paid gift tax on the earlier gifts. However, for gifts reported after August 5, 1997, this rule applies even if the donor has paid no gift tax.[57]

For gifts made in 1997 and later, it is important to adequately disclose potential gift transactions for which the gift status is unclear. The statute of limitations will not expire on a transaction unless the donor makes adequate disclosure.[58]

EXAMPLE C:12-47 ▶ Andy filed a gift tax return for 2017, reporting taxable gifts of $5.85 million made in October 2017. Andy paid gift tax. If Andy adequately disclosed all potential gifts, once the statute of limitations expires for 2017, the IRS cannot contend that, for purposes of calculating the tax on later taxable gifts, the 2017 taxable gifts exceeded $5.85 million. ◀

[56] Sec. 6501.
[57] Sec. 2504(c).
[58] Sec. 6501(c)(9).

Problem Materials

DISCUSSION QUESTIONS

C:12-1 Describe two ways in which the transfer tax (estate and gift tax) system is a unified system.

C:12-2 What was the Congressional purpose for enacting the gift-splitting provisions?

C:12-3 Determine whether the following statement is true or false: Every donor who makes a taxable gift incurs a gift tax liability. Explain your answer.

C:12-4 Under what circumstances must the amount of the unified credit usually available be reduced (by a maximum amount of $6,000) even though the donor has never claimed any unified credit?

C:12-5 Does the exemption from the gift tax for direct payment of tuition encompass payments of nonrelatives' tuition? Explain.

C:12-6 Steve is considering the following transactions. Explain to him which actions will constitute gifts for gift tax purposes.

a. Transferring all his ownership rights in a life insurance policy to another person
b. Depositing funds into a joint bank account in the names of himself and another party (who deposits nothing)
c. Paying half the consideration for land and having it titled in the names of Steve and his son as joint tenants with right of survivorship if the son furnishes the other half of the consideration
d. Paying a hospital for the medical expenses of a neighbor
e. Making a $1 million demand loan to an adult child and charging no interest

C:12-7 Dick wants to transfer property with a $600,000 FMV to an irrevocable trust with a bank as the trustee. Dick will name his distant cousin Earl to receive all of the trust income annually for the next eight years. Then the property will revert to Dick. In the last few years, the income return (yield) on the property has been 6%. Assume this yield is not likely to decline and that the applicable rate from the actuarial tables is 4%.

a. What will be the amount of Dick's gift to Earl?
b. Would you recommend that Dick transfer the property yielding 6% to this type of a trust? Explain. If not, what type of property would you recommend that Dick transfer to the trust?

C:12-8 Antonio would like to make a gift of a life insurance policy on his life. Explain to him what action he must take to make a completed gift.

C:12-9 In what circumstances might a potential donor be interested in making a net gift? Explain the potential income tax problem with making a net gift.

C:12-10 What is the purpose of the gift tax annual exclusion?

C:12-11 In what circumstances do gifts fail to qualify for the annual exclusion?

C:12-12 Compare and contrast a Sec. 2503(c) trust and a *Crummey* trust.

C:12-13 From a nontax standpoint, would a parent probably prefer to make a transfer to a minor child by using a Sec. 2503(c) trust or a *Crummey* trust?

C:12-14 Explain the requirements for classifying a transaction as a transfer of a qualified terminable interest property (QTIP).

C:12-15 Why do some donors consider the qualified terminable interest property (QTIP) transfer an especially attractive arrangement for making gifts to their spouses?

C:12-16 A client is under the impression that a donor cannot incur a gift tax liability if he or she makes gifts to only U.S. charitable organizations. What should you say to the client?

C:12-17 Describe to a married couple three advantages of making the gift-splitting election.

C:12-18 Both Damien and Latoya make taxable gifts of $250,000 in the current year. Will their current year gift tax liabilities necessarily be identical? Explain.

C:12-19 A donor made large taxable gifts beginning in 1999 and a taxable gift in the current year. In the intervening years, the highest gift tax rates declined. In calculating the tax on taxable gifts of previous periods, which rate schedule is applicable: the one for the year in which the donor made the earlier gifts or the one for the current period?

C:12-20 A mother is trying to decide which of the two assets listed below to give to her adult daughter.

Asset	*FMV*	*Adjusted Basis*	*Annual Net Income from the Asset*
Apartment	$600,000	$400,000	$(10,000)
Bonds	600,000	530,000	80,000

The mother's marginal income tax rate exceeds her daughter's. Describe the pros and cons of giving each of the two properties. Which option would be preferable?

C:12-21 Phil and Marcy have been married for a number of years. Marcy is very wealthy, but Phil is not. In fact, Phil, who has only $10,000 of property, is very ill, and his doctor believes that he probably will die within the next few months. Make one (or more) tax planning suggestions for the couple. Assume the year is 2017 and that Phil may die in 2017.

C:12-22 Assume the same facts as in Problem C:12-21 and that Marcy has decided to give Phil property valued at $5.48 million. Phil probably will leave the gifted property to their children under his will.

a. What are the gift tax consequences to Marcy and the estate tax consequences to Phil of the transfer (assuming the property does not appreciate before his death)?

b. Assume Marcy is trying to decide whether to give Phil stock with an adjusted basis of $1,285,000 or land with an adjusted basis of $2.8 million. Each asset is valued at $5.48 million. Which asset would you recommend she give and why?

C:12-23 Carlos has heard about the unified transfer tax system and does not understand how making gifts can be beneficial. Explain to Carlos how a lifetime gift fixes (freezes) the gifted property's value for transfer tax purposes.

C:12-24 Describe for a client five advantages and two disadvantages of disposing of property by gift instead of at death.

C:12-25 In general, what is the due date for the gift tax return? What are two exceptions?

C:12-26 In 2007, Frank made an installment sale of real property to Stu, his son, for $1 million with payments due over a 10-year period. Frank did not file a gift tax return. For 2015, Frank reported taxable gifts so large that he used all of his unified credit then available. In 2017, the IRS audits Frank's 2015 income tax return and discovers the sale. The IRS then contends that the property Frank sold was worth $2.5 million in 2007 and that Frank made a $1.5 million gift to Stu in 2007.

a. Can the IRS collect the gift tax on the 2007 gift? If not, will the 2007 gift affect the tax due on gifts that Frank makes in the future?

b. Will Frank potentially incur any penalty? Explain.

ISSUE IDENTIFICATION QUESTIONS

C:12-27 Kwambe is thinking of making a substantial gift of stock to his fiancée, Maya. The wedding is scheduled for October 1 of the current year. Kwambe already has exhausted his unified credit. He also is considering giving $28,000 cash this year to each of his three children by a previous marriage. What tax issues should Kwambe consider with respect to the gifts he plans to make to Maya and his three children?

C:12-28 Janet (who has made no taxable gifts) is considering transferring assets valued at $9 million to an irrevocable trust (yet to be created) for the benefit of her son, Gordon, age 15, with Farmers Bank as trustee. Her attorney has drafted a trust agreement that provides that Gordon is to receive income in the trustee's discretion for the next 20 years and that at age 35 the trust assets will be distributed equally between Gordon and his sister Joanna. Janet anticipates that her husband will consent to gift splitting. What tax issues should Janet and her husband consider with respect to the trust?

C:12-29 Melvin funds an irrevocable trust with Holcomb Bank as trustee and reserves the right to receive the income for seven years. He provides that at the end of the seventh year the trust assets will pass outright to his adult daughter, Pamela, or to Pamela's estate should Pamela not be alive. Melvin transfers assets valued at $1 million to the trust; the assets at present are producing income of about 2.5% per year. Assume that the Sec. 7520 rate per the actuarial tables for the month of the transfer is 4%. What tax issues should Melvin consider regarding the trust?

PROBLEMS

C:12-30 *Calculation of Gift Tax.* In 2017, Sondra makes taxable gifts aggregating $300,000. Her only other taxable gifts amount to $200,000, all of which she made in 1997.

a. What is Sondra's 2017 gift tax liability?

b. What is her 2017 gift tax liability under the assumption that she made the $200,000 of taxable gifts in 1974 instead of 1997?

C:12-31 *Calculation of Gift Tax.* Amir made taxable gifts as follows: $800,000 in 1975, $1.2 million in 1999, and $600,000 in 2017. What is Amir's gift tax liability for 2017?

C:12-32 *Determination of Taxable Gifts.* In the current year, Beth, who is single, sells stock valued at $40,000 to Linda for $18,000. Later that year, Beth gives Linda $12,000 in cash.

a. What is the amount of Beth's taxable gifts?

b. How would your answer to Part a change if Beth instead gave the cash to Patrick?

C:12-33 *Determination of Taxable Gifts.* In the current year, Kent gives $42,000 cash to each of his eight grandchildren. His wife makes no gifts during the current year.

a. What are Kent's taxable gifts, assuming Kent and his wife do *not* elect gift splitting?

b. How would your answer to Part a change if the couple elects gift splitting?

C:12-34 *Determination of Taxable Gifts.* In the current year, David gives $180,000 of land to David, Jr. In the current year, David's wife gives $200,000 of land to George and $44,000 cash to David, Jr. Assume the couple elects gift splitting for the current year.

a. What are the couple's taxable gifts?
b. How would your answer to Part a change if David's wife gave the $44,000 of cash to Ollie (instead of to David, Jr.)?

C:12-35 *Determination of Taxable Gifts.* Yolanda and Xavier, spouses, have four adult children, Andy, Betty, Cathy, and Danny. In 2017, they made a number of gifts. Yolanda gave Andy cash of $40,000 and Betty stock valued at $60,000. Xavier gave Cathy stock valued at $38,000 and deposited $80,000 in a bank account in the names of Xavier and Danny, joint tenants with right of survivorship. Later in the year, Xavier withdrew $10,000 from the account, and Danny withdrew $8,000. Xavier gave stock valued at $70,000 to his alma mater, State Technological Institute. Calculate the amount of taxable gifts for each spouse if they elect gift splitting.

C:12-36 *Recognition of Transactions Treated as Gifts.* In the current year, Emily, a widow, engages in the following transactions. Determine the amount of the completed gift, if any, arising from each of the following occurrences.

a. Emily names Lauren the beneficiary of a $100,000 life insurance policy on Emily's life. The beneficiary designation is not irrevocable.
b. Emily deposits $50,000 cash into a checking account in the joint names of herself and Matt, who deposits nothing to the account. Later that year, Matt withdraws $15,000 from the account.
c. Emily pays $22,000 of nephew Noah's medical expenses directly to County Hospital.
d. Emily transfers the title to land valued at $60,000 to Olive as sole owner.

C:12-37 *Calculation of Gift Tax.* Refer to the facts of Problem C:12-36 and assume the current year is 2017. Emily's prior gifts are as follows:

Year	*Amount of Taxable Gifts*
1974	$ 500,000
1998	1,000,000

What is Emily's 2017 gift tax liability?

C:12-38 *Recognition of Transactions Treated as Gifts.* In the current year, Marge (age 67) engages in the following transactions. Determine the amount of the completed gift, if any, arising from each of the following events. Assume 4% is the applicable interest rate.

a. Marge transfers $100,000 of property in trust and irrevocably names herself to receive $8,000 per year for four years and daughter Joy (age 37) to receive the remainder.
b. Marge pays her grandson's $15,000 tuition to State University.
c. Marge gives the same grandson stock valued at $72,000.
d. Marge deposits $150,000 into a revocable trust. Later in the year, the bank trustee distributes $18,000 of income to the named beneficiary, Gail.

C:12-39 *Recognition of Transactions Treated as Gifts.* Determine the amount of the completed gift, if any, arising from each of the following occurrences.

a. A parent sells real estate valued at $1.8 million to an adult child, who pays $1 million in consideration.
b. A furniture store holds a clearance sale and sells a customer a $5,000 living room suite for $1,500.
c. During the year, a father purchases food and clothing costing $8,500 for his minor child.
d. A citizen contributes $1,500 cash to a political organization.
e. Zeke lends $600,000 interest free to his son Henry, who signs a demand note on August 1. Assume 6% is the applicable interest rate and the note remains unpaid at year-end.

C:12-40 *Determination of Unified Credit.* In March 1976, Sue made a taxable gift of $200,000. In arriving at the amount of her taxable gift, Sue elected to deduct the $30,000 specific exemption then available. In 2017, Sue makes her next gift; the taxable amount is $6.5 million.

a. What unified credit can Sue claim on her 2017 return?
b. What unified credit can Sue claim on her 2017 return if she made the 1976 gift in December instead of March?

C:12-41 *Valuation of Gifts.* On September 1 of the current year, Mario irrevocably transfers a $100,000 whole life insurance policy on his life to Mario, Jr. as owner. On September 1, the policy's interpolated terminal reserve is $30,000. Mario paid the most recent annual premium ($1,800) on June 1. What is the amount of the gift Mario made in the current year?

C:12-42 *Determination of Gift Tax Deductions.* In June, Tina makes cash gifts of $700,000 to her husband and $100,000 to the City Art Museum. What are the amounts of the deductions available for these gifts when calculating Tina's income tax and gift tax liabilities if she does not elect gift splitting?

C:12-43 *Determination of Annual Exclusion.* For each of the following transactions that occur in the current year, indicate the amount of the annual exclusion available. Explain your answer.

a. Tracy creates a trust in the amount of $300,000 for the benefit of her eight-year-old daughter, May. She names a bank as trustee. Before May reaches age 21, the trustee in its discretion is to pay income or corpus (trust assets) to May or for her benefit. When May reaches age 21, she will receive the unexpended portion of the trust income and corpus. If May dies before reaching age 21, the unexpended income and corpus will be paid to her estate or a person (or persons) she appoints under a general power of appointment.
b. Assume the same facts as in Part a except May is age 28 when Tracy creates the trust and the trust agreement contains age 41 wherever age 21 appears in Part a.
c. Assume the same facts as in Part b except the trust instrument allows May to demand a distribution by December 31 of each year equal to the lesser of the amount of the annual exclusion for federal gift tax purposes or the amount transferred to the trust that year.

C:12-44 *Determination of Annual Exclusion.* During 2017, Will gives $40,000 cash to Will, Jr. and a remainder interest in a few acres of land to his friend Suzy. The remainder interest is valued at $32,000. Will and his wife, Helen, elect gift splitting, and during the current year Helen gives Joyce $8,000 of stock. What is the total amount of the annual gift tax exclusions available to Will and Helen?

C:12-45 *Availability of Annual Exclusion.* Bonnie, a widow, irrevocably transfers $1 million of property to a trust and names a bank as trustee. For as long as Bonnie's daughter Carol is alive, Carol is to receive all the trust income annually. Upon Carol's death, the property is to be distributed to Carol's children. Carol is age 32 and currently has three children. How many gift tax exclusions does Bonnie receive for the transfer?

C:12-46 *Calculation of Gift Tax.* In earlier years, neither Hugo nor Wanda, his wife, made any taxable gifts. In 2016, Hugo gave $14,000 cash to each of his nieces, nephews, and grandchildren, 30 persons in total. In 2017, Wanda gives $34,000 of stock to each of the same people. What is the *minimum* legal gift tax liability *before* reduction for the unified credit for each spouse for each year?

C:12-47 *Calculation of Marital Deduction.* Hugh makes the gifts listed below to Winnie, his wife, age 37. What is the amount of the marital deduction, if any, attributable to each?

a. Hugh transfers $500,000 to a trust with a bank named as trustee. All the income must be paid to Winnie monthly for life. At Winnie's death, the property passes to Hugh's sisters or their estates.
b. Hugh transfers $300,000 to a trust with a bank named as trustee. Income is payable at the trustee's discretion to Winnie annually until the earlier of her death or her remarriage. When payments to Winnie cease, the trustee must distribute the property to Hugh's children by a previous marriage or to their estates.

C:12-48 *Calculation of the Marital Deduction.* In the current year, Louise makes the transfers described below to Lance, her husband, age 47. Assume 4% is the applicable interest rate. What is the amount of her marital deduction, if any, attributable to each transfer?

a. In June, she gives him land valued at $45,000.
b. In October, she gives him a 12-year income interest in a trust with a bank named as trustee. She names their daughter to receive the remainder interest. She funds the irrevocable trust with $400,000 in assets.

C:12-49 *Charitable Contribution Deduction.* Tien (age 70) transfers a remainder interest in a vacation cabin (with a total value of $100,000) to a charitable organization and retains a life estate in the cabin for herself.

a. What is the amount of the gift tax charitable contribution deduction, if any, attributable to this transfer? Assume that 4% is the applicable interest rate.

b. How will your answer to Part a change if Tien instead gives a remainder interest in a valuable oil painting (worth $100,000) to the organization?

C:12-50 *Calculation of Gift Tax.* In 2017, Homer and his wife, Wilma (residents of a non–community property state) make the gifts listed below. Homer's previous taxable gifts consist of $100,000 made in 1975 and $1.4 million made in 1996. Wilma has made no previous taxable gifts.

Wilma's current year gifts were	
to Art	$400,000
to Bart	6,000
Homer's current year gifts were	
to Linda	$600,000
to a charitable organization	100,000
to Norma (future interest)	200,000

a. What are the gift tax liabilities of Homer and Wilma for 2017 if they elect gift splitting and everyone except Norma receives a present interest?
b. How would the gift tax liabilities for each spouse in Part a change if they do not elect gift splitting?

C:12-51 *Calculation of Gift Tax.* In 2017, Henry and his wife, Wendy, made the gifts shown below. All gifts are of present interests. What is Wendy's gift tax payable for 2017 if the couple elects gift splitting and Wendy's previous taxable gifts (made in 1995) total $1 million?

Wendy's current gifts were	
to Janet	$80,000
to Cindy	70,000
to Henry	50,000
Henry's current gifts were	
to Janet	30,000

C:12-52 *Basis Rules.* In June 2016, Karen transferred property with a $75,000 FMV and a $20,000 adjusted basis to Hal, her husband. Hal dies in March 2017; the property has appreciated to $85,000 in value by then. His gross estate is $1 million.
a. What is the amount of Karen's taxable gift for 2016?
b. What gain would Hal have recognized if he sold the property for $95,000 in July 2016?
c. If Hal wills the property to Dot, his daughter, what basis would Dot have?
d. How would your answer to Part c change if Hal instead willed the property to Karen?
e. How would your answer to Part d change if Hal did not die until August 2017?

C:12-53 *Basis Rules.* Siu is considering giving her son stock in Ace Corporation or Gold Corporation. Each has a current FMV of $500,000, and each has the same estimated future appreciation rate. Siu's basis in the Ace stock is $100,000, and her basis in the Gold stock is $450,000. Assume Siu has total assets of $7 million. Which stock would you suggest that she give away and why, or does it make any difference?

C:12-54 *Below-Market Loans.* On October 1, Sam lends Tom $10 million. Tom signs an interest-free demand note. The loan is still outstanding on December 31. Explain the income tax and gift tax consequences of the loan to both Sam and Tom. Assume that the federal short-term rate is 5%.

COMPREHENSIVE PROBLEM

C:12-55 In 2017, Ginger Graham, age 46 and wife of Greg Graham, engaged in the transactions described below. Determine Ginger's gift tax liability for 2017 if she and Greg elect gift splitting and Greg gave their son Stevie stock valued at $80,000 during 2017. Ginger's grandmother Mamie died November 12, 2016, and Mamie's will bequeathed $250,000 to Ginger. On March 4, 2017, Ginger irrevocably disclaimed the $250,000 in writing, and, as a result, the property passed instead to Ginger's sister Gertie. In 2017, Ginger gave $100,000 cash to her alma mater, State University. In 1996, Ginger gave ownership of a life insurance policy on her own life to her daughter, Denise, and in 2017 Ginger paid the $22,000 annual premium on the policy. In 2016, Ginger deposited $45,000 into a bank account in the name of herself and son Stevie, joint tenants with rights of survivorship.

Stevie deposited nothing. Neither party made a withdrawal until 2017, when Stevie withdrew $30,000. In 2017, Ginger created a trust with County Bank as trustee and transferred $300,000 of stock to the irrevocable trust. She named her husband Greg (age 47) to receive all the trust income semi-annually for life and daughter Drucilla to receive the remainder. In 2017, she gave a remainder interest in her beach cottage to the American Red Cross and kept the right to use the cottage rent free for the rest of her life. The fair market value of the cottage was $70,000.

Other information: Ginger's earlier *taxable* gifts are $175,000, all made in 1996. Ginger will make whatever elections are necessary to minimize her current gift tax liability. Assume the Sec. 7520 interest rate is 4%.

TAX STRATEGY PROBLEMS

C:12-56 *Determination of Taxable Gifts.* George and Martha, spouses, made a number of gifts during 2017. Their accountant is trying to help them decide whether to elect gift splitting. If they elect gift splitting, each spouse will have $4 million of taxable gifts. If they do not elect gift splitting, George's taxable gifts will be $2 million, and Martha's will be $6 million. For simplicity, assume all gifts are of remainder interests. George has not made any earlier taxable gifts, but Martha made $250,000 of taxable gifts in 2009. Calculate the amount of gift tax each spouse will owe if they elect gift splitting and if they do not elect gift splitting for 2017. What do you recommend they do concerning the election to split gifts?

C:12-57 Ilene Ishi is planning to fund an irrevocable charitable remainder annuity trust with $100,000 of cash. She will designate her sister, age 60, to receive an annuity of $5,000 per year for 15 years and State University to receive the remainder at the end of the fifteenth year. The valuation of the charitable portion of the transfer, according to Reg. Sec. 25.2522(c)-3(d)(2)(i), is to be determined under Reg. Sec. 1.664-2(c), an income tax regulation. Regulation Sec. 1.664-2(c) provides that, in valuing the remainder interest, the donor may elect to use the Sec. 7520 interest rate for either of the two months preceding the month of the transfer as an alternative to using the rate for the actual month of transfer. Otherwise, the value will be determined by using the Sec. 7520 rate for the month of the transfer. Assume that in the month of the transfer the interest rate was 4% but that in the two preceding months the rate was 4.2%. Should the donor elect to calculate the value of the remainder interest by using the interest rate for one of the two preceding months? Explain your answer. Note: The 4.2% rate does not appear in the excerpts from the actuarial tables, but the absence of such rate from the tables will not preclude you from answering this question.

TAX FORM/RETURN PREPARATION PROBLEMS

C:12-58 Use the information shown below to prepare a 2016 gift tax return (Form 709) for Joel Bruton. Pages 4 and 5 of the form are not applicable. Joel and his wife Janis, both U.S. citizens, want to elect gift splitting. They reside at 117 Panther Place, South City, NC 28000. Joel had not been married prior to his marriage to Janis in 1966. For simplicity, assume that the Sec. 7520 rate is 4%. Joel's transactions, all in July, are as shown below.

	Value on Date of Gift	*Adjusted Basis*
1. Stock given to daughter Belinda	$ 78,000	$ 60,000
2. Apartment building and land given to daughter Belinda	2,476,000	1,900,000
3. Tuition to university, paid for grandson Jacob	24,000	
4. Pottery collection given to Atlanta Art Museum	120,000	100,000
5. Stocks given to trust for benefit of wife Janis (age 67) for life with remainder to Belinda. All of the income is to be distributed quarterly to Janis	3,000,000	2,430,000

During the year Janis gave $40,000 cash to Belinda and $200,000 of stock to her sister Jeanette Johnson. Janis had a $120,000 adjusted basis in the stock. Joel made a $1 million taxable gift in 2000. It was the first and only earlier gift.

C:12-59 Ned Norris, a widower, engaged in the transactions described below during 2016. He made only one earlier taxable gift, $1.2 million in 2014. Use this information to prepare a 2016 gift tax return (Form 709) for Mr. Norris, who resides at 11616 Starstruck Blvd., Southern City, CA 90068. Pages 4 and 5 of the form are not applicable to him.

- Transfer of title to unimproved land to son Nathan, age 31, fair market value of $2 million and adjusted basis of $300,000.
- Payment of tuition ($35,000) to Private College and payment of off-campus apartment rent ($18,000) to Tall Tower, LLC for the benefit of daughter Natalie, age 21.
- Transfer of title to vacation beach house to County Hospital, fair market value of $525,000 and adjusted basis of $320,000.
- Payment of $17,000 life insurance premium on an insurance policy on his own life. He made a gift of the insurance policy to Nathan four years ago.

CASE STUDY PROBLEMS

C:12-60 Your client, Karen Kross, recently married Larry Kross. Karen is age 72, quite wealthy, and in reasonably good health. To date, she has not made any taxable gifts, but Larry made taxable gifts totaling $900,000 in 1998. Karen is considering giving each of her five college-age grandchildren approximately $34,000 of cash for them to use to pay their college expenses of tuition and room and board for the year. In addition, she is considering giving her three younger grandchildren $3,000 each to use for orthodontic bills. Karen wants to give her daughter property valued at $400,000. She is trying to choose between giving her daughter cash or stock with a basis of $125,000. She would like to give her son $400,000 of property also, but prefers to tie the property up in a discretionary trust with a bank as trustee for the son for at least 15 years. An agricultural museum approached Karen about making a contribution to it and, as a result, she is contemplating deeding her family farm to the museum but retaining a life estate in the farm.

Required: Prepare a memorandum to the tax partner of your firm that discusses the transfer tax and income tax consequences of the proposed transactions described above. Also, make any recommendations that you deem appropriate.

C:12-61 Morris Jory, a long-time tax client of the firm that employs you, has made substantial gifts during his lifetime. Mr. Jory transferred Jory Corporation stock to 14 donees in December 2016. Each donee received shares valued at $14,000. Two of the donees were Mr. Jory's adult children, Amanda and Peter. The remaining 12 donees were employees of Jory Corporation who are not related to Mr. Jory. Mr. Jory, a widower, advised the employees that within two weeks of receiving the stock certificates they must endorse such certificates over to Amanda and Peter. Six of the donees were instructed to endorse their certificates to Amanda and six to Peter. During 2016, Mr. Jory also gave $35,000 cash to his favorite grandchild, Robin. Your firm has been engaged to prepare Mr. Jory's 2016 gift tax return. In early 2017, you meet with Mr. Jory, who insists that his 2016 taxable gifts are only $21,000 ($35,000 to Robin − $14,000 annual exclusion). After your meeting with Mr. Jory, you have concerns about his position regarding the amount of his 2016 taxable gifts and have scheduled a meeting with your firm's senior tax partner, who has advised Mr. Jory for more than 20 years. In preparation for the meeting, prepare a summary of the tax and ethical considerations (with supporting authority where possible) regarding whether you should prepare a gift tax return that reports the taxable gifts in accordance with Mr. Jory's wishes.

TAX RESEARCH PROBLEMS

C:12-62 Your manager advises you that clients Mike and Winona Marsh, residents of Bath, Maine, acquired beachfront property in Maine in 2002 and titled the property in their names as joint tenants with right of survivorship. Under Maine law, either joint tenant can sever the joint tenancy unilaterally. Mike died in July 2017, survived by Winona and their two adult children. His will provided that all his property passes to Winona if she survives him. Otherwise it passes to the children equally. In September 2017, Winona executed a written disclaimer of the one-half interest in the beachfront property that otherwise would pass to her by survivorship. As a result, this interest passed to the two children equally. Winona and the children represent that Winona has not accepted the interest in the property or any of its benefits. Your manager requests that you research the issue of whether Winona made a gift to the children when she disclaimed and that you address your conclusions in a memo. She recommends that you search only in private letter rulings.

C:12-63 In July of the current year, Horace Hiatt, a widower, transferred $14,000 worth of publicly traded stock to an irrevocable trust with Benton National Bank as trustee. He named his granddaughter, Heather, then age 15, the beneficiary. The trust instrument provides that, until Heather reaches age 21, the trustee is to distribute amounts of income and/or principal to her as it "shall deem to be in the best interest of Heather." In addition, the trust instrument states that, if Heather dies before reaching age 21, the trust assets are to be distributed in accordance with Heather's appointment under a general power of appointment. The trust instrument provides further that the trust assets, including undistributed income, will be paid over to Heather upon her attaining age 21. However, if Heather does not ask for such property within 60 days of being notified of her right to ask for it, the trust is to continue until Heather reaches age 45, and the trustee is to continue to have the distribution powers it received at inception. Your manager asks you to research the effect, if any, on the eligibility for the gift tax annual exclusion resulting from the language stating that the trust will continue until age 45 if Heather does not ask for the trust assets within a certain time frame. Your manager suggests that she seems to recall reading a 2006 letter ruling on this issue and asks that you try to locate it and that you also try to locate applicable higher authority, if any. Draft a memo to your manager addressing the availability of the annual exclusion.

C:12-64 Janet Mason timely filed a 2015 gift tax return to report the gift on June 3, 2015, of closely held stock in Mason Meat Co., Inc. The tax return, which your firm prepared, reflected a value of $1,500 per share (determined by an appraiser) and a taxable gift of $6.3 million. This was Janet's first taxable gift, and she exhausted her unified credit then available of $2,117,800. On October 22, 2016, Janet's father, Mason Meat's CEO and founder, died unexpectedly at age 59. In addition, two months prior to her father's death the firm had recalled much of its meat from distributors and supermarkets because of contamination in the meat plant. The meat plant closed for six weeks while the problem was corrected. An appraiser valued the stock for her father's estate at $1,000 per share. Janet, a new client, would like for your firm to prepare an amended gift tax return and value her gift at $1,000 per share because of the decline in value resulting from the two events described. She would like a refund of the gift tax she paid and have some of her unified credit restored. Prepare a memo that addresses whether Janet should be entitled to a refund of the gift tax paid and restoration of some of her unified credit.

C:12-65 Consult the case *Estate of Edward S. Redstone*, 145 T.C. No. 11 (2016), a rather complicated case, and answer the following uncomplicated questions:

a. When did the alleged gift occur, and when did the IRS issue a notice of deficiency?
b. Why was the IRS able to argue that gift tax was owed, given the year the alleged gift occurred?
c. How much monetary compensation did Edward Redstone receive for the shares transferred to his children, Ruth Ann and Michael?
d. What did the Tax Court decide, and what was its rationale?

C:12-66 On August 3, 2014 Ginger Grayson, a widow, transferred $55,000 to each of two Sec. 529 plans (qualified tuition programs), one for grandson Greg Grayson and one for granddaughter Gayle Grayson. Her tax preparer, not a CPA, prepared a Form 1040 (individual income tax return) for Ginger for 2014 and 2015. Ginger has engaged the CPA firm for which you work to prepare her 2016 individual income tax return. In a conversation with Ginger, you learned about her 2014 transfers to the two Sec. 529 plans and inquired whether a gift tax return was prepared for 2014 to report the transfers to the Sec. 529 plans. She checked her files and responded that the tax preparer stated that no gift tax return was necessary. The preparer's rationale was that the transfers to the Sec. 529 plans could be treated as gifts in the amount of $11,000 ($55,000/5 years) per grandchild per year and, as a result, the gifts would be fully covered by the gift tax annual exclusion. Your supervisor requested that you prepare a memo addressing whether the transfers to the two Sec. 529 plans in 2014 are fully excludible from gift tax and whether a gift tax return should have been prepared for 2014. Your supervisor suggests that you consult authorities and sources listed below. The *Beyer* case is very long; therefore, concern yourself only with the portion of the case under the heading "Mr. Beyer's Gift Tax Returns" and the part of the opinion entitled "Section 529 Plans."

- IRC Sec. 529(c)
- *Estate of Edward G. Beyer,* T.C. Memo 2016-183
- Form 709 (United States Gift Tax Return), instructions for Schedule A, Line B

C:12-67 ***Internet Research Problem.*** Your manager wants you to participate in delivering a staff training course on the basics of gift taxation. Your assignment is to discuss *Crummey* trusts. You want to increase your knowledge of some of the advantages and disadvantages of such trusts. Conduct research on the Internet and summarize the advantages and disadvantages. Also indicate which site(s) is (are) the source(s) of your information.

C:12-68 ***Internet Research Problem.*** What was the Sec. 7520 rate for May, June, and July 2016?

CHAPTER

13

THE ESTATE TAX

LEARNING OBJECTIVES

After studying this chapter, you should be able to

1. Explain the formula for the estate tax
2. Describe the methods for valuing interests in the gross estate
3. Recognize which interests are includible in the gross estate
4. Identify the deductions available for estate tax purposes
5. Calculate the estate tax liability
6. Explain tax provisions that alleviate liquidity problems
7. Summarize the basic concepts of the generation-skipping transfer tax
8. Recognize tax planning opportunities for estates
9. Comply with the filing requirements for estate tax returns

CHAPTER OUTLINE

Gift taxes and estate taxes are part of a unified system that taxes the transfer of wealth. Thus, they fundamentally differ with income and property taxes. Chapter C:12 discussed their history and purposes.

As previously noted, the term *gift taxes* applies to lifetime transfers and the term *estate taxes* applies to dispositions of property resulting from the transferor's death. This chapter discusses the structure of the federal estate tax and examines the types of interests and transactions that cause inclusions in the decedent's gross estate. It also discusses the various deductions and credits affecting the federal estate tax liability and the rules concerning the taxable gifts that affect the estate tax base, an important issue because of the unified nature of the tax levied at death.

The Economic Growth and Tax Relief Reconciliation Act of 2001 (the 2001 Act) was an important landmark in the history of the estate and gift tax. It provided phased-in increases to the unified credit and phased-in reductions to the unified tax rate schedule beginning with 2002. In addition, it provided that the estate and generation-skipping transfer taxes would not apply, effective January 1, 2010. However, the 2001 Act further provided that, in the absence of additional legislation, the rules for gift, estate, and generation-skipping taxes would revert on January 1, 2011, to what they were before the 2001 Act.

Thus, as of January 1, 2010, the estate tax was automatically repealed but was scheduled to return in 2011 at pre-2001 Act levels. In addition, a decedent's assets, except for a limited amount, were not permitted to be stepped-up to fair market value. Rather, the basis of the assets transferred to beneficiaries was determined using a modified carryover basis system. In December 2010, Congress enacted the Tax Relief, Unemployment Insurance Reauthorization, and Job Creation Act of 2010 (hereinafter referred to as the Tax Relief Act), which reinstated the estate tax retroactive to January 1, 2010 along with setting the basis of assets to fair market value at the date of death. However, for decedents who died in 2010, it allowed the executor to choose between (1) no estate tax with a modified carryover basis or (2) the estate tax with a $5 million applicable exclusion amount, a top rate of 35%, and FMV bases for the estate's assets. Thus, estates below the $5 million threshold could step up the assets' bases to FMV without incurring any estate tax liability. A step-up occurs when the estate's assets have a FMV exceeding their bases. A step-down will occur for assets whose bases exceed their FMV.

The Tax Relief Act set the maximum estate and gift tax rates at 35% for 2011 and 2012 and the amount that could be transferred tax free in either context at $5 million for 2011 and $5 million indexed to $5.12 million for 2012. The American Taxpayer Relief Act of 2012 (ATRA 2012) increased the top estate and gift tax rate from 35% to 40% beginning in 2013 and retained a nontaxable amount of $5 million, indexed to $5.25, $5.34, $5.43, $5.45, and $5.49 million for 2013, 2014, 2015, 2016, and 2017, respectively.

ESTATE TAX FORMULA

OBJECTIVE 1

Explain the formula for the estate tax

The tax base for the federal estate tax is the *total* of the decedent's taxable estate (i.e., the gross estate less the deductions discussed below) and adjusted taxable gifts (post-1976 taxable gifts). After the gross tax liability on the tax base is determined, various credits—including the unified credit—are subtracted to arrive at the net estate tax payable. The estate tax formula appears in Figure C:13-1.

REAL-WORLD EXAMPLE

In 2015, the total gross estate for all returns filed was $167.4 billion with almost half of this amount made up of real estate and stock holdings.

GROSS ESTATE

As illustrated in Figure C:13-1, calculation of the decedent's estate tax liability begins with determining which items are included in the gross estate. Such items are valued at either the decedent's date of death or the alternate valuation date.[1] As a transfer tax, the estate tax is levied on dispositions that are essentially testamentary in nature. Transactions are viewed as being essentially **testamentary transfers** if the transferor's control or enjoyment of the property in question ceases at death, not before death.[2]

[1] Under Sec. 2032, the alternate valuation date is the earlier of six months after the date of death or the date the property is disposed of. See pages C:13-7 and C:13-8 for details.

[2] An example of a transaction that is essentially **testamentary** in nature is a situation where the donor transfers property in trust but reserves a lifetime right to receive the trust income and, thus, continues to enjoy the economic benefits.

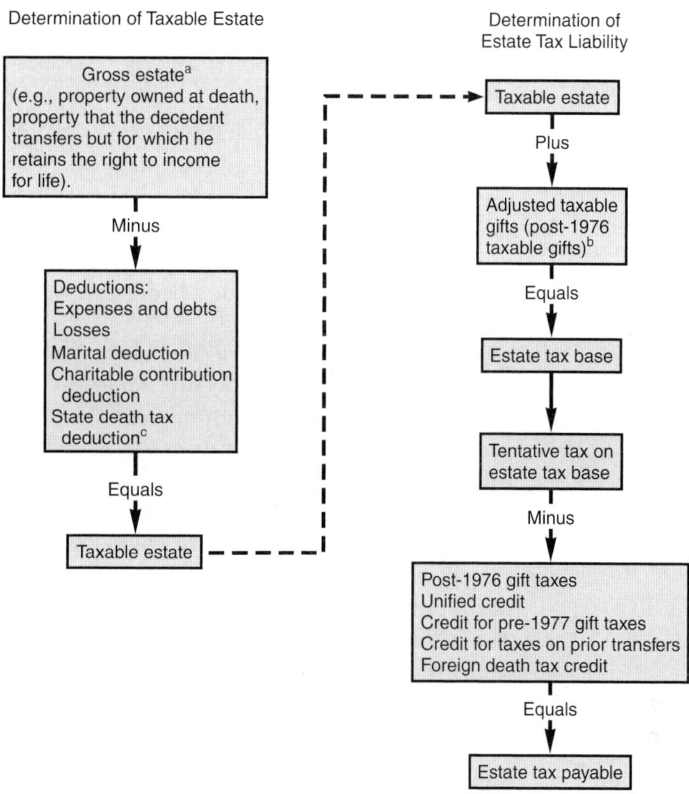

FIGURE C:13-1 ▶ ESTATE TAX FORMULA

Inclusions in the gross estate extend to a much broader set of properties than merely assets to which the decedent holds title at the time of death. Making a lifetime transfer that generates a taxable gift does not guarantee that the donor removes the transferred property from his or her gross estate. Although an individual usually removes property from his or her gross estate by giving it to another before death, the donor's gross estate must include the gifted property if the donor retains either the right to receive the income generated by the transferred property or control over the property for the donor's lifetime.

EXAMPLE C:13-1 ▶

In the current year, Ted transfers stocks to an irrevocable trust with a bank named as trustee. Under the terms of the trust agreement, Ted is to receive the trust income annually for the rest of his life and Ted's cousin Ed (or Ed's estate) is to receive the remainder. In the current year, Ted made a taxable gift of the remainder interest (but not the income interest) in the trust. If, for example, Ted already has used his entire unified credit, he incurs a gift tax liability. When Ted dies, the entire value of the trust is included in Ted's gross estate, even though Ted has made a taxable gift and does not have legal title to the property. Because the shift in the right to the income does not occur until Ted's death, the transfer is testamentary in nature. ◄

SELF-STUDY QUESTION

Six years ago Barb transferred $500,000 in trust, income for life to herself, remainder to her cousin. What part, if any, of the value of the trust's assets will be included in Barb's estate?

ANSWER

The value of the entire trust will be included in Barb's estate, because she retained the income from the trust until her death.

The categories of items included in the gross estate and their valuation are examined in detail later in this chapter. Once the components of the gross estate have been determined and valued, the deductions from the gross estate are calculated.

DEDUCTIONS

The IRC authorizes five categories of items that may be deducted in arriving at the amount of the taxable estate:

- Expenses and debts
- Casualty and theft losses

- Transfers to the decedent's spouse
- Transfers to charitable organizations
- State death taxes

Deductible expenses include funeral expenses and expenses of administering the decedent's property. As is true for gift tax purposes, there is no ceiling on the marital deduction. Thus, the death of the first spouse is free of estate taxes if the decedent's spouse receives all the decedent's property, or all the property except for an amount equal to the basic exclusion amount or exemption equivalent.[3] Property passing to charitable organizations qualifies, in general, for a charitable contribution deduction, with no ceiling on the amount of such deductions.

ADDITIONAL COMMENT

In this chapter and Chapter C:12, the terms *basic exclusion amount* and *exemption equivalent* are used interchangeably.

ADJUSTED TAXABLE GIFTS AND TAX BASE

Under the unified transfer tax concept, adjusted taxable gifts are added to the taxable estate to determine the amount of the estate tax base. Section 2001(b) defines adjusted taxable gifts as taxable gifts made after 1976 *other than* gifts included in the gross estate. Because very few gifts are included in the gross estate, almost every post-1976 taxable gift is classified as an adjusted taxable gift.

Adjusted taxable gifts are valued at their date-of-gift values. Therefore, any post-gift appreciation escapes both the gift tax and estate tax. Allowable deductions and exclusions are subtracted from the gift's value in determining taxable gifts and, thus, the adjusted taxable gifts amount. Increasing the taxable estate by adjusted taxable gifts potentially forces the estate into a higher marginal tax rate.

EXAMPLE C:13-2 ▶ In 2004, Amy made $5 million of taxable gifts, none of which were included in her gross estate. In 2017, Amy died with a taxable estate of $4 million. The property Amy gave away in 2004 appreciated to $7 million in value by her date of death. In 2005, Amy gave stock valued at $8,000 to one of her children. Amy made no taxable gift and incurred no transfer tax on the 2005 transaction. The stock had appreciated to $70,000 when Amy died. Amy's estate tax base is calculated as follows:

ADDITIONAL COMMENT

Income earned on gifted property is the donee's and is not included in the donor's estate.

Taxable estate	$4,000,000
Plus: Adjusted taxable gifts (valued at date-of-gift values)	5,000,000
Estate tax base	$9,000,000

The $2 million of post-gift appreciation on the property gifted in 2004 escapes transfer taxation. Amy's $9 million tax base includes the property gifted in 2004, whose value was "frozen" at its date-of-gift value. The 2005 gift did not affect Amy's estate tax base because the 2005 *taxable* gift was zero (because of the annual exclusion). ◀

TENTATIVE TAX ON ESTATE TAX BASE

Once the amount of the tax base has been determined, the next step is to calculate the tax on this base using the unified tax rates, which are reproduced on the inside back cover of this textbook. In 2007 through 2009, a maximum tax rate of 45% applied to tax bases exceeding $1.5 million for both estate and gift tax purposes. For 2010 through 2012, the top estate and gift tax rate was 35%, applicable to tax bases exceeding $500,000. If, however, an estate's executor so elected for 2010, the estate tax did not apply that year, but the 35% top tax rate nevertheless applied to 2010 gifts. Beginning in 2013 the maximum rate rose to 40%, and it applies to transfers above $1 million.

EXAMPLE C:13-3 ▶ Assume the same facts as in Example C:13-2. The gross tax on Amy's $9 million tax base is $3,545,800. The estate was taxed at a 40% marginal tax rate, the highest rate applicable in the year Amy died. ◀

REDUCTION FOR POST-1976 GIFT TAXES

Adjusted taxable gifts, in effect, are not taxed twice because Sec. 2001(b)(2) allows a reduction to the estate tax for gift taxes imposed on post-1976 taxable gifts. If the rate schedule for the year of death differs from the schedule applicable for the year of the gift, the tax on post-1976 taxable gifts is determined by using the rate schedule in effect for the year of

[3] The estate tax basic exclusion amount (or exemption equivalent) ($5 million for 2011, $5.12 million for 2012, $5.25 million for 2013, $5.34 million for 2014, $5.43 million for 2015, $5.45 million for 2016, and $5.49 million for 2017), as explained in Chapter C:12, is the size of the tax base for which the estate tax liability is exactly cancelled by the unified credit, $1,730,800 in 2011, $1,772,800 in 2012, $2,045,800 in 2013, $2,081,800 in 2014, $2,117,800 in 2015, $2,125,800 in 2016, and $2,141,800 in 2017.

death. The unified credit subtracted from the gift tax is recalculated to arrive at what the credit *would have been* if the tax rates in effect at the date of death had been in effect at the time of the gift. The rule regarding rates works to the disadvantage of decedents who made taxable gifts and paid taxes at a higher rate than the rate in effect on the date of death. This recalculation approach ensures that the estate pays tax at the current marginal tax rate applicable for the decedent's amount of taxable estate and adjusted taxable gifts.

EXAMPLE C:13-4 ▶ Assume the same facts as in Examples C:13-2 and C:13-3. Recall that in 2004 Amy made $5 million of taxable gifts. For 2004, the tax on $5 million of taxable gifts was $2,220,800. Amy was entitled to a $345,800 unified credit on the $1 million exemption equivalent amount and paid $1,875,000 of gift taxes. Amy's 2004 gifts were taxed at a 48% marginal rate. For the year of Amy's death (2017), the marginal rate for $5 million of transfers is 40%. Consequently, the reduction for gift taxes on post-1976 taxable gifts is limited to the amount of gift taxes that would be payable if the 2017 rate schedule were in effect in the year of the gift. This amount is calculated as follows:

Tax on $5 million at 2017 rates	$1,945,800
Minus: Unified credit for 2004 (the year of the gift)	(345,800)
Tax that would have been payable on $5 million if 2017 rates were in effect	$1,600,000

Note that the only changes to the gift tax computation are that the 2017 transfer tax rates are used. The credit applicable for the year of the gift (and not the credit for the year of death) is subtracted. This amount is recalculated (when necessary) to take into consideration the tax rates in effect for the year of the donor's death. Because the tax on the first $1 million was the same in 2004 as it is in 2017, the unified credit subtracted is the same amount as the credit used on the 2004 tax return. ◀

EXAMPLE C:13-5 ▶ From Examples C:13-3 and C:13-4, Amy's estate tax, before reduction for any credits, is calculated as follows:

Tax on $9 million tax base (Example C:13-3)	$3,545,800
Minus: Tax that would have been payable on $5 million of post-1976 taxable gifts, at 2017 rates (Example C:13-4)	(1,600,000)
Estate tax, before reduction for credits (discussed below)	$1,945,800 ◀

SELF-STUDY QUESTION

Taxpayer made $3 million of taxable gifts in 1992 and paid gift taxes of $1,098,000 (gross tax of $1,290,800 minus the unified credit of $192,800). Taxpayer died in 2017 with a taxable estate of $100,000. At 2017 rates and a credit recalculated at 2017 rates, the gift taxes payable on $3 million would be $953,000 ($1,145,800 – $192,800). Determine the amount of her estate tax liability.

ANSWER

The unified transfer tax base was $3.1 million, the sum of the $3 million of 1992 taxable gifts and the $100,000 estate. The 2017 tax on $3.1 million is $1,185,800. The unified credit of $2,141,800 and the subtraction for gift taxes of $953,000 reduce the tax liability to zero.

UNIFIED CREDIT

As shown in the inside back cover, the unified credit has varied over the years since its inception in 1977. The credit enables a certain size tax base, referred to as the exemption equivalent or basic exclusion amount, to be completely free of transfer taxes. For 2009, the unified credit was the equivalent of the tax on $3.5 million for estates and $1 million for gifts. The Tax Relief Act did not revise the amount in effect for 2010 for gift tax purposes. It, however, increased the basic exclusion amount to $5 million for estate tax purposes for the years 2010 and 2011, and for gift tax purposes for 2011. As a result, the unified credit rose to $1,730,800. In addition, this amount was indexed in 2012 to a $5.12 million amount and a $1,772,800 credit. For 2013 and later, the basic exclusion amount remains at $5 million, indexed annually for inflation. In 2017, the inflation-adjusted amount is $5.49 million, resulting in a $2,141,800 unified credit for 2017.

The estate tax computation permits an estate to subtract the entire unified credit applicable for the year of death (reduced by any phaseout for certain pre-1977 gifts) regardless of how much unified credit the decedent claimed for gift tax purposes. As a conceptual matter, however, only one unified credit is available. Under the unification concept, the estate tax is computed on a tax base consisting of the taxable estate plus the adjusted taxable gifts. The tentative tax on the tax base is reduced not by the amount of the "gross" tax on the adjusted taxable gifts, but by the "gross" tax on such gifts reduced by the unified credit. Ignoring changes in the amount of the unified credit, this computation achieves the same result as allowing the unified credit amount to be subtracted only once against all of a person's transfers but allowing a reduction to the estate tax for the gift tax liability unreduced by the unified credit.

ADDITIONAL COMMENT

Three additional credits are available for estates. See Figure C:13-1 and pages C:13-24 and C:13-25.

THE GROSS ESTATE: VALUATION

OBJECTIVE 2

Describe the methods for valuing interests in the gross estate

TYPICAL MISCONCEPTION

The basis of inherited property is the FMV of the property on the decedent's date of death, which could be higher or lower than the decedent's basis. This change is referred to as a step-up or a step-down in basis. Many taxpayers hear so much about step-up that they forget that a step-down can occur. However, see pages C:12-27 and C:12-28 for carryover basis rules applicable to deaths in 2010.

ETHICAL POINT

The executor may need to engage a qualified appraiser to value interests in closely held corporations and real estate. Because appraisals are subjective, two appraisers may arrive at different values. Using the highest appraisal may mean additional estate taxes, but it will provide a greater step-up in basis. Using too low an appraisal may subject the estate to undervaluation penalties (see page C:13-35).

DATE-OF-DEATH VALUATION

All property included in the gross estate is valued at either its fair market value (FMV) on the date of death or the alternate valuation date. Each item included in the gross estate must be valued as of the same date. In other words, the executor (called the personal representative in some states) cannot value some items as of the date of death and others as of the alternate valuation date.

Fair market value is defined as "the price at which the property would change hands between a willing buyer and a willing seller, neither being under any compulsion to buy or to sell and both having reasonable knowledge of relevant facts."[4] In general, the FMV of a particular asset on a certain date is the same regardless of whether the property is being valued for gift or estate tax purposes. Life insurance on the life of the transferor is an exception to this rule. Upon the death of the insured, the policy is valued at its face value, whereas it is valued at a lesser amount while the insured is alive. Generally, this lesser amount is either the cost of a comparable contract or the policy's interpolated terminal reserve plus the unexpired portion of the premium.

For certain types of property, Treasury Regulations contain detailed descriptions of the valuation approach. However, the valuation of interests in closely held businesses is described in only very general terms. Judicial decisions and revenue rulings provide additional guidance for valuation of assets. Valuation rules for several interests are discussed below. For purposes of this discussion, it is assumed that date-of-death valuation is elected.

Listed Stocks. Stocks traded on a stock exchange are valued at the average of their highest and lowest selling prices on the date of death.[5] If no sales occur on the date of death, but sales do take place within a few days of such date, the estate tax value is a weighted average of the high and low sales prices on the nearest trade dates before and after the date of death. The average is weighted inversely in relation to the number of days separating the sales dates and the date of death.

EXAMPLE C:13-6 ▶ Juan, who died on November 8, 2017, owned 100 shares of Jet Corporation stock. Jet stock, traded on the New York Stock Exchange, traded at a high of $120 and a low of $114 on November 8. On Juan's estate tax return, the stock was valued at $117 per share, the average of $120 and $114. The total value of the block of Jet stock was $11,700 (100 × $117). ◀

EXAMPLE C:13-7 ▶ Susan, who died on May 3, 2017 owned 100 shares of Top Corporation stock, traded on the New York Stock Exchange. No sales of Top stock occurred on May 3. The sales occurring closest to May 3 took place two business days before May 3 and three business days after May 3. On the earlier date, the stock traded at a high of $500 and a low of $490, with an average of $495. On the later date, the high was $492 and the low was $490, for an average of $491. The date-of-death per-share valuation of the stock is computed under the inverse weighted average approach, as follows:

$$\frac{[3 \times \$495] + [2 \times \$491]}{5} = \$493.40$$

The total value of the block of Top stock is $49,340 (100 × $493.40). ◀

In certain circumstances, the decedent may own such a large block of stock that the price at which the stock trades in the market may not represent the FMV per share for the decedent's number of shares. In such circumstances, Treasury Regulations allow a departure from the traditional valuation rule for stocks. These regulations, referred to as the blockage regulations, state that

[4] Reg. Sec. 20.2031-1(b).

[5] Reg. Sec. 20.2031-2(b).

> In certain exceptional cases, the size of the block of stock to be valued in relation to the number of shares changing hands in sales may be relevant in determining whether selling prices reflect the fair market value of the block of stock to be valued. If the executor can show that the block of stock to be valued is so large in relation to the actual sales on the existing market that it could not be liquidated in a reasonable time without depressing the market, the price at which the block could be sold as such outside the usual market, as through an underwriter, may be a more accurate indication of value than market quotations.[6]

Interests in Firms Whose Stock Is Not Publicly Traded. Often, the decedent owns stock in a firm whose shares are not publicly traded. Treasury Regulations do not specifically address the valuation rules for this type of an interest. However, detailed guidelines about relevant factors, including book value and earning capacity, are found in Rev. Rul. 59-60.[7] If the stock is a minority interest in a closely held firm, the courts often grant a discount for the minority interest.

SELF-STUDY QUESTION

Compare a situation where capitalization of earnings might be used instead of or in addition to comparable sales when valuing real estate.

ANSWER

Capitalization of earnings might be used instead of or in addition to comparable sales in the valuation of an apartment or office building. Comparable sales would be used for valuing a personal residence.

Real Estate. Perhaps surprisingly, Treasury Regulations do not specifically address the valuation approach for real estate. Thus, the general valuation principles concerning a price that would be acceptable to a willing buyer and a willing seller must be implemented without the benefit of more specific guidance. Appraisal literature discusses three techniques for valuing real property: comparable sales, reproduction cost, and capitalization of earnings.[8] Unfortunately, for some properties, it may be difficult to locate a comparable real estate sale. The reproduction cost, of course, is not applicable to valuing land. Capitalization of earnings often is used in valuing commercial real property. At times, an appraiser may use all three approaches.

Annuities, Interests for Life or a Term of Years, Reversions, Remainders. Actuarial tables are used to value annuities, interests for life or a term of years, reversions, and remainders included in the gross estate.[9] The same tables apply for both estate and gift tax purposes. (See Chapter C:12 for a discussion of the use of these tables.) The following example illustrates a situation when the actuarial tables must be used to value an inclusion in the decedent's estate.

EXAMPLE C:13-8 ▶ Tony gives property to a trust with a bank named as trustee and his cousin named to receive all of the trust income for the next 15 years (i.e., a term certain interest). At the end of the fifteenth year, the property reverts to Tony or his estate. Tony dies exactly four years after creating the trust, and the trust property is valued at $100,000 at Tony's death. At Tony's death, the trust has 11 years to continue until the property reverts to Tony's estate. The inclusion in Tony's estate is the value of a reversionary interest following a term certain interest with 11 remaining years. If 4% is the applicable rate, the reversionary interest is valued at $64,958 (0.649581 × $100,000) from Table B of the actuarial tables included in Appendix H. ◄

ALTERNATE VALUATION DATE

Section 2032 authorizes the executor to elect to value all property included in the gross estate at its FMV on the alternate valuation date. Congress enacted this provision in response to the stock market crash of 1929 to make sure that an entire estate could not be confiscated for taxes because of a sudden, substantial drop in values.

In general, the **alternate valuation date** is six months after the date of death. However, if the property is distributed, sold, exchanged, or otherwise disposed of within six months of the date of death, the alternate valuation date is the date of sale or other disposition.

EXAMPLE C:13-9 ▶ Ron died on March 3. Ron's estate included two items: stock and land. The estate still owned the stock on September 3, but the executor sold the land on August 20. If Ron's executor elected the alternate valuation date, the stock was valued as of September 3. The land, however, was valued as of August 20 because it was disposed of before the end of the six-month period. Of course, the value of land generally would change very little, if any, in such a short time period. ◄

6 Reg. Sec. 20.2031-2(e). As examples of cases dealing with the blockage discount, see *Horace Havemeyer v. U.S.*, 33 AFTR 1069, 45-1 USTC ¶10,194 (Ct. Cls., 1945); *Estate of Charles M. Prell*, 48 T.C. 67 (1967); and *Estate of David Smith*, 57 T.C. 650 (1972). The *Smith* case extended the blockage concept to large holdings of works of art.

7 1959-1 C.B. 237.

8 For a discussion of techniques for appraising real estate, see The Appraisal Institute, *The Appraisal of Real Estate*, 11th ed. (Arlington Heights, IL: The Appraisal Institute, 1996).

9 Section 7520 provides that the interest rate potentially changes every month. Regulation Sec. 20.7520-1(a)(2) provides these tables. An excerpt from these tables is included in Appendix H.

If the executor elects the alternate valuation date, generally any changes in value that occur *solely* because of a "mere lapse of time" must be ignored in determining the property's value.[10] In a limited number of situations, one must concentrate on the meaning of the phrase "the mere passage of time." For example, if the executor elects the alternate valuation date to value a patent, he or she must ignore any change in value attributable to the fact that the patent's remaining life is six months shorter on the alternate valuation date than it was on the date of death. Changes in value resulting from the invention of a competing patented product are relevant.

ADDITIONAL COMMENT

The limitation on the use of alternate valuation is especially important now that the exemption equivalent is $5 million, adjusted annually for inflation.

The alternate valuation date election can be made only if it decreases the value of the gross estate *and* the estate tax liability (after reduction for credits).[11] As a result of this provision, electing the alternate valuation date cannot produce a higher total step-up in basis. Congress enacted this strict rule because the alternate valuation date formerly offered a substantial tax planning advantage in situations where, because of the unlimited marital deduction, no estate tax was owed. If the property appreciated between the date of death and the alternate valuation date, the recipient could receive an increased basis if the executor elected the alternate valuation date.[12] Because of the unlimited marital deduction, the estate formerly could achieve an additional step-up in basis without increasing the estate tax liability.

Question: Joan died on December 1, 2017. Her estate consisted of three assets: an apartment building valued at $3.2 million on December 1, 2017, stock valued at $3.7 million on December 1, and $400,000 of cash. On June 1 of the next year, 1, the values were as follows: apartment building—$3.5 million, stock—$3.1 million, and cash of $400,000. Joan willed all her property to her son, who anticipates owning the property for a long time. The deductions for Joan's estate were negligible. Is there an estate tax benefit in electing the alternate valuation date? Is there an income tax benefit in electing the alternate valuation date?

Solution: An estate tax benefit results from using the alternate valuation date. The estate tax liability would be lower because the taxable estate would be $300,000 smaller if the alternate valuation date value ($7 million minus deductions) were used instead of the date of death value ($7.3 million minus deductions). Some income tax benefit also results from using the alternate valuation date. By using the alternate valuation date value, the tax basis for calculating cost recovery on the apartment building is $300,000 higher, ignoring any allocation of value to the land. However, a related detriment occurs because the basis of the stock is $600,000 lower with the alternate valuation date. If the son sells the stock soon after June 1, the $600,000 capital loss that would arise by using the date of death value would permit Joan's son to sell a number of highly-appreciated assets and offset up to a $600,000 capital gain with the $600,000 capital loss.

The Gross Estate: Inclusions

OBJECTIVE 3

Recognize which interests are includible in the gross estate

As Figure C:13-1 illustrates, the process of calculating the decedent's estate tax liability begins with determining the components of the gross estate. The **gross estate** is analogous to gross income. Once the components of the gross estate have been identified, they must be valued. As previously mentioned, the gross estate encompasses a much wider array of items than merely those to which the decedent held legal title at death. For example, under certain statutory provisions, referred to as the *transferor sections,* the gross estate includes items previously transferred by the decedent. For decedents other than nonresident aliens, the fact that property is located in a foreign country does not preclude it from being included in the gross estate. Table C:13-1 provides an overview of the inclusions in the gross estate.

[10] Reg. Sec. 20.2032-1(f).
[11] Sec. 2032(c).
[12] Sec. 1014(a).

▼ TABLE C:13-1
Inclusions in the Gross Estate

IRC Section	Type of Property or Transaction Included
2033	Property in which the decedent had an interest
2035	Gift taxes on property given away within three years of death plus certain property (primarily life insurance) given away within three years of death
2036	Property that the decedent transferred during life but in which the decedent retained economic benefits or the power to control enjoyment
2037	Property that the decedent transferred during life but for which the decedent has too large a reversionary interest
2038	Property that the decedent transferred during life but over which the decedent held the power to alter, amend, revoke, or terminate an interest
2039	Annuities
2040	Jointly owned property
2041	Property over which the decedent possessed a general power of appointment
2042	Life insurance on the decedent's life
2044	QTIP trust for which a marital deduction was claimed by the decedent's spouse

COMPARISON OF GROSS ESTATE WITH PROBATE ESTATE

The gross estate is a federal tax law concept, and the probate estate is a state law concept. To oversimplify, the **probate estate** can be defined as encompassing property that passes subject to the will (or under an intestacy statute) and is subject to court administration. Often, a decedent's gross estate is substantially larger than his or her probate estate. For example, suppose that at the time of death, a decedent owned a life insurance policy on his own life with his daughter as the beneficiary. The policy is not a part of the decedent's probate estate because the policy proceeds are payable directly to the named beneficiary (the daughter), but it is included in the gross estate.

Question: Karl died, and his executor included the following properties in Karl's gross estate: life insurance payable to the beneficiary, Karl's wife; savings account solely in Karl's name; land titled in the names of Karl and his son as joint tenants with right of survivorship; and a trust created under the will of Karl's mother. Karl had an income interest in the trust for his lifetime and complete power to designate the owners of the property on his death. With the exception of the trust assets (willed to his children), Karl's will left all his property to his beloved cousin, Karla. Which assets passed under the terms of Karl's will? Which assets did Karla receive?

Solution: This scenario illustrates the difference between the property included in a decedent's gross estate and in the probate estate. Karl's gross estate was larger than his probate estate. Only two assets included in his gross estate—the savings account and the trust property—passed under the terms of Karl's will. Karla received only the savings account because Karl willed the trust property to his children. The life insurance passed outside the will to the named beneficiary, the spouse, and the land passed outside the will to the surviving joint tenant, the son.

SELF-STUDY QUESTION

Which of the following properties will be included in (1) the probate estate, (2) the gross estate, (3) both the probate and gross estate, or (4) neither estate?

1. Real property held in joint tenancy with the decedent's spouse. (The answer is 2.)
2. Real property held as a tenant in common with the decedent's spouse. (The answer is 3.)
3. A life insurance policy owned by the decedent in which the decedent's spouse is named the beneficiary. (The answer is 2.)
4. A life insurance policy always owned by the decedent's spouse in which the decedent's children are named the beneficiaries. (The answer is 4.)

PROPERTY IN WHICH THE DECEDENT HAD AN INTEREST

Section 2033, sometimes called the *generic section,* provides that the gross estate includes the value of all property the decedent beneficially owned at the time of death. Its broad language taxes such items as a personal residence, an automobile, stocks, and any other asset titled in the decedent's name. Because the rule refers to beneficial ownership, however, its scope extends beyond assets to which the decedent held legal title. For example, such items as remainder interests also are included in the gross estate. In addition, income earned but uncollected prior to death is included.

EXAMPLE C:13-10 ▶ At the time of his death, Raj held the following assets in his name: personal residence, mountain cabin, Zero Corporation stock, checking account, and savings account. Raj beneficially owned each of these items when he died. Under Sec. 2033, each item was included in Raj's gross estate. ◀

EXAMPLE C:13-11 ▶ Ken's will named Ann to receive trust income for life and Raj or Raj's estate to receive the trust remainder upon Ann's death. Raj's gross estate, therefore, included the value of the remainder interest if Raj predeceased Ann because Raj's will controlled the passage of the remainder interest Raj beneficially owned. The transfer was associated with Raj's death, and, hence, was subject to the estate tax. ◀

DOWER OR CURTESY RIGHTS

Certain state laws provide wealth protection to surviving spouses through **dower** or **curtesy** rights. Dower is a widow's interest in her deceased husband's property, and curtesy is a widower's interest in his deceased wife's property. These rights entitle the surviving spouse to a certain portion of the decedent spouse's estate, even though the decedent may have willed a smaller portion to the spouse. Because the decedent spouse does not have complete control over the portion of his or her estate that is subject to dower or curtesy rights, some might think that the gross estate excludes the portion of the estate that the surviving spouse is entitled to receive. Thus, Congress made it crystal clear that the decedent's gross estate is not reduced for the value of the property in which the surviving spouse has a dower or curtesy interest or some other statutory interest.[13]

ADDITIONAL COMMENT

Any property that passes outright to the decedent's spouse, due to dower or curtesy rights under state law, is eligible for the marital deduction and will not increase the unified tax base.

EXAMPLE C:13-12 ▶ The laws of a certain state provide that widows are entitled to receive one-third of their deceased husband's property. The husband's gross estate includes his widow's dower rights (one-third interest) in his property. ◀

SELF-STUDY QUESTION

When Dorothy died on April 10, she owned Z Corporation bonds, which paid interest on April 1 and October 1, and stock in X and Y Corporations. X Corporation had declared a dividend on March 15 payable to stockholders of record on April 1. Y Corporation had declared a dividend on March 31 payable to stockholders of record on April 15. Dorothy's estate received the interest and dividends on the payment dates. Are any of the interest or dividends includible in Dorothy's gross estate?

ANSWER

The X Corporation dividend is included because the date of record preceded Dorothy's death. The Y Corporation dividend is not included because the date of record was after her death. The Z Corporation bond interest included is the interest that accrued between the April 1 payment date and the April 10 date of death.

TRANSFEROR PROVISIONS

Sections 2035 through 2038 are called the *transferor provisions*. They apply if, prior to death, the decedent made a transfer of a type specified in the IRC section in question, *and* the decedent did not receive adequate consideration in money or money's worth for the transferred interest. If one of the transferor provisions applies, the gross estate includes the transferred property at its date-of-death or alternate valuation date value.

Gifts Made Within Three Years of Death. Section 2035(a) specifies the circumstances in which a gift that a decedent makes within three years of death triggers an inclusion in the gross estate. The scope of this provision, which is relatively narrow, encompasses the following two types of transfers the donor-decedent made within three years before death:

- A life insurance policy on the decedent's life that would have been taxed under Sec. 2042 (life insurance proceeds received by the executor or for the benefit of the estate) had the policy not been given away, or
- An interest in property that would have been taxed under Sec. 2036 (transfers with a retained life estate), Sec. 2037 (transfers taking effect at death), or Sec. 2038 (revocable transfers) had it not been transferred.

Of these situations, the most common involves the insured's gifting a life insurance policy on his or her own life and dying within three years of the transfer. With new insurance policies, the potential for an inclusion can be avoided if the decedent never owns the new policy. In other words, instead of the insured purchasing a new policy and then giving it to a transferee as owner, the other party should buy the new policy. A common planning

[13] Sec. 2034.

technique involves a transfer of cash by an individual to a trust, and the trust (a life insurance trust) using the cash to purchase an insurance policy on the transferor's life.

EXAMPLE C:13-13 ► On April 1, 2014, Roy transferred to Sally ownership of a $400,000 life insurance policy on his own life purchased in 1997. Sally is the policy's beneficiary. Roy died on February 3, 2017. Because Roy died within three years of giving away the policy, the policy was included in Roy's gross estate. The estate tax value of the policy is its $400,000 face value. If Roy had died on April 2, 2017, the policy transfer would have fallen outside the three-year rule, and the policy would not have been included in Roy's gross estate. ◄

EXAMPLE C:13-14 ► Roy gave stock to Troy on May 1, 2016. Roy died on February 3, 2017. The stock was worth $80,000 on the gift date and $125,000 at the time of Roy's death. The gifted property was not included in Roy's gross estate because it is not life insurance on Roy's life, nor is it property that would have been taxed in Roy's estate under Secs. 2036 through 2038 had he kept such property. ◄

Gross-Up Rule. The donor-decedent's gross estate is increased by any gift tax that he or she, or his or her estate pays on any gift the decedent or his or her spouse makes during the three-year period ending with the decedent's death.[14] This provision, known as the gross-up rule, applies to the gift tax triggered by a gift of any type of property during the three-year look-back period.

The purpose of the gross-up rule is to foreclose the opportunity that existed under pre-1977 law to reduce one's gross estate (and thereby one's taxable estate) by removing the gift tax on "deathbed" gifts from the gross estate. Because the donor's estate received a credit for some or all of the gift tax paid, under the pre-1977 rules, a person on his or her deathbed in effect could prepay a portion of his or her estate tax and at the same time reduce his or her gross estate by the amount of the gift tax.

The gross-up rule, as illustrated in the two examples below, reinstates the estate to the position it would have been in had no gift tax liability been incurred.

EXAMPLE C:13-15 ► In December 2015, Cheron made her first gift, a $6 million taxable gift of stock, and paid a gift tax of $228,000 ($2,345,800 gross tax − $2,117,800 unified credit). Cheron died in March 2017. Cheron's gross estate did not include the stock, but it did include the $228,000 gift tax paid because she made the gift within three years of her death. ◄

EXAMPLE C:13-16 ► In December 2015, Hal gave Jody stock having a $12,028,000 FMV, and he and Wanda, his wife, elected gift splitting. Each was deemed to have made a $6 million [($12,028,000 ÷ 2) − $14,000 annual exclusion] taxable gift, and each paid $228,000 ($2,345,800 gross tax − $2,117,800 unified credit) of gift tax. Wanda died in March 2017. Wanda's gross estate included the $228,000 in gift tax she paid on the portion of her husband's gift that she was deemed to have made within three years of her death. Her cash balance declined because of paying the gift tax, and the gross-up for the tax reinstated her estate to the position it would have been in had she paid no gift tax. ◄

SELF-STUDY QUESTION

Refer to Example C:13-16. Assume that Hal, the spouse who actually made the gift, paid Wanda's $228,000 gift tax as well as his own $228,000 gift tax. Would Wanda's $228,000 gift tax be included in her gross estate?

ANSWER

No. It would not be included because tax paid from Hal's account did not reduce Wanda's cash balance.

Transfers with Retained Life Estate. Section 2036, although titled "Transfers with Retained Life Estate," extends beyond taxing solely lifetime transfers made by the decedent in which he or she retained a life estate (the right to income or use for life). The two primary types of transfers taxed under Sec. 2036 are those for which the decedent

- Kept possession or enjoyment of the property or the right to its income
- Retained the power to designate the person who is to possess or enjoy the property or to receive its income

Thus, Sec. 2036 applies when the transferor kept the income or enjoyment *or* the right to control other individuals' income or enjoyment.

The direct or indirect retention of voting rights in stock of a controlled corporation that the decedent transferred also can cause the gifted stock to be included in the

14 Sec. 2035(b).

transferor's gross estate.[15] A controlled corporation is one in which the decedent owned (directly, indirectly, or constructively), or had the right to vote, stock that possessed at least 20% of the voting power.[16]

The retention of income, control, or voting rights for one of the three retention periods listed below causes the transferred property to be included in the transferor's gross estate. The three periods are

- The transferor's lifetime
- A period that cannot be determined without referring to the transferor's death (e.g., the transferor retained the right to quarterly payments of income, but payments ceased with the last quarterly payment before the transferor's death)
- A period that does not end, in fact, before the transferor's death

An implied agreement or understanding is sufficient to trigger inclusion. For example, if a mother gives a residence to her daughter and continues to occupy the residence alone and rent-free, the residence probably will be included in the mother's gross estate under the argument that the parties had an implied understanding allowing the mother to reside in the residence for life without paying rent.

If Sec. 2036 applies to a transfer and if the decedent's retention of enjoyment or control extends to all the transferred property, 100% of the transferred property's value is included in the transferor's gross estate.[17] However, if the transferor keeps the right to only one-third of the income for life and retains no control over the remaining two-thirds, his estate includes just one-third of the property's date-of-death value. The following three examples illustrate some of the transactions that cause Sec. 2036 to apply.

EXAMPLE C:13-17 ▶ In 2009, David (age 30) transferred an office building to Ellen but retained the right to collect all the income from the building for life. David died in 2017. Because David retained the income right for life, the Sec. 2036 inclusion applied. The amount included was 100% of the building's date-of-death value. ◀

EXAMPLE C:13-18 ▶ Assume the same facts as in Example C:13-17 except that David retained the right to income for only 16 years. David died eight years after the transfer; therefore, David had the right to receive the income for the remaining eight-year period. Because the retention period did not *in fact* end before David's death, his gross estate included 100% of the property's date-of-death value. ◀

EXAMPLE C:13-19 ▶ Tracy created a trust with a bank as trustee and named Alice, Brad, and Carol to receive the trust income for their joint lives and Dick to receive the remainder upon the death of the first among Alice, Brad, or Carol to die. Tracy retained some control by reserving the right to designate the portion of the income to be paid to each income beneficiary each year. Only the transfer to Dick was a completed transfer and subject to gift taxes. Tracy predeceased the other parties. Because her control over the flow of income did not end before her death, the date-of-death value of the trust assets was included in Tracy's gross estate even though a portion of the transfer was subject to gift taxes. If Tracy had instead "cut the string" and not kept control over the income flow, she could have removed the trust property from her estate. ◀

SELF-STUDY QUESTION

Refer to Example C:13-19. Assume the same facts except that the trustee was directed to distribute its annual income equally to Alice, Brad, and Carol for their joint lives. Also assume that Tracy named Dick the remainderman. Was the value of the trust included in Tracy's gross estate?

ANSWER

No, because Tracy retained no power to control the enjoyment of the property.

Reversionary Interests. If, under the terms of the transfer, the chance exists that the property will pass back to the transferor the transferor has a **reversionary interest.** Under Sec. 2037, the transferor's gross estate includes earlier transferred property if the transferor stipulates that another person must survive him or her to own the property and the value of the decedent's reversionary interest exceeds 5% of the value of the transferred property. Actuarial techniques are used to value the reversionary interest.[18] Section 2037 does not apply if the value of the reversionary interest does not exceed the 5% *de minimis* amount.

EXAMPLE C:13-20 ▶ Beth transferred an asset to Tammy for life and then to Doug for life. The asset is to revert to Beth, if Beth is still alive, upon the death of either Tammy or Doug, whoever dies second. If Beth is not alive upon the death of the survivor of Tammy and Doug, the asset is to pass to Don or to

---

15 Sec. 2036(b)(1).

16 Sec. 2036(b)(2).

17 Reg. Sec. 20.2036-1(a).

18 The **reversionary interest** is the interest that will return to the transferor. Often, it will return only if certain contingencies occur. The value of Beth's reversionary interest in Example C:13-20 is a function of the present value of the interest Beth would receive after the deaths of Tammy and Doug, valued as from actuarial tables (see Appendix H), and coupled with the probability that Tammy and Doug would die before Beth.

a charitable organization if Don is not alive. Thus, Don must survive Beth to receive the property. Beth predeceases Tammy and Doug, and there is an inclusion in her estate if the value of her reversionary interest exceeds 5% of the property's value. The amount included is not the value of Beth's reversionary interest, but rather the date-of-death value of the asset less the value of Tammy's and Doug's intervening life estates. ◀

ADDITIONAL COMMENT

Sections 2036 through 2038 draw back into the gross estate certain previously transferred property and include it at its FMV on the date of the decedent's death. For income tax purposes, if the property has appreciated in value, donees will obtain a stepped-up basis rather than a carryover gift tax basis for property included in the gross estate.

Revocable Transfers. Section 2038 covers the rules for revocable transfers (i.e., revocable trusts). However, this provision also taxes all transfers over which the decedent has, at the time of his or her death, the power to change the enjoyment of property by altering, amending, revoking, or terminating an interest. Revocable trusts, sometimes called living trusts, are popular arrangements from a non-tax standpoint because assets held by a revocable trust pass outside of probate. Advantages of avoiding probate include lower probate costs and easier administration for real property located in a state that is not the decedent's state of domicile. In addition, unlike a will, a revocable trust is not a matter of public record.

Section 2038 can apply even though the decedent does not originally retain powers over the property. The crucial factor is that the transferor possesses the powers at the time of death regardless of whether the transferor retained such powers originally. The estate includes only the value of the interest that is subject to the decedent's power to change. Sections 2038 and 2036 overlap greatly, and if one amount is taxable under one section and a different amount is taxable under the other section, the gross estate includes the larger amount. Two types of transfers taxed by Sec. 2038 are illustrated in the following examples.

EXAMPLE C:13-21 ▶ Joe funded a revocable trust and named his son to receive the income for life and his grandson to receive the property upon the son's death. Because the trust was revocable, Joe could change the terms of the trust or take back the trust property during his lifetime. Joe's power to revoke the transfer extended to the entire trust. Thus, Joe's gross estate included the date-of-death value of the entire trust. ◀

EXAMPLE C:13-22 ▶ Vicki created a trust and irrevocably named Gina to receive the income for life and Matt to receive the remainder. Vicki, however, retained the right to substitute Liz (for Matt) as remainderman. When Vicki died, she had the authority to change the enjoyment of the remainder. Thus, the value of the trust's remainder interest was includible in Vicki's estate. ◀

ANNUITIES AND OTHER RETIREMENT BENEFITS

Section 2039 explicitly addresses the estate tax treatment of annuities. Even if this section had not been enacted, some annuities probably would have been taxable under the general language of Sec. 2033 because the decedent would have been viewed as having an interest in the property. For an annuity to be included in the gross estate, it must involve payments made under a contract or an agreement. In addition, the decedent must be receiving such payments at the time of his or her death or must have the right to collect such payments alone or with another person. If the annuity simply ceases with the death of the decedent in question, nothing is to be received by another party and nothing is included in the gross estate. For the payments to be included in the decedent's estate, they must be payable for the decedent's life, a period that may not be determined without referring to the decedent's date of death, or for a period that does not actually end before the decedent's death.

SELF-STUDY QUESTION

Reggie purchased an annuity and elected to collect benefits for 15 years. If Reggie dies before the end of the 15-year term of the annuity, his estate will be entitled to the remaining payments. Assume Reggie died after receiving nine payments. Will the value of the remaining six payments be included in Reggie's estate?

ANSWER

Yes. Section 2039 requires that the cost of a comparable contract of six payments be included in his gross estate.

Annuities Not Related to Employment. A person's purchase of an annuity designed to pay benefits to the purchaser and then to a named survivor upon the purchaser's death, or to both parties simultaneously and then to the survivor, is a form of wealth shifting. The survivor receives wealth that originates with the purchaser. This type of transfer differs from most other wealth transfers because it involves a series of annuity payments instead of a transfer of a tangible property.

The amount included in the gross estate with respect to annuities or other retirement benefits is a fraction (described below) of the value of the annuity or lump-sum payment to be received by the surviving beneficiary. Annuities are valued at the cost of a comparable contract.[19] To determine the inclusion in the gross estate, this cost is multiplied by a fraction that represents the portion of the purchase price the decedent contributed.

EXAMPLE C:13-23 ▶ Twelve years ago, Jim purchased a joint and survivor annuity and selected the payment option of benefits to be paid to himself and his son concurrently and then to the survivor for life. Jim and his son started collecting payments four years before Jim died, survived by his son. At the time of Jim's death, the cost of a comparable contract providing the same benefits was $180,000. Because Jim provided all the consideration to purchase the annuity, his gross estate included 100% of the $180,000 cost of a comparable contract. This annuity arrangement represents a shifting of wealth from Jim to his son upon Jim's death. ◀

SELF-STUDY QUESTION

On his retirement at age 65, Winslow elected to take a joint and survivor annuity from his qualified pension plan. The plan provided Winslow and his wife with a monthly pension of $7,500 until the death of the survivor. Winslow died seven years later. What amount (if any) was included in Winslow's gross estate if his wife survived?

ANSWER

The gross estate included the cost of a comparable contract providing $7,500 a month for the rest of the spouse's life. The younger the spouse, the higher the cost.

Employment-Related Retirement Benefits. Recall that, to determine the amount of an annuity includible in the decedent's gross estate, the cost of a comparable contract is multiplied by a fraction representing the portion of the purchase price contributed by the decedent. Section 2039(b) states that contributions from the decedent's employer (or former employer) are treated as contributions made by the decedent, provided such payments are made as a result of the employment relationship. Thus, 100% of the benefits from an employment-related annuity are included in the gross estate.

EXAMPLE C:13-24 ▶ Pat was employed by Wheel Corporation at the time of his death. Wheel Corporation maintains a qualified retirement plan to which it makes 60% of the contributions and its employees contribute 40%. Pat's spouse is to receive an annuity valued at $350,000 from the retirement plan. Because the employer's contributions are considered to have been made by the employee, Pat is deemed to have provided all the consideration for the retirement benefits. Consequently, Pat's gross estate includes 100% of the annuity's $350,000 date-of-death value. ◀

JOINTLY OWNED PROPERTY

Section 2040 addresses the estate tax treatment of jointly owned property (i.e., property owned in a joint tenancy with right of survivorship or tenancy by the entirety arrangement).[20] An important characteristic of this form of ownership is that, upon the death of one joint owner, the decedent's interest passes automatically (by right of survivorship) to the surviving joint owner(s). Thus, the property is not part of the probate estate and does not pass under the will. Section 2040 contains two sets of rules, one for property jointly owned by spouses and one for all other jointly owned properties.

Ownership Involving Persons Other than Spouses. When persons other than spouses or persons in addition to spouses own property as joint owners, the amount includible is determined by the consideration-furnished test.[21] Under this test, property is included in a joint owner's gross estate in accordance with the portion of the consideration he or she furnished to acquire the property. Obviously, this portion can range between 0% and 100%.

---

[19] Reg. Sec. 20.2031-8(a).

[20] Both joint tenancies with right of survivorship and tenancies by the entirety have the feature of survivorship. When one joint owner dies, his or her interest passes by right of survivorship to the remaining joint owner(s). Only spouses may use the tenancy by the entirety arrangement, whereas any persons may own as joint tenants with right of survivorship. A joint tenancy with right of survivorship may be severed by the action of any joint owner, whereas a tenancy by the entirety arrangement continues unless severed by the joint action of both joint owners.

The following definitions are from Henry Campbell Black, *Black's Law Dictionary*, Rev. 6th ed., Ed. by Joseph R. Nolan and Jacqueline M. Nolan-Haley (St. Paul, MN: West Publishing Co., 1990), p. 1465.

Joint tenancy with right of survivorship: The primary incident of joint tenancy is survivorship, by which the entire tenancy on the decease of any joint tenant remains to the survivors, and at length to the last survivor.

Tenancy by the entirety: A tenancy which is created between husband and wife and by which together they hold title to the whole with right of survivorship so that upon death of either, other takes whole to exclusion of deceased heirs. It is essentially a "joint tenancy" modified by the common-law theory that husband and wife are one person, and survivorship is the predominant and distinguishing feature of each. Neither party can alienate or encumber the property without the consent of the other.

[21] Sec. 2040(a).

EXAMPLE C:13-25 ▶ Seven years ago, Fred and Jack provided $10,000 and $30,000 of consideration, respectively, to purchase real property titled in the names of Fred and Jack as joint tenants with right of survivorship. Fred died and was survived by Jack. The real property was valued at $60,000. Fred's gross estate included $15,000 (0.25 × $60,000) because Fred furnished 25% of the consideration to acquire the property. If Jack instead predeceased Fred when the property was worth $60,000, his estate would have included $45,000 (0.75 × $60,000). ◀

ADDITIONAL COMMENT

The tracing rule is easy to understand but difficult to implement. Suppose a joint tenancy between a parent and a child was created and the parent paid for the property. The child died, and the parent is senile. Nothing should be included in the child's gross estate, but the burden of proof to keep a portion of the property out of the estate is on the estate.

If part of the consideration furnished by one joint tenant is originally received gratuitously from another joint tenant, the consideration is attributable to the joint tenant who made the gift. If all joint owners acquire their interests by gift, devise, bequest, or inheritance, the decedent joint owner's estate includes his or her proportionate share of the date-of-death value of the jointly owned property.

EXAMPLE C:13-26 ▶ Ray gave stock valued at $50,000 to Sam. Three years later Sam transferred this stock (now valued at $60,000) as partial consideration to acquire real property costing $120,000. Ray furnished the remaining $60,000 of consideration. The real property was titled in the names of Ray and Sam as joint tenants with right of survivorship. Because Sam received the asset that he used for consideration as a gift from Ray (the other joint tenant), Sam is treated as having furnished no consideration. If Sam dies before Ray, Sam's estate will include none of the real property's value. If Ray predeceases Sam, however, Ray's estate will include the entire date-of-death value. ◀

SELF-STUDY QUESTION

Fred and Myrtle, husband and wife, held title to their home in joint tenancy with right of survivorship. Fred died in an airplane crash. What part of the value of the residence was included in Fred's gross estate? Who will own the residence if Fred willed all his property to their children?

Ownership Involving Only Spouses. If spouses are the only joint owners, the property is classified as a **qualified joint interest**. Section 2040(b)(1) provides that, in the case of qualified joint interests, the decedent's gross estate includes one-half the value of the qualified joint interest. The 50% inclusion rule applies automatically regardless of the relative amount of consideration provided by either spouse.

EXAMPLE C:13-27 ▶ Wilma provided all the consideration to purchase stock costing $80,000. She registered the stock in her name and her husband's name as joint tenants with right of survivorship. The estate of the first spouse to die, regardless of which spouse it is, will include 50% of the value of the jointly owned stock. Upon the second spouse's death, all the property will be included in that spouse's gross estate because the property no longer is jointly owned property. ◀

ANSWER

One-half the value of the residence was included in Fred's gross estate. Myrtle will own the residence after Fred's death because Fred's interest passed to her by right of survivorship.

GENERAL POWERS OF APPOINTMENT

Section 2041 requires inclusion in the gross estate of certain property interests that the decedent never owned in a legal sense. Inclusion occurs because the decedent had the power to designate who eventually would own the property. The authority to designate the owner—a significant power—is called a power of appointment. Powers of appointment can be general or special (i.e., more restricted). By default, a power that is not general is classified as special.

Only a general power of appointment results in an addition to the gross estate. If a general power was created before October 22, 1942, however, no inclusion occurs unless the decedent exercised the power. For a post-1942 general power of appointment, inclusion occurs regardless of whether the power is exercised. A general power of appointment exists if the holder can exercise the power in favor of him- or herself, his or her estate or creditors, *or* the creditors of his or her estate. Being exercisable in favor of the decedent's estate means there is no restriction on the powerholder's ability to specify the person(s) to receive the property. The power may be exercisable during the decedent's life, by his or her will, or both.

EXAMPLE C:13-28 ▶ Kathy died in 2007, and her will created a trust from which Doris is to receive the income for life. In addition, Doris was granted the power to designate by will the person or persons to receive the trust's assets. Doris has a testamentary general power of appointment. The trust's assets are included in Doris's gross estate regardless of whether Doris exercises the power. If Kathy had instead died in 1940, Doris would have had a pre-1942 power of appointment. Such powers are taxed only if exercised. ◀

If a powerholder can exercise a power for only specified purposes and/or in favor of only certain persons such as children, the power is a special power. Appointment powers that can be exercised solely for purposes of the decedent's health, support, maintenance, or education are governed by a so-called "ascertainable standard" and also are free of estate tax consequences.

EXAMPLE C:13-29 ▶ Assume the same facts as in Example C:13-28 except that Kathy's will merely empowered Doris to name which of her descendants shall receive the trust assets. Doris now has only a special power of appointment because she does not have the power to leave the property to whomever she desires (e.g., the power to appoint the property to her estate). Because Doris's power of appointment (limited to her descendents) is only a special power, the value of the trust is not included in Doris's gross estate. ◀

LIFE INSURANCE

Section 2042 addresses the estate tax treatment of life insurance policies on the decedent's life. Life insurance policies owned by the decedent on the lives of others are taxed under the general language of Sec. 2033. According to Sec. 2042, a decedent's gross estate includes the value of policies on his or her own life if the proceeds are receivable by the executor or for the benefit of the estate, or if the decedent had any "incidents of ownership" in the policy at the time of death. Treasury Regulations list the following powers as a partial inventory of the incidents of ownership:

TYPICAL MISCONCEPTION

Many taxpayers who own life insurance policies on their own lives mistakenly believe that their estates will not owe estate taxes on the life insurance proceeds if they name someone other than their estate as the beneficiary. Life insurance will be included in the gross estate of the decedent if, at the time of death, the decedent held *any* (one) of the incidents of ownership in the policy.

- To change the beneficiary
- To surrender or cancel the policy
- To borrow against the policy
- To pledge the policy for a loan
- To revoke an assignment of the policy[22]

Examples in the regulations pertaining to incidents of ownership involve economic rights over the insurance policies. Judicial decisions also have been important in defining what constitutes incidents of ownership. In some jurisdictions, the phrase has been interpreted to be broader than simply relating to economic powers.[23]

If the decedent could have exercised the incidents of ownership only in conjunction with another party, the policy nevertheless is included in the gross estate. Moreover, it is the legal power to exercise ownership rights, not the practical ability to do so, that leads to an inclusion. The Supreme Court in the *Estate of Marshal L. Noel* emphasized the importance of the decedent-insured's legal versus practical powers in a situation where the insured was killed in a plane crash and the policies he owned on his life were on the ground in the possession of his spouse. The Court held that the decedent possessed incidents of ownership and thus the policies were includible in his gross estate.[24]

EXAMPLE C:13-30 ▶ Tracy purchased an insurance policy on her life, and several years later she transferred all her incidents of ownership in the policy to her daughter. Seven years after the transfer, Tracy died. Tracy's niece has always been the policy's beneficiary. The policy was not included in Tracy's gross estate because Tracy did not have any incidents of ownership in the policy at the time of her death, nor was her estate the beneficiary. (Also, she did not give the policy away within three years of death.) ◀

EXAMPLE C:13-31 ▶ Assume the same facts as in Example C:13-30 except that Tracy's estate instead was the policy's beneficiary. Because Tracy's estate was designated as the beneficiary, the policy was included in her gross estate and valued at its face value. ◀

It is not sufficient to consider only Sec. 2042 in determining whether a life insurance policy on the decedent's life is includible in the gross estate. Recall from the discussion earlier in this chapter that a life insurance policy is includible in a decedent's gross estate if the individual makes a gift of the life insurance policy on his or her own life within three years of dying.[25]

EXAMPLE C:13-32 ▶ Two years prior to his death, Peng gave all his incidents of ownership in a life insurance policy on his own life to his son, Phong. The face value of the policy is $400,000. Phong was

[22] Reg. Sec. 20.2042-1(c)(2).

[23] See, for example, *Estate of James H. Lumpkin, Jr. v. CIR*, 31 AFTR 2d 73-1381, 73-1 USTC ¶12,909 (5th Cir., 1973), wherein the court held that the right to choose how the proceeds were to be paid—in a lump sum or in installments—was an incident of ownership.

[24] *CIR v. Estate of Marshal L. Noel*, 15 AFTR 2d 1397, 65-1 USTC ¶12,311 (USSC, 1965).

[25] The gifted insurance policy is included under Sec. 2035(a)(2).

always the beneficiary. Because Peng died within three years of giving Phong the policy, Peng's gross estate included the policy, valued at its $400,000 date-of-death value. The potential problem of making a transfer of a life insurance policy within three years of death could have been avoided had Phong been the original owner of the policy. In that case, Peng would not have made a transfer and need not have been concerned with the three-year rule. ◀

TAX STRATEGY TIP

A very wealthy individual may be concerned that his or her estate will not have sufficient cash to pay its estate taxes. The individual could buy life insurance so his or her estate will have sufficient cash. However, if the individual owns the policy or names his or her estate the beneficiary, the proceeds of the policy will be taxed in the gross estate. In this case, the individual should have his or her children (or an irrevocable life insurance trust) buy the life insurance and name themselves the beneficiaries, even if the individual has to provide the funds for the premiums (by making gifts). If the children are the beneficiaries, they can use the policy proceeds to buy an asset from the estate so the estate can raise cash needed to pay the estate taxes.

CONSIDERATION OFFSET

Property is included in the gross estate at its FMV on the date of death or alternate valuation date. Section 2043 allows an offset against the amount included in the gross estate for consideration received in certain transactions.[26] This offset is allowed only if the decedent received some, but less than adequate, consideration in connection with an earlier transaction. The gross estate is reduced by an offset for the partial consideration received. The offset is for the actual dollars received, not for the pro rata portion of the cost paid by the decedent. This offset, called the consideration offset, serves the same function as a deduction in that it reduces the taxable estate. If the decedent receives consideration equal to the value of the property transferred, the property in question is not included in the gross estate. No offset is permitted if the property is excluded from the decedent's gross estate.

The consideration offset prevents a double counting of property in the decedent's estate. For example, if an individual makes a transfer that is includible in the gross estate and receives partial consideration in return, the consideration received is included in the gross estate unless it has been consumed. Sections 2035 through 2038 also require the transferred property to be included in the gross estate, even though the transferor does not own it at the date of death.

EXAMPLE C:13-33 ▶ Two years ago, Steve transferred a $300,000 life insurance policy on his life to Earl. The policy was worth $75,000 at the time of transfer, but Earl paid Steve only $48,000 consideration for the policy. Steve dies in the current year with the $48,000 still in his savings account. Steve's gross estate includes both the amount in the savings account and the $300,000 face value of the insurance policy. Under Sec. 2043, Steve's gross estate is reduced by the $48,000 consideration received on the transfer of the insurance policy. The insurance policy on Steve's life would be excluded from Steve's estate if Steve survived the transfer by more than three years, and no consideration offset would be permitted because the insurance is not included in the gross estate. ◀

RECIPIENT SPOUSE'S INTEREST IN QTIP TRUST

Recall from Chapter C:12 that a gift tax marital deduction is available for transferring qualified terminable interest property (QTIP) to one's spouse. A QTIP interest involves a transfer entitling the recipient spouse to all the income for life. The estate tax rules for QTIP interests are explained on page C:13-22. Claiming a marital deduction with respect to QTIP interests is voluntary. If the donor or the executor elects to claim a marital deduction for QTIP interests transferred to the spouse during life or at death, the transferred property generally is included in the recipient spouse's gross estate.[27] A QTIP interest included in the gross estate, like other property included in the gross estate, is valued at its date-of-death or alternate valuation date value.

The gross estate of the surviving spouse excludes the QTIP interest if the transferor spouse does not elect to claim a marital deduction. If the recipient spouse has a life estate, has no general power of appointment, and was not the transferor, no IRC sections other than Sec. 2044 (dealing with QTIPs) include the property in the gross estate.

QTIP interests for which a marital deduction was elected are not included in the gross estate if the recipient spouse disposes of all or a portion of his or her income interest during his or her lifetime. However, Sec. 2519 treats dispositions of all or a portion of a spouse's income interest in a QTIP as a transfer of all interests in the QTIP other than the qualifying income interest. Thus, such dispositions are subject to the gift tax.

---

[26] Section 2043 provides a consideration offset for items included in the gross estate under Secs. 2035 through 2038 and Sec. 2041.

[27] Sec. 2044.

EXAMPLE C:13-34 ▶ Henry died, and his will created a $3 million QTIP trust for his widow, Wendy, age 75. Henry's executor elected to claim a marital deduction for the QTIP trust. Wendy died five years later. By then, the assets in the QTIP trust had appreciated to $3.8 million. Wendy's gross estate included the QTIP trust, valued at $3.8 million. If Henry's executor had not claimed a marital deduction for the QTIP trust, the value of the trust would have been excluded from Wendy's estate. If Henry's executor had made a partial QTIP election for 70% of the trust, only 70% of the $3.8 million value would have been in Wendy's gross estate. ◀

DEDUCTIONS

OBJECTIVE 4

Identify the deductions available for estate tax purposes

As mentioned earlier in this chapter, deductions from the gross estate fall into five categories. Three of these categories (debts and funeral and administration expenses, casualty and theft losses, and state death taxes) allow the tax base to reflect the net wealth passed to the decedent's heirs, legatees, or devisees. Two other deduction categories reduce the estate tax base for transfers to the surviving spouse (the marital deduction) or to charitable organizations (the charitable contribution deduction). No deduction is available, however, for the amount of wealth diverted to the federal government for estate taxes. The aggregate amount of the deductions is subtracted from the gross estate amount to determine the taxable estate. Each deduction category is examined below. Table C:13-2 provides an overview of the estate tax deductions.

SELF-STUDY QUESTION

Compare the tax treatment for a mortgage compared with the accrued interest on a mortgage on a principal residence.

ANSWER

A mortgage and the accrued interest are deductible on the estate tax return as debts, and the accrued interest is also deductible on the estate's income tax return when paid.

DEBTS AND FUNERAL AND ADMINISTRATION EXPENSES

Section 2053 authorizes deductions for mortgages and other debts owed by the decedent, as well as for the decedent's funeral and administration expenses. Mortgages and all other debts of the decedent are deductible provided they represent bona fide contracts for an adequate and full consideration in money or money's worth. Even personal debts relating to an expenditure for which no income tax deduction would be allowable are deductible. Interest, state and local taxes, and trade or business expenses accrued at the date of death are deductible on both the estate tax return (as a debt of the decedent) and on the estate's income tax return (as an expense known as a deduction in respect of a decedent) when they are paid. (See Chapter C:14 for a discussion of the income tax implications.)

Examples of administration expenses include executor's commissions, attorneys' fees, court costs, accountants' fees, appraisers' fees, and expenses of preserving and distributing the estate. The executor must decide whether to deduct administration expenses on the estate tax return (Form 706) or the estate's income tax return (Form 1041). Such expenses cannot be deducted twice, although a portion may be deducted on the estate tax return and the rest on the estate's income tax return.

▼ **TABLE C:13-2**
Estate Tax Deductions

IRC Section	Type of Deduction
2053	Funeral and administration expenses[a] and debts
2054	Casualty and theft losses[a]
2055	Charitable contributions[b]
2056	Marital deduction[b]
2058	State death taxes[c]

[a]Administration expenses and losses are deductible on the estate tax return or on the estate's income tax return.
[b]No limit on deductible amount.
[c]Available as a deduction (instead of a credit) after 2004.

ADDITIONAL COMMENT

In addition to the 39.6% top income tax rate, an estate or trust can incur an incremental 3.8% on net investment income. The 3.8% rate applies to the lesser of undistributed net investment income or the excess (if any) of the entity's AGI over the dollar amount at which the highest tax bracket begins ($12,500 in 2017). Net investment income includes, among other things, interest, dividends, annuities, royalties, rents, and net gains from the disposition of certain property, all reduced by allocable deductions.

An estate that owes no estate tax (e.g., because of the unlimited marital deduction or the unified credit) should deduct administration expenses on its income tax return because no tax savings will result from a deduction on the estate tax return. If an estate owes estate taxes, its marginal estate tax rate will be 40% because this rate applies to tax bases exceeding $1 million. The highest income tax rate for an estate is 39.6% plus potentially 3.8% on net investment income. Thus, at times, the tax savings will be greater if the administration expenses are deducted on the income tax returns.

Funeral expenses are deductible only on the estate tax return. The estate may deduct any funeral expenses allowable under local law including "[a] reasonable expenditure for a tombstone, monument, or mausoleum, or for a burial lot, either for the decedent or his family, including a reasonable expenditure for its future care." The transportation costs of the person bringing the body to the burial place also are deductible as funeral expenses.[28]

EXAMPLE C:13-35 ▶ At Ed's date of death, he owed a $75,000 mortgage on his residence, plus $280 of interest accrued thereon, and $320 of personal expenditures charged to a credit card. The estate's administration expenses were $32,000. His funeral expenses totaled $12,000. Under Sec. 2053, Ed's estate could deduct $75,600 ($75,000 + $280 + $320) for debts and $12,000 for funeral expenses. The $32,000 of administration expenses are deductible on the estate tax return, on the estate's income tax return for the year in which they are paid, or some on each return. As Chapter C:14 points out, Ed's estate receives an income tax deduction for the accrued mortgage interest whenever it is paid. ◀

TAX STRATEGY TIP

The executor should elect to deduct any casualty or theft loss, when such loss is allowable, from the estate tax return if the marginal estate tax rate exceeds the estate's marginal income tax rate.

LOSSES

Section 2054 authorizes a deduction for losses incurred from theft or casualty while the estate is being settled. Just as in the context of the income tax, examples of casualties include fires, storms, and earthquakes. Any insurance compensation received affects the amount of the loss. If the alternate valuation date is elected, the loss may not be used to reduce the alternate value and then used again as a loss deduction. As with administration expenses, the executor must decide whether to deduct the loss on the estate tax return or the estate's income tax return. No double deduction is allowed for these losses, and the nondeductible floor applicable for income tax purposes does not exist for estate tax purposes.

EXAMPLE C:13-36 ▶ Sam dies on May 3, and one of the items included in Sam's gross estate is a mountain cabin valued at $125,000. The uninsured cabin is totally destroyed in a landslide on August 18. If the date-of-death valuation is chosen, the cabin is included in the gross estate at $125,000. The executor must choose between claiming a Sec. 2054 loss deduction on the estate tax return or a Sec. 165 casualty loss deduction on the estate's income tax return. ◀

EXAMPLE C:13-37 ▶ Assume the same facts as in Example C:13-36 except that Sam's executor elects the alternate valuation date. The cabin is valued at zero when determining the value of the gross estate. No loss deduction is available for the casualty on the estate tax return. Likewise, the estate cannot claim an income tax deduction for the casualty loss because the property's adjusted basis in its hands is zero. ◀

CHARITABLE CONTRIBUTION DEDUCTION

Section 2055 authorizes a deduction for transfers to charitable organizations. The rules concerning eligible donee organizations are the same as for gift tax purposes.

Because the estate tax charitable contribution deduction is unlimited, a decedent could eliminate his or her estate tax liability by willing all his or her property (or all property except for an amount equal to the exemption equivalent) to a charitable organization. Similarly, a decedent could eliminate an estate tax liability by willing an amount equal to the exemption equivalent to the children and the rest of the estate to the surviving spouse and a charitable organization (e.g., in equal shares).[29] People who desire to leave some property to a charity at their death should be encouraged to consider giving the property before death, so they can obtain an income tax deduction for the gift and also reduce their gross estate by the amount of the gift.

---

[28] Reg. Sec. 20.2053-2.

[29] Another way the estate could owe no taxes is if all of the property, or all of the property except for the exemption equivalent, is shielded from taxation by the marital deduction.

Computing the Deduction. In certain circumstances, computation of the estate tax charitable contribution deduction can be somewhat complicated. Suppose the decedent (a widow) has an $11 million gross estate and no Sec. 2053 or 2054 deductions. The decedent's will specifies that her son is to receive $8 million and a charitable organization is to receive the residue (the rest not explicitly disposed of). Assume that state law specifies that death taxes are payable from the residue. Because $8 million of property passes to the decedent's child, the estate will definitely owe some estate taxes. The charitable organization will receive $3 million, less the estate taxes payable from the residue. The estate tax liability depends on the amount of the charitable contribution deduction, which in turn depends on the amount of the estate tax liability. Simultaneous equations are required to calculate the charitable contribution deduction.[30]

EXAMPLE C:13-38 ▶ Ahmed, a widower, died with a gross estate of $9 million. Ahmed willed State University $1 million and the residue of his estate to his children. Under state law, death taxes are payable from the residue. In this scenario, Ahmed's estate receives a charitable contribution deduction for $1 million because the estate taxes were charged against the children's share (the residue). ◀

Split-Interest Transfers. If the decedent's will provides for a split-interest transfer (i.e., a transfer of interests to both an individual and a charitable organization), the rules concerning whether a charitable contribution deduction is available are very technical. Basically, the rules are the same as for gift tax purposes (discussed in Chapter C:12).

EXAMPLE C:13-39 ▶ Jane dies with a gross estate of $8 million. In 2005, she gave City Art Museum a remainder interest in her personal residence but retained the right to live there rent-free for the rest of her life. Upon Jane's death, no other individuals have an interest in the residence. Jane received an income tax deduction in 2005 for the value of the remainder interest and incurred no gift tax liability. Under Sec. 2036, Jane's gross estate includes her residence (in which she retained a life estate), valued at $350,000 at her death. Her estate receives a $350,000 charitable contribution deduction.

Her lifetime transfer triggers no added estate tax cost. The residence is included in her gross estate, but the inclusion is a wash because of the estate tax charitable contribution deduction allowed for the value of the residence. ◀

MARITAL DEDUCTION

The fourth category of deductions is the marital deduction for certain property passing to the surviving spouse.[31] Because the marital deduction is unlimited, the decedent's estate does not owe any federal estate taxes if all the items includible in the gross estate (or all items except an amount equal to the exemption equivalent) pass to the surviving spouse.[32] If the surviving spouse is not a U.S. citizen, a marital deduction is available only if the decedent's property passes to a special trust called a qualified domestic trust.

The marital deduction helps provide equal treatment for decedents of common law and community property states because marital property is treated differently under each type of state law. In community property states, for example, a large portion of the assets acquired after marriage constitute community property (i.e., property owned equally by each spouse). On the other hand, in common law states, one spouse may own the majority of the assets acquired after marriage. Thus, with no marital deduction and no portability election (discussed on Page C:13-24), the progressive estate tax rates could cause the combined estate tax liability to be higher for a couple living in a noncommunity property state. Nevertheless, a marital deduction is available to decedents who own nothing but community property.

TAX STRATEGY TIP

The marital deduction defers the estate tax until the death of the surviving spouse and protects against liquidity problems when the first spouse dies. Moreover, the surviving spouse can reduce the overall estate tax through personal consumption and a lifetime gifting program.

Under the Supreme Court's 2013 decision in *U.S. v. Windsor*,[33] same-sex spouses qualify for the marital deduction. In *Obergefell v. Hodges et al.*,[34] the Supreme Court concluded that all states must allow same-sex couples to marry and must recognize marriages of same-sex couples validly performed in other states.

---

[30] The simultaneous equation problem generally does not occur if a charity receives a bequest of a specific dollar amount. See Reg. Sec. 20.2055-3 for a discussion of death taxes payable from charitable transfers.

[31] Sec. 2056.

[32] Some states have not adopted an unlimited marital deduction; therefore, some estates may owe state death taxes even though no federal liability would otherwise exist. Payment of a substantial amount of state taxes will reduce the amount passing to the spouse as a marital deduction and can cause federal taxes to be owed.

[33] 111 AFTR2d 2013-2385, 2013-2 USTC 50,400 (USSC, 2013). Also see page C:12-5. Reg. Sec. 301.7701-18(b)(1) states that, in general, "a marriage of two individuals is recognized for federal tax purposes if the marriage is recognized by the state, possession, or territory of the United States in which the marriage is entered into, regardless of domicile." *Obergefell* (decided in 2015) requires states to recognize such marriages.

[34] 15 AFTR2d 2015-2309, 2015-1 USTC ¶50,357 (USSC, 2015).

Only certain transfers to the surviving spouse are eligible for the marital deduction. The estate does not receive a marital deduction unless the interest conveyed to the surviving spouse will be included in the recipient spouse's gross estate or will be subject to the gift tax if transferred while the surviving spouse is alive.

The following three tests must be met before an interest qualifies for the marital deduction:

- The property must be included in the decedent's gross estate.
- The property must pass to the recipient spouse in a qualifying manner.
- The interest conveyed must not be a nondeductible terminable interest.

Test 1: Inclusion in the Gross Estate. No property passing to the surviving spouse is eligible for the marital deduction unless the property is included in the decedent's gross estate. The reason for this rule is obvious: Assets excluded from the gross estate cannot generate a deduction.

EXAMPLE C:13-40 ► Gail is insured under a life insurance policy for which her husband, Al, is the beneficiary. Gail's sister always had the incidents of ownership in the policy. Even though the insurance proceeds are payable to Al, Gail's estate receives no marital deduction for the insurance. The policy is excluded from Gail's gross estate because she had no incidents of ownership, her estate was not the beneficiary, and the policy was not transferred within three years of her death. Gail held the title to the personal residence in which she and Al lived. She willed the residence to Al, and the residence qualifies for the marital deduction. ◄

Test 2: The Passing Requirement. Property is not eligible for the marital deduction unless it passes to the decedent's spouse in a qualifying manner. According to Sec. 2056(c), property is deemed to pass from one spouse to the other if the surviving spouse receives the property because of

- A bequest or devise under the decedent's will
- An inheritance resulting from the decedent dying intestate
- Dower or curtesy rights
- An earlier transfer from the decedent
- Right of survivorship
- An appointment by the decedent under a general power of appointment or in default of appointment
- A designation as the beneficiary of a life insurance policy on the decedent's life

In addition, a surviving spouse's interest in a retirement benefit plan is considered to have passed from the decedent to the survivor to the extent the retirement benefits are included in the gross estate.[35]

Test 3: The Terminable Interest Rule. The third statutory test (also applicable for gift tax purposes) requires that the recipient-spouse's interest *not* be classified as a nondeductible terminable interest.[36] A terminable interest is one that ceases with the passage of time or the occurrence of some event. Some terminable interests qualify for the marital deduction, however, because only *nondeductible* terminable interests fail to generate a marital deduction. Nondeductible terminable interests have the following features:

- An interest in the property must pass or have passed from the decedent to a person other than the surviving spouse, and such person must have paid less than adequate consideration in money or money's worth.
- The other person may possess or enjoy any part of the property after the termination of the surviving spouse's interest.

[35] Reg. Sec. 20.2056(e)-1(a)(6).

[36] Nondeductible terminable interests also are precluded from eligibility for the marital deduction for gift tax purposes.

Thus, if the decedent makes a transfer granting the surviving spouse the right to receive all the income annually for life and a general power of appointment over the property, the property is eligible for the marital deduction. As discussed below, the QTIP provisions allow a marital deduction for certain transfers that otherwise would be disqualified under the nondeductible terminable interest rule.

EXAMPLE C:13-41 ▶ Louis wills a copyright with a ten-year remaining legal life to his wife, Tina, age 42. His will also sets up a trust for the benefit of Tina, whom he entitles to receive all of the income semiannually until the earlier of her remarriage or her death. Upon Tina's remarriage or death, the trust property is to be distributed to the couple's children or their estates. Both the copyright and the trust are terminable interests. The copyright is eligible for the marital deduction because it is not a nondeductible terminable interest; the copyright simply ends at the expiration of its legal life. No person other than Tina receives an interest in the copyright. No marital deduction is available for the trust because it is a nondeductible terminable interest. Upon the termination of Tina's interest, which will occur if she remarries, the children will possess the property, and they will receive their interests from Louis without paying adequate consideration. ◀

SELF-STUDY QUESTION

A decedent, by will, creates a trust with income to the surviving spouse for 25 years, the remainder to their children. The surviving spouse's life expectancy is 16 years. Does the property qualify for the marital deduction?

ANSWER

The property does not qualify because the surviving spouse's interest terminates at the end of a specified number of years. The spouse's shorter life expectancy is irrelevant.

QTIP Transfers. Section 2056(b)(7) authorizes a marital deduction for transfers of qualified terminable interest property (called QTIP transfers). The QTIP provisions are somewhat revolutionary compared with earlier law because they allow a marital deduction in situations where the recipient spouse holds no power to designate which parties eventually receive the property.

Qualified terminable interest property is defined as property that passes from the decedent, in which the surviving spouse has a qualifying income interest for life, and to which an election applies. A spouse has a qualifying income interest for life if the following are true:

- He or she is entitled to all the income from the property, payable at least annually.
- No person has a power to appoint any portion of the property to anyone other than the surviving spouse unless the power cannot be exercised during the spouse's lifetime (e.g., it is exercisable only at or after the death of the surviving spouse).

Claiming the marital deduction with respect to QTIP transfers is not mandatory, and partial elections also are allowed. In the event the executor elects to claim a marital deduction for 100% of the QTIP transfer, the marital deduction is for the entire amount of the QTIP transfer. In other words, the deduction is not limited to the value of the surviving spouse's life estate.

If the marital deduction is elected in the first spouse's estate, the property is taxed in the surviving spouse's estate under Sec. 2044 or is subject to the gift tax in such spouse's hands if disposed of during the spouse's lifetime.[37] Thus, as with other interspousal transfers, the QTIP provisions allow a postponement of the taxable event until the second spouse dies or disposes of the interest by gift. If the taxable event is postponed, the property is valued at its FMV as of the date the second spouse transfers the property by gift or at death.

SELF-STUDY QUESTION

How does the donor spouse or decedent spouse who establishes a QTIP trust control the disposition of the trust corpus?

ANSWER

The donor or decedent spouse states in the trust instrument or in his or her will who will receive the remainder interest on the death of the recipient spouse.

EXAMPLE C:13-42 ▶ Tom died several years ago, survived by his wife, Mary. Tom's will called for setting up a $1 million trust from which Mary receives all the income quarterly for the rest of her life. Upon Mary's death, the property is to be distributed to Tom's children by a previous marriage. If Tom's executor elected to claim a marital deduction, Tom's estate received a $1 million marital deduction. At Mary's death, the trust assets are valued at $2.2 million. Section 2044 includes $2.2 million in Mary's gross estate. If Tom's executor forgoes electing the marital deduction, Mary's gross estate excludes the value of the trust. In either event, the trust assets will be taxed in the estate of one of the spouses, but not both. ◀

ADDITIONAL COMMENT

Refer to Example C:13-42. The executor may elect QTIP status for less than the entire property in the trust. For example, the executor might elect QTIP treatment for only 60% of the $1 million placed in the trust. On Mary's death, 60% of $2.2 million, or $1.32 million, is included in Mary's gross estate.

State Death Taxes. For estates of decedents dying after 2004, Sec. 2058 allows a deduction for state death taxes. Eligible taxes include estate, inheritance, legacy, and succession taxes paid to a state or the District of Columbia. The taxes must be paid no later than four years after the filing of the estate tax return. The amount of the deduction is the amount paid and, unlike the state death tax credit formerly available, is not restricted to a maximum amount.

---

[37] Section 2519 states that, if a recipient spouse disposes of a qualifying income interest for life for which the donor or the executor elected a marital deduction under the QTIP rules, the recipient spouse is treated as having made a gift of everything except the qualifying income interest. Under the generic gift rules of Sec. 2511, the gift of the income interest is treated as a gift.

Computation of Tax Liability

OBJECTIVE 5

Calculate the estate tax liability

As mentioned earlier, the estate tax base is the aggregate of the decedent's taxable estate and his or her adjusted taxable gifts. Figure C:13-1 earlier in this chapter illustrates how the estate tax formula combines these two concepts.

TAXABLE ESTATE AND TAX BASE

The gross estate's value is reduced by the deductions to arrive at the amount of the taxable estate. Under the unification provisions effective after 1976, the estate tax base consists of the taxable estate plus the adjusted taxable gifts, defined as *all taxable* gifts made *after 1976 other than* gifts included in the gross estate. If the decedent elects gift splitting (discussed in Chapter 12), the decedent's adjusted taxable gifts equal the amount of the taxable gifts the individual is deemed to have made after applying the gift-splitting provisions. Adjusted taxable gifts can arise from consenting to gift splitting, even though the decedent never actually gives away any property.

Adjusted taxable gifts are valued at date-of-gift values; therefore, any post-gift appreciation is exempt from the transfer taxes. The estate tax computations for decedents who never made gifts exceeding the excludable amount reflect no adjusted taxable gifts.

SELF-STUDY QUESTION

Verda died penniless in 2017. Because of consenting to gift splitting, her taxable gifts for 1999 were $1.75 million. She paid $457,000 of gift taxes on these gifts. What was her unified tax base?

ANSWER

Her unified tax base was $1.75 million, the amount of her lifetime taxable gifts. Note that the gifts are valued at what they were worth on the date of the gift.

TENTATIVE TAX AND REDUCTION FOR POST-1976 GIFT TAXES

The tentative tax is computed on the estate tax base, which is the sum of the taxable estate and the adjusted taxable gifts, if any.[38] The unified transfer tax rates are found in Sec. 2001(c) and are reproduced on the inside back cover. The tentative tax is reduced by the decedent's post-1976 gift taxes. In determining the tax on post-1976 taxable gifts, the effect of gift splitting is taken into consideration. That is, the amount of the post-1976 gift taxes is usually the levy imposed on the taxable gifts the decedent is deemed to have made after applying any gift-splitting election.

If the tax rates change between the time of the gift and the time of death, the subtraction for gift taxes equals the amount of gift taxes that *would have been payable* on post-1976 gifts had the rate schedule applicable in the year of death been in effect in the year of the gift. In addition to the "as if" computation for the gross tax amount, current rates are used to calculate the unified credit to be subtracted in determining the amount of gift tax that would have been payable.

SELF-STUDY QUESTION

Refer to the previous self-study question. What was the amount of the unified tax before credits? After credits?

ANSWER

The unified tax before credits was $645,800. This tax was reduced by the unified credit of $2,141,800 and by post-1976 gift taxes, which leaves zero tax due. Verda's unified tax base of $1.75 million was below the $5.49 million exemption equivalent for 2017.

UNIFIED CREDIT

The excess of the tentative tax over the post-1976 gift taxes is reduced by the unified credit. The amount of this credit has changed over the years (see inside back cover). If a decedent died in 2010 and the executor opted to incur the estate tax and obtain a FMV basis, the unified credit was $1,730,800, the tax on $5 million at a 35% top rate. In both the estate and gift tax context for 2011, the unified credit was $1,730,800, the tax on $5 million at a 35% top rate. In 2012, the $5 million amount became indexed for inflation, and the credit that year was $1,772,800, the tax on $5.12 million at the top rate of 35%. Beginning in 2013, the top rate rose to 40%, and the credit for 2013 was $2,045,800, the tax on $5.25 million. For 2015, the credit was $2,117,800, the tax on $5.43 million, for 2016 the credit was $2,125,800, the tax on $5.45 million, and for 2017 the credit is $2,141,800, the tax on $5.49 million. The unified credit never generates a refund; the most relief it can provide is to eliminate an estate's federal estate tax liability.

Section 2010(c) provides that the unified credit otherwise available for estate tax purposes must be reduced in certain situations. Before 1977, a $30,000 lifetime exemption was available for the gift tax. Donors could claim some or all of this exemption whenever they desired. For post-1976 years, Congress repealed the exemption and replaced it with the unified credit. If the decedent claimed any portion of the $30,000 exemption against gifts made after September 8, 1976, and before January 1, 1977, the unified credit must be reduced by 20% of the exemption claimed.

---

38 Sec. 2001(b).

EXAMPLE C:13-43 ▶ Carl died in 2017 with a tax base of $6 million. In October 1976, Carl made his first taxable gift and claimed the $30,000 exemption to reduce the amount of his taxable gifts. Thus, Carl's $2,141,800 unified credit is reduced by $6,000 (0.20 × $30,000). If Carl claimed the exemption by making a gift on or before September 8, 1976, his estate would have been entitled to the full $2,141,800 credit. ◀

PORTABILITY BETWEEN SPOUSES OF EXEMPTION AMOUNT

Prior to 2011, both a husband and wife had estate tax exemption amounts that could be used only by that individual. For example, in 2009, when the exempt amount was $3.5 million, the husband could use $3.5 million at his death, and the wife could use $3.5 million at her death. This situation was the case even if one spouse's estate tax base was much smaller than $3.5 million and the other spouse's estate was considerably larger than $3.5 million. For many years, a number of larger estates used a technique called "credit shelter trusts" or "bypass trusts" to make sure that $3.5 million (the 2009 amount) or the relevant amount for the year of death passed in such a way as to take advantage of the unified credit. The Tax Relief Act added flexibility and made the basic exclusion amount portable between spouses for 2011 and 2012, and ATRA 2012 made this provision permanent. As a result, any nontaxable amount that remains unused at the first spouse's death can be used by the second spouse. This concept, called portability, applies only if the executor elects it. If a surviving spouse was predeceased by more than one spouse who died after 2010, the surviving spouse can use the unused exemption amount of only the last deceased spouse. The portable amount is called the "deceased spousal unused exclusion amount." As a result of the Supreme Court's decision in *Windsor*, same-sex spouses qualify for the benefits of portability.

EXAMPLE C:13-44 ▶ Joe died early in 2012 with a taxable estate of $2.12 million. He is survived by his spouse, Joanne. Joe's executor elected portability. Thus, Joe's remaining $3 million ($5,120,000 − $2,120,000) basic exclusion amount is added to Joanne's $5 million (ignoring indexing), so she now has an exclusion amount of $8 million (again ignoring indexing). The amount portable from Joe is not indexed. ◀

EXAMPLE C:13-45 ▶ Joanne from the previous example married Karl late in 2012. Karl died in July 2013 with a taxable estate of $12 million. Thus, Karl has no unused exemption. If Joanne dies in December 2017, her basic exclusion amount will be $5.49 million as she cannot use Joe's remaining basic exclusion amount because Joe is not Joanne's last deceased spouse. ◀

OTHER CREDITS

The IRC authorizes three additional credits: a gift tax credit on pre-1977 gifts, a credit for another decedent's estate taxes paid on prior transfers, and a credit for foreign death taxes. (Prior to 2005, the IRC also allowed a state death tax credit.) These credits apply less often than the unified credit. Like the unified credit, these credits cannot exceed the amount of the estate tax actually owed.

Pre-2005 State Death Tax Credit. For many years, all states levied some form of death tax: an inheritance tax, an estate tax, or both. Many states enacted a simple system whereby the state death tax liability equaled the credit for state death taxes allowed on the federal estate tax return.

Prior to 2005, Sec. 2011 allowed a credit calculated in accordance with the table contained in Sec. 2011(b). As mentioned earlier, beginning in 2005, a deduction replaced the credit. Consequently, if a jurisdiction had earlier imposed a state death tax that was equal to the credit allowed on the federal return for state death taxes, no state death tax will be owed after 2004 *unless* that jurisdiction changes its tax rules.

EXAMPLE C:13-46 ▶ John died in 2017 with a taxable estate of $6 million. He resided in a state whose statute imposes an estate tax equal to the credit available on the federal return for state death taxes, his estate owed nothing to the state. In effect, his state no longer has an estate tax. On the other hand, if he resided in a state that levies an inheritance tax based on the value of the property the various heirs receive, his estate received a deduction (not a credit) for the inheritance tax paid. ◀

Credit for Pre-1977 Gift Taxes. Section 2012(a) authorizes a credit for gift taxes paid by the decedent on pre-1977 gifts that must be included in the gross estate. Remember that Sec. 2001(b)(2) allows a reduction for gift taxes paid on post-1976 gifts, but the IRC does not refer to this item as a credit.

In general, the credit for pre-1977 gift taxes equals the amount of gift taxes paid with respect to transfers included in the gross estate. Because of a ceiling rule, however, the amount of the credit sometimes is lower than the amount of gift taxes paid. A discussion of the ceiling computation is beyond the scope of this text.

Credit for Tax on Prior Transfers. The credit available under Sec. 2013 for the estate taxes paid on prior transfers reduces the cost of having property taxed in more than one estate in quick succession. Without this credit, the overall tax cost could be quite severe if the legatee dies soon after the original decedent. The credit applies if the person who transfers the property (i.e., the transferor-decedent) to the decedent in question (i.e., the transferee-decedent) dies no more than ten years before, or within two years after, the date of the transferee-decedent's death. The potential credit is the smaller of the federal estate tax of the transferor-decedent attributable to the transferred interest or the federal estate tax of the transferee-decedent attributable to the transferred interest.

To determine the final credit, the potential credit is multiplied by a percentage that varies inversely with the period of time separating the two dates of death. If the transferor dies no more than two years before or after the transferee, the credit percentage is 100%. As specified in Sec. 2013(a), the other percentages are as follows:

Number of Years by Which Transferor's Death Precedes the Transferee's Death	*Credit Percentage*
More than 2, but not more than 4	80
More than 4, but not more than 6	60
More than 6, but not more than 8	40
More than 8, but not more than 10	20

EXAMPLE C:13-47 ▶ Mary died on March 1, 2012. All of Mary's property passed to Debra, her daughter. Debra died on June 1, 2017. All of Debra's property passed to her son. Both Mary's and Debra's estates paid federal estate taxes. Debra's estate was entitled to a credit for a percentage of some, or all, of the taxes paid by Mary's estate. Because Mary's death preceded Debra's death by five years and three months, the credit for the tax paid on prior transfers was 60% of the potential credit. ◀

EXAMPLE C:13-48 ▶ Ed died on August 7, 2015. One of the items included in Ed's estate was a life insurance policy on Sam's life. Sam gave Ed all his incidents of ownership in this policy on December 13, 2014. Sam died on June 15, 2017, within three years of making a gift of the insurance policy on his own life. The policy was included in Sam's gross estate under Sec. 2035. Because Sam died within two years of Ed's death, Ed's estate was entitled to a credit for 100% of the potential credit and an amended return had to be filed to claim this credit. ◀

SELF-STUDY QUESTION

What is the effect of the maximum credit provision for the foreign death tax credit?

ANSWER

The effect is to tax the property located in the foreign country at the higher of the U.S. estate tax rate or the foreign death tax rate.

Foreign Death Tax Credit. Under Sec. 2014, the estate is entitled to a credit for some or all of the death taxes paid to a foreign country for property located in that foreign country and included in the gross estate. The maximum credit is the smaller of the foreign death tax attributable to the property located in the foreign country that imposed the tax or the federal estate tax attributable to the property located in the foreign country and taxed by such country.

COMPREHENSIVE ILLUSTRATION

The following comprehensive illustration demonstrates the computation of the estate tax liability.

ADDITIONAL COMMENT

This illustration pertains to 2016 because tax forms for that year are the latest available at the time this textbook was published.

Background Data. Herman Estes died on October 13, 2016. Herman, a Florida resident, was survived by his widow, Ann, and three adult children. During his lifetime, Herman made two gifts, as follows:

- In 1978, he gave his daughter, Dotty, $203,000 cash. He claimed a $3,000 annual exclusion available then and thus made a $200,000 taxable gift on which he paid a $20,800 gift tax, after claiming the $34,000 unified credit.
- In April 2015, he gave his son, Johnny, stock then worth $6,514,000. Herman claimed a $14,000 annual exclusion and thus made a $6.5 million taxable gift. He claimed the available unified credit of $2,083,800 ($2,117,800 − $34,000) and paid $487,200 ($2,571,000 − $2,083,800) gift tax. On October 13, 2016, the stock was worth $6.75 million.

Property discovered after Herman's death appears below. All amounts represent date-of-death values.

- Checking account containing $19,250.
- Savings account containing $75,000.
- Land worth $440,000 held in the names of Herman and Ann, joint tenants with right of survivorship (JTWROS). Herman provided all the consideration to buy the land in January 1993.
- Life insurance policy 123-A with a face value of $200,000. Herman had incidents of ownership; son Johnny is the beneficiary.
- A personal residence titled in Herman's name worth $325,000.
- Stock in Ajax Corporation worth $4.4 million.
- Qualified pension plan to which Herman's employer made 60% of the contributions and Herman made 40%. Ann is to receive a lump-sum distribution of $240,000.
- A trust created under the will of Herman's mother, Amelia, who died in 1999. Herman was entitled to receive all the income quarterly for life. In his will, Herman could appoint the trust assets to such of his descendants as he desired. The trust assets are valued at $375,000.

At his death, Herman owes a $25,200 bank loan, including $200 accrued interest. Balances due on his various credit cards total $6,500. Herman's funeral expenses are $15,000, and his administration expenses are $70,000. Assume the maximum tax savings will occur by deducting the administration expenses on the estate tax return instead of on the estate's income tax return.

Herman's will contains the following provisions:

- "To my wife, Ann, I leave my residence, my savings account, and $10,000 from my checking account."
- "I leave $200,000 of property in trust with First Bank as trustee. My wife, Ann, is to receive all the income from this trust fund quarterly for the rest of her life. Upon Ann's death, the trust property is to be divided equally among our three children."
- "To the American Cancer Society I leave $10,000."
- "I appoint the property in the trust created by my mother, Amelia Estes, to my daughter, Dotty."
- "The residue of my estate is to be divided equally between my sons, Johnny and Billy."

Calculation of Tax Liability. Table C:13-3 illustrates the computation of Herman's estate tax liability. These same facts are used for the sample Estate Tax Return (Form 706) included in Appendix B. For illustration purposes, it is assumed that the executor elects to claim the marital deduction on the QTIP trust and that the laws for Florida levy death taxes equal to the maximum federal credit for state death taxes. As mentioned earlier, after 2004 an estate receives a deduction instead of a credit for state death taxes. Thus, because the federal government does not allow a credit for state death taxes, Herman's estate owes nothing to the state.

▼ **TABLE C:13-3**
Comprehensive Estate Tax Illustration

Gross estate:	
Checking account (Sec. 2033)	$ 19,250
Savings account (Sec. 2033)	75,000
Land held in joint tenancy with wife (0.50 × $400,000) (Sec. 2040)	220,000
Life insurance (Sec. 2042)	200,000
Personal residence (Sec. 2033)	325,000
Ajax stock (Sec. 2033)	4,400,000
Qualified pension plan (Sec. 2039)	240,000
Gross-up for gift tax paid on 2015 gift (Sec. 2035)	487,200
Total gross estate	$5,966,450
Minus:	
Debts (Sec. 2053):	
Bank loan, including $200 accrued interest	(25,200)
Credit cards	(6,500)
Funeral expenses (Sec. 2053)	(15,000)
Administration expenses (Sec. 2053)	(70,000)
Marital deduction (Sec. 2056):	
Residence (under will)	(325,000)
Cash from checking account (under will)	(10,000)
Savings account (under will)	(75,000)
QTIP trust (under will)	(200,000)
Land (JTWROS)	(220,000)
Qualified pension plan (beneficiary)	(240,000)
Charitable contribution deduction (Sec. 2055)	(10,000)
Total reductions to gross estate	($1,196,700)
Taxable estate	$4,769,750
Plus adjusted taxable gifts (Sec. 2001(b)):	
1978 taxable gifts	200,000[a]
2015 taxable gifts	6,500,000[a]
Estate tax base	$11,469,750
Tentative tax on tax base (2016 tax rates) (Sec. 2001)	$4,533,700
Minus:	
Reduction for post-1976 gift taxes (Sec. 2001(b))	(508,000)[b]
Unified credit (Sec. 2010)	(2,125,800)
Estate tax payable	$ 1,899,900

[a]Valued at date-of-gift fair market values.
[b]If rates differ at the time of death from the time of the gift, the reduction for gift taxes is recalculated using the rates for the year of death, and the unified credit applied in determining the gift taxes also is recalculated using the rates for the year of death. In this illustration, the rates are the same for each year. Thus, in this scenario, the $508,000 subtraction is the total of the gift taxes paid, $20,800 plus $487,200.

ADDITIONAL COMMENT

In 2016, the top *income* tax rate is 39.6% plus, potentially, 3.8% on net investment income, and the top *estate* tax rate is 40%. Ann, the surviving spouse, will not benefit from portability from Herman's estate because Herman's tax base exceeded $5.45 million.

Note that these factors affect the computation set out in Table C:13-3:

- Herman had only a special power of appointment over the assets in the trust created by his mother because he could will the property only to his descendants. Therefore, the trust property is not included in his estate.
- Assets that pass to the surviving spouse outside the will, such as by survivorship and by beneficiary designation, can qualify for the marital deduction.
- Adjusted taxable gifts (added to the taxable estate) include only post-1976 taxable gifts.
- Because the highest marginal income tax rate for the estate is assumed to be lower than its 40% marginal estate tax rate and because the estate owes a tax liability (even with the available credits), administration expenses should be deducted on the estate tax return.

LIQUIDITY CONCERNS

OBJECTIVE 6

Explain tax provisions that alleviate liquidity problems

Liquidity is one of the major problems facing individuals planning their estates and executors eventually managing the estates. Individuals often use life insurance to help address this problem. In general, the entire amount of the estate tax liability is due nine months after the decedent's death. Certain provisions, however, allow the executor to pay some or all of the estate tax liability at a later date. Deferral of part or all of the estate tax payments and two other provisions aimed at alleviating a liquidity problem are discussed below.

DEFERRAL OF PAYMENT OF ESTATE TAXES

Reasonable Cause. Section 6161(a)(1) authorizes the Secretary of the Treasury to extend the payment date for the estate taxes for a *reasonable period,* defined as a period of not longer than 12 months. Moreover, the Secretary of the Treasury may extend the payment date for a maximum period of ten years if the executor shows reasonable cause for not being able to pay some, or all, of the estate tax liability on the regular date.[39]

Whenever the executor pays a portion of the estate tax after the regular due date, the estate owes interest on the portion of the tax for which it postpones payment. In general, the interest rate, which is governed by Sec. 6621, is the same as that applicable to underpayments. The interest rate on underpayments potentially fluctuates quarterly with changes in the rate paid on short-term U.S. Treasury obligations.[40]

Remainder or Reversionary Interests. If the gross estate includes a relatively large remainder or reversionary interest, liquidity problems could result if the estate had to pay the entire estate tax liability soon after the decedent's death. For example, the estate might include a remainder interest in an asset in which a healthy, 30-year-old person has a life estate. The estate might not gain possession of the assets until many years after the decedent's death. Section 6163 permits the executor to elect to postpone payment of the tax attributable to a remainder or reversionary interest until six months after the other interests terminate, which in the example would be after the person currently age 30 died. In addition, upon being convinced of reasonable cause, the Secretary of the Treasury may grant an additional extension of up to three years.

TAX STRATEGY TIP

A person who owns a substantial interest in a small business might prefer to gift property other than the business interest. He or she may want to retain the business interest so that his or her estate will qualify for the five-year deferral, ten-installment option of Sec. 6166. See Tax Planning Considerations for further details.

Interests in Closely Held Businesses. Section 6166 authorizes the executor to pay a portion of the estate tax in as many as ten annual installments in certain situations. Executors may elect to apply Sec. 6166 if

- The gross estate includes an interest in a closely held business, and
- The value of the closely held business exceeds 35% of the value of the adjusted gross estate.

Closely held businesses are defined as proprietorships and partnerships or corporations having no more than 45 owners.[41] If a corporation or partnership has more than 45 owners, it nevertheless can be classified as closely held if the decedent's gross estate includes 20% or more of the capital interest (in the partnership) or 20% or more of the value of the voting stock (in the corporation).[42]

The adjusted gross estate is defined as the gross estate less *allowable* Sec. 2053 and 2054 deductions. Consequently, in determining whether the estate meets the 35% requirement, all administration expenses and casualty and theft losses are subtracted, regardless of whether the executor elects to deduct them on the estate tax return or the estate's income tax return.

Once the election is chosen, the following provisions apply:

- The portion of the estate tax that can be paid in installments is the ratio of the value of the closely held business interest to the value of the adjusted gross estate.

---

[39] Sec. 6161(a)(2).
[40] Sec. 6621. The interest rate is discussed in Chapter C:15.
[41] Sec. 6166(b)(1).
[42] Ibid.

- The first of the ten allowable installments generally is not due until five years after the due date for the return. (This provision defers the last payment for as many as 15 years.)
- Interest on the tax due is payable annually, even during the first five years.

Some or all of the installment payments may accrue interest at a rate of only 2%. The maximum amount of deferred tax to which the 2% rate applies is (1) the tax on the total of $1 million of value (as indexed) and the exemption equivalent amount less (2) the unified credit. In no event, however, may the amount exceed the tax postponed under Sec. 6166.[43] The $1 million amount is indexed for inflation with inflation adjustments rounded to the next lowest $10,000; for 2017, this amount is $1.49 million. The interest rate on any additional deferred tax is 45% of the rate applicable to underpayments. The downside is the interest paid is not deductible as interest expense on the estate's income tax return or as an administrative expense on the estate tax return.

STOCK REDEMPTIONS TO PAY DEATH TAXES

Sometimes an estate's major asset is stock in a closely held corporation. In this situation, the corporation may have to redeem some of the corporate stock to provide the estate sufficient liquidity to pay death taxes. As discussed in Chapter C:4, stock redemptions generally receive sale or exchange treatment only if they meet certain requirements under Sec. 302, such as being substantially disproportionate or involving a complete termination of the shareholder's interest. Without exchange treatment and assuming sufficient earnings and profits, the redeemed shareholder (e.g., the estate) would recognize a dividend equal to the entire redemption proceeds rather than a capital gain equal to the difference between the redemption proceeds and the stock's adjusted basis. Because of the applicable capital gain tax rate on dividends, the primary benefit of sale or exchange treatment is being able to apply basis against proceeds. To reduce the income tax cost upon a shareholder's death, Sec. 303 allows exchange treatment to an estate on a redemption that does not meet the requirements of Sec. 302 for such treatment. This treatment minimizes any gain recognized because the stock's adjusted basis, which is subtracted from the redemption proceeds, was stepped up to its FMV upon the decedent's death.

To qualify for Sec. 303 treatment, the stock in the corporation redeeming the shares must make up more than 35% of the value of the decedent's gross estate, less any *allowable* Sec. 2053 and 2054 deductions. The maximum amount of redemption proceeds eligible for exchange treatment is the total of the estate's death taxes and funeral and administration expenses, regardless of whether they are deducted on the estate tax return or the estate's income tax return.

SELF-STUDY QUESTION

Why might an heir to farmland want an estate to forego the special valuation method of Sec. 2032A?

ANSWER

The heir may contemplate selling the land and prefer the higher basis he or she would get if FMV is used rather than the special farmland value, especially if the estate taxes are payable out of the residual estate and the heir does not share in that residual.

SPECIAL USE VALUATION OF FARM REAL PROPERTY

In 1976, Congress became concerned that farms sometimes had to be sold to generate funds to pay estate taxes. This situation was attributable, in part, to the FMV of farm land in many areas being relatively high, perhaps because of suburban housing being built nearby. Congress enacted Sec. 2032A, which allows real property used for farming or in a trade or business other than farming to be valued using a formula approach that attempts to value the property at what it is worth for farming purposes. The lowest valuation permitted is $750,000 less than the property's FMV, but the $750,000 became indexed after 1998 with adjustments rounded to the next lowest $10,000. For 2017 the indexed amount is $1.12 million.

The estate must meet a number of requirements before the executor can elect the special valuation rules.[44] Moreover, if during the ten-year period after the decedent's death the new owner of the property disposes of it or no longer uses it as a farm, in general, an additional tax equal to the estate tax savings that arose from the lower Sec. 2032A valuation is levied.

43 Sec. 6601(j).

44 For example, the farm real and personal property must make up at least 50% of the adjusted value of the gross estate, and the farm real property must make up 25% or more of the adjusted value of the gross estate.

Generation-Skipping Transfer Tax

OBJECTIVE 7

Summarize the basic concepts of the generation-skipping transfer tax

The Tax Reform Act of 1976 enacted a third transfer tax—the generation-skipping transfer tax (GSTT)—to fill a void in the gift and estate tax structure. In 1986, Congress repealed the original GSTT retroactive to its original effective date and replaced it with a revised GSTT. The revised GSTT generally applies to *inter vivos* transfers made after September 25, 1985, and transfers at death made after October 22, 1986.

For years, a popular estate planning technique, especially among the very wealthy, involved giving individuals in several generations an interest in the same property. For example, a decedent might set up a testamentary trust creating successive life estates for a child and a grandchild and a remainder interest for a great grandchild. Under this arrangement, an estate tax would be imposed at the death of the person establishing the trust but not again until the great grandchild's death. The GSTT's purpose is to ensure that some form of transfer taxation is imposed one time a generation. It accomplishes its purpose by subjecting transfers that escape gift or estate taxation for one or more generations to the GSTT.

Originally, every grantor was entitled to a $1 million exemption from the GSTT, but the exemption became indexed for inflation (with adjustments rounded to the next lowest $10,000) for estates of decedents dying after 1998.[45] Beginning in 2004, Congress changed the exemption to the same amount as the "applicable exclusion amount" for estate tax purposes, which was $3.5 million in 2009. With the increase in the unified credit beginning in 2011, the exemption rose to $5 million in 2011 and now is $5.49 million in 2017. The grantor elects when, and against which transfers, to apply this exemption. Appreciation on the property for which the exemption is elected is also exempt from the GSTT.

The GSTT is levied at a flat rate, the highest estate tax rate.[46] The tax applies to direct skip gifts and bequests and to taxable terminations of and taxable distributions from generation-skipping transfers. A **generation-skipping transfer** involves a disposition that

- Provides interests for more than one generation of beneficiaries who are in a younger generation than the transferor, or
- Provides an interest solely for a person two or more generations younger than the transferor.[47]

The recipient must be a skip person, a person two or more generations younger than the decedent (or the donor). For family members, generation assignments are made according to the family tree, regardless of the differences in age. Transfers to skip persons outside of a trust are known as direct skips because they skip one or more generations.

EXAMPLE C:13-49 ▶ Tom transfers an asset directly to his grandson, Tom, III. This is a direct skip type of generation-skipping transfer because the transferee (Tom, III) is two generations younger than the transferor (Tom). ◀

The termination of an interest in a generation-skipping arrangement is known as a taxable termination.[48] This event triggers imposition of the GSTT. The tax is levied on the before-tax amount transferred, and the trustee pays the tax.

EXAMPLE C:13-50 ▶ Tom created a trust with income payable to his son, Tom, Jr., for life and a remainder interest distributable to Tom, III upon the death of Tom, Jr. (his father). This is a generation-skipping transfer because Tom, Jr., and Tom, III are one and two generations younger, respectively, than the transferor (Tom). A taxable termination occurs when Tom, Jr., dies. ◀

[45] Sec. 2631(a).
[46] Sec. 2641.
[47] Sec. 2611.
[48] Sec. 2612(a).

EXAMPLE C:13-51 ▶ The trust in Example C:13-50 was worth $2 million when Tom, Jr., died in 2017. Assume Tom had used his GSTT exemption against other transfers. The amount of the taxable termination was $2 million. The tax was $800,000 (0.40 × $2,000,000). The trustee paid the tax and distributed the $1.2 million of remaining assets to the beneficiary (Tom, III). ◀

In the case of a direct skip, the amount subject to the GSTT is the value of the property received by the transferee.[49] The transferor is liable for the tax. If the direct skip occurs *inter vivos*, the GSTT paid by the transferor is treated as an additional transfer subject to the gift tax.[50] As a result, the total transfer tax liability (GSTT plus gift tax) can approach the value of the property the donee received.

EXAMPLE C:13-52 ▶ In 2017, Susan gave $1 million to her granddaughter. Assume Susan had used her entire unified credit and was in the 40% marginal gift tax bracket; ignore the annual exclusion and the exemption. The GSTT was $400,000 (0.40 × $1,000,000). The amount subject to the gift tax was the value of the property transferred ($1 million) plus the GSTT paid ($400,000). Thus, the gift tax is $560,000 (0.40 × $1,400,000). It cost Susan $960,000 ($400,000 + $560,000) to shift $1 million of property to her granddaughter. ◀

TAX PLANNING CONSIDERATIONS

OBJECTIVE 8

Recognize tax planning opportunities for estates

The effectiveness of many of the pre-1977 transfer tax-saving strategies was diluted by the unification of the transfer tax system in general and by the adoption of a unified rate schedule and the concept of adjusted taxable gifts in particular. To some extent, provisions that allow a larger tax base to be free of estate taxes and permit most interspousal transfers to be devoid of transfer tax consequences counterbalance unification. This section discusses various tax planning considerations that tax advisors should explore to reduce the transfer taxes applicable to a family unit.

WHAT WOULD YOU DO IN THIS SITUATION?

You are a CPA specializing in wealth transfer taxation. One of your clients is an unmarried resident of Aspen, Colorado and his health has recently taken a downhill turn. His doctor told him to consider putting his affairs in order.

This client is a merchant who owns a number of assets with FMVs totaling approximately $5.7 million. His largest asset is his Victorian era store building. Based on comparable sales in the area, your client's building appears to have a fair market value of approximately $760,000. Because your client is in poor health, he does not use all the store space and occasionally rents out some space to other vendors. During the ski season, the full price fair market rental value of the space would be over $1,000 per week. Incidentally, your client's only child has indicated that he is not interested in moving to Aspen but plans to continue the rental practices initiated by his father.

The estate probably will have no deductions. Would you propose to the client that this asset be listed in the estate as Special Use Value property pursuant to Sec. 2032A? Would it be ethical to propose a valuation method based on the historical below-market income generated by this property for the client's estate tax return? Using the historical income stream, the capitalized value would be $460,000, and his estate would be lower by $300,000. No tax would be owed because of an overall valuation of $5.4 million instead of $5.7 million.

[49] Sec. 2623.

[50] Sec. 2515.

TAX STRATEGY TIP

Prospective donors should weigh the opportunities for reducing transfer taxes through the use of lifetime gifts against the income tax disadvantage of foregoing the step up in basis that occurs by retaining the property until death. On the other hand, unless the donee is the donor's spouse, income taxes on the income produced by the gifted property often can be reduced if shifted to a donee in a lower tax bracket.

USE OF *INTER VIVOS* GIFTS

One of the most significant strategies for reducing transfer taxes is a well-designed, long-term gift program. As long as the gifts to each donee do not exceed the annual exclusion, there will be no additions to the gross estate and no adjusted taxable gifts. A donor may pass thousands of dollars of property to others free of any transfer tax consequences if he or she selects enough donees and makes gifts over a substantial number of years. If taxable gifts do occur, the donor removes the post-gift appreciation from the estate tax base. Moreover, if the donor lives more than three years after the date of the gift, the gift tax paid is removed from the gross estate.

USE OF EXEMPTION EQUIVALENT

ADDITIONAL COMMENT

As mentioned earlier, the basic exclusion amount ($5.49 million in 2017) is portable between spouses. Thus, any amount that remains unused at the first spouse's death can be used by the second spouse. However, this benefit applies only if the executor elects portability.

The exemption equivalent (or basic exclusion amount) allows a certain amount of property—$5.49 million in 2017—to pass to people other than the decedent's spouse without any estate taxes being extracted therefrom. Recall that a donor can transfer property to a spouse tax-free without limit. Because the spouse presumably will die before any children or grandchildren (i.e., individuals to whom people often will property), a very wealthy person should contemplate leaving at least an amount equal to the exemption equivalent to people other than his or her spouse. (If one leaves this amount of property in trust, the trust is often called a credit shelter or bypass trust.) This technique precludes the decedent from wasting some or all of the exemption equivalent and thereby prevents the property from being taxed when the surviving spouse dies. Taking advantage of the portability provision (discussed on page 13-24) is another opportunity for making use of the decedent's exemption equivalent.

Making full use of the exemption equivalent enables a husband and wife to transfer to third parties an aggregate of $10.98 million (using 2017 amounts) without incurring any estate taxes. The strategy of making gifts to an ill spouse, who is not wealthy, to keep the donee-spouse's exemption equivalent from being wasted was discussed earlier (see Chapter C:12). Under this technique, the wealthier spouse makes gifts to the other spouse free of gift taxes because of the marital deduction. The recipient spouse then has an estate that can be passed tax-free to children, grandchildren, or other individuals because of the exemption equivalent. This strategy no longer is the only planning technique because the portability rule allows the deceased spouse's unused exemption equivalent to shift to the surviving spouse.

STOP & THINK

Question: Sol made $600,000 in taxable gifts in 2006 but did not have to pay any gift tax. Sol died in 2017, when the gifted property was worth $825,000. Sol's taxable estate (gross estate minus estate tax deductions) was $5.49 million. Did the exemption equivalent enable Sol's estate to owe zero tax?

Solution: No. In concept, the unified credit of $2,141,800, which cancels out the tax on the $5.49 million taxable estate because of the $5.49 million exemption equivalent (in 2017), is available only once. Sol's total transfers—by gift and at death—exceeded $5.49 million. Calculation of Sol's estate tax payable would be as follows:

Taxable estate	$5,490,000
Plus: Adjusted taxable gifts	600,000
Estate tax base	$6,090,000
Tentative tax on estate tax base	$2,381,800
Minus:	
Post-1976 gift tax (on $600,000 gift)	–0–
Unified credit	(2,141,800)
Estate tax payable	$ 240,000

The $240,000 represents the tax on the incremental $600,000, the amount over and above the $5.49 million *aggregate* taxable amount that could be passed free of transfer taxes (both gift and estate).

WHAT SIZE MARITAL DEDUCTION IS BEST?

To reiterate, the tax law imposes no ceiling on the amount of property eligible for the marital deduction. Even so, the availability of an unlimited marital deduction does not necessarily mean that a person should use it. From a tax perspective, wealthier people should consider leaving an amount equal to the exemption equivalent to someone other than the spouse. Alternatively, they could leave the spouse an income interest in property equal to the exemption equivalent along with the power to invade such property for reasons of health, support, maintenance, or education and forego the QTIP election. These powers do not cause an inclusion in the gross estate. Making use of the exemption equivalent has become less important because the portability election allows the surviving spouse to use the decedent's unused exemption equivalent.

In certain circumstances, it may be preferable for an amount exceeding the exemption equivalent to pass directly to third parties. It might be beneficial for the first spouse's estate to pay some estate taxes if the surviving spouse already has substantial property and has a relatively short life expectancy, especially if the decedent spouse's assets are expected to rapidly increase in value.

STOP & THINK

Question: Tarik died in 2017 at age 78. He was survived by his wife, Saliah, and several children and grandchildren. Saliah is 54 and in excellent health. Tarik's adjusted gross estate was $8 million, and his will left $5.49 million outright to his children and the rest to a trust for Saliah. The trust is eligible for the QTIP election. An investment advisor believes that the trust assets will likely appreciate annually at the rate of at least 10%. Name two advantages and one disadvantage of electing the marital deduction on the entire trust.

Solution: One advantage is that the tax on the trust property will be deferred, perhaps for a long time, given the wife's age and health. Another advantage is that, because no tax is owed at Tarik's death, the trust assets remain intact to appreciate and produce more income for Saliah. That is, there is no current capital drain to pay transfer taxes. A disadvantage is that, because of the anticipated appreciation and the long time before Saliah's estimated death, the amount taxed in Saliah's estate will likely be much greater than the residue (here, $2.51 million) Tarik willed to Saliah. Note that Tarik took full advantage of his unified credit.

USE OF DISCLAIMERS

Because the IRC does not treat a **qualified disclaimer** as a gift, disclaimers can be valuable estate planning tools (see Chapter C:12). For example, if a decedent wills all his or her property to the surviving spouse, such spouse could disclaim an amount at least equal in size to the exemption equivalent and thereby enable the decedent's estate to take full advantage of the unified credit. However, in the absence of the spouse's disclaiming, the portability election keeps the exemption equivalent from being wasted. In a different scenario, a decedent's children might disclaim some bequests if, as a result of their disclaimer, the property would pass to the surviving spouse. This approach might be desirable if a large estate otherwise would receive a relatively small marital deduction. A disclaimer also could be appropriate if the disclaimant is elderly and in poor health and wishes to preclude the property from being taxed again relatively soon. (Of course, the credit for tax on prior transfers would provide some relief from double taxation.) Bear in mind, however, that the person making the qualified disclaimer has no input concerning which individuals receive the disclaimed property.

ROLE OF LIFE INSURANCE

Life insurance is an important asset with respect to estate planning for the following reasons:

- It can help provide the liquidity for paying estate taxes and other costs associated with death.
- It has the potential for a large increase in value. If the insured gives away his or her incidents of ownership in the policy and survives the gift by more than three years, the estate benefits by keeping the policy's increased value out of the estate.

Assume an individual is contemplating purchasing a new insurance policy on his or her life and transferring it to another individual as a gift. The insured must live for more than three years after making the gift to exclude the face amount of the policy from his or her gross estate. Should the insured die within three years of gifting the policy, the donor's gross estate includes the policy's face amount. If a third party instead purchases the policy, the insured will not make a gift of the policy, and the three-year rule will not be of concern.

QUALIFYING THE ESTATE FOR INSTALLMENT PAYMENTS

TAX STRATEGY TIP

The estate can defer payment of estate taxes as much as 14 years if the estate's executor makes a timely Sec. 6166 election. The interest charged on the deferred taxes is at a favorable rate.

It can be quite beneficial for an estate owning an interest in a closely held business to qualify for installment payment of estate taxes under Sec. 6166. In a sense, the estate can borrow a certain amount of dollars from the government at 2% and the rest at a higher, but still favorable, rate. The closely held business interest must comprise more than 35% of the adjusted gross estate, defined as the gross estate less Sec. 2053 and Sec. 2054 deductions.

Retaining closely held business interests and gifting other assets will increase the likelihood of the estate's being able to elect the installment payments. However, closely held business interests often have a potential for great appreciation. Consequently, from the standpoint of reducing the size of the estate by freezing values, they are good candidates for gifts.

Individuals cannot make gifts to restructure their estates and thereby qualify for Sec. 6166 if they postpone restructuring until soon before their death. If the decedent makes gifts within three years of dying, the closely held business interest must make up more than 35% of the adjusted gross estate with both of the following calculations:

1. Calculate the ratio of the closely held business to the actual adjusted gross estate.
2. Redo the calculations after revising the ratio to include (at date-of-death values) any property given away within three years of death.

EXAMPLE C:13-53 ▶ Joe died in 2017. Joe's gross estate included a closely held business interest valued at $2 million and other property valued at $3.6 million. Joe's allowable Sec. 2053 and 2054 deductions totaled $100,000. In 2015, partly in hopes of qualifying his estate for Sec. 6166 treatment, Joe made gifts of listed securities of $300,000 (at 2017 valuations) and paid no gift tax on the gifts. The two tests for determining whether Joe's estate qualified for Sec. 6166 are as follows:

Excluding gifts:	$2,000,000 ÷ $5,500,000 = 36.36%
Including gifts:	$2,000,000 ÷ $5,800,000 = 34.48%

Joe's estate could not elect Sec. 6166 treatment because it met the greater than 35% test in only one of the two computations. ◀

WHERE TO DEDUCT ADMINISTRATION EXPENSES

Another tax planning opportunity concerns the choice of where to deduct administration expenses: on the estate tax return, on the estate's income tax return, or some in each place. The executor should claim the deduction where it will yield the greatest tax savings. For 2017 the top tax rate is 40% for estate tax purposes and 39.6% for income tax purposes. In addition, an estate could owe an incremental 3.8% tax on its undistributed net investment income. Thus, for some estates, the tax savings will be slightly higher if the expenses are deducted on the income tax return. However, some decedents may have made bequests to certain persons or charitable organizations based on the size of the adjusted gross or taxable estate. In such circumstances, the tax return on which the administration expenses are deducted will affect the amount of the adjusted gross and taxable estates and the amount that some beneficiaries of the estate receive. If no estate taxes are owed because of the exemption equivalent or the marital and/or charitable contribution deduction, administration expenses should be deducted on the estate's income tax return.

Compliance and Procedural Considerations

OBJECTIVE 9

Comply with the filing requirements for estate tax returns

FILING REQUIREMENTS

Section 6018 indicates the circumstances in which estate tax returns are necessary. In general, no return is necessary unless the value of the gross estate plus adjusted taxable gifts exceeds the exemption equivalent (also known as the basic exclusion amount). An exception applies, however, if the decedent made any post-1976 taxable gifts or claimed any portion of the $30,000 specific exemption after September 8, 1976, and before January 1, 1977. In such circumstances, a return must be filed if the value of the gross estate exceeds the amount of the exemption equivalent reduced by the total of the decedent's adjusted taxable gifts and the amount of the specific exemption claimed against gifts made after September 8, 1976, and before January 1, 1977.

To elect the portability of the deceased spouse's unused exemption equivalent, the executor must file an estate tax return even though a return would not otherwise be required. In such situations the executor must calculate the unused amount but is allowed to make a good faith estimate of the value of the gross estate. If a return is filed, but for some reason the executor does not want to take advantage of portability, the executor must check a box on the estate tax return to denote the decision to opt out of the portability election.

Section 6035 requires executors who must file an estate tax return to furnish to the IRS and anyone receiving an interest in property included in the gross estate a statement denoting the value shown on the estate tax return. This rule is effective for estate tax returns filed after July 31, 2015.

A completed sample Estate Tax Return (Form 706) appears in Appendix B. The facts on which the return is based are the same as for the comprehensive illustration appearing on pages C:13-25 through C:13-27.

DUE DATE

REAL-WORLD EXAMPLE

The IRS reports that 11,917 estate tax returns were filed in 2015, down from 45,070 in 2005. This decrease is primarily a result of the increase in the basic exclusion amount that sets the threshold for filing Form 706.

Estate tax returns (Form 706) generally must be filed within nine months after the decedent's death.[51] The Secretary of the Treasury is authorized to grant a reasonable extension of time for filing.[52] The maximum extension period is six months. Obtaining an extension does not extend the time for paying the estate tax. Section 6601 imposes interest on any portion of the tax not paid by the due date of the return, determined without regard to the extension period. Thus, to avoid interest, the estate must pay the tax by the original due date.

VALUATION

One of the most difficult tasks of preparing estate tax returns is valuing the items included in the gross estate. Some items (e.g., one-of-a-kind art objects) may truly be unique. For many properties the executor should arrange for appraisals by experts.

If the value of any property reported on the return is 65% or less of the amount determined to be the proper value during an audit or court case, a 20% undervaluation penalty is imposed.[53] The penalty is higher if a gross valuation misstatement occurs; that is, the estate tax valuation is 40% or less than the amount determined to be the proper value.[54] A penalty of 20% is imposed on underpayments resulting from claiming "any inconsistent estate tax basis," defined as a basis claimed on a return that exceeds the basis under Sec. 1014(f).[55] Chapter C:12 discusses these penalties in more detail.

ELECTION OF ALTERNATE VALUATION DATE

The executor may value the gross estate on the alternate valuation date instead of on the date of death by making an irrevocable election on the estate tax return. The election does not necessarily have to be made on a timely return, but no election is possible if the return is filed more than a year after the due date (including extensions).

[51] Sec. 6075(a).
[52] Sec. 6081(a).
[53] Sec. 6662(g).
[54] Sec. 6662(h).
[55] Secs. 6662(c) and (k). This provision is effective for estate tax returns filed after July 31, 2015.

Problem Materials

DISCUSSION QUESTIONS

C:13-1 In general, at what amount are items includible in the gross estate valued? (Answer in words.) Indicate one exception to the general valuation rules and the reason for this exception.

C:13-2 A client requests that you explain the valuation rules used for gift tax and estate tax purposes. Explain the similarities and differences of the two sets of rules.

C:13-3 Compare the valuation for gift and estate tax purposes of a $150,000 group term life insurance policy on the transferor's life.

C:13-4 Explain how shares of stock traded on a stock exchange are valued. What is the blockage rule?

C:13-5 Assume that the properties included in Alex's gross estate have appreciated during the six-month period immediately after his death. May Alex's executor elect the alternate valuation date and thereby achieve a larger step-up in basis? Explain.

C:13-6 Explain to an executor an advantage and a disadvantage of electing the alternate valuation date.

C:13-7 A decedent transferred land to an adult child by gift two years before death. Is the land included in the decedent's gross estate? In the estate tax base?

C:13-8 From a tax standpoint, which of the following alternatives is more favorable for a client's estate?

a. Buying a new insurance policy on his life and soon thereafter giving it to another person

b. Encouraging the other person to buy the policy with funds previously received from the client

Explain your answer.

C:13-9 Explain the difference between the estate tax treatment for gift taxes paid on gifts made two years before death and on gifts made ten years before death.

C:13-10 A client is considering making a very large gift. She wants to know whether the gross-up rule will apply to the entire amount of gift taxes paid by both her and her spouse if the spouses elect gift splitting and she dies within three years of the gift. Explain.

C:13-11 A widow owns a valuable eighteenth-century residence that she would like the state historical society to own someday. Explain to her the estate tax consequences of the following two alternatives:

a. Deeding the state historical society a remainder interest in the residence and reserving the right to live there rent free for the rest of her life.

b. Giving her entire interest in the house to the society and moving to another home for the rest of her life.

C:13-12 When does the consideration furnished test apply to property that the decedent held as a joint tenant with right of survivorship?

C:13-13 Describe two circumstances in which life insurance on a decedent's life is includible in the gross estate under Sec. 2042. If insurance policies on the decedent's life escape being included under Sec. 2042, are they definitely excluded from the gross estate? Explain.

C:13-14 Indicate two situations in which property that has previously been subject, at least in part, to gift taxation is nevertheless included in the donor-decedent's gross estate.

C:13-15 Joe's will required property to be put in trust with a bank as trustee. His will named his sister Tess to receive the trust income annually for life and empowered Tess to will the property to whomever she so desires. In addition, Tess may require that the trustee make distributions of principal to her for her health or support needs. Tess plans to leave the property by will to two of her three children in equal shares. Tess seeks your advice about whether the trust will be included in her gross estate. Respond to Tess.

C:13-16 Determine the accuracy of the following statement: The gross estate includes a general power of appointment possessed by the decedent only if the decedent exercised the power.

C:13-17 Carlos died six years before his wife Maria died. His will called for the creation of a trust to be funded with $1 million of property. The bank trustee was required to distribute all the trust income semiannually to Maria for the rest of her life. Upon her death, the trust assets were to be distributed to the couple's children. When Maria died, the trust assets had appreciated to $1.7 million. Are the trust assets included in Maria's gross estate? Explain.

C:13-18 List the various categories of estate tax deductions, and compare them with the categories of gift tax deductions. What differences exist?

C:13-19 Compare the tax treatment of administration expenses with that of the decedent's debts.

C:13-20 Judy died and was survived by her husband, Jason, who received the following interests as a result of his wife's death. Does Judy's estate receive a marital deduction for them? Explain.

a. $400,000 of life insurance proceeds; Jason is the beneficiary; Judy held the incidents of ownership.

b. Outright ownership of $700,000 of land held by Judy and Jason as joint tenants. Jason provided all the consideration to purchase the land.

C:13-21 Compare the credits available for estate tax purposes with the credits available for gift tax purposes. What differences exist?

C:13-22 Explain to a client the tax policy reason Congress allowed estates to make installment payments of the portion of the estate taxes attributable to closely held business interests.

C:13-23 Assume that Larry is wealthier than Jane, his wife, and that he is likely to die before her. From an overall tax standpoint (considering transfer taxes and income taxes), is it preferable for Larry to transfer property to Jane *inter vivos* or at death, or does it matter? Explain.

C:13-24 Bala desires to freeze the value of his estate. Explain which of the following assets you would recommend that Bala transfer during his lifetime (more than one asset may be suggested):

a. Life insurance on his life
b. Cash
c. Corporate bonds (assume interest rates are expected to rise)
d. Stock in a firm with a bright future
e. Land in a boom town

C:13-25 Refer to Problem C:13-24. Explain the negative tax considerations (if any) with respect to Bala's making gifts of the assets that you recommended.

C:13-26 From a tax standpoint, describe an advantage a very wealthy married person would achieve by disposing of an amount equal to the exemption equivalent (basic exclusion amount) to individuals other than his or her spouse?

C:13-27 In general, when is the estate tax due? What are some exceptions?

ISSUE IDENTIFICATION QUESTIONS

C:13-28 Henry Arkin (a widower) is quite elderly and is beginning to engage in some estate planning. His goal is to reduce his transfer taxes. He is considering purchasing land with a high potential for appreciation and having it titled in the names of himself and his grandson as joint tenants with rights of survivorship. Henry would provide all of the consideration, estimated to be about $14 million. What tax issues should Henry Arkin consider with respect to the purchase of the land?

C:13-29 Annie James died early in 2017. All her property passed subject to her will, which provides that her surviving husband, Dave James, is to receive all the property outright. Her will further states that any property Dave disclaims will pass instead to their children in equal shares. Annie's gross estate is $6.3 million, and her Sec. 2053 deductions are $300,000. Dave, who is in poor health, already owns about $5 million of property. What tax issues should Dave James consider with respect to the property bequeathed to him by his wife?

C:13-30 Assume the same facts as in Problem C:13-29 except that Annie's will leaves all her property to a QTIP trust for Dave for life with the remainder to their children. What tax issues should Dave James and the estate's executor consider with respect to the property that passes to the QTIP trust?

C:13-31 Jeung Hong, a widower, died in March 2017. His gross estate was $6.5 million and, at the time of his death, he owed debts of $60,000. His will made a bequest of $200,000 to his undergraduate alma mater and left the rest of his property to his children. His administrative expenses were $75,000. What tax issues should the estate's CPA consider when preparing Jeung's estate tax return and his estate's income tax return?

PROBLEMS

C:13-32 *Valuation.* Beth died on May 3, 2017. Her executor elected date-of-death valuation. Beth's gross estate included, among other properties, the items listed below. What is the estate tax value of each item?

a. 4,000 shares of Highline Corporation stock, traded on a stock exchange on May 3, 2017 at a high of 30, a low of 25, and a close of 26.
b. Life insurance policy on the life of Beth having a face value of $600,000. The cost of a comparable policy immediately before Beth's death was $187,430.
c. Life insurance policy on the life of Beth's son having a face value of $100,000. The interpolated terminal reserve immediately before Beth's death was $14,000. Unexpired premiums were $920.
d. Beach cottage appraised at a FMV of $175,000 and valued for property tax purposes at $152,000.

C:13-33 *Valuation.* Mary died on April 3, 2017. As of this date, Mary's gross estate was valued at $6.5 million. On October 3, Mary's gross estate was valued at $5.8 million. The estate neither distributed nor sold any assets before October 3, 2017. Mary's estate had no deductions or adjusted taxable gifts. What was Mary's *lowest* possible estate tax liability?

C:13-34 *Estate Tax Formula.* Sue died on May 3, 2017. On October 1, 2015, Sue gave her son Tom land valued at $7,014,000. Sue applied a unified credit of $2,117,800 against the gift tax due on this transfer. On Sue's date of death the land was valued at $9.4 million.
a. With respect to this transaction, what amount was included in Sue's gross estate?
b. What is the amount of Sue's adjusted taxable gifts attributable to the 2015 gift?

C:13-35 *Transferor Provisions.* Val died on May 13, 2017. On July 3, 2015, she gave a $400,000 life insurance policy on her own life to son Ray. Because the value of the policy was relatively low, the transfer did not cause any gift tax to be payable.
a. What amount was included in Val's gross estate as a result of the 2015 gift?
b. What amount was included in Val's gross estate if the property given was land instead of a life insurance policy?
c. Refer to Part a. What amount would have been included in Val's gross estate if she instead gave Ray the policy on April 30, 2014?

C:13-36 *Transferor Provisions.* In December 2015, Jody transferred stock having an $8,114,000 FMV to her daughter Joan. Jody paid $1,068,000 ($3,185,800 − $2,117,800) of gift taxes on this transfer. When Jody died in January 2017, the stock was valued at $9 million. Jody made no other gifts during her lifetime. With respect to this gift transaction, what amount was includible in Jody's gross estate, and what amount was reportable as adjusted taxable gifts?

C:13-37 *Transferor Provisions.* In December 2015, Curt and Kate elected gift splitting to report $16,228,000 of gifts of stocks Curt made to Curt, Jr. Each paid gift taxes of $1,068,000 by spending his or her own funds. Kate died in January 2017 and was survived by Curt. Her only taxable gift was the one reported for 2015. When Kate died in 2017, the stock had appreciated to $18.8 million. With respect to the 2015 gift, what amount was included in Kate's gross estate, and what amount was reportable as adjusted taxable gifts?

C:13-38 *Transferor Provisions.* John died in 2017. What amount, if any, was included in his gross estate in each of the following situations:
a. In 1997, John created a revocable trust, funded it with $400,000 of assets, and named a bank as trustee. The trust instrument provided that the income is payable to John annually for life. Upon John's death, the assets were to be divided equally among John's descendants. When John died at the age of 72, the trust was still revocable. The trust assets were then worth $480,000.
b. In 2005, John transferred title to his personal residence to a charitable organization but retained the right to live there rent free for 20 years. The residence was worth $150,000 on the transfer date. At John's death, the residence was worth $230,000.
c. In 2000, John created an irrevocable trust, funded it with $200,000 of assets, and named a bank as trustee. According to the trust agreement, all the trust income was to be paid out annually for 25 years. The trustee, however, is to decide how much income to pay each year to each of the three beneficiaries (John's children). Upon termination of the trust, the assets are to be distributed equally among John's three children (now adults) or their estates. The trust's assets were worth $500,000 when John died.
d. In 1997, John created an irrevocable trust with a bank named as trustee. He designated his brother Al as the beneficiary of all the income for life. Upon Al's death, the property is to be distributed equally among Al's descendants. The trust assets were worth $400,000 when John died.

C:13-39 *Transferor Provisions.* Twelve years ago, Latoya transferred property to an irrevocable trust with a bank trustee. Latoya named Al to receive the trust income annually for life and Pat or Pat's estate to receive the remainder upon Al's death. Latoya reserved the power to designate Mike or Mike's estate (instead of Pat or Pat's estate) to receive the remainder. Upon Latoya's death in August 2017, the trust assets were valued at $200,000; Al was age 50; Mike, age 27; and Pat, age 32. Assume a 4% rate for the actuarial tables.
a. How much, if any, is included in Latoya's gross estate?
b. How much would have been included in Latoya's gross estate if she had *not* retained any powers over the trust?

C:13-40 *Annuities.* Maria died two years after her retirement. At the time of her death at age 67, she was covered by the two annuities listed below.

- An annuity purchased by Maria's father providing benefits to Maria upon her attaining age 65. Upon Maria's death, survivor benefits are payable to her sister. The sister's total benefits are valued at $45,000.

- An annuity purchased by Maria's former employer under a qualified plan to which only the employer contributed. Benefits became payable to Maria upon her retirement. Upon Maria's death a survivor annuity valued at $110,000 is payable to her son.

a. What is the amount of the inclusion in Maria's gross estate with respect to each annuity?
b. How would your answer for the first annuity change if Maria had instead purchased the annuity?
c. How would your answer for the second annuity change if the employer had instead made 70% of the contributions to the qualified plan and Maria had made the remaining 30%?

C:13-41 *Jointly Owned Property.* Ten years ago, Art purchased land for $60,000 and immediately titled it in the names of Art and Bart, joint tenants with right of survivorship. Bart paid no consideration. In 2017, Art died and was survived by Bart, his brother. The land's value had appreciated to $300,000.

a. What was the amount of the inclusion in Art's gross estate?
b. Assume Bart died (instead of Art). What amount would have been included in Bart's gross estate?
c. Assume that Art died in January 2017 and Bart died in November 2017, when the land was worth $320,000. What amount was included in Bart's gross estate?

C:13-42 *Jointly Owned Property.* Five years ago, Andy and Sandy, siblings, pooled their resources and purchased a warehouse. Andy provided $50,000 of consideration, and Sandy furnished $100,000. Andy died and was survived by Sandy. The property, which they had titled in the names of Andy and Sandy, joint tenants with right of survivorship, was valued at $450,000 when Andy died. What amount was includible in Andy's gross estate?

C:13-43 *Jointly Owned Property.* Fifteen years ago, Mrs. Cobb purchased land costing $80,000. She had the land titled in the names of Mr. and Mrs. Cobb, joint tenants with right of survivorship. Mrs. Cobb died and was survived by Mr. Cobb. At Mrs. Cobb's death, the land's value was $200,000.

a. What amount was included in Mrs. Cobb's gross estate?
b. What amount, if any, of the marital deduction could Mrs. Cobb's estate claim for the land?
c. Later, Mr. Cobb died, and the land was worth $240,000 at his death. What amount was included in his gross estate?

C:13-44 *Powers of Appointment.* Tai was the sole income beneficiary for life of each of the trusts described below. For each trust, indicate whether and why it was includible in Tai's gross estate.

a. A trust created under the will of Tai's mother, who died in 1996. Upon Tai's death, the trust assets are to pass to those of Tai's descendants whom Tai directs by his will. Should Tai fail to appoint the trust property, the trust assets are to be distributed to the Smithsonian Institution. Tai willed the property to his twin daughters in equal shares.
b. An irrevocable *inter vivos* trust created in 2001 by Tai's father. The trust agreement authorizes Tai to appoint the property to whomever he so desires. The appointment could be made only by his will. In his will, Tai appointed the property to an elderly neighbor.
c. An irrevocable trust created by Tai's uncle in 2005. The trust instrument authorized Tai to demand that the trustee distribute trust assets to himself for his health and/or maintenance needs. Any property remaining in the trust at Tai's death will pass in accordance with the trust instrument to Tai's descendants in equal shares.
d. A trust created under the will of Tai's great-grandmother, who died in 1941. Her will authorizes Tai to appoint the property by his will to whomever he so desires. In default of appointment, the property is to pass to Tai's descendants in equal shares. Tai's will did not mention this trust.
e. Assume the same facts as in Part b except Tai's will did not mention the trust property.

C:13-45 *Life Insurance.* Joy died on November 5, 2017. Soon after Joy's death, the executor discovered the following insurance policies on Joy's life.

Policy Number	*Owner*	*Beneficiary*	*Face Value*
123	Joy	Joy's husband	$400,000
757	Joy's son	Joy's estate	225,000
848	Joy's son	Joy's son	300,000
414	Joy's daughter	Joy's husband	175,000

Joy transferred ownership of policies 757 and 848 to her son in 2009. She gave ownership of policy 414 to her daughter in 2015. Indicate the amount includible in Joy's gross estate for each policy.

C:13-46 *Life Insurance.* Refer to Problem C:13-45. What is the net addition to Joy's *taxable estate* with respect to the insurance policies if all the property passing under Joy's will was left to Joy's son?

C:13-47 *Deductions.* When Yuji died in March 2017, his gross estate was valued at $8 million. He owed debts totaling $300,000. Funeral and administration expenses were $12,000 and $120,000, respectively. The marginal estate tax rate exceeded his estate's marginal income tax rate. Yuji willed his church $300,000 and his spouse $1.1 million. Calculate Yuji's taxable estate.

C:13-48 *Marital Deduction.* Assume the same facts as in Problem C:13-47 except that Yuji's will also provided for setting up a trust to be funded with $400,000 of property with a bank named as trustee. His wife is to receive all the trust income semiannually for life, and upon her death the trust assets are to be distributed equally among Yuji's children and grandchildren.

a. What was the amount of Yuji's taxable estate? Provide two possible answers.
b. Assume Yuji's widow died in December 2017. With respect to Yuji's former assets, explain which items will be included in the widow's gross estate. Provide two possible answers, but you need not indicate amounts.

C:13-49 *Marital Deduction.* Assume the same facts as in Problem C:13-48 and that before Yuji's death in 2017 his wife already owned property valued at $300,000. Assume that each asset owned by each spouse increased 8% in value by the surviving spouse's date of death later in 2017 and that Yuji's executor elected to claim the maximum marital deduction possible. Assume there were no state death taxes. From a tax standpoint, was the executor's strategy of electing the marital deduction on the QTIP trust a wise decision? Support your answer with computations.

C:13-50 *Portability of Exemption.* Sam Snider died February 14, 2016, survived by his spouse Janet and several children. Sam had not made any taxable gifts. Sam's gross estate was $7 million. In each of the following independent situations, indicate the amount of Sam's basic exclusion amount that is portable to Janet and that can be used by Janet's estate if Sam's executor makes the appropriate election.

a. Sam's deductions, including the marital deduction, total $3.7 million; Janet dies in 2017.
b. Sam's deductions, including the marital deduction, total $1.1 million; Janet dies in 2017.
c. Sam's deductions, including the marital deduction, total $6 million; Janet dies in 2021.
d. Sam's deductions, including the marital deduction, total $5.5 million. Janet remarries late in 2016. Her new spouse dies early in 2017 with a $9 million taxable estate, and Janet dies late in 2017.

C:13-51 *Adjusted Taxable Gifts.* Will, a bachelor, died in 2017. At that time, his sole asset was cash of $6 million. Assume no debts or funeral and administration expenses and no charitable bequests. His gift history was as follows:

Date	*Amount of Taxable Gifts*	*FMV of Gift Property at Date of Death*
October 1987	$270,000	$290,000
October 1991	90,000	45,000

a. What was Will's estate tax base?
b. How would your answer to Part a change if Will made the first gift in 1974 (instead of 1987)?

C:13-52 *Estate Tax Base.* Bess, a widow, died in October 2017. Her gross estate, which totaled $7 million, included a $100,000 life insurance policy on her life that she gave away in 2015. The taxable gift that arose from giving away the policy was $15,000. In December 2014, Bess made a $740,000 taxable gift of stock whose value increased to $790,000 by the time Bess died. She owed debts of $80,000 at the time of her death.

a. What was her estate tax base?
b. What unified credit could her estate claim?

C:13-53 *Estate Tax Base.* Maria Martinez died in 2017, survived by her spouse, Sergio, and two adult children. Her gross estate, all of which passed under her will, was valued at $7.2 million. She had Sec. 2053 deductions of $100,000. Her will left $200,000 to her church, 20% of her gross estate to her spouse, and the rest to her children in equal shares. She made taxable gifts of $20,000 in 1975 and $500,000 in 1999. The gifted assets have increased in value to $120,000 and $715,000, respectively. Calculate her taxable estate, her adjusted taxable gifts, and her estate tax base.

C:13-54 *Estate Tax Calculation.* Joseph Jernigan died in 2017 with a taxable estate of $4.1 million. He was survived by his spouse Josephine and several children. He made taxable gifts of $100,000 in 1974 and $650,000 in 2000. The property given in 1974 was valued at $425,000 when he died, and the property given in 2000 was valued at $400,000 when he died. Determine his estate tax base, his estate tax before subtraction of the unified credit, the amount of unified credit available to his estate, the reduction for post-1976 gift taxes, and his estate tax payable. Also, indicate the amount, if any, of his basic exclusion amount that is portable to Josephine.

C:13-55 *Installment Payments.* Elaine died on May 1, 2017. Her gross estate consisted of the following items:

Cash	$ 40,000
Stocks traded on a stock exchange	4,200,000
Personal residence	550,000
25% capital interest in a 60-person partnership	3,100,000

Elaine's Sec. 2053 deductions totaled $200,000. She had no other deductions.

a. What percentage of Elaine's federal estate taxes can be paid in installments under Sec. 6166? When is the first installment payment due?

b. Could Elaine's estate elect Sec. 6166 treatment if the stocks were valued at $6.2 million instead of $4.2 million?

C:13-56 *State Death Taxes.* Giovanni died in 2017 with a gross estate of $6.9 million and debts of $30,000. He made post-1976 taxable gifts of $100,000, valued at $80,000 when Giovanni died. His estate paid state death taxes of $110,200. Calculate his estate tax base.

COMPREHENSIVE PROBLEMS

C:13-57 Bonnie died on June 1, 2017, survived by her husband, Abner, and two sons, Carl and Doug. Bonnie's only lifetime taxable gift was made in October 2015 in the taxable amount of $6.25 million. She did not elect gift splitting. By the time of her death, the value of the gifted property (stock) had declined to $5.1 million.

Bonnie's executor discovered the items shown below. Amounts shown are the FMVs of the items as of June 1, 2017.

Cash in checking account in her name	$ 199,750
Cash in savings account in her name	430,000
Stock in names of Bonnie and Doug, joint tenants with right of survivorship. Bonnie provided all the consideration ($3,000) to purchase the stock.	25,000
Land in names of Bonnie and Abner, joint tenants with right of survivorship. Abner provided all the consideration to purchase the land.	360,000
Personal residence in only Bonnie's name	450,000
Life insurance on Bonnie's life. Bonnie was owner, and Bonnie's estate was beneficiary (face value)	5,000,000
Trust created under the will of Bonnie's mother (who died in 2000). Bonnie was entitled to all the trust income for life, and she could will the trust property to whomever she desired. She willed it to her sons in equal amounts.	700,000

Bonnie's debts, as of her date of death, were $60,000. Her funeral and administration expenses were $9,000 and $71,000, respectively. Her estate paid state death taxes of $65,000. The executor elected to deduct the administration expenses on the estate tax return.

Bonnie's will included the following:

> I leave my residence to my husband Abner.
>
> $250,000 of property is to be transferred to a trust with First Bank named as trustee. All of the income is to be paid to my husband, Abner, semiannually for the rest of his life. Upon his death the property is to be divided equally between my two sons or their estates.
>
> I leave $47,000 to the American Cancer Society.

Assume the executor elected to claim the maximum marital deduction possible. Compute the following with respect to Bonnie's estate:

a. Gross estate
b. Taxable estate
c. Adjusted taxable gifts
d. Estate tax base and basic exclusion amount portable to Abner
e. Tentative tax on estate tax base
f. Federal estate tax payable

C:13-58 Assume the same facts as in Problem C:13-57 except the joint tenancy land was held in the names of Bonnie and her son Doug, joint tenants with right of survivorship. Also assume that Bonnie provided 55% of the consideration to buy the land and that Bonnie's executor did not elect to claim the marital deduction on the QTIP trust. Assume further that, because of the annual exclusion, no taxable gift arose on the purchase of the joint tenancy land.

TAX STRATEGY PROBLEMS

C:13-59 Gaylord Gunnison (GG) died January 13, 2017, and his gross estate consisted of three properties—cash, land, and stock in a public company. The amount of cash on the date of his death was $2.9 million, which went into the estate. On January 13, 2017, the land had a fair market value of $1 million, and the stock had a fair market value of $2 million. On July 13, 2017, the fair market values of the land and stock were $1.1 million and $1.6 million, respectively, and the cash remained at $2.9 million. Assume, for simplicity, that the estate has no deductions and GG made no taxable gifts. GG willed all of his property to his daughter, Gilda, who anticipated that, beginning in July 2017, the stock would appreciate at the rate of 9% per year before taxes. She anticipates selling the stock on or about July 13, 2023. Assume that the land's fair market value will remain at $1.1 million through 2023 and that she anticipates retaining the land for the rest of her life.

Considering both income tax and estate tax effects, compare after-tax wealth using the alternate valuation date or the date of death to value the estate. Which date should the executor have elected? For simplicity, assume that the cash is not invested. (Incidentally, the factor for the future value, six years hence, at 9% is 1.677.) Prepare a worksheet on which you calculate the amount of after-tax wealth using the two possible valuation dates. Assume that the gain will be taxed at a 20% capital gains rate and will be subject to the 3.8% tax on net investment income (i.e., at a 23.8% rate).

C:13-60 Steve Silver, a new client, owns stock in HyTeche, Inc., which recently had an initial public offering. In early 2017, his stock is valued at $8 million. His only other asset is $9 million of cash. Unfortunately, he has a terminal illness and has a life expectancy of less than a year. He believes that the stock's value will escalate to about $10 million by the time of his death. Steve, a widower, wants his daughter Sylvia to end up with the stock. He wants you to do a projection of his total transfer tax cost (gift and estate) if he gives the stock to Sylvia immediately compared with his total transfer tax cost if he leaves the stock to Sylvia under his will. He explains that Sylvia is not likely to sell the stock. Thus, the stock's basis is a moot issue. Prepare projections for the total transfer tax cost of gifting now versus passing on at death under the assumption that he will die in late 2017 when the stock will be worth $10 million.

C:13-61 Matt Patterson died in early 2017 with a $4.5 million gross estate and no deductions other than a potential marital deduction. He bequeathed all his property to his spouse, Nancy, with the provision that, if Nancy predeceases him, the couple's two adult children will receive the entire property in equal amounts. Nancy survived Matt, but she has a recently diagnosed terminal illness. Nancy's own assets have an estimated $6.1 million fair market value as of Matt's date of death. Her estate will likely have only a minimal amount of deductions. Her current will leaves her property 50% each to the two children. Your manager will soon meet with Nancy, who wants to discuss the implications of disclaiming Matt's bequest to her. Your manager requests that you prepare projections of the combined estate tax liability of Matt and Nancy if Nancy disclaims and does not disclaim. Assume the assets do not appreciate by Nancy's date of death. Nancy requested the projections be based on the assumption that her death will occur near the end of 2017, at the latest.

TAX FORM/RETURN PREPARATION PROBLEMS

C:13-62 Prepare an estate tax return (Form 706) for Marcia Miller, who died July 23, 2016. Marcia (born April 2, 1930) resided at 117 Brandywine Way, Eastern City, PA 19000 and was a lifelong Pennsylvania resident. Her first husband, Arthur Adams, died in 1995. In June 1999, she married Matt Miller, a U.S. citizen, who survived her. Marcia has three children (Andy, Annie, and Archie Adams) from her first marriage.

Date of death values of the properties discovered at Marcia's death are listed below.

- Principal residence with a value of $420,000. Purchased by Marcia in 2001 and titled in the names of Matt and Marcia Miller, joint tenants with right of survivorship.
- Household furnishings acquired by Marcia during her first marriage and valued at $62,000 when she died.
- $1 million cash in a money market account in Marcia's name. On her date of death, there also was $2,200 of accrued interest in the account.
- $17,000 checking account at Keystone State Bank in the names of Marcia and Matt as tenants in common.
- Stock portfolio in Marcia's name with fair market value at her death of $5.6 million.
- $1 million life insurance policy. Marcia purchased the policy in 1990 and held incidents of ownership. Beneficiary is Marcia's estate.
- QTIP trust established at Franklin State Bank by Arthur Adams. His executor claimed a 60% marital deduction on the trust, valued then at $750,000. Marcia received all the income monthly for life, and the remainder is to go to the three Adams children in equal shares. The trust was valued at $1.8 million at Marcia's death.
- Trust at Quaker State Bank with value of $500,000. The trust was created under the will of Marcia's uncle, Josh Judson, who died in 1992. Marcia was entitled to receive all the income annually for life and was granted the power to will the property to such of her descendants as she so desired with the specification that, if she did not exercise the power, the property would pass to Josh's former housekeeper, Yvonne Jones.

Marcia's will included the following provisions:

- I bequeath to my spouse Matt all of my tangible, personal property.
- To First Lutheran Church I leave $50,000.
- To a trust with PHL Bank I leave $200,000. Matt is to receive all the trust income quarterly for life, and the remainder is to be divided equally at his death among my three children or their estates.
- I leave my sister Annette $100,000, but if she disclaims this amount, it will go instead to my beloved spouse.
- I appoint the property in the trust at Quaker State Bank to Annie Adams (my daughter).
- The rest of my property I leave to Andy Adams (my first born).

Other pertinent information follows:

- As of her date of death, Marcia owed her country club $800.
- The cost of Marcia's funeral and tombstone totaled $15,000.
- Her accountant's, attorney's, and executor's fees are estimated to be $120,000.
- Annette made a qualified disclaimer of the $100,000 bequest.
- Marcia's executor, Hy Phee, will make whatever elections will result in the lowest estate tax payable. During her life, Marcia never made any taxable gifts and never consented to gift splitting.
- Assume that, under state law, taxes and any other costs associated with death are payable from the estate's residue and that the state death tax owed is equal to the state death tax credit available on the federal estate tax return.

C:13-63 Prepare an estate tax return (Form 706) for Adam Zugg of 45 Cornfield Place, Midwest City, IL 60000. Adam died October 31, 2016. He was survived by his wife,

Callie, and their son, Zebulon. At the time of his death, Adam was employed by a farm equipment distributor as its office manager. The executor reports that he has discovered the property listed below.

Checking account, Adam and Callie, joint tenants with right of survivorship	$ 10,200
Stocks in public companies in the name of Adam	1,300,000
Undeveloped land (not leased or farmed) in the name of Adam	4,400,000
Qualified retirement plan funded by Adam's employer	800,000
Face value of term life insurance policy on Adam's life	2,000,000
Automobile in Adam's name	22,000

Other information includes the following:
1. Adam owned the life insurance policy, and his estate is the beneficiary.
2. Callie is the beneficiary of the retirement plan.
3. Adam willed his stocks to Callie and the rest of his property to Zebulon.
4. Adam owed $13,200 on a car loan.
5. The estate's administrative expenses were $32,000, and his funeral expenses were $8,000.
6. Assume that the estate paid state estate taxes of $45,000.
7. Adam made his only taxable gift, $6 million taxable amount, in December 2013 and paid all the gift taxes from an account solely in his name.
8. Assume the estate's marginal income tax rate will be 33%.

CASE STUDY PROBLEMS

C:13-64 Your long-time client, Harold (Hal) Holland will meet with your supervising partner next week for an estate planning appointment. Hal has been married to Winona Holland for 25 years. Hal is age 68 and retired. Winona, age 60, retired early to spend more time with Hal. They are residents of Topeka, Kansas. Hal is a U.S. citizen, and Winona is a citizen of Australia. Winona has indicated she plans to return to Australia if Hal predeceases her. Your supervising partner has requested that you identify any potential pitfalls in Hal's current estate plan so she can bring them to his attention.

Hal has stated that, in addition to providing some wealth transfers to his wife Winona, he wants to treat his three children by his prior marriage (Gina, Halbert, and Julianna) approximately equally in terms of total wealth received from him by gift plus as a result of his death.

Hal and Winona prepared and submitted via e-mail the list of assets shown below.

- Principal residence in Topeka titled in the names of Hal and Winona, joint tenants with right of survivorship; purchased with $280,000 of consideration furnished solely by Winona; fair market value of $400,000.
- Household furnishings in the Topeka house; fair market value of $34,000. Winona owned almost all of these furnishings before she married Hal.
- Portfolio of publicly traded stocks in Hal's name; fair market value of $7.12 million.
- Mountain cabin and land in Vail, Colorado. Hal purchased the property in 1998 for $60,000; fair market value is $460,000. Hal never visits the cabin, but son Halbert spends every summer and several weeks during the winter at the cabin.
- Stock (12 shares) in Harold's Hammocks, Inc. (a closely held C corporation) transferred to the Oz State Bank Revocable Trust in 1992; fair market value of $226,000, and basis of $15,000. Hal acquired the 12 shares in 1988 in a Sec. 351 transaction. Daughters Julianna and Gina own the remaining stock, 44 shares each, which Hal gifted to them in 2010.
- Individual retirement account at ToKan State Bank. The account consists of the funds rolled directly into the IRA from the non-contributory qualified retirement plan of Hal's former employer when Hal retired. Fair market value of the IRA is $540,000. Hal has not yet received any distributions. He is the IRA beneficiary, and Winona is the contingent beneficiary if Hal predeceases her.
- Cash of $825,000 in checking and savings accounts in Hal's name.
- Mutual fund shares in the names of Hal and daughter Julianna, joint tenants with right of survivorship. Hal provided all the consideration ($9,000); fair market value of $64,000. He intended to use the money to help finance Julianna's education, but she received a full scholarship.

- Stock in Dolrah, Inc. (a firm that elected S corporation status in 1990 upon its formation). The stock is in Hal's name, and he is one of six stockholders; fair market value of his shares was $79,000.

Hal's current will reads as follows:

> To my wife, Winona, I leave outright $500,000 of stock from my portfolio of publicly traded stocks, and all of my stock in Dolrah, Inc.
>
> To my grandchild, Halbert, Jr., I leave $5,750,000 of publicly traded stock from my portfolio.
>
> I leave the rest of my estate outright in equal shares to my children, Gina, Halbert, and Julianna.

Required:
Prepare a memo to your supervising partner to help her prepare for the appointment with Hal. In the memo, advise the partner of any pitfalls (problems) you have identified that she should discuss with Hal. You need not make any calculations of estate tax liabilities.

C:13-65 Your client is Jon Jake, the executor of the Estate of Beth Adams, a widow. Mrs. Adams died 11 years after the death of her husband, Sam. Mr. Jake seeks assistance in the preparation of the estate tax return for Mrs. Adams, whose estate consists primarily of real estate. Mrs. Adams's estate will be divided equally among her three adult children except for $50,000 willed to charity. The real estate has been appraised at $6.8 million by her son-in-law (who is married to one of Mrs. Adams's three children), a real estate appraiser. You have a number of real estate clients and have considerable familiarity with property values for real estate located in the same general area as the estate's property. Your "gut feeling" is that the appraised values may be somewhat understated. As a tax advisor, what responsibilities do you have for making additional inquiries? What information should you provide Mr. Jake concerning possible penalties?

TAX RESEARCH PROBLEMS

C:13-66 Arthur Zolnick died at age 84 on June 7, 2016. In March 2008, he transferred $4 million of stock to a charitable remainder annuity trust (CRAT) from which he named himself to receive $200,000 per year for life. He designated a charitable organization to receive the remainder interest after his death and appointed his nephew Luther as trustee. Luther never distributed cash to Arthur because Arthur indicated he had no need for additional funds that "would just add to my gross estate." At Arthur's date of death, the value of the assets in the CRAT had risen to $8.3 million. Another firm prepared Arthur's estate tax return, on which it claimed a charitable contribution deduction for the CRAT. The IRS proposed disallowing the deduction. Arthur's executor has engaged your firm to address whether a charitable contribution deduction should be available.

C:13-67 In May 2008, Jasper Mason died, survived by his spouse Amber Mason and four adult children. His gross estate was valued at $3 million, and he had Sec. 2053 deductions of $120,000. His will left the personal residence on which the mortgage had been paid off to Amber. Its value was $450,000. The will stated that the rest of Jasper's property was to pass to a trust at Seaman's Bank with Amber to receive all the trust income semi-annually for life and the four children to receive the remainder in equal shares. Amber was the beneficiary of a $1 million life insurance policy included in Jasper's gross estate. The insurance policy was the only non-probate asset. Jasper made no post-1976 taxable gifts. A CPA with a small firm that does not specialize in taxation prepared the estate tax return for Jasper's estate and elected to claim the marital deduction for the trust. The firm with whom you are employed has been engaged to prepare the estate tax return for Amber, who died in May 2017. The Seaman's Bank trust has increased in value to $3 million as of Amber's date of death. Amber owned assets valued at $4 million in her own name. Your manager asks you to research whether the Seaman's Bank trust has to be included in Amber's gross estate. He is hoping that it does not because, even if the marital deduction had not been claimed for the trust, Jasper's estate still would not have owed any tax. Draft a memo to your manager reporting the results of your research. Confine your research to IRS pronouncements.

C:13-68 Sam and Taylor, residents of New Jersey, entered into a domestic partnership in New Jersey in October 2004. However, they never obtained a marriage license. Sam died in

March 2017, survived by Taylor. Sam's gross estate totals $10.2 million, he owed debts of $100,000, and funeral and administrative expenses are estimated to be about $50,000. Sam willed $300,000 to his alma mater and the rest of his estate to Taylor. All of his property passed under his will. What is the amount of his taxable estate? Cite the authority supporting your decision concerning the availability of a marital deduction.

C:13-69 George Tanner died October 2, 2016, survived by his son Thomas and his daughter Gigi Tanner Stewart and her children, Sam and Cindy. George was the sole stockholder of Tanner, Inc., a C corporation. Gigi served as president of Tanner from its inception until early January 2017. However, she never had an employment agreement or a noncompete agreement with Tanner, Inc. George was not involved with the business; he simply provided the funding. Gigi executed all of Tanner's contracts with its customers and was very involved with the business. George's will left half of the Tanner stock to Gigi and the other half to Thomas. In late December 2016, Gigi and Thomas had major disagreements, and soon thereafter Gigi formed a C corporation (GTS, Inc.) to compete with Tanner, Inc. Because of the personal relationships Gigi had with Tanner's customers, almost all of them broke their contracts with Tanner and began doing business with GTS. Preparation of George's estate tax return is underway, and one of the estate's major assets is the Tanner stock. A question has arisen whether the valuation of the Tanner stock should take into account the value of Gigi's personal goodwill, given the absence of an employment agreement or a noncompete agreement. If so, the value of her personal goodwill would adversely affect the value otherwise determined for the stock. Your supervisor requested that you research this issue and present your results in a memo so she can discuss the valuation issue with the person who is preparing an appraisal of the Tanner stock.

C:13-70 *Internet Research Problem.* Philip Seymour Hoffman died in February 2014, survived by three children (Cooper, Tallulah, and Willa) and their mother Marianne O'Donnell. His estate was estimated to have a net value of $35 million. Perform a Google search using the words "Philip Seymour Hoffman will" and read the February 20, 2014 article by Deborah L. Jacobs from *Forbes*. Answer the following questions:

a. When did he execute his will?
b. Whom does his will name to receive his property?
c. What marital deduction will his estate receive?
d. If his will provides for a disclaimer, summarize its terms.
e. If Hoffman owned a $10 million life insurance policy on his own life, who will receive the insurance proceeds?

C:13-71 *Internet Research Problem.* Soon you will be meeting with a client who is considering moving to one of several other states and who currently does not have a will. You want to do some research regarding how property often passes if the decedent dies intestate (without a will). The client is married, has no children, has one living parent, and has an estate of approximately $3 million. Go to http://www.uniformlaws.org and consult Section 2-102 of the Uniform Probate Code on the site. This section describes the "model" rules for property dispositions if this client dies intestate. Prepare a brief memo about what you learn regarding the client's situation.

C:13-72 *Internet Research Problem.* Your firm has prepared the estate tax return (Form 706) for the Estate of Belinda Baker, a widow who died January 13, 2017. Besides substantial amounts of cash, mostly in certificates of deposit, she owned ABC stocks valued at $3.2 million, TUV stocks valued at $4.5 million, and 200 acres of undeveloped land valued at $5 million in total. Her will specifies that her three children (Barbara, Benjamin, and Boyd) are to share equally in her estate and that her executor is authorized to decide which person receives which asset(s) so long as each one receives, in total, assets with the same aggregate values. Consult Form 8971 (Information Regarding Beneficiaries Acquiring Property From a Decedent) and the related instructions. According to the instructions to Form 8971, what information should the executor report for each beneficiary in this type of situation?

CHAPTER

14

INCOME TAXATION OF TRUSTS AND ESTATES

LEARNING OBJECTIVES

After studying this chapter, you should be able to

1. Describe the basic concepts concerning trusts and estates
2. Distinguish between the accounting concepts of principal and income
3. Calculate the income tax liability of a trust or an estate
4. Explain the significance of distributable net income
5. Calculate the taxable income of a simple trust
6. Calculate the taxable income of a complex trust and an estate
7. Recognize the significance of income in respect of a decedent
8. Explain the effect of the grantor trust provisions
9. Identify tax planning opportunities in trust and estate income taxation
10. Comply with procedural rules for trust and estate income taxation

CHAPTER OUTLINE

Chapters C:12 and C:13 examined two components of the transfer tax system: the gift tax and the estate tax. This chapter returns to income taxation by exploring the basic rules for taxing trusts and estates, two special tax entities often called **fiduciaries**. Income generated by property owned by an estate or a **trust** is reported on an income tax return for that entity. In general, the tax rules governing estates and trusts are identical. Unless the text states that a rule applies to only one of these entities, the discussion concerns both estates and trusts. Subchapter J (Secs. 641–692) of the IRC contains the special tax rules applicable to estates and trusts, and this chapter describes its basic provisions.

This chapter also discusses principles of fiduciary accounting, a concept that influences the tax consequences. The chapter focuses on determining the fiduciary's taxable income and the amount taxable to the beneficiaries. It includes comprehensive examples concerning the computations of taxable income, and Appendix B displays completed tax returns (Form 1041) for both a simple and a complex trust. The chapter also explores the circumstances that cause the grantor (transferor) to be taxed on the trust's income.

BASIC CONCEPTS

OBJECTIVE 1

Describe the basic concepts concerning trusts and estates

INCEPTION OF TRUSTS

Often a very wealthy person (one concerned with gift and/or estate taxes) will create trusts for tax and/or other reasons (e.g., conserving assets). A person may create a trust at any point in time by transferring property to the trust. A **trustee** (named by the transferor) administers the trust property for the benefit of the beneficiary. The trustee may be either an individual or an institution, such as a bank, and a trust may have more than one trustee.

If the transfer occurs during the transferor's lifetime, the trust is called an **inter vivos trust**, meaning among the living. The transferor is known as the **grantor** or the **trustor**. A trust created under the direction of a decedent's will is called a **testamentary trust** and contains assets formerly held by the decedent's estate. A trust may continue to exist for whatever time the trust instrument or the will specifies, subject to the constraints of the **Rule Against Perpetuities.**[1]

INCEPTION OF ESTATES

REAL-WORLD EXAMPLE

The IRS reports that 3.2 million fiduciary income tax returns were filed in 2015.

Estates originate only upon the death of the person whose assets are being administered. The estate continues in existence until the executor[2] (i.e., the person(s) named in the will to manage the property and distribute the assets) or administrator (where the decedent died without a will) completes his or her duties. An executor's or administrator's duties include collecting the assets, paying the debts and taxes, and distributing the property. The time needed to perform the duties may vary from a year or two to over a decade, depending on many factors (e.g., whether anyone contests the will).

Because the estate is a separate tax entity, continuing the estate's existence results in an additional personal exemption and achieves having some income taxed to yet another taxpayer, but the estate's income tax rates are very compressed. Nevertheless, the decedent's survivors sometimes can reduce their personal income taxes by preserving the estate's existence as a separate taxpayer. Treasury Regulations provide, however, that if the IRS considers that the administration of an estate has been unreasonably prolonged, it will view the estate as terminated for federal tax purposes after a reasonable period for performance of the administrative duties has expired.[3] In such a situation, the income is taxed directly to the individuals entitled to receive the estate's assets, and sometimes these individuals face a marginal tax rate that is higher than the estate tax rate.

---

[1] The Rule Against Perpetuities addresses how long property may be tied up in trust and is the "principle that no interest in property is valid unless it vests not later than twenty-one years, plus period of gestation, after some life or lives in being which exist at time of creation of interest." Legal-dictionary.thefreedictionary.com. Some states have abolished the Rule Against Perpetuities.

[2] In some states, this individual is called a personal representative.

[3] Reg. Sec. 1.641(b)-3(a).

REASONS FOR CREATING TRUSTS

A myriad of reasons—both tax and nontax—exist for creating trusts. A discussion of some of these reasons follows.

KEY POINT

A trust is a contract between two parties: the grantor and the trustee. The grantor gives the trustee legal title to property, which the trustee holds for the benefit of a third party(ies), the beneficiary(ies). The trustee, acting in a fiduciary capacity, manages the property for the duration of the trust. Beneficiaries may have an income interest, which means that they receive part or all of the trust's income, or they may have a remainder interest, which means that they will receive the trust property on some specified future date. A beneficiary may hold both an income interest and a remainder interest. The grantor may also be a beneficiary and/or the trustee.

Tax Saving Aspects of Trusts. If the trust is irrevocable, meaning the grantor cannot alter the distribution terms or require the trustee to return the assets, one of the primary tax purposes for establishing the trust traditionally was to achieve income splitting, whereby the income from the trust assets was taxed to at least one taxpayer (i.e., the trust or the beneficiary) at a lower marginal tax rate than that of the grantor. Today's compressed fiduciary tax rate schedules, under which the top rate of 39.6% (in 2017) occurs at an income level above $12,500, often make achieving income tax reduction difficult. Sometimes the trust instrument grants the trustee discretion in "sprinkling" the income among several beneficiaries or accumulating it within the trust. In such circumstances, the trustee may consider the tax effects of making a distribution of income to one beneficiary instead of another or retaining income in the trust.

Individuals also have created trusts to minimize their estate taxes. As discussed in Chapter C:13, for the transferor to exclude the property conveyed to the trust from the gross estate, the transferor must not retain the right to receive the trust income or the power to control which other people receive the income or have, at the time of death, the power to alter the identity of anyone named earlier to receive such assets.[4]

Nontax Aspects of Trusts. Reduction of taxes is not always the foremost reason for establishing trusts. Individuals, some of whom are very wealthy, often use trusts, including Sec. 2503(c) trusts and *Crummey* trusts, when minors are the donees so that a trustee can manage the assets. (See Chapter C:12 for a discussion of such trusts.) Even when the donee is an adult, donors sometimes may prefer that the assets be managed by a trustee deemed to have better management skills than the donee. Other donors may want to avoid conveying property directly to a donee if they fear the donee would soon consume most of the assets. In addition, donors sometimes use trusts to protect assets from creditors.

The creation of a **revocable trust** (i.e., one in which the grantor may demand that the assets be returned) does not yield any income or estate tax savings for the grantor. Nevertheless, donors often establish revocable trusts, including ones in which the grantor is also the beneficiary, for nontax purposes such as having the property managed by another person or an institution with superior management skills. Use of a revocable trust reduces probate costs because assets in a revocable trust avoid probate. Such a strategy is especially important in states where probate costs are high. In this text, a trust is deemed to be an **irrevocable trust** unless explicitly denoted as being revocable.

ADDITIONAL COMMENT

Estates and trusts potentially owe the 3.8% incremental tax on net investment income, but the inception point for this tax is at a much lower amount than it is for individuals. The tax is levied on the lesser of (1) the entity's undistributed net investment income or (2) its modified adjusted gross income (MAGI) in excess of the amount at which the top tax rate of 39.6% begins ($12,500 in 2017). MAGI is AGI reduced by the personal exemption, expenses that would not have been incurred if the property were not held by an estate or trust, and the distribution deduction. Net investment income includes, among other things, interest, dividends, annuities, royalties, rents, and net gains from certain property dispositions, all reduced by allocable deductions.

BASIC PRINCIPLES OF FIDUCIARY TAXATION

Throughout the rest of this chapter, you should keep several basic principles of **fiduciary taxation** in mind. These features (discussed below) apply to all trusts other than grantor trusts, a type of trust where generally the grantor instead of the trust or the beneficiary pays tax on the income. (See pages C:14-30 through C:14-33 for a description of the tax treatment of grantor trusts.)

Trusts and Estates as Separate Taxpayers. An estate or a trust is a separate taxpaying entity that files a Form 1041, and if it has any taxable income, it pays an income tax. The 2017 tax rates applicable to estates and trusts appear on the inside back cover. These rates, which are indexed annually for inflation, are very compressed in comparison with the rates for individuals. As is true for individuals, an estate's or trust's long-term capital gains and qualified dividends are taxed at a maximum rate of 15% or 20% depending on the entity's tax bracket. Also, see the adjoining Additional Comment.

[4] Sec. 2036, relating to retention of income or control, and Sec. 2038, relating to the power to alter the identity of beneficiaries.

EXAMPLE C:14-1 ▶ For calendar year 2017, a trust reports taxable income of $15,000, all from interest on corporate bonds. Its tax liability is $4,223, ignoring the 3.8% tax on net investment income. In contrast, an unmarried individual not qualifying as a head of household would owe taxes of $1,784 on $15,000 of taxable income. Assuming that MAGI also is $15,000, the additional tax on the trust net investment income is $95 [($15,000 − $12,500) × 0.038]. ◀

No Double Taxation. Unlike the situation for corporations, no double taxation of income earned by an estate or trust (a fiduciary taxpayer) occurs because an estate or trust receives a deduction for the income it distributes to its beneficiaries. The beneficiaries, in turn, report the taxable portion of their receipts as income on their individual returns. Thus, the current income is taxed once, to the fiduciary or to the beneficiary or some to each, depending on how much is distributed. In total, all the estate or trust's current income is taxed, sometimes some to the fiduciary and the remaining amount to the beneficiary. One of the primary purposes of the Subchapter J rules is to address exactly where the estate or trust's current income is taxed.

EXAMPLE C:14-2 ▶ In the current year, the Lopez Trust receives corporate bond interest of $25,000, $15,000 of which the trustee in its discretion distributes to Lupe. Lupe is taxed on $15,000, the amount of the distribution. The trust is taxed on the income it retains or accumulates, $10,000 in this case, less a $100 personal exemption (discussed on pages C:14-9 and C:14-10). ◀

Conduit Approach. A conduit approach governs fiduciary income taxation. Under this approach, the distributed income has the same character in the hands of the beneficiary as it has to the trust. Thus, if the trust distributes nontaxable interest income on state and local bonds, the income retains its tax-free character at the beneficiary level.

EXAMPLE C:14-3 ▶ In the current year, the Lopez Trust receives $15,000 of dividends and $10,000 of nontaxable interest. It distributes all of its receipts to its beneficiary, who is deemed to receive $15,000 of dividend income and $10,000 of nontaxable interest. The preferential 15% tax rate applies to the dividends if the beneficiary's tax bracket exceeds 15%. However, if the beneficiary has low AGI and taxable income, and is in the 15% or lower tax bracket, the 0% tax rate will apply to the dividends. ◀

SELF-STUDY QUESTION

King Trust receives interest on a savings account and distributes it to Anne. Because the trust is treated as a conduit, the interest is reported by Anne as taxable interest. Why might this be important?

ANSWER

For purposes of the 3.8% tax on net investment income and the limitation on the investment interest deduction, the interest from the trust is part of Anne's investment income. For purposes of the passive loss limitations, it is classified as portfolio income.

Similarity to Rules for Individuals. Section 641(b) states "[T]he taxable income of an estate or trust shall be computed in the same manner as in the case of an individual, except as otherwise provided in this part." Sections 641–683 appear in this part (Part I) of Subchapter J. Thus, the tax effect for fiduciaries is the same as for individuals if the provisions of Secs. 641–683 do not specify rules that differ from those applicable for individual taxpayers. Sections 641–683 do not provide any special treatment for interest income from state and local bonds or for state and local tax payments. Consequently, an estate or trust receives an exclusion for state and local bond interest and the same deductions as individuals for state and local taxes. On the other hand, Sec. 642(b) specifies the amount of the personal exemption for fiduciaries. Thus, this subsection preempts the Sec. 151 rule concerning the amount of the personal exemption for individuals.

PRINCIPLES OF FIDUCIARY ACCOUNTING

OBJECTIVE 2

Distinguish between the accounting concepts of principal and income

To better understand the special tax treatment of fiduciary income, especially the determination of to whom the estate or trust's current income is taxed, one needs a general knowledge of the principles of fiduciary accounting. Receipts and disbursements are classified in either the income or principal (corpus) account.

THE IMPORTANCE OF IDENTIFYING INCOME AND PRINCIPAL

When computing taxable income, we generally are concerned with whether a particular item is included in or deducted from gross income. When answering fiduciary tax questions, however, we also need to consider whether an item is classified as principal (corpus) or income for fiduciary accounting purposes. For example, certain items (e.g., interest on state bonds) may constitute fiduciary accounting gross income but are not included in calculating gross income for tax purposes. Other items (e.g., capital gains) are included in gross income but generally classified as principal for fiduciary accounting purposes. If the trust instrument stipulates that the trustee can distribute only income prior to the termination of the trust, the amount of fiduciary accounting income sets the ceiling on the current distribution that the trustee can make to a beneficiary.

One of the most difficult aspects of feeling comfortable with the fiduciary taxation rules is appreciating the difference between fiduciary accounting income and income in the general tax sense. To understand and apply the IRC, one has to know in which context the word *income* is used. Section 643(b) provides guidance for this matter by providing that the word *income* refers to income in the fiduciary accounting context unless other words, such as "distributable net," "undistributable net," "taxable," or "gross," modify the word *income*. In this text, the term **net accounting income** is used to refer to the excess of accounting gross income over expenses charged to accounting income.

Under state law, the definitions in the trust instrument that classify items as principal or income preempt any definitions contained in state statutes. In the absence of definitions in the trust instrument, the applicable state statute controls. For purposes of defining principal and income, many states follow the Uniform Principal and Income Act of 2000 (hereafter referred to as the Uniform Act) in its entirety or with minor modifications.[5]

SELF-STUDY QUESTION

A trust agreement provides that all trust income is to be distributed to Janet until her thirty-fifth birthday, at which time the trust is to terminate and distribute all of its corpus to Joe. The trust owns only stock. If the trust sells the stock, is Janet entitled to a distribution equal to the gain?

ANSWER

This question stresses the importance of differentiating between income and principal. The trustee must follow the definitions of income and corpus stated in the trust agreement, or if not there, under state law. Janet receives no distribution if the proceeds are classified as corpus unless the trustee under the Uniform Act makes an adjustment and moves money from corpus to income.

The Uniform Act allows the trustee to make adjustments between the principal and income accounts to the extent the trustee deems them necessary (such as to increase the amount distributable), provided certain additional requirements are met. A trustee, however, will not always deem adjustments necessary. The rationale behind allowing adjustments is grounded in modern portfolio theory. By allowing trustees to transfer cash from the principal to the income account, the Uniform Act enables a trustee to apply prudent investor standards when making investment decisions. If dividends are low because of growth stock investments, the Uniform Act allows the trustee to adjust and transfer some cash to the income account, thereby increasing the amount distributable to a beneficiary entitled to receive nothing but income.

The categorization of a receipt or disbursement as principal or income generally affects the amount that can be distributed and the amount taxed to the fiduciary or the beneficiary. A trustee cannot distribute a receipt that constitutes gross income for tax purposes if it constitutes principal under the fiduciary accounting rules unless the trust instrument authorizes the trustee to distribute principal or unless, under the Uniform Act, the trustee makes adjustments by transferring some cash from principal to income. For example, if a gain is classified as principal and the trustee can distribute only income, in the absence of an adjustment, the trust is taxed on the gain.

EXAMPLE C:14-4 ▶ In the current year, the Bell Trust collects $18,000 of dividends, classified as accounting income. In addition, it sells stock for a $40,000 capital gain. The trust instrument states that the gain is allocated to principal and does not allow the trustee to make adjustments. The trust instrument requires the trustee to distribute all the trust's income to Beth annually until she reaches age 45. The trust assets are to be held and paid to Beth on her forty-fifth birthday (five years from now). The trustee must distribute $18,000 to Beth in the current year. The capital gain cannot be distributed currently because it is allocated to principal, and the trustee is not empowered to make distributions of principal this year. The trust will pay tax on the gain. ◀

PRINCIPAL AND INCOME: THE UNIFORM ACT

Income Receipts. The Uniform Act defines *income* as amounts received "as current return from a principal asset." It lists income as including rent, interest, and dividends.

[5] The *Uniform Principal and Income Act* (2000) is a model set of rules proposed by the National Conference of Commissioners on Uniform State Laws. States can voluntarily adopt such provisions verbatim or in amended form.

The rules provide details for receipts from the disposition of minerals and other natural resources. A portion (90%) of the receipts from royalties is added to principal so the trustee can use funds to buy other assets to replace income from the depleting assets. The remainder of the royalties constitutes income.

Principal Receipts. ***Principal*** is defined in the Uniform Act as "property held in trust for distribution to a remainder beneficiary when the trust terminates." Among the categories of receipts included in principal are the following: consideration received on the sale or other transfer of principal property, capital gain dividends (from mutual funds), life insurance proceeds, and 90% of royalties received from natural resources.

Expenditures. The Uniform Act provides guidance for expenditures also. Among the important charges that reduce income are the following:

- Ordinary expenses, including regularly recurring property taxes, insurance premiums on property, interest, and ordinary repairs
- One-half the regular compensation of the trustee
- Income tax payable by the trustee levied on receipts classified as income

Some of the significant expenditures chargeable to principal are

- Principal payments on debts
- One-half the regular compensation of the trustee
- Tax based on receipts allocated to principal even if the tax is described as an income tax

As with income, provisions in the trust instrument regarding allocation of principal payments take precedence over state law or the Uniform Act.

EXAMPLE C:14-5 ▶ The governing instrument for the Wang Trust does not define income and principal. The state in question has adopted the Uniform Act. In the current year, the trust reports the following receipts and disbursements:

Dividends	$12,000
Proceeds from sale of stock, including $20,000 of gain	70,000
Trustee's fee	1,000
CPA's fee for preparation of tax return	300

The trust's net accounting income is $11,200 ($12,000 − $500 − $300). The gain on the sale of stock and the remaining sales proceeds constitute corpus. One-half the trustee's fee is charged to income. If the trustee can distribute nothing but income, the maximum distribution is $11,200. ◀

SELF-STUDY QUESTION

Wilson Trust, which owns a commercial building, is required to distribute all of its income each year. The building is leased on a net lease, so the trust's only expense is depreciation. The rental income is $25,000, and the depreciation is $11,000. If depreciation is charged to income, the distribution to the income beneficiary will be $14,000, and the trustee will set aside $11,000 of the income for the remainderman. What is the impact if depreciation is chargeable to principal?

ANSWER

The income distribution will be $25,000. If the trust holds the building to the end of its useful life, the building will theoretically "turn to dust" overnight, and the remainderman would receive no funds to restore the building because the trust had no depreciation reserve.

CATEGORIZATION OF DEPRECIATION

The Uniform Act does not provide specific mandates regarding depreciation. Rather, it states that a "trustee may transfer to principal a reasonable amount of the net cash receipts from a principal asset that is subject to depreciation." Thus, the trustee has freedom to decide whether to charge depreciation against income. The Drafting Committee for the Uniform Act indicated that it believed the trustee should have discretion about how to handle depreciation. It added that a "purpose served by transferring cash from income to principal for depreciation is to provide funds to pay the principal of an indebtedness secured by the depreciable property." If depreciation is charged against income, it reduces accounting income and thereby the maximum amount the trustee can distribute to the beneficiary if it can distribute only income. If depreciation is charged against principal, the maximum amount that can be distributed to the income beneficiaries is not reduced by the depreciation deduction. This result is advantageous to the income beneficiary. (See page C:14-9 for a discussion of the tax treatment of depreciation.)

A statement in the trust instrument concerning the accounting treatment for depreciation overrides the discretion granted to the trustee by the Uniform Act.

EXAMPLE C:14-6 ▶ Park Trust, whose trust instrument is silent with respect to depreciation, collects rental income of $17,000 and pays property taxes of $1,000. Its depreciation expense is $4,000. If the trustee does not transfer an amount for depreciation to principal, the trust's net accounting income is $16,000 ($17,000 − $1,000). If the trust instrument mandates current distribution of all the income, the beneficiary receives $16,000. If the trustee transfers $4,000 to principal, the income distribution is limited to $12,000. ◀

Topic Review C:14-1 summarizes the treatment under the Uniform Act of the major receipts and expenditures of fiduciaries. The discussion in the rest of the chapter assumes the Uniform Act governs the trust and that the trustee makes no adjustments from principal to income.

Formula for Taxable Income and Tax Liability

OBJECTIVE 3

Calculate the income tax liability of a trust or an estate

With three major exceptions, the formula for determining a fiduciary's taxable income and income tax liability is very similar to the formula applicable to individuals. A fiduciary's deductions are not divided between deductions *for* and *from* adjusted gross income (AGI). Instead, a fiduciary's deductions are simply deductible in arriving at taxable income. A fiduciary receives no standard deduction. A type of deduction unique to fiduciaries—the distribution deduction—is available in computing a fiduciary's taxable income. Figure C:14-1 illustrates the formula for computing a fiduciary's taxable income and tax liability.

Gross Income

The items included in a trust or estate's gross income are the same as those included in an individual's gross income. However, the categorization of a fiduciary's income is not identical for tax and accounting purposes. For example, a gain usually constitutes principal for accounting purposes, but it is part of gross income for tax purposes.

EXAMPLE C:14-7 ▶ In the current year, Duke Trust receives $8,000 interest on corporate bonds, $20,000 interest on state bonds, and a $50,000 capital gain. The trust reports gross income of $58,000 ($8,000 + $50,000). Its accounting income is $28,000 ($8,000 + $20,000) because tax-exempt interest is accounting income, and the gain is generally part of principal. ◀

Deductions for Expenses

Fiduciaries incur numerous deductible expenses that parallel those of individuals and include interest, taxes (e.g., state and local income taxes and property taxes), fees for tax return preparation, expenses associated with producing rental income, and trade or business expenses. In addition, fiduciaries may deduct some or all of the trustee's fee under Sec. 212 as an expense incurred for the management of property held for the production of income.

TOPIC REVIEW C:14-1

Classification of Receipts and Expenditures as Principal or Income Under the Uniform Act of 2000

Income Account	Principal Account
Income:	Receipts:
Rent	Consideration (including gains) received upon disposition of property
Interest	Capital gain dividends from mutual funds
Dividends	90% of royalties
10% of royalties	Life insurance proceeds
Expenses:	Expenditures:
One-half of the trustee's fees	One-half of the trustee's fees
Ordinary expenses (e.g., property taxes, insurance, interest, and ordinary repairs)	Principal payments on debt
Taxes levied on accounting income	Taxes levied on gains and other items of principal

Note that the Uniform Act gives the trustee discretion whether to charge depreciation to income.

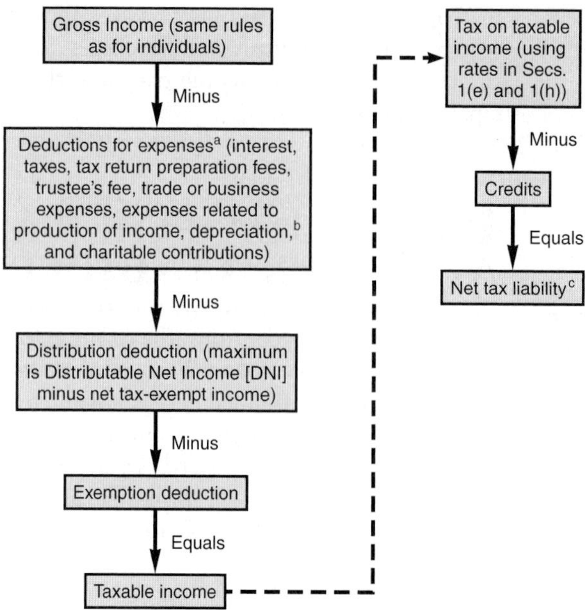

[a]No deduction is available for expenses allocable to tax-exempt income.

[b]When the trust instrument is silent, depreciation is allocated for tax purposes between the fiduciary and the beneficiary according to the portion of income attributable to each.

[c]Trusts and estates are subject to the alternative minimum tax (AMT). The AMT may be owed by a trust or estate in addition to the income tax levy described in this figure. The AMT is calculated in the same way as for individual taxpayers. Trusts and estates, however, are allowed only a $24,100 statutory exemption in 2017. The phase-out for the exemption begins at $80,450.

FIGURE C:14-1 ▶ FORMULA FOR DETERMINING THE TAXABLE INCOME AND TAX LIABILITY OF A FIDUCIARY

Individuals can deduct miscellaneous itemized deductions only to the extent they exceed 2% of AGI. For estates and trusts, Sec. 67(e) provides that a hypothetical AGI amount is determined in the same fashion as for an individual *except* that (1) expenses paid or incurred in connection with the administration of the estate or trust *that would not have been incurred if the property were not held in such trust or estate,* (2) the personal exemption, and (3) the distribution deduction are treated as deductible for hypothetical AGI. Thus, these deductions, such as the cost of preparing a fiduciary return, are not subject to the 2% floor. Controversy arose about whether investment counsel fees paid by trusts were subject to the 2% floor. The Supreme Court in *Knight*[6] concluded that, to escape the 2% rule, the costs must be "uncommon, unusual, or unlikely" for an individual to incur. It emphasized that individuals commonly engage investment advisers and concluded that the fees in question were subject to the 2% floor. For tax years beginning after 2014, Reg. Sec. 1.67-4 provides that, in general, investment advisory fees are subject to the 2% floor but that "certain incremental costs of investment advice beyond the amount that would be charged to an individual investor are not subject to the 2% floor." This regulation addresses bundled fees for various services that lack details of the amount billed for each service and are not computed on an hourly basis by stating, "only the portion of that fee that is attributable to investment advice is subject to the 2% floor." For simplicity, this chapter assumes that all trustee fees are exempt from classification as a miscellaneous itemized deduction.

An executor can deduct administration expenses on the estate's income tax return if he or she does not deduct such items on the estate tax return. Unlike the situation for individuals,

[6] *Knight v. Comm.*, 101 AFTR 2d 2008-544, 2008-1 USTC ¶50,332 (USSC, 2008). Prior to the Supreme Court's decision, the Treasury Department issued Prop. Reg. 1.67-4, which adopted a harsher position than that of the Supreme Court. It provided that miscellaneous expenses incurred by estates and trusts need to be expenses *unique* to estates and trusts to avoid the 2% floor rule. In 2014, the Treasury Department issued final Treasury Regulations described above.

a fiduciary's charitable contribution deduction is not limited. The IRC does not allow a deduction, however, unless the trust instrument authorizes a charitable contribution.[7]

A depreciation or depletion deduction is available to an estate or trust only to the extent it is not allowable to beneficiaries under Secs. 167(d) or 611(b).[8] According to Sec. 167(d), the depreciation deduction for trusts is apportioned between the income beneficiaries and the trust pursuant to the terms of the trust instrument. If the instrument is silent, the depreciation is divided between the parties on the basis of the trust income allocable to each. For estates, however, the depreciation always must be apportioned according to the share of the income allocable to each party. The Sec. 611(b) rules for depletion parallel those described above for the allocation of depreciation.

EXAMPLE C:14-8 ▶ In the current year, Nunn Trust distributes 20% of its income to Bob and 50% to Clay. It accumulates the remaining 30%. The trust's current year depreciation is \$10,000. The trust instrument is silent concerning the depreciation deduction, and the trustee exercised discretion to charge depreciation to principal. Even though net accounting income and the maximum distributable amount are not reduced by the depreciation deduction, Bob receives a \$2,000 (0.20 × \$10,000) depreciation deduction, and Clay receives a \$5,000 (0.50 × \$10,000) depreciation deduction. The remaining \$3,000 (0.30 × \$10,000) of depreciation is deducted in calculating the trust's taxable income. ◀

DISTRIBUTION DEDUCTION

Simple Trusts. Some trusts must distribute all their income currently and are not empowered to make charitable contributions. Treasury Regulations refer to such trusts as **simple trusts.**[9] According to Sec. 651(a), these trusts receive a distribution deduction for the income required to be distributed currently, that is, 100% of the trust income. No words modify the word *income;* therefore, *income* means accounting income. If the accounting income that must be distributed exceeds the trust's distributable net income, the distribution deduction may not exceed the distributable net income (see discussion beginning on page C:14-10). As used in this context, distributable net income does not include any tax-free income (net of related deductions) that the trust earned.[10] The amount deductible at the trust level is taxed to the beneficiaries, and they are taxed on all of that income, irrespective of the amount actually distributed.

KEY POINT

If a trust *must* distribute all of its income currently, has no charitable beneficiary, *and* does *not* distribute corpus during the year, it is a simple trust for that year. *Income* as used here, is accounting net income.

Complex Trusts. Trusts that are not required to distribute all their income currently are referred to as **complex trusts.**[11] The distribution deduction for complex trusts and all estates is the sum of the income required to be distributed currently and any other amounts (such as discretionary payments) properly paid, credited, or required to be distributed for the year. As is the case for simple trusts, the distribution deduction may not exceed the trust or estate's distributable net income (reduced by its tax-exempt income net of any related deductions).[12] The complex trust or estate's beneficiaries report, in the aggregate, gross income equal to the amount of the distribution deduction.[13]

EXAMPLE C:14-9 ▶ Green Trust must distribute 25% of its income annually to Amy. In addition, the trustee in its discretion may distribute additional income to Amy or Brad. In the current year, the trust has net accounting income and distributable net income of \$100,000, none from tax-exempt sources. The trust makes a \$25,000 mandatory distribution to Amy and discretionary distributions of \$10,000 each to Amy and Brad. The trust's distribution deduction is \$45,000 (\$25,000 + \$10,000 + \$10,000). Amy and Brad report trust income of \$35,000 and \$10,000, respectively, on their individual returns. ◀

PERSONAL EXEMPTION

One of the differences between the rules for individuals and for fiduciaries is the amount of the personal exemption. Under Sec. 151, individuals are allowed personal exemptions. Section 642(b) authorizes an exemption for fiduciaries that applies in lieu of the amount for individuals. A trust or estate, however, receives no exemption in the year of its termination.

---

[7] Sec. 642(c)(1).
[8] Sec. 642(e).
[9] Reg. Sec. 1.651(a)-1.
[10] Sec. 651(b).
[11] Reg. Sec. 1.661(a)-1.
[12] Secs. 661(a) and (c).
[13] Sec. 662(a).

Estates are entitled to a $600 exemption. The exemption amount for trusts differs, depending on the terms of the trust. If the trust instrument requires that the trustee distribute all the income annually, the trust receives a $300 exemption. Otherwise, $100 is the exemption amount. Some trusts may be required to make current distributions of all their income in certain years, whereas in other years they may be directed to accumulate the income or to make distributions at the trustee's discretion. For such trusts the exemption amount is $300 in some years and $100 in other years.

EXAMPLE C:14-10 ▶ Marion Gold establishes a trust in 2012 with Jack Silver as the beneficiary. The trust instrument instructs the trustee to make discretionary distributions of income to Jack during the years 2012 through 2016. Beginning in 2017, the trustee is to pay all the trust income to Jack currently. For 2012 through 2016, the trust's exemption was $100. Beginning in 2017, it rises to $300. ◀

Recall that a trust receives a distribution deduction for income currently distributed to its beneficiaries. At first blush, it appears that the distribution deduction balances out the income of trusts that must distribute all their income currently, and such trusts receive no tax benefits from their exemption deduction. True, the exemption produces no tax savings for such trusts if they have no gains credited to principal. Tax savings do result from the personal exemption, however, if the trust has undistributed gains. The exemption reduces the amount of gain otherwise taxed at the trust level.

EXAMPLE C:14-11 ▶ Rizzo Trust must distribute all of its income currently. Capital gains are characterized as principal. In the current year, Rizzo Trust has $25,000 of interest income from corporate bonds and a $10,000 capital gain. It has no expenses. It receives a distribution deduction of $25,000 and a $300 personal exemption. Its taxable income is $9,700 ($25,000 + $10,000 − $25,000 − $300), which represents the capital gain less the personal exemption. ◀

SELF-STUDY QUESTION

A trust, although not required to do so, distributes all of its income in the current year. In the same year, it has a long-term capital gain. The trust agreement allocates the gain to principal. The trust does not distribute principal, and none of its beneficiaries are charities. Is the trust a simple trust? What is its personal exemption?

ANSWER

It is a complex trust because it is not required to distribute all of its income. The exemption is $100 because distributions are discretionary.

The personal exemption amount for individuals is adjusted annually for changes in the consumer price index, but no comparable provision exists for the personal exemption for fiduciaries. On the other hand, the tax rate schedules for both fiduciaries and individuals are indexed for inflation.

CREDITS

In general, the rules for tax credits for fiduciaries are the same as those for individuals, but a fiduciary generally does not incur expenditures of the type that trigger some of the personal credits, such as the credit for household and dependent care expenses. Trusts and estates are allowed a foreign tax credit determined in the same manner as for individual taxpayers except that the credit is limited to the amount of foreign taxes not allocable to the beneficiaries.[14]

U.S. PRODUCTION ACTIVITIES DEDUCTION

The 2004 Jobs Act added a new deduction for businesses engaged in U.S. production activities for tax years beginning after 2004. Chapter C:3 describes the corporate version of this deduction, but the deduction also applies to individuals. In the fiduciary context, the deduction can arise when a sole proprietor dies, and his or her business passes to an estate or trust. To the extent income is distributed from the estate or trust, the U.S. production activities deduction applies at the beneficiary level. Thus, the estate or trust will need to determine each beneficiary's share of the business's qualified production activities income and report these amounts to the beneficiaries. Further discussion of this topic with respect to estates and trusts is beyond the scope of this text.

DISTRIBUTABLE NET INCOME

OBJECTIVE 4

Explain the significance of distributable net income

As stated earlier in this chapter, the primary function of Subchapter J is to determine to whom—the fiduciary, the beneficiary, or some to each—the estate or the trust's current income is to be taxed. **Distributable net income (DNI)** plays a key role in determining the amount taxed to each party. In fact, DNI has been called the pie to be cut for tax purposes.[15]

[14] Sec. 642(a)(1).

[15] M. Carr Ferguson, James L. Freeland, and Richard B. Stephens, *Federal Income Taxation of Estates and Beneficiaries* (Boston, MA: Little, Brown, 1970), p. 1x.

SIGNIFICANCE OF DNI

DNI sets the ceiling on the amount of distributions taxed to the beneficiaries. As mentioned earlier, beneficiaries are taxed on the lesser of the amount of the distributions they receive or their share of DNI (reduced by net tax-exempt income).

Just as the total amount taxed to the beneficiaries equals the fiduciary's distribution deduction, DNI represents not only the maximum that can be taxed to the beneficiaries but also the maximum that can be deducted at the fiduciary level. Recall from the preceding section that the distribution deduction is the smaller of the amount distributed or the fiduciary's DNI. The distribution deduction, however, may not include any portion of tax-exempt income (net of any related deductions) deemed to have been distributed.

DNI also determines the character of the beneficiaries' income. Under the conduit approach, each beneficiary's distribution is deemed to consist of various categories of income (net of deductions) in the same proportion as the total of each class of income bears to the total DNI. For example, if 40% of the trust's income consists of dividends, 40% of each beneficiary's distribution is deemed to consist of dividends.

EXAMPLE C:14-12 ▶ Southern Trust has $30,000 of DNI for the current year. Its DNI includes $10,000 of rental income and $20,000 of corporate bond interest. The trust instrument requires that each year the trustee distribute 30% of the trust's income to Jose and 70% to Petra. Because the trust has no tax-exempt income and must distribute all of its income, it receives a $30,000 distribution deduction.

Jose reports $9,000 (0.30 × $30,000) of trust income, and Petra reports $21,000 (0.70 × $30,000) of trust income. Because rents make up one-third ($10,000 ÷ $30,000) of DNI, the composition of the income reported by Jose and Petra is one-third rental income and two-thirds corporate bond interest. ◀

SELF-STUDY QUESTION

What functions does distributable net income (DNI) serve?

ANSWER

1. It establishes the maximum amount on which the beneficiaries may be taxed.
2. It establishes the maximum amount the trust or estate may deduct as a distribution deduction.
3. It establishes the character of the income or expense in DNI that flows to the beneficiaries (income or expense flows to the beneficiaries in proportion to the part each different type of income or expense bears to DNI).

DEFINITION OF DNI

Section 643(a) defines *DNI* as the fiduciary's taxable income, adjusted as follows:

- No distribution deduction is subtracted.
- No personal exemption is subtracted.
- Capital gains are not included and capital losses are not subtracted unless such gains and losses are allocated to accounting income instead of to principal.
- Extraordinary dividends and taxable stock dividends are not included if they are allocable to principal.
- An addition is made for tax-exempt interest (minus the expenses allocable thereto).

Because one purpose of DNI is to set a ceiling on the distribution deduction, the distribution deduction is not subtracted from taxable income in determining DNI. If capital gains and extraordinary dividends are allocated to corpus, they are excluded from DNI because they cannot be distributed. Tax-exempt interest is part of accounting income and can be distributed even though it is excluded from gross income. Consequently, DNI includes tax-exempt income (net of the nondeductible expenses allocable to such income). Even though net tax-exempt income is included in DNI, no distribution deduction is available for the portion of the distribution deemed to consist of tax-exempt income.

KEY POINT

A significant difference between net accounting income and DNI is that DNI is reduced by certain expenses charged to principal. These expenses do not decrease net accounting income, nor do they decrease the amount of money that can be distributed.

Aside from complicated scenarios, net accounting income and DNI are the same, with one other exception. Any expenses (e.g., trustee's fees) charged to principal reduce DNI even though they do not lessen net accounting income. The trustee's fees (whether charged to income or to principal) are deductible in arriving at taxable income. Reducing DNI by the expenses charged to principal provides a tax advantage for the income beneficiary because these fees lessen the amount taxable to the beneficiary. However, such fees do not decrease the money that can be distributed to the beneficiary.

MANNER OF COMPUTING DNI

The amount of taxable income is in large measure a function of the distribution deduction, and the distribution deduction depends on the amount of DNI. The distribution deduction cannot exceed DNI. Thus, the Sec. 643(a) definition of DNI, which involves starting with a fiduciary's taxable income and then making adjustments, is not a workable definition from a practical standpoint because the computation is circular. The distribution deduction must be computed to arrive at the amount of income taxable to the fiduciary, and the distribution deduction depends, in part, on the amount of DNI.

However, there are two practical means of determining DNI. The first approach, as illustrated below, begins with taxable income exclusive of the distribution deduction and makes the adjustments (other than the distribution deduction) to taxable income that the IRC specifies.

EXAMPLE C:14-13 ▶ In the current year, Darby Trust reports the following results. The trust must distribute all of its income annually and cannot distribute capital gains. The trust instrument requires charging all trustee's fees to principal.

	Amounts Allocable to	
	Income	*Principal*
Corporate bond interest	$20,000	
Rental income	30,000	
Gain on sale of investment land		$40,000
Property taxes	5,000	
Trustee's fee charged to corpus		2,000
Distribution to beneficiary	45,000	

The trust's taxable income exclusive of the distribution deduction is computed as follows:

Corporate bond interest	$20,000
Rental income	30,000
Capital gain	40,000
Minus: Property taxes	(5,000)
Trustee's fee	(2,000)
Personal exemption	(300)
Taxable income exclusive of distribution deduction	$82,700

Now that taxable income exclusive of the distribution deduction has been determined, DNI can be computed in the following manner:

Taxable income exclusive of distribution deduction	$82,700
Plus: Personal exemption	300
Minus: Capital gain	(40,000)
DNI	$43,000 ◀

A second method that often can be used to determine DNI is to calculate net accounting income and reduce such amount by expenses charged to corpus (e.g., the trustee's fee). In some complicated situations, however, DNI would not be correctly arrived at under this approach, but the discussion of such situations is beyond the scope of this book.

EXAMPLE C:14-14 ▶ Assume the same facts as in Example C:14-13. The following steps illustrate the second approach to calculating the DNI amount.

Corporate bond interest	$20,000
Rental income	30,000
Minus: Property taxes	(5,000)
Net accounting income	$45,000
Minus: Trustee's fee charged to corpus	(2,000)
DNI	$43,000 ◀

Although the beneficiary receives a cash distribution of $45,000 (net accounting income), he or she reports only $43,000 (DNI) as income. The beneficiary receives $2,000 tax-free. Thus, an income beneficiary benefits from trustee's fees charged to principal by getting to report a smaller amount of gross income than the amount of cash he or she receives. The trust's distribution deduction cannot exceed $43,000 (DNI) even though the amount paid to the beneficiary exceeds this amount.

Topic Review C:14-2 summarizes the DNI concept.

Question: Wei is the beneficiary of a two unrelated simple trusts. From which trust would Wei receive the larger amount of after-tax cash?

- Trust A collects corporate bond interest of $40,000 and pays a trustee's fee of $1,000, all charged to corpus.
- Trust B collects corporate bond interest of $40,000 and pays a trustee's fee of $800, all charged to income.

Solution: Wei would receive $40,000 in cash from Trust A but pay federal income taxes on only $39,000, which is the trust's DNI. The trust's distribution is based on net accounting income, which is not reduced by the trustee's fee charged to corpus. Wei's gross income is based on the trust's DNI, which is reduced by the trustee's fee. Wei would receive $39,200 in cash from Trust B. He would pay federal income taxes on the same $39,200 amount, which is the trust's DNI. The trustee's fee paid by Trust B reduces both net accounting income and DNI. Even though the trust's economic income is larger with Trust B, because of the lower trustee's fee, Wei would have a larger amount of after-tax cash flow from Trust A.

DETERMINING A SIMPLE TRUST'S TAXABLE INCOME

OBJECTIVE 5

Calculate the taxable income of a simple trust

The term *simple trust* does not appear in the IRC. Treasury Regulations interpreting Secs. 651 and 652—the statutory rules for trusts that distribute current income only—introduce the term *simple trust.* The provisions of Secs. 651 and 652 govern only trusts whose trust agreements require that all income be distributed currently and do not authorize charitable contributions. Moreover, such provisions are inapplicable if the trust makes distributions of principal.

Some trust instruments may require trusts to pay out all their income currently in certain years but permit them to retain a portion of their income in other years. In some of the years in which the instrument mandates distribution of all the income, it also permits distributions of principal. These trusts are simple trusts in some years and complex trusts in others. The amount of the personal exemption, however, turns not on whether the trust is simple or complex but on whether it must pay out all its income currently. Suppose, for

TOPIC REVIEW C:14-2

The Distributable Net Income (DNI) Concept

SIGNIFICANCE OF DNI

DNI, exclusive of net tax-exempt interest included therein, sets the ceiling on:

1. The distribution deduction, and
2. The aggregate amount of gross income reportable by the beneficiaries.

CALCULATION OF DNI

Taxable income, exclusive of distribution deduction[a]	
Plus:	Personal exemption
Minus:	Capital gains (or plus deductible capital losses)[b]
Plus:	Tax-exempt interest (net of allocable expenses)
Distributable net income (DNI)[c]	

[a]Gross income (dividends, taxable interest, rents, and capital gains) minus deductible expenses and the personal exemption.
[b]In certain situations beyond the scope of this textbook, the trustee's exercise of the power to adjust can result in the inclusion of capital gains in DNI.
[c]Frequently, DNI is the same amount as net accounting income minus trustee's fees charged to corpus.

▼ **TABLE C:14-1**
Trust Classification Rules and the Size of the Exemption

Situation	Classification	Exemption Amount
Required to pay out all of its income, makes no charitable contributions, distributes no principal	Simple	$300
Required to pay out all of its income, makes no charitable contributions, distributes principal	Complex	$300
Required to pay out all of its income, authorized to make charitable contributions, distributes no principal	Complex	$300
Authorized to make discretionary distributions of income, but not principal, makes no charitable contributions	Complex	$100
Authorized to make discretionary distributions of both income and principal, makes no charitable contributions	Complex	$100

example, a trust must pay out all of its current income and one-fourth of its principal. Because the trust distributes principal, it is a complex trust. It claims a $300 personal exemption because of the mandate to distribute all of its income. Table C:14-1 highlights the trust classification rules and the $300 or $100 exemption dichotomy.

ALLOCATION OF EXPENSES TO TAX-EXEMPT INCOME

Recall that expenses related to producing tax-exempt income are not deductible.[16] Thus, if a trust with income from both taxable and tax-exempt sources incurs expenses that are not directly attributable to the production of taxable income, a portion of such expenses may not be deducted. Regulation Secs. 1.652(b)-3 and 1.652(c)-4(e) address the issue of the allocation of deductions. An expense directly attributable to one type of income, such as a repair expense for rental property, is allocated thereto. Expenses not directly related to a particular item of income, such as a trustee's fee for administering the trust's assets, may be allocated to any type of income included in computing DNI, provided a portion of the expense is allocated to nontaxable income. Regulation Sec. 1.652(b)-3 sets forth the following formula for determining the amount of indirect expenses allocable to nontaxable income:

$$\frac{\text{Tax-exempt income (net of expenses directly attributable thereto)}}{\text{Accounting income (net of all direct expenses)}^{17}} \times \text{Expenses not directly attributable to any item of income} = \text{Indirect expenses allocable to nontaxable income}$$

EXAMPLE C:14-15 ▶ In the current year, the Mason Trust reports the following results:

Dividends	$16,000
Interest from corporate bonds	6,000
Tax-exempt interest from state bonds	18,000
Capital gain (allocated to corpus)	20,000
Trustee's fee, all allocated to corpus	4,000

[16] Sec. 265(a)(1).

[17] A discrepancy exists in the Treasury Regulations with respect to how to allocate expenses to tax-exempt income. According to Reg. Sec. 1.652(b)-3(b), the denominator is accounting income net of direct expenses. Regulation Sec. 1.652(c)-4(e), however, shows computations where the denominator is accounting income unreduced by direct expenses. The text uses the latter approach.

SELF-STUDY QUESTION

A trust can allocate indirect expenses arbitrarily (after the appropriate allocation is made to tax-exempt income). Hill Trust has rental income, taxable interest income, and dividend income. Its sole beneficiary has unused passive rental losses of her own. To which income would you suggest allocating the trustee's fee?

ANSWER

If possible, the trust should take into consideration the tax status of its beneficiaries. The trust should maximize passive rental income and not allocate the fee to its rental income. Moreover, because of the low tax rate on dividends, the trust should allocate the fee against interest income.

Accounting gross income is \$40,000 (\$16,000 + \$6,000 + \$18,000). The trustee's fee is an indirect expense that must be allocated to the tax-exempt income as follows:

$$\frac{\$18,000}{\$40,000} \times \$4,000 = \$1,800$$

Thus, the Mason Trust cannot deduct \$1,800 of its \$4,000 trustee's fee. The remaining \$2,200 may be allocated to dividends or corporate bond interest in whatever amounts the return preparer selects. Because of the low tax rate on dividends, allocating the fee to the higher taxed interest income would reduce taxes. The 3.8% tax on net investment income also is a factor for consideration in making the allocation. ◀

DETERMINATION OF DNI AND THE DISTRIBUTION DEDUCTION

As mentioned above, DNI is defined as taxable income with several adjustments, including a subtraction for capital gains credited to principal. As described earlier, a practical technique for determining DNI involves beginning with taxable income exclusive of the distribution deduction. Once DNI has been determined, both the distribution deduction and the trust's taxable income can be calculated.

A simple trust must distribute all of its net accounting income currently. Thus, a simple trust generally receives a distribution deduction equal to the amount of its net accounting income.[18] The following two exceptions modify this general rule:

- The distribution deduction may not exceed DNI. Therefore, if a trust has expenses that are charged to corpus (as in Example C:14-13), the distribution deduction is limited to the DNI amount because DNI is smaller than net accounting income.
- Because tax-exempt income is not included in the trust's gross income, no distribution deduction is available for tax-exempt income (net of the expenses allocable thereto) included in DNI.[19]

TAX TREATMENT FOR BENEFICIARY

The aggregate gross income reported by the beneficiaries equals the trust's net accounting income, subject to the constraint that the aggregate of their gross income amount does not exceed the trust's DNI. If DNI is lower than net accounting income and the trust has more than one beneficiary, each beneficiary's share of gross income is the following fraction of total DNI:[20]

$$\frac{\text{Income required to be distributed to such beneficiary}}{\text{Income required to be distributed to all beneficiaries}}$$

The income received by the beneficiaries retains the character it had at the trust level. Thus, if the trust receives tax-exempt interest, the beneficiaries are deemed to have received tax-exempt interest. Unless the trust instrument specifically allocates particular types of income to certain beneficiaries, each beneficiary is viewed as receiving income consisting of the same fraction of each category of income as the total of such category bears to total DNI.

EXAMPLE C:14-16 ▶ In the current year, Crane Trust collects \$22,000 of tax-exempt interest and \$66,000 of dividends and pays \$8,000 of trustee's fees from corpus. Its net accounting income is \$88,000, and its DNI is \$80,000: \$20,000 of net tax-exempt interest and \$60,000 of net dividends. The trust instrument requires distribution of one-eighth of the income annually to Matt and the remaining seven-eighths of the income to Pat. The cash distributions to Matt and Pat are \$11,000 and \$77,000, respectively. The distribution deduction and the aggregate gross income of the beneficiaries are limited to \$60,000 (\$80,000 DNI − \$20,000 net tax-exempt interest). Matt and Pat will report gross income of \$7,500 (0.125 × \$60,000) and \$52,500 (0.875 × \$60,000), respectively. Dividends make up 75% (\$60,000 ÷ \$80,000) of DNI and 100% (\$60,000 ÷ \$60,000) of taxable DNI. Therefore, all of Matt's and Pat's *gross* income is deemed to consist of dividends. Matt and Pat also are deemed to receive \$2,500 (0.125 × \$20,000) and \$17,500 (0.875 × \$20,000), respectively, of tax-exempt interest. ◀

[18] Sec. 651(a).
[19] Sec. 651(b).
[20] Sec. 652(a).

Because a simple trust must distribute all of its income currently, trustees cannot defer the taxation of trust income to the beneficiaries by postponing distributions until the next year. Beneficiaries of simple trusts are taxed currently on their pro rata share of taxable DNI regardless of the amount distributed to them during the year.[21]

SHORTCUT APPROACH TO PROVING CORRECTNESS OF TAXABLE INCOME

A shortcut approach may be used to verify the correctness of the amount calculated as a simple trust's taxable income. Because a simple trust must distribute all of its income currently, the only item taxable at the trust level should be the amount of gains (net of losses) credited to principal, reduced by the personal exemption. The taxable income calculated under the shortcut approach should equal the taxable income determined under the formula illustrated in Figure C:14-1. The steps of the shortcut approach are as follows:

1. Start with the excess of gains over losses credited to principal.
2. Subtract the $300 personal exemption.

EXAMPLE C:14-17 ▶ In the current year, West Trust, which must distribute all of its income currently, reports $25,000 of corporate bond interest, a $44,000 long-term capital gain, a $4,000 long-term capital loss, and no expenses. Under the shortcut approach, the test-check calculation of its taxable income is $39,700 [($44,000 – $4,000) – $300 personal exemption]. On its tax return, the trust reports $25,000 of gross income from interest, $40,000 from net long-term capital gains, a $25,000 distribution deduction, a $300 exemption, and $39,700 of taxable income. ◀

EFFECT OF A NET OPERATING LOSS

If a trust incurs a net operating loss (NOL), the loss does not pass through currently to the beneficiaries unless the loss arises in the year the trust terminates, but the trust can carry the NOL back and forward. In determining the amount of the NOL, deductions are not allowed for charitable contributions or the distribution deduction.[22] In the year a trust terminates, any loss that would otherwise qualify for a loss carryover at the trust level passes through to the individual return(s) of the beneficiary(ies) succeeding to the trust's property.[23]

EXAMPLE C:14-18 ▶ In 2017, the year it terminates, New Trust incurs a $10,000 NOL. It also has a $40,000 NOL carryover from 2015 and 2016. At termination, New Trust distributes 30% of its assets to Kay and 70% to Liz. Because 2017 is the termination year, Kay may report a $15,000 (0.30 × $50,000) NOL on her 2017 return, and Liz may report a $35,000 (0.70 × $50,000) NOL on her 2017 return. Before 2017, the beneficiaries cannot report any of the trust's NOLs on their returns. ◀

EFFECT OF A NET CAPITAL LOSS

The maximum capital loss that a trust can deduct is the lesser of $3,000 or the excess of its capital losses over capital gains.[24] Because simple trusts must distribute all of their accounting income currently and the distribution deduction reduces their taxable income to zero, they receive no current tax benefit from capital losses that exceed capital gains. Nevertheless, the trust's taxable income for the year of the loss is reduced by its net capital loss, up to $3,000. In determining the capital loss carryover, capital losses that produced no tax benefit are available as a carryover to offset capital gains realized by the trust in subsequent years. In addition, if all of the capital loss carryovers have not been absorbed by capital gains before the trust's termination date, the remaining capital loss is passed through pro rata in the termination year to the beneficiaries succeeding to the trust's property.[25]

---

[21] Reg. Sec. 1.652(a)-1.

[22] Reg. Sec. 1.642(d)-1(b).

[23] Reg. Sec. 1.642(h)-1. A trust is never categorized as a simple trust in the year it terminates because in its final year it always makes distributions of principal.

[24] Sec. 1211(b).

[25] Reg. Sec. 1.642(h)-1.

EXAMPLE C:14-19 ►

SELF-STUDY QUESTION

Why do Treasury Regulations allow unused NOLs and capital losses to be used by the remainderman on the termination of a trust? See previous page.

ANSWER

Losses have reduced the corpus of the trust. Because the remainderman's interest has been reduced by these losses, it is reasonable to allow the trust to pass these losses through to the remainderman at the end of its life.

Lev Trust, which must distribute all of its income currently, sold two capital assets before it terminates. In Year 1, it sold an asset at a $20,000 loss. In Year 2, it sold an asset for a $6,000 gain. In Year 3, it terminates and distributes its assets equally between its two beneficiaries, Joy and Tim. The trust is not a simple trust in Year 3 because it distributes principal that year. Because the $20,000 loss provided no benefit on the Year 1 return, the carryover to Year 2 was $20,000, and $6,000 of it offset Year 2's $6,000 capital gain. The remaining $14,000 carries over to Year 3. Because Year 3 is the termination year, a $7,000 (0.50 x $14,000) capital loss passes through to both Joy's and Tim's individual returns for Year 3. Joy realizes a $12,000 capital gain by selling assets in Year 3. Joy offsets the $7,000 trust loss against her own gain. Tim sells no assets in Year 3. Therefore, Tim deducts $3,000 of the loss from the trust against his other income. His remaining $4,000 loss carries over to Year 4. ◄

Topic Review C:14-3 describes how to calculate a trust's taxable income.

COMPREHENSIVE ILLUSTRATION: DETERMINING A SIMPLE TRUST'S TAXABLE INCOME

ADDITIONAL COMMENT

This illustration pertains to 2016 because tax forms for that year are the latest available at the time this textbook was published.

The following comprehensive illustration reviews a number of the points discussed previously. The facts for this illustration are used to complete the 2016 Form 1041 for a simple trust that appears in Appendix B.

Background Data. Zeb Brown established the Bob Adams Trust by a gift in 2003. The trust instrument requires that the trustee (First Bank) distribute all of the trust income at least annually to Bob Adams for life and that trustee's fees be paid from principal. Capital gains are credited to principal and cannot be distributed. The 2016 results of the trust are as follows:

	Amounts Allocable to	
	Income	*Principal*
Dividends	$30,000	
Rental income from land	5,000	
Tax-exempt interest	15,000	
Rental expenses (realtor's commission on rental income)	1,000	
Trustee's fee		$ 1,200
Fee for preparation of tax return	500	
Capital gain on sale of stock[a]		12,000
Distribution of net accounting income to Bob	48,500	
Payments of estimated tax		2,600

[a]The trust sold the stock in October for $15,000, having acquired it four years earlier.

TOPIC REVIEW C:14-3

Calculation of Trust Taxable Income

Gross income[a]
Minus: Deductions for expenses[a]
Distribution deduction[b]
Personal exemption ($300 or $100)
Taxable income

[a]Rules for calculating these amounts are generally the same as for individual taxpayers.
[b]Deduction cannot exceed the amount of DNI from taxable sources.

Trustee's Fee. As mentioned earlier, a portion of the trustee's fee is nondeductible because it must be allocated to tax-exempt income. The trust receives $50,000 ($30,000 + $5,000 + $15,000) of gross accounting income, of which $15,000 is tax-exempt. Therefore, $360 [($15,000 ÷ $50,000) × $1,200] of the trustee's fee is allocated to tax-exempt income and is nondeductible. The entire return preparation fee is deductible because no such fee would have been incurred had the trust's income been entirely from tax-exempt sources.

Distribution Deduction and DNI. One of the key amounts affecting taxable income is the distribution deduction. Taxable income exclusive of the distribution deduction is the starting point for determining the amount of DNI, a number crucial in quantifying the distribution deduction. The trust's taxable income, exclusive of the distribution deduction, is calculated as follows:

Dividends		$30,000
Rental income		5,000
Capital gain on sale of stock		12,000
Minus:	Rental expenses	(1,000)
	Deductible portion of trustee's fee ($1,200 – $360)	(840)
	Fee for tax return preparation	(500)
	Personal exemption	(300)
Taxable income, exclusive of distribution deduction		$44,360

DNI now can be calculated by making the adjustments shown below to taxable income, exclusive of the distribution deduction.[26]

Taxable income, exclusive of distribution deduction		$44,360
Plus:	Personal exemption	300
Minus:	Capital gain on sale of stock	(12,000)
Plus:	Tax-exempt interest ($15,000), net of $360 of allocable expenses	14,640
DNI		$47,300

Recall that the distribution deduction cannot exceed the DNI, as reduced by tax-exempt income (net of any allocable expenses). Nor can it exceed net accounting income of $48,500 ($30,000 + $5,000 + $15,000 – $1,000 – $500). The distribution deduction may be computed as follows:

Smaller of:	Net accounting income ($48,500) or DNI ($47,300)		$47,300
Minus:	Tax-exempt interest	$15,000	
	Minus: Allocable expenses	(360)	(14,640)
Distribution deduction			$32,660

Trust's Taxable Income and Tax. Once the amount of the distribution deduction is determined, the trust's taxable income and tax can be calculated as illustrated in Table C:14-2.

Categorizing a Beneficiary's Income. Because income reported by the beneficiary retains the character it had at the trust level, the amount of each category of income received by the beneficiary must be determined. Bob is deemed to have received dividends, rents, and tax-exempt interest. Rental expenses are charged entirely against rental income. The deductible portion of the trustee's fee and the tax return preparation fee can be allocated in full to rents or dividends, or some to each. However, because of the low tax rate

[26] Another way of determining the amount of DNI in this scenario is to reduce the net accounting income of $48,500 by the $1,200 of expenses charged to principal. The resulting amount is $47,300.

on dividends, the fees should be allocated against the higher taxed rents. Consequently, the character of Bob's income is determined as follows:

	Dividends	*Rents*	*Tax-Exempt Interest*	*Total*
Accounting income	$30,000	$5,000	$15,000	$50,000
Minus: Expenses:				
Rental expenses		(1,000)		(1,000)
Trustee's fee		(840)	(360)	(1,200)
Tax return preparation fee		(500)		(500)
DNI	$30,000	$2,660	$14,640	$47,300

Bob reports $30,000 of dividend income and $2,660 of rental income on his individual return. His dividend income is taxed at the low rate applicable to dividends.

DETERMINING TAXABLE INCOME FOR COMPLEX TRUSTS AND ESTATES

OBJECTIVE 6

Calculate the taxable income of a complex trust and an estate

The caption to Subpart C of Part I of Subchapter J (Secs. 661–664) reads "Distribution for Estates and Trusts Accumulating or Distributing Corpus." In general, the rules applicable to estates and these trusts (complex trusts) are the same. The IRC does not contain the term *complex trust*, but according to Treasury Regulations, "A trust to which subpart C is applicable is referred to as a 'complex' trust."[27] Recall from the discussion about simple trusts that a trust that must distribute all of its income currently can be classified as a

ADDITIONAL COMMENT

The short-cut approach to computing taxable income used in Table C:14-2 consists of reducing the income allocated to corpus by the personal exemption.

▼ TABLE C:14-2

Comprehensive Illustration: Determining a Simple Trust's Taxable Income and Tax Liability

Gross income:	
Dividends	$30,000
Rental income	5,000
Capital gain on sale of stock	12,000[a]
Minus: Expense deductions:	
Rental expenses	(1,000)
Deductible portion of trustee's fee	(840)
Tax return preparation fee	(500)
Minus: Distribution deduction	(32,660)
Minus: Personal exemption	(300)
Taxable income	$11,700[b]
Tax liability on taxable income (2016 rates)	$ 1,373[c]
Minus: Estimated tax payments	(2,600)
Tax owed (refunded)	$ (1,227)

[a]The stock sale took place in October and involved stock purchased four years earlier.
[b]The short-cut approach to verifying taxable income is as follows:

Long-term capital gain	$12,000
Minus: Personal exemption	(300)
Taxable income	$11,700

[c]The taxable income consists of a long-term capital gain, which, in 2016, is taxed at a maximum rate of 0% on the first $2,550 and 15% on the rest. The trust in this situation has no income taxed at the top rate and, thus, is not subject to the 3.8% tax on net investment income.

[27] Reg. Sec. 1.661(a)-1.

complex trust for a particular year if it also pays out some principal during the year. Trusts that can accumulate income are categorized as complex trusts, even in years in which they make discretionary distributions of all their income. A trust is a complex trust also if the trust instrument provides for amounts to be paid to, or set aside for, charitable organizations (see Table C:14-1).

Many of the rules are the same for simple and complex trusts, but some differences exist. Different rules apply to determine the distribution deduction for the two types of trusts. The rules for determining an estate's distribution deduction are the same as those applicable to complex trusts. The personal exemption, however, is $600 for an estate and $300 or $100 for a complex trust. The $300 amount applies for years in which a trust must pay out all of its income; otherwise, the exemption is $100.

TAX STRATEGY TIP

Trust managers can reduce overall taxes by carefully planning the amount and timing of distributions. See Tax Planning Considerations later in text for details.

DETERMINATION OF DNI AND THE DISTRIBUTION DEDUCTION

Section 661(a) defines the distribution deduction for complex trusts and estates as the sum of the total current income *required* to be paid out currently plus any other amounts "properly paid or credited or required to be distributed" (i.e., discretionary distributions) to the beneficiary during the year. If the fiduciary can make mandatory distributions from either the income or the principal account, distributions are treated as "current income required to be paid" if paid out of the trust's income account; thus, some of the income is taxed to the beneficiary. Like simple trusts, the amount of the trust's DNI limits the amount of the distribution deduction.

EXAMPLE C:14-20 ▶ In the current year, Able Trust has net accounting income and DNI of $30,000, all from taxable sources. It makes a $15,000 mandatory distribution of income to Kwame and a $4,000 discretionary distribution to Kesha. Its distribution deduction is computed as follows:

Income required to be distributed currently	$15,000
Plus: Other amounts properly paid, etc.	4,000
Tentative distribution deduction	$19,000
DNI	$30,000
Distribution deduction (lesser of tentative distribution deduction or DNI)	$19,000 ◀

As is the case for simple trusts, an additional constraint applies to the amount of the distribution deduction. No distribution deduction is allowed with respect to tax-exempt income (net of allocable expenses).

EXAMPLE C:14-21 ▶ Assume the same facts as in Example C:14-20 except that net accounting income and DNI consist of $20,000 of corporate bond interest and $10,000 of tax-exempt interest. Because one-third ($10,000 ÷ $30,000) of the DNI is from tax-exempt sources, tax-exempt income is deemed to make up one-third of the distributions. Thus, the distribution deduction is only $12,667 (0.667 × $19,000). ◀

If a trust makes charitable contributions, DNI is not reduced by the charitable contribution deduction when determining the maximum distribution deduction available for mandatory distributions. However, DNI is reduced by the charitable contribution deduction when calculating the deduction for discretionary distributions.

EXAMPLE C:14-22 ▶ Assume instead that Kwamsha Trust has net accounting income (all from taxable sources) and DNI (exclusive of the charitable contribution deduction) of $16,000. The trust makes a $15,000 mandatory distribution to Kwame and a $4,000 mandatory distribution to Kesha. In accordance with its trust instrument, the trust pays $3,000 to a charitable organization.

Tentative distribution deduction (required distributions of $15,000 + $4,000)	$19,000
DNI (excluding charitable contribution deduction)	16,000
Distribution deduction (lesser of tentative distribution deduction or DNI)	16,000

If the distributions to both Kwame and Kesha were discretionary, the $3,000 charitable contribution would be deductible by the trust and, in determining the maximum distribution deduction, would reduce DNI to $13,000, thereby limiting the distribution deduction to $13,000. Thus, in total, the beneficiaries would report $3,000 ($16,000 − $13,000) less gross income than if their distributions were mandatory. ◀

TAX TREATMENT FOR BENEFICIARY

KEY POINT

Distributions to beneficiaries retain the character that the income has at the fiduciary level; for example, the character of rents, interest, dividends, or tax-exempt income flows through to the beneficiary.

General Rules. In general, the amount of distributions from estates or complex trusts includible in a beneficiary's gross income equals the sum of income required to be distributed currently to the beneficiary plus any other amounts properly paid or credited, or required to be distributed (i.e., discretionary distributions) to the beneficiary during the year.[28] This general rule has three exceptions, all discussed later in this section.

Because distributed income retains the character it has at the fiduciary level, beneficiaries do not include distributions of tax-exempt income in their gross income. Each beneficiary's distribution is deemed to consist of tax-exempt income in the proportion that total tax-exempt income bears to total DNI.[29] Thus, if 30% of DNI is from tax-exempt income, 30% of each beneficiary's distribution is deemed to consist of tax-free income.

Even in the absence of distributions of principal, mandatory payments to beneficiaries sometimes exceed DNI because at times accounting income exceeds DNI. When the total income required to be distributed currently exceeds DNI (before reduction for the charitable contribution deduction), each beneficiary reports as gross income the following ratio of DNI attributable to taxable sources:

$$\frac{\text{Income required to be distributed currently to this beneficiary}}{\text{Aggregate income required to be distributed to all beneficiaries currently}^{30}}$$

In calculating the portion of DNI includible in the gross income of each beneficiary who receives mandatory distributions, DNI is not reduced for the charitable contribution deduction.

EXAMPLE C:14-23 ▶ In the current year, Yui Trust reports net accounting income of $125,000 but DNI of only $95,000 because of certain expenses charged to principal. The trust must distribute $100,000 of income to Tai and $10,000 to Tien. It makes no discretionary distributions or charitable contributions but is a complex trust because it is not required to distribute all of its income. Because the trust's mandatory distributions of $110,000 exceed its DNI of $95,000, the amount each beneficiary reports as gross income is as follows:

Beneficiary	*Gross Income*
Tai	$86,364 = ($100,000 ÷ $110,000) × $95,000
Tien	$8,636 = ($10,000 ÷ $110,000) × $95,000

◀

Exception—The Tier System. Some trust instruments require mandatory distributions to some beneficiaries and allow discretionary distributions to the same and/or other beneficiaries. If the sum of current income required to be distributed currently and all other amounts distributed (e.g., discretionary payments of income or any payments of corpus) exceed DNI, the amount taxable to each beneficiary is calculated under a tier system. Beneficiaries to whom income distributions must be made are commonly called **tier-1 beneficiaries.**[31] All other beneficiaries are known as **tier-2 beneficiaries.** An individual who receives both mandatory and discretionary payments in the same year can be both a tier-1 and a tier-2 beneficiary.

Under the tier system, tier-1 beneficiaries are the first to absorb income. The total income taxed to this group is the lesser of the aggregate mandatory distributions or DNI, which is determined without reduction for charitable contributions. If required income distributions plus all other payments exceed DNI, each tier-2 beneficiary includes in income a fraction of the remaining DNI, the DNI minus the income required to be distributed currently. Section 662(a)(2) states that the fraction for each beneficiary is as follows:

$$\frac{\text{Other amounts properly paid or required to be distributed to the beneficiary}}{\text{Aggregate of amounts properly paid or required to be distributed to } \textit{all} \text{ beneficiaries}}$$

[28] Sec. 662(a).
[29] Sec. 662(b).
[30] Sec. 662(a)(1).

[31] The terms *tier-1* and *tier-2* do not appear in the IRC or Treasury Regulations.

EXAMPLE C:14-24 ▶ In the current year, Eagle Trust reports net accounting income and DNI of $80,000, all from taxable sources. The trust instrument requires the trustee to distribute $30,000 of income to Holly currently. In addition, the trustee makes $60,000 of discretionary distributions, $15,000 to Holly and $45,000 to Irene. The trust distributes $90,000 total and pays $10,000 of the $60,000 discretionary distributions from corpus. The gross income reported by each beneficiary is determined as follows.

1. Gross income from mandatory distributions:	
Lesser of:	
a. Amount required to be distributed, or	$30,000
b. DNI	80,000
Amount reportable by Holly	30,000
2. Gross income from other amounts paid:	
Lesser of:	
a. All other amounts paid, or	60,000
b. DNI minus amount required to be distributed ($80,000 − $30,000)	50,000
Amount reportable by Holly and Irene	50,000
3. Total amount reportable (1) + (2b) = (3)	80,000

The portions of the $50,000 remaining DNI from Step 2 to be reported by each beneficiary are calculated under a pro rata approach as follows:

Holly: $50,000 × ($15,000 ÷ $60,000) = $12,500
Irene: $50,000 × ($45,000 ÷ $60,000) = $37,500

A recapitulation of the beneficiaries' gross income is as follows:

	Amount Reported by	
Type of Distribution	*Holly*	*Irene*
Mandatory distributions	$30,000	$ -0-
Discretionary distributions	12,500	37,500
Total	$42,500	$37,500 ◀

Tier-1 beneficiaries generally have gross income equal to their total distributions if they receive no tax-exempt interest, whereas tier-2 beneficiaries are more likely to receive a portion of their distributions tax-free. Thus, tier-2 beneficiaries potentially receive more favorable tax treatment than tier-1 beneficiaries.

SELF-STUDY QUESTION

What is the ultimate effect of the separate share rule?

ANSWER

It has the effect of treating a trust or estate as two or more separate entities, each with its own DNI. This "separate" DNI is allocated to the specific beneficiary of each separate share of the trust or estate.

Exception—Separate Share Rule. Some trusts and estates with more than one beneficiary can be treated as consisting of more than one entity in determining the amount of the distribution deduction and the beneficiaries' gross income.[32] In calculating the fiduciary's income tax liability, however, these trusts or estates are treated as one entity with the result that taxable income is taxed under one rate schedule. Entities eligible for this treatment, known as the **separate share rule**, have governing instruments requiring that distributions be made in substantially the same manner as if separate entities had been created.[33] If the separate share rule applies, the amount of the income taxable to a beneficiary can differ from the amount taxable under the general rules. Because of this rule, beneficiaries often report gross income lower than the distributions they receive.

EXAMPLE C:14-25 ▶ Bart Berry created the Berry Trust for the benefit of Dale and John. According to the trust instrument, no income is to be distributed until a beneficiary reaches age 21. Moreover, income is to be divided into two equal shares. Once a beneficiary reaches age 21, the trustee may make discretionary distributions of income and principal to such beneficiary, but distributions may not exceed a beneficiary's share of the trust. Each beneficiary is to receive his remaining share of the trust assets on his thirtieth birthday. Earlier distributions of income and principal must be taken into account in determining each beneficiary's final distribution.

On January 1 of the current year, Dale reaches age 21; John is age 16. In the current year, the trust has DNI and net accounting income of $50,000, all from taxable sources.

[32] Sec. 663(c).

[33] Reg. Sec. 1.663(c)-3(a).

The trustee distributes $25,000 of income (Dale's 50% share) and $80,000 of principal to Dale. The trustee makes no distribution of income or corpus to John. Under the separate share rule, the trust's distribution deduction and Dale's gross income inclusion cannot exceed his share of DNI, or $25,000. Dale receives the remaining $80,000 distribution tax-free. Berry Trust pays tax on John's separate share of the income (all accumulated), or $25,000, less the personal exemption. In the absence of the separate share rule, Dale would be taxed on $50,000 (the lesser of DNI or his total distributions). ◀

Exception—Specific Bequests. Recall that a beneficiary is taxed on other amounts properly paid, credited, or required to be distributed,[34] subject to the constraint that the maximum amount taxed to all beneficiaries is the fiduciary's DNI. Thus, a beneficiary can be required to report gross income even though he or she receives a distribution, including a non-cash distribution, paid from the principal account.

EXAMPLE C:14-26 ▶ Doug died last year, leaving a will that stated, "I bequeath all my property to my sister Tina." During the current year, Doug's estate reports $50,000 of DNI, all from taxable sources. Also during the current year, the executor distributes Doug's coin collection, valued at $22,000, to Tina. The adjusted basis of the coin collection also is $22,000, its value at the date of death. The distribution of the coin collection is classified as an "other amount properly paid" and, even though the executor distributes nothing from the income account, Tina must report $22,000 of gross income. If the coin collection's adjusted basis and FMV exceed $50,000 (DNI), Tina's gross income would be only $50,000, the DNI amount. ◀

ADDITIONAL COMMENT

The executor of an estate should carefully consider the timing of property distributions if the property being distributed is not the subject of a specific bequest. If possible, property (other than specific bequests) should be distributed in a year when the trust has little or no DNI to minimize the beneficiary's gross income.

On the other hand, a distribution of property does not trigger a distribution deduction at the estate level or the recognition of gross income at the beneficiary level if such property constitutes a bequest of a specific sum of money or of specific property to be paid at one time or in not more than three installments.[35] If Doug's will in Example C:14-26 instead includes specific bequest language (e.g., "I bequeath my coin collection to Tina"), Tina would not report any gross income upon receiving the coin collection.

More income is generally taxed at the estate level (and less at the beneficiary level) if the decedent's will includes numerous specific bequests. If the estate has a lower marginal income tax rate than its beneficiaries' marginal tax rates, the optimal tax result is to have the income taxed to the estate because the tax liability is lower.

EXAMPLE C:14-27 ▶ Dick died last year and bequeathed $100,000 cash to Fred and devised his residence, valued at $300,000, to Gary. The executor distributes the cash and the residence in the current year, when the estate has $80,000 of DNI, all from taxable sources. Because the cash and residence constitute specific bequests, the estate receives no distribution deduction and the beneficiaries report no gross income. Most of the income will be taxed to the estate at the top tax rate. ◀

Question: Sally is the sole beneficiary of her uncle Harry's estate. Uncle Harry's will made a specific bequest of the rare book collection to Sally. Another part of his will left Sally the rest of his estate. In the current year, the estate had DNI of $36,000, all from dividends and corporate interest, and the estate's executor distributed to Sally $12,200 of cash and her uncle Harry's rare book collection, valued at $5,400 on both date of death and date of distribution. How much gross income should Sally report from the estate during the current year? What is the amount of the estate's distribution deduction?

Solution: Sally does not have to report gross income as a result of receiving the specific bequest of the book collection. Because Sally's $12,200 cash distribution does not exceed the estate's $36,000 DNI, Sally should report gross income equal to the cash distributed to her ($12,200). The estate's distribution deduction equals the amount included in Sally's gross income ($12,200). If Harry had not specifically willed the books to Sally, the distribution of the books would be taxable to Sally because the $17,600 ($12,200 + $5,400) distributed by the estate is less than the estate's DNI.

[34] Sec. 662(a)(2).

[35] Sec. 663(a)(1).

KEY POINT

Generally, the tax consequences of both NOLs and net capital losses are the same for estates, complex trusts, and simple trusts.

EFFECT OF A NET OPERATING LOSS

As with simple trusts, an NOL of an estate or complex trust can be carried back and carried forward. In the year the trust or estate terminates, any remaining NOL passes through to the beneficiaries who succeed to the assets. In addition, in its year of termination the estate passes through to its beneficiaries any excess of current nonoperating expenses (e.g., executor's fees) over current income. If the estate incurs NOLs over a series of years, a tax incentive exists for terminating the estate as early as possible so the loss can pass through to the beneficiaries.

EFFECT OF A NET CAPITAL LOSS

The tax effect of having capital losses that exceed capital gains generally is the same for estates and complex trusts as for simple trusts. As for an individual taxpayer, the maximum capital loss deduction is the lesser of $3,000 or the excess of its capital losses over capital gains.[36] Simple trusts, however, receive no immediate tax benefit when capital losses exceed capital gains because no income is retained against which to offset the capital loss. Estates and complex trusts often do not distribute all their income and, thus, have taxable income against which they can offset a capital loss.

EXAMPLE C:14-28 ▶ Last year, Green Trust reported $30,000 of net accounting income and DNI, all from taxable sources. It made discretionary distributions totaling $7,000 to Amy. It sold one capital asset at an $8,000 long-term capital loss. The trust deducted $3,000 of capital losses in arriving at last year's taxable income. The trust carries over the remaining $5,000 capital loss to the current year. If in the current year, Green Trust sells a capital asset for a $7,000 long-term capital gain, it will offset the $5,000 loss carryover against the $7,000 capital gain. ◀

ADDITIONAL COMMENT

This illustration pertains to 2016 because tax forms for that year are the latest available at the time this textbook was published.

COMPREHENSIVE ILLUSTRATION: DETERMINING A COMPLEX TRUST'S TAXABLE INCOME

The comprehensive illustration below reviews a number of points discussed earlier. A sample Form 1041 for a complex trust appears in Appendix B; it is prepared for 2016 on the basis of the facts in this illustration.

Background Data. Ted Tims established the Cathy and Karen Stephens Trust in 2003. Its trust instrument empowers the trustee (Merchants Bank) to distribute income in its discretion to Cathy and Karen for the next 20 years. The trust will then be terminated, and the trust assets will be divided equally between Cathy and Karen, irrespective of the amount of distributions each has previously received. In other words, no separate shares are to be maintained. The trust instrument states that capital gains are part of principal and that trustee's fees are to be paid from principal.

The 2016 income and expenses of the trust appear below. With the exception of the information concerning distributions and payments of estimated tax, the amounts are the same as in the comprehensive illustration for a simple trust discussed previously in the chapter. As before, the holding period for the stock sold in October was four years.

	Amounts Allocable to	
	Income	*Principal*
Dividends	$30,000	
Rental income from land	5,000	
Tax-exempt interest	15,000	
Rental expenses (realtor's commissions on rental income)	1,000	
Trustee's fee		$ 1,200
Fee for preparation of tax return	500	
Capital gain on sale of stock		12,000
Distribution of net accounting income to:		
Cathy	14,000	
Karen	7,000	
Payments of estimated tax		5,360

Trustee's Fee. Recall that some of the trustee's fee must be allocated to tax-exempt income, with the result that this portion is nondeductible. Of the trust's gross accounting income of $50,000 ($30,000 + $5,000 + $15,000), $15,000 is from tax-exempt sources.

36 Sec. 1211(b).

Consequently, the nondeductible trustee's fee is $360 [($15,000 ÷ $50,000) × $1,200]. The remaining $840 of the fee is deductible, as is the $500 tax return preparation fee.

Distribution Deduction and DNI. Recall that the primary function of the Subchapter J rules is to provide guidance for calculating the amounts taxable to the beneficiaries and to the fiduciary. One of the crucial numbers in the process is the distribution deduction, which requires knowledge of the DNI amount. Taxable income, exclusive of the distribution deduction, is the starting point for calculating DNI and is computed as follows:

Dividends	$30,000
Rental income	5,000
Capital gain on sale of stock	12,000
Minus: Rental expenses	(1,000)
Deductible portion of trustee's fee	(840)
Fee for tax return preparation	(500)
Personal exemption	(100)
Taxable income, exclusive of distribution deduction	$44,560

DNI is calculated by adjusting taxable income, exclusive of the distribution deduction, as follows:

Taxable income, exclusive of distribution deduction	$44,560
Plus: Personal exemption	100
Minus: Capital gain on sale of stock	(12,000)
Plus: Tax-exempt interest (net of $360 of allocable expenses)	14,640
DNI	$47,300

The distribution deduction is the lesser of (1) amounts required to be distributed, plus all other amounts properly paid or credited, or required to be distributed, or (2) DNI. This lesser-of amount must be reduced by tax-exempt income (net of allocable expenses). Thus, DNI, exclusive of net tax-exempt income, is calculated as follows:

DNI	$47,300
Minus: Tax-exempt income (net of $360 of allocable expenses)	(14,640)
DNI, exclusive of net tax-exempt income	$32,660

In no event may the distribution deduction exceed $32,660, the DNI, exclusive of net tax-exempt income. The DNI ceiling has no practical significance in this example, however, because the trust distributed only $21,000.

ADDITIONAL COMMENT

This example dealing with a complex trust clearly illustrates the computational complexity when there are multiple categories of income and multiple beneficiaries.

Because a portion of the payments to each beneficiary is deemed to consist of tax-exempt income, the distribution deduction is less than the $21,000 distributed. Each beneficiary's share of tax-exempt income is determined by dividing DNI into categories of income. In this categorization process, the rental expenses are direct expenses that must be charged against rental income, and $360 of the trustee's fees must be charged against tax-exempt income. In this example, the deductible trustee's fee and the tax return preparation fee are charged against rental income. Alternatively, they could be charged against dividend income or pro rata against each income category, but an allocation to dividend income would be disadvantageous because dividends are taxed at a preferential rate. As with the simple trust illustrated earlier, total DNI of $47,300 consists of the following categories:

	Dividends	*Rents*	*Tax-Exempt Interest*	*Total*
Accounting income	$30,000	$5,000	$15,000	$50,000
Minus: Expenses:				
Trustee's fee		(840)	(360)	(1,200)
Rental expenses		(1,000)		(1,000)
Tax return preparation fee		(500)		(500)
DNI	$30,000	$2,660	$14,640	$47,300

Because there are two beneficiaries and three categories of income, we must calculate the amount of each beneficiary's distribution attributable to each income category. These steps were not needed in the simple trust illustration because the simple trust had only one beneficiary.

Category of Income	*Proportion of DNI*
Dividends	63.4249% = \$30,000 ÷ \$47,300
Rental income	5.6237% = \$ 2,660 ÷ \$47,300
Tax-exempt income	30.9514% = \$14,640 ÷ \$47,300
Total	100.0000%

As shown above, 30.9514% of each beneficiary's distribution represents tax-exempt interest and is ineligible for a distribution deduction. The amount of the distribution deduction (which cannot exceed the \$32,660 DNI, exclusive of net tax-exempt income) is determined as follows:

Total amount distributed	\$21,000
Minus: Net tax-exempt income deemed distributed (0.309514 × \$21,000)	(6,500)
Distribution deduction	\$14,500

The distributions received by the beneficiaries are deemed to consist of three categories of income in the amounts shown below.

Components of Distributions	*Cathy*	*Karen*	*Total*
Dividends (63.4249%)	\$ 8,879	\$4,440	\$13,319
Plus: Rental income (5.6237%)	788	393	1,181
Gross income (69.0486%)	\$ 9,667	\$4,833	\$14,500
Plus: Tax-exempt interest (30.9514%)	4,333	2,167	6,500
Total income (100%)	\$14,000	\$7,000	\$21,000

Trust's Taxable Income. Once the taxable and tax-exempt distributions have been quantified, the trust's taxable income can be calculated. Table C:14-3 illustrates this calculation. Unlike the simple trust situation, no short-cut approach exists for verifying taxable income for complex trusts and estates except in the years when they distribute all their income.

Trust's Tax on Net Investment Income. The trust has investment income of \$47,000 (\$30,000 dividends + \$5,000 rents + \$12,000 capital gain) and net investment income of \$44,660 (\$47,000 − \$2,340). Of this amount, \$14,500 is distributed, resulting in an undistributed amount of \$30,160 (\$44,660 − \$14,500). For purposes of the tax on net investment income, the trust's adjusted gross income (AGI) is deemed to consist of investment income less deductions for expenses, the distribution deduction, and the personal exemption. This AGI amount is \$30,060 (\$47,000 − \$2,340 − \$14,500 − \$100). Thus, AGI exceeds the amount at which the 39.6% tax bracket begins in 2016 by \$17,660 (\$30,060 − \$12,400). Because the AGI in excess of the point at which the 39.6% rate begins is the smaller amount, the tax on net investment income is \$671 (\$17,660 × 0.038).

Additional Observations. A few additional observations are in order concerning the Stephens Trust:

- ▶ If the entity is an estate instead of a trust, all amounts except the personal exemption are the same. The estate's personal exemption would be \$600 instead of \$100.
- ▶ Assume that (1) the trust owns a building instead of land and incurs \$2,000 of depreciation expense, charged in the trustee's discretion against principal. Because approximately 56% of the trust's income is accumulated (i.e., \$26,300 of its \$47,300 DNI), \$1,120 (0.56 × \$2,000) of the depreciation is deductible by the trust and its taxable income is \$1,120 lower. The remaining \$880 (0.44 × \$2,000) is deductible on the

▼ TABLE C:14-3
Comprehensive Illustration: Determining a Complex Trust's Taxable Income and Tax Liability

Gross income:	
Dividends	$30,000
Rental income	5,000
Capital gain on sale of stock	12,000
Minus: Expense deductions:	
Rental expenses	(1,000)
Deductible portion of trustee's fee	(840)
Tax return preparation fee	(500)
Minus: Distribution deduction	(14,500)
Minus: Personal exemption	(100)
Taxable income	$30,060
Tax on taxable income (2016 rates)[a]	$ 5,217
Plus: 3.8% tax on net investment income[b]	671
Total tax liability	$ 5,888
Minus: Estimated taxes	(5,360)
Tax owed	$ 528

[a]The $12,000 long-term capital gain and the $16,681 of dividends retained by the trust ($28,681 in total) are taxed at the lower rates. The $16,681 amount is $30,000 minus the $13,319 dividends distributed, as calculated on page C:14-26. The tax liability is calculated as follows:

Tax on ordinary, non-dividend income [0.15 × $1,379 (where $1,379 = $30,060 − $12,000 − $16,681)]	$ 207
Plus: Tax on capital gains and dividends at 0% [0.0 × $1,171 (where $1,171 = $2,550 − $1,379)]	−0−
Tax on capital gains and dividends at 15% [0.15 × $9,850 (where $9,850 = $12,400 income taxed at rates below 39.6% − $2,550 income already taxed)]	1,478
Tax on remaining capital gains and dividends at 20% [0.20 × $17,660 ($28,681 − $1,171 – $9,850)]	3,532
Tax on taxable income	$5,217

[b]$17,660 × 0.038 (See page C:14-26.)

beneficiaries' returns and is divided between them according to their pro rata share of the total distributions. Cathy deducts $587 [$880 × ($14,000 ÷ $21,000)], and Karen deducts $293 [$880 × ($7,000 ÷ $21,000)]. In summary, the depreciation is deductible as follows $1,120 to the trust, $587 to Cathy, and $293 to Karen.

▶ If the trustee had charged against income an amount equal to the depreciation expense for tax purposes, accounting income would have been reduced by the depreciation. In addition, the entire $2,000 of depreciation would have been deducted on the trust return, and DNI would have been $45,300 instead of $47,300.

Income in Respect of a Decedent

OBJECTIVE 7

Recognize the significance of income in respect of a decedent

DEFINITION AND COMMON EXAMPLES

Section 691 specifies the tax treatment for specific types of income known as income in respect of a decedent. **Income in respect of a decedent (IRD)** is gross income that the decedent earned before death but was not includible on the decedent's income tax return for the tax year ending with the date of death or for an earlier tax year because the decedent (a cash basis taxpayer) had not collected the income. Because most individuals use the cash method of accounting, IRD generally consists of income earned, but not actually or constructively received, prior to death. Common examples of IRD include the following:

- Interest earned, but not received, before death
- Salary, commission, or bonus earned, but not received, before death
- Dividends collected after the date of death, for which the record date precedes the date of death
- The gain portion of principal collected on a pre-death installment sale

SELF-STUDY QUESTION

Roger, a cash basis taxpayer, is a physician. At the time of Roger's death, patients owe him $150,000. These accounts receivable are "property" in which Roger has an interest at the time of his death and are included in his gross estate. Why are the accounts receivable income in respect of a decedent?

ANSWER

They are income Roger earned while alive, but did not report as income under his accounting method. They constitute income to his estate (or his heirs) when they are collected. Thus, they are income in respect of a decedent (IRD).

SIGNIFICANCE OF IRD

Double Taxation. Recall from Chapter C:13 that a decedent's gross estate includes property to the extent of his or her interest therein. The decedent has an interest in any income earned but not actually or constructively received before death. Thus, the decedent's gross estate includes income accrued as of the date of death. If the decedent used the cash method of accounting, the decedent did not include this accrued income in gross income because he or she had not yet collected it. The income is taxed to the party (i.e., the estate or a named individual) entitled to receive it. Thus, IRD is taxed under both the transfer tax system and the income tax system. Income also is taxed under two systems if the decedent collects a dividend check, deposits it into his or her bank account, and dies before consuming the cash. In the latter case, the dividend is included in the decedent's individual income tax return, and the cash (from the dividend check) is included in the decedent's gross estate. The individual income taxes owed on the dividend income are deductible as a debt on the estate tax return.

EXAMPLE C:14-29 ▶ Doug dies on July 1. Included in Doug's gross estate is an 8%, $1,000 corporate bond that pays interest each September 1 and March 1. Doug's gross estate also includes accrued interest for the period March 2 through July 1 of $27 ($1,000 × 0.08 × 4/12). On September 1, Doug's estate collects $40 of interest, of which $27 constitutes IRD. The calendar year income tax return for Doug's estate includes $40 of interest income, consisting of $27 of IRD and $13 earned after death. ◀

SELF-STUDY QUESTION

Karl receives his April paycheck on May 1 and deposits the paycheck in his savings account. He dies on May 10. He made no withdrawals from the account before his death. On June 1, Karl's employer pays Karl's estate one-third of Karl's May salary (the amount earned prior to his death on May 10). What are the tax consequences?

ANSWER

Karl's gross estate will include his savings account, which includes a deposit of his April paycheck. Karl's final income tax return will include his salary through April 30. His May 1 check is subject to both the individual income and the estate tax. The income taxes owed on the April salary are deductible as a debt on his estate tax return.

Karl's gross estate will include the one-third of his May salary. His estate's income tax return also will report this amount as income. The salary is income in respect of a decedent, so the estate will receive some relief under Sec. 691(c) from the double tax on the May salary.

Deductions in Respect of a Decedent. Section 691(b) authorizes **deductions in respect of a decedent** (DRD). Such deductions include trade or business expenses, expenses for the production of income, interest, taxes, depletion, etc. that are accrued before death but are not deductible on the decedent's final income tax return because the decedent used the cash method of accounting. Because these accrued expenses have not been paid before death, they are deductible as debts on the estate tax return. In addition, the accrued expenses are deductible on the estate's income tax return when paid by the estate (if they are for deductible expenses). Thus, a double benefit can be obtained for DRD.

EXAMPLE C:14-30 ▶ Dan dies on September 20. At the time of his death, Dan owes $18,000 of salaries to the employees of his proprietorship. The executor pays the total September payroll of $29,000 on September 30. The $18,000 accrued amount is deductible as a debt on the estate tax return. As a trade or business (Sec. 162) expense, the salaries also constitute DRD. The $18,000 of DRD and any other salaries paid are deductible on the estate's income tax return for the period in which paid. ◀

Section 691(c) Deduction. The Sec. 691(c) deduction provides some relief for the double taxation of IRD. This deduction equals the federal estate taxes attributable to the net IRD included in the gross estate. The total Sec. 691(c) deduction is the excess of the decedent's actual federal estate tax over the federal estate tax that would be payable if the net IRD were excluded from the decedent's gross estate. Net IRD means IRD minus deductions in respect of a decedent (DRD). If the IRD is collected in more than one tax year, the Sec. 691(c) deduction for a particular tax year is determined by the following formula:[37]

$$\text{Sec. 691(c) deduction for the year} = \text{Total Sec. 691(c) deduction} \times \frac{\text{Net IRD included in gross income for the year}}{\text{Total Net IRD}}$$

[37] Sec. 691(c)(1).

EXAMPLE C:14-31 ▶ Latoya (a widow) died in 2016, and her estate tax base was $6 million. Latoya's gross estate included $300,000 of IRD, primarily from gains on installment sales. Her estate had no DRD. The estate collects $250,000 of the IRD during its 2017 tax year. The Sec. 691(c) deduction for Latoya's estate for 2017 is calculated as shown below.

Actual 2016 federal estate tax on base of $6 million	$220,000[a]
Minus: 2016 federal estate tax on base of $5.7 million determined by excluding net IRD from gross estate	(100,000)[b]
Total Sec. 691(c) deduction	$120,000
Sec. 691(c) deduction available in 2017 [($250,000 ÷ $300,000) × $120,000]	$100,000 ◀

[a][$345,800 + ($6,000,000 − $1,000,000) × 0.40] − $2,125,800
[b][$345,800 + ($5,700,000 − $1,000,000) × 0.40] − $2,125,800

No Step-Up in Basis. Most property received as the result of a decedent's death acquires a basis equal to its FMV on the date of death or the alternate valuation date. Property classified as IRD, however, retains the basis it had in the decedent's hands.[38]

This carryover basis rule for IRD items is especially unfavorable when the decedent sells a highly appreciated asset soon before death, collects a relatively small portion of the sales price before death, and reports the sale under the installment method of accounting. For example, if the gain is 80% of the sales price, 80% of each principal payment in the post-death period will continue to be characterized as gain. If the sale instead had occurred after the date of death, the gain would equal the post-death appreciation (if any) because the step-up in basis rules would apply to the asset.

EXAMPLE C:14-32 ▶ On June 3 of last year, Joel sold a parcel of investment land for $40,000. The land had a $10,000 adjusted basis in Joel's hands. The buyer paid $8,000 down and signed a $32,000 note at an interest rate acceptable to the IRS. The note is payable June 3 of the current year. Joel, a cash basis taxpayer, uses the installment method for reporting the $30,000 ($40,000 − $10,000) gain. The gross profit ratio is 75% ($30,000 gain ÷ $40,000 contract price). Joel died accidentally on June 13 of last year with a gross estate of $1 million. Joel's final individual income tax return reported a gain of $6,000 (0.75 × $8,000). The estate reports a gain of $24,000 (0.75 × $32,000) on its current year income tax return because it collects the $32,000 balance on June 3 of the current year. Had the sale contract been entered into immediately after Joel's death, the gain would have been zero because the land's basis would have been its $40,000 FMV at the date of death. ◀

SELF-STUDY QUESTION

Roger (a cash basis taxpayer) died leaving $150,000 of accounts receivable. What basis does his estate have in these accounts receivable?

ANSWER

Zero. The accounts receivable constitute IRD. If they were stepped-up in basis, they would never be subject to an income tax.

Question: Isaac, a cash basis, calendar year taxpayer, died on May 12 of the current year. On which income tax return—Isaac's or his estate's—should the following income and expenses be reported? Assume the estate's tax year is the calendar year.

- Dividends declared in January and paid in February
- Interest income on a corporate bond that pays interest each June 30 and December 31
- Rent collected in June for a vacation home rented to tenants for the month of March, but the tenants were allowed to pay after occupying the property
- Balance due on Isaac's state income taxes for the previous year, paid in July because the return was extended
- Federal estimated income tax for the previous year that Isaac paid in January

Solution: Income received before death and deductible expenses paid before death (in this case the dividends and nothing more) should be reported on Isaac's individual return. Income received after his death, even though earned before his death, is to be reported on the estate's income tax return. The same is true for deductible expenses paid by the estate. Items to be reported on the estate's income tax return include the interest income, the rental income, and the state income taxes. The federal estimated income taxes paid are not deductible on the federal income tax return of either taxpayer. The amount paid, however, reduced the cash Isaac owned at his date of death and thereby his gross estate.

[38] Sec. 1014(c).

GRANTOR TRUST PROVISIONS

OBJECTIVE 8

Explain the effect of the grantor trust provisions

This portion of the chapter examines the provisions affecting a special type of trust known as a **grantor trust**, which is governed by Secs. 671–679. As discussed previously, income of a regular (or nongrantor) trust or an estate is taxed to the beneficiary to the extent distributed and to the fiduciary to the extent accumulated. In the case of a grantor trust, however, the trust's grantor (creator) is taxed on some or all of the trust's income even if such income is distributed to a third-party beneficiary. In certain circumstances, a person other than the grantor or the beneficiary (e.g., a person with powers over the trust) must pay taxes on the trust's income.

PURPOSE AND EFFECT

The grantor trust rules require grantors who do not give up enough control or economic benefits when they create a trust to pay a price by being taxed on part or all of the trust's income. A grantor must report some or all of a trust's income on his or her individual tax return if he or she does not part with enough control over the trust assets or give up the right to income produced by the assets for a sufficiently long time period. For transfers after March 1, 1986, the grantor generally is taxed on the trust's income if the trust property will eventually return to the grantor or the grantor's spouse.[39] According to the Tax Court, the grantor trust rules have the following purpose and result:

> This subpart [Secs. 671–679] enunciates the rules to be applied where, in described circumstances, a grantor has transferred property to a trust but has not parted with complete dominion and control over the property or the income which it produces. . . .[40]

Sections 671–679 use the term *treated as owner* instead of taxed. Section 671 specifies that when a grantor is treated as owner, the income, deductions, and credits attributable to the portion of the trust for which the grantor is treated as owner are reported directly on the grantor's tax return and not on the trust's return. The fiduciary tax return contains only the items attributable to the portion of the trust for which the grantor is not treated as the owner.

ADDITIONAL COMMENT

Many trust provisions can cause the grantor trust rules to apply. A trust need *not* be a revocable trust to be a grantor trust.

Unfortunately, the rules governing when the grantor has given up enough to avoid being taxed on the trust's income do not agree completely with the rules concerning whether the transfer is complete for gift tax purposes or the transferred property is excluded from the donor's gross estate. In certain circumstances, a donor can make a taxable gift and still be taxed on the income from the transferred property. For example, if a donor transfers property to a trust with the income payable annually to the donor's cousin for six years and a reversion of the property to the donor at the end of the sixth year, the donor makes a gift, subject to the gift tax, of the value of a six-year income interest. Under the grantor trust rules, however, the donor is taxed on the trust's income because the property reverts to the donor within too short a time period.

Retention of certain powers over property conveyed in trust can cause the trust assets to be included in the donor's gross estate even though these powers do not result in the donor being taxed on the trust income. Assume a donor to a trust reserves the discretionary power to pay out or accumulate trust income until the beneficiary (a grandchild) reaches age 21. The trust assets, including any accumulated income, are to be distributed to the beneficiary on his or her twenty-first birthday. The donor is not taxed on the trust income because he can exercise his powers only until the beneficiary reaches age 21. If the donor dies before the beneficiary attains age 21, however, the donor's gross estate will include the trust property because the donor retained control over the beneficiary's economic benefits (see discussion of Sec. 2036 in Chapter C:13).

[39] For trusts created before March 2, 1986, the grantor was treated as the owner with respect to the trust's capital gains but not its ordinary income if the property returned to the grantor after a period of more than ten years. In such a situation, the grantor is taxed on the capital gains and the trust and/or the beneficiary on the ordinary income. The trusts usually terminated slightly more than ten years after their funding. Thus, few (if any) of these trusts exist today.

[40] *William Scheft*, 59 T.C. 428, at 430-431 (1972).

REVOCABLE TRUSTS

The grantor of a revocable trust can control assets conveyed to the trust by altering the terms of the trust (including changing the identity of the beneficiaries) and/or withdrawing assets from the trust. Often the grantor also is a beneficiary. Sec. 676 provides that the grantor is treated as the owner of the trust and therefore is taxed on the income generated by the trust. As Chapter C:12 points out, a transfer of assets to a revocable trust is an incomplete transfer and not subject to the gift tax.

EXAMPLE C:14-33 ▶ In the current year, Tom transfers property to a revocable trust and names Ann to receive the income for life and Beth to receive the remainder. The trust's income for the current year consists of $15,000 of dividends and an $8,000 long-term capital gain. The trustee distributes the dividends to Ann but retains the gain and credits it to principal. Because the trust is revocable, the dividend and capital gain income are taxed directly to Tom on his current year individual tax return. Nothing is taxed to the trust or its beneficiaries. ◀

ADDITIONAL COMMENT

A common use of the revocable trust is to avoid probate for the property held by the trust. On the death of the grantor, who also is the beneficiary, the trustee of the revocable trust distributes the trust property in accordance with the trust agreement. Because the trustee holds legal title to the property, he or she can distribute the property without the trust assets going through the probate process. The trust assets are included in the gross estate because the trust is revocable.

POST-1986 REVERSIONARY INTEREST TRUSTS

The 1986 Tax Reform Act amended Sec. 673(a) for transfers made after March 1, 1986, to provide that, generally, the grantor is treated as the owner of the trust and is taxed on the accounting income of the trust if he or she has a reversionary interest in either income or principal. Under Sec. 672(e), a grantor is treated as holding any interest held by his or her spouse. These rules have two exceptions.

The first exception makes the grantor trust rules inapplicable if, as of the inception of the trust, the value of the reversionary interest, as valued under the actuarial tables, does not exceed 5% of the value of the trust. The second exception applies if the reversion will occur only if the beneficiary dies before reaching age 21 and the beneficiary is a lineal descendant of the grantor.

EXAMPLE C:14-34 ▶ In the current year, Paul establishes a trust with income payable to his elderly parents for 15 years. The assets of the trust will then revert to Paul. The value of Paul's reversionary interest exceeds 5%. Because Paul has a reversionary interest valued at above 5% and the transfer arose after March 1, 1986, Paul is taxed currently on the trust's accounting income and capital gains. ◀

EXAMPLE C:14-35 ▶ In the current year, Paul transfers property to a trust with income payable to his daughter Ruth until Ruth reaches age 21. On Ruth's twenty-first birthday, she is to receive the trust property outright. In the event Ruth dies before reaching age 21, the trust assets will revert to Paul. Paul is not taxed on the accounting income because his reversion is contingent on the death of the beneficiary (a lineal descendant) before age 21. ◀

RETENTION OF ADMINISTRATIVE POWERS

Under Sec. 675, the grantor is taxed on the accounting income and gains if he or she or his or her spouse holds certain administrative powers. Such powers include, but are not limited to, the following:

- The power to purchase or exchange trust property for less than adequate consideration in money or money's worth
- The power to borrow from the trust without adequate interest or security except where the trustee (who is someone other than the grantor) has a general lending power to make loans irrespective of interest or security
- The power exercisable in a role other than as trustee to (1) vote stock of a corporation in which the holdings of the grantor and the trust are significant from the standpoint of voting control and (2) reacquire the trust property by substituting other property of equal value.

RETENTION OF ECONOMIC BENEFITS

Section 677 taxes the grantor on the portion of the trust with respect to which the income may be

- Distributed to the grantor or his or her spouse,
- Held or accumulated for future distribution to the grantor or his or her spouse, or
- Used to pay premiums on life insurance policies on the life of the grantor or his or her spouse

Using trust income to provide support for a beneficiary who is a child the grantor is legally obligated to support yields obvious economic benefits to the grantor. A grantor is taxed on any trust income distributed and used to support individuals the grantor is legally obligated to support (e.g., children). However, the mere existence of the discretionary power to use trust income for support does not cause the grantor to be taxed. Taxation turns on whether the trust income is actually used for support.

The next example concerns use of trust income to support the grantor's minor child.

EXAMPLE C:14-36 ▶ Hal creates a trust and empowers the bank trustee to distribute income to his minor son, Louis, until the son reaches age 21. When Louis reaches age 21, the trust assets including accumulated income are to be paid over to the child. In the current year, when Louis is age 15, the trustee distributes $5,000 that is used to support Louis and $8,000 that is deposited into Louis's savings account. The remaining $12,000 of income is accumulated. Hal (the grantor) is taxed on the $5,000 used to support his son. Louis (the son) includes $8,000 in his gross income, and the trust pays tax on $12,000 less its $100 exemption. Note, however, that the kiddie tax rules apply to Louis's income of $8,000. ◀

The following example deals with the payment of premiums on an insurance policy on the grantor's life.

EXAMPLE C:14-37 ▶ Maria is the grantor of the Martinez Trust, one of whose assets is a life insurance policy on Maria's life. The trust instrument requires that $1,000 of trust income be used to pay the annual insurance premiums and that the rest be distributed to Maria's adult son Juan. Section 677 requires Maria (the grantor and insured) to be taxed on $1,000 , the amount paid for premiums. The remaining income is taxed to Juan under the general trust rules. ◀

ADDITIONAL COMMENT

If the grantor were a parent of the insured, the income required to be used for paying life insurance premiums would not be taxed to the grantor because the insured is not the grantor or the grantor's spouse.

CONTROL OF OTHERS' ENJOYMENT

Section 674 taxes the grantor on trust income if he or she, his or her spouse, or someone without an interest in the trust (e.g., a trustee) has the power to control others' beneficial enjoyment such as by deciding how much income to distribute. Many exceptions, including one for independent trustees, exist for the general rule.

EXAMPLE C:14-38 ▶ Otto is grantor and trustee of a trust over which the trustee has complete discretion to pay out the income or corpus in any amount he deems appropriate to some or all of the three adult beneficiaries, Kay, Fay, and May (none related to Otto). In the current year, the trustee distributes all the income to Kay. Otto, the grantor, is taxed on the income. If instead the trustee were independent, Kay would be taxed on the income she received. ◀

Under Sec. 678, an individual other than the trust's grantor or beneficiary can be required to report the trust income. This individual is taxed on the trust income if he or she has the power under the trust instrument to vest the trust principal or the income in him- or herself, provided such power is exercisable solely by such individual.

Topic Review C:14-4 summarizes the grantor trust rules.

WHAT WOULD YOU DO IN THIS SITUATION?

You, a CPA, have prepared the income tax returns for the Candy Cain Trust, an irrevocable trust, since the inception of the trust five years ago. The grantor is Able Cain, another client and the father of Candy Cain, the income beneficiary. First Bank, the trustee, is authorized to distribute income at its discretion to Candy, who reached age 18 August of last year. Last year, the trust's DNI of $4,000, all from interest on corporate bonds, was distributed to Candy in June to pay her medical bills incurred in an accident earlier in the year. You advised Mr. Cain that he must include the $4,000 trust distribution on his individual tax return because the distribution was used to satisfy his obligation to support Candy until age 18. Candy began working after her high school graduation and used her earned income to provide over half of her own support. Mr. Cain reminds you of how many clients he has referred to you and demands that you report the distribution as taxable to Candy so the income will be taxed at her low rates instead of at his rate, the highest marginal rate. How will you react to Mr. Cain's request?

TOPIC REVIEW C:14-4

Grantor Trust Rules

Factual Situation	Tax Treatment
1. Trust is revocable.	Ordinary income (including dividends) and capital gains are taxed to grantor.
2. Irrevocable trust is funded on or after March 2, 1986, with income payable to third-party beneficiary for 25 years after which property reverts to grantor; the value of the reversionary interest exceeds 5% of the value of the trust.	Ordinary income (including dividends) and capital gains are taxed to grantor.
3. The grantor of an irrevocable trust retains administrative powers described in the IRC.	Ordinary income (including dividends) and capital gains are taxed to grantor.
4. The income of an irrevocable trust is disbursed to meet the grantor's obligation to support his or her children.	Ordinary income (including dividends) used for support are taxed to grantor.
5. The income of an irrevocable trust is disbursed to pay the premium on a life insurance policy on the life of the grantor or the grantor's spouse.	Ordinary income (including dividends) and capital gains are taxed to grantor to the extent they may be used to pay the premiums.

Tax Planning Considerations

OBJECTIVE 9

Identify tax planning opportunities in trust and estate income taxation

Many tax planning opportunities exist with respect to estates and trusts, including the ability to shift income to the fiduciary and/or the beneficiaries and the opportunity for executors or trustees of discretionary trusts to consider the tax consequences of the timing of distributions. These and other tax planning considerations are discussed below.

ABILITY TO SHIFT INCOME

Before 1987, one of the primary tax advantages of using trusts was the ability to shift income from the grantor to the trust or the beneficiary. Four changes have made the tax advantages of shifting income difficult to achieve. First, the tax rate schedules for fiduciaries are very compressed. In fact, an estate or trust has only $2,550 (in 2017) of income subject to the 15% tax rate, and the 39.6% rate begins at $12,500. Second, unearned income exceeding $2,100 (in 2017) of children under age 18 (and in some cases age 18 through 23) is taxed at the higher of the parents' or the child's tax rate, even if distributed from a trust or estate. Third, dividend income is eligible for a low or zero tax rate regardless of whether it is taxed to the grantor, the beneficiary, or the trust. Fourth, the taxpayer may owe the 3.8% tax on net investment income. Depending on whether the trust income is distributed or retained, it is taxed to the trust or the beneficiary or a portion to each. Because the trust is a separate taxpayer, income taxed to the trust is taxed under the trust's rate schedule. If the beneficiary has income from other sources, the income shifted from the trust to the beneficiary is not necessarily taxed in the lowest tax bracket. An income tax savings nevertheless can occur whenever a portion of the shifted income is taxed at a rate lower than the rate the grantor would pay on such income.

ADDITIONAL COMMENT

In 2017, the first $2,550 of trust income is taxed at 15%. A complex trust pays no tax on $100 of income (because of its personal exemption) and only 15% on the next $2,550 of income. If the trust distributes income to a child subject to the kiddie tax rules who is a dependent and has no other unearned income, the child pays no tax on the first $1,050 of that income and pays taxes at his or her own rate on the next $1,050. The rest is taxed at the parents' rates. If the parents are always in the top income tax bracket, nontrivial income tax savings still can be achieved by using a trust to spread non-dividend income over different taxpayers. In such scenarios, a Sec. 2503(c) trust (trust for minors) is commonly used.

TIMING OF DISTRIBUTIONS

Individuals managing estates and discretionary trusts can reduce taxes by carefully planning the timing of distributions. From a tax standpoint, the executor or trustee should consider the beneficiary's income from other sources and make distributions in amounts that equalize the marginal tax rates of the beneficiary and the fiduciary. If the trust is a **sprinkling trust** (a discretionary trust with several beneficiaries), the trustee can accomplish tax savings for the beneficiaries by making distributions to the beneficiaries who have the lowest marginal tax rate that year. Of course, nontax reasons might require a trustee to distribute income to other beneficiaries as well. A special 65-day

KEY POINT

Given that one often cannot determine the exact amount of income a trust (or any other entity) has earned until after the end of the tax year, the importance of the 65-day rule for distribution planning becomes readily apparent.

rule allows trustees of complex trusts and estates to treat distributions made during the first 65 days of the new tax year as if they had been made on the last day of the preceding tax year. If the trustee or executor does not make the election, the distributed income is deducted by the fiduciary and taxed to the beneficiary in the year of the actual distribution.

PROPERTY DISTRIBUTIONS

Under the general rule affecting property distributions, the trust receives a distribution deduction equal to the lesser of the fiduciary's adjusted basis in the property or the property's FMV.[41] If the trust distributes appreciated property, however, the trustee can elect to recognize a gain on the distribution equal to the excess of the property's FMV over its adjusted basis on the distribution date. If the trustee does not make the election, the trust recognizes no gain when it distributes the property.

If the trustee elects to recognize the gain, the distribution deduction equals the property's FMV. The beneficiary, in turn, takes a basis equal to the property's adjusted basis to the trust plus the gain the trust recognized on the distribution. If the beneficiary likely will sell the property soon after distribution, the election provision allows the trustee to choose where the appreciation will be taxed, at the trust level or the beneficiary level. If the distribution involves appreciated capital gain property, the capital gain the trust recognizes can offset the trust's current capital loss and carryovers from prior tax years.

EXAMPLE C:14-39 ▶ Todd Trust owns a number of assets, including an asset with a FMV of $35,000 and an adjusted basis of $12,000. In the current year, the trust distributes the asset to its sole beneficiary, Susan. The trust does not make any other distributions to Susan. If the trustee elects to recognize gain of $23,000, the trust receives a distribution deduction of $35,000, the FMV of the asset. If, for example, the trust has a $23,000 capital loss, it can offset the loss against the gain. Susan includes $35,000 of income in her tax return and obtains a $35,000 basis in the asset. Thus, if she sells the asset for $35,000, she will report no gain. If the trustee had not elected to recognize gain on the in-kind distribution, the distribution deduction would have been $12,000, the asset's adjusted basis to the trust. Susan's basis in the asset also would have been $12,000, and she would have reported $12,000 income from the trust. ◀

CHOICE OF YEAR-END FOR ESTATES

Distributions from an estate or trust are taxed to the beneficiaries in the beneficiaries' tax year in which the fiduciary's year ends.[42] Congress in 1986 required all trusts (even existing fiscal-year trusts) other than tax-exempt and wholly charitable trusts to use a calendar year as their tax year to eliminate their ability to defer the taxation of trust distributions to beneficiaries by choosing a noncalendar year.[43] Estates, however, are completely free to choose a year-end as long as the tax year does not exceed 12 months.

EXAMPLE C:14-40 ▶ Molly Madison died on February 7, 2016. Madison Estate adopted a fiscal year ending January 31. During the period February 7, 2016, through January 31, 2017, Madison Estate distributes $30,000 to Bob, a calendar year beneficiary. The estate's DNI exceeds $30,000. Bob reports $30,000 of estate income on his individual return for 2017, Bob's tax year during which the estate's tax year ended. By choosing the January 31 year-end (instead of a calendar year-end), the executor postpones the taxation of income to Bob from 2016 to 2017. ◀

ADDITIONAL COMMENT

For 2017, 39.6% is the top tax rate for income tax purposes, and 40% is the highest estate tax rate. Also, both the estate and individuals can owe an additional 3.8% tax on net investment income.

DEDUCTION OF ADMINISTRATION EXPENSES

Chapter C:13 points out that the executor elects where to deduct administration expenses, i.e., on the estate tax return, the estate's income tax return, or some on each return. Unlike the situation for deductions in respect of a decedent, Sec. 642(g) denies a double deduction for administration expenses. Such expenses should be deducted where they will yield the greatest tax savings. Of course, if the surviving spouse receives all the

---

41 Sec. 643(e)(2).

42 Secs. 652(c) and 662(c).

43 Sec. 644.

decedent's property or all except for an amount equal to the exemption equivalent, deducting administration expenses on the estate tax return will produce no tax savings because the estate will owe no estate taxes.

COMPLIANCE AND PROCEDURAL CONSIDERATIONS

OBJECTIVE 10

Comply with procedural rules for trust and estate income taxation

FILING REQUIREMENTS

General Rule. Every estate that has gross income of at least $600 for the tax year must file an income tax return (Form 1041-U.S. Income Tax Return for Estates and Trusts). A trust income tax return (generally Form 1041) is required for every trust that has taxable income or has gross income of $600 or more.[44] In addition, every estate or trust that has a nonresident alien as a beneficiary must file a return.[45]

ETHICAL POINT

Individual beneficiaries report their share of income from trusts and estates on their Form 1040. CPAs have a responsibility to monitor clients' beneficial interests in trusts and estates to prevent underreporting. Some clients may unintentionally forget to disclose income from a simple trust if they received no cash distributions from the fiduciary during the year.

DUE DATE FOR RETURN AND TAX

The due date for fiduciary returns (Form 1041) is the same as for individuals, the fifteenth day of the fourth month following the end of the tax year.[46] If an extension is desired, Form 7004 must be filed. The automatic extension period is five and a half months for tax years beginning after 2015.

Both trusts and estates generally must make estimated tax payments using the general rules applicable to individual taxpayers.[47] The IRC, however, exempts estates from making estimated tax payments for their first two tax years. If the fiduciary's tax liability exceeds the estimated tax payments, the balance of the tax is due on or before the due date for the return.[48] Estimated tax payments for a trust or an estate should be accompanied by Form 1041-ES (Estimated Income Tax for Fiduciaries).

DOCUMENTS TO BE FURNISHED TO IRS

Although the executor or the trustee need not file a copy of the will or the trust instrument with the return, at times the IRS may request a copy of such documents. If the IRS makes such a request, the executor or the trustee also should transmit the following:

- A statement signed under penalty of perjury that the copy is true and complete
- A statement naming the provisions of the will or trust agreement that the executor or the trustee believes control how the income is to be divided among the fiduciary, the beneficiaries, and the grantor (if applicable)

SAMPLE SIMPLE AND COMPLEX TRUST RETURNS

Appendix B contains samples of simple and complex trust returns (Form 1041). The Appendix also illustrates completed Schedules K-1 for the reporting of distributed income, etc. to the beneficiaries. One copy of Schedule K-1 for each beneficiary is filed with Form 1041. In addition, each beneficiary receives a copy of his or her Schedule K-1, so that he or she knows the amount and type of gross income to report for the distributions received as well as other pertinent information.

In the two sets of facts illustrated in the sample returns, the trusts do not owe the alternative minimum tax (AMT). Trusts that owe the AMT report it on Schedule I of Form 1041.

[44] Secs. 6012(a)(3) and (4). A special grantor trust rule, however, permits a revocable trust's income to be reported on the grantor's tax return. See Reg. Sec. 1.671-4(b).

[45] Sec. 6012(a)(5).

[46] Sec. 6072(a).

[47] Sec. 6654(l).

[48] Sec. 6151(a).

PROBLEM MATERIALS

DISCUSSION QUESTIONS

C:14-1 Explain to a client in laymen's language what portion of the income of an estate or trust is subject to taxation at the fiduciary level.

C:14-2 Given the tax rate schedule for trusts, what reasons (tax and/or nontax) exist today for creating a trust?

C:14-3 List some major differences between the taxation of individuals and trusts.

C:14-4 Explain to a client the significance of the income and principal categorization scheme used for fiduciary accounting purposes.

C:14-5 List some common examples of principal and income items under the Uniform Act.

C:14-6 A client asks about the relevance of state law in classifying items as principal or income. Explain the relevance.

C:14-7 A trust instrument provides that, for life, Irene is entitled to receive distributions of income only and Beth is to receive the remainder interest. The trust sells property at a gain. Income and corpus are classified in accordance with the Uniform Act. Is the gain classified as income? Explain.

C:14-8 Refer to Question C:14-7. Which taxpayer (the trust, Irene, or Beth) pays the tax on the gain?

C:14-9 A trust owns an asset on which depreciation is claimed. The trust distributes all of its income to its sole income beneficiary. Whose taxable income is reduced by the depreciation?

C:14-10 What is the amount of the personal exemption for trusts and estates?

C:14-11 A client inquires about the significance of distributable net income (DNI). Explain.

C:14-12 a. Are net accounting income and DNI always the same amount?
b. If not, explain a common reason for a difference.
c. Are capital gains usually included in DNI?

C:14-13 Assume that a trust collects rental income and interest income on tax-exempt bonds. Will a portion of the rental expenses, such as repairs, have to be allocated to tax-exempt income and thereby become nondeductible? Explain.

C:14-14 a. Describe the shortcut approach for verifying that the amount calculated as a simple trust's taxable income is correct.
b. Can a shortcut verification process be applied for trusts and estates that accumulate some of their income? Explain.

C:14-15 When does the NOL of a trust or estate produce tax deductions for the beneficiaries?

C:14-16 The Mary Morgan Trust, a simple trust governed by the Uniform Act, sells one capital asset in the current year. The sale results in a loss.
a. When will the capital loss produce a tax benefit for the trust or its beneficiary? Explain.
b. Would the result necessarily be the same for a complex trust? Explain.

C:14-17 Describe the tier system for taxing trust beneficiaries.

C:14-18 Determine the accuracy of the following statement: Under the tier system, beneficiaries who receive mandatory distributions of income are more likely to be taxed on the entire distributions they receive than are beneficiaries who receive discretionary distributions.

C:14-19 a. Describe to a client what income in respect of a decedent (IRD) is.
b. Describe to the client one tax disadvantage and one tax advantage that occur because of the classification of a receipt as IRD.

C:14-20 Describe three situations that cause trusts to be subject to the grantor trust rules.

C:14-21 Can a client escape the grantor trust rules by providing in a trust instrument that income is payable to a nephew for 20 years and that the trust assets pass at the end of 20 years to the client's spouse?

C:14-22 Amelia, a widow, is in the top marginal income tax bracket and has considerably more income than she can spend. She is considering creating a trust for the benefit of her adult son Jason but is reluctant to make it irrevocable, at least presently. If she funds a revocable trust that must distribute all of its income to Jason, will Jason be taxed on the income? How may this trust help reduce the size of Amelia's gross estate?

C:14-23 What is the benefit of the 65-day rule?

C:14-24 a. When are fiduciary income tax returns due?
b. Must estates and trusts pay estimated income taxes?

ISSUE IDENTIFICATION QUESTIONS

C:14-25 Art Rutter sold an apartment building in May 2017 for a small amount of cash and a note payable with payments beginning in 2018. Principal and interest payments are due annually on the note in April of 2018 through 2022. Art died in August 2017. He willed all his assets to his daughter Amelia. Art's gross estate is about $6 million, and his estate tax deductions are very small. What tax issues should the executor of his estate consider with respect to reporting the sale of the building and the collection of the installments?

C:14-26 For the first five months of its existence (August through December 2017), the Estate of Amy Ennis had gross income (net of expenses) of $7,000 per month. For January through July 2018, the executor estimates that the estate will have gross income (net of expenses) totaling $5,000. The estate's sole beneficiary is Amy's uncle, Joe, an unmarried, calendar year taxpayer. Joe incurred a large NOL from his sole proprietorship years ago, and $34,000 of the NOL carryover remains but expires at the end of 2017. During 2017, Joe's only income was $10,000 from part-time employment. What tax issues should the executor of Amy's estate consider with respect to distributions of the estate's income?

C:14-27 Raj Kothare funded an irrevocable simple trust in May of last year. The trust benefits Raj's son for life and grandson upon the son's death. One of the assets he transferred to the trust was Webbco stock, which had a $35,000 FMV on the transfer date. Raj's basis in the stock was $39,000, and he paid no gift tax on the transfer. The stock's value has dropped to $27,000, and the trustee thinks that now (October of the current year) might be the time to sell the stock and recognize the loss. For the current year, the trust will have $20,000 of income exclusive of any gain or loss. What tax and non-tax issues should the trustee consider concerning the possible sale of the stock?

PROBLEMS

C:14-28 *Calculation of the Tax Liability.* A complex trust has taxable income of $29,900 in 2017. The $29,900 includes $5,000 of rental income and $25,000 of taxable interest income, reduced by the $100 personal exemption. The trust makes no distributions during the year. What is the trust's total tax liability? Compare this tax to the amount of tax an unmarried individual filing single would pay on the same amount of rental and interest income (with no other income). Assume the individual claims the standard deduction.

C:14-29 *Determination of Taxable Income and Tax Liability.* Suellen Symmes died on January 15, 2017. Her estate elected a November 30 year end. The executor projects that the estate will receive interest income of $50,000 by November 30, 2017, and will have no other gross income. In addition, it will have no deductions other than the personal exemption. The beneficiary of the estate is Thomas Symmes, a calendar year taxpayer who is projected to have $195,000 of taxable income in 2017, not including any distributions from the estate. Compare the overall tax costs for the estate and Thomas if (1) the executor distributes $37,250 to Thomas prior to November 30, 2017, or (2) the estate makes no distributions before November 30, 2017. Thomas is unmarried and files as a single taxpayer.

C:14-30 *Determination of Taxable Income.* A simple trust has the following receipts and expenditures for the current year. The trust instrument classifies gains, losses, and trustee's fees as part of principal.

Dividends	$20,000
Long-term capital gain	15,000
Trustee's fees	1,500
Distribution to beneficiary	20,000

a. What is the trust's taxable income under the formula approach of Figure C:14-1?
b. What is the trust's taxable income under the short-cut approach?

C:14-31 *Determination of Taxable Income.* Refer to Problem C:14-30. How would your answer to Part a change if the trust in addition received $8,000 interest from tax-exempt bonds, and it distributed $28,000 instead of $20,000?

C:14-32 *Determination of Taxable Income and Tax Liability.* A simple trust has the following receipts and expenditures for 2017. The trust instrument is silent with respect to capital gains, and state law concerning trust accounting income follows the Uniform Act. Assume the trustee's fee is charged equally to income and to principal.

Corporate bond interest	$40,000
Tax-exempt interest	9,000
Long-term capital gain	5,000
Trustee's fee	2,000
Distribution to beneficiary	48,000

a. What is the trust's taxable income under the formula approach of Figure C:14-1?
b. What is the trust's tax liability?

C:14-33 *Determination of Taxable Income.* During the current year, a simple trust has the following receipts and expenditures. The Uniform Act governs the accounting classification.

Corporate bond interest	$60,000
Long-term capital gain	20,000
Trustee's fees	3,000

a. What amount must be distributed to the beneficiary?
b. What is the trust's taxable income under the shortcut approach?

C:14-34 *Determination of Distribution Deduction.* A trust has net accounting income of $24,000 and incurs a trustee's fee of $1,000 in its principal account. What is its distribution deduction under the following situations:
a. It distributes $24,000, and all of its income is from taxable sources.
b. It distributes $24,000, and it has tax-exempt income (net of allocable expenses) of $2,000.
c. It distributes $10,000, and all of its income is from taxable sources.

C:14-35 *Determination of Beneficiary's Income.* A complex trust is authorized to make discretionary distributions of income and principal to its two beneficiaries, Roy and Sandy. Separate shares are not required. For the current year, it has DNI and net accounting income of $80,000, all from taxable sources. It distributes $60,000 to Roy and $40,000 to Sandy. How much gross income should each beneficiary report?

C:14-36 *Determination of Beneficiary's Income.* Refer to Problem C:14-35. How would your answer change if the trust instrument required that $10,000 per year be distributed to Sandy, and the trustee also made discretionary distributions of $60,000 to Roy and $30,000 to Sandy with separate shares not required?

C:14-37 *Determination of Beneficiary's Income.* A complex trust is required to distribute $20,000 and $30,000 annually to its beneficiaries, Bart and Thelma, respectively. In addition, it can distribute other amounts at its discretion. In Year 1, it had DNI of $62,000 and distributed $20,000 to Bart and $47,000 to Thelma. All of its income is from dividends. In Year 2, it had DNI of $66,000 and distributed $25,000 to Bart and $36,000 to Thelma. Again, all of its income is from dividends. Determine the amount of income each beneficiary should report with respect to the distributions for each year.

C:14-38 *Determination of Accounting Income and Distribution.* The Trotter Trust has the receipts and expenditures listed below for the current year. Assume the Uniform Act governs an item's classification as principal or income. The trustee's fee is charged one-half to principal and one-half to income. What is the trust's net accounting income and the maximum amount it can distribute? Assume the trust instrument precludes distributing principal currently.

Dividends	$15,000
Interest on tax-exempt bonds	7,000
Loss on sale of capital asset	(9,000)
Rental income from land	6,000
Property taxes on rental property	1,000
Trustee's fee	1,800

C:14-39 *Determination of Taxable Income.* Refer to Problem C:14-38. Assume the trustee must pay out all of its income currently to its beneficiary, Julio.

a. What is the deductible portion of the trustee's fee?
b. What is the trust's taxable income exclusive of the distribution deduction?
c. What is the trust's DNI?
d. What is the trust's taxable income using the formula approach of Figure C:14-1?

C:14-40 *Determination of Taxable Income.* Refer to Problem C:14-39. How would your answers change if the trust were a discretionary trust that distributes $12,000 to its beneficiary, Julio?

C:14-41 *Calculation of Deductible Expenses.* The George Grant Trust reports the receipts and expenditures listed below. What are the trust's *deductible* expenses?

U.S. Treasury interest	$25,000
Rental income	9,000
Interest from tax-exempt bonds	6,000
Property taxes on rental property	2,000
CPA's fee for tax return preparation	800
Trustee's fee	1,900

C:14-42 *Tax Treatment of Capital Losses.* A simple trust had a long-term capital loss of $10,000 for 2016 and a long-term capital gain of $15,000 for 2017. Its net accounting income and DNI are equal. Explain the tax treatment for the 2016 capital loss assuming the trust is in existence at the end of 2018.

C:14-43 *Tax Treatment of Capital Losses.* Refer to Problem C:14-42. How would your answer change if instead the trust were a complex trust that makes no distributions in 2016 and 2017? Assume the trust earns $8,000 of corporate bond interest income each year.

C:14-44 *Revocable Trusts.* A revocable trust created by Amir realizes $30,000 of rental income and a $5,000 capital loss. It distributes $22,000 to Ali, its beneficiary. How much income is taxed to the trust, the grantor, and the beneficiary?

C:14-45 *Reversionary Interest Trusts.* Holly funded the Holly Marx Trust in January 2017. The entire trust income is payable to her adult son, Jack for 20 years. At the end of the twentieth year, the trust assets are to pass to Holly's husband. In the current year, the trust realizes $30,000 of dividend income and a $15,000 long-term capital gain. How much income is taxed to the trust, the grantor, and the beneficiary in the current year?

C:14-46 *Reversionary Interest Trusts.* Refer to Problem C:14-45. Explain how your answers would change for each independent situation indicated below:

a. At the end of the trust term, the property passes instead to Holly's nephew Nathan.
b. Holly creates the trust in October 2017 for a term of 25 years, after which the property will revert to her.

C:14-47 *Income in Respect of Decedent.* The following items are relevant for the first income tax return for the Ken Kimble Estate. Mr. Kimble, a cash method of accounting taxpayer, died on July 1, 2017.

Dividends	$10,000
Interest on corporate bonds	18,000
Collection on installment note from sale of investment land	24,000

The record dates were June 14 for $6,000 of the dividends and October 31 for the remaining $4,000 of dividends. The bond interest is payable annually on October 1. Mr. Kimble's basis in the land was $8,000. He sold it in May of 2016 for a total sales and contract price of $48,000 and reported his gain under the installment method. Ignore interest on the installment note. What amount of IRD should be reported on the estate's calendar year income tax return?

C:14-48 *Income in Respect of Decedent.* Julie Brown died on May 27 of the current year. She was employed before her death at a gross salary of $4,000 per month. Her pay day was the last day of each month, and her employer did not pro rate her last monthly salary payment. She owned preferred stock that paid quarterly dividends of $800 per quarter each March 31, June 30, September 30, and December 31. The record date for the June dividend was June 10. Assume her estate chooses a calendar year as its tax year. What amount of gross income should be reported on the estate's first income tax return? Identify the items of IRD included in gross income.

C:14-49 *Property Distributions.* In the current year, Maddox Trust, a complex trust, distributed an asset with a $42,000 adjusted basis and a $75,000 FMV to its sole beneficiary, Marilyn Maddox-Mason. The trustee elected to recognize gain on the distribution. Marilyn received no other distributions from the trust during the year. The distributable net income for the year was $87,000, and none of it was from tax-exempt sources.

a. What is the trust's distribution deduction?
b. On her individual income tax return, how much gross income should Marilyn report from the trust?
c. What is Marilyn's basis in the asset distributed in kind from the trust?

C:14-50 *Income Recognition by Beneficiary.* Joan died April 17, 2016. Joan's executor chose March 31 as the tax year end for the estate. The estate's only beneficiary, Kathy, reports on a calendar year. The executor of Joan's estate makes the following distributions to Kathy:

June 2016	$ 5,000
August 2016	10,000
March 2017	12,000
August 2017	14,000

The 2016 and 2017 distributions do not exceed DNI. How much income should Kathy report on her 2016 return as a result of the distributions from the estate? On her 2017 return?

COMPREHENSIVE PROBLEM

C:14-51 Dana Dodson died October 31, 2016, with a gross estate of $6.7 million, debts of $200,000, and a taxable estate of $6.5 million. Dana made no taxable gifts. All of her property passed under her will to her son, Daniel Dodson. The estate chose a June 30 year-end. Its receipts, disbursements, and gains for the period ended June 30, 2017, were as follows:

Dividend income	$27,000
Interest income from corporate bonds	18,000
Interest income from tax-exempt bonds	9,000
Gain on sale of land	10,000
Executor's fee (charged to principal)	4,000
Distribution to Daniel Dodson	–0–

Of the $27,000 dividends received in the estate's first tax year, $7,000 were declared October 4, 2016, with a record date of October 25 and a payment date of November 4, 2016. The corporate bonds pay interest each August 31 and February 28. The estate collected $18,000 corporate bond interest in February 2017 and August 2017. The tax-exempt bonds pay interest each June 30 and December 31. The estate collected $4,500 in December 2016 and $4,500 in June 2017 from the tax-exempt bonds. Dana, a cash basis taxpayer, sold land in 2013 for a total gain of $60,000 and used installment reporting. She collected principal in 2014 and 2015 and reported gain of $30,000 on her 2014 return and $10,000 on her 2015 return. The estate collected additional principal in March 2017 and the remaining principal payment in March 2018. The gain attributable to the March 2017 and March 2018 principal collections is $10,000 per tax year. Ignore interest on the sale.

Calculate the following:

a. Deductible executor's fee.
b. Total IRD and the IRD reported on the return for the period ended June 30, 2017.
c. Total Sec. 691(c) deduction if none of the debts are DRD.
d. Section 691(c) deduction deductible on the estate's income tax return for the period ended June 30, 2017.
e. Taxable income of the estate for its tax year ended June 30, 2017.
f. Marginal income tax rate for the estate for its tax year ended June 30, 2017.

TAX STRATEGY PROBLEMS

C:14-52 Glorietta Trust is an irrevocable discretionary trust funded by Grant Glorietta. The discretionary income beneficiary for life is Grant's son, Gordon Glorietta (single). Gordon is a partner in a partnership in which he materially participates, and he has a large basis in his partnership interest. For 2017, the trust had $50,000 of corporate bond interest, net of expenses, and no other income. It made no distributions to Gordon in 2017. Assume that it is now February 22, 2018, and Gordon has just learned that his share of loss from the partnership will be $72,000. Gordon has other income for 2017 of approximately $52,000. The trustee anticipates distributing $40,000 cash to Gordon before the end of February. For the last few years, Gordon's marginal tax rate was 15%. He claims the standard deduction, has only one exemption, and files as a single individual. Discuss a tax-saving opportunity presented by this scenario. Also show a comparative analysis of the alternatives.

C:14-53 Carla plans to create a trust and transfer to it oil and gas properties producing royalty income. She will transfer no other properties. The sole income beneficiary of the trust will be Carla's son, Marshall, who is in the top marginal income tax bracket and is expected to remain there. Carla estimates that the trust, a simple trust, will receive about $30,000 of royalty income each year and have $2,000 of cash expenses each year. The situs of the trust will be a state that has enacted the latest version of the Uniform Principal and Income Act. Carla seeks your advice about the total combined income tax cost to the trust and Marshall if the Uniform Principal and Income Act governs, compared with the combined tax cost to the two taxpayers if the trust instrument states that 27.5% of the royalty income is to be allocated to principal (corpus) and the rest to income. For simplicity, use 2017 tax rates and ignore the depletion deduction that would actually be available with respect to the royalty income. In addition, ignore the 3.8% tax on net investment income. You will need to follow the instructions for Problem C:14-63 to find the rules under the Uniform Principal and Income Act.

C:14-54 Cate Cole died in 2015, and her will left her entire estate in equal shares to her two adult children, Calvin and Corrine. Both children anticipate being in the top income tax bracket for at least ten years. The Cate Cole Estate is a calendar year taxpayer. The year 2017 is almost over, and to date the estate has received $18,000 of interest income from a certificate of deposit (CD). The executor does not expect to collect any more income before the end of the year. However, in January 2018, the estate will collect $1,500 of interest income from the CD. The executor has distributed all the estate's assets except for the CD, which matures in early January 2018. The executor anticipates distributing the funds from the CD when it matures, after which he will close the estate. Because the taxable estate did not exceed the basic exclusion amount (or exemption equivalent), the executor did *not* deduct administration expenses on the estate tax return. The estate owes administration expenses totaling $25,000. Propose an income tax minimization strategy for timing, between 2017 and 2018, the payment of the administration expenses, and prepare a schedule to support your recommendation.

TAX FORM/RETURN PREPARATION PROBLEMS

C:14-55 Marion Mosley created the Jenny Justice Trust in 2005 with First Bank named as trustee. For 20 years, the trust is to pay out all its income semiannually to the beneficiary, Jenny Justice. At the end of the twentieth year, the trust assets are to be distributed to Jenny's descendants. According to the trust instrument, capital gains are credited to principal, and depreciation is charged to principal. For the current year, the irrevocable trust reports the following results:

	Amounts Allocable to	
	Income	*Principal*
Rental income	$15,000	
Corporate bond interest	27,000	
Interest on tax-exempt (non-private activity) bonds	8,000	
Long-term capital gain on sale of land		11,000[a]
Maintenance and repairs of rental property	1,500	
Property taxes on rental property	700	
CPA's fee for tax return preparation	500	
Trustee's fee		2,000
Depreciation		2,400
Estimated federal income taxes paid from principal		2,000

[a]The sales price and adjusted basis are $91,000 and $80,000, respectively. The trustee acquired the land in 2006 and the trustee sold it in November of the current year.

Prepare a Form 1041, including any needed Schedule K-1s, for the Jenny Justice Trust. Ignore the alternative minimum tax (AMT). The trustee's address is P.O. Box 100, Southwest City, TX 75000. The identification number of the trust is 74-1234567. Jenny, resides at 2 Mountain View, South City, AL 35000.

C:14-56 In 2014, Leon Lopez funded Lopez Trust #3, an irrevocable trust, at First Bank, 125 Seaview, Northwest City, WA 98112, for the benefit of his twin children, Loretta and Jorge. The trust's tax ID number is 74-1243565. The trustee, in its discretion, is to distribute income and/or principal to one or both of the beneficiaries and does not need to maintain separate shares. The trust is to terminate in 2025, when the beneficiaries reach age 35. Leon transferred corporate bonds and municipal bonds to the trust in January 2014. In 2016, the trustee distributed $8,600 to Loretta (whose address is 123 Maple Ave., Northwest City, WA 98115) and nothing to Jorge. Half of the trustee's fee is to be charged to income and half to principal; gains and losses affect principal. Other current year information for the trust is as follows:

Interest from corporate bonds	$9,200
Interest from municipal bonds	6,800
Short-term capital gain on sale of bonds	300
CPA's fee for preparation of prior year's tax return	525
Trustee's fee	800
Estimated federal income taxes paid from principal	2,400

Prepare a Form 1041 and Schedule K-1 for the trust. Ignore the alternative minimum tax.

C:14-57 Mark Meadows funded a trust in 2004 with Merchants Bank named as trustee. He paid no gift tax on the transfer. The trustee in its discretion is to pay out income, but not principal, to Mark's children, Angela and Barry, for 15 years. Then the trust will terminate, and its assets, including accumulated income, will be paid to Angela and Barry in equal amounts. (Separate shares are *not* to be maintained.) In the current year, the trustee distributes $3,000 to Angela and $9,000 to Barry. The trust paid estimated federal income taxes of $6,000 from the principal account and reported the following additional results for the current year. The trust instrument requires trustee's fees to be paid from principal.

	Amounts Allocable to	
	Income	*Principal*
Dividends	$50,000	
Interest on corporate bonds	4,000	
Interest on City of Cleveland (non-private activity) bonds	9,000	
Long-term capital loss on sale of stock		$12,000[a]
Trustee's fee		2,400
CPA's fee for tax return preparation	400	

[a]Mr. Meadows purchased the stock for $30,000 in 2000. It was valued at $44,000 when he transferred it to the trust in 2004. The price declined and the trust sold the stock for $18,000 in December of the current year.

Prepare a Form 1041, including any needed Schedule K-1s, for the trust established by Mr. Meadows. Ignore the alternative minimum tax (AMT). The trustee's address is 201 Fifth Ave., Northeast City, NY 10000. The trust's identification number is 74-1212121. Angela and Barry reside at 3 East 46th St., North City, NY 11000.

CASE STUDY PROBLEMS

C:14-58 Arthur Rich, a widower, is considering setting up an irrevocable trust (or trusts) with a bank as trustee for his three minor children. He will fund the trust at $900,000 (or $300,000 each in the case of three trusts). A friend suggested that he might want to consider a January 31 year-end for the trusts. The friend also suggested that Arthur might want to make each trust a complex discretionary trust. Arthur is a little apprehensive about the idea of a trust that would be complex. The friend warned that trust income should not be spent on support of the children.

Required: Prepare a memorandum to the tax partner of your firm concerning the above client matter. As part of your analysis, consider the following:

a. What tax reasons, if any, can you think of for having three trusts instead of one?
b. Why do you think the friend suggested a January 31 year-end?
c. What is your reaction to the friend's suggestion about the year-end?
d. Which taxpayer, the beneficiary, the grantor, or the trust, is taxed on the income from a discretionary trust?
e. To what extent do trusts serve as income-shifting arrangements?
f. What can you advise Arthur concerning his apprehension about a complex trust?
g. Why did the friend warn against spending trust income for the children's support?

C:14-59 You are preparing a current year (Year 2) individual tax return for Robert Lucca, a real estate developer and long-time client. While preparing Robert's individual tax return you learn that last year (Year 1) he received interest income from a trust his 75-year-old father created. Robert's Year 2 income from the trust is properly reflected on a Schedule K-1 prepared by the accounting firm that prepared the trust's Year 2 return. Robert prepared the trust's return for Year 1, and decided that he should not be taxed on any of the trust's income because the trust distributed nothing to him. Upon reviewing Robert's copy of the trust instrument, you learn that the instrument calls for mandatory distributions of all the income to Robert every year. Assume that the trust reported $8,000 of taxable income for Year 1 and claimed no distribution deduction and that Robert was in the highest marginal tax bracket for Year 1.

a. What responsibility do you have to correct the error made for the tax Year 1? Refer to the *Statements on Standards for Tax Services* in Appendix E.
b. Assume instead that an IRS agent has just begun to audit Robert's Year 1 individual tax return. What is your responsibility if you have discovered the error on the Year 1 trust return, and you are representing Robert in the audit?

TAX RESEARCH PROBLEMS

C:14-60 You are in the process of doing income tax projections for the Estate of Esther Simmons, who died January 3, 2017. The Estate has paid appraisal fees for having her real estate holdings appraised for estate tax valuation purposes, probate court fees, and printing costs for having notices regarding debts published in the local newspaper. Draft a memo in which you address whether these costs will be classified as miscellaneous itemized deductions subject to the 2% nondeductible floor.

C:14-61 Roy Ritter died two years ago. Among the assets he owned were Ritter Ranch, a cattle ranch consisting of 12,220 acres in Texas. In accordance with Roy's will, the ranch along with stocks producing substantial dividends passed to a testamentary trust (the Ritter Trust) with grandson Gene Ritter as trustee. The sole asset of the trust is the ranch, and unfortunately the ranch is operating at a loss. Gene is an accountant and devotes some hours to day-to-day ranching issues but does not meet the material participation test in the context of the passive activity loss (PAL) rules. Gene, in his role as trustee, employs a well-trained, full-time ranch manager and 20 "ranch hands." Ritter Trust is a new client of your firm. Write a memo in which you discuss the applicability of the PAL rules to the Ritter Trust. In particular, you should discuss whether "material participation" is measured by just the trustee's hours and activities or whether the hours and efforts of the trustee, the ranch manager, and all of the other employees should be considered. Recall that Sec. 469 is the primary IRC section for the PAL rules.

C:14-62 Ernest Jacobson created an irrevocable trust in February of last year and designated his friend Eileen Frazier as trustee. Eileen is empowered, for life, to distribute such income as she deems appropriate to herself each year. Any income not distributed to her in a given year must be retained and distributed to the remainderman Elliott Jacobson after Eileen's death. Last year, the trust received $22,000 of income, all from dividends, and Eileen distributed $4,000 of the income to herself. It is early in the second year, and your supervisor requested that you write a short memo addressing what portion, if any, of the income is taxed to the trust. She further suggested that you begin by consulting IRC Sec. 678.

C:14-63 *Internet Research Problem.* A client, Sam Curren, established the Curren Trust earlier this year. In addition to stocks and cash, the trust's assets include a life insurance policy on the life of Mr. Curren. The trust is both the owner and beneficiary of the policy. The insurance premiums are $8,250 per year. Are the premium payments classified as payments from the principal account or from the income account if the state that is the situs of the trust has adopted the latest version of the Uniform Principal and Income Act? Go to the Web site for the National Conference of Commissioners on Uniform State Laws, www.uniformlaws.org, and find the Uniform Principal and Income Act. If you type in a search request, omit the word "Uniform." Consult Section 502 of the Act and prepare a memo that addresses the classification of the insurance premium payments.

C:14-64 *Internet Research Problem.* Your manager advises you that Sam Skinner, a long-time client, died on February 13 of the current year, survived by his wife Sue Skinner and several adult children. The Skinners are residents of a non-community property state. Earlier in the current year Sam sold stock at a $40,000 long-term capital loss. To date, neither Sam nor Sue has sold any other capital assets. The estate is not likely to distribute any assets to Sue before the end of the current year. Sue owns three stocks that have appreciated in value (ABC purchased in November of the previous year with $12,000 appreciation, JKL purchased two years ago with $25,000 appreciation, and TUV purchased three years ago with $28,000 appreciation). What will be the capital gain or loss consequences for the current year's joint tax return if no additional sales of capital assets occur? Assume all three of Sue's stocks have the same predicted appreciation rate. Suggest a planning strategy for your manager to discuss with Sue next month. Your manager suggests that, as a research source, you consult a recent article in *The Tax Adviser*, a publication of the AICPA.

CHAPTER

15

ADMINISTRATIVE PROCEDURES

LEARNING OBJECTIVES

After studying this chapter, you should be able to

1. Describe the role of the IRS in our tax system
2. Discuss how returns are selected for audit and the alternatives available to taxpayers whose returns are audited
3. Explain the IRS's ruling process
4. Identify the due dates for filing tax returns and paying taxes
5. Distinguish the various types of penalties imposed by the IRS
6. Calculate the penalty for not paying estimated taxes
7. Describe the more severe penalties, including the fraud penalty
8. Recognize when the statute of limitations applies
9. Explain from whom the government may collect unpaid taxes
10. Apply the professional and governmental standards for tax practitioners

CHAPTER OUTLINE

This chapter provides an overview of the administrative and procedural aspects of tax practice, an area with which all tax advisors should be familiar. The specific matters discussed include the role of the Internal Revenue Service (IRS) in tax enforcement and collection, the manner in which the IRS chooses tax returns for audit, taxpayers' alternatives to immediately agreeing to pay a proposed deficiency, due dates for returns, taxpayer penalties, and the statute of limitations. Chapter C:1 briefly discussed the AICPA's *Statements on Standards for Tax Services* and Treasury Department *Circular 230* guidelines for tax practioners. Chapter C:15 expands the discussion on professional standards and examines additional tax practice topics, including Internal Revenue Code (IRC) penalty provisions that affect tax advisors and tax return preparers.

ROLE OF THE INTERNAL REVENUE SERVICE

OBJECTIVE 1

Describe the role of the IRS in our tax system

The IRS is part of the Treasury Department. Its chief administrative officer is the IRS Commissioner. Overseeing the activities of the IRS is a nine-member board consisting of the Secretary of the Treasury, the IRS Commissioner, a public sector representative, and six private sector representatives. All board members are appointed by the President of the United States.

ENFORCEMENT AND COLLECTION

KEY POINT

The U.S. tax structure is based on a self-assessment system. The level of voluntary compliance actually is quite high, but one of the principal purposes of the IRS is to enforce the federal tax laws and identify taxpayers who willfully or inadvertently fail to pay their fair share of the tax burden.

One of the IRS's most significant functions is enforcing tax laws.[1] The IRS is responsible for ensuring that taxpayers file returns, correctly report their tax liabilities, and pay any tax due.

Voluntary compliance with U.S. tax laws is relatively high, but a significant gap exists. As of the last study in 2016, the IRS estimated the gross tax gap to be $458 billion per year, on average, for 2008 through 2010. Enforcement efforts reduced the net tax gap to approximately $406 billion. Because some persons do not voluntarily comply, the IRS must audit selected taxpayers' returns and investigate the activities of nonfilers. In addition, because numerous ambiguities (gray areas) in the tax law exist, taxpayers and the IRS do not always agree on the proper tax treatment of transactions and events. As part of its enforcement duties, the IRS attempts to discover whether the reporting of these transactions and events differs from the way the IRS thinks they should be reported. As we point out later, taxpayers who disagree with the IRS in an audit may litigate.

The IRS must ensure that taxpayers not only report the correct tax liability, but also pay their taxes on time. For various reasons, some taxpayers file returns without paying any or all of the tax owed. The IRS's collection agents are responsible for collecting as much of the tax as possible from such persons.

INTERPRETATION OF THE STATUTE

As noted in Chapter C:1, the statutory language of the Internal Revenue Code (IRC) often is so vague that the courts and IRS must interpret it so that it can be readily applied. The IRS publishes its interpretations in revenue rulings, revenue procedures, notices, and information releases, which are available to the general public. In addition, the IRS offers guidance to specific taxpayers in the form of letter rulings, which have no precedential value for third-party taxpayers. Each of these authorities is discussed in detail in Chapter C:1.

[1] The IRS, however, does not have enforcement duties with respect to the taxes on guns and alcohol.

AUDITS OF TAX RETURNS

OBJECTIVE 2

Discuss how returns are selected for audit and the alternatives available to taxpayers whose returns are audited

The IRS operates service centers across the country, which receive and process tax returns.[2] One of the IRS's principal enforcement functions is auditing these returns. All returns are subject to some verification. One task the IRS service centers perform is checking whether amounts are properly calculated and faithfully carried from one line of a return to another. Another task is determining whether any items, such as signatures and Social Security numbers, are missing. Computers compare (or "match") by Social Security number the amounts reported on a taxpayer's return with employer- or payer-prepared documents (e.g., Forms W-2 and 1099) filed with the IRS service center.[3] To date, however, a 100% matching of these documents with tax return information has been difficult to achieve.

If the service center detects a calculation error in the tax reported on the return, it will send to the taxpayer a notice proposing an additional tax or granting a refund. If the information reported on a return is inconsistent with the information on Forms W-2 or 1099 reported by an employer or payer, the IRS asks the taxpayer to account for the discrepancy in writing or pay some additional tax.

PERCENTAGE OF RETURNS EXAMINED

REAL-WORLD EXAMPLE

Percentage examined of all returns filed in 2014:

Individuals	0.8%
C corporations	1.3%
S corporations	0.4%
Partnerships	0.5%

The IRS exams only a small fraction of all returns filed. For example, see the Real World Example in the margin. However in fiscal year 2015, for individuals with total positive income (i.e., gross income before losses and other deductions) of $1 million or more, the audit rate was 9.6%, and corporations with assets of at least $250 million faced a 21.5% audit rate. As a result of its audit activities, the IRS recommended additional taxes totaling $25.1 billion and civil penalties of $24.1 billion in that year.[4]

The examination percentages described above may be misleading because over half the returns filed are subject to a computerized matching in which the IRS compares the tax return information with documents (Forms 1099 and W-2) submitted by taxpayers and employers. Because wages, interest, alimony, pensions, unemployment compensation, Social Security benefits, and other items of income are reported to the IRS by the payers, and because state income taxes, local real estate taxes, home mortgage interest, and other items of deduction are reported to the IRS by the payees, taxpayers who report only these items on their returns effectively face a 100% audit rate. In 2015, 78% of individual examinations were by correspondence.

SELECTION OF RETURNS FOR AUDIT

Returns are chosen for audit in various ways, with many being selected under the *discriminant inventory function (DIF)* process. The IRS's objective in using the DIF process is to make the audit process as productive as possible by maximizing the number of audits that result in the collection of additional taxes. Returns with a relatively high DIF score have characteristics in common with returns for which the IRS earlier assessed a deficiency upon audit (e.g., the return may have reported a relatively high casualty loss or charitable contribution deduction). Because the IRS does not have the resources to audit all returns with a relatively high DIF score, IRS agents choose which of the higher scored returns should receive top priority for an audit. The DIF process has improved the IRS's ability to select returns for audit. In recent years, the IRS failed to collect additional taxes on approximately 10% to 15% of the individual returns audited by its revenue agents and examiners.

[2] The IRS maintains nine centers to process returns.

[3] Form W-2 reports employees' salaries and withholding tax, and Form 1099 reports income such as interest and dividends.

[4] "Examination Coverage: Recommended and Average Recommended Additional Tax Examination, by Type and Size of Return, Fiscal Year 2015," *Internal Revenue Service 2015 Data Book*, available for download at *www.irs.gov/pub/irs-soi/15databk.pdf*. Examinations are performed by revenue agents, tax auditors, and service center personnel.

HISTORICAL NOTE

Taxpayers have made several attempts to make the DIF variables public information. However, so far the courts have refused to require the IRS to provide such information. The basic thrust of the DIF program is that a return will be flagged if enough items on the return are out of the norm for a taxpayer in that particular income bracket.

The IRS developed its DIF formulas based on data gathered in its **Taxpayer Compliance Measurement Program (TCMP)**. Under the TCMP, the IRS conducted special audits of taxpayers selected at random. In these audits, the IRS examined every line item of taxpayers' returns to develop a statistical norm for the taxpayers' industry or profession as a whole. The IRS "indefinitely postponed" the TCMP in 1995, but in 2002, the IRS launched the **National Research Program (NRP)**. The NRP updates data compiled in TCMP audits and develops new statistical models for identifying returns most likely to contain errors. The NRP differs from the TCMP in two significant respects. First, it relies on pre-existing audit data as well as data compiled in ordinary, as opposed to special, audits. Second, it focuses on specific portions of a tax return, not all line-by-line items, some of which can be verified without face-to-face meetings. Like the TCMP, the NRP is based on data gathered primarily in audits of randomly selected individual tax returns.[5] Starting in 2007, the IRS began selecting 13,000 returns per year and will combine the audit results over rolling three year periods.

For business returns, the IRS conducts an audit initiative known as the Market Segment Specialization Program (MSSP). As part of this effort, the IRS publishes numerous Audit Technique Guides (ATGs) on various industries and major issues. These guides are targeted to examination agents, but also may benefit tax professionals and affected taxpayers in preparing returns. Industries covered by a separate ATG include business consulting, construction, ministry, and oil and gas. Issues covered include capitalization versus repairs, non-qualified deferred compensation, passive activity losses, real estate property foreclosure, and cancellation of debt.[6]

The IRS also conducts what are called "financial status" or "lifestyle" audits. These audits seek to identify inconsistencies between the income that a taxpayer reports and income suggested by his or her lifestyle. In the course of the audit, IRS agents review the taxpayer's overall economic situation. They may ask questions concerning where the taxpayer vacations, where his or her children go to school, and the cost and model of his or her vehicles. Although the courts generally have sanctioned the use of financial status audits, Congress has limited their use to situations in which the IRS has a reasonable indication of unreported income.

Other Methods. The IRS widely uses other methods for selecting returns for audit. Some returns are chosen because the taxpayer filed a claim for a refund of taxes paid previously, and the IRS decides to audit the tax return before refunding the requested amount. A few returns are audited because the IRS receives a tip from one taxpayer (perhaps a disgruntled former employee or ex-spouse) that another taxpayer did not file a correct return. If the IRS does collect additional taxes as a result of the audit, it will pay a reward to the individual who provided the tip. The amount of the award must be at least 15% of the additional taxes, penalties, and interest collected, but it cannot exceed 30%. The award can be reduced if the whistleblower's contribution was less than substantial. Whistleblowers can appeal to the Tax Court if the award is reduced below 15%.[7] If the tax, penalties, and interest exceed $2 million, the reward ranges from 15% to 30% of the amount collected. Sometimes, examining the return of an entity (e.g., a corporation) leads to an audit of a related party's return (e.g., a major stockholder).

Occasionally, the IRS investigates particular types of transactions or entities to ascertain taxpayer compliance with the tax law. As a result of these investigations, the IRS may select a number of returns for audit. For example, in 1989 the IRS examined 3,000 to 4,000 individual returns to determine whether taxpayers avoided classifying expenses as miscellaneous itemized deductions to escape the 2% floor. In 1997, the IRS investigated the returns of about 200,000 trusts (representing approximately 7% of total trust returns) to determine whether taxpayers had established them to avoid taxes.[8] In 2003, through a combination of audits, summons, and targeted litigation, the IRS launched an initiative

---

[5] The NRP also targets taxes other than individual taxes, including employment taxes and S corporations.

[6] https://www.irs.gov/Businesses/Small-Businesses-&-Self-Employed/Audit-Techniques-Guides-ATGs (last updated November 2016).

[7] Sec. 7623 and Reg. Sec. 301.7623-1(c).

[8] Jacob M. Schlesinger, "IRS Cracks Down on Trusts It Believes Were Set up as Tax-Avoidance Schemes," *The Wall Street Journal*, April 4, 1997, p. A2.

to identify and deter promoters of abusive tax shelters.[9] In November 2009, the IRS announced its first major employment tax research study in 25 years.

DISCLOSURE OF UNCERTAIN TAX POSITIONS

In 2010, the IRS introduced a new reporting requirement for Form 1120, specifically, Schedule UTP (Uncertain Tax Position Statement). An uncertain tax position is a tax position taken on a tax return that would result in an adjustment to a line on the tax return if the position is not sustained. Schedule UTP requires a description of each uncertain tax position for which the taxpayer recorded a reserve in its audited financial statements or for which no reserve has been recorded because of expected litigation. Taxpayers also must rank the uncertain positions and disclose whether any tax position exceeds 10% of the aggregate amount of the reserves for all tax positions. C corporations with assets exceeding $10 million that issued audited financial statements must report uncertain tax positions on Schedule UTP.

The schedule will help the IRS identify and prioritize issues for audit. The IRS hopes that Schedule UTP will make their auditors more efficient and increase taxpayer compliance. Taxpayers' primary objection is that the schedule provides a detailed roadmap of vulnerable tax positions, which would affect who was audited and what issues should be addressed. In response to this concern (in Announcement 2010-76), the IRS expanded its policy of restraint and will refrain from requesting particular documents related to uncertain tax positions and the workpapers used to complete Schedule UTP. As part of the restraint policy, the IRS will not assert that the attorney-client privilege, tax advice privilege under Sec. 7525, or the work product doctrine has been waived by providing otherwise privileged documents to financial auditors for their use in preparing financial statements. However, privilege is not created for any other document of the taxpayer or third party. Refer to "Accountant-Client Privilege" on page C:15-36.

ALTERNATIVES FOR A TAXPAYER WHOSE RETURN IS AUDITED

When the IRS notifies a taxpayer of an impending audit, the notice indicates whether the audit is a correspondence, office, or field audit. In a correspondence audit, communication, such as documenting a deduction or explaining why the taxpayer did not report certain income, is handled through the mail. In an office audit, the taxpayer and/or his or her tax advisor meet with an IRS employee at a nearby IRS office. The audit notice indicates which items the IRS will examine and what information the taxpayer should bring to the audit. Field audits are common for business returns and complex individual returns. IRS officials conduct these audits either at the taxpayer's place of business or residence or at his or her tax advisor's office.

ADDITIONAL COMMENT

This special relief rule was designed to reduce the likelihood that the IRS could harass a taxpayer by repeatedly auditing a taxpayer on the same issue.

Special Relief Rule. A special relief rule exists for repetitive audit examinations of the same item. A taxpayer who receives an audit notice can request that the IRS suspend the examination and review whether the audit should proceed if (1) the IRS audited the taxpayer's return for the same item in at least one of the two previous years and (2) the earlier audit did not result in a change to his or her tax liability. To request the suspension, the taxpayer should call the IRS official whose name and telephone number appear on the audit notice.

EXAMPLE C:15-1 ▶ In October 2017, the IRS notifies Tony that it will audit his 2015 medical expense deduction. Two years ago, the IRS audited Tony's 2013 medical expense deduction but did not assess an additional tax. Consequently, Tony may request that the IRS suspend the audit of his 2015 return regarding this issue. ◀

[9] I.R. 2003-51, April 15, 2003.

EXAMPLE C:15-2 ▶ Assume the same facts as in Example C:15-1 except the IRS audited Tony's 2013 employee business expenses. Because that audit dealt with a different item, Tony may not request a suspension. ◀

ADDITIONAL COMMENT

Taxpayers should encourage the tax practitioner to handle an IRS audit. Because taxpayers usually have a limited understanding of the complexities of the tax law and its administration, having the taxpayer present at the audit generally is not a good idea.

TYPICAL MISCONCEPTION

Taxpayers should be cautious in signing a Form 870. Once this form is executed, the taxpayer no longer is permitted to administratively pursue the items under audit.

Meeting with a Revenue Agent. Generally, the first step in the audit process is a meeting between the IRS agent and the taxpayer or the taxpayer's advisor. If the taxpayer is fortunate, the agent will agree that the return was correct as filed or, even better, that the taxpayer is entitled to a refund. In most instances, however, the agent will contend that the taxpayer owes additional taxes. Taxpayers who do not agree with the outcome of their meeting may ask to confer with the agent's supervisor. A meeting with the supervisor could lead to an agreement concerning the additional tax due.

Should the taxpayer agree and the agent's supervisor concur in the amount owed, the taxpayer must sign Form 870 (Waiver of Restrictions on Assessment and Collection of Deficiency in Tax). This form indicates that the taxpayer waives any restrictions on the IRS's authority to assess the tax and consents to the IRS's collecting it. However, signing Form 870 does not preclude the taxpayer from filing a refund claim later.

If the taxpayer agrees that he or she owes additional tax and pays the tax upon signing the Form 870 waiver, interest accrues on the tax deficiency from the due date of the return through the payment date. Interest also ceases to accrue 30 days after the taxpayer signs the Form 870 waiver but begins to accrue again when the IRS issues a notice and demand for payment. However, the IRS charges no additional interest if the taxpayer pays the tax due within 21 days of the notice and demand (ten days for $100,000 or more).

Technical Advice Memoranda. Occasionally, a highly technical issue with which an IRS agent or appeals officer has had little or no experience arises in the course of the audit. Regardless of the type of audit, the official may request advice from the IRS's national office. Sometimes, the taxpayer urges the official to seek such advice. The advice is given in a Technical Advice Memorandum, which the IRS makes public in the form of a letter ruling. If the advice is favorable to the taxpayer, the agent or appeals officer must follow it. Even if the advice is pro-IRS, the official may consider the hazards of litigation in deciding whether to compromise.

Appeal to Appeals Division. If the taxpayer does not sign the Form 870 waiver, the IRS will send the taxpayer a **30-day letter**, detailing the proposed changes in the tax-payer's liability and advising the taxpayer of his or her right to pursue the matter with the IRS appeals office. The taxpayer has 30 days from the date of the letter to request a conference with an IRS appeals officer.

If the additional tax and penalty is less than $25,000 (a small case request), taxpayers may initiate an appeal indicating the unagreed adjustments and briefly stating the reasons for the appeal. If the amount of additional tax plus penalties and interest in question exceeds $25,000, the taxpayer must submit a formal **protest letter** within the 30-day period. If the taxpayer does not respond to the 30-day letter, the IRS will follow up with a 90-day letter, discussed below.

Protest letters are submitted to an official in the appropriate IRS functional division and should include the following information:

- The taxpayer's name, address, and telephone number
- A statement that the taxpayer wishes to appeal the IRS findings to the appeals office
- A copy of the letter showing the proposed adjustments
- The tax years involved
- A list of the proposed changes with which the taxpayer disagrees and the reasons for disagreement
- A statement of facts supporting the taxpayer's position on any issue with which he or she disagrees
- The law or other authority on which the taxpayer relied[10]

[10] IRS, *Publication No. 5* [Your Appeal Rights and How to Prepare a Protest If You Don't Agree], January 1999, p. 1.

The taxpayer must declare, under penalties of perjury, that the statement of facts is true. If the taxpayer's representative prepares the protest letter, the representative must indicate whether he or she knows personally that the statement of facts is true.

KEY POINT

The appeals officer currently has the authority to settle or compromise issues with the taxpayer. To alleviate some of the workload and to make the audit process more efficient, the IRS currently is considering giving more of this settlement authority to revenue agents.

Unlike IRS agents, appeals officers generally have the authority to settle (compromise) cases after considering the hazards of litigation. For example, if the appeals officer believes that the IRS has approximately a 40% chance of winning in court, the appeals officer may agree to close the case if the taxpayer will pay an amount equal to 40% of the originally proposed deficiency. The settlement authority of appeals officers extends to questions of fact and law.

In some matters, however, an appeals officer has no settlement authority. For example, if the matter involves an appeals coordinated issue, the appeals officer must obtain concurrence or guidance from a director of appeals to reach a settlement. An **appeals coordinated issue** usually has wide impact or importance, frequently involving an entire industry or occupation group, for which the IRS desires consistent treatment. An example of an appeals coordinated issue is the income tax treatment of a sale in/lease out (SILO) transaction.[11]

If, after the appeals conference, the taxpayer completely agrees with the IRS's position, he or she signs a Form 870 waiver. However, if the appeals officer makes some concessions and the parties agree that the additional tax is less than that originally proposed, the taxpayer signs Form 870-AD (Waiver of Restrictions on Assessment and Collection). Unlike the case of a Form 870 waiver, a Form 870-AD waiver generally does not permit the taxpayer later to file a refund claim for the tax year in question. A Form 870-AD waiver is effective only if accepted by the IRS.

90-DAY LETTER

If the taxpayer and appeals officer fail to reach an agreement, or if the taxpayer does not file a written protest within 30 days of the date of the initial letter, the IRS issues a **90-day letter** (officially, a "Statutory Notice of Deficiency").[12] The 90-day letter specifies the amount of the deficiency; explains how the amount was calculated; and states that the IRS will assess it unless, within 90 days of the date of mailing, the taxpayer files a petition with the Tax Court.[13] During the 90-day period (and whether or not the taxpayer files the petition), the IRS may not assess the deficiency or attempt to collect it. After the 90-day period (and only if the taxpayer timely files the petition), the IRS still may not assess or collect the deficiency until the Court's decision becomes final.

LITIGATION

As mentioned earlier, taxpayer litigation can begin in one of three courts of first instance: the Tax Court, a U.S. district court, and the U.S. Court of Federal Claims. Before deciding where to litigate, a taxpayer should consider the precedents, if any, of the various courts. Chapter C:1 discusses the issues of precedent and "forum shopping" and provides an overview of the organization and key attributes of the federal courts. After considering the time and expense of litigation, some taxpayers decide to pay the deficiency even though they believe their position is correct.

U.S. Tax Court. Taxpayers seeking to litigate in the Tax Court must file their petition with the Tax Court within 90 days of the date on which the IRS mails the Statutory Notice of Deficiency. The Tax Court strictly enforces this time limit. Before the scheduled hearing date, taxpayers still may reach an agreement with the IRS. Going the Tax Court route has some advantages, including not having to pay the deficiency as a precondition to filing suit. If the amount in question does not exceed $25,000 for a given year, the taxpayer may use the informal small case request, an alternative not available in other courts. A potential disadvantage of this procedure is that the taxpayer may not appeal the Court's decision.

Taxpayers must pay the additional tax, plus any interest and penalties, if they lose in Tax Court and choose not to appeal their case. In some situations, the Tax Court leaves the computation of the additional tax up to the litigating parties. When this happens, the phrase "Entered Under Rule 155" appears at the end of the Tax Court's opinion.

---

[11] IRS Appeals Coordinated Issue Program Settlement Guidelines, UIL No. 9300.38-00.

[12] Upon request, the IRS may grant an extension of time for filing a protest letter.

[13] Sec. 6213(a). If the notice is addressed to a person outside the United States, the time period is 150 days instead of 90.

U.S. District Court or U.S. Court of Federal Claims. To litigate in either a U.S. district court or the U.S. Court of Federal Claims, the taxpayer must first pay the deficiency and then file a claim for a refund with the IRS. In all likelihood, the IRS will deny this claim on the ground that the IRS correctly calculated the deficiency amount and properly assessed it. Upon notice of denial or six months after filing the claim, whichever is earlier, the taxpayer may sue the IRS for a refund. In no event, however, may the taxpayer file this lawsuit two years after the IRS denies the claim.

Appeal of a Lower Court's Decision. Whichever party loses—the taxpayer or the IRS—may appeal the lower court's decision to an appellate court. If the lawsuit was filed in the Tax Court or a federal district court, the case is appealable to the circuit court of appeals with jurisdiction over the taxpayer. For individuals, the taxpayer's place of residence generally determines which court of appeals has jurisdiction. In the case of corporations, the firm's principal place of business or state of incorporation generally controls. Cases originating in the U.S. Court of Federal Claims are appealable to the Circuit Court of Appeals for the Federal Circuit; that is, all the latter cases are heard by the same circuit, irrespective of the taxpayer's residence, principal place of business, or state of incorporation.

Either the taxpayer or the government can request that the U.S. Supreme Court review an appellate court's decision by preparing a writ of certiorari. If the Supreme Court decides to hear a case, it grants **certiorari.** If the Court decides not to hear a case, it denies certiorari. In any given year, the Supreme Court hears only a few cases dealing with tax matters.

Question: Two years ago, Pete deducted an expenditure in the year he paid it. Recently, the IRS audited Pete's return for that year and contended that the expenditure is not deductible. Pete is a resident of California, which is in the Ninth Circuit. In a similar case a few years ago, the Tax Court held that the expenditure is deductible, and the IRS did not appeal the decision. In yet another similar case litigated in a U.S. district court in California, the government lost at the trial level but won on appeal to the Ninth Circuit. If Pete decides to litigate, in which forum (lower court) should he file suit, and why?

Solution: If he litigates in the Tax Court, he need not pay the proposed deficiency tax in advance. However, under the *Golsen* Rule (see Chapter C:1), the Tax Court would depart from its earlier pro-taxpayer decision and rule for the IRS. (Pete's case would be appealable to the Ninth Circuit, and the Ninth Circuit has adopted a pro-government position.) Because the court for his California district would be bound by Ninth Circuit precedent, he should not litigate in that court. This likely outcome would disappoint Pete if he believed that a jury would rule in his favor because only U.S. district courts allow for jury trials. The only forum in which he could win is the U.S. Court of Federal Claims. No precedent that this court must follow exists because neither the U.S. Supreme Court, the Court of Appeals for the Federal Circuit, nor the U.S. Court of Federal Claims has previously adjudicated the issue. (For a discussion of "forum-shopping," see Chapter C:1.)

Burden of Proof. In civil cases, the IRS has the burden of proving any factual issue relevant to a determination of the taxpayer's liability, provided the taxpayer meets four conditions.[14] First, the taxpayer introduces "credible evidence" regarding the issue. Credible evidence means evidence of a quality sufficient to serve as the basis of a court decision.[15] Second, the taxpayer complies with the recordkeeping and substantiation requirements of the IRC. These requirements include the proper documentation of meal and entertainment expenses (Sec. 274), charitable contributions (Sec. 170), and foreign controlled businesses (Sec. 6038). Third, the taxpayer "cooperates" with the reasonable requests of the IRS for witnesses, information, documents, meetings, and interviews. Cooperation includes providing

[14] See Sec. 7491.

[15] See S. Rept. No. 105-174, (PL. 105-206), pp. 45-46.

access to, and inspection of, persons and items within the taxpayer's control. It also includes exhausting all administrative remedies available to the taxpayer.[16] Fourth, the taxpayer is either a legal person with net worth not exceeding $7 million, or a natural person.

Requests for Rulings

OBJECTIVE 3

Explain the IRS's ruling process

As discussed in Chapter C:1, a taxpayer can seek to clarify the tax treatment of a transaction by requesting that the IRS rule on the transaction. The IRS will respond to certain requests by issuing a letter ruling (sometimes referred to as a private letter ruling) directly to the taxpayer. A letter ruling is a written determination that interprets and applies the tax laws to the taxpayer's specific set of facts.[17] The IRS releases letter rulings to the public but eliminates all confidential information before doing so. The IRS charges a user fee for issuing a ruling, with the 2017 fees ranging from $200 for identical accounting method changes to $218,600 for pre-filing agreements. The fee for ruling on a proposed transaction is $28,300.[18]

ADDITIONAL COMMENT

The information requirements for requesting a letter ruling are very precise (see Rev. Proc. 2016-1). In general, a tax professional experienced in dealing with the national office of the IRS should be consulted. Also, a good blueprint of what should be included in a ruling request often can be found by locating an already-published letter ruling and examining its format.

INFORMATION TO BE INCLUDED IN TAXPAYER'S REQUEST

Early each calendar year, the IRS issues a revenue procedure that details how to request a letter ruling and the information that the request must contain. Taxpayers or tax advisors should consult this procedure before requesting a ruling. Appendix B of the procedure contains a checklist the taxpayer may use to ensure that the request is in order. The IRS has issued additional guidelines concerning the data to be included in the ruling request. For example, the IRS has specified what information the taxpayer must provide in a request for a ruling on the tax effects of transfers to a controlled corporation under Sec. 351. All ruling requests must contain a statement of all the relevant facts, including the following:

- Names, addresses, telephone numbers, and taxpayer identification numbers of all interested parties
- The taxpayer's annual accounting period and method
- A description of the taxpayer's business operations
- A complete statement of the business reasons for the transaction
- A detailed description of the transaction[19]

The taxpayer also should submit copies of the contracts, agreements, deeds, wills, instruments, and other documents that pertain to the transaction. The taxpayer must provide an explicit statement of all the relevant facts and not merely incorporate by reference language from the documents. The taxpayer also should indicate what confidential data should be deleted from the ruling before its release to the public.

If the taxpayer takes a position, he or she must disclose the basis for this position and the authorities relied on. Even if the taxpayer does not argue for a particular position, he or she must furnish an opinion of the expected tax effects, along with a statement of authorities supporting this opinion. In addition, the taxpayer should disclose and discuss any authorities to the contrary. The IRS suggests that, if no authorities to the contrary exist, the taxpayer should state so.

The person on whose behalf a ruling is requested should sign the following declaration: "Under penalties of perjury, I declare that I have examined this request, including accompanying documents, and, to the best of my knowledge and belief, the request contains all the relevant facts relating to the request, and such facts are true, correct, and complete."[20]

---

[16] Ibid.

[17] Rev. Proc. 2017-1, 2017-1 I.R.B. 1, Sec. 2.01.

[18] Rev. Proc. 2017-1, 2017-1 I.R.B. 1, Appendix A.

[19] Rev. Proc. 2017-1, 2017-1 I.R.B. 1, Sec. 7.01. Certain revenue procedures provide a checklist of information to be included for frequently occurring transactions. See, for example, Rev. Proc. 83-59, 1983-2 C.B. 575, which includes guidelines for requesting rulings regarding a corporate formation under Sec. 351.

[20] Rev. Proc. 2017-1, 2017-1 I.R.B. 1, Sec. 7.01.

WILL THE IRS RULE?

In income and gift tax matters, the IRS will rule only on proposed transactions and on completed transactions for which the taxpayer has not yet filed a return.[21] In estate tax matters, the IRS generally will not rule if the estate has filed a tax return. On the other hand, the IRS will rule on the estate tax consequences of a living person.[22] If no temporary or final Treasury Regulations relating to a particular statutory provision have been issued, the following policies govern a ruling unless another IRS pronouncement holds otherwise:

- If the answer seems reasonably certain by applying the statute to the facts, but not entirely free from doubt, the IRS will rule under the usual procedures.
- If the answer does not seem reasonably certain, the IRS will rule if so doing is in the best interests of tax administration.[23]

TYPICAL MISCONCEPTION

It is easy to be confused about the difference between letter rulings, which pertain to either prospective transactions or completed transactions for which a return has not yet been filed, and Technical Advice Memoranda, which pertain to completed transactions for which the return has been filed and is under audit.

The IRS will not rule on a set of alternative ways of structuring a proposed transaction or on the tax consequences of hypothetical transactions. Generally, the IRS will not rule on certain issues because of the factual nature of the problem involved or for other reasons.[24]

From time to time, the IRS discloses, by means of a revenue procedure, the topics with respect to which it will not rule. The list of topics, however, is not all-inclusive. The IRS may refuse to rule on other topics whenever, in its opinion, the facts and circumstances so warrant.

According to Rev. Proc. 2017-3, the matters on which the IRS will not rule include the following:

- Whether property qualifies as the taxpayer's principal residence
- Whether compensation is reasonable in amount
- Whether a capital expenditure for an item ordinarily used for personal purposes (e.g., a swimming pool) has medical care as its primary purpose
- The determination of the amount of a corporation's earnings and profits.[25]

In addition, the IRS will not rule privately on issues that it proposes to address in revenue rulings, revenue procedures, or otherwise, or that the Treasury Department proposes to address in Treasury Regulations.

SELF-STUDY QUESTION

How are letter rulings different from other IRS administrative pronouncements (i.e., revenue rulings, revenue procedures, notices, and information releases)?

ANSWER

Letter rulings are written for specific taxpayers (not the general public) and have no precedential value.

WHEN RULINGS ARE DESIRABLE

Private letter rulings serve to "insure" the taxpayer against adverse, after-the-fact tax consequences. They are desirable where (1) the transaction is proposed, (2) the potential tax liability is high, and (3) the law is unsettled or unclear. They also are desirable where the IRS has issued to another taxpayer a favorable ruling regarding similar facts and issues. Because only the other taxpayer may rely on the latter ruling, *this* taxpayer may seek a ruling on which he or she may confidently rely. On the other hand, private letter rulings are undesirable where the IRS has issued to another taxpayer an unfavorable ruling regarding similar facts and issues. They also are undesirable where the IRS might publicly rule on a related matter, and the taxpayer has an interest in this matter. Private letter rulings offer insight into the IRS's thinking on the tax treatment of proposed transactions. Although third parties may not cite them as authority for the tax consequences of their transactions, they may cite them as authority for avoiding a substantial understatement penalty (discussed later in this chapter).

ADDITIONAL COMMENT

Requesting a letter ruling makes most sense for transactions that the taxpayer would not undertake without being assured of certain tax consequences. For example, certain divisive reorganizations are tax-free under Sec. 355. Taxpayers often request a ruling that a proposed transaction satisfies the intricate requirements of Sec. 355.

DUE DATES

OBJECTIVE 4

Identify the due dates for filing tax returns and paying taxes

DUE DATES FOR RETURNS

Partnerships and S corporations are due on the fifteenth day of the third month (March 15 for entities having a December 31 year-end).[26] Individuals, fiduciaries, and C corporations

[21] Ibid., Sec. 5.01.
[22] Ibid., Sec. 5.06.
[23] Ibid., Sec. 5.17.
[24] Ibid., Sec. 6.02.
[25] Rev. Proc. 2017-3, 2017-1 I.R.B. 130, Sec. 3.
[26] Sec. 6072(b).

(except those with June 30 year-ends—see below) are due on the fifteenth day of the fourth month, or April 15 for calendar year taxpayers.[27]

Until tax years beginning after 2025, C corporations with a June 30 year end are due on the fifteenth day of the third month, or by September 15.[28] This date is one month before all other C corporation returns are due, presumably to ensure that the tax revenue due on the filing deadline is paid before the federal government fiscal year-end of September 30.

EXTENSIONS

Congress realized that, in some instances, gathering the requisite information and completing the return by the designated due date is difficult. Consequently, it authorized extensions of time for filing returns. Unless the taxpayer is abroad, the extension period cannot exceed six months.[29]

Individuals. By filing Form 4868 (Application for Automatic Extension of Time to File U.S. Individual Income Tax Return), an individual taxpayer may request an automatic six-month extension of time to file the tax return.[30] The extension is automatic in the sense that the taxpayer need not convince the IRS that an extension is necessary.

EXAMPLE C:15-3 ▶ Bob and Alice, his wife, are calendar year taxpayers. By filing Form 4868, they may get an automatic extension until October 15 of the following year for filing their current year's return. However, if the fifteenth falls on Saturday, Sunday, or a holiday, the due date is the next business day. ◀

Corporations. Corporations request an automatic six-month extension by filing Form 7004 (Application for Automatic Extension of Time to File Corporation Income Tax Return) by the original due date for the return. For tax years beginning after 2015, but before 2026, C corporations with a June 30 year-end may request an automatic seven-month extension until April 15.[31]

EXAMPLE C:15-4 ▶ Lopez Corporation reports on a fiscal year ending March 31. The regular due date for its return is July 15. It may file Form 7004 and request an automatic six-month extension that postpones the due date until January 15. ◀

DUE DATES FOR PAYMENT OF THE TAX

TYPICAL MISCONCEPTION

Obtaining an extension defers the date by which the return must be filed, but it does *not* defer the payment date of the tax liability. Therefore, an extension for filing must be accompanied by a payment of an estimate of the taxpayer's tax liability. Computing this estimated tax liability can be difficult because much of the information necessary to complete the return may be incomplete or not yet available.

The granting of an extension merely postpones the due date for filing the return. It does not extend the due date for paying the tax. In general, the due date for the tax payment is the same as the unextended due date for filing the return. In addition, the first estimated tax installment for extinguishing an individual's annual income tax liability must be paid by the due date for the preceding year's return, and the remaining payments must be made, respectively, two, five, and nine months later. Taxpayers who elect to let the IRS compute their tax must pay it within 30 days of the date the IRS mails a notice of the amount payable.[32]

When individuals request an automatic extension, they should project the amount of their tax liability to the extent possible. Any tax owed, net of tax withholding and estimated tax payments, should be remitted with the extension request. In addition, if an extension for filing a gift tax return is requested (on the same form), the estimated amount of gift tax liability should be remitted. Similarly, corporations should remit with their automatic extension request the amount of tax they estimate to be due, reduced by any estimated tax already paid. The IRS, however, will not assess an underpayment penalty to a corporation if the corporation pays in at least 90% of its tax by the original due date and pays the remaining tax by the extended due date of the tax return.[33]

---

[27] Sec. 6072(a) and Sec. 6072(b). Section 6072(c) extends the due date for returns of nonresident alien individuals and foreign corporations to the fifteenth day of the sixth month after the end of their tax year.

[28] P.L. 114-41, Title II, Sec. 2006(a)(3)(B).

[29] Sec. 6081(a).

[30] Reg. Sec. 1.6081-4.

[31] Sec. 6081(b) and instructions to Form 7004.

[32] Sec. 6151(b)(1). The estimated tax payment rules for C corporations, S corporations, and trusts and estates are described in Chapters C:3, C:11, and C:14, respectively, of this volume.

[33] Reg. Sec. 301.6651-1(c)(4).

INTEREST ON TAX NOT TIMELY PAID

Interest accrues on any tax not paid by the original due date for the return even if the taxpayer extends the filing date.[34] Taxpayers incur interest charges in four situations.

- They file late, without having requested an extension, and pay late.
- They request an extension for filing but underestimate their tax liability and, thus, must pay additional tax when they file their return.
- They file in a timely manner but are not financially able to pay some, or all, of the tax.
- The IRS audits their return and determines that they owe additional taxes.

EXAMPLE C:15-5 ▶ Ann filed her Year 1 individual return in a timely manner on April 15 of Year 2, and the IRS audits it in March of Year 4. Ann is a calendar year taxpayer. The IRS contends that Ann owes $2,700 of additional taxes. Ann pays the additional taxes on March 30 of Year 4. Ann also must pay interest on the $2,700 deficiency for the period April 16 of Year 2 through March 30 of Year 4. The applicable interest rates for various segments of time appear in the schedule below. ◀

Rate Determination. The IRS fixes the interest rate that it charges taxpayers under rules provided in Sec. 6621 and announces changes in Revenue Rulings.[35] The rate varies with fluctuations in the quarterly federal short-term rate. Thus, the interest rate could change at the beginning of each calendar quarter. For noncorporate taxpayers, the interest rate on both underpayments and overpayments is three percentage points higher than the short-term federal rate. For corporate tax overpayments exceeding $10,000, the interest rate is reduced to the federal short-term rate plus one-half percentage point. For corporate underpayments exceeding $100,000, the rate is five percentage points above the federal short-term rate if the deficiency is not paid before a certain date. Rates are rounded to the nearest full percent. Recent applicable interest rates are as follows:

Period	*General Rate for Underpayments and Overpayments*
April 1, 2016, through December 31, 2016	4%
October 1, 2011, through March 30, 2016	3%
April 1, 2011, through September 30, 2011	4%
October 1, 2011, through March 31, 2012	3%
January 1, 2011, through March 31, 2011	3%
April 1, 2009, through December 31, 2010	4%
January 1, 2009, through March 31, 2009	5%

Daily Compounding. Daily compounding applies to both the interest taxpayers owe to the government and the interest the government owes to taxpayers who have overpaid their taxes. The IRS has issued Rev. Proc. 95-17 containing tables to be used for calculating interest. The major tax services have published these tables. In addition, software packages are available for interest calculations.

HISTORICAL NOTE

Probably two of the most significant changes in tax administration have been the daily compounding of interest and tying the interest rate charged to the federal short-term rate, which has resulted in a higher rate used to calculate the interest charge than in years past. Before these two changes, taxpayers who played the "audit lottery" and took aggressive positions incurred little risk.

Accrual Period. Interest usually accrues from the original due date for the return until the payment date. However, two important exceptions apply. First, if the IRS fails to send an individual taxpayer a notice within 36 months after the original due date or the date on which a return is timely filed (including extensions), whichever is later, the accrual of interest (and penalties) is suspended.[36] The suspension period begins on the

[34] Secs. 6601(a) and (b)(1).

[35] For example, see Rev. Rul. 2016-28, 2016-51 I.R.B. 805.

[36] Sec. 6404(g).

day after the 36-month period and ends 21 days after the IRS sends the requisite notice. Second, if the IRS does not issue a notice and demand for payment within 30 days after the taxpayer signs a Form 870 waiver, no interest is charged for the period between the end of the 30-day period and the date the IRS issues its notice and demand.[37] Taxpayers litigating in the Tax Court may make a deposit to reduce interest potentially owed. If the court decides that the taxpayer owes a deficiency, interest will not accrue on the deposit.

EXAMPLE C:15-6 ▶ Cindy receives an automatic extension for filing this year's return. On June 24 of the following year, she submits her return, along with the $700 balance she owes on this year's tax liability. She owes interest on $700 for the period April 16 of this year through June 24 of the following year. Interest is compounded daily based on the interest rate for underpayments determined under Sec. 6621. ◀

EXAMPLE C:15-7 ▶ After filing for an automatic extension, Hans filed his Year 1 return on August 15 of Year 2. On August 29 of Year 5, the IRS sends Hans a notice of deficiency in which it assesses interest. Because the IRS failed to send Hans the notice by August 15 of Year 5 (36 months after the date on which the return was timely filed), the accrual of interest is suspended. The suspension period begins on August 16 of Year 5 (the day after the 36-month period) and ends on September 19 of Year 5 (21 days after the IRS sends the requisite notice). ◀

EXAMPLE C:15-8 ▶ Raj filed his Year 1 individual return on March 15 of Year 2. The IRS audits the return early in Year 4, and on January 27 of Year 4, Raj signs a Form 870 waiver, in which he agrees that he owes a $780 deficiency. The IRS does not issue a notice and demand for payment until March 21 of Year 4. Raj pays the deficiency two days later. Raj owes interest, compounded daily at the Sec. 6621 underpayment rate, for the period April 16 of Year 2 (the day after the original due date) through February 26 of Year 4 (30 days after Raj signed Form 870). No interest can be assessed for the period February 27 through March 21 of Year 4 because the IRS did not issue its notice and demand for payment until more than 30 days after Raj signed the Form 870 waiver. ◀

Abatement. The IRS does not abate interest except for unreasonable errors or delays resulting from its managerial or ministerial acts.[38] A "managerial act" involves the temporary or permanent loss of records or the exercise of judgment or discretion relating to the management of personnel.[39] A "ministerial act" involves routine procedure without the exercise of judgment or discretion.[40] A decision concerning the proper application of federal law is neither a managerial nor a ministerial act.

EXAMPLE C:15-9 ▶ Omar provides documentation to an audit agent, who assures him that he will receive a copy of an audit report shortly. Before the agent has had an opportunity to act, however, the divisional manager transfers him to another office. An extended period of time elapses before the manager assigns another audit agent to Omar's case. The decision to reassign is a managerial act. The IRS may abate interest attributable to any unreasonable delay in payment resulting from this act. ◀

EXAMPLE C:15-10 ▶ Chanelle requests information from an IRS employee concerning the balance due on her current year tax liability. The employee fails to access the most current computerized database and provides Chanelle with incorrect information. Based on this information, Chanelle pays less than the full balance due. The employee's failing to access the most current database is a ministerial act. The IRS may abate interest attributable to any unreasonable delay in payment resulting from this act. ◀

FAILURE-TO-FILE AND FAILURE-TO-PAY PENALTIES

OBJECTIVE 5

Distinguish the various types of penalties imposed by the IRS

Penalties add teeth to the accounting and reporting provisions of the Internal Revenue Code. Without them, these provisions would be mere letters on the books of the legislature—words without effect. Tax-related penalties fall into two broad categories: taxpayer and preparer. As the name suggests, taxpayer penalties apply only to taxpayers, be they individuals, corporations, estates, or trusts. Preparer penalties apply only to tax return

[37] Sec. 6601(c).
[38] Sec. 6404(e).
[39] Reg. Sec. 301.6404-2(b)(1).
[40] Reg. Sec. 301.6404-2(b)(2).

REAL-WORLD EXAMPLE

In fiscal 2015, as a result of the audit process, the IRS assessed a total of $24.1 billion in civil penalties and abated about $8.9 billion for reasonable cause.

preparers, be they firms that employ tax professionals or the professionals themselves. Within these broad categories are two distinct subcategories: civil and criminal. Civil penalties are imposed on taxpayers for negligently, recklessly, or intentionally failing to fulfill their accounting or reporting obligations. Criminal penalties are imposed for maliciously or willfully failing to do so. Taxpayers may raise as a defense to some penalties "reasonable cause" and a good faith belief in the correctness of their position. Sometimes, for the defense to be valid, they also must disclose this position on their tax return. This section of the text discusses two commonly encountered penalties in income, estate, and gift taxation: failure to file and failure to pay. The IRS may assess these penalties, in addition to interest, on overdue tax liabilities. Subsequent sections of the text discuss other taxpayer and preparer penalties. Topic Review C:15-1 presents a summary of IRC penalty provisions. The Topic Review is provided here rather than later in the chapter to give readers a framework for following the discussion of the various penalties.

TOPIC REVIEW C:15-1

Overview of Penalties

Penalty	IRC Section	Applicability	Rules/Calculation	Defenses/Waiver
A. TAXPAYER—CIVIL				
Failure to file	6651(a)	All persons	*General rule:* 5% per month or fraction thereof; 25% maximum *Minimum penalty if late more than 60 days:* lesser of $205 or 100% of tax due	Reasonable cause, not willful neglect
	6651(f)	All persons	*Fraudulent reason for not filing:* 15% per month or fraction thereof; 75% maximum	
Failure to pay tax	6651(a)	All persons	*General rule:* 0.5% per month or fraction thereof; 25% maximum*	Reasonable cause, not willful neglect
Failure by individual to pay estimated tax	6654	Individuals, certain estates, trusts	*General rule:* penalty at same rate as interest rate for deficiency; imposed for period between due date for estimated tax payments and earlier of payment date or due date for return	Waiver in unusual circumstances
Failure by corporation to pay estimated tax	6655	Corporations	*General rule:* penalty at same rate as interest rate for deficiency; imposed for period between due date for estimated tax payments and earlier of payment date or due date for return	—
Negligence	6662(c)	All persons	*General rule:* 20% of underpayment attributable to negligence	Reasonable cause, good faith
Substantial understatement	6662(d)	All persons	*General rule:* 20% of underpayment attributable to substantial understatement (portion for which no substantial authority and no disclosure exists)	Reasonable cause, good faith; also, substantial authority, disclosure
Civil fraud	6663	All persons	*General rule:* 75% of portion of understatement attributable to fraud	Reasonable cause, good faith
B. TAXPAYER—CRIMINAL				
Willful attempt to evade tax	7201	All persons	*General rule:* Up to $100,000 ($500,000 for corporations) and/or up to five years in prison	—
Willful failure to collect or pay over tax	7202	All persons	*General rule:* Up to $10,000 and/or up to five years in prison	—
Willful failure to pay or file	7203	All persons	*General rule:* Up to $25,000 ($100,000 for corporations) and/or up to one year in prison	—
Willfully making false or fraudulent statements	7206	All persons	*General rule:* Up to $100,000 ($500,000 for corporations) and/or up to three years in prison	—

TOPIC REVIEW C:15-1 (CONT.)

C. PREPARER—CIVIL				
Understatement of tax by preparer	6694(a)	Tax return preparers	*General rule:* greater of $1,000 or half of preparer's income from return	Reasonable cause, substantial authority; also, disclosure
Willful attempt to understate taxes	6694(b)	Tax return preparers	*General rule:* greater of $5,000 or 75% of preparer's income from return	—
Failure to furnish copy to taxpayer	6695(a)	Tax return preparers	*General rule:* $50; $25,000 maximum	Reasonable cause, not willful neglect
Failure to sign return	6695(b)	Tax return preparers	*General rule:* $50; $25,000 maximum	Reasonable cause, not willful neglect
Failure to furnish identifying number	6695(c)	Tax return preparers	*General rule:* $50; $25,000 maximum	Reasonable cause, not willful neglect
Failure to retain copy or list	6695(d)	Tax return preparers	*General rule:* $50; $25,000 maximum	Reasonable cause, not willful neglect
Failure to file correct information returns	6695(e)	Tax return preparers	*General rule:* $50 for each failure to file a return or each failure to set forth an item in a return; $25,000 maximum	Reasonable cause, not willful neglect
Improper negotiation of checks	6695(f)	Tax return preparers	*General rule:* $500 per check	—
Aiding and abetting in understatement	6701(b)	All persons	*General rule:* $1,000 ($10,000 for corporations)	—

* If the taxpayer owes both the failure-to-file and the failure-to-pay penalties for a given month, the total penalty for such month is limited to 5% of the net tax due.

FAILURE TO FILE

Taxpayers who do not file a return by the due date generally are liable for a penalty of 5% per month (or fraction thereof) of the net tax due.[41] A fraction of a month, even just a day, counts as a full month. The maximum penalty for failing to file is 25%. If the taxpayer receives an extension, the extended due date is treated as the original due date. In determining the net tax due (i.e., the amount subject to the penalty), the IRS reduces the taxpayer's gross tax by any taxes paid by the return's due date (e.g., withholding and estimated tax payments) and tax credits claimed on the return. If any failure to file is fraudulent, the penalty rate is 15% per month up to a maximum penalty of 75%. For purposes of this provision, "fraud" is actual, intentional wrongdoing or the commission of an act for the specific purpose of evading a tax known or believed to be due.[42]

ADDITIONAL COMMENT

The most common reason given by taxpayers to support reasonable cause for failing to file a timely tax return is reliance on one's tax advisor. Other reasons include severe illness or serious accident. Reliance on a tax advisor is not always sufficient cause to obtain a waiver of the penalties.

Penalties are not levied if a taxpayer can prove that he or she failed to file a timely return because of reasonable cause (as opposed to willful neglect). According to Treasury Regulations, reasonable cause exists if "the taxpayer exercised ordinary business care and prudence and was nevertheless unable to file the return within the prescribed time."[43] Not surprisingly, much litigation deals with the issue of reasonable cause.

Note that the penalty imposed for not filing on time generally is a function of the net tax due. However, a minimum penalty applies in some cases. Congress enacted the minimum penalty provision because of the cost to the IRS of identifying nonfilers. If a taxpayer does not file an income tax return within 60 days of the due date (including any extensions), the penalty will be no less than the smaller of $205 or 100% of the tax due on the return. Taxpayers who owe no tax are not subject to the **failure-to-file penalty**. Also, the IRS may waive the penalty if the taxpayer shows reasonable cause for not filing.

[41] Rules for failure to file penalties are in Sec. 6651.

[42] *Robert W. Bradford v. CIR*, 58 AFTR 2d 86-5532, 86-2 USTC ¶9602 (9th Cir., 1996); *Chris D. Stoltzfus v. U.S.*, 22 AFTR 2d 5251, 68-2 USTC ¶9499 (3rd Cir., 1968); and *William E. Mitchell v. CIR*, 26 AFTR 684, 41-1 USTC ¶9317 (5th Cir., 1941).

[43] Reg. Sec. 301.6651-1(c)(1).

EXAMPLE C:15-11 ▶ Earl files his current year individual income tax return on July 5 of the following year. Earl requested no extension and did not have reasonable cause for his late filing, but he committed no fraud. Earl's current year return shows a balance due of $400. Under the regular rules, the late filing penalty would be $60 (0.05 × 3 months × $400). Earl's penalty is $135 because of the minimum penalty provision applicable to his failure to file the return within 60 days of the due date. ◀

In general under Sec. 6601(e)(2), interest does not accrue on any penalty paid within 21 days of the date that the IRS notifies the taxpayer of the penalty (ten days if the amount exceeds $100,000). However, interest accrues on the failure-to-file penalty, from the due date of the return (including any extensions) until the payment date.

FAILURE TO PAY

The **failure-to-pay penalty** is imposed at 0.5% per month (or fraction thereof).[44] The maximum penalty is 25%. The penalty is based on the gross tax shown on the return less any tax payments made and credits earned before the beginning of the month for which the penalty is calculated. As with the failure-to-file penalty, the IRS may waive the failure-to-pay penalty if the taxpayer shows reasonable cause.

Because the tax is due on the original due date for the return, taxpayers who request an extension without paying 100% of their tax liability potentially owe a failure-to-pay penalty. Treasury Regulations provide some relief by exempting a taxpayer from the penalty if the additional tax due with the filing of the extended return does not exceed 10% of the tax owed for the year.[45]

EXAMPLE C:15-12 ▶ Gary requests an extension for filing his current year individual income tax return. His current year tax payments include withholding of $4,500, estimated tax payments of $2,000, and $1,000 submitted with his request for an automatic extension. He files his return on June 6 of the following year, showing a total tax of $8,000 and a balance due of $500. Gary is exempt from the failure-to-pay penalty because the $500 balance due does not exceed 10% of his current year liability (0.10 × $8,000 = $800). Had Gary's current year tax instead been $9,000, he would have owed an additional tax of $1,500 and a failure-to-pay penalty of $15 (0.005 × 2 months × $1,500). ◀

The 0.5% penalty increases to 1% a month, or fraction thereof, in certain circumstances. The rate is 1% for any month beginning after the earlier of

- Ten days after the date the IRS notifies the taxpayer that it plans to levy on his or her salary or property and
- The day the IRS notifies and demands immediate payment from the taxpayer because it believes that collection is in jeopardy

EXAMPLE C:15-13 ▶ Ginny filed her Year 1 individual income tax return on April 13 of Year 2. However, Ginny did not pay her tax liability at that time. On October 7 of Year 4, the IRS notifies Ginny of its plans to levy on her property. The failure-to-pay penalty is 0.5% per month for the period April 16 of Year 2 through October 16 of Year 4. Beginning on October 17 of Year 4, ten days following the notice of levy, the penalty rises to 1% per month, or a fraction thereof. ◀

SELF-STUDY QUESTION

If a taxpayer does not have sufficient funds to pay his or her tax liability by the due date, should the taxpayer wait until the funds are available before filing the tax return?

ANSWER

No. He or she should file the return on a timely basis. This filing avoids the 5% per month failure-to-file penalty. The taxpayer still will owe the failure-to-pay penalty, but at least this penalty is only 0.5% per month.

Some taxpayers file on time to avoid the failure-to-file penalty even though they cannot pay the balance of the tax due. Barring a showing of reasonable cause, these taxpayers still will incur the failure-to-pay penalty. Because taxpayers who do not timely file a return are likely to owe additional taxes, they often owe both the failure-to-file and the failure-to-pay penalties.

The IRC provides a special rule for calculating the 5% per month failure-to-file penalty for periods in which the taxpayer owes both penalties. The 5% per month failure-to-file penalty is reduced by the failure-to-pay penalty. Thus, the total penalties for a given month will not exceed 5%. For months when the taxpayer incurs both penalties, the failure-to-file penalty is effectively 4.5% (5% − 0.5%). Note, however, that no reduction occurs if the minimum penalty for failure to file applies.

---

[44] Rules for failure to pay penalties are in Sec. 6651.

[45] Reg. Sec. 301.6651-1(c)(3) and (4).

EXAMPLE C:15-14 ▶ Tien files her current year individual income tax return on August 5 of the following year, without having requested an extension. Her total tax is $20,000. Tien pays $15,000 in a timely manner and the $5,000 balance when she files the return. Although Tien committed no fraud, she can show no reasonable cause for the late filing and late payment. Tien's penalties are as follows:

Failure-to-pay penalty:		
$5,000 × 0.005 × 4 months		$ 100
Failure-to-file penalty:		
$5,000 × 0.05 × 4 months	$1,000	
Minus: Reduction for failure-to-pay penalty imposed for same period	(100)	900
Total penalties		$1,000 ◀

EXAMPLE C:15-15 ▶ Assume the same facts as in Example C:15-14 except that Tien instead pays the $5,000 balance on November 17 of the following year. The penalties are as follows:

Failure-to-pay penalty:		
$5,000 × 0.005 × 8 months (April 16 through November 17)		$ 200
Failure-to-file penalty:		
$5,000 × 0.05 × 4 months (April 16 through August 5)	$1,000	
Minus: Reduction for failure-to-pay penalty levied for April 16 through August 5 ($5,000 × 0.005 × 4 months)	(100)	900
Total penalties		$1,100 ◀

ESTIMATED TAXES

OBJECTIVE 6

Calculate the penalty for not paying estimated taxes

ADDITIONAL COMMENT

This discussion focuses on individuals and is pertinent for individual partners as well. For a discussion of estimated taxes pertaining to corporations, see Chapter C:3.

Individuals earning only salaries and wages generally pay their annual income tax liability through payroll withholding. The employer is responsible for remitting these withheld amounts, along with Social Security taxes, to a designated federal depository. By contrast, individuals earning other types of income, as well as C corporations, S corporations, and trusts, must estimate their annual income tax liability and prepay their taxes on a quarterly basis.[46] Estates must do the same with respect to income earned during any tax year ending two years after the decedent's death.[47] Although partnerships do not pay estimated income taxes, their separate partners do if they are individuals or taxable entities. Chapters C:3, C:11, and C:14 discuss the estimated income tax requirements for C corporations, S corporations, and fiduciaries, respectively.

PAYMENT REQUIREMENTS

Individuals should pay quarterly estimated income taxes if they have a significant amount of income from sources other than salaries and wages.[48] The amount of each payment should be the same if this outside income accrues uniformly throughout the year. To avoid an estimated income tax penalty for the current year, individuals with AGI of $150,000 or less in the previous year should calculate each payment as follows:

Step 1: Determine the lesser of
- a. 90% of the taxpayer's regular tax, alternative minimum tax (if any), and self-employment tax for the current year, or
- b. 100% of the taxpayer's prior year regular tax, alternative minimum tax (if any), and self-employment tax if the taxpayer filed a return for the prior year and the year was not a short tax year.

Step 2: Calculate the total of
- a. Tax credits for the current year
- b. Taxes withheld on the current year's wages
- c. Overpayments of the prior year's tax liability the taxpayer requests be credited against the current year's tax

[46] S corporations must pay quarterly estimated taxes on their net recognized built-in gains, passive investment income, and credit recapture amounts.

[47] For example, if the decedent's death were June 15 of the current year, and the assets of the decedent's estate are not distributed by June 14 of the following year, the estate must pay estimated taxes on income earned on estate assets for the following tax year.

[48] Rules pertaining to individuals' estimated taxes are in Sec 6654.

Step 3: Multiply the excess of the amount from Step 1 over the amount from Step 2 by 25%.

Calendar year individual taxpayers should pay their quarterly installments on April 15, June 15, September 15, and January 15.

Individuals with AGI exceeding $150,000 ($75,000 for married filing separately) in the prior year can avoid the estimated tax penalty for the current year if they pay at least 90% of the current year's tax, or at least 110% of the prior year's tax.[49]

EXAMPLE C:15-16 ▶ Mike's regular tax on his current year taxable income is $35,000. Mike also owes $2,000 of self-employment tax but no alternative minimum tax. Mike's total liability last year for both income and self-employment taxes was $24,000. His AGI last year did not exceed $150,000. Taxes withheld from Mike's current year wages were $8,000. Mike did not overpay his tax last year or earn any credits this year. For the current year, Mike should have made quarterly estimated tax payments of $4,000, as calculated below.

Lesser of:	90% of current year's tax (0.90 × $37,000 = $33,300) or	
	100% of prior year's $24,000 tax liability	$24,000
Minus:	Taxes withheld from current year's wages	(8,000)
Minimum estimated tax payment to avoid penalty under general rule		$16,000
Quarterly estimated tax payments (0.25 × $16,000)		$ 4,000 ◀

ADDITIONAL COMMENT

Although it is simpler to use the amount of tax paid (or, if necessary, the applicable percentage of the amount of tax paid) in the preceding year as a safe harbor, the estimate of the current year's tax liability is preferable if the current year's tax liability is expected to be significantly less than the preceding year's tax liability.

The authority to make estimated tax payments based on the preceding year's income is especially significant for taxpayers with rising levels of income. To avoid an estimated income tax penalty, these taxpayers need to pay only an amount equal to the prior year's tax liability. Using this safe harbor eliminates the need for estimating the current year's tax liability with a high degree of accuracy.

EXAMPLE C:15-17 ▶ Peter, a single calendar year taxpayer, incurs a regular tax liability of $76,000 in the current year. Peter owes no alternative minimum tax liability nor can he claim any tax credits. No overpayments of last year's taxes are available to offset this year's tax liability. Taxes withheld evenly from Peter's wages throughout the current year are $68,000. Peter's AGI last year exceeded $150,000, and his regular tax liability was $60,000. Because Peter's $17,000 of withholding for each quarter exceeds the $15,000 minimum required quarterly payments, as calculated below, he incurs no underpayment penalty.

Lesser of:	90% of current year's (0.90 × $76,000 = $68,400) or	
	110% of prior year's $60,000 tax liability	$66,000
Minus:	Taxes withheld from current year's wages	(68,000)
Minimum estimated tax payment to avoid penalty under general rule		$ -0-

The $8,000 ($76,000 − $68,000) balance of the current's year taxes is due on or before April 15 of next year with the filing of the return or the request for extension of time to file. ◀

ADDITIONAL COMMENT

If a taxpayer is having taxes withheld and making estimated tax payments, a certain amount of tax planning is possible. Withholdings are deemed to have occurred equally throughout the year. Thus, disproportionately large amounts could be withheld in the last quarter to allow the taxpayer to avoid the underpayment penalty.

PENALTY FOR UNDERPAYING ESTIMATED TAXES

With the exceptions discussed in the next section, taxpayers who do not remit the requisite amount of estimated tax by the appropriate date are subject to a penalty for underpayment of estimated taxes. The penalty is calculated at the same rate as the interest rate applicable under Sec. 6621 to late payments of tax.[50] The penalty for each quarter is calculated on Form 2210.

The amount subject to the penalty is the excess of the total tax that should have been paid during the quarter (e.g., $6,000 [$24,000 prior year's tax liability ÷ 4] in Example C:15-16) over the sum of the estimated tax actually paid during that quarter on or before

[49] Included in the definition of *individuals* are estates and trusts. Section 67(e) defines AGI for estates and trusts. (See Chapter C:14.)

[50] Daily compounding is not applicable in calculating the penalty.

the installment date plus the withholding attributable to that quarter. Unless the taxpayer proves otherwise, the withholding is deemed to take place equally during each quarter. This rule creates a planning opportunity. Taxpayers who have not paid sufficient amounts of estimated tax in the first three quarters can avoid a penalty by having large amounts of tax withheld during the last quarter.

The penalty is assessed for the time period beginning on the due date for the quarterly installment and ending on the earlier of the date the underpayment actually is paid or the due date for the return (April 15 assuming a calendar year taxpayer). The next example illustrates the computation of the underpayment penalty.

EXAMPLE C:15-18 ▶ Assume the same facts as in Example C:15-16 except Mike pays only $3,000 of estimated tax payments on April 15, June 15, and September 15 of the current year and January 15 of next year and, for simplicity, that 6% is the Sec. 6621 underpayment rate for the entire time period. Mike files his current year return on March 30 of next year and pays the $17,000 ($37,000 − $8,000 withholding − $12,000 estimated taxes) balance due at that time. Mike's underpayment penalty is determined as follows:

TYPICAL MISCONCEPTION

Many self-employed taxpayers assume they are not liable for estimated taxes if they have sufficient itemized deductions and exemptions to create zero taxable income or a taxable loss. However, a self-employment tax liability may exist even if the individual has no taxable income. Thus, taxpayers in this situation can end up with an overall tax liability and an accompanying estimated tax penalty.

	Installment			
	First	*Second*	*Third*	*Fourth*
Amount that should have been paid ($24,000 ÷ 4)	$6,000	$6,000	$6,000	$6,000
Minus: Wage withholding	(2,000)	(2,000)	(2,000)	(2,000)
Estimated tax payment	(3,000)	(3,000)	(3,000)	(3,000)
Underpayment	$1,000	$1,000	$1,000	$1,000
Number of days of underpayment (ends March 30 of next year because earlier than April 15 of next year);	349	288	196	74
Penalty at 6% assumed annual rate for number of days of underpayment*	$ 57	$ 47	$ 32	$ 12

*Calculated as follows: Underpayment × 0.06 × (No. of days/365)

The total penalty equals $148 ($57 + $47 + $32 + $12). The $148 penalty is not deductible. ◀

Interest does not accrue on underpayments of estimated tax.[51] However, if the entire tax is not paid by the due date for the return, interest and perhaps also a failure-to-pay penalty will be levied on the unpaid amount.

EXCEPTIONS TO THE PENALTY

In certain circumstances, individuals who have not remitted the required estimated tax payments nevertheless will be exempt from the underpayment penalty. The IRS imposes no penalty if the taxpayer's tax liability exceeds by less than $1,000 taxes actually withheld from wages during the year. Similarly, the taxpayer will not owe a penalty, regardless of the underpayment amount, if the taxpayer owed no taxes for the prior tax year, the prior tax year consisted of the full 12 months, and the taxpayer was a U.S. citizen or resident alien throughout that year. The Secretary of the Treasury can waive the penalty otherwise due in the case of "casualty, disaster, or other unusual circumstances" or for newly retired or disabled individuals.[52]

EXAMPLE C:15-19 ▶ Paul's current year tax liability is $2,200, the same as last year's. His wage withholding amounts to $1,730, and Paul does not pay any estimated taxes. Paul pays the $470 balance due on March 15 of next year. Under the general rules, Paul is subject to the underpayment penalty because he does not reach either the 90% of the current year tax threshold or 100% of the prior year

[51] Sec. 6601(h).

[52] Sec. 6654(e).

tax threshold. However, because Paul's tax exceeds wage withholding by less than $1,000, he owes no penalty for underpaying his estimated tax liability. ◀

Taxpayers are exempt from the underpayment penalty in certain other circumstances, a discussion of which is beyond the scope of this text. Chapter I:14 of *Pearson's Federal Taxation: Principles* and *Comprehensive* texts, however, discusses one such circumstance where the taxpayer annualizes his or her income and bases the estimated tax payment on the annualized amount.[53] Annualizing income often is beneficial for taxpayers who realize a high percentage of their income later in the year (e.g., large year-end bonus).

Other more severe penalties

OBJECTIVE 7

Describe the more severe penalties, including the fraud penalty

In addition to the penalties for failure to file, failure to pay, and underpayment of estimated tax, taxpayers may be subject to other more severe penalties. These include the accuracy-related penalty (applicable in several contexts) and the fraud penalty, each of which is discussed below. A 20% accuracy-related penalty applies to any underpayment attributable to negligence, any substantial understatement of income tax, transactions without economic substance, and various types of errors, a discussion of which is beyond the scope of this text.[54] An accuracy-related penalty is not levied, however, if the government imposed the fraud penalty or if the taxpayer filed no return.

Negligence

ADDITIONAL COMMENT

To shift the burden of proof to the IRS, the taxpayer must introduce credible evidence regarding a factual issue relating to his or her tax liability.

The accuracy-related **negligence penalty** applies whenever the IRS determines that a taxpayer has underpaid any part of his or her taxes as a result of negligence or disregard of the rules or regulations (but without intending to defraud). The penalty is 20% of the underpayment attributable to negligence. Interest accrues on the negligence penalty at the rate applicable to underpayments.[55]

EXAMPLE C:15-20 ▶ The IRS audits Ted's individual return and assesses a $7,500 deficiency, of which $2,500 is attributable to negligence. Ted agrees to the assessment and pays the additional tax of $7,500 the following year. Ted incurs a negligence penalty of $500 (0.20 × $2,500). ◀

The IRC defines ***negligence*** as "any failure to make a reasonable attempt to comply with the provisions" of the IRC. It defines disregard of the rules or regulations as "any careless, reckless, or intentional disregard."[56] According to Treasury Regulations, a presumption of negligence exists if the taxpayer does not include in gross income an amount of income reported on an information return or does not reasonably attempt to ascertain the correctness of a deduction, credit, or exclusion that a reasonable and prudent person would think was "too good to be true."[57]

A taxpayer is careless if he or she does not diligently try to determine the correctness of his or her position. A taxpayer is reckless if he or she exerts little or no effort to determine whether a rule or regulation exists. A taxpayer's disregard is intentional if he or she knows about the rule or regulation he or she disregards.[58]

The penalty will not be imposed for any portion of an underpayment if the taxpayer had reasonable cause for his or her position and acted in good faith.[59] Failure to follow a regulation must be disclosed on Form 8275-R (Regulation Disclosure Statement), but disclosure alone is not sufficient as a defense against negligence.

---

[53] Section 6654(d)(2) allows for computation of the underpayments, if any, by annualizing income. Relief from the underpayment penalty may result from applying the annualization rules. Corporations, but not individuals, are permitted a seasonal adjustment to the annualization rules.

[54] Rules pertaining to accuracy-related penalties are in Sec. 6662.

[55] Sec. 6601(e)(2)(B).

[56] Sec. 6662(c).

[57] Reg. Sec. 1.6662-3(b)(1).

[58] Reg. Sec. 1.6662-3(b)(2).

[59] Sec. 6664(c)(1).

EXAMPLE C:15-21 ▶ The IRS audits Mario's current year individual return, and Mario agrees to a $4,000 deficiency. Mario had reasonable cause for adopting his tax return positions (which were not contrary to the applicable rules or regulations) and acted in good faith. Mario will not be liable for a negligence penalty. ◀

SUBSTANTIAL UNDERSTATEMENT

ADDITIONAL COMMENT

Theoretically, penalties are designed to deter taxpayers from willfully disregarding federal tax laws. Some taxpayers have been concerned that the IRS has used the multitude of tax penalties primarily as a source of revenue. The IRS achieved this result by "stacking" penalties (i.e., applying several penalties to a single underpayment). Recent legislation has alleviated some of this concern.

Taxpayers who substantially understate their income tax are liable for an accuracy-related penalty for their substantial understatements. The IRC defines a substantial understatement as an understatement of tax exceeding the greater of 10% of the tax required to be shown on the return or $5,000 (or $10,000 in the case of a C corporation). For a C corporation, an additional rule applies. Specifically, if 10% of the required tax exceeds $10 million, a substantial understatement exists if the understatement exceeds $10 million. The penalty equals 20% of the underpayment of tax attributable to the substantial understatement. It does not apply to understatements for which the taxpayer shows reasonable cause and good faith for his or her position.

SELF-STUDY QUESTION

How is an understatement different from an underpayment?

ANSWER

An underpayment can be larger than an understatement. Understatements do not include underpayments for which there was either substantial authority or adequate disclosure.

Understatement Versus Underpayment. The amount of tax attributable to the substantial understatement may be less than the amount of the underpayment. In general, the amount of the understatement is calculated as the amount by which the tax required to be shown (i.e., the correct tax) exceeds the tax shown on the return. Because the amount of tax attributable to certain items is not treated as an understatement, the additional tax attributed to such items is not subject to the penalty. An underpayment for an item other than a tax shelter is *not* an understatement if either of the following is true:

- ▶ The taxpayer has substantial authority (discussed below) for the tax treatment of the item.
- ▶ The taxpayer discloses, either on the return or in a statement attached to the return, the relevant facts affecting the tax treatment of the item, and the taxpayer has a reasonable basis for such treatment.

Although neither the IRC nor Treasury Regulations define "reasonable basis," Reg. Sec. 1.6662-3(b)(3) states that a "reasonable basis" standard is significantly higher than the "not frivolous" standard that usually applies to tax preparers. The latter standard involves a tax position that is not patently improper. The taxpayer meets the adequate disclosure requirement if he or she properly completes either Form 8275 or Form 8275-R and attaches it to the return, or discloses information on the return in a manner prescribed by an annual revenue procedure.[60] Large corporations required to disclose uncertain tax positions will meet the disclosure requirement by filing Schedule UTP.

EXAMPLE C:15-22 ▶ The IRS examines Val's current year individual income tax return, and Val agrees to a $9,000 deficiency, which increases her tax liability from $25,000 to $34,000. Val neither made adequate disclosure concerning the items for which the IRS assessed the deficiency nor had substantial authority for her tax treatment. Thus, Val's understatement also is $9,000. This understatement is substantial because it exceeds both 10% of her correct tax liability ($3,400 = 0.10 × $34,000) and the $5,000 minimum. Val incurs a substantial understatement penalty of $1,800 (0.20 × $9,000). ◀

EXAMPLE C:15-23 ▶ Assume the same facts as in Example C:15-22 except Val has substantial authority for the tax treatment of an item that results in a $1,000 additional assessment. In addition, she makes adequate disclosure for a second item with respect to which the IRS assesses additional taxes of $1,500. Although Val's underpayment is $9,000, her understatement is only $6,500 [$9,000 − ($1,000 + $1,500)]. The $6,500 understatement is substantial because it is more than the greater of 10% of Val's tax or $5,000. Thus, the penalty in this case is $1,300 (0.20 × $6,500). ◀

Like the negligence penalty, the substantial understatement penalty bears interest at the rate applicable for underpayments. The interest accrues from the due date of the return.

[60] Reg. Secs. 1.6662-4(f)(1) and (2). See Rev. Proc. 99-41, 1999-2 C.B. 566, Rev. Proc. 2001-11, 2001-1 C.B. 275, and Rev. Proc. 2002-66, 2002-2 C.B. 724, where the Treasury Department identifies circumstances where disclosure of a position on a taxpayer's return is adequate to reduce the understatement penalty of Sec. 6662(d) and tax preparer penalties of Sec. 6694(a).

ADDITIONAL COMMENT

Even though the substantial understatement penalty is a taxpayer penalty, tax preparers have a duty to make their clients aware of the potential risk of substantial understatement. In some situations, failure to do so has resulted in the client's attempting to collect the amount of the substantial understatement penalty from the preparer.

Concept of Substantial Authority. Treasury Regulations indicate that substantial authority

- Exists only if the weight of authorities supporting the tax treatment of an item is substantial relative to the weight of those supporting the contrary treatment, and
- Is based on an objective standard involving an analysis of law and its application to the relevant facts. This standard is more stringent than the "reasonable basis" standard that the taxpayer must meet to avoid the negligence penalty but less stringent than the "more likely than not" standard that applies to tax shelters.[61] (See discussion below.)

According to these regulations, the following are considered to be "authority": the Internal Revenue Code and other statutory provisions; proposed, temporary, and final regulations; court cases; revenue rulings; revenue procedures; tax treaties; Congressional intent as reflected in committee reports and joint statements of a bill's managers; private letter rulings; technical advice memoranda; information or press releases; notices; and any other similar documents published by the IRS in the *Internal Revenue Bulletin* and the *General Explanation of the Joint Committee on Taxation* (also known as the "Blue Book"). Conclusions reached in treatises, periodicals, and the opinions of tax professionals are not considered to be authority. The applicability of court cases in the taxpayer's district that have been overruled is not taken into account in determining the existence of substantial authority. On the other hand, the applicability of Court of Appeals cases in the taxpayer's circuit *is* taken into account in determining the existence of substantial authority.

EXAMPLE C:15-24 ▶ Authorities addressing a particular issue are as follows:

- For the government: Tax Court and Fourth Circuit Court of Appeals
- For taxpayers: U.S. District Court for Rhode Island and First Circuit Court of Appeals

The taxpayer (Tina) is a resident of Rhode Island, which is in the First Circuit. Tina would have substantial authority for a pro-taxpayer position because such a position is supported by the circuit court of appeals for Tina's geographical jurisdiction. ◀

Taxpayers should be aware that, while sparing them a substantial understatement penalty, disclosure (even with a reasonable basis for the tax treatment of the item) might raise a "red flag" that could prompt an IRS audit.

Tax Shelters and Reportable Transactions. A different set of rules applies to a tax shelter, which is any arrangement for which a significant purpose is the avoidance or evasion of federal income tax.[62] See page C:15-30 and C:15-31 for a discussion of this topic.

TRANSACTIONS WITHOUT ECONOMIC SUBSTANCE

As part of its 2010 health care legislation, Congress added a 20% accuracy-related penalty for underpayments that result from transactions lacking economic substance. Further, if the understatement results from a nondisclosed noneconomic substance transaction, the penalty is increased to 40%.[63]

Prior to 2010, the law existed in the form of a judicial doctrine (i.e., the economic substance doctrine), but the courts did not agree on what constituted economic substance. Section 7701(o)(1) states that a transaction will have economic substance if (1) the transaction changes in a meaningful way the taxpayer's economic position (apart from federal income tax effects) and (2) the taxpayer has a substantial business purpose (apart from federal income tax effects) for entering into the transaction.

CIVIL FRAUD

Fraud differs from simple, honest mistakes and negligence in that it involves a deliberate attempt to deceive. Because the IRS cannot establish intent per se, it attempts to prove

[61] Reg. Sec. 1.6662-4(d). Substantial authority is not statutorily set at a percentage, but commentators and the IRS perceive it to require a 40% chance that the position would be sustained if challenged.

[62] Sec. 6662(d)(2)(C).

[63] Secs. 6662(b)(6) and 6662(h)(2)(C).

intent indirectly by emphasizing the taxpayer's actions and the circumstances surrounding these actions. One leading authority referred to fraud cases in this manner:

> Fraud cases ordinarily involve systematic or substantial omissions from gross income or fictitious deductions or dependency claims, accompanied by the falsification or destruction of records or false or inconsistent statements to the investigating agents, especially where records are not kept by the taxpayer. The taxpayer's education and business experience are relevant.[64]

The penalty equals 75% of the portion of the underpayment attributable to fraud.[65] If the IRS establishes that any portion of an underpayment is due to fraud, the entire underpayment is treated as having resulted from fraud unless the taxpayer establishes otherwise by a preponderance of the evidence. Like the negligence penalty, the fraud penalty bears interest.

EXAMPLE C:15-25 ▶ The IRS audits Ned's individual return and claims that Ned's underpayment is due to fraud. Ned agrees to the $40,000 deficiency but establishes that only $32,000 of the deficiency is attributable to fraud. The remainder results from mistakes that the IRS did not believe were due to fraud. Ned's civil fraud penalty is $24,000 (0.75 × $32,000). ◀

The fraud penalty can be imposed on taxpayers filing income, gift, or estate tax returns. If it is imposed, the negligence and substantial understatement penalties are not assessed on the portion of the underpayment attributable to fraud.[66] With respect to a joint return, no fraud penalty can be imposed on a spouse who has not committed fraud. In other words, one spouse is not liable for the other spouse's fraudulent acts.

STOP & THINK

Question: A few years ago, Joyce filed her individual income tax return in which she reported $250,000 of taxable income. She paid all the tax shown on the return on the day she filed. She, however, fraudulently omitted an additional $100,000 of gross income and, of course, does not have substantial authority for this omission. If the IRS proves that Joyce committed fraud, will she be liable for both the civil fraud penalty and the substantial understatement penalty? What are the rates for the two penalties?

Solution: Because the penalties cannot be stacked, Joyce will not owe both penalties. If the IRS successfully proves fraud, she will owe a penalty of 75% of the tax due on the omitted income. She will not owe the 20% penalty for substantial understatements.

CRIMINAL FRAUD

REAL-WORLD EXAMPLE

In fiscal 2015, the IRS initiated 3,853 criminal investigations (down from 4,287 in 2014), and it referred 3,289 for prosecution. The IRS filed 3,208 indictments and handed down sentences in 3,092 of those cases. Of those sentenced, 80.8% were incarcerated. (Source: IRS *2015 Data Book;* see footnote 4.)

Civil and criminal fraud are similar in that both involve a taxpayer's intent to misrepresent facts. They differ primarily in terms of the weight of evidence required for conviction. Civil fraud requires proof by a preponderance of the evidence. Criminal fraud requires proof beyond a reasonable doubt. Because the latter standard is more stringent than the former, the government charges relatively few taxpayers with criminal fraud. To do so, the IRS and Justice Department must agree on the charges.

Criminal Fraud Investigations. The Criminal Investigation Division of the IRS conducts criminal fraud investigations. The agents responsible for the investigation are called **special agents.** Under IRS policy, at the first meeting of the special agent and the taxpayer, the special agent must

- Identify himself or herself as such
- Advise the taxpayer that he or she is the subject of a criminal investigation
- Advise the taxpayer of his or her rights to remain silent and consult legal counsel

---

64 Boris I. Bittker and Lawrence Lokken, *Federal Taxation of Income, Estates, and Gifts* (Boston, MA: Warren, Gorham & Lamont, 1999), vol. 4, ¶ 114–6.

65 Rules pertaining to fraud penalties are in Sec. 6663.

66 Sec. 6662(b).

ADDITIONAL COMMENT

Any time a tax professional learns a client has engaged in activities that may constitute criminal fraud, he or she immediately should refer the client to qualified legal counsel. Counsel should then hire the accountant as a consultant. Taxpayer's communications will be confidential under the attorney–client relationship. This relationship encompasses agents of the attorney.

Penalty Provisions. Sections 7201–7216 provide for criminal penalties. Three of these penalties are discussed below.

Section 7201. Section 7201 provides for an assessment of a penalty against any person who "willfully attempts . . . to evade or defeat any tax." The maximum penalty is $100,000 ($500,000 for corporations), a prison sentence of up to five years, or both.

Section 7203. Section 7203 imposes a penalty on any person who willfully fails to pay any tax or file a return. The maximum penalty is $25,000 ($100,000 for corporations), a prison sentence of no more than one year, or both. If the government charges the taxpayer with willfully failing to prepare a return, it need not prove that the taxpayer owes additional tax.

Section 7206. Persons other than the taxpayer can be charged under Sec. 7206. This section applies to any person who

> [W]illfully aids or assists in, or procures, counsels, or advises the preparation or presentation under, or in connection with any matter arising under the internal revenue laws, of a return, affidavit, claim, or other document, which is fraudulent or is false as to any material matter, whether or not such falsity or fraud is with the knowledge or consent of the person authorized or required to present such return, affidavit, claim, or document.[67]

What constitutes a material matter has been litigated extensively.[68] The maximum penalty under Sec. 7206 is $100,000 ($500,000 for corporations), a prison sentence of up to three years, or both. The government need not prove that the taxpayer owes additional tax.

STATUTE OF LIMITATIONS

OBJECTIVE 8

Recognize when the statute of limitations applies

The **statute of limitations** has the same practical implications in a tax context as in other contexts. It specifies a timeframe (called the "limitations period") during which the government must assess the tax or initiate a court proceeding to collect the tax.[69] The statute of limitations also defines the limitations period during which a taxpayer may file a lawsuit against the government or a claim for a refund.

GENERAL THREE-YEAR RULE

Under the general rule of Sec. 6501(a), the limitations period is three years after the date on which the return is filed, regardless of whether the return is timely filed. A return filed before its due date is treated as filed on the due date.

EXAMPLE C:15-26 ▶ Ali files his Year 1 individual return on March 5 of Year 2. The government may not assess additional taxes for Year 1 after April 15 of Year 5, three years after the due date. If instead Ali files his Year 1 individual return on October 7 of Year 2, the limitations period for his return expires on midnight of October 7 of Year 5, three years after Ali files his tax return. ◀

SIX-YEAR RULE FOR SUBSTANTIAL OMISSIONS

Income Tax Returns. In the case of substantial omissions, the limitations period is six years after the later of the date the return is filed or the return's due date. For income tax purposes, the six-year period is applicable if the taxpayer omits from gross income an amount exceeding 25% of the gross income shown on the return. If an item is disclosed either on the return or in a statement attached to the return, it is not treated as an omission if the disclosure adequately apprises the IRS of the nature and amount of the item. In the case of taxpayers conducting a trade or business, gross income for purposes of the 25% omission test means the taxpayer's sales revenues (not the taxpayer's gross profit).[70] Taxpayers benefit from this special definition because it renders the 25% test applicable to a gross amount (implying a higher threshold).

---

67 Sec. 7206(2).

68 See, for example, *U.S. v. Joseph DiVarco,* 32 AFTR 2d 73-5605, 73-2 USTC ¶9607 (7th Cir., 1973), wherein the court held that the source of the taxpayer's income as stated on the tax return is a material matter.

69 Rules pertaining to the statute of limitations are Sec. 6501.

70 Regulation Sec. 1.61-3(a) defines *gross income* as sales less cost of goods sold.

What Would You Do in This Situation?

After working eight years for a large CPA firm, you begin your practice as a sole practitioner CPA. Your practice is not as profitable as you had expected, and you consider how you might attract additional clients. One idea is to obtain for your clients larger refunds than they anticipate. Your reputation for knowing tax-saving tips might grow, and your profits might increase. You think further and decide that maybe you could claim itemized deductions for charitable contributions that actually were not made and for business expenses that actually were not paid. You are aware of Sec. 7206, regarding false and fraudulent statements but think that you can avoid the "as to any material matter" stipulation by keeping the deduction overstatements relatively insubstantial. Would you try this scheme for increasing your profits? If so, would you escape the scope of Sec. 7206? What ramifications might these deeds have on your standing as a CPA under the AICPA's *Statements on Standards for Tax Services* and *Code of Professional Conduct*?

EXAMPLE C:15-27 ► Peg files her Year 1 return on March 28 of Year 2. Her return shows $6,000 of interest from corporate bonds and $30,000 of salary. Peg attaches a statement to her return that indicates why she thinks an additional $2,000 receipt of income is nontaxable. However, because of an oversight, she does not report an $8,000 capital gain. Peg is deemed to have omitted only $8,000 rather than $10,000 (the $8,000 capital gain plus the $2,000 receipt) because she disclosed the $2,000 receipt. The $8,000 amount is 22.22% ($8,000/$36,000) of her reported gross income. Because the omission does not exceed 25% of Peg's reported gross income, the limitations period expires on April 15 of Year 5. ◄

EXAMPLE C:15-28 ► Assume the same facts as in Example C:15-27 except Peg does not make adequate disclosure of the $2,000 receipt. Thus, she is considered to have omitted $10,000 from gross income. The $10,000 amount is 27.77% ($10,000/$36,000) of her reported gross income. Therefore, the limitations period expires on April 15 of Year 8. ◄

EXAMPLE C:15-29 ► Rita conducts a business as a sole proprietorship. Rita's Year 1 return, filed on March 18 of Year 2, indicates sales of $100,000 and cost of goods sold of $70,000. Rita inadvertently fails to report $9,000 of interest earned on a loan to a relative. For purposes of the 25% omission test, her gross income is $100,000, not $30,000. The omitted interest is 9% ($9,000/$100,000) of her reported gross income. Because the $9,000 does not exceed 25% of the gross amount, the limitations period expires on April 15 of Year 5. ◄

KEY POINT

A 25% omission of gross income extends the basic limitations period to six years, whereas a 25% overstatement of deductions is still subject to the basic three-year limitations period. However, if fraud can be shown, there is no limitations period.

Note that the six-year rule applies only to omitted income. Thus, claiming excessive deductions will not result in a six-year limitations period. However, the statute of limitations is extended to six years in cases where gross income is understated due to an overstatement of cost or other basis of an asset sold.[71] Furthermore, if the omission involves fraud, no limitations period applies.

Gift and Estate Tax Returns. A similar six-year limitations period applies for gift and estate tax purposes. If the taxpayer omits items that exceed 25% of the gross estate value or the total amount of gifts reported on the return, the limitations period expires six years after the later of the date the return is filed or the due date. Items disclosed on the return or in a statement attached to the return that adequately apprises the IRS of the nature and amount of the item do not constitute omissions. Understatements of the value of assets disclosed on the return also are not considered omissions.

EXAMPLE C:15-30 ► John files his Year 1 gift tax return on April 3 of Year 2. The return reports a cash gift to his son of $600,000. In Year 1, John also sold land to his son for $700,000. At the time of the sale, John thought the land's FMV was $700,000. Upon audit, the IRS determines that the FMV of the land on the sale date was $900,000. Thus, John effectively gifted an additional $200,000 to his son as a result of the less than FMV, or bargain element, of the original sale. The $200,000 amount is 33⅓% ($200,000/$600,000) of all gifts reported. The limitations period expires on April 15 of Year 8. ◄

[71] Sec. 6501(e)(1)(B)(ii).

WHEN NO RETURN IS FILED

No limitations period exists if the taxpayer does not file a return. Thus, the government may assess the tax or initiate a court proceeding for collection at any time.

EXAMPLE C:15-31 ▶ Jill does not file a tax return for Year 1. No limitations period applies. Consequently, if the government discovers 20 years later that Jill did not file a return, it may assess the Year 1 tax, along with penalties and interest. ◀

OTHER EXCEPTIONS TO THREE-YEAR RULE

SELF-STUDY QUESTION

Should a taxpayer ever agree to extend the limitations period?

ANSWER

Yes. When an audit is in progress, if a taxpayer refuses to extend the limitations period, the agent may assert a deficiency for each item in question. Had the taxpayer granted an extension, perhaps many of the items in question never would have been included in the examining agent's report.

Extension of the Three-Year Limitations Period. The IRC provides other exceptions to the three-year statute of limitations rule, some of which are discussed here. The taxpayer and the IRS can mutually agree in writing to extend the limitations period for taxes other than the estate tax. In such situations, the limitations period is extended until the date agreed on by the two parties. Such agreements usually are concluded when the IRS is auditing a return near the end of the statutory period. Taxpayers often agree to extending the limitations period because they think that, if they do not do so, the IRS will assess a higher deficiency than otherwise would have been the case. Before concluding such an agreement, the IRS must notify the taxpayer that he or she may refuse to extend the limitations period or may limit the extension to particular issues.

NOL Carrybacks. For a year to which a net operating loss (NOL) carries back, the applicable limitations period is for the year in which the NOL arose.

When Fraud Is Proven.

Deficiency and Civil Fraud Penalty. If the government successfully proves that a taxpayer filed a false or fraudulent return "with the intent to evade tax" or engaged in a "willful attempt . . . to defeat or evade tax," there is no limitations period. In other words, the government may at any time assess the tax or begin a court proceeding to collect the tax and the interest thereon. In addition, if the government proves fraud, it may impose a civil penalty. If it fails to prove fraud and the normal three-year limitations period and special six-year period for 25% omissions have expired, it may not assess additional taxes. The fraud issue is significant in tax litigation because the burden of proving fraud is unconditionally on the government.

EXAMPLE C:15-32 ▶ The IRS audits Trey's 2016 return late in 2019. It also examines Trey's prior years' returns and contends that Trey had willfully attempted to evade tax on his timely filed 2013 return. Trey litigates in the Tax Court, and the Court decides the fraud issue in his favor. Because the IRS did not prove fraud, it may not assess additional taxes for 2013. Had the IRS proven fraud, the limitations period for the 2013 return would have remained open, and the IRS could have assessed the additional taxes. ◀

ADDITIONAL COMMENT

Even though a taxpayer is home free from criminal prosecution after six years of an act or omission, he or she still is subject to civil fraud penalties if fraud is proven at any time after the six-year period.

Criminal Provisions. If taxpayers are not indicted for criminal violations of the tax law within a certain period of time, they are home free. For most criminal offenses, the maximum period is six years after the commission of the offense.[72] Taxpayers cannot be prosecuted, tried, or punished unless an indictment is made within that timeframe. The six-year period begins on the date the taxpayer committed the offense, not the date he or she files the return. Taxpayers who file fraudulent returns might commit offenses related to the returns at a subsequent date. An example of an offense that some taxpayers commit after filing a return is depositing money into a new bank account under a fictitious name.

EXAMPLE C:15-33 ▶ In March of Year 2, Tony files a fraudulent Year 1 return through which he attempts to evade tax. Before filing, Tony keeps a double set of books. In Year 1, Tony deposits some funds into a bank account under a fictitious name. In Year 3, he moves to another state, and on May 5 of Year 3, he transfers these funds to a new bank account under a different fictitious name. Depositing money into the new account is an offense relating to the fraudulent return. Provided Tony commits no

[72] Sec. 6531.

additional offenses, the limitations period for indictment expires on May 5 of Year 9, six years after committing the latest fraudulent offense. ◀

SELF-STUDY QUESTION

Suppose a taxpayer incorrectly includes a receipt in a tax return and then, after the limitations period has expired for that year, correctly includes the receipt in a subsequent return. Is it equitable for the taxpayer to have to pay tax on the same income twice?

ANSWER

No. A complicated set of provisions (Secs. 1311–1314) allows, in specific situations, otherwise closed years to be opened if a position taken in an open year is inconsistent with a position taken in a closed year.

REFUND CLAIMS

Taxpayers generally are not entitled to a refund for overpayments of tax unless they file a claim for refund by the later of three years from the date they file the return or two years from the date they pay the tax.[73] The limitations period for individuals is suspended when the individual is financially disabled. A return filed before the due date is deemed to have been filed on the due date. The due date is determined without regard to extensions. In most cases, taxpayers pay the tax concurrently with filing the return. Typically, the taxpayer files a claim for a refund in the following circumstance: the IRS has audited the taxpayer's return, has proposed a deficiency, and has assessed additional taxes. The taxpayer may have paid the additional taxes two years after the due date for the return. In such a situation, the taxpayer may file a claim for a refund at any time within two years after making the additional payment (or a total of four years after the filing date). If the taxpayer does not file a claim until more than three years after the date of filing the return, the maximum refund is the amount of tax paid during the two-year period immediately preceding the date on which he or she files the claim.[74]

EXAMPLE C:15-34 ▶ Pat files his Year 1 return on March 12 of Year 2. The return reports a tax liability of $5,000, and Pat pays this entire amount when he files his return. He pays no additional tax. Pat must file a claim for refund by April 15 of Year 5, three years from the later of the date filed or the original due date without extensions. The maximum refundable amount is $5,000. ◀

EXAMPLE C:15-35 ▶ Assume the same facts as in Example C:15-34 except the IRS audits Pat's Year 1 return, and Pat pays a $1,200 deficiency on October 2 of Year 4. Pat may file a claim for refund as late as October 2 of Year 6. However, if Pat files the claim later than April 15 of Year 5, the refund may not exceed $1,200 (the amount of tax paid during the two-year period immediately preceding the filing of the claim). ◀

LIABILITY FOR TAX

OBJECTIVE 9

Explain from whom the government may collect unpaid taxes

Taxpayers are primarily liable for paying their tax. Spouses and transferees may be secondarily liable, as discussed below.

JOINT RETURNS

Ordinarily, if spouses file a joint return, their liability to pay the tax is joint and several.[75] **Joint and several liability** means that each spouse is potentially liable for the full amount due. If one spouse fails to pay any or all of the tax, the other spouse is responsible for paying the deficiency. Joint and several liability has facilitated IRS collection efforts where one spouse absconds from the country, and the other spouse remains behind.

Validity of Joint Return. To be valid, a joint return generally must include the signatures of both spouses. However, if one spouse cannot sign because of a disability, the return still is valid if that spouse orally consents to the other spouse's signing for him or her.[76] A joint return is invalid if one spouse forces the other to file jointly.

Innocent Spouse Provision. Congress has provided for **innocent spouse relief** where holding one spouse liable for the taxes due from both spouses would be inequitable.[77] Relief is available if all five of the following conditions are met:

- ▶ The spouses file a joint return.
- ▶ The return contains an understatement of tax attributable to the erroneous item(s) of an individual filing it.

---

[73] Sec. 6511(a).

[74] Under Sec. 6512, special rules apply if the IRS has mailed a notice of deficiency and if the taxpayer files a petition with the Tax Court.

[75] Sec. 6013(d)(3).

[76] Reg. Sec. 1.6012-1(a)(5).

[77] The innocent spouse provisions are in Sec. 6015.

- The other individual establishes that he or she neither knew nor had reason to know of any or all of the understatement.
- Based on all the facts and circumstances, holding the other individual liable for the deficiency would be inequitable.
- The other individual elects innocent spouse relief no later than two years after the IRS begins its collection efforts.

The degree of relief available depends on the extent of the electing spouse's knowledge. If the spouse neither knew nor had reason to know of *an understatement,* full relief will be granted. Full relief encompasses liability for taxes, interest, and penalties attributable to the full amount of the understatement. On the other hand, if the spouse either knew or had reason to know of an understatement, but not *the extent of the understatement,* only partial relief will be granted. Partial relief encompasses liability for taxes, interest, and penalties attributable to that portion of the understatement of which the spouse was unaware.

EXAMPLE C:15-36 ▶ Jim and Joy jointly filed a tax return for Year 1. Joy fraudulently reported on Schedule C two expenses: one amounting to $4,000 and the other amounting to $3,000. The IRS audits the return, assesses a $2,170 deficiency, and begins its collection efforts on June 3 of Year 3. If (1) Jim elects innocent spouse relief no later than June 3 of Year 5, (2) Jim establishes that he neither knew nor had reason to know of the understatement, and (3) holding Jim liable for the deficiency would be inequitable under the circumstances, Jim will be relieved of liability for the full $2,170. ◀

EXAMPLE C:15-37 ▶ Assume the same facts as in Example C:15-36 except Jim had reason to know the $3,000 expense was fraudulent. If (1) Jim elects innocent spouse relief no later than June 3 of Year 5, (2) Jim establishes that he neither knew nor had reason to know the *extent* of the understatement (i.e., $7,000 as opposed to $3,000), and (3) holding Jim liable for the full amount of the deficiency would be inequitable under the circumstances, Jim will be relieved of liability for that portion of the deficiency attributable to the $4,000 expense. ◀

Proportional liability is liability for only that portion of a deficiency attributable to the taxpayer's separate taxable items. A joint filer incurs proportional liability if all the following conditions are met:

- The joint filer elects proportional liability within two years after the IRS begins its collection efforts.
- The electing filer is either divorced or separated at the time of the election.
- The electing filer did not reside in the same household as the other filer at any time during the 12-month period preceding the election.
- The electing filer does not have actual knowledge of any item giving rise to the deficiency.

The electing filer bears the burden of proving the amount of his or her proportional liability. The fraudulent transfer of property between joint filers immediately before the election will invalidate it.

EXAMPLE C:15-38 ▶ Sam and Sue jointly filed a Year 1 tax return. Sam intentionally omitted to report $8,000 in gambling winnings. Sue fraudulently deducted $1,600 in business expenses. The IRS audits the return, assesses a $3,600 deficiency, and begins its collection efforts on August 19 of Year 4. Sam and Sue are subsequently divorced. If Sue (1) elects innocent spouse relief no later than August 19 of Year 6, (2) did not reside in the same household as Sam at any time during the 12-month period preceding the election, and (3) did not actually know of Sam's omission, she will be liable for only that portion of the deficiency attributable to her fraudulent deduction. ◀

Equitable Relief. Spouses unable to obtain relief under the standard innocent spouse provisions still may petition the IRS for equitable relief. The IRS uses a facts and circumstances test and, beginning in 2013, relaxed the requirements for obtaining relief, particularly in cases where one spouse was abusive or where the spouse seeking relief missed a statutory deadline.

The Effect of Community Property Laws. Community property laws are ignored in determining to whom income (other than income from property) is attributable. For example, if one spouse living in a community property state wins money by gambling, the gambling income is not treated as community property for purposes of the innocent spouse provisions. If the gambling winnings are omitted from a joint return, they are deemed to be solely the income of the spouse who gambled.

TYPICAL MISCONCEPTION

A taxpayer cannot escape paying taxes by transferring assets to a transferee (donee, heir, legatee, etc.) or a fiduciary (executor, trustee, etc.).

TRANSFEREE LIABILITY

The Internal Revenue Code authorizes the IRS to collect taxes from persons other than the taxpayer.[78] The two categories of persons from whom the IRS may collect taxes are transferees and fiduciaries. Transferees include donees, heirs, legatees, devisees, shareholders of dissolved corporations, parties to a reorganization, and other distributees.[79] Fiduciaries include executors and administrators of estates. In general, the limitations period for transferees expires one year after the limitations period for transferors. The transferors may be income earners in the case of income taxes, executors in the case of estate taxes, and donors in the case of gift taxes.

EXAMPLE C:15-39 ▶ Lake Corporation is liquidated in the current year, and it distributes all its assets to its sole shareholder, Leo. If the IRS audits Lake's return and assesses a deficiency, Leo (the distributee) is responsible for paying the deficiency. ◀

TAX PRACTICE ISSUES

OBJECTIVE 10

Apply the professional and governmental standards for tax practitioners

A number of statutes and guidelines address what constitutes proper behavior of CPAs and others engaged in tax practice, including the AICPA's *Statements on Standards for Tax Services* (see Appendix E).

STATUTORY PROVISIONS CONCERNING TAX RETURN PREPARERS

KEY POINT

As evidenced by the formidable list of possible penalties, an individual considering becoming a tax return preparer needs to be aware of certain procedures set forth in the IRC.

Sections 6694–6696 impose penalties on tax return preparers for misconduct. Section 7701(a)(36) defines a tax return preparer as a "person who prepares for compensation, or who employs one or more persons to prepare for compensation, any return of tax imposed by this title or any claim for refund of tax imposed by this title." Tax return preparers are divided into two categories: signing preparers and non-signing preparers. A signing preparer has primary responsibility for the overall substantive accuracy of the preparation of the return or refund claim. A non-signing preparer gives advice to a taxpayer or another preparer, and the advice leads to a position or entry that is a substantial portion of the return or refund claim.[80] As a result, more than one preparer can be subject to the preparer penalties. The preparer responsible for the position giving rise to the understatement is subject to preparer penalties related to that position.[81]

Section 6695 imposes penalties for

- Failure to furnish the taxpayer with a copy of the return or claim ($50 per failure)
- Failure to sign a return or claim ($50 per failure)
- Failure to furnish one's identification number ($50 per failure)
- Failure to keep a copy of a return or claim or, in lieu thereof, to maintain a list of taxpayers for whom returns or claims were prepared ($50 per failure)
- Failure to file a correct information return ($50 per failure)
- Endorsement or other negotiation of an income tax refund check made payable to anyone other than the preparer ($500 per check)
- Failure to be diligent in determining eligibility for the earned income credit ($500 per case)

The first five penalties are not assessable if the preparer shows that the failure is due to reasonable cause and not willful neglect, and the maximum penalty cannot exceed $25,000 for a return period.[82]

A preparer will owe a maximum penalty equal to $1,000 or 50% of the income derived from the return if he or she lacked substantial authority for a non-disclosed position. Substantial authority is an objective standard that involves the analysis of the law

[78] Sec. 6901.

[79] Reg. Sec. 301.6901-1(b).

[80] Reg. Sec. 301.7701-15(b).

[81] Reg. Sec. 1.6694-1(b).

[82] Regulation Sec. 1.6695-1(b)(3) states that, for the purpose of avoiding the failure-to-sign penalty, reasonable cause is "a cause which arises despite ordinary care and prudence exercised by the individual preparer."

REAL-WORLD EXAMPLE

In addition to these penalties, the IRS may suspend or bar a tax practitioner from practicing before the IRS. Each week the IRS publishes a list of suspended practitioners.

and application of the law to the relevant facts.[83] The standard is less stringent than the "more likely than not" (greater than 50%) test but more stringent than the reasonable basis standard. Reasonable basis refers to a position that is arguable and reasonably based on an acceptible authority such as the Internal Revenue Code, Treasury Regulations, court cases, and other pronouncements listed in Treasury Regulations.[84] Consequently, a tax position meets the substantial authority test if the authorities supporting the position are more substantial than authorities that take a contrary position. The preparer may avoid the penalty if the preparer has reasonable basis for the position and the position is properly disclosed. The IRS will impose no penalty if the preparer shows that he or she has reasonable cause for the understatement, and he or she acted in good faith.

If any portion of the understatement results from the preparer's willful attempt to understate taxes or from reckless or intentional disregard of rules or regulations, the penalty will be the greater of $5,000 or 50% of the income derived from the return. Treasury Regulations state that preparers are considered to have willfully understated taxes if they have attempted to wrongfully reduce taxes by disregarding pertinent information.[85] A preparer generally is deemed to have recklessly or intentionally disregarded a rule or regulation if he or she adopts a position contrary to a rule or regulation about which he or she knows, or is reckless in not knowing about such rule or regulation. A preparer may adopt a position contrary to a revenue ruling if the position has reasonable basis. In addition, a preparer may depart from following a Treasury Regulation without penalty if he or she has a good faith basis for challenging its validity and adequately discloses his or her position on Form 8275-R (Regulation Disclosure Statement).

Question: While preparing a client's tax return two days before the due date, Tevin reviews an item that arguably is deductible. He weighs the cost of researching whether he has substantial authority for the position. In so doing, he calculates that researching the issue will cost him $300 in forgone revenues and that not researching the issue will cost him $250 in preparer penalties. What should Tevin do?

Solution: Undoubtedly, Tevin should research the issue and determine whether the deduction either has substantial authority or has a reasonable basis. If he has a reasonable basis, he should disclose his position on the tax return. At stake here is not merely $300 in foregone revenues but also Tevin's professional reputation. His taking a position that does not meet the applicable standards subjects not only him as tax preparer, but also his client as taxpayer, to penalties. If the IRS imposes a penalty on the client, the client might terminate the professional relationship with Tevin or sue Tevin for negligence. Besides, Tevin may have miscalculated his own professional liability. If the IRS determines that Tevin recklessly or intentionally disregarded tax rules and regulations, it may impose a penalty of $5,000, not $250.

Tax preparers who offer advice relating to the preparation of a document, knowing that such advice will result in a tax understatement, will be liable for aiding and abetting in the understatement.[86] The penalty for aiding and abetting is $1,000 for advice given to noncorporate taxpayers and $10,000 for advice given to corporate taxpayers. If a preparer is assessed an aiding-and-abetting penalty, the preparer will not be assessed a Sec. 6694 preparer penalty for the same infraction.

REPORTABLE TRANSACTION DISCLOSURES

The IRS has continued its focus on tax shelters, including reportable and listed transactions, and has issued extensive and detailed reporting requirements on individuals who advise clients on certain aggressive tax schemes. Section 6111 sets forth the required disclosures by material advisors for reportable transactions, and Section 6112 requires material advisors to maintain a list of tax shelter clients and file information returns with the IRS.

83 Reg. Sec. 1.6662-4(d).
84 Reg. Sec. 1.6662-3(b)(3) and Reg. Sec. 1.6662-4(d)(3).
85 Reg. Sec. 1.6694-3.
86 Sec. 6701.

A reportable transaction is any transaction required to be disclosed because the IRS has determined it to have the potential for tax evasion or avoidance.[87] Reportable transactions include the following: (1) listed transactions as defined by the IRS, (2) confidential transactions, (3) transactions with contractual protection, (4) loss transactions where the losses claimed exceed certain thresholds ranging from $50,000 in a single year for individuals to $20 million for corporations over a number of years, (5) transactions of interest as designated by the IRS, and (6) patented transactions.[88]

A material advisor is any person who provides material aid, assistance, or advice with respect to any reportable transaction, and who receives gross income from the activity in excess of $50,000 if the tax benefits flow primarily to individuals or $250,000 for corporations and other entities.[89] The income thresholds are sharply reduced for listed transactions and transactions of interest ($10,000 for individuals and $25,000 for corporations).[90]

In general, a material advisor complies with the disclosure requirements by filing Form 8918 which details the transaction, the expected tax treatment, and the potential tax benefits in sufficient detail for the IRS to fully understand the transaction. Failure to make the required disclosures subjects taxpayers and material advisors to severe penalties as follows:

- *Imposed on the taxpayer:* Failure to disclose a reportable or listed transaction (ranging from $10,000 to $200,000, depending on the nature of the transaction and the status of the taxpayer)[91]
- *Imposed on the taxpayer:* Accuracy-related penalty for listed and reportable transactions (20% of the understatement for disclosed transactions; 30% for undisclosed transactions)[92]
- *Imposed on the organizer or advisor:* Failure to furnish information on reportable transactions ($50,000 in the case of tax benefits provided to individuals; $250,000 in any other case)[93]
- *Imposed on the organizer or advisor:* Failure to maintain an investor list ($10,000 per day after the twentieth business day following notice)[94]
- *Imposed on the organizer or advisor:* Tax shelter fraud (lesser of $1,000 or 100% of gross income derivable from the tax shelter)[95]

In addition, if a taxpayer fails to report information regarding a listed transaction on a required return or statement, the limitations period is extended to one year after the earlier of the date on which the information is furnished to the IRS or the date on which a material advisor meets the list maintenance requirements.[96]

ETHICAL POINT

In deciding whether to adopt a pro-taxpayer position on a tax return or in rendering tax advice, a tax advisor should keep in mind his or her responsibilities under the tax return preparer rules of the IRC, *Treasury Department Circular 230,* and the *Statements on Standards for Tax Services,* especially Statement No. 1. Statement No. 1 (reproduced in Appendix E) requires that a CPA have a good faith belief that the position adopted on the tax return is supported by existing law or by a good faith argument for extending, modifying, or reversing existing law.

RULES OF *CIRCULAR 230*

Treasury Department *Circular 230* regulates the practice of attorneys, CPAs, enrolled agents, and enrolled actuaries before the IRS. Practice before the IRS includes representing taxpayers in meetings with IRS audit agents and appeals officers. Tax professionals who do not comply with the rules and regulations of *Circular 230* can be barred from practicing before the IRS and may be subject to censure and/or monetary penalties. Such professionals are entitled to an administrative hearing before being penalized.

Circular 230 rules apply to all paid preparers (signing and non-signing), including "registered tax return preparers" (RTRP). All paid preparers must register with the IRS, pay an annual fee, and obtain a preparer tax identification number. An RTRP is limited to preparing and signing tax returns, claims for refund, and other documents to be filed with the IRS and

[87] Sec. 6707A(c).
[88] Reg. Sec. 1.6011-4 and Prop. Reg. Sec. 1.6011-4.
[89] Sec 6111(b).
[90] Reg. Sec. 301.6111-3(b)(3).
[91] Sec. 6707A.
[92] Sec. 6662A.
[93] Sec. 6111.
[94] Sec. 6708.
[95] Sec. 6700(a).
[96] Sec. 6501(c)(10).

ADDITIONAL COMMENT

The IRS amended *Circular 230* in 2011 to include additional requirements on tax return preparers who only prepare returns and do not otherwise appear before the IRS. In *Loving v. IRS*, 111 AFTR 2d 2013-589 (DC Washington D.C., 2013), the court concluded that this authority exceeded the IRS's statutory authority.

may represent a taxpayer before revenue agents, Taxpayer Advocate Service representatives, or similar employees of the IRS. However, RTRPs may not provide tax advice beyond the advice necessary to prepare the tax return and may not represent taxpayers before appeals officers, counsel, or similar IRS employees.

Among the rules governing the conduct of practitioners before the IRS are the following:[97]

- If the practitioner knows that a client has not complied with federal tax laws or has made an error in or an omission from any return, the practitioner should promptly advise the client of the error or omission. The practitioner also must advise the client of possible corrective action and the consequences of not taking such action.[98]
- Each person practicing before the IRS must exercise due diligence in preparing returns, determining the correctness of representations made to the Treasury Department, and determining the correctness of representations made to clients about tax matters.[99]

Circular 230 provides that a practitioner may not sign a return or advise a client to take a position that lacks a reasonable basis, is an unreasonable position as described in Sec. 6694(a)(2), is a willful attempt to understate tax, or is a reckless or intentional disregard of rules or regulations as described in Sec. 6694(b)(2).[100]

Circular 230 also lists best practices standards for tax advisors.[101] Such standards include the following:

- Communicate clearly with the client regarding the terms of the engagement.
- Establish the relevant facts, evaluate the reasonableness of assumptions or representations, relate the applicable law to the relevant facts, and arrive at a conclusion supported by the law and relevant facts.
- Advise the client of the implications of conclusions reached, including the applicability of accuracy-related penalties.
- Act fairly and with integrity in practice before the IRS.

Circular 230 also provides detailed substantive and format requirements for practitioners who provide written advice.[102] Accordingly, a practitioner must meet all of the following standards:

- Base the written advice on reasonable factual and legal assumptions
- Reasonably consider all relevant facts and circumstances that the practitioner knows or reasonably should know
- Use reasonable efforts to identify the facts relevant to the written advice
- Not rely on representations, statements, findings, or agreements of the taxpayer or any other person if reliance on them would be unreasonable
- Relate applicable law and authorities to the facts
- Not take into account whether or not the return will be audited or the matter will be raised in audit

Circular 230 also provides that the IRS will apply a "reasonable practitioner standard" to determine whether the requirements listed above have been met. In written advice related to tax shelters, the IRS is specifically directed to consider the additional risk caused by the practitioner's lack of knowledge of the taxpayer's particular circumstances when determining whether a practitioner has failed to comply with this section of *Circular 230*.

STATEMENTS ON STANDARDS FOR TAX SERVICES

Tax advisors confronted with ethical issues frequently turn to a professional organization for guidance. Although the guidelines set forth by such organizations are not *legally* enforceable, they carry significant moral weight, and may be cited in a negligence lawsuit as the proper "standard of care" for tax practitioners. They also may provide grounds for the termination or suspension of one's professional license. One such set of guidelines is

---

[97] *Treasury Department Circular 230* (2014), Secs. 10.21 and 10.22.
[98] Ibid., Sec. 10.21.
[99] Ibid., Sec. 10.22.
[100] Ibid., Sec. 10.34.
[101] Ibid., Sec. 10.33.
[102] Ibid., Sec. 10.37.

the *Statements on Standards for Tax Services* (SSTSs), issued by the American Institute of Certified Public Accountants (AICPA) and reproduced in Appendix E.[103] Inspired by the principles of honesty and integrity, these guidelines define standards of ethical conduct for CPAs engaged in tax practice. In the words of the AICPA:

> In our view, practice standards are the hallmark of calling one's self a professional. Members should fulfill their responsibilities as professionals by instituting and maintaining standards against which their professional performance can be measured. The promulgation of practice standards also reinforces one of the core values of the AICPA Vision—that CPAs conduct themselves with honesty and integrity.[104]

The SSTSs are professionally enforceable; that is, they may be enforced through a disciplinary proceeding conducted by the AICPA, which may terminate or suspend a practitioner from AICPA membership.

Statement No. 1 defines the circumstances under which a CPA should (or should not) recommend a tax return position to a taxpayer. It also prescribes a course of conduct that the CPA should follow when making such a recommendation. Specifically,

- A member should not recommend that a tax return position be taken with respect to any item unless the member has a good-faith belief that the position has a realistic possibility of being sustained administratively or judicially on its merits if challenged.
- [A] member may recommend a tax return position that the member concludes that the position has a reasonable basis and the member recommends that the taxpayer appropriately disclose the position.
- When recommending tax return positions and when preparing or signing a return on which a tax return position is taken, a member should, when relevant, advise the taxpayer regarding potential penalty consequences of such tax return position and the opportunity, if any, to avoid such penalties through disclosure.

The *realistic possibility standard* set forth in Statement No. 1 parallels that of Sec. 6694. Regulation Sec. 1.6694-2(b)(2) states that the relevant authorities for the realistic-possibility-of-being-sustained test are the same as those that apply in the substantial authority context. The IRS will treat a position as having met the realistic possibility of being sustained on "its merits" if a reasonable and well informed analysis by a person knowledgeable in the tax law would lead such a person to conclude that the position has approximately a one in three, or greater, likelihood of being sustained on its merits.

However, the *realistic possibility standard* set forth in Statement No. 1 differs from the IRC standard in that it allows as support for a tax return position well-reasoned articles or treatises, in addition to primary tax authorities. The IRC standard allows as support for a tax return position only primary tax authorities.

Statement No. 2 sets forth the standards when signing the preparer's declaration that the return is true, correct, and complete. Specifically,

- A member should make a reasonable effort to obtain all necessary information from the taxpayer to provide answers to all questions on the tax return.
- A request for information may necessitate a disclosure for the return to be considered complete or to avoid penalties.

Statement No. 3 addresses (1) whether tax practitioners can reasonably rely on information supplied to them by the taxpayer, (2) when they have a duty to examine or verify such information, (3) when they have a duty to make inquiries of the taxpayer, and (4) what information they should consider in preparing a tax return. Specifically,

[103] The standards were last revised in 2009, effective January 1, 2010.

[104] Letter to AICPA members by David A. Lifson, Chair, AICPA Tax Executive Committee, and Gerald W. Padwe, Vice President, AICPA Taxation Section (April 18, 2000).

- In preparing or signing a return, a member may in good faith rely, without verification, on information furnished by the taxpayer or by third parties. However, a member should make reasonable inquiries if the information furnished appears to be incorrect, incomplete, or inconsistent either on its face or on the basis of other facts known to a member.
- If the tax law or regulations impose a condition with respect to the deductibility or other tax treatment of an item . . . a member should make appropriate inquiries to determine the member's satisfaction whether such condition has been met.
- When preparing a tax return, a member should consider information actually known to that member from the tax return of another taxpayer if the information is relevant to that tax return and its consideration is necessary to properly prepare that tax return.

Note that the duty to verify arises only when taxpayer provided information appears "strange" on its face. Otherwise, the tax practitioner has no duty to investigate taxpayer facts and circumstances. The taxpayer has the ultimate responsibility for the contents of the return.

Statement No. 4 defines the circumstances in which a tax practitioner may use estimates in preparing a tax return. In addition, it cautions practitioners as to the manner in which they may use estimates. Specifically,

- A member may advise on estimates used in the preparation of a tax return, but the taxpayer has the responsibility to provide the estimated data. Appraisals or valuations are not considered estimates.
- [A] member may use the taxpayer's estimates in the preparation of a tax return if it is not practical to obtain exact data and if the member determines that the estimates are reasonable. If the taxpayer's estimates are used, they should be presented in a manner that does not imply greater accuracy than exists.

Notwithstanding this statement, the tax practitioner may not use estimates when such use is implicitly prohibited by the IRC. For example, Sec. 274(d) disallows deductions for certain expenses (e.g., meals and entertainment) unless the taxpayer can substantiate the expenses with adequate records or sufficient corroborating information. The documentation requirement effectively precludes the taxpayer from estimating such expenses and the practitioner from using such estimates.

Statement No. 5 sets forth the standards for members in recommending a tax return position that departs from the position determined in an administrative proceeding or in a court decision with respect to the taxpayer's prior return.

Statement No. 6 defines a tax practitioner's duty when he or she becomes aware of an error in the taxpayer's return or a return that is the subject of an administrative proceeding. Specifically,

- A member should inform the taxpayer promptly upon becoming aware of (1) an error in a previously filed return, (2) an error in a return that is the subject of an administrative proceeding (e.g., an IRS audit or appeals conference), or (3) a taxpayer's failure to file a required return. A member should advise the taxpayer of the potential consequences of the error and recommend the corrective measures to be taken. The member is not obligated to inform the taxing authority, and a member may not do so without the taxpayer's permission, except when required by law.
- If a member is requested to prepare the current year's return and the taxpayer has not taken appropriate action to correct an error in a prior year's return, the member should consider whether to withdraw from preparing the return and whether to continue a professional or employment relationship with the taxpayer.
- If a member is representing a taxpayer in an administrative proceeding with respect to a return that contains an error of which the member is aware, the member should request the taxpayer's agreement to disclose the error to the taxing authority.

This statement implies that the tax practitioner's primary duty is to the taxpayer, not the taxing authority. Furthermore, upon the taxpayer's failure to correct a tax related error, the practitioner may exercise discretion in deciding whether or not to terminate the professional relationship. The standard also permits the member to provide oral recommendations, but the member should document any oral advice.

Finally, Statement No. 7 addresses the quality of advice provided by the tax practitioner, what consequences presumably ensue from such advice, and whether the practitioner has a duty to update advice to reflect subsequent developments. Specifically,

- A member should use professional judgment to ensure that tax advice provided to a taxpayer reflects competence and appropriately serves the taxpayer's needs. When communicating tax advice to a taxpayer in writing, a member should comply with relevant taxing authorities' standards applicable to written tax advice. A member should use professional judgment about any need to document oral advice.
- A member should assume that tax advice provided to a taxpayer will affect the manner in which the matters or transactions considered would be reported on the taxpayer's tax returns.
- A member has no obligation to communicate with a taxpayer when subsequent developments affect advice previously provided with respect to significant matters except while assisting a taxpayer in implementing procedures or plans associated with the advice provided or when a member undertakes an obligation by specific agreement.

The statement implies that practitioner-taxpayer dealings should not be casual, nonconsensual, or open ended. Rather, they should be professional, contractual, and definite. Oral advice may be appropriate in routine matters, but written communications are recommended in important, complicated, or significant dollar value transactions. When giving tax advice, a member should consider the standards in SSTS No. 1.

TAX ACCOUNTING AND TAX LAW

Accountants and lawyers frequently deal with the same issues. These issues pertain to incorporation and merger, bankruptcy and liquidation, purchases and sales, gains and losses, compensation and benefits, and estate planning. Both types of professionals are competent to practice in many of the same areas. In some areas, however, accountants are more competent than lawyers, and in other areas, lawyers are more competent than accountants. What are these areas, and where does one draw the line?

In the realm of federal taxation, achieving a clear delineation always has been difficult. When an accountant prepares a tax return, he or she invariably delves into the intricacies of tax law. When a lawyer gives tax advice, he or she frequently applies principles of accounting. Toward clarifying the responsibilities of each, the AICPA and American Bar Association have issued the *Statement on Practice in the Field of Federal Income Taxation*.[105] This statement indicates five areas in which CPAs and attorneys are equally competent to practice and several areas in which each is exclusively competent to practice. The areas of mutual competence are as follows:

- Preparing federal income tax returns
- Determining the tax effects of proposed transactions
- Representing taxpayers before the Treasury Department
- Practicing before the U.S. Tax Court
- Preparing claims for refunds

Areas in which an accountant is exclusively competent to practice include:

- Resolving accounting issues
- Preparing financial statements included in financial reports or submitted with tax returns
- Advising clients as to accounting methods and procedures
- Classifying transactions and summarizing them in monetary terms
- Interpreting financial results

[105] Appendix A of the Joint Statement of American Bar Association and American Instituite of Certified Public Accountants, *Journal of Accountancy* (Aug. 1982).

Areas in which an attorney is exclusively competent to practice include:

- Resolving issues of law
- Preparing legal documents such as agreements, conveyances, trust instruments, and wills
- Advising clients as to the sufficiency or effect of legal documents
- Taking the necessary steps to create, amend, or dissolve a partnership, corporation, or trust
- Representing clients in criminal investigations

State bar and CPA associations have issued similar guidelines for their constituencies, and the courts generally have followed these and the national guidelines.[106]

What happens if an accountant oversteps his or her professional bounds? The transgression may constitute the **unauthorized practice of law.** The unauthorized practice of law involves the engagement, by nonlawyers, in professional activities traditionally reserved for the bar. In most states, it is actionable by injunction, damages, or both. Allegations of the unauthorized practice of law typically arise in the context of a billing dispute.[107] The CPA bills a client for professional services, and the client disputes the bill on the ground that the accountant engaged in the unauthorized practice of law. Occasionally, the court sustains the client's allegation and thus denies the accountant the amount in dispute. With this and the public interest in mind, accountants should always confine their practice to areas in which they are most competent.

ACCOUNTANT-CLIENT PRIVILEGE

ADDITIONAL COMMENT

The protected status of client prepared tax accrual workpapers is still being litigated. In 2009, the U.S. Court of Appeals for the First Circuit in *United States v. Textron Inc.*, 104 AFTR 2d 2009-5719, held that the IRS can obtain tax accrual workpapers. Given the complex issues involved and conflicts among the circuits, additional litigation is likely.

According to judicial doctrine, certain communications between an attorney and a client are "privileged," i.e., nondiscoverable in the course of litigation. In 1998, Congress extended this privilege to similar communications between a federally authorized tax advisor and a client. A federally authorized tax advisor includes a certified public accountant.

The accountant-client privilege is similar to the attorney-client privilege in two respects. First, it encompasses communications for the purpose of obtaining or giving professional advice. Second, it excludes communications for the sole purpose of preparing a tax return. The accountant-client privilege is dissimilar in three respects. First, it is limited only to *tax* advice. Second, it may be asserted only in a noncriminal tax proceeding before a federal court or the IRS. Third, it excludes written communications between an accountant and a corporation regarding a tax shelter. A tax shelter is any plan or arrangement, a significant purpose of which is tax avoidance or evasion.

EXAMPLE C:15-40 ▶ Alec, Chief Financial Officer of MultiCorp, has solicited the advice of his tax accountant, Louise, concerning a civil dispute with the IRS. Louise has advised Alec in a series of letters spanning the course of five months. An IRS appeals officer asks Louise if he can review the letters. Louise may refuse the officer's request because her professional advice was offered in anticipation of civil litigation and therefore is "privileged." ◀

EXAMPLE C:15-41 ▶ Assume the same facts as in Example C:15-40 except Louise sends Alec a letter concerning a foreign sales scheme. Because Louise communicates tax advice to a corporation concerning a "tax shelter" and because this communication is written, it is *not* privileged. ◀

The creation of an accountant-client privilege reflects Congress' belief that the selection of a tax advisor should not hinge on the question of privilege. It ensures that all tax advice is accorded the same protection regardless of the tax advisor's professional status.

---

[106] See for example *Lathrop v. Donahue*, 367 U.S. 820, 81 S. Ct. 1826 (1961), *U.S. v. Gordon Buttorff*, 56 AFTR 2d 85-5247, 85-1 USTC ¶9435 (5th Cir., 1985), *Morton L. Simons v. Edgar T. Bellinger*, 643 F.2d 774, 207 U.S. App. D.C. 24 (1980), *Emilio L. Ippolito v. The State of Florida*, 824 F. Supp. 1562, 1993 U.S. Dist. LEXIS 13091 (M.D. Fla., 1993), *In re Application of New Jersey Society of Certified Public Accountants*, 102 N.J. 231, 507 A.2d 711 (1986).

[107] See for example, *In re Bercu*, 299 N.Y. 728, 87 N.E.2d 451 (1949), and *Agran v. Shapiro*, 46 AFTR 896, 127 Cal. App.2d 807 (App. Dept. Super. Ct., 1954).

PROBLEM MATERIALS

DISCUSSION QUESTIONS

C:15-1 Describe how the IRS verifies tax returns at its service centers.

C:15-2 Name some of the IRS administrative pronouncements.

C:15-3 a. Through what programs has the IRS gathered data to develop its DIF statistical models?
b. How do these programs differ?
c. How has the IRS used these programs to select returns for audit?

C:15-4 On his individual return, Al reports salary and exemptions for himself and seven dependents. His itemized deductions consist of mortgage interest, real estate taxes, and a large loss from breeding dogs. On his individual return, Ben reports self-employment income, a substantial loss from partnership operations, a casualty loss deduction equal to 25% of his AGI, charitable contribution deductions equal to 30% of his AGI, and an exemption for himself. Al's return reports higher taxable income than does Ben's. Which return is more likely to be selected for audit under the DIF program? Explain.

C:15-5 The IRS notifies Tom that it will audit his current year return for an interest deduction. The IRS audited Tom's return two years ago for a charitable contribution deduction. The IRS, however, did not assess a deficiency for the prior year return. Is any potential relief available to Tom with respect to the audit of his current year return?

C:15-6 The IRS informs Brad that it will audit his current year employee business expenses. Brad just met with a revenue agent who contends that Brad owes $775 of additional taxes. Discuss briefly the procedural alternatives available to Brad.

C:15-7 What course(s) of action is (are) available to a taxpayer upon receipt of the following notices:
a. The 30-day letter?
b. The 90-day letter?
c. IRS rejection of a claim for a refund?

C:15-8 List the courts in which a taxpayer can begin tax-related litigation.

C:15-9 Why do taxpayers frequently litigate in the Tax Court?

C:15-10 In what situations is a protest letter necessary?

C:15-11 What information should be included in a request for a private letter ruling?

C:15-12 What conditions must the taxpayer meet to shift the burden of proof to the IRS?

C:15-13 In what circumstances will the IRS rule on estate tax issues?

C:15-14 On which of the following issues will the IRS likely issue a private letter ruling and why? In your answer, assume that no other IRS pronouncement addresses the issue and that pertinent Treasury Regulations are not forthcoming.
a. Whether the taxpayer correctly calculated a capital gain reported on last year's tax return.
b. The tax consequences of using stock derivatives in a corporate reorganization.
c. Whether a mathematical formula correctly calculates the fair market value of a stock derivative.
d. Whether the cost of an Internet course that purports to improve existing employment skills may be deducted this year as a business expense.

C:15-15 Tracy wants to take advantage of a "terrific business opportunity" by engaging in a transaction with Homer. Homer, domineering and impatient, wants Tracy to conclude the transaction within two weeks and under the terms proposed by Homer. Otherwise, Homer will offer the opportunity to another party. Tracy is unsure about the tax consequences of the proposed transaction. Would you advise Tracy to request a ruling? Explain.

C:15-16 Provide the following information relating to both individual and corporate taxpayers having a calendar year:
a. Due date for an income tax return assuming the taxpayer requests no extension.
b. Due date for the return assuming the taxpayer files an automatic extension request.

C:15-17 Your client wants to know whether she must file any documents for an automatic extension to file her tax return. What do you tell her?

C:15-18 A client believes that obtaining an extension for filing an income tax return would give him additional time to pay the tax at no additional cost. Is the client correct?

C:15-19 Briefly explain the rules for determining the interest rate charged on tax underpayments. Is this rate the same as that for overpayments? In which months might the rate(s) change?

C:15-20 In April of the current year, Stan does not have sufficient assets to pay his tax liability for the previous year. However, he expects to pay the tax by August of the current year. He wonders if he should request an extension for filing his return instead of simply filing his return and paying the tax in August. What is your advice?

C:15-21 At what rate is the penalty for underpaying estimated taxes imposed? How is the penalty amount calculated?

C:15-22 The IRS audited Tony's return, and Tony agreed to pay additional taxes plus the negligence penalty. Is this penalty necessarily imposed on the total additional taxes that Tony owes? Explain.

C:15-23 Assume that a taxpayer owes additional taxes as a result of an audit. Give two reasons why the IRS might not impose a substantial understatement penalty on the additional amount owed.

C:15-24 Upon audit, the IRS determines Maria's tax liability to be $40,000. Maria agrees to pay a $7,000 deficiency. Will she necessarily have to pay a substantial understatement penalty? Explain.

C:15-25 Distinguish between the circumstances that give rise to the civil fraud penalty and those that give rise to the negligence penalty.

C:15-26 Distinguish between the burdens of proof the government must meet to prove civil and criminal fraud.

C:15-27 Explain why the government might bring criminal fraud charges against a taxpayer under Sec. 7206 instead of Sec. 7201. Compare the maximum penalties imposed under Secs. 7201, 7203, and 7206.

C:15-28 In general, when does the limitations period for tax returns expire? List four exceptions to the general rule.

C:15-29 What is the principal purpose of the innocent spouse provisions?

C:15-30 Is the tax return preparer limited to the person who signs the return? Explain.

C:15-31 List five IRC penalties that can be imposed on tax return preparers. Does the IRC require a CPA to verify the information a client furnishes?

C:15-32 According to *Treasury Department Circular 230,* what standard should a CPA meet to properly take a position on a tax return?

C:15-33 Under the AICPA's *Statements on Standards for Tax Services*, what is the tax practitioner's professional duty in each of the following situations?

a. Client erroneously deducts $5,000 (instead of $500) on a previous year's tax return.

b. Client refuses to file an amended return to correct the deduction error.

c. Client informs tax practitioner that client incurred $200 in out-of-pocket office supplies expenses.

d. Client informs tax practitioner that client incurred $700 in business related entertainment expenses.

e. Tax practitioner learns that the exemption amount for single taxpayers has been increased by $1,000. Client is a single taxpayer.

ISSUE IDENTIFICATION QUESTIONS

C:15-34 You are preparing the tax return of Bold Corporation, which had sales of $60 million. Bold made a $1 million expenditure for which the appropriate tax treatment—deductible or capitalizable—is a gray area. Bold's director of federal taxes and chief financial officer urgently wants to deduct the expenditure. What tax compliance issues should you consider in advising her?

C:15-35 Your client, Hank Goedert, earned $100,000 of salary and received $40,000 of dividends in the current year. His itemized deductions total $37,000. In addition, Hank received $47,000 from a relative who was his former employer. You have researched whether the $47,000 should be classified as a gift or compensation and are confident that substantial authority exists for classifying the receipt as a gift. What tax compliance issues should you consider in deciding whether to include or exclude the amount in Hank's gross income?

C:15-36 The IRS audited the tax returns of Darryl Strawberry, a former major league outfielder. It contended that, between 1986 and 1990, Strawberry earned $422,250 for autograph signings, appearances, and product endorsements, but he reported only $59,685 of income. Strawberry attributed the shortfall to his receipt of cash for autograph sessions and promotional events. He allegedly concealed the cash payments in separate bank accounts of which his CPA was unaware. What tax compliance issues regarding the alleged underreporting are pertinent?

PROBLEMS

C:15-37 *Calculation of Penalties.* Amy files her current year tax return on August 13 of the following year. She pays the amount due without requesting an extension. The tax shown on her return is $24,000. Her current year wage withholding amounts to $15,000. Amy pays no estimated taxes and claims no tax credits on her current year return.

a. What penalties will the IRS likely impose on Amy (ignoring the penalty for underpayment of estimated taxes)? Assume Amy committed no fraud and that any penalty and interest period begins on April 16.

b. On what dollar amount, and for how many days, will Amy owe interest?

C:15-38 *Calculation of Penalties.* In the preceding problem, how would your answers change if Amy instead files her return on June 18 and, on September 8 pays the amount due? Assume her wage withholding tax amounts to

a. $19,000

b. $24,500

c. How would your answer to Part a change if Amy requests an automatic extension?

C:15-39 *Calculation of Penalties.* The taxes shown on Hu's tax returns for Year 1 and Year 2 are $5,000 and $8,000, respectively. Hu's wage withholding for Year 2 was $5,200, and she paid no estimated taxes. Hu filed her Year 2 return on March 18 of Year 3, but she did not have sufficient funds to pay any taxes on that date. She paid the $2,800 balance due on June 24 of Year 4. Hu's AGI for Year 1 did not exceed $150,000. Calculate the penalties Hu owes with respect to her Year 2 tax return.

C:15-40 *Calculation of Penalties.* Ted's current year return reported a tax liability of $1,800. Ted's wage withholding for the current year was $2,200. Because of his poor memory, Ted did not file his current year return until May 28 of the following year. What penalties (if any) does Ted owe?

C:15-41 *Calculation of Penalties.* Bob, a calendar year taxpayer, files his current year individual return on July 17 of the following year without having requested an extension. His return indicates an amount due of $5,100. Bob pays this amount on November 3 of the following year. What are Bob's penalties for failing to file and failing to pay his tax on time? Assume Bob committed no fraud and that any penalty period begins on April 16.

C:15-42 *Calculation of Penalties.* Carl's tax liability for last year was $19,000, and his AGI did not exceed $150,000. Carl requests an automatic extension for filing his current year individual return but does not pay any additional tax with his extension request. By April 15 of the following year, Carl has paid $20,000 of taxes in the form of wage withholding and estimated taxes. Carl files his current year return and pays the balance of the taxes due on June 18 of the following year. What penalties will Carl owe if his current year tax is $23,000? $20,800?

C:15-43 *Determination of Interest.* Refer to the preceding problem.

a. Will Carl owe interest? If so, on what amount and for how many days? Assume that any interest period begins on April 16 of a non–leap year.
b. Assume the applicable interest rate is 6%. Compute Carl's interest payable if his current year tax is $23,000. (See a major tax service for the compounding tables.)

C:15-44 *Penalty for Underpayment of Estimated Taxes.* Ed's tax liability for last year was $24,000. Ed projects that his tax for this year will be $34,000. Ed is self-employed and, thus, will have no withholding. His AGI for last year did not exceed $150,000. How much estimated tax should Ed pay for this year to avoid the penalty for underpaying estimated taxes?

C:15-45 *Penalty for Underpayment of Estimated Taxes.* Refer to the preceding problem. Assume that Ed expects his income for this year to decline and his tax liability for this year to be only $15,000. What minimum amount of estimated taxes should Ed pay this year? What problem will Ed encounter if he pays this minimum amount and his current year income exceeds last year's because of a large capital gain realized in December of this year?

C:15-46 *Penalty for Underpayment of Estimated Taxes.* Pam's prior year (Year 1) income tax liability was $23,000. Her current year (Year 2) AGI did not exceed $150,000. On April 2 of next year (Year 3), Pam, a calendar year taxpayer, timely files her current year individual return, which indicates a $30,000 income tax liability (before reduction for withholding). In addition, the return indicates self-employment taxes of $2,600. Taxes withheld from Pam's current year (Year 2) salary total $20,000; she has paid no estimated taxes.

a. Will Pam owe a penalty for not paying sufficient estimated taxes? Explain.
b. What amount (if any) per quarter is subject to the penalty, and for what period will the penalty be imposed for each quarter's underpayment?
c. How would your answers to parts a and b change if Pam's current year (Year 2) tax liability (including self-employment taxes) instead were $17,000?

C:15-47 *Penalty for Underpayment of Estimated Taxes.* Amir's projected tax liability for the current year is $23,000. Although Amir has substantial dividend and interest income, he does not pay any estimated taxes. Amir's withholding for January through November of the current year is $1,300 per month. He wants to increase his withholding for December to avoid the penalty for underpaying estimated taxes. Amir's previous year's liability (excluding withholding) is $21,000. His previous year's AGI did not exceed $150,000. What amount should Amir have withheld from his December paycheck? Explain.

C:15-48 *Negligence Penalty.* The IRS audits Tan's individual return for the current year and assesses a $9,000 deficiency, $2,800 of which results from Tan's negligence. What is the amount of Tan's negligence penalty? Does the penalty bear interest?

C:15-49 *Negligence Penalty.* The IRS audits Pearl's current year individual return and determines that, among other errors, she negligently failed to report dividend income of $8,000. The deficiency relating to the dividends is $2,240. The IRS proposes an additional $12,000 deficiency for the other errors that do not involve negligence. What is the amount of Pearl's negligence penalty for the $14,240 in deficiencies?

C:15-50 *Substantial Understatement Penalty.* Carmen's current year individual return reports a $6,000 deduction for a questionable item not relating to a tax-shelter. Carmen does not make a disclosure regarding this item. The IRS audits Carmen's return, and she consents to a deficiency. As a result, her tax liability increases from $20,000 to $21,860. Assume Carmen lacks substantial authority for the deduction.

a. What substantial understatement penalty (if any) will be imposed?
b. Will the penalty bear interest?
c. How would your answer to Parts a and b change if Carmen reported a $20,000 deduction instead of $6,000, and her tax liability increased by $6,200 to $26,200?

C:15-51 *Substantial Understatement Penalty.* Refer to Part c of the previous problem. Assume that Carmen discloses her position, which is not frivolous. How would your original answer change assuming the item does not involve a tax shelter?

C:15-52 *Fraud Penalty.* Luis, a bachelor, owes $56,000 of additional taxes, all due to fraud.

a. What is the amount of Luis' civil fraud penalty?
b. What criminal fraud penalty might the government impose on Luis under Sec. 7201?

C:15-53 *Fraud Penalty.* Hal and Wanda, his wife, are in the 35% marginal tax bracket in the current year. Wanda fraudulently omits from their joint return $50,000 of gross income. Hal does not participate in or know of her fraudulent act. Hal, however, overstates his deductions by $10,000 because of an oversight.

a. If the government successfully proves fraud in a civil suit against Wanda, what fines and/or penalties might she owe? If Hal and Wanda establish that the overstatement is not attributable to fraud, can the government impose a civil fraud penalty on Hal?
b. If the government successfully proves fraud in a criminal suit against Wanda, what fines or penalties might she owe? Could she or Hal be sentenced to prison?

C:15-54 *Statute of Limitations.* Frank, a calendar year taxpayer, reports $100,000 of gross income and $60,000 of taxable income on his Year 1 return, which he files on March 12 of Year 2. He fails to report on the return a $52,000 long-term capital gain and a $10,000 short-term capital loss. When does the limitations period for the government's collecting the tax deficiency expire if

a. Frank's omission results from an oversight?
b. His omission results from a willful attempt to evade the tax?

C:15-55 *Statute of Limitations.* Refer to the previous problem. Assume Frank subsequently commits fraud with respect to his Year 1 return as late as October 8 of Year 3. When does the limitations period for charging Frank with criminal tax fraud expire?

C:15-56 *Claim for Refund.* Maria, a calendar year taxpayer, files her Year 1 individual return on March 12 of Year 2 and pays the amount of tax due. She later discovers that she overlooked some deductions that she should have reported on the return. By what date must she file a claim for refund?

C:15-57 *Innocent Spouse Provisions.* Wilma earns no income in the current year but files a joint return with her husband, Hank. The return reports $40,000 of gross income and AGI, and $24,000 of taxable income. Hank realized $12,000 of gambling winnings (no losses) in the current year but failed to report the winnings on the return. Wilma does not know about Hank's gambling activities, much less his winnings. The IRS audits the return and assesses additional taxes. Is Wilma entitled to innocent spouse relief? Explain.

C:15-58 *Innocent Spouse Provisions.* Joe and Joan file a joint return for the current year. They are in the 35% marginal tax bracket. Unbeknownst to Joe, Joan fails to report on the return the $8,000 value of a prize she won. She, however, used the prize to buy Joe a new boat. Is Joe entitled to innocent spouse relief? Explain.

C:15-59 *Unauthorized Practice of Law.* Your client, Meade Technical Solutions, proposes to merge with Dealy Cyberlabs. In advance of the merger, you (a) issue an opinion concerning the FMV of Dealy, (b) prepare pro forma financials for the merged entity to be, (c) draft Meade shareholder resolutions approving the proposed merger, (d) file a shareholder proxy statement with the U.S. Securities and Exchange Commission, and (e) advise Meade's board of directors concerning the advantages of a Type A versus a Type B reorganization. Which of these activities, if any, constitutes the unauthorized practice of law?

C:15-60 *Unauthorized Practice of Law.* Your client, Envirocosmetics, recently has filed for bankruptcy. In the course of bankruptcy proceedings, you (a) prepare a plan of reorganization that alters the rights of preferred stockholders, (b) notify the Envirocosmetics' creditors of an impending bulk transfer of the company's assets, (c) review IRS secured claims against these assets, (d) restructure the company's debt by reducing its principal amount and extending its maturity, (e) advise the bankruptcy court as to how this restructuring will impact the company's NOLs. Which of these activities, if any, constitutes the unauthorized practice of law?

C:15-61 *Accountant-Client Privilege.* Which of the following communications between an accountant and client are privileged?

a. For tax preparation purposes only, client informs the accountant that she contributed $10,000 to a homeless shelter.
b. Client informs the accountant that he forgot to report on his tax return the $5,000 value of a prize and asks how he should correct the error.
c. Client informs the accountant that she no longer will pay alimony to her ex-husband.

C:15-62 *Accountant-Client Privilege.* Which of the following communications between an accountant and client are *not* privileged?

a. In a closed-door meeting, the accountant orally advises the client to set up a foreign subsidiary to shift taxable income to a low-tax jurisdiction.
b. In a closed-door meeting, the accountant submits to the client a plan for shifting taxable income to a low-tax jurisdiction.
c. In soliciting professional advice relating to criminal fraud, the client informs the accountant that he (the client) lied to the IRS.

COMPREHENSIVE PROBLEM

C:15-63 This year, Ark Corporation acquired substantially all the voting stock of BioTech Consultants, Inc. for cash. Subsequent to the acquisition, Ark's chief financial officer, Jonathan Cohen, approached Edith Murphy, Ark's tax advisor, with a question: Could Ark amortize the "general educational skills" of BioTech's employees? Edith researched the issue but found no primary authorities on point. She did, however, find a tax journal article, co-authored by two prominent academics, that endorsed amortizing "general educational skills" for tax purposes. The article referred to numerous primary authorities that support the amortization of "technical skills," but not "general educational skills." Edith consulted these authorities directly. Based on her research, Edith in good faith advised Jonathan that Ark could amortize the "general educational skills" over a 15-year period. In so doing, has Edith met the "realistic possibility standard" of

a. The IRC?
b. The AICPAs *Statements on Standards for Tax Services* (see Appendix E)?

TAX STRATEGY PROBLEM

C:15-64 The IRS is disputing a deduction reported on your Year 1 tax return, which you filed on April 12 of Year 2. On April 4 of Year 5, the IRS audit agent asks you to waive the statute of limitations for the entire return so as to give her additional time to obtain a Technical Advice Memorandum. The agent proposes in return for the waiver a "carrot"—the prospect of an offer in compromise—and a "stick"—the possibility of a higher penalty. Although you have substantial authority for the deduction, you consider the following alternatives: (1) waive the statute of limitations for the entire return, (2) waive the statute of limitations for the deduction only, or (3) do not waive the statute of limitations in any way, shape, or form. Which alternative should you choose, and why?

CASE STUDY PROBLEM

C:15-65 A long-time client, Horace Haney, wishes to avoid currently recognizing revenue in a particular transaction. A recently finalized Treasury Regulation provides that, in such a transaction, revenue should be currently recognized. Horace insists that you report no revenue from the transaction and, furthermore, that you make no disclosure about contravening the regulation. The IRC is unclear about whether the income should be recognized currently. No relevant cases, revenue rulings, or letter rulings deal specifically with the transaction in question.

Required: Discuss whether you, a CPA, should prepare Horace's tax return and comply with his wishes. Assume that recognizing the income in question would increase Horace's tax liability by about 25%.

TAX RESEARCH PROBLEMS

C:15-66 Art is named executor of the Estate of Stu Stone, his father, who died on February 3 of the current year. Art hires Larry to be the estate's attorney. Larry advises Art that the estate must file an estate tax return but does not mention the due date. Art, a pharmacist, has no experience in tax matters other than preparing his own tax returns. Art provides Larry with all the necessary information by June 15 of the current year. On six occasions, Art contacts Larry to check on the progress of the estate tax return. Each time, Larry assures

Art that "everything is under control." On November 15, Art contacts Larry for the seventh time. He learns that because of a clerical oversight, the return—due on November 2 of the current year—has not been filed. Larry apologizes and says he will make sure that an associate promptly files the return. The return, which reports an estate tax liability of $75,200, is filed on December 7 of the current year. Your manager requests that you prepare a memorandum addressing whether the estate will owe a failure-to-file penalty. Your manager suggests that, at a minimum, you consult

- IRC Sec. 6151(a)
- *U.S. v. Robert W. Boyle,* 55 AFTR 2d 85-1535, 85-1 USTC ¶13,602 (USSC, 1985)

C:15-67 Harold and Betty, factory workers who until this year prepared their own individual tax returns, purchased an investment from a broker last year. Although they reviewed the prospectus for the investment, the broker explained the more complicated features of the investment. Early this year, they struggled to prepare their individual return for last year but, because of the investment, found it too complicated to complete. Consequently, they hired a CPA to prepare the return. The CPA deducted losses generated from the investment against income that Harold and Betty generated from other sources. The IRS audited the return for last year and contended that the loss is not deductible. After consulting their CPA, who further considered the tax consequences of the investment, Harold and Betty agreed that the loss is not deductible and consented to paying the deficiency. The IRS also contended that the couple owes the substantial understatement penalty because they did not disclose the value of the investment on their return and did not have substantial authority for their position. Assume you are representing the taxpayers before the IRS and intend to argue that they should be exempted from the substantial understatement penalty. Your tax manager reminds you to consult Secs. 6662 and 6664 when conducting your research.

C:15-68 Gene employed his attorney to draft identical trust instruments for each of his three minor children: Judy (age 5), Terry (age 7), and Grady (age 11). Each trust instrument names the Fourth City Bank as trustee and states that the trust is irrevocable. It provides that, until the beneficiary reaches age 21, the trustee at its discretion is to pay income and/or principal (corpus) to the beneficiary. Upon reaching age 21, the beneficiary will have 60 days in which to request that the trust assets be paid over to him or her. Otherwise, the assets will stay in the trust until the beneficiary reaches age 35. The beneficiary also is granted a general testamentary power of appointment over the trust assets. If the beneficiary dies before the trust terminates and does not exercise his or her power of appointment (because, for example, he or she dies without a will), trust assets will be distributed to family members in accordance with state intestacy laws. Each trust will be funded with property valued at $100,000. Before he signs the instruments, Gene wants to obtain a ruling from the IRS concerning whether the trusts qualify for the annual gift tax exclusion. Your task is to prepare a request for a letter ruling.

A partial list of research sources is

- IRC Secs. 2503(b) and (c)
- Reg. Sec. 25.2503-4
- Rev. Rul. 67-270, 1967-2 C.B. 349
- Rev. Rul. 74-43, 1974-1 C.B. 285
- Rev. Rul. 81-7, 1981-1 C.B. 474

C:15-69 On April 15 of Year 2, Adam and Renee Tyler jointly filed a Year 1 return that reported AGI of $68,240 ($20,500 attributable to Renee) and a tax liability of $3,050. They paid this amount in a timely fashion. On their return, the Tylers claimed a $18,405 deduction for Adam's distributive share of a partnership loss. If not for the loss, the Tylers' tax liability would have been $8,358. In the previous year, Adam had withdrawn $20,000 cash from the partnership, which he used to buy Renee a new car. Although Renee, a marketing consultant, is not active in the partnership business, she has worked for the partnership as a part-time receptionist. Adam and his partner (who incidentally is Renee's brother) failed to file a partnership return for Year 1. Upon audit, the IRS discovered that the Year 1 partnership records were missing. In Year 3, Adam had a heart attack. He remains in serious condition. Unable to reach Adam, the IRS sends Renee a 30-day letter proposing a $5,308 deficiency. She intends to protest. Your supervisor has asked you to write a memorandum discussing Renee's potential liabilities and defenses. In your memorandum, you should consult the following authorities:

- IRC Secs. 6013 and 6662
- *Rebecca Jo Reser v. CIR,* 79 AFTR 2d 97-2743, 97-1 USTC ¶50,416 (5th Cir., 1997)

C:15-70 A colleague comes to you with the following investment proposal that he would like to market for Client:

- Client obtains cash of $60,000 from Bank.
- Bank loan agreement specifies that $40,000 of this amount represents principal; the remaining $20,000 represents interest.
- Client contributes the $60,000 cash to Partnership, which agrees to assume Client's $40,000 debt.
- Under Sec. 752, Partnership's debt assumption is treated as a distribution of money that reduces Client's basis in partnership interest from $60,000 to $20,000.
- Partnership invests the $60,000 in a resort hotel project.
- Before the project comes onstream, Client sells partnership interest for $15,000.

Net result: Partnership, not Client, is responsible for repayment of Bank loan. Client realizes a $5,000 capital loss without having spent any of its own funds.

Prepare a memorandum that sets forth the tax and reporting implications of this investment proposal. At a minimum, consult the following authorities:

- IRC Secs. 6707A and 6111
- Reg. Secs. 1.6011-4 and 301.6112-1
- Notice 2000-44, 2000-2 C.B. 255

C:15-71 Five years ago, Spyros Dietrich wanted to sell IMPEXT, Inc., his wholly owned import-export business. He also wanted to avoid recognizing the substantial gain that would result from his selling his IMPEXT shares on the open market. Spyros' basis in the shares ($100,000) was well below their market value ($600,000).

To avoid gain recognition, Spyros formed the SH Partnership with his brother Hussein. To capitalize the partnership, Spyros transferred all his IMPEXT shares to SH in exchange for 99 SH Partnership units. Hussein transferred $100 cash in exchange for one SH Partnership unit. Subsequently, Spyros formed Fu Yung, Inc., an S corporation, and transferred his 99 SH Partnership units to Fu Yung in exchange for 99 Fu Yung shares.

Under Sec. 708, the transfer to Fu Yung technically caused a dissolution of SH. However, Spyros and Hussein agreed to continue the SH "business" in reconstituted form as the FYH Partnership. Thereupon, FYH elected under Sec. 754 to step up its basis in the IMPEXT shares from $100,000 to $600,000. Then FYH sold the IMPEXT shares to disinterested investor Gonzalez for $615,000, thereby realizing only a $15,000 gain. Ninety-nine percent of this gain passed through to Spyros' separate return via Fu Yung and FYH.

The series of transactions went unnoticed by the IRS until the current year, when it audited Spyros' return. On that return, Spyros reported $525,000 of ordinary income and $14,850 (i.e., 99% of $15,000) of capital gain. When the IRS alleged that Spyros had substantially understated his income, Spyros raised the "statute of limitations" as a defense. Is the IRS correct in its allegation? If so, is it precluded by the statute of limitations from collecting additional taxes from Spyro?

Before answering these questions, please consult the following sources:

- IRC Secs. 708, 704, 6501
- *Brandon Ridge Partners v. U.S.*, 100 AFTR 2d 2007-5347, 2007-2 USTC ¶50,573 (DC FL, July 30, 2007)

CHAPTER

16

U.S. TAXATION OF FOREIGN-RELATED TRANSACTIONS

LEARNING OBJECTIVES

After studying this chapter, you should be able to

1. Summarize the principles underlying U.S. authority to tax foreign-related transactions
2. Determine the foreign tax credit available to U.S. taxpayers and calculate the foreign earned income exclusion available to U.S. individuals working abroad
3. Establish whether a foreign citizen is a U.S. resident or nonresident alien and calculate the U.S. tax liability of a nonresident alien
4. Apply the tax rules that pertain to foreign corporations and their U.S. shareholders
5. Identify tax planning opportunities for U.S. taxpayers engaged in foreign transactions and operations
6. Comply with procedures for foreign transactions
7. Recognize the financial statement implications of various international transactions

CHAPTER OUTLINE

When making their business decisions, taxpayers must consider the potential U.S. tax consequences of international transactions. These consequences impact whether a foreign business should be conducted directly by a U.S. corporation or indirectly through a foreign subsidiary. They also impact the placement and compensation of U.S. employees abroad. In many cases, these employees can exempt part or all of their foreign salaries and housing allowances from U.S. taxation. Such an exemption reduces the cost of employing American citizens abroad and makes their employers more competitive.

This chapter presents a general overview of the U.S. taxation of cross-border and foreign-related transactions. Coverage also includes the U.S. taxation of income derived from domestic and foreign activities conducted by U.S. citizens, resident and nonresident aliens, and domestic and foreign entities.

JURISDICTION TO TAX

OBJECTIVE 1

Summarize the principles underlying U.S. authority to tax foreign-related transactions

U.S. authority to tax foreign-related transactions is based on three factors:

- The taxpayer's country of citizenship
- The taxpayer's country of residence
- Where income is earned

The U.S. tax laws prescribe different tax treatments of income items according to the taxpayer's country of citizenship or country of organization. The United States taxes U.S. citizens and corporations[1] on their worldwide income and taxes foreign citizens and corporations primarily on income earned within U.S. territorial limits.

Individuals who are not U.S. citizens are called "aliens." The U.S. income tax laws divide aliens into two classes: resident and nonresident. A **resident alien** is an individual who resides in the United States *but* is not a U.S. citizen. A **nonresident alien** is an individual who resides outside the United States *and* is not a U.S. citizen.

TYPICAL MISCONCEPTION

Many people believe that income earned outside the United States is not subject to taxation by the United States. This belief is incorrect. U.S. citizens, resident aliens, and domestic corporations are taxed by the United States on their worldwide income.

Like U.S. citizens and domestic corporations, resident aliens are taxed on their worldwide income. In general, the same rules apply to the various classes of income they earn, whether the income is earned in the United States, a foreign country, or a U.S. possession. However, certain items of income earned in foreign countries or U.S. possessions are subject to special treatment.

- Compensation received by a U.S. citizen or resident alien who works in a foreign country for an extended period of time is eligible for a special inflation adjusted annual exclusion of up to $101,300 in 2016 and $102,100 in 2017.
- The income taxes paid by a U.S. taxpayer to a foreign country or a U.S. possession may be credited against the U.S. tax liability.

To some extent, the tax treatment accorded nonresident aliens and foreign corporations depends on whether they conducted a trade or business in the United States at some time during the year. If they did not conduct a U.S. trade or business, the nonresident aliens and foreign corporations are taxed only on their U.S.-source investment income. If they did conduct a U.S. trade or business, the nonresident aliens and foreign corporations are taxed on both their U.S.-source investment income and their U.S.-source (and certain foreign-source) income that is connected with the conduct of the U.S. trade or business. Trade or business and investment income earned outside the United States by nonresident aliens and foreign corporations generally escape U.S. taxation.

An overview of international tax issues relating to the various types of tax entities that operate in the United States is presented in Table C:16-1. This table adds structure to the following discussion of the U.S. tax rules that apply to foreign-related transactions.

[1] Secs. 7701(a)(3) and (4). A domestic corporation is a corporation created or organized under federal law or the laws of one of the 50 states or the District of Columbia. All other corporations are **foreign corporations**. A domestic corporation includes a noncorporate entity that elects under the check-the-box regulations to be taxed as a corporation. See Chapter C:2.

▼ TABLE C:16-1
Overview of International Tax Issues

Entity Form	U.S. Tax Base	U.S. Tax Issues
Individuals:		
U.S. citizen	Worldwide income	1, 2, 3
U.S. resident alien	Worldwide income	1, 2, 3
U.S. nonresident alien	U.S. territorial	3, 4
Corporations:		
U.S. parent with foreign branch	Worldwide income	1, 3
U.S. parent with foreign subsidiary	Worldwide income	1, 5, 6
Foreign parent with U.S. branch	U.S. territorial	3, 4, 6, 7
Foreign parent with U.S. subsidiary	Worldwide income	1, 3, 4, 6

U.S. Tax Issues Listing

1. Foreign tax credit
2. Foreign earned income exclusion
3. U.S. income tax liability
4. Withholding of U.S. taxes on payments by U.S. persons to non-U.S. persons
5. Deferral of U.S. taxation of foreign profits
6. Transfer pricing
7. Branch profits tax

Taxation of U.S. Citizens and Resident Aliens

OBJECTIVE 2

Determine the foreign tax credit available to U.S. taxpayers and calculate the foreign earned income exclusion available to U.S. individuals working abroad

This section examines two foreign tax provisions applicable to U.S. citizens and resident aliens: the foreign tax credit and the foreign-earned income exclusion. Both provisions alleviate the double taxation of income earned by these individuals in a foreign country.

FOREIGN TAX CREDIT

The **foreign tax credit** alleviates double taxation by allowing U.S. taxpayers to credit income taxes paid or accrued to a foreign country (including its political subdivisions such as provinces and cities) or a U.S. possession[2] against their U.S. income tax liability. The foreign tax credit reduces a U.S. taxpayer's total effective tax rate on income earned in foreign countries or U.S. possessions to the higher of the U.S. or the foreign tax rate.

Question: The United States uses the foreign tax credit as its principal mechanism for alleviating double taxation. What are the advantages and disadvantages of the foreign tax credit?

*Solution: **Advantages:*** The foreign tax credit is based on the premise that all taxable income should be subject to the same effective tax rate no matter where it is earned. Thus, it is "tax neutral" in that it advances the proposition that business decisions should not be motivated by tax considerations. The credit system requires that a taxpayer report the income, file a tax return, and apply the credit to reduce his or her U.S. tax liability. This requirement

[2] For Sec. 901 purposes, U.S. possessions include Puerto Rico, the Virgin Islands, Guam, the Northern Mariana Islands, and American Samoa. See Reg. Sec. 1.901-1(g)(4).

ensures that taxpayers report to the U.S. tax authorities their non-U.S. income taxed in a foreign jurisdiction. It also provides additional U.S. tax revenues to the extent that U.S. tax rates are higher than foreign tax rates.

Disadvantages: The reporting requirement increases compliance costs for U.S. taxpayers. The credit provides an incentive for foreign governments to raise their tax rates to the level of U.S. tax rates (in the form of "soak up taxes"). Although such increases do not alter a taxpayer's worldwide tax costs, they do increase tax revenues accruing to a foreign treasury at the expense of the U.S. Treasury.

KEY POINT

This type of double taxation results when two different jurisdictions tax the same stream of income rather than one jurisdiction taxing the same stream of income twice (such as dividends a shareholder receives from a C corporation).

Creditable Taxes. Income taxes paid or accrued to a foreign country or a U.S. possession may be credited against the U.S. tax liability. Other foreign taxes are deductible under the rules of Sec. 164, which are explained in Chapter I:7 of the companion volume, *Prentice Hall's Federal Taxation: Individuals*. The IRS regularly issues pronouncements relating to the creditability of certain foreign taxes.[3] These pronouncements save taxpayers time and effort in determining whether a specific tax is creditable. Major tax services summarize these pronouncements, as well as judicial decisions concerning creditable taxes.

REAL-WORLD EXAMPLE

The foreign tax credit is the largest U.S. tax credit. In 2013, U.S. corporations claimed $118.3 billion in foreign tax credits, which is nearly 6 times larger than their general business credits. For corporations that claimed these credits, the two credits reduced corporations' U.S. tax liability by 42%.

Eligibility for the Credit. Section 901(a) permits U.S. citizens and resident aliens to elect to claim a foreign tax credit for income taxes paid or accrued to a foreign country or a U.S. possession. This type of tax credit is known as a *direct credit.* Most taxpayers annually elect to credit their foreign income taxes against their U.S. tax liability. As discussed in the Tax Planning Consideration section of this chapter, however, taxpayers sometimes prefer to deduct their foreign income taxes from gross income.

A taxpayer who uses the accrual method of accounting claims the foreign tax credit in the year in which the tax accrues. A taxpayer who uses the cash method of accounting claims the foreign tax credit in the year in which the tax is paid unless the taxpayer makes a special election to accrue the tax (the advantages of this election are discussed in the Tax Planning Considerations section of this chapter).

ADDITIONAL COMMENT

Foreign income taxes also are deductible under Sec. 164. However, taxpayers may not both deduct and credit the same foreign income taxes. Whether a taxpayer credits or deducts the foreign income taxes requires an annual election.

Translation of the Foreign Tax Payments. Determining the credit amount necessitates translating the tax paid or accrued in a foreign currency into U.S. dollars. To do the translation, cash method taxpayers use the exchange rate as of the payment date. Accrual method taxpayers use the average exchange rate for the tax year over which the tax accrues. They may elect to translate the tax amount into U.S. dollars based on the exchange rate prevailing on the payment date, provided the tax is denominated in a currency other than that used in the taxpayer's regular course of business. (The latter currency is referred to as the taxpayer's "functional currency.") If accrual method taxpayers pay their taxes two years after the close of the tax year to which the taxes relate, they must use the exchange rate prevailing on the payment date to account for any potential currency fluctuation.[4]

EXAMPLE C:16-1 ▶ U.S. citizen Bill is a resident of Country A during the current year. Country A permits its residents to make a single tax payment on the first day of the third month following the close of the tax year. Bill's tax year for both U.S. and Country A tax reporting is the calendar year. Bill remits a 60,000 pirog payment for current year Country A taxes on March 1 of the following year. The average pirog-U.S. dollar exchange rate for the current calendar year is 1 pirog = $0.50 (U.S.). The exchange rate on the March 1 payment date is 1 pirog = $0.60 (U.S.). If Bill uses the cash method of accounting (and does not elect to accrue his foreign taxes), he can claim a $36,000 (60,000 pirogs × $0.60) foreign tax credit. If Bill uses the accrual method of accounting, he can claim a $30,000 (60,000 pirogs × $0.50) foreign tax credit based on the average dollar/pirog exchange rate for the accrual period. ◀

[3] Reg. Sec. 1.901-2. See, for example, Rev. Rul. 91-45, 1991-2 C.B. 336, relating to the creditability of the Mexican asset tax and the Mexican income tax.

[4] Temp. Reg. Sec. 1.905-3T. An amended U.S. tax return must be filed to report the increase or decrease in the credit amount if the taxpayer has filed his or her U.S. tax return by the date the foreign tax is paid. The average exchange rate translation method applies to 1998 and later tax years.

ADDITIONAL COMMENT

The numerator of the limitation fraction is U.S. taxable income from foreign sources. The foreign taxes actually paid or accrued are computed under the tax laws of the foreign jurisdiction. Because these tax laws may differ significantly from the U.S. tax laws, determining whether the fraction is a limiting factor cannot necessarily be determined by simply comparing the statutory tax rates of the two countries. One also must consider their respective tax bases.

Foreign Tax Credit Limitation.

Calculating the General Limitation. Congress enacted the foreign tax credit limitation to prevent taxpayers from crediting foreign taxes owed on income earned outside the United States against U.S. taxes owed on income earned in the United States. This limit, which corresponds to the amount of U.S. tax payable on income earned outside the United States, is calculated as follows:

$$\text{Foreign tax credit limitation} = \text{Total U.S. tax liability} \times \frac{\text{Foreign source taxable income}}{\text{Total worldwide taxable income}}$$

The foreign tax credit equals the lesser of (1) creditable taxes paid or accrued to all foreign countries and U.S. possessions or (2) the foreign tax credit limitation. The limitation permits taxpayers to offset during the same tax year excess foreign taxes paid in one country against excess limitation amounts relative to taxes paid in other countries (known as cross-crediting). However, the total foreign taxes paid or accrued on foreign source taxable income may not exceed the total U.S. tax due on such income.[5] Also, only foreign taxes allocable to the same income classes, or "baskets" (discussed later) may be cross-credited. Before claiming the foreign tax credit, individuals must reduce taxable income by nonrefundable credits allowed under Secs. 21–26.[6]

EXAMPLE C:16-2 ▶ U.S. citizen Theresa earns $10,000 of taxable income (wages) from U.S. sources and $20,000 of taxable income (wages) from Country B in the current year. Theresa pays $6,000 of taxes to Country B in the current year. Assuming a 25% U.S. tax rate, Theresa's gross U.S. tax liability is calculated as follows:

Source of Income	*Taxable Income*	*U.S. Tax Liability Before FTC*
United States	$10,000	$2,500
Country B	20,000	5,000
Total	$30,000	$7,500

Theresa's foreign tax credit limitation is determined as follows:

$$\$5{,}000 = \$7{,}500 \times \frac{\$20{,}000}{\$30{,}000}$$

Without a foreign tax credit limitation, Theresa could credit $1,000 of Country B taxes against the $2,500 of U.S. taxes assessed on her U.S. income. Accordingly, an unlimited credit would decrease her U.S. tax liability to $1,500 ($7,500 − $6,000). The foreign tax credit limitation, however, reduces the amount of foreign tax that Theresa can credit to the extent of U.S. taxes owed on the Country B income, or $5,000. This limitation ensures that Theresa pays the full $2,500 of U.S. taxes assessed on her U.S. income. The $1,000 ($6,000 − $5,000) excess credit carries back and over to other tax years as discussed below. ◀

SELF-STUDY QUESTION

Kathy Richards, a U.S. citizen, earns active business income of $100,000 in Country X, $200,000 in Country Z, and $200,000 in the United States. She pays $10,000 in taxes to X and $90,000 in taxes to Z. Assume a 35% U.S. tax rate. What is Richards's post-credit U.S. tax liability?

ANSWER

Pre-credit U.S. tax = $175,000 ($500,000 × 0.35). The credit is the lesser of the $100,000 ($10,000 + $90,000) of foreign taxes paid or the $105,000 ($175,000 × 300/500) foreign tax credit limitation. Although Richards pays taxes to Country Z at a much higher rate (45%) than the U.S. rate, all the foreign taxes are creditable because they are less than the credit limitation, which is computed on an overall basis and because the Country X tax rate is so low (10%).

Section 904(k) exempts an individual with less than $300 of creditable foreign taxes ($600 for joint filers) from the foreign tax credit limitation, provided his or her foreign source income is exclusively passive.

Determining the Income Amounts. The taxable income amount in the numerator of the credit limitation formula is determined according to the source of income ("sourcing") rules found in Secs. 861–865. These rules are summarized as follows:

- *Personal service income:* Compensation for personal services is considered to be earned in the place where the taxpayer performs the services.

[5] Sec. 904(a). An "excess" foreign tax amount is the excess of the foreign taxes paid or accrued over the foreign tax credit limitation. An "excess" limitation amount is the excess of the foreign tax credit limitation over foreign taxes paid or accrued.

[6] Sec. 904(i). The foreign tax credit is calculated in Form 1118 (see Appendix B).

- *Sales of personal property (other than inventory):* Income derived from a U.S. resident's sale of noninventory personal property (e.g., investment securities) is considered to be earned in the United States. Income derived from a nonresident's sale of such property is considered to be earned outside the United States.[7]
- *Sales of inventory:* Income derived from the sale of merchandise inventory (i.e., final goods purchased for resale) is considered to be earned in the country where the sale occurs. Income derived from the sale of manufactured inventory (i.e., goods manufactured and sold) is considered to be earned partly in the country of manufacture and partly in the country of sale.[8]
- *Sales of real property:* Income derived from the sale of real property is considered to be earned in the country where the property is located.
- *Rents and royalties:* Rents are considered to be earned in the place where the tangible property is located, and royalties in the place where the intangible property (e.g., patent, copyright, or trademark) is used. The latter rule applies to the sale of intangible property if the sale is contingent on the productivity, use, or disposition of the property.
- *Interest income:* Interest generally is considered to be earned in the debtor's country of residence. For purpose of this rule, a U.S. resident includes a foreign partnership or foreign corporation that has derived most of its income from a U.S. trade or business over the past three years.
- *Dividends:* Dividends generally are considered to be earned in the distributing corporation's country of incorporation.

In deriving foreign-source taxable income, a taxpayer allocates deductions and losses to foreign-source gross income according to the rules outlined in Reg. Sec. 1.861-8.

- For individual taxpayers, taxable income is computed without any reduction for personal exemptions.
- In general, deductions are matched with the income with which they are associated.
- Deductions not associated with a specific class of income (such as itemized deductions and the standard deduction) are allocated ratably among all classes of income.

These sourcing rules apply not only for the purpose of calculating the numerator in the foreign tax credit limitation formula, but also for other purposes, such as determining the amount of U.S.-source income subject to U.S. taxing authority and the amount of foreign earned income excludible from U.S. taxation.

Foreign Tax Credit Carrybacks and Carryovers. Excess foreign tax credits can be carried back one year and carried over ten years to a tax year in which the taxpayer has an excess foreign tax credit limitation (i.e., an unused limitation amount). The total of the foreign taxes paid or accrued in a tax year, plus any carryback or carryover to that year, cannot exceed the taxpayer's foreign tax credit limitation. When a taxpayer reports excess credits in more than one year, the excess credits are used on a first-in, first-out (FIFO) basis.[9]

EXAMPLE C:16-3 ▶ Kathy, a U.S. citizen, accrues $95,000 of creditable foreign taxes in 2017. Kathy's 2017 foreign tax credit limitation is $80,000. The $15,000 of 2017 excess credits carry back to 2016, then carry over to 2018 through 2027, until used up. The credit carryback and carryover procedure is illustrated as follows:

	2016	*2017*	*2018*
Foreign tax accrual	$ 90,000	$95,000	$100,000
Foreign tax credit limitation	100,000	80,000	95,000
Excess credits		15,000	5,000
Excess limitation	10,000		

[7] Sec. 865(a). Income derived by a nonresident alien from the sale of personal property (including inventory) attributable to an office or place of business located in the United States is considered to be earned in the United States. Section 865(g) defines the terms *resident* and *nonresident* for the purpose of personal property sales. The definition generally is based on the individual's domicile.

[8] Sec. 865(b) and Reg. Secs. 1.863-3(b) and (c). For tax purposes, an inventory sale generally occurs at the location where title passes from the buyer to the seller. The IRS may depart from this general rule where the primary purpose of the sale is tax-avoidance.

[9] Sec. 904(c).

The excess credits first carry back to 2016 and are applied to the $10,000 excess limitation. Kathy must file an amended return for 2016 to claim the $10,000 carryback. The remaining $5,000 ($15,000 – $10,000) of excess credits carry over to 2018 and are added to the $5,000 of credits generated in that year. Because in the latter year there is no excess credit limitation, the resulting $10,000 of accumulated credits carry forward to future years. Any portion of the carryover not fully used by 2027 will expire. ◀

ADDITIONAL COMMENT

U.S. corporate tax rates tend to be higher than the tax rates of many foreign jurisdictions. This fact, coupled with the imposition of separate limitation baskets, has caused U.S. multinational corporations to remain in an excess foreign tax limitation position.

Special Foreign Tax Credit Limitations. For some taxpayers, more than one foreign tax credit calculation is required. Before 2007, the Sec. 904 foreign tax credit limitation rules created nine baskets of income, for which separate foreign tax credit limitation calculations had to be made.

Beginning in 2007, the number of foreign tax credit limitation baskets was reduced to two, one for passive income and the other for general limitation income.[10] The separate baskets prevent taxpayers from cross-crediting excess foreign taxes levied on one type of income against excess limitations associated with another type of income. Without the separate baskets, taxpayers could "load up" on income items traditionally taxed at low rates (e.g., interest and dividends) to inflate the numerator in the foreign tax credit limitation formula without increasing the total amount of taxes to be credited.

Dividends received by a U.S. shareholder from a foreign corporation in which the shareholder owns at least a 10% equity stake, as well as interest, rents, and royalties received by a U.S. shareholder from a controlled foreign corporation (i.e., a majority-U.S.-owned foreign corporation) are treated as income earned in the separate baskets on a look-through basis (i.e., as if the foreign corporation were a conduit entity).

Compensation and manufacturing income fall into the general limitation basket. Taxpayers who earn only such income must make one foreign tax credit calculation. Other taxpayers must make two calculations.

Excess foreign taxes in one basket cannot offset excess limitation amounts in another basket. Because items in each basket must be accounted for separately, taxpayers generally cannot use excess credits arising from foreign taxes paid or accrued at a high rate (e.g., taxes on salary or business profits allocated to one basket) to offset U.S. taxes owed on income taxed by a foreign country at a low rate or not taxed at all (e.g., taxes on interest or dividends allocated to another basket).

EXAMPLE C:16-4 ▶ Assume the same facts as in Example C:16-2 except, in Country C, Theresa also earns $15,000 of interest income that is not subject to local taxation. The additional U.S. tax liability resulting from this interest income is $3,750 ($15,000 × 0.25). Theresa's total U.S. tax liability is $11,250 ($7,500 [from Example C:16-2] + $3,750). Two foreign tax credit limitations must be calculated for Theresa:

$$\text{Interest income } \$3{,}750 = \$11{,}250 \times \frac{\$15{,}000}{\$45{,}000}$$

$$\text{Wages } \$5{,}000 = \$11{,}250 \times \frac{\$20{,}000}{\$45{,}000}$$

SELF-STUDY QUESTION

Do any limitations restrict the carryback or carryforward of excess foreign taxes?

ANSWER

Yes. The carryback and carryover can occur only within the separate baskets. In Example C:16-4, the $1,000 of excess foreign taxes can be offset only against an excess limitation in the general limitation basket for a carryback or carryover year.

Theresa's foreign tax credit position is summarized in the following table:

Type of Income Earned	*U.S. Tax Liability Before FTC*	*Foreign Taxes Paid or Accrued*	*Foreign Tax Credit Limitation*	*U.S. Tax Liability after FTC*	*Excess Foreign Tax Payments*
Interest	$ 3,750	$ -0-	$3,750	$3,750	$ -0-
Wages	7,500	6,000	5,000	2,500	1,000
Total	$11,250	$6,000	$8,750	$6,250	$1,000

Theresa can claim a $5,000 foreign tax credit—the lesser of the $5,000 foreign tax credit limitation or the $6,000 foreign tax paid—for the Country B wages. She can claim no foreign

[10] Sec. 904(d)(1).

tax credit for the Country C interest income because she paid no foreign tax on this income. The interest income is foreign-source, and U.S. taxpayers calculate the foreign tax credit limitation based on worldwide income. Nevertheless, the $1,000 of excess taxes paid on the Country B wages cannot be used to offset the U.S. taxes owed on the Country C interest income because the interest income is included in the passive income basket and the salary income is included in the general limitation basket. Theresa can carry the excess foreign taxes allocable to the general limitation basket back to the preceding tax year then forward up to ten years, but only within that same basket. ◀

Topic Review C:16-1 summarizes the foreign tax credit provisions. A discussion of the financial statement implications of the foreign tax credit appears at the end of this chapter.

ADDITIONAL COMMENT

The foreign-earned income exclusion is calculated in Form 2555 (see Appendix B).

FOREIGN-EARNED INCOME EXCLUSION

Special income exclusions are available to individuals working in foreign countries. One such exclusion—the foreign earned income exclusion authorized under Sec. 911—is important to employers because it provides tax relief to their U.S. employees stationed in foreign countries. Many such employers reimburse their overseas employees for their incremental worldwide tax costs relative to the costs they would have incurred had they stayed in the United States. By reducing the U.S. tax liability of these employees, the Sec. 911 exclusion decreases the amount of this reimbursement and thus reduces employers' costs.

U.S. Citizens and Resident Aliens Working Abroad. The United States taxes U.S. citizens and resident aliens, including those working abroad, on their worldwide income. While working outside the country, these taxpayers may incur additional costs to maintain the same standard of living they enjoyed in the United States. In addition, they may endure inconveniences, substandard living conditions, hardships, or political hazards that warrant additional compensation in the form of special allowances. The allowances may be taxed in both the United States and the country of residence. The U.S. employer generally reimburses U.S. employees for these tax costs to relieve them of any incremental tax burden. The total compensation package can make hiring a U.S. citizen or resident alien more expensive than hiring a foreign resident or citizen with the same set of skills.

TOPIC REVIEW C:16-1

Foreign Tax Credit

- Foreign income taxes paid or accrued to a foreign country or a U.S. possession are deductible or creditable by U.S. taxpayers.
- The election to deduct or credit foreign taxes is made annually. Generally, a taxpayer will elect to credit foreign taxes because of the dollar-for-dollar tax benefit derived from a credit as opposed to a deduction.
- Cash method taxpayers can elect to accrue their foreign taxes. This election can accelerate by one year the time for claiming the credit and may reduce the need to carry back or carry over excess credits.
- A direct credit is available for foreign taxes paid or accrued by the taxpayer, as well as for foreign taxes withheld by a foreign payer.
- Foreign taxes generally are translated into U.S. dollars at the exchange rate for the date on which they are paid or the period over which they accrue, depending on the taxpayer's accounting method.
- The foreign tax credit limitation prevents crediting foreign taxes against the U.S. tax liability on U.S. source income. The amount of credit that can be claimed is the lesser of (a) the creditable taxes paid or accrued to all foreign countries and U.S. possessions, or (b) the overall foreign tax credit limitation. Excess credits may be carried back one year and then forward up to ten years. Taxpayers must account for the credit by income type, or foreign tax credit basket. An excess credit in one basket cannot offset an excess credit limitation in another basket.

ADDITIONAL COMMENT

The foreign income exclusion is elective and is made by filing Form 2555 with the income tax return (or amended return) for the first tax year for which the election is to be effective. A completed Form 2555 is reproduced in Appendix B.

To enable U.S. firms to compete abroad, the U.S. government established a policy of reducing the U.S. tax burden on U.S. citizens and resident aliens living abroad for an extended period of time. Taxpayers who are bona fide residents of a foreign country (or countries) for an entire tax year, or who are physically present in a foreign country (or countries) for 330 full days[11] out of a 12-month period, can exclude up to $101,300 in 2016 and $102,100 in 2017 of foreign-earned income from their gross income.[12] This benefit, which is known as the *foreign-earned income exclusion,* is indexed for inflation and is available to taxpayers who meet one of two tests: the bona fide residence test or the physical presence test.

KEY POINT

Whether a U.S. citizen has established foreign residency is based on all the pertinent facts and circumstances. This rule is different from the determination of whether a foreign citizen has established U.S. residency. The latter is based on either a green card or the substantial physical presence test (discussed later in this chapter).

Bona Fide Residence Test. A U.S. citizen (but not a resident alien) satisfies the bona fide residence test of Sec. 911(d)(1)(A) if he or she has resided in a foreign country (or countries) for an uninterrupted period that includes an entire tax year and has maintained a tax home in a foreign country (or countries) during the period of residence.

For Sec. 911 purposes, an individual's tax home is defined in the same way as it is for determining the deductibility of travel expenses incurred while away from home on business.[13] In other words, an individual's tax home is his or her regular or principal place of business. Temporary absences from the foreign country for trips back to the United States or to other foreign countries normally do not disqualify foreign residency.

An individual is not a bona fide resident of a foreign country if he or she submits to the taxing authorities of that country a statement claiming to be a nonresident and obtains from that country's taxing authorities an earned income exemption based on nonresident status.[14] An individual does not qualify for the foreign earned income exclusion until he or she has been a foreign resident for an *entire tax year.* At the end of that period, the individual can retroactively claim Sec. 911 benefits from the date he or she became a foreign resident.

EXAMPLE C:16-5 ▶

Mark is a U.S. citizen who uses the calendar year as his tax year. Mark is transferred by his employer to Country P, and he becomes a Country P resident upon his arrival at noon on July 15 of Year 1. At that time, Mark establishes his tax home in P's capital. Mark's residency in P is maintained until his return to the United States at 2 p.m. on January 10 of Year 5. Mark first qualifies as a bona fide resident of a foreign country on December 31 of Year 2 after residing there for a full tax year. This qualification permits Mark to claim the foreign earned income exclusion as of July 15 of Year 1. Mark can continue to claim the exclusion through January 10 of Year 5. ◀

TYPICAL MISCONCEPTION

A day is not just any 24-hour period. To count as a day, the taxpayer must be in a foreign country for a period of 24 hours beginning and ending at midnight.

SELF-STUDY QUESTION

During a 12-month period, U.S. citizen Robert's work requires him to be physically present in a foreign country for 317 days. If Robert delays his return to the U.S. by vacationing overseas for 13 more days, will he qualify for the foreign-earned income exclusion?

ANSWER

Yes. The foreign physical presence can be for any reason.

Physical Presence Test. A taxpayer who cannot satisfy the bona fide residence test still can qualify for Sec. 911 benefits by satisfying the physical presence test of Sec. 911(d)(1)(B). To do so, the taxpayer must meet two requirements:

- ▶ Be physically present in a foreign country (or countries) for at least 330 *full* days during a 12-month period.
- ▶ Maintain a tax home in a foreign country (or countries) during the period of physical presence.

The 330 days need not be consecutive, nor must the taxpayer be in the same foreign country at all times. The 12-month period may begin on any day of the calendar year. The period ends on the day before the corresponding calendar day in the twelfth succeeding month.

---

[11] A full day is a continuous 24-hour period beginning with midnight and ending with the following midnight.

[12] The IRS adjusts the exclusion each year for inflation.

[13] Sec. 911(d)(3).

[14] Sec. 911(d)(5). The Sec. 911 bona fide residence test is different from the Sec.7701(b) test used to determine whether an alien individual is a resident or nonresident of the United States. The latter test is discussed on page C:16-14.

EXAMPLE C:16-6 ▶ Assume the same facts as in Example C:16-5. The 330 days of physical presence begin with the first full day Mark is present in Country P (July 16 of Year 1) and include a total of 169 days through the end of Year 1. The 161 additional days needed to complete the 330-day period include January 1 through June 10 of Year 2. One possible 12-month period for Mark thus begins on July 16 of Year 1, and runs through July 15 of Year 2. An alternative 12-month period might be June 11 of Year 1 through June 10 of Year 2, where the 330 days of physical presence fall at the end of the period. (Note: The start and end dates of the period will differ if the 330 days encompass February 29 of a leap year.) ◀

ADDITIONAL COMMENT

Note that in Example C:16-6, Mark would prefer to use the 12-month period of June 11 of Year 1 through June 10 of Year 2, when computing the exclusion for Year 2 to have more days of the year in the qualifying period and, hence, a larger exclusion. This 12-month period places the 330 days of qualifying time at the end of the 12-month period.

Foreign Earned Income Defined. For purposes of the exclusion, earned income means wages, salaries, professional fees, and other compensation for personal services actually rendered.[15] Earned income is excludible only if it is foreign source. The sourcing rules, discussed previously in the section "Determining the Income Amounts" (see page C:16-5), are used to determine whether income is earned in the United States or a foreign country. In general, income is sourced according to where the services are performed. If the taxpayer performs services in more than one location during the tax year, he or she must allocate the income between the two or more locations based on the number of days worked at each location.[16]

Fringe benefits excluded from gross income under an IRC provision other than Sec. 911 (e.g., meals and lodging furnished for the convenience of the employer, excludible under Sec. 119) do not diminish the excludible amount. Items that generally are taxable to the recipient, but which do not comprise earned income for Sec. 911 purposes, include pensions and annuities, compensation paid by the United States or one of its agencies to an employee,[17] and amounts received more than one tax year after the tax year in which services are performed.

Amount of the Exclusion. The foreign earned income exclusion is available only for the number of days in the tax year during which the taxpayer meets either the bona fide residence test or the physical presence test. Section 911(b)(2)(A) limits the foreign earned income exclusion to the lesser of the following:

- The individual's foreign-earned income
- The amount of the daily exclusion times the number of days during the tax year that the individual qualifies for the exclusion

The 2017 annual and daily limits are $102,100 and $279.73, respectively. The 2016 annual and daily limits were $101,300 and $276.78, respectively. For 2014 and 2015, the annual limits were $99,200 and $100,800, respectively, and the daily limits were $271.78 and $276.16, respectively.

EXAMPLE C:16-7 ▶ U.S. citizen Lee, who uses the calendar year as his tax year, establishes a tax home and residency in Country A on November 1, 2015 (the 305th day of the year). Lee maintains his tax home and residency until March 31, 2017 (the 90th day), when Lee returns to the United States. While employed abroad, Lee earns salary and allowances at $15,000 monthly. Lee's exclusion is calculated as follows:

Tax Year	*Foreign Earned Income*	*Qualifying Days (1)*	*Daily Exclusion Amount (2)*	*Total Amount Excluded (3) = (1) × (2)*
2015	$ 30,000	60	$276.16	$16,570
2016	180,000	366	276.78	101,300
2017	45,000	90	279.73	25,176 ◀

Individuals satisfying the bona fide residence test can claim the exclusion for each day they "reside" in a foreign country whether or not they are physically present in that country on each day. Individuals satisfying the physical presence test can claim the exclusion for each day of a 12-month period that falls within the tax year, whether or not they are physically present in a foreign country on all 365 days. Because an individual need only be

[15] Sec. 911(d)(2).

[16] Sec. 911(b)(1)(A).

[17] Under Sec. 912, civilian officers and employees of the U.S. government who are employed abroad can exclude from gross income certain foreign area and cost-of-living allowances.

physically present in a foreign country for 330 days out of the 12-month period (365 days in a non-leap year, 366 days in a leap year) and because the exclusion applies to income earned during the full 12-month period, an individual might qualify for the exclusion for as many as 35 days before arrival in the foreign country or as many as 35 days after departure from the foreign country. Such an extension of the qualifying period in the year of arrival or departure may favor calculating the exclusion for these years based on the physical presence test.[18]

EXAMPLE C:16-8 ▶ Assume the same facts as in Example C:16-7 except Lee was physically present in Country A at all times from his arrival in 2015 to his departure in 2017. Lee's first 330 full days in Country A extend from November 2, 2015, through September 26, 2016. Lee's last 330 full days in Country A extend from May 5, 2016, through March 30, 2017. Lee's two corresponding 12-month periods extend from September 27, 2015 (the 270th day of 2015, with 96 days, inclusive, remaining), through September 26, 2016 (for a total of 366 days to reflect a leap year), and from May 5, 2016, through May 4, 2017 (the 124th day of 2017, for a total of 365 days to reflect a non-leap year). The amount of Lee's exclusion is calculated below:

Tax Year	*Foreign Earned Income*	*Qualifying Days (1)*[19]	*Daily Exclusion Amount (2)*	*Total Amount Excluded (3) = (1) × (2)*
2015	$ 30,000	96*	$276.16	$26,511
2016	180,000	366	276.78	101,300
2017	45,000	124	279.73	34,687

*Including September 27, 2015

Lee obtains a larger exclusion in 2015 and 2017 under the physical presence test because he effectively gets credit for the additional 35 days extending beyond the 330-day period, but included in the corresponding 12-month period. ◀

KEY POINT

A taxpayer may elect to use the foreign-earned income exclusion and the housing cost exclusion. Once made, the exclusion election is effective for that year and all subsequent years. See pages C:16-34 and C:16-35 for a discussion of why a taxpayer might elect out of the Sec. 911 exclusion.

Housing Cost Exclusion or Deduction. Section 911 permits a taxpayer who is eligible for the foreign earned income exclusion also to exclude or deduct a **housing cost amount** (reportable on Form 2555), which is determined as follows:

$$\text{Housing cost amount} = \text{Housing expenses} - \text{Base housing amount}$$

$$\text{Base housing amount} = 0.16 \times \text{Maximum foreign earned income exclusion} \times \frac{\text{Number of qualifying days in the tax year}}{\text{Number of days in the tax year}}$$

For 2017, the maximum foreign earned income exclusion is $102,100.[20] Thus, for taxpayers qualifying for Sec. 911 benefits for the entire tax year, the base housing amount for 2017 is $16,336 ($102,100 × 0.16), and the daily base housing amount is $44.76 ($16,336/365). The 2016 annual and daily base housing amounts were $16,208 ($101,300 × 0.16) and $44.28 ($16,208/366), respectively.

ADDITIONAL COMMENT

Employer-provided amounts include all compensation provided by the employer (salary, bonus, allowances, etc.), not just the amount identified as the housing allowance.

Housing costs include any reasonable expense paid or incurred for foreign housing for the taxpayer, his or her spouse, and any dependents during the part of the year the taxpayer qualifies for Sec. 911 benefits. Housing costs also include expenses incurred for a second home outside the United States if, because of adverse living conditions, the taxpayer must maintain a home for his or her spouse and dependents at a location other than the tax home.[21]

The exclusion is limited to 30% of the maximum foreign earned income exclusion (computed on a daily basis). Employer-provided amounts encompass any income that is foreign earned and included in the employee's gross income (without regard to Sec. 911 benefits) for

[18] Reg. Sec. 1.911-3(d).

[19] September 27, 2015, through December 31, 2015, encompasses 96 days, and January 1, 2017, through May 4, 2017, encompasses 124 days.

[20] The corresponding figure for 2016 was $101,300.

[21] Sec. 911(c)(3)(B). The IRS provides a list of countries with adverse living conditions. Individuals residing in these countries were required to leave them because of war, civil unrest, or other similar conditions that precluded the normal conduct of business. The most recent list appeared in Rev. Proc. 2004-17, 2004-1 C.B. 562, that covered tax year 2003. In addition, Notice 2016-21, 2016-12, I.R.B. 465, provides adjustments to the limitation on housing expenses on the basis of geographic differences in housing costs relative to those in the United States.

the tax year. Such amounts include, but are not limited to, salary or allowances paid by the employer (including allowances other than for housing), reimbursements to the employee for housing expenses, in-kind housing (other than that excluded under Sec. 119), and reimbursements to third parties on behalf of the employee.

EXAMPLE C:16-9 ▶ John, a U.S. citizen, is a bona fide resident of Country M for all of 2017. John, who uses the calendar year as his tax year, receives $120,000 in salary and allowances from his employer. Included in this total is a $15,000 housing allowance. In 2017, John incurred eligible housing expenses of $22,000. Thus, John's housing cost amount is $5,664 ($22,000 − $16,336). Because this amount is less than the foreign housing cost limit of $30,630 ($102,100 × 0.30), John can exclude the full housing cost amount. In addition, he can exclude $102,100 of his foreign earned income because he qualified for all of 2017. Therefore, his total exclusion is $107,764 ($5,664 + $102,100), so only $12,236 ($120,000 − $107,764) of his total compensation is subject to U.S. taxation. ◀

ADDITIONAL COMMENT

If an individual has only W-2 income (no self-employment income), he or she is eligible for only the housing cost exclusion because the entire housing cost amount is attributable to employer-provided amounts. The housing cost exclusion and deduction can both be taken only in situations where an individual has both W-2 income and self-employment income. Proration of the housing cost amount between a deduction and an exclusion is based on the relative amounts of the taxpayer's W-2 income and self-employment income.

Any portion of the housing cost amount that is not provided by an employer is a *for*-AGI deduction.[22] Thus, if an individual has only self-employment income, the entire housing cost amount is deductible. Such would be the case in Example C:16-9 if John were self-employed and the $120,000 were commission income. His $5,664 housing cost amount could be claimed only as a *for*-AGI deduction.

The housing cost deduction is limited to the taxpayer's foreign earned income minus the sum of the foreign earned income and housing cost exclusions. If the deduction for housing costs exceeds its limitation, the excess amount carries forward as a deduction in the next year (subject to that year's limitation).

Disallowance of Deductions and Credits. Section 911(d)(6) prohibits taxpayers from claiming deductions or credits relating to their excluded income. The rules used to determine the nondeductible portion of an individual's employment-related expenses and the noncreditable portion of an individual's foreign taxes are discussed below.

Employment-Related Expenses. Any employment-related expense associated with a taxpayer's excluded foreign earned income is nondeductible. By contrast, expenses relating to the employee's taxable income are deductible in full.[23] However, although foreign housing expenses may be related to excludible foreign earned income, no restriction is placed on deducting the housing cost amount.

EXAMPLE C:16-10 ▶ In 2017, Don reports $150,000 of foreign-earned income and $15,000 of foreign-employment-related expenses that are subject to the 2% of AGI floor. Don takes $12,000 of other itemized deductions not directly related to foreign earned income and not subject to the 2% of AGI floor. Don may exclude $102,100 (or 68.1%) of his foreign earned income. Based on the calculation below, the exclusion precludes Don from deducting 68.1% or $10,210 ($15,000 total expenses − $4,790 deductible expenses) of foreign-employment-related expenses. Don can deduct the full $12,000 of the other itemized deductions.

$$\text{\$4,790 (Deductible expenses)}^{a} = \text{\$15,000 (Expenses directly attributable to foreign earned income)} \times \left[1 - \frac{\text{\$102,100 (Excluded foreign earned income)}}{\text{\$150,000 (Total foreign earned income)}}\right]$$

[a] Subject to the 2% AGI floor.

The employment-related expenses are deductible only to the extent they exceed 2% of Don's $47,900 AGI ($150,000 − $102,100). Thus, Don can deduct $3,832 [$4,790 − ($47,900 × 0.02)] of employment-related expenses plus the $12,000 of other itemized deductions not subject to the 2% floor. ◀

[22] Sec. 911(c)(4)(A).

[23] Sec. 911(d)(6) and Reg. Sec. 1.911-6(a). Miscellaneous itemized expenses are subject to the 2% AGI floor whether the taxpayer is eligible for the Sec. 911 exclusion or not. The calculation of deductible and nondeductible employment-related expenses is incorporated in Form 2555 (see Appendix B).

REAL-WORLD EXAMPLE

A number of websites provide the costs of sending an employee on an overseas assignment or the cost of maintaining an employee who already is on an overseas assignment. Some sites also provide information on foreign, U.S., and state taxation. In addition, many of the sites provide cultural information and financial advice.

Foreign Income Taxes. Foreign income taxes paid or accrued on excludible foreign earned income cannot be credited or deducted for U.S. income tax purposes. Creditable foreign taxes are determined under the following formula.[24]

$$\text{Creditable taxes} = \text{Foreign income taxes paid or accrued} \times \left[1 - \frac{\text{Excludible foreign earned income (minus nondeductible foreign employment-related expenses)}}{\text{Total foreign earned income (minus expenses relating to foreign earned income) subject to foreign tax}}\right]$$

If foreign income taxes are paid or accrued on earned and other types of income, and the taxes cannot be allocated between the two amounts, the denominator of the fraction must include the total of all income subject to foreign tax (minus all related expenses).

EXAMPLE C:16-11 ▶ Assume the same facts as in Example C:16-10 except Don also incurs $33,750 of Country F income taxes on his foreign earned income. Don's $10,778 of creditable foreign taxes are 31.9% of the total foreign taxes. The creditable taxes are computed as follows:

$$\$10{,}778 = \$33{,}750 \times \left[1 - \frac{\$102{,}100 - \$10{,}210}{\$150{,}000 - \$15{,}000}\right]$$ ◀

Topic Review C:16-2 summarizes the foreign earned income and housing cost exclusions.

TOPIC REVIEW C:16-2

Foreign Earned Income and Housing Cost Exclusions

1. Only U.S. citizens can qualify under the bona fide residence test. According to this test, they must have (a) resided in a foreign country(ies) for an uninterrupted period that includes an entire tax year and (b) maintained a tax home in a foreign country(ies) during the residence period.
2. U.S. citizens and resident aliens can qualify under the physical presence test. According to this test, they must have
   (a) been physically present in a foreign country(ies) for at least 330 full days during a 12-month period and
   (b) maintained a tax home in a foreign country(ies) during the period of physical presence.
3. The exclusion equals the lesser of the taxpayer's foreign earned income or the daily exclusion ($276.78 in 2016 and $279.73 in 2017) times the number of days in the tax year that the taxpayer qualifies for the exclusion.
4. Under the bona fide residence test, qualifying days include the number of days in the tax year during which the taxpayer "resided" in a foreign country. Under the physical presence test, qualifying days encompass the full 12-month period within which at least 330 days of physical presence fall.
5. Subject to limitations, employees can exclude a housing cost amount in addition to foreign earned income. Self-employed individuals can deduct the housing cost amount. The housing cost amount equals housing expenses incurred minus the base housing amount (16% × maximum foreign earned income exclusion) for the part of the tax year during which the taxpayer qualifies for the foreign earned income exclusion.
6. Taxpayers who exclude foreign earned income may not claim deductions or credits associated with their excluded income.

[24] Reg. Sec. 1.911-6(c). This formula is incorporated in Form 2555 (see Appendix B).

Taxation of Nonresident Aliens

OBJECTIVE 3

Establish whether a foreign citizen is a U.S. resident or nonresident alien and calculate the U.S. tax liability of a nonresident alien

Whether a foreign national is a U.S. resident or a nonresident determines the U.S. tax treatment of that person's income. Under Sec. 871, U.S. taxing authority over nonresident aliens is limited to their U.S.-source investment income and any U.S. (and certain foreign) income effectively connected with the conduct of a U.S. trade or business. As a threshold issue, the foreign national's income must be sourced according to the sourcing rules previously discussed in the section "Determining the Income Amounts" (see page C:16-5).

The taxation of nonresident aliens is important for both U.S. and foreign companies that employ foreign nationals in the United States. Just like companies that employ U.S. citizens or residents abroad, companies that employ foreign citizens in the United States often assist them in complying with the U.S. tax laws and reimburse them for additional tax costs. In addition, U.S. businesses that pay U.S.-source income to nonresident aliens, foreign corporations, or foreign conduit entities (e.g., foreign partnerships) must withhold U.S. taxes on this income to avoid certain penalties.

DEFINITION OF NONRESIDENT ALIEN

With certain exceptions,[25] foreign nationals who do not satisfy the Sec. 7701(b) tests set forth below are nonresident aliens. Foreign nationals who satisfy the tests are resident aliens.

- *Lawful permanent residency test:* The foreign national must have been a lawful permanent resident of the United States at any time during the tax year. A foreign national with a "green card" is considered to be a lawful permanent resident.
- *Substantial presence test:* The foreign national must have been present in the United States for 31 or more days during the current calendar year *and* a total of 183 or more days during the current and the two preceding tax years. The 183-day prong of the test is based on a weighted average calculation, according to which the more recent the period, the greater the weight. Specifically, each day in the current year is weighted one, each day in the first preceding year is weighted one-third, and each day in the second preceding year is weighted one-sixth.

EXAMPLE C:16-12 ▶ Marco, a citizen of Country X, is present in the United States for 122 days in each of Years 1 through 3. Marco satisfies the 31-day requirement because he is present in the United States for at least 31 days in Year 3. The following table illustrates the weighting of days for purposes of the 183-day requirement:

Year	*Days Present In the United States*	*Portion of Day Counted*	*Total Days Counted*
3	122	Full day	122.00
2	122	1/3 of full day	40.67
1	122	1/6 of full day	20.33
Total			183.00

Marco is a resident alien because he satisfies both the 31-day and 183-day requirements. ◀

Even though foreign nationals satisfy the physical presence test, they are nonresident aliens if they are nominally present in the United States (i.e., physically present in the United States for less than 30 days in the current year, notwithstanding a three-year total of 183 or more days) or if they have a closer connection with a foreign country than with the United States. Under the "closer connection" rule, the individual must be present in the United States for less than 183 days in the current year, maintain a tax home in a

[25] A nonresident alien also can become a resident alien by marrying a U.S. citizen or resident alien and electing to be treated as a resident alien under Sec. 6013(g). (See the Tax Planning Considerations section of this chapter.)

foreign country for the entire year, and have maintained more significant contacts with the foreign country than with the United States.

Foreign nationals typically have dual status in their first and last years of U.S. residency. Dual status implies that the foreign national resides in the United States for part of the year and in a foreign country for the other part. Therefore, his or her tax computation is based on nonresident alien status for part of the tax year and resident alien status for the other part. An individual who satisfies the lawful permanent residency test (but not the substantial presence test) begins his or her residency period on the first day of the first year in which he or she is physically present as a lawful permanent resident in the United States. An individual who satisfies the substantial presence test in his or her first year becomes a resident on the first day of the first year in which he or she is physically present in the United States.

Foreign nationals terminate their residency on the last day of the last year in which they are lawful permanent residents. Foreign nationals who satisfy the physical presence test for a particular year maintain residency through the last day of such year (ignoring periods of nominal U.S. presence).

The United States amended its tax laws to reduce the incentive for U.S. citizens and residents to forfeit their U.S. citizenship or residency. The U.S. government can impose an expatriation tax when an individual terminates his or her U.S. citizenship or long-term residency status. The IRC sets forth a tax avoidance presumption that references the individual's average taxes for the five-year period preceding the termination, as well as the individual's net worth. The expatriation tax is based on an expanded U.S. source of income definition that applies to nonresident aliens who are liable for the additional income tax.[26] Modified estate and gift tax rules subject certain property to U.S. taxation if transferred within ten years of the event triggering the loss of citizenship or residency.[27]

INVESTMENT INCOME

Passive investment income is taxed to a nonresident alien only if it is U.S.-source. Section 871(a)(1)(A) places the following types of income in this category: interest, dividends, rents, salaries,[28] premiums; annuities; compensation; and other fixed or determinable annual or periodical gains and profits (sometimes referred to as "FDAP income"). Capital gains realized by a nonresident alien in the United States (other than in the conduct of a U.S. trade or business) are taxed to that individual only if he or she is physically present in the United States for at least 183 days during the tax year.[29] Two important exceptions to this general rule are as follows:

TYPICAL MISCONCEPTION

Foreign nationals who are U.S. residents are taxed on their worldwide income, just as U.S. citizens are. They file Form 1040. Nonresident aliens who are subject to U.S. taxation file Form 1040NR.

- Interest income earned by a nonresident alien on deposits in a U.S. bank, the foreign office of a U.S. bank, or other financial institution is exempt from U.S. taxation, provided the interest is not effectively connected with the foreign national's conduct of a U.S. trade or business.
- Portfolio interest (i.e., interest on obligations issued by U.S. persons and held by a nonresident alien as a portfolio investment) is exempt from U.S. taxation.[30]

The sale of personal property in the United States is not considered to generate fixed or determinable annual or periodic income. As a result, casual sales of inventory that are not regular, continuous, and substantial are not subject to U.S. taxation. To the extent the sales proceeds are contingent on the productivity, use, or disposition of an intangible asset (e.g., patent, copyright, trademark), gain from the sale of the asset is taxed as ordinary income. It is U.S.-source if the asset is used in the United States and foreign-source if the asset is used in a foreign country. To the extent the sales proceeds are noncontingent, the

---

[26] Sec. 877.

[27] Secs. 2107 and 2501.

[28] Compensation for personal services ordinarily is trade or business income. Salaries are trade or business income even if the foreign national does not conduct a U.S. trade or business in the tax year in which the income is reported (e.g., no services are performed in the United States in the year in which a final paycheck is collected by a cash method taxpayer) if it is attributable to an earlier tax year and would have been treated as effectively connected with the conduct of a U.S. trade or business in that year.

[29] Sec. 871(a)(2). The capital gains are reduced by U.S. capital losses, and only the net gain is taxed.

[30] Portfolio obligations include, for example, bonds issued by a U.S. corporation in the Eurobond market.

gain is capital in character. It is U.S.-source if a U.S. resident sells the asset and is foreign-source if a nonresident sells the asset.

EXAMPLE C:16-13 ▶ Paula, a citizen and resident of Country A, sells a patent to a U.S. corporation in consideration for a $2 royalty for each unit produced under the patent in the United States. In the current year, Paula receives $18,000 for 9,000 units produced. The $18,000 is a contingent payment. It is U.S.-source because the patent is used in the United States and thus is subject to U.S. taxing authority. If Paula instead received a single $18,000 payment in exchange for all rights to the patent, the $18,000 less Paula's adjusted basis in the patent would have been a capital gain. Because Paula is a foreign resident, it would have been foreign-source and thus would have escaped U.S. taxation. ◀

ADDITIONAL COMMENT

Many tax treaties reduce this flat 30% rate for specific types of income.

Investment income and capital gains earned by a nonresident alien are taxed at a flat 30% rate, applicable to the gross amount.[31] Often, this rate is reduced by tax treaty (see discussion under Tax Planning Considerations later in this chapter). The 30% rate applies to capital gains of a nonresident alien only if he or she is present in the United States for at least 183 days during a tax year. In many cases, an individual who is present in the United States for 183 or more days has already acquired resident alien status. In general, U.S. payers must withhold the tax from the gross amount and remit the tax to the IRS.[32] If the U.S. payer fails to do so, and the nonresident alien fails to pay the tax voluntarily, the U.S. payer may be liable for the tax, as well as penalties for failing to withhold.[33]

EXAMPLE C:16-14 ▶ First State Bank issues dividend checks for a domestic corporation. One of the corporation's shareholders is Kelly, a nonresident alien entitled to a $30,000 dividend. Because the dividend represents U.S.-source investment income paid to a nonresident alien, First State Bank must withhold $9,000 ($30,000 × 0.30) of U.S. tax from Kelly's payment and remit the tax to the IRS. Kelly need not report or voluntarily pay the tax to the IRS. ◀

TRADE OR BUSINESS INCOME

A nonresident alien is engaged in a U.S. trade or business if he or she, with the intent to make a profit, conducts an activity in the United States that is regular, continuous, and substantial. A partner in a partnership or a beneficiary of a trust or estate is considered to indirectly conduct a U.S. trade or business if the partnership, trust, or estate directly conducts the U.S. trade or business.

Nonresident aliens who (1) are in the United States for less than 90 days during the year; (2) are employed by a nonresident alien, foreign partnership, or foreign corporation that does not conduct a U.S. trade or business, or by a foreign office maintained by a U.S. person; and (3) do not earn more than $3,000 for their services are considered not to have conducted a U.S. trade or business. In addition, their wages are exempt from U.S. taxation because such wages are foreign source.

Nonresident aliens who invest in securities through a broker also are considered not to have conducted a U.S. trade or business. Their capital gains are exempt from U.S. taxation unless they are present in the United States for more than 183 days during the year.

Special Election for Real Estate Investors. Nonresident aliens may elect to have their U.S. real estate activities be treated as a U.S. trade or business even though the activities are passive. This election permits the nonresident aliens to claim all deductions and losses associated with the activities and thus be taxed on a net basis. If the election is not made and the activity does not constitute a trade or business, the real estate income is subject to the flat 30% withholding tax levied on a gross basis (i.e., without any reduction for deductions and losses).[34] Gains from the sale of U.S. real property interests (whether capital or ordinary) are treated as effectively connected with the conduct of a U.S. trade or business. Ownership of a U.S. real estate interest may be direct or indirect

[31] Sec. 871(a).

[32] If a nonresident alien voluntarily files a tax return, he or she can deduct casualty and theft losses related to (1) personal use property that exceed the $100/10% of AGI floor, (2) transactions entered into for a profit even if not connected with a trade or business, and (3) charitable contributions otherwise deductible under Sec. 170.

[33] Secs. 1441(a) and 1461.

[34] Sec. 871(d).

(e.g., an investment in a corporation or a partnership that owns substantial U.S. real estate).[35]

PRACTICAL APPLICATION

Paula operates a U.S. business and is a nonresident alien. Paula invests the excess cash from the business in short-term securities. The investment income is effectively connected with the business under the asset-use test because the income is derived from assets used in the business.

Effectively Connected Tests. Income is effectively connected with the conduct of a U.S. trade or business if one of two tests is met: an "asset use" test or a "business activities" test. Under the asset use test, income is effectively connected with the conduct of a U.S. trade or business if the income is derived from assets used in the business. For example, interest earned on a certificate of deposit (CD) may be either investment or business related, depending on how the CD is used. If a nonresident alien holds the CD to support the operating cycle of his or her U.S. business, the interest is derived from an asset used in the business and thus is effectively connected with the conduct of the business. Under the business activities test, income is effectively connected with the conduct of a U.S. trade or business if the activities of the business are a material factor in generating the income. For example, short-term gains realized by the U.S. branch of a foreign securities firm are effectively connected with the conduct of a U.S. business because the activities of the business (i.e., securities trading) are a material factor in generating the income. Capital gains that are effectively connected with the conduct of a U.S. trade or business under either test is taxable without regard to the number of days the individual is physically present in the United States.

Income from the sale of inventory or other personal property by a nonresident alien is U.S.-source and, therefore, taxable in the United States if the alien has a U.S. office and the sale is attributable to that office. On the other hand, the income is foreign-source and therefore exempt from U.S. taxation if the property is for foreign use or disposition and if a non-U.S. office materially participated in the sale. When a foreign national manufactures or creates personal property in the United States and then sells it abroad, a portion of the sales income is allocated to U.S. production and thus is subject to U.S. taxation. The remainder is allocated to the location where the sale occurred.

Calculating the Tax. A foreign national who conducts a U.S. trade or business may have to make two separate tax calculations. Investment income that is unrelated to the conduct of a U.S. trade or business is taxed on a gross basis at a flat 30% rate (unless reduced by a tax treaty). This tax is collected through withholding. Trade or business income is taxed at graduated rates on a net basis (i.e., reduced by all associated expenses and losses). Nonresident aliens

- Cannot use the standard deduction otherwise available to individual taxpayers
- Must itemize their deductions
- Are generally limited to a single personal exemption[36]

Individual tax rates apply to taxable income derived from an unincorporated U.S. trade or business. The trade or business income of unmarried nonresident aliens is taxed at the marginal rates for single taxpayers. Married nonresident aliens use the tax rate schedule for married individuals filing separately unless they elect to file a joint return under Sec. 6013(g) (see the Tax Planning Considerations section of this chapter). The U.S. trade or business income of nonresident aliens may be subject to the alternative minimum tax for individuals. The taxes owed on trade or business income can be reduced by any available tax credits. The taxpayer then pays the net U.S. tax liability through estimated tax installments and, if a balance remains, through a final remittance when he or she files an annual return.

EXAMPLE C:16-15 ▶ Maria, a single taxpayer, is a citizen and resident of Country D. In the current year, Maria reports $40,000 of U.S. dividends that are unrelated to Maria's U.S. trade or business and $1,000 of itemized deductions. Maria's U.S. trade or business generates $300,000 of gross income from sales activities, $20,000 of interest income, $225,000 of expenses, and $500 of tax credits.

---

[35] Secs. 897(a) and (c).

[36] Section 873(b) permits certain personal deductions (for example, casualty losses, charitable contributions, and personal exemptions) not directly related to trade or business activities.

SELF-STUDY QUESTION

In Example C:16-15, assume Maria also earned $10,000 of capital gain income on the sale of investment property she had owned in the United States. How would this change Maria's total U.S. tax liability?

ANSWER

Maria's U.S. tax liability would not increase unless the capital gain was connected with a U.S. trade or business, or it was investment gain and Maria was present in the United States for 183 days or more, and the gain was U.S. source income.

Maria's tax liability on her dividend income is $12,000 ($40,000 × 0.30), on the assumption that no U.S. tax treaty with Country D reduces the statutory 30% rate. The taxes owed on Maria's trade or business income are calculated as follows:

Gross income:	
Sales	$300,000
Interest	20,000
Total gross income	$320,000
Minus: Trade or business expenses	(225,000)
Adjusted gross income	$ 95,000
Minus: Personal exemption (2017)	(4,050)
Itemized deductions	(1,000)
Taxable income	$ 89,950
Gross tax liability (single rate schedule)	$ 18,226
Minus: Tax credits	(500)
Net tax liability	$ 17,726

Maria's total U.S. tax liability is $29,726 ($12,000 + $17,726). ◀

Topic Review C:16-3 summarizes the tax rules applicable to nonresident aliens.

TAXATION OF U.S. BUSINESSES OPERATING ABROAD

OBJECTIVE 4

Apply the tax rules that pertain to foreign corporations and their U.S. shareholders

The IRC offers numerous tax breaks to U.S. enterprises that conduct business abroad. For example, it generally exempts from U.S. taxation income earned by foreign subsidiaries of U.S. corporations unless the income is derived from a U.S. trade or business or from a U.S. investment. This exemption extends to the foreign subsidiary's U.S. owners, who generally are not taxed on their share of the subsidiary's earnings until they receive the earnings in the form of a dividend (but see discussion of controlled foreign corporations below). The remainder of this chapter examines the conduct of overseas businesses and the special tax treatment of their owners.

DOMESTIC SUBSIDIARY CORPORATIONS

The use of domestic subsidiaries to sell goods or provide services to foreign consumers offers two nontax advantages to U.S. multinationals. First, the foreign activities of the multinationals can be conducted separately from their domestic activities. Second, a subsidiary's liabilities can be separated from those of its parent corporation, thereby shielding the parent's assets from the subsidiary's creditors.

Profits from overseas business activities are taxed in the United States when earned. Losses are deductible when incurred. Because the foreign activities are conducted by a domestic corporation, they can be reported as part of a consolidated tax return that includes both the parent's and its domestic subsidiaries' operating results (see Chapter C:8 of this text). Thus, foreign losses can offset domestic profits and vice versa with respect to domestic losses.

ADDITIONAL COMMENT

The use of limited liability companies (LLCs) is popular with overseas activities. The profits and losses of an LLC pass through to its U.S. owners. In many cases, the U.S. owner of a foreign LLC is a U.S. corporation. Once the LLC becomes profitable, the U.S. owner can elect to be taxed as a C corporation under the check-the-box regulations and receive the benefits of the deferral privilege (see page C:16-20) or can continue to be treated as an LLC under its default classification.

FOREIGN BRANCHES

A domestic corporation may choose to conduct its overseas business through a foreign branch. A **foreign branch** is an unincorporated office or other fixed place of business (e.g., a manufacturing plant) maintained by a domestic entity in a foreign country. For tax purposes, a branch is treated as a legal extension of the domestic corporation. The domestic corporation reports profits attributable to the branch's foreign activities in the year in which the profits are earned, whether or not the branch remits the profits to the United States. Foreign income taxes paid or accrued on these profits are creditable against the domestic corporation's U.S. tax liability.

TOPIC REVIEW C:16-3

Taxation of Nonresident Aliens

1. Nonresident aliens are foreign nationals who do not reside in the United States. A foreign citizen can acquire U.S. resident alien status by satisfying either the lawful permanent residency test or the substantial presence test as set forth in U.S. law.
2. Foreign nationals generally have dual status in their first and last years of U.S. residency. The foreign national may be taxed as a resident alien for part of the year and as a nonresident alien for the remainder of the year. Two different tax computations for the year may be required.
3. Passive investment income (e.g., dividends, interest, rents) is taxed to a nonresident alien only if such income is U.S. source. The income is taxed at a flat 30% rate, unless reduced by tax treaty, with no allowance for deductions or exemptions.
4. Capital gains earned in the United States (other than those related to the conduct of a U.S. trade or business) are taxed at the 30% rate only if the foreign national is physically present in the United States for 183 or more days during the tax year.
5. The U.S. tax on investment income or capital gains is collected through withholding by the U.S. person who pays the income or gains to the nonresident alien.
6. The United States taxes a nonresident alien's ordinary income and capital gains that are effectively connected with the conduct of a U.S. trade or business. Related business expenses and losses are deductible from effectively connected income. In computing their U.S. tax liability, nonresident aliens can claim a single personal exemption but not a standard deduction. Graduated individual tax rates apply to the nonresident alien's U.S. taxable income. The foreign national voluntarily pays the tax owed on the effectively connected income through estimated tax payments and an annual remittance.
7. A special election to file a joint return with their U.S.-citizen or resident-alien spouse is available to nonresident aliens. If the nonresident alien makes the election, he or she is subject to U.S. taxation on his or her worldwide income.

Similarly, the domestic corporation reports losses attributable to the branch's foreign activities in the year in which the losses are incurred. Because deducting the losses reduces taxes on domestic profits, deductibility is a major advantage of conducting initial overseas activities through a branch. By using a branch, a domestic corporation can deduct start-up losses when incurred. Subject to branch loss recapture provisions, once the overseas activities become profitable, the domestic corporation can incorporate the branch in a foreign country and defer U.S. taxes on overseas profits until the profits are remitted to the United States.

FOREIGN CORPORATIONS

Conducting an overseas business through a foreign corporation offers the following four advantages:

- The foreign corporation's liabilities are separate from the assets of the parent corporation, thereby limiting the parent's losses to the extent of its capital investment in the foreign corporation.
- Unless the foreign corporation is "controlled" (see discussion of controlled foreign corporations below), the U.S. income tax on a U.S. stockholder's ratable share of the foreign corporation's earnings is deferred until the earnings are remitted to the United States.
- A domestic corporation that receives a dividend from a foreign corporation in which it owns at least 10% of the stock can claim a deemed paid tax credit for a ratable share of foreign income taxes paid or accrued by the foreign corporation.
- A domestic corporation that receives a dividend from a foreign corporation in which it owns at least 10% of the stock can claim a dividends-received deduction for the portion of any dividend paid out of the foreign corporation's undistributed profits that are effectively connected with the conduct of a U.S. trade or business. A dividends-received deduction is not available for dividends paid out of the foreign corporation's non-U.S. trade or business earnings.

The last three of these advantages, as well as the tax treatment of a foreign corporation's U.S. trade or business income, are discussed below.

ADDITIONAL COMMENT

This deferral privilege is eliminated for certain types of income of controlled foreign corporations. This topic is discussed later in the chapter.

Deferral Privilege. For U.S. tax purposes, foreign corporations are entities separate and distinct from their shareholders. The IRC effectively grants a **deferral privilege** to U.S. shareholders with respect to the foreign corporation's earnings. Under this privilege, the U.S. shareholders are not taxed on the foreign corporation's earnings until the earnings are repatriated, i.e., remitted to them as dividends.

EXAMPLE C:16-16 ▶ Adobe, a U.S. corporation, owns all the stock in Delta, a foreign corporation. In 2013, Delta reported $300,000 in after-tax profits from foreign manufacturing activities. Delta reinvested these profits outside the United States and remitted them to Adobe as a dividend in 2017. No U.S. income taxes are due on Delta's profits until 2017. This result contrasts with that for a foreign branch, whose earnings would have been taxable in the United States to Adobe in 2013. In principle, the value of the tax deferral (known as the "deferral privilege") equals the amount of U.S. taxes deferred times the time value of money for four years. ◀

TAX STRATEGY TIP

To enjoy the deferral privilege consider using a corporation rather than a branch for foreign operations.

Losses incurred by a foreign corporation cannot be deducted by any of its U.S. shareholders. Instead, the losses reduce profits earned in other years.

EXAMPLE C:16-17 ▶ Boston, a U.S. corporation, owns all the stock in Gulf, a foreign corporation. In the current year, Gulf reports $125,000 in losses. None of Gulf's current losses can be used to reduce Boston's current profits. Instead, in other years the losses can reduce Gulf's profits that might be distributed to Boston as dividends. Had the $125,000 of losses instead been incurred by a foreign branch, Boston could have used the current losses to offset its current profits. ◀

ADDITIONAL COMMENT

The deemed paid foreign tax credit is not available to individual U.S. shareholders.

Foreign Tax Credit. If a U.S. corporation conducts a foreign business through a foreign branch, it is directly liable for foreign taxes owed on the branch's earnings and can claim a direct U.S. credit for all such taxes paid or accrued. On the other hand, if a U.S. corporation conducts a foreign business through a foreign subsidiary, the foreign subsidiary is directly liable for foreign taxes owed on the subsidiary's earnings, and the U.S. corporation can claim a direct U.S. credit only for foreign taxes withheld from the subsidiary's dividend payments. Because most foreign countries impose taxes on foreign profits that are higher than taxes withheld on dividends, the foreign tax credit rules could discourage the use of foreign subsidiaries to conduct foreign businesses. To remedy this situation, Congress enacted the Sec. 902 **deemed paid credit** provisions relating to foreign income taxes paid or accrued by a foreign corporation.

For a U.S. corporation to claim a deemed paid credit, two conditions must be met:

- The foreign corporation must pay a dividend to the U.S. corporation out of the foreign corporation's earnings and profits (E&P).
- The U.S. corporation must own at least 10% of the foreign corporation's voting stock on the distribution date.[37]

TYPICAL MISCONCEPTION

The deemed paid credit is available from first- through sixth-tier foreign corporations (but not for seventh- and lower-tier corporations). The credit becomes available only as an *actual* dividend is paid from each subsidiary to its parent. The U.S. corporation claims the credit when the first-tier foreign corporation pays a dividend to the U.S. corporation.

Calculating the Deemed Paid Credit. The deemed paid credit for the domestic corporate shareholder is calculated as follows:[38]

$$\text{Deemed paid credit} = \frac{\text{Dividend paid to domestic corporation out of undistributed earnings}}{\text{Accumulated undistributed earnings}} \times \text{Creditable taxes paid or accrued by the foreign corporation}$$

[37] Secs. 902(a) and 902(b)(1)–(3). Foreign taxes paid by foreign subsidiaries of foreign corporations also qualify for the deemed paid credit.

[38] Sec. 902(a). Deemed paid foreign taxes are not deductible under Sec. 164. The calculation below pertains to post-1986 earnings and credits. Different rules apply to pre-1987 deemed paid credit calculations.

ADDITIONAL COMMENT
The foreign corporation's earnings and profits must be calculated under U.S. tax principles.

The undistributed earnings amount is not reduced by current dividends and is determined at the end of the current year. Dividends paid to all shareholders (U.S. and foreign) during the year reduce undistributed earnings at year-end. Creditable taxes also are determined at the end of the current year and include taxes paid, accrued, or deemed paid by the foreign corporation. Taxes attributable to all dividends paid during the current year reduce total taxes at year-end. The definition of "dividend" in the numerator of the fraction is the same as that for domestic corporate distributions out of E&P (see Chapter C:4).

Both the dividend received by the domestic corporation and the income equivalent of the pro rata share of foreign taxes associated with it are included in the domestic corporation's gross income.[39] This "gross up" for a pro rata share of foreign income taxes paid or accrued by the foreign corporation (equal to the amount of the deemed paid credit) precludes the domestic corporation's benefiting from both a deduction and a credit for such taxes (i.e., a deduction at the foreign corporate level and a credit at the domestic shareholder level).

EXAMPLE C:16-18 ▶ Coastal, a U.S. corporation, owns 40% of the stock in Bay, a foreign corporation. During the current year, Bay reports $200,000 of E&P, pays $50,000 in foreign income taxes, and remits $60,000 in dividends to Coastal. Bay withholds $6,000 in foreign taxes from the dividend payment. In prior tax years, Bay reported $100,000 of E&P, paid $40,000 in foreign income taxes, and paid no dividends. Based on a 34% corporate tax rate, Coastal's calculation of the deemed paid credit for the current year dividend is as follows:

$$\$18{,}000 = \frac{\$60{,}000}{\$200{,}000 + \$100{,}000} \times (\$50{,}000 + \$40{,}000)$$

The $18,000 credit amount is included in Coastal's income as a "gross up" and enters into the calculation of its U.S. tax liability:

Dividend	$60,000
Plus: Deemed paid credit gross up	18,000
Gross income	$78,000
Times: Corporate tax rate	× 0.34
Gross U.S. tax liability	$26,520
Minus: Deemed paid credit	(18,000)
Direct credit	(6,000)
Net U.S. tax liability	$ 2,520

◀

Translating the Dividend and Foreign Taxes into U.S. Dollars. Normally, a foreign corporation's books and records are maintained in the currency of the country in which the corporation operates. For U.S. tax reporting purposes, the dividend must be translated into U.S. dollars. If the distributee is a domestic corporation eligible for the deemed paid credit, the foreign corporation's E&P and foreign taxes also must be translated into U.S. dollars. The exchange rate for the date on which the dividend is included in gross income is used to translate the dividend paid by a noncontrolled foreign corporation, as well as the underlying E&P.[40] Translation of foreign taxes withheld from the dividend is based on the exchange rate in effect on the dividend payment date. For purposes of calculating the deemed paid credit, translation of foreign taxes is based on the exchange rate in effect on the date the foreign corporation pays the taxes.[41]

---

[39] Sec. 78.
[40] Reg. Secs. 1.301-1(b) and 1.902-1(g) and *The Bon Ami Co.*, 39 B.T.A. 825 (1939).
[41] Sec. 986(b).

EXAMPLE C:16-19 ▶ Houston, a U.S. corporation, owns 40% of the stock in Far East, a foreign corporation that began operations in Year 1. In Year 2, Far East pays Houston a 70,000 pira dividend. In Year 1 and Year 2, Far East earns 400,000 pira in pretax profits. It pays 30,000 and 20,000 pira in home country taxes respectively in Year 1 and Year 2. On the dividend payment date, the pira-U.S. dollar exchange rate is 1 pira = \$0.22 (U.S.). Far East paid the Year 1 and Year 2 foreign taxes when the exchange rates were 1 pira = \$0.20 (U.S.) and 1 pira = \$0.25 (U.S.), respectively. Far East's E&P is 350,000 (400,000 pretax profits − 50,000 taxes) pira. The translated dividend amount is 70,000 pira × \$0.22 = \$15,400. The translated foreign tax amount is \$11,000 [(30,000 pira × \$0.20) + (20,000 pira × \$0.25)]. The translated foreign taxes attributable to the dividend are \$2,200 [\$11,000 × (70,000 pira ÷ 350,000 pira)]. ◀

Foreign Tax Credit Baskets. U.S. corporate taxpayers that receive dividends from a 10/50 corporation must "look through" the foreign corporation to ascertain the source and character of the foreign corporation's earnings and profits out of which the dividends were paid. They then must apportion the dividends according to this source and character and assign them to one of two baskets (i.e., passive income and general limitation) into which the underlying earnings and profits would have been placed. (See the previous discussion of Special Foreign Tax Credit Limitations on page C:16-7.) To apply the Sec. 902 dividend "look through" rules, minority U.S. shareholders must rely on foreign corporations to supply them with information on the source and character of the corporation's earnings and profits.

The financial statement implications of the foreign tax credit are discussed at the end of this chapter.

ADDITIONAL COMMENT

Dividends paid by a foreign corporation out of its U.S. trade or business E&P are eligible for a dividends-received deduction.

Taxation of a Foreign Corporation's U.S. Trade or Business Income

Regular and Alternative Minimum Taxes. A foreign corporation that invests in the United States or that conducts a U.S. trade or business is taxed by the U.S. government in the same way as a nonresident alien. Section 881(a) taxes the U.S.-source investment income of a foreign corporation on a gross basis at a flat 30% rate (or lower rate specified by tax treaty). Capital gains that are not effectively connected with the conduct of a U.S. trade or business are exempt from U.S. taxation. The U.S. taxes on the investment income are collected through withholding.[42] Section 882(a) taxes that portion of the foreign corporation's income that is effectively connected with the conduct of a U.S. trade or business on a net basis at graduated rates. These earnings are not taxed to the foreign corporation's U.S. shareholders until they are distributed.

Section 245(a) allows a domestic corporation to deduct dividends (or a portion thereof) received from a foreign corporation in which it has at least a 10% stock interest. To be deductible, the dividends (or a portion thereof) must have been paid out of the foreign corporation's undistributed profits that are effectively connected with the conduct of a U.S. trade or business. The percentage (i.e., 70%, 80%, or 100%) of the effectively connected dividend amount that is deductible depends on the extent of the domestic corporation's stock ownership in the foreign corporation. The deductibility of the effectively connected dividend amount alleviates the double taxation of the foreign corporation's earnings that were previously taxed by the United States.

Branch Profits Tax. Income earned by a U.S. subsidiary of a foreign corporation is taxed twice: first, at the U.S. corporate level when earned; second, at the foreign shareholder level when distributed. The corporate level tax is assessed on a net basis at graduate rates. The U.S. subsidiary pays it voluntarily. The shareholder level tax is assessed on a gross dividend basis at a flat 30% rate, which may be reduced by treaty. The U.S. subsidiary withholds the tax and remits it to the IRS.

In a similar manner, income earned by an unincorporated U.S. branch of a foreign corporation also is taxed twice: first, at the branch level when earned; second, at the foreign corporate level when "remitted." The branch level tax is imposed on branch income

[42] Sec. 1442.

effectively connected with the conduct of a U.S. trade or business. It is assessed on a net basis at graduated rates. The corporate level tax is imposed on a "dividend equivalent amount" deemed to have been paid by the U.S. branch to the foreign corporation. This tax is assessed on a gross basis at a flat 30% rate, which may be reduced by treaty. The foreign corporation pays both of these taxes voluntarily.

The latter tax on deemed-distributed branch earnings is called the **branch profits tax.**[43] It is analogous to the 30% withholding tax on U.S. corporate dividends paid to foreign shareholders. The branch profits tax effectively places foreign corporations that conduct their U.S. business through an unincorporated U.S. branch on par with foreign corporations that conduct their U.S. business through a U.S. subsidiary. It ensures that both sets of foreign corporations are treated in the same way.

The branch profits tax equals 30% (or a lower rate specified in a tax treaty) times the dividend equivalent amount. The dividend equivalent amount equals the foreign corporation's E&P that is effectively connected with the conduct of its U.S. trade or business increased by the decrease (or decreased by the increase) in the foreign corporation's net equity investment in its branch assets during the year. Thus, the branch profits tax base is (1) increased by earnings remitted to the foreign corporation during the year as reflected by a decrease in the branch's U.S. trade or business assets and (2) decreased by earnings reinvested in branch operations during the year as reflected by an increase in the branch's U.S. trade or business assets. Under allocable interest rules, certain interest paid by a U.S. branch is taxed as if it were paid by a U.S. corporation. The interest income accruing to foreign creditors is considered to be U.S. source and hence subject to a 30% U.S. withholding tax (or a lower rate specified in a tax treaty).

CONTROLLED FOREIGN CORPORATIONS

Pre-Subpart F Rules. Before the 1962 enactment of the **controlled foreign corporation** (CFC) provisions (known as the Subpart F rules, discussed later), U.S. corporations set up majority owned foreign subsidiaries in "tax-haven" countries to minimize their U.S. tax liability on income earned from overseas operations. The typical scenario proceeded as follows:

- A U.S. manufacturer formed a sales subsidiary in a foreign country that imposed little or no corporate income tax.
- The U.S. manufacturer sold goods to foreign purchasers.
- The U.S. manufacturer shipped the goods directly to the foreign purchasers.
- The U.S. manufacturer billed the sales subsidiary for the goods at an artificially low price.
- The sales subsidiary, in turn, billed the foreign purchasers for the goods at an artificially high price.
- Through this scheme, the U.S. manufacturer effectively shifted its sale profits from the United States to the low tax jurisdiction in which the sales subsidiary operated.

A U.S. firm that performed services for foreign clients could devise a similar scheme. The following example illustrates how, absent Subpart F rules, a U.S. corporation could defer recognition of U.S. taxable income by conducting its foreign business through a foreign subsidiary as opposed to a foreign branch.

EXAMPLE C:16-20 ▶ Under pre-CFC rules, Chicago, a U.S. corporation, forms a foreign branch to conduct its overseas widget sales. The foreign country in which the branch operates imposes no income taxes. Chicago's overseas widget sales generate $1 million of profits annually. Chicago pays $340,000 ($1,000,000 × 0.34) in U.S. taxes and no foreign taxes in the year the income is earned. Had the same profit been divided equally between Chicago and Island Corporation, a newly formed foreign sales subsidiary, the worldwide tax cost would have been reduced substantially. Figure C:16-1 illustrates this result.

---

[43] Sec. 884(a).

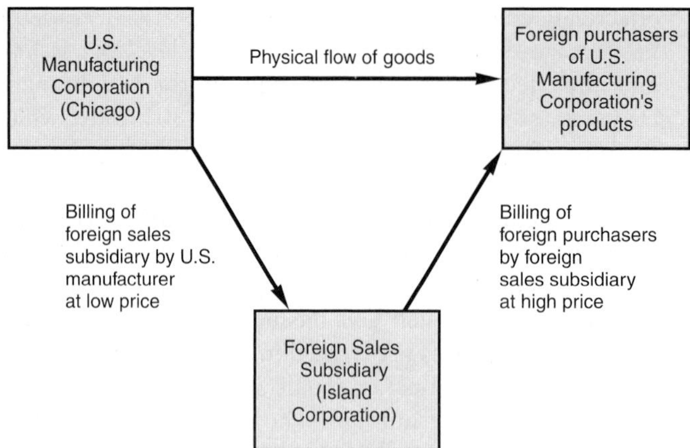

Sales made by Chicago's foreign branch:
$1,000,000 profit x 0.34 = $340,000 U.S. tax liability for Chicago. No foreign tax liability.

Sales made by Chicago. Profit divided equally between Chicago and Island Corporation in the absence of Subpart F rules:
Chicago: $500,000 profit x 0.34 = $170,000 U.S. tax liability.
Island: $500,000 profit x 0 = $0 Foreign Country tax liability (and no U.S. tax liability for Chicago until part or all of the profit is remitted to the United States.)

Sales made by Chicago. Profit divided equally between Chicago and Island Corporation in the absence of Subpart F rules:
Chicago: $500,000 profit on sales to Island x 0.34 = $170,000 U.S. tax liability.
$500,000 Subpart F income x 0.34 = $170,000 U.S. tax liability.
No U.S. tax liability when Island remits its profits to the United States.
Island: $500,000 profit x 0 = $0 Foreign Country tax liability and no U.S. tax liability.

FIGURE C:16-1 ▶ ILLUSTRATION OF USE OF FOREIGN SALES SUBSIDIARY (EXAMPLE C:16-20)

KEY POINT

The tainted income is taxable to Chicago (the CFC's U.S. parent) as a deemed paid dividend, rather than taxable directly to the CFC.

Chicago's $500,000 share of the profit results in a $170,000 ($500,000 × 0.34) U.S. tax liability. Island owes no U.S. or foreign tax on its $500,000 share of the profit. Chicago owes no U.S. tax on Island's share of the profits because the earnings have not been remitted as a dividend to its parent corporation in the United States. An attempt by Chicago to maximize its tax deferral by selling its widgets to Island at an artificially low price probably would be challenged by the IRS under the Sec. 482 transfer pricing rules (see page C:16-30). Section 482 would limit Island's profit to the portion of the $1 million total profit that it had earned, based on the value it had added to the goods. This amount may be less than the amount allocated under a 50–50 profit split method. ◀

Subpart F Rules. In the foregoing scenario, the Subpart F rules eliminate tax deferral by accelerating U.S. recognition of certain types of "tainted" income (see Figure C:16-2 for a summary of the Subpart F income categories).

EXAMPLE C:16-21 ▶ Assume the same facts as in Example C:16-20 except that Island is a CFC. Under current U.S. tax law, Island's profit on widgets manufactured by a related party outside Island's country of incorporation and resold to third parties outside Island's country of incorporation is considered tainted or Subpart F income (on the premise that positioning Island in that country was motivated primarily by tax avoidance). This profit is deemed to be distributed to Chicago on the last day of Island's tax year. Only the portion, if any, of Island's profits attributable to widget sales in Island's country of incorporation is untainted and thus deferred. If Island sells all the widgets outside its country of incorporation, its $500,000 of profits would be taxed directly to Chicago under the Subpart F rules. This result is basically the same as if Chicago had conducted its foreign sales through a foreign branch. ◀

Because of the increased tax cost associated with the Subpart F rules, U.S. businesses often arrange their overseas activities in such a way as to avoid CFC status or structure their transactions to avoid generating Subpart F income.

CFC Defined. A CFC is a foreign corporation in which more than 50% of the voting stock or more than 50% of the value of all outstanding stock is owned by U.S. shareholders

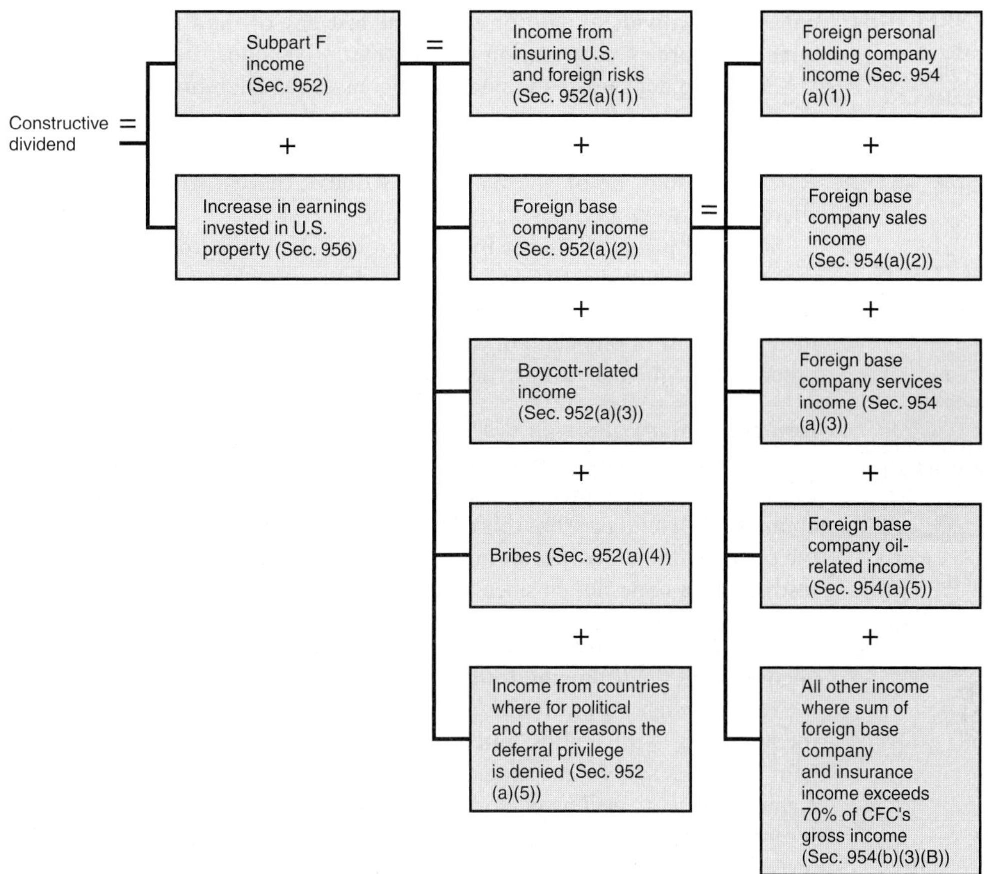

FIGURE C:16-2 ▶ TYPES OF INCOME EARNED BY A CONTROLLED FOREIGN CORPORATION (CFC) INCLUDIBLE IN THE GROSS INCOME OF ITS U.S. SHAREHOLDER(S)

on any day of the corporation's tax year.[44] A **U.S. shareholder** is a U.S. person who owns at least 10% of the foreign corporation's voting stock.[45] Ownership may be direct, indirect, or constructive. Constructive ownership is determined under the attribution rules of Sec. 318 (see Chapter C:4) with modifications specified in Sec. 958(b).

EXAMPLE C:16-22 ▶ Europa, a foreign corporation, is owned by five unrelated individuals. Al, Bill, and Connie are U.S. citizens who own 24%, 20%, and 9%, respectively, of Europa's voting and nonvoting stock. Duane and Elaine are nonresident aliens who own 40% and 7%, respectively, of Europa's voting and nonvoting stock. Only Al and Bill are considered U.S. shareholders because they are U.S. persons who own at least 10% of Europa's voting stock. Europa is not a CFC because Al and Bill together own only 44% of its voting and nonvoting stock. If Al instead were Connie's father, Connie would be a U.S. shareholder because, under the Sec. 318 family attribution rules, she would own 33% (9% directly + 24% constructively from Al) of Europa's voting stock. Europa then would be a CFC because its three U.S. shareholders together would own 53% (24% + 20% + 9%) of its voting and nonvoting stock. For purposes of the 50% rule, double counting Al's 24% interest to take into consideration both Al's and Connie's stockholdings is not permitted. ◀

Constructive Distributions of Subpart F Income. A U.S. shareholder is taxed on its ratable share of Subpart F income if the foreign corporation has been a CFC for at least 30 days during the tax year. Each U.S. shareholder reports its share as a

[44] Sec. 957(a). A CFC must adopt the same tax year as its majority U.S. shareholder if on the first day of the CFC's tax year (or other days as prescribed by the IRS) 50% or more of the voting power or value of all classes of the CFC's stock is directly, indirectly, or constructively owned by a single U.S. shareholder.

[45] Sec. 951(b). A "U.S. person" includes a U.S. citizen or resident alien, a domestic corporation, a domestic partnership, and a domestic trust or estate.

TYPICAL MISCONCEPTION

The election to be taxed as a domestic corporation allows an individual to take the deemed paid foreign tax credit. However, the election is seldom made because the income is taxed again when it is actually distributed.

constructive dividend paid on either the last day of the CFC's tax year or the last day on which the foreign corporation was a CFC.[46] The constructive dividend is included in the U.S. shareholder's gross income and increases the shareholder's basis in the CFC stock. If the U.S. shareholder is a domestic corporation, it is entitled to a deemed paid foreign tax credit for a ratable share of the CFC's foreign income taxes. If the U.S. shareholder is an individual, he or she may elect to have the constructive dividend taxed as if the shareholder were a domestic corporation.

BOOK-TO-TAX ACCOUNTING COMPARISON

A U.S. parent company's financial statements may include a foreign subsidiary's financial information in its worldwide consolidated financial statements. For tax purposes, the earnings of the foreign subsidiary are included in the parent company's U.S. federal tax return only when the earnings are repatriated to the United States or are taxed under the Subpart F rules. This deferral of the reporting of the foreign earnings for U.S. tax purposes may result in significant tax savings for the U.S. parent company.

Subpart F income falls into five categories: (1) income from insuring U.S. and foreign risks that originate outside the CFC's country of organization, (2) foreign base company income, (3) boycott-related income, (4) income equal to the amount of any bribes or other illegal payments made by or on behalf of the CFC, and (5) income from countries where for political or other reasons the deferral privilege is denied. These categories are discussed below.

Insuring U.S. and Foreign Risks. Income derived by the CFC from issuing (or reinsuring) an insurance or annuity contract is Subpart F income if the income would have been subject to tax under Subchapter L of the IRC had it been earned by a domestic (U.S.) insurance company.[47] Excluded from this rule is income earned by the CFC from insuring risks within the country of its incorporation on the premise that positioning the CFC in that country is justified by a bona fide business purpose.

Foreign Base Company Income. The broadest of all, this Subpart F income category encompasses the following four subcategories.

1. *Foreign personal holding company income* (FPHCI) includes passive investment income such as dividends, interest, royalties, annuities, and rents. FPHCI also includes gain from the sale or exchange of non-income-producing property, commodities, or foreign currency, as well as personal services contract income. It excludes rents and royalties received from a related corporation for the use of property within the CFC's country of incorporation. It also excludes income derived from the CFC's active conduct of a trade or business with an unrelated person. A special exception from the Subpart F rules applies to (1) active banking and finance income earned by a CFC predominantly or substantially engaged in a banking, financing, or similar business and (2) income from services related to the production of banking and finance income. An exception also applies to gains from property sales by security dealers. Dividends and interest are not FPHCI if received from a related corporation organized in the CFC's country of incorporation and whose principal assets are used in a trade or business in that country.[48]

EXAMPLE C:16-23 ▶ North is a CFC incorporated in Country X. North receives interest and dividends from its two foreign subsidiaries, East Corporation and West Corporation. East is incorporated in Country V and conducts all its business in that country. West is incorporated in Country X and conducts all its business in that country. Only the interest and dividends received from East are FPHCI because East is not incorporated in the same country as North. West's interest and dividends are not FPHCI because West is incorporated in Country X and conducts business within the same national market as North. ◀

KEY POINT

For foreign base company sales income to exist, the goods must be both manufactured and sold for use outside the CFC's country of incorporation. If the goods are manufactured or sold within the CFC's country of incorporation, the assumption is that a good business reason exists for operating the CFC in that country. Thus, the CFC should have no foreign base company sales income.

2. *Foreign base company sales income* includes fees and profits earned from the sale, or purchase and sale, of personal property outside the CFC's country of incorporation to or from a related party. The related party transactions that result in foreign base company sales income are[49]

- ▶ The purchase of personal property from a related person and its sale to any person
- ▶ The sale of personal property to any person on behalf of a related person (e.g., an agent on commission)
- ▶ The purchase of personal property from any person and its sale to a related person
- ▶ The purchase of personal property from any person on behalf of a related person

[46] Sec. 951(a).

[47] Sec. 953(a)(1).

[48] Sec. 954(c). Section 954(d)(3) defines "related person" for Subpart F purposes as (a) any individual, corporation, partnership, trust, or estate that controls, or is controlled by, the CFC, or (b) any corporation, partnership, trust, or estate controlled by the same persons who control the CFC. "Control" means direct, indirect, or constructive ownership of 50% or more of the total voting power or total value of the CFC's stock.

[49] Sec. 954(d)(1).

Foreign base company sales income excludes profits derived from the sale of products either manufactured in the CFC's country of incorporation, sold for use in the CFC's country of incorporation, or produced by the CFC on the premise that positioning the CFC in that country was for a bona fide business purpose, and therefore was not motivated by tax avoidance.[50]

EXAMPLE C:16-24 ▶ Dublin Corporation is a CFC organized in Country F. Dublin purchases machine tools from its U.S. parent for sale to unrelated parties. Dublin sells 70% of the tools in Country E and 30% in Country F. Only the profit earned from the sale of tools in Country E constitutes foreign base company sales income. If Dublin manufactured the machine tools, none of its profit from the Country E or Country F sales would be foreign base company sales income. ◀

ADDITIONAL COMMENT

Goods are deemed to have been manufactured by the CFC if it substantially transforms the product (such as making screws and bolts from steel rods) or if its direct labor and factory overhead account for 20% or more of the total cost of goods sold.

3. *Foreign base company services income* includes compensation for services provided for or on behalf of a related person outside the CFC's country of incorporation. In general, compensation for personal services is considered to be earned at the location where the services are performed.[51]

EXAMPLE C:16-25 ▶ Andes Corporation, organized in Country A, is 100% owned by Hi-Tech, a U.S. corporation. Hi-Tech sells industrial machines to unrelated Amazon Corporation for use in Country B. Hi-Tech assigns the portion of the sales contract covering the installation and maintenance of the machines to Andes, and Hi-Tech pays Andes for these services. Earnings derived from the installation and maintenance is foreign base company services income because Andes performs these services for a related party (Hi-Tech) outside its country of incorporation (Country A). ◀

4. *Foreign base company oil-related income* includes earnings derived from oil and gas related activities (other than the extraction of oil and gas) conducted in a foreign country. Such activities include the transport, shipping, processing, and distribution of oil and gas and any related service. Foreign base company oil-related income is not taxed under Subpart F if it is earned in the foreign country in which the oil and gas was extracted.[52]

WHAT WOULD YOU DO IN THIS SITUATION?

You are a tax manager assigned to the U.S. Manufacturing and Export Corporation (USM&E) account. USM&E manufactures machine tools for distribution throughout North and South America. USM&E sells its products to six 100%-owned foreign subsidiaries that resell the products in various North and South American markets. In reviewing USM&E's operating results, you notice that sales to the U.S. and Canadian subsidiaries account for the largest profit margin. USM&E revenues from sales to the four Central and South American subsidiaries are barely above related manufacturing costs. Upon examining prior year information, you discover that Canadian income tax rates are nearly the same as U.S. rates while the rates in the other countries are substantially lower. The sales manager at USM&E tells you that this organizational structure has been in place for years and the operations of the six sales subsidiaries are substantially identical. He also informs you that none of the other tax professionals who have worked on the account has ever questioned USM&E's sales and pricing. In reviewing USM&E's data, you discover that additional costs were incurred to ship the goods from the United States to Central and South America, but these costs do not justify the price differences between the sales made in these regions and the sales made in the United States and Canada. You suspect that a transfer pricing problem exists. What benefit can USM&E derive from its current pricing scheme? Can you advise your client about possible negative tax consequences of inappropriate pricing? Under U.S. tax laws, are any alternatives available to USM&E that might permit it to use different pricing methods or non-arm's-length transfer prices? Can USM&E obtain advice from the IRS concerning the soundness of its pricing methods?

[50] Sec. 954(d) and Reg. Sec. 1.954-3(a)(4)(i).
[51] Sec. 954(e).
[52] Sec. 954(g).

On the premise that generating certain types of income is not motivated primarily by tax avoidance, Subpart F income specifically excludes the following income items:

- Income earned by the CFC in the conduct of a U.S. trade or business. Such income is taxed directly to the CFC.[53]
- Foreign base company income or insurance income that is subject to an effective foreign tax rate greater than 90% of the maximum U.S. corporate rate.[54]
- Foreign base company income and insurance income that in total are less than the smaller of 5% of the CFC's gross income or $1 million.[55]
- Income earned by the CFC that cannot be repatriated to the United States because of currency or other restrictions.[56]

However, when foreign base company income and insurance income exceed 70% of the CFC's total gross income, all the CFC's gross income is deemed to be foreign base company income or insurance income.[57]

REAL-WORLD EXAMPLE

Countries that participate in, or cooperate with, international boycotts include Iraq, Kuwait, Lebanon, Libya, Qatar, Saudi Arabia, Syria, the United Arab Emirates, and Yemen.

Boycott-Related Income. For policy reasons, this category includes any income derived by the CFC from the participation in, or cooperation with, an international boycott against a particular nation (or group of nations). The portion of the CFC's profits that are boycott-related is determined under the rules of Sec. 999.

Bribes, Kickbacks, and Other Illegal Payments. Likewise, for policy reasons, the CFC loses its deferral privilege for the earnings equivalent of all bribes, kickbacks, and other illegal payments that it makes.

Earnings Derived in Certain Foreign Countries. U.S. shareholders of a CFC cannot defer income derived from activities in certain countries. These countries include those the U.S. government does not recognize, those with whom the U.S. Government has frozen or severed diplomatic relations, and those the U.S. Government believes support international terrorism.

Related Deductions. Subpart F income is reduced by any related deductions, the allocation of which are based on rules set forth in Reg. Sec. 1.861-8.[58]

ADDITIONAL COMMENT

Income derived from the following countries is not eligible for the deferral privilege: Iran, North Korea, Sudan, and Syria.

Increase in Earnings Invested in U.S. Property. Dividends paid by a CFC to its U.S. shareholders may be both taxed to the shareholders in the United States and subject to tax withholding in the foreign country. In the absence of special rules, the CFC could avoid the U.S. tax by either investing its earnings in U.S. property or lending funds to its U.S. shareholders, thereby affording them the beneficial use of CFC earnings without an actual earnings distribution. To close this loophole, Congress enacted a special IRC provision that taxes the U.S. shareholders on their respective pro rata shares of any increase in CFC earnings invested in U.S. property. Under this provision, each U.S. shareholder is deemed to receive a constructive distribution equal to the lesser of the shareholder's ratable share of U.S. property held by the CFC minus the CFC's E&P previously taxed as a constructive distribution, or the shareholder's ratable share of CFC earnings for the year.[59] CFC earnings previously taxed as Subpart F income may be invested in U.S. property without the shareholder's incurring additional tax liability. Such amounts, if distributed, would not constitute a dividend.

ADDITIONAL COMMENT

If the CFC guarantees an obligation of a U.S. person, it is deemed to hold that obligation. Thus, if a CFC guarantees a loan of its U.S. parent, the guarantee constitutes the acquisition of U.S. property. This result can be a tax trap for the unwary.

The U.S. property value is based on the average adjusted basis (minus any liability to which the property is subject) as of the last day of each quarter of the CFC's tax year. U.S. property includes tangible property located in the United States, stock in domestic corporations, obligations of U.S. persons, and intangibles developed by the CFC for use in the United States.[60] U.S. property excludes U.S. government obligations, U.S. bank deposits, stock in domestic corporations that are not U.S. shareholders of the CFC or more than 25% owned by a U.S. shareholder, U.S. securities acquired by CFC security dealers, obligations issued by non-corporate U.S. persons unrelated to the CFC, and U.S. property acquired before the first and after the last day on which the foreign corporation was "controlled."

[53] Sec. 952(b).
[54] Sec. 954(b)(4).
[55] Sec. 954(b)(3)(A).
[56] Sec. 964(b).
[57] Sec. 954(b)(3)(B).
[58] Sec. 954(b)(5).
[59] Sec. 951(a)(2).
[60] Sec. 956(c)(1).

EXAMPLE C:16-26 ▶ Forco is a CFC in its initial year of operation. During the current year, Forco reports $1 million of earnings, none of which is taxed as Subpart F income. On December 31, Forco invests in U.S. property worth $400,000. Because of this additional investment, which affords Forco's U.S. shareholders beneficial use of CFC income, $400,000 of Forco's earnings are no longer deferred and are taxed ratably to the shareholders. ◀

SELF-STUDY QUESTION

If $500,000 of the $1 million in Example C:16-26 had been Subpart F income (and thus currently taxed to the CFC's U.S. shareholders), would the acquisition of the U.S. property also be taxed currently?

ANSWER

The E&P invested in U.S. property is deemed to come first out of the E&P that has been previously taxed. Therefore, the U.S. shareholders would incur no additional tax liability as a result of the U.S. investment.

Distributions from a CFC. Distributions from a CFC are deemed to be made first out of any increase in earnings invested in U.S. property and the CFC's most recently accumulated Subpart F income, then out of its U.S. tax-deferred earnings, if any. Distributions of previously taxed income (i.e., the increase in earnings invested in U.S. property and Subpart F income) are tax-free to the U.S. shareholder and reduce his or her basis in CFC stock.[61]

EXAMPLE C:16-27 ▶ Bulldog, a domestic corporation, owns all the stock in Marine, a CFC. Bulldog's cost basis in the Marine stock is $600,000. Since the time Bulldog acquired the stock, Marine generated $400,000 of E&P, of which $175,000 was taxed to Bulldog as Subpart F income. Marine distributes $200,000 cash to Bulldog. Of this amount, $175,000 is deemed to be a nontaxable distribution of previously taxed Subpart F income. The remaining $25,000 is deemed to be a taxable distribution of earnings that were not previously taxed under Subpart F. After the distribution, Bulldog's basis in the Marine stock is $600,000 ($600,000 + $175,000 − $175,000). ◀

KEY POINT

Section 1248 is a backstop to the Subpart F rules in that it subjects gain from disposition of CFC stock to taxation as ordinary income to the extent that it previously has not been taxed.

Disposition of CFC Stock. Section 1248 applies to U.S. persons who own at least 10% of a foreign corporation's voting stock and who sell or exchange the stock within five years after any time the foreign corporation was a CFC. The gain recognized on the sale or exchange is taxed as a dividend to the extent of the U.S shareholder's pro rata share of the CFC's untaxed E&P. This amount is further prorated to reflect the time the U.S. person held the stock and the period during which the foreign corporation was a CFC.[62] The remaining portion of the gain is treated as capital in character. Foreign taxes associated with the dividend portion of the gain qualify for the deemed paid foreign tax credit.

EXAMPLE C:16-28 ▶ On November 1 of Year 1, Texas, a domestic corporation, purchased 200 of the 500 outstanding shares of Le Chien Corporation's stock. Texas holds the shares until March 31 of Year 2, when it sells the stock for a $60,000 gain. Le Chien is a CFC at all times while Texas owns its stock. Le Chien's E&P amounts not previously taxed to Texas under the Subpart F rules are as follows: Year 1, $60,000; Year 2, $30,000; and Year 3, $70,000. The untaxed E&P attributable to the stock sold or exchanged is determined under the following formula:

$$\text{CFC's untaxed E\&P for tax year} \times \frac{\text{Number of shares sold or exchanged}}{\text{Number of shares outstanding}} \times \frac{\text{Number of days shares are owned while corporation is a CFC}}{\text{Number of days in CFC's tax year*}} = \text{CFC's untaxed E\&P attributable to shares sold or exchanged}$$

$$\text{Year 1: } \$60{,}000 \times \frac{200}{500} \times \frac{61}{365} = \$\,4{,}011$$

$$\text{Year 2: } \$30{,}000 \times \frac{200}{500} \times \frac{365}{365} = 12{,}000$$

$$\text{Year 3: } \$70{,}000 \times \frac{200}{500} \times \frac{90}{365} = 6{,}904$$

$$\text{Total} \qquad \$22{,}915$$

* For a non-leap year, 365 days; for a leap year, 366 days. Note: For a leap year, both the numerator and denominator would increase by one digit if the holding period extends beyond February 28.

Thus, $22,915 of the gain is treated as a dividend, and $37,085 ($60,000 − $22,915) is treated as capital in character. Texas can claim a deemed paid credit for a pro rata share of foreign taxes actually paid by Le Chien on the earnings out of which the CFC paid the dividend. ◀

ADDITIONAL COMMENT

For U.S. taxpayers operating in a foreign country with a high tax rate, Sec. 1248 is a tax benefit and not a tax detriment. The combination of Sec. 1248's dividend treatment and the availability of the Sec. 902 deemed paid credit reduces the U.S. tax liability to below the U.S. tax liability if the gain were instead taxed as a capital gain.

[61] Secs. 959(c) and 961(b).

[62] Sec. 1248(a).

TYPICAL MISCONCEPTION

Section 482 applies to transactions involving two U.S. entities as well as to transactions involving a U.S. entity and a foreign entity.

Section 482 Rules and Tax Avoidance. Transactions between a domestic corporation and its foreign subsidiary, or between a foreign corporation and its U.S. subsidiary, present opportunities for tax avoidance. For example, the domestic corporation could sell goods to, or provide services for, the subsidiary at a price less than the price that would be obtained in an arm's-length dealing (see Figure C:16-1 and related text). Alternatively, the foreign subsidiary could pay a less-than-arm's-length price for the use of intangibles (such as patents or trademarks). Both transactions increase the foreign subsidiary's profits that may be deferred for U.S. tax purposes.

EXAMPLE C:16-29 ▶ Taylor, a U.S. corporation, sells widgets to its wholly owned foreign subsidiary, Wheeler Corporation. Wheeler is incorporated in, pays taxes to, and sells the widgets in Country Z. Taylor normally sells widgets at a price of $10 per unit to a U.S. wholesaler that provides services similar to those provided by Wheeler. Both the U.S. wholesaler and Wheeler incur similar costs. If Taylor sells the widgets to Wheeler at $8 per unit, Wheeler's profits increase by $2 per unit, and Taylor's profits decrease by $2 per unit. The additional profit is not Subpart F income because it is derived from sales by the CFC within its country of incorporation. Thus, the additional profit is isolated in Country Z. It is not taxed by the United States until Wheeler remits it to Taylor as a dividend. ◀

EXAMPLE C:16-30 ▶ Assume the same facts as in Example C:16-29 except Taylor instead issues a license to Wheeler to manufacture the widgets and charges a $1 per-unit royalty for each unit produced and sold. A licensing agreement between Taylor and an unrelated foreign widget producer specifies a $3 per-unit royalty payment. The reduced royalty rate increases Wheeler's profits by an additional $2 per unit. Because the profit is derived from manufacturing performed by a CFC, the additional profit is not taxed to Taylor as Subpart F income. Such profit is U.S. tax deferred until Wheeler remits it to Taylor as a dividend. ◀

Section 482 authorizes the IRS to distribute, apportion, or allocate gross income, deductions, credits or allowances between or among controlled entities to prevent tax evasion and to clearly reflect income. The IRS may use this authority under the following circumstances:

- Two or more organizations, trades, or businesses exist.
- They are owned or controlled by the same persons.
- A transaction between or among the entities does not reflect the income that would have been earned in an arm's-length transaction.

The **Sec. 482 rules** can apply to transactions between two unincorporated entities, two incorporated entities, or one incorporated entity and one unincorporated entity. The related persons can be domestic or foreign and need not be members of an affiliated group that files a consolidated return. In the two preceding examples, Sec. 482 would authorize the IRS to adjust the prices and/or profits reported by Taylor and Wheeler to reflect an arm's-length transaction.

Treasury Regulations under Sec. 482 provide guidance for determining an arm's-length standard in various types of transactions, including

- Loans or advances
- Performance of services
- Sales, transfers, or use of intangible property
- Sales, transfers, or use of tangible property
- Cost sharing arrangements[63]

These rules create safe harbors for taxpayers engaged in related party transactions. If the transaction price meets the standard set forth in the Sec. 482 Treasury Regulations, the IRS generally will not challenge it.

[63] Reg. Sec. 1.482-1 through -6 and -8.

REAL-WORLD EXAMPLE

From 1991 through December 31, 2015, the IRS entered into 2,147 advance pricing agreements (APAs) with taxpayers. APAs provide advance Sec. 482 approval for the transfer pricing procedures used by the taxpayer on transfers of tangible personal property or financial instruments. Most APAs cover a five-year period, at which time they must be renewed.

Treasury Regulations finalized in 1994 offer additional guidance. For example, Reg. Sec. 1.482-3(b)(2) states that a transaction involving the transfer of tangible property (as in Example C:16-29) between controlled taxpayers meets the arm's-length standard if the results are consistent with the outcome that would have been obtained had uncontrolled taxpayers engaged in a *comparable* transaction under *comparable* circumstances. The transaction and circumstances are comparable only if minor differences between the transactions have no effect on the amount charged, or if these differences can be reconciled through a reasonable number of adjustments to the uncontrolled transaction. If no uncontrolled transaction is comparable, the resale price, cost-plus, comparable profits, profit-split, or any other appropriate method approved by the IRS can be used.

For intangibles (as in Example C:16-30), the arm's-length price in a controlled transfer of an intangible is the same as that in a comparable uncontrolled transfer. An uncontrolled transfer is comparable to a controlled transfer if it involves similar intangible property and occurs under similar circumstances, as explained in Reg. Sec. 1.482-4(c)(2). If significant differences exist between the controlled and uncontrolled transfers that make them substantially dissimilar, the comparable profits method may not be used. The comparable profits method derives the arm's-length price paid in a controlled transfer of property from objective measures of profitability (e.g., profit level indicators such as rates of return) specific to uncontrolled persons engaged in similar business activities with other uncontrolled persons under similar circumstances. If the comparable profits method cannot be used, the taxpayer can petition the IRS to use another method.

ADDITIONAL COMMENT

Many federal government documents are available to the general public under the Freedom of Information Act (FOIA). Advance pricing arrangements (APAs), however, receive special treatment under the FOIA. APAs, both past and present, and their related background files are treated as confidential tax return information.

Section 482 permits the IRS periodically to adjust the level of payments for the use of an intangible to reflect its current revenue yield. Thus, in setting the initial royalty rate, related parties should consider projected operating results, including changes in the income stream attributed to the intangible.

A net Sec. 482 transfer pricing adjustment for the provision of services, or the sale or use of property, could constitute a substantial valuation misstatement under Sec. 6662(e)(1)(B) if it exceeds the lesser of $5 million or 10% of the taxpayer's gross receipts. If so, the IRS could impose an accuracy-related penalty equal to 20% of the tax underpayment attributable to the valuation misstatement.

INVERSIONS

In our federal system of taxation, the tax treatment of U.S. corporations differs significantly from the tax treatment of foreign corporations. Specifically, U.S. corporations are taxed on their worldwide income, both U.S.- and foreign-source. By contrast, foreign corporations are taxed almost exclusively on their U.S.-source business and investment income. Unless effectively connected with the conduct of a U.S. trade or business (or attributable to a U.S. "permanent establishment" under the terms of a treaty), the foreign-source income of foreign corporations largely escapes U.S. taxation.

This difference in tax treatment creates an incentive for U.S. corporations with substantial foreign-source income to reorganize as a foreign corporation in transactions known as **inversions**. Typically, in an inversion, a U.S. corporation (1) merges into a foreign entity or transfers substantially all of its assets to the foreign entity; (2) the owners of the U.S. business exchange stock in the U.S. corporation for equity in the foreign entity; and (3) the same owners continue to conduct their U.S. business, as well as their foreign operations, through the foreign entity. Following the merger or asset transfer, income from the U.S. business continues to be subject to U.S. taxation, but income from the foreign business largely escapes U.S. taxation.

Because inversions erode the U.S. corporate tax base, Congress added two anti-inversion provisions to Secs. 367 and 7874. Under the first provision, a foreign corporation will be deemed to be a U.S. corporation for U.S. tax purposes if (1) the foreign corporation acquired substantially all the assets of a U.S. corporation, (2) former shareholders of the

U.S. corporation own 80% or more (by vote or value) of stock in the foreign corporation by reason of their U.S. stock ownership, and (3) the foreign corporation and its affiliates do not conduct substantial business in the foreign country of incorporation.

ADDITIONAL COMMENT

Because of the recent spate of corporate inversions, the Treasury Department has stepped up its enforcement of anti-inversion provisions with additional measures to reduce or eliminate the tax advantages of these transactions.

Under the second anti-inversion provision, income recognized in an inversion transaction, as well as related taxes, cannot be offset by the U.S. corporation's otherwise available tax attributes (e.g., net operating losses or foreign tax credits) for a ten-year period if conditions (1) through (3) in the previous paragraph are met, with the substitution of 60% ownership for 80% ownership. Thus, if in the inversion, (1) the foreign corporation acquires substantially all the assets of a U.S. corporation, (2) former shareholders of the U.S. corporation own between 60% and 80% of the foreign corporation's stock by reason of their U.S. stock ownership, and (3) the foreign corporation and its affiliates do not conduct substantial business in the foreign country of incorporation, income recognized on the asset transfer cannot be reduced by the U.S. corporation's otherwise available net operating losses, and taxes owed on this income cannot be offset with the U.S. corporation's otherwise available foreign tax credits. Excepted from the rule are sales of inventory and similar property to a foreign related person.

EXAMPLE C:16-31 ▶ Gomez, Nguyen, Jones, and Ahmed own equal shares of Wilmington-Domestic, a U.S. corporation. The corporation generates $20 million of income from its U.S. business and $60 million of income from a business conducted in Country X. In an attempt to remove its foreign business income from U.S. taxing jurisdiction, Wilmington-Domestic reorganizes as Wilmington-Foreign in Country Z. In the reorganization, Gomez, Nguyen, Jones, and Ahmed exchange their stock in Wilmington-Domestic for an equal number of shares in Wilmington-Foreign, and Wilmington-Domestic merges into Wilmington-Foreign. Following the reorganization, Wilmington-Foreign conducts the U.S. and Country X businesses but conducts no business in Country Z. Under the first anti-inversion rule, Wilmington-Foreign will be treated as a U.S. corporation, and thus taxed on its worldwide income, because (1) Wilmington-Foreign acquired substantially all the assets of Wilmington-Domestic; (2) Gomez, Nguyen, Jones, and Ahmed own more than 80% of Wilmington-Foreign stock by reason of their Wilmington-Domestic stock ownership; and (3) Wilmington-Foreign conducts no business in Country Z. ◀

EXAMPLE C:16-32 ▶ Assume the same facts as in the preceding example except that only Gomez, Nguyen, and Jones exchange their stock in Wilmington-Domestic for an equal number of shares in Wilmington-Foreign (75% of the total). Under the second anti-inversion rule, any income recognized on the merger of Wilmington-Domestic into Wilmington-Foreign cannot be reduced by Wilmington-Domestic's otherwise available net operating losses, if any. Moreover, taxes owed on this income cannot be offset by Wilmington-Domestic's otherwise available foreign tax credits, if any. ◀

TAX PLANNING CONSIDERATIONS

OBJECTIVE 5

Identify tax planning opportunities for U.S. taxpayers engaged in foreign transactions and operations

DEDUCTION VERSUS CREDIT FOR FOREIGN TAXES

Taxpayers may elect annually to deduct or credit any paid or accrued foreign income taxes.[64] Nearly all taxpayers elect to credit them. The advantage of doing so is illustrated in the following example.

[64] Sec. 901(a).

EXAMPLE C:16-33 ▶ Phil, a U.S. citizen, earns $100 of foreign income. Phil pays $25 in foreign income taxes and is subject to a 28% marginal tax rate. He makes the following calculations to compare the advantages of crediting the taxes versus deducting them.

	Deduction	*Credit*
Gross income	$100	$100
Minus: Foreign tax deduction	(25)	–0–
Taxable income	$ 75	$100
Times: Marginal tax rate	× 0.28	× 0.28
Gross U.S. tax liability	$ 21	$ 28
Minus: Foreign tax credit	–0–	(25)
Net U.S. tax liability	$ 21	$ 3

If Phil deducts the foreign income taxes, his total U.S. and foreign tax liability is $46 ($25 + $21). By claiming the credit, Phil reduces his total U.S. and foreign tax liability to $28 ($25 + $3). ◀

REAL-WORLD EXAMPLE

Seldom will it be advantageous for a taxpayer to deduct foreign taxes paid when such taxes can be claimed as a foreign tax credit. Some taxpayers deduct their foreign taxes, when small in amount, because of the complexity of complying with the foreign tax credit rules (e.g., figuring out the law and filing the necessary form(s)). The complexity of the foreign tax credit rules for individual taxpayers having less than $300 ($600 for joint filers) of foreign passive income is substantially reduced because they are not subject to foreign tax credit limitation.

Some taxpayers deduct their foreign income taxes when they incur foreign losses or when they cannot credit the taxes either in the current year or in any of the one carryback or ten carryover years. The deduction provides current tax benefits where U.S. profits exceed foreign losses. If no U.S. profits are earned, the foreign taxes increase the taxpayer's NOL.

ELECTION TO ACCRUE FOREIGN TAXES

Cash method taxpayers may elect to accrue foreign taxes for credit purposes. The election permits them to credit foreign income taxes that have accrued but have not yet been paid. It does not affect the application of the cash method of accounting to other taxable items. The election is not available for the purpose of deducting foreign taxes. It is binding on all tax years and can be revoked only with IRS consent.[65]

TOPIC REVIEW C:16-4

Taxation of U.S. Persons Doing Business Abroad

TYPE OF ENTITY USED	TAX TREATMENT
Domestic subsidiary	Profits are taxed to the subsidiary (or the consolidated group) in the year earned. A direct foreign tax credit is available for foreign taxes paid or accrued. Losses are deducted in the year incurred.
Foreign branch	Foreign branches are unincorporated extensions of domestic entities. Branch profits are taxed to the entity in the year earned. A direct foreign tax credit is available for foreign taxes paid or accrued on branch profits. Branch losses are deducted in the year incurred.
Foreign corporation (less than 50% U.S.-owned)	A foreign corporation's earnings are tax deferred until repatriated to the United States. A domestic corporation can claim a deemed paid foreign tax credit with respect to dividends received from a foreign corporation in which it owns at least a 10% interest.
Controlled foreign corporation (CFC, more than 50% U.S.-owned)	Same rules as for previous entry. Subpart F income of the CFC is taxed to its U.S. shareholders in the year in which earned. The increase in CFC earnings invested in U.S. property is subject to U.S. taxation. Previously taxed income is distributed tax-free. Special rules apply to the sale or exchange of CFC stock.

[65] Sec. 905(a).

Two advantages ensue from this election.

- It accelerates use of the foreign tax credit by one or more tax years.
- It eliminates the problem of matching foreign income with foreign taxes for credit limitation purposes. In many cases, it obviates the need for a carryback or carryover of excess credits.

EXAMPLE C:16-34 In Year 1, Tulsa, a U.S. corporation and cash method taxpayer, began a business in Country Z. Z's tax laws require the use of a calendar year for tax reporting purposes. Taxes owed on income earned during the year must be paid by the first day of the third month following year-end. Tulsa conducts its foreign operations for three years before ceasing business on December 31 of Year 3. Its results are as follows:

	Year 1	*Year 2*	*Year 3*	*Year 4*
Foreign source taxable income	$1,000	$1,000	$1,000	$-0-
Foreign taxes accrued (30% rate)	300	300	300	-0-
Foreign taxes paid	-0-	300	300	300
Foreign tax credit limitation (34% U.S. corporate rate)	340	340	340	-0-
Foreign tax credit:				
Cash method	-0-	300	300	300
Accrual method	300	300	300	-0-

Under the cash method, Tulsa pays its Year 1 U.S. taxes without the benefit of a foreign tax credit. In Year 4, Tulsa generates $300 of excess credits because of the annual mismatching of foreign tax accruals and foreign tax payments. The Year 4 foreign tax payment of $300 carries back to Year 3, but only $40 of that amount can be credited because the excess limitation in Year 3 is only $40. In principle, the $260 foreign tax credit balance should carry forward to Year 5, but because Tulsa discontinued its operations at the end of Year 3, it has no U.S. tax liability in Year 5 with which to offset the $260 carryover. ◀

SPECIAL EARNED INCOME ELECTIONS

Taxpayers may revoke a previous election to exclude foreign-earned income or not make the initial election if they find themselves in one of two situations:

- They are employed in a foreign country where the foreign tax rate exceeds the U.S. tax rate (e.g., United Arab Emirates).
- They incur a substantial loss from overseas employment or in a trade or business.

In the first situation, the available foreign tax credits exceed the taxpayer's gross U.S. tax liability. The foreign-earned income exclusion diminishes the utility of the excess credits. By including foreign earned income in gross income, the taxpayer can use the entire amount of excess credits as a carryback or carryover (subject to separate basket limitations). These excess credits might be beneficial if, for example, the taxpayer earned self-employment income in another year in a foreign country where the tax rate is lower than the U.S. rate.

In the second situation, the foreign deductions of taxpayers who incur substantial losses may exceed their foreign gross income. If these taxpayers exclude part or all of their foreign-earned income from their total gross income, a pro rata portion of the related foreign expenses will be disallowed. This disallowance reduces the amount of any available NOL carryback or carryover. Including foreign earnings in the taxpayer's gross income allows the excess foreign expense portion to be deducted.

Taxpayers may not elect to exclude or deduct the housing cost amount. A qualifying taxpayer who receives only this amount (reported as W-2 income) from his or her employer must exclude it from gross income. If the taxpayer earns only self-employment income, he or she must deduct the housing cost amount. If the taxpayer earns both salary (or wages) and self-employment income, he or she must apportion the housing cost amount between an exclusion and a deduction based on the pro rata amounts of income earned.

A taxpayer can forego the foreign earned income benefits by so electing on his or her current return or on an amended return. If the taxpayer revokes the initial election, he or she may not make a new election for five years or until the IRS consents.[66] Thus, a taxpayer who revokes an election while residing in a country with a tax rate higher than the U.S. rate may not elect to exclude foreign earned income if shortly thereafter he or she moves to a country with a tax rate lower than that in the United States.

ADDITIONAL COMMENT

With certain exceptions, whenever a treaty and the IRC are in conflict, the treaty takes precedence.

TAX TREATIES

A treaty is an agreement between two or more sovereign nations. The United States has concluded tax treaties with over 100 countries. Income **tax treaties** have numerous objectives, including

- To reduce or eliminate double taxation
- To facilitate the exchange of information among taxing authorities
- To provide a mechanism for resolving disputes between residents or citizens of one country and residents or citizens of another country

In addition to income tax treaties, the United States has concluded estate and gift tax treaties, as well as Social Security tax totalization agreements.

Notwithstanding the provisions of any treaty, U.S. citizens and U.S. corporations are still taxed on their worldwide income at regular U.S. rates. A tax treaty to which the United States is a party cannot be used by U.S. citizens or U.S. corporations to reduce the scope of their income subject to U.S. taxation. On the other hand, a tax treaty can reduce the foreign taxes that U.S. citizens or U.S. corporations pay on their foreign-source investment income, and it allows them to credit against their U.S. tax liability foreign taxes paid on their foreign-source business income. Conversely, a tax treaty can reduce the U.S. taxes that foreign citizens or foreign corporations pay on their U.S.-source investment income, and it allows them to credit against their foreign tax liability U.S. taxes paid on their U.S.-source business income.

ADDITIONAL COMMENT

Tax treaties designate a competent authority to represent each country when an international tax dispute arises between the treaty partners. The U.S. competent authority is Director, International of the IRS.

The second objective is intended to prevent or eliminate tax evasion. The third objective is achieved through a "competent authority" procedure under which taxpayers of one treaty partner can settle tax disputes with taxpayers of the other treaty partner through the latter country's tax authorities.

Section 6114 requires a taxpayer who takes a position based on a treaty provision that preempts an IRC provision to disclose such position on his or her tax return or on a statement attached to the return.

SPECIAL RESIDENT ALIEN ELECTIONS

Two special elections permit nonresident aliens to be treated as resident aliens for U.S. tax purposes. The first election is usually made when a foreign national moves to the United States too late in the year to qualify as a resident (see page C:16-14). This election is available if the foreign national

- Does not qualify as a resident under the lawful residency test or substantial presence test for the calendar year for which the election is made (i.e., election year)
- Does not qualify as a resident for the calendar year preceding the election year
- Qualifies as a resident under the substantial presence test in the calendar year immediately following the election year, and was present in the United States
  - **a.** For at least 31 consecutive days in the election year and
  - **b.** For at least 75% of the days during the period beginning with the first day of the 31-consecutive-day or longer period and ending with the last day of the election year.

The election is made on the nonresident alien's tax return for the election year and may not be revoked without the IRS's consent. The election cannot be made before the foreign national has met the substantial presence test for the calendar year following the election year.[67]

---

[66] Sec. 911(e)(2).

[67] Sec. 7701(b)(4).

ADDITIONAL COMMENT

The special resident alien election is made by attaching to a joint return a statement that the Sec. 6013(g) election is being made. This election must be made within the time period designated for filing a claim for credit or refund.

Section 6013(g) permits nonresident aliens who are married to U.S. citizens or resident aliens to elect to be taxed as resident aliens. Such an election requires both spouses to agree to be taxed on their worldwide income and to provide all books, records, and information necessary to determine either spouse's tax liability. The election permits nonresident aliens to file a joint tax return with their spouses. By filing a joint return, the spouses can take advantage of the lower tax rates available to married persons filing jointly.

Another election permits nonresident aliens to be treated as resident aliens for income tax and wage withholding purposes. To qualify for the election, the foreign national must be a nonresident alien at the beginning of the tax year and a resident alien at the end of the year and must be married to a U.S. citizen or resident alien at the end of the tax year. Both spouses must make the election, which provides the same tax benefits as a Sec. 6013(g) election and eliminates nonresident alien tax treatment for part of the year and resident alien tax treatment for the remainder of the year.

COMPLIANCE AND PROCEDURAL CONSIDERATIONS

OBJECTIVE 6

Comply with procedures for foreign transactions

FOREIGN OPERATIONS OF U.S. CORPORATIONS

U.S. corporations must provide a summary of their overseas business activities on Form 1120, Schedule N (Foreign Operations of U.S. Corporations). This form reports information relating to interests in foreign partnerships, stock in controlled foreign corporations, and foreign bank and securities accounts.

REPORTING THE FOREIGN TAX CREDIT

Individual taxpayers claim the foreign tax credit on Form 1116. Corporate taxpayers claim the credit on Form 1118. Separate forms must be filed for each of the foreign tax credit limitation baskets. A completed Form 1116 is illustrated in Appendix B. This form is based on the following situation:

EXAMPLE C:16-35 ▶

Andrew Roberts is a U.S. citizen and resident who files jointly with his wife. They have no children. In 2016, he reports C$18,000 (C$ = Country X dollars) of dividend income of which C$2,700 (C$18,000 × 0.15) in income taxes are withheld on December 31, 2016. Assume that on December 31, 2016, C$1.16 equals $1 (U.S. dollars). Thus, C$18,000 translates into $15,517 (C$18,000 ÷ 1.16) of dividend income and $2,328 ($15,517 × 0.15) of income taxes. Roberts owns 3% of the distributing foreign corporation's outstanding stock. The Country X taxes are translated at the exchange rate for the date on which they were withheld (December 31, 2016). The $15,517 of gross income is reduced by an allocable portion of Andrew's deductions. As indicated on Form 1116, Andrew can claim $1,988 of the $2,328 foreign tax withheld from the dividend, as a foreign tax credit subject to Andrew's credit limitation for the passive income basket. The Roberts' taxable income before exemptions (Form 1040, Line 41) is $86,000, and their tax before credits (Form 1040, Line 44) is $11,017. ◀

ADDITIONAL COMMENT

This example pertains to 2016 because tax forms for that year are the latest available at the time this textbook was published.

REPORTING THE EARNED INCOME EXCLUSION

The elections for the foreign earned income and housing cost exclusions are made separately on Form 2555 or Form 2555-EZ. The latter form can be used by a taxpayer who meets the bona fide residence or physical presence test and maintains a tax home in a foreign country during the requisite period. In addition, the taxpayer must (1) be a U.S. citizen or resident alien, (2) have earned wages/salaries in a foreign country, (3) report total foreign earned income of no more than $101,300 in 2016 and $102,100 in 2017, (4) file a tax return for a 12-month period, (5) have earned no self-employment income, and (6) have incurred no business and/or moving expenses. Each election must be made

KEY POINT

Taxpayers who regularly reside in a foreign country generally qualify under both the physical presence and bona fide residence tests. Tax practitioners must indicate on Form 2555 which one of the two tests has been met when claiming the foreign earned exclusion. Determining whether one is a foreign resident is more difficult than merely calculating one's physical presence during the tax year. If a taxpayer fails the physical presence test, he or she should retain documentation (e.g., rent receipts, employment contract, and visas) to support bona fide residence.

on an income tax return that is timely filed (including any extensions), a later amended return filed within the appropriate limitations period, or an original income tax return filed within one year after the return's due date. Once made, the election remains in effect for that year and all subsequent years unless the IRS consents to revocation. Thus, a new election is not required when an individual either moves from one foreign country to another or moves to the United States and then returns to a foreign country years later.[68]

At the end of their first year in a foreign country, U.S. expatriates often face a dilemma. They would like to claim the foreign earned income and/or housing cost exclusion (deduction) for the current year but have not yet met either the bona fide residence or physical presence test. As a result, despite their intention to remain in the foreign country until such time as they have met one these tests, they might have to include their foreign earnings in gross income and pay U.S. taxes on an otherwise excludible amount. If in a subsequent year they eventually meet either test because of their extended stay in the foreign country, they might have to file an amended return or a refund claim to retroactively recover the foregone Sec. 911 benefits for the previous year. To avoid this result, Treasury Regulations grant these taxpayers an extension for filing their first year return until such time as they will have met either the residence or physical presence test.[69] Regulations also grant these taxpayers a general filing extension to the fifteenth day of the sixth month following the close of the tax year.[70]

Appendix B contains a completed Form 2555 based on the following situation:

EXAMPLE C:16-36 ▶

Lawrence Smith, a U.S. citizen, is employed by the Very Public Corporation in Paris, France. In 2016, he earned $60,000 in salary and received the following benefits:

Cost of living allowance	$27,000
Education allowance	8,000
Home leave stipend	6,400
Housing allowance	21,300
Total	$62,700

Smith is eligible for the Sec. 911 earned income exclusion for all of 2016 even though he spent five business days in the United States. While in the United States, he earned $1,200. For 2016, Smith can exclude up to $101,300 under the foreign earned income exclusion and an additional $5,092 ($21,300 qualifying expenses − $16,208 base housing amount) under the housing cost exclusion. This $106,392 ($101,300 + $5,092) is not reduced by any disallowed for-AGI deductions because Smith deducts all his employment-related expenses as miscellaneous itemized deductions. ◀

ADDITIONAL COMMENT

This example pertains to 2016 because tax forms for that year are the latest available at the time this textbook was published.

FILING REQUIREMENTS FOR ALIENS AND FOREIGN CORPORATIONS

A nonresident alien reports income on Form 1040-NR on or before the fifteenth day of the sixth month following the close of the tax year. If the nonresident alien's wages are subject to tax withholding, Form 1040-NR must be filed on or before the fifteenth day of the fourth month following the close of the tax year.[71]

A foreign corporation reports income on Form 1120-F, U.S. Income Tax Return of a Foreign Corporation. If the foreign corporation maintains no U.S. office or place of business, the due date for its income tax return is the fifteenth day of the sixth month following the close of its tax year. If the corporation maintains a U.S. office or place of business, the due date is the fifteenth day of the third month following the close of its tax year.

[68] Reg. Sec. 1.911-7(a).
[69] Reg. Sec. 1.911-7(c).
[70] Reg. Sec. 1.6081-5(a).
[71] Reg. Sec. 1.6072-1(c).

FINANCIAL STATEMENT IMPLICATIONS

OBJECTIVE 7

Recognize the financial statement implications of various international transactions

FOREIGN TAX CREDIT

A corporation having excess foreign taxes because of the foreign tax credit (FTC) limitation will record a deferred tax asset, possibly subject to a valuation allowance. The valuation allowance, in turn, will increase the corporation's effective tax rate. On the other hand, full use of the foreign tax credit without limitation will not affect the corporation's effective tax rate.

EXAMPLE C:16-37 ▶ Upsilon Corporation operates in the United States and in Country Low using a foreign branch. Country Low's tax rate is 20%. In the current year, Upsilon earns $1 million from its U.S. operations and $400,000 from its Country Low operations. Thus, Upsilon pays $80,000 ($400,000 × 0.20) of foreign taxes to Country Low, producing the following tax results:

U.S.-source income	$1,000,000
Foreign-source income	400,000
Taxable income	$1,400,000
Times: U.S. tax rate	0.34
U.S. tax before FTC	$ 476,000
Minus: Foreign tax credit	(80,000)
U.S. taxes payable	$ 396,000

For book purposes, Upsilon's total income tax expense is $476,000 ($396,000 U.S. + $80,000 foreign). Accordingly, Upsilon makes the following book journal entry:

Total income tax expense	476,000	
Total income taxes payable		476,000

In this case, Upsilon reports the following book results:

Net income before income tax expense	$1,400,000
Minus: Total income tax expense	(476,000)
Net income	$ 924,000
U.S. taxes ($396,000/$1,400,000)	28.29%
Foreign taxes ($80,000/$1,400,000)	5.71%
Total effective tax rate	34.00%

◀

EXAMPLE C:16-38 ▶ Assume the same facts as in Example C:16-37 except Upsilon's foreign branch is in Country High instead of Country Low. Country High imposes a 45% tax rate. In this case, Upsilon's foreign taxes are $180,000 ($400,000 × 0.45), with the FTC limited to $136,000 ($476,000 × $400,000/$1,400,000). Assuming no carryback opportunity, the $44,000 ($180,000 − $136,000) excess carries over for ten years. Upsilon's net U.S. tax is $340,000 ($476,000 − $136,000), and its total tax liability is $520,000 ($340,000 U.S. + $180,000 foreign).

For book purposes, Upsilon records a $44,000 deferred tax asset for the FTC carryover. However, if Upsilon continues to operate only in Country High, it likely will not realize the deferred tax asset because of the FTC limitation. Therefore, Upsilon also must record a $44,000 valuation allowance. Accordingly, Upsilon makes the following book journal entry:

Total income tax expense	520,000	
Deferred tax asset	44,000	
Valuation allowance		44,000
Total income taxes payable		520,000

In this case, Upsilon reports the following book results:

Net income before income tax expense	$1,400,000
Minus: Total income tax expense	(520,000)
Net income	$ 880,000

U.S. taxes ($340,000/$1,400,000)	24.28%
Foreign taxes ($180,000/$1,400,000)	12.86%
Total effective tax rate	37.14%

This effective tax rate reconciles to the 34% statutory tax rate as follows:

Statutory tax rate	34.00%
Valuation allowance ($44,000/$1,400,000)	3.14%
Total effective tax rate	37.14%

◀

EXAMPLE C:16-39 ▶ Assume the same facts as in Example C:16-38 except Upsilon plans to open second branch in Country Low. Because all income falls into the general limitation basket, Upsilon can offset the excess foreign taxes from Country High against the excess FTC limitation from Country Low and thereby use the FTC carryover within the next ten years. With these alternative facts, Upsilon need not record the valuation allowance, so its U.S. income tax expense per books reflects the entire foreign tax credit. Thus, Upsilon's U.S. tax expense is $296,000 ($476,000 − $180,000), and its foreign tax expense is $180,000, for a total of $476,000. Accordingly, Upsilon makes the following book journal entry:

Total income tax expense	476,000	
Deferred tax asset	44,000	
Total income taxes payable		520,000

In this case, Upsilon reports the following book results:

Net income before income tax expense	$1,400,000
Minus: Total income tax expense	(476,000)
Net income	$ 924,000
U.S. taxes ($296,000/$1,400,000)	21.14%
Foreign taxes ($180,000/$1,400,000)	12.86%
Total effective tax rate	34.00%

◀

DEFERRED FOREIGN EARNINGS

As discussed earlier in this chapter, a U.S. parent does not include a foreign subsidiary's earnings in its (the parent's) gross income until the subsidiary repatriates (remits) the earnings as a dividend. (An exception to this deferral privilege was discussed earlier in the text under Controlled Foreign Corporations.) Under normal income tax accounting principles, this deferred income would create a deferred tax liability.[72] However, in this situation, an exception for indefinite reinvestment applies.[73] Specifically, a reporting entity does not recognize a deferred tax liability for the excess of financial reporting basis over tax basis of an investment in a foreign subsidiary unless that temporary difference will reverse in the foreseeable future. Such a basis difference will occur if the consolidated financial statements recognize the foreign earnings but the U.S. parent's tax return does not. If the group does not invoke the indefinite reinvestment exception because it expects to repatriate the earnings in the future, the deferral and subsequent repatriation will not affect the effective tax rate. On the other hand, if the group does invoke the exception, the deferral is treated as a permanent difference that reduces the effective tax rate. However, if the subsidiary nevertheless remits the earnings in a future year, the repatriation will increase the effective tax rate. Thus, using the exception could cause wide swings in effective tax rates. These potential swings might induce management to forgo the exception or, if invoking the exception, inhibit management from repatriating the foreign earnings.

EXAMPLE C:16-40 ▶ Parent Corporation operates in the United States and in Country Low using Foreign Subsidiary in which Parent holds a 100% interest. Country Low's tax rate is 20%. In the current year, Parent earns $1 million from its U.S. operations, and Foreign earns $400,000 from its Country Low operations. Thus, Foreign pays $80,000 ($400,000 × 0.20) of foreign taxes to Country Low, and Parent incurs a $340,000 ($1,000,000 × 0.34) tax liability on its U.S.-source income. Thus, the

[72] Accounting Standards Codification (ASC) 740, which codifies SFAS No. 109.

[73] Accounting Standards Codification (ASC) 740-30-25-17, which incorporates the pre-codification APB No. 23 exception for indefinite reinvestment.

total tax liability is $420,000 ($340,000 + $80,000), and Parent defers $56,000 of U.S. taxes on the foreign earnings, computed as follows:

Gross foreign earnings	$400,000
Times: U.S. tax rate	0.34
Tax liability before FTC	$136,000
Minus: Potential deemed paid FTC	(80,000)
Deferred tax liability	$ 56,000

For book purposes, the consolidated financial statements include the foreign earnings, so the group's U.S. income tax expense is $396,000, computed as follows:

U.S.-source income	$1,000,000
Foreign-source income	400,000
Net income before income tax expense	$1,400,000
Times: U.S. tax rate	0.34
U.S. income tax expense before FTC	$ 476,000
Minus: Deemed paid FTC	(80,000)
U.S. income tax expense	$ 396,000

Consequently, the group's total income tax expense is $476,000 ($396,000 U.S. + $80,000 foreign). Assuming the group does not invoke the indefinite reinvestment exception, the group recognizes a deferred tax liability and makes the following book journal entry:

Total income tax expense	476,000	
Deferred tax liability		56,000
Total income taxes payable		420,000

In this case, the group reports the following book results:

Net income before income tax expense	$1,400,000
Minus: Total income tax expense	(476,000)
Net income	$ 924,000
U.S. taxes ($396,000/$1,400,000)	28.29%
Foreign taxes ($80,000/$1,400,000)	5.71%
Total effective tax rate	34.00%

In a subsequent year, Parent again earns $1 million from its U.S. operations, but Foreign has no earnings that year. Nevertheless, Foreign remits a $320,000 dividend to Parent out of prior year earnings from which it paid the $80,000 of foreign taxes. For tax purposes, Parent grosses up the dividend by the deemed paid FTC to $400,000 ($320,000 + $80,000) and claims the deemed paid FTC. Consequently, Parent's U.S. tax on the foreign earnings is $56,000 ($136,000 − $80,000), and its total liability is $396,000 ($340,000 + $56,000).

For book purposes, the group recognizes only the $1 million of U.S.-source earnings, so its total income tax expense is $340,000. Accordingly, the group makes the following book journal entry:

Total income tax expense	340,000	
Deferred tax liability	56,000	
Total income taxes payable		396,000

In this case, the group reports the following book results:

Net income before income tax expense	$1,000,000
Minus: Total income tax expense	(340,000)
Net income	$ 660,000
U.S. taxes ($340,000/$1,000,000)	34.00%
Foreign taxes ($0/$1,000,000)	-0-%
Total effective tax rate	34.00%

Thus, the effective tax rate is the same in each year. ◀

EXAMPLE C:16-41 ▶ Now assume the group in Example C:16-40 invokes the indefinite reinvestment exception in the first year on the assumption that it will leave the foreign earnings invested in Foreign indefinitely. Nevertheless, subsequent events lead the group to repatriate the earnings in the later year. In the first year, the group treats the $56,000 deferral as permanent. For book purposes, the consolidated financial statements include the foreign earnings, but the income tax expense does not reflect the permanent difference, so the group's U.S. income tax expense is $340,000, computed as follows:

U.S.-source income	$1,000,000
Foreign-source income	400,000
Net income before income tax expense	$1,400,000
Minus: Foreign source income treated as a permanent difference	(400,000)
Net income after permanent differences	$1,000,000
Times: U.S. tax rate	0.34
U.S. income tax expense	$ 340,000

Consequently, the group's total income tax expense is $420,000 ($340,000 U.S. + $80,000 foreign), and the group makes the following book journal entry:

Total income tax expense	420,000	
Total income taxes payable		420,000

In this case, the group reports the following book results:

Net income before income tax expense	$1,400,000
Minus: Total income tax expense	(420,000)
Net income	$ 980,000
U.S. taxes ($340,000/$1,400,000)	24.29%
Foreign taxes ($80,000/$1,400,000)	5.71%
Total effective tax rate	30.00%

This effective tax rate reconciles to the 34% statutory tax rate as follows:

Statutory tax rate	34.00%
Foreign tax treated as a permanent difference ($56,000/$1,400,000)	(4.00%)
Total effective tax rate	30.00%

In the subsequent year when Foreign remits the dividend, the group reverses the "permanent" difference, so the group's U.S. income tax expense is $476,000, computed as follows:

U.S.-source income	$1,000,000
Foreign-source income	–0–
Net income before income tax expense	$1,000,000
Plus: Reversed permanent difference	400,000
Net income after permanent differences	$1,400,000
Times: U.S. tax rate	0.34
U.S. income tax expense before FTC	$ 476,000
Minus: Deemed paid FTC	(80,000)
U.S. income tax expense	$ 396,000

The group's total income tax expense also is $396,000 because it incurred no foreign taxes in this year. Accordingly, the group makes the following book journal entry:

Total income tax expense	396,000	
Total income taxes payable		396,000

In this case, the group reports the following book results:

Net income before income tax expense	$1,000,000
Minus: Total income tax expense	(396,000)
Net income	$ 604,000

U.S. taxes ($396,000/$1,000,000)	39.60%
Foreign taxes ($0/$1,000,000)	-0-%
Total effective tax rate	39.60%

This effective tax rate reconciles to the 34% statutory tax rate as follows:

Statutory tax rate	34.00%
Reversal of foreign tax treated as a permanent difference ($56,000/$1,000,000)	5.60%
Total effective tax rate	39.60%

Thus, the effective tax rate varied from 30% in the first year to 39.6% in the subsequent year. ◀

One other point deserves mention. The foreign operations might be conducted in a high tax foreign country such that the deemed paid FTC completely eliminates the U.S. tax on the repatriated earnings. Consequently, the group would not reduce its effective tax rate by invoking the indefinite reinvestment exception. Therefore, corporations in this situation typically do not treat foreign earnings as indefinitely reinvested.

See Chapter C:3 for a general discussion of financial implications of federal income taxes.

Problem Materials

Discussion Questions

C:16-1 What three factors have the drafters of U.S. tax laws considered in determining the scope of U.S. tax jurisdiction? Explain the importance of each factor.

C:16-2 Why is it important for a foreign national to ascertain whether he or she is a resident of the United States?

C:16-3 Explain the alternatives available to individual taxpayers in accounting for foreign taxes paid or accrued on their taxable income.

C:16-4 What types of foreign taxes are eligible to be credited?

C:16-5 In what circumstances might a taxpayer prefer to deduct, rather than credit, foreign taxes?

C:16-6 Why did Congress enact the foreign tax credit limitation rules?

C:16-7 Explain how the separate basket approach to calculating the foreign tax credit has created excess foreign tax credit issues for some U.S. taxpayers.

C:16-8 What advantages does a cash method taxpayer gain by electing to accrue foreign taxes for foreign tax credit purposes?

C:16-9 What requirements must be satisfied to qualify a U.S. citizen or resident living abroad for the foreign-earned income exclusion?

C:16-10 Tony, a U.S. citizen, uses the calendar year as his tax year. Tony was transferred to Foreign Country C on June 15, 2015, and he immediately became a resident of that country. His employer transfers him back to the United States on March 10, 2017. Does Tony qualify for the foreign-earned income exclusion as a bona fide resident? If not, can he qualify in any other way?

C:16-11 Explain why a taxpayer might prefer to claim his or her foreign-earned income exclusion under the physical presence test instead of the bona fide residence test.

C:16-12 Why might a taxpayer choose to forego the foreign-earned income exclusion? If the taxpayer does so in the current tax year, what negative tax consequences might this choice have in future tax years?

C:16-13 Compare the U.S. tax treatment of a nonresident alien and a resident alien, both of whom earn U.S. trade or business and U.S. investment income.

C:16-14 Explain how a nonresident alien is taxed in the year of arrival and departure if he or she arrived in the United States on July 1, 2015, and immediately established U.S. residency, and departs from the United States on October 1, 2017, thereby terminating his or her U.S. residency.

C:16-15 How is a nonresident alien's U.S. source investment income taxed? What planning tool(s) is (are) available to reduce the tax rate below 30%? What mechanism is used to collect the tax?

C:16-16 Why is the effectively connected income concept important in taxing a nonresident alien's trade or business?

C:16-17 During the current year, Manuel, a nonresident alien, conducts a U.S. business. He earns $100,000 in sales commissions and $25,000 of interest income. What factor(s) do U.S. taxing authorities consider to determine whether the interest is investment income not subject to U.S. taxation or business income subject to U.S. taxation?

C:16-18 What are the advantages of a U.S. corporation's conducting a foreign business through a foreign branch? Through a foreign subsidiary?

C:16-19 What is the deferral privilege? What tax provisions result in the current U.S. taxation of part or all of a foreign corporation's earnings?

C:16-20 Why did Congress enact the deemed paid foreign tax credit provisions?

C:16-21 What are the "look through" rules? To whom do they apply and for what purposes? What taxable items are subject to these rules?

C:16-22 Kilarney, a foreign corporation, is incorporated in Country J and is 100%-owned by Maine, a domestic corporation. During the current year, Kilarney earns $500,000 from its Country J operations and $100,000 from its U.S. trade or business activities. None of the Country J income is Subpart F. None of Kilarney's after-tax profits are distributed as a dividend to Maine.

a. Explain how Kilarney is taxed in the U.S. and whether any of Kilarney's income is taxed to Maine.

b. How would your answer change if Kilarney earned none of its income from U.S. operations and paid a $50,000 dividend to Maine?

C:16-23 What is the branch profits tax? Explain Congressional intent behind its enactment.

C:16-24 What is a controlled foreign corporation (CFC)? How does the tax treatment of a U.S. stockholder's share of distributed and undistributed CFC profits differ from that of U.S. stockholders in a noncontrolled foreign corporation?

C:16-25 Explain the concept of Subpart F income. What major income categories are taxed under the Subpart F rules?

C:16-26 A U.S. manufacturer wants to conduct business through a foreign subsidiary organized in a low tax jurisdiction. How might it do so without being currently taxed on the subsidiary's foreign earnings?

C:16-27 How is the increase in CFC earnings invested in U.S. property measured? Explain why Congress decided to tax this amount to U.S. shareholders.

C:16-28 Explain the tax consequences to a U.S. shareholder of a CFC distribution of previously taxed Subpart F income.

C:16-29 How does the taxation of a gain recognized when a U.S. shareholder sells stock in a CFC differ from that of a gain recognized when a U.S. shareholder sells stock in a non-CFC?

C:16-30 Explain how the Sec. 482 transfer pricing and CFC rules work together to discourage a domestic corporation's use of a foreign sales subsidiary to avoid U.S. taxation.

C:16-31 What are the tax consequences of an inversion where former shareholders of the merged U.S. corporation own 85% of the voting stock in the new foreign corporation by reason of their U.S. stock ownership? Where they own 75% of this stock by reason of their U.S. stock ownership?

C:16-32 King, a U.S. corporation, owns 25% of each of two foreign corporations. King's foreign business activities are taxed at foreign tax rates that are higher than those prevailing in the United States. Consequently, King finds itself in an excess foreign tax credit position. Corporation A is located in a country that has concluded a tax treaty with the United States. The treaty reduces from 15% to 5% the withholding on dividends paid to a U.S. corporation. Corporation B is located in a non-treaty country where the withholding rate is 15%. A and B both pay local income taxes at a 20% effective tax rate. If King wants to repatriate profits, which corporation(s) should pay the dividend to minimize the repatriation cost? Can King use such a payment to reduce its excess foreign tax credits associated with its other foreign income?

ISSUE IDENTIFICATION QUESTIONS

C:16-33 Plato Toys has created a new line of plastic toys that it wants to market in Canada. The corporation's headquarters are located in Detroit, Michigan. The company currently exports about $500,000 worth of toys to Canada each year. Most of the toys are sold in the province of Ontario through a Canadian distributor. Profits on current sales average 30% of the selling price to the Canadian distributor. Plato has never had a Canadian office or plant. Because of the corporation's desire to expand its operations, Plato is planning to open branch offices in other Canadian provinces that have large population centers. If a high volume of Canadian sales materializes, the company would like to open a manufacturing facility in Canada at a future date. Your accounting firm has performed audit and tax services for Plato for a number of years. One October morning, Plato's director of taxes, Kelly Hunt, comes to your office and asks that you prepare a presentation to corporate management about the U.S. tax consequences of the company's opening additional sales offices (or a Canadian sales subsidiary). If Canadian activities sufficiently expand, the firm might send U.S. personnel to work in Canada. Plato's CFO has had reservations about transferring employees to Canada and opening branch offices. She wants you to identify possible tax and business problems, in addition to explaining whether it is necessary to operate in Canada to obtain U.S. tax breaks. Prepare a list of client-related tax and non-tax issues that you should cover in your presentation.

C:16-34 In January of the current year, George Kratzer's U.S. firm assigned him to its Brussels office. During the year, George earned salary, a cost-of-living allowance, a housing allowance, a home leave allowance that permitted him to return home once each year, and an education allowance to pay for his daughter's U.S. schooling. George and his wife, Geneva, have rented an apartment in Brussels and paid Belgian income taxes. What U.S. tax issues should George consider when preparing his tax return?

C:16-35 During the current year, Bailey, a U.S. corporation, began operating overseas. It manufactures machine tools in the United States and sells them to Canadian customers through a branch office located in Toronto. Bailey acquired a 40% investment in a Brazilian corporation from which it later received a dividend. The company received royalties from an English firm that licences machine tool patents owned by Bailey. The English firm uses the patents to manufacture machine tools that the firm sells in England. What international tax issues regarding these activities should Bailey's director of taxes consider?

C:16-36 During the current year, Sanders, a U.S. corporation, organized a foreign subsidiary in Country Z. The subsidiary purchases components from Sanders, assembles them into finished products using Country Z labor, and sells the products to unrelated wholesalers in Countries X, Y, and Z through its own sales force. Assembly costs are 25% of the wholesale price. The foreign subsidiary has paid Sanders (its parent) no dividends this year. What tax issues regarding these activities should Sanders' director of taxes consider?

PROBLEMS

C:16-37 *Translation of Foreign Tax Payments.* Arnie, a U.S. citizen who uses the calendar year as his tax year and the cash method of accounting, operates a sole proprietorship in Country Z. In Year 1, he reports 500,000 dubles of pretax profits. On June 1 of Year 2, he pays Country Z income taxes of 150,000 dubles for calendar Year 1. Duble-U.S. dollar exchange rates on various dates in Year 1 and Year 2 are as follows:

December 31, Year 1	4.00 dubles = $1 (U.S.)
Year 1 average	3.75 dubles = $1 (U.S.)
June 1, Year 2	4.25 dubles = $1 (U.S.)

a. What is the U.S. dollar amount of Arnie's foreign tax credit? In what year can Arnie claim the credit?

b. How would your answer to Part a change if Arnie elected to accrue his foreign income taxes on December 31 of Year 1, and filed his Year 1 U.S. income tax return on April 15 of Year 2?

c. What adjustment to the credit claimed in Part b would Arnie have to make when he pays his Country Z taxes on June 1 of Year 2?

C:16-38 *Foreign Tax Credit Limitation.* During the current year, Jackson, a U.S. corporation and accrual method taxpayer, engages in both U.S. and foreign business activities. All its overseas activities are conducted by a branch in Country S. The results of Jackson's current year operations are as follows:

U.S. source taxable income	$2,000,000
Foreign source taxable income	1,500,000
Accrued Country S income taxes	600,000

a. What is the amount of Jackson's foreign tax credit (assuming the corporate tax rate is 34% and income from all foreign activities fall into a single basket)?

b. Are any foreign tax credit carrybacks or carryovers available? If so, in what years can they be used?

C:16-39 *Foreign Tax Credit Limitation.* Tucson, a U.S. corporation organized in Year 1, reports the following items for a three-year period.

	Year 1	*Year 2*	*Year 3*
Foreign tax accrual	$ 100,000	$ 120,000	$ 180,000
Foreign source taxable income	400,000	300,000	500,000
Worldwide taxable income	1,000,000	1,000,000	1,000,000

The foreign source and worldwide taxable income items are determined under U.S. law.

a. What is Tucson's foreign tax credit limitation for each of the three years (assume a 34% U.S. corporate tax rate and that income from all foreign activities fall into a single basket)?

b. How are Tucson's excess foreign tax credits (if any) treated? Do any carryovers remain after Year 3?

c. How would your answers to Parts a and b change if the IRS determines that $100,000 of expenses allocated to U.S.-source income should have been allocated to foreign-source income?

d. What measures should Tucson consider if it expects its current excess foreign tax credit position to persist in the long-run?

C:16-40 *Foreign-Earned Income Exclusion.* Julia, a U.S. citizen, leaves the United States at noon on August 1, 2015, and arrives in Country P at 8:00 a.m. the next day. She immediately establishes in Country P a permanent residence, which she maintains until her return to the United States at 3:00 p.m. on April 5, 2017. Her only trips outside Country P are related to temporary employment in Country B from November 1 through December 10, 2015, and a U.S. vacation beginning at 5:00 p.m. on June 1 and ending at 10:00 p.m. on June 30, 2016. Does Julia qualify for the Sec. 911 benefits? If so, what is the amount of her foreign earned income exclusion for 2015 through 2017?

C:16-41 *Foreign-Earned Income Exclusion.* Fred, a U.S. citizen, arrives in Country K on July 15, 2015, and proceeds to a construction site in its oil fields. Once there, he moves into employer-provided housing where he is required to reside. Except for brief periods of local travel and the months of July and August 2016, when he is on vacation in the United States, he remains at the site until his departure on December 1, 2017. He provides no services while in the United States. Fred earns $10,000 per month in salary and allowances while employed overseas. In addition, while in Country K, he receives meals and lodging valued at $1,750 per month. What is the amount of Fred's Sec. 911 exclusions for 2015 through 2017?

C:16-42 *Employment-Related Expenses.* In 2017, Stuart earns $275,000 of income in Country K and incurs $23,000 of employment-related expenses in that country. The employment-related expenses are subject to the 2% of AGI floor for miscellaneous itemized deductions. Stuart incurs no other miscellaneous itemized deductions. Stuart also incurs and pays $43,805 of Country K income taxes in the current year. Determine the following amounts for Stuart: Foreign-earned income exclusion, allowable deduction for employment-related expenses, and allowable foreign tax credit.

C:16-43 *Foreign-Earned Income Exclusion.* Dillon, a U.S. citizen, resides in Country K for all of 2017. Dillon is married, files a joint return and claims two personal exemptions. The following items pertain to his 2017 activities:

Salary and allowances (other than for housing)[a]	$175,000
Housing allowance	28,000
Employment-related expenses[b]	7,500
Housing costs	30,000
Other itemized deductions	4,000
Country K income taxes	12,000

[a]All of Dillon's salary and allowances are attributable to services performed in Country K.
[b]Dillon claims the employment-related expenses as itemized deductions.

What is Dillon's net U.S. tax liability for 2017 (assume that Dillon excludes his earned income and housing cost amount)?

C:16-44 *Tax Calculation for a Nonresident Alien.* Tien is a citizen of Country C, which does not have an income tax treaty with the United States. During the current year (2016), she is a nonresident alien for U.S. tax purposes and earns the following amounts:

Dividend received from a U.S. corporation	$ 2,500
Rentals from leasing a U.S. building	13,000
Interest received from a foreign corporation	5,000

Tien does not conduct a U.S. trade or business. Her interest and depreciation expenses from leasing the building under a net lease arrangement total $7,000.

a. Assuming the real estate income is investment related, what is Tien's U.S. tax liability? How is the tax collected?
b. How would your answer to Part a change if Tien makes an election to treat the real estate activity as a U.S. trade or business?

C:16-45 *Taxation of a Nonresident Alien.* Pierre, a single nonresident alien, conducts a U.S. trade or business for 80 days during the current year. Pierre reports the following income items from his U.S. activities. Indicate how each of these items will be taxed and how the tax will be collected.

a. $25,000 of dividends earned on a U.S. portfolio stock investment unrelated to Pierre's trade or business.
b. $75,000 of sales commissions Pierre earned as an employee of a foreign corporation. Pierre generated $50,000 from sales in the United States and $25,000 from sales outside the United States.
c. A $10,000 capital gain on the sale of stock in a U.S. corporation realized by Pierre while in the United States.
d. $3,000 of interest earned on a bank account in Pierre's home country and $1,800 of interest earned on a bank account located in Jacksonville, Florida.

C:16-46 *Deemed Paid Foreign Tax Credit.* Complicity Corporation is incorporated in the United States and has a 34% tax rate. Complicity owns 33% of Detache Corporation's stock. Detache is incorporated in Country Q. During the current year, Detache reports $310,000 of current E&P, pays $82,100 in Country Q income taxes, and remits $48,000 in dividends to Complicity. In addition, Country Q withholds $7,200 in taxes from the dividend payment. Detache's accumulated E&P at the beginning of the current year is $205,000. In prior years, Detache paid $53,200 of Country Q income taxes but remitted no dividends to Complicity in those years. Determine Complicity's net U.S. tax liability resulting from the dividend payment to Complicity.

C:16-47 *Deemed Paid Foreign Tax Credit.* Paper, a U.S. corporation, owns 40% of the stock in Sud, a foreign corporation. Sud reports earnings and profits of $200,000 (before the payment of any current dividends) and foreign income taxes of $50,000. In the current year, Sud pays a total of $90,000 in dividends to all its shareholders. It withholds from the gross dividends paid to nonresident shareholders a 15% Country T income tax.

a. What gross income amount does Paper report upon receiving the dividend?
b. To what extent is Paper's U.S. tax liability increased as a result of the dividend (assume a 34% U.S. corporate tax rate)?
c. How would your answers to Parts a and b change if the foreign income taxes instead had been $80,000?

C:16-48 *Deemed Paid Foreign Tax Credit.* Duke, a U.S. corporation, owns all the stock in Taiwan, a foreign corporation. In the current year, Taiwan pays to Duke a $125,000 dividend from which $12,500 in foreign taxes are withheld. Taiwan's operating results indicate $1 million of earnings and profits (before payment of the dividend) and $300,000 of foreign income taxes. Assume Duke has no other foreign source income and its U.S. taxable income (excluding the dividend) is $1 million.

a. What is the amount of Duke's deemed paid foreign tax credit?
b. To what extent is Duke's U.S. tax liability increased as a result of the dividend (assume a 34% U.S. corporate tax rate)?
c. How would your answers to Parts a and b change if the $125,000 dividend were instead paid to U.S. citizen Donna (instead of to Duke), whose marginal tax rate is 35%? Assume the foreign-source dividend does not qualify for the 15% reduced tax rate.

C:16-49 *Translation of a Dividend.* Dayton, a U.S. corporation, owns all the stock in Fiero, a foreign corporation organized in the current year. During the year, Fiero earns 400,000 pirogs of pretax profits and accrues 100,000 pirogs of Country Z income taxes.

On August 25 of the current year, Fiero pays to Dayton a 150,000 pirog dividend on which 7,500 pirogs in Country Z taxes are withheld. On March 1 of the following year, Fiero pays 100% of its Country Z income taxes for the current year. Assume Dayton has no other foreign source income, and its U.S. taxable income (excluding the dividend) is $1 million. The pirog-U.S. dollar exchange rate on various dates are as follows:

January 1 of the current year	9.0 pirogs = $1 (U.S.)
August 25 of the current year	10.0 pirogs = $1 (U.S.)
Current year average	9.5 pirogs = $1 (U.S.)
March 1 of the following year	11.0 pirogs = $1 (U.S.)

a. For U.S. tax reporting purposes, what are Dayton's dividend and deemed paid foreign tax credit amounts in U.S. dollars?
b. What is Dayton's net U.S. tax liability as a result of the dividend?

C:16-50 *Worldwide Tax Rates.* Young Corporation conducts a business in both the United States and a foreign country. In each of the following scenarios, what is Young's worldwide (combined U.S. and foreign) tax rate relative to the branch income it earns in the foreign country? Assume that Young wants to claim the maximum foreign tax credit possible.

Scenario	*U.S. Tax Rate*	*Foreign Tax Rate*
1	34%	0%
2	34%	15%
3	34%	34%
4	34%	40%

What incentive exists for the foreign country to increase its tax rates if the United States taxes foreign income when earned? What incentive exists for a foreign country to lower its tax rates if a foreign subsidiary earns income in one year but is taxed in a later year when the income is repatriated to the United States?

C:16-51 *Section 902 Dividend Look Through Rules.* Hamilton, a U.S. corporation, reports the following results from its current year activities:

U.S.-source taxable income	$1,000,000
Foreign-source taxable income from manufacturing branch in Country M	1,000,000
Foreign taxes paid on branch income	390,000
Gross U.S. income tax liability	799,000

Hamilton owns 20% of the stock in Beauvais, a foreign corporation. Beauvais pays a $350,000 dividend to Hamilton on April 20 of the current year. Beauvais' pretax profits are $6 million, and its Country M taxes are $1.2 million. Beauvais' E&P under U.S. rules is $4 million, $3.6 million of which was derived from foreign manufacturing and $400,000 of which was earned on foreign securities. All of the foregoing figures were recorded before payment of the dividend.

a. For foreign tax credit purposes, into which of Hamilton's limitation baskets should the dividend from Beauvais be placed and in what amounts?
b. Calculate Hamilton's current year foreign tax credit.
c. How should any excess credits be treated?

C:16-52 *Definition of a CFC.* In each of the following scenarios, determine whether a foreign corporation with a single class of stock outstanding, is a controlled foreign corporation.

a. The foreign corporation's stock is owned equally by Alpha, a U.S. corporation, and Bart, a U.S. citizen, who owns no Alpha stock.
b. Assume the same facts as in Part a except Bart is a nonresident alien.
c. The foreign corporation's stock is owned 7% by Art, 49% by Phong, 29% by Colleen, and 15% by Danielle. Art, Colleen, and Danielle are U.S. citizens, and Phong is a nonresident alien. All four individuals are unrelated.
d. Assume the same facts as in Part c except Danielle is Art's daughter.

C:16-53 *Definition of Foreign Base Company Income.* Manila Corporation is organized in Country J. All of Manila's stock is owned by Simpson, a U.S. corporation. Indicate which of the following transactions generate Subpart F income.

a. Manila purchases a product from Simpson and sells it to unrelated parties in Countries J and X.

b. Manila receives a dividend from Manila-Sub, a foreign corporation organized and operating exclusively in Country J. All of Manila-Sub's stock has been owned by Manila since its incorporation.
c. Manila purchases raw materials locally, manufactures products in Country J, and sells the products to an unrelated purchaser for use in Country Z.
d. Manila services machinery manufactured by an unrelated Country J corporation. Revenues from servicing this machinery outside of Country J constitute 80% of Manila's gross income.
e. Manila purchases a product from a related U.S. corporation and sells the product to unrelated persons in Country Z.

C:16-54 *Definition of Foreign Base Company Income.* Apache, a U.S. corporation, owns 80% of the stock in Burrito, incorporated in Country Y. Burrito reports the following results for the current year:

	Gross Income	*Deductions*
Foreign base company sales income	\$300,000	\$120,000
Foreign base company services income	150,000	90,000
Dividend from Kane, a 70%-owned Country Y corporation	70,000	–0–
Rental income earned in Country Y	280,000	220,000

Kane conducts substantially all its business in Country Y.
a. What amount of income must Apache recognize as a result of Burrito's activities?
b. How would your answer to Part a change if Kane were instead a 70%-owned Country M corporation?
c. How would your answer to Part b change if foreign base company sales income before deductions were instead \$500,000?

C:16-55 *Transfer Pricing Rules.* Arrow, a U.S. corporation, annually sells one million starter motors to Bentley, a wholly owned foreign subsidiary organized in Country K. Bentley sells the starters as replacement parts through auto dealers in Country K. The statutory Country K tax rate is 20%. The U.S. tax rate is 34%.
a. What is the value of Arrow's annual U.S. tax deferral if the starters cost Arrow \$30 to produce, are sold to Bentley for \$50, and are re-sold to the auto dealers for \$70? Assume Bentley's operating expenses are \$4 million.
b. What additional benefit would accrue to Arrow annually if it reduced the sale price of each starter from \$50 to \$30? What mechanisms are likely to be used by U.S. tax authorities to address this situation?
c. How would your answer to Part a change if Bentley sold one-half of the starters to auto dealers in Country M under the same terms as it sold them to auto dealers in Country K?

C:16-56 *Sale of CFC Stock.* On April 1 of Year 1, Irvan, a U.S. corporation, acquired for \$300,000 all the stock in DeLeon, a foreign corporation. At the close of business on September 30 of Year 3, Irvan sells the DeLeon stock for \$825,000. Irvan reports \$25,000 of Subpart F income as a result of DeLeon's activities in Years 1 through 3, none of which is a leap year. DeLeon reports E&P balances for the period as follows:

Year	*E&P*
1	\$120,000
2	110,000
3	144,000

a. What are the amount and character of Irvan's gain on the sale of the DeLeon stock?
b. Can Irvan use any of DeLeon foreign taxes to reduce its U.S. tax liability on the stock gain?

COMPREHENSIVE PROBLEM

C:16-57 Allen Blay owns 100% of the stock in AB Corporation, organized ten years ago in California. AB operates a foreign branch in Country A. In the current year, AB reports \$500,000 of taxable income from U.S. activities. The branch reports a 400,000 pirog loss, which translates into a \$60,000 (U.S.) loss. Neither the branch nor the U.S. corporation paid Country A income taxes in the current year.

AB owns 50% of FC1, incorporated in Country B. Bob Haynes, a resident of Country B, owns the remaining FC1 stock. In the current year, FC1 generated 200,000 kira of Country B taxable income. The Country B corporate income tax rate is 25%. On December 31, FC1 remitted 50,000 kira of current year profits to AB. The kira-U.S. dollar exchange rate on December 31 was 1.25 kira = $1.00 (U.S.). Amounts repatriated to the United States are subject to a 15% Country B withholding tax. The United States-Country B tax treaty reduces this rate to 10%.

AB owns 100% of the stock in FC2, incorporated in Country C. FC2 purchases electronic testing equipment from AB and employs a local sales force to distribute the equipment throughout the region. Forty percent of the FC2 sales are made to customers in Country C. The remaining sales are made to customers in Country D. Total pre-tax profits from FC2's sales were 275,000 tesos in the current year. FC2 remitted none of its profits to AB. FC2 earned an additional 200,000 tesos of pre-tax profits from manufacturing electronic testing equipment from parts produced by Country C companies and selling this equipment in Countries C and D. FC2 paid 60,000 tesos of Country C taxes on income derived from its current year activities. The teso-U.S. dollar exchange rate on December 31 was 1.5 tesos = $1.00 (U.S.). FC2 remitted no profits to the United States. The profit margins on sales of electronic testing equipment in the Country C and D markets are substantially higher than those in the U.S. market.

In June of the current year, AB assigned Brad Gould to work for FC2. Brad relocated from Sunnyvale, California, to Country C under a three-year employment contract.

Required: Explain the U.S. tax consequences of each of AB's overseas activities.

TAX STRATEGY PROBLEM

C:16-58 Miami-based Florida Corporation manufactures electronic games that it has sold overseas for the past two years. Its foreign operations are conducted primarily through two distributors in South America who cater to the South American market and handle sales activities within their assigned areas. Florida has been shipping Spanish and Portuguese versions of its U.S. video games directly from Miami to its two South American distributors and billing the distributors for the shipments. All South American advertising, distribution, and billing activities are the responsibility of the two distributors.

In talking with Florida's chief financial officer (CFO), you learn that the company has been paying U.S. corporate income taxes at a 34% rate on its $2 million of profits generated from sales to the two distributors. The company has paid no foreign taxes on this profit because the sales to the two South American distributors have occurred in the United States. The CFO believes that the company can avoid foreign taxation because it has not set up a permanent establishment in any foreign country. The CFO indicates that she would like to reduce or defer the U.S. tax burden on part or all of these profits by setting up a South American subsidiary to distribute the games throughout South America. The subsidiary would be located in a South American country where the income tax rate is substantially less than the 34% U.S. corporate tax rate. She has found two countries with favorable business climates in which to establish an overseas presence. The maximum income tax rate in each country is 15%.

The CFO believes she can shift all or a large portion of the foreign sales profits to the country in which the subsidiary is established. By shifting part or all of the profits on the overseas sales to this country, the CFO hopes to defer the 34% U.S. corporate income tax until the profits are repatriated to the United States. Florida also hopes to obtain a tax holiday that would permit deferral or exemption of foreign income taxes as an incentive for investing in the foreign country. Ideally, the effective foreign tax rate would be 15% or lower.

Required: Florida's CFO would like you to advise her on alternative ways to conduct the foreign sales so as to reduce and/or defer the company's worldwide tax liability. Compare the after-tax earnings that accrue to a foreign branch and a foreign subsidiary over a five-year period. What alternative business forms can Florida use to conduct its overseas activities? For each alternative, identify the U.S. tax treatment, determine the available tax savings, and indicate whether such savings reflect a tax deferral or a permanent exclusion from U.S. income taxation. In addition, identify whether Florida must establish a foreign office or manufacturing facility in a foreign country to obtain tax reductions or deferrals.

TAX FORM/RETURN PREPARATION PROBLEMS

C:16-59 Stephen R. and Rachel K. Bates, both U.S. citizens, resided in Country K for the entire current year except when Stephen was temporarily assigned to his employer's home office in the United States. They file a joint return and use the calendar year as their tax year. The Bateses report the following current-year income and expense items:

Salary and allowances: United States	$ 20,000
Country K	150,000
Dividends: From U.S. corporation	2,000
From Country K corporation	15,000
Unreimbursed foreign business expenses (directly allocable to Country K earned income and deductible as a miscellaneous itemized deduction)	5,000
Charitable contributions paid to U.S. charities (not directly allocable to any income item)	8,000
Country K income taxes paid on April 1 of current year (in dollars)	12,500
Personal and dependency exemptions	2

Last year, the Bateses elected to accrue their foreign income taxes for foreign tax credit purposes. No foreign tax credit carryovers to the current year are available. Stephen Bates estimates the family will owe 75,000 tesos in Country K income taxes for this year on the Country K salary and dividends. The average annual exchange rate for the current year is 4 tesos to $1 (U.S.). The teso-U.S. dollar exchange rate did not change between year-end and the date the Bates paid their Country K taxes. No Country K taxes were withheld on the foreign corporation dividend.

Complete the two Form 1116s the Bateses must file with their income tax return to claim a credit for the foreign taxes paid on the salary and dividends. Use 2016 tax forms and ignore the implications of the Sec. 911 earned income exclusion, itemized deduction and personal exemption phase-outs, and alternative minimum tax provisions.

C:16-60 John Lawrence Bailey is employed in Country T by American Conglomerate Corporation. Bailey has resided with his wife and three children in Country T for seven years. He made one five-day business trip back to the United States in the current year, and $2,000 of his salary (but none of the allowances) is allocable to the U.S. business trip. Bailey reports the following tax-related information for the current year:

Income:	
Base salary	$100,000
Overseas premium in addition to base salary	15,000
Cost-of-living allowance	37,500
Housing allowance	30,000
Education allowance	16,000
Home leave travel allowance	11,000
Income tax reimbursement from employer for preceding tax year	25,000
Expenditures:	
Tuition at U.S. school	12,000
Housing expenses (rental of home and related expenses)	32,500
Itemized deductions (including $4,000 of unreimbursed employee expenses)	10,000
Foreign income taxes	12,000

Complete a 2016 Form 2555 for the Baileys' current tax year. Assume Mr. Bailey established foreign residency in 2012, and all prior tax returns were filed with a Form 2555 claiming that Mr. Bailey was a bona fide foreign resident.

CASE STUDY PROBLEMS

C:16-61 You have performed tax services for Mark Pruett, a U.S. citizen who is being transferred abroad by his employer. Mark's 2017 salary and allowances in Country M will be $210,000, which is substantially above his salary for last year. The salary differential is due to the higher cost of living in Country M and Mark's added responsibilities. Of the allowances, $30,000 is for housing although Mark's 2017 housing costs are expected to be $40,000. The Country M income tax rate is 40%. Mark's employer conducts business at a second location in Country T, where Mark probably will be transferred in three or four years. The Country T income tax rate is 20%.

The transfer date is February 1, 2017. Mark's wife and three-year-old daughter will accompany him. Mark expects to return to the United States for one week of training each year starting in September 2017. Mark takes four weeks of vacation each year. Because Mark still has family in the United States, he may spend substantial vacation time in the United States.

Required: Your tax manager has asked you to draft for her review a memorandum explaining the tax consequences of the relocation, whether Mark is entitled to the foreign earned income exclusion, and what records Mark must maintain to file his tax return for the year of transfer.

C:16-62 Ralph Sampson was hired last year by a small international trading company. You have prepared Ralph's tax returns for a number of years while he worked in the U.S. offices of a large international bank. You continue to perform tax services for Ralph while he is overseas to manage the trading company's office in Country T (a nontreaty country). Ralph has been assigned abroad since November 1 of Year 1, and has continuously resided in a company-provided apartment located in Country T's capital. His wife and child have maintained their old residence in the United States to enable Mrs. Sampson to continue her career as a university professor and their son to finish high school. During Year 1, Ralph was in Country T and other foreign countries for all of November and December. During Year 2, Ralph was in the United States for 93 days (spread out evenly throughout the four quarters of that year) and in Country T and other foreign countries for the remainder of the year. Ralph wants you to file an amended Year 1 tax return and an initial Year 2 tax return claiming on each return the maximum possible foreign earned income exclusion. (The Year 1 return originally was filed without claiming the foreign earned income exclusion because Ralph had not yet qualified for the exclusion when the return was due.) Ralph knows that he does not meet the physical presence test, but he has assured you that he meets the bona fide residence test. However, because of his heavy Year 2 travel schedule, he has not yet been able to document that he is a Country T resident.

In June of Year 3, the Sampsons' son will graduate from high school. Mrs. Sampson plans to join her son overseas and obtain a teaching position in an American school for U.S. expatriates. The Sampsons' son will spend 21/2 months of summer with his parents overseas but will return to the United States to attend the University of Tennessee. He will join his parents for an additional four weeks in December and January during the university's holiday break.

Required: Should you file the Sampson's amended Year 1 tax return and new Year 2 income tax return claiming the maximum foreign-earned income exclusion for which Ralph has asked? What information should you ask Ralph to provide before you prepare his return? What ethical issues are raised by your filing the return based on Ralph's promise to obtain the requisite information? When will Mrs. Sampson first be eligible for the foreign earned income exclusion? Under which of the two tests will she likely qualify after she begins her Country T teaching job in June of Year 3?

TAX RESEARCH PROBLEMS

C:16-63 Spike "Spitball" Weaver, a hard-throwing pitcher, was approaching the end of his major league baseball career. After becoming a free agent at the end of the Year 1 baseball season, he signed a lucrative three-year contract (which specified a substantial signing bonus) to play for the Tokyo Bombers in the fledgling World Baseball League starting in Year 2. The team's management paid 50% of the bonus in Year 1 and will pay the remaining 50% during Years 2 through 4. This league includes 12 teams, only four of which are located in the United States. Although Spike's salary is paid over a 12-month period, he resides in Japan only for the seven-month regular season, the preseason training period, and the post-season playoffs (if his team makes the playoffs). He spends the remainder of his time at his home in Fitzgerald, Georgia. The tax manager for whom you regularly work has asked you to prepare a memorandum to the file indicating what factors should be considered in allocating Spike's bonus and salary according to work performed at the U.S. and non-U.S. locations.

She suggests that at a minimum you consider

- Reg. Sec. 1.861-4
- Rev. Rul. 76-66, 1976-1 C.B. 189
- Rev. Rul. 87-38, 1987-1 C.B. 176
- *Peter Stemkowski v. CIR,* 50 AFTR 2d 82-5739, 82-2 USTC ¶9589 (2nd Cir., 1982)

C:16-64 Determine whether each of the taxes listed below may be credited against a U.S. income tax liability.

a. Saudi Arabian tax on companies producing petroleum
b. French Company Income Tax
c. Ontario (Canada) Corporations Tax
d. Japan Corporation Tax

A partial list of research sources includes:

- Research Institute of America (RIA), *United States Tax Reporter,* ¶9015.03
- Commerce Clearing House (CCH), *Standard Federal Tax Reporter,* ¶27,826.318
- Bureau of National Affairs (BNA), *Tax Management Portfolios,* individual country portfolios on Saudi Arabia, France, Canada, and Japan

For additional authority, the researcher might consult the tax treaties that the United States has concluded with each of the four countries.

TAX & FINANCIAL ACCOUNTING

C:16-65 MedTec was incorporated five years ago in Georgia. It manufactures products for doctors and hospitals in the United States. Because of lower labor costs outside the United States, MedTec establishes in Country X a foreign subsidiary that will manufacture some of its products for shipment to the United States and to foreign countries. Country X tax rates are lower than U.S. tax rates. In addition, Country X has provided special tax incentives that lead you to believe the subsidiary will pay local income taxes at a 10% rate for the first five years, and at a 25% rate for subsequent years. Only a small portion, if any, of the foreign earnings will be taxed to MedTec under Subpart F. According to financial projections, the foreign subsidiary will generate $500,000 of pre-tax profits each year. Because of MedTec's need for capital to expand its foreign operations, none of the foreign profits will be repatriated to the United States in the first ten years of operations.

Prepare a memorandum that outlines the proper financial accounting treatment of MedTec's U.S. income taxes with respect to its investment in the Country X subsidiary.

A partial list of research sources is:

- Accounting Standards Codification (ASC) 740 (Income Taxes) formerly SFAS No. 109
- IRC Sec. 951

C:16-66 AmeriCorp, a U.S. corporation based in Houston, manufactures telecommunications equipment. It sells the equipment to retailers throughout the world. To promote its Latin American sales, AmeriCorp conducts its business through three entities: TelMexico, a *sociedad anonima* organized under Mexican law and 100% owned by AmeriCorp; TelBrazilco, a *sociedade limitada*, organized under Brazilian law and 51% owned by AmeriCorp; and TelCaymanco, an ordinary nonresident company organized under Cayman Islands law and 100% owned by TelBrazilco. Foreign investors own the remaining 49% of TelBrazilco voting stock.

TelMexico routinely purchases telecommunications equipment from AmeriCorp and sells the equipment to independent retailers throughout Central America. This entity derives 20% of its revenues from equipment sales outside of Mexico. TelBrazilco manufactures telecommunications equipment in Brazil and sells the equipment to independent retailers throughout South America. This entity derives 65% of its income from equipment sales outside of Brazil. TelCaymanco purchases telecommunications equipment exclusively from TelBrazilco and sells the equipment to independent retailers throughout Europe. This entity derives 99% of its revenues from equipment sales outside the Cayman Islands. Periodically, TelMexico pays dividends to AmeriCorp, and TelCaymanco pays dividends to TelBrazilco.

AmeriCorp's chief financial officer has approached you with the following questions:

1. What are the tax implications of this organizational structure? Specifically, are the entities controlled foreign corporations, and do their activities generate Subpart F income?
2. Can AmeriCorp use the check-the-box regulations to change the tax treatment of any foreign entity?
3. What tax consequences would ensue if AmeriCorp elected to have,
   a. TelCaymanco and TelBrazilco taxed as corporations (i.e., associations)?
   b. TelBrazilco taxed as a corporation (TelCaymanco would be disregarded as a taxable entity)?

Write a memorandum that addresses these questions. At a minimum, consult the following authorities:

- Reg. Secs. 301.7701-2 and 301.7701-3

APPENDIX

TAX RESEARCH WORKING PAPER FILE

INDEX TO TAX RESEARCH FILE*

*Most accounting firms maintain a **client file** for each of their clients. Typically, this file contains copies of client letters, memoranda-to-the-file, relevant primary and secondary authorities, and billing information. In our case, the client file for Mercy Hospital would include copies of the following: (1) the December 12 letter to Elizabeth Feghali, (2) the December 9 memorandum-to-the-file, (3) Sec. 119, (4) Reg. Sec. 1.119-1, (5) the *Kowalski* opinion, (6) the *Standard Federal Tax Reporter* annotation, and (7) pertinent billing information.

Tax Research File

As mentioned in Chapter C:1 the tax research process entails six steps.

1. Determine the facts
2. Identify the issues
3. Locate applicable authorities
4. Evaluate these authorities
5. Analyze the facts in terms of applicable authorities
6. Communicate conclusions and recommendations to others.

Let us walk through each of these steps.

Determine the Facts Assume that we have determined the facts to be as follows:

> *Mercy Hospital maintains a cafeteria on its premises. In addition, it rents space to MacDougal's, a privately owned sandwich shop. The cafeteria closes at 8:00 p.m. MacDougal's is open 24 hours. Mercy provides meal vouchers to each of its 240 medical employees to enable them to remain on call in case of emergency. The vouchers are redeemable either at the cafeteria or at MacDougal's. Although the employees are not required to remain on or near the premises during meal hours, they generally do. Elizabeth Feghali, Mercy's Chief Administrator, has approached you with the following question: Is the value of a meal voucher includible in the employees' gross income?*

At this juncture, be sure you understand the facts before proceeding further. Remember, researching the wrong facts could produce the wrong results.

Identify the Issues Identifying the issues presupposes a minimum level of proficiency in tax accounting. This proficiency will come with time, effort, and perseverance. The central issue raised by the facts is the taxability of the meal vouchers. A resolution of this issue will hinge on the resolution of other issues raised in the course of the research.

Locate Applicable Authorities For some students, this step is the most difficult in the research process. It raises the perplexing question, "Where do I begin to look?" The answer depends on the tax resources at one's disposal, as well as one's research preferences. Four rules of thumb apply:

1. *Adopt an approach with which you are comfortable, and that you are confident will produce reliable results.*
2. *Always consult the IRC and other primary authorities.*
3. *Be as thorough as possible, taking into consideration time and billing constraints.*
4. *Make sure that the authorities you consult are current.*

One approach is to conduct a topical search. Begin by consulting the index to the Internal Revenue Code (IRC). Then read the relevant IRC section(s). If the language of the IRC is vague or ambiguous, turn to the Treasury Regulations. Read the relevant regulation section that elaborates or expounds on the IRC provision. If the language of the regulation is confusing or unclear, go to a commercial tax service. Read the relevant tax service paragraphs that explain or analyze the statutory and regulatory provisions. For references to other authorities, browse through the footnotes and annotations of the service. Then, consult these authorities directly. Finally, check the currency of the authorities consulted, with the aid of a citator or status (finding) list.

If a pertinent court decision or IRS ruling has been called to your attention, consult this authority directly. Alternatively, browse through the status (finding) list of a tax service for references to tax service paragraphs that discuss this authority. Better still, consult a citator or status list for references to court opinions or rulings that cite the authority. If you subscribe to a computerized tax service, conduct a keyword, citation, contents, or topical search. (For a discussion of these types of searches, see the computerized research supplement available for download at *www.pearsonhighered.com/pearsontax*.) Then, hyperlink to the authorities cited within the text of the documents retrieved. So numerous are the approaches to tax research that one is virtually free to pick and choose. All that is required of the researcher is a basic level of skill and some imagination.

Let us adopt a topical approach to the issue of the meal vouchers. If we consult an index to the IRC, we are likely to find the heading "Meals and Lodging." Below this heading are likely to be several subheadings, some pertaining to deductions, others to exclusions. Because the voucher issue pertains to an exclusion, let us browse through these subheadings. In so doing, we will notice that most of these subheadings refer to Sec. 119. If we look up this IRC section, we will see the following passage:

Sec. 119. Meals or lodging furnished for the convenience of the employer.

(a) **Meals and lodging furnished to employee, his spouse, and his dependents, pursuant to employment.**
There shall be excluded from gross income of an employee the value of any meals or lodging furnished to him . . . by, or on behalf of his employer for the convenience of the employer, but only if—

(1) **in the case of meals, the meals are furnished on the business premises of the employer . . .**

(b) **Special rules. For purposes of subsection (a)—**
(4) **Meals furnished to employees on business premises where meals of most employees are otherwise excludable.** All meals furnished on the business premises of an employer to such employer's employees shall be treated as furnished for the convenience of the employer if . . . more than half of the employees to whom such meals are furnished on such premises are furnished such meals for the convenience of the employer.

Section 119 appears to be applicable. It deals with meals furnished to an employee on the business premises of the employer. Our case deals with meal vouchers furnished to employees for redemption at employer-maintained and employer-rented-out facilities. But here, additional issues arise. For purposes of Sec. 119, are meal vouchers the same as "meals"? (Do not assume they are.) Are employer-maintained and employer-rented-out facilities the same as "the business premises of the employer"? (Again, do not assume they are.) And what does the IRC mean by "for the convenience of the employer"? Because the IRC offers no guidance in this respect, let us turn to the Treasury Regulations.

The applicable regulation is Reg. Sec. 1.119-1. How do we know this? Because Treasury Regulation section numbers track the IRC section numbers. Regulation Sec. 1.119-1 is the only regulation under Sec. 119. If we browse through this regulation, we will find the following provision:

(a) **Meals . . .**
(2) **Meals furnished without a charge**
(i) Meals furnished by an employer without charge to the employee will be regarded as furnished for the convenience of the employer if such meals are furnished for a substantial noncompensatory business reason of the employer . . .
(ii) (a) Meals will be regarded as furnished for a substantial noncompensatory business reason of the employer when the meals are furnished to the employee during his working hours to have the employee available for emergency call during his meal period . . .

(c) **Business premises of the employer.**
(1) **In general.** For purposes of this section, the term "business premises of the employer" generally means the place of employment of the employee . . .

Based on a reading of this provision, we might conclude that the hospital meals are furnished "for the convenience of the employer." Why? Because they are furnished for a "substantial noncompensatory business reason of the employer," namely, to have the employees available for emergency call during their meal periods. They also are furnished during the employees' working hours. Moreover, under Sec. 119(b)(4), if more than half the employees satisfy the "for the convenience of the employer" test, all employees will be regarded as satisfying the test. But are the meals furnished on "the business premises of the employer"? Under the regulation, the answer would depend. If the meals are furnished in the hospital cafeteria, they probably are furnished on "the business premises of the employer." The hospital is the place of employment of the medical employees. The cafeteria is part of the hospital. On the other hand, if the meals are furnished at MacDougal's, they probably are not furnished on "the business premises of the employer." MacDougal's is not the place of employment of the medical employees. Nor is it a part of the hospital. Thus, Reg. Sec. 1.119-1 is enlightening with respect to two statutory terms: "for the convenience of the employer" and "the business premises of the employer." However, it is obscure with respect to the third term, "meals." Because of this obscurity, let us turn to a tax service.

Although the index to CCH's *Standard Federal Tax Reporter* does not list "meal vouchers," it does list "cash allowances in lieu of meals" as a subtopic under Meals and Lodging. Are meal vouchers the same as cash meal allowances?—perhaps so; let us see. Next to the heading "cash allowances in lieu of meals" is a reference to CCH ¶7222.59. If we look up this reference, we will find the following annotation:

¶7222.59 **Meal allowances.**—Cash meal allowances received by an employee (state trooper) from his employer were not excludible from income. *R.J. Kowalski*, SCt, 77-2 USTC ¶9748, 434 US 77.[1]

Here we discover that, in the *Kowalski* case, the U.S. Supreme Court decided that cash meal allowances received by an employee were not excludible from the employee's income. Is the *Kowalski* case similar to our case? It might be. Let us find out. If we turn to paragraph 9748 of the second 1977 volume of *United States Tax Cases,* we will find the text of the *Kowalski* opinion. A synopsis of this opinion is present below.

In the mid-1970s, the State of New Jersey provided cash meal allowances to its state troopers. The state did not require the troopers to use the allowances exclusively for meals. Nor did it require them to consume their meals on its business premises. One trooper, Robert J. Kowalski, failed to report a portion of his allowance on his tax return. The IRS assessed a deficiency, and Kowalski took the IRS to court. In court, Kowalski argued that the meal allowances were excludible, because they were furnished "for the convenience of the employer." The IRS contended that the allowances were taxable because they amounted to compensation. The Supreme Court took up the case and sided with the IRS. The Court held that the Sec. 119 income exclusion does not apply to cash payments; it applies only to meals in kind.[2]

For the sake of illustration, let us assume that Sec. 119, Reg. Sec. 1.119-1, and the *Kowalski* case are the *only* authorities "on point." How should we evaluate them?

Evaluate Authorities Section 119 is the key authority applicable to our case. It supplies the operative rule for resolving the issue of the meal vouchers. It is vague, however, with respect to three terms: "meals," "business premises of the employer," and "for the convenience of the employer." The principal judicial authority is the *Kowalski* case. It provides an official interpretation of the term "meals." Because the U.S. Supreme Court decided *Kowalski*, the case should be assigned considerable weight. The relevant administrative authority is Reg. Sec. 1.119-1. It expounds on the terms "business premises of the employer" and "for the convenience of the employer." Because neither the IRC nor *Kowalski* explain these terms, Reg. Sec. 1.119-1 should be accorded great weight. But what if *Kowalski* had conflicted with Reg. Sec. 1.119-1? Which should be considered more authoritative? As a general rule, high court decisions "trump" the Treasury Regulations (and all IRS pronouncements for that matter). The more recent the decision, the greater its precedential weight. Had there been no Supreme Court decision and a division of appellate authority, equal weight should have been assigned to each of the appellate court decisions.

Analyze the Facts in Terms of Applicable Authorities Analyzing the facts in terms of applicable authorities involves applying the abstraction of the law to the concreteness of the facts. It entails expressing the generalities of the law in terms of the specifics of the facts. In this process, every legal condition must be satisfied for the result implied by the

[1] The researcher also might read the main *Standard Federal Tax Reporter* paragraph that discusses meals and lodging furnished by the employer (CCH ¶7222.01). Within this paragraph are likely to be references to other primary authorities.

[2] At this juncture, the researcher should consult a citator to determine whether *Kowalski* is still "good law," and to locate other authorities that cite *Kowalski.*

general rule to ensue. Thus, in our case, the conditions of furnishing "meals," "on the business premises of the employer," and "for the convenience of the employer" must be satisfied for the value of the "meals" to be excluded from the employee's income.

When analyzing the facts in terms of case law, the researcher should always draw an *analogy* between case facts and client facts. Likewise, he or she should always draw a *distinction* between case facts and client facts. Remember, under the rule of precedent, a court deciding the client's case will be bound by the precedent of cases involving *similar* facts and issues. By the same token, it will *not* be bound by the precedent of cases involving *dissimilar* facts and issues.

The most useful vehicle for analyzing client facts is the memorandum-to-the-file (see page A-6). The purpose of this document is threefold: first, it assists the researcher in recollecting transactions long transpired; second, it apprises colleagues and supervisors of the nature of one's research; third, it provides "substantial authority" for the tax treatment of a particular item. Let us analyze the facts of our case by way of a memorandum-to-the-file. Notice the format of this document; it generally tracks the steps in the research process itself.

Communicate Conclusions and Recommendations to Others For three practical reasons, research results always should be communicated to the client *in writing*. First, a written communication can be made after extensive revisions. An oral communication cannot. Second, in a written communication, the researcher can delve into the intricacies of tax law. Often, in an oral communication, he or she cannot. Third, a written communication reinforces an oral understanding. Alternatively, it brings to light an oral misunderstanding.

The written communication usually takes the form of a client letter (see page A-7). The purpose of this letter is two-fold: first, it apprises the client of the results of one's research, and second, it recommends to the client a course of action based on these results. A sample client letter is presented below. Notice the organization of this document; it is similar to that of the memorandum-to-the-file.

Memorandum-to-the-File

Date: December 9, 20X1
From: Rosina Havacek
Re: The taxability of meal vouchers furnished by Mercy Hospital to its medical staff.

Facts

[*State only the facts that are relevant to the Issue(s) and necessary for the Analysis.*] Our client, Mercy Hospital ("Mercy"), provides meal vouchers to its medical employees to enable them to remain on emergency call. The vouchers are redeemable at Mercy's onsite cafeteria and at MacDougal's, a privately owned sandwich shop. MacDougal's rents business space from the hospital. Although Mercy does not require its employees to remain on or near its premises during their meal hours, the employees generally do. Elizabeth Feghali, Mercy's Chief Administrator, has asked us to research whether the value of the meal vouchers is taxable to the employees.

Issues

[*Identify the issue(s) raised by the facts. Be specific.*] The taxability of the meal vouchers depends on three issues: first, whether the meals are furnished "for the convenience of the employer"; second, whether they are furnished "on the business premises of the employer"; and third, whether the vouchers are equivalent to cash.

Applicable Law

[*Discuss those legal principles that both strengthen and weaken the client's case. Because the primary authority for tax law is the IRC, begin with the IRC.*] Section 119 provides that the value of meals is excludible from an employee's income if the meals are furnished for the convenience of, and on the business premises of the employer. [*Discuss how administrative and/or judicial authorities expound on statutory terms.*] Under Reg. Sec. 1.119-1, a meal is furnished "for the convenience of the employer" if it is furnished for a "substantial noncompensatory business reason." A "substantial noncompensatory business reason" includes the need to have the employee available for emergency calls during his or her meal period. Under Sec. 119(b)(4), if more than half the employees satisfy the "for the convenience of the employer" test, all employees will be regarded as satisfying the test. Regulation Sec. 1.119-1 defines "business premises of the employer" as the place of employment of the employee.

[*When discussing court cases, present case facts in such a way as to enable the reader to draw an analogy with client facts.*] A Supreme Court case, *Kowalski v. CIR*, 434 U.S. 77, 77-2 USTC ¶9748, discusses what constitutes "meals" for purposes of Sec. 119. In *Kowalski*, the State of New Jersey furnished cash meal allowances to its state troopers to enable them to eat while on duty. It did not require the troopers to use the allowances exclusively for meals. Nor did it require them to consume their meals on its business premises. One trooper, R.J. Kowalski, excluded the value of his allowances from his income. The IRS disputed this treatment, and Kowalski took the IRS to Court. In Court, Kowalski argued that the allowances were excludible because they were furnished "for the convenience of the employer." The IRS contended that the allowances were taxable because they amounted to compensation. The U.S. Supreme Court took up the case and decided for the IRS. The Court held that the Sec. 119 income exclusion does not apply to payments in cash.

Analysis

[*The analysis should (a) apply applicable law to the facts and (b) address the issue(s). In this section, every proposition should be supported by either authority, logic, or plausible assumptions.*]

Issue 1: The meals provided by Mercy seem to be furnished "for the convenience of the employer." They are furnished to have employees available for emergency call during their meal breaks. This is a "substantial noncompensatory reason" within the meaning of Reg. Sec. 1.119-1.

Issue 2: Although the hospital cafeteria appears to be the "business premises of the employer," MacDougal's does not appear to be. The hospital is the place of employment of the medical employees. MacDougal's is not.

Issue 3: [*In applying case law to the facts, indicate how case facts are similar to/dissimilar from client facts. If the analysis does not support a "yes-no" answer, do not give one.*] Based on the foregoing authorities, it is unclear whether the vouchers are equivalent to cash. On the one hand, they are redeemable only in meals. Thus, they resemble meals-in-kind. On the other hand, they are redeemable at more than one institution. Thus, they resemble cash. Nor is it clear whether a court deciding this case would reach the same conclusion as the Supreme Court did in *Kowalski.* In the latter case, the State of New Jersey provided its meal allowances in the form of cash. It did not require its employees to use the allowances exclusively for meals. Nor did it require them to consume their meals on its business premises. In our case, Mercy provides its meal allowances in the form of vouchers. Thus, it indirectly requires its employees to use the allowances exclusively for meals. On the other hand, it does not require them to consume their meals on its business premises.

Conclusion

[*The conclusion should (a) logically flow from the analysis, and (b) address the issue(s).*] Although it appears that the meals acquired by voucher in the hospital cafeteria are furnished "for the convenience of the employer" and "on the business premises of the employer," it is unclear whether the vouchers are equivalent to cash. If they *are* equivalent to cash, *or* if they are redeemed at MacDougal's, their value is likely to be taxable to the employees. On the other hand, if they are not equivalent to cash, *and* they are redeemed only in the hospital cafeteria, their value is likely to be excludible.

Professional Accounting Associates
2701 First City Plaza
Suite 905
Southwest City, Texas 75019

December 12, 20X1

Elizabeth Feghali, Chief Administrator
Mercy Hospital
22650 West Haven Drive
Southwest City, Texas 75527

Dear Ms. Feghali:

[*Introduction. Set a cordial tone.*] It was great to see you at last Thursday's football game. If not for that last minute fumble, the Longhorns might have taken the Big 12 Conference championship!

[*Issue/Purpose.*] In our meeting of December 6, you asked us to research whether the value of the meal vouchers that Mercy provides to its medical employees is taxable to the employees. [*Short Answer.*] I regret to inform you that if the vouchers are redeemed at MacDougal's, their value is likely to be taxable to the employees. On the other hand, if the vouchers are redeemed in the hospital cafeteria, their value is likely to be excludible from the employee's income. [*The remainder of the letter should elaborate, support, and qualify this answer.*]

[*Steps taken in deriving conclusion.*] In reaching this conclusion, we consulted relevant provisions of the Internal Revenue Code ("IRC"), applicable Treasury Regulations under the IRC, and a pertinent Supreme Court case. In addition, we reviewed the documents on employee benefits that you submitted to us at our earlier meeting.

[*Facts. State only the facts that are relevant to the issue and necessary for the analysis.*] The facts as we understand them are as follows: Mercy provides meal vouchers to its medical employees to enable them to eat while on emergency call. The vouchers are redeemable either in the hospital cafeteria or at MacDougal's. MacDougal's is a privately owned institution that rents business space from the hospital. Although Mercy's employees are not required to remain on or near the premises during their meal hours, they generally do.

[*Applicable law. State, do not interpret.*] Under the IRC, the value of meals is excludible from an employee's income if two conditions are met: first, the meals are furnished "for the convenience of the employer" and second, they are provided "on the business premises of the employer." Although the IRC does not explain what is meant by "for the convenience of the employer," "business premises of the employer," and "meals," other authorities do. Specifically, the Treasury Regulations define "business premises of the employer" to be the place of employment of the employees. The regulations state that providing meals during work hours to have an employee available for emergency calls is "for the convenience of the employer." Moreover, under the IRC, if more than half the employees satisfy the "for the convenience of the employer" test, all the employees will be regarded as satisfying the test. The Supreme Court has interpreted "meals" to mean food-in-kind. The Court has held that cash allowances do not qualify as "meals."

[*Analysis. Express the generalities of applicable law in terms of the specifics of the facts.*] Clearly, the meals furnished by Mercy are "for the convenience of the employer." They are furnished during the employees' work hours to have the employees available for emergency call. Although the meals provided in the hospital cafeteria appear to be furnished "on the business premises of the employer," the meals provided at MacDougal's do not appear to be. The hospital is the place of employment of the medical employees. MacDougal's is not. What is unclear is whether the meal vouchers are equivalent to food-in-kind. On the one hand, they are redeemable at more than one institution and thus resemble cash allowances. On the other hand, they are redeemable only in meals and thus resemble food-in-kind.

[*Conclusion/Recommendation.*] Because of this lack of clarity, we suggest that you modify your employee benefits plan to allow for the provision of meals-in-kind exclusively in the hospital cafeteria. In this way, you will dispel any doubt that Mercy is furnishing "meals," "for the convenience of the employer," "on the premises of the employer."

[*Closing/Follow Up.*] Please call me at 475-2020 if you have any questions concerning this conclusion. May I suggest that we meet next week to discuss the possibility of revising your employee benefits plan.

Very truly yours,
Professional Accounting Associates

By: Rosina Havacek, Junior Associate

APPENDIX

B TAX FORMS

Facts for Sole Proprietorship (Schedule C)

Andrew Lawrence is the sole proprietor of a business that operates under the name Andrew Lawrence Furniture (Business Code 337000). The proprietorship is located at 1234 First Avenue, City, ST 55555. Andrew started the business with a $200,000 capital investment on June 1, 2010. The proprietorship uses the calendar year as its tax year (the same as its proprietor) and the accrual method of accounting. The following information pertains to its 2016 activities:

A trial balance is included as part of the accompanying worksheet. Notes accompanying the account balances are presented below.

1. Cost of goods sold is determined as follows:

Inventory at beginning of year	$ 64,000
Plus: Purchases	340,800
Cost of labor	143,204
Additional Sec. 263A adjustment	7,000
Other costs	90,000
Goods available for sale	$645,004
Minus: Inventory at end of year	(104,800)
Cost of goods sold	$540,204

The proprietorship values its inventory using the first-in, first-out method and historical costs. The Sec. 263A rules apply to the proprietorship. No change in valuing inventories occurred between the beginning and end of the tax year.

2. The proprietorship uses MACRS depreciation for tax purposes. The current year tax depreciation is $27,476. Of this amount, $15,000 is included in cost of goods sold and inventory. The AMT depreciation adjustment on post-1986 personal property is $1,514. This amount is reported on Andrew Lawrence's Form 6251 (Alternative Minimum Tax—Individuals), which is not reproduced here.

3. Using its excess funds, the proprietorship has purchased various temporary investments, including a 2% investment in Plaza Corporation stock, 50 shares of Service Corporation stock, and some tax-exempt municipal bonds. The proprietorship has held the Plaza stock for two years and sold it in July for $4,500 more than its $7,000 adjusted basis. Prior to the sale, Plaza paid a $1,000 dividend. The 50 shares of Service stock, which had been purchased during the year, was declared worthless during the year. The proprietorship recovered none of its $2,100 adjusted basis.

4. Employees other than Andrew Lawrence receive limited fringe benefits. One employee also receives a $2,000 contribution to an Individual Retirement Account paid by the proprietorship.

5. Miscellaneous expenses include $150 of expenses related to the production of the dividend income.

6. The proprietorship paid no estimated taxes.

7. Balance sheet information is not provided for the sole proprietorship because it is not reported on the Schedule C. Balance sheet information, however, can be found on page 4 of the C corporation tax return.

8. For additional information, see Schedule C and the worksheet on page B-6.

SCHEDULE C (Form 1040)
Department of the Treasury Internal Revenue Service (99)

Profit or Loss From Business
(Sole Proprietorship)

► Information about Schedule C and its separate instructions is at *www.irs.gov/schedulec*.
► Attach to Form 1040, 1040NR, or 1041; partnerships generally must file Form 1065.

OMB No. 1545-0074
2016
Attachment Sequence No. 09

Name of proprietor: Andrew Lawrence
Social security number (SSN): XXX-XX-XXXX

A Principal business or profession, including product or service (see instructions): Manufacturing Furniture
B Enter code from instructions ► 3 3 7 0 0 0

C Business name. If no separate business name, leave blank.
D Employer ID number (EIN), (see instr.): X X X X X X X X X

E Business address (including suite or room no.) ► 1234 Avenue
City, town or post office, state, and ZIP code: City, ST 55555

F Accounting method: (1) ☐ Cash (2) ☒ Accrual (3) ☐ Other (specify) ►

G Did you "materially participate" in the operation of this business during 2016? If "No," see instructions for limit on losses ☒ Yes ☐ No

H If you started or acquired this business during 2016, check here ► ☐

I Did you make any payments in 2016 that would require you to file Form(s) 1099? (see instructions) ☐ Yes ☒ No

J If "Yes," did you or will you file required Forms 1099? ☐ Yes ☐ No

Part I Income

		Line	Amount
1	Gross receipts or sales. See instructions for line 1 and check the box if this income was reported to you on Form W-2 and the "Statutory employee" box on that form was checked ► ☐	1	869,658
2	Returns and allowances	2	29,242
3	Subtract line 2 from line 1	3	840,416
4	Cost of goods sold (from line 42)	4	540,204
5	**Gross profit.** Subtract line 4 from line 3	5	300,212
6	Other income, including federal and state gasoline or fuel tax credit or refund (see instructions)	6	
7	**Gross income.** Add lines 5 and 6 ►	7	300,212

Part II Expenses. Enter expenses for business use of your home only on line 30.

		Line	Amount			Line	Amount
8	Advertising	8	13,000	18	Office expense (see instructions)	18	16,000
9	Car and truck expenses (see instructions)	9	4,000	19	Pension and profit-sharing plans	19	2,000
				20	Rent or lease (see instructions):		
10	Commissions and fees	10	10,400	a	Vehicles, machinery, and equipment	20a	36,000
11	Contract labor (see instructions)	11		b	Other business property	20b	
12	Depletion	12		21	Repairs and maintenance	21	
13	Depreciation and section 179 expense deduction (not included in Part III) (see instructions)	13	12,476	22	Supplies (not included in Part III)	22	
				23	Taxes and licenses	23	9,840
				24	Travel, meals, and entertainment:		
14	Employee benefit programs (other than on line 19)	14	4,000	a	Travel	24a	4,000
				b	Deductible meals and entertainment (see instructions)	24b	4,000
15	Insurance (other than health)	15					
16	Interest:			25	Utilities	25	
a	Mortgage (paid to banks, etc.)	16a		26	Wages (less employment credits)	26	52,000
b	Other	16b	8,000	27a	Other expenses (from line 48)	27a	8,650
17	Legal and professional services	17		b	**Reserved for future use**	27b	

		Line	Amount
28	**Total expenses** before expenses for business use of home. Add lines 8 through 27a ►	28	184,366
29	Tentative profit or (loss). Subtract line 28 from line 7	29	
30	Expenses for business use of your home. Do not report these expenses elsewhere. Attach Form 8829 unless using the simplified method (see instructions). **Simplified method filers only:** enter the total square footage of: (a) your home: ______ and (b) the part of your home used for business: ______. Use the Simplified Method Worksheet in the instructions to figure the amount to enter on line 30	30	115,846
31	**Net profit or (loss).** Subtract line 30 from line 29. • If a profit, enter on both **Form 1040, line 12** (or **Form 1040NR, line 13**) and on **Schedule SE, line 2.** (If you checked the box on line 1, see instructions). Estates and trusts, enter on **Form 1041, line 3.** • If a loss, you **must** go to line 32.	31	115,846

32 If you have a loss, check the box that describes your investment in this activity (see instructions).
- If you checked 32a, enter the loss on both **Form 1040, line 12,** (or **Form 1040NR, line 13**) and on **Schedule SE, line 2.** (If you checked the box on line 1, see the line 31 instructions). Estates and trusts, enter on **Form 1041, line 3.**
- If you checked 32b, you **must** attach **Form 6198.** Your loss may be limited.

32a ☐ All investment is at risk.
32b ☐ Some investment is not at risk.

For Paperwork Reduction Act Notice, see the separate instructions. Cat. No. 11334P **Schedule C (Form 1040) 2016**

Form 706 (Rev. 8-2013)

Estate of: Herman Estes

Decedent's social security number XXX XX XXXX

SCHEDULE I—Annuities

Note. Generally, no exclusion is allowed for the estates of decedents dying after December 31, 1984 (see instructions).

Note. If the value of the gross estate, together with the amount of adjusted taxable gifts, is less than the basic exclusion amount and the Form 706 is being filed solely to elect portability of the DSUE amount, consideration should be given as to whether you are required to report the value of assets eligible for the marital or charitable deduction on this schedule. See the instructions and Reg. section 20.2010-2T (a)(7)(ii) for more information. If you are not required to report the value of an asset, identify the property but make no entries in the last three columns.

		Yes	No
A	Are you excluding from the decedent's gross estate the value of a lump-sum distribution described in section 2039(f)(2) (as in effect before its repeal by the Deficit Reduction Act of 1984)? . . . . If "Yes," you must attach the information required by the instructions.		X

Item number	Description. Show the entire value of the annuity before any exclusions	Alternate valuation date	Includible alternate value	Includible value at date of death
1	Qualified pension plan issued by Buckeye Corporation. Beneficiary — Ann Estes, spouse			240,000
	Total from continuation schedules (or additional statements) attached to this schedule . .			
	TOTAL. (Also enter on Part 5—Recapitulation, page 3, at item 9.)			240,000

(If more space is needed, attach the continuation schedule from the end of this package or additional statements of the same size.)

Form 706 (Rev. 8-2013)

Estate of: Herman Estes	Decedent's social security number XXX XX XXXX

SCHEDULE J—Funeral Expenses and Expenses Incurred in Administering Property Subject to Claims

▶ Use Schedule PC to make a protective claim for refund due to an expense not currently deductible. For such a claim, report the expense on Schedule J but without a value in the last column.

Note. Do not list expenses of administering property not subject to claims on this schedule. To report those expenses, see instructions.

If executors' commissions, attorney fees, etc., are claimed and allowed as a deduction for estate tax purposes, they are not allowable as a deduction in computing the taxable income of the estate for federal income tax purposes. They are allowable as an income tax deduction on Form 1041, U.S. Income Tax Return for Estates and Trusts, if a waiver is filed to forgo the deduction on Form 706 (see Instructions for Form 1041).

	Yes	No
Are you aware of any actual or potential reimbursement to the estate for any expense claimed as a deduction on this schedule?		
If "Yes," attach a statement describing the expense(s) subject to potential reimbursement. (see instructions)		

Item number	Description	Expense amount	Total amount
	A. Funeral expenses:	15,000	
	Total funeral expenses . . . . . ▶		15,000
	B. Administration expenses:		
	1 Executors' commissions—amount estimated/agreed upon/paid. (Strike out the words that do not apply.)		
	2 Attorney fees—amount estimated/agreed upon/paid. (Strike out the words that do not apply.) . .		70,000
	3 Accountant fees—amount estimated/agreed upon/paid. (Strike out the words that do not apply.) .		
	4 Miscellaneous expenses:	Expense amount	
	Total miscellaneous expenses from continuation schedules (or additional statements) attached to this schedule		
	Total miscellaneous expenses . . . . . ▶		
	TOTAL. (Also enter on Part 5—Recapitulation, page 3, at item 14.) . . . . . ▶		85,000

(If more space is needed, attach the continuation schedule from the end of this package or additional statements of the same size.)

Form 706 (Rev. 8-2013)

Estate of: Herman Estes

Decedent's social security number XXX XX XXXX

SCHEDULE K—Debts of the Decedent, and Mortgages and Liens

► Use Schedule PC to make a protective claim for refund due to a claim not currently deductible. For such a claim, report the expense on Schedule K but without a value in the last column.

	Yes	No
Are you aware of any actual or potential reimbursement to the estate for any debt of the decedent, mortgage, or lien claimed as a deduction on this schedule?		X
If "Yes," attach a statement describing the items subject to potential reimbursement. (see instructions)		
Are any of the items on this schedule deductible under Reg. section 20.2053-4(b) and Reg. section 20.2053-4(c)?		X
If "Yes," attach a statement indicating the applicable provision and documenting the value of the claim.		

Item number	Debts of the Decedent—Creditor and nature of debt, and allowable death taxes	Amount
1	Bank loan (including $200 interest accrued through date of death)	25,200
2	American Express, Visa, and Master Card credit card debts	6,500
	Total from continuation schedules (or additional statements) attached to this schedule	
	TOTAL. (Also enter on Part 5—Recapitulation, page 3, at item 15.)	31,700

Item number	Mortgages and Liens—Description	Amount
	Total from continuation schedules (or additional statements) attached to this schedule	
	TOTAL. (Also enter on Part 5—Recapitulation, page 3, at item 16.)	

(If more space is needed, attach the continuation schedule from the end of this package or additional statements of the same size.)

Form 706 (Rev. 8-2013)

Estate of: Herman Estes	Decedent's social security number XXX XX XXXX

SCHEDULE M—Bequests, etc., to Surviving Spouse

Note. If the value of the gross estate, together with the amount of adjusted taxable gifts, is less than the basic exclusion amount and the Form 706 is being filed solely to elect portability of the DSUE amount, consideration should be given as to whether you are required to report the value of assets eligible for the marital or charitable deduction on this schedule. See the instructions and Reg. section 20.2010-2T (a)(7)(ii) for more information. If you are not required to report the value of an asset, identify the property but make no entry in the last column.

			Yes	No
1	Did any property pass to the surviving spouse as a result of a qualified disclaimer? If "Yes," attach a copy of the written disclaimer required by section 2518(b).	1		X
2a	In what country was the surviving spouse born? United States			
b	What is the surviving spouse's date of birth? 3-12-1948			
c	Is the surviving spouse a U.S. citizen?	2c	X	
d	If the surviving spouse is a naturalized citizen, when did the surviving spouse acquire citizenship? N/A			
e	If the surviving spouse is not a U.S. citizen, of what country is the surviving spouse a citizen? N/A			
3	**Election Out of QTIP Treatment of Annuities.** Do you elect under section 2056(b)(7)(C)(ii) not to treat as qualified terminable interest property any joint and survivor annuities that are included in the gross estate and would otherwise be treated as qualified terminable interest property under section 2056(b)(7)(C)? (see instructions)	3		X

Item number	Description of property interests passing to surviving spouse. For securities, give CUSIP number. If trust, partnership, or closely held entity, give EIN	Amount
	QTIP property:	
	Trust with First Bank as trustee	200,000
	All other property:	
	Residence	325,000
	Savings account	75,000
	Checking account	10,000
	Land held in joint tenancy	220,000
	Qualified pension plan	240,000
	Total from continuation schedules (or additional statements) attached to this schedule	

4	**Total** amount of property interests listed on Schedule M	4	1,070,000
5a	Federal estate taxes payable out of property interests listed on Schedule M	5a	
b	Other death taxes payable out of property interests listed on Schedule M	5b	
c	Federal and state GST taxes payable out of property interests listed on Schedule M	5c	
d	Add items 5a, 5b, and 5c	5d	
6	Net amount of property interests listed on Schedule M (subtract 5d from 4). Also enter on Part 5—Recapitulation, page 3, at item 21	6	1,070,000

(If more space is needed, attach the continuation schedule from the end of this package or additional statements of the same size.)

Form 706 (Rev. 8-2013)

Estate of: Herman Estes | **Decedent's social security number** XXX XX XXXX

SCHEDULE O—Charitable, Public, and Similar Gifts and Bequests

Note. If the value of the gross estate, together with the amount of adjusted taxable gifts, is less than the basic exclusion amount and the Form 706 is being filed solely to elect portability of the DSUE amount, consideration should be given as to whether you are required to report the value of assets eligible for the marital or charitable deduction on this schedule. See the instructions and Reg. section 20.2010-2T (a)(7)(ii) for more information. If you are not required to report the value of an asset, identify the property but make no entry in the last column.

		Yes	No
1a	If the transfer was made by will, has any action been instituted to contest or have interpreted any of its provisions affecting the charitable deductions claimed in this schedule? . . . . If "Yes," full details must be submitted with this schedule.		X
b	According to the information and belief of the person or persons filing this return, is any such action planned? . If "Yes," full details must be submitted with this schedule.		X
2	Did any property pass to charity as the result of a qualified disclaimer? . . . . If "Yes," attach a copy of the written disclaimer required by section 2518(b).		X

Item number	Name and address of beneficiary	Character of institution	Amount
1	American Cancer Society	Charity	10,000
	Total from continuation schedules (or additional statements) attached to this schedule		

3	Total			3	10,000
4a	Federal estate tax payable out of property interests listed above	4a			
b	Other death taxes payable out of property interests listed above	4b			
c	Federal and state GST taxes payable out of property interests listed above .	4c			
d	Add items 4a, 4b, and 4c			4d	
5	Net value of property interests listed above (subtract 4d from 3). Also enter on Part 5—Recapitulation, page 3, at item 22			5	10,000

(If more space is needed, attach the continuation schedule from the end of this package or additional statements of the same size.)

Form **1041** Department of the Treasury—Internal Revenue Service
U.S. Income Tax Return for Estates and Trusts 2016 OMB No. 1545-0092
▶ Information about Form 1041 and its separate instructions is at *www.irs.gov/form1041.*

A Check all that apply:	For calendar year 2016 or fiscal year beginning , 2016, and ending , 20	
☐ Decedent's estate	Name of estate or trust (If a grantor type trust, see the instructions.)	C Employer identification number
☒ Simple trust	Bob Adams Trust (Simple Trust)	XX-XXXXXXX
☐ Complex trust	Name and title of fiduciary	D Date entity created
☐ Qualified disability trust	First Bank	2003
☐ ESBT (S portion only)	Number, street, and room or suite no. (If a P.O. box, see the instructions.)	E Nonexempt charitable and split-interest trusts, check applicable box(es), see instructions.
☐ Grantor type trust		
☐ Bankruptcy estate-Ch. 7	Post Office Box 100	☐ Described in sec. 4947(a)(1). Check here
☐ Bankruptcy estate-Ch. 11	City or town, state or province, country, and ZIP or foreign postal code	if not a private foundation . . . ▶ ☐
☐ Pooled income fund	City, ST 44444	☐ Described in sec. 4947(a)(2)
B Number of Schedules K-1 attached (see instructions) ▶ 1	F Check applicable boxes: ☐ Initial return ☐ Final return ☐ Amended return ☐ Change in trust's name ☐ Change in fiduciary ☐ Change in fiduciary's name	☐ Net operating loss carryback ☐ Change in fiduciary's address

G Check here if the estate or filing trust made a section 645 election . . . . . . ▶ ☐ Trust TIN ▶

Income	1	Interest income	1		
	2a	Total ordinary dividends	2a	30,000	
	b	Qualified dividends allocable to: (1) Beneficiaries 30,000 (2) Estate or trust -0-			
	3	Business income or (loss). Attach Schedule C or C-EZ (Form 1040)	3		
	4	Capital gain or (loss). Attach Schedule D (Form 1041)	4	12,000	
	5	Rents, royalties, partnerships, other estates and trusts, etc. Attach Schedule E (Form 1040)	5	4,000	*
	6	Farm income or (loss). Attach Schedule F (Form 1040)	6		
	7	Ordinary gain or (loss). Attach Form 4797	7		
	8	Other income. List type and amount	8		
	9	**Total income.** Combine lines 1, 2a, and 3 through 8 ▶	9	46,000	
Deductions	10	Interest. Check if Form 4952 is attached ▶ ☐	10		
	11	Taxes	11		
	12	Fiduciary fees ($1,200 – $360)	12	840	
	13	Charitable deduction (from Schedule A, line 7)	13		
	14	Attorney, accountant, and return preparer fees	14	500	
	15a	Other deductions **not** subject to the 2% floor (attach schedule)	15a		
	b	Net operating loss deduction. See instructions	15b		
	c	Allowable miscellaneous itemized deductions subject to the 2% floor	15c		
	16	Add lines 10 through 15c ▶	16	1,340	
	17	Adjusted total income or (loss). Subtract line 16 from line 9 — 17: 44,660			
	18	Income distribution deduction (from Schedule B, line 15). Attach Schedules K-1 (Form 1041)	18	32,660	
	19	Estate tax deduction including certain generation-skipping taxes (attach computation)	19		
	20	Exemption	20	300	
	21	Add lines 18 through 20 ▶	21	32,960	
Tax and Payments	22	Taxable income. Subtract line 21 from line 17. If a loss, see instructions	22	11,700	
	23	**Total tax** (from Schedule G, line 7)	23	1,373	
	24	**Payments: a** 2016 estimated tax payments and amount applied from 2015 return	24a	2,600	
	b	Estimated tax payments allocated to beneficiaries (from Form 1041-T)	24b		
	c	Subtract line 24b from line 24a	24c	2,600	
	d	Tax paid with Form 7004. See instructions	24d		
	e	Federal income tax withheld. If any is from Form(s) 1099, check ▶ ☐	24e		
		Other payments: f Form 2439 ; g Form 4136 ; Total ▶	24h		
	25	**Total payments.** Add lines 24c through 24e, and 24h ▶	25	2,600	
	26	Estimated tax penalty. See instructions	26		
	27	**Tax due.** If line 25 is smaller than the total of lines 23 and 26, enter amount owed	27		
	28	**Overpayment.** If line 25 is larger than the total of lines 23 and 26, enter amount overpaid	28	1,227	
	29	Amount of line 28 to be: **a Credited to 2017 estimated tax** ▶ 1,227 ; **b Refunded** ▶	29		

Sign Here Under penalties of perjury, I declare that I have examined this return, including accompanying schedules and statements, and to the best of my knowledge and belief, it is true, correct, and complete. Declaration of preparer (other than taxpayer) is based on all information of which preparer has any knowledge.

Signature of fiduciary or officer representing fiduciary	Date	EIN of fiduciary if a financial institution	May the IRS discuss this return with the preparer shown below (see instr.)?
Tom Trusty	3-14-17	XX-XXXXXXX	☒ Yes ☐ No

Paid Preparer Use Only	Print/Type preparer's name	Preparer's signature	Date	Check ☒ if self-employed	PTIN
	Karen Certified	Karen Certified	3-14-17		
	Firm's name ▶ Karen Certified			Firm's EIN ▶	
	Firm's address ▶ One Some Place, City, ST 44444			Phone no.	

For Paperwork Reduction Act Notice, see the separate instructions. Cat. No. 11370H Form **1041** (2016)

*Line 5: Net rental income = Rental income $5,000 – Realtor's commissions $1,000 = $4,000

Note: Pages concerning the AMT are omitted because the trust does not owe the AMT.

See the Comprehensive Illustration on text page C:14-17 for tax form facts.

Form 1041 (2016) Page **2**

Schedule A **Charitable Deduction.** Don't complete for a simple trust or a pooled income fund.

1	Amounts paid or permanently set aside for charitable purposes from gross income. See instructions	1		
2	Tax-exempt income allocable to charitable contributions. See instructions	2		
3	Subtract line 2 from line 1	3		
4	Capital gains for the tax year allocated to corpus and paid or permanently set aside for charitable purposes	4		
5	Add lines 3 and 4	5		
6	Section 1202 exclusion allocable to capital gains paid or permanently set aside for charitable purposes. See instructions	6		
7	**Charitable deduction.** Subtract line 6 from line 5. Enter here and on page 1, line 13	7		

Schedule B **Income Distribution Deduction**

1	Adjusted total income. See instructions	1	44,660	
2	Adjusted tax-exempt interest ($15,000 – $360)	2	14,640	*
3	Total net gain from Schedule D (Form 1041), line 19, column (1). See instructions	3		
4	Enter amount from Schedule A, line 4 (minus any allocable section 1202 exclusion)	4		
5	Capital gains for the tax year included on Schedule A, line 1. See instructions	5		
6	Enter any gain from page 1, line 4, as a negative number. If page 1, line 4, is a loss, enter the loss as a positive number	6	(12,000)	
7	**Distributable net income.** Combine lines 1 through 6. If zero or less, enter -0-	7	47,300	
8	If a complex trust, enter accounting income for the tax year as determined under the governing instrument and applicable local law — 8			
9	Income required to be distributed currently	9	48,500	
10	Other amounts paid, credited, or otherwise required to be distributed	10		
11	Total distributions. Add lines 9 and 10. If greater than line 8, see instructions	11	48,500	
12	Enter the amount of tax-exempt income included on line 11	12	14,640	
13	Tentative income distribution deduction. Subtract line 12 from line 11	13	33,860	
14	Tentative income distribution deduction. Subtract line 2 from line 7. If zero or less, enter -0-	14	32,660	
15	**Income distribution deduction.** Enter the smaller of line 13 or line 14 here and on page 1, line 18	15	32,660	

Schedule G **Tax Computation** (see instructions)

1	**Tax:** a Tax on taxable income. See instructions	1a	1,373			
	b Tax on lump-sum distributions. Attach Form 4972	1b				
	c Alternative minimum tax (from Schedule I (Form 1041), line 56)	1c				
	d **Total.** Add lines 1a through 1c ▶			1d	1,373	
2a	Foreign tax credit. Attach Form 1116	2a				
b	General business credit. Attach Form 3800	2b				
c	Credit for prior year minimum tax. Attach Form 8801	2c				
d	Bond credits. Attach Form 8912	2d				
e	**Total credits.** Add lines 2a through 2d ▶			2e		
3	Subtract line 2e from line 1d. If zero or less, enter -0-			3	1,373	
4	Net investment income tax from Form 8960, line 21			4	-0-	**
5	Recapture taxes. Check if from: ☐ Form 4255 ☐ Form 8611			5		
6	Household employment taxes. Attach Schedule H (Form 1040)			6		
7	**Total tax.** Add lines 3 through 6. Enter here and on page 1, line 23 ▶			7	1,373	

	Other Information	Yes	No
1	Did the estate or trust receive tax-exempt income? If "Yes," attach a computation of the allocation of expenses. Enter the amount of tax-exempt interest income and exempt-interest dividends ▶ $ 15,000	X	
2	Did the estate or trust receive all or any part of the earnings (salary, wages, and other compensation) of any individual by reason of a contract assignment or similar arrangement?		X
3	At any time during calendar year 2016, did the estate or trust have an interest in or a signature or other authority over a bank, securities, or other financial account in a foreign country?		X
	See the instructions for exceptions and filing requirements for FinCEN Form 114. If "Yes," enter the name of the foreign country ▶		
4	During the tax year, did the estate or trust receive a distribution from, or was it the grantor of, or transferor to, a foreign trust? If "Yes," the estate or trust may have to file Form 3520. See instructions		X
5	Did the estate or trust receive, or pay, any qualified residence interest on seller-provided financing? If "Yes," see the instructions for required attachment		X
6	If this is an estate or a complex trust making the section 663(b) election, check here. See instructions ▶ ☐		
7	To make a section 643(e)(3) election, attach Schedule D (Form 1041), and check here. See instructions ▶ ☐		
8	If the decedent's estate has been open for more than 2 years, attach an explanation for the delay in closing the estate, and check here ▶ ☐		
9	Are any present or future trust beneficiaries skip persons? See instructions		X
10	Was the trust a specified domestic entity required to file Form 8938 for the tax year (see the Instructions for Form 8938)?		X

Form **1041** (2016)

* Line 2: Allocation of expenses: $\frac{\$15,000}{\$50,000} \times \$1,200 = \$360$ of trustee's fee allocated to tax-exempt income

** Zero because AGI of $11,700 ($44,660 – $32,660 – $300) does not exceed the beginning of the 39.6% tax bracket.

SCHEDULE D (Form 1041)

Department of the Treasury Internal Revenue Service

Capital Gains and Losses

▶ Attach to Form 1041, Form 5227, or Form 990-T.

▶ Use Form 8949 to list your transactions for lines 1b, 2, 3, 8b, 9 and 10.

▶ Information about Schedule D and its separate instructions is at *www.irs.gov/form1041*.

OMB No. 1545-0092

2016

Name of estate or trust	Employer identification number
Bob Adams Trust	XX-XXXXXXX

Note: *Form 5227 filers need to complete* ***only*** *Parts I and II.*

Part I Short-Term Capital Gains and Losses—Assets Held One Year or Less

See instructions for how to figure the amounts to enter on the lines below. This form may be easier to complete if you round off cents to whole dollars.	(d) Proceeds (sales price)	(e) Cost (or other basis)	(g) Adjustments to gain or loss from Form(s) 8949, Part I, line 2, column (g)	(h) Gain or (loss) Subtract column (e) from column (d) and combine the result with column (g)
1a Totals for all short-term transactions reported on Form 1099-B for which basis was reported to the IRS and for which you have no adjustments (see instructions). However, if you choose to report all these transactions on Form 8949, leave this line blank and go to line 1b				
1b Totals for all transactions reported on Form(s) 8949 with **Box A** checked				
2 Totals for all transactions reported on Form(s) 8949 with **Box B** checked				
3 Totals for all transactions reported on Form(s) 8949 with **Box C** checked				

4 Short-term capital gain or (loss) from Forms 4684, 6252, 6781, and 8824	4	
5 Net short-term gain or (loss) from partnerships, S corporations, and other estates or trusts	5	
6 Short-term capital loss carryover. Enter the amount, if any, from line 9 of the 2015 Capital Loss Carryover Worksheet	6	( )
7 **Net short-term capital gain or (loss).** Combine lines 1a through 6 in column (h). Enter here and on line 17, column (3) on the back ▶	7	

Part II Long-Term Capital Gains and Losses—Assets Held More Than One Year

See instructions for how to figure the amounts to enter on the lines below. This form may be easier to complete if you round off cents to whole dollars.	(d) Proceeds (sales price)	(e) Cost (or other basis)	(g) Adjustments to gain or loss from Form(s) 8949, Part II, line 2, column (g)	(h) Gain or (loss) Subtract column (e) from column (d) and combine the result with column (g)
8a Totals for all long-term transactions reported on Form 1099-B for which basis was reported to the IRS and for which you have no adjustments (see instructions). However, if you choose to report all these transactions on Form 8949, leave this line blank and go to line 8b	15,000	3,000		12,000
8b Totals for all transactions reported on Form(s) 8949 with **Box D** checked				
9 Totals for all transactions reported on Form(s) 8949 with **Box E** checked				
10 Totals for all transactions reported on Form(s) 8949 with **Box F** checked				

11 Long-term capital gain or (loss) from Forms 2439, 4684, 6252, 6781, and 8824	11	
12 Net long-term gain or (loss) from partnerships, S corporations, and other estates or trusts	12	
13 Capital gain distributions	13	
14 Gain from Form 4797, Part I	14	
15 Long-term capital loss carryover. Enter the amount, if any, from line 14 of the 2015 Capital Loss Carryover Worksheet	15	( )
16 **Net long-term capital gain or (loss).** Combine lines 8a through 15 in column (h). Enter here and on line 18a, column (3) on the back ▶	16	12,000

Schedule D (Form 1041) 2016 Page **2**

Part III **Summary of Parts I and II**
Caution: *Read the instructions* ***before*** *completing this part.*

			(1) Beneficiaries' (see instr.)	(2) Estate's or trust's	(3) Total
17	**Net short-term gain or (loss)**	17			
18	**Net long-term gain or (loss):**				
a	Total for year	18a		12,000	12,000
b	Unrecaptured section 1250 gain (see line 18 of the wrksht.)	18b			
c	28% rate gain	18c			
19	**Total net gain or (loss).** Combine lines 17 and 18a ▶	19		12,000	12,000

Note: *If line 19, column (3), is a net gain, enter the gain on Form 1041, line 4 (or Form 990-T, Part I, line 4a). If lines 18a and 19, column (2), are net gains, go to Part V, and* ***don't*** *complete Part IV. If line 19, column (3), is a net loss, complete Part IV and the* ***Capital Loss Carryover Worksheet,*** *as necessary.*

Part IV **Capital Loss Limitation**

20 Enter here and enter as a (loss) on Form 1041, line 4 (or Form 990-T, Part I, line 4c, if a trust), the **smaller** of:
a The loss on line 19, column (3) **or b** $3,000 . . . 20 ( )

Note: *If the loss on line 19, column (3), is more than $3,000,* ***or*** *if Form 1041, page 1, line 22 (or Form 990-T, line 34), is a loss, complete the* ***Capital Loss Carryover Worksheet*** *in the instructions to figure your capital loss carryover.*

Part V **Tax Computation Using Maximum Capital Gains Rates**

Form 1041 filers. Complete this part **only** if both lines 18a and 19 in column (2) are gains, or an amount is entered in Part I or Part II and there is an entry on Form 1041, line 2b(2), **and** Form 1041, line 22, is more than zero.

Caution: *Skip this part and complete the* ***Schedule D Tax Worksheet*** *in the instructions if:*

- *Either line 18b, col. (2) or line 18c, col. (2) is more than zero, or*
- *Both Form 1041, line 2b(1), and Form 4952, line 4g are more than zero.*

Form 990-T trusts. Complete this part **only** if both lines 18a and 19 are gains, or qualified dividends are included in income in Part I of Form 990-T, **and** Form 990-T, line 34, is more than zero. Skip this part and complete the **Schedule D Tax Worksheet** in the instructions if either line 18b, col. (2) or line 18c, col. (2) is more than zero.

21	Enter taxable income from Form 1041, line 22 (or Form 990-T, line 34)			21	11,700		
22	Enter the **smaller** of line 18a or 19 in column (2) but not less than zero	22	12,000				
23	Enter the estate's or trust's qualified dividends from Form 1041, line 2b(2) (or enter the qualified dividends included in income in Part I of Form 990-T)	23	-0-				
24	Add lines 22 and 23	24	12,000				
25	If the estate or trust is filing Form 4952, enter the amount from line 4g; otherwise, enter -0- ▶	25	-0-				
26	Subtract line 25 from line 24. If zero or less, enter -0-			26	12,000		
27	Subtract line 26 from line 21. If zero or less, enter -0-			27	-0-		
28	Enter the **smaller** of the amount on line 21 or $2,550			28	2,550		
29	Enter the **smaller** of the amount on line 27 or line 28			29	-0-		
30	Subtract line 29 from line 28. If zero or less, enter -0-. This amount is taxed at 0% ▶					30	2,550
31	Enter the **smaller** of line 21 or line 26			31	11,700		
32	Subtract line 30 from line 26			32	9,450		
33	Enter the **smaller** of line 21 or $12,400			33	11,700		
34	Add lines 27 and 30			34	2,550		
35	Subtract line 34 from line 33. If zero or less, enter -0-			35	9,150		
36	Enter the **smaller** of line 32 or line 35			36	9,150		
37	Multiply line 36 by 15% (0.15) ▶					37	1,373
38	Enter the amount from line 31			38	11,700		
39	Add lines 30 and 36			39	11,700		
40	Subtract line 39 from line 38. If zero or less, enter -0-			40	-0-		
41	Multiply line 40 by 20% (0.20) ▶					41	-0-
42	Figure the tax on the amount on line 27. Use the 2016 Tax Rate Schedule for Estates and Trusts (see the Schedule G instructions in the instructions for Form 1041)			42	-0-		
43	Add lines 37, 41, and 42			43	1,373		
44	Figure the tax on the amount on line 21. Use the 2016 Tax Rate Schedule for Estates and Trusts (see the Schedule G instructions in the instructions for Form 1041)			44	2,975		
45	**Tax on all taxable income.** Enter the **smaller** of line 43 or line 44 here and on Form 1041, Schedule G, line 1a (or Form 990-T, line 36) ▶					45	1,373

661113

☐ Final K-1 ☐ Amended K-1 OMB No. 1545-0092

Schedule K-1 (Form 1041) **2016**
Department of the Treasury
Internal Revenue Service

For calendar year 2016, or tax year beginning ________, 2016, and ending ________, 20 ____

Beneficiary's Share of Income, Deductions, Credits, etc.

▶ See back of form and instructions.

Part I Information About the Estate or Trust

A Estate's or trust's employer identification number
XX-XXXXXXX

B Estate's or trust's name
Bob Adams Trust

C Fiduciary's name, address, city, state, and ZIP code
First Bank
Post OfficeBox 100
City, ST 44444

D ☐ Check if Form 1041-T was filed and enter the date it was filed ________

E ☐ Check if this is the final Form 1041 for the estate or trust

Part II Information About the Beneficiary

F Beneficiary's identifying number
XXX-XX-XXXX

G Beneficiary's name, address, city, state, and ZIP code
Bob Adams
3 Jackson Highway
City, ST 44444

H ☒ Domestic beneficiary ☐ Foreign beneficiary

Part III Beneficiary's Share of Current Year Income, Deductions, Credits, and Other Items

1	Interest income	
2a	Ordinary dividends	30,000
2b	Qualified dividends	30,000
3	Net short-term capital gain	
4a	Net long-term capital gain	
4b	28% rate gain	
4c	Unrecaptured section 1250 gain	
5	Other portfolio and nonbusiness income	
6	Ordinary business income	
7	Net rental real estate income	2,660*
8	Other rental income	
9	Directly apportioned deductions	
10	Estate tax deduction	
11	Final year deductions	
12	Alternative minimum tax adjustment	
13	Credits and credit recapture	
14	Other information	A 14,640

*See attached statement for additional information.

Note. A statement must be attached showing the beneficiary's share of income and directly apportioned deductions from each business, rental real estate, and other rental activity.

For IRS Use Only

For Paperwork Reduction Act Notice, see the Instructions for Form 1041. IRS.gov/form1041 Cat. No. 11380D **Schedule K-1 (Form 1041) 2016**

*5,000 – ($1,000 + $840 + $500) = $2,660

Schedule K-1 (Form 1041) 2016 Page **2**

This list identifies the codes used on Schedule K-1 for beneficiaries and provides summarized reporting information for beneficiaries who file Form 1040. For detailed reporting and filing information, see the Instructions for Schedule K-1 (Form 1041) for a Beneficiary Filing Form 1040 and the instructions for your income tax return.

	Report on
1. Interest income	Form 1040, line 8a
2a. Ordinary dividends	Form 1040, line 9a
2b. Qualified dividends	Form 1040, line 9b
3. Net short-term capital gain	Schedule D, line 5
4a. Net long-term capital gain	Schedule D, line 12
4b. 28% rate gain	28% Rate Gain Worksheet, line 4 (Schedule D Instructions)
4c. Unrecaptured section 1250 gain	Unrecaptured Section 1250 Gain Worksheet, line 11 (Schedule D Instructions)
5. Other portfolio and nonbusiness income	Schedule E, line 33, column (f)
6. Ordinary business income	Schedule E, line 33, column (d) or (f)
7. Net rental real estate income	Schedule E, line 33, column (d) or (f)
8. Other rental income	Schedule E, line 33, column (d) or (f)
9. Directly apportioned deductions	
Code	
A Depreciation	Form 8582 or Schedule E, line 33, column (c) or (e)
B Depletion	Form 8582 or Schedule E, line 33, column (c) or (e)
C Amortization	Form 8582 or Schedule E, line 33, column (c) or (e)
10. Estate tax deduction	Schedule A, line 28
11. Final year deductions	
A Excess deductions	Schedule A, line 23
B Short-term capital loss carryover	Schedule D, line 5
C Long-term capital loss carryover	Schedule D, line 12; line 5 of the wksht. for Sch. D, line 18; and line 16 of the wksht. for Sch. D, line 19
D Net operating loss carryover — regular tax	Form 1040, line 21
E Net operating loss carryover — minimum tax	Form 6251, line 11
12. Alternative minimum tax (AMT) items	
A Adjustment for minimum tax purposes	Form 6251, line 15
B AMT adjustment attributable to qualified dividends	See the beneficiary's instructions and the Instructions for Form 6251 (codes B through I)
C AMT adjustment attributable to net short-term capital gain	
D AMT adjustment attributable to net long-term capital gain	
E AMT adjustment attributable to unrecaptured section 1250 gain	
F AMT adjustment attributable to 28% rate gain	
G Accelerated depreciation	
H Depletion	
I Amortization	
J Exclusion items	2017 Form 8801

13. Credits and credit recapture

Code	*Report on*
A Credit for estimated taxes	Form 1040, line 65
B Credit for backup withholding	Form 1040, line 64
C Low-income housing credit	See the beneficiary's instructions (codes C through R)
D Rehabilitation credit and energy credit	
E Other qualifying investment credit	
F Work opportunity credit	
G Credit for small employer health insurance premiums	
H Biofuel producer credit	
I Credit for increasing research activities	
J Renewable electricity, refined coal, and Indian coal production credit	
K Empowerment zone employment credit	
L Indian employment credit	
M Orphan drug credit	
N Credit for employer-provided child care and facilities	
O Biodiesel and renewable diesel fuels credit	
P Credit to holders of tax credit bonds	
Q Credit for employer differential wage payments	
R Recapture of credits	

14. Other information

A Tax-exempt interest	Form 1040, line 8b
B Foreign taxes	Form 1040, line 48 or Sch. A, line 8
C Qualified production activities income	Form 8903, line 7, col. (b) (also see the beneficiary's instructions)
D Form W-2 wages	Form 8903, line 17
E Net investment income	Form 4952, line 4a
F Gross farm and fishing income	Schedule E, line 42
G Foreign trading gross receipts (IRC 942(a))	See the Instructions for Form 8873
H Adjustment for section 1411 net investment income or deductions	Form 8960, line 7 (also see the beneficiary's instructions)
I Other information	See the beneficiary's instructions

Note. If you are a beneficiary who does not file a Form 1040, see instructions for the type of income tax return you are filing.

Form **1041** Department of the Treasury—Internal Revenue Service
U.S. Income Tax Return for Estates and Trusts 2016 OMB No. 1545-0092
▶ Information about Form 1041 and its separate instructions is at *www.irs.gov/form1041*.

A Check all that apply:
- ☐ Decedent's estate
- ☐ Simple trust
- ☒ Complex trust
- ☐ Qualified disability trust
- ☐ ESBT (S portion only)
- ☐ Grantor type trust
- ☐ Bankruptcy estate-Ch. 7
- ☐ Bankruptcy estate-Ch. 11
- ☐ Pooled income fund

For calendar year 2016 or fiscal year beginning , 2016, and ending , 20

Name of estate or trust (If a grantor type trust, see the instructions.): Cathy and Karen Stephens Trust (Complex Trust)

C Employer identification number: XX-XXXXXXX

Name and title of fiduciary: Merchants Bank

D Date entity created: 2003

Number, street, and room or suite no. (If a P.O. box, see the instructions.): 3000 Sun Plaza

E Nonexempt charitable and split-interest trusts, check applicable box(es), see instructions.
☐ Described in sec. 4947(a)(1). Check here if not a private foundation ▶ ☐
☐ Described in sec. 4947(a)(2)

City or town, state or province, country, and ZIP or foreign postal code: City, ST 88888

B Number of Schedules K-1 attached (see instructions) ▶ 2

F Check applicable boxes: ☐ Initial return ☐ Final return ☐ Amended return ☐ Net operating loss carryback ☐ Change in trust's name ☐ Change in fiduciary ☐ Change in fiduciary's name ☐ Change in fiduciary's address

G Check here if the estate or filing trust made a section 645 election ▶ ☐ Trust TIN ▶

Income	1	Interest income	1	
	2a	Total ordinary dividends	2a	30,000
	b	Qualified dividends allocable to: (1) Beneficiaries 13,319 (2) Estate or trust 16,681		
	3	Business income or (loss). Attach Schedule C or C-EZ (Form 1040)	3	
	4	Capital gain or (loss). Attach Schedule D (Form 1041)	4	12,000
	5	Rents, royalties, partnerships, other estates and trusts, etc. Attach Schedule E (Form 1040)	5	4,000
	6	Farm income or (loss). Attach Schedule F (Form 1040)	6	
	7	Ordinary gain or (loss). Attach Form 4797	7	
	8	Other income. List type and amount	8	
	9	**Total income.** Combine lines 1, 2a, and 3 through 8 ▶	9	46,000
Deductions	10	Interest. Check if Form 4952 is attached ▶ ☐	10	
	11	Taxes	11	
	12	Fiduciary fees ($1,200 – $360)	12	840
	13	Charitable deduction (from Schedule A, line 7)	13	
	14	Attorney, accountant, and return preparer fees	14	500
	15a	Other deductions **not** subject to the 2% floor (attach schedule)	15a	
	b	Net operating loss deduction. See instructions	15b	
	c	Allowable miscellaneous itemized deductions subject to the 2% floor	15c	
	16	Add lines 10 through 15c ▶	16	1,340
	17	Adjusted total income or (loss). Subtract line 16 from line 9 — 17: 44,660		
	18	Income distribution deduction (from Schedule B, line 15). Attach Schedules K-1 (Form 1041)	18	14,500
	19	Estate tax deduction including certain generation-skipping taxes (attach computation)	19	
	20	Exemption	20	100
	21	Add lines 18 through 20 ▶	21	14,600
Tax and Payments	22	Taxable income. Subtract line 21 from line 17. If a loss, see instructions	22	30,060
	23	**Total tax** (from Schedule G, line 7)	23	5,888
	24	**Payments: a** 2016 estimated tax payments and amount applied from 2015 return	24a	5,360
	b	Estimated tax payments allocated to beneficiaries (from Form 1041-T)	24b	
	c	Subtract line 24b from line 24a	24c	5,360
	d	Tax paid with Form 7004. See instructions	24d	
	e	Federal income tax withheld. If any is from Form(s) 1099, check ▶ ☐	24e	
		Other payments: **f** Form 2439 ; **g** Form 4136 ; Total ▶	24h	
	25	**Total payments.** Add lines 24c through 24e, and 24h ▶	25	5,360
	26	Estimated tax penalty. See instructions	26	
	27	**Tax due.** If line 25 is smaller than the total of lines 23 and 26, enter amount owed	27	528
	28	**Overpayment.** If line 25 is larger than the total of lines 23 and 26, enter amount overpaid	28	
	29	Amount of line 28 to be: **a Credited to 2017 estimated tax** ▶ ; **b Refunded** ▶	29	

Sign Here Under penalties of perjury, I declare that I have examined this return, including accompanying schedules and statements, and to the best of my knowledge and belief, it is true, correct, and complete. Declaration of preparer (other than taxpayer) is based on all information of which preparer has any knowledge.

Fred Fidus — Signature of fiduciary or officer representing fiduciary | 3-14-17 — Date | ▶ XX-XXXXXXX — EIN of fiduciary if a financial institution

May the IRS discuss this return with the preparer shown below (see instr.)? ☒ Yes ☐ No

Paid Preparer Use Only

Print/Type preparer's name	Preparer's signature	Date	Check ☒ if self-employed	PTIN
Sarah Public	Sarah Public	3-13-17		

Firm's name ▶ Sarah Public — Firm's EIN ▶
Firm's address ▶ 200 Sun Plaza City, ST 88888 — Phone no.

For Paperwork Reduction Act Notice, see the separate instructions. Cat. No. 11370H Form **1041** (2016)

*Line 5: Net Rental income = Rental income $5,000 – Rental expenses $1,000 = $4,000

Note: Pages concerning the AMT are omitted because the trust does not owe the AMT.

See the Comprehensive Illustration on text page C:14-24 for tax form facts.

Form 1041 (2016) Page **2**

Schedule A **Charitable Deduction.** Don't complete for a simple trust or a pooled income fund.

1	Amounts paid or permanently set aside for charitable purposes from gross income. See instructions	1	
2	Tax-exempt income allocable to charitable contributions. See instructions	2	
3	Subtract line 2 from line 1	3	
4	Capital gains for the tax year allocated to corpus and paid or permanently set aside for charitable purposes	4	
5	Add lines 3 and 4	5	
6	Section 1202 exclusion allocable to capital gains paid or permanently set aside for charitable purposes. See instructions	6	
7	**Charitable deduction.** Subtract line 6 from line 5. Enter here and on page 1, line 13	7	

Schedule B **Income Distribution Deduction**

1	Adjusted total income. See instructions	1	44,660
2	Adjusted tax-exempt interest ($15,000 − $360)	2	14,640
3	Total net gain from Schedule D (Form 1041), line 19, column (1). See instructions	3	
4	Enter amount from Schedule A, line 4 (minus any allocable section 1202 exclusion)	4	
5	Capital gains for the tax year included on Schedule A, line 1. See instructions	5	
6	Enter any gain from page 1, line 4, as a negative number. If page 1, line 4, is a loss, enter the loss as a positive number	6	(12,000)
7	**Distributable net income.** Combine lines 1 through 6. If zero or less, enter -0-	7	47,300
8	If a complex trust, enter accounting income for the tax year as determined under the governing instrument and applicable local law — 8: 48,500		
9	Income required to be distributed currently	9	-0-
10	Other amounts paid, credited, or otherwise required to be distributed	10	21,000
11	Total distributions. Add lines 9 and 10. If greater than line 8, see instructions	11	21,000
12	Enter the amount of tax-exempt income included on line 11	12	6,500
13	Tentative income distribution deduction. Subtract line 12 from line 11	13	14,500
14	Tentative income distribution deduction. Subtract line 2 from line 7. If zero or less, enter -0-	14	32,660
15	**Income distribution deduction.** Enter the smaller of line 13 or line 14 here and on page 1, line 18	15	14,500

Schedule G **Tax Computation** (see instructions)

1	**Tax:** a Tax on taxable income. See instructions	1a	5,217		
	b Tax on lump-sum distributions. Attach Form 4972	1b			
	c Alternative minimum tax (from Schedule I (Form 1041), line 56)	1c			
	d **Total.** Add lines 1a through 1c ▶			1d	5,217
2a	Foreign tax credit. Attach Form 1116	2a			
b	General business credit. Attach Form 3800	2b			
c	Credit for prior year minimum tax. Attach Form 8801	2c			
d	Bond credits. Attach Form 8912	2d			
e	**Total credits.** Add lines 2a through 2d ▶			2e	
3	Subtract line 2e from line 1d. If zero or less, enter -0-			3	5,217
4	Net investment income tax from Form 8960, line 21			4	671
5	Recapture taxes. Check if from: ☐ Form 4255 ☐ Form 8611			5	
6	Household employment taxes. Attach Schedule H (Form 1040)			6	
7	**Total tax.** Add lines 3 through 6. Enter here and on page 1, line 23 ▶			7	5,888

Other Information

		Yes	No
1	Did the estate or trust receive tax-exempt income? If "Yes," attach a computation of the allocation of expenses. Enter the amount of tax-exempt interest income and exempt-interest dividends ▶ $ 15,000; (see below)	X	
2	Did the estate or trust receive all or any part of the earnings (salary, wages, and other compensation) of any individual by reason of a contract assignment or similar arrangement?		X
3	At any time during calendar year 2016, did the estate or trust have an interest in or a signature or other authority over a bank, securities, or other financial account in a foreign country? See the instructions for exceptions and filing requirements for FinCEN Form 114. If "Yes," enter the name of the foreign country ▶		X
4	During the tax year, did the estate or trust receive a distribution from, or was it the grantor of, or transferor to, a foreign trust? If "Yes," the estate or trust may have to file Form 3520. See instructions		X
5	Did the estate or trust receive, or pay, any qualified residence interest on seller-provided financing? If "Yes," see the instructions for required attachment		X
6	If this is an estate or a complex trust making the section 663(b) election, check here. See instructions ▶ ☐		
7	To make a section 643(e)(3) election, attach Schedule D (Form 1041), and check here. See instructions ▶ ☐		
8	If the decedent's estate has been open for more than 2 years, attach an explanation for the delay in closing the estate, and check here ▶ ☐		
9	Are any present or future trust beneficiaries skip persons? See instructions		X
10	Was the trust a specified domestic entity required to file Form 8938 for the tax year (see the Instructions for Form 8938)?		X

Form **1041** (2016)

Line 2: Allocation of expenses: $\frac{\$15,000}{\$50,000} \times \$1,200 = \$360$ of trustee's fee allocated to tax-exempt income

SCHEDULE D (Form 1041)

Department of the Treasury
Internal Revenue Service

Capital Gains and Losses

▶ Attach to Form 1041, Form 5227, or Form 990-T.
▶ Use Form 8949 to list your transactions for lines 1b, 2, 3, 8b, 9 and 10.
▶ Information about Schedule D and its separate instructions is at *www.irs.gov/form1041*.

OMB No. 1545-0092

2016

Name of estate or trust: Cathy and Karen Stephens Trust

Employer identification number: XX-XXXXXXX

Note: *Form 5227 filers need to complete **only** Parts I and II.*

Part I Short-Term Capital Gains and Losses—Assets Held One Year or Less

See instructions for how to figure the amounts to enter on the lines below. This form may be easier to complete if you round off cents to whole dollars.	(d) Proceeds (sales price)	(e) Cost (or other basis)	(g) Adjustments to gain or loss from Form(s) 8949, Part I, line 2, column (g)	(h) Gain or (loss) Subtract column (e) from column (d) and combine the result with column (g)
1a Totals for all short-term transactions reported on Form 1099-B for which basis was reported to the IRS and for which you have no adjustments (see instructions). However, if you choose to report all these transactions on Form 8949, leave this line blank and go to line 1b .				
1b Totals for all transactions reported on Form(s) 8949 with **Box A** checked				
2 Totals for all transactions reported on Form(s) 8949 with **Box B** checked				
3 Totals for all transactions reported on Form(s) 8949 with **Box C** checked				

4 Short-term capital gain or (loss) from Forms 4684, 6252, 6781, and 8824	4	
5 Net short-term gain or (loss) from partnerships, S corporations, and other estates or trusts . . .	5	
6 Short-term capital loss carryover. Enter the amount, if any, from line 9 of the 2015 Capital Loss Carryover Worksheet	6	( )
7 **Net short-term capital gain or (loss).** Combine lines 1a through 6 in column (h). Enter here and on line 17, column (3) on the back . . . . ▶	7	

Part II Long-Term Capital Gains and Losses—Assets Held More Than One Year

See instructions for how to figure the amounts to enter on the lines below. This form may be easier to complete if you round off cents to whole dollars.	(d) Proceeds (sales price)	(e) Cost (or other basis)	(g) Adjustments to gain or loss from Form(s) 8949, Part II, line 2, column (g)	(h) Gain or (loss) Subtract column (e) from column (d) and combine the result with column (g)
8a Totals for all long-term transactions reported on Form 1099-B for which basis was reported to the IRS and for which you have no adjustments (see instructions). However, if you choose to report all these transactions on Form 8949, leave this line blank and go to line 8b .	15,000	3,000		12,000
8b Totals for all transactions reported on Form(s) 8949 with **Box D** checked				
9 Totals for all transactions reported on Form(s) 8949 with **Box E** checked				
10 Totals for all transactions reported on Form(s) 8949 with **Box F** checked.				

11 Long-term capital gain or (loss) from Forms 2439, 4684, 6252, 6781, and 8824	11	
12 Net long-term gain or (loss) from partnerships, S corporations, and other estates or trusts . . .	12	
13 Capital gain distributions	13	
14 Gain from Form 4797, Part I	14	
15 Long-term capital loss carryover. Enter the amount, if any, from line 14 of the 2015 Capital Loss Carryover Worksheet	15	( )
16 **Net long-term capital gain or (loss).** Combine lines 8a through 15 in column (h). Enter here and on line 18a, column (3) on the back . . . . ▶	16	12,000

Schedule D (Form 1041) 2016 Page **2**

Part III **Summary of Parts I and II**
Caution: *Read the instructions* ***before*** *completing this part.*

			(1) Beneficiaries' (see instr.)	(2) Estate's or trust's	(3) Total
17	**Net short-term gain or (loss)**	17			
18	**Net long-term gain or (loss):**				
a	Total for year	18a		12,000	12,000
b	Unrecaptured section 1250 gain (see line 18 of the wrksht.)	18b			
c	28% rate gain	18c			
19	**Total net gain or (loss).** Combine lines 17 and 18a ▶	19		12,000	12,000

Note: *If line 19, column (3), is a net gain, enter the gain on Form 1041, line 4 (or Form 990-T, Part I, line 4a). If lines 18a and 19, column (2), are net gains, go to Part V, and* ***don't*** *complete Part IV. If line 19, column (3), is a net loss, complete Part IV and the* ***Capital Loss Carryover Worksheet,*** *as necessary.*

Part IV **Capital Loss Limitation**

20 Enter here and enter as a (loss) on Form 1041, line 4 (or Form 990-T, Part I, line 4c, if a trust), the **smaller** of:
a The loss on line 19, column (3) **or b** $3,000 . . . 20 ( )

Note: *If the loss on line 19, column (3), is more than $3,000,* ***or*** *if Form 1041, page 1, line 22 (or Form 990-T, line 34), is a loss, complete the* ***Capital Loss Carryover Worksheet*** *in the instructions to figure your capital loss carryover.*

Part V **Tax Computation Using Maximum Capital Gains Rates**

Form 1041 filers. Complete this part **only** if both lines 18a and 19 in column (2) are gains, or an amount is entered in Part I or Part II and there is an entry on Form 1041, line 2b(2), **and** Form 1041, line 22, is more than zero.

Caution: *Skip this part and complete the* ***Schedule D Tax Worksheet*** *in the instructions if:*

- *Either line 18b, col. (2) or line 18c, col. (2) is more than zero, or*
- *Both Form 1041, line 2b(1), and Form 4952, line 4g are more than zero.*

Form 990-T trusts. Complete this part **only** if both lines 18a and 19 are gains, or qualified dividends are included in income in Part I of Form 990-T, **and** Form 990-T, line 34, is more than zero. Skip this part and complete the **Schedule D Tax Worksheet** in the instructions if either line 18b, col. (2) or line 18c, col. (2) is more than zero.

21	Enter taxable income from Form 1041, line 22 (or Form 990-T, line 34)			21	30,060		
22	Enter the **smaller** of line 18a or 19 in column (2) but not less than zero	22	12,000				
23	Enter the estate's or trust's qualified dividends from Form 1041, line 2b(2) (or enter the qualified dividends included in income in Part I of Form 990-T)	23	16,681				
24	Add lines 22 and 23	24	28,681				
25	If the estate or trust is filing Form 4952, enter the amount from line 4g; otherwise, enter -0- ▶	25	-0-				
26	Subtract line 25 from line 24. If zero or less, enter -0-			26	28,681		
27	Subtract line 26 from line 21. If zero or less, enter -0-			27	1,379		
28	Enter the **smaller** of the amount on line 21 or $2,550			28	2,550		
29	Enter the **smaller** of the amount on line 27 or line 28			29	1,379		
30	Subtract line 29 from line 28. If zero or less, enter -0-. This amount is taxed at 0% ▶					30	1,171
31	Enter the smaller of line 21 or line 26			31	28,681		
32	Subtract line 30 from line 26			32	27,510		
33	Enter the **smaller** of line 21 or $12,400			33	12,400		
34	Add lines 27 and 30			34	2,550		
35	Subtract line 34 from line 33. If zero or less, enter -0-			35	9,850		
36	Enter the **smaller** of line 32 or line 35			36	9,850		
37	Multiply line 36 by 15% (0.15) ▶					37	1,478
38	Enter the amount from line 31			38	28,681		
39	Add lines 30 and 36			39	11,021		
40	Subtract line 39 from line 38. If zero or less, enter -0-			40	17,660		
41	Multiply line 40 by 20% (0.20) ▶					41	3,532
42	Figure the tax on the amount on line 27. Use the 2016 Tax Rate Schedule for Estates and Trusts (see the Schedule G instructions in the instructions for Form 1041)			42	207		
43	Add lines 37, 41, and 42			43	5,217		
44	Figure the tax on the amount on line 21. Use the 2016 Tax Rate Schedule for Estates and Trusts (see the Schedule G instructions in the instructions for Form 1041)			44	10,199		
45	**Tax on all taxable income.** Enter the **smaller** of line 43 or line 44 here and on Form 1041, Schedule G, line 1a (or Form 990-T, line 36) ▶					45	5,217

Schedule D (Form 1041) 2016

Form **8960** — Department of the Treasury, Internal Revenue Service (99)

Net Investment Income Tax— Individuals, Estates, and Trusts

► Attach to your tax return
► Information about Form 8960 and its separate instructions is at *www.irs.gov/form8960.*

OMB No. 1545-2227 | **2016** | Attachment Sequence No. **72**

Name(s) shown on your tax return: Cathy and Karen Stephens Trust
Your social security number or EIN: XX-XXXXXXX

Part I Investment Income ☐ Section 6013(g) election (see instructions) ☐ Section 6013(h) election (see instructions) ☐ Regulations section 1.1411-10(g) election (see instructions)

Line	Description	Sub-line	Sub-amount	Line	Amount
1	Taxable interest (see instructions)			1	
2	Ordinary dividends (see instructions)			2	30,000
3	Annuities (see instructions)			3	
4a	Rental real estate, royalties, partnerships, S corporations, trusts, etc. (see instructions)	4a	4,000		
b	Adjustment for net income or loss derived in the ordinary course of a non-section 1411 trade or business (see instructions)	4b			
c	Combine lines 4a and 4b			4c	4,000
5a	Net gain or loss from disposition of property (see instructions)	5a	12,000		
b	Net gain or loss from disposition of property that is not subject to net investment income tax (see instructions)	5b			
c	Adjustment from disposition of partnership interest or S corporation stock (see instructions)	5c			
d	Combine lines 5a through 5c			5d	12,000
6	Adjustments to investment income for certain CFCs and PFICs (see instructions)			6	
7	Other modifications to investment income (see instructions)			7	
8	Total investment income. Combine lines 1, 2, 3, 4c, 5d, 6, and 7			8	46,000
Part II	**Investment Expenses Allocable to Investment Income and Modifications**				
9a	Investment interest expenses (see instructions)	9a			
b	State, local, and foreign income tax (see instructions)	9b			
c	Miscellaneous investment expenses (see instructions)	9c	1,340		
d	Add lines 9a, 9b, and 9c			9d	1,340
10	Additional modifications (see instructions)			10	
11	Total deductions and modifications. Add lines 9d and 10			11	1,340
Part III	**Tax Computation**				
12	Net investment income. Subtract Part II, line 11 from Part I, line 8. Individuals complete lines 13–17. Estates and trusts complete lines 18a–21. If zero or less, enter -0-			12	44,660
	Individuals:				
13	Modified adjusted gross income (see instructions)	13			
14	Threshold based on filing status (see instructions)	14			
15	Subtract line 14 from line 13. If zero or less, enter -0-	15			
16	Enter the smaller of line 12 or line 15			16	
17	Net investment income tax for individuals. Multiply line 16 by 3.8% (.038). **Enter here and include on your tax return** (see instructions)			17	
	Estates and Trusts:				
18a	Net investment income (line 12 above)	18a	44,660		
b	Deductions for distributions of net investment income and deductions under section 642(c) (see instructions)	18b	14,500		
c	Undistributed net investment income. Subtract line 18b from 18a (see instructions). If zero or less, enter -0-	18c	30,160		
19a	Adjusted gross income (see instructions) *	19a	30,060*		
b	Highest tax bracket for estates and trusts for the year (see instructions)	19b	12,400		
c	Subtract line 19b from line 19a. If zero or less, enter -0-	19c	17,660		
20	Enter the smaller of line 18c or line 19c			20	17,660
21	Net investment income tax for estates and trusts. Multiply line 20 by 3.8% (.038). **Enter here and include on your tax return** (see instructions)			21	671

For Paperwork Reduction Act Notice, see your tax return instructions. Cat. No. 59474M Form **8960** (2016)

*$44,660 – $14,500 – $100 = $30,060

661113

☐ Final K-1 ☐ Amended K-1 OMB No. 1545-0092

Schedule K-1 (Form 1041) **2016**

Department of the Treasury
Internal Revenue Service

For calendar year 2016, or tax year beginning ____________, 2016, and ending ____________, 20 ____

Beneficiary's Share of Income, Deductions, Credits, etc.

► See back of form and instructions.

Part I Information About the Estate or Trust

A Estate's or trust's employer identification number

XX-XXXXXXX

B Estate's or trust's name

Cathy and Karen Stephens Trust

C Fiduciary's name, address, city, state, and ZIP code

Merchants Bank
3000 Sun Plaza
City, ST 88888

D ☐ Check if Form 1041-T was filed and enter the date it was filed ____________

E ☐ Check if this is the final Form 1041 for the estate or trust

Part II Information About the Beneficiary

F Beneficiary's identifying number

XXX-XX-XXXX

G Beneficiary's name, address, city, state, and ZIP code

Cathy Stephens
13 Sunny Shores
City, ST 77777

H ☒ Domestic beneficiary ☐ Foreign beneficiary

Part III Beneficiary's Share of Current Year Income, Deductions, Credits, and Other Items

1	Interest income	
2a	Ordinary dividends	8,879
2b	Qualified dividends	8,879
3	Net short-term capital gain	
4a	Net long-term capital gain	
4b	28% rate gain	
4c	Unrecaptured section 1250 gain	
5	Other portfolio and nonbusiness income	
6	Ordinary business income	
7	Net rental real estate income	788
8	Other rental income	
9	Directly apportioned deductions	
10	Estate tax deduction	
11	Final year deductions	
12	Alternative minimum tax adjustment	
13	Credits and credit recapture	
14	Other information	A 4,333

*See attached statement for additional information.

Note. A statement must be attached showing the beneficiary's share of income and directly apportioned deductions from each business, rental real estate, and other rental activity.

For IRS Use Only

661113

☐ Final K-1 ☐ Amended K-1 OMB No. 1545-0092

Schedule K-1 (Form 1041) **2016**

Department of the Treasury
Internal Revenue Service

For calendar year 2016, or tax year beginning ____________, 2016, and ending ____________, 20 ____

Beneficiary's Share of Income, Deductions, Credits, etc.

▶ See back of form and instructions.

Part I Information About the Estate or Trust

A Estate's or trust's employer identification number

XX-XXXXXXX

B Estate's or trust's name

Cathy and Karen Stephens Trust

C Fiduciary's name, address, city, state, and ZIP code

Merchants Bank
3000 Sun Plaza
City, ST 88888

D ☐ Check if Form 1041-T was filed and enter the date it was filed ____________

E ☐ Check if this is the final Form 1041 for the estate or trust

Part II Information About the Beneficiary

F Beneficiary's identifying number

XXX-XX-XXXX

G Beneficiary's name, address, city, state, and ZIP code

Karen Stephens
1472 Ski Run
City, ST 11111

H ☒ Domestic beneficiary ☐ Foreign beneficiary

Part III Beneficiary's Share of Current Year Income, Deductions, Credits, and Other Items

1	Interest income	
2a	Ordinary dividends	4,440
2b	Qualified dividends	4,440
3	Net short-term capital gain	
4a	Net long-term capital gain	
4b	28% rate gain	
4c	Unrecaptured section 1250 gain	
5	Other portfolio and nonbusiness income	
6	Ordinary business income	
7	Net rental real estate income	393
8	Other rental income	
9	Directly apportioned deductions	
10	Estate tax deduction	
11	Final year deductions	
12	Alternative minimum tax adjustment	
13	Credits and credit recapture	
14	Other information	A 2,167

*See attached statement for additional information.

Note. A statement must be attached showing the beneficiary's share of income and directly apportioned deductions from each business, rental real estate, and other rental activity.

For IRS Use Only

For Paperwork Reduction Act Notice, see the Instructions for Form 1041. IRS.gov/form1041 Cat. No. 11380D **Schedule K-1 (Form 1041) 2016**

Form **1116** | Department of the Treasury Internal Revenue Service (99)

Foreign Tax Credit

(Individual, Estate, or Trust)

► Attach to Form 1040, 1040NR, 1041, or 990-T.

► Information about Form 1116 and its separate instructions is at *www.irs.gov/form1116.*

OMB No. 1545-0121 | 2016 | Attachment Sequence No. 19

Name: Andrew Roberts | Identifying number as shown on page 1 of your tax return: XXX-XX-XXXX

Use a separate Form 1116 for each category of income listed below. See *Categories of Income* in the instructions. Check only one box on each Form 1116. Report all amounts in U.S. dollars except where specified in Part II below.

a ☒ Passive category income
b ☐ General category income
c ☐ Section 901(j) income
d ☐ Certain income re-sourced by treaty
e ☐ Lump-sum distributions

f Resident of (name of country) ► United States

Note: If you paid taxes to only one foreign country or U.S. possession, use column A in Part I and line A in Part II. If you paid taxes to **more than one** foreign country or U.S. possession, use a separate column and line for each country or possession.

Part I Taxable Income or Loss From Sources Outside the United States (for Category Checked Above)

		Foreign Country or U.S. Possession				Total
		A	B	C		(Add cols. A, B, and C.)
g	Enter the name of the foreign country or U.S. possession ►	Country X				
1a	Gross income from sources within country shown above and of the type checked above (see instructions): Dividends				1a	15,517
b	Check if line 1a is compensation for personal services as an employee, your total compensation from all sources is $250,000 or more, and you used an alternative basis to determine its source (see instructions) ► ☐					
	Deductions and losses (**Caution:** See instructions.):					
2	Expenses **definitely related** to the income on line 1a (attach statement)					
3	Pro rata share of other deductions **not definitely related:**					
a	Certain itemized deductions or standard deduction (see instructions)					
b	Other deductions (attach statement)					
c	Add lines 3a and 3b					
d	Gross foreign source income (see instructions)					
e	Gross income from all sources (see instructions)					
f	Divide line 3d by line 3e (see instructions)					
g	Multiply line 3c by line 3f					
4	Pro rata share of interest expense (see instructions):					
a	Home mortgage interest (use the Worksheet for Home Mortgage Interest in the instructions)					
b	Other interest expense					
5	Losses from foreign sources					
6	Add lines 2, 3g, 4a, 4b, and 5	-0-			6	-0-
7	Subtract line 6 from line 1a. Enter the result here and on line 15, page 2 ►				7	15,517

Part II Foreign Taxes Paid or Accrued (see instructions)

Country	Credit is claimed for taxes (you must check one): (h) ☒ Paid (i) ☐ Accrued	Foreign taxes paid or accrued								
		In foreign currency				In U.S. dollars				
		Taxes withheld at source on:			(n) Other foreign taxes paid or accrued	Taxes withheld at source on:			(r) Other foreign taxes paid or accrued	(s) Total foreign taxes paid or accrued (add cols. (o) through (r))
	(j) Date paid or accrued	(k) Dividends	(l) Rents and royalties	(m) Interest		(o) Dividends	(p) Rents and royalties	(q) Interest		
A	12-31-16	2,700*				2,328				2,328
B										
C										

8	**Add lines A through C, column (s). Enter the total here and on line 9, page 2** ►	8	2,328

For Paperwork Reduction Act Notice, see instructions. Cat. No. 11440U Form **1116** (2016)

*Denominated in Country X currency.

See text Example C:16-35 for tax form facts.

Form 1116 (2016) Page **2**

Part III Figuring the Credit

Line	Description		Amount	
9	Enter the amount from line 8. These are your total foreign taxes paid or accrued for the category of income checked above Part I	9	2,328	
10	Carryback or carryover (attach detailed computation)	10		
11	Add lines 9 and 10	11	2,328	
12	Reduction in foreign taxes (see instructions)	12	( )	
13	Taxes reclassified under high tax kickout (see instructions)	13		
14	Combine lines 11, 12, and 13. This is the total amount of foreign taxes available for credit	14		2,328
15	Enter the amount from line 7. This is your taxable income or (loss) from sources outside the United States (before adjustments) for the category of income checked above Part I (see instructions)	15	15,517	
16	Adjustments to line 15 (see instructions)	16		
17	Combine the amounts on lines 15 and 16. This is your net foreign source taxable income. (If the result is zero or less, you have no foreign tax credit for the category of income you checked above Part I. Skip lines 18 through 22. However, if you are filing more than one Form 1116, you must complete line 20.)	17	15,517	
18	**Individuals:** Enter the amount from Form 1040, line 41; or Form 1040NR, line 39. **Estates and trusts:** Enter your taxable income without the deduction for your exemption	18	86,000	
	Caution: If you figured your tax using the lower rates on qualified dividends or capital gains, see instructions.			
19	Divide line 17 by line 18. If line 17 is more than line 18, enter "1"	19		0.180430
20	**Individuals:** Enter the amount from Form 1040, lines 44 and 46. If you are a nonresident alien, enter the amounts from Form 1040NR, lines 42 and 44. **Estates and trusts:** Enter the amount from Form 1041, Schedule G, line 1a; or the total of Form 990-T, lines 36, 37, and 39	20		11,017*
	Caution: If you are completing line 20 for separate category **e** (lump-sum distributions), see instructions.			
21	Multiply line 20 by line 19 (maximum amount of credit)	21		1,988
22	Enter the **smaller** of line 14 or line 21. If this is the only Form 1116 you are filing, skip lines 23 through 27 and enter this amount on line 28. Otherwise, complete the appropriate line in Part IV (see instructions) ▶	22		1,988

Part IV Summary of Credits From Separate Parts III (see instructions)

Line	Description		Amount	
23	Credit for taxes on passive category income	23	1,988	
24	Credit for taxes on general category income	24		
25	Credit for taxes on certain income re-sourced by treaty	25		
26	Credit for taxes on lump-sum distributions	26		
27	Add lines 23 through 26	27		1,988
28	Enter the **smaller** of line 20 or line 27	28		1,988
29	Reduction of credit for international boycott operations. See instructions for line 12	29		
30	Subtract line 29 from line 28. This is your **foreign tax credit.** Enter here and on Form 1040, line 48; Form 1040NR, line 46; Form 1041, Schedule G, line 2a; or Form 990-T, line 41a ▶	30		1,988

Form **1116** (2016)

*Tax on $86,000 – (2 x $4,050) = $77,900 of taxable income based on the 2016 tax rate schedule. The figure reported on Line 41 is net of the standard deduction or itemized deductions.

Form **2555**

Department of the Treasury
Internal Revenue Service

Foreign Earned Income

▶ Attach to Form 1040. Complete the Foreign Earned Income Tax Worksheet in the instructions for Form 1040 if you enter an amount on lines 45 or 50.

▶ Information about Form 2555 and its separate instructions is at *www.irs.gov/form2555*.

OMB No. 1545-0074

2016

Attachment Sequence No. **34**

For Use by U.S. Citizens and Resident Aliens Only

Name shown on Form 1040: Lawrence E. Smith

Your social security number: XXX-XX-XXXX

Part I General Information

1 Your foreign address (including country): 123 Rue de Harve 75000 Paris France

2 Your occupation: Financial Vice-President

3 Employer's name ▶ Very Public Corporation

4a Employer's U.S. address ▶ 90 Fifty Avenue, U.S. City, ST 10000

b Employer's foreign address ▶ 11 Rue de Nanettes/5 e'Etage, 75011 Paris France

5 Employer is (check any that apply): ▶ a ☐ A foreign entity b ☒ A U.S. company c ☐ Self d ☐ A foreign affiliate of a U.S. company e ☐ Other (specify) ▶

6a If you previously filed Form 2555 or Form 2555-EZ, enter the last year you filed the form. ▶ 2015

b If you didn't previously file Form 2555 or 2555-EZ to claim either of the exclusions, check here ▶ ☐ and go to line 7.

c Have you ever revoked either of the exclusions? . . . . . ☐ Yes ☒ No

d If you answered "Yes," enter the type of exclusion and the tax year for which the revocation was effective. ▶

7 Of what country are you a citizen/national? ▶ United States

8a Did you maintain a separate foreign residence for your family because of adverse living conditions at your tax home? See **Second foreign household** in the instructions . . . . . ☐ Yes ☒ No

b If "Yes," enter city and country of the separate foreign residence. Also, enter the number of days during your tax year that you maintained a second household at that address. ▶ N/A

9 List your tax home(s) during your tax year and date(s) established. ▶ 123 Rue de Harve, 75000 Paris France July 10, 2014

Next, complete either Part II or Part III. If an item doesn't apply, enter "NA." If you don't give the information asked for, any exclusion or deduction you claim may be disallowed.

Part II Taxpayers Qualifying Under Bona Fide Residence Test (see instructions)

10 Date bona fide residence began ▶ July 10, 2014, and ended ▶ Still a resident

11 Kind of living quarters in foreign country ▶ a ☐ Purchased house b ☒ Rented house or apartment c ☐ Rented room d ☐ Quarters furnished by employer

12a Did any of your family live with you abroad during any part of the tax year? . . . . . ☒ Yes ☐ No

b If "Yes," who and for what period? ▶ Wife and two children for entire year

13a Have you submitted a statement to the authorities of the foreign country where you claim bona fide residence that you aren't a resident of that country? See instructions . . . . . ☐ Yes ☒ No

b Are you required to pay income tax to the country where you claim bona fide residence? See instructions . ☒ Yes ☐ No

If you answered "Yes" to 13a and "No" to 13b, you don't qualify as a bona fide resident. Don't complete the rest of this part.

14 If you were present in the United States or its possessions during the tax year, complete columns **(a)–(d)** below. **Don't** include the income from column **(d)** in Part IV, but report it on Form 1040.

(a) Date arrived in U.S.	(b) Date left U.S.	(c) Number of days in U.S. on business	(d) Income earned in U.S. on business (attach computation)	(a) Date arrived in U.S.	(b) Date left U.S.	(c) Number of days in U.S. on business	(d) Income earned in U.S. on business (attach computation)
2-19-16	2-23-16	5	1,200				

15a List any contractual terms or other conditions relating to the length of your employment abroad. ▶ Indefinite

b Enter the type of visa under which you entered the foreign country. ▶ Resident

c Did your visa limit the length of your stay or employment in a foreign country? If "Yes," attach explanation . ☐ Yes ☒ No

d Did you maintain a home in the United States while living abroad? . . . . . ☒ Yes ☐ No

e If "Yes," enter address of your home, whether it was rented, the names of the occupants, and their relationship to you. ▶ 4710 68th Terrace, City, ST 54321 (rented to unrelated party)

See text Example C:16-36 for tax form facts.

Form 2555 (2016) Page **2**

Part III **Taxpayers Qualifying Under Physical Presence Test** (see instructions)

16 The physical presence test is based on the 12-month period from ► N/A through ►

17 Enter your principal country of employment during your tax year. ►

18 If you traveled abroad during the 12-month period entered on line 16, complete columns **(a)–(f)** below. Exclude travel between foreign countries that didn't involve travel on or over international waters, or in or over the United States, for 24 hours or more. If you have no travel to report during the period, enter "Physically present in a foreign country or countries for the entire 12-month period." **Don't** include the income from column **(f)** below in Part IV, but report it on Form 1040.

(a) Name of country (including U.S.)	**(b)** Date arrived	**(c)** Date left	**(d)** Full days present in country	**(e)** Number of days in U.S. on business	**(f)** Income earned in U.S. on business (attach computation)

Part IV **All Taxpayers**

Note: Enter on lines 19 through 23 all income, including noncash income, you earned and actually or constructively received during your 2016 tax year for services you performed in a foreign country. If any of the foreign earned income received this tax year was earned in a prior tax year, or will be earned in a later tax year (such as a bonus), see the instructions. **Don't** include income from line 14, column **(d),** or line 18, column **(f).** Report amounts in U.S. dollars, using the exchange rates in effect when you actually or constructively received the income.

If you are a cash basis taxpayer, report on Form 1040 all income you received in 2016, no matter when you performed the service.

	2016 Foreign Earned Income				**Amount (in U.S. dollars)**
19	Total wages, salaries, bonuses, commissions, etc.			19	58,800*
20	Allowable share of income for personal services performed (see instructions):				
a	In a business (including farming) or profession			20a	
b	In a partnership. List partnership's name and address and type of income. ►			20b	
21	Noncash income (market value of property or facilities furnished by employer—attach statement showing how it was determined):				
a	Home (lodging)			21a	
b	Meals			21b	
c	Car			21c	
d	Other property or facilities. List type and amount. ►			21d	
22	Allowances, reimbursements, or expenses paid on your behalf for services you performed:				
a	Cost of living and overseas differential	22a	27,000		
b	Family	22b			
c	Education	22c	8,000		
d	Home leave	22d	6,400		
e	Quarters	22e	21,300		
f	For any other purpose. List type and amount. ►	22f			
g	Add lines 22a through 22f			22g	62,700
23	Other foreign earned income. List type and amount. ►			23	
24	Add lines 19 through 21d, line 22g, and line 23			24	121,500
25	Total amount of meals and lodging included on line 24 that is excludable (see instructions)			25	
26	Subtract line 25 from line 24. Enter the result here and on line 27 on page 3. This is your **2016 foreign earned income** ►			26	121,500

*$60,000 salary – $1,200 U.S. source income from Part II, Line 14(d).

Form **2555** (2016)

Form 2555 (2016) Page **3**

Part V All Taxpayers

27	Enter the amount from line 26	27	121,500	
	Are you claiming the housing exclusion or housing deduction? ☐ **Yes.** Complete Part VI. ☐ **No.** Go to Part VII.			

Part VI Taxpayers Claiming the Housing Exclusion and/or Deduction

28	Qualified housing expenses for the tax year (see instructions)	28	21,300	
29a	Enter location where housing expenses incurred (see instructions) ▶ France			
b	Enter limit on housing expenses (see instructions)	29b	30,390	
30	Enter the **smaller** of line 28 or line 29b	30	21,300	
31	Number of days in your qualifying period that fall within your 2016 tax year (see instructions) . . . . **31** 366 days			
32	Multiply $44.28 by the number of days on line 31. If 366 is entered on line 31, enter $16,208 here	32	16,208	
33	Subtract line 32 from line 30. If the result is zero or less, don't complete the rest of this part or any of Part IX	33	5,092	
34	Enter employer-provided amounts (see instructions) **34** 121,500			
35	Divide line 34 by line 27. Enter the result as a decimal (rounded to at least three places), but don't enter more than "1.000"	35	× 1.00	
36	**Housing exclusion.** Multiply line 33 by line 35. Enter the result but don't enter more than the amount on line 34. Also, complete Part VIII . . . . ▶	36	5,092	
	Note: The housing deduction is figured in Part IX. If you choose to claim the foreign earned income exclusion, complete Parts VII and VIII before Part IX.			

Part VII Taxpayers Claiming the Foreign Earned Income Exclusion

37	Maximum foreign earned income exclusion	37	$101,300	00
38	• If you completed Part VI, enter the number from line 31. • All others, enter the number of days in your qualifying period that fall within your 2016 tax year (see the instructions for line 31). **38** 366 days			
39	• If line 38 and the number of days in your 2016 tax year (usually 366) are the same, enter "1.000." • Otherwise, divide line 38 by the number of days in your 2016 tax year and enter the result as a decimal (rounded to at least three places).	39	× 1.00	
40	Multiply line 37 by line 39	40	101,300	
41	Subtract line 36 from line 27	41	116,408	
42	**Foreign earned income exclusion.** Enter the **smaller** of line 40 or line 41. Also, complete Part VIII ▶	42	101,300	

Part VIII Taxpayers Claiming the Housing Exclusion, Foreign Earned Income Exclusion, or Both

43	Add lines 36 and 42	43	106,392	
44	Deductions allowed in figuring your adjusted gross income (Form 1040, line 37) that are allocable to the excluded income. See instructions and attach computation	44	-0-	
45	Subtract line 44 from line 43. Enter the result here and in parentheses on **Form 1040, line 21.** Next to the amount enter "Form 2555." On Form 1040, subtract this amount from your income to arrive at total income on Form 1040, line 22	45	106,392	

Part IX Taxpayers Claiming the Housing Deduction—Complete this part only if (a) line 33 is more than line 36 and (b) line 27 is more than line 43.

46	Subtract line 36 from line 33	46	-0-	
47	Subtract line 43 from line 27	47	15,108	
48	Enter the **smaller** of line 46 or line 47	48	-0-	
	Note: If line 47 is **more than** line 48 and you couldn't deduct all of your 2015 housing deduction because of the 2015 limit, use the housing deduction carryover worksheet in the instructions to figure the amount to enter on line 49. Otherwise, go to line 50.			
49	Housing deduction carryover from 2015 (from housing deduction carryover worksheet in the instructions)	49	-0-	
50	**Housing deduction.** Add lines 48 and 49. Enter the total here and on Form 1040 to the left of line 36. Next to the amount on Form 1040, enter "Form 2555." Add it to the total adjustments reported on that line . . . . ▶	50	-0-	

Form **2555** (2016)

APPENDIX

C MACRS TABLES

MACRS, ADS, and ACRS Depreciation Methods Summary

System	Characteristics	Depreciation Method: MACRS	Depreciation Method: ADS	Table No.[a]: MACRS	Table No.[a]: ADS
MACRS & ADS	Personal Property:				
	1. Accounting convention	Half-year or mid-quarter	Half-year or mid-quarter[b]		
	2. Life and method				
	a. 3-year, 5-year, 7-year, 10-year	200% DB or elect straight-line	150% DB or elect straight-line	1, 2, 3, 4, 5	10, 11[c]
	b. 15-year, 20-year	150% DB or elect straight-line	150% DB or elect straight-lined	1, 2, 3, 4, 5	
	3. Luxury automobile limitations			6	
	Real Property:				
	1. Accounting convention	Mid-month	Mid-month		
	2. Life and method				
	a. Residential rental property	27.5 years, straight-line	40 years straight-line	7	12
	b. Nonresidential real property	39 years, straight-line[e]	40 years straight-line	9	12

System	Characteristics	ACRS
ACRS[f]	Personal Property:	
	1. Accounting convention	Half-year
	2. Life and method	
	a. 3-year, 5-year, 10-year, 15-year	150% DB or elect straight-line
	Real Property:	
	1. Accounting convention	First of month or mid-month
	2. Life	
	a. 15-year property	Placed in service after 12/31/80 and before 3/16/84
	b. 18-year property	Placed in service after 3/15/84 and before 5/9/85
	c. 19-year property	Placed in service after 5/8/85 and before 1/1/87
	3. Method	
	a. All but low-income housing	175% DB or elect straight-line
	b. Low-income housing property	200% DB or elect straight-line

[a]All depreciation tables in this appendix are based upon tables contained in Rev. Proc. 87-57, as amended.
[b]General and ADS tables are available for property lives from 2.5–50.0 years using the straight-line method. These tables are contained in Rev. Proc. 87-57 and are only partially reproduced here.
[c]The mid-quarter tables are available in Rev. Proc. 87-57, but are not reproduced here.
[d]Special recovery periods are assigned certain MACRS properties under the alternative depreciation system.
[e]A 31.5-year recovery period applied to nonresidential real property placed in service under the MACRS rules prior to May 13, 1993 (see Table 8).
[f]ACRS was effective for years 1981–1986. ACRS tables are no longer reproduced here.

▼ TABLE 1

General Depreciation System—MACRS
Personal Property Placed in Service After 12/31/86
Applicable Convention: Half-Year
Applicable Depreciation Method: 200 or 150 Percent Declining Balance Switching to Straight Line

If the Recovery Year Is:	And the Recovery Period Is: 3-Year	5-Year	7-Year	10-Year	15-Year	20-Year
	The Depreciation Rate Is:					
1	33.33	20.00	14.29	10.00	5.00	3.750
2	44.45	32.00	24.49	18.00	9.50	7.219
3	14.81	19.20	17.49	14.40	8.55	6.677
4	7.41	11.52	12.49	11.52	7.70	6.177
5		11.52	8.93	9.22	6.93	5.713
6		5.76	8.92	7.37	6.23	5.285
7			8.93	6.55	5.90	4.888
8			4.46	6.55	5.90	4.522
9				6.56	5.91	4.462
10				6.55	5.90	4.461
11				3.28	5.91	4.462
12					5.90	4.461
13					5.91	4.462
14					5.90	4.461
15					5.91	4.462
16					2.95	4.461
17						4.462
18						4.461
19						4.462
20						4.461
21						2.231

▼ TABLE 2

General Depreciation System—MACRS

Personal Property Placed in Service After 12/31/86

Applicable Convention: Mid-Quarter (Property Placed in Service in First Quarter)

Applicable Depreciation Method: 200 or 150 Percent Declining Balance Switching to Straight Line

If the Recovery Year Is:	And the Recovery Period Is: 3-Year	5-Year	7-Year	10-Year	15-Year	20-Year
	The Depreciation Rate Is:					
1	58.33	35.00	25.00	17.50	8.75	6.563
2	27.78	26.00	21.43	16.50	9.13	7.000
3	12.35	15.60	15.31	13.20	8.21	6.482
4	1.54	11.01	10.93	10.56	7.39	5.996
5		11.01	8.75	8.45	6.65	5.546
6		1.38	8.74	6.76	5.99	5.130
7			8.75	6.55	5.90	4.746
8			1.09	6.55	5.91	4.459
9				6.56	5.90	4.459
10				6.55	5.91	4.459
11				0.82	5.90	4.459
12					5.91	4.460
13					5.90	4.459
14					5.91	4.460
15					5.90	4.459
16					0.74	4.460
17						4.459
18						4.460
19						4.459
20						4.460
21						0.557

▼ TABLE 3

General Depreciation System—MACRS
Personal Property Placed in Service After 12/31/86
Applicable Convention: Mid-Quarter (Property Placed in Service in Second Quarter)
Applicable Depreciation Method: 200 or 150 Percent Declining Balance Switching to Straight Line

If the Recovery Year Is:	And the Recovery Period Is: 3-Year	5-Year	7-Year	10-Year	15-Year	20-Year
	The Depreciation Rate Is:					
1	41.67	25.00	17.85	12.50	6.25	4.688
2	38.89	30.00	23.47	17.50	9.38	7.148
3	14.14	18.00	16.76	14.00	8.44	6.612
4	5.30	11.37	11.97	11.20	7.59	6.116
5		11.37	8.87	8.96	6.83	5.658
6		4.26	8.87	7.17	6.15	5.233
7			8.87	6.55	5.91	4.841
8			3.33	6.55	5.90	4.478
9				6.56	5.91	4.463
10				6.55	5.90	4.463
11				2.46	5.91	4.463
12					5.90	4.463
13					5.91	4.463
14					5.90	4.463
15					5.91	4.462
16					2.21	4.463
17						4.462
18						4.463
19						4.462
20						4.463
21						1.673

▼ TABLE 4

General Depreciation System—MACRS
Personal Property Placed in Service After 12/31/86
Applicable Convention: Mid-Quarter (Property Placed in Service in Third Quarter)
Applicable Depreciation Method: 200 or 150 Percent Declining Balance Switching to Straight Line

If the Recovery Year Is:	And the Recovery Period Is: 3-Year	5-Year	7-Year	10-Year	15-Year	20-Year
	The Depreciation Rate Is:					
1	25.00	15.00	10.71	7.50	3.75	2.813
2	50.00	34.00	25.51	18.50	9.63	7.289
3	16.67	20.40	18.22	14.80	8.66	6.742
4	8.33	12.24	13.02	11.84	7.80	6.237
5		11.30	9.30	9.47	7.02	5.769
6		7.06	8.85	7.58	6.31	5.336
7			8.86	6.55	5.90	4.936
8			5.53	6.55	5.90	4.566
9				6.56	5.91	4.460
10				6.55	5.90	4.460
11				4.10	5.91	4.460
12					5.90	4.460
13					5.91	4.461
14					5.90	4.460
15					5.91	4.461
16					3.69	4.460
17						4.461
18						4.460
19						4.461
20						4.460
21						2.788

▼ TABLE 5

General Depreciation System—MACRS

Personal Property Placed in Service After 12/31/86

Applicable Convention: Mid-Quarter (Property Placed in Service in Fourth Quarter)

Applicable Depreciation Method: 200 or 150 Percent Declining Balance Switching to Straight Line

If the Recovery Year Is:	And the Recovery Period Is: 3-Year	5-Year	7-Year	10-Year	15-Year	20-Year
	The Depreciation Rate Is:					
1	8.33	5.00	3.57	2.50	1.25	0.938
2	61.11	38.00	27.55	19.50	9.88	7.430
3	20.37	22.80	19.68	15.60	8.89	6.872
4	10.19	13.68	14.06	12.48	8.00	6.357
5		10.94	10.04	9.98	7.20	5.880
6		9.58	8.73	7.99	6.48	5.439
7			8.73	6.55	5.90	5.031
8			7.64	6.55	5.90	4.654
9				6.56	5.90	4.458
10				6.55	5.91	4.458
11				5.74	5.90	4.458
12					5.91	4.458
13					5.90	4.458
14					5.91	4.458
15					5.90	4.458
16					5.17	4.458
17						4.458
18						4.459
19						4.458
20						4.459
21						3.901

TAX AUTHORITY UPDATE

At the time this edition went to print, the IRS had not yet released the 2017 ceiling limits. For examples and problems in the text, we assume the limits will be the same for 2017 as they were in 2016.

▼ TABLE 6

Luxury Automobile Depreciation Limits

	Year Automobile Is Placed in Service[a] 2012–2016	2010–2011	2009	2008
Maximum Allowable Depreciation (100% Business Use):				
Year 1	$3,160[b]	$3,060[c]	$2,960[d]	$2,960[e]
Year 2	5,100	4,900	4,800	4,800
Year 3	3,050	2,950	2,850	2,850
Year 4 and Each Succeeding Year	1,875	1,775	1,775	1,775

[a]For years prior to 2008, see the Revenue Procedure for the appropriate year.

[b]$11,160 in Year 1 (2016, 2015, 2014, 2013, or 2012) if taxpayer claims bonus depreciation.

[c]$11,060 in Year 1 (2011 or 2010) if taxpayer claims bonus depreciation.

[d]$10,960 in Year 1 (2009) if taxpayer claims bonus depreciation.

[e]$10,960 in Year 1 (2008) if taxpayer claimed bonus depreciation.

▼ **TABLE 6 (continued)**

Truck and Van Depreciation Limits

	Year Truck or Van Is Placed in Service[a]								
	2016	**2015**	**2014**	**2013**	**2012**	**2011**	**2010**	**2009**	**2008**
Maximum Allowable Depreciation (100% Business Use):									
Year 1	\$3,560[b]	\$3,460[c]	\$3,460[c]	\$3,360[d]	\$3,360[d]	\$3,260[e]	\$3,160[f]	\$3,060[g]	\$3,160[f]
Year 2	5,700	5,600	5,550	5,400	5,300	5,200	5,100	4,900	5,100
Year 3	3,350	3,350	3,350	3,250	3,150	3,150	3,050	2,950	3,050
Year 4 and Each Succeeding Year	2,075	1,975	1,975	1,975	1,875	1,875	1,875	1,775	1,875

[a]For years prior to 2008, see the Revenue Procedure for the appropriate year.
[b]\$11,560 in Year 1 (2016) if taxpayer claims bonus depreciation.
[c]\$11,460 in Year 1 (2014 and 2015) if taxpayer claims bonus depreciation.
[d]\$11,360 in Year 1 (2012 and 2013) if taxpayer claims bonus depreciation.
[e]\$11,260 in Year 1 (2011) if taxpayer claims bonus depreciation.
[f]\$11,160 in Year 1 (2010 and 2008) if taxpayer claims bonus depreciation.
[g]\$11,060 in Year 1 (2009) if taxpayer claimed bonus depreciation.

TAX AUTHORITY UPDATE

At the time this edition went to print, the IRS had not yet released the 2017 ceiling limits. For examples and problems in the text, we assume the limits will be the same for 2017 as they were in 2016.

▼ **TABLE 7**

General Depreciation System—MACRS

Residential Rental Real Property Placed in Service After 12/31/86

Applicable Recovery Period: 27.5 Years

Applicable Convention: Mid-Month

Applicable Depreciation Method: Straight Line

If the Recovery Year Is:	And the Month in the First Recovery Year the Property Is Placed in Service Is: 1	2	3	4	5	6	7	8	9	10	11	12
	The Depreciation Rate Is:											
1	3.485	3.182	2.879	2.576	2.273	1.970	1.667	1.364	1.061	0.758	0.455	0.152
2	3.636	3.636	3.636	3.636	3.636	3.636	3.636	3.636	3.636	3.636	3.636	3.636
3	3.636	3.636	3.636	3.636	3.636	3.636	3.636	3.636	3.636	3.636	3.636	3.636
4	3.636	3.636	3.636	3.636	3.636	3.636	3.636	3.636	3.636	3.636	3.636	3.636
5	3.636	3.636	3.636	3.636	3.636	3.636	3.636	3.636	3.636	3.636	3.636	3.636
6	3.636	3.636	3.636	3.636	3.636	3.636	3.636	3.636	3.636	3.636	3.636	3.636
7	3.636	3.636	3.636	3.636	3.636	3.636	3.636	3.636	3.636	3.636	3.636	3.636
8	3.636	3.636	3.636	3.636	3.636	3.636	3.636	3.636	3.636	3.636	3.636	3.636
9	3.636	3.636	3.636	3.636	3.636	3.636	3.636	3.636	3.636	3.636	3.636	3.636
10	3.637	3.637	3.637	3.637	3.637	3.637	3.636	3.636	3.636	3.636	3.636	3.636
11	3.636	3.636	3.636	3.636	3.636	3.636	3.637	3.637	3.637	3.637	3.637	3.637
12	3.637	3.637	3.637	3.637	3.637	3.637	3.636	3.636	3.636	3.636	3.636	3.636
13	3.636	3.636	3.636	3.636	3.636	3.636	3.637	3.637	3.637	3.637	3.637	3.637
14	3.637	3.637	3.637	3.637	3.637	3.637	3.636	3.636	3.636	3.636	3.636	3.636
15	3.636	3.636	3.636	3.636	3.636	3.636	3.637	3.637	3.637	3.637	3.637	3.637
16	3.637	3.637	3.637	3.637	3.637	3.637	3.636	3.636	3.636	3.636	3.636	3.636
17	3.636	3.636	3.636	3.636	3.636	3.636	3.637	3.637	3.637	3.637	3.637	3.637
18	3.637	3.637	3.637	3.637	3.637	3.637	3.636	3.636	3.636	3.636	3.636	3.636
19	3.636	3.636	3.636	3.636	3.636	3.636	3.637	3.637	3.637	3.637	3.637	3.637
20	3.637	3.637	3.637	3.637	3.637	3.637	3.636	3.636	3.636	3.636	3.636	3.636
21	3.636	3.636	3.636	3.636	3.636	3.636	3.637	3.637	3.637	3.637	3.637	3.637
22	3.637	3.637	3.637	3.637	3.637	3.637	3.636	3.636	3.636	3.636	3.636	3.636
23	3.636	3.636	3.636	3.636	3.636	3.636	3.637	3.637	3.637	3.637	3.637	3.637
24	3.637	3.637	3.637	3.637	3.637	3.637	3.636	3.636	3.636	3.636	3.636	3.636
25	3.636	3.636	3.636	3.636	3.636	3.636	3.637	3.637	3.637	3.637	3.637	3.637
26	3.637	3.637	3.637	3.637	3.637	3.637	3.636	3.636	3.636	3.636	3.636	3.636
27	3.636	3.636	3.636	3.636	3.636	3.636	3.637	3.637	3.637	3.637	3.637	3.637
28	1.970	2.273	2.576	2.879	3.182	3.485	3.636	3.636	3.636	3.636	3.636	3.636
29	0.000	0.000	0.000	0.000	0.000	0.000	0.152	0.455	0.758	1.061	1.364	1.667

▼ TABLE 8

General Depreciation System—MACRS
Nonresidential Real Property Placed in Service After 12/31/86 and Before 5/13/93
Applicable Recovery Period: 31.5 Years
Applicable Convention: Mid-Month
Applicable Depreciation Method: Straight Line

If the Recovery Year Is:	And the Month in the First Recovery Year the Property Is Placed in Service Is: 1	2	3	4	5	6	7	8	9	10	11	12
	The Depreciation Rate Is:											
1	3.042	2.778	2.513	2.249	1.984	1.720	1.455	1.190	0.926	0.661	0.397	0.132
2	3.175	3.175	3.175	3.175	3.175	3.175	3.175	3.175	3.175	3.175	3.175	3.175
3	3.175	3.175	3.175	3.175	3.175	3.175	3.175	3.175	3.175	3.175	3.175	3.175
4	3.175	3.175	3.175	3.175	3.175	3.175	3.175	3.175	3.175	3.175	3.175	3.175
5	3.175	3.175	3.175	3.175	3.175	3.175	3.175	3.175	3.175	3.175	3.175	3.175
6	3.175	3.175	3.175	3.175	3.175	3.175	3.175	3.175	3.175	3.175	3.175	3.175
7	3.175	3.175	3.175	3.175	3.175	3.175	3.175	3.175	3.175	3.175	3.175	3.175
8	3.175	3.174	3.175	3.174	3.175	3.174	3.175	3.175	3.175	3.175	3.175	3.175
9	3.174	3.175	3.174	3.175	3.174	3.175	3.174	3.175	3.174	3.175	3.174	3.175
10	3.175	3.174	3.175	3.174	3.175	3.174	3.175	3.174	3.175	3.174	3.175	3.174
11	3.174	3.175	3.174	3.175	3.174	3.175	3.174	3.175	3.174	3.175	3.174	3.175
12	3.175	3.174	3.175	3.174	3.175	3.174	3.175	3.174	3.175	3.174	3.175	3.174
13	3.174	3.175	3.174	3.175	3.174	3.175	3.174	3.175	3.174	3.175	3.174	3.175
14	3.175	3.174	3.175	3.174	3.175	3.174	3.175	3.174	3.175	3.174	3.175	3.174
15	3.174	3.175	3.174	3.175	3.174	3.175	3.174	3.175	3.174	3.175	3.174	3.175
16	3.175	3.174	3.175	3.174	3.175	3.174	3.175	3.174	3.175	3.174	3.175	3.174
17	3.174	3.175	3.174	3.175	3.174	3.175	3.174	3.175	3.174	3.175	3.174	3.175
18	3.175	3.174	3.175	3.174	3.175	3.174	3.175	3.174	3.175	3.174	3.175	3.174
19	3.174	3.175	3.174	3.175	3.174	3.175	3.174	3.175	3.174	3.175	3.174	3.175
20	3.175	3.174	3.175	3.174	3.175	3.174	3.175	3.174	3.175	3.174	3.175	3.174
21	3.174	3.175	3.174	3.175	3.174	3.175	3.174	3.175	3.174	3.175	3.174	3.175
22	3.175	3.174	3.175	3.174	3.175	3.174	3.175	3.174	3.175	3.174	3.175	3.174
23	3.174	3.175	3.174	3.175	3.174	3.175	3.174	3.175	3.174	3.175	3.174	3.175
24	3.175	3.174	3.175	3.174	3.175	3.174	3.175	3.174	3.175	3.174	3.175	3.174
25	3.174	3.175	3.174	3.175	3.174	3.175	3.174	3.175	3.174	3.175	3.174	3.175
26	3.175	3.174	3.175	3.174	3.175	3.174	3.175	3.174	3.175	3.174	3.175	3.174
27	3.174	3.175	3.174	3.175	3.174	3.175	3.174	3.175	3.174	3.175	3.174	3.175
28	3.175	3.174	3.175	3.174	3.175	3.174	3.175	3.174	3.175	3.174	3.175	3.174
29	3.174	3.175	3.174	3.175	3.174	3.175	3.174	3.175	3.174	3.175	3.174	3.175
30	3.175	3.174	3.175	3.174	3.175	3.174	3.175	3.174	3.175	3.174	3.175	3.174
31	3.174	3.175	3.174	3.175	3.174	3.175	3.174	3.175	3.174	3.175	3.174	3.175
32	1.720	1.984	2.249	2.513	2.778	3.042	3.175	3.174	3.175	3.174	3.175	3.174
33	0.000	0.000	0.000	0.000	0.000	0.000	0.132	0.397	0.661	0.926	1.190	1.455

Johns and Lawrence General Partnership Reconciliation of Book and Taxable Income for Year Ending December 31, 2016

	Book Income		Adjustments		Taxable Income		Form 1065 Schedule K	
Account Name	Debit	Credit	Debit	Credit	Debit	Credit	Ordinary Income	Separately Stated Items
Sales		$869,658				$869,658	$869,658	
Sales returns & allowances	$ 29,242				$ 29,242		(29,242)	
Cost of sales	540,204				540,204		(540,204)	
Dividends		1,000				1,000		$ 1,000
Tax-exempt interest		18,000	$18,000			0		18,000
Gain on stock sale		4,500				4,500		4,500
Worthless stock loss	2,100				2,100			(2,100)
Guaranteed payments[(a)]	36,000			$36,000	0		(36,000)	
Other salaries	52,000				52,000		(52,000)	
Rentals	36,000				36,000		(36,000)	
Bad debts	4,000				4,000		(4,000)	
Interest:								
Working capital loans	8,000				8,000		(8,000)	
Purchase tax-exempt bonds	2,000			2,000	0			(2,000)
Employment taxes	8,320				8,320		(8,320)	
Taxes	1,520				1,520		(1,520)	
Repairs	4,800				4,800		(4,800)	
Depreciation[(b)]	12,000		476		12,476		(12,476)	
Charitable contributions	12,000				12,000			(12,000)
Travel	4,000				4,000		(4,000)	
Meals and entertainment[(c)]	8,000			4,000	4,000		(4,000)	
Meals and ent. nondeductible								(4,000)
Office expenses	16,000				16,000		(16,000)	
Advertising	13,000				13,000		(13,000)	
Transportation expense	10,400				10,400		(10,400)	
General and administrative	3,000				3,000		(3,000)	
Pension plans[(d)]	2,000				2,000		(2,000)	
Employee benefit programs[(e)]	4,000				4,000		(4,000)	
Miscellaneous	1,000				1,000		(850)	(150)
Net profit/Taxable income	83,572		$23,524		107,096			
Total	$893,158	$893,158	$42,000	$42,000	$875,158	$875,158	$ 79,846	

[(a)] Guaranteed payments have no net effect on taxable income. The guaranteed payments both reduce ordinary income and increase separately stated income items that are taxable.

[(b)] MACRS depreciation = $27,476 total − $15,000 allocated to COGS = $12,476

[(c)] 50% of the meals and entertainment expense is not deductible for tax purposes but must be separately stated on Schedules K and K-1.

[(d)] The pension plan expense is the same for book and tax purposes for this partnership. No pension expenses relate to pensions for the partners.

[(e)] The employee benefit expense is the same for book and tax purposes for this partnership. None relates to partner benefits.

Facts for S Corporation (Form 1120S)

The same basic facts presented for the Andrew Lawrence proprietorship are used for the S corporation except for the following:

1. Johns and Lawrence, Inc. made an S corporation election on June 13, 2010. The election was effective for its initial tax year.
2. The book income for Johns and Lawrence is presented in the attached worksheet, which reconciles book income and S corporation taxable income.
3. The $18,000 salaries paid to each employee are subject to the same employment tax requirements as when paid by the C corporation. The total employment taxes ($14,480) are the same as for the C corporation.
4. The S corporation paid no estimated federal income taxes.
5. The corporation distributed $14,106 to each of the two shareholders.
6. Other deductions include:

Travel	$ 4,000
Meals and entertainment	8,000
Minus: 50% disallowance	(4,000)
Office expenses	16,000
Transportation	10,400
General and administrative	3,000
Miscellaneous*	850
Total	$38,250

*$150 of the miscellaneous expenses are related to the production of the dividend income and are separately stated.

7. The following schedule reconciles net income for the C corporation and the S corporation:

Net income per books for C corporation	$63,412
Plus: Federal income taxes	14,000
Net income per books for S corporation	$77,412

The S corporation return can be tied back to the partnership return. The only difference between the two returns is that the S corporation pays an additional $6,160 in employment taxes with respect to the shareholder-employee salaries, as compared to the partnership's guaranteed payments. This dollar difference is reflected in the net income numbers, the ordinary income numbers, capital account balances, and total asset amounts.

8. Qualified production activities income (QPAI) equals $80,000. Employer's W-2 wages allocable to U.S. production activities equal $88,000.
9. The balance sheet for Johns and Lawrence appears on page 4 of Form 1120S.
10. For additional information, see worksheet on page B-47.

Form **1120S**

Department of the Treasury
Internal Revenue Service

U.S. Income Tax Return for an S Corporation

► Do not file this form unless the corporation has filed or is attaching Form 2553 to elect to be an S corporation.
► Information about Form 1120S and its separate instructions is at *www.irs.gov/form1120s.*

OMB No. 1545-0123

2016

For calendar year 2016 or tax year beginning , 2016, ending , 20

A S election effective date: 6-13-2010	Name: Johns and Lawrence, Inc.	D Employer identification number: XX-XXXXXXX
B Business activity code number (see instructions): 337000	TYPE OR PRINT — Number, street, and room or suite no. If a P.O. box, see instructions.: 1234 First Avenue	E Date incorporated: 6-1-2010
C Check if Sch. M-3 attached ☐	City or town, state or province, country, and ZIP or foreign postal code: City, ST 55555	F Total assets (see instructions): $ 498,324

G Is the corporation electing to be an S corporation beginning with this tax year? ☐ Yes ☐ No If "Yes," attach Form 2553 if not already filed

H Check if: (1) ☐ Final return (2) ☐ Name change (3) ☐ Address change (4) ☐ Amended return (5) ☐ S election termination or revocation

I Enter the number of shareholders who were shareholders during any part of the tax year . . . ► 2

Caution: Include **only** trade or business income and expenses on lines 1a through 21. See the instructions for more information.

Income	1a	Gross receipts or sales	1a	869,658		
	b	Returns and allowances	1b	29,242		
	c	Balance. Subtract line 1b from line 1a			1c	840,416
	2	Cost of goods sold (attach Form 1125-A)			2	540,204
	3	Gross profit. Subtract line 2 from line 1c			3	300,212
	4	Net gain (loss) from Form 4797, line 17 (attach Form 4797)			4	
	5	Other income (loss) (see instructions—attach statement)			5	
	6	**Total income (loss).** Add lines 3 through 5 ►			6	300,212
Deductions (see instructions for limitations)	7	Compensation of officers (see instructions—attach Form 1125-E)			7	36,000
	8	Salaries and wages (less employment credits)			8	52,000
	9	Repairs and maintenance			9	4,800
	10	Bad debts			10	4,000
	11	Rents			11	36,000
	12	Taxes and licenses			12	16,000
	13	Interest			13	8,000
	14	Depreciation not claimed on Form 1125-A or elsewhere on return (attach Form 4562)			14	12,476
	15	Depletion **(Do not deduct oil and gas depletion.)**			15	
	16	Advertising			16	13,000
	17	Pension, profit-sharing, etc., plans			17	2,000
	18	Employee benefit programs			18	4,000
	19	Other deductions (attach statement)			19	38,250
	20	**Total deductions.** Add lines 7 through 19 ►			20	226,526
	21	**Ordinary business income (loss).** Subtract line 20 from line 6			21	73,686
Tax and Payments	22a	Excess net passive income or LIFO recapture tax (see instructions)	22a			
	b	Tax from Schedule D (Form 1120S)	22b			
	c	Add lines 22a and 22b (see instructions for additional taxes)			22c	NONE
	23a	2016 estimated tax payments and 2015 overpayment credited to 2016	23a			
	b	Tax deposited with Form 7004	23b			
	c	Credit for federal tax paid on fuels (attach Form 4136)	23c			
	d	Add lines 23a through 23c			23d	NONE
	24	Estimated tax penalty (see instructions). Check if Form 2220 is attached ► ☐			24	
	25	**Amount owed.** If line 23d is smaller than the total of lines 22c and 24, enter amount owed			25	NONE
	26	**Overpayment.** If line 23d is larger than the total of lines 22c and 24, enter amount overpaid			26	
	27	Enter amount from line 26 **Credited to 2017 estimated tax ►**	**Refunded ►**		27	

Sign Here

Under penalties of perjury, I declare that I have examined this return, including accompanying schedules and statements, and to the best of my knowledge and belief, it is true, correct, and complete. Declaration of preparer (other than taxpayer) is based on all information of which preparer has any knowledge.

Signature of officer	Date	Title
► *Andrew Lawrence*	3-14-17	► Vice-President

May the IRS discuss this return with the preparer shown below (see instructions)? ☒ Yes ☐ No

Paid Preparer Use Only

Print/Type preparer's name	Preparer's signature	Date	Check ☒ if self-employed	PTIN
Michael Prepper	*Michael Prepper*	3-14-17		
Firm's name ► Michael S. Prepper			Firm's EIN ►	
Firm's address ► 1111 Second Street, City, ST 55555			Phone no.	

Form 1120S (2016) Page **2**

Schedule B Other Information (see instructions)

		Yes	No
1	Check accounting method: a ☐ Cash b ☒ Accrual c ☐ Other (specify) ▶		
2	See the instructions and enter the: a Business activity ▶ Manufacturing b Product or service ▶ Furniture		
3	At any time during the tax year, was any shareholder of the corporation a disregarded entity, a trust, an estate, or a nominee or similar person? If "Yes," attach Schedule B-1, Information on Certain Shareholders of an S Corporation		X
4	At the end of the tax year, did the corporation:		
a	Own directly 20% or more, or own, directly or indirectly, 50% or more of the total stock issued and outstanding of any foreign or domestic corporation? For rules of constructive ownership, see instructions. If "Yes," complete (i) through (v) below		X

(i) Name of Corporation	(ii) Employer Identification Number (if any)	(iii) Country of Incorporation	(iv) Percentage of Stock Owned	(v) If Percentage in (iv) is 100%, Enter the Date (if any) a Qualified Subchapter S Subsidiary Election Was Made

		Yes	No
b	Own directly an interest of 20% or more, or own, directly or indirectly, an interest of 50% or more in the profit, loss, or capital in any foreign or domestic partnership (including an entity treated as a partnership) or in the beneficial interest of a trust? For rules of constructive ownership, see instructions. If "Yes," complete (i) through (v) below		X

(i) Name of Entity	(ii) Employer Identification Number (if any)	(iii) Type of Entity	(iv) Country of Organization	(v) Maximum Percentage Owned in Profit, Loss, or Capital

		Yes	No
5a	At the end of the tax year, did the corporation have any outstanding shares of restricted stock?		X
	If "Yes," complete lines (i) and (ii) below.		
	(i) Total shares of restricted stock ▶		
	(ii) Total shares of non-restricted stock ▶		
b	At the end of the tax year, did the corporation have any outstanding stock options, warrants, or similar instruments?		X
	If "Yes," complete lines (i) and (ii) below.		
	(i) Total shares of stock outstanding at the end of the tax year ▶		
	(ii) Total shares of stock outstanding if all instruments were executed ▶		
6	Has this corporation filed, or is it required to file, **Form 8918,** Material Advisor Disclosure Statement, to provide information on any reportable transaction?		X
7	Check this box if the corporation issued publicly offered debt instruments with original issue discount ▶ ☐ If checked, the corporation may have to file **Form 8281,** Information Return for Publicly Offered Original Issue Discount Instruments.		
8	If the corporation: **(a)** was a C corporation before it elected to be an S corporation **or** the corporation acquired an asset with a basis determined by reference to the basis of the asset (or the basis of any other property) in the hands of a C corporation **and (b)** has net unrealized built-in gain in excess of the net recognized built-in gain from prior years, enter the net unrealized built-in gain reduced by net recognized built-in gain from prior years (see instructions) ▶ $ N/A		
9	Enter the accumulated earnings and profits of the corporation at the end of the tax year. $ -0-		
10	Does the corporation satisfy **both** of the following conditions?		
a	The corporation's total receipts (see instructions) for the tax year were less than $250,000		
b	The corporation's total assets at the end of the tax year were less than $250,000		X
	If "Yes," the corporation is not required to complete Schedules L and M-1.		
11	During the tax year, did the corporation have any non-shareholder debt that was canceled, was forgiven, or had the terms modified so as to reduce the principal amount of the debt?		X
	If "Yes," enter the amount of principal reduction $		
12	During the tax year, was a qualified subchapter S subsidiary election terminated or revoked? If "Yes," see instructions		X
13a	Did the corporation make any payments in 2016 that would require it to file Form(s) 1099?		X
b	If "Yes," did the corporation file or will it file required Forms 1099?		

Form 1120S (2016) Page 3

Schedule K — Shareholders' Pro Rata Share Items

Section	Line	Description			Line	Total amount	
Income (Loss)	1	Ordinary business income (loss) (page 1, line 21)			1	73,686	
	2	Net rental real estate income (loss) (attach Form 8825)			2		
	3a	Other gross rental income (loss)	3a				
	b	Expenses from other rental activities (attach statement)	3b				
	c	Other net rental income (loss). Subtract line 3b from line 3a			3c		
	4	Interest income			4		
	5	Dividends: **a** Ordinary dividends			5a	1,000	
		b Qualified dividends	5b	1,000			
	6	Royalties			6		
	7	Net short-term capital gain (loss) (attach Schedule D (Form 1120S))			7	(2100)	
	8a	Net long-term capital gain (loss) (attach Schedule D (Form 1120S))			8a	4,500	
	b	Collectibles (28%) gain (loss)	8b				
	c	Unrecaptured section 1250 gain (attach statement)	8c				
	9	Net section 1231 gain (loss) (attach Form 4797)			9		
	10	Other income (loss) (see instructions) Type ▶			10		
Deductions	11	Section 179 deduction (attach Form 4562)			11		
	12a	Charitable contributions			12a	12,000	
	b	Investment interest expense			12b	150	
	c	Section 59(e)(2) expenditures **(1)** Type ▶ **(2)** Amount ▶			12c(2)		
	d	Other deductions (see instructions) Type ▶			12d		
Credits	13a	Low-income housing credit (section 42(j)(5))			13a		
	b	Low-income housing credit (other)			13b		
	c	Qualified rehabilitation expenditures (rental real estate) (attach Form 3468, if applicable)			13c		
	d	Other rental real estate credits (see instructions) Type ▶			13d		
	e	Other rental credits (see instructions) Type ▶			13e		
	f	Biofuel producer credit (attach Form 6478)			13f		
	g	Other credits (see instructions) Type ▶			13g		
Foreign Transactions	14a	Name of country or U.S. possession ▶					
	b	Gross income from all sources			14b		
	c	Gross income sourced at shareholder level			14c		
		Foreign gross income sourced at corporate level					
	d	Passive category			14d		
	e	General category			14e		
	f	Other (attach statement)			14f		
		Deductions allocated and apportioned at shareholder level					
	g	Interest expense			14g		
	h	Other			14h		
		Deductions allocated and apportioned at corporate level to foreign source income					
	i	Passive category			14i		
	j	General category			14j		
	k	Other (attach statement)			14k		
		Other information					
	l	Total foreign taxes (check one): ▶ ☐ Paid ☐ Accrued			14l		
	m	Reduction in taxes available for credit (attach statement)			14m		
	n	Other foreign tax information (attach statement)					
Alternative Minimum Tax (AMT) Items	15a	Post-1986 depreciation adjustment			15a	1,514	
	b	Adjusted gain or loss			15b		
	c	Depletion (other than oil and gas)			15c		
	d	Oil, gas, and geothermal properties—gross income			15d		
	e	Oil, gas, and geothermal properties—deductions			15e		
	f	Other AMT items (attach statement)			15f		
Items Affecting Shareholder Basis	16a	Tax-exempt interest income			16a	18,000	
	b	Other tax-exempt income			16b		
	c	Nondeductible expenses			16c	6,000	*
	d	Distributions (attach statement if required) (see instructions)			16d	28,212	
	e	Repayment of loans from shareholders			16e		

Form **1120S** (2016)

*Disallowed meals and entertainment expenses ($4,000) plus interest on loan to purchase tax-exempt bonds ($2,000).

Form 1120S (2016) Page 4

Schedule K — Shareholders' Pro Rata Share Items (continued)

				Total amount	
Other Information	17a	Investment income	17a	1,000	*
	b	Investment expenses	17b		
	c	Dividend distributions paid from accumulated earnings and profits	17c		
	d	Other items and amounts (attach statement)			
Reconciliation	18	**Income/loss reconciliation.** Combine the amounts on lines 1 through 10 in the far right column. From the result, subtract the sum of the amounts on lines 11 through 12d and 14l	18		

Schedule L — Balance Sheets per Books

	Assets	Beginning of tax year (a)	(b)	End of tax year (c)	(d)
1	Cash		60,000		86,600
2a	Trade notes and accounts receivable	25,000		24,000	
b	Less allowance for bad debts	(1,000)	24,000	(1,000)	23,000
3	Inventories		64,000		104,800
4	U.S. government obligations				
5	Tax-exempt securities (see instructions)		200,000		200,000
6	Other current assets (attach statement)		7,000		
7	Loans to shareholders				
8	Mortgage and real estate loans				
9	Other investments (attach statement)				
10a	Buildings and other depreciable assets	151,600		151,600	
b	Less accumulated depreciation	(45,200)	106,400	(72,676)	78,924
11a	Depletable assets				
b	Less accumulated depletion	( )		( )	
12	Land (net of any amortization)				
13a	Intangible assets (amortizable only)				
b	Less accumulated amortization	( )		( )	
14	Other assets (attach statement)				
15	Total assets		461,400		493,324
	Liabilities and Shareholders' Equity				
16	Accounts payable		26,000		19,000
17	Mortgages, notes, bonds payable in less than 1 year		4,000		4,000
18	Other current liabilities (attach statement)		3,600		3,600
19	Loans from shareholders				
20	Mortgages, notes, bonds payable in 1 year or more		130,000		119,724
21	Other liabilities (attach statement)				
22	Capital stock		200,000		200,000
23	Additional paid-in capital				
24	Retained earnings		97,800		147,000
25	Adjustments to shareholders' equity (attach statement)				
26	Less cost of treasury stock		( )		( )
27	Total liabilities and shareholders' equity		461,400		493,324

Form **1120S** (2016)

*Investment income only if shareholders elect to tax dividends at ordinary rates under Sec. 163(d)(4)(B).

Form 1120S (2016) Page **5**

Schedule M-1 **Reconciliation of Income (Loss) per Books With Income (Loss) per Return**
Note: The corporation may be required to file Schedule M-3 (see instructions)

1	Net income (loss) per books	77,412	5	Income recorded on books this year not included on Schedule K, lines 1 through 10 (itemize): a Tax-exempt interest $ 18,000	18,000
2	Income included on Schedule K, lines 1, 2, 3c, 4, 5a, 6, 7, 8a, 9, and 10, not recorded on books this year (itemize)				
3	Expenses recorded on books this year not included on Schedule K, lines 1 through 12 and 14l (itemize): a Depreciation $ b Travel and entertainment $ 4,000 Interest on loans* $2,000	6,000	6	Deductions included on Schedule K, lines 1 through 12 and 14l, not charged against book income this year (itemize): a Depreciation $ 476	476
			7	Add lines 5 and 6	18,476
4	Add lines 1 through 3	83,412	8	Income (loss) (Schedule K, line 18). Line 4 less line 7	64,936

Schedule M-2 **Analysis of Accumulated Adjustments Account, Other Adjustments Account, and Shareholders' Undistributed Taxable Income Previously Taxed** (see instructions)

		(a) Accumulated adjustments account	**(b)** Other adjustments account	**(c)** Shareholders' undistributed taxable income previously taxed
1	Balance at beginning of tax year	86,100	11,700	
2	Ordinary income from page 1, line 21	73,686		
3	Other additions	5,500**	18,000	
4	Loss from page 1, line 21	( )		
5	Other reductions	(18,250***)	(2,000)	
6	Combine lines 1 through 5	147,036	27,700	
7	Distributions other than dividend distributions	28,212		
8	Balance at end of tax year. Subtract line 7 from line 6	118,824	27,700	

Form **1120S** (2016)

*For municipal bonds
**$1,000 + $4,500 = $5,500
***$12,000 + $4,000 + $150 +$2,100 = $18,250

671113

☐ Final K-1 ☐ Amended K-1 OMB No. 1545-0123

Schedule K-1 (Form 1120S) **2016**
Department of the Treasury
Internal Revenue Service

For calendar year 2016, or tax year beginning ________, 2016 ending ________, 20 ____

Shareholder's Share of Income, Deductions, Credits, etc.

► See back of form and separate instructions.

Part I Information About the Corporation

A Corporation's employer identification number
XX-XXXXXXX

B Corporation's name, address, city, state, and ZIP code
Johns and Lawrence, Inc.
1234 First Avenue
City, ST 55555

C IRS Center where corporation filed return
Center, ST

Part II Information About the Shareholder

D Shareholder's identifying number
XXX-XX-XXXX

E Shareholder's name, address, city, state, and ZIP code
Andrew Lawrence*
333 Third Street
City, ST 55555

F Shareholder's percentage of stock ownership for tax year . . . . 50% %

For IRS Use Only

Part III Shareholder's Share of Current Year Income, Deductions, Credits, and Other Items

Line	Item	Amount
1	Ordinary business income (loss)	36,843
2	Net rental real estate income (loss)	
3	Other net rental income (loss)	
4	Interest income	
5a	Ordinary dividends	500
5b	Qualified dividends	500
6	Royalties	
7	Net short-term capital gain (loss)	(1,050)
8a	Net long-term capital gain (loss)	2,250
8b	Collectibles (28%) gain (loss)	
8c	Unrecaptured section 1250 gain	
9	Net section 1231 gain (loss)	
10	Other income (loss)	
11	Section 179 deduction	
12	Other deductions	
A		6,000
G		75
Q		40,000
R		44,000
13	Credits	
14	Foreign transactions	
15	Alternative minimum tax (AMT) items	
A		757
16	Items affecting shareholder basis	
A		9,000
C		3,000
D		14,106
17	Other information	
A		500 **

* See attached statement for additional information.

For Paperwork Reduction Act Notice, see Instructions for Form 1120S. IRS.gov/form1120s Cat. No. 11520D **Schedule K-1 (Form 1120S) 2016**

*Schedule K-1 for Stephen Johns is similar to this one and is not reproduced here.

**Investment income only if shareholder elects to tax dividends at ordinary rates under Sec. 163(d)(4)(B).

Schedule K-1 (Form 1120S) 2016 Page 2

This list identifies the codes used on Schedule K-1 for all shareholders and provides summarized reporting information for shareholders who file Form 1040. For detailed reporting and filing information, see the separate Shareholder's Instructions for Schedule K-1 and the instructions for your income tax return.

1. Ordinary business income (loss). Determine whether the income (loss) is passive or nonpassive and enter on your return as follows:

	Report on
Passive loss	See the Shareholder's Instructions
Passive income	Schedule E, line 28, column (g)
Nonpassive loss	Schedule E, line 28, column (h)
Nonpassive income	Schedule E, line 28, column (j)
2. Net rental real estate income (loss)	See the Shareholder's Instructions
3. Other net rental income (loss)	
Net income	Schedule E, line 28, column (g)
Net loss	See the Shareholder's Instructions
4. Interest income	Form 1040, line 8a
5a. Ordinary dividends	Form 1040, line 9a
5b. Qualified dividends	Form 1040, line 9b
6. Royalties	Schedule E, line 4
7. Net short-term capital gain (loss)	Schedule D, line 5
8a. Net long-term capital gain (loss)	Schedule D, line 12
8b. Collectibles (28%) gain (loss)	28% Rate Gain Worksheet, line 4 (Schedule D instructions)
8c. Unrecaptured section 1250 gain	See the Shareholder's Instructions
9. Net section 1231 gain (loss)	See the Shareholder's Instructions

10. Other income (loss)

Code		
A	Other portfolio income (loss)	See the Shareholder's Instructions
B	Involuntary conversions	See the Shareholder's Instructions
C	Sec. 1256 contracts & straddles	Form 6781, line 1
D	Mining exploration costs recapture	See Pub. 535
E	Other income (loss)	See the Shareholder's Instructions

11. Section 179 deduction — See the Shareholder's Instructions

12. Other deductions

A	Cash contributions (50%)	See the Shareholder's Instructions
B	Cash contributions (30%)	See the Shareholder's Instructions
C	Noncash contributions (50%)	See the Shareholder's Instructions
D	Noncash contributions (30%)	See the Shareholder's Instructions
E	Capital gain property to a 50% organization (30%)	See the Shareholder's Instructions
F	Capital gain property (20%)	See the Shareholder's Instructions
G	Contributions (100%)	See the Shareholder's Instructions
H	Investment interest expense	Form 4952, line 1
I	Deductions—royalty income	Schedule E, line 19
J	Section 59(e)(2) expenditures	See the Shareholder's Instructions
K	Deductions—portfolio (2% floor)	Schedule A, line 23
L	Deductions—portfolio (other)	Schedule A, line 28
M	Preproductive period expenses	See the Shareholder's Instructions
N	Commercial revitalization deduction from rental real estate activities	See Form 8582 instructions
O	Reforestation expense deduction	See the Shareholder's Instructions
P	Domestic production activities information	See Form 8903 instructions
Q	Qualified production activities income	Form 8903, line 7b
R	Employer's Form W-2 wages	Form 8903, line 17
S	Other deductions	See the Shareholder's Instructions

13. Credits

A	Low-income housing credit (section 42(j)(5)) from pre-2008 buildings	See the Shareholder's Instructions
B	Low-income housing credit (other) from pre-2008 buildings	See the Shareholder's Instructions
C	Low-income housing credit (section 42(j)(5)) from post-2007 buildings	See the Shareholder's Instructions
D	Low-income housing credit (other) from post-2007 buildings	See the Shareholder's Instructions
E	Qualified rehabilitation expenditures (rental real estate)	See the Shareholder's Instructions
F	Other rental real estate credits	See the Shareholder's Instructions
G	Other rental credits	See the Shareholder's Instructions
H	Undistributed capital gains credit	Form 1040, line 73, box a
I	Biofuel producer credit	See the Shareholder's Instructions
J	Work opportunity credit	See the Shareholder's Instructions
K	Disabled access credit	See the Shareholder's Instructions
L	Empowerment zone employment credit	See the Shareholder's Instructions
M	Credit for increasing research activities	See the Shareholder's Instructions
N	Credit for employer social security and Medicare taxes	See the Shareholder's Instructions
O	Backup withholding	See the Shareholder's Instructions
P	Other credits	See the Shareholder's Instructions

14. Foreign transactions

Code		*Report on*
A	Name of country or U.S. possession	Form 1116, Part I
B	Gross income from all sources	Form 1116, Part I
C	Gross income sourced at shareholder level	Form 1116, Part I
	Foreign gross income sourced at corporate level	
D	Passive category	Form 1116, Part I
E	General category	Form 1116, Part I
F	Other	Form 1116, Part I
	Deductions allocated and apportioned at shareholder level	
G	Interest expense	Form 1116, Part I
H	Other	Form 1116, Part I
	Deductions allocated and apportioned at corporate level to foreign source income	
I	Passive category	Form 1116, Part I
J	General category	Form 1116, Part I
K	Other	Form 1116, Part I
	Other information	
L	Total foreign taxes paid	Form 1116, Part II
M	Total foreign taxes accrued	Form 1116, Part II
N	Reduction in taxes available for credit	Form 1116, line 12
O	Foreign trading gross receipts	Form 8873
P	Extraterritorial income exclusion	Form 8873
Q	Other foreign transactions	See the Shareholder's Instructions

15. Alternative minimum tax (AMT) items

A	Post-1986 depreciation adjustment	See the Shareholder's Instructions and the Instructions for Form 6251
B	Adjusted gain or loss	See the Shareholder's Instructions and the Instructions for Form 6251
C	Depletion (other than oil & gas)	See the Shareholder's Instructions and the Instructions for Form 6251
D	Oil, gas, & geothermal—gross income	See the Shareholder's Instructions and the Instructions for Form 6251
E	Oil, gas, & geothermal—deductions	See the Shareholder's Instructions and the Instructions for Form 6251
F	Other AMT items	See the Shareholder's Instructions and the Instructions for Form 6251

16. Items affecting shareholder basis

A	Tax-exempt interest income	Form 1040, line 8b
B	Other tax-exempt income	See the Shareholder's Instructions
C	Nondeductible expenses	See the Shareholder's Instructions
D	Distributions	See the Shareholder's Instructions
E	Repayment of loans from shareholders	See the Shareholder's Instructions

17. Other information

A	Investment income	Form 4952, line 4a
B	Investment expenses	Form 4952, line 5
C	Qualified rehabilitation expenditures (other than rental real estate)	See the Shareholder's Instructions
D	Basis of energy property	See the Shareholder's Instructions
E	Recapture of low-income housing credit (section 42(j)(5))	Form 8611, line 8
F	Recapture of low-income housing credit (other)	Form 8611, line 8
G	Recapture of investment credit	See Form 4255
H	Recapture of other credits	See the Shareholder's Instructions
I	Look-back interest—completed long-term contracts	See Form 8697
J	Look-back interest—income forecast method	See Form 8866
K	Dispositions of property with section 179 deductions	See the Shareholder's Instructions
L	Recapture of section 179 deduction	See the Shareholder's Instructions
M	Section 453(l)(3) information	See the Shareholder's Instructions
N	Section 453A(c) information	See the Shareholder's Instructions
O	Section 1260(b) information	See the Shareholder's Instructions
P	Interest allocable to production expenditures	See the Shareholder's Instructions
Q	CCF nonqualified withdrawals	See the Shareholder's Instructions
R	Depletion information—oil and gas	See the Shareholder's Instructions
S	Reserved	See the Shareholder's Instructions
T	Section 108(i) information	See the Shareholder's Instructions
U	Net investment income	See the Shareholder's Instructions
V	Other information	See the Shareholder's Instructions

Form **1125-A** (Rev. December 2012) Department of the Treasury Internal Revenue Service

Cost of Goods Sold

▶ Attach to Form 1120, 1120-C, 1120-F, 1120S, 1065, or 1065-B.
▶ Information about Form 1125-A and its instructions is at *www.irs.gov/form1125a*.

OMB No. 1545-2225

Name	Employer identification number
Johns and Lawrence, Inc.	XX-XXXXXXX

1	Inventory at beginning of year	1	64,000
2	Purchases	2	340,800
3	Cost of labor	3	143,204
4	Additional section 263A costs (attach schedule)	4	7,000
5	Other costs (attach schedule)	5	90,000
6	**Total.** Add lines 1 through 5	6	645,004
7	Inventory at end of year	7	104,800
8	**Cost of goods sold.** Subtract line 7 from line 6. Enter here and on Form 1120, page 1, line 2 or the appropriate line of your tax return (see instructions)	8	540,204

9a Check all methods used for valuing closing inventory:

(i) ☒ Cost

(ii) ☐ Lower of cost or market

(iii) ☐ Other (Specify method used and attach explanation.) ▶

b Check if there was a writedown of subnormal goods ▶ ☐

c Check if the LIFO inventory method was adopted this tax year for any goods (if checked, attach Form 970) ▶ ☐

d If the LIFO inventory method was used for this tax year, enter amount of closing inventory computed under LIFO **9d**

e If property is produced or acquired for resale, do the rules of section 263A apply to the entity (see instructions)? ☐ Yes ☒ No

f Was there any change in determining quantities, cost, or valuations between opening and closing inventory? If "Yes," attach explanation ☐ Yes ☒ No

Section references are to the Internal Revenue Code unless otherwise noted.

General Instructions

Purpose of Form

Use Form 1125-A to calculate and deduct cost of goods sold for certain entities.

Who Must File

Filers of Form 1120, 1120-C, 1120-F, 1120S, 1065, or 1065-B, must complete and attach Form 1125-A if the applicable entity reports a deduction for cost of goods sold.

Inventories

Generally, inventories are required at the beginning and end of each tax year if the production, purchase, or sale of merchandise is an income-producing factor. See Regulations section 1.471-1. If inventories are required, you generally must use an accrual method of accounting for sales and purchases of inventory items.

Exception for certain taxpayers. If you are a qualifying taxpayer or a qualifying small business taxpayer (defined below), you can adopt or change your accounting method to account for inventoriable items in the same manner as materials and supplies that are not incidental.

Under this accounting method, inventory costs for raw materials purchased for use in producing finished goods and merchandise purchased for resale are deductible in the year the finished goods or merchandise are sold (but not before the year you paid for the raw materials or merchandise, if you are also using the cash method).

If you account for inventoriable items in the same manner as materials and supplies that are not incidental, you can currently deduct expenditures for direct labor and all indirect costs that would otherwise be included in inventory costs. See the instructions for lines 2 and 7.

For additional guidance on this method of accounting, see Pub. 538, Accounting Periods and Methods. For guidance on adopting or changing to this method of accounting, see Form 3115, Application for Change in Accounting Method, and its instructions.

Qualifying taxpayer. A qualifying taxpayer is a taxpayer that, (a) for each prior tax year ending after December 16, 1998, has average annual gross receipts of $1 million or less for the 3 prior tax years and (b) its business is not a tax shelter (as defined in section 448(d)(3)). See Rev. Proc. 2001-10, 2001-2 I.R.B. 272.

Qualifying small business taxpayer. A qualifying small business taxpayer is a taxpayer that, (a) for each prior tax year ending on or after December 31, 2000, has average annual gross receipts of $10 million or less for the 3 prior tax years, (b) whose principal business activity is not an ineligible activity, and (c) whose business is not a tax shelter (as defined in section 448 (d)(3)). See Rev. Proc. 2002-28, 2002-18 I.R.B. 815.

Uniform capitalization rules. The uniform capitalization rules of section 263A generally require you to capitalize, or include in inventory, certain costs incurred in connection with the following.

- The production of real property and tangible personal property held in inventory or held for sale in the ordinary course of business.
- Real property or personal property (tangible and intangible) acquired for resale.
- The production of real property and tangible personal property by a corporation for use in its trade or business or in an activity engaged in for profit.

See the discussion on section 263A uniform capitalization rules in the instructions for your tax return before completing Form 1125-A. Also see Regulations sections 1.263A-1 through 1.263A-3. See Regulations section 1.263A-4 for rules for property produced in a farming business.

Johns and Lawrence, Inc. (S Corporation) Reconciliation of Book and Taxable Income for Year Ending December 31, 2016

	Book Income		Adjustments		Taxable Income		Form 1120S Schedule K	
Account Name	Debit	Credit	Debit	Credit	Debit	Credit	Ordinary Income	Separately Stated Items
Sales		$869,658				$869,658	$869,658	
Sales returns & allowances	$ 29,242				$ 29,242		(29,242)	
Cost of sales	540,204				540,204		(540,204)	
Dividends		1,000				1,000		1,000
Tax-exempt interest		18,000	$18,000			0		$18,000
Gain on stock sale		4,500				4,500		4,500
Worthless stock loss	2,100				2,100			(2,100)
Officers salaries[(a)]	36,000				36,000		(36,000)	
Other salaries	52,000				52,000		(52,000)	
Rentals	36,000				36,000		(36,000)	
Bad debts	4,000				4,000		(4,000)	
Interest:								
Working capital loans	8,000				8,000		(8,000)	
Purchase tax-exempt bonds	2,000			$ 2,000	0			(2,000)
Employment taxes	14,480				14,480		(14,480)	
Taxes	1,520				1,520		(1,520)	
Repairs	4,800				4,800		(4,800)	
Depreciation[(b)]	12,000		476		12,476		(12,476)	
Charitable contributions	12,000				12,000			(12,000)
Travel	4,000				4,000		(4,000)	
Meals and entertainment[(c)]	8,000			4,000	4,000		(4,000)	
Meals and ent. nondeductible								(4,000)
Office expenses	16,000				16,000		(16,000)	
Advertising	13,000				13,000		(13,000)	
Transportation expense	10,400				10,400		(10,400)	
General and administrative	3,000				3,000		(3,000)	
Pension plans[(d)]	2,000				2,000		(2,000)	
Employee benefit programs[(e)]	4,000				4,000		(4,000)	
Miscellaneous	1,000				1,000		(850)	(150)
Net profit/Taxable income	77,412			12,476	64,936			
Total	$893,158	$893,158	$18,476	$18,476	$875,158	$875,158	$ 73,686	

[(a)] Salaries for the S corporation's shareholder-employees are deductible by the S corporation and are subject to the same employee taxes imposed on nonshareholder-employees.

[(b)] MACRS depreciation = $27,476 total − $15,000 allocated to COGS = $12,476

[(c)] 50% of the meals and entertainment expense is not deductible for tax purposes but must be separately stated on the Schedules K and K-1.

[(d)] The pension plan expense is the same for book and tax purposes for this corporation. No pension expenses relate to pensions for the shareholder-employees.

[(e)] The employee benefit expense is the same for book and tax purposes for this corporation. None relates to shareholder-employee benefits.

Form **709**

Department of the Treasury
Internal Revenue Service

United States Gift (and Generation-Skipping Transfer) Tax Return

▶ Information about Form 709 and its separate instructions is at *www.irs.gov/form709*.

(For gifts made during calendar year 2016)

▶ See instructions.

OMB No. 1545-0020

2016

Part 1—General Information

1 Donor's first name and middle initial	2 Donor's last name	3 Donor's social security number
Wilma	Brown	XXX-XX-XXXX
4 Address (number, street, and apartment number)		5 Legal residence (domicile)
2 Main Street		State
6 City or town, state or province, country, and ZIP or foreign postal code		7 Citizenship (see instructions)
City, ST 22222		U.S.A.

Line	Item	Yes	No
8	If the donor died during the year, check here ▶ ☐ and enter date of death ____ , ____ .		
9	If you extended the time to file this Form 709, check here ▶ ☐		
10	Enter the total number of donees listed on Schedule A. Count each person only once. ▶ 6		
11a	Have you (the donor) previously filed a Form 709 (or 709-A) for any other year? If "No," skip line 11b	X	
b	Has your address changed since you last filed Form 709 (or 709-A)?		X
12	**Gifts by husband or wife to third parties.** Do you consent to have the gifts (including generation-skipping transfers) made by you and by your spouse to third parties during the calendar year considered as made one-half by each of you? (see instructions.) (If the answer is "Yes," the following information must be furnished and your spouse must sign the consent shown below. **If the answer is "No," skip lines 13–18.**)	X	
13	Name of consenting spouse Hugh Brown — 14 SSN XXX-XX-XXXX		
15	Were you married to one another during the entire calendar year? (see instructions)	X	
16	If 15 is "No," check whether ☐ married ☐ divorced or ☐ widowed/deceased, and give date (see instructions) ▶		
17	Will a gift tax return for this year be filed by your spouse? (If "Yes," mail both returns in the same envelope.)	X	

18 **Consent of Spouse.** I consent to have the gifts (and generation-skipping transfers) made by me and by my spouse to third parties during the calendar year considered as made one-half by each of us. We are both aware of the joint and several liability for tax created by the execution of this consent.

Consenting spouse's signature ▶ *Hugh Brown* **Date** ▶ 3-2-2017

Line	Item	Yes	No
19	Have you applied a DSUE amount received from a predeceased spouse to a gift or gifts reported on this or a previous Form 709? If "Yes," complete Schedule C		

Part 2—Tax Computation

Line	Item	Line	Amount
1	Enter the amount from Schedule A, Part 4, line 11	1	350,155
2	Enter the amount from Schedule B, line 3	2	500,000
3	Total taxable gifts. Add lines 1 and 2	3	850,155
4	Tax computed on amount on line 3 (see *Table for Computing Gift Tax* in instructions)	4	287,360
5	Tax computed on amount on line 2 (see *Table for Computing Gift Tax* in instructions)	5	155,800
6	Balance. Subtract line 5 from line 4	6	131,560
7	Applicable credit amount. If donor has DSUE amount from predeceased spouse(s), enter amount from Schedule C, line 4; otherwise, see instructions	7	2,125,800
8	Enter the applicable credit against tax allowable for all prior periods (from Sch. B, line 1, col. C)	8	68,000
9	Balance. Subtract line 8 from line 7. Do not enter less than zero	9	2,057,800
10	Enter 20% (.20) of the amount allowed as a specific exemption for gifts made after September 8, 1976, and before January 1, 1977 (see instructions)	10	
11	Balance. Subtract line 10 from line 9. Do not enter less than zero	11	2,057,800
12	Applicable credit. Enter the smaller of line 6 or line 11	12	131,560
13	Credit for foreign gift taxes (see instructions)	13	-0-
14	Total credits. Add lines 12 and 13	14	131,560
15	Balance. Subtract line 14 from line 6. Do not enter less than zero	15	-0-
16	Generation-skipping transfer taxes (from Schedule D, Part 3, col. H, Total)	16	-0-
17	Total tax. Add lines 15 and 16	17	-0-
18	Gift and generation-skipping transfer taxes prepaid with extension of time to file	18	
19	If line 18 is less than line 17, enter **balance due** (see instructions)	19	-0-
20	If line 18 is greater than line 17, enter **amount to be refunded**	20	

Attach check or money order here.

Sign Here

Under penalties of perjury, I declare that I have examined this return, including any accompanying schedules and statements, and to the best of my knowledge and belief, it is true, correct, and complete. Declaration of preparer (other than donor) is based on all information of which preparer has any knowledge.

May the IRS discuss this return with the preparer shown below (see instructions)? ☒ Yes ☐ No

▶ *Wilma Brown* — Signature of donor | 3-2-2017 — Date

Paid Preparer Use Only

Print/Type preparer's name	Preparer's signature	Date	Check ☒ if self-employed	PTIN
Sally Preparer	*Sally Preparer*	3-1-2017		
Firm's name ▶ Sally Preparer			Firm's EIN ▶	
Firm's address ▶ 110 Last Bank Tower, City, ST 22222			Phone no.	

For Disclosure, Privacy Act, and Paperwork Reduction Act Notice, see the instructions for this form. Cat. No. 16783M Form **709** (2016)

Note: Pages 4 and 5, which are not pertinent to the tax consequences, are omitted because the donor made no generation–skipping transfers and had no deceased spousal unused exclusion amount. See the Comprehensive Illustration on text page C:12-25 for tax form facts.

Form 709 (2016) Page **2**

SCHEDULE A Computation of Taxable Gifts (Including transfers in trust) (see instructions)

A Does the value of any item listed on Schedule A reflect any valuation discount? If "Yes," attach explanation . . . . Yes ☐ No ☒

B ☐ ◀ Check here if you elect under section 529(c)(2)(B) to treat any transfers made this year to a qualified tuition program as made ratably over a 5-year period beginning this year. See instructions. Attach explanation.

Part 1—Gifts Subject Only to Gift Tax. Gifts less political organization, medical, and educational exclusions. (see instructions)

A Item number	B • Donee's name and address • Relationship to donor (if any) • Description of gift • If the gift was of securities, give CUSIP no. • If closely held entity, give EIN	C	D Donor's adjusted basis of gift	E Date of gift	F Value at date of gift	G For split gifts, enter 1/2 of column F	H Net transfer (subtract col. G from col. F)
1-4	} Schedule attached		593,000	2016	756,310	78,155	678,155
Gifts made by spouse —*complete **only** if you are splitting gifts with your spouse and he/she also made gifts.*							
5	State University, stock		32,000	2016	100,000	50,000	50,000
6	Betsy Brown, daughter, land		112,000	2016	600,000	300,000	300,000

Total of Part 1. Add amounts from Part 1, column H . . . . ▶ 1,028,155

Part 2—Direct Skips. Gifts that are direct skips and are subject to both gift tax and generation-skipping transfer tax. You must list the gifts in chronological order.

A Item number	B • Donee's name and address • Relationship to donor (if any) • Description of gift • If the gift was of securities, give CUSIP no. • If closely held entity, give EIN	C 2632(b) election out	D Donor's adjusted basis of gift	E Date of gift	F Value at date of gift	G For split gifts, enter 1/2 of column F	H Net transfer (subtract col. G from col. F)
Gifts made by spouse —*complete **only** if you are splitting gifts with your spouse and he/she also made gifts.*							

Total of Part 2. Add amounts from Part 2, column H . . . . ▶

Part 3—Indirect Skips. Gifts to trusts that are currently subject to gift tax and may later be subject to generation-skipping transfer tax. You must list these gifts in chronological order.

A Item number	B • Donee's name and address • Relationship to donor (if any) • Description of gift • If the gift was of securities, give CUSIP no. • If closely held entity, give EIN	C 2632(c) election	D Donor's adjusted basis of gift	E Date of gift	F Value at date of gift	G For split gifts, enter 1/2 of column F	H Net transfer (subtract col. G from col. F)
Gifts made by spouse —*complete **only** if you are splitting gifts with your spouse and he/she also made gifts.*							

Total of Part 3. Add amounts from Part 3, column H . . . . ▶

(If more space is needed, attach additional statements.)

Form **709** (2016)

Form 709 (2016) Page **3**

Part 4—Taxable Gift Reconciliation

1	Total value of gifts of donor. Add totals from column H of Parts 1, 2, and 3			1	1,028,155
2	Total annual exclusions for gifts listed on line 1 (see instructions)			2	56,000 *
3	Total included amount of gifts. Subtract line 2 from line 1			3	972,155
Deductions (see instructions)					
4	Gifts of interests to spouse for which a marital deduction will be claimed, based on item numbers 4 of Schedule A	4	600,000		
5	Exclusions attributable to gifts on line 4	5	14,000		
6	Marital deduction. Subtract line 5 from line 4	6	586,000		
7	Charitable deduction, based on item nos. 5 less exclusions	7	36,000		
8	Total deductions. Add lines 6 and 7			8	622,000
9	Subtract line 8 from line 3			9	350,155
10	Generation-skipping transfer taxes payable with this Form 709 (from Schedule D, Part 3, col. H, Total)			10	
11	**Taxable gifts.** Add lines 9 and 10. Enter here and on page 1, Part 2—Tax Computation, line 1			11	350,155

Terminable Interest (QTIP) Marital Deduction. (see instructions for Schedule A, Part 4, line 4)

If a trust (or other property) meets the requirements of qualified terminable interest property under section 2523(f), and:

a. The trust (or other property) is listed on Schedule A, and

b. The value of the trust (or other property) is entered in whole or in part as a deduction on Schedule A, Part 4, line 4, then the donor shall be deemed to have made an election to have such trust (or other property) treated as qualified terminable interest property under section 2523(f).

If less than the entire value of the trust (or other property) that the donor has included in Parts 1 and 3 of Schedule A is entered as a deduction on line 4, the donor shall be considered to have made an election only as to a fraction of the trust (or other property). The numerator of this fraction is equal to the amount of the trust (or other property) deducted on Schedule A, Part 4, line 6. The denominator is equal to the total value of the trust (or other property) listed in Parts 1 and 3 of Schedule A.

If you make the QTIP election, the terminable interest property involved will be included in your spouse's gross estate upon his or her death (section 2044). See instructions for line 4 of Schedule A. If your spouse disposes (by gift or otherwise) of all or part of the qualifying life income interest, he or she will be considered to have made a transfer of the entire property that is subject to the gift tax. See *Transfer of Certain Life Estates Received From Spouse* in the instructions.

12 Election Out of QTIP Treatment of Annuities

☐ ◀ Check here if you elect under section 2523(f)(6) **not** to treat as qualified terminable interest property any joint and survivor annuities that are reported on Schedule A and would otherwise be treated as qualified terminable interest property under section 2523(f). See instructions. Enter the item numbers from Schedule A for the annuities for which you are making this election ▶ ______

SCHEDULE B **Gifts From Prior Periods**

If you answered "Yes," on line 11a of page 1, Part 1, see the instructions for completing Schedule B. If you answered "No," skip to the Tax Computation on page 1 (or Schedules C or D, if applicable). Complete Schedule A before beginning Schedule B. See instructions for recalculation of the column C amounts. Attach calculations.

A Calendar year or calendar quarter (see instructions)	B Internal Revenue office where prior return was filed	C Amount of applicable credit (unified credit) against gift tax for periods after December 31, 1976	D Amount of specific exemption for prior periods ending before January 1, 1977	E Amount of taxable gifts
1975	Atlanta, GA	-0-		300,000
1988	Atlanta, GA	68,000		200,000
1 Totals for prior periods	1	68,000		500,000

2	Amount, if any, by which total specific exemption, line 1, column D is more than $30,000	2	
3	Total amount of taxable gifts for prior periods. Add amount on line 1, column E and amount, if any, on line 2. Enter here and on page 1, Part 2—Tax Computation, line 2	3	500,000

(If more space is needed, attach additional statements.) Form **709** (2016)

*$14,000 each for Billy, Betsy, State University, and Hugh.

Form 709 (2016), Schedule A, Part 1

A	*B*	*C*	*D*	*E*	*F*	*G*	*H*
1	Billy Brown, son, cash		$ 80,000	2016	$ 80,000	$40,000	$ 40,000
2	Betsy Brown, daughter, jewelry		18,000	2016	30,000	15,000	15,000
3	Ruth Cain, friend, remainder interest in vacation cabin (0.46310 × 100,000)		15,000	2016	46,310	23,155	23,155
4	Trust at First Bank, income to Hugh Brown, spouse, for life. Remainder to Jeff Bass, brother, (QTIP trust)		480,000	2016	600,000	-0-	600,000
			$593,000		$756,310	$78,155	$678,155

Note: To save space, addresses are not shown here.

Form **706** (Rev. August 2013) Department of the Treasury Internal Revenue Service

United States Estate (and Generation-Skipping Transfer) Tax Return

▶ Estate of a citizen or resident of the United States (see instructions). To be filed for decedents dying after December 31, 2012.
▶ Information about Form 706 and its separate instructions is at www.irs.gov/form706.

OMB No. 1545-0015

Part 1—Decedent and Executor

1a Decedent's first name and middle initial (and maiden name, if any): Herman	1b Decedent's last name: Estes		2 Decedent's social security no.: XXX XX XXXX
3a City, town, or post office; county; state or province; country; and ZIP or foreign postal code.: County, FL 22222	3b Year domicile established: 1941	4 Date of birth: 1935	5 Date of death: 10-13-2016
6a Name of executor (see instructions): John Johnson	6b Executor's address (number and street including apartment or suite no.; city, town, or post office; state or province; country; and ZIP or foreign postal code) and phone no.: 10 Main Place City, FL 22222 Phone no.		
6c Executor's social security number (see instructions): 123 45 6789			

6d If there are multiple executors, check here ☐ and attach a list showing the names, addresses, telephone numbers, and SSNs of the additional executors.

7a Name and location of court where will was probated or estate administered | 7b Case number

8 If decedent died testate, check here ▶ ☒ and attach a certified copy of the will. | 9 If you extended the time to file this Form 706, check here ▶ ☐

10 If Schedule R-1 is attached, check here ▶ ☐ | 11 If you are estimating the value of assets included in the gross estate on line 1 pursuant to the special rule of Reg. section 20.2010-2T(a) (7)(ii), check here ▶ ☐

Part 2—Tax Computation

Line	Description			Line	Amount
1	Total gross estate less exclusion (from Part 5—Recapitulation, item 13)			1	5,966,450
2	Tentative total allowable deductions (from Part 5—Recapitulation, item 24)			2	1,196,700
3a	Tentative taxable estate (subtract line 2 from line 1)			3a	4,769,750
b	State death tax deduction			3b	
c	Taxable estate (subtract line 3b from line 3a)			3c	4,769,750
4	Adjusted taxable gifts (see instructions)			4	6,700,000
5	Add lines 3c and 4			5	11,469,750
6	Tentative tax on the amount on line 5 from Table A in the instructions			6	4,533,700
7	Total gift tax paid or payable (see instructions)			7	508,000
8	Gross estate tax (subtract line 7 from line 6)			8	4,025,700
9a	Basic exclusion amount	9a	5,450,000		
9b	Deceased spousal unused exclusion (DSUE) amount from predeceased spouse(s), if any (from Section D, Part 6—Portability of Deceased Spousal Unused Exclusion).	9b			
9c	Applicable exclusion amount (add lines 9a and 9b)	9c	5,450,000		
9d	Applicable credit amount (tentative tax on the amount in 9c from Table A in the instructions)	9d	2,125,800		
10	Adjustment to applicable credit amount (May not exceed $6,000. See instructions.)	10			
11	Allowable applicable credit amount (subtract line 10 from line 9d)			11	2,125,800
12	Subtract line 11 from line 8 (but do not enter less than zero)			12	1,899,900
13	Credit for foreign death taxes (from Schedule P). (Attach Form(s) 706-CE.)	13			
14	Credit for tax on prior transfers (from Schedule Q)	14			
15	Total credits (add lines 13 and 14)			15	
16	Net estate tax (subtract line 15 from line 12)			16	1,899,900
17	Generation-skipping transfer (GST) taxes payable (from Schedule R, Part 2, line 10)			17	
18	Total transfer taxes (add lines 16 and 17)			18	1,899,900
19	Prior payments (explain in an attached statement)			19	
20	Balance due (or overpayment) (subtract line 19 from line 18)			20	1,899,900

Under penalties of perjury, I declare that I have examined this return, including accompanying schedules and statements, and to the best of my knowledge and belief, it is true, correct, and complete. Declaration of preparer other than the executor is based on all information of which preparer has any knowledge.

Sign Here

▶ *John Johnson* Signature of executor ▶ 5-14-17 Date

▶ Signature of executor ▶ Date

Paid Preparer Use Only

Print/Type preparer's name	Preparer's signature	Date	Check ☒ if self-employed	PTIN
Mary Wilson, CPA	*Mary Wilson, CPA*	5-12-17		

Firm's name ▶ Mary Wilson, CPA | Firm's EIN ▶

Firm's address ▶ 15 Main Place, City, ST 22222 | Phone no.

For Privacy Act and Paperwork Reduction Act Notice, see instructions. Cat. No. 20548R Form **706** (Rev. 8-2013)

Note: Pages not pertinent to the tax consequences are omitted.
See the Comprehensive Illustration beginning on text page C:13-25 for tax form facts.

Form 706 (Rev. 8-2013)

Estate of: Herman Estes	Decedent's social security number XXX XX XXXX

Part 3—Elections by the Executor

Note. For information on electing portability of the decedent's DSUE amount, including how to opt out of the election, see Part 6—Portability of Deceased Spousal Unused Exclusion.
Note. Some of the following elections may require the posting of bonds or liens.

Please check "Yes" or "No" box for each question (see instructions).

			Yes	No
1	Do you elect alternate valuation?	1		X
2	Do you elect special-use valuation? If "Yes," you must complete and attach Schedule A-1	2		X
3	Do you elect to pay the taxes in installments as described in section 6166? If "Yes," you must attach the additional information described in the instructions. **Note. By electing section 6166 installment payments, you may be required to provide security for estate tax deferred under section 6166 and interest in the form of a surety bond or a section 6324A lien.**	3		X
4	Do you elect to postpone the part of the taxes due to a reversionary or remainder interest as described in section 6163?	4		X

Part 4—General Information

Note. Please attach the necessary supplemental documents. **You must attach the death certificate.** (See instructions)

Authorization to receive confidential tax information under Reg. section 601.504(b)(2)(i); to act as the estate's representative before the IRS; and to make written or oral presentations on behalf of the estate:

Name of representative (print or type)	State	Address (number, street, and room or suite no., city, state, and ZIP code)
Mary Wilson	ST	15 Main Place, City, ST 22222

I declare that I am the ☐ attorney/ ☒ certified public accountant/ ☐ enrolled agent (check the applicable box) for the executor. I am not under suspension or disbarment from practice before the Internal Revenue Service and am qualified to practice in the state shown above.

Signature	CAF number	Date	Telephone number
Mary Wilson, CPA		5-12-17	

1 Death certificate number and issuing authority (attach a copy of the death certificate to this return).
1246, County Coroner

2 Decedent's business or occupation. If retired, check here ► ☒ and state decedent's former business or occupation.
Executive

3a Marital status of the decedent at time of death:
☒ Married ☐ Widow/widower ☐ Single ☐ Legally separated ☐ Divorced

3b For all prior marriages, list the name and SSN of the former spouse, the date the marriage ended, and whether the marriage ended by annulment, divorce, or death. Attach additional statements of the same size if necessary.

4a Surviving spouse's name	4b Social security number	4c Amount received (see instructions)
Ann Estes	XXX XX XXXX	1,070,000

5 Individuals (other than the surviving spouse), trusts, or other estates who receive benefits from the estate (do not include charitable beneficiaries shown in Schedule O) (see instructions).

Name of individual, trust, or estate receiving $5,000 or more	Identifying number	Relationship to decedent	Amount (see instructions)
Johnny Estes	XXX-XX-XXXX	Son	1,291,325
Billy Estes	XXX-XX-XXXX	Son	1,091,325
Daughter, Dorothy Estes, received the corpus in the special power of appointment trust created by Amelia Estes			
All unascertainable beneficiaries and those who receive less than $5,000 ►			
Total			2,382,650*

If you answer "Yes" to any of the following questions, you must attach additional information as described.

		Yes	No
6	Is the estate filing a protective claim for refund? If "Yes," complete and attach two copies of Schedule PC for each claim.		X
7	Does the gross estate contain any section 2044 property (qualified terminable interest property (QTIP) from a prior gift or estate)? (see instructions)		X
8a	Have federal gift tax returns ever been filed? If "Yes," attach copies of the returns, if available, and furnish the following information:	X	
b	Period(s) covered: 1978, 2013 — c Internal Revenue office(s) where filed: Cincinnati, OH		
9a	Was there any insurance on the decedent's life that is not included on the return as part of the gross estate?		X
b	Did the decedent own any insurance on the life of another that is not included in the gross estate?		X

* $4,769,750 taxable estate – $487,200 gross up – $1,899,900 estate tax

Form 706 (Rev. 8-2013)

Estate of: Herman Estes — **Decedent's social security number** XXX XX XXXX

Part 4—General Information *(continued)*

If you answer "Yes" to any of the following questions, you must attach additional information as described.		Yes	No
10	Did the decedent at the time of death own any property as a joint tenant with right of survivorship in which **(a)** one or more of the other joint tenants was someone other than the decedent's spouse, and **(b)** less than the full value of the property is included on the return as part of the gross estate? If "Yes," you must complete and attach Schedule E		X
11a	Did the decedent, at the time of death, own any interest in a partnership (for example, a family limited partnership), an unincorporated business, or a limited liability company; or own any stock in an inactive or closely held corporation?		X
b	If "Yes," was the value of **any** interest owned (from above) discounted on this estate tax return? If "Yes," see the instructions on reporting the total accumulated or effective discounts taken on Schedule F or G		
12	Did the decedent make any transfer described in sections 2035, 2036, 2037, or 2038? (see instructions) If "Yes," you must complete and attach Schedule G	X	
13a	Were there in existence at the time of the decedent's death any trusts created by the decedent during his or her lifetime?		X
b	Were there in existence at the time of the decedent's death any trusts not created by the decedent under which the decedent possessed any power, beneficial interest, or trusteeship?	X	
c	Was the decedent receiving income from a trust created after October 22, 1986, by a parent or grandparent?	X	
	If "Yes," was there a GST taxable termination (under section 2612) on the death of the decedent?		X
d	If there was a GST taxable termination (under section 2612), attach a statement to explain. Provide a copy of the trust or will creating the trust, and give the name, address, and phone number of the current trustee(s).		
e	Did the decedent at any time during his or her lifetime transfer or sell an interest in a partnership, limited liability company, or closely held corporation to a trust described in lines 13a or 13b?		X
	If "Yes," provide the EIN for this transferred/sold item. ▶		
14	Did the decedent ever possess, exercise, or release any general power of appointment? If "Yes," you must complete and attach Schedule H		X
15	Did the decedent have an interest in or a signature or other authority over a financial account in a foreign country, such as a bank account, securities account, or other financial account?		X
16	Was the decedent, immediately before death, receiving an annuity described in the "General" paragraph of the instructions for Schedule I or a private annuity? If "Yes," you must complete and attach Schedule I	X	
17	Was the decedent ever the beneficiary of a trust for which a deduction was claimed by the estate of a predeceased spouse under section 2056(b)(7) and which is not reported on this return? If "Yes," attach an explanation		X

Part 5—Recapitulation.

Note. If estimating the value of one or more assets pursuant to the special rule of Reg. section 20.2010-2T(a)(7)(ii), enter on both lines 10 and 23 the amount noted in the instructions for the corresponding range of values. (See instructions for details.)

Item no.	Gross estate		Alternate value	Value at date of death
1	Schedule A—Real Estate	1		325,000
2	Schedule B—Stocks and Bonds	2		4,400,000
3	Schedule C—Mortgages, Notes, and Cash	3		94,250
4	Schedule D—Insurance on the Decedent's Life (attach Form(s) 712)	4		200,000
5	Schedule E—Jointly Owned Property (attach Form(s) 712 for life insurance)	5		220,000
6	Schedule F—Other Miscellaneous Property (attach Form(s) 712 for life insurance)	6		
7	Schedule G—Transfers During Decedent's Life (att. Form(s) 712 for life insurance)	7		487,200
8	Schedule H—Powers of Appointment	8		
9	Schedule I—Annuities	9		240,000
10	Estimated value of assets subject to the special rule of Reg. section 20.2010-2T(a)(7)(ii)	10		
11	Total gross estate (add items 1 through 10)	11		5,966,450
12	Schedule U—Qualified Conservation Easement Exclusion	12		
13	Total gross estate less exclusion (subtract item 12 from item 11). Enter here and on line 1 of Part 2—Tax Computation	13		5,966,450

Item no.	Deductions		Amount
14	Schedule J—Funeral Expenses and Expenses Incurred in Administering Property Subject to Claims	14	85,000
15	Schedule K—Debts of the Decedent	15	31,700
16	Schedule K—Mortgages and Liens	16	
17	Total of items 14 through 16	17	116,700
18	Allowable amount of deductions from item 17 (see the instructions for item 18 of the Recapitulation)	18	116,700
19	Schedule L—Net Losses During Administration	19	
20	Schedule L—Expenses Incurred in Administering Property Not Subject to Claims	20	
21	Schedule M—Bequests, etc., to Surviving Spouse	21	1,070,000
22	Schedule O—Charitable, Public, and Similar Gifts and Bequests	22	10,000
23	Estimated value of deductible assets subject to the special rule of Reg. section 20.2010-2T(a)(7)(ii)	23	
24	Tentative total allowable deductions (add items 18 through 23). Enter here and on line 2 of the Tax Computation	24	1,196,700

Form 706 (Rev. 8-2013)

Estate of: Herman Estes	Decedent's social security number XXX XX XXXX

SCHEDULE A—Real Estate

- For jointly owned property that must be disclosed on Schedule E, see instructions.
- Real estate that is part of a sole proprietorship should be shown on Schedule F.
- Real estate that is included in the gross estate under sections 2035, 2036, 2037, or 2038 should be shown on Schedule G.
- Real estate that is included in the gross estate under section 2041 should be shown on Schedule H.
- If you elect section 2032A valuation, you must complete Schedule A and Schedule A-1.

Note. If the value of the gross estate, together with the amount of adjusted taxable gifts, is less than the basic exclusion amount and the Form 706 is being filed solely to elect portability of the DSUE amount, consideration should be given as to whether you are required to report the value of assets eligible for the marital or charitable deduction on this schedule. See the instructions and Reg. section 20.2010-2T (a)(7)(ii) for more information. If you are not required to report the value of an asset, identify the property but make no entries in the last three columns.

Item number	Description	Alternate valuation date	Alternate value	Value at date of death
1	Personal residence, house and lot, located at 105 Elm Court, City, ST			325,000
	Total from continuation schedules or additional statements attached to this schedule . . .			
	TOTAL. (Also enter on Part 5—Recapitulation, page 3, at item 1.)			325,000

(If more space is needed, attach the continuation schedule from the end of this package or additional statements of the same size.)

Form 706 (Rev. 8-2013)

Estate of: Herman Estes | **Decedent's social security number** XXX XX XXXX

SCHEDULE B—Stocks and Bonds

(For jointly owned property that must be disclosed on Schedule E, see instructions.)

Note. If the value of the gross estate, together with the amount of adjusted taxable gifts, is less than the basic exclusion amount and the Form 706 is being filed solely to elect portability of the DSUE amount, consideration should be given as to whether you are required to report the value of assets eligible for the marital or charitable deduction on this schedule. See the instructions and Reg. section 20.2010-2T (a)(7)(ii) for more information. If you are not required to report the value of an asset, identify the property but make no entries in the last four columns.

Item number	Description, including face amount of bonds or number of shares and par value for identification. Give CUSIP number. If trust, partnership, or closely held entity, give EIN.	CUSIP number or EIN, where applicable	Unit value	Alternate valuation date	Alternate value	Value at date of death
1	Stock in Ajax Corporation 1,000 shares, $10 per share		4,400			4,400,000
	Total from continuation schedules (or additional statements) attached to this schedule . . .					
	TOTAL. (Also enter on Part 5—Recapitulation, page 3, at item 2.)					4,400,000

(If more space is needed, attach the continuation schedule from the end of this package or additional statements of the same size.)

Form 706 (Rev. 8-2013)

Estate of: Herman Estes

Decedent's social security number XXX XX XXXX

SCHEDULE C—Mortgages, Notes, and Cash

(For jointly owned property that must be disclosed on Schedule E, see instructions.)

Note. If the value of the gross estate, together with the amount of adjusted taxable gifts, is less than the basic exclusion amount and the Form 706 is being filed solely to elect portability of the DSUE amount, consideration should be given as to whether you are required to report the value of assets eligible for the marital or charitable deduction on this schedule. See the instructions and Reg. section 20.2010-2T (a)(7)(ii) for more information. If you are not required to report the value of an asset, identify the property but make no entries in the last three columns.

Item number	Description	Alternate valuation date	Alternate value	Value at date of death
1	Checking account			19,250
2	Savings account (includes accrued interest through date of death)			75,000
	Total from continuation schedules (or additional statements) attached to this schedule . .			
	TOTAL. (Also enter on Part 5—Recapitulation, page 3, at item 3.)			94,250

(If more space is needed, attach the continuation schedule from the end of this package or additional statements of the same size.)

Form 706 (Rev. 8-2013)

Estate of: Herman Estes

Decedent's social security number XXX XX XXXX

SCHEDULE D—Insurance on the Decedent's Life

You must list all policies on the life of the decedent and attach a Form 712 for each policy.

Note. If the value of the gross estate, together with the amount of adjusted taxable gifts, is less than the basic exclusion amount and the Form 706 is being filed solely to elect portability of the DSUE amount, consideration should be given as to whether you are required to report the value of assets eligible for the marital or charitable deduction on this schedule. See the instructions and Reg. section 20.2010-2T (a)(7)(ii) for more information. If you are not required to report the value of an asset, identify the property but make no entries in the last three columns.

Item number	Description	Alternate valuation date	Alternate value	Value at date of death
1	Life insurance policy No. 123-A issued by the Life Insurance Company of Ohio. Beneficiary — Johnny Estes			200,000
	Total from continuation schedules (or additional statements) attached to this schedule			
	TOTAL. (Also enter on Part 5—Recapitulation, page 3, at item 4.)			200,000

(If more space is needed, attach the continuation schedule from the end of this package or additional statements of the same size.)

Form 706 (Rev. 8-2013)

Estate of: Herman Estes	Decedent's social security number XXX XX XXXX

SCHEDULE E—Jointly Owned Property

(If you elect section 2032A valuation, you must complete Schedule E and Schedule A-1.)

PART 1. Qualified Joint Interests—Interests Held by the Decedent and His or Her Spouse as the Only Joint Tenants (Section 2040(b)(2))

Note. If the value of the gross estate, together with the amount of adjusted taxable gifts, is less than the basic exclusion amount and the Form 706 is being filed solely to elect portability of the DSUE amount, consideration should be given as to whether you are required to report the value of assets eligible for the marital or charitable deduction on this schedule. See the instructions and Reg. section 20.2010-2T (a)(7)(ii) for more information. If you are not required to report the value of an asset, identify the property but make no entries in the last three columns.

Item number	Description. For securities, give CUSIP number. If trust, partnership, or closely held entity, give EIN.	CUSIP number or EIN, where applicable	Alternate valuation date	Alternate value	Value at date of death
1	Land				440,000
	Total from continuation schedules (or additional statements) attached to this schedule				
1a	Totals		1a		440,000
1b	Amounts included in gross estate (one-half of line **1a**)		1b		220,000

PART 2. All Other Joint Interests

2a State the name and address of each surviving co-tenant. If there are more than three surviving co-tenants, list the additional co-tenants on an attached statement.

	Name	Address (number and street, city, state, and ZIP code)
A.		
B.		
C.		

Item number	Enter letter for co-tenant	Description (including alternate valuation date if any). For securities, give CUSIP number. If trust, partnership, or closely held entity, give EIN	CUSIP number or EIN, where applicable	Percentage includible	Includible alternate value	Includible value at date of death
1						
	Total from continuation schedules (or additional statements) attached to this schedule					
2b	Total other joint interests			2b		
3	**Total includible joint interests** (add lines 1b and 2b). Also enter on Part 5—Recapitulation, page 3, at item 5			3		220,000

(If more space is needed, attach the continuation schedule from the end of this package or additional statements of the same size.)

Form 706 (Rev. 8-2013)

Estate of: Herman Estes	Decedent's social security number XXX XX XXXX

SCHEDULE G—Transfers During Decedent's Life

(If you elect section 2032A valuation, you must complete Schedule G and Schedule A-1.)

Note. If the value of the gross estate, together with the amount of adjusted taxable gifts, is less than the basic exclusion amount and the Form 706 is being filed solely to elect portability of the DSUE amount, consideration should be given as to whether you are required to report the value of assets eligible for the marital or charitable deduction on this schedule. See the instructions and Reg. section 20.2010-2T (a)(7)(ii) for more information. If you are not required to report the value of an asset, identify the property but make no entries in the last three columns.

Item number	Description. For securities, give CUSIP number. If trust, partnership, or closely held entity, give EIN	Alternate valuation date	Alternate value	Value at date of death
A.	Gift tax paid or payable by the decedent or the estate for all gifts made by the decedent or his or her spouse within 3 years before the decedent's death (section 2035(b))	X X X X X		487,200
B.	Transfers includible under sections 2035(a), 2036, 2037, or 2038:			
	Total from continuation schedules (or additional statements) attached to this schedule . .			
	TOTAL. (Also enter on Part 5—Recapitulation, page 3, at item 7.)			487,200

SCHEDULE H—Powers of Appointment

(Include "5 and 5 lapsing" powers (section 2041(b)(2)) held by the decedent.)
(If you elect section 2032A valuation, you must complete Schedule H and Schedule A-1.)

Note. If the value of the gross estate, together with the amount of adjusted taxable gifts, is less than the basic exclusion amount and the Form 706 is being filed solely to elect portability of the DSUE amount, consideration should be given as to whether you are required to report the value of assets eligible for the marital or charitable deduction on this schedule. See the instructions and Reg. section 20.2010-2T (a)(7)(ii) for more information. If you are not required to report the value of an asset, identify the property but make no entries in the last three columns.

Item number	Description	Alternate valuation date	Alternate value	Value at date of death
1				
	Total from continuation schedules (or additional statements) attached to this schedule . . .			
	TOTAL. (Also enter on Part 5—Recapitulation, page 3, at item 8.)			

(If more space is needed, attach the continuation schedule from the end of this package or additional statements of the same size.)

Form 706 (Rev. 8-2013)

Estate of: Herman Estes

Decedent's social security number XXX XX XXXX

SCHEDULE I—Annuities

Note. Generally, no exclusion is allowed for the estates of decedents dying after December 31, 1984 (see instructions).

Note. If the value of the gross estate, together with the amount of adjusted taxable gifts, is less than the basic exclusion amount and the Form 706 is being filed solely to elect portability of the DSUE amount, consideration should be given as to whether you are required to report the value of assets eligible for the marital or charitable deduction on this schedule. See the instructions and Reg. section 20.2010-2T (a)(7)(ii) for more information. If you are not required to report the value of an asset, identify the property but make no entries in the last three columns.

		Yes	No
A	Are you excluding from the decedent's gross estate the value of a lump-sum distribution described in section 2039(f)(2) (as in effect before its repeal by the Deficit Reduction Act of 1984)? . . . . If "Yes," you must attach the information required by the instructions.		X

Item number	Description. Show the entire value of the annuity before any exclusions	Alternate valuation date	Includible alternate value	Includible value at date of death
1	Qualified pension plan issued by Buckeye Corporation. Beneficiary — Ann Estes, spouse			240,000
	Total from continuation schedules (or additional statements) attached to this schedule . .			
	TOTAL. (Also enter on Part 5—Recapitulation, page 3, at item 9.)			240,000

(If more space is needed, attach the continuation schedule from the end of this package or additional statements of the same size.)

Form 706 (Rev. 8-2013)

Estate of: Herman Estes

Decedent's social security number XXX XX XXXX

SCHEDULE J—Funeral Expenses and Expenses Incurred in Administering Property Subject to Claims

▶ Use Schedule PC to make a protective claim for refund due to an expense not currently deductible. For such a claim, report the expense on Schedule J but without a value in the last column.

Note. Do not list expenses of administering property not subject to claims on this schedule. To report those expenses, see instructions.

If executors' commissions, attorney fees, etc., are claimed and allowed as a deduction for estate tax purposes, they are not allowable as a deduction in computing the taxable income of the estate for federal income tax purposes. They are allowable as an income tax deduction on Form 1041, U.S. Income Tax Return for Estates and Trusts, if a waiver is filed to forgo the deduction on Form 706 (see Instructions for Form 1041).

	Yes	No
Are you aware of any actual or potential reimbursement to the estate for any expense claimed as a deduction on this schedule? . . . . . If "Yes," attach a statement describing the expense(s) subject to potential reimbursement. (see instructions)		

Item number	Description	Expense amount	Total amount
	A. Funeral expenses:	15,000	
	Total funeral expenses . . . . . ▶		15,000
	B. Administration expenses:		
	1 Executors' commissions—amount estimated/agreed upon/paid. (Strike out the words that do not apply.)		
	2 Attorney fees—amount estimated/agreed upon/paid. (Strike out the words that do not apply.) . .		70,000
	3 Accountant fees—amount estimated/agreed upon/paid. (Strike out the words that do not apply.) .		
	4 Miscellaneous expenses:	Expense amount	
	Total miscellaneous expenses from continuation schedules (or additional statements) attached to this schedule		
	Total miscellaneous expenses . . . . . ▶		
	TOTAL. (Also enter on Part 5—Recapitulation, page 3, at item 14.) . . . . . ▶		85,000

(If more space is needed, attach the continuation schedule from the end of this package or additional statements of the same size.)

Form 706 (Rev. 8-2013)

Estate of: Herman Estes

Decedent's social security number XXX XX XXXX

SCHEDULE K—Debts of the Decedent, and Mortgages and Liens

► Use Schedule PC to make a protective claim for refund due to a claim not currently deductible. For such a claim, report the expense on Schedule K but without a value in the last column.

	Yes	No
Are you aware of any actual or potential reimbursement to the estate for any debt of the decedent, mortgage, or lien claimed as a deduction on this schedule?		X
If "Yes," attach a statement describing the items subject to potential reimbursement. (see instructions)		
Are any of the items on this schedule deductible under Reg. section 20.2053-4(b) and Reg. section 20.2053-4(c)?		X
If "Yes," attach a statement indicating the applicable provision and documenting the value of the claim.		

Item number	Debts of the Decedent—Creditor and nature of debt, and allowable death taxes	Amount
1	Bank loan (including $200 interest accrued through date of death)	25,200
2	American Express, Visa, and Master Card credit card debts	6,500
	Total from continuation schedules (or additional statements) attached to this schedule	
	TOTAL. (Also enter on Part 5—Recapitulation, page 3, at item 15.)	31,700

Item number	Mortgages and Liens—Description	Amount
	Total from continuation schedules (or additional statements) attached to this schedule	
	TOTAL. (Also enter on Part 5—Recapitulation, page 3, at item 16.)	

(If more space is needed, attach the continuation schedule from the end of this package or additional statements of the same size.)

Form 706 (Rev. 8-2013)

Estate of: Herman Estes	Decedent's social security number XXX XX XXXX

SCHEDULE M—Bequests, etc., to Surviving Spouse

Note. If the value of the gross estate, together with the amount of adjusted taxable gifts, is less than the basic exclusion amount and the Form 706 is being filed solely to elect portability of the DSUE amount, consideration should be given as to whether you are required to report the value of assets eligible for the marital or charitable deduction on this schedule. See the instructions and Reg. section 20.2010-2T (a)(7)(ii) for more information. If you are not required to report the value of an asset, identify the property but make no entry in the last column.

			Yes	No
1	Did any property pass to the surviving spouse as a result of a qualified disclaimer? If "Yes," attach a copy of the written disclaimer required by section 2518(b).	1		X
2a	In what country was the surviving spouse born? United States			
b	What is the surviving spouse's date of birth? 3-12-1948			
c	Is the surviving spouse a U.S. citizen?	2c	X	
d	If the surviving spouse is a naturalized citizen, when did the surviving spouse acquire citizenship? N/A			
e	If the surviving spouse is not a U.S. citizen, of what country is the surviving spouse a citizen? N/A			
3	**Election Out of QTIP Treatment of Annuities.** Do you elect under section 2056(b)(7)(C)(ii) not to treat as qualified terminable interest property any joint and survivor annuities that are included in the gross estate and would otherwise be treated as qualified terminable interest property under section 2056(b)(7)(C)? (see instructions)	3		X

Item number	Description of property interests passing to surviving spouse. For securities, give CUSIP number. If trust, partnership, or closely held entity, give EIN	Amount
	QTIP property:	
	Trust with First Bank as trustee	200,000
	All other property:	
	Residence	325,000
	Savings account	75,000
	Checking account	10,000
	Land held in joint tenancy	220,000
	Qualified pension plan	240,000
	Total from continuation schedules (or additional statements) attached to this schedule	

4	**Total** amount of property interests listed on Schedule M			4	1,070,000
5a	Federal estate taxes payable out of property interests listed on Schedule M	5a			
b	Other death taxes payable out of property interests listed on Schedule M	5b			
c	Federal and state GST taxes payable out of property interests listed on Schedule M	5c			
d	Add items 5a, 5b, and 5c			5d	
6	Net amount of property interests listed on Schedule M (subtract 5d from 4). Also enter on Part 5—Recapitulation, page 3, at item 21			6	1,070,000

(If more space is needed, attach the continuation schedule from the end of this package or additional statements of the same size.)

Form 706 (Rev. 8-2013)

Estate of: Herman Estes | Decedent's social security number XXX XX XXXX

SCHEDULE O—Charitable, Public, and Similar Gifts and Bequests

Note. If the value of the gross estate, together with the amount of adjusted taxable gifts, is less than the basic exclusion amount and the Form 706 is being filed solely to elect portability of the DSUE amount, consideration should be given as to whether you are required to report the value of assets eligible for the marital or charitable deduction on this schedule. See the instructions and Reg. section 20.2010-2T (a)(7)(ii) for more information. If you are not required to report the value of an asset, identify the property but make no entry in the last column.

		Yes	No
1a	If the transfer was made by will, has any action been instituted to contest or have interpreted any of its provisions affecting the charitable deductions claimed in this schedule? . . . . If "Yes," full details must be submitted with this schedule.		X
b	According to the information and belief of the person or persons filing this return, is any such action planned? . If "Yes," full details must be submitted with this schedule.		X
2	Did any property pass to charity as the result of a qualified disclaimer? . . . . If "Yes," attach a copy of the written disclaimer required by section 2518(b).		X

Item number	Name and address of beneficiary	Character of institution	Amount
1	American Cancer Society	Charity	10,000
	Total from continuation schedules (or additional statements) attached to this schedule		

3	Total		3	10,000
4a	Federal estate tax payable out of property interests listed above	4a		
b	Other death taxes payable out of property interests listed above	4b		
c	Federal and state GST taxes payable out of property interests listed above .	4c		
d	Add items 4a, 4b, and 4c		4d	
5	Net value of property interests listed above (subtract 4d from 3). Also enter on Part 5—Recapitulation, page 3, at item 22		5	10,000

(If more space is needed, attach the continuation schedule from the end of this package or additional statements of the same size.)

Form **1041** Department of the Treasury—Internal Revenue Service
U.S. Income Tax Return for Estates and Trusts
2016 OMB No. 1545-0092

▶ Information about Form 1041 and its separate instructions is at *www.irs.gov/form1041*.

For calendar year 2016 or fiscal year beginning , 2016, and ending , 20

A Check all that apply:
- ☐ Decedent's estate
- ☒ Simple trust
- ☐ Complex trust
- ☐ Qualified disability trust
- ☐ ESBT (S portion only)
- ☐ Grantor type trust
- ☐ Bankruptcy estate-Ch. 7
- ☐ Bankruptcy estate-Ch. 11
- ☐ Pooled income fund

Name of estate or trust (If a grantor type trust, see the instructions.): Bob Adams Trust (Simple Trust)

Name and title of fiduciary: First Bank

Number, street, and room or suite no. (If a P.O. box, see the instructions.): Post Office Box 100

City or town, state or province, country, and ZIP or foreign postal code: City, ST 44444

C Employer identification number: XX-XXXXXXX

D Date entity created: 2003

E Nonexempt charitable and split-interest trusts, check applicable box(es), see instructions.
- ☐ Described in sec. 4947(a)(1). Check here if not a private foundation ▶ ☐
- ☐ Described in sec. 4947(a)(2)

B Number of Schedules K-1 attached (see instructions) ▶ 1

F Check applicable boxes: ☐ Initial return ☐ Final return ☐ Amended return ☐ Net operating loss carryback ☐ Change in trust's name ☐ Change in fiduciary ☐ Change in fiduciary's name ☐ Change in fiduciary's address

G Check here if the estate or filing trust made a section 645 election . . . ▶ ☐ Trust TIN ▶

Income	1	Interest income	1	
	2a	Total ordinary dividends	2a	30,000
	b	Qualified dividends allocable to: (1) Beneficiaries 30,000 (2) Estate or trust -0-		
	3	Business income or (loss). Attach Schedule C or C-EZ (Form 1040)	3	
	4	Capital gain or (loss). Attach Schedule D (Form 1041)	4	12,000
	5	Rents, royalties, partnerships, other estates and trusts, etc. Attach Schedule E (Form 1040)	5	4,000 *
	6	Farm income or (loss). Attach Schedule F (Form 1040)	6	
	7	Ordinary gain or (loss). Attach Form 4797	7	
	8	Other income. List type and amount	8	
	9	**Total income.** Combine lines 1, 2a, and 3 through 8 ▶	9	46,000
Deductions	10	Interest. Check if Form 4952 is attached ▶ ☐	10	
	11	Taxes	11	
	12	Fiduciary fees ($1,200 – $360)	12	840
	13	Charitable deduction (from Schedule A, line 7)	13	
	14	Attorney, accountant, and return preparer fees	14	500
	15a	Other deductions **not** subject to the 2% floor (attach schedule)	15a	
	b	Net operating loss deduction. See instructions	15b	
	c	Allowable miscellaneous itemized deductions subject to the 2% floor	15c	
	16	Add lines 10 through 15c ▶	16	1,340
	17	Adjusted total income or (loss). Subtract line 16 from line 9	17	44,660
	18	Income distribution deduction (from Schedule B, line 15). Attach Schedules K-1 (Form 1041)	18	32,660
	19	Estate tax deduction including certain generation-skipping taxes (attach computation)	19	
	20	Exemption	20	300
	21	Add lines 18 through 20 ▶	21	32,960
Tax and Payments	22	Taxable income. Subtract line 21 from line 17. If a loss, see instructions	22	11,700
	23	**Total tax** (from Schedule G, line 7)	23	1,373
	24	**Payments: a** 2016 estimated tax payments and amount applied from 2015 return	24a	2,600
	b	Estimated tax payments allocated to beneficiaries (from Form 1041-T)	24b	
	c	Subtract line 24b from line 24a	24c	2,600
	d	Tax paid with Form 7004. See instructions	24d	
	e	Federal income tax withheld. If any is from Form(s) 1099, check ▶ ☐	24e	
		Other payments: f Form 2439 ; g Form 4136 ; Total ▶	24h	
	25	**Total payments.** Add lines 24c through 24e, and 24h ▶	25	2,600
	26	Estimated tax penalty. See instructions	26	
	27	**Tax due.** If line 25 is smaller than the total of lines 23 and 26, enter amount owed	27	
	28	**Overpayment.** If line 25 is larger than the total of lines 23 and 26, enter amount overpaid	28	1,227
	29	Amount of line 28 to be: **a Credited to 2017 estimated tax** ▶ 1,227 ; **b Refunded** ▶	29	

Sign Here

Under penalties of perjury, I declare that I have examined this return, including accompanying schedules and statements, and to the best of my knowledge and belief, it is true, correct, and complete. Declaration of preparer (other than taxpayer) is based on all information of which preparer has any knowledge.

Tom Trusty — Signature of fiduciary or officer representing fiduciary | 3-14-17 — Date | ▶ XX-XXXXXXX — EIN of fiduciary if a financial institution

May the IRS discuss this return with the preparer shown below (see instr.)? ☒ Yes ☐ No

Paid Preparer Use Only

Print/Type preparer's name	Preparer's signature	Date	Check ☒ if self-employed	PTIN
Karen Certified	Karen Certified	3-14-17		

Firm's name ▶ Karen Certified — Firm's EIN ▶

Firm's address ▶ One Some Place, City, ST 44444 — Phone no.

For Paperwork Reduction Act Notice, see the separate instructions. Cat. No. 11370H Form **1041** (2016)

*Line 5: Net rental income = Rental income $5,000 – Realtor's commissions $1,000 = $4,000

Note: Pages concerning the AMT are omitted because the trust does not owe the AMT.

See the Comprehensive Illustration on text page C:14-17 for tax form facts.

Form 1041 (2016) Page 2

Schedule A **Charitable Deduction.** Don't complete for a simple trust or a pooled income fund.

1	Amounts paid or permanently set aside for charitable purposes from gross income. See instructions	1		
2	Tax-exempt income allocable to charitable contributions. See instructions	2		
3	Subtract line 2 from line 1	3		
4	Capital gains for the tax year allocated to corpus and paid or permanently set aside for charitable purposes	4		
5	Add lines 3 and 4	5		
6	Section 1202 exclusion allocable to capital gains paid or permanently set aside for charitable purposes. See instructions	6		
7	**Charitable deduction.** Subtract line 6 from line 5. Enter here and on page 1, line 13	7		

Schedule B **Income Distribution Deduction**

1	Adjusted total income. See instructions	1	44,660	
2	Adjusted tax-exempt interest ($15,000 – $360)	2	14,640	*
3	Total net gain from Schedule D (Form 1041), line 19, column (1). See instructions	3		
4	Enter amount from Schedule A, line 4 (minus any allocable section 1202 exclusion)	4		
5	Capital gains for the tax year included on Schedule A, line 1. See instructions	5		
6	Enter any gain from page 1, line 4, as a negative number. If page 1, line 4, is a loss, enter the loss as a positive number	6	(12,000)	
7	**Distributable net income.** Combine lines 1 through 6. If zero or less, enter -0-	7	47,300	
8	If a complex trust, enter accounting income for the tax year as determined under the governing instrument and applicable local law [8]			
9	Income required to be distributed currently	9	48,500	
10	Other amounts paid, credited, or otherwise required to be distributed	10		
11	Total distributions. Add lines 9 and 10. If greater than line 8, see instructions	11	48,500	
12	Enter the amount of tax-exempt income included on line 11	12	14,640	
13	Tentative income distribution deduction. Subtract line 12 from line 11	13	33,860	
14	Tentative income distribution deduction. Subtract line 2 from line 7. If zero or less, enter -0-	14	32,660	
15	**Income distribution deduction.** Enter the smaller of line 13 or line 14 here and on page 1, line 18	15	32,660	

Schedule G **Tax Computation** (see instructions)

1	**Tax: a** Tax on taxable income. See instructions	1a	1,373			
	b Tax on lump-sum distributions. Attach Form 4972	1b				
	c Alternative minimum tax (from Schedule I (Form 1041), line 56)	1c				
	d **Total.** Add lines 1a through 1c ▶			1d	1,373	
2a	Foreign tax credit. Attach Form 1116	2a				
b	General business credit. Attach Form 3800	2b				
c	Credit for prior year minimum tax. Attach Form 8801	2c				
d	Bond credits. Attach Form 8912	2d				
e	**Total credits.** Add lines 2a through 2d ▶			2e		
3	Subtract line 2e from line 1d. If zero or less, enter -0-			3	1,373	
4	Net investment income tax from Form 8960, line 21			4	-0-	**
5	Recapture taxes. Check if from: ☐ Form 4255 ☐ Form 8611			5		
6	Household employment taxes. Attach Schedule H (Form 1040)			6		
7	**Total tax.** Add lines 3 through 6. Enter here and on page 1, line 23 ▶			7	1,373	

Other Information

		Yes	No
1	Did the estate or trust receive tax-exempt income? If "Yes," attach a computation of the allocation of expenses. Enter the amount of tax-exempt interest income and exempt-interest dividends ▶ $ 15,000	X	
2	Did the estate or trust receive all or any part of the earnings (salary, wages, and other compensation) of any individual by reason of a contract assignment or similar arrangement?		X
3	At any time during calendar year 2016, did the estate or trust have an interest in or a signature or other authority over a bank, securities, or other financial account in a foreign country?		X
	See the instructions for exceptions and filing requirements for FinCEN Form 114. If "Yes," enter the name of the foreign country ▶		
4	During the tax year, did the estate or trust receive a distribution from, or was it the grantor of, or transferor to, a foreign trust? If "Yes," the estate or trust may have to file Form 3520. See instructions		X
5	Did the estate or trust receive, or pay, any qualified residence interest on seller-provided financing? If "Yes," see the instructions for required attachment		X
6	If this is an estate or a complex trust making the section 663(b) election, check here. See instructions ▶ ☐		
7	To make a section 643(e)(3) election, attach Schedule D (Form 1041), and check here. See instructions ▶ ☐		
8	If the decedent's estate has been open for more than 2 years, attach an explanation for the delay in closing the estate, and check here ▶ ☐		
9	Are any present or future trust beneficiaries skip persons? See instructions		X
10	Was the trust a specified domestic entity required to file Form 8938 for the tax year (see the Instructions for Form 8938)?		X

Form **1041** (2016)

* Line 2: Allocation of expenses: $\frac{\$15,000}{\$50,000} \times \$1,200 = \$360$ of trustee's fee allocated to tax-exempt income

** Zero because AGI of $11,700 ($44,660 – $32,660 – $300) does not exceed the beginning of the 39.6% tax bracket.

SCHEDULE D (Form 1041)

Department of the Treasury
Internal Revenue Service

Capital Gains and Losses

▶ Attach to Form 1041, Form 5227, or Form 990-T.
▶ Use Form 8949 to list your transactions for lines 1b, 2, 3, 8b, 9 and 10.
▶ Information about Schedule D and its separate instructions is at *www.irs.gov/form1041*.

OMB No. 1545-0092

2016

Name of estate or trust: Bob Adams Trust

Employer identification number: XX-XXXXXXX

Note: *Form 5227 filers need to complete* ***only*** *Parts I and II.*

Part I Short-Term Capital Gains and Losses—Assets Held One Year or Less

See instructions for how to figure the amounts to enter on the lines below. This form may be easier to complete if you round off cents to whole dollars.	(d) Proceeds (sales price)	(e) Cost (or other basis)	(g) Adjustments to gain or loss from Form(s) 8949, Part I, line 2, column (g)	(h) Gain or (loss) Subtract column (e) from column (d) and combine the result with column (g)
1a Totals for all short-term transactions reported on Form 1099-B for which basis was reported to the IRS and for which you have no adjustments (see instructions). However, if you choose to report all these transactions on Form 8949, leave this line blank and go to line 1b				
1b Totals for all transactions reported on Form(s) 8949 with **Box A** checked				
2 Totals for all transactions reported on Form(s) 8949 with **Box B** checked				
3 Totals for all transactions reported on Form(s) 8949 with **Box C** checked				

4 Short-term capital gain or (loss) from Forms 4684, 6252, 6781, and 8824	4	
5 Net short-term gain or (loss) from partnerships, S corporations, and other estates or trusts	5	
6 Short-term capital loss carryover. Enter the amount, if any, from line 9 of the 2015 Capital Loss Carryover Worksheet	6	( )
7 **Net short-term capital gain or (loss).** Combine lines 1a through 6 in column (h). Enter here and on line 17, column (3) on the back ▶	7	

Part II Long-Term Capital Gains and Losses—Assets Held More Than One Year

See instructions for how to figure the amounts to enter on the lines below. This form may be easier to complete if you round off cents to whole dollars.	(d) Proceeds (sales price)	(e) Cost (or other basis)	(g) Adjustments to gain or loss from Form(s) 8949, Part II, line 2, column (g)	(h) Gain or (loss) Subtract column (e) from column (d) and combine the result with column (g)
8a Totals for all long-term transactions reported on Form 1099-B for which basis was reported to the IRS and for which you have no adjustments (see instructions). However, if you choose to report all these transactions on Form 8949, leave this line blank and go to line 8b	15,000	3,000		12,000
8b Totals for all transactions reported on Form(s) 8949 with **Box D** checked				
9 Totals for all transactions reported on Form(s) 8949 with **Box E** checked				
10 Totals for all transactions reported on Form(s) 8949 with **Box F** checked				

11 Long-term capital gain or (loss) from Forms 2439, 4684, 6252, 6781, and 8824	11	
12 Net long-term gain or (loss) from partnerships, S corporations, and other estates or trusts	12	
13 Capital gain distributions	13	
14 Gain from Form 4797, Part I	14	
15 Long-term capital loss carryover. Enter the amount, if any, from line 14 of the 2015 Capital Loss Carryover Worksheet	15	( )
16 **Net long-term capital gain or (loss).** Combine lines 8a through 15 in column (h). Enter here and on line 18a, column (3) on the back ▶	16	12,000

Schedule D (Form 1041) 2016 Page 2

Part III Summary of Parts I and II
Caution: *Read the instructions* ***before*** *completing this part.*

			(1) Beneficiaries' (see instr.)	(2) Estate's or trust's	(3) Total
17	**Net short-term gain or (loss)**	17			
18	**Net long-term gain or (loss):**				
a	Total for year	18a		12,000	12,000
b	Unrecaptured section 1250 gain (see line 18 of the wrksht.)	18b			
c	28% rate gain	18c			
19	**Total net gain or (loss).** Combine lines 17 and 18a ▶	19		12,000	12,000

Note: *If line 19, column (3), is a net gain, enter the gain on Form 1041, line 4 (or Form 990-T, Part I, line 4a). If lines 18a and 19, column (2), are net gains, go to Part V, and* ***don't*** *complete Part IV. If line 19, column (3), is a net loss, complete Part IV and the* ***Capital Loss Carryover Worksheet,*** *as necessary.*

Part IV Capital Loss Limitation

20 Enter here and enter as a (loss) on Form 1041, line 4 (or Form 990-T, Part I, line 4c, if a trust), the **smaller** of:
a The loss on line 19, column (3) **or b** $3,000 . . . 20 ( )

Note: *If the loss on line 19, column (3), is more than $3,000,* ***or*** *if Form 1041, page 1, line 22 (or Form 990-T, line 34), is a loss, complete the* ***Capital Loss Carryover Worksheet*** *in the instructions to figure your capital loss carryover.*

Part V Tax Computation Using Maximum Capital Gains Rates

Form 1041 filers. Complete this part **only** if both lines 18a and 19 in column (2) are gains, or an amount is entered in Part I or Part II and there is an entry on Form 1041, line 2b(2), **and** Form 1041, line 22, is more than zero.

Caution: *Skip this part and complete the* ***Schedule D Tax Worksheet*** *in the instructions if:*

- *Either line 18b, col. (2) or line 18c, col. (2) is more than zero, or*
- *Both Form 1041, line 2b(1), and Form 4952, line 4g are more than zero.*

Form 990-T trusts. Complete this part **only** if both lines 18a and 19 are gains, or qualified dividends are included in income in Part I of Form 990-T, **and** Form 990-T, line 34, is more than zero. Skip this part and complete the **Schedule D Tax Worksheet** in the instructions if either line 18b, col. (2) or line 18c, col. (2) is more than zero.

21	Enter taxable income from Form 1041, line 22 (or Form 990-T, line 34)			21	11,700		
22	Enter the **smaller** of line 18a or 19 in column (2) but not less than zero	22	12,000				
23	Enter the estate's or trust's qualified dividends from Form 1041, line 2b(2) (or enter the qualified dividends included in income in Part I of Form 990-T)	23	-0-				
24	Add lines 22 and 23	24	12,000				
25	If the estate or trust is filing Form 4952, enter the amount from line 4g; otherwise, enter -0- ▶	25	-0-				
26	Subtract line 25 from line 24. If zero or less, enter -0-			26	12,000		
27	Subtract line 26 from line 21. If zero or less, enter -0-			27	-0-		
28	Enter the **smaller** of the amount on line 21 or $2,550			28	2,550		
29	Enter the **smaller** of the amount on line 27 or line 28			29	-0-		
30	Subtract line 29 from line 28. If zero or less, enter -0-. This amount is taxed at 0% ▶					30	2,550
31	Enter the **smaller** of line 21 or line 26			31	11,700		
32	Subtract line 30 from line 26			32	9,450		
33	Enter the **smaller** of line 21 or $12,400			33	11,700		
34	Add lines 27 and 30			34	2,550		
35	Subtract line 34 from line 33. If zero or less, enter -0-			35	9,150		
36	Enter the **smaller** of line 32 or line 35			36	9,150		
37	Multiply line 36 by 15% (0.15) ▶					37	1,373
38	Enter the amount from line 31			38	11,700		
39	Add lines 30 and 36			39	11,700		
40	Subtract line 39 from line 38. If zero or less, enter -0-			40	-0-		
41	Multiply line 40 by 20% (0.20) ▶					41	-0-
42	Figure the tax on the amount on line 27. Use the 2016 Tax Rate Schedule for Estates and Trusts (see the Schedule G instructions in the instructions for Form 1041)			42	-0-		
43	Add lines 37, 41, and 42			43	1,373		
44	Figure the tax on the amount on line 21. Use the 2016 Tax Rate Schedule for Estates and Trusts (see the Schedule G instructions in the instructions for Form 1041)			44	2,975		
45	**Tax on all taxable income.** Enter the **smaller** of line 43 or line 44 here and on Form 1041, Schedule G, line 1a (or Form 990-T, line 36) ▶					45	1,373

Schedule D (Form 1041) 2016

661113

☐ Final K-1 ☐ Amended K-1 OMB No. 1545-0092

Schedule K-1 (Form 1041) **2016**

Department of the Treasury
Internal Revenue Service

For calendar year 2016, or tax year beginning ________, 2016, and ending ________, 20 ____

Beneficiary's Share of Income, Deductions, Credits, etc.

▶ See back of form and instructions.

Part I Information About the Estate or Trust

A Estate's or trust's employer identification number

XX-XXXXXXX

B Estate's or trust's name

Bob Adams Trust

C Fiduciary's name, address, city, state, and ZIP code

First Bank
Post OfficeBox 100
City, ST 44444

D ☐ Check if Form 1041-T was filed and enter the date it was filed ________

E ☐ Check if this is the final Form 1041 for the estate or trust

Part II Information About the Beneficiary

F Beneficiary's identifying number

XXX-XX-XXXX

G Beneficiary's name, address, city, state, and ZIP code

Bob Adams
3 Jackson Highway
City, ST 44444

H ☒ Domestic beneficiary ☐ Foreign beneficiary

Part III Beneficiary's Share of Current Year Income, Deductions, Credits, and Other Items

1	Interest income	
2a	Ordinary dividends	30,000
2b	Qualified dividends	30,000
3	Net short-term capital gain	
4a	Net long-term capital gain	
4b	28% rate gain	
4c	Unrecaptured section 1250 gain	
5	Other portfolio and nonbusiness income	
6	Ordinary business income	
7	Net rental real estate income	2,660*
8	Other rental income	
9	Directly apportioned deductions	
10	Estate tax deduction	
11	Final year deductions	
12	Alternative minimum tax adjustment	
13	Credits and credit recapture	
14	Other information	A 14,640

*See attached statement for additional information.

Note. A statement must be attached showing the beneficiary's share of income and directly apportioned deductions from each business, rental real estate, and other rental activity.

For IRS Use Only

For Paperwork Reduction Act Notice, see the Instructions for Form 1041. IRS.gov/form1041 Cat. No. 11380D **Schedule K-1 (Form 1041) 2016**

*5,000 – ($1,000 + $840 + $500) = $2,660

This list identifies the codes used on Schedule K-1 for beneficiaries and provides summarized reporting information for beneficiaries who file Form 1040. For detailed reporting and filing information, see the Instructions for Schedule K-1 (Form 1041) for a Beneficiary Filing Form 1040 and the instructions for your income tax return.

	Report on
1. Interest income	Form 1040, line 8a
2a. Ordinary dividends	Form 1040, line 9a
2b. Qualified dividends	Form 1040, line 9b
3. Net short-term capital gain	Schedule D, line 5
4a. Net long-term capital gain	Schedule D, line 12
4b. 28% rate gain	28% Rate Gain Worksheet, line 4 (Schedule D Instructions)
4c. Unrecaptured section 1250 gain	Unrecaptured Section 1250 Gain Worksheet, line 11 (Schedule D Instructions)
5. Other portfolio and nonbusiness income	Schedule E, line 33, column (f)
6. Ordinary business income	Schedule E, line 33, column (d) or (f)
7. Net rental real estate income	Schedule E, line 33, column (d) or (f)
8. Other rental income	Schedule E, line 33, column (d) or (f)
9. Directly apportioned deductions	
Code	
A Depreciation	Form 8582 or Schedule E, line 33, column (c) or (e)
B Depletion	Form 8582 or Schedule E, line 33, column (c) or (e)
C Amortization	Form 8582 or Schedule E, line 33, column (c) or (e)
10. Estate tax deduction	Schedule A, line 28
11. Final year deductions	
A Excess deductions	Schedule A, line 23
B Short-term capital loss carryover	Schedule D, line 5
C Long-term capital loss carryover	Schedule D, line 12; line 5 of the wksht. for Sch. D, line 18; and line 16 of the wksht. for Sch. D, line 19
D Net operating loss carryover — regular tax	Form 1040, line 21
E Net operating loss carryover — minimum tax	Form 6251, line 11
12. Alternative minimum tax (AMT) items	
A Adjustment for minimum tax purposes	Form 6251, line 15
B AMT adjustment attributable to qualified dividends	See the beneficiary's instructions and the Instructions for Form 6251
C AMT adjustment attributable to net short-term capital gain	
D AMT adjustment attributable to net long-term capital gain	
E AMT adjustment attributable to unrecaptured section 1250 gain	
F AMT adjustment attributable to 28% rate gain	
G Accelerated depreciation	
H Depletion	
I Amortization	
J Exclusion items	2017 Form 8801

13. Credits and credit recapture

Code	*Report on*
A Credit for estimated taxes	Form 1040, line 65
B Credit for backup withholding	Form 1040, line 64
C Low-income housing credit	See the beneficiary's instructions
D Rehabilitation credit and energy credit	
E Other qualifying investment credit	
F Work opportunity credit	
G Credit for small employer health insurance premiums	
H Biofuel producer credit	
I Credit for increasing research activities	
J Renewable electricity, refined coal, and Indian coal production credit	
K Empowerment zone employment credit	
L Indian employment credit	
M Orphan drug credit	
N Credit for employer-provided child care and facilities	
O Biodiesel and renewable diesel fuels credit	
P Credit to holders of tax credit bonds	
Q Credit for employer differential wage payments	
R Recapture of credits	

14. Other information

A Tax-exempt interest	Form 1040, line 8b
B Foreign taxes	Form 1040, line 48 or Sch. A, line 8
C Qualified production activities income	Form 8903, line 7, col. (b) (also see the beneficiary's instructions)
D Form W-2 wages	Form 8903, line 17
E Net investment income	Form 4952, line 4a
F Gross farm and fishing income	Schedule E, line 42
G Foreign trading gross receipts (IRC 942(a))	See the Instructions for Form 8873
H Adjustment for section 1411 net investment income or deductions	Form 8960, line 7 (also see the beneficiary's instructions)
I Other information	See the beneficiary's instructions

Note. If you are a beneficiary who does not file a Form 1040, see instructions for the type of income tax return you are filing.

Form **1041** Department of the Treasury—Internal Revenue Service
U.S. Income Tax Return for Estates and Trusts **2016** OMB No. 1545-0092

▶ Information about Form 1041 and its separate instructions is at *www.irs.gov/form1041.*

A Check all that apply:
- ☐ Decedent's estate
- ☐ Simple trust
- ☒ Complex trust
- ☐ Qualified disability trust
- ☐ ESBT (S portion only)
- ☐ Grantor type trust
- ☐ Bankruptcy estate-Ch. 7
- ☐ Bankruptcy estate-Ch. 11
- ☐ Pooled income fund

For calendar year 2016 or fiscal year beginning , 2016, and ending , 20

Name of estate or trust (If a grantor type trust, see the instructions.): Cathy and Karen Stephens Trust (Complex Trust)

Name and title of fiduciary: Merchants Bank

Number, street, and room or suite no. (If a P.O. box, see the instructions.): 3000 Sun Plaza

City or town, state or province, country, and ZIP or foreign postal code: City, ST 88888

C Employer identification number: XX-XXXXXXX

D Date entity created: 2003

E Nonexempt charitable and split-interest trusts, check applicable box(es), see instructions.
☐ Described in sec. 4947(a)(1). Check here if not a private foundation . . . ▶ ☐
☐ Described in sec. 4947(a)(2)

B Number of Schedules K-1 attached (see instructions) ▶ 2

F Check applicable boxes: ☐ Initial return ☐ Final return ☐ Amended return ☐ Net operating loss carryback ☐ Change in trust's name ☐ Change in fiduciary ☐ Change in fiduciary's name ☐ Change in fiduciary's address

G Check here if the estate or filing trust made a section 645 election . . . . . . ▶ ☐ Trust TIN ▶

Income	1	Interest income	1	
	2a	Total ordinary dividends	2a	30,000
	b	Qualified dividends allocable to: (1) Beneficiaries 13,319 (2) Estate or trust 16,681		
	3	Business income or (loss). Attach Schedule C or C-EZ (Form 1040)	3	
	4	Capital gain or (loss). Attach Schedule D (Form 1041)	4	12,000
	5	Rents, royalties, partnerships, other estates and trusts, etc. Attach Schedule E (Form 1040)	5	4,000
	6	Farm income or (loss). Attach Schedule F (Form 1040)	6	
	7	Ordinary gain or (loss). Attach Form 4797	7	
	8	Other income. List type and amount	8	
	9	**Total income.** Combine lines 1, 2a, and 3 through 8 ▶	9	46,000
Deductions	10	Interest. Check if Form 4952 is attached ▶ ☐	10	
	11	Taxes	11	
	12	Fiduciary fees ($1,200 – $360)	12	840
	13	Charitable deduction (from Schedule A, line 7)	13	
	14	Attorney, accountant, and return preparer fees	14	500
	15a	Other deductions **not** subject to the 2% floor (attach schedule)	15a	
	b	Net operating loss deduction. See instructions	15b	
	c	Allowable miscellaneous itemized deductions subject to the 2% floor	15c	
	16	Add lines 10 through 15c ▶	16	1,340
	17	Adjusted total income or (loss). Subtract line 16 from line 9 — 17: 44,660		
	18	Income distribution deduction (from Schedule B, line 15). Attach Schedules K-1 (Form 1041)	18	14,500
	19	Estate tax deduction including certain generation-skipping taxes (attach computation)	19	
	20	Exemption	20	100
	21	Add lines 18 through 20 ▶	21	14,600
Tax and Payments	22	Taxable income. Subtract line 21 from line 17. If a loss, see instructions	22	30,060
	23	**Total tax** (from Schedule G, line 7)	23	5,888
	24	**Payments: a** 2016 estimated tax payments and amount applied from 2015 return	24a	5,360
	b	Estimated tax payments allocated to beneficiaries (from Form 1041-T)	24b	
	c	Subtract line 24b from line 24a	24c	5,360
	d	Tax paid with Form 7004. See instructions	24d	
	e	Federal income tax withheld. If any is from Form(s) 1099, check ▶ ☐	24e	
		Other payments: **f** Form 2439 ; **g** Form 4136 ; Total ▶	24h	
	25	**Total payments.** Add lines 24c through 24e, and 24h ▶	25	5,360
	26	Estimated tax penalty. See instructions	26	
	27	**Tax due.** If line 25 is smaller than the total of lines 23 and 26, enter amount owed	27	528
	28	**Overpayment.** If line 25 is larger than the total of lines 23 and 26, enter amount overpaid	28	
	29	Amount of line 28 to be: **a Credited to 2017 estimated tax** ▶ ; **b Refunded** ▶	29	

Sign Here Under penalties of perjury, I declare that I have examined this return, including accompanying schedules and statements, and to the best of my knowledge and belief, it is true, correct, and complete. Declaration of preparer (other than taxpayer) is based on all information of which preparer has any knowledge.

Fred Fidus | 3-14-17 | ▶ XX-XXXXXXX
Signature of fiduciary or officer representing fiduciary | Date | EIN of fiduciary if a financial institution

May the IRS discuss this return with the preparer shown below (see instr.)? ☒ Yes ☐ No

Paid Preparer Use Only

Print/Type preparer's name: Sarah Public | Preparer's signature: Sarah Public | Date: 3-13-17 | Check ☒ if self-employed | PTIN

Firm's name ▶ Sarah Public | Firm's EIN ▶

Firm's address ▶ 200 Sun Plaza City, ST 88888 | Phone no.

For Paperwork Reduction Act Notice, see the separate instructions. Cat. No. 11370H Form **1041** (2016)

*Line 5: Net Rental income = Rental income $5,000 – Rental expenses $1,000 = $4,000

Note: Pages concerning the AMT are omitted because the trust does not owe the AMT.

See the Comprehensive Illustration on text page C:14-24 for tax form facts.

Form 1041 (2016) Page **2**

Schedule A **Charitable Deduction.** Don't complete for a simple trust or a pooled income fund.

1	Amounts paid or permanently set aside for charitable purposes from gross income. See instructions	1	
2	Tax-exempt income allocable to charitable contributions. See instructions	2	
3	Subtract line 2 from line 1	3	
4	Capital gains for the tax year allocated to corpus and paid or permanently set aside for charitable purposes	4	
5	Add lines 3 and 4	5	
6	Section 1202 exclusion allocable to capital gains paid or permanently set aside for charitable purposes. See instructions	6	
7	**Charitable deduction.** Subtract line 6 from line 5. Enter here and on page 1, line 13	7	

Schedule B **Income Distribution Deduction**

1	Adjusted total income. See instructions	1	44,660
2	Adjusted tax-exempt interest ($15,000 − $360)	2	14,640
3	Total net gain from Schedule D (Form 1041), line 19, column (1). See instructions	3	
4	Enter amount from Schedule A, line 4 (minus any allocable section 1202 exclusion)	4	
5	Capital gains for the tax year included on Schedule A, line 1. See instructions	5	
6	Enter any gain from page 1, line 4, as a negative number. If page 1, line 4, is a loss, enter the loss as a positive number	6	(12,000)
7	**Distributable net income.** Combine lines 1 through 6. If zero or less, enter -0-	7	47,300
8	If a complex trust, enter accounting income for the tax year as determined under the governing instrument and applicable local law — 8: 48,500		
9	Income required to be distributed currently	9	-0-
10	Other amounts paid, credited, or otherwise required to be distributed	10	21,000
11	Total distributions. Add lines 9 and 10. If greater than line 8, see instructions	11	21,000
12	Enter the amount of tax-exempt income included on line 11	12	6,500
13	Tentative income distribution deduction. Subtract line 12 from line 11	13	14,500
14	Tentative income distribution deduction. Subtract line 2 from line 7. If zero or less, enter -0-	14	32,660
15	**Income distribution deduction.** Enter the smaller of line 13 or line 14 here and on page 1, line 18	15	14,500

Schedule G **Tax Computation** (see instructions)

1	**Tax:** a Tax on taxable income. See instructions	1a	5,217		
	b Tax on lump-sum distributions. Attach Form 4972	1b			
	c Alternative minimum tax (from Schedule I (Form 1041), line 56)	1c			
	d **Total.** Add lines 1a through 1c ▶			1d	5,217
2a	Foreign tax credit. Attach Form 1116	2a			
b	General business credit. Attach Form 3800	2b			
c	Credit for prior year minimum tax. Attach Form 8801	2c			
d	Bond credits. Attach Form 8912	2d			
e	**Total credits.** Add lines 2a through 2d ▶			2e	
3	Subtract line 2e from line 1d. If zero or less, enter -0-			3	5,217
4	Net investment income tax from Form 8960, line 21			4	671
5	Recapture taxes. Check if from: ☐ Form 4255 ☐ Form 8611			5	
6	Household employment taxes. Attach Schedule H (Form 1040)			6	
7	**Total tax.** Add lines 3 through 6. Enter here and on page 1, line 23 ▶			7	5,888

	Other Information	Yes	No
1	Did the estate or trust receive tax-exempt income? If "Yes," attach a computation of the allocation of expenses. Enter the amount of tax-exempt interest income and exempt-interest dividends ▶ $ 15,000; (see below)	X	
2	Did the estate or trust receive all or any part of the earnings (salary, wages, and other compensation) of any individual by reason of a contract assignment or similar arrangement?		X
3	At any time during calendar year 2016, did the estate or trust have an interest in or a signature or other authority over a bank, securities, or other financial account in a foreign country? See the instructions for exceptions and filing requirements for FinCEN Form 114. If "Yes," enter the name of the foreign country ▶		X
4	During the tax year, did the estate or trust receive a distribution from, or was it the grantor of, or transferor to, a foreign trust? If "Yes," the estate or trust may have to file Form 3520. See instructions		X
5	Did the estate or trust receive, or pay, any qualified residence interest on seller-provided financing? If "Yes," see the instructions for required attachment		X
6	If this is an estate or a complex trust making the section 663(b) election, check here. See instructions ▶ ☐		
7	To make a section 643(e)(3) election, attach Schedule D (Form 1041), and check here. See instructions ▶ ☐		
8	If the decedent's estate has been open for more than 2 years, attach an explanation for the delay in closing the estate, and check here ▶ ☐		
9	Are any present or future trust beneficiaries skip persons? See instructions		X
10	Was the trust a specified domestic entity required to file Form 8938 for the tax year (see the Instructions for Form 8938)?		X

Form **1041** (2016)

Line 2: Allocation of expenses: $\frac{\$15,000}{\$50,000} \times \$1,200 = \$360$ of trustee's fee allocated to tax-exempt income

SCHEDULE D (Form 1041)

Department of the Treasury
Internal Revenue Service

Capital Gains and Losses

▶ Attach to Form 1041, Form 5227, or Form 990-T.
▶ Use Form 8949 to list your transactions for lines 1b, 2, 3, 8b, 9 and 10.
▶ Information about Schedule D and its separate instructions is at *www.irs.gov/form1041*.

OMB No. 1545-0092

2016

Name of estate or trust: Cathy and Karen Stephens Trust

Employer identification number: XX-XXXXXXX

Note: *Form 5227 filers need to complete **only** Parts I and II.*

Part I Short-Term Capital Gains and Losses—Assets Held One Year or Less

See instructions for how to figure the amounts to enter on the lines below. This form may be easier to complete if you round off cents to whole dollars.	(d) Proceeds (sales price)	(e) Cost (or other basis)	(g) Adjustments to gain or loss from Form(s) 8949, Part I, line 2, column (g)	(h) Gain or (loss) Subtract column (e) from column (d) and combine the result with column (g)
1a Totals for all short-term transactions reported on Form 1099-B for which basis was reported to the IRS and for which you have no adjustments (see instructions). However, if you choose to report all these transactions on Form 8949, leave this line blank and go to line 1b .				
1b Totals for all transactions reported on Form(s) 8949 with **Box A** checked				
2 Totals for all transactions reported on Form(s) 8949 with **Box B** checked				
3 Totals for all transactions reported on Form(s) 8949 with **Box C** checked				

4 Short-term capital gain or (loss) from Forms 4684, 6252, 6781, and 8824	4	
5 Net short-term gain or (loss) from partnerships, S corporations, and other estates or trusts . . .	5	
6 Short-term capital loss carryover. Enter the amount, if any, from line 9 of the 2015 Capital Loss Carryover Worksheet	6	( )
7 **Net short-term capital gain or (loss).** Combine lines 1a through 6 in column (h). Enter here and on line 17, column (3) on the back . . . . ▶	7	

Part II Long-Term Capital Gains and Losses—Assets Held More Than One Year

See instructions for how to figure the amounts to enter on the lines below. This form may be easier to complete if you round off cents to whole dollars.	(d) Proceeds (sales price)	(e) Cost (or other basis)	(g) Adjustments to gain or loss from Form(s) 8949, Part II, line 2, column (g)	(h) Gain or (loss) Subtract column (e) from column (d) and combine the result with column (g)
8a Totals for all long-term transactions reported on Form 1099-B for which basis was reported to the IRS and for which you have no adjustments (see instructions). However, if you choose to report all these transactions on Form 8949, leave this line blank and go to line 8b .	15,000	3,000		12,000
8b Totals for all transactions reported on Form(s) 8949 with **Box D** checked				
9 Totals for all transactions reported on Form(s) 8949 with **Box E** checked				
10 Totals for all transactions reported on Form(s) 8949 with **Box F** checked.				

11 Long-term capital gain or (loss) from Forms 2439, 4684, 6252, 6781, and 8824	11	
12 Net long-term gain or (loss) from partnerships, S corporations, and other estates or trusts . . .	12	
13 Capital gain distributions	13	
14 Gain from Form 4797, Part I	14	
15 Long-term capital loss carryover. Enter the amount, if any, from line 14 of the 2015 Capital Loss Carryover Worksheet	15	( )
16 **Net long-term capital gain or (loss).** Combine lines 8a through 15 in column (h). Enter here and on line 18a, column (3) on the back . . . . ▶	16	12,000

Schedule D (Form 1041) 2016 Page **2**

Part III Summary of Parts I and II **Caution:** *Read the instructions* **before** *completing this part.*		(1) Beneficiaries' (see instr.)	(2) Estate's or trust's	(3) Total
17 Net short-term gain or (loss)	17			
18 Net long-term gain or (loss):				
a Total for year	18a		12,000	12,000
b Unrecaptured section 1250 gain (see line 18 of the wrksht.)	18b			
c 28% rate gain	18c			
19 Total net gain or (loss). Combine lines 17 and 18a ▶	19		12,000	12,000

Note: *If line 19, column (3), is a net gain, enter the gain on Form 1041, line 4 (or Form 990-T, Part I, line 4a). If lines 18a and 19, column (2), are net gains, go to Part V, and* **don't** *complete Part IV. If line 19, column (3), is a net loss, complete Part IV and the* **Capital Loss Carryover Worksheet,** *as necessary.*

Part IV Capital Loss Limitation

20 Enter here and enter as a (loss) on Form 1041, line 4 (or Form 990-T, Part I, line 4c, if a trust), the **smaller** of:
a The loss on line 19, column (3) **or b** $3,000 . . . 20 ( )

Note: *If the loss on line 19, column (3), is more than $3,000,* **or** *if Form 1041, page 1, line 22 (or Form 990-T, line 34), is a loss, complete the* **Capital Loss Carryover Worksheet** *in the instructions to figure your capital loss carryover.*

Part V Tax Computation Using Maximum Capital Gains Rates

Form 1041 filers. Complete this part **only** if both lines 18a and 19 in column (2) are gains, or an amount is entered in Part I or Part II and there is an entry on Form 1041, line 2b(2), **and** Form 1041, line 22, is more than zero.

Caution: *Skip this part and complete the* **Schedule D Tax Worksheet** *in the instructions if:*

- *Either line 18b, col. (2) or line 18c, col. (2) is more than zero, or*
- *Both Form 1041, line 2b(1), and Form 4952, line 4g are more than zero.*

Form 990-T trusts. Complete this part **only** if both lines 18a and 19 are gains, or qualified dividends are included in income in Part I of Form 990-T, **and** Form 990-T, line 34, is more than zero. Skip this part and complete the **Schedule D Tax Worksheet** in the instructions if either line 18b, col. (2) or line 18c, col. (2) is more than zero.

21	Enter taxable income from Form 1041, line 22 (or Form 990-T, line 34)			21	30,060		
22	Enter the **smaller** of line 18a or 19 in column (2) but not less than zero	22	12,000				
23	Enter the estate's or trust's qualified dividends from Form 1041, line 2b(2) (or enter the qualified dividends included in income in Part I of Form 990-T)	23	16,681				
24	Add lines 22 and 23	24	28,681				
25	If the estate or trust is filing Form 4952, enter the amount from line 4g; otherwise, enter -0- ▶	25	-0-				
26	Subtract line 25 from line 24. If zero or less, enter -0-			26	28,681		
27	Subtract line 26 from line 21. If zero or less, enter -0-			27	1,379		
28	Enter the **smaller** of the amount on line 21 or $2,550			28	2,550		
29	Enter the **smaller** of the amount on line 27 or line 28			29	1,379		
30	Subtract line 29 from line 28. If zero or less, enter -0-. This amount is taxed at 0% ▶					30	1,171
31	Enter the smaller of line 21 or line 26			31	28,681		
32	Subtract line 30 from line 26			32	27,510		
33	Enter the **smaller** of line 21 or $12,400			33	12,400		
34	Add lines 27 and 30			34	2,550		
35	Subtract line 34 from line 33. If zero or less, enter -0-			35	9,850		
36	Enter the **smaller** of line 32 or line 35			36	9,850		
37	Multiply line 36 by 15% (0.15) ▶					37	1,478
38	Enter the amount from line 31			38	28,681		
39	Add lines 30 and 36			39	11,021		
40	Subtract line 39 from line 38. If zero or less, enter -0-			40	17,660		
41	Multiply line 40 by 20% (0.20) ▶					41	3,532
42	Figure the tax on the amount on line 27. Use the 2016 Tax Rate Schedule for Estates and Trusts (see the Schedule G instructions in the instructions for Form 1041)			42	207		
43	Add lines 37, 41, and 42			43	5,217		
44	Figure the tax on the amount on line 21. Use the 2016 Tax Rate Schedule for Estates and Trusts (see the Schedule G instructions in the instructions for Form 1041)			44	10,199		
45	**Tax on all taxable income.** Enter the **smaller** of line 43 or line 44 here and on Form 1041, Schedule G, line 1a (or Form 990-T, line 36) ▶					45	5,217

Form **8960**

Department of the Treasury Internal Revenue Service (99)

Net Investment Income Tax— Individuals, Estates, and Trusts

▶ Attach to your tax return

▶ Information about Form 8960 and its separate instructions is at *www.irs.gov/form8960.*

OMB No. 1545-2227

2016

Attachment Sequence No. 72

Name(s) shown on your tax return	Your social security number or EIN
Cathy and Karen Stephens Trust	XX-XXXXXXX

Part I **Investment Income**
☐ Section 6013(g) election (see instructions)
☐ Section 6013(h) election (see instructions)
☐ Regulations section 1.1411-10(g) election (see instructions)

1	Taxable interest (see instructions)			1	
2	Ordinary dividends (see instructions)			2	30,000
3	Annuities (see instructions)			3	
4a	Rental real estate, royalties, partnerships, S corporations, trusts, etc. (see instructions)	4a	4,000		
b	Adjustment for net income or loss derived in the ordinary course of a non-section 1411 trade or business (see instructions)	4b			
c	Combine lines 4a and 4b			4c	4,000
5a	Net gain or loss from disposition of property (see instructions)	5a	12,000		
b	Net gain or loss from disposition of property that is not subject to net investment income tax (see instructions)	5b			
c	Adjustment from disposition of partnership interest or S corporation stock (see instructions)	5c			
d	Combine lines 5a through 5c			5d	12,000
6	Adjustments to investment income for certain CFCs and PFICs (see instructions)			6	
7	Other modifications to investment income (see instructions)			7	
8	Total investment income. Combine lines 1, 2, 3, 4c, 5d, 6, and 7			8	46,000

Part II **Investment Expenses Allocable to Investment Income and Modifications**

9a	Investment interest expenses (see instructions)	9a			
b	State, local, and foreign income tax (see instructions)	9b			
c	Miscellaneous investment expenses (see instructions)	9c	1,340		
d	Add lines 9a, 9b, and 9c			9d	1,340
10	Additional modifications (see instructions)			10	
11	Total deductions and modifications. Add lines 9d and 10			11	1,340

Part III **Tax Computation**

12	Net investment income. Subtract Part II, line 11 from Part I, line 8. Individuals complete lines 13–17. Estates and trusts complete lines 18a–21. If zero or less, enter -0-			12	44,660
	Individuals:				
13	Modified adjusted gross income (see instructions)	13			
14	Threshold based on filing status (see instructions)	14			
15	Subtract line 14 from line 13. If zero or less, enter -0-	15			
16	Enter the smaller of line 12 or line 15			16	
17	Net investment income tax for individuals. Multiply line 16 by 3.8% (.038). **Enter here and include on your tax return** (see instructions)			17	
	Estates and Trusts:				
18a	Net investment income (line 12 above)	18a	44,660		
b	Deductions for distributions of net investment income and deductions under section 642(c) (see instructions)	18b	14,500		
c	Undistributed net investment income. Subtract line 18b from 18a (see instructions). If zero or less, enter -0-	18c	30,160		
19a	Adjusted gross income (see instructions) *	19a	30,060*		
b	Highest tax bracket for estates and trusts for the year (see instructions)	19b	12,400		
c	Subtract line 19b from line 19a. If zero or less, enter -0-	19c	17,660		
20	Enter the smaller of line 18c or line 19c			20	17,660
21	Net investment income tax for estates and trusts. Multiply line 20 by 3.8% (.038). **Enter here and include on your tax return** (see instructions)			21	671

For Paperwork Reduction Act Notice, see your tax return instructions. Cat. No. 59474M Form **8960** (2016)

*$44,660 – $14,500 – $100 = $30,060

661113

☐ Final K-1 ☐ Amended K-1 OMB No. 1545-0092

Schedule K-1 (Form 1041) **2016**
Department of the Treasury
Internal Revenue Service

For calendar year 2016, or tax year beginning ________, 2016, and ending ________, 20 ____

Beneficiary's Share of Income, Deductions, Credits, etc.

► See back of form and instructions.

Part I Information About the Estate or Trust

A Estate's or trust's employer identification number
XX-XXXXXXX

B Estate's or trust's name
Cathy and Karen Stephens Trust

C Fiduciary's name, address, city, state, and ZIP code
Merchants Bank
3000 Sun Plaza
City, ST 88888

D ☐ Check if Form 1041-T was filed and enter the date it was filed ________

E ☐ Check if this is the final Form 1041 for the estate or trust

Part II Information About the Beneficiary

F Beneficiary's identifying number
XXX-XX-XXXX

G Beneficiary's name, address, city, state, and ZIP code
Cathy Stephens
13 Sunny Shores
City, ST 77777

H ☒ Domestic beneficiary ☐ Foreign beneficiary

Part III Beneficiary's Share of Current Year Income, Deductions, Credits, and Other Items

1	Interest income	
2a	Ordinary dividends	8,879
2b	Qualified dividends	8,879
3	Net short-term capital gain	
4a	Net long-term capital gain	
4b	28% rate gain	
4c	Unrecaptured section 1250 gain	
5	Other portfolio and nonbusiness income	
6	Ordinary business income	
7	Net rental real estate income	788
8	Other rental income	
9	Directly apportioned deductions	
10	Estate tax deduction	
11	Final year deductions	
12	Alternative minimum tax adjustment	
13	Credits and credit recapture	
14	Other information	A 4,333

*See attached statement for additional information.

Note. A statement must be attached showing the beneficiary's share of income and directly apportioned deductions from each business, rental real estate, and other rental activity.

For IRS Use Only

661113

☐ Final K-1 ☐ Amended K-1 OMB No. 1545-0092

Schedule K-1 (Form 1041) **2016**
Department of the Treasury
Internal Revenue Service

For calendar year 2016, or tax year beginning ________, 2016, and ending ________, 20 ____

Beneficiary's Share of Income, Deductions, Credits, etc.

▶ See back of form and instructions.

Part I Information About the Estate or Trust

A Estate's or trust's employer identification number
XX-XXXXXXX

B Estate's or trust's name
Cathy and Karen Stephens Trust

C Fiduciary's name, address, city, state, and ZIP code
Merchants Bank
3000 Sun Plaza
City, ST 88888

D ☐ Check if Form 1041-T was filed and enter the date it was filed ________

E ☐ Check if this is the final Form 1041 for the estate or trust

Part II Information About the Beneficiary

F Beneficiary's identifying number
XXX-XX-XXXX

G Beneficiary's name, address, city, state, and ZIP code
Karen Stephens
1472 Ski Run
City, ST 11111

H ☒ Domestic beneficiary ☐ Foreign beneficiary

Part III Beneficiary's Share of Current Year Income, Deductions, Credits, and Other Items

1	Interest income	
2a	Ordinary dividends	4,440
2b	Qualified dividends	4,440
3	Net short-term capital gain	
4a	Net long-term capital gain	
4b	28% rate gain	
4c	Unrecaptured section 1250 gain	
5	Other portfolio and nonbusiness income	
6	Ordinary business income	
7	Net rental real estate income	393
8	Other rental income	
9	Directly apportioned deductions	
10	Estate tax deduction	
11	Final year deductions	
12	Alternative minimum tax adjustment	
13	Credits and credit recapture	
14	Other information	A 2,167

*See attached statement for additional information.

Note. A statement must be attached showing the beneficiary's share of income and directly apportioned deductions from each business, rental real estate, and other rental activity.

For IRS Use Only

Form **1116** | Department of the Treasury Internal Revenue Service (99)

Foreign Tax Credit

(Individual, Estate, or Trust)

▶ Attach to Form 1040, 1040NR, 1041, or 990-T.

▶ Information about Form 1116 and its separate instructions is at *www.irs.gov/form1116.*

OMB No. 1545-0121 | 2016 | Attachment Sequence No. 19

Name: Andrew Roberts | Identifying number as shown on page 1 of your tax return: XXX-XX-XXXX

Use a separate Form 1116 for each category of income listed below. See *Categories of Income* in the instructions. Check only one box on each Form 1116. Report all amounts in U.S. dollars except where specified in Part II below.

a ☒ Passive category income | c ☐ Section 901(j) income | e ☐ Lump-sum distributions
b ☐ General category income | d ☐ Certain income re-sourced by treaty

f Resident of (name of country) ▶ United States

Note: If you paid taxes to only one foreign country or U.S. possession, use column A in Part I and line A in Part II. If you paid taxes to **more than one** foreign country or U.S. possession, use a separate column and line for each country or possession.

Part I Taxable Income or Loss From Sources Outside the United States (for Category Checked Above)

		Foreign Country or U.S. Possession				Total
		A	B	C		(Add cols. A, B, and C.)
g	**Enter the name of the foreign country or U.S. possession** ▶	Country X				
1a	Gross income from sources within country shown above and of the type checked above (see instructions): Dividends				1a	15,517
b	Check if line 1a is compensation for personal services as an employee, your total compensation from all sources is $250,000 or more, and you used an alternative basis to determine its source (see instructions) ▶ ☐					
	Deductions and losses (**Caution:** See instructions.):					
2	Expenses **definitely related** to the income on line 1a (attach statement)					
3	Pro rata share of other deductions **not definitely related:**					
a	Certain itemized deductions or standard deduction (see instructions)					
b	Other deductions (attach statement)					
c	Add lines 3a and 3b					
d	Gross foreign source income (see instructions)					
e	Gross income from all sources (see instructions)					
f	Divide line 3d by line 3e (see instructions)					
g	Multiply line 3c by line 3f					
4	Pro rata share of interest expense (see instructions):					
a	Home mortgage interest (use the Worksheet for Home Mortgage Interest in the instructions)					
b	Other interest expense					
5	Losses from foreign sources					
6	Add lines 2, 3g, 4a, 4b, and 5	-0-			6	-0-
7	Subtract line 6 from line 1a. Enter the result here and on line 15, page 2 ▶				7	15,517

Part II Foreign Taxes Paid or Accrued (see instructions)

Country	Credit is claimed for taxes (you must check one) (h) ☒ Paid (i) ☐ Accrued	Foreign taxes paid or accrued								
		In foreign currency				In U.S. dollars				
		Taxes withheld at source on:			(n) Other foreign taxes paid or accrued	Taxes withheld at source on:			(r) Other foreign taxes paid or accrued	(s) Total foreign taxes paid or accrued (add cols. (o) through (r))
	(j) Date paid or accrued	(k) Dividends	(l) Rents and royalties	(m) Interest		(o) Dividends	(p) Rents and royalties	(q) Interest		
A	12-31-16	2,700*				2,328				2,328
B										
C										

8 **Add lines A through C, column (s). Enter the total here and on line 9, page 2** ▶ 8 | 2,328

For Paperwork Reduction Act Notice, see instructions. Cat. No. 11440U Form **1116** (2016)

*Denominated in Country X currency.

See text Example C:16-35 for tax form facts.

Form 1116 (2016) Page 2

Part III Figuring the Credit

Line	Description	Box	Amount	Line	Amount
9	Enter the amount from line 8. These are your total foreign taxes paid or accrued for the category of income checked above Part I	9	2,328		
10	Carryback or carryover (attach detailed computation)	10			
11	Add lines 9 and 10	11	2,328		
12	Reduction in foreign taxes (see instructions)	12	( )		
13	Taxes reclassified under high tax kickout (see instructions)	13			
14	Combine lines 11, 12, and 13. This is the total amount of foreign taxes available for credit			14	2,328
15	Enter the amount from line 7. This is your taxable income or (loss) from sources outside the United States (before adjustments) for the category of income checked above Part I (see instructions)	15	15,517		
16	Adjustments to line 15 (see instructions)	16			
17	Combine the amounts on lines 15 and 16. This is your net foreign source taxable income. (If the result is zero or less, you have no foreign tax credit for the category of income you checked above Part I. Skip lines 18 through 22. However, if you are filing more than one Form 1116, you must complete line 20.)	17	15,517		
18	**Individuals:** Enter the amount from Form 1040, line 41; or Form 1040NR, line 39. **Estates and trusts:** Enter your taxable income without the deduction for your exemption	18	86,000		
	Caution: If you figured your tax using the lower rates on qualified dividends or capital gains, see instructions.				
19	Divide line 17 by line 18. If line 17 is more than line 18, enter "1"			19	0.180430
20	**Individuals:** Enter the amount from Form 1040, lines 44 and 46. If you are a nonresident alien, enter the amounts from Form 1040NR, lines 42 and 44. **Estates and trusts:** Enter the amount from Form 1041, Schedule G, line 1a; or the total of Form 990-T, lines 36, 37, and 39			20	11,017*
	Caution: If you are completing line 20 for separate category **e** (lump-sum distributions), see instructions.				
21	Multiply line 20 by line 19 (maximum amount of credit)			21	1,988
22	Enter the **smaller** of line 14 or line 21. If this is the only Form 1116 you are filing, skip lines 23 through 27 and enter this amount on line 28. Otherwise, complete the appropriate line in Part IV (see instructions) ▶			22	1,988

Part IV Summary of Credits From Separate Parts III (see instructions)

Line	Description	Box	Amount	Line	Amount
23	Credit for taxes on passive category income	23	1,988		
24	Credit for taxes on general category income	24			
25	Credit for taxes on certain income re-sourced by treaty	25			
26	Credit for taxes on lump-sum distributions	26			
27	Add lines 23 through 26			27	1,988
28	Enter the **smaller** of line 20 or line 27			28	1,988
29	Reduction of credit for international boycott operations. See instructions for line 12			29	
30	Subtract line 29 from line 28. This is your **foreign tax credit.** Enter here and on Form 1040, line 48; Form 1040NR, line 46; Form 1041, Schedule G, line 2a; or Form 990-T, line 41a ▶			30	1,988

Form **1116** (2016)

*Tax on $86,000 – (2 x $4,050) = $77,900 of taxable income based on the 2016 tax rate schedule. The figure reported on Line 41 is net of the standard deduction or itemized deductions.

Form **2555**

Department of the Treasury
Internal Revenue Service

Foreign Earned Income

▶ Attach to Form 1040. Complete the Foreign Earned Income Tax Worksheet in the instructions for Form 1040 if you enter an amount on lines 45 or 50.

▶ Information about Form 2555 and its separate instructions is at *www.irs.gov/form2555.*

OMB No. 1545-0074

2016

Attachment Sequence No. **34**

For Use by U.S. Citizens and Resident Aliens Only

Name shown on Form 1040: Lawrence E. Smith

Your social security number: XXX-XX-XXXX

Part I General Information

1 Your foreign address (including country): 123 Rue de Harve 75000 Paris France

2 Your occupation: Financial Vice-President

3 Employer's name ▶ Very Public Corporation

4a Employer's U.S. address ▶ 90 Fifty Avenue, U.S. City, ST 10000

b Employer's foreign address ▶ 11 Rue de Nanettes/5 e'Etage, 75011 Paris France

5 Employer is (check any that apply): a ☐ A foreign entity b ☒ A U.S. company c ☐ Self d ☐ A foreign affiliate of a U.S. company e ☐ Other (specify) ▶

6a If you previously filed Form 2555 or Form 2555-EZ, enter the last year you filed the form. ▶ 2015

b If you didn't previously file Form 2555 or 2555-EZ to claim either of the exclusions, check here ▶ ☐ and go to line 7.

c Have you ever revoked either of the exclusions? . . . ☐ Yes ☒ No

d If you answered "Yes," enter the type of exclusion and the tax year for which the revocation was effective. ▶

7 Of what country are you a citizen/national? ▶ United States

8a Did you maintain a separate foreign residence for your family because of adverse living conditions at your tax home? See **Second foreign household** in the instructions . . . ☐ Yes ☒ No

b If "Yes," enter city and country of the separate foreign residence. Also, enter the number of days during your tax year that you maintained a second household at that address. ▶ N/A

9 List your tax home(s) during your tax year and date(s) established. ▶ 123 Rue de Harve, 75000 Paris France July 10, 2014

Next, complete either Part II or Part III. If an item doesn't apply, enter "NA." If you don't give the information asked for, any exclusion or deduction you claim may be disallowed.

Part II Taxpayers Qualifying Under Bona Fide Residence Test (see instructions)

10 Date bona fide residence began ▶ July 10, 2014, and ended ▶ Still a resident

11 Kind of living quarters in foreign country ▶ a ☐ Purchased house b ☒ Rented house or apartment c ☐ Rented room d ☐ Quarters furnished by employer

12a Did any of your family live with you abroad during any part of the tax year? . . . ☒ Yes ☐ No

b If "Yes," who and for what period? ▶ Wife and two children for entire year

13a Have you submitted a statement to the authorities of the foreign country where you claim bona fide residence that you aren't a resident of that country? See instructions . . . ☐ Yes ☒ No

b Are you required to pay income tax to the country where you claim bona fide residence? See instructions . ☒ Yes ☐ No

If you answered "Yes" to 13a and "No" to 13b, you don't qualify as a bona fide resident. Don't complete the rest of this part.

14 If you were present in the United States or its possessions during the tax year, complete columns **(a)–(d)** below. **Don't** include the income from column **(d)** in Part IV, but report it on Form 1040.

(a) Date arrived in U.S.	**(b)** Date left U.S.	**(c)** Number of days in U.S. on business	**(d)** Income earned in U.S. on business (attach computation)	**(a)** Date arrived in U.S.	**(b)** Date left U.S.	**(c)** Number of days in U.S. on business	**(d)** Income earned in U.S. on business (attach computation)
2-19-16	2-23-16	5	1,200				

15a List any contractual terms or other conditions relating to the length of your employment abroad. ▶ Indefinite

b Enter the type of visa under which you entered the foreign country. ▶ Resident

c Did your visa limit the length of your stay or employment in a foreign country? If "Yes," attach explanation . ☐ Yes ☒ No

d Did you maintain a home in the United States while living abroad? . . . ☒ Yes ☐ No

e If "Yes," enter address of your home, whether it was rented, the names of the occupants, and their relationship to you. ▶ 4710 68th Terrace, City, ST 54321 (rented to unrelated party)

For Paperwork Reduction Act Notice, see the Form 1040 instructions. Cat. No. 11900P Form **2555** (2016)

See text Example C:16-36 for tax form facts.

Part III Taxpayers Qualifying Under Physical Presence Test (see instructions)

16 The physical presence test is based on the 12-month period from ▶ N/A through ▶

17 Enter your principal country of employment during your tax year. ▶

18 If you traveled abroad during the 12-month period entered on line 16, complete columns **(a)–(f)** below. Exclude travel between foreign countries that didn't involve travel on or over international waters, or in or over the United States, for 24 hours or more. If you have no travel to report during the period, enter "Physically present in a foreign country or countries for the entire 12-month period." **Don't** include the income from column **(f)** below in Part IV, but report it on Form 1040.

(a) Name of country (including U.S.)	**(b)** Date arrived	**(c)** Date left	**(d)** Full days present in country	**(e)** Number of days in U.S. on business	**(f)** Income earned in U.S. on business (attach computation)

Part IV All Taxpayers

Note: Enter on lines 19 through 23 all income, including noncash income, you earned and actually or constructively received during your 2016 tax year for services you performed in a foreign country. If any of the foreign earned income received this tax year was earned in a prior tax year, or will be earned in a later tax year (such as a bonus), see the instructions. **Don't** include income from line 14, column **(d),** or line 18, column **(f).** Report amounts in U.S. dollars, using the exchange rates in effect when you actually or constructively received the income.

If you are a cash basis taxpayer, report on Form 1040 all income you received in 2016, no matter when you performed the service.

	2016 Foreign Earned Income				**Amount (in U.S. dollars)**
19	Total wages, salaries, bonuses, commissions, etc.			19	58,800*
20	Allowable share of income for personal services performed (see instructions):				
a	In a business (including farming) or profession			20a	
b	In a partnership. List partnership's name and address and type of income. ▶			20b	
21	Noncash income (market value of property or facilities furnished by employer—attach statement showing how it was determined):				
a	Home (lodging)			21a	
b	Meals			21b	
c	Car			21c	
d	Other property or facilities. List type and amount. ▶			21d	
22	Allowances, reimbursements, or expenses paid on your behalf for services you performed:				
a	Cost of living and overseas differential	22a	27,000		
b	Family	22b			
c	Education	22c	8,000		
d	Home leave	22d	6,400		
e	Quarters	22e	21,300		
f	For any other purpose. List type and amount. ▶	22f			
g	Add lines 22a through 22f			22g	62,700
23	Other foreign earned income. List type and amount. ▶			23	
24	Add lines 19 through 21d, line 22g, and line 23			24	121,500
25	Total amount of meals and lodging included on line 24 that is excludable (see instructions)			25	
26	Subtract line 25 from line 24. Enter the result here and on line 27 on page 3. This is your **2016 foreign earned income** ▶			26	121,500

*$60,000 salary – $1,200 U.S. source income from Part II, Line 14(d).

Form 2555 (2016) Page 3

Part V **All Taxpayers**

27	Enter the amount from line 26	27	121,500
	Are you claiming the housing exclusion or housing deduction? ☐ **Yes.** Complete Part VI. ☐ **No.** Go to Part VII.		

Part VI **Taxpayers Claiming the Housing Exclusion and/or Deduction**

28	Qualified housing expenses for the tax year (see instructions)		28	21,300
29a	Enter location where housing expenses incurred (see instructions) ▶ France			
b	Enter limit on housing expenses (see instructions)		29b	30,390
30	Enter the **smaller** of line 28 or line 29b		30	21,300
31	Number of days in your qualifying period that fall within your 2016 tax year (see instructions)	31 366 days		
32	Multiply $44.28 by the number of days on line 31. If 366 is entered on line 31, enter $16,208 here		32	16,208
33	Subtract line 32 from line 30. If the result is zero or less, don't complete the rest of this part or any of Part IX		33	5,092
34	Enter employer-provided amounts (see instructions)	34 121,500		
35	Divide line 34 by line 27. Enter the result as a decimal (rounded to at least three places), but don't enter more than "1.000"		35	× 1.00
36	**Housing exclusion.** Multiply line 33 by line 35. Enter the result but don't enter more than the amount on line 34. Also, complete Part VIII ▶		36	5,092

Note: The housing deduction is figured in Part IX. If you choose to claim the foreign earned income exclusion, complete Parts VII and VIII before Part IX.

Part VII **Taxpayers Claiming the Foreign Earned Income Exclusion**

37	Maximum foreign earned income exclusion		37	$101,300 00
38	• If you completed Part VI, enter the number from line 31. • All others, enter the number of days in your qualifying period that fall within your 2016 tax year (see the instructions for line 31).	38 366 days		
39	• If line 38 and the number of days in your 2016 tax year (usually 366) are the same, enter "1.000." • Otherwise, divide line 38 by the number of days in your 2016 tax year and enter the result as a decimal (rounded to at least three places).		39	× 1.00
40	Multiply line 37 by line 39		40	101,300
41	Subtract line 36 from line 27		41	116,408
42	**Foreign earned income exclusion.** Enter the **smaller** of line 40 or line 41. Also, complete Part VIII ▶		42	101,300

Part VIII **Taxpayers Claiming the Housing Exclusion, Foreign Earned Income Exclusion, or Both**

43	Add lines 36 and 42	43	106,392
44	Deductions allowed in figuring your adjusted gross income (Form 1040, line 37) that are allocable to the excluded income. See instructions and attach computation	44	-0-
45	Subtract line 44 from line 43. Enter the result here and in parentheses on **Form 1040, line 21.** Next to the amount enter "Form 2555." On Form 1040, subtract this amount from your income to arrive at total income on Form 1040, line 22	45	106,392

Part IX **Taxpayers Claiming the Housing Deduction**—Complete this part only if **(a)** line 33 is more than line 36 and **(b)** line 27 is more than line 43.

46	Subtract line 36 from line 33	46	-0-
47	Subtract line 43 from line 27	47	15,108
48	Enter the **smaller** of line 46 or line 47	48	-0-
	Note: If line 47 is **more than** line 48 and you couldn't deduct all of your 2015 housing deduction because of the 2015 limit, use the housing deduction carryover worksheet in the instructions to figure the amount to enter on line 49. Otherwise, go to line 50.		
49	Housing deduction carryover from 2015 (from housing deduction carryover worksheet in the instructions)	49	-0-
50	**Housing deduction.** Add lines 48 and 49. Enter the total here and on Form 1040 to the left of line 36. Next to the amount on Form 1040, enter "Form 2555." Add it to the total adjustments reported on that line ▶	50	-0-

Form **2555** (2016)

APPENDIX

MACRS TABLES

MACRS, ADS, and ACRS Depreciation Methods Summary

System	Characteristics	Depreciation Method: MACRS	Depreciation Method: ADS	Table No.[a]: MACRS	Table No.[a]: ADS
MACRS & ADS	Personal Property:				
	1. Accounting convention	Half-year or mid-quarter	Half-year or mid-quarter[b]		
	2. Life and method				
	a. 3-year, 5-year, 7-year, 10-year	200% DB or elect straight-line	150% DB or elect straight-line	1, 2, 3, 4, 5	10, 11[c]
	b. 15-year, 20-year	150% DB or elect straight-line	150% DB or elect straight-lined	1, 2, 3, 4, 5 6	
	3. Luxury automobile limitations				
	Real Property:				
	1. Accounting convention	Mid-month	Mid-month		
	2. Life and method				
	a. Residential rental property	27.5 years, straight-line	40 years straight-line	7	12
	b. Nonresidential real property	39 years, straight-line[e]	40 years straight-line	9	12

System	Characteristics	ACRS
ACRS[f]	Personal Property:	
	1. Accounting convention	Half-year
	2. Life and method	
	a. 3-year, 5-year, 10-year, 15-year	150% DB or elect straight-line
	Real Property:	
	1. Accounting convention	First of month or mid-month
	2. Life	
	a. 15-year property	Placed in service after 12/31/80 and before 3/16/84
	b. 18-year property	Placed in service after 3/15/84 and before 5/9/85
	c. 19-year property	Placed in service after 5/8/85 and before 1/1/87
	3. Method	
	a. All but low-income housing	175% DB or elect straight-line
	b. Low-income housing property	200% DB or elect straight-line

[a]All depreciation tables in this appendix are based upon tables contained in Rev. Proc. 87-57, as amended.

[b]General and ADS tables are available for property lives from 2.5–50.0 years using the straight-line method. These tables are contained in Rev. Proc. 87-57 and are only partially reproduced here.

[c]The mid-quarter tables are available in Rev. Proc. 87-57, but are not reproduced here.

[d]Special recovery periods are assigned certain MACRS properties under the alternative depreciation system.

[e]A 31.5-year recovery period applied to nonresidential real property placed in service under the MACRS rules prior to May 13, 1993 (see Table 8).

[f]ACRS was effective for years 1981–1986. ACRS tables are no longer reproduced here.

▼ TABLE 1

General Depreciation System—MACRS
Personal Property Placed in Service After 12/31/86
Applicable Convention: Half-Year
Applicable Depreciation Method: 200 or 150 Percent Declining Balance Switching to Straight Line

If the Recovery Year Is:	And the Recovery Period Is: 3-Year	5-Year	7-Year	10-Year	15-Year	20-Year
	The Depreciation Rate Is:					
1	33.33	20.00	14.29	10.00	5.00	3.750
2	44.45	32.00	24.49	18.00	9.50	7.219
3	14.81	19.20	17.49	14.40	8.55	6.677
4	7.41	11.52	12.49	11.52	7.70	6.177
5		11.52	8.93	9.22	6.93	5.713
6		5.76	8.92	7.37	6.23	5.285
7			8.93	6.55	5.90	4.888
8			4.46	6.55	5.90	4.522
9				6.56	5.91	4.462
10				6.55	5.90	4.461
11				3.28	5.91	4.462
12					5.90	4.461
13					5.91	4.462
14					5.90	4.461
15					5.91	4.462
16					2.95	4.461
17						4.462
18						4.461
19						4.462
20						4.461
21						2.231

▼ TABLE 2

General Depreciation System—MACRS
Personal Property Placed in Service After 12/31/86
Applicable Convention: Mid-Quarter (Property Placed in Service in First Quarter)
Applicable Depreciation Method: 200 or 150 Percent Declining Balance Switching to Straight Line

If the Recovery Year Is:	And the Recovery Period Is: 3-Year	5-Year	7-Year	10-Year	15-Year	20-Year
	The Depreciation Rate Is:					
1	58.33	35.00	25.00	17.50	8.75	6.563
2	27.78	26.00	21.43	16.50	9.13	7.000
3	12.35	15.60	15.31	13.20	8.21	6.482
4	1.54	11.01	10.93	10.56	7.39	5.996
5		11.01	8.75	8.45	6.65	5.546
6		1.38	8.74	6.76	5.99	5.130
7			8.75	6.55	5.90	4.746
8			1.09	6.55	5.91	4.459
9				6.56	5.90	4.459
10				6.55	5.91	4.459
11				0.82	5.90	4.459
12					5.91	4.460
13					5.90	4.459
14					5.91	4.460
15					5.90	4.459
16					0.74	4.460
17						4.459
18						4.460
19						4.459
20						4.460
21						0.557

▼ TABLE 3

General Depreciation System—MACRS
Personal Property Placed in Service After 12/31/86
Applicable Convention: Mid-Quarter (Property Placed in Service in Second Quarter)
Applicable Depreciation Method: 200 or 150 Percent Declining Balance Switching to Straight Line

If the Recovery Year Is:	And the Recovery Period Is: 3-Year	5-Year	7-Year	10-Year	15-Year	20-Year
	The Depreciation Rate Is:					
1	41.67	25.00	17.85	12.50	6.25	4.688
2	38.89	30.00	23.47	17.50	9.38	7.148
3	14.14	18.00	16.76	14.00	8.44	6.612
4	5.30	11.37	11.97	11.20	7.59	6.116
5		11.37	8.87	8.96	6.83	5.658
6		4.26	8.87	7.17	6.15	5.233
7			8.87	6.55	5.91	4.841
8			3.33	6.55	5.90	4.478
9				6.56	5.91	4.463
10				6.55	5.90	4.463
11				2.46	5.91	4.463
12					5.90	4.463
13					5.91	4.463
14					5.90	4.463
15					5.91	4.462
16					2.21	4.463
17						4.462
18						4.463
19						4.462
20						4.463
21						1.673

▼ TABLE 4

General Depreciation System—MACRS
Personal Property Placed in Service After 12/31/86
Applicable Convention: Mid-Quarter (Property Placed in Service in Third Quarter)
Applicable Depreciation Method: 200 or 150 Percent Declining Balance Switching to Straight Line

If the Recovery Year Is:	And the Recovery Period Is: 3-Year	5-Year	7-Year	10-Year	15-Year	20-Year
	The Depreciation Rate Is:					
1	25.00	15.00	10.71	7.50	3.75	2.813
2	50.00	34.00	25.51	18.50	9.63	7.289
3	16.67	20.40	18.22	14.80	8.66	6.742
4	8.33	12.24	13.02	11.84	7.80	6.237
5		11.30	9.30	9.47	7.02	5.769
6		7.06	8.85	7.58	6.31	5.336
7			8.86	6.55	5.90	4.936
8			5.53	6.55	5.90	4.566
9				6.56	5.91	4.460
10				6.55	5.90	4.460
11				4.10	5.91	4.460
12					5.90	4.460
13					5.91	4.461
14					5.90	4.460
15					5.91	4.461
16					3.69	4.460
17						4.461
18						4.460
19						4.461
20						4.460
21						2.788

▼ TABLE 5

General Depreciation System—MACRS
Personal Property Placed in Service After 12/31/86
Applicable Convention: Mid-Quarter (Property Placed in Service in Fourth Quarter)
Applicable Depreciation Method: 200 or 150 Percent Declining Balance Switching to Straight Line

If the Recovery Year Is:	And the Recovery Period Is: 3-Year	5-Year	7-Year	10-Year	15-Year	20-Year
	The Depreciation Rate Is:					
1	8.33	5.00	3.57	2.50	1.25	0.938
2	61.11	38.00	27.55	19.50	9.88	7.430
3	20.37	22.80	19.68	15.60	8.89	6.872
4	10.19	13.68	14.06	12.48	8.00	6.357
5		10.94	10.04	9.98	7.20	5.880
6		9.58	8.73	7.99	6.48	5.439
7			8.73	6.55	5.90	5.031
8			7.64	6.55	5.90	4.654
9				6.56	5.90	4.458
10				6.55	5.91	4.458
11				5.74	5.90	4.458
12					5.91	4.458
13					5.90	4.458
14					5.91	4.458
15					5.90	4.458
16					5.17	4.458
17						4.458
18						4.459
19						4.458
20						4.459
21						3.901

TAX AUTHORITY UPDATE

At the time this edition went to print, the IRS had not yet released the 2017 ceiling limits. For examples and problems in the text, we assume the limits will be the same for 2017 as they were in 2016.

▼ TABLE 6

Luxury Automobile Depreciation Limits

	Year Automobile Is Placed in Service[a] 2012–2016	2010–2011	2009	2008
Maximum Allowable Depreciation (100% Business Use):				
Year 1	$3,160[b]	$3,060[c]	$2,960[d]	$2,960[e]
Year 2	5,100	4,900	4,800	4,800
Year 3	3,050	2,950	2,850	2,850
Year 4 and Each Succeeding Year	1,875	1,775	1,775	1,775

[a]For years prior to 2008, see the Revenue Procedure for the appropriate year.
[b]$11,160 in Year 1 (2016, 2015, 2014, 2013, or 2012) if taxpayer claims bonus depreciation.
[c]$11,060 in Year 1 (2011 or 2010) if taxpayer claims bonus depreciation.
[d]$10,960 in Year 1 (2009) if taxpayer claims bonus depreciation.
[e]$10,960 in Year 1 (2008) if taxpayer claimed bonus depreciation.

▼ TABLE 6 (continued)
Truck and Van Depreciation Limits

	Year Truck or Van Is Placed in Service[a]								
	2016	2015	2014	2013	2012	2011	2010	2009	2008
Maximum Allowable Depreciation (100% Business Use):									
Year 1	$3,560[b]	$3,460[c]	$3,460[c]	$3,360[d]	$3,360[d]	$3,260[e]	$3,160[f]	$3,060[g]	$3,160[f]
Year 2	5,700	5,600	5,550	5,400	5,300	5,200	5,100	4,900	5,100
Year 3	3,350	3,350	3,350	3,250	3,150	3,150	3,050	2,950	3,050
Year 4 and Each Succeeding Year	2,075	1,975	1,975	1,975	1,875	1,875	1,875	1,775	1,875

[a]For years prior to 2008, see the Revenue Procedure for the appropriate year.
[b]$11,560 in Year 1 (2016) if taxpayer claims bonus depreciation.
[c]$11,460 in Year 1 (2014 and 2015) if taxpayer claims bonus depreciation.
[d]$11,360 in Year 1 (2012 and 2013) if taxpayer claims bonus depreciation.
[e]$11,260 in Year 1 (2011) if taxpayer claims bonus depreciation.
[f]$11,160 in Year 1 (2010 and 2008) if taxpayer claims bonus depreciation.
[g]$11,060 in Year 1 (2009) if taxpayer claimed bonus depreciation.

TAX AUTHORITY UPDATE

At the time this edition went to print, the IRS had not yet released the 2017 ceiling limits. For examples and problems in the text, we assume the limits will be the same for 2017 as they were in 2016.

▼ TABLE 7
General Depreciation System—MACRS
Residential Rental Real Property Placed in Service After 12/31/86
Applicable Recovery Period: 27.5 Years
Applicable Convention: Mid-Month
Applicable Depreciation Method: Straight Line

If the Recovery Year Is:	And the Month in the First Recovery Year the Property Is Placed in Service Is: 1	2	3	4	5	6	7	8	9	10	11	12
	The Depreciation Rate Is:											
1	3.485	3.182	2.879	2.576	2.273	1.970	1.667	1.364	1.061	0.758	0.455	0.152
2	3.636	3.636	3.636	3.636	3.636	3.636	3.636	3.636	3.636	3.636	3.636	3.636
3	3.636	3.636	3.636	3.636	3.636	3.636	3.636	3.636	3.636	3.636	3.636	3.636
4	3.636	3.636	3.636	3.636	3.636	3.636	3.636	3.636	3.636	3.636	3.636	3.636
5	3.636	3.636	3.636	3.636	3.636	3.636	3.636	3.636	3.636	3.636	3.636	3.636
6	3.636	3.636	3.636	3.636	3.636	3.636	3.636	3.636	3.636	3.636	3.636	3.636
7	3.636	3.636	3.636	3.636	3.636	3.636	3.636	3.636	3.636	3.636	3.636	3.636
8	3.636	3.636	3.636	3.636	3.636	3.636	3.636	3.636	3.636	3.636	3.636	3.636
9	3.636	3.636	3.636	3.636	3.636	3.636	3.636	3.636	3.636	3.636	3.636	3.636
10	3.637	3.637	3.637	3.637	3.637	3.637	3.636	3.636	3.636	3.636	3.636	3.636
11	3.636	3.636	3.636	3.636	3.636	3.636	3.637	3.637	3.637	3.637	3.637	3.637
12	3.637	3.637	3.637	3.637	3.637	3.637	3.636	3.636	3.636	3.636	3.636	3.636
13	3.636	3.636	3.636	3.636	3.636	3.636	3.637	3.637	3.637	3.637	3.637	3.637
14	3.637	3.637	3.637	3.637	3.637	3.637	3.636	3.636	3.636	3.636	3.636	3.636
15	3.636	3.636	3.636	3.636	3.636	3.636	3.637	3.637	3.637	3.637	3.637	3.637
16	3.637	3.637	3.637	3.637	3.637	3.637	3.636	3.636	3.636	3.636	3.636	3.636
17	3.636	3.636	3.636	3.636	3.636	3.636	3.637	3.637	3.637	3.637	3.637	3.637
18	3.637	3.637	3.637	3.637	3.637	3.637	3.636	3.636	3.636	3.636	3.636	3.636
19	3.636	3.636	3.636	3.636	3.636	3.636	3.637	3.637	3.637	3.637	3.637	3.637
20	3.637	3.637	3.637	3.637	3.637	3.637	3.636	3.636	3.636	3.636	3.636	3.636
21	3.636	3.636	3.636	3.636	3.636	3.636	3.637	3.637	3.637	3.637	3.637	3.637
22	3.637	3.637	3.637	3.637	3.637	3.637	3.636	3.636	3.636	3.636	3.636	3.636
23	3.636	3.636	3.636	3.636	3.636	3.636	3.637	3.637	3.637	3.637	3.637	3.637
24	3.637	3.637	3.637	3.637	3.637	3.637	3.636	3.636	3.636	3.636	3.636	3.636
25	3.636	3.636	3.636	3.636	3.636	3.636	3.637	3.637	3.637	3.637	3.637	3.637
26	3.637	3.637	3.637	3.637	3.637	3.637	3.636	3.636	3.636	3.636	3.636	3.636
27	3.636	3.636	3.636	3.636	3.636	3.636	3.637	3.637	3.637	3.637	3.637	3.637
28	1.970	2.273	2.576	2.879	3.182	3.485	3.636	3.636	3.636	3.636	3.636	3.636
29	0.000	0.000	0.000	0.000	0.000	0.000	0.152	0.455	0.758	1.061	1.364	1.667

▼ **TABLE 8**

General Depreciation System—MACRS
Nonresidential Real Property Placed in Service After 12/31/86 and Before 5/13/93
Applicable Recovery Period: 31.5 Years
Applicable Convention: Mid-Month
Applicable Depreciation Method: Straight Line

If the Recovery Year Is:	And the Month in the First Recovery Year the Property Is Placed in Service Is:											
	1	2	3	4	5	6	7	8	9	10	11	12
	The Depreciation Rate Is:											
1	3.042	2.778	2.513	2.249	1.984	1.720	1.455	1.190	0.926	0.661	0.397	0.132
2	3.175	3.175	3.175	3.175	3.175	3.175	3.175	3.175	3.175	3.175	3.175	3.175
3	3.175	3.175	3.175	3.175	3.175	3.175	3.175	3.175	3.175	3.175	3.175	3.175
4	3.175	3.175	3.175	3.175	3.175	3.175	3.175	3.175	3.175	3.175	3.175	3.175
5	3.175	3.175	3.175	3.175	3.175	3.175	3.175	3.175	3.175	3.175	3.175	3.175
6	3.175	3.175	3.175	3.175	3.175	3.175	3.175	3.175	3.175	3.175	3.175	3.175
7	3.175	3.175	3.175	3.175	3.175	3.175	3.175	3.175	3.175	3.175	3.175	3.175
8	3.175	3.174	3.175	3.174	3.175	3.174	3.175	3.175	3.175	3.175	3.175	3.175
9	3.174	3.175	3.174	3.175	3.174	3.175	3.174	3.175	3.174	3.175	3.174	3.175
10	3.175	3.174	3.175	3.174	3.175	3.174	3.175	3.174	3.175	3.174	3.175	3.174
11	3.174	3.175	3.174	3.175	3.174	3.175	3.174	3.175	3.174	3.175	3.174	3.175
12	3.175	3.174	3.175	3.174	3.175	3.174	3.175	3.174	3.175	3.174	3.175	3.174
13	3.174	3.175	3.174	3.175	3.174	3.175	3.174	3.175	3.174	3.175	3.174	3.175
14	3.175	3.174	3.175	3.174	3.175	3.174	3.175	3.174	3.175	3.174	3.175	3.174
15	3.174	3.175	3.174	3.175	3.174	3.175	3.174	3.175	3.174	3.175	3.174	3.175
16	3.175	3.174	3.175	3.174	3.175	3.174	3.175	3.174	3.175	3.174	3.175	3.174
17	3.174	3.175	3.174	3.175	3.174	3.175	3.174	3.175	3.174	3.175	3.174	3.175
18	3.175	3.174	3.175	3.174	3.175	3.174	3.175	3.174	3.175	3.174	3.175	3.174
19	3.174	3.175	3.174	3.175	3.174	3.175	3.174	3.175	3.174	3.175	3.174	3.175
20	3.175	3.174	3.175	3.174	3.175	3.174	3.175	3.174	3.175	3.174	3.175	3.174
21	3.174	3.175	3.174	3.175	3.174	3.175	3.174	3.175	3.174	3.175	3.174	3.175
22	3.175	3.174	3.175	3.174	3.175	3.174	3.175	3.174	3.175	3.174	3.175	3.174
23	3.174	3.175	3.174	3.175	3.174	3.175	3.174	3.175	3.174	3.175	3.174	3.175
24	3.175	3.174	3.175	3.174	3.175	3.174	3.175	3.174	3.175	3.174	3.175	3.174
25	3.174	3.175	3.174	3.175	3.174	3.175	3.174	3.175	3.174	3.175	3.174	3.175
26	3.175	3.174	3.175	3.174	3.175	3.174	3.175	3.174	3.175	3.174	3.175	3.174
27	3.174	3.175	3.174	3.175	3.174	3.175	3.174	3.175	3.174	3.175	3.174	3.175
28	3.175	3.174	3.175	3.174	3.175	3.174	3.175	3.174	3.175	3.174	3.175	3.174
29	3.174	3.175	3.174	3.175	3.174	3.175	3.174	3.175	3.174	3.175	3.174	3.175
30	3.175	3.174	3.175	3.174	3.175	3.174	3.175	3.174	3.175	3.174	3.175	3.174
31	3.174	3.175	3.174	3.175	3.174	3.175	3.174	3.175	3.174	3.175	3.174	3.175
32	1.720	1.984	2.249	2.513	2.778	3.042	3.175	3.174	3.175	3.174	3.175	3.174
33	0.000	0.000	0.000	0.000	0.000	0.000	0.132	0.397	0.661	0.926	1.190	1.455

▼ **TABLE 9**

General Depreciation System—MACRS
Nonresidential Real Property Placed in Service After 5/12/93
Applicable Recovery Period: 39 years
Applicable Depreciation Method: Straight Line

If the Recovery Year Is:	**And the Month in the First Recovery Year the Property Is Placed in Service Is: 1**	**2**	**3**	**4**	**5**	**6**	**7**	**8**	**9**	**10**	**11**	**12**
	The Depreciation Rate Is:											
1	2.461	2.247	2.033	1.819	1.605	1.391	1.177	0.963	0.749	0.535	0.321	0.107
2-39	2.564	2.564	2.564	2.564	2.564	2.564	2.564	2.564	2.564	2.564	2.564	2.564
40	0.107	0.321	0.535	0.749	0.963	1.177	1.391	1.605	1.819	2.033	2.247	2.461

▼ **TABLE 10**

Alternative Depreciation System—MACRS (Partial Table)
Property Placed in Service After 12/31/86
Applicable Convention: Half-Year
Applicable Depreciation Method: 150 Percent Declining Balance Switching to Straight Line

If the Recovery Year Is:	**And the Recovery Period Is: 3**	**4**	**5**	**7**	**10**	**12**
	The Depreciation Rate Is:					
1	25.00	18.75	15.00	10.71	7.50	6.25
2	37.50	30.47	25.50	19.13	13.88	11.72
3	25.00	20.31	17.85	15.03	11.79	10.25
4	12.50	20.31	16.66	12.25	10.02	8.97
5		10.16	16.66	12.25	8.74	7.85
6			8.33	12.25	8.74	7.33
7				12.25	8.74	7.33
8				6.13	8.74	7.33
9					8.74	7.33
10					8.74	7.33
11					4.37	7.32
12						7.33
13						3.66

▼ TABLE 11

Alternative Depreciation System—MACRS (Partial Table)
Property Placed in Service After 12/31/86
Applicable Convention: Half-Year
Applicable Depreciation Method: Straight Line

If the Recovery Year Is:	And the Recovery Period Is: 3	4	5	7	10	12
	The Depreciation Rate Is:					
1	16.67	12.50	10.00	7.14	5.00	4.17
2	33.33	25.00	20.00	14.29	10.00	8.33
3	33.33	25.00	20.00	14.29	10.00	8.33
4	16.67	25.00	20.00	14.28	10.00	8.33
5		12.50	20.00	14.29	10.00	8.33
6			10.00	14.28	10.00	8.33
7				14.29	10.00	8.34
8				7.14	10.00	8.33
9					10.00	8.34
10					10.00	8.33
11					5.00	8.34
12						8.33
13						4.17

▼ TABLE 12

Alternative Depreciation System—MACRS
Real Property Placed into Service After 12/31/86
Applicable Recovery Period: 40 years
Applicable Convention: Mid-Month
Applicable Depreciation Method: Straight Line

If the Recovery Year Is:	And the Month in the First Recovery Year the Property Is Placed in Service Is: 1	2	3	4	5	6	7	8	9	10	11	12
	The Depreciation Rate Is:											
1	2.396	2.188	1.979	1.771	1.563	1.354	1.146	0.938	0.729	0.521	0.313	0.104
2 to 40	2.500	2.500	2.500	2.500	2.500	2.500	2.500	2.500	2.500	2.500	2.500	2.500
41	0.104	0.312	0.521	0.729	0.937	1.146	1.354	1.562	1.771	1.979	2.187	2.396

TAX AUTHORITY UPDATE

At the time this edition went to print, the IRS had not yet released the 2017 lease inclusion amounts. For examples and problems in the text, we assume the amounts will be the same for 2017 as they were in 2016.

▼ TABLE 13

Lease Inclusion Dollar Amounts for Automobiles (Other Than for Trucks or Vans) With a Lease Term Beginning in Calendar Year 2016

REV. PROC. 2016-23 TABLE 5 *DOLLAR AMOUNTS FOR PASSENGER AUTOMOBILES (THAT ARE NOT TRUCKS OR VANS) WITH A LEASE TERM BEGINNING IN CALENDAR YEAR 2016*

Fair Market Value of Passenger Automobile		Tax Year During Lease				
Over	Not Over	1st	2nd	3rd	4th	5th and Later
$19,000	$19,500	6	13	20	23	27
19,500	20,000	7	15	23	27	30
20,000	20,500	8	17	26	30	35
20,500	21,000	9	19	29	33	39
21,000	21,500	10	21	31	38	42
21,500	22,000	11	23	34	41	47
22,000	23,000	12	26	39	46	53
23,000	24,000	14	30	44	54	60
24,000	25,000	16	34	50	60	69
25,000	26,000	17	38	56	67	78
26,000	27,000	19	42	62	74	85
27,000	28,000	21	46	68	81	93
28,000	29,000	23	50	73	89	101
29,000	30,000	25	53	80	95	110
30,000	31,000	26	58	85	102	118
31,000	32,000	28	62	91	109	126
32,000	33,000	30	65	98	116	134
33,000	34,000	32	69	103	123	142
34,000	35,000	34	73	109	130	150
35,000	36,000	35	77	115	137	158
36,000	37,000	37	81	121	144	166
37,000	38,000	39	85	127	151	174
38,000	39,000	41	89	132	158	183
39,000	40,000	42	93	138	166	190
40,000	41,000	44	97	144	172	199
41,000	42,000	46	101	150	179	207
42,000	43,000	48	105	155	187	215
43,000	44,000	50	109	161	193	223
44,000	45,000	51	113	167	201	231
45,000	46,000	53	117	173	207	239
46,000	47,000	55	121	179	214	247
47,000	48,000	57	124	185	222	255
48,000	49,000	59	128	191	228	264
49,000	50,000	60	133	196	236	271
50,000	51,000	62	136	203	242	280
51,000	52,000	64	140	209	249	288
52,000	53,000	66	144	214	257	295
53,000	54,000	68	148	220	263	304
54,000	55,000	69	152	226	271	312
55,000	56,000	71	156	232	277	320

TAX AUTHORITY UPDATE

At the time this edition went to print, the IRS had not yet released the 2017 lease inclusion amounts. For examples and problems in the text, we assume the amounts will be the same for 2017 as they were in 2016.

▼ TABLE 13 (continued)

REV. PROC. 2016-23 TABLE 5 *DOLLAR AMOUNTS FOR PASSENGER AUTOMOBILES (THAT ARE NOT TRUCKS OR VANS) WITH A LEASE TERM BEGINNING IN CALENDAR YEAR 2016*

Fair Market Value of Passenger Automobile		Tax Year During Lease				
Over	Not Over	1st	2nd	3rd	4th	5th and Later
$ 56,000	$ 57,000	73	160	238	284	328
57,000	58,000	75	164	243	292	336
58,000	59,000	77	168	249	298	345
59,000	60,000	78	172	255	306	352
60,000	62,000	81	178	264	316	364
62,000	64,000	85	185	276	330	381
64,000	66,000	88	194	287	344	397
66,000	68,000	92	201	299	358	413
68,000	70,000	95	209	311	372	430
70,000	72,000	99	217	322	387	445
72,000	74,000	102	225	334	400	462
74,000	76,000	106	233	346	414	478
76,000	78,000	110	241	357	428	494
78,000	80,000	113	249	369	442	510
80,000	85,000	120	262	390	467	538
85,000	90,000	128	282	419	502	579
90,000	95,000	137	302	448	537	620
95,000	100,000	146	322	477	572	660
100,000	110,000	160	351	521	625	721
110,000	120,000	178	390	580	695	801
120,000	130,000	196	430	638	765	882
130,000	140,000	214	469	697	835	963
140,000	150,000	232	508	755	906	1,044
150,000	160,000	249	548	814	975	1,126
160,000	170,000	267	588	872	1,045	1,207
170,000	180,000	285	627	930	1,116	1,288
180,000	190,000	303	666	989	1,186	1,368
190,000	200,000	321	706	1,047	1,256	1,449
200,000	210,000	339	745	1,106	1,326	1,530
210,000	220,000	357	784	1,165	1,396	1,611
220,000	230,000	375	824	1,223	1,466	1,692
230,000	240,000	393	863	1,281	1,537	1,773
240,000	and over	411	902	1,340	1,607	1,854

TAX AUTHORITY UPDATE

At the time this edition went to print, the IRS had not yet released the 2017 lease inclusion amounts. For examples and problems in the text, we assume the amounts will be the same for 2017 as they were in 2016.

▼ **TABLE 14**

Lease Inclusion Dollar Amounts for Trucks and Vans With a Lease Term Beginning in Calendar Year 2016

REV. PROC. 2016-23 TABLE 6 *DOLLAR AMOUNTS FOR TRUCKS AND VANS WITH A LEASE TERM BEGINNING IN CALENDAR YEAR 2016*

Fair Market Value of Truck or Van		Tax Year During Lease				
Over	Not Over	1st	2nd	3rd	4th	5th and Later
$19,500	$20,000	3	8	12	14	16
20,000	20,500	4	10	15	17	20
20,500	21,000	5	12	17	21	25
21,000	21,500	6	14	20	25	28
21,500	22,000	7	16	23	28	32
22,000	23,000	8	19	28	33	38
23,000	24,000	10	23	33	41	46
24,000	25,000	12	26	40	47	55
25,000	26,000	14	30	46	54	63
26,000	27,000	16	34	51	62	70
27,000	28,000	17	38	58	68	79
28,000	29,000	19	42	63	76	86
29,000	30,000	21	46	69	82	95
30,000	31,000	23	50	75	89	103
31,000	32,000	25	54	80	97	111
32,000	33,000	26	58	86	104	119
33,000	34,000	28	62	92	111	127
34,000	35,000	30	66	98	117	136
35,000	36,000	32	70	104	124	143
36,000	37,000	34	73	110	132	151
37,000	38,000	35	78	115	139	160
38,000	39,000	37	82	121	146	167
39,000	40,000	39	85	128	152	176
40,000	41,000	41	89	133	160	184
41,000	42,000	42	94	139	166	192
42,000	43,000	44	97	145	174	200
43,000	44,000	46	101	151	181	208
44,000	45,000	48	105	157	187	217
45,000	46,000	50	109	162	195	224
46,000	47,000	51	113	169	201	233
47,000	48,000	53	117	174	209	240
48,000	49,000	55	121	180	216	248
49,000	50,000	57	125	186	222	257
50,000	51,000	59	129	191	230	265
51,000	52,000	60	133	197	237	273
52,000	53,000	62	137	203	244	281
53,000	54,000	64	141	209	250	290
54,000	55,000	66	144	216	257	298
55,000	56,000	68	148	221	265	305
56,000	57,000	69	153	226	272	314
57,000	58,000	71	156	233	279	321
58,000	59,000	73	160	239	285	330
59,000	60,000	75	164	244	293	338
60,000	62,000	77	170	253	304	350
62,000	64,000	81	178	265	317	366
64,000	66,000	85	186	276	331	383

TAX AUTHORITY UPDATE

At the time this edition went to print, the IRS had not yet released the 2017 lease inclusion amounts. For examples and problems in the text, we assume the amounts will be the same for 2017 as they were in 2016.

▼ TABLE 14 (continued)

REV. PROC. 2016-23 TABLE 6 *DOLLAR AMOUNTS FOR TRUCKS AND VANS WITH A LEASE TERM BEGINNING IN CALENDAR YEAR 2016*

Fair Market Value of Truck or Van		Tax Year During Lease				
Over	Not Over	1st	2nd	3rd	4th	5th and Later
$ 66,000	$ 68,000	88	194	288	345	399
68,000	70,000	92	202	299	360	414
70,000	72,000	95	210	311	374	431
72,000	74,000	99	217	324	387	447
74,000	76,000	102	226	335	401	463
76,000	78,000	106	233	347	415	480
78,000	80,000	110	241	358	430	495
80,000	85,000	116	255	379	454	524
85,000	90,000	125	274	409	489	564
90,000	95,000	134	294	437	525	605
95,000	100,000	143	314	466	560	645
100,000	110,000	156	344	510	612	706
110,000	120,000	174	383	569	682	787
120,000	130,000	192	422	628	752	868
130,000	140,000	210	462	685	823	949
140,000	150,000	228	501	744	893	1,030
150,000	160,000	246	540	803	963	1,111
160,000	170,000	264	580	861	1,033	1,192
170,000	180,000	282	619	920	1,102	1,274
180,000	190,000	300	658	979	1,172	1,354
190,000	200,000	318	698	1,036	1,243	1,435
200,000	210,000	335	738	1,095	1,313	1,516
210,000	220,000	353	777	1,154	1,383	1,597
220,000	230,000	371	816	1,212	1,454	1,678
230,000	240,000	389	856	1,270	1,524	1,759
240,000	and over	407	895	1,329	1,594	1,839

APPENDIX

D GLOSSARY

Accounting method The rules used to determine the tax year in which income and expenses are reported for tax purposes. Generally, the same accounting method must be used for tax purposes as is used for keeping books and records. The accounting treatment used for any item of income or expense and for specific items (e.g., installment sales and contracts) is included in this term.

Accounting period See Tax year.

Accumulated adjustments account (AAA) Account that must be kept by S corporations. The cumulative total of the ordinary income or loss and separately stated items for the most recent S corporation election period.

Accumulated earnings and profits The sum of the undistributed current earnings and profits balances (and deficits) from previous years reduced by any distributions that have been made out of accumulated earnings and profits.

Accumulated earnings credit Deduction that reduces the accumulated taxable income amount. It does not offset the accumulated earnings tax on a dollar-for-dollar basis. Different rules apply for operating companies, service companies, and holding or investment companies.

Accumulated earnings tax Penalty tax on corporations other than those subject to the personal holding company tax among others. It is levied on a corporation's current year addition to its accumulated earnings balance exceeding the amount needed for reasonable business purposes and not distributed to the shareholders. This tax is intended to discourage companies from retaining excessive amounts of earnings if the funds are invested in activities unrelated to business needs. The tax is 20% of accumulated taxable income.

Accumulated taxable income The tax base for the accumulated earnings tax, which is determined by taking the corporation's taxable income and increasing (decreasing) it by positive (negative) adjustments and decreasing it by the accumulated earnings credit and available dividends-paid deductions.

Accumulation distribution rules (throwback rules) Exception to the general rule that distributable net income (DNI) serves as a ceiling on the amount taxable to a beneficiary. Under the general rule, the beneficiary excludes the portion of any distribution exceeding DNI from his gross income. Accumulation distributions made by a trust are taxable to the beneficiaries in the year received.

ACE See Adjusted current earnings.

Acquiescence policy IRS policy of announcing whether it agrees or disagrees with a court decision decided in favor of the taxpayer. Such statements are not issued for every case.

Acquisitive reorganization A transaction in which the acquiring corporation obtains all or part of the stock or assets of a target corporation.

Adjusted current earnings (ACE) Alternative minimum taxable income for the tax year plus or minus a series of special adjusted current earnings adjustments specified in Sec. 56(g)(4) (special depreciation calculation, special E&P rules, etc.).

Adjusted current earnings adjustment 75% of the excess (if any) of the adjusted current earnings of the corporation over the preadjustment AMTI. A downward adjustment is provided for 75% of the excess (if any) of preadjustment AMTI over the adjusted current earnings of the corporation.

Adjusted grossed-up basis For Sec. 338 purposes, the sum of (1) the basis of a purchasing corporation's stock interest in a target corporation plus (2) an adjustment for the target corporation's liabilities on the day following the acquisition date plus or minus (3) other relevant items.

Adjusted income from rents (AIR) This amount equals the corporation's gross income from rents reduced by the deductions claimed for amortization or depreciation, property taxes, interest, and rent.

Adjusted ordinary gross income (AOGI) A corporation's adjusted ordinary gross income is its ordinary gross income reduced by (1) certain expenses incurred in connection with gross income from rents, mineral, oil and gas royalties, and working interests in oil or gas wells, (2) interest received by dealers on certain U.S. obligations, (3) interest received from condemnation awards, judgments, or tax refunds, and (4) rents from certain tangible personal property manufactured or produced by the corporation.

Adjusted taxable gift Taxable gifts made after 1976 that are valued at their date-of-gift value. These gifts affect the size of the transfer tax base at death.

Administrative pronouncement Treasury Department or IRS statement that interprets provisions of the IRC. Such pronouncements may be in the form of Treasury regulations, revenue rulings, or revenue procedures.

Advance ruling See Letter ruling.

Affiliated group A group consisting of a parent corporation and at least one subsidiary corporation.

Aggregate Deemed Sale Price (ADSP) Price at which old target is deemed to have sold all of its assets pursuant to a Sec. 338 deemed sale election.

AIR See Adjusted income from rents.

Alien An individual who is not a U.S. citizen.

Alternate valuation date The alternate valuation date is the earlier of six months after the date of death or the date the property is sold, exchanged, distributed, etc. by the estate. Unless this option is elected, the gross estate is valued at its FMV on the date of the decedent's death.

Alternative minimum tax (AMT) Tax that applies to individuals, corporations, and estates and trusts if it exceeds the taxpayer's regular tax. Most taxpayers are not subject to this tax, including corporations meeting the small corporation exception. This tax equals the amount by which the tentative minimum tax exceeds the regular tax.

Alternative minimum taxable income (AMTI) The taxpayer's taxable income (1) increased by tax preference items and (2) adjusted for income, gain, deduction, and loss items that have to be recomputed under the AMT system.

AMT See Alternative minimum tax.

AMTI See Alternative minimum taxable income.

Annotated tax service A multivolume tax commentary organized by IRC section number. The IRC-arranged subdivisions contain the IRC provision, related Treasury Regulations, publisher-provided commentary and explanations, and annotations that summarize related cases and IRS pronouncements. The service has a topical index to assist research.

Announcement Information release issued by the IRS to provide a technical explanation of a current tax issue. Announcements are aimed at tax practitioners rather than the general public.

Annual exclusion An exemption intended to relieve a donor from keeping an account of and reporting the numerous small gifts (e.g., wedding and Christmas gifts) made throughout the year. This exclusion currently is $14,000 per donee (in 2016 and 2017).

AOGI See Adjusted ordinary gross income.

Appeals coordinated issue Issue over which the appeals officer must obtain a concurrence of guidance from the regional director of appeals to render a decision.

Assignment of income doctrine A judicial requirement that income be taxed to the person that earns it.

At-risk basis Essentially the same amount as the regular partnership basis with the exception that liabilities increase the at-risk basis only if the partner is at-risk for such an amount.

At-risk rules These rules limit the partner's loss deductions to his or her at-risk basis.

Bardahl formula Mathematical formula for determining the amount of working capital that a business reasonably needs for accumulated earnings tax purposes. For a manufacturing company, the formula is based on the business's operating cycle.

Basic exclusion amount Portion of the estate and gift tax base that is completely free of transfer taxes because of the unified credit (previously called the exemption equivalent).

Boot Property that may not be received tax-free in certain nontaxable transactions (i.e., any money, debt obligations, and so on).

Bootstrap acquisition An acquisition where an investor purchases part of a corporation's stock and then has the corporation redeem the remainder of the seller's stock.

Branch profits tax Special tax levied by the U.S. government on the branch activities of a foreign corporation doing business in the United States.

Brother-sister controlled group Under the narrow 50%–80% definition, this type of controlled group exists if (1) five or fewer individuals, estates, or trusts own at least 80% of the voting stock or 80% of the value of each corporation and (2) the shareholders have common ownership of more than 50% of the voting power or 50% of the value of all classes of stock. Under the broad 50%-only definition, the five or fewer shareholders need to meet only the 50% test.

Built-in deduction A deduction that accrues in a separate return limitation year but which is recognized for tax purposes in a consolidated return year.

Built-in gain A gain that accrued prior to the conversion of a C corporation to an S corporation.

Built-in gains (Sec. 1374) tax Tax on built-in gains recognized by the S corporation during the ten-year period beginning on the date the S corporation election took effect.

Built-in loss A loss that accrued prior to the conversion of a C corporation to an S corporation.

Business purpose A judicial doctrine established by the U.S. Supreme Court that a transaction cannot be solely motivated by a tax avoidance purpose. Transactions that serve no business purpose usually are ignored by the IRS and the courts.

Capital gain property For charitable contribution deduction purposes, property upon which a long-term capital gain would be recognized if that property were sold at its FMV.

Capital interest An interest in the assets owned by a partnership.

C corporation Form of business entity taxed as a separate taxpaying entity. Its income is subject to an initial tax at the corporate level. Its shareholders are subject to a second tax if the corporation pays dividends from its earnings and profits. This type of corporation is sometimes referred to as a regular corporation.

Certiorari An appeal from a lower court (i.e., a federal court of appeals) that the U.S. Supreme Court agrees to hear. Such appeals, which are made as a writ of certiorari, generally are not granted unless (1) a constitutional issue needs to be decided or (2) a conflict among the lower court decisions must be clarified.

CFC See Controlled foreign corporation.

Charitable contribution deduction Contributions of money or property made to qualified organizations (i.e., public charities and private nonoperating foundations). For income tax purposes, the amount of the deduction depends on (1) the type of charity receiving the contribution, (2) the type of property contributed, and (3) other limitations mandated by the tax law. Charitable contributions also are deductible under the unified transfer tax (i.e., gift tax and estate tax rules).

Charitable remainder annuity trust This type of trust makes distributions to individuals for a certain time period or for life. The annual distributions are a uniform percentage (5% or higher) of the value of the trust property as valued on the date of transfer.

Charitable remainder unitrust This type of trust makes annual distributions for either a specified time period or for life. The distributions are a uniform percentage (5% or higher) of the value of the property as revalued annually.

Check-the-box regulations Treasury Regulations that permit certain entities (e.g., partnerships and limited liability companies) to select an income tax status different from their basic classification.

Circular 230 Rules and standards issued by the Treasury Department regarding practice before the IRS.

Clifford trust A trust that normally is held for a ten-year period after which the principal reverts to the grantor. The trust accounting income generally is not taxed to the grantor.

Closed-fact or tax compliance situation Situation or transaction in which the facts have already occurred. In such situations, the tax advisor's task is to analyze the facts to determine the appropriate tax treatment.

Closed transaction Situation where the property in question (e.g., property distributed in a corporate liquidation) can be valued with reasonable certainty. The gain or loss reported on the transaction is determinable at the time the transaction occurs. See Open transaction doctrine.

Closely held corporation A corporation owned by either a single individual or a small group of individuals who may or may not be family members.

Closely held C corporation For purposes of the at-risk rules, a C corporation in which more than 50% of the stock is owned by five or fewer individuals at any time during the last half of the corporation's tax year.

Combined controlled group A group of three or more corporations that are members of a parent-subsidiary or brother-sister controlled group. In addition, at least one of the corporations must be the parent corporation of the parent-subsidiary controlled group and a member of a brother-sister controlled group.

Combined taxable income The total amount of the separate taxable incomes of the individual group members of an affiliated group that is filing a consolidated tax return.

Common law state All states other than the community property states are common law states. In such states, all assets acquired during the marriage are the property of the acquiring spouse.

Community property law Law in community property states mandating that all property acquired after marriage generally is community property unless acquired by gift or inheritance. Each spouse owns a one-half interest in community property.

Community property state The eight traditional community property states (Louisiana, Texas, New Mexico, Arizona, California, Washington, Idaho, and Nevada) and Wisconsin (which adopted a similar law). These states do not follow the common law concept of property ownership.

Complex trust Trust that is not required to distribute all of its income currently.

Congressional intent What Congress *intended* by a particular statutory term, phrase, or provision as gleaned from House and Senate committee reports, records of committee hearings, and transcripts of floor debates.

Consent dividend Hypothetical dividend generally deemed paid to a personal holding company's shareholders on the last day of the corporation's tax year. Also may be paid to avoid the personal holding company tax or accumulated earnings tax.

Consolidated return year A tax year for which a consolidated return is filed or is required to be filed by an affiliated group.

Consolidated taxable income The taxable income reported on a consolidated return filed by a group of affiliated corporations. The calculation of this amount is determined by establishing each member's separate taxable income and then following a series of steps that result in a consolidated amount.

Consolidated tax return A single tax return filed by an affiliated group of includible corporations.

Consolidation A nontaxable reorganization involving two or more corporations whose assets are acquired by a new corporation. The stock, securities, and other consideration transferred by the acquiring corporation is then distributed by each target corporation to its shareholders and security holders in exchange for their stock and securities.

Constructive dividend The manner in which the IRS or the courts might recharacterize an excessive corporate payment to a shareholder to reflect the true economic benefit conferred upon the shareholder. As a result of the recharacterization, the IRS or the courts usually recast a corporate-shareholder transaction as an E&P distribution, deny the corporation an offsetting deduction, and treat all or a portion of the income recognized by the shareholder as a dividend.

Continuity of interest doctrine The judicial requirement that shareholders who transfer property to a transferee corporation continue their ownership in the property through holding the transferee corporation's stock to defer recognition of their gains.

Controlled foreign corporation (CFC) Foreign corporation that is directly or indirectly controlled by U.S. shareholders at any time during the taxable year, provided that such U.S. shareholders control more than 50% of its voting power or more than 50% of the value of the outstanding stock.

Controlled group Two or more separately incorporated businesses owned by a related group of individuals or entities. Such groups include parent-subsidiary groups, brother-sister groups, or combined groups.

Corporation A separate taxpaying entity (such as an association, joint stock company, or insurance company) that must file a tax return every year, even when it had no income or loss for the year.

Corresponding item The buyer's income, gain, deduction, or loss from an intercompany transaction, or from property acquired in an intercompany transaction.

Crummey trust Technique that allows a donor to set up a discretionary trust and obtain an annual exclusion. Such a trust arrangement allows the beneficiary to demand an annual distribution of the lesser of the annual exclusion ($14,000 in 2016 and 2017) or the amount transferred to the trust that year.

C short year That portion of an S termination year that begins on the day on which the termination is effective and continues through to the last day of the corporation's tax year.

Current distribution See Nonliquidating distribution.

Current earnings and profits Earnings and profits calculated annually by (1) adjusting the corporation's taxable income (or net operating loss) for items that must be recomputed, (2) adding back any excluded income items, income deferrals, and deductions not allowed in computing earnings and profits, and (3) subtracting any expenses and losses not deductible in computing the corporation's taxable income.

Curtesy A widower's interest in his deceased wife's property.

Deductions in respect of a decedent (DRD) Deduction accrued prior to death but not includible on decedent's final tax return because of the decedent's method of accounting.

Deemed paid credit An indirect foreign tax credit available to a domestic corporation owning at least 10% of the voting stock of a foreign corporation when the foreign corporation pays or accrues creditable foreign taxes.

Deemed sale election Election under Sec. 338 permitting an acquiring corporation that acquires a controlling interest in a target corporation's stock to step-up or step-down the basis of the target corporation's assets to their adjusted grossed-up basis via a deemed sale and purchase of its assets.

Deferral privilege A tax exemption provided U.S. taxpayers who own stock of a foreign corporation. The foreign corporation's earnings generally are not taxed in the United States until repatriated unless an exception such as the Subpart F rules applies.

Deferred tax asset A book balance sheet item that results from temporary differences that produce tax deductions in the future when the differences reverse. The amount is the applicable tax rate times the temporary difference.

Deferred tax liability A book balance sheet item that results from temporary differences that produce taxable income in the future when the differences reverse. The amount is the applicable tax rate times the temporary difference.

Deficiency dividend This type of dividend substitutes an income tax levy on the dividend payment at the shareholder level for the payment of the personal holding company tax.

DIF See Discriminant Function Program.

Discriminant Function Program (DIF) Program used by the IRS to select individual returns for audit. This system is intended to identify those tax returns that are most likely to contain errors.

Dissolution A legal term implying that a corporation has surrendered the charter it originally received from the state.

Distributable net income (DNI) Maximum amount of distributions taxed to the beneficiaries and deducted by a trust or estate.

Distributive share The portion of partnership taxable and nontaxable income, losses, credits, and so on that the partner must report for tax purposes.

Dividend A distribution of property made by a corporation out of its earnings and profits.

Dividends-paid deduction Distributions made out of a corporation's earnings and profits are eligible for this deduction for personal holding company tax and accumulated earnings tax purposes. The deduction is equal to the amount of money plus the adjusted basis of the noncash property distributed.

Dividends-received deduction This deduction attempts to mitigate the triple taxation that would occur if one corporation paid dividends to a corporate shareholder who, in turn, distributed such amounts to its individual shareholders. Certain restrictions and limitations apply to this deduction.

Divisive reorganization Transaction in which part of a transferor corporation's assets are transferred to a second, newly created corporation controlled by either the transferee or its shareholders.

DNI See Distributable net income.

Domestic corporation Corporation incorporated in one of the 50 states or under federal law.

Dower A widow's interest in her deceased husband's property.

DRD See Deductions in respect of a decedent.

E&P See Earnings and profits.

E&P adjusted basis Adjusted basis obtained by using special calculations required under the E&P rules (e.g., calculation using straight-line depreciation under the alternative depreciation system).

E&P gain The difference between an asset's FMV and its E&P adjusted basis, which may differ from an asset's tax gain.

Earnings and profits (E&P) A measure of the corporation's ability to pay a dividend from its current and accumulated earnings without an impairment of capital.

Effective tax rate Total book income tax expense divided by pre-tax book income. In footnotes to the financial statements, firms reconcile the effective tax rate to the statutory tax rate.

Electing large partnership A partnership having at least 100 partners for the preceding tax year (excluding service partners). Electing large partnerships have a simplified reporting procedure that reduces the number of income, gain, loss, deductions, and credit items passing through to the partners. This elective form is repealed after 2017.

Estate A legal entity that comes into being only upon the death of the person whose assets are being administered. The estate continues in existence until the duties of the executor have been completed.

Excess loss account A negative investment account of a member of an affiliated group that files a consolidated tax return which attaches to an investment in a lower-tier subsidiary corporation.

Excess net passive income An amount equal to the S corporation's net passive income multiplied by the fraction consisting of its passive investment income less 25% of its gross receipts divided by its passive investment income. It is limited to the corporation's taxable income.

Excess net passive income (Sec. 1375) tax Tax levied when (1) an S corporation has passive investment income for the taxable year that exceeds 25% of its gross receipts and (2) at the close of the tax year the S corporation has earnings and profits from C corporation tax years.

Exemption equivalent That portion of the tax base that is completely free of transfer taxes because of the unified credit. (Also called the applicable exclusion amount.)

Expanded affiliated group A group of corporations treated as one corporation for purposes of determining the U.S. production activities deduction allowed to the group. A 50% ownership test applies for identifying members of the group.

Failure-to-file penalty Penalty imposed for the failure to file a timely return. The penalty is assessed at 5% per month (or fraction thereof) on the amount of the net tax due. The maximum penalty for failing to file is 25%. The minimum penalty is the lesser of $205 or 100% of the tax due.

Failure-to-pay penalty Penalty imposed at 0.5% per month (or fraction thereof) on the amount of tax shown on the return less any tax payments made before the beginning of the month for which the penalty is being calculated. The maximum penalty is 25%.

Fair market value (FMV) The amount that would be realized from the sale of a property at a price that is agreeable to both the buyer and the seller when neither party is obligated to participate in the transaction.

Fiduciary A person or other entity (e.g., a guardian, executor, trustee, or administrator) who holds and manages property for someone else.

Fiduciary taxation The special tax rules that apply to fiduciaries (e.g., trusts and estates).

FMV See Fair market value.

Foreign branch An office or other establishment of a domestic entity that operates in a foreign country.

Foreign corporation A corporation that is incorporated under the laws of a country other than the United States.

Foreign tax credit Tax credit given to mitigate the possibility of double taxation faced by U.S. citizens, residents, and corporations earning foreign income.

Forum shopping The ability to consider differing precedents in choosing the forum for litigation.

Future interest Such interests include reversions, remainders, and other interests that may not be used, owned, or enjoyed until some future date.

General partner Partner or partners with (1) the authority to make management decisions and commitments for the partnership and (2) unlimited liability for all partnership debts.

General partnership A partnership with two or more partners where no partner is a limited partner.

General power of appointment Power of appointment under which the holder can appoint the property to himself, his estate, his creditors, or the creditors of his estate. Such power may be exercisable during the decedent's life, by his will, or both.

Generation-skipping transfer A disposition that (1) provides interests for more than one generation of beneficiaries who are in a younger generation than the transferor or (2) provides an interest solely for a person two or more generations younger than the transferor.

Gift tax A wealth transfer tax that applies if the property transfer occurs during a person's lifetime. A $14,000 (2016 and 2017) per donee annual exclusion is allowed.

Grantor The transferor who creates a trust.

Grantor trust Trust governed by Secs. 671 through 679. The income from such trusts is taxed to the grantor even if some or all of the income has been distributed.

Gross estate The gross estate includes items to which the decedent held title at death as well as certain incomplete transfers made by the decedent prior to death.

Guaranteed minimum Minimum amount of payment guaranteed to a partner. This amount is important if the partner's distributive share is less than his guaranteed minimum. See also Guaranteed payment.

Guaranteed payment Minimum amount of payment guaranteed to a partner in the form of a salary-like payment made for services provided to the partnership and interest-like payments for the use of invested capital. Guaranteed payments, which may be in the form of a guaranteed minimum amount or a set amount, are taxed as ordinary income. See also Guaranteed minimum.

Headnote An editorial summary of a particular point of case law that appears immediately before the text of a judicial opinion.

Hedge agreement An obligation on the part of a shareholder-employee to repay to the corporation any portion of salary disallowed by the IRS as a deduction. It also is used in connection with other corporate payments to shareholder-employees (e.g., travel and entertainment expenses).

Housing cost amount A special deduction or exclusion equal to the housing expenses incurred by a taxpayer eligible for the Sec. 911 earned income exclusion minus the base housing amount.

Income beneficiary Entity or individual that receives the income from a trust.

Income in respect of a decedent (IRD) Amount to which the decedent was entitled as gross income but which was not properly includible in computing his or her taxable income for the tax year ending with his or her date of death or for a previous tax year under the method of accounting employed by the decedent.

Income tax expense A subtraction item in the book income statement that represents a firm's current and deferred tax expense for the year. It is the total tax expense and sometimes is called the total tax provision.

Innocent spouse relief This provision exempts a spouse from penalty and liability for tax if such spouse meets certain requirements.

Intercompany item The seller's income, gain, deduction, or loss from an intercompany transaction.

Intercompany transaction Transaction that takes place during a consolidated return year between corporations that are members of the same group immediately after the transaction.

Interpretative regulations Treasury Regulations that serve to interpret the provisions of the Internal Revenue Code. Interpretative regulations are less authoritative than legislative regulations.

Inter vivos trust Transfer to a trust that is made during the grantor's lifetime.

Inversion A transaction in which a U.S. corporation reorganizes as a foreign entity for the purpose of removing foreign-source income not associated with a U.S. business from U.S. taxing jurisdiction.

IRD See Income in respect of a decedent.

Irrevocable trust Trust under which the grantor cannot require the trustee to return the trust's assets.

Joint and several liability The potential liability for the full amount of tax due. If one joint filer is unable to pay any or all of the tax, the other joint filer is liable for the deficiency. Also see Proportional liability.

Joint tenancy A popular form of property ownership that serves as a substitute for a will. Each joint tenant is deemed to have an equal interest in the property.

Judicial decisions Decision rendered by a court deciding the case that is presented to it by a plaintiff and defendant. These decisions are important sources of the tax law and can come from trial courts and appellate courts.

Legislative reenactment doctrine Rule holding that Congress's failure to change the wording in the IRC over an extended period signifies that Congress has approved the treatment provided in Treasury Regulations.

Legislative regulations Treasury Regulations that are treated as law because Congress has delegated its rulemaking authority to the Treasury Department. Such regulations may be overturned by the courts on the grounds that they exceed the scope of the delegated authority or are unreasonable.

Letter ruling A letter ruling originates from the IRS at the taxpayer's request. It describes how the IRS will treat a proposed transaction. It is binding only on the person requesting the ruling provided the transaction is completed as proposed in the ruling. Letter rulings that are of general interest are published as revenue rulings.

Life estate A property transfer in trust that results in the transferor reserving the right to income for life. Another individual is named to receive the property upon the transferor's death.

LIFO recapture tax A tax imposed on a C corporation that uses the LIFO inventory method and which elects S corporation treatment. The tax is imposed in the final C corporation tax year and is paid over a four-year period.

Limited liability company (LLC) A business entity that combines the legal and tax benefits of partnerships and S corporations. These entities are taxed as partnerships for federal tax purposes unless they elect to be taxed as corporations under the check-the-box regulations.

Limited liability partnership (LLP) Similar to a limited liability company, but formed under a separate state statute that generally applies to service companies.

Limited partner Partner who has no right to be active in the management of the partnership and whose liability is limited to his original investment plus any additional amounts he or she is obligated to contribute.

Limited partnership A partnership where one or more of the partners is designated as a limited partner and at least one partner is a general partner.

Liquidating distribution A distribution that (1) liquidates a partner's entire partnership interest due to retirement, death, or other business reason or (2) partially or totally liquidates a shareholder's stock interest in a corporation following the adoption of a plan at liquidation.

Loss corporation A corporation entitled to use a net operating loss carryover or having a net operating loss for the taxable year in which an ownership change occurs.

Majority partners The one or more partners in a partnership who have an aggregate interest in partnership profits and capital exceeding 50%.

Mandatory basis adjustment Required basis adjustment if the partnership has a substantial built-in loss at the time a partner sells his or her partnership interest or if the partnership has a decreasing basis adjustment at the time of a liquidating distribution.

Marital deduction Deduction allowed for tax-free inter-spousal transfers other than those for gifts of certain terminable interests.

Memorandum (memo) decision Decision issued by the Tax Court dealing with a factual variation on a matter where the law already has been decided in an earlier case.

Merger A nontaxable reorganization one form of which has the acquiring corporation transfer its stock, securities, and other consideration to the target corporation in exchange for its assets and liabilities. The target corporation then distributes the consideration it receives to its shareholders and security holders in exchange for their stock and securities.

Minimum tax credit (MTC) A tax credit allowed for the amount of alternative minimum tax that arose because of deferral and permanent adjustments and preference items. This credit carries over to offset regular tax liabilities in subsequent years.

MTC See Minimum tax credit.

National Research Program (NRP) An IRS program designed to develop new statistical models for identifying returns most likely to contain errors. The models are based on preexisting audit data as well as data compiled in ordinary audits.

Negligence The IRC defines negligence as (1) any failure to reasonably attempt to comply with the IRC and (2) "careless, reckless, or intentional disregard" of the rules and regulations.

Negligence penalty Penalty assessed if the IRS finds that the taxpayer has filed an incorrect return because of negligence. Generally, this penalty is 20% of the underpayment attributable to negligence.

Net accounting income The excess of accounting income over expenses for a fiduciary (i.e., an estate or trust). Excluded are any items credited to or charged against capital.

Net gift A gift upon which the donee pays the gift tax as a condition of receiving the gift.

Net operating loss (NOL) A net operating loss occurs when business expenses exceed business income for any taxable year. Such losses may be carried back two years or carried forward 20 years to a year in which the taxpayer has taxable income. The loss is carried back first and must be deducted from years in chronological order unless the taxpayer makes a special election to forgo the carryback.

New loss corporation Any corporation permitted to use a net operating loss carryover after an ownership change occurs.

News release An administrative pronouncement concerning an issue that the IRS thinks the general public will be interested in. Such releases are issued in lay terms and widely published.

Ninety (90)-day letter Officially called a Statutory Notice of Deficiency, this letter is sent when (1) the taxpayer does not file a protest letter within 30 days of receipt of the 30-day letter or (2) the taxpayer has met with an appeals officer but no agreement was reached. The letter notifies the taxpayer of the amount of the deficiency, how that amount was determined, and that a deficiency will be assessed if a petition is not filed with the Tax Court within 90 days. The taxpayer also is advised of the alternatives available to him.

NOL See Net operating loss.

Nonliquidating (current) distribution Distribution that (1) reduces, but does not eliminate, a partner's partnership interest or (2) is made with respect to a shareholder's stock interest in a corporation at a time when no plan of liquidation has been adopted and may or may not reduce the shareholder's interest in the corporation.

Nonrecourse loan Loan for which the borrower has no personal liability. Usually, the lender can look only to the secured property for satisfaction.

Nonresident alien Individual whose residence is not the United States and who is not a U.S. citizen.

Notice An interpretation by the IRS that provides guidance concerning how to interpret a statute, perhaps one recently enacted.

OGI See Ordinary gross income.

Old loss corporation Any corporation allowed to use a net operating loss carryover, or that has a net operating loss for the tax year in which an ownership change occurs, and that undergoes the requisite stock ownership change.

Open-fact or tax-planning situation Situation or transaction in which the facts have not yet occurred. In such situations, the tax advisor's task is to plan for the facts or shape them so as to produce a favorable tax result.

Open transaction doctrine Valuation technique for property that can be valued only on the basis of uncertain future payments. This doctrine determines the shareholder's gain or loss when the asset is sold, collected, or able to be valued. Assets that cannot be valued are assigned a value of zero.

Optional basis adjustment An elective technique that adjusts the basis for the underlying partnership assets up or down as a result of (1) distributions from the partnership to its partners, (2) sales of partnership interests by existing partners, or (3) transfers of the interest following the death of a partner.

Ordinary gross income (OGI) A corporation's ordinary gross income is its gross income reduced by capital gains and Sec. 1231 gains.

Ordinary income property For charitable contribution deduction purposes, any property that would result in the recognition of ordinary income if it were sold. Such property includes inventory, works of art or manuscripts created by the taxpayer, capital assets that have been held for one year or less, and Sec. 1231 property that results in ordinary income due to depreciation recapture.

Other intercompany transactions An intercompany transaction that is not a deferred intercompany transaction. See Intercompany transaction.

Parent-subsidiary controlled group To qualify as such, a common parent must own at least 80% of the voting stock or at least 80% of the value of at least one subsidiary corporation and at least 80% of each other component member of the controlled group must be owned by other members of the controlled group.

Partial liquidation Occurs when a corporation discontinues one line of business, distributes the assets related to that business to its shareholders, and continues at least one other line of business.

Partner A member of a partnership. The member may be an individual, trust, estate, or corporation. Also see General partner and Limited partner.

Partnership Syndicate, group, pool, joint venture, or other unincorporated organization that carries on a business or financial operation or venture and that has at least two partners.

Partnership agreement Agreement that governs the relationship between the partners and the partnership.

Partnership item Virtually all items reported by the partnership for the tax year, including tax preference items, credit recapture items, guaranteed payments, and at-risk amounts.

Partnership ordinary income The positive sum of all partnership items of income, gain, loss, or deduction that do not have to be separately stated.

Partnership ordinary loss The negative sum of all partnership items of income, gain, loss, or deduction that do not have to be separately stated.

Partnership taxable income The sum of all taxable items among the separately stated items plus the partnership ordinary income or ordinary loss.

Party to a reorganization Such parties include corporations that result from a reorganization and the corporations involved in a reorganization where one corporation acquires the stock or assets of the other corporation.

Passive activity limitation Separate limitation on the amount of losses and credits that can be claimed with respect to a passive activity.

Passive foreign investment company (PFIC) A foreign corporation having passive income as 75% or more of its gross income for the tax year, or at least 50% of the average value of its assets during the tax year producing or held for producing passive income.

Passive income Income from an activity that does not require the taxpayer's material involvement or participation. Thus, income from tax shelters and rental activities generally fall into this category.

Passive loss Loss generated from a passive activity. Such losses are computed separately. They may be used to offset income from other passive activities but may not be used to offset either active income or portfolio income.

Permanent difference Items reported in taxable income but not book income or vice versa. Such differences include book income items that are nontaxable in the current year and will never be taxable and book expense items that are nondeductible in computing taxable income for the current year and will never be deductible.

Personal holding company (PHC) A closely held corporation (1) that is owned by five or fewer shareholders who own more than 50% of the corporation's outstanding stock at any time during the last half of its tax year and (2) whose PHC income equals at least 60% of the corporation's adjusted ordinary gross income for the tax year. Certain corporations (e.g., S corporations) are exempt from this definition.

Personal holding company income (PHCI) Categories of income including the following: dividends; interest; annuities; royalties (other than minerals, oil and gas, computer software, and copyright royalties); adjusted income from rents; adjusted income from mineral, oil and gas royalties, or working interests in oil and gas wells; computer software royalties; copyright royalties; produced film rents; income from personal service contracts involving a 25% or more shareholder; rental income from corporate property used by a 25% or more shareholder; and distributions from estates and trusts.

Personal holding company (PHC) tax This tax equals 20% of the undistributed personal holding company income and, if applicable, is assessed in addition to the regular corporate income tax and the AMT.

Personal service corporation Corporation whose principal activity is the performance of personal services.

PHC See Personal holding company.

PHCI See Personal holding company income.

Plan of liquidation A written document detailing the steps to be undertaken while carrying out the complete liquidation of a corporation.

Plan of reorganization A consummated transaction that is specifically defined as a reorganization.

Pooled income fund A fund in which individuals receive an income interest for life and a charitable contribution deduction equal to the remainder interest for amounts contributed to the fund. The various individual beneficiaries receive annual distributions of income based upon their proportionate share of the fund's earnings.

Post-termination transition period The period of time following the termination of the S corporation election during which (1) loss and deduction carryovers can be deducted or (2) distributions of S corporation previously taxed earnings can be made tax-free.

Power of appointment The power to designate the eventual owner of a property. Such appointments may be general or specific. Also see General power of appointment.

Preadjustment AMTI Alternative minimum taxable income determined without the adjusted current earnings adjustment and the alternative tax NOL deduction.

Preferential dividend Dividends are preferential if (1) the amount distributed to a shareholder exceeds his ratable share of the distribution as determined by the number of shares owned or (2) the distribution amount for a class of stock is more or less than its rightful amount.

Preferred stock bailout A tax treatment mandated by Sec. 306 that prevents shareholders who receive nontaxable preferred stock dividends from receiving capital gain treatment upon the sale or redemption of the preferred stock.

Present interest An unrestricted right to the immediate use, possession, or enjoyment of property or the income from property (e.g., a life estate or term certain).

Previously taxed income (PTI) Income earned in a pre-1983 S corporation tax year and that was taxed to the shareholder. A money distribution of PTI can be distributed tax-free once all of a corporation's AAA balance has been distributed. See Accumulated adjustments account.

Primary citation The highest level official reporter that reports a particular case.

Principal partner Partner who owns at least a 5% interest in the partnership's capital or profits.

Private Letter Ruling See Letter ruling.

Probate estate Properties that (1) pass subject to the will or under an intestacy statute and (2) are subject to court administration are part of the probate estate.

Profits interest Interest in the partnership's future earnings.

Property Cash, tangible property (e.g., buildings and land), and intangible property (e.g., franchise rights, trademarks, and leases).

Proportional liability The liability for one's pro rata share of the amount of tax due. If one joint filer is unable to pay any or all the tax, the other joint filer is liable only for the portion of the tax attributable to his or her separate taxable items. Also see Joint and several liability.

Protest letter If the additional tax in question is more than $25,000 and the IRS audit was a field audit, the taxpayer must file a protest letter within 30 days. If no such letter is sent, the IRS will follow-up with a 90-day letter. Also see Ninety (90)-day letter.

Publicly traded partnership A partnership that is actively traded on an established securities exchange or is traded in a secondary market or the equivalent thereof. Such partnerships formed after December 17, 1987, are taxed as corporations unless they earn predominantly passive income; publicly traded partnerships that existed before that date will be treated as partnerships if they agree to pay a special excise tax on their gross income.

QTIP See Qualified terminable interest property.

Qualified disclaimer Disclaimer made by a person named to receive property under a decedent's will who wishes to renounce the property and any of its benefits. Such a disclaimer must be in written form and be irrevocable. In addition, it must be made no later than nine months after the later of the day the transfer is made or the day the recipient becomes 21 years old. The property must pass to either the decedent's spouse or another person not named by the person making the disclaimer.

Qualified joint interest If spouses are the only joint owners of a property, that property is classified as a qualified joint interest.

Qualified Subchapter S Subsidiary (QSub) An S corporation that is 100%-owned by another S corporation. The income earned by a QSub is treated and reported as if earned by its parent corporation.

Qualified Subchapter S trusts (QSSTs) A domestic trust that owns stock in one or more S corporations and distributes (or is required to distribute) all of its income to its sole income beneficiary. The beneficiary must make an irrevocable election to be treated as the owner of the trust consisting of the S corporation stock. A separate QSST election must be made for each corporation's stock owned by the trust.

Qualified terminable interest property (QTIP) QTIP property is property for which a special election has been made that makes it eligible for the marital deduction. Such property must be transferred by the donor-spouse to a donee-spouse who has a qualifying interest for life. In other words, the donor does not have to grant full control over the property to his spouse.

Reasonable business needs For accumulated earnings tax purposes, the amount that a prudent business person would consider appropriate for the business's bona fide present and future needs, Sec. 303 (death tax) redemption needs, and excess business holding redemption needs.

Recapitalization A nontaxable change in the capital structure of an existing corporation for a bona fide business purpose.

Recomputed corresponding item The corresponding item that would occur if the selling and buying group members were divisions of a single corporation.

Recourse loan Loan for which the borrower remains liable until repayment is complete. If the loan is secured, the lender can be repaid by selling the security. Any difference in the sale amount and the loan amount must be paid by the borrower.

Regular corporation See C corporation.

Regular decision Tax Court decision issued on a particular issue for the first time.

Regular tax A corporation's tax liability for income tax purposes reduced by foreign tax credits allowable for income tax purposes.

Remainder interest The portion of an interest in property retained by a transferor who is not transferring his entire interest in the property.

Remainderman The person entitled to the remainder interest.

Reorganization A corporate acquisition or division that meets specific requirements to qualify as nontaxable transaction. Reorganizations are classified as Type A, B, C, D, E, F, or G.

Resident alien An individual whose residence is the United States but who is not a U.S. citizen.

Revenue procedure Issued by the national office of the IRS and reflects the IRS's position on procedural aspects of tax practice issues. Revenue procedures are published in the Cumulative Bulletin.

Revenue ruling Issued by the national office of the IRS and reflects the IRS's interpretation of a narrow tax issue. Revenue rulings, which are published in the Cumulative Bulletin, have less weight than Treasury Regulations.

Reverse triangular merger Type of nontaxable transaction in which a subsidiary corporation is merged into a target corporation, and the target corporation stays alive as a subsidiary of the parent corporation.

Reversionary interest An interest in property that might revert back to the transferor under the terms of the transfer. If the amount of reversionary interest is 5% or less, it is not included in the gross estate.

Revocable trust Trust under which the grantor may demand that the assets be returned.

Rule against perpetuities The requirement that no property interest vest more than 21 years, plus the gestation period, after some life or lives in being at the time the interest is created.

S corporation Election that can be made by small business corporations that allows them to be taxed like partnerships rather than like C corporations. Small business corporations are those that meet the 100-shareholder limitation, the type of shareholder restrictions, and the one class of stock restriction.

Secondary citation Citation to a secondary source (i.e., an unofficial reporter) for a particular case.

Section 306 stock Preferred stock received as a stock dividend or a part of a nontaxable reorganization. Sec. 306 stock is subject to the special preferred stock bailout rules when sold or redeemed. See Preferred stock bailouts.

Section 382 loss limitation rules Limitation that principally prevents trafficking in NOLs. Applies to corporate acquisitions, stock redemptions, and reorganizations when a more than 50 percentage point change in ownership occurs. The NOL that can be used in a tax year is limited to the value of the loss corporation's stock times a federal long-term tax exempt rate.

Section 444 election Personal service corporations, partnerships, and S corporations that are unable to otherwise elect a fiscal year instead of their required tax year, under Sec. 444 can elect a fiscal year as their taxable year.

Section 482 rules The IRS has the power under Sec. 482 to distribute, apportion, or allocate income, deductions, credits, or allowances between or among controlled entities to prevent tax evasion and to clearly reflect the income of the entities.

Section 2503(c) trust Trust created for children under age 21 that need not distribute all of its income annually. The undistributed interest passes to the beneficiary when he or she attains age 21 or to his or her estate should he or she die before age 21.

Security A security includes (1) shares of stock in a corporation; (2) a right to subscribe for, or the right to receive, a share of stock in a corporation; and (3) a bond, debenture, note, or other evidence of indebtedness issued by a corporation with interest coupons or in registered form.

Separate return limitation year Any separate return year except (1) a separate return year of the group member designated as the parent corporation for the consolidated return year to which the tax attribute is carried or (2) a separate return year of any corporation that was a group member for every day of the loss year.

Separate return limitation year (SRLY) rules Limitation on the amount of net operating loss and other deduction and loss amounts from a separate return year that can be used by an affiliated group in a consolidated return year to the member's contribution to consolidated taxable income.

Separate return year A tax year for which a corporation files a separate return or joins in the filing of a consolidated return with a different affiliated group.

Separate share rule Rule permitting a trust with several beneficiaries to treat each beneficiary as having a separate trust interest for purposes of determining the amount of the distribution deduction and the beneficiary's gross income.

Separate taxable income (loss) The taxable income (loss) of an individual corporate member of an affiliated group filing a consolidated tax return. This amount is used to calculate the group's combined taxable income.

Short-period tax return A tax return covering a period of less than 12 months. Short period returns are commonly filed in the first or final tax year or when a change in tax year is made.

Short-term trust Trust whose period is long enough for the grantor to escape being taxed on the trust's accounting income. A *Clifford* trust is a short-term trust.

Simple trust Trust that must distribute all of its income currently and is not empowered to make a charitable contribution.

Small business trust A type of trust that can own stock in a small business corporation that has made an S election to be taxed as an S corporation.

Small cases procedure A Tax Court procedure for adjudicating tax-related claims of $25,000 or less. Small cases procedure decisions are not appealable and have no precedential value.

Sole proprietorship Form of business owned by an individual who reports all items of income and expense on Schedule C (or Schedule C-EZ) of his individual return.

Special agents The IRS agents responsible for criminal fraud investigations.

Spin-off A nontaxable distribution in which a parent corporation distributes the stock and securities of a subsidiary to its shareholders without receiving anything in exchange.

Split-interest transfer A transfer made for both private (i.e., an individual) and public (i.e., a charitable organization) purposes.

Split-off A nontaxable distribution in which a parent corporation distributes a subsidiary's stock and securities to some or all of its shareholders in exchange for part or all of their stock and securities in the parent corporation.

Split-up A nontaxable distribution in which a parent corporation distributes the stock or securities of two or more subsidiaries to its shareholders in exchange for all of their stock and securities in the parent corporation. The parent corporation then goes out of existence.

Sprinkling trust A discretionary trust with several beneficiaries.

S short year That portion of an S termination year that begins on the first day of the tax year and ends on the day preceding the day on which the termination is effective.

SSTS See Statements on Standards for Tax Services.

Statements on Standards for Tax Services (SSTS) Ethical standards of practice and compliance set by the Tax Division of the American Institute of Certified Public Accountants. The AICPA enforces these standards, and thus they have a great deal of influence on ethics in tax practice.

Statute of limitations A period of time as provided by law after which a taxpayer's return may not be changed either by the IRS or the taxpayer. The limitations period is generally three years from the later of the date the tax return is filed or its due date. A fraudulent return has no statute of limitations.

Step transaction doctrine A judicial doctrine that the IRS can use to collapse a multistep transaction into a single transaction (either taxable or nontaxable) to prevent the taxpayers from arranging a series of business transactions to obtain a tax result that is not available if only a single transaction is used.

S termination year A tax year in which a termination event occurs on any day other than the first day of the tax year. It is divided into an S short year and a C short year.

Stock dividend A dividend paid in the form of stock in the corporation issuing the dividend.

Stock redemption The acquisition by a corporation of its own stock in exchange for property. Such stock may be cancelled, retired, or held as treasury stock.

Stock rights Rights issued by a corporation to its shareholders or creditors that permit the purchase of an additional share(s) of stock at a designated exercise price with the surrender of one or more of the stock rights.

Subpart F income A series of income categories deemed distributed to the U.S. shareholders of a controlled foreign corporation on the last day of its tax year. Subpart F income includes income from insurance of U.S. and foreign risks, foreign base company income, boycott-related income, bribes, and income from countries where for political reasons, etc. the deferral privilege is denied.

Substantially appreciated inventory This type of inventory includes (1) items held for sale in the normal course of partnership business, (2) other property that would not be considered a capital asset or Sec. 1231 property if it were sold by the partnership, and (3) any other property held by the partnership that would fall into the above classification if it were held by the selling or distributee partner.

Target corporation The corporation that transfers its assets as part of a taxable or nontaxable acquisition. Also may be known as the acquired or transferor company.

Tax attributes Corporations have various tax items, such as earnings and profits, deduction and credit carryovers, and depreciation recapture potential, that are called tax attributes. The tax attributes of a target or liquidating corporation are assumed by the acquiring or parent corporation, respectively, in acquisitive reorganizations and tax-free liquidations.

Tax matters partner Partner who is designated by the partnership or who is the general partner having the largest profits interests at the close of the partnership's tax year.

Taxpayer Compliance Measurement Program (TCMP) A stratified random sample used to select tax returns for audit. The program is intended to test the extent to which taxpayers are in compliance with the law.

Tax preference items Designated items that increase taxable income to arrive at AMTI. Unlike AMT adjustments, tax preference items do not reverse in later years and reduce AMTI.

Tax research The process of solving a specific tax-related question on the basis of both tax law sources and the specific circumstances surrounding the particular situation.

Tax services Multivolume commentaries on the tax law. Generally, these commentaries contain copies of the Internal Revenue Code and the Treasury Regulations. Also included are editorial comments prepared by the publisher of the tax service, current matters, and a cross-reference to various government promulgations and judicial decisions. Most tax services now are available on the Internet.

Tax treaties Bilateral agreements entered into between two nations that address tax and other matters. Treaties provide for modifications to the basic tax laws involving residents of the two countries (e.g., reductions in the withholding rates).

Tax year The period of time (usually 12 months) selected by taxpayers to compute their taxable income. The tax year may be a calendar year or a fiscal year. The election is made on the taxpayer's first return and cannot be changed without IRS approval. The tax year may be less than 12 months if it is the taxpayer's first or final return or if the taxpayer is changing accounting periods.

TCMP See Taxpayer Compliance Measurement Program.

Technical advice memorandum Such memoranda are administrative interpretations issued by the national office of the IRS in the form of a letter ruling. Taxpayers may request them if they need guidance about the tax treatment of complicated technical matters being audited.

Temporary differences Items that are included in book income in the current year but that were included in taxable income in the past or will be included in the future. Book income items that are nontaxable in the current year even though they were taxed in the past or will be taxed in the future and book expenses that are not currently deductible even though that status was different in the past or will be different in the future are categorized as temporary differences.

Temporary regulations Regulations issued by the Treasury Department relating to an IRC provision. Such regulations are effective for a limited period of time, usually three years. Issuance of temporary regulations is not preceded by a public hearing on their substance. Temporary regulations have the same precedential value as final regulations.

Tentative minimum tax (TMT) Tax calculated by (1) multiplying 20% times the corporation's alternative minimum taxable income less a statutory exemption amount and (2) deducting allowable foreign tax credits.

Term certain interest A person holding such an interest has a right to receive income from property for a specified term but does not own or hold title to such property. The property reverts to the grantor at the end of the term.

Terminable interest A property interest that ends when some event occurs (or fails to occur) or when a specified amount of time passes.

Testamentary Of, pertaining to, or of the nature of a testament or will.

Testamentary transfers A transferor's control or enjoyment of a property ceases at death.

Testamentary trust Trust created under the direction of a decedent's will and funded by the decedent's estate.

Thirty (30)-day letter A report sent to the taxpayer if the taxpayer does not sign Form 870 (Waiver of Statutory Notice) concerning any additional taxes assessed. The letter details the proposed changes and advises the taxpayer of his or her right to pursue the matter with the Appeals Office. The taxpayer then has 30 days in which to request a conference.

Throwback dividends For accumulated earnings tax and personal holding company tax purposes, these are distributions made out of current or accumulated earnings and profits in the first two and one-half months after the close of the tax year.

Tier-1 beneficiary Beneficiary to whom a distribution must be made.

Tier-2 beneficiary Beneficiary who receives a discretionary distribution.

TMT See Tentative minimum tax.

Topical tax service A multivolume tax commentary organized by topic. Topics might include, for example, deferred compensation, Type A reorganizations, or S corporations. These volumes are an excellent place to begin research in an unfamiliar area.

Transferor corporation The corporation that transfers its assets as part of a reorganization. Also may be known as acquired or target corporation.

Triangular merger A type of merger transaction where the parent corporation uses a subsidiary corporation to serve as the acquiring corporation.

Triangular reorganization A type of reorganization (i.e., Type A, B, or C) where the parent corporation uses a subsidiary corporation to serve as the acquiring corporation. Also see Triangular merger.

Trust An arrangement created either by will or by an inter vivos declaration whereby trustees take title to property for the purpose of protecting it or conserving it for the beneficiaries.

Trustee An individual or institution that administers a trust for the benefit of a beneficiary.

Trustor The grantor or transferor of a trust.

Type A reorganization Type of corporate reorganization that meets the requirements of state or federal law. It may take the form of a consolidation, merger, triangular merger, or reverse triangular merger.

Type B reorganization Reorganization characterized by a stock-for-stock exchange. The target corporation remains in existence as a subsidiary of the acquiring corporation.

Type C reorganization A transaction that requires the acquiring corporation to obtain substantially all the target corporation's assets in exchange for its voting stock and a limited amount of other consideration. The target corporation generally is liquidated.

Type D reorganization This type of reorganization may be either acquisitive or divisive. In the former, substantially all the transferor corporation's assets (and possibly some or all of its liabilities) are acquired by a controlled corporation. The target corporation is liquidated. The latter involves the acquisition of the part or all of the transferor corporation's assets (and liabilities) by a controlled subsidiary corporation(s). The transferor corporation may either remain in existence or be liquidated.

Type E reorganization This type of reorganization changes the capital structure of a corporation. The corporation remains in existence.

Type F reorganization The old corporation's assets or stock are transferred to a single newly formed corporation in this type of transaction. The "old" corporation is liquidated.

Type G reorganization This type of reorganization may be either acquisitive or divisive. In either case, part or all the target or transferor corporation's assets (and possibly some or all of its liabilities) are transferred to another corporation as part of a bankruptcy proceeding. The target or transferor corporation may either remain in existence or be liquidated.

Unauthorized practice of law The engagement of nonlawyers in professional activities traditionally relegated to the legal profession. Such activities include preparing legal documents, formalizing business entities, and representing clients in criminal investigations.

Unified credit The unified credit enables a tax base of a certain size (i.e., the exemption equivalent or applicable exclusion amount) to be completely free of transfer taxes. It may be subtracted only once against all of a person's transfers—throughout one's lifetime and at death. See Exemption equivalent and Applicable exclusion amount.

Unified rate schedule Progressive rate schedule for estate and gift taxes. These rates are effective for gifts made after 1976 and deaths occurring after 1976.

Unrealized receivable Right to payment for goods and services that has not been included in the owner's income because of its method of accounting.

Unreported decisions District court decisions that are not reported in official reporters. Such decisions may be reported in secondary reporters that report only tax-related cases.

U.S. production activities deduction A deduction equal to 9% times the lesser of (1) qualified production activities income for the year or (2) taxable income before the U.S. production activities deduction. The deduction, however, cannot exceed 50% of the corporation's W-2 wages allocable to U.S. production activities for the year.

U.S. shareholder For controlled foreign corporation purposes, a U.S. person who owns at least 10% of the foreign corporation's voting stock.

Valuation allowance A contra-type account that represents the portion of a deferred tax asset that likely will not be realized.

Voting trust An arrangement whereby the stock owned by a number of shareholders is placed under the control of a trustee for purposes of exercising the voting rights possessed by the stock. This practice increases the voting power of the minority shareholders.

Wealth transfer taxes Estate taxes (i.e., the tax on dispositions of property that occur as a result of the transferor's death) and gift taxes (i.e., the tax on lifetime transfers) are wealth transfer taxes.

Writ of certiorari See Certiorari.

APPENDIX

E AICPA STATEMENTS ON STANDARDS FOR TAX SERVICES NOS. 1–7

Note: The AICPA released revised Statements on Standards for Tax Services (SSTS) effective on January 1, 2010. These statements are enforceable standards of tax practice for AICPA members. Changes to Statements No. 1 and 7 (formerly No. 8) were substantive in nature. As a result, Interpretations No. 1-1 and 1-2 relating to former Statement No. 1 are currently being updated. The new statements as well as the old statements can be found on the AICPA website at www.aicpa.org.

PREFACE

1. Standards are the foundation of a profession. The AICPA aids its members in fulfilling their ethical responsibilities by instituting and maintaining standards against which their professional performance can be measured. Compliance with professional standards of tax practice also reaffirms the public's awareness of the professionalism that is associated with CPAs as well as the AICPA.

2. This publication sets forth enforceable tax practice standards for members of the AICPA, Statements on Standards for Tax Services (SSTSs or statements). These statements apply to all members providing tax services regardless of the jurisdictions in which they practice. Interpretations of these statements may be issued as guidance to assist in understanding and applying the statements. The SSTSs and their interpretations are intended to complement other standards of tax practice, such as Treasury Department Circular No. 230, *Regulations Governing the Practice of Attorneys, Certified Public Accountants, Enrolled Agents, Enrolled Actuaries, Enrolled Retirement Plan Agents, and Appraisers before the Internal Revenue Service*; penalty provisions of the Internal Revenue Code; and state boards of accountancy rules.

3. The SSTSs are written in as simple and objective a manner as possible. However, by their nature, practice standards provide for an appropriate range of behavior and need to be interpreted to address a broad range of personal and professional situations. The SSTSs recognize this need by, in some sections, providing relatively subjective rules and by leaving certain terms undefined. These terms are generally rooted in tax concepts and, therefore, should be readily understood by tax practitioners. Accordingly, enforcement of these rules, as part of the AICPA's Code of Professional Conduct Rule 201, *General Standards*, and Rule 202, *Compliance With Standards* (AICPA, *Professional Standards*, vol. 2, ET sec. 201 par. .01 and ET sec. 202 par. .01), will be undertaken on a case-by-case basis. Members are expected to comply with them.

History

4. The SSTSs have their origin in the Statements on Responsibilities in Tax Practice (SRTPs), which provided a body of advisory opinions on good tax practice. The guidelines as originally set forth in the SRTPs became more important than many members had anticipated when the guidelines were issued. The courts, the IRS, state accountancy boards, and other professional organizations recognized and relied on the SRTPs as the appropriate articulation of professional conduct in a CPA's tax practice. The SRTPs became *de facto* enforceable standards of professional practice, because state disciplinary organizations and courts regularly held CPAs accountable for failure to follow the guidelines set forth in the SRTPs.

5. The AICPA's Tax Executive Committee concluded it was appropriate to issue tax practice standards that would become a part of the AICPA's *Professional Standards*. At its July 1999 meeting, the AICPA Board of Directors approved support of the executive committee's initiative and placed the matter on the agenda of the October 1999 meeting of the AICPA's governing Council. On October 19, 1999, Council approved designating the Tax Executive Committee as a standardsetting body, thus authorizing that committee to promulgate standards of tax practice. As a result, the original SSTSs, largely mirroring the SRTPs, were issued in August 2000.

6. The SRTPs were originally issued between 1964 and 1977. The first nine SRTPs and the introduction were promulgated in 1976; the tenth SRTP was issued in 1977. The original SRTPs concerning the CPA's responsibility to sign the tax return (SRTP No. 1, *Signature of Preparers*, and No. 2, *Signature of Reviewer: Assumption of Preparer's Responsibility*) were withdrawn in 1982 after Treasury Department regulations were issued adopting substantially the same standards for all tax return preparers. The sixth and seventh SRTPs, concerning the responsibility of a CPA who becomes aware of an error, were revised in 1991. The first interpretation of the SRTPs, Interpretation No. 1-1, "Realistic Possibility Standard," was approved in December 1990. The SSTSs and Interpretation No. 1-1, "Realistic Possibility Standard," of SSTS No. 1, *Tax Return Positions*, superseded and replaced the SRTPs and their Interpretation No. 1-1, effective October 31, 2000. Although the number and names of the SSTSs, and the substance of the rules contained in each of them, remained the same as in the SRTPs, the language was revised to both clarify and reflect the enforceable nature of the SSTSs. In addition, because the applicability of these standards is not limited to federal income tax practice (as was the case with the SRTPs), the language was changed to indicate the broader scope. In 2003, in connection with the tax shelter debate, SSTS Interpretation No. 1-2, "Tax Planning," of SSTS No. 1 was issued to clarify a member's responsibilities in connection with tax planning; that interpretation became effective December 31, 2003.

7. When the original SSTSs were issued, an effort was made to keep to a minimum any changes in the language of the SSTSs from that of the predecessor SRTPs. This was done to alleviate concerns regarding the enforceability of standards that differed from the SRTPs under which members had been practicing. Since the issuance of the original SSTSs, members have asked for clarification on certain matters, such as the duplication of the language in SSTS No. 6, *Knowledge of Error: Return Preparation*, and No. 7, *Knowledge of Error: Administrative Proceedings*. Also, certain changes in federal and state tax laws have raised concerns regarding the need to revise SSTS No. 1. As a result, in 2008, the original SSTS Nos. 1–8 were updated, effective January 1, 2010. The original SSTS Nos. 6–7 were combined into the revised SSTS No. 6, *Knowledge of Error: Return Preparation and Administrative Proceedings*. The original SSTS No. 8, *Form and Content of Advice to Taxpayers*, was renumbered SSTS No. 7. In addition, various revisions were made to the language of the original SSTSs.

Ongoing Process

8. The following SSTSs and any interpretations issued thereunder reflect the AICPA's standards of tax practice and delineate members' responsibilities to taxpayers, the public, the government, and the profession. The statements are intended to be part of an ongoing process of articulating standards of tax practice for members. These standards are subject to change as necessary or appropriate to address changes in the tax law or other developments in the tax practice environment.

9. Members are encouraged to assess the adequacy of their practices and procedures for providing tax services in conformity with these standards. This process will vary according to the size of the practice and the nature of tax services performed.

10. The Tax Executive Committee promulgates the SSTSs and their interpretations. Acknowledgment is also due to the many members who have devoted their time and efforts over the years to developing and revising the AICPA's standards.

STATEMENT ON STANDARDS FOR TAX SERVICES NO. 1, *TAX RETURN POSITIONS*

Introduction

1. This statement sets forth the applicable standards for members when recommending tax return positions, or preparing or signing tax returns (including amended returns, claims for refund, and information returns) filed with any taxing authority. For purposes of these standards

a. a *tax return position* is (i) a position reflected on a tax return on which a member has specifically advised a taxpayer or (ii) a position about which a member has knowledge of all material facts and, on the basis of those facts, has concluded whether the position is appropriate.
b. a *taxpayer* is a client, a member's employer, or any other third-party recipient of tax services.

2. This statement also addresses a member's obligation to advise a taxpayer of relevant tax return disclosure responsibilities and potential penalties.

3. In addition to the AICPA, various taxing authorities, at the federal, state, and local levels, may impose specific reporting and disclosure standards with regard to recommending tax return positions or preparing or signing tax returns.[1] These standards can vary between taxing authorities and by type of tax.

Statement

4. A member should determine and comply with the standards, if any, that are imposed by the applicable taxing authority with respect to recommending a tax return position, or preparing or signing a tax return.

5. If the applicable taxing authority has no written standards with respect to recommending a tax return position or preparing or signing a tax return, or if its standards are lower than the standards set forth in this paragraph, the following standards will apply:

a. A member should not recommend a tax return position or prepare or sign a tax return taking a position unless the member has a good-faith belief that the position has at least a realistic possibility of being sustained administratively or judicially on its merits if challenged.
b. Notwithstanding paragraph 5(a), a member may *recommend a tax return position* if the member (i) concludes that there is a reasonable basis for the position and (ii) advises the taxpayer to appropriately disclose that position. Notwithstanding paragraph 5(a), a member may *prepare or sign a tax return* that reflects a position if (i) the member concludes there is a reasonable basis for the position and (ii) the position is appropriately disclosed.

[1]A member should refer to the current version of Internal Revenue Code Section 6694, Understatement of taxpayer's liability by tax return preparer, and other relevant federal, state, and jurisdictional authorities to determine the reporting and disclosure standards that are applicable to preparers of tax returns.

6. When recommending a tax return position or when preparing or signing a tax return on which a position is taken, a member should, when relevant, advise the taxpayer regarding potential penalty consequences of such tax return position and the opportunity, if any, to avoid such penalties through disclosure.

7. A member should not recommend a tax return position or prepare or sign a tax return reflecting a position that the member knows

a. exploits the audit selection process of a taxing authority, or
b. serves as a mere arguing position advanced solely to obtain leverage in a negotiation with a taxing authority.

8. When recommending a tax return position, a member has both the right and the responsibility to be an advocate for the taxpayer with respect to any position satisfying the aforementioned standards.

Explanation

9. The AICPA and various taxing authorities impose specific reporting and disclosure standards with respect to tax return positions and preparing or signing tax returns. In a given situation, the standards, if any, imposed by the applicable taxing authority may be higher or lower than the standards set forth in paragraph 5. A member is to comply with the standards, if any, of the applicable taxing authority; if the applicable taxing authority has no standards or if its standards are lower than the standards set forth in paragraph 5, the standards set forth in paragraph 5 will apply.

10. Our self-assessment tax system can function effectively only if taxpayers file tax returns that are true, correct, and complete. A tax return is prepared based on a taxpayer's representation of facts, and the taxpayer has the final responsibility for positions taken on the return. The standards that apply to a taxpayer may differ from those that apply to a member.

11. In addition to a duty to the taxpayer, a member has a duty to the tax system. However, it is well established that the taxpayer has no obligation to pay more taxes than are legally owed, and a member has a duty to the taxpayer to assist in achieving that result. The standards contained in paragraphs 4–8 recognize a member's responsibilities to both the taxpayer and the tax system.

12. In reaching a conclusion concerning whether a given standard in paragraph 4 or 5 has been satisfied, a member may consider a well-reasoned construction of the applicable statute, well-reasoned articles or treatises, or pronouncements issued by the applicable taxing authority, regardless of whether such sources would be treated as *authority* under Internal Revenue Code Section 6662, *Imposition of accuracy-related penalty on underpayments*, and the regulations thereunder. A position would not fail to meet these standards merely because it is later abandoned for practical or procedural considerations during an administrative hearing or in the litigation process.

13. If a member has a good-faith belief that more than one tax return position meets the standards set forth in paragraphs 4–5, a member's advice concerning alternative acceptable positions may include a discussion of the likelihood that each such position might or might not cause the taxpayer's tax return to be examined and whether the position would be challenged in an examination. In such circumstances, such advice is not a violation of paragraph 7.

14. A member's determination of whether information is appropriately disclosed by the taxpayer should be based on the facts and circumstances of the particular case and the disclosure requirements of the applicable taxing authority. If a member recommending a position, but not engaged to prepare or sign the related tax return, advises the taxpayer concerning appropriate disclosure of the position, then the member shall be deemed to meet the disclosure requirements of these standards.

15. If particular facts and circumstances lead a member to believe that a taxpayer penalty might be asserted, the member should so advise the taxpayer and should discuss with the taxpayer the opportunity, if any, to avoid such penalty by disclosing the position on the tax return. Although a member should advise the taxpayer with respect to disclosure, it is the taxpayer's responsibility to decide whether and how to disclose.

16. For purposes of this statement, preparation of a tax return includes giving advice on events that have occurred at the time the advice is given if the advice is directly relevant to determining the existence, character, or amount of a schedule, entry, or other portion of a tax return.

STATEMENT ON STANDARDS FOR TAX SERVICES NO. 2, *ANSWERS TO QUESTIONS ON RETURNS*

Introduction

1. This statement sets forth the applicable standards for members when signing the preparer's declaration on a tax return if one or more questions on the return have not been answered. The term *questions* includes requests for information on the return, in the instructions, or in the regulations, whether or not stated in the form of a question.

Statement

2. A member should make a reasonable effort to obtain from the taxpayer the information necessary to provide appropriate answers to all questions on a tax return before signing as preparer.

Explanation

3. It is recognized that the questions on tax returns are not of uniform importance, and often they are not applicable to the particular taxpayer. Nevertheless, there are at least three reasons why a member should be satisfied that a reasonable effort has been made to obtain information to provide appropriate answers to the questions on the return that are applicable to a taxpayer:

a. A question may be of importance in determining taxable income or loss, or the tax liability shown on the return, in which circumstance an omission may detract from the quality of the return.
b. A request for information may require a disclosure necessary for a complete return or to avoid penalties.
c. A member often must sign a preparer's declaration stating that the return is true, correct, and complete.

4. Reasonable grounds may exist for omitting an answer to a question applicable to a taxpayer. For example, reasonable grounds may include the following:

a. The information is not readily available and the answer is not significant in terms of taxable income or loss, or the tax liability shown on the return.
b. Genuine uncertainty exists regarding the meaning of the question in relation to the particular return.
c. The answer to the question is voluminous; in such cases, a statement should be made on the return that the data will be supplied upon examination.

5. A member should not omit an answer merely because it might prove disadvantageous to a taxpayer.

6. A member should consider whether the omission of an answer to a question may cause the return to be deemed incomplete or result in penalties.

7. If reasonable grounds exist for omission of an answer to an applicable question, a taxpayer is not required to provide on the return an explanation of the reason for the omission.

STATEMENT ON STANDARDS FOR TAX SERVICES NO. 3, *CERTAIN PROCEDURAL ASPECTS OF PREPARING RETURNS*

Introduction

1. This statement sets forth the applicable standards for members concerning the obligation to examine or verify certain supporting data or to consider information related to another taxpayer when preparing a taxpayer's tax return.

Statement

2. In preparing or signing a return, a member may in good faith rely, without verification, on information furnished by the taxpayer or by third parties. However, a member should not ignore the implications of information furnished and should make reasonable inquiries if the information furnished appears to be incorrect, incomplete, or inconsistent either on its face or on the basis of other facts known to the member. Further, a member should refer to the taxpayer's returns for one or more prior years whenever feasible.

3. If the tax law or regulations impose a condition with respect to deductibility or other tax treatment of an item, such as taxpayer maintenance of books and records or substantiating documentation to support the reported deduction or tax treatment, a member should make appropriate inquiries to determine to the member's satisfaction whether such condition has been met.

4. When preparing a tax return, a member should consider information actually known to that member from the tax return of another taxpayer if the information is relevant to that tax return and its consideration is necessary to properly prepare that tax return. In using such information, a member should consider any limitations imposed by any law or rule relating to confidentiality.

Explanation

5. The preparer's declaration on a tax return often states that the information contained therein is true, correct, and complete to the best of the preparer's knowledge and belief based on all information known by the preparer. This type of reference should be understood to include information furnished by the taxpayer or by third parties to a member in connection with the preparation of the return.

6. The preparer's declaration does not require a member to examine or verify supporting data; a member may rely on information furnished by the taxpayer unless it appears to be incorrect, incomplete, or inconsistent. However, there is a need to determine by inquiry that a specifically required condition, such as maintaining books and records or substantiating documentation, has been satisfied and to obtain information when the material furnished appears to be incorrect, incomplete, or inconsistent. Although a member has certain responsibilities in exercising due diligence in preparing a return, the taxpayer has the ultimate responsibility for the contents of the return. Thus, if the taxpayer presents unsupported data in the form of lists of tax information, such as dividends and interest received, charitable contributions, and medical expenses, such information may be used in the preparation of a tax return without verification unless it appears to be incorrect, incomplete, or inconsistent either on its face or on the basis of other facts known to a member.

7. Even though there is no requirement to examine underlying documentation, a member should encourage the taxpayer to provide supporting data where appropriate. For example, a member should encourage the taxpayer to submit underlying documents for use in tax return preparation to permit full consideration of income and deductions arising from security transactions and from pass-through entities, such as estates, trusts, partnerships, and S corporations.

8. The source of information provided to a member by a taxpayer for use in preparing the return is often a pass-through entity, such as a limited partnership, in which the taxpayer has an interest but is not involved in management. A member may accept the information provided by the pass-through entity without further inquiry, unless there is reason to believe it is incorrect, incomplete, or inconsistent, either on its face or on the basis of other facts known to the member. In some instances, it may be appropriate for a member to advise the taxpayer to ascertain the nature and amount of possible exposure to tax deficiencies, interest, and penalties by taxpayer contact with management of the pass-through entity.

9. A member should make use of a taxpayer's returns for one or more prior years in preparing the current return whenever feasible. Reference to prior returns and discussion of prior-year tax determinations with the taxpayer should provide information to determine the taxpayer's general tax status, avoid the omission or duplication of items, and afford a basis for the treatment of similar or related transactions. As with the examination of information supplied for the current year's return, the extent of comparison of the details of income and deduction between years depends on the particular circumstances.

STATEMENT ON STANDARDS FOR TAX SERVICES NO. 4, *USE OF ESTIMATES*

Introduction

1. This statement sets forth the applicable standards for members when using the taxpayer's estimates in the preparation of a tax return. A member may advise on estimates used in the preparation of a tax return, but the taxpayer has the responsibility to provide the estimated data. Appraisals or valuations are not considered estimates for purposes of this statement.

Statement

2. Unless prohibited by statute or by rule, a member may use the taxpayer's estimates in the preparation of a tax return if it is not practical to obtain exact data and if the member determines that the estimates are reasonable based on the facts and circumstances known to the member. The taxpayer's estimates should be presented in a manner that does not imply greater accuracy than exists.

Explanation

3. Accounting requires the exercise of professional judgment and, in many instances, the use of approximations based on judgment. The application of such accounting judgments, as long as not in conflict with methods set forth by a taxing authority, is acceptable. These judgments are not estimates within the purview of this statement. For example, a federal income tax regulation provides that if all other conditions for accrual are met, the exact amount of income or expense need not be known or ascertained at year end if the amount can be determined with reasonable accuracy.

4. When the taxpayer's records do not accurately reflect information related to small expenditures, accuracy in recording some data may be difficult to achieve. Therefore, the use of estimates by a taxpayer in determining the amount to be deducted for such items may be appropriate.

5. When records are missing or precise information about a transaction is not available at the time the return must be filed, a member may prepare a tax return using a taxpayer's estimates of the missing data.

6. Estimated amounts should not be presented in a manner that provides a misleading impression about the degree of factual accuracy.

7. Specific disclosure that an estimate is used for an item in the return is not generally required; however, such disclosure should be made in unusual circumstances where nondisclosure might mislead the taxing authority regarding the degree of accuracy of the return as a whole. Some examples of unusual circumstances include the following:

a. A taxpayer has died or is ill at the time the return must be filed.
b. A taxpayer has not received a Schedule K-1 for a pass-through entity at the time the tax return is to be filed.
c. There is litigation pending (for example, a bankruptcy proceeding) that bears on the return.
d. Fire, computer failure, or natural disaster has destroyed the relevant records.

STATEMENT ON STANDARDS FOR TAX SERVICES NO. 5, *DEPARTURE FROM A POSITION PREVIOUSLY CONCLUDED IN AN ADMINISTRATIVE PROCEEDING OR COURT DECISION*

Introduction

1. This statement sets forth the applicable standards for members in recommending a tax return position that departs from the position determined in an administrative proceeding or in a court decision with respect to the taxpayer's prior return.

2. For purposes of this statement, *administrative proceeding* includes an examination by a taxing authority or an appeals conference relating to a return or a claim for refund.

3. For purposes of this statement, *court decision* means a decision by any court having jurisdiction over tax matters.

Statement

4. The tax return position with respect to an item as determined in an administrative proceeding or court decision does not restrict a member from recommending a different tax position in a later year's return, unless the taxpayer is bound to a specified treatment in the later year, such as by a formal closing agreement. Therefore, the member may recommend a tax return position or prepare or sign a tax return that departs from the treatment of an item as concluded in an administrative proceeding or court decision with respect to a prior return of the taxpayer provided the requirements of Statement on Standards for Tax Services (SSTS) No. 1, *Tax Return Positions*, are satisfied.

Explanation

5. If an administrative proceeding or court decision has resulted in a determination concerning a specific tax treatment of an item in a prior year's return, a member will usually recommend this same tax treatment in subsequent years. However, departures from consistent treatment may be justified under such circumstances as the following:

a. Taxing authorities tend to act consistently in the disposition of an item that was the subject of a prior administrative proceeding but generally are not bound to do so. Similarly, a taxpayer is not bound to follow the tax treatment of an item as consented to in an earlier administrative proceeding.
b. The determination in the administrative proceeding or the court's decision may have been caused by a lack of documentation. Supporting data for the later year may be appropriate.

c. A taxpayer may have yielded in the administrative proceeding for settlement purposes or not appealed the court decision, even though the position met the standards in SSTS No. 1.

d. Court decisions, rulings, or other authorities that are more favorable to a taxpayer's current position may have developed since the prior administrative proceeding was concluded or the prior court decision was rendered.

6. The consent in an earlier administrative proceeding and the existence of an unfavorable court decision are factors that the member should consider in evaluating whether the standards in SSTS No. 1 are met.

STATEMENT ON STANDARDS FOR TAX SERVICES NO. 6, *KNOWLEDGE OF ERROR: RETURN PREPARATION AND ADMINISTRATIVE PROCEEDINGS*

Introduction

1. This statement sets forth the applicable standards for a member who becomes aware of (a) an error in a taxpayer's previously filed tax return; (b) an error in a return that is the subject of an administrative proceeding, such as an examination by a taxing authority or an appeals conference; or (c) a taxpayer's failure to file a required tax return. As used herein, the term *error* includes any position, omission, or method of accounting that, at the time the return is filed, fails to meet the standards set out in Statement on Standards for Tax Services (SSTS) No. 1, *Tax Return Positions*. The term *error* also includes a position taken on a prior year's return that no longer meets these standards due to legislation, judicial decisions, or administrative pronouncements having retroactive effect. However, an error does not include an item that has an insignificant effect on the taxpayer's tax liability. The term *administrative proceeding* does not include a criminal proceeding.

2. This statement applies whether or not the member prepared or signed the return that contains the error.

3. Special considerations may apply when a member has been engaged by legal counsel to provide assistance in a matter relating to the counsel's client.

Statement

4. A member should inform the taxpayer promptly upon becoming aware of an error in a previously filed return, an error in a return that is the subject of an administrative proceeding, or a taxpayer's failure to file a required return. A member also should advise the taxpayer of the potential consequences of the error and recommend the corrective measures to be taken. Such advice and recommendation may be given orally. The member is not allowed to inform the taxing authority without the taxpayer's permission, except when required by law.

5. If a member is requested to prepare the current year's return and the taxpayer has not taken appropriate action to correct an error in a prior year's return, the member should consider whether to withdraw from preparing the return and whether to continue a professional or employment relationship with the taxpayer. If the member does prepare such current year's return, the member should take reasonable steps to ensure that the error is not repeated.

6. If a member is representing a taxpayer in an administrative proceeding with respect to a return that contains an error of which the member is aware, the member should request the taxpayer's agreement to disclose the error to the taxing authority. Lacking such agreement, the member should consider whether to withdraw from representing the taxpayer in the administrative proceeding and whether to continue a professional or employment relationship with the taxpayer.

Explanation

7. While performing services for a taxpayer, a member may become aware of an error in a previously filed return or may become aware that the taxpayer failed to file a required return. The member should advise the taxpayer of the error and the potential consequences, and recommend the measures to be taken. Similarly, when representing the taxpayer before a taxing authority in an administrative proceeding with respect to a return containing an error of which the member is aware, the member should advise the taxpayer to disclose the error to the taxing authority and of the potential consequences of not disclosing the error. Such advice and recommendation may be given orally.

8. It is the taxpayer's responsibility to decide whether to correct the error. If the taxpayer does not correct an error, a member should consider whether to withdraw from the engagement and whether to continue a professional or employment relationship with the taxpayer. Although recognizing that the taxpayer may not be required by statute to correct an error by filing an amended return, a member should consider whether a taxpayer's decision not to file an amended return or otherwise correct an error may predict future behavior that might require termination of the relationship.

9. Once the member has obtained the taxpayer's consent to disclose an error in an administrative proceeding, the disclosure should not be delayed to such a degree that the taxpayer or member might be considered to have failed to act in good faith or to have, in effect, provided misleading information. In any event, disclosure should be made before the conclusion of the administrative proceeding.

10. A conflict between the member's interests and those of the taxpayer may be created by, for example, the potential for violating Code of Professional Conduct Rule 301, *Confidential Client Information* (AICPA, *Professional Standards*, vol. 2, ET sec. 301 par. .01) (relating to the member's confidential client relationship); the tax law and regulations; or laws on privileged communications, as well as by the potential adverse impact on a taxpayer of a member's withdrawal. Therefore, a member should consider consulting with his or her own legal counsel before deciding upon recommendations to the taxpayer and whether to continue a professional or employment relationship with the taxpayer.

11. If a member believes that a taxpayer may face possible exposure to allegations of fraud or other criminal misconduct, the member should advise the taxpayer to consult with an attorney before the taxpayer takes any action.

12. If a member decides to continue a professional or employment relationship with the taxpayer and is requested to prepare a tax return for a year subsequent to that in which the error occurred, the member should take reasonable steps to ensure that the error is not repeated. If the subsequent year's tax return cannot be prepared without perpetuating the error, the member should consider withdrawal from the return preparation. If a member learns that the taxpayer is using an erroneous method of accounting and it is past the due date to request permission to change to a method meeting the standards of SSTS No. 1, the member may sign a tax return for the current year, providing the tax return includes appropriate disclosure of the use of the erroneous method.

13. Whether an error has no more than an insignificant effect on the taxpayer's tax liability is left to the professional judgment of the member based on all the facts and circumstances known to the member. In judging whether an erroneous method of accounting has more than an insignificant effect, a member should consider the method's cumulative effect, as well as its effect on the current year's tax return or the tax return that is the subject of the administrative proceeding.

14. If a member becomes aware of the error while performing services for a taxpayer that do not involve tax return preparation or representation in an administrative proceeding, the member's responsibility is to advise the taxpayer of the existence of the error and to recommend that the error be discussed with the taxpayer's tax return preparer. Such recommendation may be given orally.

STATEMENT ON STANDARDS FOR TAX SERVICES NO. 7, *FORM AND CONTENT OF ADVICE TO TAXPAYERS*

Introduction

1. This statement sets forth the applicable standards for members concerning certain aspects of providing advice to a taxpayer and considers the circumstances in which a member has a responsibility to communicate with a taxpayer when subsequent developments affect advice previously provided. The statement does not, however, cover a member's responsibilities when the expectation is that the advice rendered is likely to be relied on by parties other than the taxpayer.

Statement

2. A member should use professional judgment to ensure that tax advice provided to a taxpayer reflects competence and appropriately serves the taxpayer's needs. When communicating tax advice to a taxpayer in writing, a member should comply with relevant taxing authorities' standards, if any, applicable to written tax advice. A member should use professional judgment about any need to document oral advice. A member is not required to follow a standard format when communicating or documenting oral advice.

3. A member should assume that tax advice provided to a taxpayer will affect the manner in which the matters or transactions considered would be reported or disclosed on the taxpayer's tax returns. Therefore, for tax advice given to a taxpayer, a member should consider, when relevant (*a*) return reporting and disclosure standards applicable to the related tax return position and (*b*) the potential penalty consequences of the return position. In ascertaining applicable return reporting and disclosure standards, a member should follow the standards in Statement on Standards for Tax Services No. 1, *Tax Return Positions*.

4. A member has no obligation to communicate with a taxpayer when subsequent developments affect advice previously provided with respect to significant matters, except while assisting a taxpayer in implementing procedures or plans associated with the advice provided or when a member undertakes this obligation by specific agreement.

Explanation

5. Tax advice is recognized as a valuable service provided by members. The form of advice may be oral or written and the subject matter may range from routine to complex. Because the range of advice is so extensive and because advice should meet the specific needs of a taxpayer, neither a standard format nor guidelines for communicating or documenting advice to the taxpayer can be established to cover all situations.

6. Although oral advice may serve a taxpayer's needs appropriately in routine matters or in welldefined areas, written communications are recommended in important, unusual, substantial dollar value, or complicated transactions. The member may use professional judgment about whether, subsequently, to document oral advice.

7. In deciding on the form of advice provided to a taxpayer, a member should exercise professional judgment and should consider such factors as the following:

a. The importance of the transaction and amounts involved
b. The specific or general nature of the taxpayer's inquiry
c. The time available for development and submission of the advice
d. The technical complexity involved
e. The existence of authorities and precedents
f. The tax sophistication of the taxpayer
g. The need to seek other professional advice
h. The type of transaction and whether it is subject to heightened reporting or disclosure requirements
i. The potential penalty consequences of the tax return position for which the advice is rendered
j. Whether any potential applicable penalties can be avoided through disclosure
k. Whether the member intends for the taxpayer to rely upon the advice to avoid potential penalties

8. A member may assist a taxpayer in implementing procedures or plans associated with the advice offered. When providing such assistance, the member should review and revise such advice as warranted by new developments and factors affecting the transaction.

9. Sometimes a member is requested to provide tax advice but does not assist in implementing the plans adopted. Although such developments as legislative or administrative changes or future judicial interpretations may affect the advice previously provided, a member cannot be expected to communicate subsequent developments that affect such advice unless the member undertakes this obligation by specific agreement with the taxpayer.

10. Taxpayers should be informed that *(a)* the advice reflects professional judgment based upon the member's understanding of the facts, and the law existing as of the date the advice is rendered and *(b)* subsequent developments could affect previously rendered professional advice. Members may use precautionary language to the effect that their advice is based on facts as stated and authorities that are subject to change.

11. In providing tax advice, a member should be cognizant of applicable confidentiality privileges.

These Statements on Standards for Tax Services were unanimously adopted by the assenting votes of the 17 members of the 18-member Tax Executive Committee who participated in the August 6, 2009, Tax Executive Committee meeting.

Note: *Statements on Standards for Tax Services are issued by the Tax Executive Committee, the senior technical body of the AICPA designated to promulgate standards of tax practice. Rule 201, General Standards, and Rule 202, Compliance With Standards, of the Code of Professional Conduct (AICPA, Professional Standards, vol. 2, ET sec. 201 par. .01 and ET sec. 202 par. .01), require compliance with these standards.*

APPENDIX

F

COMPARISON OF TAX ATTRIBUTES FOR C CORPORATIONS, PARTNERSHIPS, AND S CORPORATIONS

APPENDIX F: COMPARISON OF TAX ATTRIBUTES FOR C CORPORATIONS, PARTNERSHIPS, AND S CORPORATIONS

Tax Attribute	C Corporation	Partnership	S Corporation
I. General Characteristics			
1. Application of the separate entity versus conduit (flow through) concept.	*Entity:* The corporation is treated as a separate taxpaying entity. If the corporation distributes income to shareholders in the form of dividends, the shareholders are subject to a second tax on such amounts. Shareholders also are subject to a second tax if they sell their stock.	*Conduit:* The partners report their distributive share of partnership ordinary income and separately stated items on their tax returns. Most elections, such as depreciation methods, accounting period and methods, are made at the partnership level. Special tax rules apply to electing large partnerships.	*Conduit:* Similar to the partnership form of organization. However, the S corporation may be subject to tax at the corporate level on excess net passive income, or built-in gains under special circumstances.
2. Period of existence.	Continues until dissolution; not affected by stock sales by shareholders.	Termination can occur by agreement, or by death, retirement, or disaffiliation of a partner.	Same as for C corporation.
3. Transferability of interest.	Stock can be transferred easily; corporation may retain right to buy back shares.	Addition of new partner or transfer of partner's interest generally requires approval of other partners.	Same as for C corporation.
4. Liability exposure.	Shareholders generally liable only for capital contributions.	General partners are personally, jointly, and severally liable for partnership obligations. Limited partners usually are liable only for capital contributions.	Same as for C corporation.
5. Management responsibility.	Shareholders may be part of management or may hire outside management.	All general partners participate in management. Limited partners generally do not participate.	Because of limited number of shareholders, shareholders usually are part of management.
II. Election and Restrictions			
1. Restrictions on: a. Type of owners.	No restriction.	No restriction.	Limited to individuals, estates, charitable organizations, and certain kinds of trusts.
b. Number of owners.	No restriction.	No restriction.	Limited to 100 shareholders, where a family counts as one shareholder.
c. Type of entity.	Includes domestic or foreign corporations, unincorporated entities known as associations, and certain kinds of trusts. A publicly traded partnership is taxed as a corporation unless more than 90% of its income is qualifying passive income. Grandfathered publicly traded partnerships can avoid corporate taxation by paying an excise tax. Partnerships, LLCs, and proprietorships can elect to be taxed as a corporation under the check-the-box regulations.	Includes a variety of unincorporated entities including limited liability company and limited liability partnership forms. Certain joint undertakings are excluded from partnership status.	Domestic corporations and unincorporated entities (e.g., associations) are eligible. A partnership, LLC, or proprietorship that elects to be treated as an S corporation automatically is considered to have elected to be treated as a corporation under the check-the-box regulations.

APPENDIX F: COMPARISON OF TAX ATTRIBUTES FOR C CORPORATIONS, PARTNERSHIPS, AND S CORPORATIONS

Tax Attribute	C Corporation	Partnership	S Corporation
d. Special tax classifications.	No restriction.	No restriction.	S corporation cannot be a former Domestic International Sales Corporation, or have elected the special Puerto Rico and U.S. Possessions tax credit. Certain financial institutions and insurance companies also are ineligible.
e. Investments made by entity.	No restriction.	No restriction.	S corporation can own 80% or more of a C corporation but cannot file a consolidated tax return with the C corporation.
f. Capital structure.	No restriction.	No restriction.	Limited to a single class of stock that is outstanding. Differences in voting rights are disregarded. Special "safe harbor" rules are available for debt issues.
g. Passive interest income.	No restriction.	No restriction.	Passive investment income cannot exceed 25% of gross receipts for three consecutive tax years when the corporation also has Subchapter C E&P at the end of the year.
2. Election and shareholder consent.	No election required.	No election required.	Election can be made during the preceding tax year or first 2 1/2 months of the tax year. Shareholders must consent to the election.
3. Termination of election.	Not applicable.	The partnership can terminate if it does not carry on any business, financial operation, or venture or if a sale or exchange of at least 50% of the profits and capital interests occurs within a 12-month period.	Occurs if one of the requirements is failed after the election is first effective or if the passive investment income test is failed for three consecutive tax years. IRS can waive invalid elections and permit inadvertent terminations not to break the S election.
4. Revocation of election.	Not applicable.	Not applicable.	Election may be revoked only by shareholders owning more than one-half of the stock. Must be made in first 2 1/2 months of tax year or on a prospective basis.
5. New election.	Not applicable.	Not applicable.	Not permitted for five-year period without IRS consent to early reelection.

APPENDIX F: COMPARISON OF TAX ATTRIBUTES FOR C CORPORATIONS, PARTNERSHIPS, AND S CORPORATIONS

Tax Attribute	C Corporation	Partnership	S Corporation
III. Accounting Periods and Elections			
1. Taxable year.	Calendar year or fiscal year is permitted. Personal service corporations are restricted to using a calendar year unless IRS grants approval to use a fiscal year. A special election is available to use a fiscal year resulting in a three-month or less income deferral if the corporation meets a series of minimum distribution requirements.	Generally use tax year of majority or principal partners. Otherwise use of the least aggregate deferral year is required. Can use a fiscal year that has a business purpose for which IRS approval is obtained. An electing partnership may use a fiscal year resulting in a three-month or less income deferral if an additional required payment is made.	Can use a fiscal year that has a business purpose for which IRS approval is obtained. An S corporation may use a fiscal year resulting in a three-month or less income deferral if an additional required payment is made. If neither of the above applies, a calendar year must be used.
2. Accounting methods.	Elected by the corporation. Use of cash method of accounting is restricted for certain personal service corporations and C corporations having $5 million or more annual gross receipts.	Elected by the partnership. Restrictions on the use of the cash method of accounting apply to partnerships having a C corporation as a partner or that are tax shelters.	Elected by the S corporation. Restrictions on the use of the cash method of accounting apply to S corporations that are tax shelters.
IV. Taxability of Profits			
1. Taxability of profits.	Ordinary income and capital gains are taxed to the corporation. Profits are taxed a second time when distributed.	Ordinary income and separately stated income and gain items pass through to the partners at the end of the partnership's tax year whether or not distributed.	Same as partnership.
2. Allocation of profits.	Not applicable.	Based on partnership agreement. Special allocations are permitted.	Based on stock ownership on each day of the tax year. Special allocations are not permitted.
3. Character of income.	Distributed profits (including tax-exempt income) are dividends to extent of earnings and profits (E&P).	Items receiving special treatment (e.g., capital gains or tax-exempt income) pass through separately to the partner and retain same character as when earned by the partnership.	Same as partnership.
4. Maximum tax rate for earnings.	15% on the first $50,000; 25% from $50,000 to $75,000; 34% from $75,000 to $10 million. The rate is 35% for taxable income above $10 million. A 5% surcharge applies to taxable income between $100,000 and $335,000, and a 3% surcharge applies to taxable income between $15 million and $18,333,333. Special rules apply to controlled groups. Personal service corporations are taxed at a flat 35% rate.	Rates of tax applicable to noncorporate partners from 10% through 39.6% are levied on pass-through income from the partnership. An additional 3.8% tax may apply to net investment income. C corporation rates apply to corporate partners.	Same as partnership except for certain special situations where a special corporate tax applies to the S corporation.

APPENDIX F: COMPARISON OF TAX ATTRIBUTES FOR C CORPORATIONS, PARTNERSHIPS, AND S CORPORATIONS

Tax Attribute	C Corporation	Partnership	S Corporation
5. Special tax levies.	Can be subject to accumulated earnings tax, personal holding company tax, and corporate alternative minimum tax.	Not applicable.	Can be subject to built-in gains tax, excess net passive income tax, and LIFO recapture tax.
6. Income splitting between family members.	Only possible when earnings are distributed to shareholder. Dividends received by shareholder under age 18 (or, in some cases, ages 18 through 23) are taxed at parents' marginal tax rate.	Transfer of partnership interest by gift will permit income splitting. Subject to special rules for transactions involving family members requiring payment of reasonable compensation for capital and services. Income received by partner under age 18 is taxed at parents' marginal tax rate.	Transfer of S corporation interest by gift will permit income splitting. Special rules apply to transactions involving family members requiring payment of reasonable compensation for capital and services. Income received by shareholder under age 18 is taxed at parents' marginal tax rate.
7. Sale of ownership interest.	Gain is taxed as capital gain; from 50% to 100% of gain may be excluded under Sec. 1202 qualified small business stock rules. The 100% exclusion applies for Sec. 1202 stock acquired after September 27, 2010. Loss is eligible for Sec. 1244 treatment.	Gain may be either ordinary income or capital gain depending on the nature of underlying partnership assets. Losses usually are capital.	Gain is capital in nature but is not eligible for special Sec. 1202 small business stock rules. Loss is eligible for Sec. 1244 treatment.
V. Treatment of Special Income, Gain, Loss, Deduction, and Credit Items			
1. Capital gains and losses.	Long-term capital gains are taxed at regular tax rates. Capital losses offset capital gains; excess losses carried back three years and forward five years.	Passed through to partners (according to partnership agreement).	Passed through to shareholders (on a daily basis according to stock ownership).
2. Section 1231 gains and losses.	Eligible for long-term capital gain or ordinary loss treatment. Loss recapture occurs at the corporate level.	Passed through to partners. Loss recapture occurs at the partner level.	Same as partnership.
3. Dividends received from domestic corporation.	Eligible for 70%, 80%, or 100% dividends-received deduction.	Passed through to noncorporate partners, subject to the applicable capital gains tax rate if qualified, possibly including an additional 3.8% on net investment income. Corporate partners may be eligible for the dividends-received deduction.	Same as partnership except S corporation cannot have corporate shareholders.
4. U.S. production activities deduction.	Deduction equals a 9% times the lesser of (1) qualified production activities income for the year or (2) taxable income before the U.S. production activities deduction. The deduction, however, cannot exceed 50% of the corporation's W-2 wages allocable to U.S. production activities for the year.	Passed through to partners. Limitations apply at partner level.	Same as partnership.
5. Organizational expenditures.	Deduct up to $5,000 and amortize balance over 180 months.	Same as C corporation.	Same as partnership.
6. Charitable contributions.	Limited to 10% of taxable income.	Passed through to partners. Limitations apply at partner level.	Same as partnership.
7. Expensing of asset acquisition costs.	Limited to the Sec. 179 limits in effect for the year property is placed in service.	Limited to the Sec. 179 limits in effect for the year property is placed in service for the partnership and for each partner.	Same as partnership.

APPENDIX F: COMPARISON OF TAX ATTRIBUTES FOR C CORPORATIONS, PARTNERSHIPS, AND S CORPORATIONS

Tax Attribute	C Corporation	Partnership	S Corporation
8. Expenses owed to related parties.	Regular Sec. 267 rules apply to payments and sales or exchanges made to or by the corporation and certain other related parties (e.g., controlling shareholder and corporation or members of a controlled group).	Regular Sec. 267 rules can apply. Special Sec. 267 rules for passthrough entities apply to payments made by the partnership to a partner.	Same as partnership.
9. Employment-related tax considerations.	An owner-employee may be treated as an employee for Social Security tax and corporate fringe benefit purposes. The corporate qualified pension and profit-sharing benefits available to owner-employees are comparable to the plan benefits for self-employed individuals (partners and sole proprietors).	A partner is not considered an employee of the business. Therefore, the partner must pay self-employment tax on the net self-employment income from the business. Corporate fringe benefit exclusions such as group term life insurance are not available (i.e., the premiums are not deductible by the business and are not excludable from the partner's income). Fringe benefits may be provided as nontaxable distribution or as taxable compensation.	Corporate fringe benefit exclusions generally are not available to S corporation shareholders. Fringe benefits usually are provided as nontaxable distribution or taxable compensation. S corporation shareholders may be treated as employees, however, for Social Security tax payments and qualified pension and profit sharing plan rules.
10. Tax preference items and AMT adjustments.	Subject to the corporate alternative minimum tax at the corporate level.	Passed through to partners and taxed under the alternative minimum tax rules applicable to the partner.	Same as partnership.
VI. Deductibility of Losses and Special Items			
1. Deductibility of losses.	Losses create net operating loss (NOL) that carry back two years (unless an extended carryback period applies) or forward 20 years or capital loss that carry back three years or forward five years.	Ordinary losses and separately stated loss and deduction items pass through to the partners at the end of the partnership tax year. May create a personal NOL.	Same as partnership.
2. Allocation of losses.	Not applicable.	Based on partnership agreement. Special allocations are permitted.	Based on stock ownership on each day of the tax year. Special allocations are not permitted.
3. Shareholder and entity loss limitations.	Passive losses may be restricted under the passive activity limitation if the C corporation is closely held.	Limited to partner's basis for the partnership interest. Ratable share of all partnership liabilities is included in basis of partnership interest. Excess losses carry over indefinitely until partnership interest again has a basis. Subject to at-risk, passive activity, and hobby loss restrictions.	Limited to shareholder's basis for the stock interest plus basis of S corporation debts to the shareholder. Excess losses carry over indefinitely until shareholder again has basis for stock or debt. Subject to the at-risk, passive activity, and hobby loss restrictions.
4. Basis adjustments for debt and equity interests.	Not applicable.	Basis in partnership interest reduced by loss and deduction passthrough. Subsequent profits increase basis of partnership interest.	Basis in S corporation stock reduced by loss and deduction passthrough. Once basis of stock has been reduced to zero, any other losses and deductions reduce basis of debt (but not below zero). Subsequent net increases restore basis reductions to debt before increasing basis of stock.

APPENDIX F: COMPARISON OF TAX ATTRIBUTES FOR C CORPORATIONS, PARTNERSHIPS, AND S CORPORATIONS

Tax Attribute	C Corporation	Partnership	S Corporation
5. Investment interest deduction limitation.	Not applicable.	Investment interest expenses and income pass through to the partners. Limitation applies at partner level.	Same as partnership.
VII. Distributions			
1. Taxability of nonliquidating distributions to shareholder.	Taxable as dividends if made from current or accumulated E&P. Additional distributions first reduce shareholder's basis for stock, and distributions exceeding stock basis trigger capital gain recognition.	Nontaxable unless money, money equivalents, or marketable securities received by the partner exceeds his or her basis for the partnership interest.	Nontaxable if made from the accumulated adjustment account or shareholder's basis for his or her stock. Taxable if made out of accumulated E&P or after stock basis has been reduced to zero.
2. Taxability of nonliquidating distributions to distributing entity.	Gain (but not loss) recognized as if the corporation had sold the property for its FMV immediately before the distribution.	No gain or loss recognized by the partnership except when a disproportionate distribution of Sec. 751 property occurs.	Gain (but not loss) recognized and passed through to the shareholders as if the corporation had sold the property for its FMV immediately before the distribution. Gain may be taxed to the S corporation under one of the special tax levies.
3. Basis adjustment to owner's investment for distribution.	None unless the distribution exceeds E&P.	Amount of money or adjusted basis of distributed property reduces basis in partnership interest.	Amount of money or FMV of distributed property reduces basis of stock except when distribution is made out of accumulated E&P.
VIII. Other Items			
1. Tax return.	Form 1120. Schedule M-3 may be required.	Form 1065 (Information Return). Schedule M-3 may be required.	Form 1120S (Information Return). Schedule M-3 may be required.
2. Due date.	April 15 for calendar year C corporations. March 15 if the corporation has a December 31 year-end.	March 15 for calendar year partnerships.	March 15 for calendar year S corporations.
3. Extensions of time permitted.	Six months, generally. Seven months for December 31 year-end corporations.	Six months.	Six months.
4. Estimated tax payments required.	Yes—April 15, June 15, September 15, and December 15 for calendar year C corporations.	No—Estimated taxes are required of the partners for passed through income, etc.	Yes—Applies to built-in gains tax and excess net passive income tax.
5. Audit rules.	IRS audits corporation independently of its shareholders.	Special audit rules apply requiring audit of partnership and requiring partners to take a position consistent with the partnership tax return.	Special rules require consistent tax treatment for Subchapter S items on the corporation and shareholder returns.

APPENDIX

G RESERVED

APPENDIX H

ACTUARIAL TABLES

TRANSFERS MADE AFTER APRIL 30, 2009
EXCERPT FROM TABLE S
SINGLE LIFE REMAINDER FACTORS

	INTEREST RATE								
AGE	**2%**	**4%**	**6%**	**8%**	**AGE**	**2%**	**4%**	**6%**	**8%**
25	.36464	.14924	.06960	.03724	58	.64573	.43790	.31103	.23053
26	.37134	.15440	.07288	.03929	59	.65553	.45041	.32348	.24197
27	.37819	.15980	.07639	.04153	60	.66534	.46310	.33625	.25380
28	.38520	.16542	.08012	.04396	61	.67515	.47595	.34933	.26603
29	.39233	.17126	.08406	.04656	62	.68494	.48892	.36267	.27862
30	.39959	.17730	.08820	.04933	63	.69470	.50200	.37625	.29155
31	.40698	.18355	.09255	.05229	64	.70443	.51519	.39010	.30484
32	.41449	.19002	.09712	.05543	65	.71411	.52849	.40420	.31850
33	.42213	.19671	.10192	.05878	66	.72385	.54203	.41872	.33273
34	.42988	.20360	.10693	.06231	67	.73359	.55575	.43363	.34749
35	.43774	.21070	.11217	.06605	68	.74331	.56963	.44887	.36272
36	.44572	.21803	.11764	.06999	69	.75299	.58360	.46438	.37837
37	.45381	.22557	.12335	.07416	70	.76260	.59764	.48013	.39443
38	.46201	.23334	.12932	.07856	71	.77215	.61176	.49614	.41090
39	.47032	.24133	.13554	.08320	72	.78162	.62593	.51237	.42776
40	.47873	.24954	.14201	.08807	73	.79098	.64009	.52876	.44494
41	.48724	.25797	.14873	.09319	74	.80019	.65417	.54523	.46235
42	.49585	.26662	.15572	.09856	75	.80923	.66813	.56169	.47991
43	.50457	.27552	.16301	.10422	76	.81807	.68192	.57810	.49754
44	.51338	.28465	.17057	.11016	77	.82671	.69553	.59444	.51525
45	.52228	.29400	.17843	.11640	78	.83515	.70894	.61068	.53298
46	.53129	.30360	.18659	.12294	79	.84337	.72213	.62680	.55071
47	.54037	.31343	.19505	.12980	80	.85135	.73507	.64272	.56836
48	.54955	.32351	.20383	.13699	81	.85910	.74773	.65844	.58590
49	.55882	.33383	.21294	.14453	82	.86660	.76009	.67391	.60330
50	.56819	.34442	.22242	.15247	83	.87385	.77214	.68909	.62050
51	.57766	.35528	.23226	.16080	84	.88084	.78385	.70396	.63745
52	.58722	.36641	.24249	.16957	85	.88757	.79521	.71849	.65412
53	.59687	.37781	.25309	.17876	86	.89402	.80619	.73264	.67046
54	.60658	.38945	.26406	.18837	87	.90021	.81679	.74638	.68642
55	.61635	.40131	.27537	.19838	88	.90612	.82700	.75971	.70200
56	.62613	.41335	.28697	.20875	89	.91176	.83681	.77259	.71714
57	.63593	.42555	.29887	.21947	90	.91713	.84620	.78500	.73181

Source: Reg. Sec. 20.2031-7(d)(7), as supplemented by IRS Pub. 1457: Actuarial Values, Table S.

EXCERPT FROM TABLE B
TERM CERTAIN REMAINDER FACTORS

	INTEREST RATE			
YEARS	**2%**	**4%**	**6%**	**8%**
1	.980392	.961538	.943396	.925926
2	.961169	.924556	.889996	.857339
3	.942322	.888996	.839619	.793832
4	.923845	.854804	.792094	.735030
5	.905731	.821927	.747258	.680583
6	.887971	.790315	.704961	.630170
7	.870560	.759918	.665057	.583490
8	.853490	.730690	.627412	.540269
9	.836755	.702587	.591898	.500249
10	.820348	.675564	.558395	.463193
11	.804263	.649581	.526788	.428883
12	.788493	.624597	.496969	.397114
13	.773033	.600574	.468839	.367698
14	.757875	.577475	.442301	.340461
15	.743015	.555265	.417265	.315242
16	.728446	.533908	.393646	.291890
17	.714163	.513373	.371364	.270269
18	.700159	.493628	.350344	.250249
19	.686431	.474642	.330513	.231712
20	.672971	.456387	.311805	.214548
21	.659776	.438834	.294155	.198656
22	.646839	.421955	.277505	.183941
23	.634156	.405726	.261797	.170315
24	.621721	.390121	.246979	.157699
25	.609531	.375117	.232999	.146018

Source: Reg. Sec. 20.2031-7(d)(6), Table B, as supplemented by IRS Pub. 1457: Actuarial Values, Table B.

APPENDIX

I INDEX OF CODE SECTIONS

APPENDIX

J INDEX OF TREASURY REGULATIONS

APPENDIX

K INDEX OF GOVERNMENT PROMULGATIONS

APPENDIX

L INDEX OF COURT CASES

APPENDIX

M SUBJECT INDEX

2017
TAX RATE SCHEDULES

ESTATES AND TRUSTS [§1(e)]:

If taxable income is:	The tax is:
Not over $2,550	15% of taxable income.
Over $2,550 but not over $6,000	$382.50 plus 25% of the excess over $2,550
Over $6,000 but not over $9,150	$1,245.00 plus 28% of the excess over $6,000
Over $9,150 but not over $12,500	$2,127.00 plus 33% of the excess over $9,150
Over $12,500	$3,232.50 plus 39.6% of the excess over $12,500

CORPORATIONS [§11(b)]

If Taxable Income Is:		The Tax Is:	
Over—	But Not Over—		Of the Amount Over—
$ 0	$ 50,000	15%	$ 0
50,000	75,000	$ 7,500 + 25%	50,000
75,000	100,000	13,750 + 34%	75,000
100,000	335,000	22,250 + 39%	100,000
335,000	10,000,000	113,900 + 34%	335,000
10,000,000	15,000,000	3,400,000 + 35%	10,000,000
15,000,000	18,333,333	5,150,000 + 38%	15,000,000
18,333,333		6,416,667 + 35%	18,333,333

UNIFIED CREDIT AMOUNT FOR ESTATE AND GIFT TAX

Year of Gift/Year of Death	Amount of Credit	Basic Exclusion Amount (Exemption Equivalent)
January through June, 1977	$ 30,000 (6,000)[b]	$ 120,666 (30,000)[b]
July through December, 1977	30,000	120,666
1978	34,000	134,000
1979	38,000	147,333
1980	42,500	161,563
1981	47,000	175,625
1982	62,800	225,000
1983	79,300	275,000
1984	96,300	325,000
1985	121,800	400,000
1986	155,800	500,000
1987 through 1997	192,800	600,000
1998	202,050	625,000
1999	211,300	650,000
2000 and 2001	220,550	675,000
2002 and 2003	345,800	1,000,000
2004 and 2005	555,800 (345,800)[a]	1,500,000 (1,000,000)[a]
2006, 2007, and 2008	780,800 (345,800)[a]	2,000,000 (1,000,000)[a]
2009	1,455,800 (345,800)[a]	3,500,000 (1,000,000)[a]
2010	1,730,800[b] (330,800)[a]	5,000,000[b] (1,000,000)[a]
2011	1,730,800	5,000,000
2012	1,772,800	5,120,000
2013	2,045,800	5,250,000
2014	2,081,800	5,340,000
2015	2,117,800	5,430,000
2016	2,125,800	5,450,000
2017	2,141,800	5,490,000

[a] The numbers in parentheses represent the credit and exemption equivalent amounts for the gift tax.
[b] This amount applied if the executor opted to have the estate subject to the estate tax and FMV basis rule in 2010.